MW01098385

OF

# SOLDIERS FROM NORTH CAROLINA

## IN THE

# AMERICAN REVOLUTION

WITH AN APPENDIX CONTAINING
A COLLECTION OF MISCELLANEOUS
RECORDS

GENEALOGICAL PUBLISHING CO., INC.

*Baltimore*                                    *1988*

Originally Published by
The North Carolina Daughters of the American Revolution
Durham, 1932
Reprinted by Genealogical Publishing Co., Inc.
Baltimore, 1967, 1972, 1977, 1984, 1988
Library of Congress Catalogue Card Number 67-28097
International Standard Book Number 0-8063-0091-4
*Made in the United States of America*

# FOREWORD

For years there has seemed an urgent need for a concrete one-volume publication giving the names and records of the men serving in the Revolution from each of the thirteen original states comprised in our Republic. Students particularly regret the lack of such a reference book. Patriotic souls, proud of the sacrifice their forefathers made in this struggle, have openly expressed a desire that such data be collected and made more accessible to the reading public generally.

The Daughters of the American Revolution have been most eager to uphold the ideals of their Revolutionary ancestors, and to pass on to future generations a knowledge of the part these men played in those trying years, 1776-1783. With their usual enthusiasm the North Carolina Daughters, at the request and instigation of the National Board in April, 1929, undertook such a compilation for their own state. That same month the plan was presented before the Executive Board Meeting in Raleigh, and met with hearty approval. Mrs. R. Duke Hay, Historian, sought the coöperation of the State Historical Commission, and the resources of the state archives were placed at her command. A committee of three was appointed to work with the Historian: viz., Mrs. J. R. Briggs, Mrs. R. T. Gowan of Raleigh, and Mrs. Wm. Ray Snow of Winston-Salem. These met in Raleigh the 3rd of July, 1929, at the Historical Building, with Dr. A. R. Newsome, Chairman of the State Historical Commission. Requirements and the matter of research were gone into most rigidly and searchingly.

At the end of that day the project appeared an Herculean task, with difficulties undreamed of on all sides. The source material from which to gather a complete list of soldiers of that period was scattered. County seats and private homes held important documents, newspapers and old letters which would have aided wonderfully. Could the task have been tackled a hundred years ago, it would have been easier. Destructive court house fires had taken heavy toll, and the aging process of time had made many pages of State records almost illegible. Names of men who fought as bravely as any recorded in the present list could not be deciphered, and thus it appeared no complete compilation, at this late date, was possible. But it is a fact much invaluable material *was* preserved and this encouraged the workers to persist in the undertaking.

The compilers of this book and the North Carolina Daughters of the American Revolution generally wish to extend their appreciation for the loan of the Margaret Gregory Overman fund, without which this publication would probably not have been possible.

In such a work as this, devised as it is for posterity, the aim primarily must be for accuracy and authenticity, therefore only such records and documents as have the *State* and *National* stamp of recognition have been employed. It has been a labor of love, there is no claim for originality, since all materials used have been copied. Errors there may be, but such are the records. Human hands have done the best they could with the matter available.

One big question in the outset was the approximate number of men North Carolina furnished from 1776-1783. Deductions are purely problematical, since enlistments ranged from three months to three years, and many were reënlisted. Ashe's History, page 721, estimates 22,000 different names on the muster rolls of the North Carolina troops. Here was the definite task of finding these names and such records as remain, with the resultant records of approximately 36,000 names. It was deemed advisable to apportion the work among the members of the committee.

Mrs. Chas. R. Whitaker, Regent at the time, secured from Washington a copy of "U. S. War Department Report of Pensions" 1835. A work of unquestioned authority, however it was not classified as to states. The loan was for such limited time that Mrs. Whitaker personally undertook the task of weeding out the North Carolina names. This proved a contribution of more than 1,400 names with references.

Mrs. J. A. Briggs and Mrs. R. T. Gowan, of Raleigh, were untiring in their work of compiling Revolutionary accounts, comptroller records, and thereby adding many thousand names.

Mrs. Wm. Ray Snow, of Winston-Salem, literally sat up with the work, going again and again to Raleigh, keeping untiringly at the tedious work of research through dust-covered boxes of unclassified material, sorting, deciphering and copying. She has had a part in every phase of the work and much praise is due her.

The Historian took for her big task the work of copying the 10 Regiments with their records, artillery, company rosters, and various miscellaneous records; Pierce's Register, and Army Accounts in Vol. XVII, State Records.

No more faithful, efficient and self-sacrificing co-workers could have been found to assist a historian in the undertaking than this splendid committee. Each and all have wrought nobly, proving the fact of their rich heritage from forefathers, who in their wise vision planted the tree of Constitutional Freedom, whose sweet spirits have been, are now and shall be enjoyed by their descendants so long as cherished ideals and memories keep alive a just spirit of pride and patriotism.

We are deeply indebted to the Joseph K. Ruebush Company, publishers of "King's Mountain Men," by Katherine Keogh White, for the privilege of including in this volume the names of North Carolina men who participated in the battle of King's Mountain.

Remembering that "Tree of Freedom, was planted by Virtue, raised by Toil, and nurtured by the Blood of Heroes," the North Carolina Daughters of the American Revolution dedicate this volume to the memory of those heroes of the eight most tragic, yet glorious years of our national history. Heroes they are whose names we preserve and love, and the unknown heroes whose names we do not know, but whom we also love and venerate.

GERTRUDE SLOAN HAY (MRS. R. DUKE),<br>
*Historian.*

Winston-Salem, N. C.
December, 1931.

# COMMITTEE ON COMPILATION AND PUBLICATION

*State Regent, 1928-1931*

Harriett Reed Whitaker (Mrs. Chas. R.)
Southern Pines

*State Historian, 1929-1933*

Gertrude Sloan Hay (Mrs. R. Duke)
Winston-Salem, N. C.

Maude Reynolds Snow (Mrs. Wm. Ray)..............Winston-Salem
Louisa Hall Briggs (Mrs. J. A.)..........................Raleigh
Olivia Barkley Gowan (Mrs. R. T.)......................Raleigh

# CONTENTS

# ROSTER

OF

## SOLDIERS FROM NORTH CAROLINA

IN THE

## AMERICAN REVOLUTION

# PIERCE'S REGISTER

## From Seventeenth Report of the National Society
## Daughters American Revolution

The general index of the register is preserved in MSS. in the Library of Congress
N. C. Certificates 89,501 to 91,938

A

[Page 150]

No.

90271. Abbott, John
89932. Abute, John
90455. Acock, Simon
89912. Adams, David
90057. Adams, William
90423. Adams, William
91417. Adams, William
89901. Adams, Zachariah
91057. Adcock, Edward
90302. Adkins, Richard
91161. Adkins, Samuel
89502. Aiken, Gideon
91533. Aikens, Gideon
90875. Aiken, Gideon
90593. Airs Ezekial
90276. Akins, Gideon
91022. Albrith, John
90036. Albrooks, William
90953. Albrooks, William
90620. Alderman, Daniel
89877. Adams, Phil
90604. Alderman, John
91163. Aldridge, Francis
89793. Alduson, Robert
90763. Alexander, Ezekial
91601. Alexander, William
91844-6. Alexander, William
91936. Alexander, William
90947. Alexon, Peter
90714. Allen, Elijah
89846. Allen, James
90752. Allen, Jonathan
91003. Allen, Joheph
91436. Alsbrook, Claburn
89815. Allsbrood, Jesse
89501. Ambrose, David
90820. Ambrose, David
91468. Ambrose, David
90374. Anderson, George
90405. Anderson, Thomas
89720. Ashlock, Jesse
89780. Andrews, Alfred
90176. Andrews, Joseph

No.

90982. Angel, Thomas
90525. Aram, Elijah
91110. Archdeacon, Richd.
91619-21. Armstrong, John
91921. Armstrong, John
91893. Armstrong, Thomas
91646-8. Armstrong,William
91899. Armstrong, William
90475. Arnel, William
90770. Arnold, Aaron
90750. Arrington, John
90610. Arters, Stephen
90595. Artis, John
91397. Ashe, Charles
91733-5. Ashe, Samuel
91913. Ashe, Samuel
89673. Ashue, Charles
90101. Askins, John
90125. Aspey, John
91388. Atkins, Benj.
91453. Atkinson, James
91354. Atkinson, Joel
91086. Atwood, John
91168. Audler, Etancis
91427. Avery, George
91078. Avery, Isam

B

91331. Bacchus, Joseph
90584. Bacchus, William
91583. Bacot, Peter
91862. Bacot, Peter
90254. Baggott, John
90522. Bailes, John
90301. Bailey, Archibald
91667. Bailey, Benjamin
91668. Bailey, Benj.
91669. Bailey, Benj.
91905. Bailey, Benj.
89508. Bailey, John
90825. Bailey John
91473. Bailey, John
90182. Bailey, Stephen
90216. Baits, James
89756. Baker, Benjamin

[ 3 ]

| No. | |
|---|---|
| 90285. | Baker, James |
| 90137. | Baker, John |
| 91355. | Baker, John |
| 90077. | Baker, Joseph |
| 91439. | Baker, Joseph |
| 91056. | Baldwin, Edward |
| 89966. | Ball, Hosea |
| 90815. | Baxter, Lemuel |
| 89506. | Baxter, Samuel |
| 90879. | Barko, Leyman |
| 89945. | Ballard, Dudley |
| 91325. | Ballard, Jacob |
| 91649-50. | Ballard, Kedar |
| 91561. | Ballard, Kedar |
| 90272. | Ballard, Lewis |
| 90484. | Ballard, Wyatt |
| 91426. | Balstaff, Frederick |
| 90586. | Barce, John |
| 90536. | Barker, Isaac |
| 91527. | Barko, Leyman |
| 91005. | Barnes, Moses |
| 91194. | Barnet, Sion |
| 90118. | Barnhill, David |
| 90464. | Barrett, Joseph |
| 90180. | Bass, Hardy |
| 90940. | Bateman, William |
| 89627. | Bates, Luke |
| 90924. | Bates, Luke |
| 91571. | Bates, Luke |
| 91787-9. | Banot, Peter |
| 91344. | Baxley, Joseph |
| 91464. | Baxter, Samuel |
| 91060. | Baxter, Thomas |
| 90012. | Baxter, William |
| 89968. | Beasley, William |
| 89510. | Bynum, Drury |
| 89923. | Bynum, Elijah |
| 89727. | Butler, Lawrence |
| 90072. | Beaverhouse, Abraham |
| 91292. | Belew, John |
| 90048. | Bell, George |
| 91326. | Bell, James |
| 90587. | Bell, Josiah |
| 91590. | Bell, Robert |
| 91829. | Bell, Robert |
| 91830. | Bell, Robert |
| 91831. | Bell, Robert |
| 91891. | Bell, Robert |
| 91678. | Bell, Samuel |
| 90767. | Bell, William |
| 89843. | Bennet, Richard |
| 90930. | Benton, Dempsey |
| 89688. | Benton, John |
| 90114. | Benton, Josiah |

| No. | |
|---|---|
| 90694. | Benton, Nathan |
| 90412. | Berry, James |
| 90111. | Best, John |
| 90737. | Betts, Mathias |
| 90711. | Betts, William |
| 90220. | Bexley, James |
| 90335. | Bibbe, Solomon |
| 89850. | Bilbe, Edward |
| 90309. | Billops, Richard |
| 89818. | Billups, Thomas |
| 81141. | Bingham, John |
| 91521. | Binham, Drury |
| 90784. | James Block |
| 91261. | James Block |
| 90801. | Blacke, Given |
| 90591. | Blanchard, Micajah |
| 89895. | Blaxton, Henry |
| 89794. | Bletcher, Jacob |
| 89635. | Blount, Frederick |
| 90855. | Blount, Frederick |
| 91503. | Blount, Frederick |
| 91573. | Blount, Reading |
| 91754. | Blount, Reading |
| 91755. | Blount, Reading |
| 91756. | Blount, Reading |
| 91877. | Blount, Reading |
| 90121. | Blount, Thomas |
| 90239. | Blunt, Benjamin |
| 91605. | Blythe, Joseph |
| 91760. | Blythe, Joseph |
| 91761. | Blythe, Joseph |
| 91762. | Blythe, Joseph |
| 91938. | Blythe, Joseph |
| 91426. | Boga, Benjamin |
| 91406. | Boyakin, James |
| 91193. | Boid, Benjamin |
| 91275. | Boling, Thomas |
| 90908. | Bond, James |
| 89512. | Bond, James |
| 91320. | Bond, Richard |
| 89959. | Boon, David |
| 89772. | Boon, Elisha |
| 90040. | Boston, Andrew |
| 90041. | Boston, Christopher |
| 90389. | Boweles, Benjamin |
| 90897. | Bowers, Jiles |
| 91531. | Bowers, Jiles |
| 90224. | Bowers, Solomon |
| 90173. | Boyce, John |
| 81999. | Boyd, Thomas |
| 91652. | Bradley, Gee |
| 91653. | Bradley, Gee |
| 91654. | Bradley, Gee |
| 91900. | Bradley, Gee |

*No.*

90948. Brady, John
90200. Brady, Benjamin
91198. Bragwell, John
90119. Branch, Burrell
90061. Brannen, Thomas
91390. Brantley, Amos
91433. Brantley, John
91231. Braswell, George
90230. Brawn, Solomon
91557. Bryan, Dempsey
91661. Brevard, Alexander
91662. Brevard, Alexander
91663. Brevard, Alexander
91903. Brevard, Alexander
91595. Brevard, Joseph
91915. Brevard, Joseph
91802. Breevard, Joseph
91803. Breevard, Joseph
91804. Breevard, Joseph
91420. Brewer, William
90719. Brewer, Henry
89714. Briant, Hezekiah
89938. Brickles, William
90031. Briggs, Robert
89511. Bright, Charles
89984. Bright, Charles
90874. Bright, Charles
91522. Bright, Charles
90558. Bright, Jesse
90457. Bright, John
90627. Bright, Simon
91386. Brintley, Micharl
89700. Bristow, Philemon
91403. Brockley, William
90214. Brothers, David
90250. Brown, Arthur
91106. Brown, Benjamin
91007. Brown, Isaac
89745. Brown, James
90161. Brown, James
90249. Brown, James
89749. Brown, John
91249. Brown, John
89629. Brown, Joseph
90821. Brown, Joseph
91469. Brown, Joseph
89504. Brown, Thomas
90837. Brown, Thomas
91485. Brown, Thomas
90297. Brown, Warner
91105. Brown, Warren
89622. Brown, William
90853. Brown, William
91501. Brown, William

*No.*

89916. Browning, Elijah
89872. Browning, Mark
91339. Brumager, Edward
90766. Bryan, Kedar
89987. Bryant, Charles
90904. Bryant, Dempsey
90017. Bryant, James
90066. Bryant, John
90958. Bryant, John
91380. Bryant, John
91434. Bryant, John
89509. Bryant, William
90844. Bryant, William
91492. Bryant, William
89648. Bryon, Dempsey
91706. Budd, Samuel
91707. Budd, Samuel
91708. Budd, Samuel
91884. Budd, Samuel
91876. Bull, Thomas
90944. Bullock, Nathan
91293. Bunch, Clement
89670. Bunkley, Michael
90128. Bunkley, Thomas
90935. Bunn, Jesse
90408. Burke, David
90400. Burke, Elihu
89668. Burket, Uriah
91422. Burnes, David
91502. Burnet, William
90056. Burnett, James
90105. Burnett, John
90854. Burnett, William
89951. Burnhill, James
91267. Burroughs, Aaron
90407. Burruss, John
90332. Burton, John
91604. Bush, William
91796. Bush, William
91797. Bush, William
91798. Bush, William
91866. Bush, William
90733. Busley, William
98819. Butts, Archibald

C

91217. Cain, Richard
91333. Callahan, Martin
91688. Callendar, Thomas
91689. Callendar, Thomas
91690. Callendar, Thomas
9163. Callendar, Thomas
90618. Calvet, Stephen
90222. Cameron, Alexander

*No.*
90720. Cameron, Daniel
89952. Campbell, Israel
90289. Campbell, Jesse
91589. Campbell, John
91823. Campbell, John
91824. Campbell, John
91825. Campbell, John
91932. Campbell, John
90648. Campbell, Niel
89518. Campbell, Walter
90422. Campbell, William
91584. Campen, James
91805. Campen, James
91806. Campen, James
91807. Campen, James
91885. Campen, James
90905. Campen, John
91552. Campen, John
90098. Canady, Thomas
90636. Cannon, Edward
91438. Capel, Charles
90395. Caps, Francis
90268. Card, William
90725. Carleton, David
90724. Carleton, John
90575. Carmack, John
91099. Carrel, Hardy
90569. Carrol, Benjamin
89624. Carrol, William
89878. Carroll, John
91580. Carter, Benjamin
91778. Carter, Benjamin
91779. Carter, Benjamin
91780. Carter, Benjamin
90009. Carter, Isaac
90996. Carter, Isaac
91489. Carter, John
91081. Carter, Moses
89835. Carter, Sewel
89834. Carter, William
90693. Cartwright, Joseph
89994. Cason, Cannon
91063. Cason, Thomas
90704. Casteen, Wm.
90841. Caste, John
89658. Caswell, Thomas
90386. Cavender, James
90373. Cavender, William
90293. Chance, Philemon
89516. Chandler, Thomas
91927. Chapman, Samuel
89710. Chappel, Samuel
90280. Chaulton, George
90028. Chavers, Drury

*No.*
90449. Chaves, Caesar
90378. Cheavus, William
91462. Chester, David
89513. Chester, David
90813. Chester, David
90991. Chester, John
90106. Chubbuck, Jeremiah
91908. Claddenin, John
91817. Claike, Thos.
91818. Claike, Thos.
91819. Claike, Thos.
91727. Clandennin, John
91728. Clandennin, John
91729. Clandennin, John
89520. Clark, Isaac
90891. Clark, Isaac
91567. Clark, Isaac
91588. Clark, Thomas
91528. Clarke, Isaac
90082. Clarke, Thomas
90740. Clarke, Thomas
91607. Clarke, Thomas
91608. Clarke, Thomas
91609. Clarke, Thomas
91931. Clarke, Thomas
90555. Clarkson, Thomas
90999. Clay, David
90029. Clayton, Lambert
91227. Clifton, Cloid
90549. Clowen, Wm.
90551. Clower, Daniel
90708. Clubb, Samuel
89799. Coats, Benjamin
90582. Cobb, Henry
91289. Cofield, Samuel
90121. Cogdell, William
90454. Cogen, Robert
90969. Colbreath, Archibald
90568. Cole, Abner
90179. Cole, Charles
89575. Cole, Martin
90909. Cole, Martin
91555. Cole, Martin
89647. Cole, William
90903. Cole, William
91550. Cole, William
91769. Coleman, Benjamin
91770. Coleman, Benjamin
91771. Coleman, Benjamin
91880. Coleman, Benjamin
89991. Coleman, John
90665. Coleman, Joseph
90190. Coleman, Levi
90366. Collins, Hezekiah

*No.*
90560. Collins, Jeremiah
90523. Collins, John
90580. Collins, John
90939. Collins, John
91162. Collins, John
91208. Collins, Shadrack
91577. Colman, Benjamin
90772. Colsan, James
91109. Colsan, James
90895. Colter, Levy
91201. Colwell, David
90376. Combs, George
89649. Compen, John
90383. Conn, John
91402. Connaway, William
91155. Conner, Benjamin
91243. Conner, Dorsey
89934. Conner, James
90519. Conner, John
90441. Conway, Francis
89662. Cook, Allen
91166. Cooke, William
90432. Cooker, Joseph
90260. Cooksey, Hazekiah
90263. Cooksey, Thomas
90470. Coombs, Robert
91048. Coomer, Hugh
90027. Cooper, Benjamin
90033. Cooper, Frederick
91291. Copelin, Job
89980. Cornelius, John
90697. Corroner, Christopher
91318. Cotants, John
90775. Cotree, Mathew
91530. Cotter, Levi
91274. Cox, Jesse
90404. Cox, John
90732. Cox, John
91640. Craddock, John
91641. Craddock, John
91642. Craddock, John
91882. Craddock, John
90283. Crane, Stephen
90211. Creamor, James
90640. Cremortice, William
91268. Crews, Ethelred
90643. Crice, Theophilus
91721. Croucher, Anthony
91722. Croucher, Anthony
91723. Croucher, Anthony
90168. Croven, Peter
90046. Crow, James
90963. Crumpton, James
91269. Crumpton, Thomas

*No.*
91890. Crutcher, Anthony
91224. Cunagin, William
89972. Cunningham, William

**D**
90103. Daniel, Jeptha
91350. Daniel, Job
91664. Daves, John
90629. Davis, Aaron
91323. Davis, Archibald
90109. Davis, Joel
90726. Davis, John
91337. Davis, John
91365. Davis, Joseph
89838. Davis, Micajah
91061. Davis, Robert
90397. Davis, Thomas
90030. Davis, William
90747. Davis, William
91424. Dawsey, William S.
90024. Dawson, John
91430. Deal, John
89911. Davis, James
89521. Dean, Abraham
90253. Dean Moses
89646. Dean Philip
90901. Dean, Philip
91549. Dean, Philip
89654. Dean Robert
90165. Dean, Robert
91147. DeGunsalis, Ferdinand
90380. Dempsey, Allen
91215. Depriest, James
91416. Derraberry, Andrew
90154. Dickins, James
91400. Dickins, Thomas
91042. Dickson, Michael
90777. Diddin, Jacob
90403. Dillard, James
91739. Dixon, Charles
91740. Dixon, Charles
91741. Dixon, Charles
90994. Dixon, Chasell
90241. Dixon, Jeremiah
91857. Dixon, Tilman
91700. Dixon, Tilmon
91701. Dixon, Tilmon
91702. Dixon, Tilmon
91550. Dixon, Wayne
91602. Dixon, Wayne
91851. Dixon, Wayne
91852. Dixon, Wayne
91934. Dixon, Wayne
90023. Dobbins, James

No.
91047. Dobbins, Wm.
91136. Dobson, Joseph
91631. Doherty, George
91632. Doherty, George
91633. Doherty, George
91923. Doherty, George
91922. Donoho, Thomas
89801. Dollar, Jonathan
91287. Donalson, Jacob
91628. Donoho, Thomas
91629. Donoho, Thomas
91630. Donoho, Thomas
91188. Dotey, Isaac
90878. Douglas, William
89524. Douglass, Wm.
91526. Douglas, William
91133. Dowdle, John
90606. Downing, Thomas
90633. Dubust, Jacob
89754. Donally, Hugh
91041. Dodd, Thomas
89721. Ducast, Ezekial
91736. Dudley, Thomas
91737. Dudley, Thomas
91738. Dudley, Thomas
91914. Dudley, Thomas
90968. Due, John
90948. Dukes, John
89805. Duncan, George
89522. Dunick, Peter
91389. Dunnagan, David
89713. Dunstan, Charles
91027. Durden, Mills
90360. Durham, Humphrey
89671. Durham, William

**E**

90044. Eagle, Thomas
91119. Earhart, Philip
91930. Eaton, James
89962. Edwards, David
93091. Edwards, John
89960. Edwards, John, Sr.
89527. Edwards, John, Jr.
90487. Elder, William
89823. Ellis, Bartholemu
89589. Ellis, Aaron
90090. Ellis, James
90443. Elixon, Peter
90785. Eller, John
90778. Eller, Joseph
90647. Ellis, Robt.
91197. Ellunes, James
89674. Elmes, Charles

No.
90313. Elmes, James
90163. Elmore, James
91262. Elsmore, Ephraim
91068. Emlin, David
91064. Emmery, William
90146. Enax, David
90315. Enderkin, Francis
90282. Engrum, Tobias
20328. Enman, William
90626. Essoms, Thomas
90689. Esters, John
89948. Estridge, Ephriam
89652. Etherage, John
90918. Etherage, John
91563. Etherage, John
91239. Etherington, William
90615. Enganus, William
90381. Euing, George
89864. Evans, Charles
90672. Evans, John
90291. Elliot, Zacheriah
89808. Evans, Maurice
89736. Evans, Reuben
91679. Evans, Thomas
91680. Evans, Thomas
91681. Evans, Thomas
91928. Evans, Thomas
92029. Evans, Nel
90245. Ewell, Caleb
90156. Eweman, Christopher
90709. Ezell, Timothy

**F**

89530. Faithfood, William
91513. Faithful, William
90865. Faithful, William
89970. Fain, William
90554. Farebee, Thomas
91376. Farmer, Jesse
89532. Faulks, James
90574. Faulks, James
91516. Faulks, James
90868. Faulks, John
91691. Faun, William
91692. Faun, William
91693. Faun, William
91619. Faun, William
89958. Fauner, Benjamin
89957. Fauner, William
91600. Fenner, Richard
91838. Fenner, Richard
91831. Fenner, Richard
91840. Fenner, Richard
91889. Fenner, Richard

*No.*
91634. Fenner, Richard
91635. Fenner, Richard
91636. Fenner, Richard
91887. Fenney, Thomas
90578. Fentice, Moses
91892. Fergus, James
89914. Ferguson, Irom
91460. Ferguson, Peter
89917. Ferguson, Robert
90189. Ferrel, James
91305. Farrel, Clement
89774. Ferrell, John
90334. Ferrill, Gabriel
90950. Fields, John
90603. Fight, Conrod
91303. Finney, Samuel
91592. Finney, Thomas
91841. Finney, Thomas
91842. Finney, Thomas
91843. Finney, Thomas
89528. Fist, Thomas
86689. Flannagan, Dennis
90139. Flemming, James
93101. Floch, Lewis
91216. Flood, Benjamin
90458. Flood, Enoch
91265. Flood, Frederick
89781. Flowers, William
90331. Flye, Charles
90686. Folk, James
91039. Follock, Jesse
91270. Folly, John
90003. Forbes, William
91593. Ford, John
91847. Ford, John
91848. Ford, John
91849. Ford, John
91912. Ford, John
91038. Fortune, William
91111. Fortune, William
90089. Foster, Richard
89990. Foster, William
91315. Foster, William
89879. Fountain, David
89894. Fountain, James
89529. Fowler, Abraham
90846. Fowler, Abraham
91496. Fowler, Abraham
90986. Fowler, George
90382. Frederick, Christopher
90467. Freeman, Howell
90474. Freeman, Moses
90673. Freeman, Roger
91150. Froger, John

*No.*
90803. Frost, Miller
91370. Fryer, William
90049. Fryes, John
91054. Fuller, John
90998. Fulsher, Cason
91236. Furnavil, Richard
91213. Futral, Joseph

**G**

89751. Gagens, Michael
90656. Gailor, James
89539. Gainer, Samuel
90886. Gainer, Samuel
91541. Gainer, Samuel
90178. Gallimore, John
90152. Gallimore, William
91407. Gandy, Ephriam
89734. Ganess, Wiley
89807. Ganis, Bigford
90306. Gardner, Thomas
90327. Garland, William
89763. Garns, James
90588. Garrett, Samuel
90461. Garris, Hardy
91160. Garrisen, Stephen
89870. Gatlin, Edward
91297. Gatlin, Jesse
89857. Gay, Allen
89830. Gay, Babel
89898. Gay, Henry
90350. Gay, James
91404. Gay, James
89899. Gay, Richard
91449. Gay, William
91154. Gazloy, Charles
90893. George, Britain
91534. George Britain
89537. George Britain
91080. George Lewis
91591. Gerrard, Charles
91835. Gerrard, Charles
91836. Gerrard, Charles
91837. Gerrard, Charles
91886. Gerrard, Charles
90431. Gibbson, David
89535. Gibson, Collin
89986. Gibson, Henry
90471. Gilbert, John
89258. Gilham, Thomas
91311. Gill, Alexander
89650. Gill, John
90911. Gill, John
91557. Gill, John
91094. Gill, Robert

No.
91117. Gillespie, Isaac
89534. Gilmore, Thomas
90579. Ginn, Elijah
89743. Ginn, Hardy
90728. Ginn, Jacob
90437. Ginn, James
91184. Ginnings, George
89803. Gist, Robert
89536. Glandor, Major
89836. Glover, John
89885. Glover, John
90256. Godet, John
90037. Gonzelos, Ferdinand
91157. Good, John
91450. Gooden, Martin
91134. Gooden, Robertson
91212. Gooden, Willie
90743. Gooding, Thomas
89788. Goodson, Israel
90727. Goodson, John
89859. Goodwin, John
89765. Goon, William
90486. Gordon, Sol
90710. Graff, Anthony
90406. Graham, Arthur
90387. Graham, Francis
90952. Graham, Francis
89773. Graham, John
90634. Graham, John
90867. Graham, John
91515. Graham, John
89664. Graham, William
89892. Grant, Giles
91089. Grant, John
91603. Graves, Francis
91793. Graves, Francis
91794. Graves, Francis
91795. Graves, Francis
91910. Graves, Francis
90476. Gray, Cox
89666. Gray, Henry
89641. Grayham, John
91875. Green, James W.
91853. Green, James W.
91854. Green, James W.
91855. Green, James W.
89907. Green, Sutton
91458. Green, William
90026. Greenman, Caleb
90781. Grice, Gabriel
90207. Griffin, Dempsey
90393. Griffin, Edward
90122. Griffin, Ezekial
90203. Griffin, James

No.
90790. Griffin, James
91558. Griffin, William
90913. Griffin, William
90357. Grindstaff, Micharl
91095. Grinnage, John
91401. Grissell, Willie
90547. Guard, Joshua
89686. Guin, Roland
91167. Guinn, Samuel
89538. Gurley, Joseph
89882. Gurley, Joseph
90896. Gurley, Joseph
91532. Gurley, Joseph

H
91250. Haddock, Andrew
91582. Hadley, Joshua
91784. Hadley, Joshua
91785. Hadley, Joshua
91786. Hadley, Joshua
91860. Hadley, Joshua
91283. Hadley, William
90843. Hadsock, Peter
91491. Hadsock, Peter
90339. Hagenton, Jesse
86983. Hailey, Caleb
86984. Hailey Caleb
86735. Haines, John
90007. Hair, James
91576. Hall, Clement
91763. Hall, Clement
91764. Hall, Clement
91765. Hall, Clement
91879. Hall, Clement
89996. Hall, James
90341. Hall, James
90356. Hall, Jesse
89746. Hall, John
91129. Hall, John
91321. Hall, John
90445. Hall, Joshua
90478. Hall, William
90212. Halloway, Thomas
89995. Hambleton, Stewart
90218. Hallaway, Thomas
89995. Hambleton, Stewart
41410. Hammock, Samuel
89656. Hammon, Isaac
90676. Hammond, Isaac
90202. Hammontre, Griffin
91660. Handy, Levin
89729. Haney, Anthony
91392. Harden, Lewis
89547. Hardick, Richard

*No.*
90462. Hardick, Richard
90197. Harding, Israel
89630. Hardrock, Peter
90861. Hardwick, Richard
91509. Hardwick, Richard
91091. Hargrave, Hezekiah
91715. Hargrave, Hezekiah
91716. Hargrave, Hezekiah
91717. Hargrave, Hezekiah
91871. Hargrave, Hezekiah
90559. Harman, James
91613. Harney, Selbey
91614. Harney, Selbey
91615. Harney, Selbey
91896. Harney, Silbey
91448. Harper, Jett
90231. Harper, John
90155. Harper, Moses
90235. Harper, Moses
89677. Harper, Soseph
89669. Harper, William
91045. Harris, Benjamin
91127. Harris, Edward
89922. Harris, Elijah
90310. Harris, Henry
91348. Harris, Jesse
89889. Harris, Nelson
89848. Harris, Robert
90765. Harris, Thomas
90010. Harrison, Francis
89769. Harrison, Henry
90769. Harrison, Henry
89928. Harrison, Thomas
89852. Harrison, William
89544. Hart, Adam
90836. Hart, Adam
91484. Hart, Adam
91234. Hart, Samuel
90316. Harvey, Absolom
90892. Harvey, Joshua
91533. Harvey, Joshua
90020. Hassell, Joseph
90459. Hatch, Alexander
91169. Hawkins, Ephraim
91258. Hawkins, Lorton
91811. Hayes, Robert
91812. Hayes, Robert
91813. Hayes, Robert
91870. Hayes, Robert
91358. Hayes, William
90259. Haynes, William
91587. Hayse, Robert
89954. Headright, John
89933. Hedgeforth, John

*No.*
91409. Hedgepathe, Abraham
90247. Hem, John
90227. Henderson, Robert
90032. Hendricke, Albert
91276. Hendricks, Samuel
90695. Henry, William
91001. Hensley, William
91071. Henson, William
90961. Herrington, Jiles
91226. Herrington, Samuel
90107. Herrington, Thomas
90929. Herrington, Thomas
90195. Hester, John
90688. Hester, Joseph
90018. Hews, James
90993. Hickman, Jacob
89690. Hicks, Micajah
91240. Hicks, Micajah
91088. Highfield, Hezekiah
90002. Hill, Jesse
90201. Hill, John
91599. Hill, John
91832. Hill, John
91833. Hill, John
91834. Hill, John
91935. Hill, John
90371. Hill, Richard
90346. Hill, Robert
89777. Hill, Samuel
91122. Hill, Solomon
89543. Hill, Thomas
90696. Hill, William
90362. Hilton, Arnold
91444. Hind, Daniel
89724. Hinde, John
91396. Hinds, Benjamin
89703. Hinds, Lewis
90590. Hobbs, Jacob
90166. Hobbs, Joseph
90305. Hodgepeth, Peter
90217. Hodges, William
90745. Hogg, Andrew
90757. Hogg, Gideon
91625. Hogg, Thomas
91626. Hogg, Thomas
91627. Hogg, Thomas
91897. Hogg, Thomas
91145. Holland, Bazil
91446. Holland, Daniel
90639. Holland, Henry
91159. Hollinghead, Benjamin
91174. Hollinghead, Thomas
91052. Hollis, James
89541. Holly, Benjamin

No.
90649. Holly, John
91597. Holmes, Hardy
91820. Holmes, Hardy
91821. Holmes, Hardy
91822. Holmes, Hardy
91918. Holmes, Hardy
90532. Holmes, John
90533. Holmes, Josiah
91345. Holston, Bazel
90370. Holt, Thomas
89712. Honey, John
91082. Hood, Charles
91083. Hood, William
90209. Hooder, John
91255. Hope, William
90292. Hopkins, Joseph
90365. Hopper, John
90277. Horn, Henry
90349. Hornsby, Thomas
90149. Howard, Edward
90104. Howard, Joseph
89924. Howard, William
89925. Howard, Willis
90183. Howell, Dempsey
89655. Howey, Joshua
91445. Howry, Burrell
90237. Hubbard, John
90153. Huddleton, Robert
90949. Hudson, Miles
90348. Huffey, John
89747. Huggins, James
89768. Huggins, Luke
91260. Hughes, William
91108. Hughes, Willis
89546. Hukins, James
90822. Hukins, James
91537. Hukins, James
90420. Hunsucker, Abraham
90094. Hunter, Asa
91044. Hurley, David
89623. Hurley, John
90675. Hurley, John
90869. Hurley, John
91517. Hurley, John
91040. Hurley, Joseph
90126. Huse, Joseph
90354. Hutchens, Edward
90099. Hutson, Miles
90434. Hutway, John

I

91125. Ijmes, Vachil
91637. Ingles, John
91638. Ingles, John
91639. Ingles, John

No.
91881. Ingles, John
89550. Ives, James
90849. Ives, James
91497. Ives, James
91586. Ivey, Curtis
91790. Ivey, Curtis
91791. Ivey, Curtis
91792. Ivey, Curtis
91929. Ivey, Curtis
89548. Ivey, David
90005. Ivey, Reuben

J

89551. Jack ......
91074. Jackson, Coleby
90213. Jackson, James
91415. Jacobs, Josiah
91306. Jacobs, Primas
90534. Jacobs, Zachariah
90581. James, Benjamin
89865. James, Jeremiah
91429. James, William
89738. Jarvis, John
91123. Jarvis, John
89906. Jeffrey, Drewry
90147. Jeffries, Jacob
90281. Jenneson, Absolom
90623. Jero, Alexander
90278. Jessey, John
90110. Johnson, Absolam
89555. Johnson, Crawford
89862. Johnson, Daniel
90127. Johnson, John
90540. Johnson, John
91865. Johnson, Joseph
90824. Johnston, Crawford
91472. Johnston, Crawford
90754. Johnston, Ephraim
90964. Johnston, Frederick
90566. Johnston, William
89552. Joiner, Benjamin
90829. Joiner, Benjamin
91478. Joiner, Benjamin
90483. Jones, Abraham
91032. Jones, Abraham
89904. Jones, Benjamin
90473. Jones, Britain
90638. Jones, David
91185. Jones, Francis
90093. Jones, Frederick
90266. Jones, Frederick
89905. Jones, Freeman
89876. Jones, Griffith
90096. Jones, Henry
90388. Jones, Isaac

*No.*
89696. Jones, James
90311. Jones, James
90325. Jones, James
89786. Jones, John
90482. Jones, John
90614. Jones, Jonathan
89549. Jones, Josiah
90921. Jones, Josiah
91568. Jones, Josiah
91103. Jones, Moses
89927. Jones, Nathan
91334. Jones, Nathan
89789. Jones, Nathan
91685. Jones, Samuel
91686. Jones, Samuel
91687. Jones, Samuel
91895. Jones, Samuel
90227. Jones, Thomas
90304. Jones, William
90516. Jones, William
90275. Jones, Zachariah
89554. Jordan, Caleb
90823. Jordan, Caleb
90846. Jordan, Fountain
90295. Jordan, Zeblin
91471. Jorden, Caleb
91494. Jorden, Fountain
90565. Jorden, Nathan
90299. Jordon, Stephen

**K**

90616. Kates, Thomas
90499. Kean, Jacob
90613. Kean, Saucer
91360. Keay, James
91443. Keay, William
90018. Keel, Charles
90257. Keel, Hardy
90658. Keen, William
90805. Keener, John
90796. Keener, Martin
91278. Kellehan, Isaac
91062. Kelley, James
90945. Kellum, George
90932. Kellum, John
91346. Kelly, John
90799. Kenedy, John
91372. Kenedy, John
90637. Kenedy, Richard
91381. Kent, Levy
91366. Kersey, James
90538. Ketter, Nehemiah
91207. Kidds, John
91251. Kilpatrick, Hugh
90186. Kilyan, Jacob

*No.*
90131. Kilyon, John
90300. King, Anthony
90322. King, David
89557. King, Edward
90915. King, Edward
91049. King, Edward
91560. King, Edward
91093. King, Vincent
90608. King, Woody
90133. Kittle, Jacob
90485. Knight, Absolom
90286. Knight, George
89556. Knight, Miles
90910. Knight, Miles
91556. Knight, Miles

**L**

89558. Lacho, Francis
91313. Lackey, Thomas
91581. Lamb, Abner
91799. Lamb, Abner
91800. Lamb, Abner
91801. Lamb, Abner
91872. Lamb, Abner
89778. Lain, Jacob
89562. Lamb, Gibbs
90888. Lamb, Gibbs
91543. Lamb, Gibbs
89560. Leach, John
90679. Lead, Alende M.
89563. Lewis, Isaac
90744. Lamb, John
90655. Land, Henry
90087. Land, John
90594. Lane, Benjamin
90563. Lane, Citizen
90570. Lane, Timothy
91008. Lane, William
91028. Larcy, Patrick
91463. Larbe, Francis
90814. Larbo, Francis
90609. Lassiter, Jesse
91378. Lassiter, James
90229. Laston, Camas
90248. Laughinghouse, John
91096. Law, John
90333. Lawbun, James
90450. Lawrence, Joseph
91724. Lawrence, Nat
91894. Lawrence, Nath
89730. Lawrence, William
90735. Lawson, William
91481. Leach, John
91387. Lee, Aaron
90941. Lee, James

*No.*
89561. Lee, John
90831. Lee, John
91474. Lee, John
90312. Lee, Richard
90833. Leech, John
90946. Leggett, Abraham
90507. Leigh, Lewis
90812. Leighton, William
91219. Lepard, William
91025. Lesley, John
89831. Lethgo, William
88917. Letour, Conrad
89900. Lett, James
90025. Lewis, David
90079. Lewis, Frederick
89884. Lewis, Hardy
90862. Lewis, Isaac
91510. Lewis, Isaac
90320. Lewis, James
90550. Lewis, Jones
90683. Lewis, Jonathan
90399. Lewis, Marshall
89890. Lewis, Richard
90261. Lewis, Richard
89701. Lewis, Thomas
90442. Lilley, Lewis
91221. Linden, Patrick
91050. Lindsey, James
90287. Litter, George
90288. Litter, William
91058. Littleton, William
91124. Loller, John
91412. Long, James
89226. Long, John
90415. Long, John
89564. Long, Wiliam
90822. Long, William
91470. Long, William
90055. Loomax, William
91916. Loomis, Jonathan
89654. Love, Samuel
89499. Loveday, Thomas
91138. Low, Thomas
91036. Loyesey, Boling
90321. Lucas, Thomas
91034. Lucas, Thomas
90876. Lucey, Burrel
91524. Lucey, Burrel
89559. Lucy, Bunel
91069. Ludwick, Lewis
89500. Lynn, David
91939. Lynn, David
91302. Lyons, William
91572. Lytle, Archibald
91757. Lytle, Archibald

*No.*
91752. Lytle, Archibald
91753. Lytle, Archibald
91581. Lytle, William
91781. Lytle, William
91782. Lytle, William
91783. Lytle, William
91920. Lytle, Archibald
91926. Lytle, William

M

90767. McAffee, John
90644. McCall, Benjamin
91059. M'Callister, John
90793. McCarthy, James
90433. M'Caskey, Allan
89514. M'Cay, Daniel
90039. M'Clannen, Thomas
90788. McClenchorn, Malcom
91204. M'Clund, John
89760. M'Clunney, William
90786. M'Cormic, Archibald
91367. M'Coy, John
90866. M'Craw, Roger
91514. M'Craw, Roger
91114. M'Culloh, Francis
90517. McDaniel, Hugh
89525. McDonald, Arthur
90885. McDonald, Arthur
91540. McDonald, Arthur
90653. M'Donald, Col.
90716. M'Donald, Daniel
90116. M'Dugald, Dugald
90243. M'Durmid, Malcomb
90687. M'Farland, Morgan
90839. M'Farter, Daniel
89531. M'Fater, Daniel
91487. M'Fater, Daniel
89726. M'Gee, Thomas
89737. M'Ginnis, Daniel
90242. M'Gounds, John
89519. M'Graw, Roger
90809. McIntyre, Charles
90808. McIntyre, Gilbert
90225. M'Intyre, James
90920. M'Intire, William
91562. M'Intire, William
91340. McIntosh, Morticae
90680. M'Kay, John
90662. M'Kee, William
89632. M'Kenny, Robert
90847. M'Kenny, Robert
91004. M'Kensey, Alexander
89651. M'Kensey, William
90668. M'Kensie, Hugh
90635. M'Ketham, John

No.
91495. M'Kinney, Robert
90518. M'Kinsey, William
90917. M'Kinsey, William
91561. M'Kinsey, William
89714. M'Knight, Andrew
91606. M'Lain, William
90021. M'Lamore, John
90780. M'Lane, Hugh
91031. M'Laren
90669. M'Laughlin, Alexander
90679. M'Lead, Alenonde
90797. M'Leod, John
91673. M'Nees, John
91674. M'Nees, John
91675. M'Nees, John
91907. M'Nees, John
90804. M'Neil, Hector
91574. M'Ree, Griffith J.
91757. M'Ree, Griffith J.
91758. M'Ree, Griffith J.
91759. M'Ree, Griffith J.
91898. M'Ree, Griffith J.
90642. M'Ree, John
91118. M'Swine, William
89608. M'Vay, Eli
90850. M'Vay, Ely
91498. Ely
89607. M'Vay, John
89942. Mabery, Benjamin
91187. Madra, Darling
89762. Madross, John
90095. Mainer, Josiah
91170. Mainis, Frederick
91087. Malottee, Jacob
91222. Manders, William
90810. Manley, Allen
91295. Manley, Littleton
90150. Manley, Moses
91431. Manley, Moses
91294. Manley, William
91241. Manning, John
90792. Manuel, Jasse
90244. Marlin, James
90674. Maroney, Anthony
91181. Marritt, Drury
89855. Marsh, Barnett
91709. Marshal, Dixon
91710. Marshal, Dixon
91711. Marshal, Dixon
89840. Marshall, Adam
91867. Marshall, Dixon
90062. Martin, Absolam
91223. Martin, Gabriel
91361. Martin, Jeile

90232. Martin, Joshua
90444. Mashum, William
89764. Mason, Patrick
89571. Mason, Philip
91566. Mason, Philip
90236. Mason, William
91158. Massey, Joseph
91172. Massey, Philip
90088. Maston, Thomas
91459. Mathews, Jacob
90764. Mathews, John
90169. Mathias, James
89701. Mathias, Moses
90761. Mathias, Stephen
90355. Matterson, George
90067. Mathews, Daniel
90345. Mathews, Riot
91165. Matzlear, John
90573. May, Joseph
91290. Meaner, Henry
90273. Medlin, Shadrack
90794. Meek, John
91393. Meeks, William
90047. Meggs, James
89860. Melteri, Jethro
89771. Melton, Benjamin
91019. Meredith, William
90524. Messick, Aaron
91242. Michel, Abner
91248. Michell, Willial
89573. Middleton, Solomon
90835. Middleton, Solomon
91483. Middleton, Solomon
90016. Midget, William
90411. Miller, Benedic
91189. Miller, Conrad
91271. Miller, Conrad
91146. Miller, George
89643. Miller, Henry
90898. Miller, Henry
91546. Miller, Henry
90562. Miller, John
90123. Miller, Martin
90258. Miller, Martin
90798. Miller, Peter
91343. Mills, Jacob
91676. Mills, James
91677. Mills, James
91678. Mills, James
91917. Mills, James
90436. Mills, John
90063. Mires, David
90102. Misser, John
90739. Mitchell, Charles
91457. Mitchell, Drewry

*No.*
90730. Mitchell, George
89953. Mitchell, John
90035. Mitchell, John
91375. Mitchell, Oliver
89929. Mitchell, Theophilus
89867. Mitchell, William
89976. Mitchell, William
90734. Molden, Humphrey
91235. Monk, James
90084. Moody, Thomas
91205. Moon, Sampson
89711. Mooney, William
91814. Moor, James
91815. Moor, James
91816. Moor, James
90771. Moor, John
90205. Moor, Lemuel
90641. Moor, Willis
91029. Moore, Elijah
91682. Moore, Elijah
91683. Moore, Elijah
91684. Moore, Elijah
90491. Moore, George
91000. Moore, James
91014. Moore, James
91596. Moore, James
91873. Moore, James
90234. Moore, Jesse
91015. Moore, Simeon
90124. Moore, William
90069. Morgan, Benjamin
89570. Morgan, Bennet
90816. Morgan, Bennet
91465. Morgan, Bennet
91441. Morgan, Isaac
89866. Morgan, John
90140. Morgan, John
90391. Morgan, Reuben
89566. Morgan, Sampson
90863. Morrin, Morris
90192. Morris, Abraham
89567. Morris, Coffin
90990. Morris, Nathan
90424. Morris, William
91175. Morris, Witt
89569. Morrison, Alexander
90013. Morriston, John
90065. Morton, William
89572. Mott, Benjamin
91466. Mott, Benjamin
89574. Mott, Edgerton
90817. Motte, Benjamin
91535. Motte, Edgerton
90880. Motte, Edgerton
91142. Moy, John

*No.*
91092. Muckleya, William
91186. Mullen, Michael
91655. Mumford, Joseph
91656. Mumford, Joseph
91657. Mumford, Joseph
91901. Mumford, Joseph
89897. Munger, Jesse
91616. Murfee, Hardy
91617. Murfee, Hardy
91618. Murfee, Hardy
91856. Murfee, Hardy
91309. Murfree, James
90632. Murphy, Archibald
90759. Murphy, Patrick
89963. Murry, Alexander, L.
89682. Murry, Morgan
90469. Musknock, George
91253. Myers, George

**N**

90171. Neal, Christopher
90196. Neal, Philip
91622. Nelson, John
91623. Nelson, John
91624. Nelson, John
89903. Nettles, Shadreck
90630. Newark, Nicholas
89628. Newbury, Mathew
90758. Newby, Mathew
90818. Newby, Mathew
91467. Newby, Mathew
90666. Newman, Joseph
91085. Newton, Edward
90552. Newton, Edward
90526. Newton, Joseph
89719. Newton, Levi
90811. Newton, Patrick
90504. Nicheus, Malicha
90225. Nicholas, William
89886. Nichols, Henry
90503. Nichols, John
90585. Nichols, Joseph
91097. Nichols, William
89813. Nicholson, Isaac
89804. Nisio, Nicholas
90091. Nithucut, William
90174. Nobles, Hezekiah
90983. Nobles, John
90368. Nothern, Solomon
90463. Nowell, Josiah
90329. Nube, Francis
90426. Nusom, Thomas
89576. Nuson, Nathreldred

**O**

90542. Oberton, John
90075. O'Bryan, Richard

*No.*
90011. Odder, Peter
90115. Oliver, John
91335. Oliver, William
91383. Olphin, William
90451. Omery, Jacob
91411. O'Neal, Benjamin
91272. O'Neale, John
89874. Orange, William
90973. Order, Peter
91362. Osborne, Jesse
90398. Osborne, Squire
91299. Osbourne, Morgan
90997. Osteen, William
90448. Outlaw, James
90731. Overton, John
90746. Owen, John
89839. Owens, Etheldred
89896. Owens, Enoch

P

89967. Padgett, John
91553. Pafford, William
89583. Paford, William
90175. Page, Benjamin
91017. Page, Solomon
90776. Palmer, Thomas
91023. Palmore, Elisha
91352. Parish, Edward
91079. Parker, Abraham
90654. Parker, Amos
90753. Parker, Amos
90774. Parker, Arthur
91239. Parker, James
89578. Parker, Jepteth
89784. Parkes, William
91220. Parkes, William
90294. Parks, Andrew
89891. Parks, Hugh
90298. Parks, Peter
90181. Parrott, Nathaniel
90303. Parry, John
89946. Parum, William
89915. Pasens, James
90717. Pasmore, David
91594. Pasteur, Thomas
91808. Pasteurs, Thomas
91809. Pasteurs, Thomas
91810. Pasteurs, Thomas
91869. Pasteurs, Thomas
89828. Pate, Coride
89827. Pate, Edward
91452. Patrick, Spencer
90460. Pattaway, James
91107. Patten, John
90651. Patterson, Duncan

*No.*
90330. Patterson, William
91610. Patton, John
91611. Patton, John
91612. Patton, John
90187. Panks, John
90065. Paul, Philip
90906. Payford, William
90453. Pearce, Edmund
91697. Pearl, James
91698. Pearl, James
91699. Pearl, James
91864. Pearl, James
90435. Pearse, Ephraim
90113. Pearson, Thomas
89581. Pendleton, Benjamin
90782. Penrice, Francis
90556. Penrice, Samuel
90506. Perkins, David
90384. Perkins, Thomas
90142. Petiford, William
91053. Petrie, Peter
91013. Pettie, John
90185. Pettiford, Elias
90148. Pettiford, Philip
89988. Pettijohn, Abraham
90034. Pettis, James
91076. Phillips, Aaron
91328. Phillips, William
91384. Philips, Zachariah
90001. Pierce, Israel
90419. Pierson, Richard
91225. Piland, Peter
90427. Pinkston, William
90059. Pinneger, Martin
90194. Pitman, John
91210. Pitts, James
89580. Platt, John
90852. Platt, John
91500. Platt, John
91177. Pollock, Jesse
89757. Potis, Lewis
91192. Potter, Daniel
90172. Pouh, Henry
40417. Powell, George
90715. Powell, William
90352. Powers, Absolom
90567. Powers, James
90367. Powers, Jesse
90369. Powers, Moses
90375. Pratt, Thomas
90840. Pravey, Nehemiah
91488. Pravey, Nehemiah
89735. Prevet, John
90975. Price, Abner
90167. Price, Edward

No.
90466. Price, Lewis
90919. Price, William
91564. Price, William
89691. Privet, Peter
91075. Privet, William
90748. Procter, Aaron
91414. Proctor, William

Q

90452. Quillany, Shadrack
90078. Quinn, David

R

89930. Raifield, Caleb
91575. Raiford, Robert
91766. Raiford, Robert
91767. Raiford, Robert
91768. Raiford, Robert
91878. Raiford, Robert
90045. Ralph, Thomas
90318. Raper, James
90951. Rahter, Hardy
89913. Ratley, Benjamin
90269. Rawson, Daniel
10667. Ray, Archibald
91182. Rayma, John
90030. Razor, Christopher
90159. Read, Benjamin
91247. Reams, William
90228. Reasoner, John
89672. Reaves, Frederick
90571. Reddick, Abraham
91670. Reed, Jesse
91671. Reed, Jesse
91672. Reed, Jesse
91906. Reed, Jesse
90120. Reed, William
91012. Reel, Joshua
90314. Retley, Micajah
91456. Reynolds, William
85996. Rhea, Joseph
91924. Rhodes, Joseph T.
91578. Rhodes, Joseph, Tho
91772. Rhodes, Joseph, Tho
91773. Rhodes, Joseph, Tho
91774. Rhodes, Jose, Tho
90592. Rhodes, Nathan
90495. Ribber, Daniel
89883. Richards, Curtis
90631. Richards, Nicholas
90967. Richardson, Andrew
90429. Richardson, Ellis
89837. Richardson, John
89854. Richardson, Richard
90464. Richardson, William
89887. Ricks, Benjamin
91152. Rictor, Lewis

No.
89729. Riddle, James
90749. Riggins, James
89973. Riggins, William
90559. Rigsby, James
90070. Riles, William
90670. Riley, Edmund
91046. Riley, William
91121. Riley, William
90791. Rinehart, Jacob
90721. Rising, David
89587. Rivers, Benjamin
90890. Rivers, Benjamin
91545. Rivers, Benjamin
90162. Rix, William
90970. Roberson, John
90392. Roberts, Moses
89640. Roberts, Richard
90619. Roberts, Richard
90860. Roberts, Richard
91508. Roberts, Richard
91115. Roberts, William
90501. Robertson, John
90043. Robertson, Mark
89723. Robertson, Thomas
90270. Robertson, Upsher
90972. Robeson, John
90136. Robinson, Mark
90006. Robinson, Willoughby
90756. Rochee, Amos
90646. Rochell, Aaron
91324. Roe, Jessee
91416. Roger, Daniel
89800. Rogers, Dunstan
90050. Rogers, James
89820. Rogers, Parker
90928. Rogers, Parker
90685. Rogers, William
90700. Rogers, William
90472. Rolany, Daniel
90160. Rolls, James
91130. Roman, Thomas
90223. Roper, George
89961. Ross, James
91009. Roundtree, Jesse
90204. Rowe, Jesse
90344. Rowland, William
91353. Rozier, Daniel
91369. Rozier, David
90943. Rozier, John
90684. Runnels, Ephraim
90409. Russ, Epaphros
91113. Rutherford, Thomas
89822. Rutland, Randolph
89821. Rutland, Reding
89634. Ryal, William

*No.*

91499. Ryal, William
90851. Ryal, William
89586. Ryan, Cornelius
90914. Ryan, Cornelius
91559. Ryan, Cornelius
89584. Ryon, Patrick

**S**

90377. Sailor, George
89591. Salmon, Vincent
90834. Salmon, Vincent
91482. Salmon, Vincent
90401. Sampson, Isaac
89989. Sanderlin, Josiah
90962. Sanderlin, Robert
91057. Sanders, Henry
89659. Sanders, Robt.
91273. Sanders, Samuel
91742. Sanders, William
91743. Sanders, William
91744. Sanders, William
91330. Sanders, William
89589. Santee, Caesar
90827. Santee, Caesar
91476. Santee, Caesar
90019. Santee, Michael
89941. Saunders, John
90496. Saunders, Thomas
91408. Savage, Micajah
90468. Savage, Moses
90737. Savage, Thomas
90428. Sawyer, Joseph
90989. Scarborough, Nathan
90372. Scarborough, Samuel
90602. Scarborough, Shadrick
90661. Scarlet, Thomas
90071. Scorborough, Stephen
90712. Scorlet, James
90718. Scorlet, William
90296. Scott, Dannis
91209. Scott, Dennis
91026. Scott, Drury
89871. Scott, Emanuel
91437. Scott, Isaac
90337. Scott, Isam
89126. Scott, James
91428. Scott, James
90611. Scott, Saul
90974. Scott, Thomas
90705. Screws, Joseph
91263. Screws, William
91425. Scrugs, Richard
90358. Scudder, Abner
90800. Scurlock, James
91748. Scurlock, James

*No.*

91749. Scurlock, James
91750. Scurlock, James
91937. Scurlock, James
90760. Seaborne, Joseph
90279. Seagraves, John
91077. Seagreaves, John
90064. Searly, Christopher
89775. Sears, Asia
89695. Searsey, Asa
90857. Seayers, Robert
91505. Seayers, Robert
89679. Sebriel, Joshua
90489. Seburn, Joseph
89680. Segraves, Jacob
90738. Sellers, Jordan
89766. Sellis, Thomas
90528. Sessams, Asel
89637. Seyers, Robert
91579. Sharpe, Anthony
91775. Sharpe, Anthony
91776. Sharpe, Anthony
91777. Sharpe, Anthony
91925. Sharpe, Anthony
89596. Sharpe, Benjamin
90883. Sharpe, Benjamin
91538. Sharpe, Benjamin
91712. Shaw, Daniel
91713. Shaw, Daniel
91714. Shaw, Daniel
91868. Shaw, Daniel
90660. Shaw, Duncan
90933. Shearer, Frederick
90768. Sheffield, William
89731. Shelton, James
89594. Shepherd, John
90872. Shepherd, John
91520. Shepherd, John
90074. Shepherd, William
90942. Shepherd, William
91002. Shepherd, Willoughby
90068. Sherod, Benjamin
91132. Shippard, Bird
90416. Shoemaker, Randal
90596. Shrode, Adam
90199. Shurley, Thomas
90807. Shy, Jesse
89592. Sidle, Jesse
89971. Sikes, Henry
90505. Sikes, James
91347. Silas, Thomas
91100. Silvester, Nathan
91148. Simkins, Joseph
90479. Simmonds, Alexander
90520. Simmonds, Jeremiah
90645. Simmons, John

| No. | | No. | |
|---|---|---|---|
| 89979. | Simmonds, John | 90988. | Smith, Stephen |
| 90117. | Simmons, Willis | 89718. | Smith, Thomas |
| 91300. | Simons, Felix | 89965. | Smith, William |
| 89902. | Simons, John | 90233. | Smith, William |
| 90992. | Simpkins, John | 90324. | Smith, William |
| 89636. | Simpson, John | 91442. | Snell, Allen |
| 90856. | Simpson, John | 90512. | Snider, Anthony |
| 91504. | Simpson, John | 89935. | Snider, Christain |
| 90514. | Simpson, Richard | 89694. | Solomon, Lazarus |
| 89597. | Simpson, Samuel | 90240. | Solomon, William |
| 90889. | Simpson, Samuel | 89414. | Southall, Furney |
| 91544. | Simpson, Samuel | 91322. | Spain, Thomas |
| 90513. | Simpson, William | 90957. | Spearman, George |
| 90238. | Sinclair, William | 90430. | Spearpoint, Joseph |
| 90184. | Sink, Paul | 89944. | Spears, Kindred |
| 90338. | Sippo, Hill | 91391. | Spears, Willis |
| 90877. | Sisk, James | 90385. | Speers, Joseph |
| 91525. | Sisk, Janes | 90246. | Spelmore, Aaron |
| 90576. | Skinner, Evan | 90465. | Spelmore, Jacob |
| 91418. | Skinner, John | 90021. | Spewell, Godfrey |
| 90545. | Skipper, James | 89863. | Spires, Thomas |
| 90762. | Slade, Frederick | 91090. | Springfield, Michael |
| 90177. | Slade, James | 90092. | Springs, Micajah |
| 91055. | Slade, Nathan | 90262. | Squires, Andrew |
| 91718. | Slade, Stephen | 89847. | Stacks, Benjamin |
| 91719. | Slade, Stephen | 89893. | Stallion, Moses |
| 91720. | Slade, Stephen | 91423. | Stamy, John |
| 91888. | Slade, Stephen | 90956. | Standley, James |
| 91808. | Slade, Thomas | 90440. | Stanfield, James |
| 90692. | Slaughter, John | 91598. | Steed, Jesse |
| 90690. | Slaughter, Rob't. | 91826. | Steed, Jesse |
| 89697. | Smart, John | 91827. | Steed, Jesse |
| 89921. | **Smith, Aaron** | 91828. | Steed, Jesse |
| 89985. | Smith, Benjamin | 91874. | Steed, Jesse |
| 91191. | Smith, Burrel | 90707. | Steel, William |
| 91021. | Smith, Ezekial | 90741. | Steelman, William |
| 90132. | Smith, Henry | 90494. | Stephens, Benjamin |
| 89997. | Smith, Isaac | 90447. | Stephens, Hugh |
| 90702. | Smith, Jacob | 89702. | Sterling, Elihu |
| 91200. | Smith, Jacob | 89707. | Stevens, Henry |
| 89593. | Smith, James | 89706. | Stevens, James |
| 90541. | Smith, James | 91286. | Stevens, Thomas |
| 90922. | Smith, James | 91180. | Stewart, Charles |
| 91569. | Smith, James | 91643. | Stewart, Charles |
| 90703. | Smith, Jeremiah | 91644. | Stewart, Charles |
| 90701. | Smith, Job | 91645. | Stewart, Charles |
| 89744. | Smith, John | 91883. | Stewart, Charles |
| 90527. | Smith, John | 90206. | Stewart, Daniel |
| 91139. | Smith, John | 91037. | Stewart, Dempsey |
| 91327. | Smith, John | 91104. | Stewart, Dempsey |
| 91211. | Smith, Peter | 91301. | Stewart, James |
| 89841. | Smith, Richard | 91316. | Still, John |
| 91341. | Smith, Richard | 91153. | Stilliard, Peter |
| 91178. | Smith, Samuel | 89716. | Stillwel, Jacob |

No.
90042. Stiwall, Frederick
90755. Stokely, Peter
90546. Stokely, Peter
90058. Stone, John
90802. Strange, William
89733. Stricking, Frederick
89931. Strickland, John
91016. Stringer, Hezekiah
89639. Stringer, John
90509. Stringer, John
90871. Stringer, John
91519. Stringer, John
90252. Stringer, Mingar
90215. Stringer, Noah
90722. Stuart, Daniel
90729. Stuart, John
91385. Sturdevant, Charles
90624. Suggs, Aleygood
90625. Suggs, Ezekial
89223. Suit, Jesse
90598. Sulivant, Owen
90130. Sullivan, James
89588. Sullivan, John
91694. Summers, John
91695. Summers, John
91696. Summers, John
91859. Summers, John
91230. Sumner, Francis
89709. Sumner, George
90060. Surls, Thomas
89875. Sweat, Abraham
89645. Sweat, David
90900. Sweat, David
91548. Sweat, David
90342. Swinney, Thomas
89920. Syas, Jesse
90135. Sykes, Dempsey
90960. Sykes, James
89684. Sweetman, William
89590. Sykes, Sampson
90838. Sykes, Sampson
91486. Sykes, Sampson
91033. Sylvester, Nathan

T
91120. Taddss, James
89840. Tailton, James
89947. Talton, Joseph
91314. Talton, Joseph
91338. Tann, Drury
90193. Tanner, Jinnings
91329. Tarber, Samuel
91858. Tatum, Howell
91730. Tatum, James
91731. Tatum, James

No.
91732. Tatum, James
91911. Tatum, James
89999. Taxey, Nathaniel
89603. Tayborn, Joel
90830. Tayborn, Joel
89943. Taybourn, Burrell
91479. Taybourn, Joel
91280. Taylor, Abel
89660. Taylor, Abraham
89600. Taylor, Benjamin
90414. Taylor, Emanuel
91281. Taylor, James
89849. Taylor, John
91279. Taylor, John
90521. Taylor, Lewis
90054. Taylor, Samuel
91349. Taylor, Valentine J.
90985. Taylor, William
91116. Terry, Pompey
90308. Thackston, William
89869. Thomas, Amasa
89642. Thomas, Caleb
90859. Thomas, Caleb
91507. Thomas, Caleb
90144. Thomas, James
89810. Thomas, Philemon
90076. Thomas, Philip
89856. Thomas, Samuel
90251. Thomas, Stephen
89819. Thomas, Thomas
89598. Thomas, William
90845. Thomas, William
91493. Thomas, William
90607. Thompson, George
90004. Thompson, Jesse
90353. Thompson, John
91065. Thompson, John
91131. Thompson, John
89881. Thompson, Nicholas
89667. Thompson, Samuel
91066. Thompson, William
91202. Thompson, William
91018. Thristin, William
90597. Tice, Henry
90605. Tice, James
91284. Tillery, Jacob
90083. Tillman, William
90410. Tilly Jacob
90073. Tilman, Aaron
90188. Tinon, James
89964. Tins, Jonathan
89761. Tipper, William
91073. Tippet, George
90979. Talbert, John
90481. Tomlinson, Aaron

*No.*
89626. Toney, Anthony
90923. Toney, Anthony
91570. Toney, Anthony
90336. Toney, John
91440. Torbush, Robert
90537. Townley, Philemon
90477. Trader, Jonathan
89604. Trapp, Elijah
91126. Trent, William
90488. Trotman, Thomas
90319. Tucker, Curell
89599. Tucker, Gray
89625. Tucker, James
90912. Tucker, James
90561. Tucker, John
91006. Tucker, John
90015. Turner, Arthur
89806. Turner, David
89687. Twigg, David
89601. Tyack, Thomas
89661. Tyer, Thomas
91413. Tyler, Moss
89602. Tyler, Owen
90881. Tyler, Owen
91536. Tyler, Owen
90497. Tyler, Thomas
91382. Tyner, Daniel
90959. Tyner, William
91398. Tyser, Ellis

**U**
89663. Uell, William
90907. Underdoo, Dempsey
91554. Underdoo, Dempsey
89605. Undudoo, Dempsey
91143. Unger, Lawrence

**V**
90100. Vallo, Nicholas
91231. Vance, David
90583. Varden, David
90361. Vaughn, William
91238. Vessire, Lemuel
91067. Viccory, Luke
91190. Vick, Jacob
89704. Vick, Joseph
91256. Vicker, Thomas
91298. Vickery, Marmiduke
89608. Vickry, John
90198. Vines, John
90530. Vines, John
90531. Vines, Samuel
89609. Vose, Joseph
90902. Vose, Joseph

**W**
90081. Waddle, James
91264. Wade, John

*No.*
91098. Wadsworth, William
91199. Waide, Elisha
91356. Wainwright, Obediah
90085. Walden, John
89888. Walker, Jeremiah
89939. Walker, John
90938. Walker, William
91266. Wall, Jonathan
90480. Wall, Richard
90773. Wallace, Thomas
89615. Wallis, George
90129. Wallis, James
90145. Wallis, John
91214. Walter, Nathaniel
90977. Walters, Jeremiah
90916. Walters, Solomon
91703. Walton, William
91704. Walton, William
91705. Walton, William
91861. Walton, William
90577. Warberton, Solomon
91310. Warbuton, Thomas
91512. Warbuton, Thomas
91176. Ward, William
89978. Ward, Willis
90146. Warf, George
90364. Warren, Archibald
90363. Warren, John
90364. Warren, Archibald
90363. Warren, John
91342. Warren, Samuel
90086. Warwick, Wiat
89617. Waters, Solomon
89620. Waters, Solomon
91565. Waters, Solomon
91368. Watkins, Benjamin
90787. Watson, Alexander
89638. Watson, Lott
90858. Watson, Lott
91506. Watson, Lott
90789. Watson, Neal
90143. Watt, James
90413. Weaks, Dixon
90601. Weathers, Willis
89853. Weaver, Benjamin
89845. Weaver, Daniel
90226. Weaver, Edward
89992. Webb, Jacob
90543. Webb, John
91196. Webb, Lewis
89998. Webb, Rice
91351. Webb, Samuel
90681. Weeks, Levi
91330. Welch, Noel C.
90112. Welch, Thomas

No.
90894. Welch, William
91529. Welch, William
89612. Wells, John
90842. Wells, John
91490. Wells, John
89614. Welsh, William
91135. Welsh, James
90539. West, Merideth
90955. West, Samuel
89873. West, William
90151. Westbrok, William
90826. Westerdale, Francis
91475. Westerdale, Francis
90723. Western, John
89613. Westudale, Francis
90899. Whaley, Ezekial
91547. Whaley, Ezekial
90657. Wheeler, Asa
89705. Wheeler, Benjamin
91159. Wheeler, David
89621. White, Benjamin
90832. White, Benjamin
90981. White, Benjamin
91480. White, Benjamin
90446. White, Church
91031. White, Churchill
90995. White, David
90742. White, Edgar
91377. White, George
90170. White, Hampton
89616. White, Jacob
91405. White, John
90138. White, Philip
91379. White, William
91070. Whitehead, John
90980. Whitehouse, Anthony
90934. Whitfield, Willis
91457. Whitley, Micajah
91237. Whittaker, Robert
91252. Widener, Samuel
91102. Wiggins, Arthur
91277. Wiggins, James
89949. Wiggins, Elisha
89611. Wiggins, Levi
91477. Wiggins, Levi
90828. Wiggins, Levy
91101. Wiggins, Mathews
90652. Wiggins, William
89940. Wilburn, Zachariah
89676. Wilder, William
90000. Wiley, James
91307. Wilford, Archibald
91374. Wilford, Archibald
91371. Wilford, James
90134. Wilkins, Elijah

No.
90599. Wilkins, George
90671. Wilkins, Kinchen
90219. Wilkins, Thomas
91359. Wilkins, Thomas
90307. Wilkinson, John
91909. Wilkinson, Reuben
89610. William, Peter
89919. Williams, Allenby
89190. Williams, Benjamin
91447. Williams, Benjamin
91419. Williams, Colden
90650. Williams, David
91308. Williams, Dudley
89633. Williams, Edward
90544. Williams, Edward
89619. Williams, Francis
90887. Williams, Francis
91542. Williams, Francis
91285. Williams, Jeremiah
90713. Williams, John
91933. Williams, Nath
91745. Williams, Nathan
91746. Williams, Nathan
91747. Williams, Nathan
90080. Williams, Nicholas
90553. Williams, Robert
90108. Williams, Samuel
90267. Williams, Stephen
90954. Williams, Stephen
91229. Williams, William
90510. Williamson, Charles
91336. Williamson, Francis
90340. Williamson, William
90265. Williford, Theophilus
89978. Willing, Evan
90664. Willson, James
90402. Willson, Robert
90053. Willson, Thomas
91183. Willson, Thomas
89683. Willson, William
90208. Willson, William
91144. Wilson, John
91288. Wilton, James
89857. Winburn, Philip
91450. Winder, Levin
91451. Winder, William
91452. Winder, William
91453. Winder, William
91454. Winder, William
90438. Winley, James
91164. Winne, Zachariah
90418. Winters, Moses
89832. Wise, Jesse
89790. Witley, Micajah

*No.*
91303. Witt, Burgess
91445. Wood, Bennet
89618. Wood, Charles
91539. Wood, Charles
90884. Wood, Charles
90284. Wood, Isaac
89699. Wood, John
90264. Wood, John
90157. Wood, Sampson
90706. Wood, William
91024. Wood, Willis
89910. Woodard, Henry
89693. Woodle, Geremiah
91332. Woodle, John
89692. Woodle, Joseph
89937. Woodrough, Edw. H.
91245. Woodward, David

*No.*
91020. Woodward, Edward
90359. Workman, Peter
91228. Worrel, John
91435. Worsley, Leman
90617. Wright, Abraham
91203. Wright, Ewel

Y

90783. Yarborough, David
91658. Yarborough, Edward
91659. Yarborough, Edward
91660. Yarborough, Edward
91902. Yarborough, Edward
91432. Yates, Thomas
91282. Yeates, David
91233. Yorden, John
91149. Young, Michael

# HEITMAN'S REGISTER

[Pages 45, 46, 47]

NOTE—The records of the North Carolina regiments are very meager, owing to the constant and arduous campaigns in the Carolinas, etc., with frequent loss of all their baggage and records. Hence the following list is incomplete, and arrangement defective.

## FIRST NORTH CAROLINA LINE

Col. James Moore, 1st Sept. 1775 to 1st Mch. 1776.
Col. Francis Nash, 10th Apr. 1776 to 5th Feb. 1777.
Col. Thomas Clark, 5th Feb. 1777 to close of war.
Lt. Col. Francis Nash, 1st Sept. 1775 to 10th Apr. 1776.
Lt. Col. Thomas Clark, 10th Apr. 1776 to 5th Feb. 1777.
Lt. Col. Wm. Davis, 5th Feb. 1777 to 1st June 1778.
Lt. Col. Robert Mebane, 1st June 1778 to 8th June 1779.
Lt. Col. Hardy Murfree, 1st Apr. 1778 to July 1782.
Lt. Col. John B. Ashe, 2nd Nov. 1778 to ........
Lt. Col. Wm. L. Davidson, 9th June 1779 to 1st Feb. 1781.
Major Wm. Davis, 10th Apr. 1776 to 5th Feb. 1777.
Major Caleb Granger, 5th Feb. 1777 to 26th Apr. 1777.
Major John Walker, 26th Apr. 1777 to 22nd Dec. 1777.
Major James Emmet, 22nd Dec. 1777 to 1st June, 1778.
Major John B. Ashe, 1st June, 1778 to 2nd Nov. 1778.
Major John Nelson, 6th Feb. 1782 to close of war.

## SECOND NORTH CAROLINA LINE

Col. Robert Howe, 1st Sept. 1775 to 1st Mch. 1776.
Col. Alexander Martin, 10th Apr. 1776 to 22nd Nov. 1777.
Col. John Patten, 22nd Nov. 1777 to 1st Jan. 1783.
Lt. Col. Alexander Martin, 1st Sept. 1775 to 10th Apr. 1776.
Lt. Col. John Patten, 10th Apr. 1776 to 22nd Nov. 1777.
Lt. Col. Selley Harney, 22nd Nov. 1777 to 6th Feb. 1782.
Major John Patten, 1st Sept. 1775 to 10th Apr. 1776.
Major John White, 20th Apr. 1776 to 1st Feb. 1777.
Major Hardy Murfree, 1st Feb. 1777 to 1st Apr. 1778.
Major Reading Blount, 6th Feb. 1782 to close of war.

## THIRD NORTH CAROLINA LINE

Col. Jethro Summer, 15th Apr. 1776 to 9th Jan. 1779.
Lt. Col. Wm. Ashton, 15th Apr. 1776 to 4th Oct. 1777.
Lt. Col. Lott Brewster, 25th Oct. 1777 to 15th Mch. 1778.
Lt. Col. Henry Dixon, 12th May 1778 to 20th June 1779.
Lt. Col. Robert Mebane, 7th June 1779 to close of war.
Major Samuel Lockhart, 15th Apr. 1776 to 12th Oct. 1777.
Major Henry Dixon, 8th July 1777 to 12th May, 1778.
Major Pinketham Eaton, 22nd Nov. 1777 to 24th May 1781.
Major James Emmet, 15th Feb. 1778 to 1st June 1778.
Major Thomas Hogg, 1st June 1778 to ........
Major Griffith J. McRae, 11th Sept. 1781 to close of war.

[ 25 ]

FOURTH NORTH CAROLINA LINE

Col. Thomas Polls, 16th Apr. 1776 to 28 June 1778.
Lt. Col. James Thackston, 15th Apr. 1776 to 1st Jan. 1781.
Major Wm. L. Davidson, 15th Apr. 1776 to 4th Oct. 1777.
Major John Armstrong, 6th Oct. 1777 to 17th July 1782.
Major John Nelson, 3rd Feb. 1778 to 6th Feb. 1782.
Major George Doherty, 13th Oct. 1781 to . . Feb. 1782.
Major Thomas Donahoe, 6th Feb. 1782 to close of war.

FIFTH NORTH CAROLINA LINE

Col. Edward Buncombe, 15th Apr. 1776 to 19th Oct. 1777.
Lt. Col. Henry Irwin, 15th Apr. 1776 to 4th Oct. 1777.
Lt. Col. Wm. L. Davidson, 4th Oct. 1777 to 9th June 1779.
Major Levi Dawson, 15th Apr. 1776 to 19th Oct. 1777.
Major Thomas Hogg, 12th Oct. 1777 to 1st June 1778.
Major Reading Blount, 12th May 1778 to 6th Feb. 1782.

SIXTH NORTH CAROLINA LINE

Col. John A. Lillington, 15th Apr. 1776 to 6th May 1776.
Col. Gideon Lamb, 26th Jan. 1777 to 1st June 1778.
Lt. Col. Wm. Taylor, 15th Apr. 1776 to 1st June 1781.
Lt. Col. Archibald Lytle, 1st Feb. 1781 to close of war.
Major Gideon Lamb, 15th Apr. 1776 to 26th Jan. 1777.
Major John B. Ashe, 26th Jan. 1777 to 1st June 1778.
Major Thomas Donahue, 13th Oct. 1781 to 6th Feb. 1782.
Major George Doherty, 17th July 1782 to close of war.

SEVENTH NORTH CAROLINA LINE

Col. James Hogun, 26th Nov. 1776 to 9th Jan. 1779.
Lt. Col. Robert Mebane, 26th Nov. 1776 to 1st June 1778.
Major Lott Brewster, 26th Nov. 1776 to 25th Oct. 1777.
Major Wm. Fenner, 24th Oct. 1777 to 1st June 1778.

EIGHTH NORTH CAROLINA LINE

Col. James Armstrong, 26th Nov. 1776 to 1st June 1778.
Lt. Col. James Ingram, 26th Nov. 1776 to 8th July 1777.
Lt. Col. Samuel Lockhart, 12th Oct. 1777 to 19th Oct. 1777.
Lt. Col. Levi Dawson, 19th Oct. 1777 to 1st June 1778.
Major Selby Harney, 26th Nov. 1776 to 22nd Nov. 1777.

NINTH NORTH CAROLINA LINE

Co. John P. Williams, 7th Apr. 1777 to 1st June 1778.
Lt. Col. John Luttrell, 27th Nov. 1776 to 1st June 1778.
Major Wm. Polk, 27th Nov. 1776 to . . . . . . . . . .

TENTH NORTH CAROLINA LINE

Col. Abraham Shepard, 17th Apr. 1777 to 1st June 1778.
Lt. Col. Adam Perkins, 17th Apr. 1777 to 1st June 1778.
Major . . . . . ., . . . . . ., . . . . . ., . . . . .

(It appears that a new Tenth North Carolina was organized in 1779 as a State Regiment.)

# ALPHABETICAL LIST OF OFFICERS OF THE CONTINENTAL ARMY BY HEITMAN

Including many officers of the Militia during the war of the Revolution, 1775 to 1783, showing the various ranks they held, how long they served, when and where wounded, taken prisoners, exchanged, died, etc., and all cases in which thanks, swords, or medals were awarded by Congress.

*Pages*

64. Aitkin, James, Chaplain 4th N. C., 5th Apr. 1777; in service in July 1777; name also spelled Atkin.
64. Albarty, Fred'k., Ensn. N. C. Reg., 1781; died Aug. 29th, 1831.
65. Alderson, Simeon, Capt. 5th N. C., 17th Apr. 1776; retired June 1, 1778.
65. Alderson, Thomas, Ensn. 5th N. C., 3d May 1776 to ......
65. Alexander, Charles, 2nd Lt. 4th N. C., Nov. 1776, 1st Lt. 20 Jan. 1776 to ......
65. Alexander, Hezekiah, Paymaster 4th N. C., 16th Apr. 1776, 1st Lt. 20 Jan. 1777; retired 1st June 1778.
66. Alexander, Robert, Capt. N. C. Militia, 1776.
66. Alexander, William, Ensn. 10th N. C., May 10, 1781, Lt. Sept. 8, 1781; transferred to 4th N. C. Feb. 6, 1782 and served to close of war.
66. Alexander, William Lee, Capt. of a N. C. Regt. in 1779 and 1780.
67. Allen, Charles, Ensn 2nd N. C. Oct. 20, 1775, Lt. June 8, 1776, Capt. .., 1777, transferred 15th N. C. June 1, 1778, and served to ......
68. Allen, John, Lt. 5th N. C. Oct. 1, 1776 to ......
68. Allen, Richard, Capt. N. C. Militia at King's Mtn. Oct. 1780; died Oct. 10, 1832.
68. Allen, Thomas, Capt. 1st N. C. Sept. 1, 1775; resigned, Aug. 15, 1776.
69. Allen, Thomas, 1st Lt. 3rd N. C. Mch. 17, 1778; taken prisoner at Charlestown May 12, 1780; died in prison 26th Aug. 1780.
69. Allen, Walter, Ensn. 5th N. C. Mch. 28, 1777, Lt. 4th Oct. 1777 to ......
70. Amis, Thomas, Commissary 3rd N. C. Dec. 22, 1776 to ......
70. Amis, William, Commissary 3rd N. C. May 6, 1776, retired Dec. 1, 1776.
71. Anderson, Simon, Capt. 5th N. C. Apr. 16, 1776 to ......
72. Andrews, Richard, Ensn. 2nd N. C. Nov. 1, 1777, 2nd Lt. .. Mch. 1778; taken pris. at Ft. Fayette, June 1st, 1779, exchanged Mch. 26, 1781; 1st Lt. May 10, 1780; wounded at Eutaw Springs, Sept. 8, 1781, and rendered no subsequent service.
74. Armstrong, Andrew, Lt. 6th N. C. Apr. 16, 1776, Capt. Oct. 12, 1777, served to ......
74. Armstrong, James, Capt. 2nd N. C. Sept. 1, 1775, Col. 8th N. C. Nov. 26, 1776, retired June 1, 1778, Col of a N. C. State Regt., wounded at Stono Ferry, June 20, 1779.
74. Armstrong, James, Lt. N. C. Dragoons, Oct. 1777 to Jan. 1781.
74. Armstrong, John, Col. N. C. Militia, wounded at Stono Ferry June 20, 1779.
75. Armstrong, John, Ensn. 2nd N. C. Sept. 1, 1775, May 4th N. C. Oct. 6, 1777; Deputy Adjutant Gen. to Gen. Gates Aug. 3rd, 1780; wounded at Stono Ferry June 20, 1779, Lt. Col. 1st N. C. July 17, 1782, retired Jan. 1, 1783.
75. Armstrong, Thomas, 1st Lt. 5th N. C. Apr. 16, 1776, Capt. Oct. 25, 1777, wounded and taken prisoner at Fort Fayette June 1, 1779, exchanged Dec. 1779, taken prisoner at Charleston May 12, 1780, exchanged July 1781, Aid-de-camp to Gen. Sumner Feb. 11, 1782 to close of war, Brevet Majr. Sept. 30, 1783.
75. Armstrong, William, Ensn. 1st N. C. Jan. 4, 1776, 2nd Lt. Apr. 10, 1776, 1st Lt. Jan. 1, 1777, Capt. Aug. 20, 1777, wounded at Ramsour's Mill, June 20, 1780, transferred to 3rd N. C. Feb. 6, 1782, retired Jan. 1, 1783.

*Pages*
77. Ashe, John, Brig. Gen. N. C. State Troops.   His command was defeated at Briar Creek, Mch. 3, 1779, was betrayed into hands of enemy at Wilmington, N. C., Feb. 1, 1781, suffered severe confinement until he died Oct. 24, 1781.
77. Ashe, John, Jr., Capt. 4th N. C. Apr. 16, 1776 to . . . . . . .
77. Ashe, John Baptista, Capt. 6th N. C., Apr. 16, 1776; major 6th N. C. Jan. 26, 1777, transferred to 1st N. C. 1st June 1778, Lt. Col. Nov. 2, 1778; served to . . . . . . ; died Nov. 27, 1802.
77. Ashe, Samuel, Lt. and paymaster, 1st N. C. Sept. 1, 1775; resigned Apr. 16, 1776, Capt. 1st Troops N. C. Dragoons, Lt. Troops Mch. 7, 1777 to 1st Jan. 1781; died 1814.
77. Ashe, Samuel, Jr., Ensn. 1st N. C. .., 1779; taken prisoner at Charleston May 12, 1780; exchanged June 14, 1781; Lt. Jan. 23, 1781; . . . . in 3rd N. C. in Feb. 1782; served to close of war; died 3 Nov. 1835.
77. Ashton, William, Lt. Col. 3rd N. C. Apr. 15, 1776; resigned Oct. 25, 1777.
77. Atkin, James, see Aitkin.
78. Avery, Waitstill, Col. N. C. Militia 1778 to close of war; died 1821.
80. Bacot, Peter, Ensn., 1st N. C. Sept. 19, 1776; 2nd Lt. Feb. 8, 1777; 1st Lt. Oct. 4, 1777; taken prisoner at Charlestown, May 12, 1780; exchanged June 14, 1781; Capt. Sept. 8, 1781; served to close of war; died Aug. 13, 1821.
80. Bagley, James, Lt. N. C. Militia, 1780-1781.
80. Bailey, Benjamin, Ensn., 7th N. C. Nov. 28, 1776, Lt. Dec. 22, 1776; transfd. to 1st N. C. June 1, 1778, Capt. Sept. 8, 1781; transfd. to 3rd N. C. Jan. 1, 1782; retired Jan. 1, 1783.
81. Baird, James, Capt. N. C. Militia, 1776.
82. Baker, John, Surgeon's Mate 3rd N. C. 1777 and 1778.
82. Baker, John, 1st Lt. 7th N. C. Nov. 28, 1776, Capt. July 6, 1777; retired June 1, 1778; Col. N. C. Militia; wounded at Bulltown Swamp, Nov. 19, 1778.
82. Baker, Peter, Lt. 1st N. C. Feb. 8, 1777 to . . . . . . .
84. Ball, Hosea, Ensn. N. C. Militia, 1779.
84. Ballard, Kedar, 1st Lt. 3rd N. C. Apr. 16, 1776, Capt. Oct. 4, 1777; Regimental paymaster, Oct. 10, 1779; taken prisoner at Charleston May 12, 1780; prison parole Aug. 1781; retired Jan. 1, 1783; died Jan. 15, 1834.
86. Barber, John, Capt. N. C. Militia, 1776.
86. Barber, William, Lt. 1st N. C. Apr. 19, 1776 to . . . . . . .
88. Barnes, Thomas, Ensn. N. C. Militia in 1780.
89. Barret, William, Capt. 3rd N. C. Apr. 16, 1776, to . . . . . . ; 1st Lt. 3rd. Cont. Dragoons Apr. 10, 1778; Capt. May .., 1779; retained in Baylor's Consolidated Regt. of Dragoons Nov. 9, 1782, served to close of war; died 1815.
89. Barrow, Jacob, Lt. 7th N. C. Dec. 22, 1776 to . . . . . . .
89. Barrow, Samuel, Lt. 7th N. C. Nov. 28, 1776 to . . . . . . .
90. Barton, John, Capt. N. C. Militia, at King's Mt'n. in Oct. 1780; died 1827.
92. Baxter, Andrew, Jr., Lt. N. C. Militia; wounded at Camden, May 10, 1781; died 1814.
94. Beattie, Thomas, Major N. C. Militia, 1776.
95. Beavans, Robert, 1st Lt. 2nd N. C. May 1776; on roll for Aug. 1776.
97. Beeks, William, Lt. & Adjutant 7th N. C. Nov. 22, 1777; retired June 1, 1778.
97. Beene, Jesse, Capt. N. C. Militia at King's Mtn. 1780 (name also spelled Bean).
97. Beeson, Edward, Capt. N. C. Militia, .., 1779.
97. Bell, Green, Capt. 7th N. C. Nov. 28, 1776 to . . . . . . .
98. Bell, Robert, Ensn. 10th N. C. May 18, 1781, Lt. Sept. 8, 1781; transfd. to 2nd N. C. Feb. 6, 1782; served to close of war.
98. Bell, Robert, Lt. 1st N. C. on roll for .. Nov. 1777.
101. Berryhill, William, Lt. 1st N. C. Sept. 1, 1775 to . . . . . . .
101. Bertie, Thomas, Ensn. 8 N. C. Nov. 28, 1776 to . . . . . . .

*Pages*

101. Bethel, William, Capt. N. C. Militia at Guilford, Mch. 15, 1781.
102. Bickerstaff, John, Ensn. 2nd N. C. June 8, 1776 to . . . . . . .
105. Blackly, Ebenezer, Surgeon's Mate 10th N. C., on roll for July 1778.
107. Blanton, Rowland, Ensn. 7th N. C. Nov. 28, 1776, to . . . . . . .
108. Blount, Jacob, Paymaster, N. C. Militia, 1777.
108. Blount, James, Capt. 2nd N. C. Sept. 1, 1775 to . . . . . .
108. Blount, Jess, Commissary 8th N. C. Dec. 11, 1776 to . . . . . . .
108. Blount, Reading, Capt. 3rd N. C. Apr. 16, 1777; Maj. 5th N. C. May 12, 1778; transfd. to 2nd N. C. June 1, 1778; transfd. to 1st N. C. Jan. 1, 1781; served to close of war. Died Oct. 12, 1807.)
108. Blount, Thomas, Lieut. 5th N. C. 28th Apr. 1777, to . . . . . . .
108. Blount, William, Paymaster 3rd N. C. Dec. 11, 1778, to . . . . . . (Died Mch. 21, 1800.)
108. Blunt, Whitmal, Lt. 4th N. C. Nov. 20, 1776 to . . . . . . .
108. Blyth, Joseph, Surgeon, 1st N. C. July 12, 1776; taken prisoner at Charleston, May 12, 1780; exchgd. June 14, 1781; in 4th N. C. Feb. 1782 & served to close of war.
109. Blyth, Samuel, Ensign, 1st N. C. Mch. 28, 1776; 2nd Lt. July 7, 1776; resigned, May 16, 1778.
109. Broadley, George, Capt. 3rd N. C. Sept. 19, 1778, to . . . . . .; in service Jan. 1780.
113. Bowman, Joshua, 2nd Lt. 1st N. C. Sept. 1, 1775; 1st Lt. Nov. 15, 1775; Capt. Sept. 18, 1776; wounded at Charleston, May 12, 1780; killed at Ramseur's Mill June 20, 1780.
114. Boyd, Adam, Ensn. 1st N. C. Jan. 4, 1776; 2nd Lt. Mch. 3, 1776; Chaplain 2nd N. C. Oct. 1777; Brigade Chaplain, Aug. 18, 1778 to June 1780. (Died 1800.)
114. Boyd, Hugh, Surgeon 4th N. C. Apr. 17, 1776 to . . . . . . .
116. Bradford, William, Jr., Lt. Col. Deputy Quartermaster General in 1778.
117. Bradley, Gee, 1st Lt. 3rd N. C. May 12, 1776; Capt. Sept. 19, 1778; taken pris. in Charleston May 12, 1780; exchanged June 1781; retired 1st Jan. 1783.
117. Bradley, Richard, Paymaster 3rd N. C. Mch. 5, 1777; retired June 1, 1778.
118. Brandon, John, Capt. N. C. Militia at King's Rev. in Oct. 1780.
118. Brandon, William, Lt. 1st N. C. Sept. 1, 1775; resigned Mch. 8, 1776.
119. Brevard, Alexander, Ensn. 4th N. C. Nov. 27, 1776; 1st Lt. Dec. 9, 1776; transf'd. to 1st N. C. June 1, 1778; Capt. Oct. 20, 1780; transf'd. to 4th N. C. Feb. 6, 1782; retired Jan. 1, 1783; served as Col. N. C. Militia in 1779. (Died 1829.)
119. Brevard, Ephraim, Surgeon 1st N. C. . . . .; taken pris. at Charleston, May 12, 1780. (Died 1783.)
119. Brevard, Joel, Capt. 9th N. C. Nov. 28, 1776; resigned June 1, 1778.
119. Brevard, John, 1st Lt. 9th N. C. Nov. 28, 1776 to . . . . . . .
119. Brevard, Joseph, Ensn. 10th N. C. May 9, 1781; Lt. Aug. 1, 1781; transf'd. to 2nd N. C. Feb. 12, 1782; Regimental Quartermaster, Mch. 13, 1782; served to close of war.
120. Brewster, Lott, Maj. 2nd N. C. Nov. 27, 1776; Lt. Col. 3rd N. C. Oct. 25, 1777; resigned Mch. 15, 1778.
120. Brice, Peter, Ensn. 9th N. C. Nov. 28, 1776 to . . . . . . .
120. Brickell, Thomas, Capt. 7th N. C. Nov. 28, 1776 to . . . . . .; appears to have been taken prisoner, but when and where taken not stated.
121. Bright, Simon, Capt. 2nd N. C. Sept. 1, 1775; resigned May 3, 1776.
121. Brinkley, John, Capt. N. C. Militia, 1780-1781.
121. Brinkley, William, Capt. 3rd N. C. Apr. 16, 1776; retired June 1, 1778.
125. Brown, James S., Lt. Col. N. C. Militia; was prisoner in 1778; where and when taken not stated.
125. Brown, John, Ensn. 1st N. C. Nov. 15, 1775; 2nd Lt. Jan. 4, 1776; Capt. Apr. 26, 1777; was at King's Mtn. in Oct. 1780; on list for June 1778, he is dropped with remark transferred to one of the Dragoon Regiments of N. C.

*Pages*

126. Brown, Morgan W., 1st Lt. 9th N. C. Nov. 28, 1776; resigned Oct. 12, 1777; served as a volunteer and was taken prisoner at Charleston May 12, 1780. (Died 1840.)

128. Bryan, Benjamin, Ensn. 2nd N. C. Apr. 27, 1777; 2nd Lt. 7th N. C., July 15, 1777; retired June 1, 1778.

128. Bryan, Hardy, Commissary 7th N. C. Dec. 11, 1776 to ........

128. Bryan, John, Capt. N. C. Militia; killed at his home by Tories Mch. 12, 1782.

129. Bryant, John, Jr., Lt. 7th N. C. Nov. 28, 1776 to ........

129. Bryer, Benjamin, Ensn. 7th N. C. Apr. 27, 1777; 2nd Lt. July 15, 1777; retired June 1, 1778.

129. Buck, Stephen, Ensn. N. C. Militia, 1780-1781.

130. Budd, Samuel, 1st Lt. 2nd N. C. Nov. 11, 1777; Capt. .. 1779; taken pris. at Charleston, May 12, 1780; exchanged June 14, 1781; retired 1st Jan. 1783.

131. Buford, William, 2nd Lt. 2nd N. C. May 15, 1777; 1st N. C. Dragoons July 16, 1777; was a Capt. 1781; was wounded at Stono Ferry, Sept. 8, 1781; and served to close of war. (Died 1810.)

132. Bull, Thomas, Surgeon's Mate 10th N. C. Dec. 1780 to 1783.

132. Bullock, Daniel, Lt. 9th N. C. Nov. 28, 1776 to ........

132. Buncombe, Edward, Col. 5th N. C. Apr. 15, 1776; died Nov. 1777, while a prisoner, of wounds received at Germantown, Oct. 4, 1777.

136. Bush, John, Ensn. 8th N. C. Nov. 28, 1776; 1st Lt. Aug. 5, 1777; transferred 5th N. C. June 1, 1778; Adjutant Aug. 7, 1781; served to ........

136. Bush, William, Ensn. 8th N. C. Apr. 10, 1777; 2nd Lt. Aug. 15, 1777; transferred to 1st N. C. June 1, 1778, 1st Lt. Feb. 1, 1779; Capt. 1781, and served to close of war. (Died 1821.)

137. Butler, John, Brigadier Gen. N. C. Militia, 1780-1781.

138. Bynum, Turner, Capt. N. C. Militia, 1781.

140. Callahan, John, Lt. N. C. Militia at King's Mtn. Oct. 1780.

140. Callender, Thomas, Ensn. 1st N. C. June 6, 1776; 2nd Lt. Jan. 1, 1777; 1st Lt. July 8, 1777; Capt. Lt. Mch. 30, 1780; taken prisoner at Charlestown May 12, 1780; exchanged June 14, 1781; Capt. May 12, 1780; retired Jan. 1, 1783. (Died Aug. 20, 1828.)

141. Campbell, Arthur, Col. N. C. Militia in 1780.

141. Campbell, James, Ensn. 4th N. C. Dec. 11, 1776; Lt. 10 N. C. Apr. 19, 1777; 1st Lt. Dec. 21, 1777; Quartermaster Sept. 10, 1778; transferred to 2nd N. C. June 1, 1778; Capt. Dec. 14, 1778; wounded and taken prisoner at Stono Ferry June 20, 1779; exchanged June 14, 1781, and served to close of war (name also spelled Campen.)

141. Campbell, John, 1st Lt. 10 N. C. Apr. 20, 1777; transferred to 4th N. C. June 1, 1778; Capt. Apr. 5, 1779; retired Jan. 1, 1783.

141. Campbell, John, 2nd Lt. 2nd Continental Artillery June 29, 1781; and served to June 1783.

143. Cannon, Lewis, Lt. 10th N. C. Apr. 19, 1777 to ........

145. Carpenter, Peter, Ensn. 8th N. C. Nov. 28, 1776 to ........

146. Carroway, Gideon, Lt. 8th N. C. Nov. 28, 1776 to ........

146. Carroll, Butler, Ensn. 10th N. C. mentioned in 1777.

146. Carson, Andrew, Privt. and Capt. N. C. Partisan Rangers under Gen. Davidson, 1776-1782. (Died Jan. 29, 1841.)

146. Carter, Benjamin, 1st Lt. 4th N. C. Dec. 22, 1776; Capt. 1 Jan., 1779; transferred to 2nd N. C. Feb. 6, 1782, and served to close of war. (Died Jan. 20, 1830.)

147. Caruthers, Andrew, Lt. N. C. Militia at King's Mtn. Oct. 1780. (Died 1818.)

148. Caswell, Richard, Col. N. C. Partisan Rangers, 1776 to 1777; Maj. Gen. N. C. Militia 1780 to close of war; was also Gov. of N. C. at sometime. (Died Nov. 20, 1789.)

*Pages*

148. Caswell, William, Ensn. 2nd N. C. Sept. 1, 1775; Capt. 5th N. C. Apr. 16, 1776 to . . . . . . .
148. Caustaphan, James, Ensn. 7th N. C. Nov. 28, 1776 to . . . . . . .
151. Chapman, Samuel, 2nd Lt. 8th N. C. Nov. 28, 1776; 1st Lt. Aug. 1, 1777; transfr'd. to 4th N. C. June 1, 1778; Capt. Apr. 5, 1779, and served to close of war.
151. Charlton, William, Ensn. 10th N. C. Mch. 14, 1779; 2nd Lt. Sept. 1779; wounded Stono Ferry, June 20, and died June 21, 1779.
152. Cheese, John, Ensn. 1st N. C. June 12, 1776; 2nd Lt. Jan. 20, 1777; resigned Apr. 1, 1777.
152. Cheesboro, John, Paymaster 6th N. C. July 3, 1777; Ensn. Apr. 25, 1778; retired June 1, 1778.
153. Child, Francis, 1st Lt. 6th N. C. Apr. 16, 1776; Capt. Jan. 26, 1777; transferred to 3rd N. C. June 1, 1778; taken prisoner at Charleston May 12, 1780.
153. Child, James, Ensn. 1st N. C. Sept. 1, 1775 to . . . . . . .
153. Childs, James, Ensn. 1st N. C. Sept. 1, 1775 to . . . . . . .
154. Childs, Thomas, Capt. N. C. Militia in 1780. (Died Sept. 15, 1820.)
154. Christman, Nathaniel, Capt. N. C. Militia; was a prisoner; exchanged 7th June, 1782; when and where taken not stated.
154. Christman, Richard, Capt. N. C. Militia in 1780.
154. Chronicle, William, Maj. N. C. Partisan Rangers; killed at King's Mtn. Oct. 7, 1780.
157. Clark, Jonathan, Lt. N. C. Militia, 1779-1780.
158. Clark, Thomas, Maj. 1st N. C. Sept. 1, 1775; Lt. Col. Apr. 10, 1776; Col. Feb. 5, 1777; wounded Stono Ferry June 20, 1779; taken pris. at Charleston, May 12, 1780; retired Jan. 1, 1783. (Died Dec. 25, 1792.)
158. Clark, Thomas, Ensn. 9th N. C. Nov. 28, 1776; Lt. Feb. 1, 1777; transfr'd. to 4th N. C. July 1st, 1778; Capt. Feb. 10, 1779; served to . . . . . . .
158. Clark, Thomas, Capt. N. C. Artillery Co. Jan. 1, 1777; last record of him is June 1779.
160. Clendenin, John, Ensn. 3rd N. C. Apr. 15, 1776; 2nd Lt. Oct. 29, 1777; 1st Lt. Dec. 23, 1777; Regimental Quartermaster Dec. 14, 1779; taken prisoner at Charleston, May 12, 1780; exchgd. June 14, 1781; served to close of war. Brevet Capt. Sept. 30, 1783, (name also spelled Clendinin and Clending).
160. Cleveland, Benjamin, Ensn. 2nd N. C., Sept. 1, 1775; Lt. Jan. 1776; Capt. Nov. 23, 1776; retired 1st June, 1778; Col. N. C. Militia, Aug. 1778, to close of war, died . . . . Oct. 1806.
160. Cleveland, Larkin, Lt. N. C. Militia; wounded at Lovelady Ford, N. C., Sept. 30, 1780.
160. Cleveland, Robert, Capt. N. C. Militia at King's Mtn. Oct. 1780. (Died 1812.)
161. Clinch, James, Ensn. 2nd N. C. Sept. 1, 1775 to . . . . . . .
163. Coffield,. Benjamin, Adjutant 6th N. C. May 17, 1777 to July 1, 1778.
164. Coleman, Benjamin, Capt. 5th N. C. Apr. 30, 1777, transferred to 2nd N. C. June 1, 1778; taken pris. at Charleston May 12, 1780.
164. Coleman, Charles, Regimental Quartermaster, 4th N. C. Oct. 14, 1777 to . . . . . . .
165. Coleman, John, Ensn. 9th N. C. Nov. 28, 1776 to . . . . . . .
165. Coleman, Theophelus, Lt. 7th N. C. Nov. 28, 1776 to . . . . . . .
165. Coles, William T., Capt. 4th N. C. Apr. 16, 1776 to . . . . . .; was in service July 1776.
165. Collier, John, Col. N. C. Militia, 1780-1781.
167. Conger, Stephen, Adjutant 1st N. C. Jan. 29, 1778; retired June 1, 1778.
169. Cook, George, 2nd Lt. 10th N. C. Apr. 19, 1777; 1st Lt. July 10, 1777; transferred to 1st N. C. June 1, 1778; taken prisoner at Charleston May 12, 1780.

*Pages*
169. Cook, James, Ensn. 2nd N. C. Sept. 1, 1775; Capt. 3rd N. C. Apr. 16, 1776; retired June 1, 1778.
169. Cook, Richard D., Capt. 9th N. C. Nov. 28, 1776; retired June 1, 1778.
170. Cooley, Samuel, Surgeon 5th N. C. Apr. 17, 1776; retired June 1, 1778; Surgeon Virginia Militia in 1780.
171. Cooper, Soloman, Lt. 10th N. C. Jan. 20, 1778 to ......
171. Cooper, William, Lt. 5th N. C. Apr. 16, 1776 to ......
171. Coots, James, Lt. 4th N. C. Nov. 20, 1776 to ......
172. Cotgrave, Arthur, 1st Lt. 2nd N. C. Mch. 26, 1778; taken prisoner at Charleston, May 12, 1780; exchanged June 14, 1781, and served to close of war.
172. Cotton, Josiah, Capt. 7th N. C. Nov. 28, 1776; retired June 1, 1778.
172. Cotton, Thomas, Capt. N. C. Militia in 1780.
173. Council, Arthur, Capt. 6th N. C. Apr. 16, 1776; died .. April, 1777.
173. Council, Robert, Ensn. 1st N. C. Jan. 4, 1776; 2nd Lt. July 7, 1776; resigned Sept. 10, 1776; Ensn. 1st N. C. Mch. 28, 1777; 2nd Lt. July 8, 1777; Capt. Co. of N. C. Dragoons July 1, 1778, and served to close of war.
173. Covington, James, Lt. 9th N. C. Nov. 28, 1776 to ......
173. Covington, William, Adjutant 4th N. C. Mch. 28, 1777 to ......
173. Cowan, David, Lt. 10th N. C. Mch. 20, 1779; Capt. 1781, and served to ......
173. Cowan, Thomas, Capt. N. C. State Troops, wounded at Eutaw Springs Sept. 8, 1781. (Died 1817.)
173. Cowan, Thomas, Capt. N. C. Militia 1780-1781; (Died 1817.)
174. Craddock, John, Ensn. 2nd N. C. May 3, 1776; 2nd Lt. May 16, 1776; 1st Lt. Jan, 1777; Capt. Lt. Dec. 21, 1777; wounded and taken prisoner at Charleston May 12, 1780; pris. on parole until retired Jan. 1, 1783.
174. Crafton, Bennett, Adjutant 6th N. C. Apr. 15, 1776 to ......
175. Craighead, ...., Capt. N. C. Militia; wounded at Hanging Rock Aug. 6, 1780.
176. Craik, Thomas, Deputy Commissary Gen. Nov. 23, 1776 to ......
177. Craven, James, Ensn. 1st N. C. June 12, 1776; 2nd Lt. Jan. 1, 1777; 1st Lt. July 28, 1777; dishonorably discharged Nov. 20, 1779.
177. Crawford, Charles, Capt. 2nd N. C. Sept. 1, 1775; retired June 1, 1778.
177. Crawford, David, Ensn. 1st N. C. June 10, 1777; Lt. ....; wounded at Hanging Rock, Aug. 6, 1780.
177. Crawford, William, Ensn. 1st N. C. 4th Jan. 1776; 2nd Lt. Mch. 28, 1776; resigned Aug. 5, 1776.
177. Creecy, John, Lt. N. C. Militia, 1780-1781.
177. Crenshaw, Arthur, Ensn. 2nd N. C. ....; taken prisoner at Charleston, May 12, 1780; exchanged June 14, 1781; served to ......
179. Crutcher, Anthony, Ensn. 5th N. C. Feb. 27, 1780; Lt. May 18, 1781; transferred to 2nd N. C. Feb. 6, 1782; served to close of war.
182. Curtis, John, Lt. 5th N. C. Oct. 1, 1776 to ......
182. Curtis, Joshua, Ensn. 4th N. C. July 1, 1777; resigned Feb. 21, 1778.
182. Curtis, Reuben, Ensn. 2nd N. C. in 1777.
182. Curtis, Thomas Ensn. 8th N. C. Nov. 28, 1776 to ......
184. Daly, Joshua, 1st Lt. 7th N. C. Dec. 19, 1776; Capt. Oct. 12, 1777; retired June 1, 1778.
184. Dance, Etheldred, Ensn. .... N. C. Reg. in 1781; (Died Feb. 4, 1828.)
185. Daniel, James, Lt. 9th N. C. Nov. 28, 1776 to ......
185. Daniel, Stephen, Ensn. 1st N. C. Jan. 4, 1776; resigned June 3, 1776.
186. Darnall, Henry, Lt. and Adjutant 5th N. C. Apr. 15, 1776; Capt. Oct. 1, 1776; retired June 1, 1778.
186. Daves, John, Quartermaster 2nd N. C. June 7, 1776; Ensn. Sept. 30, 1776; 1st Lt. Oct. 4, 1777; wounded at Stony Point, July 16, 1779; taken pris. at Charleston May 12, 1780; exchanged June 1781; transferred to 3rd N. C. Jan. 1, 1781; Capt. Sept. 8, 1781; retired Jan. 1, 1783. (Died Oct. 12, 1804.)

*Pages*
186. Daves, John, Ensn. 10th N. C. May 6, 1781 to . . . . . .
186. Davidson, George, Capt. 1st N. C. Sept. 1, 1775; resigned Feb. 5, 1777.
186. Davidson, Thomas, Lt. N. C. Militia, 1780-1781.
186. Davidson, William Lee, Maj. 4th N. C. Apr. 15, 1776; Lt. Col. 5th N. C. Oct. 4, 1777; transferred to 3rd N. C. June 1, 1778; transferred to 1st N. C. June 9, 1779; served also as Brig. Gen. N. C. Militia . . . .; killed at Cowan's Ford Feb. 1, 1781.
187. Davie, William Richardson, Entered the Army in 1776, as a Volunteer; Lt. of Dragoons Pulaski Legion, Apr. 5, 1779; Capt. . . May 1779; wounded at Stono Ferry, June 20, 1779; Col. N. C. Cavalry State Troops, Sept. 5, 1780, and served to close of war; Brig. Gen. U. S. Army July 19, 1798; honorably dischgd. June 15, 1800. (Died Nov. 18, 1820.)
187. Davis, Abraham, Adjutant 7th N. C. Dec. 22, 1776; resigned Nov. 21, 1777. (Name also spelled Dawes.)
189. Davis, William, Capt. 1st N. C. Sept. 1, 1775; Maj. Apr. 10, 1776; Lt. Col. 1st N. C. Feb. 5, 1777; retired June 1, 1778.
189. Dawes, Abraham. See Davis.
189. Dawes, Josiah, Regimental Quartermaster 7th N. C. July 10, 1777 to . . . . . . .
189. Dawson, Henry, Capt. 2nd N. C. Nov. 29, 1776; resigned Oct. 11, 1777.
189. Dawson, Levi, Maj. 5th N. C. Apr. 15, 1776; Lt. Col. 8th N. C. Oct. 19, 1777; retired June 1, 1778.
192. De Keyser, Lehancius, Adjutant 1st N. C. Sept. 16, 1775; 2nd Lt. Jan. 4, 1776; 1st Lt. Feb. 3, 1776; resigned Dec. 10, 1776.
193. Dellinger, John, Capt. N. C. Militia, 1776.
193. de Medici, Cosmo. See Medici.
193. Dennis, William, 1st Lt. 8th N. C. Nov. 28, 1776; Capt. Sept. 30, 1777; retired June 1, 1778.
194. Dent, William, Commissary 9th N. C. Dec. 11, 1776 to . . . . . . .
196. Dickenson, Richard, Ensn. 6th N. C. Apr. 12, 1777; Lt. Oct. 12, 1777; transferred to 1st N. C. June 1, 1778; cashiered Nov. 20, 1779.
196. Dickerson, Nathaniel, Lt. 9th N. C. Nov. 28, 1776 to . . . . . . .
197. Dickey, John, Capt. N. C. Militia 1779-1781. (Died 1808.)
197. Diggs, Anthony, Lt. 5th N. C. Aug. 20, 1777; retired June 1, 1778.
198. Dillon, James, 2nd Lt. 7th N. C. Jan. 1, 1777; 1st Lt. Oct. 12, 1777; transferred to 2nd N. C. June 1, 1778; killed at Eutaw Springs Sept. 8, 1781.
198. Dillon, John, Lt. 10th N. C. . . Feb. 1779 to . . . . . . .
198. Dixon, Charles, Ensn. 6th N. C. Apr. 2, 1777; Paymaster, Jan. 19, 1778; transferred to 3rd N. C. July 1, 1778; Lt. Feb. 8, 1779; wounded at Eutaw Springs Sept. 8, 1781; transferred to 4th N. C. Feb. 6, 1782; retired Jan. 1, 1783.
198. Dixon, Henry, Capt. 1st N. C. Sept. 1, 1775; arranged to 8th N. C. Jan. 1777; Maj. 3rd N. C. Oct. 4, 1777; Lt. Col. May 12, 1778; wounded at Stono Ferry June 20, 1779; transferred to 2nd N. C. Feb. 6, 1782; died July 17, 1782.
198. Dixon, Joseph, Maj. N. C. Militia at Kings Mtn. Oct. 1780. (Died Apr. 14, 1825.)
198. Dixon, Tilghman, 1st Lt. 1st N. C. Oct. 20, 1775; Capt. Feb. 5, 1777; taken prisoner at Charleston May 12, 1780; exchanged June 14, 1781; retired Jan. 1, 1783.
199. Dixon, Wynne, Ensn. 10th N. C. Mch. 1, 1781; 2nd Lt. July 5, 1781; transferred to 1st N. C. Feb. 1782; served to close of war. (Died Nov. 24, 1829.)
199. Dobbins, Hugh, Lt. 9th N. C. . . ., 1777 to June 1, 1778.
199. Dobson, . . . ., Capt. N. C. Militia, killed at Ramsour's Mill June 20, 1780.
199. Doherty, George, 1st Lt. 6th N. C. Apr. 16, 1776; Capt. Oct. 28, 1776; transferred to 4th N. C. June 1, 1778; Maj. Oct. 13, 1781; and served to June 1783.
200. Donoho, Thomas, 1st Lt. 6th N. C. Apr. 16, 1776; Capt. Sept. 10, 1776; Maj. Oct. 13, 1781; in 4th N. C. Feb. 6, 1782; served to close of war. (Died 1825.)

34        ROSTER OF NORTH CAROLINA SOLDIERS

*Pages*
202. Douglas, Robert, Lt. of Kingsbury's Co. N. C. Artillery July 19, 1777; omitted July 1778.
202. Douglas, William, Regimental Quartermaster 4th N. C. Feb. 10, 1777 to ......
203. Dowal, David, Capt. N. C. Militia, 1776.
205. Dudley, Guilford, Lt. Col. N. C. Militia, 1780-1781.
206. Dudley, Thomas, Musician 6th N. C. in 1776; Ensn. May 1778; transferred to 3rd N. C. June 1, 1778; 2nd Lt. June 20, 1779; 1st Lt. Mch. 1, 1781; wounded at Eutaw Springs Sept. 8, 1781, served to close of war.
207. Duncan, Robert, Regimental Paymaster, 4th N. C. Dec. 1, 1777, retired June 1, 1778.
210. Eagle, Joseph, Ensn. 4th N. C. Jan. 1, 1776; resigned Mch. 20, 1776.
210. Earl, William, Capt. N. C. Militia 1780-1781.
210. Easton, Seth, Lt. 7th N. C. Nov. 28, 1776 to ......
210. Eaton, Pinketham, Capt. 3rd N. C. Apr. 16, 1776; Maj. 8th N. C. 22, 1777; retired June 1, 1778; Col. N. C. Militia; wounded at Briar Creek Mch. 3, 1779; and was killed at Fort Grierson May 24, 1781.
211. Eborne, John, Lt. 5th N. C. Oct. 1, 1776 to ......
211. Eborne, Thomas, Lt. 5th N. C. Apr. 16, 1776 to ......
212. Edmunds, Nicholas, Capt. 3rd N. C. in 1777; served to ......
215. Elmer, Eli, 1st Lt. Clark's Co. N. C. Artillery Jan. 1, 1777; resigned Feb. 13, 1780.
216. Ely, Eli, 1st Lt. 7th N. C. Dec. 11, 1776; Capt. Oct. 12, 1777; retired June 1, 1778.
216. Ely, Samuel, Capt. 7th N. C. Dec. 17, 1776; resigned Feb. 17, 1778.
217. Emmet, James, Capt. 3rd N. C. Apr. 16, 1776; Maj. 1st N. C. Dec. 22, 1777; retired June 1, 1778.
217. Enloe, John, Capt. 5th N. C. Apr. 16, 1776; resigned Oct. 25, 1777.
218. Espy, Samuel, Capt. N. C. Militia; wounded at King's Mtn. Oct. 7, 1780; (Died Dec. 29, 1838.)
219. Evans, Thomas, Ensn. 2nd N. C. June 6, 1776; 2nd Lt. July 19, 1776; 1st Lt. May 15, 1777; Adjutant Nov. 22, 1778; taken prisoner at Tappan Sept. 28, 1778; exchanged Nov. 4, 1780; retained in 1st N. C. Jan. 1, 1781; Capt. June 1st, 1781; transferred to 4th N. C. Feb. 6, 1782; and served to close of war.
220. Ewell, William, Lt. 5th N. C. Apr. 20, 1777 to ......; name also spelled Hewell.
221. Faircloth, William, Lt. 10th N. C. Jan. 20, 1778; retired June 1, 1778.
221. Falls, ...., Capt. N. C. Partisan Rangers ....; killed at Ramseur's Mill, June 20, 1780.
223. Fawn, William, 2nd Lt. 3rd N. C. Apr. 15, 1777; 1st Lt. Oct. 4, 1777; Capt. Lt. Mch. 30, 1780; wounded and taken prisoner at Charleston May 12, 1780; Capt. ....; retired Jan. 1, 1783.
223. Fear, Edmund, Capt. N. C. Militia at King's Mtn. Oct. 1780.
224. Fenner, Richard, Ensn. 2nd N. C. Jan. 10, 1779; taken prisoner at Charleston May 12, 1780; exchanged June 14, 1781; Lt. May 12, 1781; and served to close of war.
224. Fenner, Robert, Lt. 2nd N. C. Jan. 1, 1776; Capt. May 20, 1777; taken prisoner at Charleston May 12, 1780; served to close of war; Brevet Maj. Sept. 30, 1783.
224. Fenner, William, 1st Lt. 2nd N. C. Sept. 1, 1775; Capt. May 1, 1776; Major 7th N. C. Oct. 24, 1777; retired June 1, 1778.
225. Fergus, Janus, Surgeon 1st N. C. May 24, 1776; resigned .... Apr. 1777; Surgeon's Mate 1st N. C. Feb. 21, 1782; Surgeon Aug. 20, 1782, and served to close of war.
225. Ferrell, Micajah, Ensn. 9th N. C. Nov. 28, 1776 to ......
225. Ferrebee, Joseph, Lt. 10th N. C. May 5, 1777 to ......
225. Ferrebee, William, Lt. 7th N. C. Nov. 28, 1776; transferred to 4th N. C. June 1, 1778; Capt. July 1, 1781; retired Jan. 1, 1783.

*Pages*
225. Ferrell, Luke L., Lt. 10th N. C. ...., 1778 to .......
225. Ferrell, William, Ensn. 8th N. C. Sept. 8, 1777; 2nd Lt. Oct. 10, 1777; transfr'd. to 2nd N. C. June 1, 1778 and served to ......
227. Finney, Thomas, Ensn. 2nd N. C. Nov. 12, 1777; Lt. Jan. 23, 1781; taken prisoner at Charleston May 12, 1780; exchanged June 14, 1781, served to close of war.
231. Foakes, Yelverton, Lt. and Regimental Quartermaster 1st N. C. Feb. 3, 1776; resigned Aug. 1, 1776.
231. Foard, Hezekiah, Chaplain 5th N. C. Apr. 20, 1777; retired June 1, 1778.
231. Forbes, Arthur, Col. N. C. Militia; wounded at Guilford Mch. 15, 1781; and died in April 1781.
231. Forbes, John, Capt. N. C. Militia in 1781; killed at Guilford Mch. 15, 1781.
232. Foreman, Caleb, Lt. 8th N. C. Nov. 28, 1776 to .......
233. Forney, Peter, Capt. N. C. Rangers, serving in S. C. 1780-1781 (D. 1834.)
235. Fowkes, Yelverton, Quartermas't'r. 1st N. C. Feb. 3, 1776; resign'd. Aug. 1, 1776.
236. Francis, ...., Capt. N. C. Partisan Rangers; killed at Shallow Ford, Feb. 6, 1781.
236. Franklin, Jesse, 1st Lt. Capt. and Maj. N. C. Militia 1776-1782. (Died Sept. .., 1823.)
236. Franklin, John, Capt. N. C. Militia at King's Mtn. Oct. 1780. (D. Sept. 20, 1823.)
241. Gakae, James, Surgeon 1st N. C. Dec. .., 1775; resigned May 1776.
241. Gamble, Edmund, Ensn. 1st N. C. Mch. 28, 1776; 2nd Lt. July 7, 1776; 1st. Lt. Jan. 20, 1777; transferred to N. C. Dragoons State Regt. June 1, 1778, and served to close of war.
243. Gardner, James, Capt. 2nd N. C. May 1776; resigned May 15, 1777.
243. Gardner, William, Ensn. 2nd N. C. Sept. 1, 1775 to ......; 2nd Lt. Oct. 20, 1775, and served to .......
244. Gaston, Alexander, Capt. N. C. Militia; murdered by Tories Aug. 20, 1781. Where not stated.
244. Gaston, Robert, Capt. 2nd N. C. Feb. 1776 to .......
244. Gatling, Levi, Ensn. 10th N. C. .., 1777; Lt. Feb. 12, 1778; cashiered Aug. 25, 1778.
245. Gee, Howell, Ensn. 7th N. C. Apr. 15, 1777; Lt. Nov. 1777; Capt. ...., and served to .......
245. Gee, James, 1st Lt. 2nd N. C. Sept. 1, 1775; Capt. May 3, 1776; died Nov. 12, 1777.
245. Geikee, James, Surgeon 1st N. C. Dec. .. 1775, resigned May .. 1776.
245. Gerrard, Charles, Ensn. 5th N. C. Apr. 30, 1777; 2nd Lt. Dec. 19, 1777; 1st Lt. 2nd N. C. June 1, 1778; taken prisoner at Charleston May 12, 1780; exchanged June 14, 1781; transferred to 1st N. C. Jan. 1, 1781; served to close of war.
247. Gibson, Thomas, Ensn. of a N. C. Reg. Feb. 20, 1780; taken prisoner at Charleston May 12, 1780; exchanged June 14, 1781.
248. Gillespie, Robert, Ensn. 4th N. C. .... 1777; Lt. Aug. .. 1777; served to ......
250. Glechan, John, Capt. 7th N. C. Nov. 28, 1776; resigned Oct. 11, 1777.
250. Glover, William, 1st Lt. 6th N. C. Apr. 16, 1776; Capt. May 7, 1776. Retired June 1, 1778.
250. Godfrey, William, Lt. 8th N. C. Nov. 28, 1776; resigned Aug. 15, 1777.
252. Goodin, Christopher, Lt. 6th N. C. Apr. 16, 1776; transferred to 3rd N. C. June 1, 1778; Capt. Jan. .. 1779; killed at Eutaw Springs, Sept. 8, 1781.
252. Goodloe, Robert, Capt. N. C. Militia 1779-1781. (D. 1797.)
252. Goodman, William, Capt. 4th N. C. Oct. 1, 1776; killed at Eutaw Springs Sept. 8, 1781.
252. Goodwin, John, Lt. N. C. Militia, 1781.
253. Gordon, Charles, Maj. N. C. Partisan Rangers ..; wounded at King's Mtn. Oct. 7, 1780; (D. Mch. 24, 1799.)

*Pages*
255. Graham, George, Ensn. 1st N. C. Sept. 1, 1775; 2nd Lt. Jan. 4, 1776; resigned Apr. 15, 1776; served subsequently as Capt. of N. C. Rangers.
255. Graham, Joseph, served as Lt. & Capt. N. C. Rangers from Sept. 1778; Maj. N. C. Partisan Rangers 1780; wounded at Charlotte Sept. 26, 1780. (D. Nov. 12, 1836.)
256. Graham, Richard, Lt. 2nd N. C. June 8th, 1776; Capt. Jan. 1778; retired June 1, 1778.
256. Graham, William, Col. N. C. Militia, 1776-1781, (D. May 3, 1835.)
256. Grainger, Caleb, Capt. 1st N. C. Sept. 1, 1775; Maj. Feb. 5, 1777; resigned Apr. 26, 1777.
256. Grainger, John, 1st Lt. 2nd N. C. Sept. 1, 1775 to ......
256. Granberry, George, Capt. 3rd N. C. Apr. 16, 1776 to ......
256. Granberry, John, Lt. 3rd N. C. .. 1777 to ......
256. Granberry, Thomas, Capt. 3rd N. C. Apr. 16, 1776; was taken prisoner; when and where not stated. (D. May 20, 1830.)
257. Grant, Reuben, Ensn. 6th N. C. Apr. 16, 1776; Lt. June 6, 1776; served to ......
257. Grant, Thomas, Ensn. 6th N. C. Apr. 16, 1776 to ...... (D. 1828.)
257. Graves, Francis, Reg. Quartmstr. 8th N. C. Sept. 1, 1777; Lt. 10th N. C. Oct. 26, 1777; transfd. to 3rd N. C. June 1, 1778; 1st Lt. July 14, 1779; transfd. to 1st N. C. .. July 1780; taken prisoner at Charleston May 12, 1780, exchanged June 14, 1781; and served to close of war.
258. Gray, John, Capt. 3rd N. C. Apr. 16, 1776; retired June 1, 1778.
259. Green, James W., Surgeon's Mate 10th N. C. June 10, 1778; Surgeon Dec. 7, 1779; taken prisoner at Charleston May 12, 1780; exchanged June 14, 1781; transfd. to 1st N. C. Feb. 6, 1782; served to close of war.
260. Green, Joseph, Commissary 8th N. C. Dec. 11, 1776 to ......
260. Green, William, Capt. 1st N. C. Sept. 1, 1775; resigned Jan. 4, 1776.
260. Green, William, Ensn. 6th N. C. June 6, 1776; 2nd Lt. Oct. 28, 1776; 1st Lt. Aug. 27, 1777; served to ......
261. Greensbury, Thomas, Capt. 3rd N. C. Apr. 16, 1776; resigned Dec. 28, 1779.
261. Greer, Robert, 2nd Lt. 8th N. C. Nov. 28, 1776; 1st Lt. Apr. 24, 1777; retired June 1, 1778.
262. Gregory, Dempsey, Capt. 10th N. C. Apr. 19, 1777; resigned May 22, 1778.
262. Gregory, Isaac, Brig. Gen. N. C. Militia, wounded at Camden Aug. 16, 1780.
264. Groves, William, 1st Lt. 5th N. C. Apr. 16, 1776; Capt. Aug. 17, 1777; retired June 1, 1778. (Name also spelled Graves.)
265. Guion, Isaac, Surgeon 1st N. C. Sept. 1, 1775; resigned Dec. .. 1775; Commissary & Paymaster 7th N. C. Mch. 11, 1776; retired July 1, 1778.
265. Gurley, William, Capt. 8th N. C. Nov. 28, 1776 to ......
266. Hadley, Joshua, 1st Lt. 6th N. C. Apr. 1, 1776; transfrd. to 1st N. C. June 1, 1778; Capt. June 13, 1779; wounded at Eutaw Springs Sept. 8, 1781; served to close of war. (D. Feb. 8, 1830.)
266. Hair, John L., Lt. 1st N. C. Aug. 16, 1777 to ......
267. Hall, Clement, 1st Lt. 2nd N. C. Sept. 1, 1775; Capt. Apr. 19, 1777; Brevet Majr. Sept. 30, 1783; served to close of war.
267. Hall, James, Capt. 9th N. C. .. 1777 to ......; Lt. Col. N. C. Militia; killed at Cowan's Ford, Feb. 1, 1781.
268. Hall, Robert, Surgeon 3rd N. C. Apr. 17, 1776; resigned Feb. 28, 1777.
268. Hall, Thomas, Ensn. 1st N. C. Dec. 24, 1776; 2nd Lt. Feb. 8, 1777; resigned Apr. 3, 1777.
268. Hall, William, Capt. N. C. Militia, 1779-1781; served as Col. and Brig. Gen. Tennessee Militia during war of 1812. (D. June 3, 1825.)
269. Halling, Solomon, Surgeon 4th N. C. in 1779 to close of war.
269. Hambright, Frederick, Capt. N. C. Militia, 1776; Lt. Col. N. C. Riflemen Militia, wounded at King's Mtn. Oct. 7, 1780. (D. Mch. .. 1817.)

*Pages*
270. Hamilton, Hanse, Surgeon 7th N. C. Apr. .. 1777 to ......
271. Hammond, George, Lt. N. C. Militia; wounded at Eutaw Springs Sept. 8, 1781.
271. Hampton, Andrew, Capt. N. C. Militia in 1776, Col. N. C. Militia at King's Mtn. Oct. 1780; (Died Oct. 8, 1805.)
272. Handcock, William, Ensn. 6th N. C. Apr. 28, 1777; 2nd Lt. Aug. 1, 1777; resigned Aug. 27, 1777.
274. Hardy, William, Paymaster Battalion N. C. Light Dragoons Sept. 10, 1777 to .....
274. Hargrave, William, Ensn. 10th N. C. Jan. 16, 1778, transfrd. 1st N. C. June 1, 1778; Lt. Mch. 30, 1780; taken at Charleston May 12, 1780, exchanged June 14, 1781; retired Jan. 1, 1783.
274. Harjett, Fredrick, Capt. 8th N. C. Nov. 28, 1776 to ......
275. Harney, Selby, Maj. 8th N. C. Nov. 26, 1776; Lt. Col. Nov. 6, 1777; transfrd. to 2nd N. C. June 1, 1778; taken pris. at Charleston May 12, 1780; exchanged ....; transfrd to 3rd N. C. Feb. 6, 1782; Col. Sept. 30, 1783, & served to close of war.
275. Harper, Andrew, Brigade-Major to Gen. Hogun in 1779.
275. Harper, Jonathan, Lt. Col. N. C. Militia, 1780-1781.
276. Harris, Thomas, Capt. 4th N. C. Apr. 16, 1776; reported as Maj. in 1781; served to ...... (D. Aug. 31, 1826.)
276. Harris, West, Lt. 9th N. C. Nov. 28, 1776; Lt. N. C. Dragoons .., 1777 to Jan. 1780.
277. Harrison, Richard, Maj. N. C. Militia in 1780.
277. Harrison, William, Ensn. 7th N. C. Dec. 11, 1776; 2nd Lt. Dec. 19, 1776; 1st Lt. July 15, 1777; Capt. .., 1779; served to close of war. (D. July 18, 1831.)
277. Hart, Anthony, 2nd Lt. 3rd N. C. Apr. 16, 1777; 1st Lt. Nov. 22, 1777; taken pris. at Charleston, May 12, 1780; exchgd. June 14, 1781; Capt. 1781; served to close of war.
277. Hart, John, 2nd Lt. 6th N. C. May 7, 1776; 1st Lt. ....; Capt. 6th Aug. 1779, and served to .....
277. Hart, Nathaniel, Capt. N. C. Rangers; killed by Indians at Blue Lick Springs, Kentucky, Aug. 19, 1782.
278. Hart, Samuel, Lt. 9th N. C. Nov. 28, 1776 to ......
278. Hart, Thomas, Commissary 6th N. C. Apr. 23, Oct. 28, 1776.
278. Harvey, James, Paymaster, 7th N. C. Dec. 11, 1776 to ......
278. Harvey, John, Capt. N. C. Militia at King's Mtn. in Oct. 1780.
280. Hawkins, Philemon, Col. N. C. Militia, 1776-1781. (D. 1801.)
282. Hays, James, Lt. 7th N. C. Nov. 28, 1776 to ......
282. Hays, Robert, Ensn. 4th N. C. Aug. 16, 1777; 2nd Lt. Jan. 1, 1778; transfrd. to 1st N. C. June 1, 1778; 1st Lt. Feb. 16, 1780; taken pris. at Charleston, May 12, 1780; exch'gd. June 14, 1781; served to close of war.
284. Henderson, Michael, Capt. 9th N. C. Nov. 28th, 1776 to ......
285. Henderson, Pleasant, Lt. 6th N. C. Apr. 16, 1776 to ......; Maj. N. C. Militia, 1780-1781. (D. 1842.)
285. Henderson, Richard, Capt. in N. C. Militia, 1780-1781.
286. Herndon, Benjamin, Maj. N. C. Militia at King's Mtn. Oct. 1780. (D. Dec. 31, 1819.)
287. Herndon, Joseph, Capt. N. C. Militia at King's Mtn. Oct. 1780.
287. Herritage, John, 1st Lt. 2nd N. C. Sept. 1, 1775; Capt. May 3, 1776; resigned May 15, 1777.
287. Herron, Armwell, Capt. 10th N. C. Apr. 19, 1777; retired June 1, 1778.
287. Hewell, William, Lt. 5th N. C. Apr. 20, 1777 to ...... Name also spelled Ewell.
287. Hewes, Joseph, a signer of the Dec. of Independence. D. Nov. 10, 1779.
288. Hickman, William, Lt. 4th N. C. .., 1777 to ......
289. Hicks, William, Ensn. 9th N. C. Nov. 28, 1776 to ......; was Capt. N. C. Militia in 1781.

*Pages*

290. Hill, John, Ensn. 10th N. C. Apr. 4, 1781; Lt. July 5, 1781; transfrd. to 4th N. C. Feb. 6, 1782; served to close of war.
290. Hill Williams, Lt. 1st N. C. Sept. 1, 1775 to . . . . . . .
291. Hilton, William, 2nd Lt. 6th N. C. Apr. 1, 1777; 1st Lt. Oct. 12, 1777; transfrd. to 1st N. C. July 1, 1778; killed at Stony Point, July 15, 1779.
293. Hodges, John, Ensn. 5th N. C. May 4, 1776; Lt. Oct. 1, 1776; was in service as a Capt. in 1780 and 1781; served to . . . . . .
293. Hodgton, Alvery, Lt. & Adjt. 3rd N. C. in 1777, and served to . . . . . . .
294. Hogg, Thomas, 1st Lt. 1st N. C. Sept. 1, 1775; Capt. Apr. 10, 1776; Maj. 5th N. C. Sept. 19, 1777; transfrd. to 3rd N. C. June 1st, 1778; taken pris. at Charleston May 12, 1780; exchgd. Mch. 1781, and served to close of war; Brevet Lt. Col. Sept. 30, 1783.
294. Hogun, James, Maj. Georgia Militia in 1776; Col. 7th N. C. Nov. 26, 1776; transfrd. to 3rd N. C. June 1, 1778; Brig. Gen. Cont. Army, Jan. 9, 1779; taken pris. at Charleston May 12, 1780 and died in Captivity Jan. 4, 1781.
296. Holland, James, Lt. and Capt. N. C. Militia, 1776-1781.
296. Holland, Spier, Ensn. 5th N. C. Mch. 24th, 1776; 1st Lt. Oct. 25, 1777, and served to . . . . . . .
297. Hollingsworth, Charles, Lt. 4th N. C. . ., 1777 to . . . . . . .
297. Hollowell, Samuel, Lt. 8th N. C. Sept. 20, 1777; retired June 1, 1778.
297. Holmes, Hardy, 2nd Lt. 1st N. C. Nov. . ., 1776; 1st Lt. . ., 1777 to . . . . . . ; Capt. . . .; wounded at Eutaw Springs, Sept. 8, 1781; served to close of war.
300. Hooper, William, a signer of the Dec. of Indpndce. D. Oct. 11, 1790.
302. Houston, Christopher, Capt. N. C. Rangers 1776-1782. (D. May 12, 1837.)
302. Houston, James, Capt. N. C. Rangers, 1777-1780; wounded at Ramsour's Mill, June 20, 1780. (D. Aug. 2, 1819.)
304. Howe, Robert, Col. 2nd N. C. Sept. 1, 1775; Brig. Gen. Cont. Army, Mch. 1, 1776; Maj. Gen. Oct. 20, 1777; and served to close of war. (D. Nov. 12, 1785.)
304. Howell, Elias, Ensn. 8th N. C. Nov. 12, 1776; 2nd Lt. July 12, 1777; retired July 1, 1778.
309. Hunt, Jesse, Capt. N. C. Militia, 1778.
310. Hunter, James, Maj. N. C. Militia at Guilford in March 1781.
313. Inglas, John, 1st Lt. 2nd N. C. May 3, 1776; Capt. Oct. 24, 1777; taken pris. at Charleston May 12, 1780; exchgd. June 1781; served to close of war; Brevt Maj. Sept. 30, 1783.
313. Ingram, James, Lt. Col. 8th N. C. Nov. 27, 1776; resigned July 8, 1777.
313. Irwin, Henry, Lt. Col. 5th N. C. Apr. 15, 1776; killed at Germantown Oct. 4, 1777.
313. Irwin, John, Ensn. 1st N. C. Mch. 28, 1777; 2nd Lt. Apr. 4, 1777; resigned Aug. 28, 1777; Col. N. C. Militia in 1780-1781.
313. Isaacs, Elisha, Col. N. C. Militia . .; wounded and taken pris. at Camden Aug. 16, 1780; exchgd. July 1781.
315. Ivey, Curtis, Ensn. 5th N. C. Apr. 23, 1777; 1st Lt. Oct. 10, 1777; transfrd. to 3rd N. C. June 1, 1778; Capt. Feb. 1, 1779; transfrd. to 4th N. C. Feb. 6. 1782; served to close of war. Name also spelled *Ivory*.
317. Jacobs, John, Ensn. 6th N. C. June 2, 1776; 2nd Lt. Nov. 1, 1776; resigned Mch. 1, 1778.
317. James, John, Capt. 6th N. C. Apr. 16, 1776 to . . . . . .
318. Jarvis, John, Capt. 10th N. C. Apr. 19, 1777 to . . . . . .
318. Jarvis, Samuel, Col. N. C. Militia in 1780.
320. Johnson, James, Regimental Quartermaster, 6th N. C. Apr. 2, 1777; retired June 1, 1778; Capt. N. C. Militia at King's Mtn. . . ., Oct. 1780. (D. July 23, 1805) (?)
321. Johnson, Joshua, Lt. 9th N. C. Nov. 28, 1776 to . . . . . . .

*Pages*
321. Johnson, Samuel, Lt. 10th N. C. ...; wounded at King's Mtn. Oct. 7, 1780. (Died Sept. 15, 1834.)
322. Johnston, Gilbert, Capt. N. C. Rangers under Marion in 1780 & 1781. (D. 1794.)
323. Johnston, Hugo, Capt. N. C. Militia; wounded at Wiggins Mill, Geo. Apr. 1781. (D. 1794.)
322. Johnston, James, Capt. N. C. Militia, 1776, and at King's Mtn. in 1780. (D. July 23, 1805.) (?)
322. Johnston, John, Capt. N. C. Militia, 1779-1781.
322. Johnston, Jones, Col. N. C. Militia; killed at Stono Ferry, June 20, 1779.
322. Johnston, Joseph, Ensn. 9th N. C. Nov. 28, 1776; transfrd. to 1st N. C. June 1, 1778; 1st Lt. Feb. 1, 1779; taken pris. at Charleston, May 12, 1780; exchngd. June 1781; served to close of war.
322. Johnston, Launcelot, Surgeon 9th N. C. Dec. 22, 1776; retired June 1, 1778; Surgeon N. C. Militia in 1779-1780. (D. Sept. 19, 1832.)
323. Johnston, William, Capt. N. C. Militia at King's Mtn. Oct. 1780.
323. Jones, Allen, Lt. Col. & Col. & Brig.-Gen. N. C. Militia, 1775-1782. (D. Nov. 10, 1798.)
324. Jones, Daniel, Capt. 3rd N. C. May 12, 1776; retired June 1, 1778.
324. Jones, David, 1st Lt. 4th N. C. Nov. 27, 1776; omitted Jan. 1, 1778.
324. Jones, John, Col. N. C. Partisan Rangers, ....; wounded at Pacolett River, N. C. July 14, 1780.
325. Jones, Maurice, Lt. 6th N. C. June 15, 1776 to ......
325. Jones, Philip , Lt. 8th N. C. Nov. 28, 1776; Capt. Lt. of Kingsbury's Independent Co. N. C. Artillery, July 19, 1777; taken pris. at Charleston May 12, 1780.
325. Jones, Samuel, Ensn. 8th N. C. Nov. 28, 1776; 1st Lt. 10th N. C. Oct. 4, 1777; transfrd. to 3rd N. C. June 1, 1778; Capt. Sept. 11, 1781; retired Jan. 1, 1783.
325. Jones, Samuel, Ensn. 2nd N. C. ..... (D. July 7, 1778.)
325. Jones, Thomas, Ensn. 7th N. C. Apr. 7, 1777; Lt. Aug. 15, 1777; retired June 1, 1778.
325. Jones, Timothy, Lt. 10th N. C. Apr. 19, 1777; retired June 1, 1778.
326. Jones, Wm., Brig.-Gen. N. C. Militia, 1780-1781.
327. Karr, James, Lt. of a N. C. Reg. in 1781. (D. Mch. 13, 1823.)
327. Keais, Nathaniel, Capt. 2nd N. C. Sept. 1, 1775; retired June 1, 1778.
329. Kennedy, Robert, Capt. N. C. Militia at King's Mtn. Oct. 1780.
329. Kennedy, Thomas, Capt. N. C. Militia; wounded at Ramsour's Mill, June 20, 1780. (D. June 19, 1836.)
329. Kennon, John, Lt. 6th N. C. Apr. 16, 1776 to ....
330. Kennon, William, Lt. and Commissary 1st N. C. Sept. 1, 1776; resigned Apr. 1777.
331. Kilby, William, Ensn. 2nd N. C. June 6, 1776. (D. Apr. 6, 1777.)
331. Kilby, Wm. Tyler, Ensign 2nd N. C. June 6, 1776, (D. Apr. 6, 1777.)
332. King, James, Ensn. 1st N. C. June 1, 1776; 2nd Lt. Aug. 15, 1776; 1st Lt. Apr. 3, 1777; Capt. Mch. 30, 1780; taken pris. at Charleston May 12, 1780, and died in captivity.
333. Kingsbury, John, Capt. Independent Co. N. C. Artillery, July 19, 1777; taken pris. at Charleston May 12, 1780.
336. Knott, William, Lt. 4th N. C. ...., 1777 to ......
336. Koen, Caleb, Lt. 10th N. C. Apr. 19, 1777 to ......
337. Lacey, John. Ensn. 2nd N. C. May 20, 1779 to ......
337. Lackey, Christopher, 2nd Lt. 5th N. C. May 3, 1776; 1st Lt. .., 1777; transfrd. to 3rd N. C. June 1, 1778; served to ......
338. Lamb, Abner, Ensn. 1st N. C. .., 1780; Lt. June 1, 1781; wounded at Eutaw Springs, Sept. 8, 1781; served to close of war.
338. Lamb, Gideon, Maj. 6th N. C. Apr. 15, 1776; Lt. Col. May 6, 1776; Col. Jan. 26, 1777; retired June 1, 1778.

*Pages*
339. Lane, Isaac, Lt. N. C. Militia at King's Mtn. in Oct. 1780.
340. Langford, Alloway, Ensn. 8th N. C. Feb. 8, 1777; 2nd Lt. Aug. 1, 1777; 1st Lt. Oct. 12, 1777; retired June 1, 1778.
340. Lanier, David, Lt. N. C. Militia in 1780.
340. Lanier, James, Ensn. 8th N. C. Nov. 28, 1776; 2nd Lt. Aug. 26, 1777; retired June 1, 1778.
340. Lanier, William, Ensn. N. C. Militia, 1780.
341. Lasiter, Jethro, Ensn. 7th N. C. Nov. 28, 1776; 2nd Lt. Dec. .., 1776; 1st Lt. Oct. 12, 1777; retired June 1, 1778.
342. Lawrence, Nathaniel, Ensn. 3rd N. C. June 1, 1777; taken pris. at Fort Fayette, June 1, 1779; exchanged Apr. 18, 1781; retained at Lt. 2nd N. C. to rank from Jan. 23, 1781; retired Jan. 1, 1783.
347. Lemmy, Joseph, Ensn. 1st N. C. Jan. 4, 1776; 2nd Lt. Jan. 18, 1776; died July 1776. Name also spelled McLemmy.
347. Lenear, James, Ensn. 8th N. C. Nov. 28, 1776; resigned Oct. 12, 1777. Name also spelled Lenoir.
347. Lenoir, William, Capt. N. C. Rangers, .., 1776; wounded at King's Mtn. Oct. 7, 1780; (D. May 6, 1839.)
349. Lewis, James Martin, Lt. N. C. Militia; wounded at King's Mtn., Oct. 7, 1780.
349. Lewis, Joel, Lt. 10th N. C. Aug. 1, 1779; Capt. 4th N. C. ..; wounded at King's Mtn. Oct. 7, 1780; was a Maj. in 1782, and served to ..... (D. Nov. 22, 1816.)
349. Lewis, Joseph, Lt. 8th N. C. Nov. 28, 1776; resigned Oct. 10, 1777.
349. Lewis, Micajah, Capt. 1st N. C. July 25, 1777; transfrd. to 4th N. C. June 1, 1778; Major ....; wounded at King's Mtn. Oct. 7, 1780; died Feb. 28, 1781, of wounds received at Pyle's defeat, Feb. 25, 1781.
350. Lewis, William, Lt. 9th N. C. Mch. 1777 to .....
350. Ligman, John, Capt. N. C. Militia, 1780-1781.
350. Lillington, John, Lt. 1st N. C. Sept. 1, 1775; resigned May .., 1776; Col. N. C. Militia, 1779-1782.
350. Lillington, John Alexander, Col. 6th N. C. Apr. 15, 1776; resigned May 16, 1776; Brig.-Gen. N. C. Militia, 1776-1783. (D. 1786.)
352. Linton, Wm. 2nd Lt. 3rd N. C. July 24, 1776; 1st Lt. Apr. 14, 1777, and served to ...... (D. Feb. 28, 1827.)
352. Liscombe, John, Ensn. 6th N. C. Apr. 28, 1777 to ......
355. Locke, Francis, Col. N. C. Militia 1779-1781. (D. Jan. 8, 1823.)
355. Locke, George, Lt. N. C. Militia; killed at Charlotte Sept. 26, 1780.
355. Lockhart, Samuel, Maj. 3rd N. C. Apr. 15, 1776; Lt.-Col. 8th N. C. Oct. 12, 1777; resigned Oct. 19, 1777; was taken pris. at Charleston May 12, 1780, is then called Col.
356. Long, Nehemiah, Lt. 5th N. C. Oct. 4, 1776 to ......
356. Long, Nicholas, Col. N. C. Militia in 1775; Col. Deputy Quartermaster, General Southern Department, May 7, 1776 to ....; Col. 43rd U. S. Infantry Aug. 4, 1813; honorably dischg'd. June 15, 1815. (D. Aug. 22, 1819.)
356. Loomis, Abner, Ensn. 8th N. C. Feb. 8, 1776; 2nd Lt. Aug. 27, 1777; resigned Nov. 15, 1777.
356. Loomis, Jonathan, Surgeon, 8th N. C. Nov. 26, 1776; transfrd. to 3rd N. C. June 1, 1778; taken pris. at Charleston, May 12, 1780; exchanged June 14, 1781; served to close of war.
357. Looney, David, Major N. C. Militia 1779-1782. (D. 1810.)
357. Lord, William, Paymstr. 1st N. C. Dec. 12, 1776; resigned Mch. 5, 1777; Lt. 10th N. C. Aug. 1, 1779, and served to .....
358. Love, Amos, Lt. 6th N. C. Apr. 16, 1776, to .....
358. Love, David, Surgeon N. C. Brigade Aug. 18, 1779 to Aug. 1, 1781; was taken pris., when and where not stated.

*Pages*
359. Lowe, John, Lt. 10th N. C. Apr. 19, 1777; retired June 1, 1778. (D. 1826.)
359. Lowe, Philip, Ensn. 2nd N. C. Sept. 1st, 1775; Lt. May 3, 1776; resigned Feb. 1, 1777; Maj. 4th Georgia June 18, 1778; Lt. Col. .., 1780; retired Oct. 1, 1780.
360. Lumos, Jonathan, Surgeon 3rd N. C. Nov. 26th, 1776; retired Jan. 1, 1783.
361. Luton, James, Ensn. 2nd N. C. Apr. 1, 1777; resigned Mch. 3, 1778.
361. Luttrell, John, Lt. Col. 9th N. C. Nov. 27, 1776; retired June 1, 1778.
361. Lynch, John, Lt. 7th N. C. Nov. 28, 1776 to . . . . .
363. Lytle, Archibald, Capt. 6th N. C. Apr. 16, 1776; Lt. Col. 6th N. C. Jan. 26, 1777; wounded at Stono Ferry, June 20, 1779; taken pris. at Charleston May 12, 1780; exchgd. Feb. 9, 1782; Col. Sept. 30, 1783; served to close of war.
363. Lytle, Micajah, Lt. 3rd N. C. May 3, 1776 to . . . . .
363. Lytle, William, Ensn. 9th N. C. Dec. 6, 1776; Lt. Apr. 16, 1777; transfrd. to 1st N. C. June 1, 1778; Capt. Jan. 28, 1779; transfrd. to 4th N. C. Feb. 6, 1782; served to close of war. (D. 1829.)
363. Mac & Mc. (Mc arranged as if spelled Mac.)
363. McAllister, Neil, Ensn. 1st N. C. Sept. 1, 1775; 2nd Lt. Jan. 4, 1776; 1st Lt. June 29, 1776; resigned June 20, 1777.
364. McCann, John, Lt. 6th N. C. Apr. 16, 1776; killed Oct. 4, 1777, at Germantown, Pa.
364. McCarthy, Florence, Ensn. 4th N. C. May 1, 1777 to . . . . . . .
364. McCauley, Matthew, Lt. 10th N. C. Apr. 19, 1777 to . . . . . . .
364. McClammy, Joseph, Ensn. 2nd N. C., Oct. 20, 1775 to . . . . . .
365. McClelland, Daniel, Capt. in a N. C. Regm't in 1780 & 1781.
366. McClure, James, Ensn. N. C. Militia, wounded at Hanging Rock Aug. 6, 1780.
366. McClure, William, Surgeon 6th N. C. Apr. 17, 1776; transfrd. to 2nd N. C. June 1, 1778; transfrd. to 1st N. C. .., 1780; taken pris. at Charleston May 12, 1780; exchanged June 14, 1781; served to close of war. (D. Oct. 25, 1828.)
367. McCrory, Thomas, Capt. 9th N. C. Nov. 28, 1776 to . . . . . .
368. McDougall, James, Cornet 3rd Continental Dragoons Jan. 8th, 1777 to . . . . . .
368. McDowell, Charles, Col. N. C. Militia, 1779-1781. (D. Mch. 31, 1815.)
369. McDowell, Joseph, Sr., Major N. C. Militia at King's Mtn. Oct. 1780, and at Cowpens in Jan. 1781; served subsequently as Col. and Brig.-Gen. in N. C. Militia. (D. Aug. 11, 1801.)
369. McDowell, Joseph, Capt. N. C. Militia 1780-1781; (was cousin of Joseph McDowell, Sr.); died Feb. 27, 1795.
369. McFadden, James, Capt. N. C. Militia, 1776.
370. McGibbony, Patrick, Ensn. 4th N. C., Nov. 27, 1776; Lt. Dec. 9, 1776; served to . . . . . .
370. McGlaughlan, John, Capt. 7th N. C. Nov. 28, 1776 to . . . . . .
371. McIlwaine, Stringer, Lt. 2nd N. C. in 1777.
372. McKinney, James, Ensn. 5th N. C. May 9, 1776 to . . . . . .
373. McKissick, Daniel, Capt. N. C. Militia; wounded at Ramsour's Mill, June 20, 1780.
373. McLane, John, Capt. 4th N. C. Apr. 16, 1776 to . . . . . .
373. McLane, Wm., Surgeon's Mate 10th N. C. Jan. 1, 1783 to close of war. (D. Oct. 25, 1828.)
373. McLaughlan, John, Lt. 1st N. C. May 6, 1776; Capt. 1780, and served to . . . . . .
373. McLean, William, Surgeon's Mate 1st N. C. in 1779 to 1781; name also spelled McLane. (D. Oct. 25, 1823.)
374. McNaughton, John, 2nd Lt. 8th N. C. Nov. 28, 1776; 1st Lt. Aug. 5, 1777; retired June 1, 1778.
374. McNees, John, 2nd Lt. 3rd N. C. Mch. 8, 1777; 1st Lt. Nov. 20, 1777; taken pris. at Charleston May 12, 1780; exchgd. June 14, 1781; transfrd. to 1st N. C. Jan. 1, 1781; was in 3rd N. C. Feb. 1782, and served to close of war.

*Pages*
375. McNeil, Hector, 1st Lt. 1st N. C., Sept. 1, 1775; deserted Feb. 3, 1776.
375. Mason, John, 1st Lt. 7th N. C. Nov. 28, 1776; Capt. Dec. 11, 1776; retired June 1, 1778.
375. McRee, Griffith John, Capt. 6th N. C. Apr. 16, 1776; transfrd. to 1st N. C. June 1, 1778; taken pris. at Charleston May 12, 1780; Maj. 3rd N. C. Sept. 11, 1781, and served to close of war; Capt. of Artillerists and Engineers, June 2, 1794; resigned 29th Apr. 1798. (D. Oct. 3, 1801.)
376. McReynolds, Robert, Ensn. 10th N. C. Apr. 19, 1777 to ......
376. McRory, James, Ensn. 9th N. C. May 2, 1777 to ......
376. McSheehy, Miles, Adjutant 9th N. C. Feb. 12, 1777 to ......
377. Magness, Wm., Capt. N. C. Militia, 1776-1777.
377. Mallett, Daniel, Commissary 4th N. C. Apr. 23, 1776 to ......
377. Mallett, Peter, Commissary 6th N. C. Oct. 28, 1776; of the 5th N. C. Apr. 23, 1777 to June 1, 1778, when retired.
380. Marshall, Dixon, Ensn. 1st N. C. Mch. 28, 1777; 2nd Lt. Apr. 26, 1777; 1st Lt. July 1779; taken pris. at Charleston May 12, 1780; exchgd. June 14, 1781; served to close of war. (D. Aug. 22, 1824.)
381. Martin, Alexander, Lt. Col. 2nd N. C. Sept. 1, 1775; Col. May 7, 1776; resigned Nov. 22, 1777. (D. Nov. 12, 1807.)
381. Martin, James, 1st Lt. 2nd N. C. May 3, 1776; Capt. 5th N. C. Apr. 20, 1777; retired June 1, 1778; Col. N. C. Militia 1780-1781.
382. Martin, Samuel, 1st Lt. 2nd N. C. June 8, 1776; Capt. June .., 1780; served to ...... (D. Nov. 26, 1836.)
383. Mason, Richard, Ensn. 2nd N. C. Sept. 4th, 1778; Lt. .. 1779; Capt. 1781, and served to close of war.
384. Masterson, James, Ensn. N. C. Militia in 1780.
385. May, James, Capt. 8th N. C. Nov. 28, 1776; resigned Aug. 5, 1777.
387. Mebane, Robert, Lt. Col. 7th N. C. Nov. 28, 1776; transfrd. to 1st N. C. June 1, 1778; Lt. Col. Commandant 3rd N. C. June 7, 1779; taken pris. at Charleston May 12, 1780.
387. Medaris, John, 1st Lt. 3rd N. C. Apr. 15, 1777; Capt. Dec. 23, 1777; tranfrd. to 1st N. C. Feb. 6, 1782; and served to close of war. Brevet Maj. Sept. 30, 1783.
387. Medici, Cosmode, Capt. Independent Co. N. C. Light Horse Mch. 3, 1777; Company dischgd. Jan. 1, 1779.
389. Mercer, John, Ensn. 7th N. C. Nov. 28, 1776; resigned Nov. 22, 1777.
389. Meredith, Wm., Capt. N. C. Militia at King's Mtn., Oct. 1780.
390. Messick, Jacob, Ensn. 8th N. C. Nov. 28, 1776; Lt. Apr. 24, 1777; retired June 1, 1778.
392. Miller, James, Lt. N. C. Militia in 1777; Capt. N. C. Militia at King's Mtn. Oct. 1780.
394. Mills, Benjamin, 1st Lt. 8th N. C. Nov. 28, 1776; resigned July 12, 1777; 1st Lt. N. C. Dragoons July 15, 1777, and served to Jan. 1781.
394. Mills, James, 1st Lt. 8th N. C. Nov. 28, 1776; transfrd. to 1st N. C. June 1778; appears to have been a Capt. in 10th N. C. in 1779, and is reported to have been killed in a skirmish in Mch. 1781.
395. Mitchell, George, Capt. 6th N. C. Apr. 16, 1776 to ......
396. Mitchels, Nathaniel, Regimental Quartermaster 3rd N. C. ....; dismissed Oct. 31, 1778.
396. Montford, Joseph, 1st Lt. 3rd N. C. Apr. 16, 1776; Capt.-Lt. Feb. 1777; Capt. Jan. 9, 1779; taken pris. at Charleston May 12, 1780; exchanged and served to close of war; Capt. 1st U. S. Infantry June 3, 1790; killed Apr. 27, 1792 by Indians near Fort Jefferson, Ohio.
398. Moore, Alfred, Capt. 1st N. C. Sept. 1, 1775; resigned Mch. 8, 1777. (D. Oct. 15, 1810.)

*Pages*
398. Moore, Dempsey, 1st Lt. 6th N. C. Apr. 16, 1776; resigned **Aug. 27, 1777.**
398. Moore, Elijah, 1st Lt. 10th N. C. Oct. 12, 1777; transfrd. to 1st N. C. June 1, 1778; Capt. Sept. 11, 1781; transfrd. to 4th N. C. Feb. 6, 1782; retired Jan. 1, 1783.
399. Moore, Isaac, Capt. 10th N. C. Apr. 19, 1777; transfrd. to 1st N. C. June 1, 1778; (D. July 10, 1778.)
399. Moore, James, Col. 1st N. C. Sept. 1, 1775; Brig.-Gen. Continental Army, Mch. 1, 1776. (D. Apr. 9, 1777.)
399. Moore, James, Ensn. 1st N. C. .., 1780; Lt. July 1, 1781; wounded at Eutaw Springs Sept. 8, 1781; did not rejoin regiment.
399. Moore, Maurice, Ensn. 1st N. C. Sept. 1, 1775; 2nd Lt. Jan. 4, 1776; killed Jan. 18, 1776 at . . . . . .
399. Moore, Robert, Ensn. 9th N. C. Nov. 28, 1776; was a Capt. in 1778 and 1779.
399. Moore, Roger, Capt. 4th N. C. Apr. 16, 1776; resigned Nov. . ., 1776.
400. Moore, Stephen, Lt. Col. N. C. Militia, taken pris. at Charleston May 12, 1780.
400. Moore, William, Surgeon's Mate, 10th N. C. Jan. 19, 1778; resigned May . . ., 1778.
400. Morehead, James, Lt. 10th N. C. Mch. 23, 1779 to . . . . . .
401. Morgan, Benjamin, Ensn. 3rd N. C. Nov. 28, 1776 to . . . . . .
404. Moseley, William, Paymstr. 6th N. C. Dec. 11, 1776; resigned May 1777.
405. Moslander, Abel, Lt. 4th N. C. Jan. 25, 1777 to . . . . . .
405. Mossam, Richard, Ensn. 10th N. C. Sept. 4, 1778 to . . . . . .
407. Mumford, Joseph, Capt. 1st N. C. Jan. 9, 1779; taken pris. at Charleston, May 12, 1780.
408. Murfree, Hardy, Capt. 2nd N. C. Sept. 1, 1775; Maj. Feb. 1, 1777; Lt. Col. 1st N. C., Apr. 1, 1778, & served July 1782. (D. Apr. 6, 1809.)
408. Murphy, Archibald, Col. N. C. Militia in 1777. (D. 1817.)
408. Murray, William, Ensn. 4th N. C. Apr. 1, 1777 to . . . . . .
409. Myrick, John, Ensn. 7th N. C. Nov. 28, 1776; Lt. Dec. 11, 1776 to . . . . . .
409. Nash, Clement, 1st Lt. 2nd N. C. May 3, 1776; resigned Feb. 1, 1777; Capt. 3rd Georgia, Apr. 10, 1777; was taken prisoner at Briar Creek Mch. 3rd, 1779; exchanged . . . .; taken pris. at Charleston May 12, 1780.
409. Nash, Francis, Lt. Col. 1st N. C. Sept. 1, 1775; Col. Apr. 10, 1776; Brig.-Gen. Continental Army Feb. 5, 1777; died Oct. 7, 1777 of wounds received at Germantown Oct. 4, 1777.
410. Neal, Andrew, Lt. N. C. Militia, 1776.
410. Neal, William, Lt. 9th N. C. Nov. 28th, 1776 to . . . . .; was a Capt. N. C. Militia at King's Mt'n. in Oct. 1780.
410. Neale, Henry, Ensn. 1st N. C. Sept. 1, 1775; 2nd Lt. Jan. 4, 1776; 1st Lt. Mch. 28, 1776; Capt. Feb. 5, 1777; resigned Apr. 3, 1777; name also spelled Neill.
410. Nelson, Alexander, Ensn. 4th N. C. July 1, 1777 to . . . . . .
410. Nelson, John, Capt. 4th N. C. Apr. 16, 1776; Maj. 1st N. C. Feb. 3, 1778; taken pris. at Charleston May 12, 1780; exchanged Mch. 1781, transferred to 1st N. C. Feb. 1782; retired Jan. 1, 1783.
414. Nicholson, Robert, 1st Lt. 10th N. C. Apr. 19, 1777; transfr'd. to 1st N. C. June 1, 1778; resigned June 25, 1779. (Died May 21, 1819.)
415. Nixon, Thomas, Capt. 8th N. C. Nov. 28, 1776; resigned Sept. 20, 1777.
415. Noble, Wm. Lt. 7th N. C. Nov. 28, 1776, to . . . . . .
417. Nuthall, Nathaniel, Ensn. 9th N. C. May 20, 1777; Adjutant May 26, 1777; transferred to 3rd N. C., June 1, 1778; dismissed Oct. 31, 1778.
419. Oldham, John, Capt. N. C. Militia at Guilford in March 1781. (D. 1831.)
419. Oliver, John, Ensn. 2nd N. C. Sept. 1, 1775 to . . . . . .
420. O'Neal, Charles, Ensn. 3rd N. C. Apr. 18, 1777; 2nd Lt. July 20, 1777; retired July 1, 1778.

*Pages*

421. Orrell, Thomas, Ensn. 10th N. C. Mch. 14, 1778; retired June 1, 1778.
421. Osborn, Alexander, Col. N. C. Militia, 1775-1776. (D. 1776.)
422. Outlaw, Edward, Ensn. 6th N. C. Apr. 16, 1776 to ......
422. Owen, Stephen, Ensn. 8th N. C. Jan. 1777; Lt. Aug. 15, 1777; retired June 1, 1778.
422. Owens, John, Lt. 6th N. C. May 7, 1776 to ......
424. Palmer, Joseph, Ensn. 5th N. C. June 6, 1776 to ......
426. Parker, Kedar, 2nd Lt. 6th N. C. May 7, 1776; 1st Lt. Sept. 19, 1776; retired June 1, 1778.
426. Parkinson, James, 1st Lt. 2nd N. C. May 1777. (D. Mch. 26, 1778.)
428. Pasteur, John, Lt. 6th N. C. July 2, 1776 to ......
428. Pasteur, Thomas, Ensn. 4th N. C. July 15, 1777; 2nd Lt. Dec. 29, 1777; transfrd. to 1st N. C. June 1, 1778; Regimental Adjutant June 26, 1779; 1st Lt. Nov. 10, 1779; taken pris. at Charleston May 12, 1780; exchgd. Dec. 1780; and served to close of war; Lt. Infantry U. S. Army June 3, 1790; Capt. 1st U. S. Infantry, Mch. 5, 1792; assigned to 1st Sub. Legion Sept. 4, 1792; assigned to 1st U. S. Infantry Nov. 1, 1796; Major 2nd Infantry Apr. 11, 1803. (D. July 29, 1806.)
428. Pasteur, William, Paymaster 4th N. C. Dec. 12, 1776 to ......
428. Pasteur, William, Surgeon 2nd N. C. Sept. 1, 1775 to June 1776.
429. Patten, John, Maj. 2nd N. C. Sept. 1, 1775; Lt. Col. Apr. 10, 1776; Col. Nov. 22, 1777; taken pris. at Charleston May 12, 1780; retired Jan. 1, 1783.
429. Patten, William, Surgeon 2nd N. C. Sept. 1, 1775 to ......
431. Payne, Michael, Capt. 2nd N. C. Sept. 1, 1775 to ......
432. Pearce, George, Ensn. 9th N. C. Nov. 28, 1776 to ......
432. Pearce, James, Capt. N. C. Militia in 1780. (D. Apr. 1, 1833.)
432. Pearl, James, Ensn. 8th N. C. Nov. 28, 1776; Lt. Oct. 29, 1777; transfrd. to 1st N. C. June 1, 1778; Capt. July 17, 1780; retired Jan. 1, 1783.
435. Penn, John, a Signer of the Declaration of Independence. Died Sept. 14, 1788.
436. Perkins, Adam, Lt. Col. 10th N. C. Apr. 7, 1777 to ......
437. Perry, George, Maj. N. C. Militia in 1776.
437. Phifer, Caleb, Col. N. C. Militia, 1776-1777. (D. 1811.)
439. Phifer, Martin, Capt. Independent Company N. C. Light Horse, Mch. 1777 to Apr. 1780. (D. 1837.)
440. Phillips, Joseph, Capt. 4th N. C. Apr. 16, 1776 to ......
441. Pickett, Thomas, Ensn. 1st N. C. Oct. 20, 1775 to Jan. 1776.
441. Pickett, William, Capt. 1st N. C. Sept. 1, 1775 to Jan. 4, 1776, when his company was broken up.
442. Pike, Benjamin, 1st Lt. 6th N. C. Apr. 16, 1776; Capt. Apr. 28, 1777; (D. Oct. 12, 1777.)
442. Pilley, John, Ensn. 2nd N. C. Dec. 11, 1776 to ......
443. Pitts, John, Capt. N. C. Militia in 1780.
444. Polk, Charles, Lt. 4th N. C. Apr. 25, 1777 to ......
444. Polk, Thomas, Col. N. C. Regiment, 21 Dec., 1775; Col. 4th N. C. Apr. 16, 1776; resigned June 28, 1778; Brig.-Gen. N. C. Militia 1781 to close of war. (D. 1793.)
445. Polk, William, Maj. 9th N. C. Nov. 27, 1776; wounded at Germantown Oct. 4, 1777; retired June 1, 1778; Col. N. C. Militia and State Troops, 1779-1781. (D. Jan. 4, 1834.)
446. Pope, Henry, Ensn. 1st N. C. Sept. 1, 1775; Capt. 8th N. C. Nov. 28, 1776; retired June 1, 1778.
447. Porter, James, Maj. N. C. Militia ....; died Oct. 16, 1780 of wounds received at King's Mtn. Oct. 7, 1780.
448. Porter, Robert, Capt. N. C. Militia, 1776-1779.
448. Porterfield, Dennis, Ensn. 6th N. C. Apr. 16, 1776; Lt. Apr. 2, 1777; transfrd. to 1st N. C. June 1, 1778; Capt. Feb. 1, 1779; killed Sept. 8, 1781, at Eutaw Springs.

*Pages*

450. Powell, Isaac, Lt. N. C. Militia, 1780-1781.
450. Powers, James, 2nd Lt. 7th N. C. Nov. 28, 1776; 1st Lt. Apr. 20, 1777; transfrd. to 3rd N. C. June 1, 1778; served to . . . . . (D. 1818.)
450. Poynter, John, Capt. 7th N. C. Nov. 28, 1776 to . . . . .
454. Pugh, Whitmill, Ensn. 2nd N. C. Sept. 1, 1775 to . . . . . .
454. Purviance, James, Capt. N. C. Militia, 1779-1781.
455. Pyatt, Peter, Lt. 10th N. C. Mch. 30, 1781 to . . . . . .
456. Quinn, Michael, 1st Lt. 8th N. C. Nov. 28, 1776; Capt. Aug. 1, 1777; retired June 1, 1778.
457. Raiford, John 2nd Lt. 2nd N. C. . ., 1777; resigned Feb. 1st, 1778.
457. Raiford, Peter, Capt. in 1st N. C. in 1779; served to . . . . . .
457. Raiford, Robert, Capt. 8th N. C. Nov. 28, 1776; transfrd. to 2nd N. C. June 1, 1778; served to close of war; Brevet Maj. Sept. 30, 1783.
457. Raindtree, Reuben, Lt. 10th N. C. Apr. 19, 1777; omitted Jan. 1, 1778.
457. Ramsay, Allen, Lt. 7th N. C. Dec. 19, 1776; omitted Jan. 1778.
457. Ramsay, Matthew, Capt. 9th N. C. Nov. 28, 1776; transferred to 4th N. C. June 1, 1778; resigned Nov. 1781.
457. Ramsey, Ambrose, Col. N. C. Militia in 1780.
459. Read, James, Ensn. 1st N. C. Jan. 4, 1776; 2nd Lt. July 6, 1776; 1st Lt. July 7, 1776; Capt. July 8, 1777 to . . . . .; Col. N. C. Militia; taken pris. at Charleston May 12, 1780. (D. 1803.)
460. Read, Jesse, 2nd Lt. 6th N. C. Oct. 20, 1776; 1st Lt. Oct. 25, 1777; transfrd. to 2nd N. C. June 1st, 1778; transfrd. to 3rd N. C. Jan. 1, 1781; taken pris. at Eutaw Springs Sept. 8, 1781; Capt. Oct. 15, 1781; served to close of war.
460. Reddick, John, Lt. N. C. Militia, 1780-1781.
460. Redpith, John, Lt. 4th N. C. Aug. 20, 1777; died Oct. 13, 1777 of wounds received at Germantown Oct. 4, 1777.
461. Reed, George, Capt. N. C. Militia; killed at Hanging Rock Aug. 6, 1780.
461. Reed, Samuel, Capt. N. C. Militia 1780-1781. (D. 1810.)
462. Reese, George, Lt. 9th N. C. Nov. 28, 1776 to . . . . . .
463. Respess, John, Ensn. 8th N. C. Nov. 28, 1776; resigned Apr. 24, 1777.
463. Reynolds, Elisha, Lt. N. C. Militia at King's Mtn. in Oct. 1780. (D. Dec. 13, 1836.)
464. Rhodes, Joseph, Lt. 8th N. C. Nov. 28, 1776; Capt. Aug. 5, 1777; retired June 11, 1778.
464. Rice, Hezekiah, 1st Lt. 1st N. C. Sept. 1, 1775; Capt. Nov. 28, 1776; omitted Jan. 1778.
464. Rice, Jeptha, Quartermstr. Sergt. 9th N. C. Nov. 28, 1776; Ensn. Mch. 15, 1777; retired June 1, 1778.
465. Rice, John, Adjutant 1st N. C. Dec. 10, 1776; Ensn. Mch. 28, 1777; 2nd Lt. Apr. 3, 1777; 1st Lt. 1st Continental Dragoons June 1, 1778, and served to Nov. 9, 1782. (D. June 30, 1830.)
466. Richardson, John, Ensn. 10th N. C. Feb. 1777; omitted Jan. 1, 1778.
466. Richardson, Joseph, Ensn. 6th N. C. Jan. 1777; 2nd Lt. Aug. 27, 1777; retired June 1, 1778.
467. Ridley, William, Surgeon, 3rd N. C. Apr. 21, 1777; resigned Nov. 21, 1777.
469. Roberts, John (N. C. and Va.), Lt. 5th N. C. Mch. 28, 1777; retired June 1, 1778; Capt. Va. Convention Guards Jan. 11, 1779; Maj. Mch. 5, 1779; retired May 1, 1781. (D. Nov. 30, 1843.)
469. Robertson, Charles, Maj. N. C. Rangers . . .; wounded at Wofford's Iron Works Aug. 8, 1780.
471. Robinson, Septimus, Ensn. 1st N. C. Mch. 28, 1776; 2nd Lt. July 7, 1776. (D. Dec. 10, 1776.)
471. Rochel, John, Capt. 3rd N. C. Nov. 28, 1776; omitted Jan. 1778.

*Pages*
471. Rochel, Lodowick, 1st Lt. 3rd N. C. Nov. 28, 1776; resigned Nov. .., 1777.
471. Rochester, Nathaniel, Paymstr. N. C. Militia in 1775 & 1776; Col. N. C. Militia & Commissary-Gen. of Military Stores in N. C. May 10, 1776 to 1782.
472. Rogers, John, Jr., Paymstr. 5th N. C. Dec. 11, 1776 to .....
472. Rogers, Patrick, Regimental Quartermstr. 1st N. C. Nov. 3, 1776; Ensn. Mch. 28, 1777; 2nd Lt. Apr. 3, 1777; (D. Apr. 19, 1778.)
473. Rolston, Isaac, Ensn. 2nd N. C. June 8, 1776; 1st Lt Jan. 1777; retired June 1, 1778.
473. Rolston, Robert, Ensn. 1st N. C. Sept. 1, 1775; 2nd Lt. Jan. 4, 1776; 1st Lt. Mch. 28, 1776; Capt. Mch. 8, 1777; resigned Aug. 29, 1777.
474. Ross. Francis, Lt. 9th N. C. Nov. 28, 1776 to ......
475. Roulledge, William, 1st Lt. 4th N. C. Jan. 25, 1777; resigned Aug. 20, 1777.
475. Rountree, Reuben, Lt. 10th N. C. Apr. 19, 1777 to ......
475. Rowan, John, Lt. N. C. Militia, 1780. (D. July 27, 1825.)
475. Rowan, Robert, Capt. 1st N. C. Sept. 1, 1775; resigned June 29, 1776.
477. Rushworm, William, Lt. 3rd N. C. Apr. 16, 1777; omitted Jan. 1, 1778; Cornet N. C. Dragoons, 1778-1780.
477. Russell, George, Lt. N. C. Militia at King's Mtn. Oct. 1780.
478. Rutherford, Griffith, Brig.-Gen. N. C. Militia; wounded and taken pris. at Camden Aug. 16, 1780; exchgd. June 14, 1781. (D. Dec. .., 1799.)
478. Rutherford, John, Maj. N. C. Militia; killed at Eutaw Springs, Sept. 8, 1781.
480. Salter, James, Commissary 2nd N. C. Dec. 19, 1776 to ......
480. Salter, Robert, Commissary 2nd N. C. Apr. 23, 1776; resigned Dec. 1, 1776.
480. Sanders, Richard, Capt. N. C. Militia, 1782.
482. Saunders, Jesse, Capt. 6th N. C. Apr. 16, 1776; resigned May 1776.
482. Saunders, William, Ensn. 6th N. C. Apr. 2, 1777; transfrd. to 1st N. C. June 1, 1778; Lt. Feb. 6, 1779; Capt. Feb. 8, 1779; transfrd. to 4th N. C. Feb. 6, 1782; retired Jan. 1, 1783.
483. Sawyer, Levi, 2nd Lt. 2nd N. C. May 15, 1776; resigned Mch. 16, 1778.
483. Sawyer, William, Ensn. 2nd N. C. May 15, 1776 to ......
487. Scull, John Gambier, Ensn. 1st N. C. June 1, 1776; 2nd Lt. Nov. 21, 1776; 1st Lt. Apr. 26, 1777; was a Capt. in 1780, and served to close of war.
487. Scurlock, James, Lt. 10th N. C. Sept. 1, 1780; Capt. Sept. 11, 1781; transfrd. to 4th N. C. Feb. 6, 1782; retired Jan. 1, 1783.
487. Seawell, Benjamin, Col. N. C. Militia, 1780-1781.
489. Sevier, John, Col. N. C. Militia 1777, to close of war; Brig.-Gen. U. S. Army, July 19, 1798; honorably dischgd. June 15, 1800. (D. Sept. 24, 1815.)
490. Sevier, Robert, Capt. N. C. Militia; mortally wounded at King's Mtn. Oct. 7, 1780.
490. Sevier, Valentine, Capt. N. C. Militia at King's Mtn. in Oct. 1780. (D. Feb. 23, 1800.)
491. Sharp, Anthony, 1st Lt. 9th N. C. Nov. 28, 1776; Capt. Aug. 24, 1777; transfrd. to 1st N. C. June 1, 1778; transfrd. to 4th N. C. Feb. 6, 1782; and served to close of war; Brevet Maj. Sept. 30, 1783.
491. Sharp, John, Ensn. of Capt. Pemberton's Company N. C. Rangers; in service Oct. 1780.
491. Sharpe, Anthony, Capt. 1st N. C. ....; in service in 1779.
491. Sharpe, Joseph, Capt. N. C. Militia, 1780-1781.
491. Shaw, Daniel, Ensn. 6th N. C. Apr. 2, 1777; 2nd Lt. Oct. 11, 1777; transfrd. to 1st N. C. June 1, 1778; 1st Lt. Oct. 1, 1779; Regimental Quartermaster June 1, 1778; taken pris. at Charleston May 12, 1780; exchgd. June 14, 1781, and served to close of war.
492. Shelby, Moses, Capt. N. C. Militia; wounded at King's Mtn. Oct. 7, 1780, and again wounded at Augusta, Ga., in Apr. 1781.

*Pages*
493. Shepard, Abraham, Col. 10th N. C. Apr. 17, 1777; retired June 1, 1778.
494. Shepherd, William, 1st Lt. 10th N. C. .., 1777; Capt. Jan. 20, 1778; retired June 1, 1778.
495. Shipman, James, Capt. N. C. Militia, 1779-1780.
496. Shute, Thomas, Ensn. 10th N. C. Apr. 19, 1777; retired June 1, 1778; (D. Jan. 15, 1819.)
498. Simons, Peter, Capt. 5th N. C. Apr. 16, 1776 to . . . . .
498. Singletary, Joseph, Lt. N. C. Militia, 1777.
498. Singletary, William, Lt. 8th N. C. Nov. 28, 1776; resigned Oct. 26, 1777.
498. Singleton, Richard, Capt. N. C. Militia in 1776.
498. Singleton, Robert, Ensn. 10th N. C. 1777; omitted May 1778.
498. Sitgreaves, John, Lt. N. C. Militia in 1776. (D. Mch. 4, 1802.)
499. Slade, Stephen, Quartermstr.-Sergt. 2nd N. C. May 12, 1776; Regimental Quartermstr. Jan. 1, 1778; Ensn. Sept. 5, 1778; Lt. Jan. 11, 1780; exchgd. June 14, 1781; 1st Lt. Jan. 13, 1781, and served to close of war.
499. Slade, William, Ensn. 4th N. C. Jan. 2, 1777; 2nd Lt. Apr. 26, 1777; transfrd. to 1st N. C. June 1, 1778; Regimental Adjutant June 1, 1778; resigned Feb. 18, 1780. (D. 1791.)
499. Slaughter, John, Capt. 5th N. C. in 1779.
500. Sledge, Arthur, Ensn. 7th N. C. Dec. 19, 1776 to . . . . . .
500. Sloan, Archibald, Lt. N. C. Militia, 1780-1781.
500. Slocum, Ezekiel, Lt. N. C. Militia in 1776.
501. Smith, . . . . . ., Capt. N. C. Partisan Rangers, . . . .; killed at Ramsour's Mill, June 20, 1780.
503. Smith, Jabez., Ensn. 5th N. C., Jan. 1777; 2nd Lt. Sept. 1, 1777; retired June 1, 1778.
504. Smith, John, Ensn. 9th N. C. Nov. 28, 1776 to . . . . . .
506. Smith, Minor, Capt. N. C. Militia; wounded at King's Mtn. Oct. 7, 1780; is also reported as being from Virginia.
506. Smith, Robert, 1st Lt. 2nd N. C. Sept. 1, 1775; Capt. 4th N. C. Apr. 16, 1776; transfrd. to 3rd Continental Dragoons Jan. 9, 1777; retired Nov. 4, 1778.
507. Smith, Samuel, Ensn. 2nd N. C. May 3, 1776 to . . . . . .
509. Snowden, Nathaniel, Lt. 10th N. C. June 5, 1778 to . . . . . .
509. Snowden, William, Lt. 7th N. C. Nov. 28, 1776 to . . . . . .
509. Southerland, Ransom, Commissary 4th N. C. Apr. 23, 1776 to . . . . .
509. Spain, Augustin, Capt. N. C. Militia 1780-1781.
510. Speed, . . . . . ., Capt. N. C. Militia, wounded at Stono Ferry, June 20, 1779.
511. Spicer, John, Capt. 2nd N. C. Dec. 11, 1776 to . . . . . .
512. Spratt, Thomas, Lt. 9th N. C. Nov. 28, 1776 to . . . . . .
513. Spycer, James, Paymstr. 5th N. C. in 1777, and 1778; name also spelled Spicer.
514. Standin, Thomas, Ensn. 2nd N. C. Oct. 20, 1775; Lt. May 3, 1776; Capt. Jan. 1777; resigned May 15, 1777.
516. Stedman, Benjamin, Capt. 5th N. C. Apr. 16, 1776; omitted Jan. 1, 1778.
516. Steed, Jesse, Ensn. 10th N. C. June 1, 1781; Regimental Quartermstr July 13, 1781; Lt. Sept. 8, 1781; transfrd. to 1st N. C. Feb. 6, 1782; retired Jan. 1, 1783.
519. Stevenson, Silas, 1st Lt. 10th N. C. Nov. 28, 1776; Capt. Apr. 19, 1777; retired June 1, 1778.
520. Stewart, Charles, 1st Lt. 5th N. C. July 23, 1777; transfrd. to 2nd N. C. June 1, 1778; Capt. Lt. Jan. 1, 1779; taken pris. at Charleston May 12, 1780; exchgd. June 14, 1781; Capt. May 18, 1781; killed at Eutaw Springs, Sept. 8, 1781.
520. Stewart, George, Lt. 9th N. C. Nov. 28, 1776 to . . . . . .
520. Stewart, Joseph, Lt. 9th N. C. Nov. 28, 1776 to . . . . . .
520. Stewart, Nicholas, Lt. 2nd N. C. Apr. 30, 1777 to . . . . . .
521. Stinson, James, Capt. N. C. Militia at King's Mtn. in Oct. 1780.

*Pages*
527. Suggs, George, Lt. 5th N. C. Nov. 1776 to ......
527. Summers, John, Ensn. 1st N. C. Mch. 28, 1776; 2nd Lt., July 7, 1776; 1st Lt. Feb. 5, 1777; Capt. July 10, 1778; taken pris. at Williamson's plantation, July 12, 1780; retired Jan. 1, 1783.
527. Sumner, Jethro, Col. 3rd N. C. Apr. 15, 1776; Brig.-Gen. Continental Army, Jan. 9, 1779, and served to close of war. (D. Mch. 18, 1785.)
528. Sutton, James, 2nd Lt. 2nd N. C. Dec. 16, 1776; resigned Mch. 10, 1778.
529. Swan, Nimrod, Regimental Quartermaster, 5th N. C. June 18, 1777; omitted Jan. 1, 1778.
530. Sykes, William, Ensn. N. C. Militia in 1781.
533. Tarrant, Manlove, Ensn. 2nd N. C. May 3, 1776; Lt. June 8, 1776; Capt. Oct. 24, 1777; retired June 1, 1778.
533. Tartanson, Francis, Capt. 8th N. C. Jan. 16, 1777; resigned Sept. 10, 1778.
533. Tate, James, Chaplain, 1st N. C. Oct. 13, 1775; Brigade Chaplain N. C. Troops, June 1, 1778, and served to close of war.
533. Tate, Joseph, 1st Lt. 2nd N. C. Sept. 1, 1775; Capt. May 16, 1776. (D. June 2, 1777.)
533. Tatum, Absolom, 1st Lt. 1st N. C. Sept. 1, 1775; Capt. June 29, 1776; resigned Sept. 19, 1776.
533. Tatum, Howell, Ensn. 1st N. C. Sept. 1, 1775; 2nd Lt. Jan. 4th, 1776; 1st Lt. Mch. 28, 1776; Capt. Apr. 3, 1777; taken pris. at Charleston May 12, 1780; exchgd. June 14, 1781; resigned May 20, 1782.
533. Tatum, James, Ensn. 9th N. C. Aug. 12, 1777; 2nd Lt. Jan. 1, 1778; transfrd. to 3rd N. C. June 1, 1778; 1st Lt. Dec. 14, 1779; taken pris. at Charleston May 12, 1780, and was a pris. on parole to close of war. (D. Sept. 10, 1821.)
534. Taylor, Christopher, Capt. N. C. Militia at King's Mtn. Oct. 1780.
534. Taylor, John, Ensn. 1st N. C. Sept. 1, 1775 to ......
534. Taylor, John, Lt. and Paymstr. 8th N. C. July 24, 1777; omitted Jan. 1, 1778.
534. Taylor, Philip, Capt. 6th N. C. Apr. 16, 1776; retired June 1, 1778.
535. Taylor, William, Lt. Col. 6th N. C. May 7, 1776 to ......
537. Thackston, James, Lt. Col. 4th N. C. Apr. 15, 1776; retired Jan. 1, 1781.
539. Thomas, John, Ensn. 9th N. C. Nov. 28, 1776 to ......
541. Thompson, Lawrence, 1st Lt. 1st N. C. Sept. 1, 1775; Capt. Aug. 15, 1776; retired June 1, 1778.
541. Thompson, Samuel, Lt. 6th N. C. Apr. 16, 1776 to ......
541. Thompson, William, Capt. N. C. Militia in 1778-1779.
544. Tillery, John, Lt. 3rd N. C. ...., 1777; omitted Jan. 1, 1778.
544. Tinning, ......, Col. N. C. Militia, 1779-1780.
545. Toole, Henry Irwin, Capt. 2nd N. C. Sept. 1, 1775; resigned Apr. 1776.
546. Toschey, William, Ensn. 2nd N. C. May 3, 1776 to ......
548. Triplett, Charles, Ensn. 1st N. C. Sept. 19, 1776; died Dec. 1776.
549. Trousdale, James, Capt. N. C. Militia, 1780-1781. (D. 1818.)
551. Turbee, William, Lt. 3rd N. C. July 6, 1777. (In service Jan. 1780,)
551. Turner, Berryman, Ensn. 1st N. C. Sept. 1, 1775 to ......
551. Turner, Jacob, Capt. 3rd N. C. Apr. 16, 1776; killed at Germantown Oct. 4, 1777.
552. Turner, Robert, Lt. 10th N. C. Feb. 1778; retired June 1, 1778.
554. Usher, William, Surgeon, 3rd N. C. Dec. 4, 1776 to Mch. 1777.
554. Vail, Edward, 1st Lt. 2nd N. C. Sept. 1, 1775; Capt. Aug. 21, 1776; cashiered Dec. 21, 1777; name also spelled Veal.
555. Vance, David, Ensn. 2nd N. C. Apr. 20, 1776; 1st Lt. June 8, 1776; retired June 1, 1778; Capt. N. C. Militia at King's Mtn. in October 1780, and in the South Carolina Campaign in 1781. (D. 1813.)
555. Vance, John Carlow, 1st Lt. of Capt. Kingsbury's Company N. C. State Artillery, July 19, 1777; taken pris. at Charleston May 12, 1780; exchanged June 14, 1781.

*Pages*
556. Vanoy, Andrew, Capt. 10th N. C. Apr. 19, 1777; retired June 1, 1778.
559. Varcaze, James, Lt. 10th N. C. Mch. 17, 1778; retired June 1, 1778.
559. Varner, Robert, Ensn. 1st N. C. Mch. 28, 1776; 2nd Lt. July 7, 1776; 1st Lt. Mch. 8, 1777; cashiered Oct. 1, 1779.
559. Vaughan, Benjamin, Capt. N. C. Militia in 1776.
559. Vaughan, James, 1st Lt. 7th N. C. Nov. 28; 1776; Capt. July 6, 1777; resigned Aug. 27, 1777.
560. Verner, James, Capt. Lt. 1st N. C. May 8, 1777, and served to ...... (In service Jan. 1780.)
560. Vernon, Richard, Lt. and Capt. N. C. Militia, 1779-1781.
561. Visson, Henry, Ensn. 2nd N. C. Sept. 1, 1775 to ......
562. Wade, Joseph J., Capt. 9th N. C. Nov. 28, 1776; omitted Jan. 1, 1778.
565. Walker, Felix, Lt.-Col. N. C. Militia, at King's Mtn. Oct. 1780. (D. 1829.)
565. Walker, John, Capt. 1st N. C. Sept. 1, 1775; Maj. Apr. 26, 1777; Lt.-Col. and Aid-de-Camp to Gen. Washington Feb. 17, 1777; resigned Dec. 22, 1777. (D. Dec. 2, 1809.)
565. Walker, Joseph, Capt. 7th N. C. Nov. 28, 1776; omitted Jan. 1, 1778.
565. Walker, Solomon, Ensn. 6th N. C. Apr. 16, 1776; 2nd Lt. Apr. 20, 1777; resigned Aug. 27, 1777.
566. Walker, William, Lt. 2nd N. C. ......; taken pris. at Charleston May 12, 1780; exchgd. June 14, 1781.
566. Wall, James, 1st Lt. of Capt. Kingsbury's Company N. C. Artillery July 19, 1777; resigned July 20, 1779.
566. Wallace, James, Lt. 10th N. C. Nov. 30, 1778; omitted July 1, 1779.
567. Wallis, James, Ensn. 3rd N. C. Nov. 30, 1778 to ......
567. Walsh, John, Capt. 8th N. C. Nov. 28, 1776; omitted Jan. 1, 1778.
567. Walton, William, 2nd Lt. 7th N. C. Apr. 20, 1777; transfrd. to 1st N. C. June 1, 1778; 1st Lt. Aug. 15, 1778; taken pris. at Charleston May 12, 1780, and made his escape; Capt. Aug. 1, 1781; retired Jan. 1, 1783. (D. 1816.)
568. Ward, Edward, Capt. 8th N. C. Nov. 28, 1776; resigned Aug. 1, 1777.
568. Ward, William, Capt. 5th N. C. Apr. 16, 1776 to ......
573. Washington, Robert, Adjutant 3rd N. C. Apr. 15, 1776 to ......
574. Washington, William, Ensn. 9th N. C. Aug. 15, 1777; retired Jan. 1, 1778.
574. Waters, James, Ensn. 1st N. C. Dec. 24, 1776; 2nd Lt. Mch. 29, 1777; resigned Apr. 23, 1777.
575. Waters, Samuel, Ensn. 1st N. C. Dec. 24, 1776; 2nd Lt. Mch. 29, 1777; resigned Apr. 23, 1777.
575. Waters, William, Ensn. 1st N. C. Sept. 19, 1776; 2nd Lt. Feb. 5, 1777; 1st Lt. Sept. 19, 1777; on roll for June 1778; is reported as transferred to Cavalry Regiment June 1, 1778.
576. Watson, Thomas, 1st Lt. 7th N. C. Nov. 28, 1776; resigned Apr. 12, 1777.
577. Webb, Elisha, Ensn. 7th N. C. Nov. 28, 1776 to ......
578. Webb, John, Commissary 3rd N. C. Apr.,23, 1776 to ......
583. Whedbee, Richard, 2nd Lt. 7th N. C. May 1, 1777; 1st Lt. Aug. 15, 1777; dismissed Jan. 15, 1778.
585. Whitaker, Hudson, Ensn. 7th N. C. Dec. 22, 1776 to .....; Capt. ....; wounded at Hickory Hill, June 28, 1779.
586. White, Isaac, Lt. N. C. Militia at King's Mtn. Oct. 1780. (D. 1821.)
586. White, James, Capt. N. C. Militia, 1779-1781. (D. 1821.)
586. White, Joseph, Capt. N. C. Militia at King's Mtn. in Oct. 1780.
586. White, Matthew, Lt. 6th N. C. Nov. 2, 1776; killed at Germantown Oct. 4, 1777.
587. White, Thomas, 1st Lt. 6th N. C. Apr. 16, 1776; Capt. Jan. 20, 1777; retired June 1, 1778.
587. White, William, Ensn. 7th N. C. Apr. 17, 1777; omitted Nov. .., 1777.

*Pages*
588. Whitehall, Alexander, Capt. N. C. Militia in 1780.
593. Wilkinson, Reuben, Lt. 4th N. C. Dec. 20, 1776; retired June 1, 1778.
593. Wilkinson, Reuben, Ensn. 3rd N. C. May 1, 1779; Lt. .., 1780; retired July 21, 1782.
594. Williams, Benjamin, 1st Lt. 2nd N. C. Sept. 1, 1775; Capt. July 19, 1776; and served to . . . . . ; was in service Jan. 1780.
594. Williams, Daniel, 1st Lt. 6th N. C. Apr. 16, 1776; Capt. Apr. 1, 1777; retired June 1, 1778; Capt. N. C. Militia, 1780-1781. (D. 1823.)
595. Williams, James, 1st Lt. 4th N. C. June 2, 1776; Capt. Apr. 3, 1777. (D. May 2, 1778.)
595. Williams, John, 1st Lt. 2nd N. C. Sept. 1, 1775; retired June 1, 1778.
595. Williams, John P., Capt. 5th N. C. Apr. 16, 1776; Col. 9th N. C. Nov. 26, 1776; retired June 1, 1778.
595. Williams, Joseph, Lt. Col. N. C. Militia, 1777-1780. (D. 1827.)
596. Williams, Nathaniel B., 2nd Lt. 8th N. C. Nov. 28, 1776; retired June 1, 1778; 1st Lt. 10th N. C. Jan. 23, 1781; transfrd. to 4th N. C. Feb. 6, 1782, and served to close of war.
596. Williams, Ralph, Lt. 9th N. C., Nov. 28, 1776; omitted Jan. 1, 1778.
596. Williams, Robert, Surgeon 3rd N. C. June 1778 to 1781. (D. Oct. 12, 1840.)
596. Williams, Samuel, Capt. N. C. Militia at King's Mtn. in Oct. 1780.
596. Williams, Theophilus, Ensn. 6th N. C. Apr. 2, 1777; omitted Jan. 1, 1778.
597. Williams, William, Ensn. 2nd N. C. Dec. 11, 1776 to . . . . . .
597. Williams, William, 1st Lt. and Adjutant 4th N. C. Sept. 1, 1775; wounded at Germantown Oct. 4, 1777; Capt. Invalid Regiment Apr. 1, 1778, and served to Apr. 23, 1783.
597. Williams, William B., Maj. 1st N. C. June 13, 1776 to . . . . . .
598. Wilson, James, Capt. 10th N. C. Apr. 19, 1777; resigned May 25, 1778.
599. Wilson, Robert, Surgeon, 6th N. C. June 8, 1776 to . . . . . .
599. Wilson, Whitfield, Regimental Quartermstr. 3rd N. C. Apr. 24, 1777; resigned Oct. 1, 1777.
599. Winborne, John, Lt. 7th N. C. Nov. 28, 1776. (D. Nov. .., 1777.)
601. Winston, Joseph, Maj. N. C. Militia at King's Mtn. Oct. 1780. (D. Apr. 28, 1815.)
601. Witherspoon, David, Lt. N. C. Militia at King's Mtn. in Oct. 1780. (D. 1828.)
602. Withrow, James, Capt. N. C. Militia, at King's Mtn. in Oct. 1780.
602. Womack, William, Regimental Quartermstr, 1st N. C. Jan. 1778; retired June 1, 1778.
603. Wood, Matthew, 1st Lt. 3rd N. C. July 24, 1776; Capt. Nov. 22, 1777; retired June 1, 1778. (D. Oct. 28, 1832.)
603. Wood, Samuel, Capt. N. C. Militia at King's Mtn. in Oct. 1780.
603. Wood, Solomon, Lt. 8th N. C. Nov. 28, 1776 to . . . . . .
604. Woodhouse, John, Ensn. 2nd N. C. Sept. 1, 1775 to . . . . . .
606. Wooten, Shadrach, Ensn. 5th N. C. Nov. 28, 1776 to . . . . . .
606. Worth, Joseph, Ensn. 2nd N. C. Oct. 20, 1775; 1st Lt. May 3, 1776. (Died Apr. 6, 1777.)
607. Wright, Daniel, Capt. N. C. Militia, 1779-1780.
609. Yancey, Charles, Lt. 9th N. C. Nov. 28, 1776 to . . . . . .
609. Yarborough, Edward, Ensn. 3rd N. C. May 8, 1776; Lt. Apr. 16, 1777; Capt.-Lt. Jan. 9, 1777; Capt. May 10, 1779; retired Jan. 1, 1783.
611. Zollikoffer, John Conrad, Capt. N. C. Militia, 1778-1780. (D. 1796.)

# ROSTER OF THE CONTINENTAL LINE FROM NORTH CAROLINA

Reference: North Carolina State Records, Clark, Vol. XVI, 1782-1783

Copy of a Register showing the names alphabetically (in Regiments) rank, dates of commission and enlistment, periods of service, and occurrences, taken from the original muster and pay rolls of the North Carolina Line of the late Army of the United States.

### 1ST REGIMENT—COL. THOS. CLARK

| Name and Rank | Company | Dates of Enlistment and Commission | Period of Service | Occurrences |
|---|---|---|---|---|
| **A** P. 1002-3 | | | | |
| Atkins, David, Sergt.... | Bowman's | 1777 | | Dischgd. Nov. 1777 |
| Armstrong, Wm., Lt.... | Hogg's | " | | Capt. 29 Aug. '77 |
| | | | | Deranged 1 Jan, '83 |
| Angline, Cornelius, Pt... | Dixon's | " | 3 yrs. | Died July 1777 |
| Adams, Niper, Pt...... | " | " | | Died 27 July 1777 |
| Adcock, George, Pt.... | Reid's | | 2½ yrs. | Died 21 Aug. '78 |
| Allen, Jesse, Sergt...... | Child's | 16 Apr. '76 | " | P.C.June'78, Sergt.Sep'78 |
| | | | | Dischgd. 10 Nov. '78 |
| Apperson, Wm., Pt.... | Brown's | 13 June " | " | Dischgd. 16 Mar. '79 |
| **B** (P. 1009) | | | | |
| Bradley, Richd., Capt... | | 5 Mar. '77 | | Omtd June '78 |
| Brown, John, Capt...... | | 26 Apr. " | | Omtd June '78 |
| Brennon, Chrisn, Pt.... | Brown's | 1777 | 2½ yr.W | Corpl. Apr. '78 |
| | | | | Omtd June '78 |
| Bryley, Charles, Pt..... | " | " | " | Killed 17 Sept. '77 |
| Bagnel, John, Pt....... | | 1777 | 2½ yrs. | Omtd Feb. '78 |
| Burrow, Wyly, Pt..... | Tatum's | " | W | Corpl.Mar.'78,Pt.July '78 |
| Barnard, Peter, Pt..... | Dixon's | | " | Destd. 14 Sep. '78 |
| Bowman, Joshua, Capt.. | | 18 Sept. '76 | | Killed 30 Mar. '80 |
| Blythe, Samuel, 1 Lt.... | Bowman's | 5 Feb. '77 | | Resigned 16 Apr. '78 |
| Baker, Peter, 2 Lt...... | " | 8 Feb. '77 | | |
| Bell, John, Musc...... | " | 1777 | " | P. C. June '78 |
| Blue, Neil, Pt......... | " | " | W | Corpl. 1 July '79 |
| | | | | Destd 7 Dec. '79 |
| Barnes, Britton, Pt..... | " | " | " | Omtd Sep. '77, Destd. |
| Berry, John, Pt........ | " | " | | Omtd Sep. '77, Destd. |
| Bozar, Thomas, Pt..... | Thompson's | " | W | |
| Brown, Collins, Pt..... | Dixon's | " | " | Died 14 Apr. '78 |
| Barber, Wm., Pt....... | " | " | " | Pris. 14 Apr. '79 |
| | | | | News Nov. '79 |
| Bailey, H. Wm., Sergt... | Hogg's | 5 Nov. '76 | 3 yr. W | Pt. 22 Oct. '77—Sergt 21 |
| | | | | Mar.'79. Omtd Nov. '79 |
| Brown, Thos., Sergt..... | " | 1 Aug. '76 | 3 yrs. | Pt. May '78 |
| | | | | Omtd Mar. '79 |
| Bowman, Robt., Pt..... | Dixon's | | W | Destd in 1776 |
| Blake, Wm............ | Rolston's | | " | Sergt. Oct. '77,Pt.May'78 |
| | | | | Corpl. Nov. '79, Sergt 10 |
| | | | | Feb. '80 |
| Batey, Hugh, Pt....... | " | | " | Corpl. Nov.'77, Died 6 |
| | | | | Aug. '78 |
| Bowlin, Jereh, Pt...... | " | | " | Destd 4 Aug. 1777 |
| Bowlin, Baxter, Pt..... | " | Nov. '77 | " | Omtd Jan. '78 |
| Boyd, Adam.......... | | Oct. " | " | Omtd Nov. '79 |
| | | | | News in '79 |

| Name and Rank | Company | Dates of Enlistment and Commission | Period of Service | Occurrences |
|---|---|---|---|---|
| Browne, Wm., Pt....... | Tatum's | 1 Sep. '77 | 3 yrs W | |
| Barko, Wyllis, Pt....... | Dixon's | 23 Sep. " | 3 yrs. | Dead Nov. '78 |
| Bryan, Randle, Pt...... | Bowman's | 1 Oct. '76 | 3 yrs. | Omtd Nov. '79 |
| Bradley, Richd., Corpl. . | Reid's | 9 Aug. '77 | " | |
| Burges, Isaac, Pt....... | Sharp's | 15 Aug. '77 | " | Died 10 July '78 |
| C (P. 1025) | | | | |
| Cross, Martin, Drummer | Brown's | 1777 | | {Fife Major. '79, Destd. 9<br>Dec. '79 |
| Clark, Isaac, Pt........ | " | | | |
| Carmichael, Robt., Pt... | " | | | |
| Costen, Henry, Pt..... | " | | | |
| Clark, Jacob, Pt....... | " | | | |
| Cubert—Drummer..... | " | | " | Omtd Jan. '78 |
| Campbell, Wm., Pt..... | " | 10 Sep. '76 | " | |
| Cole, Martin, Pt....... | " | '77 | " | Omtd Jan. '78 |
| Churn, Jno., Pt......... | Tatum's | " | W | |
| Conner, Chas., Pt...... | " | " | " | Omtd June '78 |
| Conolly, Jno., Pt...... | " | " | " | Omtd Jan. '78 |
| Caper, Robt., Pt....... | Dixon's | " | " | {Pt. Oct. '77. Died 25<br>Oct. '77 |
| Council, Robbenon..... | Bowman's | " | | 1st Lt. 20 Aug. '77 |
| Christopher, Simon, Pt.. | " | | W | Omt. Feb. '78 |
| Ceeley, Tobias, Pt..... | " | | | Destd Sep. '77 |
| Curry, Robt., Pt...... | " | 28 May '76 | | Destd 15 June '77 |
| Cox, Wm., Pt......... | " | 22 Aug. " | | Destd 31 Aug. '77 |
| Carney, Anth'y, Sergt... | Thompson's | 1777 | | {Dischg.20 Jan.'78.Mustd.<br>Pt.Mar.'78.Omtd July'79 |
| Condon, Jno........... | " | Oct. " | | Omtd Jan. '78 |
| Callender, Thos., Lt..... | Dixon's | 1 Jan. '77 | | {Pris. 12 Mar.'80. Capt.'80<br>Deranged 1 Jan. '83 |
| Colley, Wm., Corpl..... | " | 1777 | | {Sergt. 1 Jan. '78. Sergt.<br>Maj. 19 Mar. '78 |
| Craven, Jas., Lt........ | Hogg's | " | | Dismissed 20 Nov. '79 |
| Cook, Jno., Pt......... | " | " | 3 yrs. | Destd Jan. '77 |
| Chester, David, Sergt... | Rolston's | 23 Oct. '76 | W | {Irner Sgt. '79. Mustd.Sgt.<br>Jan. '82 |
| Clark, Thos., Col...... | | 5 Feb. '77 | | {Pris. 12 May '80.<br>Deranged 1 Jan. '83 |
| Christmas, Jos. D. Maj.. | | 1 Sep. '75 | W | Pt. July '79 |
| Conger, Step'n, S. Maj.. | | 10 Oct. '76 | 3 yrs. | { Act'g Adj't Sept. '77.<br>Omtd '78 |
| Cole, Martin, Sgt. Maj.. | | 18 Nov. '76 | " | {Transf'd to Gen. Guards<br>19 Mar.'78. Mustd. Sgt.<br>for War in 1782 |
| Cox, Wm. Armon...... | | 10 June '76 | | Omtd Nov. 1777 |
| Cochran, Jno., Pt...... | Armstrong's | 19 May '79 | 2½ Yrs. | |
| Cartwright, Robt., Pt... | " | 10 Nov. '77 | W | |
| Cartwright, Thos., Pt... | " | 20 Sep. '77 | W | Corpl. July '79 |
| Chalk, Wm., Pt........ | Tatum's | 29 Dec. '76 | 3 yrs. | Sergt. March 1780 |
| Clinton, Jno., Sergt..... | Reid's | 19 Apr | 2½ yrs. | {Pt. June 1778, Dischgd.<br>28 Oct. '78 |
| Cole, Robt., Pt........ | Sharp's | | 3 yrs. | Died 28 April '78 |
| Carter, Jno., Pt....... | " | 30 May '77 | " | |
| D (P. 1039) | | | | |
| Disarn, Francis, Pt...... | Brown's | 1777 | | Died 12 Mch 1778 |
| Dixon, Tilman, Capt.... | | 5 Feb. " | | {Mustd. Pris. '81, Exchg.<br>Mar.'81.Derang'd1Jan.83 |

| Name and Rank | Company | Dates of Enlistment and Commission | Period of Service | Occurrences |
|---|---|---|---|---|
| Dolohide, Silas, Pt...... | Dixon's | 1777 | W | Dest'd 19 Jan. 1780 |
| Dunsee, Edward, Sergt.. | Bowman's | " | | Dest'd 28 Sept. 1777 |
| Dorner, John, Pt....... | " | " | | Dest'd 28 Aug. 1777 |
| Davis, Benj., Pt....... | Thomson's | Nov. " | W | Dischd 28 Feb. '78 |
| Davis, Jas, Pt......... | " | 15 June " | " | Mustd. Aug. '78 |
| Dixon, Henry, Capt..... | " | 1 Sept. '75 | | Maj. 1777. See 3rd Reg. |
| Douglas, Wm., Pt...... | Dixon's | 1777 | W | |
| Dennis, Robt., Pt...... | " | " | " | In 9th Reg. 1777 |
| Donaldson, Francis, Pt.. | " | " | " | Detchd 6 May '77 |
| Dyches, Isom, Pt...... | Ralston's | " | " | |
| Davis, Wm., I.t. Col.... | | 5 Feb. " | | Omtd June 1778 |
| Dupree, Jas. Arms...... | | 10 June '76 | | Omtd Nov. '77 |
| Dondalout, Henry, Pt... | Tatum's | 26 Jan. '77 | 3 yrs. | {Corpl. Feb. '79, Dischgd 27 Jan. '80 |
| Douge, Jas., Pt........ | Ely's | | | Died 3 May 1778 |
| Dellong, Francis, Musc.. | Dixon's | 13 Sep. " | 3 yr. W | |
| Davis, Jas., Pt........ | Bowman's | | | Dischgd 28 May '78 |
| Dickinson, Geo., Pt..... | Reid's | 8 Aug. '78 | 3 yr. W | Destd 11 May '79 |
| Duncan, Jesse, Pt...... | " | May '76 | 2½ yrs. | Dischgd 28 May '79 |
| Douglas, Jno., Pt...... | " | " | " | {Omitd Sept. '78, Unfit for Service |
| Donaldson, David, Pt... | Sharp's | 15 Feb. '78 | 3 yrs. | Destd 20 May '79 |
| Dowell, Jas., Pt....... | Brown's | May " | W | |
| E    (P. 1049) | | | | |
| Edge, Thos., Pt....... | Thompson's | 1777 | W | Dischgd 28 Feb. '78 |
| Erwin, Jno., Ensn...... | Dixon's | " | | Resigned 25 Aug. '77 |
| Ethridge, Jno., Pt...... | " | " | W | |
| Ecret, Robt., Fife Maj. . | | 1 Sep. '75 | | Omtd Jan. '78 |
| Everet, Jno., Pt........ | Tatum's | | | Dead Aug '78 |
| F    (P. 1055) | | | | |
| Fikes, Jas., Sergt...... | Thompson's | 1777 | W | Died Jan. 1778 |
| Furguson, Jno., Pt...... | Dixon's | " | " | |
| Fowler, Dan'l, Pt...... | Armstrong's | 1 June '76 | 3 yrs. | Dischgd 28 June '79 |
| G    (P. 1062) | | | | |
| Griffin, Josh, Pt........ | Brown's | 1777 | W | Died 4 Mar. '78 |
| Griffis, Allen, Pt........ | Tatum's | " | " | Omtd Jan '78 |
| Gambell, Edm'd, Lt..... | Thompson's | 20 Jan. '77 | | Omtd June '78 |
| Gandip, Jno., Musc..... | " | " | W | {Pt. Feb. '78. Mustd. June '78 |
| Gibson, Jno., Pt........ | " | " | " | Omtd Feb. '78 |
| Green, Wm., Pt........ | Thompson's | 1777 | W | Omtd Jan. '78 |
| Goldsmith, Jesse, Musc.. | Dixon's | " | " | Pt. June '78 |
| Griffiths, Jno., Pt....... | " | " | " | {Trans. Mar. '78 to his Excy Guards, Mus.N. '79 |
| Grifford, Jas., Pt....... | " | " | " | Missing 12 Sept. '77 |
| Glover, Thos., Pt....... | " | " | " | Executed 24 Oct. '78 |
| George, Brittian, Pt..... | " | " | " | |
| Grimes, Elisha, Pt...... | Hogg's | " | 3 yrs. | Destd 28 May '77 |
| Gough, Wm., Corpl..... | " | 11 Nov. " | " | {Pt. Sept. '77. Omtd Feb. '79. Mustd Nov. '79 |
| Germany, Thos., Pt..... | Tatum's | 4 Sept. " | " | |
| Gilston, Sam'l, Sergt.... | Ely's | 6 Oct. " | " | Ir. Mr. Sergt 17 June '79 |
| Gregory, Wm., Sergt.... | Reid's | 12 June " | " | Omtd Nov. '79 |
| Gunter, Joel, Pt........ | Child's | 6 Dec. '76 | 2½ yrs. | Dischgd 29 Jan. '80 |
| H    (P. 1072) | | | | |
| Harrison, Jas., Pt....... | Brown's | 1777 | 3½ yr. W | |
| Hall, Thos., Lt......... | Dixon's | 8 Feb. " | | Resigned 10 Apr. '77 |

| Name and Rank | Company | Dates of Enlistment and Commission | Period of Service | Occurrences |
|---|---|---|---|---|
| Hamilton, Jno., Sergt... | Bowman's | 1777 | | {Omtd Jan. '78. Must 1 {Jan. '79, in 4th Reg. |
| Henry, Jno., Pt........ | " | " | W | |
| Holt, Thos., Pt........ | " | " | | Omtd Nov. '77 |
| Hancock, Isaac, Corpl... | Dixon's | " | W | {Sergt. 12 Oct. '77 {Pt. 1 Feb. '80 |
| Horseford, Jas.......... | " | " | " | Corpl. 1 Feb. '80 |
| Hochammer, Philip, Pt.. | Dixon's | 1777 | | {Dest. 12 Oct '77. Mustd. {Apr. '78 |
| Haynes, Wm., Pt...... | " | " | " | Died 23 Mar. '78 |
| Harris, Jno., Pt........ | " | " | " | Omtd Jan. '78 |
| Hopper, Wm., Q. M. Sgt. | " | 28 Sep. '76 | " | {Sergt. 20 Sep. '77. Q. M. {Sergt. Dec. '77. Dischg 11 {June '78 |
| Hogg, Thos., Capt...... | | 1 Mar. '76 | " | Maj. 4 Oct.'77 in5thReg. |
| Harris, Peter, Agt Am'r. | | 10 June " | | Omtd Sep. 1777 |
| Hale, Thos., D.M.M.G.. | | 20 June '77 | | Omtd Sep. 1777 |
| Heimbergh, Fred, Sergt. | | 15 Mar. '78 | | |
| Haynes, Jno., Pt........ | Armstrong's | | | Dischgd June '78 |
| Hood, Wm., Pt........ | | | | Died 14 Feb. '78 |
| Horton, Jas., Pt........ | Tatum's | May '78 | W | Died 3 June '78 |
| Horton, Levy, Pt....... | " | " | " | |
| Haddock, Andrew, Sgt. . | Reid's | | 2½ yrs. | Dischgd 8 Apr. '78 |
| Hall, Jas., Pt........... | " | 1 Jan. '77 | 3 yrs. | Dischgd 1 Feb. '80 |
| Hair, Jno. L., Lt........ | Sharp's | 16 Aug. " | | Omtd June '78 |
| Holley, Joseph, Lt...... | " | 9 June " | " | Died 1 Sep. '78 |
| Hedspeth, Mar'duke,Pt. | Child's | 1778 | W | |
| Harrell, Jno., Pt........ | Brown's | 14 Apr. '76 | 2½ yrs. | Dischgd 6 Oct. '78 |
| I (P. 1086) | | | | |
| Ingraham, Jno., Sergt... | Dixon's | 1777 | W | Destd Sep. '77 |
| Irwin, Jas., Musc...... | Hogg's | 1 Jan. " | 3 yrs. | Pt. Jan. '78 |
| J (P.1086) | | | | |
| Johnson, Willeby, Pt.... | Thompson's | '77 | W | Destd Sep. '77 |
| Johnson, Thos., Pt...... | " | " | " | Destd Jan. '80 |
| Jones, Thos., Pt........ | Hogg's | " | 3 yrs. | Omtd June '78 |
| Jacobs, Peter, Pt....... | " | 1 Jan. " | 3 yrs W | |
| Johnson, Jas., Pt...... | Ralston's | " | W | Omtd Sept. '77 |
| Jones, Wm., Pt......... | Tatum's | 21 Sep. " | 3 yrs. | Destd 28 June '79 |
| Jordon, Robt., Pt...... | Reid's | " | " | Died 24 Aug. '78 |
| Jones, Jno., Sergt...... | Child's | 8 Sep. " | " | |
| K (P. 1095) | | | | |
| Kelly, Wm., Pt......... | Brown's | 1777 | W | Omtd June '78 |
| King, Jas., Lt.......... | Tatum's | 3 Apr. " | | {Capt. 1 Apr. '80 {Died 8 Sep. '80 |
| Kennedy, Isaac, Pt..... | Bowman's | " | | Destd Aug '77 |
| Kittle, Jacob, Pt........ | Armstrong's | 9 Oct. " | 3 yrs. | |
| Kelley, Jno., Pt........ | Ely's | | " | |
| Keith, Jno., Pt........ | Reid's | | W | Musc. Sick 10 Feb. '80 |
| L (P. 1100) | | | | |
| Lucy, Fred'k, Pt........ | Tatum's | 1777 | W | |
| Linch, Lawne, Pt....... | " | " | " | |
| Lawson, Richard, Pt.... | Dixon's | " | | Killed 4 Oct. '77 |
| Lewis, Wm., Pt........ | " | " | | Musc Sep.'77. Pt. June'78 |
| Lamb, Gibbs, Pt........ | " | " | | Corpl. 1 Apr. '82 |
| Lucas, Edw'd, Pt...... | Dixon's | 1777 | W | {Destd 18 Feb. '78.Mustd {June '78 in 2nd Reg. {Omtd Feb. '79 |

| Name and Rank | Company | Dates of Enlistment and Commission | Period of Service | Occurrences |
|---|---|---|---|---|
| Ledum, Jno., Pt........ | Dixon's | 14 Oct. '77 | 3 yrs. | Omtd May '79 |
| Lock, Jno., Sergt...... | Bowman's | 25 Apr. '76 | 2½ yrs. | {Pt. June '78. Dischgd Oct. '78 |
| Lapsley, Jas., Pt....... | " | | | Destd 15 Aug. '77 |
| Logan, Wm., Pt........ | Sharp's | 15 Dec. '77 | 3 yr. W | |
| M  (P. 1108) | | | | |
| Manchester, Isaac, Fifer. | Brown's | 1777 | W | Destd 21 May '79 |
| Mott, Dan'l, Pt........ | " | " | " | Omtd July '79 |
| Mott, Edge, Pt......... | " | " | " | Corpl. Nov. '79 Pt. '82 |
| McCoy, Rich'd, Pt..... | " | " | " | Destd Aug. '78 |
| McGibbon, Neil, Pt.... | " | " | " | Omtd Aug. '78 |
| Mills, Joseph, Sergt.... | " | " | " | {Pt. Jan. '78 Omtd Feb. '78 |
| Marshall, Dixon, 2nd Lt. | " | 26 Apr. '77 | " | Deranged 1 Jan. '83 |
| McCobb, Jas., Pt...... | | Nov. '77 | " | |
| McCarthur, Alex., Pt.... | | 10 Mar. " | 3 yrs. | |
| Morrison, Alex., Sergt... | Tatum's | | | {Pt. 14 Aug.'77. Sergt Oct. '77. Dischgd May '83 |
| Mash, Jno., Pt........ | " | | | Under Sentence Aug. '77 |
| Millegan, Jas., Lt...... | " | 29 Aug. " | " | {From Hogg's Co. Omtd May '78 |
| McBride, Duncan, Pt... | Bowman's | | W | |
| Mash, Jno., Pt........ | " | | | Destd Aug. '77 |
| Mash, Ely, Pt......... | " | | | Destd Aug. '77 |
| Marshall, Dixon, Ensn. . | Thompson's | 28 Mar. " | " | See above |
| Morgan, Wm., Corpl.... | " | | " | |
| Martin, Joel, Pt........ | " | | | Omtd Aug. '78 |
| Martin, Robt., Corpl.... | Dixon's | 13 Dec. '76 | 3 yrs.. | Destd 1 Feb. '80 |
| Melton, Wm., Pt........ | " | | W | Corpl. 1 Nov. '77 |
| Merriam, Philip, Pt..... | " | | " | Omtd Feb. '79 |
| Mellegan, Jas., Ensn.... | Hoggs' | | | See above |
| Mooney, Thos., Pt..... | " | | 3 yrs. | Destd Jan. '77 |
| McNeal, Arch'd., Pt.... | Dixon's | | W | Destd 1 Jan. '77 |
| Mingo—Asse Armourer. | " | 10 June '76 | | Omtd Sep. '77 |
| Morris, Philem, Pt...... | Tatum's | 11 Jan. '78 | 3 yrs. | |
| Merchant, Caleb, Pt.... | " | 10 Sep. '77 | " | Trans. to 6 Reg. '79 |
| Marshall, Emanuel, Pt.. | " | Mar. '78 | " | Died 5 Apr. '78 |
| Marshall, Wyllis, Sergt.. | Dixon's | 16 Jan. '77 | " | {Pt. Nov. '78 Omtd May '79 |
| McDoug,Jas.or Sam'l,Pt. | " | Apr. '78 | " | Omtd Mar. '79 |
| McCullock, Alex., Pt.... | Reid's | 10 Oct. '77 | | |
| Mitchell Abner, Pt...... | Child's | | 2½ yrs. | Dischgd 1 Nov. '78 |
| McGee, Peter, Pt...... | " | May '78 | W | {Corpl. Mar. '79 Sergt. Nov. '79 |
| N  (P. 1123) | | | | |
| Needham, Thos., Sergt.. | Tatum's | 1777 | W | {Pt.Sep.'77. Serg. Dec.'77 Omtd Jan. '78 |
| Norton, Wm., Musc..... | Bowman's | " | | Pt. Feb.'78. Dead Sep.'78 |
| Norton, Jacob, Musc.... | Hogg's | " | W | {Pt. June '78 Died 28 July '78 |
| Newman, Reuben, Pt... | Reid's | 1 May '76 | 2½ yrs. | Dischgd 10 Nov. '78 |
| O  (P. 1128) | | | | |
| Orr, Chas., Pt......... | Brown's | '77 | W | {Corpl. 1 Sep. '77 Died 20 June '78 |
| Oliver, Abisha, Pt....... | Thompson's | '77 | | Omtd Jan '78 |
| O'Bar, Daniel, Pt....... | Dixon's | | W | |
| O'Bar, Robt., Pt........ | " | | " | |

| Name and Rank | Company | Dates of Enlistment and Commission | Period of Service | Occurrences |
|---|---|---|---|---|
| O'Bar, Mich'l, Pt...... | Dixon's | | W | Omtd Jan. '78 |
| **P**  (P. 1132) | | | | |
| Porter, Wm., Pt........ | Brown's | 1777 | | Died 5 Mar. '78 |
| Parker, Jas., Pt........ | " | " | W | Destd 10 Sep.'78. Mustd Nov.'78. Destd 28 June79 |
| Peavey, Thos., Pt...... | Dixon's | " | " | Omtd Jan. '78 |
| Parks, Jno., Pt........ | " | 1779 | | Destd 7 Jan. '80 |
| Pew, Arthur, Pt........ | Tatum's | 20 Feb. '78 | 3 yrs. | |
| Phillips, Mich'l, Pt...... | Dixon's | 9 Sep. '77 | " | |
| Parker, Sam'l, Pt...... | " | 1 Dec. '78 | " | Omtd Mar. '79 |
| Patrick, Benj., Musc.... | Reid's | | | Omtd June '78 |
| Price, Samuel.......... | Sharp's | 15 Nov. '77 | 3 yrs. | |
| Peck, Fred'k, Pt....... | " | 1 Dec. " | " | |
| Power, Wm., Pt....... | | 13 May '77 | " | Dischgd 30 Nov. '78 |
| **R**  (P. 1142) | | | | |
| Rice, Jno., Lt.......... | Brown's | 8 Apr. '77 | | Omtd June '78 |
| Royals, Joseph, Pt...... | " | " | | Died 6 Mar. '78 |
| Rogers, Pat'k, 2nd Lt... | Tatum's | 3 Apr. " | | Died 19 Apr. '78 |
| Roberts, Sam'l, Musc. .. | " | " | 3 yrs. | Died 3 Apr. '78 |
| Richards, Geo., Pt...... | Dixon's | | | Omtd Apr. '78 |
| Rozer, Jordan, Pt....... | Thompson's | | | Destd 1 Feb. 1780 |
| Rozer, Chas., Pt....... | " | | | Destd 28 Mar. '83 |
| Rowell, Jesse, Pt....... | " | | | |
| Reed, Jas., 1st Lt....... | Dixon's | 7 July '76 | | Capt. 8 July '77 and Pris. 1 June'78. Pris.12 May'80 |
| Rice, Thos., Sergt...... | " | 1777 | | Died 5 Sep. '77 |
| Rolston, Robt., Capt.... | | 8 Mar. " | | Omtd Oct. '77 |
| Roark, Jas., Pt......... | Rolston's | 9 Sep. '76 | W | |
| Roback, Wm., Musc.... | " | | | Omtd July '78 |
| Roberts, Jno., Pt...... | " | | " | |
| Ralph, Jno., Pt......... | Ely's | | | Died 4 Apr. '78 |
| Robertson, Jno., Pt..... | Reid's | | | Omtd Feb. '78 |
| Runnals, Joseph, Pt..... | Child's | | | Corpl. 8 Nov. '79 |
| Rodgers, Arthur, Pt..... | Brown's | 24 May '76 | 2½ yrs. | Died 22 Oct. '78 |
| Roberts, Wm., Pt....... | " | 1 Jan '77 | W | Omtd Aug. ?? Destd '79 |
| **S**  (P. 1152) | | | | |
| Scull, Jno., Lt.......... | Brown's | 26 Apr. '77 | | |
| Spillards, Jese, Pt...... | " | 1777 | 3 yr. W | Destd Mar. '83 |
| Smith, Wm., Sergt...... | " | 1 Aug. " | 3 yrs. | |
| Stanton, Jno., Sergt..... | Tatum's | 1777 | W | Pt. June '78 Sergt. Mar. '80 |
| Smith, Henry, Pt....... | " | " | " | |
| Stevens, Joseph, Pt..... | " | 5 Mar. " | " | |
| Summers, Jno., Lt...... | Dixon's | 5 Feb. '77 | | Capt. 10 July '78 Mustd 12 May '80 Deranged 1 Jan. '83 |
| Southerland, Geo., Pt... | " | " | | Sergt. Oct. '77 Omtd Jan. '78 |
| Stevens, Thos., Pt...... | Bowman's | " | | Destd Aug. '77 |
| Summers, Jno., 1st Lt... | " | " | | Supposed in Dixon's Co. above |
| Spikes, Joseph, Pt...... | Thompson's | " | W | Destd 12 Sep. '77 Mustd Nov. '77 |
| Stewart, Chas., Sergt.... | " | " | | Omtd Jan. '78 |
| Summers, Jas., Musc.... | Dixon's | " | " | F. Maj. 1 June'78. Pt. Dec. '78. Sergt. 1 Feb. '80 |
| Stillwell, Jacob, Musc... | " | | | Dischgd 1 Feb. '78 |

| Name and Rank | Company | Dates of Enlistment and Commission | Period of Service | Occurrences |
|---|---|---|---|---|
| Simpson, Jno., Pt....... | Dixon's | 1777 | W | |
| Smith, Owen, Pt........ | " | " | | Died 17 Aug. '77 |
| Smith, Joseph, Corpl.... | " | | 3 yrs. | ⌠Destd 24 Mar. '77. **Mustd**<br>⌡Pt. May '78 |
| Southerland, Wm., Pt... | " | | " | Omtd Sep. '77 |
| Strader, Geoe., Pt...... | " | | W | Destd 1776 |
| Sheppard, Jno., Pt...... | Ralston's | | " | |
| Stewart, Wm., Pt...... | " | | " | Omtd Sep. '77 |
| Stillwell, David, Pt..... | | | | |
| Shields, Wm., Wag.Mak. | " | | | Omtd Sep. '77 |
| Springs, Sdrh, Asst. Or.. | | 10 Jan. '76 | | ⌠Springs Sedgwick **Ar.**<br>⌡Omtd Nov. '77 |
| Smith, Thos........... | | " | | Omtd Sep. '77 |
| Sawyer, Henry, Pt...... | Tatum's | | 3 yrs. | Died Aug. '78 |
| Smith, Geor., Pt....... | Dixon's | 6 Oct. '77 | 3 yr. W | Sergt. Nov. '78 |
| Saxton, Jerch, Pt...... | Bowman's | | W | Died 25 Apr. '79 |
| Stroud, Jno., Pt........ | Sharp's | 15 May " | 3 yrs. | Omtd Aug. '78 |
| Steem, Wm., Pt........ | " | 7 Jan. " | 3 yrs. | Omtd Feb. '79 |
| T (P. 1160) | | | | |
| Turner, John, Sergt..... | Brown's | 1 Aug. '77 | | Pt. June 1778 |
| Turner, Wm., Pt...... | " | 1777 | | Died 24 May '78 |
| Townley, Wm., Pt..... | " | " | | Omtd Feb. '78 |
| Tatum, Howell, Capt. .. | | 3 Apr. " | | Resigned 20 May '82 |
| Tapp, Geo., Pt......... | Tatum's | 1777 | W | Dischgd 10 Dec. '78 |
| Tailor, Wm., Pt........ | " | | | Destd 25 July '77 |
| Trantham, Martin, Pt... | Bowman's | | | Omtd Dec. '77 |
| Thompson, Lawr., Capt. | | 15 Aug '76 | | Omtd Jan. '78 |
| Thomas, Lem'l, Pt...... | Dixon's | 1777 | W | |
| Tate, Jas., Chaplain.... | | 13 Oct. '75 | | ⌠Omtd 1 June '78. Said to<br>⌡be transf'd to 4th Reg. |
| Thomas, Abisha,<br>  D. 2. M. G......... | | 1 May '76 | | Omtd Nov. '77 |
| Tatum, Jno., Pt........ | Ely's | | 3 yrs. | Dischgd 10 May '79 |
| Trowell, Wm., Musc.... | Bowman's | 1778 | W | ⌠Pt June '78<br>⌡Destd 13 June '83 |
| Thrift, Mills........... | Child's | " | " | Died May 1779 |
| V (P. 1177) | | | | |
| Vaughn, Jas., Pt........ | Brown's | 1777 | | |
| Varner, Robt., Pt...... | Dixon's | 8 Mar. " | | |
| Ventress, Lem'l, Pt..... | Tatum's | 25 Dec " | 3 yrs. | Dischgd 1 Sep. '78 |
| Vaugh, Rich'd, Pt...... | Child's | | 2½ yrs. | Died 2 June '78 |
| Vize, Henry, Pt........ | " | 1778 | " | |
| W (P. 1180) | | | | |
| Welch, Wm., Corpl.... | Brown's | 1777 | W | Destd 28 Sep. '77 |
| Wesbrook, Wm., Pt.... | " | " | 3 yrs. | Destd 12 Feb. '79 |
| Wotlon, Chrisn., Pt..... | Tatum's | " | W | |
| Williams, Jno., Pt...... | " | " | " | |
| Williams, Thos., Pt..... | " | " | " | |
| Ward, Thos........... | Dixon's | " | 3 yrs. | Omtd June '78 |
| Wearing, Jas., Pt...... | Bowman's | 30 June " | | Destd 2 July '77 |
| Waters, Wm., Lt....... | Thompson's | 5 Feb. " | | Omtd June '78 |
| Wood, Jno., Pt......... | " | 4 Apr. " | W | Sergt. Jan. Pt. June '78 |
| Wynne, Knibb, Sergt... | Dixon's | 1777 | " | Omtd Jan. '78 |
| William, David, Sergt... | " | " | | Dischgd 27 Sep. '77 |
| Wynne, Jones, Pt...... | " | " | W | |
| Watkins, Shad'k, Pt.... | " | " | " | |
| Wilson, Jno., Pt........ | " | " | " | Died 21 Feb. '78 |

| Name and Rank | Company | Dates of Enlistment and Commission | Period of Service | Occurrences |
|---|---|---|---|---|
| Weeks, Sylvanus, Pt.... | Dixon's | 1777 | W | Died 15 Mar. '78 |
| Wynne, Wm., Pt....... | " | " | " | Omtd Jan. '78 |
| Walters, Jno., Musc..... | Hogg's | " | " | Dm. Maj. July '79 |
| Walton, Rich'd, Pt...... | " | " | 3 yrs. | Omtd Sep. '78 |
| Waters, Sam'l, Lt....... | Ralston's | 29 Mar. '77 | | Resigned May '77 |
| Woodward, Jno., Pt..... | " | | W | |
| Walker, John, Maj...... | | 26 Apr. '77 | " | Resigned 22 Dec. '77 |
| Williams, Wm., B. Maj.. | | 13 June '76 | | {Omtd Nov.'77. See him in 4 th Reg. |
| Walker, Thos., D. W. M. Gl........ | | 5 Apr. '77 | " | Omtd Sep. '77 |
| Wilkins, Joshua, Pt..... | Tatum's | 15 Aug. '77 | 3 yrs. | |
| Wyatt, Jno., Sergt...... | Ely's | | " | Died 29 Apr. '77 |
| Wharton, Lem'l, Pt..... | Dixon's | 1 Dec. 76 | " | |
| White, Stephen, Sergt... | Reid's | | " | Died 28 June 78 |
| White, Wm., Pt........ | " | | | Died 31 Mar. 78 |
| White, Henry, Pt....... | " | 9 May 76 | 2½ yrs. | Dischgd 10 Nov. 78 |
| Williamson, Henry, Pt. . | " | May 76 | 3 yrs. | Dischgd 27 May 79 |
| **Y** (P. 1194) | | | | |
| Young, Jas., Pt........ | Bowman's | 1777 | | {Omtd July 79 Mustd Nov 79 |
| York, Wm............. | Dixon's | " | W | |
| **Z** (P. 1195) | | | | |
| Zakel, James, Pt........ | Granberry's | 2 Apr. '76 | W | Pris. 1 June '79 |

## 2ND REGIMENT—COL. ALEXANDER MARTIN

| Name and Rank | Company | Dates of Enlistment and Commission | Period of Service | Occurrences |
|---|---|---|---|---|
| **A** (P. 1003) | | | | |
| Adams, Lanier, Pt...... | William's | 1777 | | Omtd Jan. 1778 |
| Allen, Chas., Capt...... | | " | | Omtd Jan. '78 |
| Ambrose, David....... | Allen's | " | W | Pt. Apr. '78. Musc. '81 |
| Alexander, William..... | " | " | " | Died 14 Mar. '78 |
| Allen, William......... | " | " | | Died Jan. 7, '78 |
| Andrews, Rich'd, 2nd Lt. | Gee's | " | | {Pris. 1 June '79. Musc. '81. Resigned '82 |
| Alexander, Joseph, Pt... | Fenner's | Apr. " | 3 yrs. | Destd. 1 Jan. '80 |
| Alexander, Wm., Musc.. | " | " | | Pt. Sep. '77 |
| Alderson, Simon, Pt..... | Vail's | " | W | {Sergt. 20 May '79 Pris. 1 June '79 |
| Armstrong, John, Capt.. | | 1 Sep. '75 | | {Maj. 4 Oct. '77 in 4th Reg. |
| **B** (P. 1010) | | | | |
| Baxter, Sam'l, Sergt..... | William's | 22 Nov. '76 | | {Pt. 1 Jan.'78. Pris. 1 June '79. Corpl. Nov. '79. Musc. Sergt. Jan. '82 |
| Bull, Mich'l, Musc..... | " | | 3 yrs. | Pt. Jan. '78 Died Jan. '79 |
| Bruties, Pt............ | " | | | Omtd Jan. '78 |
| Bruce, Thos., Pt....... | " | | | Omtd Jan. '78 |
| Budd, Sam'l, Lt........ | Allen's | | W | {Omtd June '78 Pris. 8 Sep. '81 Capt. Deranged 1 Jan. '83 |
| Bogle, Arch'd, Sergt..... | " | | W | |
| Bone, Jas., Corpl....... | " | 15 Jan. '77 | 3 yrs.W | {Pt. Jan. '78 Died 17 June '83 |
| Bryan, Wm., Musc..... | " | " | W | Pt. June '78 |
| Best, Thos., Pt........ | " | " | " | Deserted 17 Feb. '80 |

| Name and Rank | Company | Dates of Enlistment and Commission | Period of Service | Occurrences |
|---|---|---|---|---|
| Bates, Frederick, Pt..... | Allen's | '77 | | |
| Bell, Benj., Corpl....... | Hall's | " | | Died 17 Apr. '78 |
| Bosen, Jacob, Sergt..... | Martin's | 29 Nov. '76 | W | |
| Branch, Job, Corpl...... | " | " | | {Pt. June '78 / Dischgd 29 Jan. '08 |
| Bright, Chas., Pt...... | " | 7 Aug. '77 | 3 yrs.W | {Corpl. Nov. '78 / Sergt. 21 Feb. '79 |
| Beal, Jno., Pt......... | " | " | 2½ yrs. | Died 16 May '78 |
| Berry, Solom, Sergt..... | Gee's | " | 3 yrs. | Pt. 31 Jan. '80 |
| Brown, Joseph, Pt..... | " | 9 Nov. '76 | " | {Musc. Corpl. for War / Sep. '82 |
| Berry, John, Pt........ | " | '77 | " | {Corpl. Dec. '78. Sergt. / Nov. '79. Pt. 10 Feb. '80 |
| Beaman, Jereh, Pt..... | " | " | W | |
| Bullock, Balaam, Pt.... | " | " | " | {Pris. 1 June '79 / Musc. Nov. '79 |
| Borows, John, Pt...... | Fenner's | " | | Omtd Apr. '78 |
| Buford, Wm., 2nd Lt.... | Vail's | 15 May '77 | | Resigned Aug. '77 |
| Bateman, Jona., Pt..... | " | " | " | Died 8 Apr. '78 |
| Bailey, Josh., Pt....... | " | 1 Dec. '76 | 3 yrs. | {Sergt. 1 July '79 / Dischgd 16 Feb. '80 |
| Barnes, Jas., Pt........ | Armstrong's | " | W | {Sergt. Aug.'77. Pt. 1 July / '78. Destd 25 Oct. '78 |
| Babb, Josh............ | " | 19 June '76 | 3 yrs. | Musc.Apr.'78.Pt. June'78 |
| C   (P. 1026) | | | | |
| Cheshire, H'dy., Dm. Maj.......... | | 1777 | | Omtd Nov. '77 |
| Cary, Jno., Pt.......... | William's | " | | Omtd Jan. '78 |
| Craddock, John, Lt..... | " | " | W | {Capt. 21 Dec. '77. Pris. 12 / May '80. Deranged 1 / Jan. '83 |
| Campin, Jas., Lt....... | " | " | | |
| Colihorn, Robt., Pt..... | Allen's | " | W | Dead 16 May '78 |
| Cole, Geoe., Pt........ | " | " | " | Dischgd 30 Jan. '80 |
| Cashway, Josh, Pt..... | Hall's | " | | Pris. 1 June '79 |
| Carman, Stepn, Corpl... | Martin's | " | " | {Sergt. Oct. '77 / Destd 20 Feb. '79 |
| Collins, Sam'l, Musc.... | " | " | 3 yrs. | Died 18 Apr. '78 |
| Cotgrave, Arthur, Lt.... | " | " | | Resigned 1 Aug. '82 |
| Chamberlain, Chris., Pt. | " | " | | Died 22 May '78 |
| Christain, Jas., Pt...... | " | 19 May " | 3 yrs. | |
| Cheshire, H'y, Musc.... | Gee's | " | | Omtd Nov. '77 |
| Curry, Jno., Pt......... | " | " | W | Dischgd 10 Nov. '78 |
| Collins, Jno., Pt....... | " | 18 Mar. '76 | 2 yrs. | Dischgd 30 Sep. '78 |
| Cox, Joseph, Pt........ | Fenner's | " | " | {Corpl. Jan. '78 / Died 23 Apr. '78 |
| Campbell, Pat'k, Pt..... | " | 18 Aug. " | " | {Sergt. Sep. '77 / Dischgd 1 May '79 |
| Cook, Joseph, Pt...... | " | '77 | | Omtd Sep. '77 |
| Calf, Robt., Pt........ | " | " | | {Mustd Sep. '77 / Omtd June '78 |
| Curtis, Reuben, Ensn. .. | " | " | | Omtd Jan. '78 |
| Carson, Jno., Sergt...... | Armstrong's | 18 Mar. '76 | W | {Pt. Nov. '78 / Pris. 1 June '79 |
| Cook, Stephen, Pt...... | " | 20 Dec. " | 3 yrs. | Died Nov. 19, '79 |
| Curtis, Barth., Volnt.... | " | '77 | | Omtd Dec. '77 |

| Name and Rank | Company | Dates of Enlistment and Commission | Period of Service | Occurrences |
|---|---|---|---|---|
| **D** (P. 1040) | | | | |
| Davis, John, 2nd Lt..... | | 1777 | | Lt. Oct.'77. Capt. 8 Sep. '81. Deranged 1 Jan. '83 |
| Davis, Thos., Sergt..... | Hall's | " | | Sergt. Maj. Nov. '77. Pt. Feb.'78. Sergt. Nov. '78 |
| Dring, Thos., Pt........ | Allen's | " | | Died 11 Sep. '77 |
| Davis, Wm., Corpl..... | Hall's | 7 Nov. '76 | W | Pt. June '78 Corpl. 1 Apr. '79 |
| Dodge, Jonah, Musc.... | " | 1777 | | Destd 10 Feb. '79 |
| Davis, Asa, Musc....... | " | " | " | Pt. June '78 |
| Deal, Isaac, Pt........ | " | " | | Destd 1 Jan. '79 |
| Deal, Wm., Pt........ | " | " | | Died Mar. 5, '78 |
| Dawson, Math., Pt.... | " | " | | Trans. 1 Jan. '79 to the Invalids |
| Dudley, Jno............ | " | " | " | Sergt. Sep.'77. Pt. Jan. '78. Destd 15 Jan. '80 |
| Daughtry, Dempsy, Pt.. | " | " | | Omtd Jan. '78 |
| Deal, Reuben, Pt...... | Martin's | " | 3 yrs. | Died 28 Apr. '78 |
| Drake, Cove, Sergt..... | Gee's | " | 2½ yrs. | Dischgd 2 Aug. '78 from his Excy. Guards |
| Dillard, Sampson, Corpl. | " | | W | Pt. Dec. '78 |
| Dunbar, Dunn, Corpl... | " | 12 Jan. '76 | " | Pt. Nov. '78 Destd 30 Apr. '79 |
| Davis, Fred'k, Pt...... | " | 12 Dec. " | 3 yrs. | Dischgd 31 Jan. '80 |
| Drew, Wm., Pt........ | " | '77 | W | |
| Davis, Jno., Pt........ | Vail's | " | | |
| Davis, Zach, Pt........ | Fenner's | 3 Nov. '76 | 3 yrs. | |
| Day, Jno., Pt.......... | Armstrong's | '77 | W | Died Jan. 14, '78 |
| **E** (P. 1049) | | | | |
| Edmons, Abel, Pt...... | William's | 1 Feb. '77 | 3 yrs. | Dischgd 1 Feb. '80 |
| Emory, Stephen, Pt.... | " | 1 " " | " | Died Oct, '78 |
| Evans, Thos., 1st Lt.... | Martin's | 19 July '76 | | Adj't 22 Nov.'78 Capt. June '81. Deranged 1 Jan. '83 |
| Ellis, Robt., Pt........ | Fenner's | 3 Sep. '76 | 3 yrs. | |
| Edwards, Jno., Pt...... | Armstrong's | 1 June '76 | " | Died 15 Feb. '78 |
| **F** (P. 1055) | | | | |
| Finney, Thos., Sergt. Maj.......... | | 1777 | | 2nd Lt. 12 Nov. '77 |
| Finner, Rich'd P., Mr... | | " | | Ensn. 10 Jan. '80 Lt. 12 May '81 |
| Fields, Lewis, Pt........ | Hall's | " | | Destd Aug.'77. Mustd Sep.'78. Destd Nov. '78. Wag. Mast. 22 Aug. '79. Omtd Oct. '79 |
| Fryar, Josiah, Pt...... | Gee's | " | W | Died June 18, '78 |
| Foisett, Robt., Pt...... | " | 20 Nov. '76 | 3 yrs. | |
| Felps, Garret, Pt...... | " | '77 | | 30 Jan. '78 |
| Foxa, John, Pt........ | " | " | | |
| Fenner, Wm., Capt..... | | " | | Maj. 24 Oct.'77, 7 Reg. |
| Flounder, Robt., 1st Lt.. | Fenner's | 1 Jan. '76 | | Capt. 4 Oct. '77 P. Mr. 1 June '78 Deranged 1 Jan. '83 |
| Flood, Alex, Pt........ | | 4 July '77 | 3 yrs. | Mustd Jan. '78 |
| **G** (P. 1062) | | | | |
| Geedin, Isaac, Fife Maj. | | 7 Nov. '76 | 3 yrs. | Musc. Dec. '77 Pt. Nov. '78 |

| Name and Rank | Company | Dates of Enlistment and Commission | Period of Service | Occurrences |
|---|---|---|---|---|
| Griffin, Edmond, Pt..... | William's | 7 Nov. '76 | 3 yrs. | Trans. to his Excy's Guards '78. Dischgd 31 Jan. '80 |
| Glover, Sam'l, Sergt.... | Allen's | '77 | W | Pt. July '79 Died 23 Feb. '80 |
| Glass, Jas., Pt.......... | Hall's | " | | Destd Aug. '77 |
| Gee, Jas., Capt......... | | " | | Died 12 Nov. '77 |
| Gallop, Mathew, Corpl.. | Gee's | " | | Pris. June '79. See Lyile's Coy. Mustd in '81 |
| Gregory, Thos., Pt...... | " | " | | |
| Goslin, Ambrose, Pt..... | Fenner's | " | | Died Sep. 1, '77 |
| Gamberlin, Jas., Corpl.. | Vail's | 14 Dec. '76 | 3 yrs. | Pt. June'78.Pris.June'79. Mustd Nov. '79 Dischgd 30 Jan. '80 |
| Glasgow, Caleb, Pt...... | " | '77 | W | Dischgd Sep. '78 |
| Gurley, Simon, Pt...... | " | " | " | Died 6 May '78 |
| Garret, Thos., Pt....... | " | " | " | Destd 11 Dec. '79 |
| Gallop, Isaac, Pt....... | " | 22 May " | 3 yrs. | |
| Glenn, Tobias, Musc.... | Armstrong s | " | In 4th Reg. Dec. 77 | |
| Grant, David, Pt...... | " | " | W | Destd 1 Jan. 80 |
| H   (P. 1073) | | | | |
| Harney, Selby, Lt. Col.. | | 22 Nov. '77 | | Mustd Pris. '81 Mustd Jan. '82 Deranged 1 Jan. '83 |
| Harvey, John, Pt....... | William's | 17 Sep. '76 | 3 yrs. | Destd 1 Jan. '80 |
| Huste, John, Pt........ | " | Nov. " | " | |
| Harvey, Joshua, Pt..... | Allen's | | W | Pris. 1 June'79.Mustd '83 |
| Hall, Clement, Capt. ... | | 19 Apr. '77 | | |
| Howell, John, Pt....... | Hall's | 17 June " | 3 yrs. | |
| Harris, Wm., Pt........ | Martin's | 7 Nov. '76 | " | |
| Harris, Jno., Pt........ | " | '77 | | Omtd Nov. '77. Mustd Apr.'77. Dischgd May'78 |
| Howard, Pat'k, Pt...... | Gee's | " | W | Destd time not known and Mustd Jan. '78 |
| Humphreys, Dan'l, Pt.. | " | 18 Mar. '76 | 2½ yrs. | Dischgd 30 Sep. '78 |
| Huling, Jacob, Sergt..... | Fenner's | '77 | | Pt. Sep. '77 |
| Hair, Robt., Pt......... | " | " | | Destd Dec. '77 |
| Hoskins, Eben'z., Pt.... | Armstrong's | 1 Apr. " | W | Destd 1 Sep. '78 |
| Hazle, Thos., Pt....... | " | " | " | Died 28 Feb. '78 |
| I   (P. 1086) | | | | |
| Ingles, Jno., Lt. & Adj't. | | 1777 | | Capt. 12 Nov.'77. Pris. 12 May '80 Deranged 1 Jan. '83 |
| Irwin, Nich's, Pt....... | Hall's | 7 Oct. '76 | W | Destd 29 Apr. '79 |
| Ingles, Jno., 1st Lt...... | Gee's | '77 | | Capt. Nov.'77 (See above) |
| J   (P. 1088) | | | | |
| Jones, Brinson, Corpl. .. | William's | '77 | | Dead June '78 |
| Jolly, Malachi, Pt...... | " | " | | In 8 Reg. Dec. '77(John Moore in his stead) |
| Jennet, Solomon, Pt..... | " | 1 Feb. " | 3 yrs. | |
| Jewell, Sm'l............ | " | 27 Jan. " | " | |
| Jacob, Jno., Lt......... | Allen's | 1 Nov. '76 | | Omtd Feb. '78 |
| Jennings, Thos., Pt..... | " | 20 Dec. " | W | Corpl. 30 Apr. '79 Distg 30 Jan. '80 |
| Jackson, Robt., Pt...... | " | 1 June '77 | 3 yrs. | Pris. 1 June '79 Mustd Nov. '79 |

| Name and Rank | Company | Dates of Enlistment and Commission | Period of Service | Occurrences |
|---|---|---|---|---|
| Johnson, Henry, Musc. . | Hall's | '77 | W | {Corpl. May '78<br>{Destd 1 Apr. '79 |
| Jenkins, Dempsey...... | `"` | 19 June `"` | 3 yrs. | |
| Jones, Robt........... | `"` | `"` | `"` | Omtd Jan. '79 |
| James, Noah, Corpl..... | Gee's | 7 Nov. '76 | `"` | |
| Johnson, John, Pt...... | Fenner's | 20 Nov. `"` | `"` | Omtd Feb. '78 |
| Johnson, Benj., Corpl... | Vail's | 26 Dec `"` | `"` | Dischgd 30 Jan. '80 |
| Jordon, Nath'l., Pt...... | Armstrong's | `"` | W | Died 24 Jan. '78 |
| K (P. 1095) | | | | |
| Kelly, Wm., Pt......... | Brown's | 1777 | W | Omtd June '78 |
| King, Jas., Lt.......... | Tatum's | 3 Apr. `"` | | {Capt. 1 Apr. '80<br>{Died 8 Sep. '80 |
| Kennedy, Isaac, Pt..... | Bowman's | `"` | | Destd Aug. '77 |
| Kettle, Jacob, Pt....... | Armstrong's | 9 Oct. `"` | 3 yrs. | |
| Kelly, Jno., Pt........ | Ely's | | `"` | |
| Keith, Jno., Pt......... | Reid's | | W | Musc. Sick 10 Feb. '80 |
| L (Pp. 1100-1101) | | | | |
| Litten, Abell, Pt....... | Gee's | 1 Dec. '76 | 3 yrs. | {Musc. Nov. '77<br>{Dm. Maj. 1 Nov. '78 |
| Linch, John, Sergt...... | `"` | '77 | `"` | {Pt. Feb.'78. Trans.1 July<br>'79 to 2nd Virga. Reg. |
| Leach, Jno., Corpl...... | Fenner's | 25 Nov. '76 | 2½ yrs. | {Sergt. 1 Nov.'77. Pt. Jan.<br>'78. Mustd '81 |
| Linton, Theheu, Sergt... | `"` | '77 | | {Pt. Nov. '77<br>{Died 3 Dec. '77 |
| Little, Jno., Pt......... | `"` | 25 Sep. '76 | 3 yrs. | Destd 15 Aug. '78 |
| Lacey, Jno., Sergt....... | Vail's | '77 | W | {Sergt. Maj. Feb.'78 Sergt.<br>June'78. Ensn. 20 May'79<br>Resigned in '79 |
| Latham, Phineas, Sergt.. | `"` | `"` | `"` | {Pt. 24 May'79. Pris. June<br>'79. Mustd Nov. '79 |
| Low, Geo., Pt......... | `"` | `"` | `"` | Destd 15 Aug. '78 |
| M (P. 1109) | | | | |
| Martin, Alex., Col...... | | 1777 | | Resigned 22 Nov. '77 |
| Murfree, Hardy, Maj. .. | | 1 Feb. `"` | | {Lt. Col. 1 Apr. '77<br>{Deranged 1 Jan. '83 |
| McClure, Wm., Surg.... | | 1 May '76 | | |
| Mason, Philip, Dr.Maj.. | | '77 | W | |
| Martin, Sam'l, Lt....... | William's | `"` | | Resigned Aug. '77 |
| Morning, Jno., Pt....... | `"` | `"` | | Omtd Jan. '78 |
| Marshall, Robt., Pt..... | `"` | `"` | | Destd Aug. '77 |
| Moore, John, Pt....... | `"` | Dec. `"` | | {For Malachi Jolly,<br>{Died 31 Dec. '78 |
| Montague, Bryan, Pt. .. | Allen's | `"` | | Omtd Jan. '78 |
| McDonald, Thos., Pt.... | `"` | `"` | W | |
| Montague, Sam'l, Pt.... | `"` | `"` | | Omtd Jan. '78 |
| Morgan, Bennet, Sergt.. | Hall's | 7 Nov. '76 | 3 yrs. | |
| Martin, Henry, Corpl... | `"` | `"` `"` | `"` | Pt. June '78 |
| Martin, James, Capt.... | | 20 Apr. '77 | | Omtd Jan. '78 |
| Miller, James, Pt....... | Martin's | `"` | 3 yrs. | Omtd Feb. '78 |
| Moore, Ralph, Pt....... | `"` | 1 June `"` | `"` | {Or Moon, Omtd Nov.'77<br>{Mustd Oct. '78. Died 20<br>Dec. '78 |
| Mitchel, Wm., Pt...... | `"` | 2 `"` `"` | `"` | {Musc. Feb. '78. Pt. June<br>{Musc. July '79 |
| Mathews, Jacob, Musc.. | Gee's | `"` | W | Pt. June '78 |
| Molbone, Malachi, Pt... | `"` | `"` | `"` | Destd 10 July '79 |

| Name and Rank | Company | Dates of Enlistment and Commission | Period of Service | Occurrences |
|---|---|---|---|---|
| Marchant, John, Pt..... | Fenner's | '77 | W | Died 20 Apr. '78 |
| McPherson, Abell, Sergt. | " | " | " | Q. M. Sergt. 20 Dec. '79 |
| Mason, Philip, Musc.... | Vail's | " | " | See Dm. Maj. above |
| Messick, Joseph, Pt..... | " | " | " | Destd 10 July '79 |
| McGuire, Silas, Pt...... | " | " | " | Died 1 July '78 |
| McIlwane, Stringer, Lt.. | Armstrong's | " | " | Omtd Oct. '77 |
| Mexico, Abue, Corpl.... | " | " | " | {Pt. June '78 / Died 20 June '78 |
| McConnel, Philip, Pt.... | | " | " | Dischgd 10 Sep. '78 |
| McDowell, Geo., Pt..... | | " | " | Destd 8 Mar. '78 |
| **N (P. 1123)** | | | | |
| Nicholas, Geo.or Jno.,Pt. | Hall's | 1777 | | Omtd Jan. '78 |
| Nicholas, Sam'l, Sergt... | Gee's | " | | Died 22 July '77 |
| Negrove, Fred'k, Musc.. | Fenner's | " | | Omtd Jan. '78 |
| Nash, Joseph, Pt....... | Vail's | " | W | Destd 15 Mar. '79 |
| Negroe, Benj'n, Musc... | Armstrong's | " | | Dischgd Dec. '77 |
| Nicholas, Geo., Pt..... | " | " | " | {Destd 1 Mar.'78. Mustd / May '78. Destd17Mar.'79 |
| **O (P. 1128)** | | | | |
| Osborn, Joseph, Pt...... | Gee's | 1777 | W | Destd 10 Aug. '78 |
| **P (P. 1132)** | | | | |
| Pattin, Jno., Lt. Col.... | | 1777 | | {Col. 22 Nov.'77. Pris. 12 / May '80. Deranged 1 / Jan. '83 |
| Parkinson, Jas., Lt...... | William's | " | | Died 26 Mar. '78 |
| Pierce, Thos., Pt....... | " | " | 3 yrs. | Died 2 Jan. '78 |
| Philip, Geo., Pt........ | Allen's | " | W | |
| Pollard, Wm., Pt....... | Martin's | " | | Omtd Sep. '77 |
| Patterson, Jno., Pt..... | Gee's | " | W | Destd 1 May '79 |
| Powers, David, Pt..... | Fenner's | " | | Died 3 May '78 |
| Pyot, Thos., Pt........ | " | " | | Omtd Jan. '78 |
| Parr, Noah, Pt........ | Vail's | " | | Pt. Aug. '78 |
| Pond, Jno., Pt......... | Armstrong's | " | | {Destd 28 June '79. Mustd / Nov.'79. Destd 5 Feb.'80 |
| **R (P. 1142-3)** | | | | |
| Reff, Chas., Sergt...... | William's | 1777 | | Destd Nov. '77 |
| Ring, Jas., Musc....... | " | " | | Died 13 Sep. '77 |
| Ring, Jas. Sen., Pt...... | " | " | | Died 1 Dec. '77 |
| Richardson, Jno., Pt.... | Allen's | " | W | {Corpl. July '78. Destd 30 / Apr. '79 |
| Rolston, Isaac, Lt...... | Hall's | | | Omtd Apr. '78 |
| Roberts, Rich'd, Pt..... | " | 10 July " | 3 yrs. | Pris. 1 June '79 |
| Raiford, Jno, Lt....... | " | " | | Resigned Jan. '78 |
| Runner, Corns, Sergt.... | Martin's | " | W | {Corpl. Oct. '77. Died 29 / Apr. '78 |
| Richards, Wm., Pt. .... | " | " | " | |
| Roe, Sam'l, Pt........ | Gee's | 9 Apr. '76 | 2½ yrs. | Dischgd 10 Nov. '78 |
| Ridgeway, Jno., Pt..... | " | '77 | W | Dest 6 Dec. 79 |
| Raper, Robt., Pt....... | Fenner's | " | | |
| Raper, Jno., Pt........ | " | 22 Dec '76 | 3 yrs. | {Musc. July '79. Dischgd / 1 Feb. '80 |
| Royal, Jas., Corpl...... | " | '77 | | Died 6 Mar. '78 |
| Raper, Caleb, Pt...... | Vail's | | | Omtd Oct. '77 |
| Royal, Wm., Pt........ | Armstrong's | 26 June '77 | 3 yrs. | Omtd Apr. '78 |
| **S (P. 1153)** | | | | |
| Spicer, Jno............ | | 1777 | | Omtd Nov. '77 |

| Name and Rank | Company | Dates of Enlistment and Commission | Period of Service | Occurrences |
|---|---|---|---|---|
| Slade, Stephen, Qr. Mr. Sergt....... | | 1777 | | {Qr. Mr. 1 Jan. '78.Ensn. Sep. '78. Lt. 11 Jan. '81 Deranged 1 Jan. '83 |
| Sanders, Wm., Pt....... | Williams's | 1 Feb. " | 3 yrs. | Dischgd 1 Feb. '80 |
| Smith, Wm., Pt........ | " | 18 Dec. '76 | " | Dischgd 30 Jan. '80 |
| Sebron, Joseph, Pt..... | " | 1 Feb. '77 | " | {Dischgd Nov. '78, (Unfit For Service) |
| Stevenson, Wm., Pt..... | " | 1 Jan. " | " | |
| Sanders, Andrew, Pt.... | " | 1 Feb. " | " | {Corpl. 13 Nov.'78. Pris. 1 Jne'79.Dischgd 1 Feb.'80 |
| Scott, Thos., Pt........ | " | 16 June " | " | Music Jan. '78 |
| Stradley, Edward, Corpl. | Allen's | " | W | Pt. 15 May '79 |
| Smith, Jno., Pt........ | " | 17 July '76 | 3 yrs.W | Pris. 1 June '79 |
| Smith, Jere., Pt........ | " | '77 | W | Dischgd 30 June '80 |
| Squires, Skidmore, Pt... | " | 20 Nov. " | 3 yrs. | Destd 14 Feb. '79 |
| Smith, Jno., Pt........ | Hall's | " | " | Died 27 Feb. '78 |
| Smith, Jno. Jr., Pt..... | " | 7 Nov. '76 | " | Destd 17 Feb. '80 |
| Sanderlin, Levy, Pt.... | " | '77 | 2½ yrs. | {Destd 25 Dec.'77.Mustd Jan.'79. 5 Reg. Corpl. June '79 |
| Steelman, Jno., Pt...... | " | " | | Destd Aug. '77 |
| Sessions, Jno., Pt....... | " | | | Omtd Nov.'77. Mustd '79 |
| Smith, Redick, Musc.... | Martin's | 5 Dec. '76 | | {Pt. June '78 Corpl. July '79 |
| Simmons, Jas., Pt....... | " | '77 | 3 yrs. | |
| Simmons, Malachi, Pt... | " | " | " | Died 1 May '78 |
| Sewells, Dan'l, Pt...... | " | " | W | Died 14 Apr. '78 |
| Squires, Jno., Pt....... | " | 22 May " | 3 yrs. | |
| Smith, Wm., Pt........ | Gee's | " | W | Died 28 Feb. '78 |
| Siborn, Wm., Pt....... | " | " | " | |
| Sanderlin, Jno., Pt...... | " | " | " | Destd 25 Dec. '77 |
| Shepard, Jno., Pt...... | " | " | " | |
| Spear, David, Sergt.... | " | 26 Dec. '76 | 3 yrs. | {Sergt. Maj. 1 June '78 Reduced 1 Feb. '79 |
| Smith, Caleb, Pt........ | " | '77 | W | |
| Smith, Wm., Sergt..... | Fenner's | 7 Dec. '76 | 3 yrs. | Pt. Aug. '78 |
| Shackler, Philip, Corpl.. | " | 23 Mar. " | W | Pt. Jan. '78 |
| Spires, Absolm, Pt..... | " | 20 Nov. " | 3 yrs. | |
| Sawyer, Wm., Ensn.... | Vail's | 15 May '76 | | {Omtd Sep.'77, Supposed Levy Sawyer, 2 Lt., Armstrong's Co. |
| Spain, Eps, Corpl...... | " | '77 | W | {Sergt. 1 Dec.'77.Pt. June '78. Sergt Oct.'78. Pt. 1 Jan. '80 |
| Sterling, Isaac, Pt..... | Vail's | " | " | {Sergt. Dec. '77 Died 5 Apr. '78 |
| Scott, Jas., Pt......... | " | | | Omtd Nov. '77 |
| Scandrett, Jas., Sergt... | Armstong's | 10 Aug. '76 | 2½ yrs. | Omtd Feb. '79 |
| Sawyer, Levy, 2nd Lt... | " | '77 | | Resigned 1 Mar. '78 |
| Steward, Wm., Musc.... | " | 27 June " | 3 yrs. | {Pt. Mar. '78 Destd 1 Jan. '80 |
| T   (P. 1168) Tiffin, Thos., Sergt..... | William's | 26 Oct. '76 | 3 yrs. | {Pt. 1 Jan. '78 Dischgd 31 Jan. '80 |
| Turner, Benj., Pt...... | " | '77 | | Died 1 Dec. '77 |
| Thorogood, Francis, Pt.. | Allen's | " | W | Corpl. 15 July '79 |

| Name and Rank | Company | Dates of Enlistment and Commission | Period of Service | Occurrences |
|---|---|---|---|---|
| Truit, Franklin, Pt...... | Hall's | '77 | W | |
| Tillman, Belitha, Pt.... | " | " | | Omtd Nov. '77 |
| Talton, Jas., Pt......... | " | " | | Omtd Jan. '78 |
| Thom, Thos., Pt........ | Martin's | " | 3 yrs. | Died July 20, '78 |
| Taylor, Jno., Pt........ | Gee's | " | W | |
| Tellet, Avery, Pt...... | " | " | " | {Pris. 1 June '79 / Mustd Nov. '79 |
| Tarrant, Manlove, 1 Lt. | Vail's | 15 May " | | {Capt. 24 Oct. '77 / Omtd June '78 |
| Thomas, Jno., Pt...... | Armstrong's | 3 Mar. " | W | |
| Truit, Stephen, Pt..... | | 1 July " | 3 yrs. | |
| U  (P. 1176) | | | | |
| Upton, Jno., Pt......... | Allen's | 14 Dec. '76 | 3 yrs. | Corpl. Feb. '79 |
| V  (P. 1179) | | | | |
| Vance, David, Lt....... | Hall's | 20 Apr. '76 | | Omtd June '78 |
| Vail, Edw'd, Capt..... | | 21 Aug. " | | Cashiered 21 Dec. '77 |
| Vick, Isaac, Pt......... | | 16 Sep. '77 | 3 yrs. | |
| W  (P. 1181) | | | | |
| Williams, Benj., Capt... | | 1777 | | Resigned 1 Jan. '79 |
| Williams, Chas., Pt.... | William's | " | | Died 15 May '78 |
| Washington, Wm.,Sergt. | Allen's | " | | Omtd Nov. '77 |
| Webb, Chas., Corpl.... | " | " | W | Pt. Feb. '79 |
| Wooten, Wm., Pt....... | " | " | | Died 21 Apr. '78 |
| Watson, Thos., Sergt.... | Hall's | " | | Omtd Jan. '78 |
| Williams, Jno., Lt....... | Martin's | 21 Apr. " | | Omtd Apr. '78 |
| White, Dempsey, Pt.... | " | 20 Mar. '76 | 2½ yrs. | Destd 1 Nov. '78 |
| Weeks, Hardy, Pt..... | " | '77 | | Destd Aug. '77 |
| Waymouth, Corbin, Pt.. | Gee's | 18 Dec. '76 | 3 yrs. | {Corpl. Nov.'78. Pris. 1 / June'79. Dischgd1Jan.'80 |
| White, Jno., Pt........ | " | '77 | W | Died 16 May '78 |
| Wiggins, Absolm, Pt.... | " | " | " | Omtd Jan. '78 |
| Westerdale, Francis Musc.............. | Fenner's | 30 Mar. '76 | 3 yrs. | {Pt. June '78. Mustd War / Jan. '82 |
| Webster, Rich'd, Pt..... | " | 23 Dec. '76 | " | |
| Wilson, Aaron, Pt...... | " | '77 | | {Pris. Sep.'77. Mustd June / '78. Destd 15 June '79 |
| Willis, Geo., Pt........ | " | 10 Oct. '76 | 3 yrs.W | {Pris. 1 June '79 / Mustd Nov. '79 |
| Webb, Joshua, Pt...... | " | 20 May '77 | 3 yrs. | |
| Waldron, Thos., Musc... | Vail's | '77 | W | Pt. June'78 |
| Williams, Frans., Pt..... | | " | " | Pris. 2 June'79. Mustd '82 |
| White, Rich'd, Pt....... | Armstrong's | 2 Oct. '76 | 2½ yrs. | {Pris. 1 June '79 / Mustd Nov. '79 |

### 3RD REGIMENT—COL. JETHRO SUMNER

| Name and Rank | Company | Dates | Period | Occurrences |
|---|---|---|---|---|
| A  (P. 1003) | | | | |
| Ashton, Wm., Lt. Col... | | 15 Apr. '76 | | Resigned 25 Oct. '77 |
| Acock, Moses, Pt....... | Turner's | '77 | 2½ yrs. | Dead May, '78 |
| Acock, Robt., Pt...... | " | 20 Apr. '76 | " | Dischgd 10 Nov. '78 |
| Aged, Benj'n, Pt....... | " | 11 May " | " | Dischgd 10 Nov. '78 |
| Ammis, Jas., Pt........ | Granberry's | 25 May " | " | Dischgd 10 Nov. '78 |
| Angel, Benj'n, Pt...... | Emmet's | " | " | Dischgd Mar. '78 |
| B  (P. 1011) | | | | |
| Brewster, Lott, Lt. Col.. | | 25 Oct. '77 | | Resigned 15 Mar. '78 |
| Braoley, Rich'd, Mr. P.. | | " | | See him in 1st Reg. |

| Name and Rank | Company | Dates of Enlistment and Commission | Period of Service | Occurrences |
|---|---|---|---|---|
| Barrow, James, Drum... | Eaton's | '77 | | { Dr. Maj. Sep. '77 <br> { Omtd Sep. '78 |
| Bridges, Benj., Pt....... | Turner's | 20 Apr. '76 | 2½ yrs. | Dischgd Oct. '78 |
| Bennet, Pt............ | " | 8 May '76 | " | { Sergt. Oct. 25,'78. Corpl. <br> { June '78. Dischgd 10 <br> { Nov. '78 |
| Brandon, Wm., Pt...... | " | 1 May '77 | 3 yrs. | Omtd Jan. '78 |
| Ballard, Keedar, Lt..... | Emmet's | 16 Apr. '76 | 2½ yrs. | { Capt. Nov.'77. M. 1. Oct. <br> { '79. Pris. 12 May'80. <br> { Deranged 1 Jan. '83 |
| Bartholomew, Jno., Pt.. | Turner's | | " | Dischgd Oct. '78 |
| Butts, Jona, Sergt....... | Granberry's | '76 | " | Dischgd Oct. 17, '77 |
| Butts, Jacob, Sergt..... | " | " | " | Omtd Oct. '77 |
| Butts, Job., Corpl...... | " | " | " | Dischgd Oct. '78 |
| Bailey, Lewis, Pt....... | " | 10 Apr. " | " | Dischgd Oct. '78 |
| Bilberry, Nath., Pt..... | " | 20 Apr. " | " | Omtd Jan. '78 |
| Brinkley, Wm., Capt.... | | " | | Omtd Jan. '78 |
| Bradley, James, Capt... | | 16 Apr. '77 | | Omtd June '78 |
| Baler, Norris, Pt....... | Eaton's | 18 Apr. '76 | " | { Dischgd 30 Nov. '78 <br> { F'od. 20 Feb. '80 |
| Bennett, Moses, Pt..... | " | | " | Dischgd 10 Nov. '78 |
| Bradley, Gee, Lt........ | Eaton's | | | { Capt. 19 Sep.'78. Pris. 12 <br> { May '80. Deranged <br> { 1 Jan. '83 |
| Bugg, Wm., Pt......... | Emmet's | 25 May " | 2½ yrs. | Dischgd 10 Nov. '78 |
| Benton, Keedar, Pt..... | " | 16 Apr. " | " | Dischgd 16 Oct. '78 |
| Bargoner, Jno., Pt...... | " | " | " | Dischgd 10 Nov. '78 |
| Benton, Jesse, Sergt..... | " | 11 May " | " | Omtd Oct. '77 |
| Blanchet, Jno., Musc.... | " | 11 Oct. " | " | { Mustd 2nd Reg. 27 Mar. <br> { for W. |
| **C** (P. 1027) <br> Coleman, Chas., <br> Qr. Mast. Sergt...... | | '77 | | { Qr. Mast. 14 Oct. '77 <br> { Omtd Sep. '78 |
| Christian, Jno., Fife.... | Emmet's | 11 May '76 | 2½ yrs. | { Fife Maj. 17 Aug.'77. Pt. <br> { June'78. Dischgd Oct.'78 |
| Carter, Giles, Pt....... | Turner's | 1 Mar. '77 | 3 yrs. | |
| Champion, Thos., Pt.... | " | 18 Apr. '76 | 2½ yrs. | Dischgd Nov. 10, '78 |
| Clark, Jno., Pt........ | " | | " | Dischgd Oct, 10, '78 |
| Curry, Thompson, Corpl. | Granberry's | 4 May " | " | { Sergt. Nov. '77 <br> { Dischgd Oct. '78 |
| Cone, W., Pt.......... | " | '77 | " | Died 16 Sep. '77 |
| Carey, Andrew H., Sergt. | Eaton's | Apr. '76 | " | Dead Sep. '77 |
| Cordle, Rich'd, Pt...... | " | 1 Nov. " | " | Omtd June '79 |
| Cannon, Benj., Musc.... | " | Apr. " | " | Died May 1, '78 |
| Clendenin, Jno., Ensn... | Emmet's | 15 Apr. " | | { Lt. 23 Dec.'77. Qr. Mast. <br> { 14 Dec.'79. Pris. 8 Sep.'81 <br> { Deranged 1 Jan. '83 |
| Copeland, Rich'd, Pt.... | " | 17 May " | 2½ yrs. | Dischgd Oct. '78 |
| Clifton, Rich'd, Pt..... | " | " | W | Died Feb. '78 |
| **D** (P. 1041) <br> Dixon, Henry, Maj..... | | 8 July '77 | | { Lt. Col. 12 May '78 <br> { Died 17 July '82 |
| Davis, Sam'l, Pt........ | Turner's | " | 2½ yrs. | Dischgd Oct. '78 |
| Dondon, Sm'l, Pt....... | " | " | " | Pris. 11 Sep. '77 |
| Dixon, Geo., Musc...... | Granberry's | July '76 | " | Omtd June '78 |
| Doley, Nath'l, Sergt. ... | " | June " | " | Omtd June '78 |

| Name and Rank | Company | Dates of Enlistment and Commission | Period of Service | Occurrences |
|---|---|---|---|---|
| Dunning, Jas., Pt....... | Emmet's | 15 May '76 | 2½ yrs. | Dischgd Oct. '78 |
| E  (P. 1050) | | | | |
| Edwards, Benj., Pt..... | Turner's | '77 | 2½ yrs. | Omtd June '78 |
| Elloms, Chas., Pt...... | " | 28 Oct. '76 | | Dischgd 1 May '79 |
| Eaton, Pinketham, Capt. | | 16 Apr. " | | Maj. 22 Nov.'77. Omtd Jan.'78. Mustd Jan. '79 in 5th Reg. |
| Edmunds, Nicholas, Capt............. | | '77 | | Omtd Jan. '78 |
| Emmet, Jas., Capt..... | | 16 Apr. '76 | | Maj. Feb. '78 / Omtd June '78 |
| F  (P. 1056) | | | | |
| Fawn, Wm., Lt........ | Turner's | 15 Apr. '77 | | Pris. 12 May '80. Capt. Deranged 1 Jan. '83 |
| Fryar, Wm., Pt........ | Emmet's | 3 May '76 | 2½ yrs. | Dischgd 10 Nov. '78 |
| G  (P. 1063) | | | | |
| Goodridge, Mat'w, Sergt. | Turner's | 25 Apr. '76 | 2½ yrs. | Destd Oct. '77 |
| Granberry, Thos, Capt.. | | 16 Apr. " | " | Resigned 27 Dec. '77 |
| Gee, Wm., Corpl....... | Granberry's | 23 Apr. " | " | Sergt. Nov.'77. Pt. June '78. Dischagd Oct. '78 |
| Glover, Jno., Pt....... | " | 27 Apr. " | " | Dischgd 10 Nov. '78 |
| Garland, Elisha, Pt..... | Eaton's | 4 Jan. '77 | " | Dischgd Oct. '78 |
| Garland, Jno........... | Eaton's | 29 Apr. '76 | 2½ yrs. | Omtd 10 Nov. '78 |
| Granberry, Jno., Lt..... | " | '77 | | Omtd May |
| Green, Josiah, Pt...... | Emmet's | " | | Omtd Sep. '77 |
| H  (P. 1073-4) | | | | |
| Hodgton, Alvery, Lt. and Adj........ | | '77 | | Omtd Jan. '78 |
| Hudson, Isaac, Sergt. Maj.......... | | 24 May " | 2½ yrs. | Omtd Sep. '78 |
| Hudson, Chamberlain, Corpl............. | Turner's | 7 May '76 | | Sergt. 25 Oct.'79. Pt. June '78. Dischgd Oct. '78 |
| Hutston, Abin, Pt...... | " | | | |
| Hastings, Wylie, Pt.... | " | 27 Jan. '77 | 3 yrs. | |
| Howell, Henry, Pt...... | Granberry's | " | 2½ yrs. | Destd Aug. '77 |
| Harrison, Jas., Pt...... | " | 20 Apr. '76 | " | Dischgd Oct. '77 |
| Hart, Anthony, Lt..... | " | '77 | | See 2nd Reg. Com. P. 1064 |
| Hall, Delany, Pt........ | Brinkley's | " | " | Died 13 Mar. '78 |
| Hood, Arch'd, Pt...... | " | 2 May '76 | " | Dischgd Oct. '78 |
| Hitchcock, Fred'k, Pt... (P. 1074) | " | 20 Apr. '76 | " | Dischgd Oct. '78 |
| Hull, Jackson, Pt...... | " | '77 | 3 yrs. | Dead Jan. '78 |
| Hart, Anthony, Lt..... | Eaton's | 16 Apr. " | | And Adj. June '78 Resigned 1 Apr. '82 |
| Hart, Thos., Pt........ | " | " | 2½ yrs. | Dead June '78 |
| Hardy, Thos., Pt...... | " | " | " | Dischgd Oct. '78 |
| Harris, Geo., Pt....... | Emmet's | " | | Missing 4 Oct. '78 |
| Hern, Drury, Pt........ | " | 15 May '76 | | Dischgd 10 Nov. '78 |
| J  (P. 1089) | | | | |
| Jeffries, Thos. Pt...... | Turner's | '77 | 2½ yrs. | Omtd Jan. '78 |
| Jones, Rich'd, Pt....... | " | 15 Apr. '76 | " | Dischgd Oct. '78 |
| Jones, Jacob, Pt....... | Granberry's | 20 Apr. " | " | Dischgd 10 Nov. '78 |
| Judge, Jas., Pt......... | " | | | Dischgd Oct. '78 |
| Jones, Thos., Pt....... | " | 10 May '76 | | Dischgd Nov. '78 |
| Jumper, Rich'd, Pt..... | Eaton's | | 12 Mo. | Omtd Jan. '78 |

| Name and Rank | Company | Dates of Enlistment and Commission | Period of Service | Occurrences |
|---|---|---|---|---|
| Johnson, Thos., Pt...... | Eaton's | | 12 Mo. | Died 20 May '78 |
| Jones, Dan'l, Capt...... | | | | Omtd June '78 |
| Jones, Josiah, Pt........ | Emmet's | 17 Apr. '76 | 2½ yrs. | Dischgd Oct. '78 |
| Jones, Hesk., Pt........ | " | 11 Apr. " | " | Dischgd 16 Oct. '78 |
| **K** (P. 1095) | | | | |
| Knight, Reuben, Musc.. | Emmet's | 16 Apr. '76 | 2½ yrs. | {Pt. June '78 |
| | | | | {Dischgd 1 Feb. '80 |
| King, Jno., Pt......... | " | '77 | W | Omtd June '78 |
| Kippey, Peter, Pt...... | | | | {Mustd Jan. '78 |
| | | | | {Omtd Feb. '78 |
| **L** (P. 1101) | | | | |
| Lockhart, Sam'l, Maj.. . | | 15 Apr. '76 | | Lt. Col. '77 in 8th Reg. |
| Linton, Wm., Lt........ | Turner's | 24 July '76 | | Resigned 1 Nov. '78 |
| Lane, Jesse, Pt......... | " | 1 Mar. '77 | 3 yrs. | |
| Lackey, Chri'r., Lt..... | Granberry's | '77 | " | Omtd Dec. '77 |
| Lacy, Burwell, Pt...... | " | " | | Corpl. 1 Apr. '82 |
| Lucey, Isom, Pt....... | Emmet's | " | | |
| Lucus, Valentine, Pt..... | " | 22 Apr. '76 | | Dischgd Oct. '78 |
| **M** (P. 1110) | | | | |
| Metissick, Thos, Corp... | Turner's | 25 Apr. '76 | 2½ yrs. | {Pt. June '78 |
| | | | | {Dischgd 30 Oct. '78 |
| Mathews, Edw'd, Musc. | " | | " | Dischgd 10 Aug. '78 |
| Medlin, Shadrack, Pt. .. | " | | " | A.W.O.L. Jan. '78 |
| Meacon, Jas., Pt........ | " | | | Omtd Sep. '77 |
| Massey, John, Pt....... | " | | | Dischgd 3 Feb. '78 |
| Meacon, Wm., Pt...... | " | | | Omtd Sep. '77 |
| Montford, Joseph, Lt. .. | Granberry's | 16 Apr. " | | {Capt. Jan. 9,'79. Pris. 12 |
| | | | | {May '80. Deranged |
| | | | | {1 Jan. '83 |
| McMullen, Jas., Musc... | " | 10 May '76 | " | Dischgd 10 Nov. '78 |
| Manning, Timothy, Pt.. | " | '77 | | |
| Medearis, John, Lt..... | Eaton's | 15 Apr. " | | {Capt. 23 Dec. '77 |
| | | | | {Omtd in '82 |
| Marshall, Geo., Pt...... | " | 22 Apr. '76 | W | Destd 10 July '79 |
| Massey, Thos., Sergt.... | Everett's | '77 | 2½ yrs. | Died 12 Mar. '78 |
| McDonald, Gus, Musc.. | " | 1 May '76 | 3 yrs. | Dischgd 1 May '76 |
| McDonald, Thos., Pt.... | " | " " | " " | Dischgd 1 May '76 |
| **N** (P. 1123) | | | | |
| Neil, Jno., Pt......... | Turner's | '77 | 2 ½ yrs. | Died Nov. '77 |
| Nunnery, Henry, Pt..... | Granberry's | 5 May '76 | " | Dischgd Oct. '78 |
| Norton, Wm., Pt....... | Eaton's | '77 | 3 yrs. | Died Jan. '78 |
| **O** (P. 1128) | | | | |
| Owen, Omery, Pt....... | Turner's | | | Died Jan. '78 |
| O'Neal, Chas., Ensn..... | Granberry's | 18 Apr. '77 | 2½ yrs. | {Lt. 20 July '77 |
| | | | | {Omtd June '78 |
| Oram, Jno., Pt........ | " | " | " | Died 11 Mar. '78 |
| Orr—, Pt............. | Emmet's | " | | Omtd Sep. '77 |
| **P** (P. 1133) | | | | |
| Penticost, Dancey, Sergt. | | 20 Apr. '76 | 2½ yrs. | {Qr. Mast. Sergt Nov.'77 |
| | | | | {Omtd Sep. '78 |
| Powell, Jno., Corpl...... | Turner's | 16 Apr. " | " | Pt. '78. Dischgd Oct. '78 |
| Philips, David, Pt...... | " | 16 Apr. " | " | Dischgd Oct. '78 |
| Potaway, Macaja, Pt.... | Granberry's | 20 Apr. " | " | Dischgd Oct. '78 |
| Potter, Jno., Pt........ | " | | | Dischgd Oct. '78 |
| Pulley, Isom, Pt....... | " | 5 May " | " | Dischgd Oct. '78 |

| Name and Rank | Company | Dates of Enlistment and Commission | Period of Service | Occurrences |
|---|---|---|---|---|
| Prichel, Jno., Pt........ | Granberry's | '77 | 2½ yrs. | Omtd 7 Sep. '77 |
| Pulley, Jas., Musc...... | " | 12 May '76 | " | Pt. June '78 / Dischgd 12 Nov. '78 |
| Parkerson, Jno., Corpl.. | Eaton's | 16 Apr. " | " | Sergt. 1 Aug.'77. Corpl. June'78. Pt. 15 July '79 |
| Perry, Jerry, Pt....... | " | 29 Apr. " | " | Dischgd 10 Nov. '78 / Corpl. From Feb to June '78 |
| Portress, Jno., Pt...... | " | '77 | " | Died 1 May '78 |
| Polson, Jno., Corpl..... | Emmet's | 11 May '76 | " | Sergt. Oct. '77 / Dischgd 16 Oct. '78 |
| **R (P. 1143)** | | | | |
| Ridley, Wm., Surgn..... | | 21 Apr. '77 | | Absent no leave Nov. '77 |
| Richards, Jos., Sergt.... | Turner's | 25 Apr. '76 | | Pris. 4 Oct. '77 |
| Rotley, Jno., Pt........ | | '77 | 3 yrs. | Died 30 July '78 |
| Roberts, Kitchin, Pt.... | Brinkley's | " | 2½ yrs. | Died 10 Mar. '78 |
| Roper, Jas., Pt......... | " | 7 Apr. " | 3 yrs. | |
| Rushworm, Wm., Lt.... | Eaton's | 16 Apr. " | | Omtd Jan. '78 |
| Raifield, Spencer, Pt.... | " | 10 May '76 | 2½ yrs. | Dischgd 10 Nov. '78 |
| Robinson, Ruben, Pt.... | Emmet's | '77 | | Died 4 Sep. '77 |
| **S (P. 1154)** | | | | |
| Sumner, Jethro, Col..... | | 15 Apr. '76 | | Brig. Gen. 9 Jan. '79 |
| Savage, Mich'l, Pt...... | Turner's | Apr. " | 2½ yrs. | Dischgd Oct. '78 |
| Sherrin, Jacob, Pt...... | " | '77 | | Corpl. 7 Nov. '77 / Died 20 May '78 |
| Solsberry, Benj'n, Pt.... | " | 26 Oct. '76 | " | Dischgd Oct. '78 |
| Shoementon, Hezk., Pt.. | Granberry's | 20 Dec. " | " | Dischgd Nov. '78 |
| Swenet, Jas., Pt........ | " | '77 | " | Destd Aug. '77 |
| Smith, Thos., Pt....... | " | " | " | Destd Aug. '77 |
| Strickler, Jno., Pt...... | " | 15 Mar. " | " | Dischgd 10 Nov. '78 |
| Smith, Simon, Pt...... | " | 20 Apr. '76 | " | Dischgd 10 Nov. '78 |
| Stevens, Lewis, Pt..... | " | 5 May " | " | Dischgd 10 Nov. '78 |
| Sturt, Henry, Pt........ | " | 15 May " | " | Dischgd 10 Nov. '78 |
| Sweat, Wm., Pt........ | Eaton's | 20 Apr. " | " | Dischgd 10 Nov. '78 |
| Scott, Jno............. | " | '77 | | Omtd June '78. Mustd Jan. '79 in 4th Reg. |
| Smith, Wm., Pt........ | " | " | | Died 31 Mar. '78 |
| Santy, Caesar, Pt...... | " | 22 Feb. '77 | | Pris. 1 June '79 / Mustd '81 for War |
| Spells, Henry, Pt...... | " | 5 May '76 | | Dischgd 1 Dec. '78 |
| Simpson, Sm'l, Pt...... | " | '77 | 2½ y. W | Corpl. 1 Apr.'79. Pt. '82 |
| Skinner, Jno., Corpl..... | " | 1 May '76 | | Pt. June '78 / Dischgd 1 Nov. '78 |
| Sypress, Robt., Sergt.... | Emmet's | 15 May " | | Dischgd Oct. '78 |
| Smith, Wm., Pt........ | " | 22 Dec. " | | Dischgd 1 Feb. '80 |
| **T (P. 1169)** | | | | |
| Turner, Jacob, Capt..... | | 16 Apr. '76 | | Killed 4 Oct. '77 |
| Turner, Bryan, Sergt.... | Turner's | 22 Apr. '77 | | Destd 15 Oct. '77 |
| Threat, Fred'k, Pt...... | " | 5 May '76 | 2½ yrs. | Dischgd Oct. '78 |
| Toby, Wm., Pt........ | Eaton's | 4 May " | W | Corpl. Oct. '77. Pt. June '78. Pris. 1 June '79 |
| Tillery, Jno., Lt........ | " | '77 | | Omtd Jan. '78 |
| Tulston, Wm., Pt....... | Emmet's | " | | Destd Aug. '77 |
| Thurston, Wm., Pt...... | " | 16 Apr. '76 | 2½ yrs | Dischgd 16 Oct. '78 |
| **W (P. 1181-2)** | | | | |
| Wilson, Whitfield Qr. Mast.......... | | 24 Apr. '77 | | Promoted 14 Oct. '77 / Omtd Jan. '78 |

| Name and Rank | Company | Dates of Enlistment and Commission | Period of Service | Occurrences |
|---|---|---|---|---|
| Wood, Mathew, Lt...... | Turner's | 24 July '76 | | Capt. 22 Nov. '77 Omtd Jan. '78 |
| Wheeler, Sam'l, Pt...... | " | 18 Apr. " | 2½ yrs. | Dischgd 10 Nov. '78 |
| Williamson, Wm., Pt.... (P. 1182) | " | 16 Apr. " | " | Dischgd 10 Nov. '78 |
| Willis, Augustor, Sergt.. | Eaton's | 24 Sep. " | " | Omtd June '78 |
| Welch, Basil, Pt........ | " | 1 Nov. " | " | Dischgd 1 Dec. '78 |
| Whitley, Haniford...... | " | 22 Apr. " | " | Dischgd 10 Nov. '78 |
| Wiggins, Willis, Corpl... | Emmet's | 11 Apr. " | " | Sergt. Oct.'77. Corpl. June'78.Dischgd 17 Oct. '78 |
| Wiggins, Henry, Pt..... | " | '77 | " | Omtd June '78 |
| Wiggins, Noah, Pt...... | " | " | " | Dischgd 11 May '78 |
| White, Jno............ | " | " | " | Died 12 Apr. '78 |
| Y (P. 1194) | | | | |
| Yarborough, Ruben,,Sgt. | Turner's | 25 Apr. '76 | 2½ yrs. | Dischgd 30 Oct. '78 |
| Young, Jno., Corpl...... | " | 1 Aug. " | | Pt. June '78 Dischgd 31 Oct. '78 |
| Yarborough, Edd., Lt... | " | 16 Apr. '77 | | Capt. Jan. '79 Deranged 1 Jan. '83 |

## 4TH REGIMENT—COL. THOS. POLK

| Name and Rank | Company | Dates of Enlistment and Commission | Period of Service | Occurrences |
|---|---|---|---|---|
| A (P. 1004) | | | | |
| Atkins, James, Chaplain | | 5 Apr. '77 | | Resigned 10 Aug. '77 |
| Anderson, James, Dm. Maj.......... | | 25 Jan. " | | Died 12 June '78 |
| Armstrong, John, Maj... | | 4 Oct. " | | Lt. Col. 17 July '78 Deranged 1 Jan. '83 |
| Andrews, Abiel, Lt...... | William's... | " | W | Omtd Jan. '78 |
| Alexander, Chas., Lt.... | Lewis' | 20 Jan. " | | Omtd Jan. '78 |
| B (P. 1012) | | | | |
| Ballentine, Jas., Sergt. Maj.......... | | 20 Apr. '77 | | Omtd Jan. '78 |
| Bishop, Chris., Musc.... | Williams' | " | 2½ yrs. | Dischgd 8 Nov. '77 |
| Bracher, Sam'l, Pt...... | " | " | 1½ yrs. | Dischgd Nov. '77 |
| Benton, Jesse, Pt...... | " | " | W | Omtd Feb. '78 |
| Bootle, Thos., Pt....... | Philips' | 20 May '76 | " | Destd 26 Oct.'77. Mustd Feb.'78. Dischgd 26 May '79 |
| Betts, Mathew, Pt...... | " | " | 2½ yrs. | Dischgd 25 Nov. '77 |
| Brown, Joseph, Pt..... | " | 4 Apr. '77 | 3 yrs. | Destd 10 Sep. '78 |
| Brevard, Alex., Lt...... | Goodman's | 9 Dec. '76 | | Capt. Oct. 20, '80 Deranged 1 Jan. '83 |
| Belew, Chas., Pt........ | Philips' | 20 May " | 2½ yrs. | Sergt. Apr. '78 Omtd Dec. '78 |
| Beseley, John, Corpl.... | Goodman's | '77 | 3 yrs. | |
| Bonny, Gideon, Corpl... | " | " | " | |
| Bush, Chany, Pt...... | " | " | | Died 2 Jan. '78 |
| Boggs, Jno........ | " | " | | Dischgd 15 July '79 |
| Burges, Geo., Pt...... | " | 15 July '76 | 3 yrs. | Dischgd 28 Jan. '80 |
| Burges, Peter, Pt...... | " | 1 Jan. '77 | " | Destd 3 Feb. '80 |
| Boggs, Ezkl., Pt........ | " | 1 Jan. " | " | Dischgd 25 July '79 |
| Bryly, Wm., Pt......... | Harris' | 26 July '76 | " | Time Out 31 Oct. '77 |
| Burtson, Jesse, Pt...... | " | '76 | | Time Out 31 Oct. '77 |

| Name and Rank | Company | Dates of Enlistment and Commission | Period of Service | Occurrences |
|---|---|---|---|---|
| Barksdale, Henry, Sergt. | Lewis' | 20 Apr. '76 | 3 yrs. | Corpl. June '78. Sergt 10 Nov. '78. Dischgd 1 May '79 |
| Boon, Joseph, Pt....... | " | " | 2½ yrs. | Omtd Jan. '78 |
| Barrow, Jno., Pt....... | Lewis' | 20 Apr. '76 | 2½ yrs. | Dischgd 10 Nov. '78 |
| Boyes, Jesse, Pt....... | " | 22 Apr. " | " | Dischgd 10 Nov. '78 |
| Bryant, John, Pt...... | " | 4 July " | 3 yrs. | Sergt. 1 Nov.'77. Pt. Apr. '78. Omtd Jan. '79 |
| Beafield, Stephen, Pt.... | " | " | " | Died 1 Feb. '78 |
| Bird, Moses, Musc...... | " | " | " | Omtd Jan. '78 |
| Burus, Jno., Sergt...... | Smith's | 20 May " | 3 yrs.W | Pt. June '78. Sergt. 10 Nov. '78. Destd 25 Dec. '79 |
| Brown, Peter, Pt...... | " | " | " | Omtd May '78 |
| Biddlehizer, Lewis, Pt... | " | 17 June '77 | " | Omtd Feb. '79 |
| Bullock, Thos., Sergt.... | Nelson's | '77 | " | Omtd Feb. '78 |
| Bullock, Martin, Corpl.. | " | 20 Feb. " | " | Pt. June '78 Dest. Dec. '78 |
| Bradley, Jas., Pt....... | " | " | " | Dischgd May '79 |
| Baker, Thos., Pt........ | " | 14 Feb. " | " | Destd 10 Dec. '79 |
| Benton, David, Pt...... | " | 15 June '76 | " | Dischgd 15 June '79 |
| C (P. 1029) | | | | |
| Covington, Wm., Adj... | | 28 Mar. '77 | | Died 13 Apr. '78 |
| Conger, Jona, Qr. Mast. Sergt...... | | 25 Jan. " | | Promoted 11 Sep. '77 |
| Curry, Jno., Pt........ | Williams' | " | W | Missing 16 Sep. '77 |
| Cox, Philip, Pt........ | " | " | 1 yr. | Dischgd Aug. '77 |
| Cortslow, Thos., Pt..... | " | " | " | Dischgd Aug. '77 |
| Clack, Wm., Pt........ | Philips' | 20 May '76 | 3 yrs. | Sergt. Sep.'77. Pt. June '78. Pris. 14 Apr. '79 |
| Crab, Benj., Sergt...... | Goodman's | 1 Dec. " | 2½ yrs. | Dischgd 18 Nov. '78 |
| Crump. Edward, Pt..... | " | 1 Mar. " | 3 yrs. | Destd 24 Mar. '79 |
| Cullum, Israel, Pt...... | " | '77 | " | Died 7 July '77 |
| Cavender, Wm., Pt..... | " | Sep. " | | Time Out 31 Oct. '77 |
| Caswell, Thos., Pt...... | " | 15 July '76 | 3 yrs. | Corpl. Dec. '78 Dischgd 16 June '79 |
| (P. 1028) | | | | |
| Chetry, Alex., Pt...... | " | " " | | Dead May '78 |
| Campbell, Martin, Pt... | " | 1 June '77 | | |
| Coots, Jas., Lt........ | " | 20 Nov. '76 | 3 yrs.W | Omtd June '78 |
| Coplin, Reuben, Corpl... | Harris' | | | Time Out 31 Oct. '77 |
| Clarke, Jno........... | " | '77 | | Corpl. Sep. Dischgd 1 Nov. '77 |
| Curbo, Jas., Pt........ | " | 6 May '76 | 3 yrs. | Destd 1 Jan. '80 |
| Curbo, Wm., Pt....... | " | 20 Apr. " | " | Dischgd 10 May, '79 |
| Coleman, Wm., Pt...... | " | '77 | | Destd Aug. '77 |
| Cole, Wm. I., Capt..... | " | 20 Apr. '76 | | Omtd Jan. '78 |
| Carter, Benj'n, 1st Lt... | Cole's | 22 Nov. " | | Cap. 1 Jan. '79 |
| Crider, Jacob, Corpl.... | " | '77 | 3 yrs. | Destd 3 Oct. '77 |
| Collins, Josh, Musc..... | " | " | " | Destd 15 Feb. '78 |
| Cooper, Jno., Corpl..... | " | | | Died 16 Apr. '78 |
| Cooper, Wm., Pt....... | Lewis' | 20 Apr. '76 | 2½ yrs. | Dischgd 10 Nov. '78 |
| Charney, David, Pt..... | Smith's | | | Omtd Sep. '77 |
| Curtis, Joshua, Ensn.... | Nelson's | | | |
| Caruthers, James, Corpl. | " | 1 May " | 3 yrs. | Pt. June '78 Dischgd 10 May '79 |
| Coulson, Hy., Pt...... | " | June 7 " | " | Dischgd 1 June '79 |

| Name and Rank | Company | Dates of Enlistment and Commission. | Period of Service | Occurrences |
|---|---|---|---|---|
| Cummings, Jno., Pt..... | Nelson's | | 3 yrs. | Omtd Feb. '79 |
| Carruthers, Thos., Pt. .. | " | 27 Apr. '76 | " | Dischgd 2 May, '79 |
| Clark, Jno., Corpl...... | " | Oct. '77 | " | Pt. June '78 |
| Curtis, Peter, Musc..... | " | " | " | Destd Sep. '77 |
| D  (P. 1041) | | | | |
| Davidson, Wm., Maj.... | | 15 Apr. '76 | | Lt. Col. Oct. '77 in 5 Reg. |
| Douglas, Wm., Qr. Mast. | | 10 Feb. '77 | | Omtd Jan. '78 |
| Duncan, Robt., P. Mast. | | " | | Omtd Jan. '78 |
| Dillard, John, Sergt..... | Williams' | " | 2½ yrs. | Omtd Sep. '77 |
| Dilliard, Wm., Pt...... | " | 15 May '76 | 2½ yrs. | Dischgd 10 Nov. '78 |
| Downs, Jno., Pt....... | " | | W | {Corpl. 10 Nov. '78 {Sergt. Jan. '80 |
| Dignam, Thos., Pt...... | " | | | Dischgd 10 Nov. '78 |
| Dailey, Jereh, Pt....... | " | | | Dischgd 10 Nov. '78 |
| Dillard, Osborn, Pt..... | " | | | Omtd Sep. '77 |
| Darley, Jno., Pt........ | " | | | Omtd Apr. '78 |
| Douglas, Jno., Pt....... | " | | | |
| Dodson, Chas., Pt...... | Philips' | " | " | |
| Davidson, Josh, Pt..... | Goodman's | 20 Apr. " | 2½ yrs. | Dischgd 10 Nov. '78 |
| Daviees, John, Pt....... | " | 1 July '77 | 3 yrs. | {Destd Dec.'77. Mustd in {Aug. Destd 22 Sep. '78 |
| Dodd, David, Sergt..... | Harris' | 4 May '76 | " | {Pt. June '78. Corpl Aug. {'78. Dischgd 15 May '79 |
| Dodd, Jesse, Pt........ | " | " | W | {Omtd Sep.'77. MustdJan. {'78. Dischgd 15 Nov. '79 |
| Davis, Hugh, Pt....... | Cole's | 10 June '77 | 3 yrs. | Destd 7 Dec. '79 |
| Derrum, Nath'l, Pt..... | Nelson's | 20 June '76 | " | Dischgd 20 June '79 |
| Dixon, Jereh, Pt....... | " | '77 | " | |
| Donally, John, Pt...... | " | 7 May '76 | " | Omtd Oct. '78 |
| F  (P. 1056) | | | | |
| Freeman, Dn'l, Pt...... | Williams' | 3 May '76 | 2½ yrs. | Dischgd 10 Nov. '78 |
| Faulkner, Francis, Pt. .. | Philips' | 25 May " | 3 yrs. | {Sergt. Sep.'77. Pt. June {'78. Dischgd 25 May '79 |
| Filsby, Rich'd, Musc.... | Nelson's | 14 Feb. '77 | " | {Pt. June '78. Mustd Oct. {'78. Time Out Feb. '80 |
| E  (P. 1050) | | | | |
| Eslick, Jas., Pt........ | Williams' | '77 | 3 yrs. | Omtd Feb. '78 |
| Earl, Jas., Pt.......... | " | " | " | Omtd Sep. '77 |
| Eldridge, Levy, Pt...... | Philips' | " | W | Destd 20 Nov. '77 |
| Evans, Joseph, Pt...... | Goodman's | " | 3 yrs. | {Pt. June '78 {Dead Apr. '78 |
| Ellison, Andrew, Pt..... | Cole's | 7 May '76 | " | Pris. 14 Apr. '79 |
| Evans, Jno., Pt........ | Smith's | 10 Apr. " | " | Dischgd 1 May '79 |
| Erwin, Jno., Pt........ | " | '77 | " | Omtd Sep. '77 |
| Eves, Wm., Pt......... | " | " | " | Dischgd 10 Aug. '77 |
| Eliot, Jno., Pt......... | " | " | " | Omtd Sep. '77 |
| G  (P. 1064) | | | | |
| Glenn, Tobias, Musc.... | Williams' | Dec. '77 | | {From 2nd Reg. Omtd {July '78 |
| Goodman, Wm., Capt... | " | 1 Oct. '76 | | {Omtd June '78. Mustd {Jan. '79 in 4th Reg. |
| Gillispie, Robt., Ensn. .. | Goodman's | '77 | | Lt. Aug. '77 Omtd Jan.'78 |
| Glenn, Geo., Pt........ | " | 15 May " | | Omtd Nov. '79 |
| Garrick, Black., Musc... | Smith's | " | | Omtd Jan. '78 |
| Gilmore, Thos., Pt...... | " | 16 May " | | |
| Griswit, Thos., Pt...... | " | " | | Dead Jan. '78 |
| Goff, Thos., Pt........ | " | " | | Omtd Sep. '77 |

| Name and Rank | Company | Dates of Enlistment and Commission | Period of Service | Occurrences |
|---|---|---|---|---|
| **H** (P. 1074) | | | | |
| Harrison, Geo., Pt..... | Philips' | 20 May '76 | 2½ yrs. | Omtd Jan. '79 |
| Hickman, Wm., Lt..... | Goodman's | '77 | | Resigned 25 Aug. '77 |
| Howell, Edw'd, Corpl... | " | 6 May '76 | " | Dischgd 10 Nov. '78 |
| Henry, John, Pt........ | " | | " | Dead Jan. '78 |
| Harris, Thos., Capt.... | | 16 Apr. " | | Omtd Jan. '78 |
| Hurley, Jno., Pt....... | Harris' | '77 | | Dead July '77 |
| Howard, Geo., Pt...... | " | 5 May '76 | 3 yrs. | Dist 15 May '79 |
| Hughes, Jno., Sergt.... | " | 20 Dec. " | 3 yrs. | Distchgd 25 June '79 |
| Holland, Reason, Pt..... | " | Oct. '77 | W | {Omtd Dec. '77 \ See him in 5th Reg. |
| Hyde, Andrew, Musc.... | " | 20 June " | 3 yrs. | Pt. Dec.'77. Omtd Sep.'78 |
| Hudson, Thos., Pt..... | Lewis' | '77 | W | Omtd Sep. '78 |
| Harmon, Robt., Musc... | Smith's | 30 Dec. '76 | 3 yrs.W | {Pt. June '78 \ Dead 17 Apr. '79 |
| Hurton, Hugh, Pt...... | " | 5 July " | " | Dischgd 5 July '79 |
| Hughes, Jno., Pt....... | " | 1 May " | " | {Corpl. Oct. '77. Pt. June \ '78. Dischgd 14 May '79 |
| Hood, Geo., Sergt...... | Nelson's | | " | Dischgd 7 May '78 |
| **J** (P. 1089) | | | | |
| Johnson, Wm., Pt...... | Williams' | '77 | | Omtd Sep. '77 |
| Johnson, Reuben, Pt.... | Philips' | " | W | |
| Jarvis, Levy, Pt....... | " | 25 May '76 | 2½ yrs. | Omtd Dec. '78 |
| Johnson, Crawford, Pt.. | Cole's | 11 Apr. " | W | |
| Jones, David, 1st Lt.... | Nelson's | 3 Apr. '77 | | {Omtd Jan. '78. Mustd \ Jan. '79 4th Reg. |
| Jackson, Wm., Pt...... | " | 1 May '76 | 3 yrs. | Dischgd 1 May '79 |
| **K** (P. 1096) | | | | |
| Knott, Wm., Lt....... | Philips' | '77 | | {Omtd Jan. '78. Mustd \ Feb. '79 5th Reg. |
| King, Joseph, Musc.... | Goodman's | 1 Jan. " | 3 yrs. | {Pt. Jan. '78 \ Dischgd 28 Jan. '80 |
| Kilgo, Jas., Musc....... | Harris' | " | | Time Out 31 Oct. '77 |
| Kidwell, Elisha, Pt..... | Cole's | 1 May '76 | 3 yrs. | Omtd Apr. '79 |
| Knop, Adm., Pt....... | " | '77 | 12 Mo. | Dischgd 10 Aug. '77 |
| Kirk, Jno., Pt.......... | Nelson's | 19 May " | 3 yrs. | |
| **L** (P. 1102) | | | | |
| Lorain, Henry, Sergt.... | William's | '77 | W | {Corpl. June '78 \ Died 13 July '78 |
| Loyd, Leonard........ | Philips' | " | " | Omtd Jan. '78 |
| Lufman, John.......... | Goodman's | 30 July '76 | 3 yrs. | Dischgd 31 July '79 |
| Lipscomb, Wyllis, Pt.... | " | 30 July " | 3 yrs. | Dischgd 31 July '79 |
| Logan, Philip, Musc. ... | Cole's | 24 Apr. " | 2½ yrs. | Dischgd 10 Nov. '78 |
| Linsey, Walter, Pt..... | | '77 | | Destd 12 Sep. '77 |
| Lewis, Macaja, Capt.... | | 29 July " | | {Retired from Service 23 \ Jan. '81 |
| Low, Wm., Musc....... | Lewis' | 21 Apr. '76 | 3 yrs. | Dischgd 1 May '79 |
| Lille, Lewis, Pt........ | " | | | Dischgd 13 Aug. '79 |
| Larry, Cornelius, Pt..... | " | | W | Destd 23 June '79 |
| Laferty, John, Pt...... | Smith's | 10 June " | 3 yrs. | Dischgd 15 June '79 |
| Linn, Robt., Pt........ | Nelson's | 19 May " | " | Dischgd 16 May '79 |
| **M** (P. 1110-11) | | | | |
| Moslander, Abel, Lt..... | William's | 25 Jan. '77 | | Omtd Jan. '78 |
| Mathews, Chas., Pt..... | " | " | 18 Mo. | Dischgd 1 Nov. '77 |
| Murray, Wm., Ensn. ... | " | 1 Apr. " | | {Destd Jan. '78. Mustd \ Jan. '79 in 4th Reg. |
| Miller, Josiah, Pt....... | Goodwin's | 20 July '76 | 3 yrs.W | Omtd Nov. '79 |

| Name and Rank | Company | Dates of Enlistment and Commission | Period of Service | Occurrences |
|---|---|---|---|---|
| Martin, Rich'd, Pt...... | Goodwin's | 7 May '76 | 2½ yrs. | Dischgd 10 Nov. '78 |
| Moore, Thos., Pt...... | " | 1 Nov. " | " | Dischgd 10 Nov. '78 |
| Mahaney's, Wm., Pt.... | " | 28 July " | 3 yrs. | Dischgd 25 July '79 |
| Medum, Jno., Pt....... | " | " | " | Omtd Dec. '77 |
| McGibbony, Pat'k, Lt... | Harris | 9 Dec. " | | Omtd June '78. Mustd Jan. '79 4th Reg. |
| McGill, Jas., Pt........ | " | '77 | | Dischgd 28 July '77 |
| Martin, Rich'd, Pt...... | " | " | W | Omtd June '78 |
| Manora, Nich., Pt...... | " | " | 3 yrs. | Destd 6 June '77 |
| McCarthy, Florence, Ensn.............. | Cole's | 1 May '76 | | Omtd Jan. '78 |
| Moore, Wm., Sergt..... | " | 20 Sep. " | | Omtd Feb. '78. Said to be promoted |
| McCloud, Dan'l, Pt.... (P. 1111) | " | 5 May " | 3 yrs. | Dischgd 10 May '79 |
| Moore, Nath'l, Pt...... | Cole's | '77 | 1 yr. | Dischgd 10 Aug. '77 |
| Mitchell, Fred'k, Pt.... | " | " | " | Dischgd |
| McMullen, Jerome, Pt. . | " | " | W | Omtd Apr. '78 |
| McCullough, John, Pt... | " | 8 Feb. " | 3 yrs. | Pris. 14 Apr. '79 Mustd Nov. '79 |
| Mitchell, Job, Pt....... | Lewis' | | 2½ yrs. | Omtd Sep. '77 |
| Murray, Chas, Sergt.... | Smith's | 1 May '76 | 3 yrs. | Pt. Oct. '77 Dischgd 10 Nov. '78 |
| Murray, John, Pt...... | " | '77 | " | Sergt. Oct. '77 |
| Morrow, Sam'l, Corpl... | " | 1 May '76 | " | Pt. June '78 Dischgd 14 May '79 |
| McGlauhlin, John, Pt... | " | 6 May " | " | Dischgd 14 May '79 |
| Martin, Arch'd, Pt...... | " | '77 | " | Omtd Sep. '77 |
| McOllister, Dan'l, Pt.... | " | " | | Dischgd 11 Aug. '77 |
| McDaniel, Hugh, Sergt.. | Nelson's | " | 3 yrs. | Omtd Feb. '78 |
| McClelland, Jas., Sergt.. | " | 1 May '76 | " | Dischgd 1 May '79 |
| Mitchell, Arthur, Pt..... | " | '77 | " | Omtd Jan. '78 |
| Mattlock, John, Pt..... | " | 18 Apr. '76 | " | Corpl. Feb. '78. Sergt. Dec. '78. Dischgd 1 May '79 |
| Mitchell, Josh, Pt....... N (P. 1124) | " | 6 May " | " | Dischgd 14 May '79 |
| New, Wm., Pt.......... | Williams' | '77 | | Dischgd Nov. '77 |
| Nicholson, Isaac, Pt..... | Phillips' | " | | Des'd 24 June '79 |
| Needham, Jno., Pt...... | Goodman's | 1 June " | | |
| Nevy, Fred'k, Pt....... | Cole's | " | | Omtd Jan. '78 |
| Nooning, Wm., Pt...... | Lewis' | " | | Died 2 June '78 |
| Newbern, Thos., Pt..... | " | 23 Apr. '76 | | Dischgd 10 Nov. '78 |
| Nelson, Alex., Ensn..... | Smith's | 1 July '77 | | Omtd Jan. '78. Mustd Jan. '79 in 4th Reg. |
| Nelson, John, Capt..... | " | " | | Maj. 3 Feb. '78. Pris 12 May '80. Deranged 1 Ja. '83 |
| Nelson, Robt., Pt....... | Nelson's | 2 May '76 | 3 yrs. | Dischgd May '79 |
| Nash, Jno., Pt.......... | " | 19 Nov. " | " | Corpl. Dec. '78. Sergt. May'79. Dischgd Nov.'79 |
| Newport, Jas., Pt....... P (P. 1133) | " | '77 | " | Destd 16 Sep. '77 |
| Polk, Thos., Col........ | | 15 Apr. '76 | | |
| Pearce, Jacob, Pt....... | Williams' | '77 | W | Omtd Jan. '78 |
| Pritchett, Edw'd, Pt.... | " | " | " | |
| Pemel, Jno., Pt........ | | " | " | Died Nov. '77 |

| Name and Rank | Company | Dates of Enlistment and Commission | Period of Service | Occurrences |
|---|---|---|---|---|
| Philips, Joseph, Capt.... | Philips' | 16 Apr. '76 | | Omtd Jan. '78 |
| Philips, Rich'd, Pt..... | " | 10 May " | 3 yrs. | Dischgd 20 May '79 |
| Patrick, Wm., Pt...... | " | '77 | 2½ yrs. | Destd 26 Oct. '77 |
| Patrick, Jno., Pt....... | " | " | " | Destd 26 Oct. '77 |
| Patrick, Andrew, Pt..... | " | 1 Apr. " | 3 yrs. | Dischgd 10 Nov. '78 |
| Parr, Isaac, Sergt...... | Goodman's | 24 Dec. '76 | 2½ yrs. | |
| Partree, Emanuel, Pt.... | " | '77 | 3 yrs. | Died 4 Oct. '77 |
| Parks, Hugh, Pt........ | " | 20 May '76 | " | Dischgd 20 May '79 |
| Parker, Thos., Pt....... | " | 30 July '76 | " | Dischgd 31 July '79 |
| Pasture Thos, Ensn..... | Harris' | 15 July '77 | | Lt. 29 Dec.'78. Adjt. 26 June '79. Pay. Mast. 19 Oct. '82 |
| Pierce, Wm........... | Cole's | " | 3 yrs. | Invalid Aug. '77 |
| Proudfoot, Jno., Pt..... | " | 20 May " | W | |
| Prescott, Aaron, Pt..... | Lewis' | " | 2½ yrs. | Died 4 Nov. '77 |
| Prescott, Chas., Pt..... | " | " | W | Died 15 Aug. '77 |
| Polk, Chas., Lt........ | Smith's | 25 Apr. " | | Omtd Jan. '78 |
| Prewet, Joshua, Pt..... | Nelson's | 1 June '76 | 3 yrs. | Dischgd 1 June '79 |
| Prewet, Ransom, Pt.... | " | " | " | Dischgd 1 June '79 |
| R  (P. 1144) | | | | |
| Routledge, Wm., Lt..... | Williams' | 25 Jan. '77 | | Resigned 20 Aug. '77 |
| Ross, Jno., Pt......... | " | " | W | |
| Richards, Chas., Pt..... | " | " | 12 Mo. | Dischgd Aug. '77 |
| Robinson, Hugh, Pt..... | Philips' | " | W | Corpl. Sep. '77 Destd 6 Oct. '77 |
| Rigsby, Fred'k, Pt...... | Philips' | 9 May '76 | 3 yrs. | Corpl. Oct. '77. Pt. June '78. Dischgd 10 May '79 |
| Reeves, Sam'l, Pt....... | " | 10 May " | | Trans. to his Excellency's Guards |
| Rainey, Jas, Sergt...... | Goodman's | 26 Apr. " | 3 yrs. | Pt. June '78 Dischgd 1 May '79 |
| Rayburn, Geo., Pt...... | " | 25 July " | | Dischgd 25 July '79 |
| Ramsey, Joel, Pt....... | " | 20 May " | | Dischgd 20 May '79 |
| Riggans, Powell, Pt..... | " | 20 May " | | Dischgd 20 May '79 |
| Ryan, Hercules, Pt..... | " | 1 May '77 | | Died 24 Nov. '77 |
| Rinefield, Henry, Pt.... | Harris' | " | 3 yrs. | Dischgd 18 Oct. '77 |
| Redpith, Jno., Lt....... | Cole's | 20 Aug. " | " | Died 13 Oct. '77 |
| Reed, Wm., Pt......... | " | " | W | Omtd Nov. '79 |
| Ryan, Pat'k, Pt........ | " | 27 June " | " | Corpl. Apr. '79. Sergt. July '79. Died 6 Sep. '82 |
| Rough, Peter, Pt....... | " | " | 3 yrs. | Died 15 Mar. '78 |
| Rearding, Jereh, Pt..... | " | 20 May " | " | |
| Robinson, Jacob, Pt..... | " | 6 May '76 | " | Dischgd 1 May '79 |
| Raby, Cader, Pt........ | Lewis' | | 2½ yrs. | Destd 26 Oct. '77 |
| Raby, Adam, Pt........ | " | | " | Omtd Sep. '77 |
| Ralph, Lewis, Sergt.... | Smith's | 12 Feb. '77 | 3 yrs. | Pt. Feb. '78 Omtd Nov. '79 |
| Richards, Chas, Pt...... | Nelson's | | W | Omtd Jan. '78 |
| Rose, Wm., Pt........ | " | 23 Apr. '76 | 3 yrs. | Sergt. May '78 Pt. June '78 |
| S  (P. 1155) | | | | |
| Sellers, Henry, Sergt.... | Philips' | 1 May '76 | 3 yrs. | Dischgd 25 Dec. 79 |
| Shepard, Wm., Pt....... | " | | | Omtd Apr. '78 |
| Simmons, Isler, Sergt.... | Goodman's | 1 Oct. " | " | Pt. Aug. '78 Dischgd Nov. 10, '79 |
| Smith, Thos., Pt....... | " | 25 July " | " | Dischgd 25 July '79 |

| Name and Rank | Company | Dates of Enlistment and Commission | Period of Service | Occurrences |
|---|---|---|---|---|
| Smith, Sm'l, Pt........ | Goodman's | 20 May '76 | | { Corpl. 1 Dec. '78 <br> { Dischgd 20 May '79 |
| Smith, Clem, Pt....... | " | 25 July " | 3 yrs. | Dischgd 20 July '79 |
| Simpson, Smith........ | " | '77 | " | Omtd June '78 |
| Street, Jno., Sergt...... | Harris' | " | | Time Out 31 Oct. '77 |
| Stokes, Young, Pt...... | " | " | | Time Out 31 Oct. '77 |
| Stokes, Drury, Pt....... | " | " | | Time Out 31 Oct. '77 |
| Swearingham, Van., Pt.. | " | " | | Time Out 31 Oct. '77 |
| Saxton, Jas., Sergt...... | Cole's | 7 May " | | { Pt. Jan. '78 <br> { Pris. 14 Apr. '79 |
| Spearpoint, Joseph, Pt. . | " | " | | Omtd Mar. '78 |
| Spindler, Boston, Pt..... | " | 2 Oct. " | | |
| Smiter, Valente, Pt..... | " | " | 3 yrs. | Destd 12 Oct. '77 |
| Smith, Robt., Capt..... | " | 16 Apr. '76 | | Omtd Jan. '78 |
| Scanthing, Pat'k, Pt.... | Smith's | 26 Apr. " | " | Dischgd 1 May '79 |
| Simmons, Benj., Pt..... | " | | " | Omtd Jan. '78 |
| Shaw, Robt., Pt....... | " | | | Dischgd 10 Aug. '77 |
| Syrus, Jas., Pt......... | Nelson's | | | Dischgd 13 Oct. '77 |
| Smith, Jno., Pt........ | " | | " | { Mustd Jan. '78 <br> { Omtd June '78 |
| (P. 1154) | | | | |
| Standfast, Wm., Sergt... | Williams' | '77 | | { Qr. Mr. Sergt. 11 Sep. '77 <br> { Sergt. Aug. '78. Destd 1 <br> { Jan. '80. Pt. 1 Apr. '79 |
| Steed, Jesse, Sergt...... | " | " | 2½ yrs. | Omtd Jan. '78 |
| Sill, Thos., Pt......... | " | " | W | Omtd Sep. '77 |
| Seymore, Sol., Corpl..... | " | 1 May '76 | | { Pt. June '78 <br> { Dischgd 10 Nov. '78 |
| Slade, Wm., Lt........ | Philips' | 1 May '77 | | { And Adjt. June '78. 1 Lt. <br> { 25 June '79. Resigned 18 <br> { Feb. '80 |
| Smith, Benj., Sergt..... | " | 20 May '76 | 3 yrs. | { Pt. June '78 <br> { Dischgd 25 May '79 |
| T   (P. 1169) | | | | |
| Thaxton, Jas., Lt. Col... | | 15 Apr. '76 | | { Retired from Service <br> { Jan. '81 |
| Tipper, Jno., Pt....... | Williams' | 10 May " | 2½ yrs. | Dischgd 10 Nov. '78 |
| Timbrel, Jno., Pt...... | " | '77 | | Omtd Sep. '77 |
| Thompson, Jno., Pt.... | " | " | | Dischgd Aug. '77 |
| Taylor, Jno., Musc...... | Philips' | " | 3 yrs. | Omtd June '78 |
| Tilley, Lewis, Pt....... | " | 1 Apr. " | " | |
| Tucker, Rich'd, Pt..... | Goodman's | 25 July '76 | " | |
| Thompson, John, Pt..... | Cole's | '77 | 1 yr. | Dischgd 10 Aug. '77 |
| Thompson, Dan'l, Musc. | Nelson's | 14 Feb. " | 3 yrs. | { Pt. Feb. '79 <br> { Dischgd Feb. '79 |
| U   (P. 1176) | | | | |
| Usher, Wm., Surg...... | | 24 Apr. '77 | | Resigned 1 Nov. '77 |
| W   (P. 1182) | | | | |
| Williams, Jas., Capt..... | | 3 Apr. '77 | | Died 2 May '78 |
| Wade, Dan'l, Musc..... | Williams' | " | W | Omtd Feb. '78 |
| White, Geo., Pt........ | " | " | " | |
| Williamson, Wm., Pt... | " | " | 18 Mo. | Dischgd Nov. '77 |
| Waters, Isaac, Pt...... | " | " | " | Dischgd Nov. '77 |
| Wile, Martin, Pt........ | Philips' | " | | Destd 26 Oct. '77 |
| Williams, Wm., Lt...... | Harris' | 9 Dec. '76 | 3 yrs. | { Omtd Jan. '78 <br> { See 5th Reg. |

| Name and Rank | Company | Dates of Enlistment and Commission | Period of Service | Occurrences |
|---|---|---|---|---|
| Wright, Adam, Musc.... | Harris' | '77 | W | {Omtd Mar. '78 <br> {Mustd Jan. '79 |
| Wright, Thos., Pt...... | | 29 Apr. '76 | 3 yrs. | Dischgd 10 May '79 |
| Watts, Andrew, Pt...... | | '77 | " | Died 19 Feb. '78 |
| Weaver, Lewis, Corpl. .. | Cole's | " | " | Omtd Sep. '77 |
| Watson, Jas., Pt....... | " | " | " | Destd 22 Sep. '77 |
| Wren, Wm., Pt......... | " | 13 May '76 | " | Corpl. 10 Feb. '80 |
| Wilkinson, Reuben, Lt. . | Lewis' | 20 Dec. " | | Resigned 21 July '82 |
| Wills, Willis, Pt....... | " | '77 | " | Died 16 Nov. '77 |
| White, Ezx'l, Pt....... | " | 4 May '76 | " | Dischgd 14 May '79 |
| Whitmel, Blunt, Lt..... | Smith's | 20 Nov. " | | Omtd Jan. '78 |
| Wilson, Geo., Musc..... | " | '77 | " | Omtd Jan. '78 |
| Webb, Jno., Pt......... | | " | | Dischgd 16 Aug. '77 |
| Wright, Jno., Pt....... | | " | | Omtd Sep. '77 |
| Ward, Jno., Pt......... | Nelson's | 16 May '76 | 3 yrs.W | |
| Willard, Maj., Pt...... | " | 16 May " | " | |
| Ward, Drewry, Pt..... | " | 16 May " | " | Dischgd 16 May '79 |

## 5TH REGIMENT—COL. EDWARD BUNCOMBE

| Name and Rank | Company | Dates of Enlistment and Commission | Period of Service | Occurrences |
|---|---|---|---|---|
| **A** (P. 1004) | | | | |
| Allen, Thos., 2nd Lt. ... | Stedman's | 1777 | | |
| Armstrong, Thos., 1 Lt.. | Williams' | 16 Apr. '76 | | {Capt. 25 Oct. '77. Pris. 1 <br> {June '79. Mustd '81 <br> {A.D.C. 28 Mar. '82 |
| Arthur, Jno. L., Pt...... | Caswell's | 27 Mar. '77 | 3 yrs. | Corpl. Nov. '79 |
| Ammons, Jordan, Pt.... | " | 20 Apr. " | W | |
| Angel, Thos., Pt....... | " | 12 May " | | {Pris. 1 June '79 <br> {Mustd Nov. '79 |
| Anderson, Jas., Pt..... | " | | 2½ yrs. | Died 14 Nov. '77 |
| Anderson, Thos., Musc.. | " | 18 Dec. '76 | 3 yrs. | {Pt. Jan. '78 <br> {Destd 30 Apr. '79 |
| Allen, John, Lt........ | " | 1 Oct. " | | {Omtd Jan. '78 <br> {Died Sep. '80 |
| Arnold, Arthur, Pt...... | Blount's | | W | Omtd Feb. '78 |
| Allen, Walter, Ensn..... | " | 28 Mar. '77 | | {Lt. 1 Oct. '77 <br> {Omtd 4 Oct. '78 |
| Atkins, Benj'n, Pt..... | " | " | 3 yrs. | Omtd June '78 |
| Allison, Achis, Pt....... | Darnal's | " | W | {Pris. 1 June '79 <br> {Mustd Nov. '79 |
| Anderson, Wilson, Corpl. | Enloe's | " | 3 yrs. | Dead 15 Mar. '78 |
| Albertson, Henry....... | " | " | " | Destd 29 Feb. '80 |
| Anderson, John........ | " | " | " | Destd 29 Feb. '80 |
| Alderson, Simon, Capt. . | " | 16 Apr. '76 | | Omtd Sep. '77 |
| Aldridge, Joseph, Pt..... | Alderson's | 18 Dec. " | " | Dischgd 20 May '79 |
| Abbitt, Ezekial, Musc... | " | " | " | Omtd Jan. '78 |
| **B** (P. 1013) | | | | |
| Buncombe, Edw'd, Col.. | | 15 Apr. '76 | | {Pris. 4 Oct. '77 <br> {Omtd Jan. '78 |
| Boyd, Adam, Chaplain.. | | 1 Oct. '77 | | {Omtd June '78 <br> {Mustd in '79 |
| Brownlay, Robt., Corpl.. | Stedman's | " | W | Sergt. Nov. '78 |
| Burk, Jacob, Pt........ | " | " | " | |
| Barnes, Wm., Pt....... | " | " | 3 yrs. | Missing 4 Oct. '77 |
| Bowers, Wm., Pt...... | " | " | W | Dead June '78 |

| Name and Rank | Company | Dates of Enlistment and Commission | Period of Service | Occurrences |
|---|---|---|---|---|
| Banks, Wm., Pt........ | Stedman's | | | { Corpl. 10 Nov. '78 <br> { Destd 1 Apr. '79 |
| Blount, Thos., 1st Lt.... | " | 28 Apr. '77 | | Omtd Jan. '78 |
| Braboy, Jacob, Pt...... | Williams' | 9 May '76 | 2½ yrs. | Dischgd 10 Nov. '78 |
| Boon, Whylis, Pt....... | " | | " | Omtd Feb. '78 |
| Bailey, Benj'n, 2nd Lt. . | " | 1 Oct. " | | { Capt. Sep. 8, '81 <br> { Deranged 1 Jan. '83 |
| Brooks, Asa, Sergt...... | Caswell's | '77 | 3 yrs. | { Qr. Mr. Sergt. Jan. '78 <br> { Died 3 June '78 |
| Benson, Bailey, Pt...... | " | " | " | Dischgd 8 Feb. '80 |
| Burtonshell, Joshua, Pt.. | " | " | " | Destd Nov. '77 |
| Blount, Reading, Capt. . | | 16 Apr. '76 | | Maj. '82 |
| Bradley, Sam'l, Pt...... | Blount's | | " | Omtd June '78 |
| Broom, Mason, Pt...... | " | 2 Apr. " | 2½ yrs. | Dischgd Oct. '78 |
| Burnet, David, Pt...... | " | | W | Omtd Feb. '78 |
| Brown, Thos., Pt....... | " | | " | |
| Bond, Rich'd, Pt....... | " | | 2½ yrs. | Omtd Feb. '78 |
| Burges, Absalom, Sergt.. | Darnal's | '77 | W | { Pris. 1 June '79 <br> { Mustd Nov. '79 |
| Brown, David, Pt...... | " | " | " | Dischgd Apr. '78 |
| Belch, Philip, Pt........ | " | " | 3 yrs. | Died 21 Nov. '77 |
| Brand, Jno., Pt........ | " | " | 2½ yrs. | Destd Aug. '77 |
| Blocksom, Sovvain, Pt. . | Enloe's | 29 Nov. '76 | 3 yrs. | Dischgd 30 Jan. '80 |
| Bullock, Jno., Pt....... | " | 20 Apr. " | 2½ yrs. | Dischgd 10 Nov. '78 |
| Butler, Clareys, Pt..... | " | 20 Apr. " | | Dischgd 10 Nov. '78 |
| Benham, Drury, Corpl. . | " | 16 Dec. " | | { Sergt. Sep. '77. Pt. June <br> '78. Corpl. 15 May '79 <br> { Sergt. 25 July '79 |
| Baker, Jno., Pt........ | " | '77 | | Destd 15 Mar. '77 |
| Blake, Chris., Pt........ | Alderson's | " | 2½ yrs. | Died 30 Apr. '78 |
| Blount, Jas., Pt........ | " | " | " | Dischgd 6 Oct. '77 |
| Blurton, Henry, Sergt... | Coleman's | " | " | Omtd Jan. '78 |
| Brady, Jas., Pt........ | " | " | " | { Corpl. 1 Sep. '77 <br> { Omtd Jan. '78 |
| Blurton, Edw'd, Pt..... | " | " | " | Omtd Jan. '78 |
| C   (P. 1028) | | | | |
| Cooley, Sam'l, Surg..... | | 16 Apr. '76 | | Omtd Jan. '78 |
| Carter, John, Pt........ | Stedman's | '77 | W | |
| Coggins, Jas., Pt....... | " | " | | |
| Crutcher, H'y., Ensn.... | " | 20 Aug. " | | Resigned 11 Dec. '77 |
| Carter, Sam'l, Pt....... | Williams' | 26 Apr. '76 | 2½ yrs. | { Corpl. Nov. '77. Pt. Apr. <br> '78. Dischgd 16 Oct. '78 |
| (P. 1029) | | | | |
| Church, Wm., Pt...... | " | 12 May " | | Dischgd 12 Nov. '78 |
| Cooper, Jer'h, Pt...... | " | '77 | 2½ yrs. | Omtd Apr. '78 |
| Cooper, Nath., Pt...... | " | 5 May '76 | " | Dischgd 10 Nov. '78 |
| Clark, Abner, Pt....... | " | '77 | " | Died 28 Jan. '78 |
| Craig, Geo., Pt........ | " | " | " | Died Nov. '77 |
| Carter, Robt., Pt...... | " | 4 May '76 | " | Dischgd 10 Nov. '78 |
| Cornelius, Isaac, Pt.... | " | '77 | " | Dischgd 10 Nov. '78 |
| Collins, Jno., Pt....... | " | " | " | Dischgd 1 Mar. '79 |
| Charles, Winoke, Pt.... | " | Dec. " | " | Destd 28 Aug. '77 |
| Cornelius, Isaac, Pt.... | " | 16 Apr. '76 | " | Omtd Jan. '77 |
| Caswell, Wm., Capt.... | | 16 Apr. " | " | Omtd Jan. '77 |
| Cole, Thos., Corpl...... | Caswell's | 26 Nov. " | 3 yrs. | { Pt. June '78 <br> { Dischgd 8 Feb. '80 |

| Name and Rank | Company | Dates of Enlistment and Commission | Period of Service | Occurrences |
|---|---|---|---|---|
| Carmady, Jas., Corpl. .. | Caswell's | '77 | 3 yrs. | Pt. Jan. '78 / Died 12 May '78 |
| Carvin, Thos., Pt....... | " | 26 Nov. '76 | | |
| Cox, Wm., Pt......... | " | 16 Apr. " | 2½ yrs. | Omtd Sep.'77. MustdOct. '78. Dischgd 10 Nov. '78 |
| Caps, Wm., Pt......... | " | '77 | " | |
| Cummings, Benj'n, Pt... | Blount's | | | Dead 5 May '78 |
| Clagburn, Shubal, Pt.... | " | 28 Oct. '76 | | Corpl. Dec. '77 / Pt. Nov. '78 |
| Cooper, Wm., Lt....... | Darnal's | 16 Apr. " | | Omtd Oct. '77 |
| Cotanch, Malachi, Pt. .. | " | 11 Jan. '77 | W | Destd 30 Jan. '80 |
| Cooper, Josh, Pt....... | | 1 Nov. '76 | 3 yrs. | Pris. 1 June '79. Mustd Nov. '79, "re-enlisted" |
| Cherry, Dan'l, Pt...... | " | '77 | 1 yr. | Died 18 Oct. '77 |
| Cason, Wm., Pt........ | Enloe's | | | Died 5 Mar. '78 |
| Curtis, Jno., Lt........ | Alderson's | 16 Oct. '76 | | Omtd Sep. '77 |
| Carter, Edw'd, Sergt.... | " | '77 | | Omtd Jan. '78 |
| Coble, Shadrock, Pt..... | " | " | | Killed 4 Oct. '77 |
| Corbett, Alex'r, Pt...... | " | " | W | Destd 28 Aug. '77 |
| Coleman, Benj'n, Capt.. | | 30 Apr. " | | |
| Crutches, Anth'y, Sergt. | Coleman's | 14 May " | 3 yrs. | Ensn. 27 Feb. '80. Lt. 18 May'81. Deranged 1 Jan. '83 |
| Carrell, Benj., Pt...... | " | " | 2½ yrs. | Died Aug. '77 |
| **D** (P. 1042) | | | | |
| Dawson, Levy, Maj..... | | 15 Apr. '76 | | Lt. Col. 19 Oct. '77 in 8th Reg. |
| Davidson, Wm. L., 1st Lt. Col......... | | 4 Oct. '77 | | 1st Reg. '79. Retired 1 Jan. '81 |
| Daniel, Jno., Corpl...... | Stedman's | " | W | Pt. '77. Died 30 Dec. '77 |
| Deggs, Anth'y, Ensn.... | Williams' | 20 Mar. " | | Lt. 20 Aug. '77. Omtd Jan. '78 |
| Davis, Wyllis, Pt...... | " | " | 2½ yrs. | Omtd June '78 |
| Davis, Aaron, Pt....... | " | - " | " | Omtd Jan. '78 |
| Dempsey, Squire, Pt.... | " | " | " | Died 17 May '78 |
| Diggins, Edw'd, Pt..... | Caswell's | " | " | Destd Nov. '77 |
| Draper, Roger, Pt....... | Blount's | | " | Died 16 Apr. '78 |
| Darnal, Henry, Capt.... | | 1 Oct. '76 | | Omtd Jan. '78 |
| Duggin, Thos., Pt...... | Darnal's | '77 | " | Missing 4 Oct. '77 |
| Duggin, Jesse......... | | " | " | Killed 4 Oct. '77 |
| Dean, Benj'n, Pt....... | Enloe's | 2 Apr. " | 3 yrs. | Mustd 27 of Mar for W |
| Dennis, Hezekiah, Pt.... | Alderson's | " | " | Died 12 Jan. '78 |
| **E** (P. 1051) | | | | |
| Eburn, Thos., Lt....... | Stedman's | 16 Apr. '76 | | Omtd Oct. '77 |
| Elks, Wm., Pt......... | " | '77 | W | Omtd Feb. '78 |
| Edulus, Thos., Musc.... | | " | 2½ yrs. | Omtd Jan. '78 |
| Eburn, Jno., Lt......... | Williams' | 1 Oct. '76 | | Omtd Jan. '78 |
| Ewell, Wm., Lt........ | Blount's | 20 Apr. '77 | | Omtd Jan.'78 |
| Early, Jas., Pt......... | Darnal's | " | W | Destd Aug. '77 |
| Enloe, John, Capt..... | | 16 Apr. '76 | | Omtd Oct. '77 |
| Erwin, Jas., Pt........ | | " | | Destd Sep. '78 |
| **F** (P. 1056) | | | | |
| Ford, Hezekiah, Chap'n. | | 20 Apr. '77 | | Omtd Sep. '77 |
| Flury, Wm., Sergt...... | Stedman's | " | W | Died 16 Mar. '78 |
| Frazzle, Dan'l, Sergt.... | Williams' | 23 Apr. '76 | 2½ yrs. | Pt. Apr. '78 / Dischgd Oct. '78 |

| Name and Rank | Company | Dates of Enlistment and Commission | Period of Service | Occurrences |
|---|---|---|---|---|
| Farmer, Wm., Pt...... | Williams' | 29 Apr. '76 | 2½ yrs. | Dischgd 24 Oct. '78 |
| Fooks, Jno., Pt........ | Caswell's | 24 May " | " | Dischgd 1 Dec. '78 |
| Fooks, Jas., Pt........ | " | '77 | " | Omtd Oct. '77 |
| Fowler, Abin, Pt........ | Blount's | 6 May '76 | W | |
| G (P. 1064) | | | | |
| Giles, Jno., Qr. Mast. Sergt..... | | 22 Aug. '77 | " | Omtd Jan. '78 |
| Gaskins, Wm., Sergt.... | Stedman's | " | W | Pt. Aug. '78 Corpl. Mar. '79 |
| Green, Jno., Pt........ | " | " | 3 yrs. | Died 20 Aug. '77 |
| Garet, James, Pt....... | " | " | W | Omtd Feb. '78 |
| Gerald, Chas., Ensn..... | Williams' | 30 Apr. " | | Lt. 19 Dec. '76 |
| Groves, Wm., 1st Lt.... | Caswell's | 16 Apr. " | | Capt. 17 Aug. '77 Omtd Jan. '78 |
| Griffin, Jas., Corpl...... | Blount's | 1 Dec. '76 | 3 yrs. | Dischgd 1 Feb. '80 |
| Glanhan, Jer'h, Sergt... | Darnal's | '77 | W | Died 21 Apr. '78 |
| Garret, Dan'l, Corpl.... | " | " | | Dischgd 15 Oct. '77 |
| Gaddy, Thos., Pt...... | " | 21 May '76 | W | Corpl. Aug. '77 Pt. June '78 |
| Gainer, Sam'l......... | " | '77 | 3 yrs.W | |
| Gladhan, Dan'l........ | " | " | 3 yrs. | Omtd Jan. '78 |
| Garret, Thos.......... | " | " | 2½ yrs. | Destd Aug. '77 |
| Goldsbury, Wm., Pt..... | Enloe's | " | 3 yrs. | Omtd June '78 |
| H (P. 1074) | | | | |
| Hogg, Thos., Maj...... | | 4 Oct. '76 | | Deranged 1 Jan. '83. See 1st Reg. |
| Holland, Spear, Ensn.... | Stedman's | 24 Mar. " | | Lt. 25 Oct. '77. Omtd Jan. '78 |
| Hammon, John B. Sergt. | " | 7 May " | 2½ yrs. | Dischgd 10 Nov. '78 |
| Harris, Jas., Pt........ | " | 27 May " | W | |
| Harris, Stephen, Pt..... | " | '77 | 2½ yrs. | Omtd Sep. '77 |
| Hamilton, Jno., Pt..... | " | " | W | |
| Hodges, Jno., Lt....... | Williams' | 1 Oct. '76 | | Omtd Jan. '78 |
| Howard, Solomon,Sergt. | " | 28 Apr. " | 2½ yrs. | Pt. Jan. '78 Dischgd Oct. '78 |
| Holden, Jas., Corpl..... | " | '77 | " | Omtd Jan. '78 |
| Hollenbeck, Jno., Corpl.. | " | " | " | Pt. Nov. '77 Omtd Feb. '78 |
| Holmes, Shadrock, Pt... | " | " | " | Omtd Feb. '78 |
| Hooks, Epha'm, Pt..... | " | 9 May '76 | " | Dischgd 9 Nov. '78 |
| Hicks, Jno., Pt........ | " | '77 | " | |
| Hicks, Jas., Pt......... | " | " | " | Omtd Feb. '78 |
| Hoggard, Wm., Pt...... | " | 29 Apr. '76 | " | Dischgd 29 Oct. '78 |
| Hill, Thos., Pt......... | " | 26 Apr. '76 | " | Corpl. Nov. '77 Dischgd Oct. '78 |
| Holland, Josiah, Pt..... | " | '77 | | Died June '77 |
| I (P. 1087) | | | | |
| Irwin, Henry, Lt. Col... | | 15 Apr. '76 | | Killed 4 Oct. '77 |
| Ivy, Curtis, Ensn....... | Williams' | 23 Apr. '77 | | Lt. 10 Oct. '77 |
| Ivy, Jas., Pt.......... | Alderson's | 15 Nov. '76 | 3 yrs.W | |
| Inglish, Joseph, Musc... | " | '77 | 3 yrs. | Died 17 Dec. '77 |
| J (P. 1090) | | | | |
| Jones, Chas., Pt....... | Williams' | '77 | 2½ yrs. | Died 2 Mar. '78 |
| James, Edwin, Pt....... | " | 4 May '76 | " | Dischgd 6 Oct. '78 |
| Jenkins, Abr'n, Corpl.... | " | 22 Apr. " | " | Sergt. 15 May '78. Corpl. June '78. Dischgd Oct.'78 |
| Jenkins, Robt., Pt..... | " | 29 Apr. " | " | Dischgd 29 Oct. '78 |

| Name and Rank | Company | Dates of Enlistment and Commission | Period of Service | Occurrences |
|---|---|---|---|---|
| Jones, John, Pt........ | Caswell's | '77 | 2½ yrs. | Killed 4 Oct. '77 |
| Jenkins, Wm., Pt...... | Blount's | " | " | Omtd Apr. '78 |
| Johnson, John, Pt..... | " | " | 2½ yrs. | Omtd Feb. '78 |
| Jones, Jas., Pt......... | Enloe's | 18 Nov. '76 | 3 yrs. | |
| Jacobs, Joshua, Pt..... | Alderson's | '77 | " | Killed 11 Sep. '77 |
| Johnson, Holland, Sergt. | " | 20 May '76 | " | ⎰Corpl. Jan. '78. Pt. July ⎱'78. Dischgd 20 May '79 |
| Jones, Jones Lytleton,Pt. | " | '77 | " | Died 20 Sep. '77 |
| Jeffrey, Jno., Pt....... | Coleman's | " | 2½ yrs. | |
| K (P. 1096) | | | | |
| Kennedy, Archibald, Sergt. Maj......... | | 1 Aug. '77 | | Omtd Sep. '77 |
| Knight, Morgan........ | Blount's | " | | Omtd Feb. '78 |
| Kennedy, Benj'n, Sergt.. | Darnal's | " | | ⎰Omtd Jan. '78 ⎱Mustd Jan. 5th Reg. |
| Kennedy, Geo., Pt..... | " | " | | Destd Aug. '77 |
| Kennedy, Jno., Pt..... | " | " | | Destd Aug. '77 |
| Killingswith, Jno., Musc. | " | " | W | Pt. Jan. '78 |
| L (P. 1102) | | | | |
| Lott, Job, Pt.......... | Williams' | 1777 | 2½ yrs. | Died June '77 |
| Lewis, Amos, Pt........ | Blount's | 14 May '76 | " | Dischgd 4 Nov. '78 |
| Lodge, Lewis, Pt...... | " | 1 Oct. " | 3 yrs. | Omtd Feb. '78 |
| Long, Nehemh, Lt..... | " | 1 Oct. " | | Omtd Jan. '78 |
| Loyd, Burrel, Pt....... | Darnal's | '77 | W | Omtd Feb. '79 |
| Ligget, Dan'l, Pt....... | " | " | 2½ yrs. | ⎰Destd Aug. '77 ⎱Mustd Jan. '79 5th Reg. |
| Laughinghouse, Thos.Pt. | Enloe's | " | 3 yrs. | Omtd Jan. '78 |
| Lisk, Jas., Pt.......... | " | " | " | Omtd Jan. '78 |
| Lucas, Mathew, Pt..... | Coleman's | " | W | Killed 4 Oct. '77 |
| M (P. 1111) | | | | |
| Miller, Henry, Maj..... | | 8 Mar. '77 | 3 yrs. | ⎰Omtd between Jan. and ⎱Sep. '79 |
| McDowal, Peter, Pt..... | Stedman's | " | W | Destd 1 Nov. '79 |
| McGuire, Mich'l, Pt.... | " | " | " | Dischgd 25 Apr. '78 |
| Maddry, John, Corpl.... | Williams' | 13 May '76 | 2½ yrs. | Destd 13 Nov. '78 |
| Martin, Jas., Musc..... | " | 15 July " | " | ⎰Pt. Jan.'78. Mustd May ⎰'78. Pt. June '78. Dischgd ⎱10 Nov. '78 |
| Morris, Rich'd, Pt..... | " | 17 Aug. " | " | |
| Morris, Jno., Pt....... | " | " | " | Dischgd 16 June '78 |
| Morgan, Chas., Corpl... | " | | | ⎰Sergt. Nov. '77. Pt. Jan. ⎰'78. See Blount's Co., 3rd ⎱Reg. |
| McNees, Jno., 2nd Lt... | " | 8 Mar. '77 | | ⎰Capt. 2 Nov. '82. ⎱Deranged Jan. 1, '83 |
| Murphy, Thos, Pt...... | Caswell's | " | 2½ yrs. | Died 3 Feb. '78 |
| (P. 1112) | | | | |
| McElroy, Sm'l, Pt..... | " | '77 | " | Omtd Feb. '78 |
| Moore, Jos., Corpl..... | Blount's | 2 May '76 | " | ⎰Pt. Sep. '77. Dischgd ⎱Oct. '78 |
| Miller, Henry.......... | " | | W | Corpl. Feb.'80. Sergt in'82 |
| Moore, Fred'k, Pt..... | " | | " | |
| Moore, Thos., Pt...... | Blount's | | | Dischgd 10 Nov. '78 |
| Moore, Jacob, Pt...... | " | | | Died 28 Apr. '78 |
| Moye, Geo., Pt........ | " | | | Dischgd 10 Nov. '78 |
| Morris, Jas., Corpl..... | Darnal's | '77 | | Pt. Jan.'78. Omtd Feb.'78 |
| Morris, Benj'n, Pt..... | " | " | | Omtd Feb. '78 |

| Name and Rank | Company | Dates of Enlistment and Commission | Period of Service | Occurrences |
|---|---|---|---|---|
| McAllister, Jas., Pt..... | Darnal's | '77 | | Died 7 Mar. '78 |
| McAltree, Barnabas, Pt. | " | " | | Omtd Sep. '78 |
| Moore, Wm., Pt........ | " | " | 2½ yrs. | Destd Aug. '77 |
| Moulborn, Sol'n, Sergt. . | Enloe's | " | 3 yrs. | Died 27 Feb. '78 |
| Maulborn, David, Sergt. | " | " | " | Dischgd 30 Jan. '80 |
| Meeks, Robt., Corpl..... | Anderson's | 8 Dec. '76 | " | Pt. Jan. '78 |
| | | | | Dischgd 1 Mar. '80 |
| Mathews, John, Pt...... | " | 25 Dec. " | " | Corpl. Mar., Pt. June. Corpl. 28 Aug. '78. Dischgd 1 Jan. '80 |
| McCoy, John, Pt....... | " | '77 | 2½ yrs. | Died 10 Mar. '78 |
| Moons, Shad'k, Pt..... | " | " | 3 yrs. | Died 5 Oct. '77 |
| Moseley, Thos., Pt..... | " | " | " | Omtd Mar. '78 |
| Middleton, Daniel, Pt... | " | " | " | Omtd Feb. '78 |
| Moore, Lemuel, Pt..... | " | " | " | Music Nov. '77. Pt. Jan. '78. Musc. Feb. '78. Died Apr. 26, '78 |
| Meeks, Wm., Pt........ | " | " | " | |
| **N** (P. 1124) | | | | |
| Nobles, Hez'k., Musc.... | Williams' | 5 May '76 | 2½ yrs. | Pt. Sep. '77 Dischgd Oct. '78 |
| Newsom, Rand'l, Musc.. | Caswell's | '77 | 3 yrs. | Omtd Jan. '78 Mustd '79 |
| Nash, Francis, Pt...... | " | " | " | Died 1 Mar. '78 |
| Nelson, Wm., Pt........ | Enloe's | " | " | Died 15 Aug. '78 |
| Nichols, Jas., Pt........ | Alderson's | 18 Apr. '76 | 2½ yrs. | Dischgd 30 Oct. '78 |
| **O** (P. 1129) | | | | |
| Owens, Jno., Pt........ | Caswell's | '77 | 3 yrs. | Died 2 Feb. '78 |
| O'Guien, Jno., Pt....... | Darnal's | " | 2½ yrs. | Destd Aug. '77 |
| **P** (P. 1134) | | | | |
| Paul, Stephen, Pt...... | Stedman's | '77 | | Died 27 Sep. '77 |
| Pierce, Wm., Pt........ | Williams' | " | | Omtd Feb. '78 |
| Ponder, Wm., Pt....... | " | 30 June '77 | 3 yrs. | Musc. Sep.'77. Pt. Sep.'78 |
| Pierce, Thos., Pt........ | " | " | 2½ yrs. | Died Oct. '78 |
| Peoples, Wm., Pt...... | Caswell's | 1 Apr. '76 | " | Dischgd 1 Oct. '78 |
| Parker, Arthur, Pt..... | " | 16 Apr. " | " | Dischgd 10 Nov. '78 |
| Parish, John, Pt........ | " | 1 Sep. " | 3 yrs. | Destd 20 Nov. '79 |
| Procter, Wm., Pt....... | Blount's | 15 May " | 2½ yrs. | Dischgd 10 Nov. '78 |
| Padget, Solomon, Pt.... | Darnal's | '77 | | Destd Aug. '77 |
| Paramore, Amos, Corpl.. | Enloe's | " | 3 yrs. | |
| Pilchard, Jno., Pt...... | " | " | " | Omtd Jan. '78 |
| Pope, Sm'l, Pt.......... | Alderson's | " | 2½ yrs. | |
| Private, Miles, Pt...... | " | 15 Nov. '76 | 3 yrs. | Omtd Feb. '78 |
| Phillips, Bush, Pt...... | Coleman's | '77 | 2½ yrs. | Omtd Sep. '77 |
| Patterson, Jno., Pt..... | " | " | | Mustd 4th Reg. Jan. '79 for 3 yrs. |
| **R** (Pp. 1144-45) | | | | |
| Reid, Jese, Lt.......... | Stedman's | 20 Oct. '76 | | Pris. Sep.'81. Capt. 1 Apr. '82. Deranged 1 Jan. '83 |
| Rue, Chas., Pt......... | " | '77 | **W** | Omtd Dec. '77 |
| Rhodes, Chas., Sergt.... | William's | 14 May '76 | 2½ yrs. | Dischgd 25 Oct. '78 |
| Ryan, Thos, Musc...... | " | 1 Oct. " | " | Dischgd 30 Oct. '78 |
| Rhodes, Isaac, Pt...... | " | 28 Oct. " | " | Dischgd 28 Oct. '78 |
| (P. 1145) | | | | |
| Rickerson, Jese, Pt...... | Caswell's | 27 Mar. '77 | 3 yrs. | |
| Robert, John, Lt........ | " | " | " | Omtd June '78 |
| Roberts, Thos., Sergt.... | Blount's | " | " | Mustd Pt. '79 by name of Thos. Robertson |

| Name and Rank | Company | Dates of Enlistment and Commission | Period of Service | Occurrences |
|---|---|---|---|---|
| Robertson, Jacob, Sergt. | Blount's | '77 | 2½ yrs. | Pt. Sep.'77. Omtd Dec.'77 |
| Reasons, Wm., Musc.... | " | 10 Sep. '76 | 3 yrs. | Pt. Jan.'78. Destd June '79. See him re-enlisted for 18 Mo. |
| Russell, Major, Pt..... | " | 6 Dec. " | W | |
| Robertson, Benj'n, Pt... | " | 17 Aug. " | 3 yrs. | Music No. '78. Omtd June '79 |
| Russell, Jno., Pt........ | " | '77 | 2½ yrs. | Died 8 Jan. '78 |
| Recford, Morris, Pt..... | Coleman's | " | " | Corpl. Oct. '77 / Omtd Jan. '78 |
| Rogers, Eli, Pt........ | " | 12 Aug. " | 3 yrs. | Corpl. 1 Mar. '80 |
| **S** (Pp. 1155-56) | | | | |
| Swan, Nimrod, Qr. Mr.. | | 18 June '77 | | Omtd Jan. '78 |
| Stedman, Benj'n, Capt.. | | 16 Apr. '76 | | Omtd Jan. '78 |
| Sanders, Duss, Pt...... | Stedman's | 1777 | W | Missing 11 Sep. '77 |
| Smith, Jabez, Ensn..... | " | | | Lt. Sep.'77. Omtd Jan.'78 |
| Stollings, Jas., Pt...... | Williams' | " | 2½ yrs. | Omtd Feb. '78 |
| Sanders, Jas., Pt....... | " | | " | Died 17 Sep. '78 |
| Sykes, Adam, Pt....... | " | | 3 yrs. | Omtd Feb.'78 |
| Scollar, Isaac, Pt...... | " | | 2½ yrs. | Killed 4 Oct. '77 |
| (P. 1156) | | | | |
| Sanders, Jas., Pt........ | " | Dec. '77 | " | Omtd Jan. '78 |
| Stewart, Chas., Lt...... | Caswell's | 23 July '77 | | Pris. 12 May '80.Capt. Deranged 1 Jan. '83 |
| Stringer, Sam'l, Sergt.... | " | " | | Destd 1 Oct. '78 |
| Smith, Thos., Corpl..... | " | 26 Nov. '76 | | Sergt. Aug. '78. Pt. 19 Nov.'79. Dischgd 8 Feb. '80 |
| Seymore, Phelix, Pt..... | " | 26 Nov. " | 3 yrs. | Dischgd 8 Feb. '80 |
| Stringer, Josiah, Pt..... | Blount's | 6 Nov. '77 | " | Corpl.Nov.'78. Sergt.June '79. Dischgd 1 Feb. '80 |
| Shockley, Isaac, Pt..... | " | | 2½ yrs. | Died 5 Nov. '77 |
| Smithwick, Wm., Corpl. | Darnal's | " | W | Sergt. Oct. '77. Corpl. Jan. '78. Sergt Nov. '79 |
| Sellinger, Absolem, Pt... | " | " | " | Died 3 May '78 |
| Smithwick, Edd or Edw'd, Pt......... | " | " | " | Omtd Feb. '78 |
| Smith, Wm., Pt....... | " | " | 3 yrs. | Destd Aug. '77 |
| Simpson, Joseph, Pt..... | " | " | 2½ yrs. | Destd Aug. '77 |
| Smith, David, Pt...... | " | 20 Nov. '76 | W | |
| Spain, Augustus, Sergt.. | Enloe's | '77 | 3 yrs. | Omtd Feb. '78 |
| Smith, Thos., Pt........ | " | 24 Oct '76 | " | |
| Smith, Wm., Pt....... | Alderson's | '77 | " | Omtd Feb. '78 |
| Swindle, Jese, Pt...... | " | " | " | Omtd Mar. '78 |
| **T** (P. 1170) | | | | |
| Taylor, Jas, Sergt. Maj.. | | 28 Mar. '77 | | Omtd Jan. '78 |
| Tyak, D. Thos., Fife Maj........... | | 21 June " | W | Mustd Musc. Jan. '82 |
| Thomas, Ashia, Pt...... | Williams' | 29 Apr. '76 | 2½ yrs. | Dischgd 10 Nov. '78 |
| Thomas, Thos., Pt...... | " | 14 May " | " | Dischgd 10 Nov. '78 |
| Todwine, Coleman, Sgt.. | Caswell's | '77 | 3 yrs. | Omtd Jan. '78 |
| Taylor, Jas. Jr., Pt...... | " | | " | |
| Taylor, Abue, Pt...... | " | | | |
| Taylor, Jas. Sr., Pt..... | " | | 2½ yrs. | Omtd Feb. '78 |
| Thomas, John, Musc... | Blount's | | W | Pt. Dec. '77 |
| Taylor, Joseph, Pt..... | " | | 2½ yrs. | Dischgd 30 Jan. '79 |
| Truelock, Sutton, Pt.... | " | 12 Aug. '76 | 3 yrs. | |

| Name and Rank | Company | Dates of Enlistment and Commission | Period of Service | Occurrences |
|---|---|---|---|---|
| Trainer, Arthur, Sergt... | Darnal's | 15 Nov. '76 | W | Omtd Sep. '77. Mustd Pt. Jan. '78. Pris. 1 June '79 |
| Thompson, Goodwin, Pt. | " | '77 | 3 yrs. | Died 22 Aug. '77 |
| Tyson, Jas., Corpl..... | Alderson's | 9 Dec '76 | " | |
| Tyson, Henry, Corpl.... | " | " " | " | Pt. June '78 Dischgd 30 Jan. '80 |
| Tharp, Bishop, Pt...... | " | '77 | " | Omtd Mar. '78 |
| Talton, Wm., Pt........ | Coleman's | " | 2½ yrs. | Omtd Jan. '78 |
| V   (P. 1177) | | | | |
| Verrier, Jas., Adj't..... | | 1 Oct. '76 | | Ensn. 20 Aug. '77. Lt. June '78. Resigned Nov. 22, '78 |
| Vance, David, Pt...... | Williams' | 29 Apr. " | 2½ yrs. | Dischgd 10 Nov. '78 |
| Vance, Elijah, Pt...... | " | 12 May " | " | Dischgd 10 Nov. '78 |
| W   (P. 1183) | | | | |
| Watson, Robt., Pt..... | Stedman's | 16 May '76 | W | Destd 20 Apr. '79 |
| Williams, P. Jno. Capt.. | | 10 Apr. " | | Omtd Jan. '78 |
| West, Joseph, Sergt..... | Williams' | 12 May " | 2½ yrs. | Pt. Nov. '77. Sergt. Jan.'78. Pt. 20 May '78. Dischgd Oct. '78 |
| Whitley, Arthur, Pt.... | " | 2 May " | " | Dischgd 10 Nov. '78 |
| Whitley, Wm., Pt...... | " | '77 | " | Died 2 Nov. '77 |
| Williams, Thos., Pt.... | " | " " | " | Died 20 July '77 |
| Watson, Mich'l, Pt..... | Caswell's | 26 Nov. " | 3 yrs. | |
| Williamson, Chas., Pt... | " | " " | " | Pris. 1 June '79 |
| Williams, Thos., Pt.... | " | " | 2½ yrs. | Omtd June '78 |
| Wamble, Benj'n, Pt.... | " | 16 Apr. '76 | " | Dischgd 10 Nov. '78 |
| Wilcox, Geo., Corpl..... | Blount's | | 3 yrs. | Died 4 Nov. '77 |
| Warner, Jno., Pt........ | " | 6 Apr. " | 2½ yrs. | Dischgd Oct. '78 |
| Williams, Sam'l, Musc.. | Darnal's | 10 Nov. " | W | Pt. June '78 |
| White, Malachi, Pt..... | " | '77 | | Omtd July '79 Mustd Nov. '79 |
| Webb, Joseph, Pt...... | " | " | | Omtd Feb. '78 |
| Ward, Job, Pt......... | " | " | | Omtd Feb. '78 |
| Wiley, Stephen, Pt...... | " | " | 2½ yrs. | Omtd Sep. '77 |
| Woolard, Jesse, Pt..... | " | " | W | Pris. 1 June '79. Mustd Nov. '79. Mustd 27 Mar. '80 |
| Warren, Edw'd, Pt...... | " | " | | |
| Warren, Wm., Pt...... | " | | 2½ yrs. | Dischgd Apr. '78 |
| White, Dan'l, Musc..... | Enloe's | | 3 yrs. | Pt. Oct. '77. Musc. Jan. '78. Pt. Apr. '78. Dischgd 10 Nov. '78 |
| Wiggins, Thos, Pt...... | " | | " | Died 27 Apr. '78 |
| Wood, Jno., Sergt...... | Alderson's | 20 Oct. '76 | " | |
| Weat, Nath'l, Pt........ | " | '77 | " | Dead 30 Nov. '77 |
| Williamson, Jno., Pt.... | " | " | 2½ yrs. | Omtd Feb. '78 |
| Willson, Wm., Pt....... | " | " | 3 yrs. | Omtd Feb. '78 |
| Williams, Elisha, Pt..... | " | 18 Dec '76 | " | Dischgd 20 May '79 |
| Woesley, Bryan, Pt..... | " | 15 Apr. '77 | " | |
| Williamson, Robt., Pt... | " | " | | Omtd Feb. '78 |
| Wise, Jno., Pt......... | Coleman's | " | 2½ yrs. | Omtd Jan. '78 Mustd Corpl. Jan. '79 |
| Ward, Thos., Pt........ | " | " | W | Destd 22 July '77 |
| Warren, Zebn., Musc.... | | | " | Died 15 Feb. '78 |

## 6TH REGIMENT—COL. GIDEON LAMB

| Name and Rank | Company | Dates of Enlistment and Commission | Period of Service | Occurrences |
|---|---|---|---|---|
| **A** (P. 1005) | | | | |
| Ashe, John B., Maj..... | | 26 Jan '77 | | Lt. Col. 2 Nov. '78 |
| Arthur, Wm., Sergt..... | Taylor's | " | 2½ yrs. | Destd 25 Aug. '77 |
| Adams, Eze'cl, Pt....... | Donohoe's | " | " | Destd 25 Aug. '77 |
| Alexander, Levy, Pt..... | " | " | " | Dead Aug. '77 |
| Adkinson, Jno., Corpl... | White's | 24 Apr. '76 | " | {Pt. June '78 / Omtd Nov. '78 |
| Armstrong, Andrew, Lt.. | McRees' | 19 Sep. " | | Omtd Dec. '77 |
| **B** (P. 1014) | | | | |
| Beausnaut, Jos., Sergt... | Donohoe's | 1777 | 2½ yrs. | Omtd Jan. '78 |
| Burus, Sterral, Pt....... | " | " | W | Destd Aug. '77 |
| Barker, Jesse, Pt........ | " | " | " | Dest Aug. '77 |
| Barker, Dan'l, Pt...... | " | " | " | Dest Aug. '77 |
| Barnes, Hez'l, Pt...... | " | 16 Apr. '76 | 2½ yrs. | {Corpl. Sep. '77 / Dischgd 10 Nov. '78 |
| Burges, Joseph......... | " | '77 | | Dead Aug. '77 |
| Braunon, Jos., Pt...... | White's | 15 Apr. '76 | 3 yrs. | {Sergt. Nov. '77. Pt. Sep. / '78. Dischgd 17 May '79 |
| Brown, Jos., Pt........ | " | 8 May " | " | Dischgd 10 May '79 |
| Baker, Wm., Pt........ | " | 26 Jan. " | " | Dischgd 1 Apr. '79 |
| Burnsides, David, Sergt. | Doherty's | | | Omtd Jan. '78 |
| Brantley, Jno., Pt...... | " | 1 May '76 | " | Dischgd Nov. '78 |
| Belsire, Thos., Pt....... | " | | W | {Missing 4 Oct. '77 / Mustd July '78 |
| Blount, Jno., Pt........ | " | | " | Dead 24 Jan. '78 |
| Berry, Robt., Pt........ | " | '77 | " | Omtd July '79 |
| Blanks, Nich'ls, Pt..... | " | 2 May '76 | " | Dischgd 10 Nov. '78 |
| Boyd, Jno., Sergt...... | McRees' | '77 | | {P. C. June '77 / Sergt. Nov. '79 |
| Brees, Thos., Pt........ | Child's | 2 May " | 3 yrs. | {Corpl. Feb. '78 / Pt. June '78 |
| **C** (P. 1030) | | | | |
| Caffield, Benj., Adj..... | | 17 May '77 | | Omtd Jan. '78 |
| Cheesborough, Jno., P. Ner............. | | 3 July " | | {Ensn. 23 Apr. '79 / Omtd July '79 |
| Cook, Jno., Corpl...... | Taylor's | " | 2½ yrs. | Omtd Nov. '78 |
| Cummings, Geo., Sergt.. | Donoho's | 16 Apr. '76 | " | {Pt. Dec. '77. Sergt. Mar. / '78. Pt. Oct. '78. Dischgd / 3 Nov. '79 |
| Campbell, Wm., Corpl. . | " | '77 | W | Died Feb. '80 |
| Carter, Jno., Sergt..... | " | 25 June '76 | " | Dischgd 16 May '79 |
| Casidy, Jno., Pt........ | " | '77 | 2½ yrs. | Died 28 Jan. '78 |
| Carter, Jno., Jr. Pt..... | " | " | W | |
| Craft, Stephen, Pt...... | " | " | 2½ yrs. | Omtd Jan. '78 |
| Craft, Jas., Pt......... | " | " | " | Omtd Jan. '78 |
| Cleaner, Jacob, Sergt.... | White's | 6 May '76 | " | {Pt. May '78 / Dischgd 20 Oct. '78 |
| Cates, Mathew, Pt...... | " | 30 June " | " W | |
| Conver, Jno., Pt....... | " | 15 Aug. " | " | Time Out Feb. '80 |
| Craig, Gerald, Sergt..... | Doherty's | 24 May " | " | {Pt. June '78 / Omtd Oct. '78 |
| Carter, Hibbard, Pt..... | " | | W | Died 11 Apr. '78 |
| Carroll, Wm., Pt...... | " | | " | Omtd Jan. '78 |
| Campbell, Jno., Pt..... | " | | " | Omtd Feb. '78 |

| Name and Rank | Company | Dates of Enlistment and Commission | Period of Service | Occurrences |
|---|---|---|---|---|
| Claben, Chas., Pt...... | Doherty's | | W | Missing 11 Sep. '77 |
| Clarke, Neil, Pt........ | McRee's | | | Omtd June '78 |
| Craige, Arch'd, Pt...... | " | | | Killed 4 Oct. '77 |
| Corinth, Wm.......... | " | Oct. '77 | " | Died 27 Feb. '78 |
| Collins, Math'w, Pt..... | " | " | " | Dischgd 4 June '78 |
| Childs, Francis, Capt.... | | 26 Jan. " | | {Returned from Service {Jan. '81 |
| **D** (P. 1042) | | | | |
| Davis, Granville, Sergt.. | Taylor's | 22 Apr. '76 | 2½ yrs. | {Pt. Aug. '78 {Omtd Sep. '78 |
| Davis, Arch'd, Pt...... | " | | " | Omtd Feb. '78 |
| Douglas, Jno., Pt...... | " | | W | Omtd Feb. '77 |
| Donoho, Thos., Capt.... | | 10 Sep. " | | {Maj. 13 Oct. '81 {Deranged 1 Jan. '83 |
| Dudley, Thos., Musc.... | Donoho's | '77 | W | {Omtd Jan. '78. See him {forward as Lt. |
| Dixon, Henry, Pt...... | " | | 2½ yrs. | Died Aug. '77 |
| Davis, Cyrus, Corpl..... | " | 29 Apr. '76 | " | {Pt. June '78 {Dischgd 9 Sep. '78 |
| Davis, Sam'l, Musc..... | White's | " | " | {Corpl. Nov. '77 {Omtd Jan. '78 |
| Dowling, Dennis, Pt.... | " | " | " | Omtd Nov. '77 |
| Doherty, Geo. Capt..... | | 28 Oct. '76 | | {Promoted May 17 July {'82. Deranged 1 Jan. '83 |
| Dickenson, Rich'd, Ensn.............. | Doherty's | 2 Apr. '77 | | {Lt. 10 Oct. '77. Dismissed {Service 20 Nov. '79 |
| Dudley, Geo., Corpl..... | " | " | | Dischgd 27 Oct. '77 |
| Dixon, Chas., Ensn..... | McRees' | 2 Apr. " | | {P. M. 19 Jan. '78.do 8 Feb {'79. Deranged 1 Jan. '83 |
| Davis, Wm., Pt........ | White's | " | 2½ yrs. | {Destd May '78. Mustd {5th Reg. Dischgd Apr.'79 |
| Dennis, Abner, Pt...... | Williams' | " | " | Died Sep. '78 |
| Dennis, Wm., Pt...... | " | 16 Apr. '76 | " | Dischgd 10 Nov. '78 |
| Desern, Fred'k, Pt..... | Childs' | '77 | W | Dischgd 20 Jan. '80 |
| Dixon, Jno., Pt........ | " | " | 3 yrs. | Omtd Sep. '78 |
| Dixon, Joel, Pt........ | " | 2 June " | " | |
| **E** (P. 1051) | | | | |
| Ellis, Jno., Pt.......... | Donoho's | '77 | W | Destd Aug. '77 |
| Evans, Thos., Pt....... | White's | Oct. " | 2½ yrs. | Died 30 Apr. '78 |
| Elkins, Josh, Corpl...... | Doherty's | | W | Missing 4 Oct. '77 |
| Elkins, Shad'k, Musc.... | " | 23 Mar. " | " | {Pt. June '78 {Destd 1 Jan. '80 |
| Edwards, John, Corpl... | Childs' | " | | Omtd Feb. '78 |
| **F** (P. 1057) | | | | |
| Franklin John, Fife Maj. | | 1 July '77 | | {Omtd Mch. '78, Musc. {Nov.'79,Destd 11 Dec.'79 |
| Freeman, Nath'l, Corpl.. | Doherty's | 1777 | W | Pt. Jan. '78 |
| Forrester, Thos., Pt..... | McRees' | " | | Killed 4 Oct. '77 |
| Flinn, David, Pt....... | Childs' | " | 3 yrs. | Destd Sep. '78 |
| Farrow, Thos., Pt...... | " | " | | Died 8 Feb. '78 |
| **G** (P. 1065) | | | | |
| Griffin, Robt., S. Maj... | | 15 May '77 | | Omtd Nov. '78 |
| Goodin, Chris'n., Lt..... | Taylor's | 19 Sep. '76 | | {Omtd Jan.'78, Mustd.Jan. {'79 as Capt. in 5 Reg. |
| Goodman, Sam'l, Corpl.. | " | 12 May " | 2½ yrs. | {Pt. June '78, Corpl. Sep. {'78, Omtd Nov. '78 |

| Name and Rank | Company | Dates of Enlistment and Commission | Period of Service | Occurrences |
|---|---|---|---|---|
| Gouch, Jno., Pt........ | Taylor's | | W | |
| Gouch, Wm, Pt....... | " | | " | Omtd Feb. '78 |
| Garland, Humphy, Pt... | " | | | Omtd Jan. '78 |
| Green Wm., Lt........ | " | 28 Oct. " | | Omtd Sep. '78 |
| Gibson, Wm., Musc.... | " | 6 May '77 | W | {Pt. Apr. '78, <br> Omtd June '78 |
| Gilbert, Peter, Pt...... | Donoho's | | " | Destd Aug. '77 |
| Griffin, Jas., Pt........ | " | | " | Destd Aug. '77 |
| Geary, Geo., Pt........ | " | 16 Apr. '76 | " | Dischg 10 Nov. '78 |
| Geary, Josh, Pt........ | " | '77 | 2½ yrs. | Dead Aug. '77 |
| Grant, Wm., Pt........ | " | " | " | Dead Aug. '77 |
| Garvy, Mathew, Pt..... | Doherty's | " | W | Dead Mar. '78 |
| Godfrey, Clemt., Pt.... | " | 18 Dec. '76 | W | |
| Gunn, Alexr., Sergt..... | McRees' | '77 | " | Omtd Jan. '78 |
| Gordon, Alexr., Pt..... | " | " | " | Destd 10 Jan. '80 |
| Godfrey, Wm., Pt..... | " | " | " | {Omtd Jan.'78, Mustd <br> Corpl. Jan.'79, 5 Reg. for <br> 3 yrs. |
| Grissom, Robt., Musc... | Childs' | 1 June '76 | 3 yrs. | {Pt. Oct. '78, <br> Destd 6 June '79 |
| Garvey, Thos., Pt..... | " | 2 " " | W | |
| **H (P. 1076)** | | | | |
| Hyman, Joseph, Pt..... | Taylor's | 1777 | W | Omtd June '78 |
| Harris, John, Pt....... | " | " | " | Omtd Nov. '77 |
| Hopkins, Richd., Pt.... | " | 9 May '76 | 2½ yrs. | Omtd Nov. '78 |
| Hadley, Joshua, Lt..... | " | 1 Apr. '77 | | Capt. 13 June '79 |
| Hubbard, Elisha, Sergt.. | " | Nov. '77 | W | Omtd Dec. '77 |
| Herbert, Wm., Sergt.... | Donoho's | " | " | {Omtd Jan. '78, Mustd <br> Jan. '79 in 4 Reg. |
| Hadnot, West, Sergt.... | " | " | " | {Pt. Nov. '77, <br> Omtd Nov. '78 |
| Hurley, Wm., Corpl..... | " | " | 2½ yrs.. | Omtd Feb. '78 |
| Hammonds, Edw., Corp. | " | " | W | Destd Aug. '77 |
| Howard, Wm., Pt....... | " | " | 2½ yrs. | Destd Aug. '77 |
| Haycraft, Mark, Pt..... | " | " | " | Destd Aug. '77 |
| Haslip, Chas., Pt...... | " | " | " | Omtd Sep. '77 |
| Huggin, Jeff, Pt........ | " | " | " | Omtd Sep. '77 |
| Hopkins, Isaac, Pt..... | " | " | " | {Destd Aug. '77, Mustd <br> Feb. '79 in 5 Reg. |
| Hammond, Judah, Pt... | " | " | " | Dead Aug. '77 |
| Hudson, Thos., Sergt.... | " | " | " | Died 3 Apr. '78 |
| Hurt, Wm., Pt........ | " | " | " | Killed 4 Oct. '77 |
| Hilton, Wm., Lt........ | White's | 1 Apr. '77 | | {Omtd June '78, Mustd <br> Jan. '79 in 5 Reg. |
| Hart, Sm'l, Musc...... | " | 6 May " | 2½ yrs. | {Pt. July '78, <br> Omtd Nov. '78 |
| Hewings, Thos., Pt..... | " | " | 3 yrs. | Omtd Oct. '77 |
| Hicks, Henry, Pt....... | " | " | 2½ yrs. | Dead Dec. '77 |
| Higgins, Thos., Pt..... | Doherty's | " | W | Died 27 Mar. '78 |
| Humphreys, Randle, Pt.. | McRees' | " | " | |
| Hewet, Ebenezer, Pt.... | " | 2 Apr. " | " | |
| Harris, Goodman, Pt.... | Williams' | 9 May '76 | 2½ yrs. | Dischgd 10 Nov. '78 |
| Hays, Thos., Pt....... | " | 9 May " | 3 yrs. | Dischgd 10 Nov. '78 |
| Higgins, Peter, Pt..... | " | '77 | 2½ yrs. | Died 24 Mar. '78 |
| Hancock, Wm., Lt..... | Pikes' | 28 Apr. " | | Resigned 28 Aug. '77 |

| Name and Rank | Company | Dates of Enlistment and Commission | Period of Service | Occurrences |
|---|---|---|---|---|
| Hopkins, Isaac, Pt...... | Pikes' | 10 May '77 | 3 yrs. | Omtd Jan. '78, Mustd Jan. '79 |
| J (P. 1090) | | | | |
| Johnson, Jos., Qr. Mast. | | 2 Apr. '77 | | Omtd Jan. '78 |
| Jones, Sam'l, Lt........ | Donoho's | 1 Jan. " | | Died July '78 (There appears to be two of the same name, one promoted to Capt. in '81. See Ford |
| Jameson, Thos., Pt..... | White's | | | Omtd Nov. '78 |
| Jarvis, Thos., Sergt..... | Donoho's | | | Omtd Jan. '78 |
| Jackson, Zacka., Sergt... | " | 13 June '76 | | Trans.22 Mar.'78 to Gen'l Guards,dischgd 13 July'79 |
| Jackson, John, Pt...... | " | | | Destd 12 July '79 |
| Jones, Thos., Pt........ | " | | | Omtd Jan.'79, Mustd Jan. '79 in 5 Reg. and Destd Apr. '79 |
| Johnson, Benj., Pt..... | Williams' | 9 May " | 2½ yrs. | Dischgd 10 Nov. '78 |
| Johnson, Littleton, Sergt | Childs' | | | Omtd Feb. '78 |
| K (P. 1097) | | | | |
| Kee, Jona, Musc........ | Donoho's | 1777 | W | Pt. June '78, Dischgd 21 Aug. '78 |
| Kees, Joseph, Sergt..... | " | 5 May '76 | 2½ yrs. | Pt. Nov. '77, Time Out Nov. '78 |
| Kelly, Jas., Pt.......... | " | '77 | 3 yrs. | Died 15 Apr. '78 |
| Kelly, Edwd., Pt....... | " | " | W | |
| Kinkaid, Wm., Pt...... | Doherty's | " | 2½ yrs. | Omtd Nov. '78 |
| King, Jas., Pt.......... | Williams' | " | | |
| L (P. 1103) | | | | |
| Lamb, Gideon, Col..... | | 26 Jan '77 | | Retired from Service Jan. 1781 |
| Little, Arch'd, Lt. Col.. | | " | | Not Mustd from Jan. '78, till 7 Nov. '82 |
| Little, Wm., Lt........ | Taylor's | 16 Apr. '76 | | Capt. Jan. 28th '79 |
| Loyd, Thos., Sergt...... | Donoho's | 1777 | 2½ yrs. | Omtd Jan. '78 |
| Later, Ambroze, Pt..... | " | " | " | Destd Aug. '77 |
| Lock, Wm., Pt......... | " | " | " | Died 22 May '78 |
| Leathers, Moses, Pt..... | White's | 27 Apr. '76 | " | Omtd Nov. '78 |
| Legar, Jas., Pt......... | Doherty's | 11 Dec. '" | 3 yrs. | Omtd Nov. '79 |
| Laws, Jno., Pt.......... | " | | 2½ yrs. | Sergt. Feb. '78, Died 7 Mar. '78 |
| Lott, Geo., Pt.......... | " | | W | |
| Landus, Jno., Pt....... | McRees' | | " | |
| Liscombe, Jno., Ensn.... | Williams' | 28 Apr. '77 | | Omtd Jan. '78 |
| M (P. 1112) | | | | |
| Mixom, Chas., Ensn.... | Taylor's | 2 Apr. '77 | | Omtd Sep. '77 |
| McElroy, Wm., Pt..... | " | | W | Omtd Aug. '78 |
| Morse, Farrell, Pt..... | " | | 2½ yrs. | Died 13 Mar. '78 |
| Moore, Dempsey, Lt.... | Donoho's | 28 Oct. '76 | | Omtd Sep. '77 |
| McIntire, Wm., Pt..... | " | '77 | W | |
| McDowel, David, Pt.... | " | " | 2½ yrs. | Omtd Jan. '78 |
| Mallery, Levy......... | " | " | W | Destd 10 Oct. '78 |
| Medows, Abm., Pt..... | " | " | | Destd 18 Feb. '80 |
| Melton, Jona, Pt...... | " | 16 Apr. '76 | 2½ yrs. | Dischgd 10 Nov. '78 |
| Morton, W............ | " | | " | Destd Aug. '77 |
| Morgan, John.......... | White's | 26 Apr. " | | Dischgd 10 May '79 |
| Mount, Rich'd, Pt..... | " | 31 May " | | Omtd Mar. '79 |
| McCann, John, Lt...... | Doherty's | 1 Jan. '77 | | Killed 4 Oct. '77 |

| Name and Rank | Company | Dates of Enlistment and Commission | Period of Service | Occurrences |
|---|---|---|---|---|
| McDonald, Arthur, Pt... | Doherty's | '77 | W | Corpl. 1 Dec.'78, Pt. '82 |
| McBride, Duncan, Pt... | " | " | 2½ yrs. | {Corpl. Nov. '77, Omtd Nov. '78 |
| McCoy, Dan'l......... | " | | W | |
| McDonald, Hugh, Pt.... | " | | 2½ yrs. | Omtd Nov. '78 |
| McDonald, Alex'r, Pt... | " | | 3 yrs. | {Corpl. 20 May '79, Time Out Jan. '80 |
| McRee, J. Griffith, Capt. | " | 16 Apr. '76 | | {Pris.'81, Exchgd Mar.'81, Major 11 Sep. '81 |
| McCoy, John, Pt...... | McRee's | '77 | W | |
| McFalter, Dan'l, Pt.... | " | " | | {Destd 17 May '78, Mustd '81 |
| McDonald, Malcolm, Pt. | " | " | | Omtd June '78 |
| N (P. 1125) | | | | |
| Nelson, Robt., Qr. Mster Sergt..... | | 1 Jan. '77 | | Omtd Jan. '78 |
| Noble, Wm., Sergt..... | Donoho's | " | 2½ yrs. | {Omtd Jan. '78, Mustd '79 in 4 Reg. |
| Norkell, Wm., Pt...... | McRees' | " | W | Destd 1 Nov. '77 |
| O (P. 1129) | | | | |
| Owens, Daniel, Pt..... | Donoho's | '77 | 2½ yrs. | Destd Aug. '77 |
| Owen, David, Pt...... | McRees' | " | " | Died 28 Apr. '78 |
| Owen, Francis, Pt..... | " | " | " | Omtd Nov. '78 |
| P (P. 1135) | | | | |
| Pendleton, Edmund, Sgt. | Taylor's | 1777 | 2½ yrs. | Omtd Feb. '78 |
| Parker, Jesse, Pt....... | " | 26 Apr. '76 | W | {Corpl. Jan. '79, Mustd Sergt. Nov. '79 |
| Pendergrass, David, Pt.. | " | 30 Apr. " | 2½ yrs. | Dischgd 10 Nov. '78 |
| Perry, Jno., Pt........ | " | | " | Omtd Sep. '77 |
| Prescott, Willoughby,Pt. | Donoho's | | 3 yrs. W | |
| Perry, Jno............ | " | 16 Apr. " | 3 yrs. | Dischgd 10 Nov. '78 |
| Pierson, Thos......... | " | | 2½ yrs. | Omtd Sep. '77 |
| Pitchet, Oliver........ | " | | " | Destd Aug. '77 |
| Pierce, Theops......... | White's | | 3 yrs. | Died 21 May '78 |
| Potter, Dan'l.......... | Doherty's | | W | {Corpl. Nov. '77, Sergt. May '78, Dischgd 21 Mar. '79 |
| Parker, Keder, Lt...... | McRees' | 19 Sep. " | | {Omtd Dec. '77, Mustd Jan. '79 in 4 Reg. |
| Pevier, Jas., Pt........ | " | '77 | W | Omtd June '78 |
| Pike, Benj., Capt...... | | 28 Apr. " | | Died 11 Oct. '77 |
| Potterfield, Dennis, Lt. . | Childs' | 2 Apr. " | | {Omtd Jan.'78, Mustd Jan. '79 in 5 Reg., Capt. 1 Feb. '79 |
| Pritchard, Jese, Sergt. .. | " | " | | Died Feb. '78 |
| Perry, Wm., Pt........ | " | " | | Died 13 Mar. '78 |
| Plumpus, Tinity, Pt..... | " | " | | Omtd Nov. '77 |
| R (P. 1145) | | | | |
| Richards, Jacob, Pt..... | White's | 1777 | 2½ yrs. | {Sergt. Oct., Sergt. Majr. Nov. '77, Omtd Jan. '78 |
| Riggin, Jno., Pt........ | Taylor's | " | W | Omtd June '78 |
| Rochester, Nich's, Pt.... | " | " | 2½ yrs. | Omtd Sep. '77 |
| Rochester, Wm., Pt.... | " | 10 May '76 | " | {Omtd Sep.'77, Mustd Sep. '78, Dischgd 21 Mar. '79 |
| Ramsey, Wm., Pt...... | " | " | " | Destd Aug. '77 |
| Rose, Jno., Pt......... | " | " | " | Destd Aug. '77 |

| Name and Rank | Company | Dates of Enlistment and Commission | Period of Service | Occurrences |
|---|---|---|---|---|
| Robb, Wm., Corpl...... | White's | 24 Apr. '76 | 2½ yrs. | {Pt. Nov. '77, Omtd Nov. '78 |
| Roberts, Reuben, Pt.... | " |  | 3 yrs. | Omtd June '78 |
| Robertson, Jese, Pt.... | " | 24 Sep. " | " | Omtd Nov. '79 |
| Robertson, Edw'd, Pt... | Doherty's |  |  | {Sergt. Feb, Died 8 May '78 |
| Ray, Benj'n, Pt....... | " |  | W |  |
| Rule, Jas., Pt......... | " |  | " | Missing 4 Oct. '77 |
| Russell, Jno., Pt....... | Williams' | " | " | Omtd Feb. '78 |
| S   (P. 1156) |  |  |  |  |
| Shores, David, Pt....... | Taylor's | 9 May '76 | 2½ yrs. | Omtd Nov. '77 |
| Smith, Jno., Pt........ | " |  | W | Omtd Sep. '78 |
| Seagrove, Jno., Pt..... | " | 7 May " | 2½ yrs. | Omtd Nov. '78 |
| Saunders, Wm., Ensn. .. | Donoho's | 2 Apr. '77 |  | {Lt. 8 Feb. '79, Deranged 1 Jan. '83 |
| Stranges, Jas., Musc. ... | " |  | W | Pt. June '78 |
| Scanthen, Wm., Pt...... | " |  | 2½ yrs. | Omtd Nov. '78 |
| Sharp, Benj'n, Pt....... | White's | 13 May '76 | 3 yrs. W | Sergt. Sep. '78, Pt. '82 |
| Sutherland, Jno., Pt..... | " |  | 2½ yrs. | Omtd Oct. '77 |
| Staples, Robt., Musc.... | Doherty's |  | W | {Omtd Jan.'78, Mustd Jan. '79 in 5 Reg. |
| Stevenson, Benj'n, Pt... | " |  | " | Died Feb. '79 |
| Smith, Thos., Pt....... | " |  | " | Omtd Jan. '78 |
| Sawyer, Thos., Pt...... | " | 24 Apr. '77 | 3 yrs. | Destd 6 Feb. '80 |
| (P. 1157) |  |  |  |  |
| Smith, Job, Pt........ | " |  | W | {Sergt. Sep. '77, Omtd Jan. '78 |
| Simpson, Benj., Pt..... | " |  |  | Omtd Apr. '78 |
| Slaven, Sam'l, Musc..... | McRees' |  | " | Died 15 Apr. '78 |
| Sellers, Dan'l, Pt...... | " |  | " |  |
| Stafford, Jno., Pt...... | " |  | 2½ yrs. | Omtd Nov. '78 |
| Shaw, Dan'l, Ensn...... | Williams' | 2 Apr. '77 |  | {2 Lt. 11 Oct.'77, Qr. Mr. 1 June '78, Deranged 1 Jan. '83 |
| T   (P. 1170) |  |  |  |  |
| Taylor, Philip, Capt. ... |  | 16 Apr. '76 |  | {Omtd June '78, Mustd '79 in 5 Reg. |
| Thomas, Philip, Pt...... | Taylor's |  | W | Omtd Sep. '77 |
| Tilley, Avery, Pt....... | Donoho's |  | 2½ yrs. | Destd Aug. '77 |
| Thomas, Rich'd, Pt..... | White's |  | " | Dischgd 7 June '78 |
| Thurnell, Jno., Pt...... | Doherty's |  | W | Dead Nov. '78 |
| Terrall, Richmond, Pt... | McRees' |  | " |  |
| V   (P. 1178) |  |  |  |  |
| Vickory, Henry, Pt..... | Taylor's | '77 | 2½ yrs. | Died 18 June '77 |
| Vanpelt, Peter, Pt...... | Donoho's | " | " | Destd Aug. '77 |
| Vowells, Wm., Pt....... | White's | 1 May '76 | 3 yrs. W |  |
| W   (P. 1184) |  |  |  |  |
| Wilson, Robt., Surgn.... |  | 16 Apr. '76 |  | Died 28 Oct. '77 |
| West, Levey, Musc..... | Donoho's | '77 |  | {Dr. Maj. Sep. '77, Omtd Jan. '78 |
| Wood, Chas., Pt........ | Taylor's | " | W | Corpl. May '79, Pt. '82 |
| Weatherspoon, Laure,Pt. | " | " |  | Destd 5 July '77 |
| Williams, Theo., Ensn... | " | 2 Apr. " |  | Omtd Jan '78 |
| Waid, And'w, Pt....... | " | 25 Apr. '76 | 2½ yrs. | Omtd Nov. '78 |
| Williams, Sol'n, Corpl... | Donoho's | 1777 | " | Omtd Sep. '77 |
| Ward, Jas., Pt........ | " | " | W | Destd Aug. '77 |
| Waters, Jno., Pt....... | " | " | 2½ yrs. | Destd Aug. '77 |

| Name and Rank | Company | Dates of Enlistment and Commission | Period of Service | Occurrences |
|---|---|---|---|---|
| Weeks, Silas, Pt....... | Donoho's | '77 | 2½ yrs. | Died 22 May '78 |
| Weeks, Levy, Pt........ | " | 3 May '76 | " | Dischgd 10 Nov. '78 |
| Weeks, Theophilus, Pt. . | " | " | " | Destd Aug. '77, Mustd Jan.'78, Dischgd 10 Nov. '78 |
| Windslow, Silvester, Pt.. | " | '77 | | Destd Aug. '77 |
| White, Thos., Capt..... | " | 20 Jan. " | | Omtd Jan. '78, Mustd in '79, 5 Reg. |
| Woodman, Edwd., Pt... | White's | 18 Apr. '76 | 2½ yrs. | Omtd Nov. '78 |
| Warren, Mathew, Pt.... | " | | 3 yrs. | Died 9 Feb. '78 |
| Webley, Sam'l, Pt..... | Doherty's | | W | Died 8 Dec. '77 |
| Williams, Geo., Corpl. .. | " | 28 June " | 2½ yrs. | Pt. June '78, Dischgd 14 Jan. '79 |
| White, Jno., Sergt...... | McRees' | '77 | " | Died 6 Jan. '78 |
| Walker, Moses, Pt..... | " | Oct. " | " | Omtd Feb. '78 |
| Williamson, Dan'l, Capt. | | 1 Apr. " | | Omtd Jan. '79, Mustd Jan. '79 |
| White, Mathew, Lt..... | Williams' | '77 | | Omtd Nov. '77 |
| Walker, Solomon, Lt.... | Pikes' | 28 Apr. " | | Resigned 28 Aug. '77 |
| Williamson, Geo., Pt.... | Childs' | " | W | Destd 3 Sep. '78 |
| Weeks, Cornes, Sergt.... | " | " | 3 yrs. | Omtd Dec. '77, Say dischgd Apr. '79 |
| **Y**   (P. 1194) | | | | |
| Yates, John, Pt......... | White's | | 2½ yrs. | Omtd Feb. '78 |
| Young, Isaac, Pt...... | Childs' | | " | Died Feb. 13th '78 |
| Young, Wm., Pt....... | " | | " | Died Feb 13th '78 |
| Yarborough, Rich'd, Pt. | Montfort's | 20 July '78 | 9 mo. | |
| Yoeman, Harris, Pt..... | Quinn's | " | " | |
| Yates, Sam'l, Pt....... | Ballard's | " | " | |
| Yet, Jas., Pt.......... | " | | | See Jas. Jew |
| Young, Jno., Pt....... | " | 1779 | 3 yrs. | |
| Yates, Wm., Pt........ | McRees' | 9 May '81 | | Omtd Aug. '81 Sick |
| Yewman, Christ'r, Pt. .. | Donoho's | 25 " " | 12 mo. | See Ewman Waltons Co. |
| Yarborough, David, Pt.. | Bailey's | 18 June '82 | " | |
| Yates, Thos., Pt........ | Bacot's | 1782 | 18 mo. | |
| Yordon, Philip, Pt..... | Carter's | " | " | |
| Yoeman, Harris, Pt..... | Raiford's | " | " | Destd 11 June '83 |
| Young, Mich'l, Pt..... | Sharp's | " | " | |
| Yates, David, Pt....... | Lytle's | " | " | |
| Yarborough, Jas., Pt.... | | | | Mustd dead 1779 |

### 7TH REGIMENT—COL. JAMES HOGUN

| Name and Rank | Company | Dates of Enlistment and Commission | Period of Service | Occurrences |
|---|---|---|---|---|
| **A**   (P.1077) | | | | |
| Archer, Dempsey, Pt.... | Ely's | Nov. '77 | 3 yrs. | Dead 14 Feb. '78 |
| Alexander, Benj., Pt.... | Walker's | " | " | Dischgd 27 Feb. '80 |
| Alsworth, Joseph, Pt.... | | " | " | Destd 17 Sep. '77 |
| Ames, John, Pt......... | McGlanhan's | " | " | Died 15 Nov. '77 |
| Ames, Thos., Pt....... | " | 1 Feb. " | " | Destd 12 Feb. '79 |
| Anderson, William, ..... | " | " | " | Destd Apr. '77 |
| **B**   (Pp. 1014-15) | | | | |
| Bryan, John, Musc...... | McGlanhan's | '77 | 3 yrs. | Destd Aug. '77 |
| Brewster, Lott, Majr.,.. | | 24 Nov. '76 | | Lt. Col. 25 Oct. '77 in 3rd Reg. |
| Beeks, Wm., Maj. Sergt. | | '77 | | Adj't. Dec. '77 |
| Brickall, Mathias " " | | Dec. " | | Omtd Jan. '78 |

| Name and Rank | Company | Dates of Enlistment and Commission | Period of Service | Occurrences |
|---|---|---|---|---|
| Brewer, Benj., Pt....... | Dawson's | '77 | 3 yrs. | Dead 25 Oct. '77 |
| Bennet, Jas., Pt........ | " | | " | Dead July '77 |
| Brown, Thos., Pt....... | " | | " | Destd Apr. '77 |
| Brickell, Thos., Capt.... | " | 28 Nov. '76 | " | Omtd Jan. '78 |
| Brickell, Mathew, Sergt. | Brickell's | 8 Dec. " | 3 yrs. | Omtd Jan. '78 |
| Bryant, Jno., Sergt...... | " | 28 Jan. '77 | | Omtd Oct. '77 |
| Branton, Eph'm, Pt..... | " | " | W | {Corpl. Oct. '77, Died 12 Mar. '78 |
| Barker, Jas., Pt........ | " | " | " | Destd July '77 |
| Burnham, Jesse, Pt..... | " | " | " | Destd Apr. '77 |
| Bush, Wm., Pt........ | | " | W | Destd Apr. '77 |
| Baker, Jno., Lt......... | Walker's | 28 Nov.'76 | | {Capt. to July '77, and P. Mr. June '78, Omtd '79 |
| Brown, Benj., Corpl..... | " | '77 | 3 yrs. | Died Feb. '78 |
| Bryan, Jno............. | " | " | " | Destd 17 Sep. '77 |
| Bennett, Jas., Pt........ | " | " | " | Died 26 Jan. '76 |
| Barho, Thos., Corpl..... | Poynter's | 10 Jan. " | " | {Pt. Jan. '78, Corpl. June '78, Destd 11 Dec. '79 |
| Barlow, Christ, Pt...... | " | 19 Dec. '76 | " | Omtd Feb. '78 |
| Bartley, Henry, Pt...... | " | 13 Mar. '77 | " | Omtd Feb. '78 |
| *Bryan, Benj., Ensn..... | McGlanhan's | 27 Apr. " | | Omtd Nov. '77 |
| Billops, Thos., Musc.... | " | 11 Mar. " | 3 yrs. | |
| (*Brickler's perhaps) | | | | |
| **C** (P. 1031) | | | | |
| Cooper, Henry, Sergt.... | McGlanhan's | 1777 | | {Qr. Mr. Sergt. 18 Dec.'77, Sergt. June '78, Qr. Mr. Sergt. 12 Feb. '79 |
| Carr, Solmn, Pt....... | " | " | 3 yrs. | Dischgd 1 Feb. '80 |
| Canstanphin, Jas., Ensn. | Dawson's | 28 Nov. '76 | | Omtd Oct. '77 |
| Cobb, Wm., Pt........ | " | '77 | " | Died Jan. 26, '78 |
| Chalco, Wm., Pt....... | Brickell's | " | W | Destd Apr. '77 |
| Crether, Jereh, Pt...... | " | " | " | Died 14 Mar. '78 |
| Carter, Wm., Pt....... | Walker's | " | 3 yrs. | Died 17 Apr. '78 |
| Conn, David, Pt..... | " | " | " | Omtd Sep. '77 |
| Chesson, Joshua, Pt.... | " | 4 Feb " | " | Dischgd 8 Feb. '80 |
| Cail, Amo, Pt......... | Vaughn's | 1 Feb. " | " | Died Dec. '77 |
| Corbin, Arthur, Pt..... | " | 2 Dec. '76 | " | Dischgd 1 Feb. '80 |
| Cooper, Jno., Pt........ | McGlanhan's | '77 | " | Died July '77 |
| Cooper, Josiah, Pt...... | " | " | " | Died 29 Nov. '77 |
| Cowan, Robt., Pt...... | | 7 Jan. " | " | {Distd Apr. '77, Mustd June '78, Corpl. Nov.'78, Sergt. Sept. '79 |
| Connor, Wm., Pt...... | " | " | " | Died 21 Apr. '78 |
| Connor, Jacob, Pt..... | " | " | " | Died 6 Feb. '78 |
| **D** (P. 1043) | | | | |
| Daws, Abrm., Adjt..... | | 22 Dec. '76 | | Resigned 22 Nov. '77 |
| Daws, Jonah, Qr. Mr.... | | 10 July '77 | | Omtd Jan. '78 |
| Duke, Buckner, Pt...... | Macon's | " | 3 yrs. | Destd Aug. '77 |
| Dawson, Hy., Capt..... | | 28 Nov. '76 | | Omtd Jan. '78 |
| Duke, Jas., Pt......... | Dawson's | 25 Dec. '77 | " | |
| Daniel, Josh, Musc...... | " | " | " | Dead July '77 |
| *Dayley, Joshua, Lt..... | Pointer's | 12 Dec. '76 | | {Capt. 12 Oct. '77, Omtd Jan. '78 |
| Dillon, Benj., Ensn..... | Walker's | 28 Nov. " | | {Lt. 12 Oct.'77, Omtd Jan. '78, Mustd 4th Reg. Feb. '79 |

| Name and Rank | Company | Dates of Enlistment and Commission | Period of Service | Occurrences |
|---|---|---|---|---|
| Davenport, Asahel, Cpl. | Walker's | '77 | 3 yrs. | Pt. Oct. '77, Omtd Dec. '77 |
| Douge, Jas., Sergt...... | Pointer's | 16 Jan " | " | Dischgd 28 Jan. '80 |
| Dailey, Jno., Sergt...... | " | 8 Jan. " | " | Pt. Jan. '78, Died Dec. 15, '78 |
| Davis, David, Pt....... | " | 15 Jan. " | " | Destd Aug. '77 |
| Doniho, Henry, Pt...... | McGlanhan's | 26 Jan. " | " | Destd Apr. '77 |
| Druge, Griffin, Corpl.... | Pointer's | May " | " | |
| Douge, Joab, Musc..... | " | 11 May " | " | |
| **E** (P. 1051) | | | | |
| Ely, Eli, Lt............ | Macon's | 11 Dec. '76 | | Capt. 12 Oct. '77, Omtd Jan. '78 |
| Ely, Leml., Capt...... | | 28 Nov. " | | Resigned 14 Feb. '78 |
| Easton, Seth, Lt....... | Brickell's | " | | Resigned Aug. '77 |
| Ellis, Wm., Pt......... | " | '77 | W | Destd Apr. '77 |
| Evans, Geo., Pt....... | Walker's | 20 Dec. '76 | 3 yrs. | Destd Aug. '77, Mustd and distd Sep. '79 |
| Eastmead, John, Pt..... | " | 1777 | " | Died Aug. '77 |
| **F** (P. 1057) | | | | |
| Fenner, Wm., Maj...... | | 25 Oct. '77 | | Omtd Sep. '78 |
| Ferrabee, Wm., Lt..... | Macon's | 28 Nov. '76 | | Capt. 1 July '81, Resigned '82 |
| Frazer, Alex'r, Sergt.... | Brickell's | 8 Dec. " | | Destd Aug. '77 |
| Fenton, Joshua, Pt..... | " | 1777 | W | Died 24 Mar. '78 |
| Forbus, Joshua, Sergt... | Walker's | " | 3 yrs. | Transf'd Apr. '78 to his X. C. L. N. C'y guards, Dischgd 18 Dec. '79 |
| Finley, Abm., Pt....... | " | 23 Dec. '76 | " | |
| Freeman, Sam'l, Pt..... | " | '77 | " | |
| Fox, Wm., Sergt....... | Pointer's | 11 Jan. " | " | Omtd May '78 |
| Ford, Elias, Pt........ | McGlanhan's | 11 Apr. " | " | Corpl. Sep. '77, Sergt. 7 Nov. '78 |
| **G** (P. 1066) | | | | |
| Ginon, Isaac, P. M..... | | 1777 | | Omtd Jan. '78 |
| Gee, Howell, Ensn...... | Macon's | 15 Apr. " | | Lt. Nov. '77, Omtd Jan. '78 |
| Gibbs, Joel, Pt........ | " | " | 3 yrs. | Mustd Nov. '77, Mtd '78 |
| Griffin, Wm., Pt........ | Dawson's | " | " | Omtd Feb. '78 |
| Garnes, Anth'y, Pt..... | Ely's | 14 July " | " | |
| Godfrey, Francis, Pt.... | Brickell's | " | W | Dead 28 Nov. '77 |
| Green, Abm., Pt....... | " | " | " | Destd Apr. '77 |
| Goodwin, Tiney,...... | " | " | 3 yrs. | Destd 25 July '77 |
| Green, Abm., Pt....... | " | " | W | Omtd Jan. '78 |
| Greenwood, Jno., Sergt.. | Walker's | " | 3 yrs. | Prisoner 11 Sep. '77 |
| Goodwin, Wm., Pt...... | | 10 Mar. " | 3 yrs. W | |
| Garrel, Jno., Sergt..... | Pointer's | 10 Jan " | 3 yrs. | Omtd Jan. '78 |
| Grandy, Obdh., Pt..... | " | 18 Jan " | " | Omtd Sep. '77 |
| Gerrel, Wm., Pt....... | " | 10 Jan. " | " | Omtd Sep. '77 |
| Griffith, Edwd, Sergt.... | Vaughn's | 28 Dec. '76 | | Died Jan. '77 |
| Griffin, Isaac, Musc.... | " | 1 Mar. '77 | 3 yrs. | Sergt. Nov. '77 |
| Gold, David, Pt....... | McGlanhan's | 7 Jan. " | " | Died Oct. '78 |
| Gideon, Lewis, Pt...... | " | " | " | Destd Apr. '77 |
| Garnes, Jeffrey, Pt..... | Ely's | Nov. " | " | Died 22 Jan. '78 |
| **H** (P. 1077) | | | | |
| Hogan, Jas., Col....... | | 24 Nov. '76 | | Omtd* between Jan. and Sep.'79, Died 4 Jan. '81 |
| Hamilton, Hanse, Surgn. | | Apr. '77 | | Died Jan. '78 |

| Name and Rank | Company | Dates of Enlistment and Commission | Period of Service | Occurrences |
|---|---|---|---|---|
| Harvey, Jas., P. M..... | | 28 Nov. '76 | | Died Oct. '77 |
| Hardison, Hardy, Q.M. Sergt.......... | | 14 Apr. '77 | | Died 18 Dec. '77 |
| Harrison, Wm., Lt...... | Mason's | 19 Dec. '76 | | Omtd Jan. '78 |
| Hays, Jas., 2nd Lt...... | Dawson's | 28 Nov. " | | Omtd Oct. '77 |
| Haynes, Chrisr., Sergt... | " | 15 Apr. '77 | 3 yrs. | Dischgd 3 Nov. '77 |
| Haynes, Bythell, Sergt. . | " | 9 Apr. " | " | Destd 17 Sep. '77 |
| Hathaway, Jno., Pt..... | " | " | " | Omtd Feb. '78 |
| Hall, Jas., Pt.......... | " | " | | Omtd Oct. '77 |
| Hobbs, Moses, Pt....... | " | " | " | Omtd Feb. '78 |
| Harrison, Jas., Sergt.... | Ely's | " | " | Died Aug. '77 |
| Howell, Fred'k, Pt..... | " | 6 Aug. " | 3 yrs. W | {Omtd July '79, Mustd Nov. '79 |
| (*Because promoted to Brig. Gen. 9 Jan. 1779) J (P. 1091) | | | | |
| Jones, Thos., Ensn...... | Macon's | 17 Apr. '77 | | {Lt. 15 Aug. '77, Resigned 17 May '78 |
| Jackson, Edwd., Pt..... | " | 29 Mar. " | 3 yrs. | Died 30 Apr. '79 |
| Jackson, Basil, Pt...... | Brickell's | " | W | |
| Jones, Wm., Pt......... | " | " | " | Destd Apr. '77 |
| Jones, Jona, Corpl..... | Pointer's | 10 Jan. " | 3 yrs. | Dischgd 29 Jan. '80 |
| Jethro, Josiah, Corpl.... | Vaughn's | 13 Feb. " | " | Omtd Jan. '78 |
| Jones, Jno., Pt........ | " | 14 Jan. " | " | Died 12 Sep. '78 |
| Josea, Wm., Pt........ | " | 2 Mar. " | " | Destd Aug. '77 |
| K (P. 1097) | | | | |
| Kilpatrick, Robt., Musc. | Dailey's | 9 Aug. '77 | 3 yrs. W | |
| L (P. 1103) | | | | |
| Lassiter, Jethro, Ensn... | Dailey's | 28 Nov. '76 | | {Lt. 12 Oct. '77, Omtd Nov. '78 |
| Linch, Jno., Lt......... | Ely's | " | | Omtd Nov. '78 |
| Laden, Thos........... | Brickell's | 11 Apr. '77 | 3 yrs. | |
| Long, Jno., Pt......... | " | " | " | Died 24 Feb. '78 |
| Lewis, Wm., Musc...... | Walker's | 19 Dec. '76 | " | Dr. Maj.'79, Dischgd '79 |
| Leftyear, Uriah, Pt..... | " | 19 Mar. '77 | 3 yrs. W | Destd 26 Mar. '79 |
| Lewis, Joshua, Pt....... | " | " | 3 yrs. | Omtd Jan. '78 |
| Love, Thos., Pt........ | Pointer's | 20 Mar. " | " | Omtd Feb. '79 |
| Lumberly, Simon, Pt.... | Vaughan's | 13 Mar. " | " | Died Feb. 78 |
| Luten, Lemuel, Corpl.... | McGlanhan's | " | " | Died Sep. '77 |
| M (P. 1113) | | | | |
| Mebane, Robt., Lt. Col. | | 24 Nov. '76 | | {Col. 9 Feb. '79, Killed Oct. '81 |
| Macon, John, Capt..... | | 12 Dec. " | | Omtd Jan. '78 |
| Moore, John, Lt........ | Ely's | 28 Nov. " | | Omtd Nov. '77 |
| Miller, John, Corpl..... | Brickell's | 1777 | W | Died 4 Mar. '78 |
| Modlin, Jereh, Pt...... | " | " | " | Omtd Feb. '78 |
| Modlin, Benj., Pt...... | " | " | " | |
| McKabe, Joshua, Pt.... | Walker's | " | 3 yrs. | Died Feb. '78 |
| Maun, Thos., Pt....... | " | 18 Dec. '76 | " | {Corpl. Mar. '79, Destd 14 Feb. '80 |
| Morrisett, Henry, Pt.... | " | '77 | " | Died 28 Mar. '78 |
| Mercer, John, Ensn..... | " | 28 Nov. '76 | " | Resigned 22 Nov. '77 |
| McCuller, Joseph, Sergt. | " | '77 | " | Died 3 Apr. '78 |
| Morgan, Jos., Pt....... | " | 18 Dec. '76 | " | {Corpl. Dec.'76, Pt. June '78, Dischgd 29 Jan. '80 |
| Morrison, Isaac, Pt..... | Pointer's | 8 Mar. '77 | " | {Destd 5 Dec.'77, Mustd Sep.'78, Destd Nov. '78 |
| Mauning, Chas., Pt..... | Vaughan's | 3 Jan. " | " | Destd 12 Sep. '77 |

| Name and Rank | Company | Dates of Enlistment and Commission | Period of Service | Occurrences |
|---|---|---|---|---|
| McGlanhan, John, Capt. | Vaughan's | 28 Nov. '76 | | Resigned 12 Oct.'77 |
| Monk, Israel, Pt....... | McGlanhan's | 1777 | | Destd Apr. '77 |
| (P. 1114) | | | | |
| Monk, Nollingham, Pt. . | | 13 June " | 3 yrs. | Dischgd 19 Jan. '80 |
| Moss, Robt., Pt........ | | " | " | Omtd Feb. '78 |
| N  (P. 1125) | | | | |
| Nosworthy, Sam'l, Pt... | Macon's | 1777 | 3 yrs. | Omtd Jan. '78 |
| Norris, Thos., Pt....... | Walker's | " | " | { On Bd the Gallies Nov.'77 / Destd 28 July '78 |
| Northgroves, Wm., Msc. | Pointer's | 19 Jan. " | " | Destd 9 May '77 |
| Nichols, Jno., Pt....... | McGlanhan's | 11 Mar " | " | |
| O  (P. 1129) | | | | |
| Outlaw, Lewis, Pt....... | Brickell's | 1777 | W | Omtd Oct. '77 |
| Overton, Joab, Corpl.... | Pointer's | 4 Feb. " | 3 yrs. | { Pt. June '78, / Died 29 Apr. '79 |
| Odin, Robt., Corpl...... | McGlanhan's | " | " | { Pt. Sep. '77, / Died 25 Dec. '77 |
| P  (P. 1135) | | | | |
| Platt, Sam'l, Sergt. Mr.. | | 16 May '77 | | Omtd Dec. '77 |
| Pound, Sam'l, Pt....... | Macon's | " | 3 yrs. | Destd Aug. '77 |
| Peal, Dan'l, Pt......... | Brickell's | 26 Dec. '76 | 3 yrs. W | |
| Pierce, Wm., Pt........ | " | '77 | W | Destd Apr. '77 |
| Powers, Jas., Lt........ | " | 28 Nov. '76 | | { Omtd between Jan. and / Sep. '79 |
| Parker, Wm., Sgt. Maj.. | | '77 | 3 yrs. | { Pris. 11 Sep. '77, Mustd / Pt. and Destd May '79 in / 5 Reg. |
| Parks, Sam'l, Pt........ | Walker's | " | " | Died 27 Nov. '77 |
| Pointer, John, Capt..... | | 28 Nov. '76 | | Omtd Jan. '78 |
| Portlock, Caleb, Pt..... | Pointer's | 1 Sep. '77 | 3 yrs. | |
| Price, Micajah, Pt...... | McGlanhan's | " | " | Died 15 Nov. '77 |
| R  (P. 1146) | | | | |
| Robertson, Henry, Musc. | Dawson's | 1777 | 3 yrs. | Died 6 Feb. '78 |
| Robins, Jas., Pt........ | " | 1 Jan. " | " | Dischgd 1 Feb. '80 |
| Robins, John, Pt....... | " | " | " | Omtd Jan. '78 |
| Reed, Joseph, Sergt..... | Brickell's | 20 Jan. " | " | Died Aug. '77 |
| Redner, Geo., Musc..... | " | " | 3 yrs. | Died 4 Nov. '77 |
| Ramsay, Allen, Lt...... | Walker's | 19 Dec. '76 | " | Omtd Jan. '78 |
| Roe, Lemuel, Corpl..... | Pointer's | 4 Jan. '77 | " | { Pt. Nov. '77, / Dischgd 1 Feb. '80 |
| Rose, John, Pt......... | " | " | " | Destd 16 Apr. '77 |
| Ramsay, Mills, Pt...... | Vaughan's | 1 Jan. " | " | Died 2 Jan. '78 |
| Rasko, Tettle, Pt...... | " | 14 Jan. " | " | { Corpl. Jan. '78, / Died 24 Feb. '78 |
| Ray, Stephen, Pt....... | McGlanhan's | " | " | Died 31 Mar. '78 |
| S  (P. 1157) | | | | |
| Smith, Wm., Sergt...... | Macon's | 20 Feb. '77 | 3 yrs. | Died 9 Apr. '78 |
| Smith, Drew, Pt........ | Dawson's | " | " | Destd 25 Oct. '77 |
| Seals, Jno., Pt......... | " | " | " | Died Oct. '77 |
| Sowel, Zadock, Pt...... | " | 8 Jan. " | 3 yrs. W | |
| Smith, John, Musc...... | Dailey's | Nov. " | 3 yrs. | Died 24 Feb. '78 |
| Soddin, Jno., Pt....... | Brickell's | " | W | { Claimed by Capt. Greg- / ory Sep. '77 |
| Smith, Sm'l, Pt........ | " | " | 3 yrs. | |
| Sawyer, Miller, Musc. .. | Walker's | 16 Dec. '76 | 3 yrs. W | |
| Sanders, Joseph, Pt..... | " | '77 | 3 yrs. | Omtd Oct. '77 |
| Snell, Jas., Pt......... | | 14 Apr. " | " | |

| Name and Rank | Company | Dates of Enlistment and Commission | Period of Service | Occurrences |
|---|---|---|---|---|
| Sanders, Isaac......... | Walker's | '77 | 3 yrs. | Died May '78 |
| Simpson, Andrew, Pt.... | " | 21 May " | " | {Corpl. June '78, Sergt. July '79 |
| Salter, Jno............. | " | May " | " | {Music Dec. '77, Destd Jan. '80 |
| Sykes, Zedekiah, Pt..... | Pointer's | 4 Feb. " | | Dischgd 8 Feb. '80 |
| Sawyer, Willis......... | " | 13 Jan. " | | Dead May '78 |
| Schoolfield, Benj., Pt.... | " | 15 Jan. " | | Died 27 Jan. '78 |
| Spense, Jabez., Pt...... | " | " | | Omtd Oct. '77 |
| Simmons, Anthy., Pt.... | " | 14 Feb. " | | Omtd Sep. '77 |
| Smith, Wm., Pt........ | McGlanhan's | " | " | Destd Apr. '77 |
| Smith, Malachi, Pt..... | " | " | " | Destd Apr. '77 |
| T   (P. 1171) | | | | |
| Tow, Chris'r, Corpl..... | Brickell's | 1777 | W | {Destd 1 Sep. '77, Mustd Feb. and died 1 Apr. '78 |
| Troy, Jas., Pt.......... | Walker's | " | 3 yrs. | Omtd Apr. '78 |
| Thompson, Edwd., Pt... | " | " | " | Died 3 Feb. '78 |
| Turner, Jno., Pt....... | Vaughan's | 13 Feb. " | " | Destd Oct. '77 |
| Taylor, Thos., Pt...... | " | 14 Mar. " | " | Destd Aug. '77 |
| Todd, Thos., Musc...... | McGlanhan's | " | " | Died Sep. '77 |
| Todd, Wm., Pt......... | " | 1 Jan " | 3 yrs. W | {Omtd Feb.'78, Mustd July '78, Corpl. 1 Feb. '80 |
| Todd, Ephm., Pt...... | " | " | " | Omtd Feb. '78 |
| Todd, Jas., Pt......... | " | " | " | Died |
| Thomson, Andrew, Pt... | " | " | " | {Omtd Oct. '78, said to be Transfd. |
| U   (P. 1176) | | | | |
| Upton, Josiah, Pt...... | Pointer's | 4 Feb. '77 | 3 yrs. | Omtd Apr. '78 |
| Upton, Willis, Pt...... | " | 14 Feb. " | " | Died 1 July '78 |
| V   (P. 1178) | | | | |
| Vaughan, West, Pt..... | Dailey's | | | Died 20 Feb. '78 |
| Vandeford, Noah, Pt.... | Walker's | | | Died 5 Mar. '78 |
| Venters, Moses, Pt..... | Pointer's | | | Dischgd 28 Jan. '80 |
| Vaughan, Jas., Capt..... | | 28 Nov. '76 | | Resigned Aug. '77 |
| W   (Pp. 1184-85) | | | | |
| Witherington, Wm., Sgt. | Dawson's | 13 June '77 | 3 yrs. | {Pt. June '78, Dischgd 1 Feb. '80 |
| Williams, Jno., Pt...... | " | " | " | Omtd Jan. '78 |
| Whedbey, Rich'd, Lt.... | Brickell's | 28 Nov. " | " | Omtd Jan. '78 |
| Walter, Dempsey, Pt.... | " | " | W | Missing 4 Oct. '77 |
| Ward, Wm., Pt........ | " | " | " | Destd Apr. '77 |
| Wiggins, Wm., Pt...... | " | " | " | Destd Apr. '77 |
| Walker, Joseph, Capt. .. | Walker's | 28 Nov. '76 | | Omtd Jan. '78 |
| Winburn, Jno., Lt...... | " | 28 Nov. " | | Omtd Nov. '77, Dead |
| Woods, Wm., Fifer..... | " | 1777 | 3 yrs. | Destd 17 Sep. '77 |
| Williams, Thophis, Pt... | " | " | " | {Corpl. Sep., Sergt. Nov. '77, Died Mar. '78 |
| Williams, Zadock, Pt.... | " | 23 Dec. '76 | " | Dischgd 29 Jan. '80 |
| Winborne, Henry, Pt.... | " | 24 May '77 | " | |
| Witherington, Jos., Pt... | " | 6 May " | " | |
| Wakefield, Wm., Musc.. | Pointer's | 23 Jan. " | | {Pt. Nov. '77, Dischgd 28 Jan. '80 |
| Walter, Wm., Pt....... | Brickell's | | | Omtd Oct. '77 |
| Williams, Benj., Pt..... | Pointer's | | | Sergt. 1 May '79 |
| Walton, Wm., Lt...... | " | 17 Apr. '77 | | {Capt. 1 Aug. '81, Deranged 1 Jan. '83 |
| White, Wm., Ensn...... | " | " | | Omtd Nov. '77 |

| Name and Rank | Company | Dates of Enlistment and Commission | Period of Service | Occurrences |
|---|---|---|---|---|
| Wiggins, Jas., Sergt..... | Vaughan's | 1 Jan. '77 | 3 yrs. | Destd 19 Sep. '77 |
| Williams, Jno., Pt....... | " | 21 Feb. " | " | Dischgd 1 Mar. '80 |
| Welburne, Robt., Pt.... | " | 18 Mar. " | " | Corpl. Mar. '78 |
| Washington, Eth'd, Musc.............. | " | 12 July " | 3 yrs. W | |
| Watson, Thos., Lt...... | McGlanhan's | 28 Nov. '76 | | Resigned 12 Apr. '77 |
| White, Wm., Sergt..... | " | 10 Dec. " | | Dischgd 27 Jan. '80 |
| White, Jas., Pt........ | " | '77 | 3 yrs. | Died 27 Jan. '78 |
| White, Jno., Pt........ | " | 4 Jan. " | " | Dead Aug. '78 |
| Williams, Wm., Pt..... | " | 16 May '76 | " | {Destd Aug. '77, Mustd Jan.'78, Dischgd Nov. '78 |
| Wharton, Jas., Pt...... | " | 6 Apr. '77 | " | |

## 8TH REGIMENT—COL. JAMES ARMSTRONG

| Name and Rank | Company | Dates of Enlistment and Commission | Period of Service | Occurrences |
|---|---|---|---|---|
| **A** (P. 1005) Armstrong, James, Col. . | | 26 Nov. '76 | | {Retired from Service Jan. '81 |
| **B** (P. 1015) Bush, Wm., Ensn....... | Tartarson's | 10 Apr. '77 | | {1 Lt. 15 Aug. '77, Adj't. 12 May '81 |
| Blackleach, Thos. Sergt. | Walsh's | " | | Pt. Jan.'78, Omtd Feb.'78 |
| Bencham, Hodges, Sgt... | Tartarson's | " | 3 yrs. | Dead 30 Mar. '78 |
| Bush, Jno., Lt......... | Walsh's | 8 Feb. " | | {And Adj't. 2 Aug. '77, Omtd Jan. '78 |
| Bryan, Wm., Sergt..... | " | " | W | Pt. Apr. '78 |
| Boyce, Seth, Pt........ | " | " | | Died 5 Oct. '77 |
| Boon, Wm., Pt........ | " | 1 Jan. " | 3 yrs. | |
| Broadbent, Rich'd, Pt... | " | " | " | Destd 11 Feb. '79 |
| Broadsher, Jno., Pt..... | " | " | " | Died 28 Jan. '78 |
| Boothe, Jno., Pt....... | Raiford's | 19 Feb. " | " | Omtd Feb. '78 |
| Bourke, Chas., Pt...... | " | 27 May " | " | {Pris. 2 June '79, Mustd Nov. '79 |
| Bundy, Jas., Pt........ | Tartarson's | 13 Mar " | 3 yrs. | Corpl. June '78 |
| Bullock, Moses, Pt..... | " | " | | Omtd Sep. '77 |
| Bullock, Jno., Pt....... | " | " | | Omtd Sep. '77 |
| **C** (Pp. 1031-32) Clark, Jas., Corpl....... | Walsh's | 1 Feb. '77 | 3 yrs. | {Pt. June '78, Corpl. Mar. '79, Dischgd 1 Feb. '80 |
| Carmack, Jas., Corpl.... | " | " | | {Pt. Jan. '78, Omtd Feb. '78 |
| Conver, Wm., Musc.... | " | " | | Omtd Jan. '78 |
| Collins, Thos., Pt...... | " | " | | Omtd Jan. '78 |
| Calaghan, Cornl's, Pt. .. | " | 14 Feb. " | | {Pris. 1 June '79, Dischgd 14 Feb. '80 |
| Carter, Isaac, Pt....... | " | 1 Sep. " | | {Pris. 1 June '79, Dischgd 20 Feb. '80 |
| Card, Jno., Pt......... | " | " | | Died 4 Oct. '77 |
| Collins, Jno., Sergt...... | Raiford's | 11 Feb. '76 | 3 yrs. | |
| Collins, Benj., Pt...... | " | 8 Sep. " | " | {Corpl. Nov. '77, Pt. June '78, Dischgd 16 Feb. '80 |
| Cahoon, Jona, Musc.... | | 1 Mar. '77 | W | Pt. Jan.'78, Omtd Feb. '78 |
| Chapman, Sam'l, Lt..... | Tartarson's | 28 Nov. '76 | | {Resigned 2 Nov. '82 (Capt. from 5 Apr. '79) |
| Cook, Francis, Musc.... | " | 29 Mar. '77 | 3 yrs. | Pt. June '78 |
| Colnell, Jno., Pt....... | " | 12 Mar. '77 | " | |

| Name and Rank | Company | Dates of Enlistment and Commission | Period of Service | Occurrences |
|---|---|---|---|---|
| Coops, Wm., Pt........ | Tartarson's | '77 | | Omtd Sep. '77 |
| D (P. 1044) | | | | |
| Dawson, Levy, Lt. Col.. | | 19 Oct. '77 | | Omtd Jan. '78 |
| Dye, Hopkins, Pt....... | Walsh's | 5 Jan. " | 3 yrs. | Dischgd 31 Jan. '80 |
| Delaney, John, Pt..... | " | 1 Apr. " | " | {Pris. 1 June '79 / Mustd Nov. '79 |
| Dyson, Thos., Pt...... | " | 19 Jan. " | " | Musc. 1 Feb. '80 |
| Delaney, Antich?, Sergt. | " | " | " | Pt. Nov.'78, Omtd Sep.'78 |
| Duffell, Thos., Pt....... | Raeford's | 17 Mar. " | | |
| Dennis, Wm., Lt........ | Tartarson's | 28 Nov. " | | {Capt. 20 Sep. '77, / Omtd Jan. '78 |
| Dennis, Jno., Pt....... | " | " | | Gone Home 25 Nov. '77 |
| E (P. 1052) | | | | |
| Etheridge, Dan'l, Corpl. | Walsh's | | | {Destd Oct. '77, Joined 1 / Dec.'77, Died 19 Jan. '78 |
| Eliot, Jabez,.......... | Quinn's | 10 Nov. '76 | 3 yrs. | Dischgd 5 Jan. '79 |
| F (P. 1057) | | | | |
| Fox, Francis, Pt....... | Walsh's | 8 Feb. '77 | 3 yrs. | Dischgd 20 Feb. '80 |
| Foreman, Caleb, Lt.... | Raiford's | 28 Nov. '76 | | Omtd Jan. '78 |
| G (P. 1066) | | | | |
| Graves, Francis, Qr. Mr. | | 1 Sep. '77 | | And Lt. 26 Oct. '77 |
| Greer, Robt., Lt........ | Walsh's | 28 Nov. '76 | | Omtd June '78 |
| Gilaspy, David, Pt..... | " | '77 | | {Omtd June '78, Mustd / Jan.'79 in 5 Reg., Dischgd / 14 Mar. '80 |
| Gifford, Jas, Sergt...... | Raiford's | 30 Dec. '76 | | {Pt. June '78, / Destd 1 Dec. '79 |
| Gilbert, Jos., Pt........ | Tartarson's | '77 | | Omtd Feb. '78 |
| H (P. 1077) | | | | |
| Harvey, Selby, Maj.... | | 26 Nov. '76 | | {Lt. Col. 22 Nov. '77, / See him in 2 Reg. |
| Hall, David, Sergt...... | Walsh's | '77 | | {Pt. Jan. '78, Sergt. Feb. / '79, Pt. Aug. '79, Dischgd / 1 Feb. '80 |
| Hart, Jno., Pt......... | " | " | | Omtd Feb. '78 |
| Huggins, Jas., Pt...... | " | 4 Dec. '76 | 3 yrs. W | |
| Hughes, Henry, Corpl... | " | 28 June '77 | 3 yrs. | {Pt. Jan. '78, Corpl. June, / Pt. Sep. '78 |
| Herrington, Peter, Corpl. | Tartarson's | " | " | Pt. Jan.'78, Omtd Feb. '78 |
| Hayes, Jno., Pt........ | Quinn's | Nov. " | | {Omtd Jan. '78, Supposed / the same mustd in Hall's / Co. in '82 |
| Hollowell, Sam'l, Lt..... | " | 20 Sep. " | | Omtd Jan. '78 |
| J (P. 1091) | | | | |
| Jackson, Thos., Pt...... | Walsh's | | | Omtd Feb. '78 |
| Johnson, Rich'd, Pt..... | " | | 3 yrs. | {Sergt. July '79, / Dischgd 9 Feb. '80 |
| Jolly, Malachi, Pt....... | Raiford's | Dec. '77 | | {From 2 Reg. Mustd Sergt. / Jan. '79 in 4 Reg. |
| Jones, Philip, Lt....... | | | | {Returned Pri 12 May '80 / from War Office |
| K (P. 1097) | | | | |
| Kelly, Pat'k, Pt........ | Tartarson's | 1777 | 3 yrs. | Died 26 Nov. '77 |
| L (P. 1104) | | | | |
| Lockhart, Jas. or Sam'l, Lt. Col............. | | Sep. '77 | | {From 3 Reg., Omt'd / Oct. '77 |

| Name and Rank | Company | Dates of Enlistment and Commission | Period of Service | Occurrences |
|---|---|---|---|---|
| Loomis, Jona, Serg't.... | | 26 Nov. '76 | | Resigned 19 Aug. '82 |
| Leony, Mich'l, Sgt. Maj. | | Dec      '77 | | Omtd Jan. '78 |
| Langford, Alloway, Ensn | Walsh's | 8 Feb.    " | | {Lt. 1 Aug. '77,<br>Omtd Jan. '78 |
| Lanier, Jas., Ensn....... | Tartarson's | 28 Nov. '76 | | Resigned 12 Oct. '77 |
| Lolley, Wm., Pt......... | " | '77 | | Destd 20 Aug. '77 |
| **M** (P. 1114) | | | | |
| Middleton, Sam'l, Sergt. | Walsh's | 1777 | | Pris. Feb., Omtd June '78 |
| McNalty, John, Pt...... | " | " | | Omtd Jan. '78 |
| Mezick, Jacob, Lt...... | " | 24 Apr.   " | | Died 11 Dec. '77 |
| Milton, John, Pt........ | " | Nov.     " | | Omtd Jan. '78 |
| Mashborne, Edw'd, Pt. . | Raiford's | 9 Feb.    " | 3 yrs. | Omtd Feb. '78 |
| Maddin, Bryan, Pt...... | " | 16 June  " | W | Omtd Jan. '78 |
| Moore, John, Pt........ | " | | 3 yrs. | In 2 Reg. Dec. '77 |
| Moseley, John, Pt...... | Tartarson's | 21 Feb.   " | " | {Pris. 1 June '79<br>Discharged 20 Feb. '80 |
| Martin, Joel, Pt........ | " | " | | Omtd Sep. '77 |
| **N** (P. 1125) | | | | |
| Nolley, Dixon, Pt...... | Walsh's | 1777 | | Died 10 Jan. '78 |
| Niel, Dan'l, Pt......... | Raiford's | 24 Feb.   " | 3 yrs. | Omtd Mar. '78 |
| Niel, Jno., Pt.......... | Tartarson's | " | " | Omtd Jan. '78 |
| **O** (P. 1130) | | | | |
| Oran (or Owens) Jas. Pt. | Walsh's | 1777 | | Omtd Feb. '77 |
| Owens, Stephen, Lt..... | | 15 Aug.   " | | Omtd June '77 |
| Owens, Jacob, Pt....... | | " | | Omtd Feb. '79 |
| O'Kelly, Pat'k, Pt...... | | " | W | Omtd Sep. '78 |
| **P** (P. 1136) | | | | |
| Pate, Wm., Corpl....... | Walsh's | 29 June '77 | 3 yrs. | {Destd 17 Oct. '77, Joined<br>1 Dec. '77, Corpl. Feb. '79,<br>Dischgd 31 Jan. '80 |
| Parsons, Jesse, Pt...... | " | | | Pris. 4 Oct. '77 |
| Parsons, Sam'l, Corpl. .. | " | | | {Pt. Jan. '78,<br>Died 19 Mar. '78 |
| Parsons, Roger, Pt..... | " | | 3 yrs. | Omtd Feb. '79 |
| Parsons, Nathan, Pt. ... | " | | | Pris. 4 Oct. '77 |
| Pettit, Gideon, Musc.... | Raiford's | 5 Apr. | | {Omtd Jan. '78,<br>Mustd May '79 in 5 Reg. |
| Potter, Sam'l, Pt....... | " | '77 | | Dead Sep. '77 |
| Pridgion, Thos., Corpl... | " | " | 3 yrs. | Pt. Feb.'78, Died Oct. '78 |
| Proctor, Joshua, Pt..... | " | " | | Omtd Mar. '78 |
| Palmer, Robt., Pt...... | Tartarson's | " | | Omtd Feb. '78 |
| Pearl, Jos., Lt......... | Dennis' | 29 Oct.   " | | {Capt. 17 July '82,<br>Deranged 1 Jan. '83 |
| **Q** (P. 1141) | | | | |
| Quinn, Mich'l, Lt....... | Walsh's | 28 Nov. '76 | | {Capt. 1 Aug. '77,<br>Resigned 14 Dec. '79 |
| **R** (P. 1146) | | | | |
| Rhein, Peter, Sergt...... | Walsh's | 10 Feb. '77 | 3 yrs. | {Qr. Mr. Sergt. Nov. '77,<br>Sergt. Jan. '78, Pt. 4 July<br>'79, Dischgd 10 Feb. '80 |
| Rhodes, Wm., Sergt.... | " | " | | Pt. Jan.'78, Omtd Feb.'78 |
| Rowe, Jese, Musc....... | " | " | | Omtd Jan. '78 |
| Rowe, Geo., Pt......... | " | " | | Omtd Jan. '78 |
| Rhodes, Henry, Pt...... | " | " | | Omtd Jan. '78 |
| Raiford, Robt., Capt.... | " | 28 Nov. '76 | | |
| Rollins, Robt., Sergt.... | Tartarson's | '77 | 3 yrs. | Omtd Nov. '77 |

| Name and Rank | Company | Dates of Enlistment and Commission | Period of Service | Occurrences |
|---|---|---|---|---|
| **S** (P. 1158) | | | | |
| Stanley, Robt., Sergt.... | Walsh's | 1777 | | Pt. Jan.'78, Omtd Feb.'78 |
| Singleton, Henry, Pt.... | " | 22 Feb. " | 3 yrs. W | |
| Standley, Jos., Pt...... | " | | | Omtd Jan. '78 |
| Skipper, Joseph, Pt..... | " | | | Died 19 Dec. '77 |
| Spain, Thos., Musc..... | Tartarson's | 10 Feb. " | 3 yrs. | {Pt. June '78, Musc. Nov. '78 |
| Spain, Wm., Musc...... | " | 10 Mar. " | | |
| Stevenson, Jos., Sergt... | " | | " | Dead 12 Feb. '78 |
| Stewart, Geo., Sergt..... | " | | " | Omtd Sep. '77 |
| Storry, Wm., Pt....... | " | | " | Omtd Sep. '77 |
| Simmons, Benj., Pt.... | Quinn's | | W | Sergt. 3 Reg. Oct. '79 |
| Sumner, Francis, Pt..... | " | 15 May " | 2½ yrs. | |
| **T** (P. 1171) | | | | |
| Taylor, Jno., P. Mr..... | | 24 July '77 | | Omtd Jan. '78 |
| Thurrell, Abm., Pt...... | Walsh's | 2 July ' | 3 yrs. | Died Jan. '79 |
| Towning, Jas., Pt....... | " | 15 Dec. " | | |
| Turner, Mathias, Corpl.. | Raiford's | | 2½ yrs. | Pt. Jan.'78, Omtd Feb.'79 |
| Turner, Dan'l, Corpl.... | " | | " | Pt. Nov. '77, Died Jan.'78 |
| Tartarson, Francis, Cpt. | | 16 Jan. " | | Resigned 19 Sep. '78 |
| Tyson, Abm., Sergt..... | Tartarson's | | 3 yrs. | {Pt. June '78, Omtd Feb. '79 |
| **V** (P. 1178) | | | | |
| Varey, Benj., Pt........ | William's | 1777 | | Destd 1 Oct. '77 |
| **W** (Pp. 1185-86) | | | | |
| Walsh, Jno., Capt...... | | 28 Nov. '76 | | Omtd Jan. '78 |
| Wilson, Jno., Pt........ | Walsh's | 1 Jan. '77 | 3 yrs. | Corpl. Nov. '78 |
| Williams, B. Nath'l, Lt.. | " | 28 Nov. '76 | | Deranged 1 Jan. '83 |
| Wise, Jno., Musc....... | Raiford's | '77 | | {Pt. Jan. '78, Died 6 Mar. '77 |
| Wiseheart, Wm., Pt..... | " | | | Omtd Mar. '78 |
| Walsh, Robt., Pt....... | " | | | Omtd Feb. '78 |
| Whitehouse, Joel, Pt.... | " | | " | {Pris. 1 June '79, Mustd Nov. '79 |
| Williams, Robt., Sergt... | Tartarson's | " | " | Corpl. June '78, Pt. Apr. '78, Dischgd 1 Feb. '80 |
| Wallace, Geo., Musc.... | " | 1 Apr. " | 3 yrs. W | Fife Maj. Dec. '82 |
| Willowby, Jno., Pt...... | " | " | 3 yrs. | Died 14 Feb. '78 |
| Wotton, Wm., Sergt..... | Quinn's | " | | Died 1 May '78 |

## 9TH REGIMENT—COL. JOHN WILLIAMS

| Name and Rank | Company | Dates of Enlistment and Commission | Period of Service | Occurrences |
|---|---|---|---|---|
| **A** (P. 1006) | | | | |
| Avery, James, Pt...... | McCrory's | 1777 | W | Destd 28 Dec. '77 |
| Arbuckle, John, Pt..... | " | " | 3 yrs. | Destd 2 Dec. '77 |
| Austin, Absolem, Pt.... | " | " | " | Died 7 Mar. '78 |
| Ammons, Jas., Pt...... | Wade's | 10 May " | 3 yrs. W | Omtd July '79 |
| Anthony, Jas., Pt....... | Rice's | 4 May " | " | |
| **B** (P. 1016) | | | | |
| Brown, Morgan, Lt..... | Cook's | 28 Nov. '76 | | Resigned 12 Oct. '77 |
| Bond, Elisha, Pt....... | " | 1 Jan. '77 | 3 yrs. | Dischgd 27 Jan. '80 |
| Bond, Thos., Pt....... | " | " | " | Died 13 Dec. '77 |
| Britnal, Jas., Pt....... | " | 28 Mar. " | " | |
| Bruce, Geo., Pt........ | " | 15 Mar. " | " | |
| Britton, Jas., Pt........ | " | 1 Dec. '76 | " | Dischgd 1 Feb. '80 |
| Beck, Fred'k, Pt........ | " | '77 | " | Destd 10 Oct. '77 |

| Name and Rank | Company | Dates of Enlistment and Commission | Period of Service | Occurrences |
|---|---|---|---|---|
| Brown, David, Pt....... | Cook's | 8 Jan. '77 | 3 yrs. | Killed or taken Oct. 4, '77, Mustd '78, Died 18 Nov. '78 |
| Bullock, Dan'l, Pt..... | " | 23 Mar. " | | Corpl. Nov.'77, Sergt. Jan. '78, Pt. June '78 Omtd Nov. '79 |
| Bay, And'w, Sergt. Maj. | | 1 May " | W | Omtd Jan. '78 |
| Bayne, John, Pt........ | McCrory's | | 3 yrs. | Omtd Feb. '79 |
| Black, John, Pt........ | " | | W | Destd Nov. '77 |
| Brown, Wm., Pt........ | " | | 3 yrs. | |
| Bullock, Dan'l, Pt..... | Ramsay's | | | Omtd Jan. '78 |
| Britton, Philip, Musc. .. | Wade's | | " | Pt. Jan. '78, Dischgd 27 Jan. '80 |
| Barrlow, Robt., Pt..... | " | | " | Died 12 Mar. '78 |
| Blalock, Wm., Pt...... | " | | " | Destd 6 Aug. '77 |
| Brevard, Jno., Pt....... | | | | Omtd Jan. '78 |
| Brandon, Thos., Pt..... | Brevard's | 12 Jan. '77 | 3 yrs. | Dischgd 27 Jan. '80 |
| C  (P. 1032) | | | | |
| Cook, D. Rich'd., Capt.. | | 28 Nov. '76 | | Omtd Jan. '78 |
| Clark, Thos., Ensn..... | Cook's | " | | Lt. Feb. '79 |
| Christain, Jas., Sergt.... | " | '77 | 3 yrs. | Dischgd 29 Jan. '78 |
| Cozzart, David, Sergt.. | " | 18 Dec. '76 | " | Pt. Feb. '78, Dischgd 27 Jan. '80 |
| Clifton, Wm., Sergt..... | " | 24 Dec. " | " | Omtd Jan. '78 |
| Cook, Thos., Sergt..... | " | '77 | " | Omtd Dec. '77 |
| Carrier, Jno., Pt........ | " | 5 May " | 3 yrs. W | Corpl. Nov. '79 |
| Copland, Ripley, Pt..... | Ramsay's | 10 Mar. " | " | Dischgd 15 Mar. '80 |
| Chappel, Sam'l, Pt..... | Wade's | 25 Dec. '76 | " | Dischgd 1 Feb. '80 |
| Coles, Alex'r, Pt....... | " | | " | Corpl. Jan. '78, Died 4 Apr. '78 |
| Conaway, John, Pt...... | Brevard's | 19 June '77 | " | Sergt. Jan.'78, Corpl. June '78, Pt. Aug. '78, Destd 15 Dec. '79 |
| D  (P. 1044) | | | | |
| Doherty, John, Pt..... | Cook's | 1777 | 3 yrs. | Destd Aug. '77 |
| Dennis, Robt., Pt....... | " | " | | Died 6 Mar. '78 |
| Dobbins, Hugh, Lt..... | McCrory's | " | | Omtd June '78 |
| Daniel, Jos., Lt......... | Wade's | 28 Nov. '76 | | Resigned Nov. '77 |
| Dickerson, Neth., Lt.... | " | " | | Omtd June '78, Mustd May '79, 5 Reg. |
| E  (P. 1052) | | | | |
| Epps, Jno., Pt......... | Cook's | 1777 | 3 yrs. | Dischgd 27 Jan. '80 |
| Epps, Wm., Pt........ | " | 24 Jan. '77 | " | Dischgd 27 Jan. '80 |
| Easter, David, Pt...... | " | " | " | Died 22 Feb. '78 |
| F  (P. 1058) | | | | |
| Fagety, Jas., Pt........ | Cook's | 25 Dec. '76 | 3 yrs. | Corpl. Nov.'77, Pt. Jan. '79, Dischgd 27 Jan. '80 |
| Francisco, Thos., Pt..... | " | '77 | " | Died 23 Mar. '78 |
| Ford, Wm., Pt........ | " | " | " | Omtd Feb. '78 |
| Ferrell, Jas., Pt........ | McCrory's | 16 Dec. " | " | Corpl. Jan.'78, Pt. June'78 |
| Fee, Thos., Pt......... | " | " | " | Deserted 30 June '79 |
| Fossett, Edw'd, Pt...... | " | " | | Omtd June '78 |
| Fowler, Wm., Pt........ | " | " | | Died 16 Mar. '78 |
| Ferrell, Micajah, Ensn. . | Wade's | 28 Nov. '76 | | Resigned Nov. '78 |
| G  (P. 1067) | | | | |
| Graham, Wm., Sergt.... | Cook's | '77 | 3 yrs. | Supposed dead Nov. '77 |
| Green, Sol'm, Musc..... | " | " | " | Destd Aug. '77 |

| Name and Rank | Company | Dates of Enlistment and Commission | Period of Service | Occurrences |
|---|---|---|---|---|
| Garret, Wm., Pt....... | Brevard's | '77 | 3 yrs. | Omtd Feb. '78 |
| H  (P. 1078) | | | | |
| Harris, Edw., Pt....... | Cook's | 10 Jan. '77 | 3 yrs. | Omtd Sep. '78 |
| Howell, Silas, Pt....... | " | " | " | Destd Aug. '77 |
| Hays, Jno............. | " | " | " | Destd Aug. '77 |
| Howard, Isaac, Pt..... | " | 15 Feb. " | " | Dischgd 8 Mar. '80 |
| Howell, Stephen, Musc.. | McCrory's | 28 Jan. " | " | {Mustd Pt. May '78, Died 8 July '78 |
| Hooker, Robt., Pt..... | " | " | " | Destd Nov. '77 |
| Hicks, C. Tubel, Sergt. . | Wade's | | | Died 27 Jan. '78 |
| Hogan, Proser, Musc.... | " | | 3 yrs. W | {Pt. June '79, Musc. Nov. '79, Pt. 1 Mar. '80 |
| Hall, Jas., Pt........... | " | | 3 yrs. | Omtd Jan. '78 |
| Hall, Jos., Capt........ | | May " | | Omtd Jan. '78 |
| Hicks, Thos., Musc..... | Rice's | " " | " | Omtd Jan. '78 |
| J  (P. 1091) | | | | |
| Johnson, Edw'd, Pt..... | McCrory's | 1777 | 3 yrs. | Destd Nov. '77 |
| Johnson, Joshua, Lt..... | Ramsay's | 28 Nov. '76 | | Resigned 15 May '82 |
| K  (P. 1097) | | | | |
| Knight, Sam'l, Sergt.... | Brevard's | 30 May '77 | 3 yrs. | Pt. 21 May '78 |
| L  (P. 1104) | | | | |
| Lewis, Jno., Pt......... | Cook's | 1777 | 3 yrs. | Killed 4 Oct. '77 |
| Lewis, Wm., Lt......... | Rice's | Mar. " | | {Omtd Jan. '78, Mustd June '79, 4 Reg. |
| Lutzell, Jno., Lt. Col.... | | 24 Nov. '76 | | Omtd Jan. '78 |
| M  (P. 1115) | | | | |
| McRory, Jas., Sergt..... | Cook's | 15 Apr. '76 | 3 yrs. | {Ensn. 2 May '79, Omtd Jan. '78 |
| May, Major, Corpl...... | " | 10 Dec. '77 | " | Died 27 Nov. '77 |
| Miller, Gilbert, Pt..... | • | '77 | " | Omtd Sep. '77 |
| Miller, Martin, Pt..... | " | 22 Dec. '76 | " | {Music Sep. '77, Pt. Feb. '78, Dischgd 27 Jan. '80 |
| Mallison, Jno., Pt...... | " | '77 | " | {Sergt. Nov. '77, Omtd Jan. '78 |
| May, Thos., Pt......... | " | 1 Dec. '76 | " | Dischgd 27 Jan. '80 |
| McRory, Thos., Capt. .. | " | 28 Nov. '76 | " | Died 2 Nov. '77 |
| McKinley, Dan'l, Sergt.. | McCrory's | '77 | | Omtd Jan. '78 |
| McClure, Francis, Pt.... | " | " | 3 yrs. | Destd Nov. '77 |
| McGaw, Neil, Pt...... | " | " | W | Destd Nov. '77 |
| McCleyea, Jno., Musc... | " | 28 July " | 3 yrs. W | Pt. Aug.'78, Music Sep.'78 |
| Morgan, John, Pt....... | Wade's | " | 3 yrs. | {Music Feb. '78, Died 10 July '78 |
| Morris, Edw'd, Sergt.... | Brevard's | " | " | {Reduced 3 June '78, Destd 15 June '78 |
| McSheby, Miles, Adj't. . | | 12 Feb. | | Omtd Jan. '78 |
| N  (P. 1126) | | | | |
| Niel, Wm., Lt......... | Brevard's | 28 Nov. '76 | | Omtd Jan. '78 |
| Nuthall, Nath., Qr. Mr.. | | 20 May '77 | | {And Ensn., dismissed Service 4 Nov. '78 |
| O  (P. 1130) | | | | |
| O'Bryan, Dennis, Pt.... | Cook's | '77 | 3 yrs. | {Drawn out of the Regt. Aug. '77 |
| P  (P. 1136) | | | | |
| Pyatt, Peter, Sergt...... | Cook's | 1777 | 3 yrs. | {Qr. Mr. Sergt. 15 June '78, Dischgd 15 June '79 |
| Perkins, Ab'm, Pt...... | Ramsay's | " | " | Died 5 Mar. '78 |
| Polk, Wm., Maj........ | | 28 Nov. '76 | " | Omtd Jan. '78 |

| Name and Rank | Company | Dates of Enlistment and Commission | Period of Service | Occurrences |
|---|---|---|---|---|
| **R** (P. 1147) | | | | |
| Ramage, Alex., Corpl.... | Cook's | 1 Jan. '77 | 3 yrs. | {Sergt. Jan. '78, Pt. Feb. '78, Died 19 Mar. '79 |
| Rickets, Thos., Musc.... | " | " | | {Omtd Sep. '77, Mustd '79 in 5 Reg. |
| Rickets, Reason, Pt..... | " | 6 Jan. " | | {Corpl. Jan. '78, Pt. June '78, Hanged 21 Nov. '79 |
| Richards, Jas., Pt...... | " | " | | {Destd Aug. '77, Mustd '78, Dischgd 10 Nov. '78 |
| Roberts, Vincent, Pt.... | " | " | " | |
| Rowland, Wm., Pt..... | | | | Died 11 Mar. '78 |
| Ramsay, Mathew, Capt. | | | | Resigned before '82 |
| Rochel, Jno., Pt....... | | | | Omtd Jan. '78 |
| Rice, Hezk............ | | | | Omtd Jan. '78 |
| Rochel, Louise, Lt..... | | | | Resigned Nov. '77 |
| Ricely, Jeptha, Ensn.... | | | | Not Mustd after Jan. '78 |
| Rainey, Jas., Pt........ | Rice's | '77 | 3 yrs. | Omtd Nov. '79 |
| Renney, Peter, Sergt.... | " | 23 June " | " | |
| **S** (P. 1158) | | | | |
| Scandling, Mich'l, Musc. | Cook's | 1777 | W | {Pt. Nov. '77, Destd Feb. '79 |
| Seymore, Wm., Pt..... | " | " | " | Dischgd 28 Jan. '80 |
| Sharp, Anty., Lt........ | McCrory's | 28 Nov. '76 | | Capt. 24 Aug. '77 |
| Stewart, Jos., Pt........ | " | '77 | 3 yrs. | Dischgd 20 Dec. '77 |
| Siscoe................ | | | | See Francisco |
| **T** (P. 1172) | | | | |
| Tucker, Thos., Corpl.... | Cook's | 1777 | 3 yrs. | Omtd Jan. '78 |
| Thomas, Wm., Pt...... | " | " | " | Dead Aug. '77 |
| Thrift, Solomon, Pt..... | " | " | " | Died 15 June '78 |
| Thrift, Ab'm, Pt........ | " | 17 Jan. " | " | |
| Thomson, Thos., Pt.... | " | " | | Destd Aug. '77 |
| Thomas, Benj., Pt...... | McCrory's | " | W | Omtd Jan. '78 |
| Tatum, Jas., Ensn...... | Brevard's | 12 Aug. " | | {Lt. 1 Jan.'78, Pris. 12 May '80, Deranged 1 Jan. '88 |
| Templelon, Thos., Sergt. | | " | | {Omtd Jan. '78, Mustd May '79 in 5 Reg. |
| **V** (P. 1178) | | | | |
| Vandyke, Chas., Pt..... | Cook's | '77 | 3 yrs. | Died 3 Apr. '78 |
| **W** (P. 1186) | | | | |
| Walker, Jno., Sergt..... | Cook's | 20 Jan. '77 | 3 yrs. | {Qr. Mr. Sergt 20 Sep. '77, Omtd Jan. '78 |
| White, Dan'l, Corpl.... | " | 24 Dec. '76 | " | Destd 10 Oct. '77 |
| Watson, Philip, Pt...... | " | 16 Jan. '77 | " | Dischgd 27 Jan. '80 |
| Watts, Wm., Pt....... | " | " | " | Died 9 Sep. '77 |
| Witty, Jas., Pt........ | McCrory's | 21 May " | W | {Destd Nov. '77, Mustd May '78 |
| Warwick, Thos., Pt..... | " | " | 3 yrs. | Omtd Jan. '78 |
| Wade, I. Joseph, Capt. . | | 28 Nov. '76 | | Omtd Jan. '78 |
| Washington, Wm., Ensn. | Wade's | 15 Aug. '77 | | Omtd Jan. '78 |
| Williams, Ralph, Lt..... | " | 28 Nov. '76 | | Omtd Jan. '78 |
| Worneck, Wm., Sergt. .. | | '77 | 3 yrs. | {Qr. Mr. 14 Jan. '78, Omtd June '78 |
| Williams, John, Col..... | | 24 Nov. '76 | | Omtd Jan. '78 |

## 10TH REGIMENT—COL. ABRAHAM SHEPARD

| Name and Rank | Company | Dates of Enlistment and Commission | Period of Service | Occurrences |
|---|---|---|---|---|
| **A** (P. 1006) | | | | |
| Adcock, Joshua, Pt..... | Wilson's | 6 May '77 | 3 yrs. | |
| Adcock, John, Pt....... | " | " " | " | |
| Adams, Arthur, Pt...... | Shepard's | 12 Aug. " | " | |
| Arnold, John, Pt....... | Stephenson's | 21 Apr. " | " | Omtd Jan. '78 |
| Alcock, Wm., Pt........ | " | 31 Aug. " | " | Destd 20 Jan. '78 |
| Adkins, Thos., Pt...... | Gregory's | 22 May " | " | |
| Adams, Jno., Sergt...... | Hearon's | 5 July | " | Pt. June '78, Died 10 July '78 |
| Albertson, Caleb, Pt.... | Moore's | 10 May " | " | Omtd Jan. '78 |
| Adkinson, John, Pt..... | Van Noy's | 26 May " | " | Mustd June '78, Pt. Sep. '78 |
| Avent, Jas., Pt......... | | 15 May '76 | 2½ yrs. | Dischgd 10 Nov. '78 |
| Allen, Joseph, Sergt..... | | 3 July '77 | 2 yrs. | Lt. 31 Mar. '82 |
| Adkins, Benj., Pt....... | | 10 Dec. " | 3 yrs. | |
| Amsley, James, Pt...... | | | 3 yrs. W | Mustd Sep. '78 |
| Alsbrook, Amos, Pt..... | Montford's | 20 July '78 | 9 mo. | |
| Adams, Philip, Pt....... | " | 20 " " | " | |
| Ammons, Thos., Pt..... | " | " " | " | |
| Abbot, John, Musc..... | Hogg's | " " | " | |
| Aldridge, Thos., Pt..... | Quinn's | " " | " | |
| Anderson, Wm., Pt..... | Blount's | " " | " | Sergt. 25 Oct. '78, reinlisted, Corpl. 20 May '79 for 18 Mo. |
| Asbett, Jas., Pt........ | " | " " | " | |
| Axum, Philip, Pt...... | Ballard's | " " | " | |
| Allen, Hardy, Pt....... | " | " " | " | |
| Adkins, Gideon, Musc... | " | 16 June " | W | |
| Altman, Garret, Pt..... | Bradley's | 20 July " | 9 mo. | |
| Aldridge, Gess, Pt...... | " | " " | " | |
| Avarette, Thos., Sergt... | Child's | " " | 9 mo. | Died 28 Nov. '78 |
| Antory, John, Corpl.... | Ballard's | 22 June '79 | W | |
| Anderson, Isaac, Pt..... | " | " | 9 mo. | |
| Alexander, John, Pt..... | " | " | " | |
| Addleman, John, Pt..... | " | " | " | |
| Abbot, John, Pt........ | Quinn's | 24 June " | 3 yrs. | |
| Allen, Joseph, Pt....... | " | " | W | |
| Anderson, Geo., Pt..... | " | " | 9 mo. | |
| Andrews, Isaac, Pt..... | Blount's | 5 June " | " | |
| Allen, Wm., Pt........ | | " | W | |
| Adkerson, Rich'd, Pt.... | | " | 9 mo. | |
| Alexander, Wm., Ensn. . | | 10 May '81 | | |
| Ashley, John, Sgt. Mgr.. | | 5 May " | | |
| Anderson, John, Pt..... | McRees' | 28 Apr. " | 12 mo. | |
| Adams, Wm., Pt....... | " | 6 June " | " | |
| Airs, Patt, Pt......... | " | 28 Apr. " | " | |
| Albrooks, Wm., Pt...... | " | 28 Apr. " | " | Left Service 28 Apr. '82 |
| Alsbrook, Jesse, Corpl... | Raiford's | 25 Apr. " | " | Time expired 25 Apr. '82 |
| Askins, John, Pt........ | Doherty's | May " | " | Time expired 25 May '82 |
| Allen, Jas., Pt......... | Raiford's | 25 Apr. " | " | Dischgd 14 Feb. '82 |
| Addams, Philip, Pt...... | " | 2 May " | " | Time out 2 May '82 |
| Apsley, John, Sergt..... | | 15 May " | " | Left service 5 May '82, See above Sergt. Maj |
| Ashlock, Jesse, Pt....... | Dixon's | 15 May " | 12 mo. | Left service 21 May '82 |
| Adams, Zach'l, Pt....... | Lytle's | | | |

| Name and Rank | Company | Dates of Enlistment and Commission | Period of Service | Occurrences |
|---|---|---|---|---|
| Adams, David, Pt...... | Lytle's | 6 June '81 | 12 Mo. | Left service 6 June '82 |
| Abute, John, Pt....... | " | | | |
| Ammons, Wood, Pt..... | " | 12 Apr. " | " | Destd 5 July '82 |
| Allens, Arthur, Pt...... | " | " " | " | Destd 7 July '82 |
| Allen, Walter, Sergt.... | Sharp's | | " | |
| Andrews, Joseph, Pt.... | Walton's | 25 Apr. " | 12 mo. | Time out 1 Apr. '82 |
| *This name illegible and | partly worn a | way by age o | f paper. | |
| Amos, John, Pt......... | Rhodes' | 1781 | 12 mo. | Time out Apt. 12, '82 |
| Andrews, Alfred, Corpl.. | Armstrong's | " | " | Dischgd 27 Mar. '82 |
| Anderson, Robt., Pt..... | " | " | " | Left service 22 May '82 |
| Alexander, Anth'y, Pt... | Bailey's | 3 Apr. " | " | Left service 3 Apr. '82 |
| Anderson, Thos., Pt..... | Brevard's | " | " | Left service 28 May '82 |
| Adams, William, Pt..... | " | " | " | Left service 1 May '82 |
| Anderson, Geo........ | " | " | " | Left service 12 Apr. '82 |
| Aaronheart, Jno., Pt.... | " | " | " | Left service 28 Apr. '82 |
| Ashe, Sam'l, Lt......... | Hall's | 23 Jan. " | " | Deranged 1 Jan. '83 |
| Airs, Ezl., Pt.......... | " | " | " | Left service 21 Apr. '82 |
| Armstrong, Benj., Pt.... | " | " | " | Destd 1 Apr. '82 |
| Artis, John, Pt......... | " | " | " | Left service 1 Nov. '82 |
| Addleman, Jno., Pt..... | " | " | " | Left service 29 Sep. '82 |
| Arters, Stephen, Pt..... | " | " | " | Time out 21 Nov. '82 |
| Abbot, John, Sergt..... | Yarborough's | " | " | Time out 22 Apr. '82 |
| Adkins, Gideon, Musc... | " | " | " | Time out 1 Apr. '82 |
| Adkins, Rich'd, Pt...... | " | " | " | Time out 17 Apr. '82 |
| Acock, Sam'l, Pt....... | Carter's | April " | " | Time out 25 Apr. '82 |
| **B** (P. 1016) | | | | |
| Burton, Julius, Corpl.... | Wilson's | 12 May '77 | 3 yrs. W | Pt. June '78 |
| Brown, Thos., Pt...... | " | 20 May " | W | |
| Brower, Henry, Pt..... | " | " " | | |
| Brooks, Thos., Pt...... | " | 1 July " | | |
| Bryant, Ambrose, Pt.... | " | 16 June " | | Omtd June '78 |
| Brown, Pond, Sergt..... | Shephard's | 12 May " | 3 yrs. | Destd 1 May '79 |
| Barfield, Marmask, Cpl. | " | 4 May " | | Pt. June '78, Destd 17 Sep. '78 |
| Barfield, Jas., Pt....... | " | 20 June " | | Prisoner in June '79, Mustd Nov. '79 |
| Butts, Arch'd, Pt...... | " | 1 Apr. '78 | | Mustd Oct. '78, Destd 15 June '83 |
| Butts, Wm., Pt........ | " | 23 July '77 | | |
| Brown, Moses, Pt...... | " | 28 July " | | |
| Bates, Luke, Pt....... | " | 27 Apr. " | | |
| Bird, Hardy, Pt....... | " | 1 July " | 3 yrs. | Pris. 1 June '79, Mustd Nov. '79 |
| Bass, Ezdras, Pt....... | " | 22 Apr. " | | Omtd June '78 |
| Bryant, Wm., Pt...... | " | 12 July " | " | Omtd Aug. '78 |
| Brown, Thos., Pt...... | " | 25 Aug. " | " | Omtd June '78 |
| Burnett, Wm., Pt...... | " | 5 Sep. " | " | Destd 15 Jan. '80 |
| Bateman, Peter, Pt..... | " | 12 July " | | Omtd June '79, Reinlisted Nov. '79 |
| Bryan, Thos., Musc..... | Stephenson's | 1 June " | " | Pt. June '78, Mustd July '79 |
| Black, Martin, Pt...... | " | 16 May " | " | |
| Boyd, John, Pt........ | " | 14 June " | " | Died 22 Mar. '78 |
| Boyd, Wm., Pt........ | " | " " | " | |
| Badget, Sam'l, Pt...... | " | 24 Aug. " | " | Destd 20 Jan. '78 |
| Ballentine, Malachi, Pt.. | Jarvis' | 2 June " | 3 yrs. W | Musc 8 Mar. '79 |
| Brable, Jas............ | " | 17 May " | | |

| Name and Rank | Company | Dates of Enlistment and Commission | Period of Service | Occurrences |
|---|---|---|---|---|
| Bennett, Jacob, Pt...... | Jarvis' | 8 Sep. '77 | | |
| Bennett, Benj., Pt..... | | 16 June " | | Omtd June, '78 |
| Barco, Jno., Musc...... | Gregory's | 24 May " | 3 yrs. | Pt. June '78 |
| Burus, Wm., Pt........ | " | 20 May " | " | Musc June '78, Destd 10 Feb. '79 |
| Barco, Leaman, Pt...... | " | 9 June " | " | Corpl. Apr. '82 |
| Barker, Wm., Lt........ | Moore's | 19 Apr. " | " | Omtd June '78 |
| Boswell, Wm., Sergt.... | " | 11 June " | " | Pt. June '78, Corpl. Oct. '78 |
| Brains, Mich'l, Pt...... | " | 20 June " | " | Died 9 Sep. '77 |
| Bartie, Jno............ | " | 5 Aug. " | " | Destd 1 Jan. '83 |
| Brooks, Geo., Sergt..... | Vanoy's | 2 June " | " | Pt. June '78, Corpl. Oct. '78, Sergt. Feb. '79 |
| Blanchett, Thos., Sergt.. | " | 21 June " | " | Pt. June '78 |
| Blanchett, Fred'k, Musc. | " | 20 Aug. " | " | |
| Ballentine, Alex., Pt..... | | | W | Sergt. May '79, Pt. Jan. '80 |
| Brown, Robt.......... | | 30 Aug. " | 3 yrs. | Dischgd 16 Sep. '78 |
| Boyce, Arthur, Qr. Mr. Sergt....... | | June '78 | | Sergt. June '79, Destd 2 Dec. '79 |
| Blackley, E., Surg. Mt.. | | 20 Apr. " | | Omtd Aug. '78 |
| Berry, Amos, Pt....... | | | W | Joined 10 Jan. '78, Died 10 Apr. '78 |
| Bray, Cornelius, Pt.... | | | | Joined Apr. '78 |
| Bissell, Enos, Pt....... | | 10 Sep. '77 | | |
| Bridget, Wm., Pt...... | | | | Joined 11 May '78, Dead July '78 |
| Barrow, Jas., Pt........ | | 10 May '76 | 2½ yrs. | Dischgd 10 Nov. '78 |
| Brown, Jas., Pt........ | | 1 July '77 | 3 yrs. | Destd 1 Jan. '80 |
| Browning, Geo., Corpl... | | 1 July " | " | Sergt. Jan. '79 |
| Baker, Wm., Pt....... | | | " | Omtd Feb. '79 |
| Baker, Wm., Pt....... | | | | Omtd Feb. '79 |
| Brooks, Jno., Pt....... | | 15 May '76 | 2½ yrs. | Dischgd 10 Nov. '78 |
| Brewer, Benj'n, Pt..... | | | " | Died 1 Aug. '78 |
| Burgess, Philip, Pt..... | | | W | Mustd, June '78 |
| Barco, Wyllis, Pt...... | | 17 Dec. '77 | 3 yrs. | |
| Brazle, Bird, Pt....... | | 5 May '76 | 2½ yrs. | Dischgd Oct. '78 |
| Bogart, Tunis, Pt....... | Fenner's | 1 Mar. '79 | W | |
| Brazel, Jno., Pt....... | | | | Mustd May '78 |
| Burges, John, Pt....... | | | 3 yrs. | Mustd Jan. '78 |
| Brandon, Wm., Pt...... | | | " | Omtd Feb. '78 Mustd Jan.'78, Omtd June '78, Mustd Jan. '79 5 Reg. |
| Bishop, Moses, Sergt.... | Colonel's | 20 July '78 | 9 mo. | |
| Brown, Sam'l, Pt....... | " | " " | " | |
| Brinkley, Mitch'l, Pt.... | " | " " | " | Omtd Oct. '78 |
| Beavous, Geo., Pt...... | Montford's | '78 | " | |
| Bagley, Isaac, Corpl..... | Hogg's | 20 July " | " | |
| Braddy, Henry, Pt...... | " | " " | " | |
| Blago, Moses, Pt...... | " | " " | " | |
| Blunt, Thos., Pt....... | " | " " | " | |
| Brown, Thos., Pt....... | " | " " | " | |
| Braddy, Benj., Pt...... | " | " " | " | |
| Blango, Benj., Pt...... | " | " " | " | |
| Benton, Edom., Pt..... | " | " " | " | Died 7 Nov. '78 |
| Burwick, Edw'd, Pt..... | " | " " | " | Destd 2 Aug. '78 |
| Bruington, Benj., Pt.... | Quinn's | 20 July " | " | |

| Name and Rank | Company | Dates of Enlistment and Commission | Period of Service | Occurrences |
|---|---|---|---|---|
| Bootey, Caudel, Pt. | Quinn's | 20 July '78 | 9 Mo. | |
| Bryant, Darby, Pt. | " | " " " | " | |
| Bryant, Thos., Pt. | " | June " | " | Destd 14 June '78 |
| Brittle, Benj., Pt. | Lt. Col. | 20 July " | " | |
| Badgett, Jesse, Corpl. | " | " " | " | |
| Bass, Council, Musc. | " | " " | " | |
| Boyd, Jas., Pt. | " | " " " | " | Mustd Mar. '80 |
| Battes, John, Pt. | " | " " " | " | |
| Boyd, Sam'l, Pt. | " | " " " | " | |
| Bass, Uriah, Pt. | " | " " " | " | |
| Brevard, Adam, Pt. | " | " " | " | |
| Brantley, Brittin, Corpl. | Baker's | " " | | |
| Burch, Jno., Musc. | " | " " | | |
| Bell, Elias, Pt. | " | 20 July " | | |
| Buck, Ab'm, Pt. | " | " " | | |
| Butler, John, Pt. | " | 5 May '76 | 2½ yrs. | Omtd '79 |
| Butler, Isaac, Pt. | " | " " | | Dischgd 8 May '79 |
| Broadwell, David, Pt. | " | 4 May " | | Omtd '79 |
| Baker, Enos, Pt. | " | 20 July '78 | | |
| Boon, Elisha, Pt. | " | " | | |
| Bailey, Robt., Pt. | " | " | | |
| Brantley, John, Pt. | " | " | | |
| Backingham, Wm., Pt. | " | " | | Died 25 Nov. '78 |
| Brazil, Benj., Pt. | " | | | Destd 9 July '78 |
| Baker, Wm., Musc. | Blount's | 20 July '78 | " | |
| Butler, Wm., Pt. | " | " " | | |
| Butler, Jos., Pt. | " | " | | |
| Barber, Jno., Pt. | " | " | | |
| Blanchets, Jos., Pt. | " | " | | |
| Bryant, Wm., Pt. | " | 26 Apr. '76 | 2½ yrs. | Omtd in '79 |
| Boon, Lewis, Pt. | " | 20 July '78 | 9 mo. | |
| Britt, Arthur, Pt. | " | " | " | Died Oct. 28, '78 |
| Bolton, Richard, Sergt. | Ballard's | " | " | |
| Broadstreet, Jas., Corpl. | " | " | " | |
| Brewer, Lewis, Pt. | " | " | " | |
| Boon, David, Pt. | " | " | " | |
| Bozman, Ethelredge, Pt. | " | " | " | Omtd Oct. '78 |
| Brown, Sam'l, Pt. | " | " | " | Omtd Oct. '78 |
| Baney, Lyon, Pt. | " | " | " | Omtd Oct. '78 |
| Barbere, Isaac, Pt. | " | " | " | |
| Bird, Benj., Pt. | " | " | " | Omtd Oct. '78 |
| Bozman, Jesse, Pt. | " | " | " | Omtd Oct. '78 |
| Boyd, Joseph, Corpl. | Bradley's | " | " | |
| Breacher, John, Corpl. | " | " | " | |
| Bernell, Neheh, Pt. | " | " | " | |
| Barrow, Dan'l, Pt. | " | " | " | |
| Bennett, Wm., Pt. | " | " | " | |
| Butler, Joel, Pt. | " | " | | |
| Burke, Meredy, Pt. | " | " | " | |
| Blockwell, James, Pt. | " | " | " | |
| Boon, Jas., Pt. | " | " | " | |
| Bowers, Giles, Pt. | " | " | " | Destd Oct. '78 |
| Brown, John, Sergt. | Childs' | " | " | |
| Beach, Robt., Pt. | " | " | " | |
| Bateman, Nary, Pt. | " | " | " | |
| Bullock, Dan'l, Pt. | " | " | " | |
| Barnhill, Henry, Pt. | " | " | " | |

| Name and Rank | Company | Dates of Enlistment and Commission | Period of Service | Occurrences |
|---|---|---|---|---|
| Bennet, Wm., Pt. | Child's | 20 July '78 | 9 Mo. | |
| Brinton, John, Pt. | " | " | " | Destd 1 Aug. '78 |
| Blythe, Joseph, Sergt. | | " | " | |
| Bailey, Wm., Corpl. | Bradley's | 21 June '79 | 18 mo. | |
| Blanton, Levy, Pt. | " | 2 " " | " | |
| Brock, Jas., Pt. | " | 30 " " | " | |
| Brantley, Jno., Pt. | " | 30 " " | " | |
| Bass, Moses, Pt. | " | 5 July " | W | Destd Sep. '79 |
| Brigman, Thos., Pt. | " | 22 Jan. '80 | | |
| Burnett, Chas., Pt. | Montford's | | W | |
| Basket, Wm., Pt. | " | | 18 mo. | |
| Beeney, Joseph, Pt. | " | | " | Omtd Oct. '79 |
| Bation, David, Pt. | " | | W | Destd Sep. '79 |
| Brewer, Robt., Pt. | " | 1779 | | Omtd Oct. '79 |
| Blount, Thos., Pt. | Ballard's | 29 June " | 18 mo. | |
| Burshaw, Jno., Pt. | " | 30 " " | " | Destd 26 Sep. '79 |
| Burden, Thos., Pt. | " | 18 " " | W | Destd 27 Oct. '79 |
| Bunbardy, Jno., Pt. | " | 22 " " | " | Destd 3 Oct. '79 |
| Burdenton, John, Pt. | " | 29 " " | " | Destd 19 Nov. '79 |
| Brayboy, John, Pt. | " | 27 Aug. '78 | 3 yrs. | Destd 29 Oct. '79 |
| Bennet, Solomon, Pt. | " | 29 June '79 | | Destd 5 Aug. '79 |
| Bright, Job, Pt. | " | " " | | Corpl. Dec. '79 |
| Barber, Wm., Pt. | " | " " | | |
| Bates, Edw'd, Pt. | " | " " | | |
| Biby, Thos., Pt. | " | " " | 9 mo. | Dischgd 1 Dec. '79 |
| Barnes, Thos., Pt. | Quinn's | 24 May " | 18 mo. | Corpl. '80 |
| Burrows, Sam'l, Pt. | " | 24 June " | " | Omtd Oct. '79 |
| Bass, Aaron, Pt. | " | " " | " | Destd Dec. '79 |
| Brown, Jos., Pt. | " | 10 June " | " | Destd Oct. '79 |
| Baggot, Allen, Pt. | " | 5 " " | " | Omtd Oct. '79 |
| Barnes, Wm., Pt. | " | 24 " " | W | |
| Beaver, John, Corpl. | Blount's | 1 Mar. " | 9 mo. | Dischgd 1 Dec. '79 |
| Beasley, Sam'l, Pt. | " | 20 May '77 | 3 yrs. | |
| Bagley, Natham, Pt. | " | 5 Aug. '79 | W | Destd Oct. '79 |
| Bailey, Wm., Pt. | " | " " | | Destd Sep. '79 |
| Brannon, Jese, Pt. | " | " " | | Died 25 Aug. '79 |
| Brown, Jas, Pt. | | " " | | Destd Sep. '79 |
| Bell, Robt, Ensn. | Raiford's | 18 May '81 | " | Lt. 8 Sep. '81 |
| Brevard, Joseph, Ensn. | | 9 " " | | Lt. 1 Aug. '81 |
| Boston, Chrisn., Pt. | McRees' | 28 Apr. " | 12 mo. | Left service 28 Apr. '82 |
| Boston, Andrew, Pt. | " | " " | " | Left service 28 Apr. '82 |
| Briggs, Robt. | " | 9 May " | " | {Sergt. Aug. '81, Left service 9 May '82 |
| Bell, Geo., Pt. | " | 25 Apr. " | " | Left service 25 Apr. '82 |
| Barnet, Jno. or Jas., Pt. | " | 1 June " | " | Left service 1 June '82 |
| Brandon, Thos. | " | 28 Apr. " | " | Left service 28 Apr. '82 |
| Bird, Jacob, Pt. | " | " " | " | Destd 18 June '81 |
| Billings, Ab'm, Pt. | " | " " | " | Destd 13 July '81 |
| Bryan, John, Pt. | " | 20 May " | " | Left service 25 May '82 |
| Billips, Thos., Musc. | Raiford's | 15 Apr. " | " | Left service 15 Apr. '82 |
| Brown, Henry, Pt. | " | 6 June " | " | Dead Oct. '81 |
| Bass, Dred, Pt. | " | 18 May " | " | {Transferred Aug. '81 to the Legion |
| Bennet, Reuben, Pt. | " | 5 May " | " | Time out 5 May '82 |
| Bubby, Edw'd, Pt. | " | 2 June " | " | Time out 3 June '82 |
| Browning, Mark, Pt. | " | 23 Apr. " | " | Time out 25 Apr. '82 |
| Baker, John, Pt. | Donoho's | 25 May " | " | Left service 25 May '82 |

| Name and Rank | Company | Dates of Enlistment and Commission | Period of Service | Occurrences |
|---|---|---|---|---|
| Bass, Hardy, Pt....... | Donoho's | 14 June '81 | 12 Mo. | Left service 14 June '82 |
| Bailey, Stephen, Pt..... | " | " | " | Left service 14 June '82 |
| Brinkley, Thos., Pt..... | " | " | " | {Sergt. Jan. '82, Left service 19 May '82 |
| Booling, Wm., Pt....... | " | " | " | Omtd in '81 |
| Bass, Rich'd, Pt....... | " | 18 May " | 3 yrs. | Omtd in '81 |
| Barrot, Joseph, Pt...... | " | 14 June " | 12 mo. | {Destd 19 July '81, Mustd Jan., Left ser. 14 June '82 |
| Brown, Jos., Pt........ | " | :" | " | Left service 14 June '82 |
| Butler, Lawrence, Pt.... | Dixon's | 1 June " | " | Died 24 Mar. '82 |
| Bryan, Hez'h, Pt...... | " | 15 " " | " | Left service 16 June '82 |
| Brown, Jas., Pt........ | " | 25 Apr. " | " | Left service 16 June '82 |
| Brown, Jno., Pt....... | " | " | " | Left service 26 May '82 |
| Burnet, Wm., Pt....... | " | " | W | Left service 25 Apr. '82 |
| Baker, Benj., Pt....... | " | 15 " | 12 mo. | Left service 25 Apr. '82 |
| Blount, Edmond, Pt.... | " | " " | " | Omtd in '81 |
| Busler, Jno., Pt........ | " | " " | " | Left service 25 Apr. '82 |
| Bibby, Absolom, Pt..... | " | 18 May " | " | Left service 21 May. '82 |
| Butler, Jethro, Pt...... | " | 15 Apr. " | " | Left srevice 25 Apr. '82 |
| Boon, Elisha, Pt....... | " | 4 May " | " | Time out 4 may '82 |
| Brown, Collin, Corpl.... | Lytle's | 12 Oct. '80 | 3 yrs. | Omtd in '81 |
| Blackstone, Henry, Mus. | " | 20 June " | 12 mo. | |
| Binum, Wm., Pt........ | " | 12 Apr. '81 | | Left service 12 Apr. '82 |
| Brittle or Britton, Wm., Pt................. | " | " " " | " | Left service 5 Apr. '82 |
| Ballard, Dudley, Pt.... | " | " " " | " | Left service 12 Apr. '82 |
| Brownum, Elizah, Pt.... | " | 6 June " | " | Left service 6 June '82 |
| Bonner, Wm., Corpl..... | Sharp's | 15 Apr. " | " | Omtd in '81 |
| Brady, Benj., Corpl..... | " | " | " | {Sergt. Jan., Left service 15 Apr. '82 |
| Brown, Solomon, Pt.... | " | 2 May " | " | {Destd 22 Apr. '81, Musc. Jan., Left service 21 May '82 |
| Brown, Arthur, Pt..... | " | 15 Apr. " | " | Left service 15 Apr. '82 |
| Blount, Benj., Pt....... | " | " | " | {Left service 15 Apr. '82, Musc. Mar. '82, Destd June '83 |
| Bates, James, Pt....... | " | " | " | Left service 15 Apr. '82 |
| Bexley, James, Pt...... | " | 5 Apr. " | " | Left service 5 Apr. '82 |
| Baggett, John, Pt...... | " | " | " | Left service 5 Apr. '82 |
| Bowers, Solomon, Pt.... | " | " | " | Left service 15 Apr. '82 |
| Brown, Jas, Pt......... | " | 15 " " | " | Dischgd 14 Feb. '82 |
| Boyce, John, Pt........ | " | " | 3 yrs. | Died 25 July '82 |
| Baggett, Drew, Musc. .. | Dixon's | 12 Ms, No d'bt | | Timeout 25 May '82 |
| Barnhill, James, Pt..... | Lyle's | " | | Time out 10 June '82 |
| Boon, David, Pt....... | " | " | | Time out 19 May '82 |
| Brothers, David, Pt. ... | Sharp's | " | | Time out 15 Apr. '82 |
| Bailey, John, Pt....... | Doherty's | | W | Mustd Jan. '82 |
| Barker, Joseph, Pt...... | " | 12M81 No d. | | Time out 25 May '82 |
| Burnett, John, Pt...... | " | " | | Time out 25 May '82 |
| Burt, John, Pt......... | " | " | | Time out 25 May '82 |
| Benton, Josh., Pt...... | " | " | | Time out 25 May '82 |
| Barnhill, David, Pt..... | " | " | | Time out 25 May '82 |
| Branch, Burrell, Pt..... | " | " | | Time out 25 May '82 |
| Blount, Thos., Pt....... | " | " | | Time out 25 May '82 |
| Burket, Uriah, Corpl.... | Rhode's | " | | Time out Apr. '82 |

| Name and Rank | Company | Dates of Enlistment and Commission | Period of Service | Occurrences |
|---|---|---|---|---|
| Brinkley, Mich'l, Pt..... | Rhode's | 12M81 No d. | | Dischgd 23 Jan. '82 |
| Boyd, Benj., Pt........ | " | " | | Dischgd 23 Jan. '82 |
| Benton, John, Pt....... | " | " | | Dischgd 17 Feb. '82 |
| Brisler, Philemon, Pt.... | " | " | | Time out 14 May '82 |
| Bable, John, Pt........ | Armstrongs' | | W | Mustd Jan. '82 |
| Boya, Dempsey, Capt... | " | " | | Time 1st Nov. '82 |
| Boya, Wm., Pt........ | " | " | | Left service 1 Oct. '82 |
| Bletcher, Jacob, Pt..... | " | " | | Left service 23 Dec. '82 |
| Bishop, Wm., Pt....... | " | " | | Left sevice 1 Dec. '82 |
| Bolton, Benj., Pt....... | " | " | | Left service 1 Dec. '82 |
| Ball, Hosea, Sergt....... | Bailey's | 17 May '81 | 12 mo. | Left service 17 May '82 |
| Beverhouse, Ab'm...... | " | June " | " | Left service 26 June '82 |
| Beesley, Wm., Corpl.... | " | 17 May " | " | Time out 17 May '82 |
| Bright, Chas., Pt....... | " | 1 Apr. " | " | Time out 1 Apr. '82 |
| Bryant, Chas., Pt...... | " | " | " | {Re-enlisted 1 Mar. '82 in {Lee's Legion |
| Baxter, Wm., Pt....... | " | 12 Apr. " | " | Left service 12 Apr. '82 |
| Brant, Jas, Pt......... | " | 17 May " | " | Left service 17 May '82 |
| Boyles, Benj., Pt...... | Brevard's | " | " | Left service 12 Apr. '82 |
| Boyles, Wm., Pt....... | " | " | " | Left service 12 Apr. '82 |
| Burk, Elihu, Pt........ | " | " | " | Left service 7 June '82 |
| Burrus, John, Pt....... | " | " | " | Left service 28 Apr. '82 |
| Burk, David, Pt....... | " | " | " | Left service May '82 |
| Berry, James, Pt...... | " | " | " | Left service 25 Apr. '82 |
| Bright, Jesse, Corpl..... | Hall's | " | 12 mo. | Left service 10 July '82 |
| Bachus, Wm., Pt....... | " | " | " | Left service 1 Aug. '82 |
| Barko, John, Pt........ | " | " | " | Left service 10 July '82 |
| Bell, Josiah, Pt........ | " | " | " | Left service 10 July '82 |
| Blanchard, Michaja, Pt.. | " | " | " | Left service 1 Aug. '82 |
| Bentley, Thos., Pt...... | " | " | " | Left service 1 Apr. '82 |
| Ballard, Lewis, Corpl.... | Yarborrow's | " | " | Left service 22 Apr. '82 |
| Baker, James, Pt....... | " | " | " | Left service 22 Apr. '82 |
| Burns, Fred'k, Pt...... | " | " | " | Left service 15 Apr. '82 |
| Brown, Warren, Pt..... | " | " | " | Left service 1 May '82 |
| Bealey, Arch'd, Pt..... | " | " | " | Left service 17 June '82 |
| Billips, Rich'd, Pt..... | " | " | " | Left service 22 Apr. '82 |
| Banks, Wm., Pt....... | " | " | " | Left service 1 Apr. '82 |
| Burton, John, Pt...... | " | " | " | Time out 1 May '82 |
| Bibby, Solomon, Pt.... | " | " | " | Omtd 1 Apr. '82 |
| Brinkle, Wm., Forage Mr.......... | " | " | " | Omtd 1 Apr. '82 |
| Burns, Jesse, Pt....... | " | " | " | Pris. 1 Apr. '82 |
| Bright, John, Pt....... | Carter's | " | " | Time out 10 Apr. '82 |
| Bibber, Dan'l, Pt...... | " | 6 June " | " | Time out 6 June '82 |
| Ballard, Wyatt, Pt..... | " | " | " | Time out 7 Apr. '82 |
| Benton, Nathan, Pt..... | Jones' | 1 Jan. '82 | " | |
| Betts, Wm., Pt........ | " | 6 Mar. " | " | |
| Brown, Henry, Pt..... | " | 9 Jan. " | " | For Brewer |
| Beesley, William, Pt.... | " | 2 Jan. " | " | |
| Baker, Isaac, Pt........ | " | 1 Oct. '81 | " | |
| Betts, Mathias, Pt...... | " | 14 Sep. " | " | |
| Brookin, Thos., Sergt.... | Mill's | 7 Jan. '82 | 3 yrs | Died 5 Aug. '82 |
| Bailee, Jno., Pt........ | " | 7 Feb. '81 | 12 mo. | Time out 7 Jan. '82 |
| Bracker, Isaac, Pt...... | " | " | " | Died 18 Sep. '82 |
| Bright, Simon, Pt....... | Coleman's | 1 Jan. '82 | " | |
| Bell, Wm., Pt......... | " | 15 May '81 | " | {Re-enlisted 1 Aug. '82 for {12 mos. |

| Name and Rank | Company | Dates of Enlistment and Commission | Period of Service | Occurrences |
|---|---|---|---|---|
| Bell, Sm'l, Pt......... | Coleman's | 7 Feb. '82 | 12 mo. | |
| Blackstone, Henry, Pt... | " | 1 Apr. " | " | Mustd 1 Sep. '82 |
| Bradley, Rich'd, Pt..... | Hall's | | | {Mustd 1 Apr. '82, Omtd Sep. '82 |
| Bryan, Keeder, Pt...... | " | 1 Feb. " | " | |
| Blount, Fred'k, Pt...... | " | 15 July " | W | |
| Brewer, Rice, Pt....... | Jones' | 1 Jan. '81 | 12 mo. | |
| Bailey, Rich'd, Pt...... | " | Dec. " | " | Dischgd Oct. '82 |
| Brantley, Jno., Pt...... | " | 1 Aug. '82 | " | Dischgd 1 Aug. '82 |
| Brown, Benj., Pt....... | Bailey's | 17 Sep. " | 18 mo. | |
| Banks, Joseph, Pt...... | " | 13 Sep. " | " | |
| Baker, Dempsey, Pt.... | " | 10 Sep. " | " | Destd 21 June '83 |
| Bryant, John, Pt....... | " | 7 Sep. " | " | |
| Brown, Warren, Pt..... | " | 7 Sep. " | " | |
| Black, Jas., Pt......... | " | 1 Sep. " | 12 mo. | |
| Black, Giren, Pt....... | " | 1 Aug. " | " | |
| Bond, Rich'd, Sergt..... | Hadley's | " | 18 mo. | |
| Ballard, Joal, Corpl..... | " | " | " | |
| Bell, Jas., Corpl........ | " | " | " | |
| Bachus, Josh, Pt....... | " | " | " | |
| Baxley, Josh, Pt ....... | " | " | " | {Or Backsley, Died 6 June '83 |
| Baker, John, Pt........ | " | " | " | |
| Bussell, Wm., Pt....... | " | " | " | |
| Brummager, Edw'd, Pt.. | " | " | " | |
| Bryant, John, Pt....... | " | " | " | |
| Bakot, Peter, Capt..... | " | 8 Sep. '81 | | |
| Brintley, Mich'l, Sergt. . | Bacot's | '82 | " | |
| Bransley, Amos, Corpl. . | " | " | " | |
| Brewer, Moses, Pt...... | " | " | " | |
| Brantley, John, Pt..... | " | " | " | |
| Burgess, Bryant, Pt.... | " | " | " | |
| Brocky, Wm., Pt....... | " | " | " | |
| Boyaken, Jas., Pt...... | " | " | " | |
| Brewer, Wm., Pt...... | " | " | " | |
| Batstaff, Fred'k, Pt.... | " | " | " | |
| Barrer, Moses, Pt...... | " | " | " | |
| Burns, David, Pt...... | " | " | " | |
| Black, Guin, Pt....... | " | " | " | |
| Boyd, Benj., Corpl..... | Carter's | " | " | |
| Bennett, Sion, Corpl.... | " | " | " | |
| Bracell, Geo., Pt........ | " | " | " | |
| Bagwell, John, Pt...... | " | " | " | |
| Berry, James, Pt...... | " | " | " | Destd 25 Dec. '82 |
| Bowers, Giles, Pt...... | Raiford's | " | W | Destd 8 June '83 |
| Benton, Dempsey, Pt. .. | " | " | 18 mo. | |
| Bennett, John, Pt...... | " | " | " | Destd 11 June '83 |
| Bunn, Jesse, Pt....... | " | " | " | |
| Bateman, Wm., Pt..... | " | " | " | |
| Bullock, Nathan, Pt.... | " | " | " | |
| Brady, John, Pt........ | " | " | " | |
| Brown, John, Pt....... | " | " | " | Destd 10 June '83 |
| Bryant, Dempsey, Musc. | Sharp's | " | W | |
| Bingham, John, Pt..... | " | " | 18 mo. | |
| Bucoe, Ab'm, Pt....... | " | " | " | Destd 13 June '83 |
| Black, Geo., Sergt...... | Lytle's | " | " | Destd 10 Dec. '82 |
| Black, Jas., Pt......... | " | " | " | |

| Name and Rank | Company | Dates of Enlistment and Commission | Period of Service | Occurrences |
|---|---|---|---|---|
| Burris, Aaron, Pt....... | Lytle's | '82 | 18 mo. | |
| Boling, Thos., Pt....... | " | " | " | |
| Belew, John, Pt........ | " | " | " | |
| Brown, John, Sergt..... | " | " | " | |
| Bunch, Clement, Pt..... | " | " | " | |
| Baldwin, Edw'd, Pt..... | Brevard's | " | " | |
| Baxter, Thos., Pt...... | " | " | " | |
| Blamer, John, Corpl..... | Evan's | " | " | Died 13 June '83 |
| Brown, Isaac, Pt....... | " | " | " | |
| Black, Martin, Pt...... | " | " | " | |
| Bailey, Josh., Pt....... | " | " | " | Omtd Jan. '83 transf'd. |
| Barnes, Moses, Pt..... | " | " | " | {Mustd '82, Resigned 19 Aug. '82 |
| Bull, Thos., Surg. Mate. | | | | |
| Bright, Wyllis, Pt...... | | | | Musc. Destd Sep. '79 |
| Burnham, Sam'l, Pt.... | | | | Ditto |
| Bright, Wm., Pt....... | | | | Ditto |
| Bido, John, Pt........ | | | | Ditto |
| Brice, John, Pt........ | | | | Ditto |
| Berry, Caleb, Pt....... | | 1779 | 3 yrs. | |
| Boons, Wm., Pt........ | | | | Mustd Destd Sep. '79 |
| Boon, Jno., Pt.......... | Mill's | Jan. '82 | 12 mo. | |
| Burris, Geo., Pt....... | Raiford's | | | {Mustd Dec. '82, Destd 2 Apr. '83 |
| Baker, Josh, Pt........ | Bacot's | | | {Mustd Dec. '83, Died 18 June '83 |
| Bogas, Benajah, Pt..... | Carter's | | | Mustd Dec. '82 |
| Bowen, Stephen, Sergt. . | Sharp's | 28 July '78 | 3 yrs. | |
| Blount, Warren, Sergt... | " | 10 Mar. | 9 mo. | |
| Bryan, David, Pt....... | " | " | " | |
| Bruington, Joshua, Pt... | " | " | " | |
| Bullard, Thos., Pt...... | " | " | " | |
| Braddy, John, Pt....... | " | " | " | |
| Baker, Josh., Pt........ | " | " | " | |
| Brewer, Joshua, Pt..... | " | " | " | |
| Bachus, Josh., Pt....... | Armstrong's | 25 May '78 | 3 yrs. | Mustd June '79 |
| Burnham, Sam'l, Pt..... | Lt. Col. | " | " | Mustd June '79 |
| Bright, Wyllis, Pt...... | | 22 May " | " | Mustd Feb. '79 |
| Beasley, Sam'l, Pt...... | Medaria's | | 9 mo. | Mustd Jan. '79 |
| Berry, Caleb, Pt....... | " | | 3 yrs. | Mustd Jan. '79 |
| Bedo, John, Pt......... | " | | " | Mustd Feb. '79 |
| Bowen, Stephen, Sergt. . | Sharp's | | " | Mustd Feb. See above |
| Bailey, Isaac, Pt....... | " | | " | {Mustd Feb. '79, Destd 22 Apr. '79 |
| Bird, Moses, Musc...... | Taylor's | | 2½ yrs. | Mustd Jan. '79 |
| Birgay, Wm., Pt........ | " | | " | {Mustd Jan. '79, Corpl. May '79 |
| Burns, David, Pt...... | " | | " | {Mustd Jan. '79, Dischgd Apr. '79 |
| Brock, John, Pt........ | " | | W | Mustd Jan. '79 |
| Brown, Jas., Pt......... | " | | 2½ yrs. | Mustd Jan. '79 |
| Browning, Wm., Pt..... | " | | 3 yrs. | {Mustd Jan. '79, Sergt. Apr. '79 |
| Boomer, Wm., Pt...... | Eaton's | | " | Mustd Jan. '79 |
| Bowen, Jas., Pt......... | " | | " | Mustd Jan. '79 |
| C (P. 1033) | | | | |
| Carter, David, Corpl.... | Wilson's | 20 Aug. '77 | | Died July '78 |

| Name and Rank | Company | Dates of Enlistment and Commission | Period of Service | Occurrences |
|---|---|---|---|---|
| Collins, Chas., Pt....... | Wilson | 6 May '77 | | |
| Cocker, Hy., Pt........ | " | 1 July " | 3 yrs. | or Coker |
| Coats, Benj., Pt........ | " | 1 Sep. " | | |
| Cooper, Solomon, Pt.... | Shepard's | 20 Jan. '78 | | Omtd June '78 |
| Clark, Ab'm, Pt......... | " | 3 May '77 | | Omtd June '78 |
| Cotton, Elijah, Pt...... | " | 1 July " | | |
| Caraway, Thos., Pt...... | " | 5 May " | 3 yrs. W | |
| Candy, Wm., Pt........ | " | 16 Feb. '78 | 3 yrs. | Destd 14 Sep. '78 |
| Cox, Edw'd, Musc...... | " | 12 June '77 | | Omtd Jan. '78 |
| Cox, Thos., Pt......... | " | " | 3 yrs. W | Corpl. 1 Nov. '82, Destd 13 June '83 |
| Clements, Jno., Sergt.... | Stephenson's | 21 Apr. " | " | Pt. June '78 |
| Clark, Orsborn, Sergt.... | " | 1 June " | 3 yrs. | Do |
| Cook, John, Corpl. | " | 21 Apr. " | " | Omtd Feb. '79 |
| Clark, Thos., Pt....... | " | " | " | Destd Apr. '78 |
| Carter, Isaac, Pt........ | " | 1 Sep. " | 3 yrs. W | Destd 13 June '83 |
| Cummings, Shad'k, Pt... | " | 12 " " | " | Destd 1 Mar. '83 |
| Capps, Wm., Pt........ | " | 14 June " | 3 yrs. | |
| Charleton, Wm., Pt..... | " | 3 " " | " | Prisner 1 June, '79 / Mustd Nov. '79 |
| Cox, Wm., Pt......... | " | " | " | Dead Nov. '78 |
| Curry, Robt., Pt....... | " | 27 " " | " | Destd Apr. '78 |
| Connor, Jno., Pt........ | " | 28 " " | " | Died Dec. '78 |
| Cummings, Jno., Pt..... | " | 25 July " | " | Died Oct. '78 |
| Cook, Geo., Lt......... | Jarvis' | 19 Apr. " | | Died May '80 |
| Carrall, Butler, Ensn.... | " | | | Omtd June '78 |
| Carlton, Jas., Corpl..... | " | 5 May '77 | | Pt. June '78 |
| Creef, Thos., Musc...... | " | 14 " " | | Do |
| Callum, Fred'k, Pt..... | " | 17 " " | 3 yrs. | Died 12 Jan. '79 |
| Caton, Thos., Pt....... | " | 12 June " | " | Corpl. 1 Dec. '78, Pt. 20 Mar. '79 |
| Cox, Jesse, Pt......... | " | 10 June " | " | Sergt. 15 June '79, Omtd Nov. '79 |
| Campbell, Thos., Pt.... | " | 18 June " | | |
| Campbell, Solomon, Pt.. | " | 4 Aug. " | | Dead Apr. '78 |
| Cartwright, Josiah, Pt... | Gregory's | 31 May " | 3 yrs. | |
| Cook, Sanders, Pt...... | " | " " | " | |
| Cannon, Lewis, Lt...... | Heron's | 19 Apr. " | | Omtd '78, Mustd in 5th Reg. May '79 |
| Chance, Stephen, Musc. | " | 1 July " | " | Pt. June '78 |
| Chance, Philemn, Pt.... | " | " " | " | Pris'r. 1 June '79, Mustd Nov. '79 |
| Chew, Malachi, Pt...... | Moore's | 28 June " | 3 yrs. W | Corpl. May '79, Sergt. Nov. '79 |
| Campbell, Jas., Lt...... | Vanois' | 19 Apr. " | | Lt. and Qr. Mr. 10 Sep. '79, Capt. 14 Dec. '79 |
| Chumney, Robt., Pt.... | " | 27 June " | 3 yrs. | |
| Covry, Shad'k, Pt...... | " | 30 May " | " | |
| Curry, Duncan, Pt...... | " | 24 Oct. " | " | |
| Chumney, Jno., Pt...... | " | 27 June " | | Omtd June '78 |
| Clampett, Govey, Pt.... | " | 1 Apr. " | 3 yrs. | Omtd Mar. '79 |
| Coulter, Levy, Pt....... | Maj. Ash's | 1 Feb. '77 | 2½ y. W | |
| Cates, Matthias, Corpl.. | " | 30 June '76 | 3 yrs. | Pt. Aug. '78 |
| Clements, Custis, Pt.... | " | 1 July '77 | " | |
| Cotton, Jno., Pt........ | " | 13 June " | " | Destd June '79 |
| Cottle, Jno., Pt......... | Coleman's | | | Omtd Aug. '78 |
| Copeland, Keeder, Pt. .. | " | 11 Sep. " | " | |

| Name and Rank | Company | Dates of Enlistment and Commission | Period of Service | Occurrences |
|---|---|---|---|---|
| Carrol, Douglas, Pt..... | | | 3 yrs. | Mustd June '78 |
| Connor, Jno., Pt........ | | 18 July '77 | " | |
| Calahan, Humphy, Pt... | | | W | {Mustd Aug. '78, Destd 6 Oct. '78 |
| Creekman, Mathia, Pt. | | | " | Mustd Mar. '79 |
| Creed, Hazard, Pt...... | Montfort's | 20 July '78 | 9 mo. | |
| Cleveland, Jas., Pt...... | " | " | " | |
| Cain, Wm., Pt......... | " | " | " | |
| Crawford, Jas., Pt...... | " | " | " | |
| Christie, Jno., Pt....... | " | " | " | |
| Cooley, Jeffy, Pt........ | " | " | " | {Destd 21 July '78, Mustd 5 Reg. Jan. '79 for 3 yrs. |
| Charlescroft, Stephen, Pt. | Hogg's | 1 May '76 | 2½ yrs. | Dischgd 2 Nov. '78 |
| Carol, Britton, Pt....... | " | 20 July '78 | 9 mo. | |
| Charles, Wynnick, Pt. .. | " | " | " | |
| Carraway, Jno., Pt...... | Quinn's | " | " | |
| Caster, Jno., Pt........ | " | " | " | |
| Caster, Jacob, Pt....... | " | " | " | |
| Campbell, Geo., Pt..... | " | " | " | |
| Custis, Thos., Pt....... | " | " | " | Dischgd 24 July '78 |
| Cummings, Edw'd, Pt... | " | 20 July '78 | " | |
| Cornet, Bird, Pt....... | Lt. Col. | " | " | |
| Clark, Jno., Pt......... | " | " | " | |
| Carter, Jno., Pt........ | " | " | " | Died 18 Nov. '78 |
| Casten, Francis, Pt..... | Baker's | " | " | |
| Carol, Jno., Pt......... | " | '78 | " | Destd 23 July '78 |
| Clark, H., Pt........... | Blount's | 20 July " | " | |
| Cooper, Nath'l, Pt...... | " | " | " | |
| Clanghorn, Timothy, Pt. | " | " | " | |
| Coward, Eph'm, Pt..... | " | " | " | |
| Chamberlain Malachi, Pt. | " | " | " | |
| Cobb, Nath'l, Pt........ | " | " | " | |
| Cook, Robt., Pt........ | " | " | " | |
| Coward, Zad'k, Pt...... | " | " | " | |
| Collins, Jno., Pt........ | " | " | " | Omtd Oct. '78 |
| Chapell, Edw'd, Pt...... | Ballard's | " | " | |
| Curl, Jno., Pt.......... | " | " | " | |
| Collins, Shad'k, Pt...... | " | " | " | |
| Chitham, Thos., Pt..... | " | " | " | |
| Choves, Solm'n, Pt..... | " | " | " | |
| Crabb, Hilly, Pt........ | " | " | " | |
| Cooley, Wm., Pt........ | Bradley's | " | " | |
| Cooley, Gab'l, Pt....... | " | " | " | |
| Corbit, Rich'd., Pt...... | " | " | " | |
| Chester, Jno., Pt....... | " | " | " | |
| Cockburn, Jno., Pt...... | " | " | " | |
| Cherry, Joshua, Pt...... | Child's | 20 July '78 | " | |
| Cotanch, Jno., Pt....... | " | " | " | {Mustd Dead in Lyle's Co'y '82 |
| Corey, Jno., Pt......... | " | " | " | |
| Carey, Arthur, Pt....... | " | " | " | |
| Coats, Ezek'l, Pt....... | " | " | " | |
| Clark, Isaac, Pt........ | " | 20 Feb. '77 | 3 yrs. W | |
| Colbreath, Dan'l, Pt.... | Bradley's | 20 May '78 | W | Destd 16 Oct. '79 |
| Carter, Jno., Pt........ | " | 30 June '79 | 18 mo. | |
| Cominel, Frans., Pt..... | " | 30 " " | 3 yrs. | Destd Dec. '79 |
| Cross, Anth'y, Pt....... | " | 14 " " | " | Omtd Oct. '79 |

| Name and Rank | Company | Dates of Enlistment and Commission | Period of Service | Occurrences |
|---|---|---|---|---|
| Chardick, Benj., Pt.... | Bradley's | 20 June '79 | W | Destd Sep. '79 |
| Cain, Jos., Pt......... | " | 27 Aug. '78 | 3 yrs. | |
| Case, Jos., Pt......... | " | " | " | |
| Cole, Wm., Pt......... | " | 25 Dec. '77 | " | {Dischgd before the 30 Mar. '80 |
| Carbett, Jas., Corpl.... | Montfort's | 29 June '79 | " | |
| Close, Geo., Pt........ | " | 26 May " | 18 mo. | Omtd Oct. '79 |
| Connor, Wm., Pt...... | " | 1 July " | " | Destd 10 Nov. '79 |
| Clemmens, Jno., Pt..... | " | " | " | |
| Cornelison, Jno., Pt..... | " | 1 Mar. " | 9 mo. | Dischgd 1 Dec. '79 |
| Crawley, David, Sergt... | " | " | " | Omtd Dec. '79 |
| Clifton, Dan'l, Sergt. ... | Quinn's | 5 June " | 18 mo. | |
| Cain, Jno., Pt......... | " | 24 " " | " | |
| Caesar, Francis, Pt.... | " | 19 " " | W | Destd Dec. '79 |
| Copland, Jas., Pt...... | " | " " | 9 mo. | Dischgd Dec. '79 |
| Copland, Rich'd, Pt.... | " | " " | " | Do |
| Chase, Blake, Pt....... | " | 21 May '78 | 3 yrs. | |
| Capps, Dempsey, Pt.... | Blount's | 20 May '77 | " | |
| Curby, Wm., Pt........ | " | 5 Aug. '77 | W | Destd Oct. '79 |
| Calvard, Jno., Pt...... | " | 3 " " | 18 mo. | Do |
| Copland, Rich'd, Pt.... | " | 5 " " | W | Do |
| Carter, Ab'm, Pt...... | " | 1779 | 9 mo. | Omtd Oct. '79 |
| Cole, Jesse, Pt........ | " | " | " | Destd Sep. '79 |
| Cooley, Gab'l, Pt...... | " | " | " | Died Sep. '79 |
| Campbell, Jno., Lt...... | " | 20 Apr. " | | |
| Clayton, Lambt., Sergt.. | McRee's | 28 Apr. '81 | 12 mo. | Left service 28 Apr. '82 |
| Cooper, Fred'k, Pt..... | " | " | " | {Corpl. Aug. '81, Left service 28 Apr. '82 |
| Crow, Jas., Pt......... | " | " | " | Left service 28 Apr. '82 |
| Chambers, Jas., Pt..... | " | " | " | Omtd after Apr. '82 |
| Charborough, Stephn, Pt | " | 6 June '81 | " | Left service 26 June '82 |
| Cannon, Bind., Pt..... | " | 8 May " | " | Destd 1 June '81 |
| Curtis, Moses, Pt...... | " | 9 " " | " | Destd 28 May '81 |
| Carter, Wm., Pt....... | Raiford's | 28 Apr. " | " | Time out 26 Apr. '82 |
| Childas, Wm., Corpl.... | " | 5 May " | " | {Pt. 5 Jan. '82, Time out 5 May '82 |
| Carter, Sewall, Pt...... | " | 1781 | | Time out 1 Apr. '82 |
| Carrel, Jno., Pt........ | " | 11 June " | 12 mo. | Time out 11 June '82 |
| Connor, Wm., Pt...... | Donoho's | 14 " " | " | Omtd in '81 |
| Chavons, Drury, Pt.... | " | " " | " | Do |
| Cole, Chas., Pt........ (P. 1036) | " | 18 May " | " | Left service 18 May '82 |
| Coleman, Levy, Pt...... | " | 25 Apr. " | " | Left service 25 May '82 |
| Campbell, Jas., Pt...... | Dixon's | " " | " | Omtd in '81 |
| Chappell, Sam'l, Sergt... | " | 24 Apr. " | " | Left service Apr. 25, '82 |
| Carns, Joshua, Pt...... | " | 15 May " | " | Omtd in '81 |
| Cleaton, Coleman, Pt. .. | " | " " | " | Left service 28 May '82 |
| Carmicarl, Duncan, Pt. . | " | " " | " | Do |
| Carvin, Wm., Pt........ | " | 12 May " | " | Destd 20 July '81 |
| Caton, Frank, Pt...... | " | 15 May " | " | Destd 18 July '81 |
| Connor, Jas., Pt....... | Lytle's | 7 Apr. " | " | Left service 7 Apr. '82 |
| Copland, John, Pt...... | Sharp's | 2 May " | " | Omtd in '81 |
| Craimor, Jas., Pt...... | " | 15 Apr. " | " | Left service 15 Apr. '82 |
| Carney, Jno., Pt....... | " | 5 " " | " | Omtd in '81 |
| Cammeron, Alex'r, Pt... | " | 24 " " | " | Left service 24 Apr. '82 |
| Crover, Peter, Pt...... | Walton's | '81 | | {Left service May '82, Time out |

| Name and Rank | Company | Dates of Enlistment and Commission | Period of Service | Occurrences |
|---|---|---|---|---|
| Clower, Jno., Pt........ | Walton's | '81 | | Do |
| Campbell, Irael, Pt..... | Lytle's | " | | {Left service 12 May '82, Time out |
| Chandler, Thos., Pt..... | " | " | W | Mustd Jan. '82 |
| Cooksey, Hezk., Pt..... | Sharp's | " | | Time out 2 Feb. '83 |
| Cooksey, Thos., Musc... | " | " | | Do |
| Carr, Jas., Sergt........ | Doherty's | " | Time out | 25 May '82 |
| Clark, Thos., Musc..... | " | " | | Do |
| Canady, Thos., Pt...... | " | " | | Do |
| Chubbuck, Jereh, Pt. ... | " | " | | Do |
| Campbell, Walter, Pt.... | " | " | W | Mustd Jan. '82 |
| Craford, Jno., Pt....... | Rhode's | " | | Time out 25 Apr. '82 |
| Cronester, Jas., Pt...... | Armstrong's | | " | Mustd Jan. '82 |
| Crosbey, Wm., Pt..... | " | | " | {Mustd Jan. '82, Destd 7 May '82 |
| Coats, Benj., Pt........ | " | " | 12 mo. | Left service 23 Dec. '82 |
| Cason, Hilly, Corpl..... | Bailey's | 12 June '80 | 3 yrs. | Died 12 Aug. '82 |
| Cunningham, Wm., Pt. . | " | 15 May '81 | 12 mo. | Left service 15 May '82 |
| Cornelius, Jno., Pt..... | " | 2 May " | " | Left service 15 May '82 |
| Case, Jona, Pt......... | " | 17 May " | " | Left service May 17, '82 |
| Coleman, Jno., Pt...... | " | 15 May " | " | Left service May 15, '82 |
| Cason, Canon, Pt...... | " | 12 June '80 | 3 yrs. | |
| Carter, Isaac, Pt....... | " | 25 May '81 | 12 mo. | Left service 25 May '82 |
| Cooper, Benj., Pt....... | " | 17 May " | " | Do    17 May '82 |
| Chavers, Drury, Pt.... | " | 25 May " | " | Do    25 May '82 |
| Collins, Hez'k, Pt...... | Brevard's | " | | Do    25 May '82 |
| Cavender, Wm., Pt.... | " | " | | Do    25 May '82 |
| Combs, Geo., Pt........ | " | " | | Do     9 May '82 |
| Chavers, Wm., Pt...... | " | " | | Do    12 Apr. '82 |
| Conn, Jno., Pt.......... | " | " | | Do    28 May '82 |
| Cavender, Jas., Pt..... | " | " | | Do    25 May '82 |
| Capps, Francis, Pt..... | " | " | | Do    12 Apr. '82 |
| Cheshire, Jno., Pt...... | " | " | | Do    28 May '82 |
| Cox, Jno., Pt.......... | " | " | | Do    28 Apr. '82 |
| Cogdill, Wm., Pt....... | " | " | | Do    25 Apr. '82 |
| Campbell, Wm., Pt.... | " | " | | Do    28 Apr. '82 |
| Coker, Josh., Pt........ | " | " | | {Transf'd 20 Mar. '82, to Virga. Artillery |
| Clarkson, Thos., Sergt... | Hall's | " | 12 mo. | Left service 21 Apr. '82 |
| Collins, Jereh, Corpl. ... | " | " | " | Do    16 Aug. '82 |
| Cale, Abner, Pt......... | " | 1781 | " | Do    16 Aug. '82 |
| Carroll, Benj., Pt...... | " | " | 12 mo. | Do    10 Nov. '82 |
| Carroll, Wm., Pt...... | " | " | " | { Do    10 Nov. '82  Mustd W. Jan. '82 |
| Carmack, Jno., Pt..... | " | " | " | Do     1 Nov. '82 |
| Collins, Jno., Pt........ | " | " | " | Do     1 Aug. '82 |
| Cob, Henry, Pt........ | " | " | " | Do     1 Sept. '82 |
| Carter, Dan'l, Pt...... | " | " | " | Destd 1 Apr. '82 |
| Carpenter, Thos., Pt.... | " | " | " | Left service 12 Apr. '82 |
| Card, Wm., Sergt...... | Yarboro's | " | " | Time out 22 Apr. '82 |
| Charleton, Geo., Pt.... | " | " | " | Omtd 1 Apr. '82 |
| Crane, Stephen, Pt..... | " | " | " | Time out 22 Apr. '82 |
| Chance, Phileman, Pt... | " | " | " | {Corpl. Apr. '82, Time out 1 Oct. '83 |
| Campbell, Jesse, Pt..... | " | " | " | Time out 22 Apr. '82 |
| Clifton, Wm., Pt....... | " | " | " | Do    22 Apr. '82 |
| Caraway, Francis, Corpl. | Carter's | 12 May '82 | " | Do    25 Apr. '82 |

| Name and Rank | Company | Dates of Enlistment and Commission | Period of Service | Occurrences |
|---|---|---|---|---|
| Chavers, Caezer, Pt..... | Carter's | 19 May '82 | 12 mo. | Do    25 Apr. '82 |
| Coggin, Robt., Pt...... | " | 1781 | " | Do    7 Apr. '82 |
| Cross Stephen, Pt...... | " | 19 May " | " | Do    19 Apr. '82 |
| Combs, Robt., Pt...... | " | 2 " " | ". | Do    2 Apr. '82 |
| Cadle, Zack'h, Pt...... | " | 19 July " | " | Destd 15 Oct. '82 |
| Cake, Phillip, Sergt..... | Jones' | 1 Feb. '80 | W | Destd 1 Apr. '82 |
| Cartwright, Joseph, Pt. . | " | 1 Jan. '82 | 13 mo. | |
| Carroner, Chris'r, Pt.... | " | 15 " " | " | |
| Casteen, Wm., Pt....... | " | 3 Feb. " | " | Died 14 Sep. '82 |
| Clubb, Sam'l, Pt........ | " | 6 Mar. " | " | |
| Cameron, Dan'l, Pt..... | " | 4 Jan. " | " | |
| Cox, John, Pt.. ........ | " | 19 Oct. '81 | " | |
| Carter, John, Pt........ | " | 1 Feb. " | W | |
| Criswell, Thos., Pt..... | " | 8 Mar. '82 | " | |
| Cannon, Jno., Pt....... | Mill's | 7 Feb. " | 12 mo. | Died 25 Aug. '82 |
| Collens, Jno., Pt........ | " | 6 " " | " | |
| Chamberlin, Dixon, Pt. . | " | 7 " " | " | |
| Clower, Dan'l, Pt....... | " | 13 Jan. " | " | |
| Clower, Wm., Pt....... | " | " " " | " | |
| Calvert, Stephen, Corpl. | Coleman's | 18 Dec. '81 | " | Pt. Apr. '82 |
| Connon, David or Edw'd, Pt............ | " | " | " | |
| Canady, Rich'd, Pt..... | " | 15 Apr. " | " | |
| Crumety, Wm., Pt...... | " | 5 Dec. " | " | |
| Campbell, Neil, Pt..... | " | 25 Nov. " | " | |
| Coleman, Jno., Pt...... | " | 10 Feb. '82 | " | |
| Cookey, Isaac, Pt....... | Hall's | 1 Apr. " | " | |
| Cason, Hilly, Pt........ | Jones' | " " | " | Time out |
| Cook, Allen, Pt........ | " | 5 Mar. " | W | |
| Clark, Thos., Pt........ | " | 20 Feb. " | 12 mo. | |
| Civil, David, Pt........ | " | 1 Mar. " | " | |
| Cason, Cannon, Pt..... | " | 1 Jan. " | " | |
| Carleton, David, Pt.... | " | 7 Dec. '81 | " | Time out Jan. 1, '83 |
| Carleton, John, Pt..... | " | " " " | " | Time out Jan. 1, '83 |
| Coxey, Thos., Pt....... | Mill's | 1782 | " | Time out Jan. 1, '83 |
| Curry, Jno., Pt........ | " | 4 Oct. " | " | { Do    4 Oct. '83, Qr. Mr. Sergt Dec. '82 |
| Colston, Jas., Pt....... | Bailey's | 13 May " | 3 yrs. | |
| Cunningham, Wm., Pt. . | " | 7 Sep. " | 18 mo. | |
| Carrin, Emanuel, Pt.... | " | " " " | " | |
| Conaway, Wm., Pt..... | Bacot's | 1782 | " | |
| Cappell, Chas., Pt..... | " | | " | |
| Connor, Wm., Pt...... | Carter's | | " | |
| Clifton, Clay, Pt........ | " | | " | |
| Collins, Shad'k, Pt..... | " | | " | |
| Cain, Rich'd, Pt........ | " | | " | |
| Colwell, David, Pt...... | " | | " | |
| Connor, Doshey, Pt.... | " | | " | Died 14 June 83 |
| Conn, Benj., Pt........ | Raiford's | | W | Destd 2 Apr. '83 |
| Collins, Jno., Pt....... | " | | 18 mo. | |
| Crumpton, Jas., Pt...... | " | | " | |
| Cale, Wm., Musc...... | Sharp's | | W | |
| Cook, Wm., Pt........ | " | | 18 mo. | |
| Connor, Benj., Pt...... | " | | " | |
| Campbell, Angus, Pt.... | " | | " | |
| Collins, Jno., Pt....... | " | | " | Died 26 Mar. '83 |
| Campen, Jno., Pt....... | " | | W | |

| Name and Rank | Company | Dates of Enlistment and Commission | Period of Service | Occurrences |
|---|---|---|---|---|
| Crews, Ethelred, Pt..... | Lytle's | 1782 | 18 mo. | |
| Crumpton, Thos., Pt.... | " | " | " | |
| Cox, Jese, Pt.......... | " | " | " | |
| Cofield, Sam'l, Pt...... | " | " | " | |
| Coplin, Job, Pt........ | " | " | " | Died 7 Mar. '82 |
| Comber, Hugh, Corpl... | Brevard's | " | " | |
| Childers, Robt., Musc... | " | " | " | Destd Mar. '83 |
| Cayson, Thos., Pt...... | " | " | " | |
| Carter, Henry, Pt...... | " | " | " | |
| Carter, Moses, Pt...... | " | " | " | |
| Croe, Wm., Pt......... | " | " | " | Dischgd 1 Mar. '83 |
| Connor, Mordicai, Pt.... | " | " | " | |
| Carrell, Hardy, Pt...... | Rhode's | 1 Dec. '82 | " | |
| Colbreath, Arch'd, Sergt. | Evans' | " | " | |
| Chester, Jno., Pt....... | " | " | " | |
| Carter, Isaac, Pt....... | " | " | " | Destd 11 June '83 |
| Clay, David, Pt........ | " | " | " | |
| Combs, Jno., Pt........ | " | " | " | Destd 21 June '83 |
| Crable, Dan'l, Pt...... | " | " | 3 yrs. | Mustd. Destd Sep. '97* |
| Coroband, Wyllis, Pt.... | | | | Do |
| Corbet, James, Corpl.... | Sharp's | 14 Dec. '78 | 3 yrs. | |
| Childers, Wm., Pt...... | " | 1 Nov. " | 9 mo. | |
| Crabb, Jairah, Pt...... | " | " | " | |
| Cowan, David, Lt...... | Ramsay's | 20 Mar '79 | | |
| Curling, Wm., Pt....... | Armstrong's | | W | Mustd Jan. '79 |
| Calahan, Wm., Corpl.... | Taylor's | | 3 yrs. | Do |
| Chace, Blake, Pt....... | Eaton's | 22 May '78 | " | Do |
| Charleton, Wm., Ensn... | " | 14 Mar. '79 | | Said to be Lt. 25 May'78 |
| Carter, Stephen, Pt..... | Sharp's | 26 Aug. '78 | W | Destd Jan. '79 |
| **D** (P. 1038) | | | | |
| Davis, Rich'd, Pt....... | Wilson's | 15 May '77 | | |
| Davis, Case, Pt......... | " | 1 Oct. " | | |
| Davis, Benj., Pt........ | Shephard's | 2 May " | 3 yrs. | |
| Dean, Sterling, Pt...... | " | 5 July " | 3 yrs. W | (Pris. 1 June '79, Mustd Nov. '79 |
| Doming, Speakman, Pt.. | " | 20 June " | | |
| Downing, Rich'd, Pt.... | " | " | 3 yrs. | |
| Defnel, Wm., Corpl..... | Stephenson's | 21 Apr. " | " | Pt. June '78 |
| Defnel, David, Pt...... | " | 21 Apr. " | " | |
| Dew, John, Pt.......... | " | | | |
| Dove, Wm., Pt........ | " | | | |
| Docan, John, Pt........ | | | | Omtd June '78 |
| Daug, Zacha, Musc..... | Jarvis' | 13 May " | " | Pt. Aug. '78 |
| Daug, Peter, Pt........ | " | 7 | " | Omtd Sep. '78 |
| Dunn, Jeffrey, Pt...... | " | 11 Nov. " | " | Died 12 Jan. '79 |
| Dunn, Jacob, Pt........ | " | Dec. " | | |
| Dunn, Malachi, Pt...... | " | " | " | Dead Dec. '78 |
| Davis, Elisha, Sergt..... | Gregory's | 31 May " | " | Pt. June '78 |
| Dawley, David, Corpl... | Heron's | 29 Apr. " | " | (Pt. June '78, Corpl. Nov. '79 |
| Donaldson, Spencer, Musc............... | Moore's | 18 May " | " | |
| Dugan, Francis, Musc... | " | 14 Aug. " | 3 yrs. W | Mustd 27 Mar. '80 |
| Deal, John, Pt......... | " | 5 Aug. " | 3 yrs. | |
| Drischall, David, Musc.. | Vannois' | 9 Aug. " | 3 yrs. W | Pt. June '78 |
| Daughty, Jese, Pt...... | " | " '78 | W | Destd 8 Jan. '80 |
| Dukes, Hardmond, Pt... | | 1 May '76 | 2½ yrs. | Dischgd Nov. '78 |

| Name and Rank | Company | Dates of Enlistment and Commission | Period of Service | Occurrences |
|---|---|---|---|---|
| Dukes, William, Pt.... | | 6 May '76 | 2½ yrs. | Do |
| Dasher, Chris'n, Pt.... | | 31 Mar. '78 | 3 yrs. | |
| DeEll, Wm., Pt....... | | 1 May '79 | W | Omtd Nov. '79 |
| Dolly, Caleb, Sergt.... | | 3 Feb. '78 | " | {Pt. June '78, / Destd June '79 |
| Dobey, Nath'l, Pt..... | | 23 Apr. '76 | | Dischgd 10 Nov. '78 |
| Dukemore, Marina, Pt.. | | | | {Joined Apr. '78, / Omtd June '78 |
| Davis, Jno., Pt........ | | | | {Mustd Jan. '78, / Dead May '78 |
| Dunnick, Peter, Sergt... | | | W | {Mustd 11 May '78, Corpl. / June '78, Sergt. 24 May'79 / Transf'd Apr. '82 |
| Durham, Jno., Musc.... | | 28 June '77 | 3 yrs. W | |
| Davis, Josiah, Pt...... | | 25 Apr. '76 | 2½ yrs. | Dischgd 30 Oct. '78 |
| Dunnigan, Thos., Pt.... | | | W | Mustd Jan. '78 |
| Denny, Ab'm, Pt...... | | | 3 yrs. | |
| Davidson, Thos., Pt.... | | | " | {Mustd June '78, / Dischgd 1 Oct. '78 |
| Dowdy, Geo., Pt...... | | 1778 | | Died Apr. '78 |
| Drake, Ely, Pt........ | Monfort's | 20 July " | 9 mo. | |
| Duncan, Wm., Pt...... | Hogg's | 20 Apr. '76 | 2½ yrs. | Dischged 19 Oct. '78 |
| Duncan, Geo., Pt...... | " | " | " | Dischgd 19 Oct. '78 |
| Dempsey, Jno., Pt..... | | 20 July '78 | 9 mo. | Destd 21 July '78 |
| Davenport, Wm., Pt.... | Quinn's | " | " | |
| Dean, Jno., Pt........ | " | " | " | |
| Doherty, Rich'd, Pt.... | | " | " | |
| Duberry, Solomon, Pt... | Lt. Colol. | " | " | |
| Davis, Sam'l, Pt....... | " | | | |
| Dean, Rich'd, Pt...... | Baker's | " | " | |
| Dempsey, Wm., Pt..... | " | | " | Destd 30 Aug. '78 |
| Dudley, Ambrose, Pt.... | | 1778 | " | Destd 9 July '78 |
| Doddriel, Jas., Pt...... | Blount's | 20 July " | " | Corpl. 3 Oct. '78 |
| Dunning, Uriah, Pt.... | | " " | " | Sergt. 25 Oct. '78 |
| Dixon, Retson, Pt...... | Ballard's | " " | " | |
| Davis, Aaron, Pt...... | " | " " | " | |
| Dunn, Jacob, Pt........ | " | " " | " | |
| Dickenson, Wm., Pt.... | " | " " | " | Destd 24 July '78 |
| Dempsey, Heszk'h, Pt.. | " | '78 | " | Destd 30 Aug. '78 |
| Davis, Bartley, Pt..... | Bradley's | 20 July " | " | |
| Dawtry, Lewis, Pt..... | " | " | " | |
| Durden, Cornelius, Pt.. | " | " | " | |
| Dawtry, Thos., Pt..... | " | " | " | |
| Durden, Benj., Pt..... | " | 20 Apr. " | " | Destd Oct. '78 |
| Darnald, Anth'y, Pt.... | | " | " | |
| Dixon, Wm., Pt....... | Childs' | | " | Destd 2 Aug. '78 |
| Daniel, Thos., Pt...... | " | | 3 yrs. | Destd 26 Oct. '79 |
| Dubois, Nich., Pt...... | Bradley's | 18 June '79 | " | Destd 27 May '83 |
| Danolson, Jesse, Pt..... | Monfort's | 5 " " | W | Destd Sep. '79 |
| Durnegan, Jno., Pt..... | " | 4 " " | " | |
| Dunson, Wm., Pt...... | " | 4 July " | 18 mo. | |
| Davis, Jas., Pt........ | Ballard's | 1 " " | W | Destd 19 Oct. '79 |
| Davis, John, Pt........ | " | 30 June " | " | |
| Dikons, Edw'd........ | Quinn's | 2 June " | " | Omtd Oct. '79, Corpl. '80 |
| Dawtry, Jacob........ | " | " | 3 yrs. | |
| Davis, Stephen........ | | " | " | |

| Name and Rank | Company | Dates of Enlistment and Commission | Period of Service | Occurrences |
|---|---|---|---|---|
| Dedrick, Jacob......... | Blount's | | 18 mo. | Joined Dec. '79 Pulaski's Legion |
| Dunn, Nich............ | " | 7 June " | W | |
| Dunham, Jno.......... | " | 25 June " | 18 mo. | |
| Denson, Wm........... | | " | 9 mo. | Died 1 Sep. '79 |
| Dennis, Wm........... | | " | | Died 1 Sep. '79 |
| Dudley, Thos., Lt....... | | 20 June " | | Deranged 1 Jan. '83, Promoted from Musc. 6 Reg. Lt. '82 |
| Dixon, Wynn, Ensn..... | | 1 Mar. '81 | | |
| Davis, Jehu, Ensn...... | | 6 May " | | |
| Davis, Wm., Sergt...... | McRee's | 28 Apr. " | 12 mo. | Left service 25 Apr. '82 |
| Davidson, Jno., Pt..... | " | 25 May " | " | Left service 25 May '82 |
| Dixon, Robt., Pt....... | " | 28 Apr. " | " | Destd 1 June '81 |
| Dixon, Joseph, Pt....... | " | 2 May " | W | Transf'd in '82, not known where |
| Duke, Wm., Sergt..... | Raiford's | 5 May " | 12 mo. | Pt. Feb. 1, '82, |
| Davis, Micajah, Pt..... | " | " " | " | Left service 27 Apr. '82 Promoted 8 Jan. '82, |
| Duke, Sherard, Pt..... | " | " | " | Left service 23 Apr. '82 Died Oct. '81 |
| Davidson, Jas., Pt..... | | 15 Apr. " | " | Destd Aug. '81, Joined 25 Dec. '81, Omtd Jan. '82, See Hardy Lewis |
| Dowdy, Francis, Pt..... | " | 19 May " | " | Destd Nov. '81 |
| Dickings, Jas., Pt...... | Donoho's | 25 " " | " | Left service 25 May '82 |
| Dunstand, Chas., Corpl. | Dixon's | 12 " " | " | Do    21 May '82 |
| Duert, Hezh., Pt....... | | 15 " " | " | Do |
| Davey, Jas., Pt......... | Lytle's | 9 July " | " | Omtd in '82 |
| Davis, Jos., Pt......... | " | 6 June " | " | Left service 6 June '82 |
| Daniels, Jno., Pt....... | " | 12 Apr. " | | Destd 6 July '81 |
| Duncan, Peter, Sergt.... | Sharp's | 30 May " | | Omtd in '81 |
| Doiland, Benj., Pt...... | " | 21 May " | | Do |
| Dixon, Wm., Pt....... | " | 15 Apr. " | | Do |
| Dean, Moses, Pt....... | " | | | Dischgd 1 Feb. '82 |
| Dixon, Jereh, Pt....... | " | " | | Left service 15 Apr. '82 |
| Davis, Burrel, Pt....... | " | 20 June " | | Omtd in '81 |
| Dean, Robt., Pt....... | Walton's | " | | Mustd War 1 Sep. '82 Dead 11 Nov. '82 |
| Dixon, Wynn, Lt....... | Lytle's | 5 July " | | |
| Daniel, Jepha, Pt...... | Doherty's | " | | Time out 26 May '82 |
| Davis, Joel, Pt......... | | " | | Do    3 July '82 |
| Durham, Wm., Pt..... | Rhode's | 5 July '81 | | Time out 12 Apr. '82 |
| Dean, Ab'm, Pt....... | Armstrong's | " | W | Mustd Jan. '82 |
| Davidson, Jas., Pt..... | " | " | | Time out 21 Apr. '82 |
| Drake, Axom, Pt...... | " | " | | Left service 1 Apr. '82 |
| Dollar, Jona, Pt....... | " | " | | Do    1 July '82 |
| Dixon, Thos., Pt....... | Bailey's | 25 May " | 12 mo. | Do    26 July '82 |
| Duncan, Geo., Pt...... | " | 2 " " | " | Do    29 May '82 |
| Dobbins, Jas., Pt...... | " | 25 " " | " | Do    25 May '82 |
| Davenport, Eph'm, Pt. . | Brevard's | | " | Do    2 May '82 |
| Dawson, Jno., Pt...... | " | | " | Do    25 May '82 |
| Durham, Humphrey, Pt. | " | | " | Do    Do |
| Demry, Allen, Pt....... | " | | " | Do    Do |
| Dillard, Jas., Pt....... | " | | " | Left service 9 May '82 |
| Davis, Leonard, Pt..... | " | | W | Mustd Jan. '82 |
| Davis, Thos., Pt........ | " | | | Left service 7 July '82 |

| Name and Rank | Company | Dates of Enlistment and Commission | Period of Service | Occurrences |
|---|---|---|---|---|
| Davis, Thos., Pt........ | Hall's | '81 | 12 mo. | {Destd 1 Apr. '82, Mustd War Dec. '82, Destd 15 Jan. '83 |
| Downing, Thos., Pt..... | " | '82 | " | Time out 29 Jan. '83 |
| Duke, John, Pt........ | Carter's | 19 May '81 | " | Do 19 May '82 |
| Davis, Edw'd, Pt...... | Jones' | 12 Dec. " | " | |
| Davis, Jno............ | " | 3 Oct. " | " | {Corpl. Apr. '82, Time out 1 Oct. '82 |
| (P. 1047) | | | | |
| Demry, Jehu.......... | Mills' | 20 Jan. '82 | W | Mustd 1 Apr. '82 |
| (P. 1048) | | | | |
| Davis, Aaron......... | Coleman's | 12 Dec. '81 | 12 mo. | |
| Debush, Jacob........ | " | 15 Apr. " | " | |
| Doude, Jno........... | Hall's | | W | {Mustd Sep. '82, Destd 1 June '83 |
| Davis, Wm., Pt........ | Jones' | 1 Mar '82 | 12 mo. | |
| Davis, Thos........... | " | 1 Feb. " | " | Destd 1 Apr. '82 |
| Daniels, Thos, Corpl... | Mills' | " | " | Time out 1 Mar. '83 |
| Dedrick, Jacob, Pt..... | Hadley's | 27 Aug. " | " | Or Bailey's Co. |
| Davis, John, Pt....... | " | | 18 mo. | |
| Daniels, Joab, Pt...... | " | | " | |
| Davis, Joseph......... | " | | " | |
| Davis, Arch'd, Musc.... | " | | 3 yrs. | Pt. Dec. '82 |
| Donagin, David, Sergt.. | Bacot's | " | 18 mo. | |
| Dickons, Thos., Pt..... | " | " | " | |
| Denrebesy, And'w, Pt... | " | " | " | |
| Dawby, I. Wm., Pt..... | " | " | " | |
| Deal, Jno............. | " | " | " | |
| Doty, Isaac, Sergt..... | Carter's | " | " | |
| Douglas, Wm., Corpl.... | Raiford's | " | W | |
| Dobson, Joseph....... | Sharp's | " | 18 mo. | |
| Dowdle, Jno.......... | " | " | " | |
| Donaldson, Jacob...... | Lythes | " | " | |
| Dodd, Thos., Sergt..... | Brevard's | " | " | |
| Dixon, Mich'l, Sergt.... | " | " | " | |
| Dobbins, Wm., Corpl.... | " | " | " | Died 28 June '83 |
| Davis, Robt., Pt........ | " | " | " | |
| Due, John, Sergt....... | Evans' | " | " | |
| Dickenson, Henry...... | " | " | " | |
| Dixon, Caswell, Pt..... | " | " | " | |
| Durdon, Mills, Pt...... | " | " | " | |
| (P. 1040) | | | | |
| Dean, Philip, Pt........ | Coleman's | 1782 | W | Mustd Jan. '79 |
| Downing, Wm......... | | | 3 yrs. | Mustd Sep. '82 |
| Davis, Lee, Pt......... | | | | Mustd Sep. '82 |
| Davis, Thos., Pt....... | | | | Mustd, destd Sep. '79 |
| Dego, Eve, Pt......... | | | " | Mustd Jan '79 |
| Dean, Philip, Pt....... | | | | Mustd, destd Sep. '79 |
| Delerase, Peter, Pt..... | | | | Do |
| Dupriest, Jas., Pt...... | | | | Mustd Dec. '82 |
| Donally, Hugh........ | Dixon's | 25 Apr. '81 | 12 mo. | Died 24 Jan.'82 |
| Dupriest, Jas., Pt...... | Sharp's | 1 Nov. '78 | 9 mo. | |
| Davis, Stephen, Pt..... | " | | 3 yrs. | Mustd Jan. '79 |
| Drury, Morgan........ | McRee's | | | Mustd Nov. '79 |
| Drury, John, Pt....... | " | | | Do |
| Delidge, Peter, Pt...... | Lt. Colo's | | 3 yrs. | Mustd Jan. '79 |
| Davidson, Emanuel, Pt.. | Sharp's | 14 Dec. '78 | | Mustd Feb. '79 |

| Name and Rank | Company | Dates of Enlistment and Commission | Period of Service | Occurrences |
|---|---|---|---|---|
| Delany, Mich'l, Pt..... | Doherty's | | 3 yrs. | ⎰Mustd Feb. '79, ⎱Destd 10 Apr. '79 |
| Duncan, Elijah........ | Taylor's | | " | ⎰Mustd Feb. '79, ⎱Destd Apr. '79 |
| Dillard, Jno., Lt........ | Eaton's | | " | Mustd Feb. '79 |
| Davis, Joshua.......... | Colonels' | 10 June '79 | 18 mo. | |
| E  (Pp. 1052-54) | | | | |
| Eager, Jno., Pt......... | Wilson's | 1 Oct    '77 | 3 yrs. | |
| Everington, Edw'd, Pt.. | Gregory's | 21 May  " | " | |
| Eastman, Benj., Pt..... | " | 21 July  " | " | ⎰Sergt. June '78, ⎱Pt. 7 Nov. '78 |
| Elliott, Joseph, Pt...... | Moore's | 21 May  " | " | Destd Apr. '78 |
| Elliott, Jno., Sergt...... | Van Noy's | 16 June  " | " | ⎰Pt. June '78, Pris. June '79, ⎱Mustd Nov. '79 |
| Emboey, Jno., Pt...... | " | 25 July  " | " | ⎰Prisn. 1 June '79 ⎱Mustd Nov. '79 |
| Ellis, John, Pt.......... | | 27 Apr. '76 | 2½ yrs. | Dischgd 1 July '79 |
| Ewell, Stephen, Pt..... | | 6 June   '77 | 3 yrs. | |
| Ewell, Nath'l, Pt...... | | 29 Aug.  " | " | Dischgd 15 Sep. '78 |
| Edwards, Brown, Pt.... | Montfort's | 20 July  " | 9 mo. | |
| Evans, Burrell, Pt..... | " | " | " | |
| Edwards, Stephen, Pt... | " | " | " | |
| Equals, Wm., Pt....... | Hogg's | " | " | ⎰Reinlisted 15 May '79, ⎱Sergt. for 3 yrs. |
| Eason, Wm., Pt....... | " | " | " | |
| Eggerton, Jesse, Pt..... | " | " | " | |
| Edens, Jno., Pt......... | Baker's | " | " | |
| Evans, Chas., Pt....... | " | " | " | |
| Evans, Jno., Pt........ | " | 1778 | " | Destd 23 July '78 |
| Evans, Chas., Pt....... | Blount's | 20 July  " | " | |
| Edoc, Jas., Pt.......... | Ballard's | " | " | |
| Ellison, Corn'ls, Pt..... | " | " | " | |
| Edmonds, David, Pt.... | " | " | " | |
| Ellick, Joshua, Pt...... | " | " | " | |
| Edwards, Lemuel....... | " | " | " | Omtd Oct. '78 |
| Elmore, Morgan........ | Bradley's | " | 18 mo. | |
| Ellis, Absalom, Pt..... | " | " | " | |
| Elmore, Daniel......... | " | | " | |
| Ewell, Wm., Sergt..... | Childs' | | " | |
| Edwards, Solomon, Pt... | " | | " | |
| Evans, Rich'd, Pt....... | Bradley's | | " | |
| Emory, Jno., Pt........ | Montfort's | | 9 mo. | Dischgd 1 Dec. '79 |
| Evans, Jas............. | " | | 18 mo. | Do |
| Everidge, Isaac, Musc... | Ballard's | | 3 yrs. | |
| Edenton, Nicholas, Sgt.. | Quinn's | | 9 mo. | Dischgd Jan. '80 |
| Eagle, Geo., Pt........ | McRee's | | 12 mo. | Left service 10 Apr. '82 |
| Ellis, Barth'w, Pt...... | Raiford's | | " | Do      2 May '82 |
| Edwards, Simon, Pt.... | " | | " | Do      4 May '82 |
| Easeley, Roderick, Pt... | " | | " | Do    14 May '82 |
| Ellis, Aaron, Pt........ | " | | " | Time out 19 May '82 |
| Evens, Chas., Pt....... | " | | " | Do    15 Apr. '82 |
| Ellis, Jno., Pt......... | " | | W | |
| Erricks, David, Pt...... | Donoho's | | 12 mo. | Left service 14 June '82 |
| Elmore, Jas., Pt....... | " | | " | Do    25 May '82 |
| Evans, Reubens, Pt..... | Dixon's | | " | Do    26 May '82 |
| Ellis, Thos., Pt......... | " | | " | Do    25 Apr. '82 |
| Everet, Matthew, Pt.... | Lytle's | | " | Omtd in '81 |

| Name and Rank | Company | Dates of Enlistment and Commission | Period of Service | Occurrences |
|---|---|---|---|---|
| Edwards, Jno. | Lytle's | 12 Apr. '78 | 12 mo. | {Destd July '81, Mustd Jan., Left ser. 12 Apr. '82 |
| Esterlege, Eph'm, Pt. | " | 5 " " | " | Left service 5 Apr. '82 |
| Ewmen, Chris'r, Pt. | Walton's | 25 " " | " | Time out 25 May '82 |
| Edwards, Jno. Jr., Pt. | Lytle's | | W | Mustd Jan. '82 |
| Ewell, Calleb, Pt. | Sharp's | 1781 | 12 mo. | Time out 15 Apr. '82 |
| Ellis, Jas., Pt. | Doherty's | " | " | Do    25 May '82 |
| Elmes, Chs., Pt. | Rhode's | " | " | Do    12 Apr. '82 |
| Evans, Murin, Pt. | Armstrong's | " | " | Left service 1 Oct. '82 |
| Edwards, David, Sergt. | Bailey's | 25 Apr. " | " | 25 Apr. '82 |
| Ewing, Geo., Pt. | Brevard's | " | " | Do    28 Apr. '82 |
| Elliot, Zach'r, Pt. | Yarborough's | " | " | 10 July 82 |
| Elleums, Jas., Pt. | " | " | " | 22 Apr. '82 |
| Enderkin, Francis, Pt. | " | " | " | Time out 22 May '82 |
| Euman, Wm., Pt. | " | " | " | Do    22 Apr. '82 |
| Engram, Tobias, Pt. | Carter's | " | " | Do        Do |
| Ellison, Peter, Pt. | " | 19 May " | " | 19 May '82 |
| Elder, Wm. | " | 1 " " | " | 1 June '82 |
| Ezell, Timothy, Pt. | Jones' | 6 Mar. '82 | " | |
| Essins, Thos., Pt. | Coleman's | 13 Dec. '81 | " | |
| Ellis, Robt., Pt. | " | 1 Jan. '82 | " | |
| Evans, Jno., Pt. | " | 13 " " | " | |
| Engavis, Wm., Sergt. | " | 10 Dec. '81 | " | |
| Esteridge, Thos., Pt. | Jones' | 1 Mar. '82 | " | |
| Edwards, Jno., Pt. | " | Oct '81 | " | Time out 1 Oct. '82 |
| Eller, Joseph, Pt. | Bailey's | 15 Jan. '82 | " | |
| Eller, John, Pt. | " | " | " | |
| Edmonson, Jno., Pt. | Hadley's | 1 Aug. " | 18 mo. | Destd 13 May '83 |
| Edwards, Lem'l, Pt. | Bacot's | " | " | Dischgd 10 Jan. '82 |
| Edgner, Math's, Pt. | " | " | W | Destd 15 June '83 |
| Edlow, Jno., Pt. | Carter's | 1 Aug. '81 | 18 mo. | |
| Ellums, Jas., Pt. | " | " | " | Corpl. Dec. '82 |
| Evans, John | Raiford's | " | " | Destd 11 June '83 |
| Edwards, Jno., Pt. | Sharp's | " | " | Destd 30 Apr. '83 |
| Ethrington, Wm., Pt. | Lytle's | " | " | |
| Edmons, Wm., Pt. | " | " | " | Destd 5 May '83 |
| Elsmore, Ep'm, Pt. | " | " | " | |
| Emory, Wm., Pt. | Brevard's | " | " | |
| Emley, David, Pt. | " | " | " | Transf'd 20 Apr. '83 |
| Emason, Henry, Pt. | " | " | " | Destd 23 June '83 |
| Earhart, Philip, Pt. | " | " | " | Transf'd Mar. '83 |
| Eckles, Wm., Sergt. (P. 1054) | Evans' | " | " | |
| Emerson, Sam'l, Pt. | Col. Summers' | " | W | Mustd Jan. '79 |
| **F** (Pp. 1058-61) | | | | |
| Ferrell, Enoch, Pt. | Wilson's | 8 Aug. '77 | | |
| Ford, Ab'm, Pt. | " | 10 May " | | |
| Faircloth, Wm., Lt. | Shephard's | 20 Jan. '78 | | Omtd June '78 |
| Fillips, Jno., Pt. | " | 26 Aug. '77 | | Do |
| Flood, Wm., Pt. | " | 5 July " | 3 yrs. | |
| Fillips, Josh., Pt. | " | 26 Aug. " | | Do |
| Fail, Thos., Pt. | " | 1 May " | | Do |
| Fonville, Isaac, Corpl. | Stephenson's | 21 Apr. " | 3 yrs. | |
| Fornes, Wm., Pt. | " | 28 June " | " | |
| Ferebee, Joseph, Lt. | Jarvis' | | | |
| Fletcher, Wm., Sergt. | " | 5 May '77 | 3 yrs. | Died 20 Jan. '79 |

| Name and Rank | Company | Dates of Enlistment and Commission | Period of Service | Occurrences |
|---|---|---|---|---|
| Fletcher, Thos., Pt..... | Lytle's | | 12 mo. | Pt. Jan. '79 |
| Fisher, Jas., Pt........ | " | | " | Destd 6 Feb. '80 |
| Fenton, Thos., Pt...... | " | | | |
| Flora, Lazars, Pt...... | " | | | |
| Flora, Rich'd, Pt...... | " | | | |
| Foster, Robt., Pt...... | | | | |
| Foy, Patrick, Pt....... | | 29 Jan '77 | 3 yrs. W | Corp. Nov.'78, Pt. Jan.'79 |
| Flinn, Wm., Pt........ | | | 3 yrs. | {Joined 14 May '78, \Died 6 July '78 |
| Ferrell, Wm., Lt....... | | 8 Sep. " | | Killed 10 May '80 |
| Fleetwood, Francis, Pt. . | | | " | Destd 15 July '78 |
| Falconer, Jas., Pt...... | | | " | {Mustd June '78, Corpl. \Nov. '78, Sergt. 15 July'79 |
| Flood, Benj., Pt....... | | 10 July " | " | |
| Ford, John, Ensn...... | | 3 Nov. '78 | | Lt. '80 |
| Fleming, John, Qr. Mr. Sergt....... | Colonel's | 20 July " | 9 mo. | |
| Freeman, Jese, Pt...... | Quinn's | 20 " " | " | |
| Frazier, Thos., Pt...... | " | | " | |
| Forms, Jno., Pt........ | " | 14 May '76 | 2½ yrs. | Omtd '79 |
| Floyd, Jno., Pt........ | Lt. Colos' | 20 July '78 | 9 mo. | |
| Floyd, Buckner, Pt.... | " | " " | " | |
| Futrell, Joseph, Pt..... | " | | " | |
| Ford, Jno., Sergt...... | " | 1 Sep. " | " | See Ensign above* |
| Fisher, Jno., Pt........ | Baker's | 20 July '78 | " | |
| Finch, Isom, Pt........ | " | | " | |
| Foster, David, Pt...... | " | | " | |
| Farmer, Jno., Pt....... | Blount's | " | " | Corpl. Oct. '78 |
| Fountain, Solomon, Pt. . | Ballard's | " | " | |
| Fearless, Elisha, Pt.... | Bradley's | " | " | Omtd Oct. '78 |
| Ferrell, Wm., Pt....... | " | " | " | |
| Freeman, Wm., Pt..... | Childs' | " | " | |
| Fields, Jno., Pt........ | " | " | " | |
| Faircloth, Jno., Sergt... | Bradley's | 20 May " | W | |
| Fosdick, West, Pt...... | " | | | Destd Sep. '79 |
| Fling, Thos., Pt....... | " | 20 June '79 | 18 mo. | |
| Furney, Peter.......... | " | 1 " " | 3 yrs. | Omtd Oct. '79 |
| Ford, Lewis, Pt........ | Montford's | 18 " " | 18 mo. | |
| Fisher, Wm., Pt........ | " | 1 Mar. " | 9 mo. | Dischgd 1 Dec. '79 |
| Foster, Wm., Pt....... | Ballard's | 15 June " | 18 mo. | |
| Fontain, Jese, Pt....... | Quinn's | 1779 | 9 mo. | Dischgd Dec. '79 |
| Farmer, Henry, Pt...... | Blount's | 7 June " | W | Destd Dec. '79 |
| Fauning, Peter, Pt..... | " | 1 July " | " | Do |
| Faison, Jas., Pt........ | " | 7 May '78 | 3 yrs. | |
| Farmer, Jno........... | " | 1 Aug. '79 | W | Destd Dec. '79 |
| Field, Timothy........ | | 1777 | 9 mo. | Dead Sep. '79 |
| Frieze, Jno., Pt........ | McRee's | 28 Apr. '81 | 12 mo. | Left service 28 Apr. '82 |
| Fauney, Jno., Corpl.... | Raiford's | 19 May '81 | " | {Transf'd Sep. '81 to S. C. \Line |
| Fleming, Wm., Pt...... | Donoho's | 14 June " | " | Omtd in '81 |
| Fleming, Jas., Pt...... | " | " " " | " | Left service 14 June '82 |
| Ferrell, Jas., Pt........ | " | 25 May " | " | Do    25 May '82 |
| Flinn, Jno., Pt......... | Dixon's | May " | " | 21 May '82 |
| (P. 1059-60) | | | | |
| Fearle, Ansol, Corpl.... | Lytle's | 6 Apr. '81 | 12 mo. | Omtd in '81 |
| Furguson, Isom, Pt..... | " | 11 June " | " | Left service 21 June '82 |
| Furguson, Robt., Pt.... | " | " " | " | Do |

| Name and Rank | Company | Dates of Enlistment and Commission | Period of Service | Occurrences |
|---|---|---|---|---|
| Futrel, Dempsey, Pt.... | Lytle's | 12 Apr. '81 | 12 mo. | Destd 7 July '81 |
| Fountain, Jos., Pt...... | " | " " | " | {Corpl. Jan., / Left service 12 Apr. '82 |
| Farmer, Benj., Pt...... | " | 1 June " | " | Left service 1 June '82 |
| Farmer, Wm., Pt....... | " | " | | Do |
| Fountain, David, Pt.... | Raiford's | 1781 | | Time out 12 June '82 |
| Fist, Sam'l, Pt......... (P. 1060) | Walton's | " | W | |
| Ferrell, Jno., Pt....... | Dixon's | " | 12 mo. | Time out before Apr. '82 |
| Fuller, Geo., Pt........ | " | " | " | Time out May 21, '82 |
| Freazer, Dan'l, Pt..... | Sharp's | " | " | Do Sep. 1, '82 |
| Foster, Rich'd, Pt...... | Doherty's | " | " | Do May, 25, '82 |
| Filman, Wm., Musc..... | " | " | " | Do May 25, '82 |
| Flowers, Wm., Pt...... | Armstrong's | " | " | Left service 15 Sep. '82 |
| Fann, Wm., Corpl..... | Bailey's | 12 Apr. " | " | Do 12 Apr. '82 |
| Foster, Wm., Corpl..... | " | 2 May " | " | Do 2 May '82 |
| Forbes, Wm., Corpl.... | " | 24 Apr. " | " | Do 24 Apr. '82 |
| Freeman, Edw'd, Corpl. | Brevard's | " | " | Do 11 July '82 |
| Frederick, Chrisn., Corpl. | " | " | " | Do 28 Apr. '82 |
| Fereby, Robt., Sergt.... | Hall's | " | " | Do 10 July '82 |
| Fox, Joseph, Sergt..... | " | " | " | Do Do |
| Forehand, Jarvis, Pt.... | " | " | " | Do 21 Apr. '82 |
| Folks, Jas., Pt......... | " | " | " | Died 14 Sep. '82 |
| Fentice, Moses, Pt...... | " | " | " | Time out 20 July '82 |
| Fight, Conrod, Pt...... | " | " | " | Time out 27 Dec. '82 |
| Fly, Chas., Pt......... | Yarborough's | " | " | Omtd 1 Apr. '82 |
| Ferrell, Gab'l, Pt...... | " | " | " | Do Do |
| Flood, Enoch, Pt...... | Carter's | 12 Apr. " | " | Time out 10 Apr. '82 |
| Freeman, Howell, Pt.... | " | 25 " " | " | Do 25 Apr. '82 |
| Faithfull, Wm., Pt..... | " | " | W | Do Do |
| Folks, Jas., Pt......... | Jones' | 1 Jan. '82 | 12 mo. | Mustd Jan. '81 |
| Freeman, Moses, Pt..... | Carter's | 25 Apr. " | " | Mustd War 1 Apr. '82 |
| Freeman, Roger, Pt..... | Coleman's | 1 Jan. " | " | |
| Fowler, Ashly, Pt...... | | | | |
| Foster, Wm., Pt........ | Bailey's | 27 Aug. " | 18 mo. | |
| Fields, Jno., Pt........ | " | 10 Sep. " | " | |
| Frost, Miller, Pt....... | " | 1 Jan. " | 12 mo. | |
| Furguson, Peter, Pt.... | " | 1 Aug. " | 18 mo. | |
| Fryar, Willis, Pt........ | Hadley's | 10 Sep. " | " | |
| Farmer, Jas., Pt........ | " | " " | " | |
| Farmer, Jesse, Pt...... | " | | " | |
| Foster, David, Pt...... | Bacot's | 1782 | " | Destd 19 June '83 |
| Forbush, Robt., Pt..... | " | " | " | Died 15 June '83 |
| Florida, Francis, Pt.... | " | " | " | Destd 27 Jan. '83 |
| Francis, Sam'l, Pt...... | Carter's | " | " | Destd 10 Apr. '83 |
| Futrell, Josh, Pt....... | " | " | " | |
| Farrow, Thos., Pt...... | " | " | " | Destd 14 June '83 |
| Flood, Sam'l, Pt....... | " | " | " | |
| Farnavil, Rich'd, Pt.... | " | " | " | |
| Frailey, Jno., Corpl..... | Sharp's | " | " | |
| Felton, Sam'l, Corpl..... | Lytle's | " | " | Destd 31 Mar. '83 |
| Flood, Fred'k, Pt...... | " | " | " | |
| Foley, Jno., Pt......... | " | " | " | |
| Ferrell, Clem't, Pt..... | " | " | " | |
| Fuller, Jno., Pt........ | Brevard's | " | " | |
| Faddles, Jas., Pt....... | " | " | " | Died 17 Dec. '83 |
| Fowler, Geo., Pt........ | Evan's | " | " | |

| Name and Rank | Company | Dates of Enlistment and Commission | Period of Service | Occurrences |
|---|---|---|---|---|
| Fulcher, Cason, Pt..... | Evan's | 1782 | 18 mo. | |
| Francis, Ant'y, Pt...... | " | " | " | |
| Fortune, Wm., Pt...... | " | " | " | Transf'd 1 Dec. '82 |
| Fergus, Jas., Sugn. Mt.. | | 21 Feb. '82 | | {Surgeon 20 Aug. '82, Omtd in '83 |
| Futch, Martin, Pt..... | Lytle's | | | {Mustd Dec. '82, Destd 11 June '83 |
| Fussell, Sam'l, Pt...... | Sharp's | 26 Aug. '78 | W | Died 5 Apr. '79 |
| Faircloth, Jno., Pt..... | " | 10 Nov. " | 9 mo. | |
| Francis, Jno., Pt........ | | | | Mustd Nov. '79 |
| Fountain, Jesse, Pt..... | Rhode's | | 3 yrs. | Mustd Apr. '79 |
| Ferrell, Jno., Pt....... | Taylor's | | " | Mustd Jan. '79 |
| Ferrell, Luke, Pt........ | White's | | | Mustd Jan. '79 |
| Fuller, Wm., Pt........ | Carter's | 20 May '78 | W | |
| **G** (P. 1067) | | | | |
| Gray, Jas., Sergt....... | Wilson's | 15 May '77 | | |
| Guttery, Hy., Pt........ | " | 1 Nov. " | | Died Oct. '78 |
| Giligan, Jno., Pt....... | " | 1 Apr. '78 | | Destd 22 Apr. '78 |
| Ginew, Wm., Pt....... | " | 6 Nov. '77 | | Omtd June 1 |
| Glandon, Major, Pt.... | Shepard's | 30 Sep. " | 3 yrs. W | |
| Grant, Elijah, Pt...... | " | 20 Aug. " | " | {Prisn. 1 June '79, Mustd Nov. '79 |
| Gothrop, Jno., Pt...... | " | 25 May " | | Dischgd Sep. '78 |
| Gatlin, Levy, Ensn...... | Stevenson's | | | {Lt. 12 Feb. '78, dismissed service Aug. '78 |
| Griffin, Ezek'l, Pt...... | " | 21 Apr. " | 3 yrs. | Omtd June '78 |
| Guard, Jno., Pt........ | " | 24 June " | " | Died 23 Mar. '78 |
| Gamewell, Wm., Pt..... | Jarvis' | 13 " " | " | |
| Greggs, Chas., Pt...... | " | 18 May " | 3 yrs. W | |
| Gregory, Demp'y, Capt. | " | 19 Apr. " | | Resigned 20 May '78 |
| Gray, Wm., Pt........ | Gregory's | 10 June " | " | |
| Grogin, Jas., Pt........ | " | 24 May " | " | Omtd Feb. '79 |
| Griffith, Isaac, Pt...... | " | 21 May " | " | Dischgd Sergt. 1 Mar.'80 |
| Griffin, Dan'l, Pt...... | Heron's | 30 May " | " | Omtd June '78 |
| Gray, M. Wm., Pt..... | " | 27 Apr. " | " | |
| Garvis, Sykes, Pt...... | " | 4 May " | " | Destd 19 June '83 |
| Garvis, Pigford, Pt..... | " | " | 3 yrs. | Music June '78 |
| Gray, Sam'l, Pt........ | " | 2 June " | " | {Do Prisr., 1 June '79 Mustd Nov. '79 |
| Gilleham, Howell, Pt.... | Moore's | 6 May " | 3 yrs. W | Sergt. May '79 |
| Grinder, Jno., Pt...... | | '78 | | Died 29 June '79 |
| Green, Wm., Pt........ | Armstrong's | July '77 | 3 yrs. | |
| Gardner, Dempsey, Pt. . | | '78 | W | Prisr. 1 June '79 |
| Gregory, Isaac, Pt..... | | | 3 yrs. | Mustd Apr. '78 |
| Gilbert, Jno., Pt....... | | | | {Mustd, dead or destd 6 May '78 |
| Gilbert, Jas., Pt........ | | | | Omtd Feb. '79 |
| Green, W. Jas., Sur. Mt. | | 10 June '78 | | {Surgeon 7 Dec. '79, Pris. 12 May '80 |
| Gunnel, Jno., Pt....... | | | W | {Mustd Jan. '79, Destd 30 Jan. '80 |
| Gunn, Jas., Pt.......... | | | 3 yrs. | Mustd '78, Omtd Feb. '78 |
| Green, Wilson, Corpl.... | | | " | {Mustd '78, Died Apr. 18, '78 |
| Graves, Francis, Lt. .... | | 26 Oct. '77 | | {And Qr. Mr. 6 Nov. '78 See him in 8th Reg. |
| Good, Jno., Pt......... | Montfort's | 20 July '78 | 9 mo. | |

| Name and Rank | Company | Dates of Enlistment and Commission | Period of Service | Occurrences |
|---|---|---|---|---|
| Good, Wm., Pt. | Montford's | 20 July '78 | 9 mo. | |
| Gray, Henry, Pt. | " | " | " | |
| Green, Thos., Pt. | Hogg's | " | " | |
| Griffin, Jesse, Pt. | Quinn's | " | " | |
| Goodat, Jno., Pt. | " | " | " | |
| Gaskin, Joseph, Pt. | " | " | " | |
| Gray, Cocks, Pt. | " | " | " | |
| Gotson, Jas., Pt. | Lt. Col. | " | " | |
| Gay, Wm., Pt. | " | " | " | |
| Grant, Wm., Pt. | " | " | " | |
| Gibson, Chas., Pt. | " | " | " | |
| Gums, Isaac, Pt. | " | " | " | |
| Godwin, John, Corpl. | " | " | " | |
| Gro, Jas., Pt. | Baker's | " | " | Died 16 Nov. '78 |
| Gregory, Robt., Pt. | Blount's | " | " | |
| Glisson, Arthur, Pt. | " | " | " | |
| Gray, Isom, Pt. | Ballard's | " | " | |
| Grant, Eph'm, Corpl. | Bradley's | " | " | |
| Gardner, Geo., Pt. | " | " | " | |
| Gay, Simon, Pt. | " | " | " | |
| Ginn, Hardy, Pt. | " | " | " | |
| Gamalion, Ab'm, Pt. | " | " | " | |
| Grant, John, Pt. | " | " | " | Died 16 Nov. '78 |
| Goodridge, Lewis, Pt. | " | " | " | Dischgd 5 Dec. '78 |
| Griffin, Martin, Pt. | Childs' | " | " | |
| Gurganus, Reuben, Pt. | " | " | " | |
| Gale, Geo., Pt. | Bradley's | 25 June '79 | 18 mo. | Dead Dec. '79 |
| Gainer, Stephen, Pt. | " | 1 Aug. '78 | 3 yrs. | |
| Grogan, John, Pt. | Montfort's | 24 June '79 | W | Destd 8 Nov. '79 |
| Gee, Jesse, Pt. | | 1 Mar. " | 9 mo. | Dischgd 1 Dec. '79 |
| Goren, John, Corpl. | Ballard's | 29 June " | W | |
| Geniens, Miles, Pt. | " | 21 June " | 18 mo. | |
| Gardner, Thos., Pt. | " | 1 July " | " | Destd 1 Oct. '79 |
| Goodwin, Edw'd, Pt. | Quinn's | 24 June " | W | |
| Godfrey, Ant'y, Pt. | Blount's | 2 Dec. " | 3 yrs. | |
| Gibson, Jacob, Pt. | " | 20 June " | 18 mo. | |
| Gray, Wm., Pt. | | " | 9 mo. | Omtd Oct. '79 |
| Gonsalez, de-Ferdinando, Corpl. | McRee's | 28 Apr. '81 | 12 mo. | Pt. Aug. '81, Left service 28 Apr. '82, re-enlisted '82 for 18 Mos. |
| Green, Fred'k, Pt. | " | 9 May " | " | Destd 1 July '81 |
| Gray, Babel, Pt. | Raiford's | 17 May " | 12 mo. | Left service 17 May '82 |
| Glover, John, Pt. | " | 2 May " | " | Do 2 May '82 |
| Gay, Joshua, Pt. | " | 9 June " | " | Do 17 May '82 |
| Gay, Allen, Pt. | " | 2 June " | " | Do 3 May '82 |
| Goodwin, John, Pt. | " | 19 May " | " | Dischgd 14 Feb. '82 |
| Gatlin, Edw'd, Pt. | " | 11 " " | " | Left service 17 May '82 |
| Gilmore, Wm., Pt. | Donoho's | 14 June " | " | Do 14 June '82 |
| Gallimore, John, Corpl. | " | " " " | " | Pt. Jan. '82, Left service 14 June '82 |
| Gregory, Jas., Pt. | " | " " " | " | Omtd in '81 |
| Goslin, Simon, Pt. | Dixon's | 15 May " | " | Left service 21 May '82 |
| Garvis, Wylley, Pt. | " | 12 " " | " | Do 26 May '82 |
| Garnes, Gab'l, Pt. | " | 25 " " | " | Omtd in '81 |
| Goin, Wm., Pt. | " | " " " | " | Left service 21 May '82 |
| Giun, Hardy, Pt. | " | 25 Apr. " | " | Do 25 Apr. '82 |

| Name and Rank | Company | Dates of Enlistment and Commission | Period of Service | Occurrences |
|---|---|---|---|---|
| Gaunt, Giles, Corpl.... | Lytle's | 6 June '81 | 12 mo. | Do        12 Apr. '82 |
| Gay, Henry, Pt........ | Lytle's | 15 Apr. '81 | 12 mo. | Left service 12 Apr. '82 |
| Gay, Rich'd, Pt........ | " | " " " | " | Do            Do |
| Gay, Solomon, Pt...... | " | " " " | " | Omtd in '81 |
| Green, Sutton, Pt...... | " | 16 June " | " | Left service 16 June '82 |
| Grindstaff, Michs., Pt... | " | 6 " " | " | Do        6 June '82 |
| Griffin, Wm........... | " | " | W | From Gee's Co. 2 Reg. |
| Garland, Henry, Pt.... | " | 2 Apr. " | | Destd 5 July '81 |
| Glover, Allen, Pt....... | " | 12 " " | | Destd 7 July '81 |
| Glover, Benj., Pt...... | " | " " " | W | {Destd 7 July '81, Mustd Jan. '82 |
| Griffin, Dempsey, Pt.... | Sharp's | 20 June " | 12 mo. | Left service 20 June '82 |
| Godett, John, Pt....... | " | 5 Apr. " | " | Do        5 Apr. '82 |
| Gurley, Joseph, Pt..... | Raiford's | 1781 | " | {Time out 13 Sep., re-enlisted for the war |
| Gerns, Jas., Pt........ | Dixon's | " | " | Time out 15 Apr. reinl'd |
| Graham, John, Pt...... | " | " | " | Do before    Do |
| Graham, Peter, Pt..... | " | " | " | Do            Do |
| Griffin, Jas., Corpl..... | Sharp's | " | " | Do    12    Do |
| Gilgo, Fibin, Pt....... | " | " | " | Do    15    Do |
| Griffin, Ezk'l, Pt....... | Doherty's | " | " | Do    1 Sep. Do |
| Grayham, Wm., Sergt... | Rhode's | " | " | Do    17 June Do |
| Gray, Henry, Sergt.... | " | " | " | Dischgd 21 Jan., reinl'd |
| Giun, Roland, Pt...... | " | " | " | Time out 16 July '82 |
| Goods, Israel, Pt....... | Armstrong's | " | " | Do    1 July '82 |
| Garland, Thos., Pt..... | " | " | " | Do    1 Dec. '82 |
| Gist, Robt., Pt........ | " | " | " | Do    1 Dec. '82 |
| Garris, Begford, Pt..... | " | " | " | Dischgd 21 Jan. '82 |
| Galesby, David, Pt..... | " | " | " | Left service 1 July '82 |
| Gibson, Henry, Pt..... | Bailey's | 17 May '81 | " | Do        17 May, '82 |
| Garner, Dempy, Pt.... | " | " | | Do        1 Apr. '82 |
| Greenman, Caleb, Pt... | " | 1 June " | " | Do        1 June '82 |
| Gay, Jas., Sergt....... | Brevard's | " | | Do        28 Apr. '82 |
| Gibson, Colin, Corpl... | " | " | W | Mustd Jan. '82 |
| Grindstaff, Mich'l, Cpl. | " | " | | Left service    7 June '82 |
| Griffin, Edw'd, Pt..... | " | " | | Do        11 July '82 |
| Griffin, Edw'd, Pt..... | " | " | | Do        11 July '82 |
| Gragham, Arthur, Pt.... | " | " | | Do        15 June '82 |
| Gibson, David, Pt...... | " | " | | Destd Apr. '82 |
| Graham, Francis, Pt... | " | " | 12 mo. | Left service 28 Apr. '82 |
| Garret, Sam'l, Pt...... | Hall's | " | " | Time out 1 Aug. '82 |
| Garner, Thos., Pt...... | Yarborough's | " | " | Do        1 June '82 |
| Garland, Wm., Pt..... | " | " | " | Do        22 Apr. '82 |
| Gunn, Jas., Sergt...... | Carter's | 15 Apr. " | " | Do        10 Apr. '82 |
| Garris, Hardy, Pt...... | " | 25 Apr. " | " | Do        25 Apr. '82 |
| Gaskins, Wm., Pt...... | " | 12 May " | " | Do        25 Apr. '82 |
| Gilbert, Jno., Pt....... | " | 19 " " | " | Do        19 May '82 |
| Gray, Cox, Pt......... | " | 25 Apr. " | " | Do        25 Apr. '82 |
| Gordon, Solomon, Pt... | " | 12 " " | " | Do        25 Apr. '82 |
| Goldin, And'w, Pt..... | " | " | W | {Mustd Aug., Destd 17 Aug. '81 |
| Graft, Ant'y, Pt....... | Jones' | 6 Mar. '82 | 12 mo. | |
| Goodson, Jno., Pt...... | " | 11 Dec. '81 | " | |
| Ginn, Jacob, Pt....... | " | " | " | {Dischgd 1 Dec. '82 by the name of Elijah Ginn |
| Guard, Joshua, Pt..... | Mills' | 7 Feb. '82 | " | |
| Graham, Jno., Pt...... | Coleman's | 13 Dec. '81 | W | |

| Name and Rank | Company | Dates of Enlistment and Commission | Period of Service | Occurrences |
|---|---|---|---|---|
| Greece, Thoplus, Pt..... | Coleman's | 10 Jan. '82 | 12 mo. | |
| Gaylor, Jas., Pt........ | " | 1 Jan. " | " | |
| Goodwin, Thos., Pt..... | Jones' | 15 Mar. " | " | |
| Gatree, Mat'w, Pt...... | Bailey's | 17 Aug. " | " | |
| Grice, Gab'l, Pt....... | " | 15 Aug. " | " | |
| Griffin, Jas., Pt........ | " | 1 " " | " | |
| Gill, Alex'r, Pt........ | " | " | 18 mo. | Died 18 June '83 |
| Green, Hobart, Pt..... | Hadley's | " | " | Destd 29 Apr. '83 |
| Glass, Levy, Pt........ | " | 20 Aug " | " | |
| Gammond, Jesse, Pt.... | Bacot's | 1782 | " | |
| Gay, Jas., Pt.......... | " | " | " | |
| Gandy, Eph'm, Pt..... | " | " | " | |
| Gidcomb, Josh, Pt..... | " | " | " | Destd 15 June '83 |
| Gay, Wm., Pt......... | " | " | " | |
| Grissel, Willy, Pt...... | " | " | " | |
| Godden, Martin, Pt.... | " | " | " | |
| Gooden, Wyly, Pt...... | Carter's | " | " | |
| Goodson, Uzal, Pt..... | Raiford's | " | " | Destd 10 June '83 |
| Gargas, Job., Pt....... | " | " | " | Destd 11 June '83 |
| Graham, Francis, Pt... | " | " | " | |
| German, Emory, Pt.... | Sharp's | " | " | Destd 5 May '83 |
| Goodwin, Robertson, Pt. | " | " | " | |
| Guin, Sam'l, Pt........ | " | " | " | |
| Goseley, Chas., Pt..... | " | " | " | |
| Garrison, Stephen, Pt.. | " | " | " | |
| Good, Jno., Pt......... | " | " | 12 mo. | |
| Ginnings, Geo., Pt..... | " | " | " | Died Jan. '83 |
| Gill, Jno., Pt.......... | Lytle's | " | W | |
| Gatlin, Jese, Pt........ | " | " | 18 mo. | |
| George, Lewis, Pt...... | Brevard's | " | " | |
| Gilespy, Isaac, Pt...... | " | " | " | Transf'd Mar. '83 |
| Grant, Jno., Pt........ | " | " | " | |
| Gill, Robt., Pt......... | " | " | " | Died 20 June '83 |
| Grinage, Jno., Pt...... | " | " | " | Destd 7 Dec. '82 |
| Green, Jas., Pt........ | " | " | " | Destd 8 June '83 |
| Gardner, Jno., Corpl.... | Evans' | " | " | |
| Green Randolph, Pt..... | " | | | |
| Garrison, Stephen, Pt.. | | | 3 yrs. | Mustd Aug. '79 |
| Glass, Lemuel, Pt...... | | | | {Mustd Aug. '79, Destd Aug. '79 |
| Gregory, Thos., Pt..... | Sharp's | 10 Nov. '78 | 9 mo. | |
| Grimes, Wm., Pt....... | Dixon's | | | Mustd Nov. '79 |
| Gibson, Thos., Ensn.... | Lt. Col's | 20 Feb. '80 | | Died Jan. '82 |
| Giun, Wm., Pt........ | Coll's | " | 2½ yrs. | {Mustd Feb. '79, Destd Apr. '79 |
| Grisham, Major, Pt.... | Lewis' | " | W | Mustd '79 |
| German, Benj., Pt..... | Coll's | " | 3 yrs. | Mustd '79 |
| Glasscow, Sam'l, Pt.... | Lt. Col's | " | | Mustd Jan. '79 |
| Gardner, Jno., Pt...... | Taylor's | " | W | {Mustd Jan. '79, Destd same Mustd |
| Greer, Jno., Pt........ | White's | " | 3 yrs. | {Mustd Jan. '79, Destd June '79 |

H (P. 1078)

| Name and Rank | Company | Dates of Enlistment and Commission | Period of Service | Occurrences |
|---|---|---|---|---|
| Hawkins, Wm., Pt...... | Wilson's | 12 May '77 | 3 yrs. W | |
| Hooper, Anth'y, Pt.... | " | 16 " " | 3 yrs. | |
| Hargrave, Wm., Ensn... | Shephard's | 20 Jan. '78 | | {Lt. 30 Mar. '80, Pris. 12 May '80, dergd 21 Jan. '80 |

| Name and Rank | Company | Dates of Enlistment and Commission | Period of Service | Occurrences |
|---|---|---|---|---|
| Hay, Ab'm, Pt......... | Shephard's | 4 May '77 | 3 yrs. | |
| Handley, Wm., Pt...... | " | 28 July " | 3 yrs. W | |
| Hayes, Isaac, Pt....... | " | 12 June " | 3 yrs. | {Mustd War Jan. '82, Dead Sep. '82 |
| Harril, Peter, Sergt..... | " | 20 May " | | Pt. Sep. '78, Sergt. Nov. '78, Pris. 1 June '79, Mustd Nov. '79 |
| Hitchcock, Zack'h, Pt... | " | 4 June " | " | Destd 1 Feb. '80 |
| Hartley, Joseph, Sergt... | Stevenson's | 27 June " | " | Pt. June '78 |
| Harper, Robt., Pt...... | " | 21 Apr. " | " | Omtd June '78 |
| Halstead, Lem'l, Corpl. . | Jarvis' | 5 May " | " | {Pt. June '78, Dead 12 Jan. '79 |
| (P. 1078) | | | | |
| Halstead, Jolly, Pt...... | " | 28 May " | " | |
| Harrison, Jesse, Corpl... | Gregory's | 21 Aug. " | " | Pt. June '78 |
| (P. 1079) | | | | |
| Hanners, Henry, Corpl. . | " | 18 Sep. " | " | {Pt. June '78, Died 3 Aug. '78 |
| Harrison, Jno., Musc.... | " | 24 May " | " | {Pt. June '78, Dischgd Sep. 9, '78 |
| Harrison, Dempsy, Pt... | " | 21 Aug. " | " | Corpl. '79 |
| Herron, Armwell, Capt.. | | 19 Apr. " | | Omtd June '78 |
| Herron, Matt'w, Corpl. . | Heron's | 8 July " | 3 yrs. W | {Pt. June '78, Pris. 1 June Mustd Nov. '79 |
| Hudler, Lem'l, Pt...... | " | 7 July " | 3 yrs. | Died 19 Apr. '78 |
| Haycraft, Mark, Pt..... | " | 13 July " | " | {Pris. 1 June '79, Mustd Nov. '79 |
| Holmes, Robt., Sergt.... | Moore's | 8 May " | " | {Pris. 14 Apr. '79, Dischgd 1 Feb. '80 |
| Harris, Harry, Pt...... | " | 7 June " | " | |
| Hertsock, Peter, Pt..... | " | 25 June " | " | Mustd Jan. '82, for War |
| Hendricks, Thos., Pt.... | " | 30 June " | " | Dead Oct. '78 |
| Harris, Hugh, Pt...... | | 20 May '76 | " | {Corpl. 10 Nov. '78, Dischgd 20 May '79 |
| Hodges, Benj., Sergt.... | | 23 Aug. '77 | 3 yrs. W | |
| Hill, Jno., Pt.......... | | 20 Sep. '78 | 20 mo. | Dischgd 28 Jan. '80 |
| Hayes, Robt., Ensn..... | | 16 Aug. '77 | | Lt. 9 Oct. '77 |
| Henderson, Arch'd, Mus. | | 3 Feb. '78 | W | {Pt. June '78, Mussick Sep. '78 |
| (P. 1079) | | | | |
| Habbet, Ezek'l, Pt..... | | | 2½ yrs. | Dischgd 1 May '78 |
| Hargrave, Jno., Pt..... | | 19 May '77 | 3 yrs. | |
| Harrick, Elisha, Pt..... | | 20 May '76 | 2½ yrs. | Dischgd 16 Jan. '79 |
| Hartley, Jno., Pt...... | Coleman's | | | Died 20 June '78 |
| Harrard, Jas., Pt....... | | 13 May '77 | 3 yrs. | |
| Holloman, Kinchan, Pt.. | | 4 May '76 | 2½ yrs. | Dischgd 10 Nov. '78 |
| Hill, Jno, Pt........... | | 17 Mar. '76 | 3 yrs. | Dischgd 1 Feb. '80 |
| Hayes, Theoe., Pt...... | | 3 Mar. '77 | | |
| Herman, Jno., Pt....... | | Jan. '78 | | Omtd June '78 |
| Hatchcock, Isom, Pt.... | Montfort's | 20 July '78 | 9 mo. | |
| Hobgood, Jno., Pt...... | " | " | " | |
| Hardin, Lewis, Pt....... | " | " | " | |
| Hatcock, Edw'd, Pt..... | " | " | " | |
| Harris, Thos., Corpl..... | Hogg's | 28 Apr. '76 | 2½ yrs. | Dischgd 1 Nov. '78 |
| Hawkins, Loeston, Pt. .. | " | 20 July '78 | 9 mo. | |
| Howard, Edw'd, Corpl. . | Quinn's | " | " | |
| Hill, Wm., Corpl....... | " | " | " | |

| Name and Rank | Company | Dates of Enlistment and Commission | Period of Service | Occurrences |
|---|---|---|---|---|
| Hawley, Wm., Pt...... | Quinn's | 20 July '78 | 9 mo. | |
| Hale, Joseph, Pt....... | " | " | " | |
| Hobbs, Peter, Pt...... | " | " | " | |
| Hoover, Henry, Pt..... | " | " | " | Died 2 Nov. '78 |
| Hoover, Sam'l, Pt...... | " | " | " | |
| Hamb, Wm., Pt...... | " | " | " | |
| Haywood, Edw'd, Pt.... | " | " | " | |
| Horton, Jno., Corpl..... (P. 1079) | Lt. Cols. | 1 Oct. '78 | " | |
| Hatchcock, Wm., Pt.... | " | 20 July '78 | " | |
| Hardison, Jesse, Sergt... (P. 1080) | Baker's | " | " | |
| Harris, Ab'm, Pt....... | " | " | " | |
| Hooks, Willowby, Pt.... | " | " | " | |
| Hall, Edw'd, Pt....... | " | " | " | |
| Hunt, David, Pt....... | " | " | " | |
| Harrison, Wm., Pt...... | " | " | " | Destd 2 Aug. '78 |
| Horpus, Basford, Pt.... | | 1778 | | Destd 9 July '78 |
| Holmes, Shad'k, Pt..... | Blount's | 14 May '76 | 2½ yrs. | {Sergt. 1 July '78, Dischgd 25 Oct. '78 |
| Hopkins, Dan'l, Corpl... | " | 20 July '78 | 9 mo. | |
| Hoggart, Jno., Pt....... | " | " | " | |
| Heal, Elisha, Pt....... | " | " | " | |
| Hubbard, Jas., Pt...... | " | " | " | |
| Hoggart, Pat'k, Pt...... | " | " | " | |
| Hair, Wm., Pt......... | Ballard's | " | " | |
| Hearn, Jas., Pt........ | " | " | " | |
| Hare, Nich'ls, Pt....... | " | " | " | |
| Hawkins, Henry, Pt..... | " | " | " | |
| Hawkins, Rich'd, Pt..... | " | " | " | |
| Howington, Wm., Pt.... | " | 5 May '76 | 2½ yrs. | Omtd in '79 |
| Howell, Jno., Pt........ | " | 1778 | | Died 28 Sep. '78 |
| Hinson, Elizah, Sergt.... | Bradley's | 20 July '78 | 9 mo. | |
| Hill, Moses, Pt........ (P. 1080) | " | " | " | |
| Hutchins, Robt., Pt..... | " | " | " | |
| Harper, Fred'k, Pt...... | " | " | " | |
| Hudson, Jno., Pt...... | " | " | " | |
| Harris, Abner, Pt....... | " | " | " | |
| Hardison, Joseph, Pt.... | " | " | " | |
| Hearn, Benj., Pt....... | " | " | " | Dischgd 7 May '79 |
| Harris, Jese, Pt........ | " | " | " | |
| Hinsen, David, Pt...... | " | " | " | |
| Hodges, Wm., Pt...... | " | 30 July '79 | 18 mo. | Destd 20 Oct. '79 |
| Hudley, Joseph, Pt..... | " | 20 June " | W | Died 28 Jan. '80 |
| Hair, Thos., Pt........ | " | 20 May '78 | " | Destd 16 Oct. '79 |
| Hoby, Wm., Pt......... | " | 20 July '79 | " | Destd Sep. '79 |
| Harrison, Dan'l, Pt..... | " | 20 Aug. '77 | 3 yrs. | |
| Harbut, Benj., Pt....... | Montfort's | 26 July '79 | W | |
| Hodges, Joseph, Pt..... | " | 1 June " | 18 mo. | Omtd Oct. '79 |
| Hewett, Jeremh, Pt.... | " | 24 " " | 2 yrs. | Destd Sep. '79 |
| Hall, Thos., Pt........ | " | 1 Mar. " | 9 mo. | Dischgd 1 Dec. '79 |
| Hastings, Carter, Musc.. | Ballard's | 1 July " | 18 mo. | |
| Hewlett, Chas., Pt...... | " | " | " | |
| Huddy, Wm., Pt........ | " | 1779 | 3 yrs. | |
| Hood, Eph'm, Pt...... | Quinn's | 7 June " | 18 mo. | |
| Hinton, Jonas, Pt....... | " | 1 June " | " | |

| Name and Rank | Company | Dates of Enlistment and Commission | Period of Service | Occurrences |
|---|---|---|---|---|
| Heathcock, Aaron, Pt... | Quinn's | 22 June '79 | 2 yrs. | |
| Hogun, David, Pt...... | " | 24 " " | W | Omtd Oct.'79, Must in'80 |
| Hall, Jas., Pt.......... | " | 1779 | 9 mo. | Dischgd Dec. '79 |
| (P. 1080) | | | | |
| Hicksman, Chas., Pt.... | " | " | " | Dischgd Dec. '79 |
| Hudson, Jno., Pt...... | " | " | " | Do |
| Holloway, David, Corpl. | Blount's | 1 Mar. " | " | Do |
| Hawthorn, Jno., Musc... | " | " | " | Do |
| (P. 1081) | | | | |
| Hutchins, Jesse, Pt...... | " | 26 July " | 3 yrs. | |
| Harp, Rich'd, Pt...... | " | 1 Mar. " | 9 mo. | Dischgd 1 Dec. '79 |
| Hopkins, Joseph, Pt..... | " | 25 June " | W | Destd Oct. '79 |
| Honycutt, Jno., Pt..... | " | 5 Aug. " | " | Destd Oct. '79 |
| Hall, Nathan, Musc..... | | " | 9 mo. | Died 24 Aug. '79 |
| Hide, Sal., Pt.......... | | " | " | Omtd Oct. '79 |
| Hill, Wm., Pt.......... | | " | " | Do |
| Hill, Joseph, Pt........ | | " | " | Died 15 Aug. '79 |
| Hussar, Francis, Pt..... | | " | " | Omtd Oct. '79 |
| Hickman, Corbin, Pt.... | | " | " | Do |
| Hicks, Hasell, Pt...... | | " | " | Destd Sep. '79 |
| Hall, Jesse, Pt........ | | " | " | Do |
| Haygood, Wm., Pt..... | | " | " | Omtd Oct. '79 |
| Hill, Jno., Ensn........ | | 4 Apr. " | " | Lt. 5 July '81 |
| Hendrick, Albert, Corpl. | McRee's | 28 " " | 12 mo. | {Sergt. Aug. '81, Left service 28 Apr. '82 |
| Hays, Jno., Pt......... | " | 9 May " | " | Destd 1 June '81 |
| Harmond, Jno., Pt..... | " | 28 Apr. " | " | Dead Sep. '81 |
| Hilbert, Jno., Pt........ | Raiford's | 4 May " | " | Dead Dec. '81 |
| Harris, Robt., Pt...... | " | 5 " " | " | Left service 28 Apr. '82 |
| Harrison, Wm., Pt..... | " | 18 " " | " | Do        18 May '82 |
| (P. 1081) | | | | |
| Hewes, Joseph, Sergt.... | Donoho's | 25 May '79 | 12 mo. | Do        25 May '82 |
| Hester, Jno., Pt....... | " | 14 June " | " | {Pt. Jan., Left service 16 June '82 |
| Howell, Dempsy, Pt..... | " | 2 May " | " | Left service  2 May '82 |
| Howard, Edw'd, Pt..... | " | 14 June '81 | " | Do        14 June '82 |
| Huttliston, Robt., Pt.... | " | " | " | Do        14 June '82 |
| Hopper, Moses, Pt..... | " | 25 May " | " | Do        25 May '82 |
| Hart, Adam, Pt........ | " | " | W | |
| Hainey, Jno., Corpl..... | Dixon's | 15 May " | 12 mo. | Do        21 May '82 |
| Hester, Benj., Pt...... | " | " | " | Omtd in '81 |
| Hainey, Anth'y, Corpl. . | " | " | " | Left service 21 May '82 |
| Hill, Geo., Pt.......... | " | 12 May " | " | Omtd in '81 |
| Hancock, Henry, Pt.... | " | 25 Apr. " | " | Do |
| Hall, Jno., Pt.......... | " | " | " | Left service 25 Apr. '82 |
| Huggins, Jas., Pt...... | " | " | " | Do        25 Apr. '82 |
| Huggins, Luke, Pt..... | " | " | " | Do        25 Apr. '82 |
| Huggins, Mich'l, Pt..... | " | " | " | Do        25 Apr. '82 |
| Hickman, Corbin, Pt.... | " | 12 May " | " | Do        26May '82 |
| Harvey, Joshua, Pt..... | " | " | W | {Transf'd 29 July '81 to Coll. Lee's |
| Holdin, Wm., Pt....... | " | 12 May " | | {Transf'd 29 July '81 to Coll. Lee's |
| (P. 1081) | | | | |
| Hunter, Geo., Pt...... | " | 12 Apr. '81 | | Destd 20 July '81 |
| Harris, Nelson, Sergt.... | Lytle's | 18 Sep. '80 | 12 mo. | Left service 12 Apr. '82 |
| Hassle, Stephen, Pt.... | " | 5 Apr. '81 | " | Omtd in '81 |

| Name and Rank | Company | Dates of Enlistment and Commission | Period of Service | Occurrences |
|---|---|---|---|---|
| Hampton, Zacha., Pt.... | Lytle's | 6 June '81 | 12 mo. | Do |
| Hafner, Jacob, Pt...... | " | 1 June " | " | |
| (P. 1082) | | | | |
| Harris, Elizah, Pt...... | " | 1 June " | " | Left service  1 June '82 |
| Howard, Wm., Pt...... | " | 12 Apr. " | " | Do       12 Apr. '82 |
| Howard, Wilson, Pt.... | " | " | " | Do       12 Apr. '82 |
| Hodges, Wyllis, Pt...... | " | " | " | Do       12 Apr. '82 |
| Hodges, Jas., Pt....... | " | " | " | Omtd in '81 |
| Harrison, Thos., Pt.... | " | " | " | Left service 12 Apr. '82 |
| Headright, Jno., Pt.... | " | 1 June '81 | " | Do       1 June '82 |
| Hodges, Robt., Pt...... | " | 12 Apr. " | | Destd 5 July '81 |
| Holly, Jacob, Pt....... | " | " | W | |
| Hedspeth, Jno., Pt..... | " | 12 Apr. " | 12 mo. | Left service 12 Apr. '82 |
| Harding, Israel, Sergt... | Sharp's | 15 " " | " | Do       15 Apr. '82 |
| Hamontree, Griffith, Cpl. | " | " | " | Do       15 Apr. '82 |
| Hern, Howell, Pt...... | " | 21 May " | | Omtd in '81 |
| Harding, Ab'm, Pt...... | " | 15 Apr. " | | Omtd in '81 |
| Hodgs, Wm., Pt....... | " | 15 June '81 | " | Left service 15 June '82 |
| Hewell, Caleb, Pt...... | " | 5 Apr. " | " | Omtd in '81 |
| Hern, Jno., Pt......... | " | " | | Died 20 Feb. '82 |
| Hardy, Joseph, Pt..... | " | " | | Omtd in '81 |
| (P. 1082) | | | | |
| Harper, Jno., Pt....... | " | | | |
| Hill, Green, Pt........ | " | | | |
| Harper, Nathan, Pt..... | " | | | |
| Hill, Jno., Pt.......... | " | 5 Apr. '81 | 12 mo. | ⎰Corpl. Jan., Left service 5 Apr. '82 |
| Hooker, Jno., Pt....... | " | " | " | Left service 5 Apr. '82 |
| Hobbs, Joseph, Pt..... | Walton's | 1781 | | Do       1 July '82 |
| Hills, Sam'l, Pt........ | Dixon's | " | | Time out 1 Apr. '82 |
| Holly, Benj., Pt....... | Lytle's | | W | Mustd War Jan. '82 |
| Hataway, Thos., Pt.... | Sharp's | " | | |
| Hubbard, Jno., Pt..... | " | | 12 mo. | Time out   8 Sep. '82 |
| Haines, Wm., Pt....... | " | | " | Do       3 Feb. '83 |
| Hunter, Asa, Pt........ | Doherty's | | " | Do       25 May '82 |
| Hutson, Miles, Pt...... | " | | " | Do       25 Apr. '82 |
| Howard, Joseph, Pt.... | " | | " | Do       25 May '82 |
| Herrington, Thos., Pt. .. | " | | " | Do       25 May '82 |
| Hill, Thos., Pt......... | " | | W | ⎰Mustd Jan. '82, Omtd 1 Apr. '82 |
| Harper, Wm., Pt....... | Rhode's | " | 12 mo. | Time out 14 June '82 |
| Hardy, Joseph, Pt..... | " | " | " | Do       25 Apr. '82 |
| Harper, Joseph, Pt..... | " | " | " | Do       14 May '82 |
| Hicks, Micaja, Pt...... | " | " | " | Do       25 Apr. '82 |
| Hinds, Lewis, Pt....... | " | " | " | Do       16 July '82 |
| Hanberry, Jesse, Pt..... | Armstrong's | " | " | Do       1 Nov. '82 |
| (P. 1082) | | | | |
| Harrison, Henry, Pt..... | Armstrong's | 31 Dec. '81 | " | Died 20 Sep. '82 |
| Helderman, Nicholas, Pt | " | " | W | |
| Hamilton, Stewart, Pt... | Bailey's | 25 May " | 12 mo. | Left service 25 May '82 |
| Hall, Jas., Pt......... | " | 15 Apr. " | " | Do       15 Apr. '82 |
| Hill, Jese, Pt.......... | " | 2 May " | " | Do       2 May '82 |
| Hair, Jas., Pt.......... | " | " | | Do       2 May '82 |
| Hews, Jas., Pt......... | " | 25 May " | | Do       25 May '82 |
| Harrison, Francis, Pt.... | " | 15 Apr. " | | Do       15 Apr. '82 |
| (P. 1083) | | 2 May " | | |
| Hassel, Joseph, Pt..... | " | | 12 mo. | Do       2 May '82 |

| Name and Rank | Company | Dates of Enlistment and Commission | Period of Service | Occurrences |
|---|---|---|---|---|
| Hornsby, Thos., Qr. Mr. Sergt........ | Brevard's | 1781 | 12 Mo. | Do        28 Apr. '82 |
| Hardy, Robt., Sergt..... | " | " | " | Do        28 May '82 |
| Hutchins, Edw'd, Sergt.. | " | " | " | Do        11 July '82 |
| Hall, Jesse, Corpl....... | " | " | " | Do         9 May '82 |
| Hilton, Arnold, Pt...... | " | " | " | Do        25 May '82 |
| Hopper, Jno., Pt........ | " | " | " | Do         9 May '82 |
| Holt, Thos., Pt......... | " | " | " | Do        12 Apr. '82 |
| Hill, Rich'd, Pt........ | " | " | " | Do        12 Apr. '82 |
| Hunsucker, Ab'm, Pt. .. | " | " | " | Do         7 June '82 |
| Harvey, John, Sergt.... | " | " | " | Transf'd 9 Jan. '82 to Pena Line |
| Hobbs, Reuben, Pt...... | Hall's | " | " | Time out 1 Aug. '82 |
| Hobbs, Jacob, Pt...... | " | " | " | Time out 1 Aug. '82 |
| Hays, John, Pt........ | " | | W | Mustd Jan. '82, see him in 8 Reg. |
| (P. 1083) | | | | |
| Harmon, James, Corpl. . | Hall's | 1781 | 12 mo. | Time out 16 Aug. '82 |
| Horn, Henry, Musc..... | Yarboro's | " | " | Do        22 Apr. '82 |
| Harris, Henry, Musc.... | " | " | " | Do        10 Apr. '82 |
| Hopkins, Joseph, Musc.. | " | " | " | Do        15 Apr. '82 |
| Hedspeth, Peter, Musc.. | " | " | " | Do         7 May '82 |
| Harvey, Absolom, Musc. | " | " | " | Omtd 1 Apr. '82 |
| Hagenton, Jese, Musc... | " | " | " | Time out 10 Apr. '82 |
| Hall, Jas., Musc........ | " | " | " | Time out 10 Apr. '82 |
| Hill, Robt., Musc...... | " | " | " | Omtd 1 Apr. '82 |
| Hussey, John, Musc..... | " | " | " | Time out 22 Apr. '82 |
| Hall, Josua, Musc....... | Carter's | 25 Apr. " | " | Do        25 Apr. '82 |
| Hoard, Micajah, Musc.. | " | 15 Apr. " | " | Do        25 Apr. '82 |
| Hack, Alex'r, Musc..... | " | "    " | " | Do        10 Apr. '82 |
| Hardick, Rich'd, Musc.. | " | 31 July " | " | Do        25 July '82, re-enlisted War Apr. '82 |
| Hall, Wm., Musc...... | | 12 Apr. " | " | Time out 7 Apr. '82 |
| Hester, Joseph, Musc. .. | Jones' | 1 Jan. '82 | " | |
| Hester, John, Musc..... | " | "    " | " | |
| Henry, Wm., Musc.... | " | 25 "    " | " | |
| Hill, Wm., Musc....... | " | 2 Jan. " | " | |
| Hammon, Isaac, Musc. . | " | 1 Aug. '81 | W | |
| Holmes, Hardy, Lt...... | " | 1781 | | |
| (P. 1083) | | | | |
| Hayes, Southy, Pt...... | Mill's | 7 Feb. '82 | 12 mo. | |
| Hunt, John, Pt......... | " | 6 "    " | " | |
| Holmes, John, Pt...... | " | 18 Dec. '81 | " | |
| Holmes, Josiah, Pt...... | " | "    " | " | |
| Holland, Henry, Pt..... | Coleman's | 14 Sep. " | " | |
| Holly, John, Pt........ | " | 10 Jan. '82 | " | Died 16 Sep. '82 |
| Hurley, John, Pt....... | " | "    " | " | |
| Hammon, Isaac, Pt.... | " | 1 Nov. '81 | " | Dead 1 Aug. '82 |
| Hogg, Gideon, Pt....... | " | 1 Jan. '82 | | |
| Harris, Thos., Pt...... | Hall's | 1 Mar. " | | |
| (P. 1084) | | | | |
| Hurley, John, Pt...... | " | | W | Mustd Sep. '82 |
| Hicks, Dempsy, Pt..... | " | | " | Mustd Sep. '82, Destd 10 Dec. '82 |
| Hogg, Andrew, Pt...... | Jones' | 8 Feb. " | 12 mo. | |
| Haws, John, Sergt...... | Mills' | Jan. " | " | Time out 1 Jan. '83 |
| Hutchison, Elizah, Pt... | Bailey's | 1 Aug. " | 18 mo. | Destd 5 May '83 |

| Name and Rank | Company | Dates of Enlistment and Commission | Period of Service | Occurrences |
|---|---|---|---|---|
| Hews, Willis, Pt....... | | 17 Sep. '82 | 18 Mo. | |
| Hicks, Henry.......... | | 4 Feb. " | 12 mo. | |
| Holston, Salathiel, Sgt... | Hadley's | 1 Aug. " | 18 mo. | Destd 18 June '83 |
| Hall, John, Pt.......... | " | " | " | |
| Halten, Brazil, Pt...... | " | " | " | |
| Harris, Jese, Pt....... | " | " | " | |
| Hays, Wm., Pt........ | " | " | " | |
| Harding, Lewis, Corpl... | Bacot's | 1782 | " | |
| Hines, Benjamin, Pt..... | " | " | " | |
| (P. 1084) | | | | |
| Hammock, Sam'l, Pt.... | " | " | " | |
| Holland, Daniel, Pt..... | " | " | " | |
| Henry, Burrel, Pt...... | " | " | " | |
| Harper, Jett, Pt........ | " | " | " | |
| Hedgpeth, Ab'm, Pt. ... | " | " | " | |
| Hull, Nathaniel, Pt..... | Carter's | " | " | Destd 21 June '83 |
| Hicks, Micaja, Pt....... | " | " | " | |
| Hart, Samuel, Pt....... | " | " | " | |
| Herrington, Samuel, Pt.. | " | " | " | |
| Hughes, Samuel, Pt..... | " | " | " | |
| Hutson, David, Pt...... | " | " | " | Destd 26 Nov. '82 |
| Hollin, Jeremiah, Pt..... | " | " | " | Destd 9 June '83 |
| Henderson, Robt., Sergt. | Raiford's | " | " | |
| Harrington, Thos., Cpl.. | " | " | " | |
| Harrington, Giles, Pt... | " | " | " | |
| Hand, Joseph, Pt...... | " | " | " | |
| Heath, William, Pt..... | " | " | " | |
| Hutson, Miles, Pt....... | " | " | " | |
| Hall, John, Corpl....... | Sharp's | " | " | |
| Hawkins, Ep'm, Pt..... | " | " | " | |
| Hyner, Lewis, Pt..... | " | " | " | Destd 17 June '83 |
| Holland, Brazil, Pt..... | " | " | " | |
| Hollenhead, Benj., Pt... | " | " | " | |
| Hollenhead, Thos., Pt.. | " | " | " | |
| (P. 1084) | | | | |
| Haddock, And'w, Sergt.. | Lytle's | 1782 | 18 mo. | |
| Haddock, Richard, Pt... | " | " | " | |
| Hawkins, Lorton, Pt.... | " | " | " | |
| Hews, William, Pt...... | | " | " | |
| Hendrick, Sam'l, Pt.... | | " | " | |
| Hadley, William, Pt..... | | " | " | |
| Harris, Henry, Pt...... | | " | " | |
| Hurley, Joshua, Sergt... | Brevard's | " | " | |
| Hurley, David, Pt...... | " | " | " | Pt. Mar. '83 |
| Henson, Wm., Pt...... | " | " | " | |
| (P. 1085) | | | | |
| Hood, Chas, Pt........ | " | " | " | |
| Hood, Wm., Pt........ | " | " | " | |
| Highfield, Hezk., Pt.... | " | " | | |
| Hargrave, Hezk., Pt. ... | " | " | " | |
| Hill, Solomon, Pt...... | " | " | " | Transf'd Mar. '83 |
| Harris, Benj., Pt....... | Rhode's | 1 Aug. " | " | Sergt. 1 Aug. '83 |
| Hickman, Jacob, Pt..... | Evans' | 1782 | " | |
| Hensley, Wm., Pt...... | " | " | " | |
| Hutson, Miles, Pt...... | | 1779 | 3 yrs. | |
| Hall, Joshua, Pt....... | | " | " | |
| Harris, David, Pt...... | | " | | Mustd, Destd Sep. '79 |

| Name and Rank | Company | Dates of Enlistment and Commission | Period of Service | Occurrences |
|---|---|---|---|---|
| Hatcher, David, Pt..... | | 1779 | | Mustd, Dead Sep. '79 |
| Harbourd, Jno., Pt..... | | " | | Mustd, Destd Sep. '79 |
| Hussey, Jno., Pt....... | | | 3 yrs. | Mustd Aug. '79 |
| (P. 1085) | | | | |
| Hinds, Dan'l, Pt....... | Bacot's | | | Mustd Dec. '82 |
| Hope, Wm., Musc...... | Lytle's | | | Do |
| Harris, Edw'd, Sergt.... | Sharp's | | | Do |
| Hollis, Jas., Musc....... | Rhode's | | | Do |
| Hutson, Miles, Pt....... | Sharp's | 14 Dec. '78 | W | |
| Huggins, Nehemh, Pt... | " | | 3 yrs. | |
| Hedgeman, Geo., Pt. ... | " | 10 Nov. '78 | | |
| Hedgeman, Lewis, Pt... | " | " | | |
| Hair, Thos., Pt......... | " | " | | |
| Hicks, Chas., Pt....... | " | 1 Nov. '78 | | |
| Harvey, Jas., Pt........ | " | " | | |
| Harp, Mattw, Sgt. Mjr.. | Armstrong's | | W | Mustd Jan. '79 |
| Hall, Davis, Pt......... | Lt. Col's | | | Do |
| Hall, Joshua, Pt....... | " | | | Do |
| Hall, Futrill, Pt........ | Taylor's | | | Do |
| Harback, Jno., Pt...... | Eaton's | | W | Do |
| I (P. 1087) | | | | |
| Ivy, David, Musc....... | Wilson's | 12 May '77 | 3 yrs. W | Waggoner in '81 |
| Ingraham, Jno., Pt..... | | June '79 | W | Sergt. 1 Jan. '80 |
| Inman, Wm., Pt....... | Bradley's | 1 Aug. " | " | |
| Ivey, Reubin, Pt...... | Bailey's | 25 May '81 | 12 mo. | Left service 25 May '82 |
| Inglish, Jno., Pt....... | Hall's | | W | {Mustd Apr. '82, |
| | | | | Destd 13 June '83 |
| Isdall, Geo., Pt........ | Lytle's | 1782 | 18 mo. | Destd 5 May '83 |
| J (P. 1092) | | | | |
| Jordan, John, Pt........ | Shepard's | 5 May '77 | | Died 17 Mar. '78 |
| Jarvis, John, Capt...... | | | | Omtd June '78 |
| Jarvis, Willoughby, Pt.. | Jarvis' | 14 May " | | Corpl. June, Pt. Aug. '78 |
| Jones, Timothy, Lt..... | Gregory's | 19 Apr. " | | Resigned Apr. '78 |
| Jennings, John, Corpl... | " | 21 May " | 3 yrs. | Pt. June '78 |
| Jones, Wm., Pt........ | Heron's | 22 July " | " | |
| Jason, Henry, Pt...... | Van Noy's | 29 May " | | Omtd June '78 |
| Jacobs, Benj., Pt....... | | 16 Feb. " | 2½ yrs. | Corpl. 19 May '79 |
| Jennings, Wm., Pt...... | Major's | 6 Nov. " | " | Dead Oct '78 |
| Jones, John, Pt......... | | 14 Jan " | " | Died 15 Oct. '78 |
| James, Wm., Pt........ | | 1 Dec. " | " | Died 31 Oct. '78 |
| Jones, Thos., Pt........ | | 28 Sep. " | W | Sergt. 1 Jan. '80 |
| Johnson, Dan'l, Pt..... | | 16 Sep. " | 3 yrs. W | |
| Johnson, Henry, Pt.... | | 29 " " | 3 yrs. | Musician Nov. '79 |
| Jones, Phillip, Pt...... | | 4 " " | " | |
| Johnson, Brutus, Musc.. | | | | {Mustd Jan., and died 15 |
| | | | | Feb. '78 |
| Jones, Wm., Pt........ | | 2 July " | " | |
| Joiner, Henry, Sergt. ... | Colonel's | 20 " '78 | 9 mo. | |
| Joiner, Ely, Pt......... | " | " | " | |
| Johnson, Balaam, Pt.... | Hogg's | " | " | |
| Johnson, Solomon, Pt... | " | | | Dead 15 Sep. '78 |
| Jackson, Jereh, Pt...... | Quinn's | 16 Oct. '78 | 3 yrs. | {See him for war in Quinn's |
| | | | | Co'y in '79 |
| Johnson, Josh., Sergt.... | " | 20 July " | 9 mo. | |
| (P. 1092) | | | | |
| Jones, Isom, Pt......... | Lt. Col's | 20 July '78 | 9 mo. | |
| Johnson, Dempsy, Pt.... | " | " | " | |

| Name and Rank | Company | Dates of Enlistment and Commission | Period of Service | Occurrences |
|---|---|---|---|---|
| Johnson, Barns, Pt...... | Lt. Col's | 20 July '78 | 9 mo. | |
| Jonican, David, Pt...... | " | " | " | |
| Jackson, Edw'd, Pt..... | Baker's | " | " | |
| Jones, Peter, Pt........ | " | " | " | |
| Joiner, Nath'l, Pt....... | " | '78 | | Destd 14 July '78 |
| James, David, Pt....... | Blount's | 20 July " | | |
| James, Jereh, Pt........ | " | " | " | |
| James, Thos., Pt........ | " | " | " | |
| Jackson, Fred'k, Pt..... | Ballard's | " | " | |
| Jones, Josiah, Musc..... | Bradley's | " | " | Mustd for War Jan. '82 |
| Johnson, Mathias, Pt. .. | Child's | " | " | |
| James, Mecaja, Pt...... | " | " | " | |
| Jones, Broton, Pt....... | Bradley's | 10 June '79 | 18 mo. | Omtd Oct. '79 |
| Jack, Francis, Pt....... | Montfort's | 19 " " | " | Do |
| Jew, James, Pt........ | " | 1 Mar. " | 9 mo. | Dischgd 1 Dec. '79 |
| Johnson, Henry, Sergt... | Ballard's | 1 June " | 3 yrs. | ⎰Transf'd Mar. '80 to 2nd ⎱Reg. |
| Jordan, Caleb, Pt....... | " | 29 " " | W | ⎰Destd 5 Aug. '79, ⎱Mustd Jan. '82 |
| Jeanes, Nathan, Pt...... | " | 1779 | | Dischgd 1 Dec. '79 |
| Johnson, James, Pt..... | " | " | | Do |
| Jones, John, Pt........ | " | | 3 yrs. | Dischgd 1 Feb. '80 |
| Jackson, Jereh, Pt...... (P. 1093) | Quinn's | 24 June " | W | Omtd Oct.'79,Mustd in'80 |
| Johnson, Thos., Pt..... | " | 1779 | 9 mo. | Dischgd Dec. '79 |
| Jenks, Thos, Corpl...... | " | " | " | Do |
| Johnson, Wm., Pt...... | Blount's | 1 July " | W | |
| Jones, Wm., Pt........ | " | 1 June '78 | 3 yrs. | |
| Jones, Hardy, Pt....... | " | 17 Oct. " | " | |
| Josnes, David, Pt....... | | '79 | 9 mo. | Omtd Oct. '79 |
| Jeffrey, Jno., Pt....... | | " | " | Died 15 Aug. '79 |
| Johnson, Dan'l, Pt...... | Raiford's | 17 May '81 | 12 mo. | Left service 15 May, '82 |
| Jones, Griffith, Pt...... | " | " | " | Artificer '82 |
| James, Jereh, Pt........ | " | " | " | Left service 15 Apr. '82 |
| Johnson, John, Pt....... | Donoho's | 14 June " | " | ⎰Sergt. Jan., ⎱Left service in June '82 |
| Jenkins, Elijah......... | " | 15 Apr. " | " | Omtd in '81 |
| Jeffries, Jacob, Pt....... | " | 25 May " | " | Left service 25 May '82 |
| Jennings, James, Pt..... | " | " | " | Omtd in '81 |
| Johnson, Jese, Pt...... | " | 14 June " | " | Left service 14 June '82 |
| Jarvis, John, Pt........ | Dixon's | 12 May " | " | Do    12 June '82 |
| Jones, Berry, Pt........ | Lytle's | 9 July " | " | Do    26 June '82 |
| Jones, Freeman, Pt..... | " | " | " | Do    26 June '82 |
| Jeffrey, Drewry, Pt..... | " | " | " | Do    26 June '82 |
| Johnson, Jacob, Pt...... | Walton's | 1781 | " | Do    1 Apr. '82 |
| Jones, Nathan, Pt...... | Lytle's | " | " | Do    12 Apr. '82 |
| Jackson, Jas., Pt....... | Sharp's | " | " | Do    21 Aug. '82 |
| Jones, Thos., Pt........ | " | " | " | Time out 16 July '82 |
| Jones, Fred'k, Pt...... (P. 1093) | " | " | " | Do    5 Aug. '82 |
| Joiner, Benj., Pt........ | Doherty's | | W | Mustd Jan. '82 |
| Jones, Fred'k, Pt....... | " | 1781 | 12 mo. | Time out 25 May'82 |
| Jones, Henry, Pt....... | " | " | " | Do    Do |
| Johnson, Absolom, Pt... | " | " | " | Do    Do |
| Jones, Jas., Pt.......... | Rhode's | " | " | Dischgd 17 Feb. '82 |
| Jones, John, Pt........ | Armstrong's | " | " | Left service  1 Nov. '82 |
| Jones, Isaac, Pt........ | Brevard's | " | | Do    10 May '82 |

| Name and Rank | Company | Dates of Enlistment and Commission | Period of Service | Occurrences |
|---|---|---|---|---|
| Jordan, Nathan........ | Hall's | 1781 | 12 mo. | Do    16 Aug. '82 |
| Johnson, Wm.......... | " | " | " | Do    16 Aug. '82 |
| James, Benj........... | " | " | " | Do    16 Aug. '82 |
| Jacobs, Henry......... | " | " | " | Do    1 Aug. '82 |
| Jones, Zacha., Corpl..... | Yarboro's | " | " | Do    1 July '82 |
| Jesse, John, Musc...... | " | " | " | Do    22 Apr. '82 |
| Jordon, Zeb'l, Pt...... | " | | | Do    1 May '82 |
| Jordon, Stephen, Pt.... | " | | | Do    1 May '82 |
| Jones, Wm., Pt......... | " | | | Do    22 May '82 |
| Jones, Jas., Pt......... | " | | | Do    13 Apr. '82 |
| Jones, Jas., Pt......... | " | | | Do    27 Apr. '82 |
| Jones, Britton, Pt...... | Carter's | 25 Apr.  " | " | Do    25 Apr. '82 |
| Johnson, Solomon, Pt.. | Jones' | 15 June " | " | |
| Johnson, Eph'm, Pt..... | " | " | | |
| Johnson, Soasby, Pt.... | " | | | |
| Jones, Sam'l, Capt..... | | 11 Sep.  " | 12 mo. | {Lt. from 4 Oct. '77, Deranged 1 Jan. '83 |
| (P. 1094) | | | | |
| Jones, Wm., Pt......... | Mill's | 5 Feb.  '82 | 12 mo. | |
| Jones, Jno., Pt......... | " | 6  "   " | " | |
| Jones, Ab'm, Pt....... | " | " | " | |
| Jacobs, Zacha, Pt...... | " | 18 Dec. '81 | " | |
| Jacobs, Hezk., Pt...... | " | " | " | |
| Johnson, John, Pt...... | | 1 Jan. '82 | " | |
| Jacobs, Wm. Pt....... | | 20 Feb. '82 | W | |
| Jones, Jona, Capt....... | Coleman's | 12 Dec. '81 | 12 mo. | |
| Jones, David, Pt........ | " | " | " | |
| Jones, Benj., Pt........ | Hall's | | W | |
| Jones, Phillip.......... | | 1781 | 12 mo. | Left service 25 July '82 |
| Jordon, Fountain....... | " | 1 Feb. '82 | " | Time out 1 Nov. '82 |
| Jones, Phillip.......... | Mill's | " | " | Mustd War Sep. '82 |
| James, Wm........... | Bailey's | 10 Sep.  " | 18 mo. | Time out 1 Mar. '83 |
| Jackson, Wm.......... | " | 1 Aug.  " | " | |
| Jones, Moses.......... | " | 17 Sep.  " | " | |
| Jones, Wm............ | Hadley's | 1 Aug  " | " | |
| Jacobs, Joshua........ | Bacot's | " | " | |
| Jaene, Sherrod........ | Carter's | " | " | Destd 21 June '83 |
| Johnson, Fred'k........ | Raiford's | " | " | |
| Jimes, Vachel, Sergt..... | Sharp's | " | " | |
| Jones, Ezek'l, Pt....... | " | " | | |
| Jones, Francis......... | | " | " | Transf'd 27 Dec. '82 |
| Jacobs, Primus........ | Lytle's | " | " | |
| Jackson, Colby........ | Brevard's | " | " | |
| (P. 1094) | | | | |
| Jarvis, Jno............ | Brevard's | 1782 | 18 mo. | Died 29 Nov. '82 |
| Jordon, Rives, Corpl.... | Evans' | " | " | Destd 4 June '82 |
| Jones, Ab'm, Pt....... | " | " | | Omtd Jan. dead |
| Jarmin, Benj., Pt...... | Colonel's | | 3 yrs. | {Mustd Jan. '79 vide Benj. German |
| Jones, John, Pt........ | Raiford's | 27 May '78 | W | Mustd Feb. '79 |
| K  (P. 1098) | | | | |
| Kelly, Chas., Sergt..... | Wilson's | 4 Aug '77 | 3 yrs. | {Pt. June '78, Corpl. 1 Aug. '78, Sergt. 26 Feb. '79 |
| King, Jas., Pt......... | Stevenson's | 1 Aug.  " | 3 yrs. W | |
| Koen, Caleb, Lt....... | | 19 Apr.  " | | |
| King, Enoch, Pt....... | Moore's | 25 June  " | " | |
| King, Jno., Pt......... | | 4 Oct.  " | " | |

| Name and Rank | Company | Dates of Enlistment and Commission | Period of Service | Occurrences |
|---|---|---|---|---|
| Kail, Jno., Pt......... | | 16 Apr. '77 | 2½ yrs. | Dischgd 31 Dec. '78 |
| Kelly, Thos., Pt....... | | | W | Destd 12 Sep. '78, Mustd, dischgd Jan. '79 |
| Koen, Jno., Sergt...... | | 30 May " | 3 yrs. | Corpl. June '78 |
| Keller, Mich'l, Pt...... | | 6 June " | " | |
| Knight, Miles, Pt...... | | 1 Nov. " | 2½ y.W | Pris. 1 June '79, Sergt. 16 Feb. '80 |
| King, Mason, Pt........ | Hogg's | 20 July '78 | 9 mo. | Destd 21 July '78 |
| Keel, Hardy, Sergt...... | Baker's | 26 Dec. '76 | 3 yrs. | |
| Kitchen, Benj., Sergt.... (P. 1098) | " | 20 July '78 | 9 mo. | |
| Kelly, Wm., Pt........ | " | " | " | |
| King, Thos., Pt........ | " | " | " | |
| Kail, Jacob, Pt........ | Blount's | " | " | |
| Kirk, Roger, Pt........ | Ballard's | " | " | |
| King, Edw'd, Pt........ | Bradley's | " | " | Mustd War in '82 in Hadley's Co'y |
| Killet, Joseph, Pt....... | Bradley's | " | " | Destd Oct. '78 |
| Kite, Jas., Pt........... | Child's | " | " | |
| Kelly, Jas., Pt......... | Bradley's | 20 May '78 | W | Destd Sep. '79 |
| Kittle, Benj., Pt....... | Montfort's | 10 Aug. '79 | 18 mo. | Destd Sep. '79 |
| Kenny, Robt., Pt...... | Ballard's | 1 July " | " | Destd 1 Oct. '79 |
| Kickman, Corbin, Pt.... | Quinn's | 1777 | | Dischgd 22 Nov. '79 |
| Kennedy, Wm., Sergt... | Ramsay's | " | 9 mo. | Omtd Oct. '79 |
| King, Jas., Pt......... | " | " | | Dead Sep. '79 |
| Kent, Thos., Pt....... | | " | " | Dead Sep. '79 |
| Kent, Thos., Pt....... | | " | " | Omtd Oct. '79 |
| Kennedy, Benj., Pt..... | | " | " | Omtd Oct. '79 |
| Kesley, Rich'd, Pt...... | McRee's | 11 June '81 | 12 mo. | Left service 11 June '82 |
| Kellion, Jno., Pt........ | Donoho's | 25 May '82 | " | Corpl. Jan., Left service 25 May '82 |
| Kellion, Jacob, Pt...... | " | " | " | Left service 25 May '82 |
| Kettle, Jacob or Jno., Corpl.............. | " | " | " | Sergt. Jan., Left service 25 May '82 |
| Kenny, Thos., Pt...... | Lytle's | 6 June '81 | " | Omtd in '81 |
| Keel, Hardy, Pt........ (P. 1098) | Sharp's | 15 Apr. " | " | Left service 15 Apr. '82 |
| Keel, Chas., Pt........ | Bailey's | 1 June '81 | 12 mo. | Left service 1 June '82 |
| Keen, Saucer, Pt....... | Hall's | Feb. '82 | " | Time out 22 Feb. '83 |
| King, Woody, Pt...... | " | 1781 | " | Do    21 Apr. '82 |
| Kite, Geo., Pt.......... | Yarborough's | " | " | Do    22 Apr. '82 |
| King, Anth'y, Pt...... | " | " | " | Do    1 May '82 |
| King, David, Pt....... | " | " | " | Do    23 May '82 |
| Kean, Jacob, Pt........ | Mill's | 4 Feb. '82 | " | Do    23 May '82 |
| Keeter, Nehemh, Pt..... | " | 18 Dec. '81 | " | Died 6 Sep. '82 |
| Keen, Wm., Pt......... (P. 1099) | Coleman's | 10 Jan '82 | " | |
| Keates, Thos., Sergt. ... | " | 10 Jan. " | " | Corpl. 1 Apr. '82, Pt. Sep. '82 |
| Kittrell, Jona, Pt....... | Mill's | 8 Mar. " | " | |
| Keener, Martin, Pt.... | Bailey's | 1 Aug. " | " | |
| Kennedy, Jno., Pt...... | " | " | " | |
| Keener, Jno., Pt....... | " | " | " | |
| Kinsey, Wm. .......... | Hadley's | " | 18 mo. | |
| Kellahan, Martin....... | " | " | " | |
| Kelly, Jno., Pt........ | " | " | " | |
| King, Edw'd, Pt........ | Brevard's | " | " | |

| Name and Rank | Company | Dates of Enlistment and Commission | Period of Service | Occurrences |
|---|---|---|---|---|
| Key, Jas., Pt........... | Hadley's | 1 Aug. '82 | 18 mo. | |
| Kersey, Jas., Pt........ | " | 20 " " | " | |
| Kennedy, Jno., Pt...... | " | 10 Sep. " | " | |
| Kent, Levy, Pt........ | " | 1 Aug. " | " | |
| Key, Wm., Pt.......... | Bacot's | 1782 | " | |
| Kids, Jno., Pt.......... | Carter's | " | " | |
| (P. 1099) | | | | |
| Kellum, Jno., Pt....... | Raiford's | " | 18 mo. | Died 28 June '83 |
| Kellum, Geo., Pt...... | " | " | " | |
| Kime, David, Pt........ | Sharp's | " | " | |
| Kilpatrick, Hugh, Pt.... | Lytle's | " | " | |
| Kingston, Sam'l, Pt.... | " | " | " | Destd 12 June '83 |
| Kellihan, Isaac, Pt..... | " | " | " | |
| King, Vincen., Pt....... | Brevard's | " | " | |
| Kelly, Jas., Pt......... | " | " | " | |
| Kennedy, Mich'l, Pt.... | Armstrong's | | 3 yrs. | Mustd June '79 |
| Kight, Demsy, Pt....... | Lt. Col's | | " | Mustd Jan. '79 |
| Kight, Chas., Pt........ | " | | " | Mustd Jan. '79 |
| L  (P. 11044) | | | | |
| Low, Jno., Lt.......... | Wilson's | 19 Apr. '77 | | Omtd Jan. '78 |
| Lambert, Aaron, Pt..... | Stevenson's | 21 " " | 3 yrs. | |
| Lester, Wm., Pt....... | " | 24 " " | " | Dischgd Apr. '78 |
| Lewis, Edw'd, Pt....... | " | 7 May " | " | Dead May '79 |
| Lewis, Elisha, Pt....... | " | 29 June " | " | Omtd Feb. '79 |
| Lewis, Jona, Pt......... | " | 1 Aug. " | " | Pris. 1 June '79 |
| Luts, Jno., Pt.......... | Jarvis' | 25 May " | | Corpl. June '78, Died 10 Nov. '78 |
| (P. 1105) | | | | |
| Lane, Jacob, Corpl...... | Moore's | 2 Aug. " | 3 yrs. | Pt. June '78 |
| Lippincott, Wm., Musc.. | " | 8 May " | 3 yrs. W | |
| Lollard, Jno., Pt....... | " | 18 Mar. '78 | 3 yrs. | |
| Low, Rich'd, Pt........ | | | " | Dischgd 14 June '78 |
| Lucas, Ambrose, Pt.... | | 14 Apr. '76 | 2½ y.W | Destd 1 Feb. '80 |
| Love, Thos., Pt........ | | June '77 | 3 yrs. | |
| Lane, Thos., Pt......... | Coleman's | 1 May " | " | |
| Lewis, W. Sam'l, Pt.... | | | " | Mustd May '78, Omtd June '78 |
| Lawrence, Nath'l, Lt.... | Fenner's | 1 June '78 | | Pris. 1 June '79, Deranged 1 Jan. '83 |
| Lane, Jethro, Pt........ | | 26 June '77 | 3 yrs. | |
| Lasiter, Jacob, Pt...... | | | | Mustd Feb. and died 16 Mar. '78 |
| Lucas, Famoth, Pt..... | Montforth's | 20 July '78 | 9 mo. | |
| Lewis, Morgan, Pt...... | " | " | " | |
| Lewis, Jno., Pt......... | " | " | " | |
| Lewis, Chas., Pt........ | Hogg's | " | " | |
| Lewis, Eph'm, Pt....... | " | " | " | |
| Lasiter, Josiah, Pt..... | " | " | " | Dead 15 Sep. '78 |
| Lambeth, Jno., Pt...... | Quinn's | " | " | |
| Lucas, Rich'd, Pt....... | " | " | " | Omtd Oct. '78 |
| Lewis, Joshua, Pt....... | Lt. Col's | " | " | |
| Lemon, Land, Pt...... | " | " | " | |
| Lane, Jethro, Pt........ | " | " | " | |
| Lewis, Jacob, Pt........ | Baker's | " | " | |
| Lucas, Chas., Pt........ | " | " | " | |
| Lucas, Arthur, Pt...... | " | " | " | |

| Name and Rank | Company | Dates of Enlistment and Commission | Period of Service | Occurrences |
|---|---|---|---|---|
| Lacey, Jno., Pt......... | Baker's | 20 July '78 | 9 mo. | Destd 30 Aug. '78 |
| Lee, Ab'm, Pt.......... | Blount's | " | " | |
| Leggett, Lewis, Pt...... | " | " | " | |
| Lawrence, Joseph, Pt.... | " | " | " | |
| Lewis, Nathan, Pt...... | Ballard's | " | " | |
| Long, Jas., Pt......... | " | " | " | |
| Langston, Elisha, Pt.... | " | " | " | |
| Lee, Jesse, Pt......... | " | " | " | Omtd Oct. '78 |
| Lee, Bryan, Pt......... | " | " | " | Omtd Oct. '78 |
| Lee, Chas., Pt......... | " | " | " | Omtd Oct. '78 |
| Lovet, Moses, Pt....... | Bradley's | " | " | |
| Lambert, Jno., Pt....... | Child's | " | " | |
| Loyd, Jesse, Pt........ | " | " | " | |
| Loyd, Henry, Pt....... | " | " | " | |
| Lewis, Wyllis, Corpl. ... | " | " | " | |
| Lee, Wm., Musc....... | Bradley's | 15 June '79 | W | |
| Lee, Wm., Pt.. ....... | " | 20 May '78 | " | Destd Sep. '79 |
| Liner, Thomas, Pt...... | " | 22 " '79 | 18 mo. | {Destd 28 Oct. '79, Mustd Dec. '79 |
| Lockhart, Jno., Sergt.... | Montfort's | 24 " '79 | " | Qr. Mr. Sergt. 15 Dec. '79 |
| Lawhorn, Sam'l, Pt..... | " | 26 July " | " | |
| Lasiter, Jas., Pt....... | " | 15 June " | " | Omtd Oct. '79 |
| Linch, Thos., Pt....... (P. 1106) | " | 10 Aug. " | " | Omtd Oct. '79 |
| Larouse, Joshua, Pt..... | " | 18 June '79 | 3 yrs. | Omtd Oct. '79 |
| Labiel, Francis, Pt...... | Ballard's | " | W | Omtd Oct. '79 |
| Lovell, Jno., Pt........ | " | 29 June " | " | Destd 14 Nov. '79 |
| Lewis, Joshua, Pt....... | " | 1 July " | 18 mo. | Destd 29 Oct. '79 |
| Lohar, Jno., Sergt...... | " | 20 June " | 9 mo. | |
| Lane, Jas., Pt......... | | 29 " " | W | Destd 5 Aug. '79 |
| Lane, Isaac, Pt........ | | 29 " " | W | Destd 22 Aug. '79 |
| Lowe, Jas., Pt......... | Quinn's | 1779 | 3 yrs. | |
| Litten, Isaac, Sergt..... | Blount's | 20 June '77 | " | |
| Little, John, Pt........ | " | 1 Mar. '79 | 9 mo. | Dischgd 1 Dec. '79 |
| Low, Ab'm, Pt........ | " | 10 May " | 18 mo. | |
| Lomax, Wm., Pt....... | " | " " | W | Omtd Nov. '79 |
| Lewis, Marshall, Pt.... | " | 22 June " | " | Destd Oct. '79 |
| Lovell, Wm., Pt....... | " | 5 " " | " | Dest Oct. '79 |
| Lucas, Billing, Pt....... | | " | 9 mo. | Died 5 Sep. '79 |
| Lomax, Wm., Pt....... | McRee's | 9 May '81 | 12 mo. | Left service 9 May '82 |
| Lanfield, Joseph, Pt.... | " | " | " | Destd 2 July '81 |
| Lyerly, Chrisr., Pt..... | " | 28 Apr. " | " | Left service 28 Apr. '82 |
| Lee, Wm. Jr., Pt...... | " | " | " | Destd 2 July '81 |
| Lasiter, Luke, Pt....... | Raiford's | 13 June " | " | Left service 25 June '82 |
| Lethgo, Wm., Pt...... | " | 9 Apr. " | " | Died 1 Apr. '82 |
| Link, Paul, Pt......... | Donoho's | 25 May " | " | Left service 21 May '82 |
| Lawrence, Wm., Pt..... | Dixon's | 12 " " | | Do          Do |
| Leept, Edm'd, Pt...... | " | " | | (Leet) Do          Do |
| Lasiter, Jonas or Jas., Pt. (P. 1106) | " | " | | Do          20 May '82 |
| Lee, Thos., Pt......... | " | 29 Apr. '81 | 12 mo. | Do          25 Apr. '82 |
| Lewis, Benj., Pt....... | " | " | " | Do          Do |
| Lee, Phillip, Pt........ | " | 12 May " | " | {Trans'd 29 July '81, to Col. Lee's |
| Liles, Jno., Pt......... | " | " | " | Do          Do |
| Lovin, Arthur, Pt...... | " | 24 Apr. '81 | " | Destd 15 July '81 |
| Lett, Jas., Pt.......... | Lytle's | 20 June '80 | 3 yrs. | |

| Name and Rank | Company | Dates of Enlistment and Commission | Period of Service | Occurrences |
|---|---|---|---|---|
| Lewis, Rich'd, Sergt..... | Lytle's | 1 June '81 | 12 mo. | |
| Lindenham, Isaac, Pt. ... | " | 20 June '80 | 3 yrs. | |
| Laughinghouse, Jno., Pt. | Sharp's | 15 Apr. '81 | | Dischgd 14 Feb. '82 |
| Little, Thos., Pt........ | " | " | | Omtd in '81 |
| Lafton, Canon, Pt...... | " | 15 June '81 | 12 mo. | Time out 15 June '82 |
| Lewis, Hardy, Pt....... | Raiford's | Jan. '80 | " | {(In lieu of Jas. Davison) Time out 15 Apr. '82 |
| Lennihan, Jno., Pt..... | Lytle's | 1781 | " | Time out 28 May '82 |
| Little, Guin, Pt........ | " | " | " | Do    12 Apr. '82 |
| Lewis, Rich'd, Pt...... | Sharp's | " | " | Do    10 Oct. '82 |
| Lewis, Fred'k, Corpl.... | Doherty's | " | " | Do    25 May '82 |
| Land, Jno., Pt......... | " | " | " | Do    25 May '82 |
| Laighton, Wm., Pt..... | " | " | 3 yrs. | |
| Lewis, Thos., Pt........ | Rhode's | " | | Time out 16 May '82 |
| Larks, Francis, Sergt.... | Armstrongs' | | W | Mustd Jan. '82 |
| Lain, Jacob, Corpl..... | " | " | 12 mo. | Time out 1 Nov. '82 |
| (P. 1106) | | | | |
| Louis, David, Pt....... | Bailey's | 12 Apr. '81 | 12 mo. | Left service 12 Apr. '82 |
| Lamb, Abner, Pt...... | " | | | Lt. 1 June '81 |
| Long, Jno., Pt......... | Brevard's | 1781 | 12 mo. | Left service 21 July '82 |
| (P. 1107) | | | | |
| Lewis, Marshall, Pt..... | " | " | " | Do    28 Apr. '82 |
| Lane, Cityzen, Pt...... | Hall's | " | " | Time out  1 Aug '82 |
| Lilly, Isaac, Pt........ | " | " | " | Do    16 Aug. '82 |
| Lane, Timothy, Pt..... | " | " | " | Do    1 Aug. '82 |
| Lane, Benj., Pt........ | " | " | " | Do    16 Aug. '82 |
| Lasiter, Jese, Pt....... | " | " | " | Do    12 Apr. '82 |
| Litter, Geo., Pt........ | Yarborough's | " | " | Do    22 Apr. '82 |
| Litter, Wm., Pt....... | " | " | " | Do    22 Apr. '82 |
| Lee, Rich'd, Pt........ | " | " | " | Omtd 1 Apr. '82 |
| Lewis, Jas., Pt........ | " | " | " | Omtd 1 Apr. '82 |
| Lucas, Thos., Pt....... | " | " | " | Omtd 1 Apr. '82 |
| Lashorn, Jas., Pt...... | " | " | " | Omtd 1 Apr. '82 |
| Lille, Lewis, Pt........ | Carter's | 19 May '81 | " | Time out 19 Apr. '82 |
| Lawrence, Joseph, Pt.... | | 25 Apr. '82 | " | Do    25 Apr. '82 |
| Lewis, Jona, Corpl..... | | 5 Apr. '81 | " | Do    1 Oct. '82 |
| Love, Sam'l, Pt........ | | 8 Mar. '82 | " | Do    1 Mar. '82 |
| Lawson, Wm., Pt...... | | 5 Oct. '82 | " | Do    1 Oct. '82 |
| Leigh, Lewis, Sergt...... | Mill's | 2 Feb. " | " | Died 17 July 82 |
| Lewis, Jno., Pt........ | " | 13 Jan. " | " | |
| Land, Henry, Pt....... | Coleman's | " | " | Time out 1 July '83 |
| Lewis, Isaac, Pt....... | Hall's | Apr. " | W | |
| (P. 1107) | | | | |
| Long, Wm., Pt........ | " | " | " | Corpl. 1 Nov. '82 |
| Lamb, Jno., Pt........ | Mill's | Jan. " | 12 mo. | Time out Jan. '83 |
| Lackey, Thos., Pt...... | Bailey's | 4 Nov. " | | |
| Lasiter, Jas., Pt....... | Hadley's | 10 Sep. " | | |
| Lee, Aaron, Sergt...... | Bacot's | " | " | |
| Long, Jas., Pt......... | | " | " | |
| Leopard, Wm., Pt..... | Carter's | " | " | |
| Lindon, Pat'k, Pt...... | " | " | " | |
| Lambert, Enoch, Sergt.. | Raiford's | " | " | |
| Lee, Jas., Pt.......... | " | " | " | |
| Leggett, Abs'm, Pt..... | " | " | " | |
| Lollar, Jno., Sergt...... | Sharp's | " | " | |
| Low, Thos., Pt........ | " | " | " | |
| Lambley, Phillip, Pt.... | " | " | " | |

| Name and Rank | Company | Dates of Enlistment and Commission | Period of Service | Occurrences |
|---|---|---|---|---|
| Leir, Jas., Pt.......... | Sharp's | '82 | 12 mo. | Destd 14 May '83 |
| Lyon, Wm., Pt......... | Lytle's | " | " | |
| Linsey, Jas., Corpl...... | Brevard's | " | " | |
| Loving, Jno., Pt....... | " | " | " | Destd 23 June '83 |
| Littleton, Wm., Pt..... | " | " | " | |
| Ludwick, Lewis, Pt.... | " | " | " | |
| Law, Jno., Pt.......... | " | " | " | |
| Lewis, Benj., Pt....... | Evan's | " | " | Destd 8 June '83 |
| Lane, Wm., Pt......... | " | " | " | |
| Lucas, Thos., Pt....... | " | " | " | Omtd Jan. '83. Transf'd |
| Larey, Pat'k, Pt....... (P. 1107) | " | " | " | Omtd Jan. '83, Transf'd |
| Lovesy, Boling, Pt..... | " | 1782 | 18 mo. | |
| Lesley, Jno., Pt........ | Coleman's | 1 Aug. '82 | " | |
| Low, Wm., Pt......... | " | 1779 | 3 yrs. | |
| Long, Henry, Pt....... | " | " | 9 mo. | |
| Lord, Wm., Pt........ | Eaton's | | | Mustd in '79 |
| Lewis, Joel, Pt........ | Gorden's | | | Mustd in '79 |
| **M**  (P. 1115) | | | | |
| McColley, Mat'w, Lt.... | Wilson's | 19 Apr. '77 | | Omtd June '78 |
| McCollister, Joseph, Pt . | " | 15 July " | | |
| McFailin, Alex'r, Pt.... | " | 4 Nov. " | | Destd Jan. '80 |
| Morse, Francis, Pt..... | " | 3 Apr. '78 | | Destd 20 Apr. '78 |
| McRevels, Robt., Ensn . | | 19 Apr. '77 | | Omtd Aug. '78 |
| McCollester, John, Pt... | | 8 Aug. " | 12 mo. | Omtd Aug. '78 |
| Martin, Jas., Sergt...... | Sheppard's | 4 " " | 3 yrs. | |
| Mitchell, John, Pt..... | " | 15 " " | | Omtd June '78 |
| Matchet, Edw'd, Pt.... | " | 28 July " | 3 yrs. W | |
| Mills, Elisha, Pt....... | Stevenson's | 9 June " | 3 yrs. | |
| Mahaus, Sam'l, Sergt. .. (P. 1116) | Jarvis' | 12 May " | " | Corpl. June '78 |
| Miller, John, Pt........ | " | 8 " " | " | Dischgd 1 Sep. '78 |
| Morris, John, Pt....... | Gregory's | 15 July " | " | |
| May, Gardner, Musc.... | Heron's | 22 May " | " | {Pt. June '78, Corpl. Nov. '78, Prisr, 1 June '79 |
| Morgan, Rich'd........ | " | 26 July " | " | Died 23 Sep. '78 |
| Miller, Dan'l, Pt....... | " | 14 Aug. " | " | |
| Moore, Isaac, Capt..... | | 19 Apr. " | " | Died 10 July '78 |
| Mullen, Wm., Corpl..... | Moore's | 14 Aug. " | " | Pt. June '78 |
| Modlin, Elisha, Pt...... | " | 3 May " | " | Mustd 27 Mar. '80 |
| Mundin, Joseph, Pt.... | " | 17 " " | " | Died 20 Dec. '77 |
| Modlin, Thos., Pt...... | " | " | " | {Corpl. Aug. '78, Pt. Mar. '79 |
| Modlin, Miles, Pt...... | " | " | " | Omtd Sep. '78 |
| Modlin, Zebulon, Pt.... | " | " | " | |
| Modlin, Ezek'l, Pt..... (P. 1116) | " | 1 Dec. " | | Died 20 Apr. '78 |
| Mullen, Richard, Pt. ... | Moore's | 12 Aug. '77 | 3 yrs. | |
| Mires, John, Pt........ | Vannoy's | 21 " " | " | |
| Mason, John, Pt....... | " | 1 July " | | Omtd June '78 |
| McDaniel, Joseph, Pt... | " | " | 3 yrs. W | Omtd Nov. '79 |
| Myre, Henry, Pt...... | Colonel's | 1 Aug. '78 | 2½ yrs. | Destd July '79 |
| Martin, Joshua, Pt..... | | 14 May '76 | 3 yrs. | Dischgd 31 July '79 |
| Martin, Richard, Pt.... | | 8 Aug. " | " | Dischgd 1 Apr. '79 |
| Minshew, John, Pt..... | | | | {Mustd Apr. '78, died **14** May '78 |
| Moore, Marmaduke, Pt. | | 1 Nov. '77 | 3 yrs. W | |

| Name and Rank | Company | Dates of Enlistment and Commission | Period of Service | Occurrences |
|---|---|---|---|---|
| Messer, Benj., Pt...... | | | 3 yrs. | Trans. to Invalids Nov.'79 |
| Moore, Joseph, Musc.... | Fenner's | | 3 yrs. | {Mustd Jan. '78, died 16 Mar. '78 |
| McDowell, Jesse, Pt..... | " | 1 June " | | Pt. June '78 |
| Myhan, Wm., Pt...... | " | | 2½ yrs. | Died 18 July '78 |
| Maples, Marmaduke, Pt. | | 7 " " | 3 yrs. | Corpl. Jan. '79 |
| Marlow, Demsy, Pt..... | | 1 July " | " | |
| Man, John, Pt........ | | | " | {Mustd June '78, Omtd Feb. '79 |
| Mardray, Darlin, Pt.... | | 26 Apr. '76 | 2½ yrs. | Dischgd 10 Nov. '78 |
| Mullin, Malone, Pt..... | | 27 " " | | Dischgd 10 Oct. '78 |
| McGraw, Joseph, Pt.... | | | 3 yrs. | {Mustd June '78, Omtd Oct. '78 |
| McKeel, Mich'l, Pt..... | | 4 May '76 | 2½ yrs. | Dischgd 1 Aug. '79 |
| Mossom, Rich'd, Ensn.. (P. 1116) | Hall's | 4 Sep. '78 | | |
| Maudley, Wm., Pt...... | | | 3 yrs. | Mustd Jan. '79 |
| Moore, W., Surg. Mate . | | 19 Jan. '78 | | Omtd Sep. '78 |
| McKiel, Thos., Pt..... | | | " | {Mustd Jan. '78, Omtd June '78 |
| McDonald, Jona, Pt.... | | 1778 | | Died 20 Feb. '78 |
| Mitchell, Beth'w, Pt.... | | | 3 yrs. | {Mustd Jan. '78, Omtd Mar. '78 |
| Moore, Reuben, Pt..... | Montfort's | 20 July '78 | 9 mo. | |
| Manning, Thos., Pt..... | " | | | |
| Meigs, Thos., Pt....... (P. 1117) | " | | | |
| Merrit, Joel, Pt........ | " | | | |
| Mitchell, Jacob, Pt..... | " | | | |
| Montcrief, Maxwell, Pt.. | " | | | |
| Moreland, Bartlet, Pt... | " | | | |
| Micham, Paul, Pt....... | " | | | |
| Murphy, Dan'l, Pt...... | Hogg's | | | |
| Moore, John, Pt....... | " | | | |
| Mushaw, John, Pt..... | " | | | |
| Moore, Mat'w, Pt..... | " | | | |
| Mitchell, Oliver, Pt.... | " | | | |
| Moore, Wm., Pt....... | " | | | |
| Miller, Abel, Pt........ | " | | | |
| Maddry, Brylan, Pt.... | " | | | Omtd Oct. '78 |
| McCumber, Humpy, Pt. | Quinn's | | | |
| McAlpin, Robt., Pt..... (P. 1117) | " | | | |
| McComber, Benj., Pt. .. | " | | | Dischgd 23 July '78 |
| Murrel, Matt'w, Sergt... | Lt. Col's | 20 July '78 | 9 mo. | |
| Murrell, Barnabas, Musc | " | 1 Sep. " | " | |
| Morgan, Timothy, Pt... | " | 20 July " | " | |
| Monger, Robt., Pt...... | " | " " | " | |
| Moore, Wm., Pt....... | " | " " | " | |
| Messley, Josiah, Pt..... | " | " " | " | |
| Mauley, Sothy, Pt...... | " | " " | " | |
| McFashin, Caleb, Pt.... | Baker's | " " | " | Died 4 Nov. '78 |
| Mason, John, Pt....... | " | " " | " | Died 24 Nov. '78 |
| Morris, Wm., Pt........ | " | " " | " | Died 24 Nov. '78 |
| Monnyhan, John, Pt.... | " | " " | " | |
| Mitchell, Wm., Pt..... | " | 25 Apr. '76 | 2½ yrs. | Omtd in '79 |

| Name and Rank | Company | Dates of Enlistment and Commission | Period of Service | Occurrences |
|---|---|---|---|---|
| Morgan, Chas., Pt...... | Blount's | 14 May '76 | 2½ yrs. | { Sergt. Nov. '77, dischgd 25 Oct. '78 |
| McDaniel, Jas., Pt...... | " | 20 July '78 | 9 mo. | |
| Matthews, Joseph, Pt... | Ballard's | " | " | |
| Malaby, Wm., Pt....... | Bradleys | " | " | |
| Manning, John, Pt...... | " | " | " | |
| Mills, John, Musc....... | Child's | " | " | |
| Morris, Benj., Pt....... | " | " | " | |
| Mount, Jereh, Pt....... | " | " | " | |
| Moseley, Wm., Pt.... ɩ. | " | " | " | |
| Mays, Shad'k, Pt....... | " | " | " | |
| Moon, Sampson, Pt..... | " | " | " | |
| (P. 1117) | | | | |
| McComber, Humph., Pt. | Bradley's | 27 June '79 | 18 mo. | |
| Murphy, Pat'k, Pt...... | " | 3 May " | " | |
| Mitchell, Jas., Pt...... | " | 2 June " | " | |
| Maltimore, Wm., Pt.... | " | 10 " " | " | |
| McCoy, Reuben, Pt.... | " | 1 July " | " | |
| Miller, John, Pt........ | " | 30 June " | | |
| Moore, Jesse, Pt........ | Montfort's | 20 " " | " | |
| McClaskey, Geo., Pt... | " | 23 " " | " | Destd Sep. '79 |
| McConnough, Dougal,Pt | " | " " " | | |
| McMullin, Mich'l, Corpl | " | 2 " " | 3 yrs. | |
| Murphy, Wm., Pt...... | " | 24 " " | W | Destd 3 Nov. '79 |
| Moss, Rich'd, Pt........ | Ballard's | '79 | 3 yrs. | |
| (P. 1118) | | | | |
| Marton, Jacob, Pt..... | " | " | | |
| Mathews, Gilbert, Pt... | Quinn's | 6 June " | 20 mo. | |
| Morgan, Wm., Pt...... | " | " | 3 yrs. | |
| Myers, Philip, Pt...... | " | " | 9 mo. | Dischgd Dec. '79 |
| Madry, John, Pt........ | " | " | " | Dischgd Dec. '79 |
| McBane, Dan'l, Sergt... | Blount's | 4 Aug. " | W | |
| Martin, Wm., Pt....... | " | " | 9 mo. | Dischgd 1 Dec. '79 |
| Monto, Fred'k, Pt..... | " | 25 July " | W | Destd 17 Dec. '79 |
| McDonald, Sam'l, Pt.... | " | 12 June " | 18 mo. | Destd Oct. '79 |
| McPherson, Othmiel, Pt. | " | 5 Aug. " | W | Do |
| McPherson, Wm., Pt.... | " | " | " | Do |
| Matthews, Jas., Pt...... | " | " | " | Do |
| Murphy, Moses, Pt..... | " | " | " | Do |
| (P. 1118) | | | | |
| Murphy, Solomon, Pt... | Blount's | 5 Aug. '79 | W | Do |
| Mitchell, Jesse, Pt...... | " | " | " | Do |
| McKean, John, Pt...... | " | 1 July " | " | Died 15 Oct. '79 |
| Myers, Wm., Pt....... | | " | 9 mo. | Omtd Oct. '79 |
| Moore, Cuffee, Pt...... | | " | " | Died 17 Aug. '79 |
| Minson, Mas., Pt...... | | " | " | Omtd Oct. '79 |
| Mollet, Thos., Pt...... | | " | " | Destd Sep. '79 |
| Moore, Elizah, Lt...... | | 12 Oct. " | " | { Capt. 13 Oct. '81, deranged 1 Jan. '83 |
| Mitchell, John, Pt..... | McRee's | 15 May '81 | " | Left service 15 May '82 |
| McLeland, Wm., Pt.... | " | 28 Apr. '81 | " | Do   28 Apr. '82 |
| Murphy, Jas., Pt....... | " | " " | " | Dead Oct. '81 |
| Meggs, Jas., Pt........ | " | 15 May " | 12 mo. | Left service 15 May '82 |
| McKenny, Robt. Pt..... | " | 28 Apr. " | " | { Do   28 Apr. '82, Mustd War Sep. '82 |
| Martin, Ab'm, Pt....... | | 25 " " | " | Left service 28 Apr. '82 |

| Name and Rank | Company | Dates of Enlistment and Commission | Period of Service | Occurrences |
|---|---|---|---|---|
| Marlow, Robt, Pt....... | McRees | 20 May '81 | 12 mo. | Destd 28 May '81, mustd for War Jan. '82, destd June '83 |
| Myres, David, Pt...... |  | 9 " '81 | " | Destd 2 July '81, mustd Jan., and left service May '82 |
| Minyard, John, Pt..... | " | 20 " '81 | " | Destd July'81, mustd Aug. Left service 9 May '82 |
| (P. 1118) |  |  |  |  |
| McCann, John, Pt...... | McRee's | 20 May '81 | 12 mo. | Destd 9 July '81 |
| McDowell, John, Pt..... | " | 18 " " | " | Destd 10 June '81 |
| McKay, John, Pt....... | Raiford's | 4 " " | " | Killed 8 Sep. '81 |
| Mabray, John, Pt...... | " | 5 " " | " | Tr. Aug. 31 to the Legion |
| Mann, John, Pt...... | " | 25 " " | " | Left service 25 May '82 |
| Morgan, John, Pt...... | " | 19 " " | " | Do   19 Apr. '82 |
| Moses, Ab'm, Pt........ | " | 18 " " | " | Do   18 May '82 |
| Marshall, Adam, Pt..... | " | 4 " " | " | Do   4 May '82 |
| Muster, John, Pt...... | " | " | W | Omtd in '81 |
| March, Barnet, Pt..... | " | 19 May " | 12 mo. | Left service 19 May '82 |
| Metters, Jethro, Pt..... | " | " | | Do   19 May '82 |
| Michel, Wm., Pt....... | " | 19 Apr. " | | Do   15 Apr. '82 |
| (P. 1119) |  |  |  |  |
| Michel, Ezk'l, Pt....... | " | 15 June " | | Destd 30 Aug. '81 |
| Morris, Ab'm, Musc..... | Donoho's | 15 Apr. " | 12 mo. | Left service 15 Apr. '82 |
| Morgan, Jno., Pt...... | " | 14 June " | " | Do   14 June '82 |
| Matthews, Jas., Pt..... | " | " | " | Do   Do |
| Manly, Moses or Morris, Pt.......... | " | 2 May " | " | Do   2 May '82 |
| McDonald, Larkins, Pt.. | " | 14 June " | " | Do   14 June '82 |
| Mooney, Wm., Corpl.... | Dixon's | 15 May " | " | Sergt. before Jan., Left service 21 May '82 |
| McGehee, Thos., Pt..... | " | 28 " " | " | Do   1 June '82 |
| McGinnis, Dan'l, Pt. ... | " | 12 " " | " | Trans. 7 Feb.'82 to P. line |
| Madara, Jno., Pt...... | " | 18 " " | " | Dischgd 18 Jan. '82 |
| Mason, Pat'k, Pt...... | " | 15 " " | " | Left service 21 May '82 |
| Mitchell, Jese, Pt...... | " | 15 Apr. " | " | Do   25 Apr. '82 |
| (P. 1119) |  |  |  |  |
| McClainey, Wm., Pt.... | " | 15 May " | 12 mo. | Do   21 May '82 |
| Mungoe, Jese, Pt....... | Lytle's | 12 Apr. " | | |
| Medlock, Nath'l, Pt..... | " | | | |
| Moore, Dan'l, Pt....... | " | | | |
| Morris, Wm., Pt........ | " | | | |
| Mitchell, Theophilus, Pt. | " | 12 Apr. " | " | Dead before Apr. '82 |
| Morgan, Sampson, Pt... | " | " | | Destd 8 July '81, Mustd Jan. '82 for War |
| Morris, Griffin, Pt..... | " | " | | Destd 6 July '81, Mustd Jan. '82 for War |
| Mabury, Benj., Pt...... | " | " | 12 mo. | Left service 12 Apr. '82 |
| Martin, Jno., Pt........ | " | 11 June " | W | |
| Mitchell, Jno., Sergt.... | " | 12 Apr. " | 12 mo. | Pt. Jan., left service 12 Apr. '82 |
| McDermid, Malcom, Pt. | Sharp's | 1 July " | " | Left service 1 July '82 |
| McGaunds, Jno., Pt..... | " | 15 Apr. " | " | Do   15 Apr. '82 |
| Messer, Jereh, Pt...... | " | " | | Omtd in '81 |
| Moore, Lem'l, Pt....... | " | " | 12 mo. | Left service 15 Apr. '82 |
| Martin, Joshua, Pt...... | " | " | " | Dead or destd 31 Jan. '82 |
| Moore, Jese, Pt........ | " | " | " | Left service 5 Apr. '82 |

| Name and Rank | Company | Dates of Enlistment and Commission | Period of Service | Occurrences |
|---|---|---|---|---|
| Morgan, Benj., Pt...... | McRee's | 5 Apr. '81 | 12 mo. | Do 1 Sep. '82 |
| Matthews, Dan'l, Pt.... | | 6 May " | " | Do 6 May '82 |
| McKnight, Andw, Corpl. | Dixon's | 1781 | | Time out 21 May '82 |
| Moore, Jas............. | Lytle's | | | Lt. 1 July '81 |
| Moran, Wm., Pt........ | Sharp's | " | | Time out 12 Apr. '82 |
| (P. 1119) | | | | |
| Martin, Jas., Pt........ | Sharp's | " | | Time out 12 Apr. '82 |
| McQuillin, Walter, Pt... | | " | | Died 1 Dec. '81 |
| Millen, Martin, Pt..... | | " | | Time out 1 Aug. '82 |
| Moody, Thos., Pt...... | Doherty's | " | | Do 25 May '82 |
| Masten, Thos., Pt..... | " | " | | Do Do |
| Mainer, Josiah, Pt..... | " | " | | Do Do |
| Messer, Jno., Pt........ | " | " | | Do 20 July '82 |
| McDougal, Dougal, Pt.. | " | " | | Time out 25 May '82 |
| Moore, Wm., Pt........ | " | " | | Dischgd 31 Jan. '82 |
| Murray, Morgan, Pt.... | Rhode's | " | | Left service 1 Apr. '82 |
| Moring, Maurice, Pt.... | Armstrong's | | W | Mustd Jan. '82 |
| (P. 1120) | | | | |
| Mills, Dan'l, Pt........ | " | " | | Dischgd 17 Jan. '82 |
| Manley, Allen, Pt...... | " | " | 3 yrs. | Left servicee 1 Apr. '82 |
| Mathis, Moses, Pt...... | " | " | " | Do 23 Apr. '82 |
| Middleton, Solomon, Pt. | " | " | W | |
| Murray, L. Alex'r, Sgt.. | Bailey's | 2 May " | 12 mo. | Left service 2 May '82 |
| Mitchell, Wm., Pt..... | " | 12 Apr. " | " | Do 12 Apr. '82 |
| Morrison, Jno., Pt..... | " | 25 May " | " | Do 25 May '82 |
| Medgett, Wm., Pt..... | " | 17 " " | " | Do 17 May '82 |
| Merritt, Thos., Pt..... | " | 1 July " | " | Do 1 July '82 |
| Matterson, Geo., Corpl. | Brevard's | 1781 | " | Do 28 Apr. '82 |
| Morgan, Reubin, Pt.... | " | " | " | Do 12 Apr. '82 |
| Miller, Benedict, Pt.... | " | " | " | Do 28 Apr. '82 |
| Morris, Wm., Pt........ | " | " | " | Do 9 June '82 |
| Moore, Thos., Pt....... | " | " | " | Do 7 June '82 |
| (P. 1120) | | | | |
| McClaskey, Allen, Pt.... | " | " | " | Dischgd 12 Mar. '82 |
| May, Joseph, Pt........ | Hall's | " | " | Time out 10 July '82 |
| Miller, Jno., Musc...... | " | " | " | Do 10 July '82 |
| Medlin, Shadrack, Corpl. | Yarborough's | " | " | Do 22 Apr. '82 |
| Matthews, Reps., Pt.... | " | " | " | Do 22 Apr. '82 |
| Mills, Jno., Sergt....... | Carter's | 12 May " | " | Do 2 May '82 |
| Mashburn, Wm., Pt..... | " | 19 " " | " | Do 19 May '82 |
| Moor, Geo., Pt......... | " | 18 Oct. " | " | Do 18 Oct. '82 |
| Muskinock, Geo., Pt.... | " | 5 June " | " | Do 6 June '82 |
| McRay, Jno., Sergt..... | Jones' | 24 Mar. " | " | |
| McDonald, Findley, Sgt. | " | 14 June '82 | | Pt. Apr. '82 |
| Mott, Benj., Corpl...... | " | 1 Feb. '80 | W | Sergt. Apr. '82 |
| McFarlane, Morgan, Pt. | " | 1 Jan. '82 | 12 mo. | |
| McDonald, Dan'l, Pt.... | " | 1 Feb. " | " | |
| Mitchell, Geo., Pt...... | " | 1 Oct. '81 | " | |
| Mitchell, Chas., Pt..... | " | 25 Dec. " | " | |
| Malden, Hump'y, Pt.... | " | 5 Apr. " | " | |
| Mills, Jas., Capt....... | | | | ⎰Mustd June '79, ⎱Deranged 1 Jan. '83 |
| McDonald, Hugh, Pt.... | Mill's | 2 Feb. '82 | 12 mo. | |
| McKinsey, Wm., Pt..... | " | 1 " " | " | |
| McVay, Eli, Pt......... | | 17 " " | " | Mustd War Sep. '82 |
| Messick, Aaron, Pt..... | | 6 " " | " | |
| McLamore, Jno., Pt..... | Coleman's | 15 Dec. '81 | " | |

| Name and Rank | Company | Dates of Enlistment and Commission | Period of Service | Occurrences |
|---|---|---|---|---|
| Mumford, Chas., Pt..... (P. 1120) | Coleman's | 11 Feb. '82 | 12 mo. | |
| McKithen, Duncan, Pt.. | " | 26 Dec. '81 | " | |
| Murphy, Arch'd, Pt..... | " | 18 " " | " | |
| McKithen, Jno., Pt..... | " | 20 " " | | |
| Moore, Wyllis, Pt....... | " | 8 Nov. " | | |
| McKee, Jno., Pt....... | " | 1 Jan. '82 | | |
| McGraw, Roger, Pt..... | " | 25 Dec. '81 | | Mustd War '82 |
| McCall, Dan'l, Pt...... | " | 1 Nov. " | 12 mo. | |
| McDonald, Call, Pt..... | " | 15 Jan. '82 | " | |
| McKee, Wm., Pt...... | " | 16 May '81 | " | |
| Moneyham, Thos., Pt... | " | 27 Nov. " | | |
| McVay, Jno., Pt........ | " | 14 Jan. '82 | W | Died 6 Sep. '82 |
| McKinsey, Hugh, Pt.... (P. 1121) | " | 4 " " | 12 mo. | |
| McCloud, Alex'r, Pt.... | " | 5 " " | " | Died Oct. '82 |
| McLaughlin, Alex'r, Pt.. | " | " " " | " | |
| Maroney, Anth'y, Pt.... | " | 15 Feb. " | " | |
| Mathias, Stephen, Pt.... | Hall's | 1 Apr. | " | |
| Matthews, Jno., Pt..... | " | 1 Mar. " | " | |
| Malphus, Henry, Pt..... | " | " | " | |
| McAffee, Azariah or Jno., Pt........... | " | 1 Feb. " | " | |
| Myson, Zach'l, Pt...... | " | 1 Dec. '81 | " | |
| Morgan, Sampson, Pt... | " | 1781 | " | Time out 1 Nov. '82 |
| Moore, Shad'k, Pt..... | " | " | " | Do   1 Oct. '82 |
| Moore, Jno., Pt....... | " | | | {Mustd Apr. '82, Omtd Sep. '82 |
| McCan, Hugh, Pt..... (P. 1121) | " | 1 Sep. '82 | W | Destd 13 June '83 |
| McDaniel, And'w, Pt... | Jones' | 1 Oct '81 | 12 mo. | |
| McKay, Dougal, Q. Mr. Sergt......... | | | | Time out 1 Feb. '83 |
| McSwain, McAm., Pt.. | Mill's | Oct. '82 | 12 mo. | |
| Merrideth, Wm., Corpl.. | Bailey's | 18 Sep. " | 18 mo. | Pt. Dec. '82 |
| Manley, Moses, Pt..... | " | 7 " " | " | |
| Martin, Gabriel, Pt..... | " | 17 " " | " | |
| McLain, Hugh, Pt...... | " | 20 Aug. " | 12 mo. | |
| McCormick, Arch'd, Pt. | " | " | " | |
| McClenahan, Malcome, Pt................. | " | " | " | |
| Manewell, Jese, Pt...... | " | 15 July '82 | " | |
| Moor, Wm., Pt........ | " | 2 Apr. " | " | |
| McCarthy, Jas., Pt..... | " | 2 Mar. " | " | |
| Meck, Jno., Pt........ | " | 1 Aug. " | " | |
| McLeod, Jno., Pt...... | " | 4 Sep. " | " | |
| Miller, Peter, Pt....... | " | 9 Aug. " | " | |
| McNeal, Hector, Pt.... | " | 16 June " | " | |
| McIntire, Gilbert, Pt.... | " | 20 Aug. " | " | |
| McIntire, Chas., Pt..... | " | " | " | |
| McKensey, Jas., Pt..... | Hadley's | 1 Aug. '82 | 18 mo. | Destd 24 June '82 |
| McIntosh, Murdock, Pt. | " | " | | |
| Mills, Jacob, Pt........ | " | " | | |
| McDonald, Benj., Pt.... | " | " | | Destd 20 June '83 |
| Martin, Jese, Pt....... (P. 1121) | " | 10 Aug. '82 | 18 mo. | |
| McKey, Jno., Pt........ | Hadley's | 1 Aug. '82 | 18 mo. | |

| Name and Rank | Company | Dates of Enlistment and Commission | Period of Service | Occurrences |
|---|---|---|---|---|
| Mitchell, Oliver, Pt..... | Hadley's | 10 Sep. '82 | 18 mo. | |
| McKinsey, Wm., Pt..... | " | 20 Aug. " | W | Mustd Dec. '82 |
| Meeks, Wm., Corpl..... | Bacot's | 1782 | 18 mo. | |
| Morgan, Isaac, Pt...... | " | " | " | |
| Maddry, Darling, Sergt. | Carter's | " | " | |
| Miller, Christo., Pt...... | " | " | " | |
| Mitchell, Abner, Pt..... | " | " | " | |
| Manders, Wm., Pt..... | " | " | " | |
| McLoud, Jno., Pt....... | " | " | " | |
| Manning, Jno., Pt..... | " | " | " | |
| McDonnock, Jno., Pt... | " | " | " | Destd 18 May '83 |
| May, Mich'l, Pt....... | " | " | " | Destd 4 Apr. '83 |
| Monk, Jas., Pt........ | " | " | " | |
| (P. 1122) | | | | |
| Mitchell, Wm., Pt..... | " | " | " | |
| McDonald, Jas., Pt.... | " | " | " | |
| Moon, Sampson, Pt.... | " | " | " | |
| McIntire, Jas, Sergt..... | Raiford's | " | " | |
| McKenney, Sam'l, Pt... | " | " | " | Destd 11 June '83 |
| Morris, Wm., Sergt..... | Sharp's | " | " | Destd 19 Apr. '83 |
| Mabry, Philip, Pt...... | " | " | " | Destd 30 Apr. '83 |
| Morris, Jno., Pt....... | " | " | " | Destd 19 Apr. '83 |
| Manis, Fred'k, Pt...... | " | " | " | Destd 27 Feb. '83 |
| Mesey, Philip, Pt...... | " | " | " | |
| Miller, Geo., Pt....... | " | " | " | |
| (P. 1122) | | | | |
| Martin, Mich'l, Pt...... | Sharp's | 1782 | 18 mo. | Destd 26 May '83 |
| May, Jno., Pt......... | " | " | " | |
| Metchler, Jno., Pt..... | " | " | " | |
| Morris, Witt, Pt....... | " | " | " | |
| Messey, Joseph, Pt..... | " | " | " | Died 22 June '83 |
| Merritt, Drury, Pt..... | " | " | " | |
| Mullen, Mich'l, Pt..... | " | " | " | Died 8 Dec. '82 |
| Miers, Geo., Corpl...... | Lytle's | " | " | |
| Miller, Conrad, Pt..... | " | " | " | |
| Maynor, Henry, Pt..... | " | " | " | |
| Marley, Wm., Pt...... | " | " | " | |
| Manley, Littleton, Pt. .. | " | " | " | |
| Murphy, Jas., Pt...... | " | " | " | |
| McMahan, Barnet, Pt... | Brevard's | " | " | Destd 25 Mar. '83 |
| McAllister, Jno., Pt..... | " | " | " | |
| McCullough, Frans., Pt. | " | " | " | Transf'd Mar. '83 |
| McGennis, Jno., Pt..... | " | " | " | Destd Mar. '83 |
| Mallot, Jacob, Pt...... | " | " | " | |
| McSwine, Wm., Pt..... | " | " | " | Transf'd Mar. '83 |
| McElya, Wm., Pt...... | " | " | " | |
| Morton, Wm., Sergt..... | Evan's | " | " | |
| Morris, Nathan, Pt..... | " | " | " | |
| Moore, Elijah, Pt...... | " | " | " | |
| Moore, Jas., Pt........ | " | " | " | |
| McCarran, Dan'l, Pt.... | " | " | " | |
| (P. 1122) | | | | |
| McKinsey, Alex'r, Pt.... | Evan's | 1782 | 18 mo. | |
| Moore, Simion, Pt...... | " | " | " | |
| McLain, Wm., Sgt. Mt.. | | 1 Jan '83 | | |
| Morris, Wm., Pt........ | Coll. | 1 Dec. '79 | | |
| Malone, Isaac, Pt....... | Ballard's | | | Mustd Feb. '80 |

| Name and Rank | Company | Dates of Enlistment and Commission | Period of Service | Occurrences |
|---|---|---|---|---|
| Moglin, Freeman, Pt.... | Colonel's | | 2½ yrs. | Mustd Feb. '79 |
| Morehead, Jas., Lt...... | Lytle's | 23 Mar '79 | | |
| Miller, Wm., Pt........ | Medearis' | 20 Dec. '78 | 3 yrs. | |
| McKinley, Jno., Pt..... | Taylor's | | 2½ yrs. | {Mustd Jan. '79, {Dischgd Apr. '79 |
| McMullen, Mich'l, Pt... | " | | 3 yrs. | Mustd Jan. '79 |
| Morrisett, Peter, Corpl.. N   (P. 1126) | Carter's | 21 May '78 | W | |
| Nelson, Jesse, Pt........ | Shepard's | 12 May '77 | 3 yrs. | |
| Newell, Nathan, Pt..... | " | 29 Aug. '77 | | Omtd Jan. '78 |
| Nicholson, Robt., Lt.... | Moore's | 19 Apr.  " | | Resigned 4 July '79 |
| Norman, Thos., Pt..... | " | 17 June  " | 3 yrs. | |
| Nixon, Jno., Corpl...... | | 15 May '78 | " | Pt Mar. Destd 20 Apr.'79 |
| Nichols, Wm., Pt....... | | 4 Nov. '77 | " | {Pris. 2 June '79, {Mustd Nov. '79 |
| Nicholas, Jno., Pt....... | Hogg's | 17 Mar. '77 | " | |
| Nicholson, Jno., Pt..... | " | 20 July  " | 9 mo. | |
| Nelson, Arthur, Pt...... | Quinn's | " | | Died 24 Oct. '78 |
| Norwood, Wm., Pt..... | " | | | Omtd 24 Oct. '78 |
| Newsom, Boothe, Pt.... | Lt. Col's | 20 July '78 | 9 mo. | |
| Norwood, Jno., Pt...... | " | " | " | |
| Newton, Jesse, Pt....... | Blount's | " | " | |
| Nichols, Jacob, Sergt.... | Ballard's | " | " | |
| Norvel, Enos, Pt........ | " | " | " | |
| Nowles, Rich'd, Sergt... | Bradley's | " | " | |
| Newell, Jno., Pt........ | " | " | " | |
| Newsom, Aaron, Pt..... | " | " | " | Died 30 Oct. '78 |
| Nobles, Jas., Pt......... | Childs' | " | " | |
| Newham, Francis, Pt.... | Montfort's | 1 July '79 | 18 mo. | Destd 22 Oct. '79 |
| Night, Jesse, Pt........ | " | 28 May '77 | 3 yrs. | |
| North, Jas., Pt........ | Ballard's | 20 June '79 | W | Omtd Oct. '79 |
| Newsom, Nathelrid, Pt.. (P. 1126) | Quinn's | 24  "   " | " | |
| Newsom, Robt., Pt..... | " | 31 May  " | 3 yrs. | |
| Night, Absolom, Pt..... | Blount's | 23 June  " | W | {Destd Oct. '79, {Left service 16 Apr. '82 |
| Nicholson, Isaac, Sergt.. | Raiford's | 16 Apr. | 18 mo. | Sergt. Maj. Dec. '81 |
| Newton, Levy, Pt....... | Dixon's | 15 May  " | " | Left service 21 May '82 |
| Nettles, Jesse, Pt....... | Lytle's | 9 July  " | " | Omtd in '81 |
| Nettles, Shadrack, Pt... | " | " | " | Left service 26 June '82 |
| Neil, Philip, Sergt...... | Sharp's | 5 Apr. '81 | " | Do      5 Apr. '82 |
| Nobles, Drury, Pt...... | " | 15 Apr.  " | | Do    15 Apr. '82 |
| Nichols, Henry, Pt...... | Raiford's | 15  "   " | | Do         Do |
| Neal, Chris'r, Pt....... | Walton's | 1781 | | |
| Nobles, Ezl., Pt........ | " | " | | |
| Nicholas, Wm., Pt...... | Sharp's | " | | Time out 23 May '82 |
| Newton, Pat'k, Sergt.... | Doherty's | " | 3 yrs. | Omtd Apr. '82 |
| Nithercut, Wm., Pt..... | " | | | Time out 25 May '82 |
| Nonnery, Anderson, Pt.. | " | " | W | Mustd Jan. '82 |
| Nisco, Nich's, Pt....... | Armstrong's | " | | Left servie 25 Apr. '82 |
| Nobles, Benj., Pt....... | Bailey's | 15 May  " | 12 mo. | Do    15 May '82 |
| Newsom, Thos., Pt...... | Brevard's | " | " | Dischgd 12 Mar. '82 |
| Nothern, Solomon, Pt... | " | " | " | Left service 8 Apr. '82 |
| Nichols, Joseph, Pt..... | Hall's | " | " | Do    1 Aug. '82 |
| Nube, Francis, Pt....... | Yarborough's | " | " | Dischgd 25 Feb. '82 |
| Neckins, Malachi, Pt.... | Carter's | 19 May '81 | " | Time out 19 May '82 |
| Night, Absolom, Pt..... | " | " | " | Do    1 July '82 |

| Name and Rank | Company | Dates of Enlistment and Commission | Period of Service | Occurrences |
|---|---|---|---|---|
| Nowel, Josiah, Pt....... | Carter's | '81 | 12 mo. | Do       1 Jan. '83 |
| Newsom, Edw'd, Pt..... (P. 1127) | Mill's | 4 Feb. '82 | " | |
| Nicholas, Jno., Pt...... | " | 6 Feb. '82 | " | |
| Newton, Joseph, Pt.... | " | 7  "    " | " | |
| Newton, Edw'd, Pt..... | " | 7  "    " | " | |
| Newman, Joseph, Pt.... | Coleman's | 9 Feb.  " | " | |
| Newark, Nicholas, Pt... | " | 1 Nov. '81 | " | |
| Newly, Matt'w, Sergt... | Hall's | 12 Mar '82 | W | |
| Naswoethy, Sam'l, Pt... | Mill's | 27 Feb.  " | 12 mo. | |
| Nookes, Asbel, Pt...... | Carter's | " | 18 mo. | Destd 3 June '83 |
| Nevill, Geo., Pt........ | Lytle's | " | " | Destd 16 Mar. '83 |
| Neil, Jno., Pt......... | | " | 18 mo. | |
| Newton, Edw'd, Pt..... | Brevard's | " | " | Died 25 June '83 |
| Nichols, Wm., Pt...... | Rhode's | 1 Aug.  " | " | |
| Nobles, Jno., Pt........ | Evans' | 1782 | " | |
| Newham, Francis, Pt... | " | " | " | Destd 20 Apr. '83 |
| Nikins, Edw'd, Pt...... | Lt. Col's | | 3 yrs. | Mustd Jan '79 |
| Newsom, Rand'h, Musc. | Taylor's | | " | Do |
| Newby, Mathew, Pt.... O    (P. 1130) | " | | " | Do |
| O'Neal, Jas., Pt....... | Williams' | 12 May '77 | 3 yrs. | |
| Organ, Wm., Pt....... | " | 8 Aug.  " | " | Dischgd 21 Aug. '78 |
| Oliver, Jno., Pt........ | Stevenson's | 22 Apr.  " | " | Dischgd 6 June '78 |
| Overton, Pt........... | Moore's | 30 June  " | " | |
| Overton, Lem'l, Pt..... | " | 30 June  " | " | |
| Oldridge, Wm., Pt..... | | 19 Apr. '76 | 2½ yrs. | |
| Oyler, Jno., Pt........ | | 14 Feb. '77 | 3 yrs. | Dischgd 22 Oct. '78 |
| Owens, Jno., Pt........ | | 29 Mar.  " | " | |
| O'Neal, Jno., Pt....... | Coleman's | 18 Feb.  " | | |
| Oligood, Henry, Pt..... | | | | { Mustd Jan. '78, { Omtd Jan. '78 |
| Orange, Wm., Pt....... | Montfort's | 20 July '78 | 9 mo. | Feb. '78 |
| Odum, Aaron, Pt...... | Hogg's | " | " | |
| *Osborne, Jno., Pt..... | Baker's | " | " | |
| O'Neal, Wm., Pt....... | Ballard's | " | " | |
| O'Banion, Wm., Pt..... | Bradley's | 20 July '76 | 2½ yrs. | Dischgd 6 Nov. '78 |
| Owens, Jno., Pt........ | " | 10 June '79 | 18 mo. | |
| Owens, Thos., Pt....... | " | 20 June  " | " | |
| Odum, Lewis, Pt....... | Montfort's | 9 Aug.  " | " | Omtd Oct. '79 |
| Overton, Jas., Pt...... | " | 1 Mar.  " | 3 yrs. | |
| Owens, Bailey, Pt...... | Ballard's | 1779 | " | Dischgd 1 Dec. '79 |
| Owens, Thos., Pt....... | " | " | " | Do |
| O'Donnelly, Benj., Pt... | Quinn's | 7 June  " | 18 mo. | Omtd Oct. '79 |
| O'Donnelly, Daniel, Pt.. | Blount's | 24 June  " | W | { (Quinn's Co'y) Destd { Dec. '79 |
| Overton, Daniel, Pt..... | Raiford's | 20 Jan.  " | 3 yrs. | (Blount's) |
| Owen, Ethelred, Pt..... | " | 4 May '81 | 12 mo. | Left service 4 May '82 |
| Orange, Wm........... | Dixon's | 14 June  " | | { (Raiford's) Time out 14 { Dec. '82 |
| *O'Neal, Isom......... | Hogg's | 20 July '78 | 9 mo. | { (Dixon's) Left sevice 24 { Jan., dead. |
| O'Donnally, Hugh, Pt... | Lytle's | 15 Apr. '81 | | Left service 6 June '82 |
| Overturie, Jno., Pt...... | " | 6 June  " | " | { (Lytle's) Left service 12 { Apr. '82 |
| Owen, Enoch, Pt....... | Doherty's | 12 Apr.  " | " | |

| Name and Rank | Company | Dates of Enlistment and Commission | Period of Service | Occurrences |
|---|---|---|---|---|
| (P. 1131) | | | | |
| O'Bryan, Rich'd, Sergt.. | Doherty's | 12 Apr. '81 | 12 mo. | Do       25 May '82 |
| Oliver, Jno., Pt......... | " | " | " | Do       25 May '82 |
| Odder, Peter, Pt........ | Bailey's | 25 May " | " | Do       25 May '82 |
| Osborn, Squire, Pt..... | Brevard's | " | " | Do       28 Apr. '82 |
| Outlaw, Jas., Pt........ | Carter's | 25 Apr. " | " | Do       25 Apr. '82 |
| O'Merry, Jacob........ | " | 3 June " | " | Do       3 June '82 |
| Overton, Jona, Pt....... | Jones' | 17 Nov. " | " | |
| Overton, Jno., Pt....... | Mills' | 7 Jan. '82 | " | Died 9 Sep. '82 |
| Owens, Jno............ | Jones' | 12 Feb. '82 | " | |
| Oliver, Wm., Pt........ | Hadley's | 1 Aug. '82 | 18 mo. | |
| Osborn, Jesse, Pt...... | " | 1 Aug. " | " | |
| Olfin, Wm............ | " | 1783 | " | |
| O'Neal, Benj., Pt....... | Bacot's | 1782 | " | |
| Osborn, Benj., Pt...... | " | | " | Destd 19 June '83 |
| Oiler, Francis, Pt....... | Sharp's | | " | |
| Osborn, Morgan, Pt.... | Lytle's | | " | Dischgd 31 Dec. '82 |
| Osteen, Wm., Pt........ | Evans' | | " | |
| Order, Peter, Pt....... | " | | " | |
| O'Bryant, Jno.......... | Bacot's | | " | Mustd Dec. '82 |
| Owles, Piram, Pt....... | Madero's | | 3 yrs. | Mustd Feb. '79 |
| Orrell, Thos., Ensn...... | | 14 Mar. '78 | | |
| P   (P. 1136) | | | | |
| Pasmore, David, Pt..... | Wilson's | 15 May '77 | | |
| Paden, Thos., Pt....... | " | 20 " " | 3 yrs. | |
| Pope, Wm., Sergt....... | Shephard's | 5 " " | " | Pt. June '78 |
| Pope, Sam'l, Sergt..... | " | 5 May " | " | Pt. June '78, Deranged 30 June '79 |
| Pinkum, Philip, Corpl... | " | 12 Aug. " | " | Pt. June '78, Pris. 1 June '79, Mustd and Destd 6 Dec. '79 |
| Paramore, Jas., Pt..... | " | 5 May " | | Died 20 Oct. '78 |
| Phelps, Jas., Pt........ | " | 12 May " | | Music Nov. '79 |
| (P. 1137) | | | | |
| Phelps, Keeder, Pt...... | Shephard's | 12 May '77 | 3 yrs. W | Music June '78 |
| Perkins, Isaac, Pt...... | Stevenson's | 16 " " | 3 yrs. | |
| Prescott, Thos., Pt..... | " | 21 Apr. " | " | Died 20 Mar. '78 |
| Parker, Hillery, Pt..... | Jarvis' | 12 May " | | Died 3 Nov. '78 |
| Pair, Wm., Pt.......... | " | 26 Dec. '76 | | |
| Poyner, Peter.......... | " | 9 May " | 3 yrs. | Omtd Nov. '79 |
| Palmore, Joseph, Pt..... | Gregory's | 21 June " | | Died 13 July '78 |
| Petyjohn, Thos., Corpl.. | Moore's | 7 May " | | Died 19 Jan. '79 |
| Pratt, Zeba, Pt........ | " | " | | Mustd 27 Mar. '80 |
| Poor, Wm., Pt......... | Vanois' | 23 June " | " | |
| Price, Jos............. | " | 25 July '77 | | Taken away by his master 12 Apr. '78 |
| Pendergrass, Jno., Pt.... | | 20 May '76 | 3 yrs. | Dischgd 20 May '79 |
| Peters, Chs., Pt........ | Coleman's | 1778 | | |
| Pierce, Jas., Pt......... | " | 24 Aug '77 | 3 yrs. W | |
| Peacock, Jno., Pt...... | | | 3 yrs. | Joined 11 May '78 |
| Poe, David, Pt......... | | 15 May '76 | 2½ yrs. | Dischgd 10 Nov. '78 |
| Pierce, Hardy, Pt....... | | | | Mustd June '78, Died Oct '78 |
| Purdy, Jas., Pt........ | | 24 May '77 | 3 yrs. | |
| (P. 1137) | | | | |
| Phillips, Joseph, Pt.... | | 1 July '77 | 3 yrs. | Pris. 1 June '79, Mustd Nov. '79 |

| Name and Rank | Company | Dates of Enlistment and Commission | Period of Service | Occurrences |
|---|---|---|---|---|
| Powell, Wm., Pt....... | | 5 Oct. '81 | 12 mo. | Dischgd 29 Mar. '82 |
| Peal, Pearson, Pt...... | | 22 June " | " | {Corp. Aug. '78, Sergt. 1 Feb. '80 |
| Philips, Jno., Pt....... | | 1 Sep. " | " | Dischgd 11 Sep. '78 |
| Powell, Thos., Pt...... | | 31 Aug. " | " | Corpl. 1 June '79 |
| Parkinson, Jacob, Pt.... | | | W | From Va. Reg. 1 July '79 |
| Powers, Absolom, Corpl. | Montfort's | 20 July '78 | 9 mo. | |
| Powell, Jos., Pt........ | " | " | " | |
| Pully, Wassdon, Pt..... | " | " | " | |
| Parham, Wm., Pt...... | " | " | " | |
| Parham, Drury, Pt..... | " | " | " | |
| Partin, Benj., Pt....... | " | " | " | |
| Phillips, Wm., Pt...... | " | June " | " | Omtd July '78 |
| Pritchet, Joshua, Pt..... | Hogg's | 30 July " | 9 mo. | |
| Perdue, Caleb, Pt...... | " | " | " | |
| Person, Jona, Pt....... | " | " | " | |
| Prior, Thos., Pt........ | Quinn's | " | " | |
| Price, Mat'w, Pt....... | " | " | " | |
| Potter, Peleg, Pt....... | " | " | " | Destd 29 July '78 |
| Parthis, Hardy, Pt..... | Lt. Col's | | " | |
| Parker, Dan'l.......... | " | | " | |
| Pee, Jona............. | Baker's | | " | |
| Pearson, Thos., Pt..... | " | | " | |
| Pitt, Thos............. | " | | " | |
| Priest, Wm............ | " | | " | |
| Phillips, Jno.......... | Ballard's | 1778 | 9 mo. | |
| Perrett, Needham...... | " | " | " | |
| Proctor, Wm.......... | " | " | " | |
| Parker, Joseph......... | Bradley's | " | " | |
| (P. 1138) | | | | |
| Pettis, Stephen......... | " | 20 July '78 | " | |
| Pollard, Matt'w........ | " | " | " | |
| Parrish, Jacob, Pt..... | " | " | " | |
| Plumley, Geo., Pt...... | " | " | " | |
| Page, Ab'm, Pt........ | " | " | " | Died 26 Sep. '78 |
| Price, Jas., Pt......... | Child's | " | " | |
| Price, Wm., Pt........ | " | " | " | |
| Pardmore, Jno., Pt..... | " | " | " | |
| Parks, Wm., Pt........ | Bradley's | 29 Apr. '77 | W | Destd 15 Oct. '79 |
| Porter, Jas., Pt........ | " | 24 May '79 | 18 mo. | |
| Parrish, Ab'm, Pt...... | | 22 Jan. '80 | | |
| Pool, Jas., Pt......... | Montfort's | 28 June '79 | W | Destd 22 Nov. '79 |
| Pavy, Thos., Pt........ | " | 24 " " | " | |
| Punal, Ab'm, Pt....... | " | 5 Nov. '78 | 3 yrs. | |
| Parmer, Jno., Pt....... | " | 1 Mar. '79 | 9 mo. | Dischgd 1 Dec. '79 |
| Pierce, Israel, Pt....... | Ballard's | 15 June " | 18 mo. | |
| Peters, Jno., Pt........ | " | 18 " " | W | Destd Feb. '80 |
| Pell, Gilbert, Pt....... | Quinn's | '79 | | Destd Sep. '79 |
| Perkins, Rich'd, Pt..... | Ballard's | 24 " " | | |
| Petigrew, Ance, Pt..... | " | 15 Sep. '76 | | |
| (P. 1138) | | | | |
| Parsons, Jas., Pt....... | " | 22 June '79 | W | Destd Oct. '79 |
| Payne, Thos., Pt....... | " | 30 Aug. " | " | Do |
| Powell, Wm., Pt....... | " | 9 " " | " | Do |
| Peevel, Jno., Pt....... | | '79 | 9 mo. | Omtd Oct. '79 |
| Philips, Henry, Pt..... | | " | " | Died 19 Aug. '79 |
| Powers, Wm., Pt....... | | June " | | Dischgd 1 Aug. '79 |

| Name and Rank | Company | Dates of Enlistment and Commission | Period of Service | Occurrences |
|---|---|---|---|---|
| Penigar, Martin, Pt..... | McRee's | 28 Apr. '81 | 12 mo. | Left service 28 Apr. '82 |
| Pittia, Jas., Pt.......... | " | 11 June " | " | {Corpl. Aug. '81, Left service 11 June '82 |
| Peck, Joseph, Pt....... | " | 28 Apr. " | " | Tr. Aug. '81 to Legion |
| Philips, Thos., Pt...... | " | 20 May " | " | Destd 1 June '81 |
| Paul, Philip, Pt........ | " | " " | " | Left service 25 May '82 |
| Pucket, Solomon, Pt.... | " | 15 June '81 | " | Destd 1 Aug. '81 |
| Pervas, Tiberius, Corpl.. | Raiford's | 10 May " | " | Left service 18 May '82 |
| Powell, Axom, Pt....... | " | 2 " " | " | Do 2 May '82 |
| Pate, Edw'd, Pt........ | " | 4 " " | | Do 4 May '82 |
| Pate, Cordie, Pt....... | " | 4 " " | " | Do 4 May '82 |
| Philips, Lovin, Pt...... | " | 19 " " | " | {Transf'd Oct. '81 to So. Carolina Line |
| Page, Benj., Corpl...... | Donoho's | 14 June '81 | " | {Pt. Jan., Left service 14 June '82 |
| Parrott, Nath'l, Pt...... | " | " | " | Left service 14 June '82 |
| Pettiford, Wm., Pt...... | " | " | " | Do Do |
| Perkerson, Drury, Pt.... (P. 1138) | " | " | " | Omtd in '81 |
| Pettiford, Philip, Pt..... | Donoho's | 14 June '81 | 12 mo. | Left service 14 June '82 |
| Pettiford, Elias, Pt...... | " | " " | " | Do Do |
| Philips, Zacha, Pt...... | " | 25 May " | " | Do 25 May '82 |
| Parks, Jno., Pt......... | " | " " " | " | Do Do |
| Parker, Leonard, Sergt.. | Dixon's | 15 " " | " | Omtd in '81 |
| Parsons, Jas., Corpl.... | " | 15 " " | " | Left service 21 May '82 |
| Prebit, Jno., Pt........ (P. 1139) | " | 12 " " | " | Do 26 May '82 |
| Portis, Lewis, Pt........ | " | 15 " " | " | Do 25 Apr. '82 |
| Powell, Lewis, Pt...... | Lytle's | 25 Nov. '80 | " | Omtd in '81 |
| Pierce, Lewis, Pt...... | " | 12 Apr. '81 | " | Destd 7 July '81 |
| Parum, Wm., Pt...... | " | 5 Apr. " | | Left service 5 Apr. '82 |
| Pethosell, Thos., Pt..... | Sharp's | 2 May " | | Omtd in '81 |
| Platt, Jno., Pt......... | " | 10 Apr. '78 | W | |
| Pierce, Ruben, Pt...... | | 15 Apr. '81 | | Omtd in '81 |
| Porter, Joshua, Pt...... | | | | Do |
| Porter, Wm., Pt....... | | | | Do |
| Purser, Joseph, Pt...... | | | | Do |
| Pitman, Jno., Pt........ | Walton's | 1781 | | Left service 9 June '82 |
| Price, Edw'd, Pt....... | " | " | | Do 1 July '82 |
| Porks, Henry, Pt...... | " | " | | Do 2 June '82 |
| Pyeatt, Peter, Lt....... | Dixon's | 30 Mar '82 | | |
| Pierce, Jas., Pt......... | Lytle's | '81 | | Time out 12 Apr. '82 |
| Parks, Hugh, Sergt..... | " | " | | Do 10 June '82 |
| Poulston, Jonas, Pt..... (P. 1139) | " | " | | Left service 1 Oct. '82 |
| Pierson, Thos., Pt...... | Doherty's | '81 | | Time out 25 May '82 |
| Parks, Wm., Pt........ | Rhode's | " | | Do 12 Apr. '82 |
| Privat, Peter, Pt....... | " | " | | Left service 1 Apr. '82 |
| Perry, Robt., Pt........ | Armstrong's | | W | Mustd Jan. '82 |
| Parks, Wm., Pt........ | " | " | 12 Mo. | Time out 1 Oct. '82 |
| Pettijohn, Ab'm, Pt..... | Bailey's | 24 Apr. " | " | Left service 24 Apr. '82 |
| Pearse, Israel, Pt...... | " | 2 May " | " | Do 2 May '82 |
| Pharas, Ablm., Pt...... | " | 17 " " | " | Do 17 May '82 |
| Powers, Absolom, Sergt. | Brevard's | " | | Do 12 May '82 |
| Powers, Jesse.......... | " | 1781 | | Do 12 May '82 |
| Powers, Moses......... | " | " | | Do 12 May '82 |
| Praet, Thos., Pt........ | " | " | | Do 28 May '82 |

| Name and Rank | Company | Dates of Enlistment and Commission | Period of Service | Occurrences |
|---|---|---|---|---|
| Perkins, Thos., Pt...... | Brevard's | 1781 | | Do      28 Apr. '82 |
| Pendleton, Benj., Pt... | " | " | W | Mustd Jan. '82 |
| Powell, Geo., Pt........ | " | " | | Left service 25 Apr. '82 |
| Pinkstone, Wm., Pt..... | " | " | | Dischgd 20 Feb. '82 |
| Pierson, Rich'd, Pt..... | " | " | | Left service 24 May '82 |
| Penrice, Sam'l, Sergt.... | Hall's | | 12 mo. | Do      16 Aug. '82 |
| Powers, Jos., Pt........ | | | " | Do      10 July '82 |
| Pough, Stephen, Pt.... | " | | " | Mustd War Sep. '82, Destd 10 Dec. '82 |
| Penrice, Francis, Pt..... | " | | " | Time out 16 Apr. '82 |
| Parks, Andrew, Pt..... | Yarboro's | | " | Omtd 1 Apr. '82 |
| Parks, Peter, Pt........ | " | | " | Time out 1 May '82 |
| Perry, Jno., Pt........ | " | | " | Do      17 May '82 |
| Patterson, Wm., Pt..... | " | | " | Dischgd 25 Feb. '82 |
| Pierce, Eph'm, Sergt.... | Carter's | 12 May '81 | " | Time out 2 May '82 |
| Phillips, David, Pt..... | " | 7 Apr. " | " | Do       2 Apr. '82 |
| Pierce, Edw'd, Pt...... | " | 12 May " | " | Do      25 Apr. '82 |
| Petteway, Jas., Pt...... | " | 25 Apr. " | " | Do      25 May '82 |
| Price, Lewis, Pt....... | " | 15  "    " | " | Do      25 Apr. '82 |
| Potter, Edw'd, Pt...... | " | 3 June '81 | " | Pris. 8 Sep. '82 |
| Powell, Wm., Pt........ | Jones' | 4 Feb. '82 | " | |
| Pasmore, David, Pt.... | " | 2 Dec. '81 | " | |
| Perkins, David, Sergt... (P. 1140) | Mill's | 6 Feb. '82 | " | Pt. Apr. '82 |
| Pavey, Nebemh, Musc.. | " | "  "  " | " | War. Sep. '82 |
| Pipkin, Wm............ | " | " | " | Died 9 Aug. '82 |
| Petterson, Duncan, Pt... | Coleman's | 15 Jan. '82 | W | |
| Parker, Amos, Pt....... | " | 13 "   " | 12 mo. | |
| Poe, Henry, Pt........ | Hall's | | W | Mustd Sep. '82, Destd 30 Nov. '82 |
| Proctor, Aaron, Pt..... | Jones' | 1 Feb. '82 | 12 mo. | |
| Pridgeon, Francis, Pt.... | Mills' | 1 Dec. '81 | " | |
| Parker, Arthur, Sergt.... | Bailey's | 1 July '82 | " | |
| Page, Solomon, Corpl... | " | 10 Sep. " | 18 mo. | Pt. Jan. '83 |
| Pyland, Peter, Pt...... | " | 17  "   " | " | Pt. Dec. '82 |
| Petty, Jno., Pt........ | " | 10 Sep. " | " | |
| Palmer, Thos., Pt...... | " | 13 Sep. " | 12 mo. | |
| Penris, Francis, Pt..... | " | 7 Jan. " | " | Time out 7 Jan. '83 |
| Philip, Wm., Pt........ | Hadley's | 1 Aug. " | 18 mo. | Died 6 June '83 |
| Parish, Edw'd, Pt...... | " | "   " | " | Died 16 Jan. '83 |
| Philips, Zacha, Pt...... | " | "   " | " | Died 18 May '83 |
| Powell, Stephen, Pt.... | " | 1 Aug. '82 | | |
| Powell, Lewis. ........ | " | 10 Sep. " | | |
| Price, Wm., Pt........ | Bacot's | 1782 | 18 mo.W | |
| Patrick, Spencer....... | | " | " | |
| Potter, Dan'l, Corpl..... | Carter's | " | " | Sergt. Dec. '82 |
| Payford, Wm., Musc.... | " | " | W | |
| Parks, Jas., Pt........ | " | " | 18 mo. | |
| Parks, Wm., Pt........ | " | " | " | |
| Pitts, Jas., Pt......... | " | " | " | |
| Pudney, Jereh, Pt....... | Raiford's | " | " | Destd 11 June '82 |
| Prozer, Jno., Pt........ | Sharp's | " | " | |
| Pevy, Sam'l, Musc...... | Lytle's | " | " | Destd 16 Mar. '83 |
| Ponder, Thos., Sergt.... | Brevard's | " | " | |
| Patrie, Peter, Pt....... | " | " | " | |
| Poe, Simeon, Pt....... | " | " | " | Destd 23 June '83 |
| Pattin, Jno........... | " | " | " | |

| Name and Rank | Company | Dates of Enlistment and Commission | Period of Service | Occurrences |
|---|---|---|---|---|
| Prival, Wm. .......... | Brevard's | 1782 | 18 mo. | |
| Philips, Aron ......... | " | " | " | |
| Parker, Ab'm ......... | " | " | " | |
| Purvis, Jos., Pt........ | Evans' | " | " | Destd 21 June '83 |
| Polmore, Elijah, Pt..... | " | " | " | |
| Pollock, Jesse, Pt...... | " | " | " | Transf'd Dec. '83 |
| Pearse, Abner, Pt...... | " | " | " | |
| Padget, Jno., Corpl..... | Bailey's | 2 May '81 | 12 mo. | Time out 2 May '82 |
| Proctor, Francis, Pt..... | Bacot's | | " | Mustd Dec. '82 |
| (P. 1140) | | | | |
| Patterson, Tilman, Sergt | Sharp's | 1 Nov. '78 | " | |
| Porch, Jas., Pt......... | " | " | " | |
| Powell, Jacob, Corpl.... | " | " | " | |
| Phips, John, Pt........ | " | 10 Nov. " | " | |
| Parnel, Ab'm, Pt....... | Major's | | W | Mustd Jan. '79 |
| Powers, Wm., Pt....... | Lytle's | | 3 yrs. | Mustd June '79 |
| Pendergrass, Job, Pt.... | Rhode's | | " | Mustd Apr. '79 |
| Patrick, Dan'l, Pt...... | Raiford's | 11 Sep. '78 | 3 yrs. | |
| Perkins, Adam, Pt...... | Lt. Col's | | W | Mustd Jan. '79 |
| Pendleton, Hiram, Pt. .. | " | 22 May '78 | | |
| Q   (P. 1141) | | | | |
| Quinn, Thos., Pt........ | Shepard's | 29 Aug. '77 | 3 yrs. | {Prisr. 1 June '79, Mustd Nov. '79 |
| Quinby, Eleazer, Pt..... | | 4 July '76 | " | Dischgd 30 July '79 |
| Quinn, David, Corpl.... | Doherty's | 1781 | 12 mo. | Time out 25 May '82 |
| Quilina, Shad'k, Pt..... | Carter's | " | " | Do    30 July '82 |
| Quinn, Francis, Pt...... | Bascot's | 1782 | 18 mo. | {Transf'd Dec. '82 to Penn. Line. |
| R   (P. 1147) | | | | |
| Rice, Jeptha, Qr. Mr. Sgt | | 15 May '81 | | |
| Randall, Andrews, Sergt. | Wilson's | "  "  '77 | 3 yrs. W | {Pt. 1 July '78, Sergt. 1 Jan. '79 |
| Rice, Timothy Corpl.... | " | 10 Oct. " | 2½ yrs. | {Pt. June '78 Omtd June '79 |
| (P. 1147) | | | | |
| Richards, Jona, Pt...... | " | 10 May '77 | | Omtd June '78 |
| Reasons, Thos., Pt...... | Shepard's | 15 Aug. " | 3 yrs. | |
| Roberts, Rich'd, Pt..... | " | 12 July " | | Omtd June '78 |
| Roberts, Ishmael, Pt.... | " | 3 June " | | Do |
| Rutter, Joseph, Pt...... | " | 25 Aug. " | | Died 28 May '78 |
| Robeson, Wm., Pt...... | Stevenson's | 21 Apr. " | 3 yrs. | {Destd Apr. '78, Mustd June '78, Sergt. Aug. '78, Destd '49 |
| Roland, Godfrey, Pt.... | Jarvis' | 4 Sep. " | | Omtd June '78 |
| Richardson, Jno., Ensn. | Gregory's | 1 Oct. " | | Do |
| Raindtree, Ruben, Lt.... | Heron's | 19 Apr. " | | Do |
| Robets, Jas., Pt........ | " | 24 July " | | |
| Redicks, Isaac, Pt...... | Moore's | 7 June " | | |
| Rogers, Jno., Pt........ | " | 4 May " | 3 yrs. W | |
| Razor, Jno., Pt......... | | 29 Mar. '78 | " | Pris. 14 Apr. '79 |
| (P. 1148) | | | | |
| Reardon, Dodley, Pt.... | Coleman's | 25 Aug. '77 | 3 yrs. | Dischgd 4 Dec. '78 |
| Reed, Moses, Pt........ | " | 4 May " | " | |
| Reed, Jas., Pt.......... | | 10 Sep. " | " | |
| Rogers, Stephen, Pt..... | | 17 Aug. " | " | |
| Right, Levy, Pt........ | | 7 May " | " | |

| Name and Rank | Company | Dates of Enlistment and Commission | Period of Service | Occurrences |
|---|---|---|---|---|
| Risk, Wm., Pt........ | | | | Mustd June '78, Omtd Aug. '78 |
| Roark, Nich's, Pt...... | | 1 Jan. '77 | 3 yrs. | Pris. 1 June '79, Mustd Nov. '79, Dischgd 31 Jan. '80 |
| (P. 1148) | | | | |
| Roberts, Thos., Sgt. Maj | | 20 July '78 | 9 mo. | |
| Reeves, Jese, Pt....... | Colol's | " | " | Corpl. Oct. '78 |
| Ryles, David, Pt....... | Hogg's | " | " | |
| Robison, Noah, Pt..... | " | " | " | |
| Ruff, Robt., Pt........ | " | " | " | |
| Reed, Sam'l, Sergt...... | Quinn's | " | " | |
| Ridgeway, Joseph, Pt... | " | " | " | |
| Reed, Jas., Pt......... | " | " | " | |
| Ross, Chas., Pt........ | " | " | " | Dischgd 13 July '78 |
| Remes, Joshua, Pt...... | Lt. Col's | 20 July '78 | " | |
| Roberts, James, Pt..... | " | " | " | |
| Rowell, And'w, Pt..... | " | " | " | |
| Rowell, Isaac, Pt...... | " | " | " | |
| Rhodes, Wm., Pt...... | Baker's | " | " | |
| Reed, Fred'k, Pt....... | " | " | " | |
| Richardson, Jas., Pt.... | " | " | " | |
| Ray, Dan'l, Pt........ | " | 1778 | | Destd 9 July '78 |
| Ractliff, Wm., Pt...... | " | " | | Destd 14 July '78 |
| Reddit, Constant, Corpl. | Blount's | 20 July '78 | 9 mo. | Sergt. 25 Oct. '78 |
| Ragly, Blake, Pt....... | " | " | " | |
| Robinson, Hardy, Pt.... | " | " | " | |
| Russell, Wm., Pt...... | Bradley's | " | " | |
| Ritto, Josiah, Pt....... | " | " | " | |
| Reasons, Wm., Pt...... | " | 1 June '79 | 18 mo. | See him in 5 Regt. |
| (P. 1148) | | | | |
| Roberts, Thos., Pt...... | Bradley's | 2 June '79 | 18 mo. | |
| Rape, F. Jno., Pt....... | Montfort's | 4 " " | W | Destd Sep. '79 |
| Rock, Jack, Pt........ | " | 18 " " | " | |
| Rooks, Hardiman, Pt... | " | 10 Aug. " | 18 mo. | Destd Sep. '79 |
| Ram, Jacob, Pt........ | " | 12 June " | W | Do |
| Rice, Benj., Pt......... | " | 23 " " | " | Do |
| Reynolds, Jas., Pt...... | " | 26 May '78 | 3 yrs. | |
| Ross, Thos., Pt........ | " | 1 Mar. '79 | 9 mo. | Dischgd 1 Dec. '79 |
| Raws, Lawrence, Pt..... | Ballard's | 1 July " | W | |
| Ritto, Peter, Musc...... | " | 22 June " | " | Pt. Oct. '79, Destd 4 Jan. '80 |
| Rowland, Fred'k, Corpl. | " | 1779 | 9 mo. | Dischgd 9 Dec. '79 |
| Rowe, Chas., Pt....... | " | " | " | Do |
| Richardson, Lewis, Pt... | " | " | | Supposed Rich'ds Lewis destd 1 Mar. '82 |
| Rakes, Jas., Sergt....... | Quinn's | 24 June '79 | 18 mo. | Destd Sep. '79 |
| Rogers, Silvester, Pt.... | " | " | 3 yrs. | |
| (P. 1149) | | | | |
| Ravell, Nath'l, Pt...... | " | " | 18 mo. | Destd Sept. '79 |
| Redley, Hardy, Pt..... | " | " | W | Omtd Oct. '79 |
| Russell, Wm., Pt...... | " | " | " | |
| Russell, Jas., Sergt...... | Blount's | 1 May " | 2½ yrs. | |
| Richmond, Jno., Pt..... | " | 1 June " | W | |
| Robinson, Jno., Pt...... | " | 1779 | " | Destd Dec. '79 |
| Ryan, Wm., Pt......... | " | 7 Jan. " | " | Destd Oct. '79 |
| Razor, Chrisr., Pt...... | McRee's | 28 Apr. '81 | 12 mo. | Left service 28 Apr. '82 |

| Name and Rank | Company | Dates of Enlistment and Commission | Period of Service | Occurrences |
|---|---|---|---|---|
| Robeson, Mark, Pt...... | McRee's | 28 Apr. '81 | 12 mo. | Do          Do |
| (P. 1149) | | | | |
| Ralph, Thos., Pt.......... | McRee's | 9 May '81 | 12 mo. | Left service 9 May '82 |
| Rogers, Jas., Pt........ | | 28 Apr. " | " | Do          28 Apr. '82 |
| Ramsay, Dan'l, Pt..... | | 25 May " | " | Died Oct. '81 |
| Riel, Jno., Pt........... | " | 28 Apr. " | " | Transf'd to the Legion Aug. '81 |
| Ryan, Thos., Pt........ | " | " | " | Destd 1 June '81 |
| Rogers, Parker, Musc... | Raiford's | 1 May '81 | " | Left service 1 May '82 |
| Rutland, Reding, Pt.... | " | 2 "  " | " | Do          2 May '82 |
| Rutland, Randolph, Pt.. | " | " | " | Do          Do |
| Robertson, Jas., Pt..... | " | 13 June " | " | Do          13 June '82 |
| Russell, Urias, Pt....... | " | 4 May " | " | Died Oct. '81 |
| Richards, Curtis, Pt..... | " | 18 "  " | " | Left service 18 May '82 |
| Richardson, Jno., Pt.... | " | 10 June " | " | Do          10 June '82 |
| Richardson, Rich'd, Pt.. | " | 19 May " | " | Left service 19 May '82 |
| Rochester, Wm., Corpl.. | Donoho's | 14 June " | " | Omtd in '81 |
| Roberson, Mark, Pt..... | " | " | " | Left service 14 June '82 |
| Reed, Benj., Pt......... | " | " | " | Do          Do |
| Rall, Jas., Pt........... | " | " | " | Do          19 May '82 |
| Riggins, Powell, Pt..... | " | | " | Do          25 May '82 |
| Reeks, Wm., Pt........ | " | 14 June " | " | Do          2 May '82 |
| Riddle, Jas., Pt......... | Dixon's | 15 May " | " | Do          21 May '82 |
| Robertson, Thos., Pt.... | " | " | " | Do          Do |
| Ratley, Benj........... | Lytle's | 6 June " | " | Do          6 June '82 |
| Rafle, Caleb........... | " | 12 Apr. " | " | Do          12 Apr. '82 |
| Robison, Jno........... | " | " | " | Omtd in '81 |
| (P. 1149) | | | | |
| Revell, Lazarus........ | Lytle's | 2 Apr. '81 | | Destd 5 July '81, Mustd Jan. '82 for War, Destd 10 Oct. '82 |
| Rush, Absolom, Pt..... | " | 5 June " | | Destd 1 July '81 |
| Rowland, Jno., Pt..... | " | " | | Omtd in '81 |
| Roberts, Moses, Pt..... | Sharp's | 21 May " | | See him in Brevard's Co'y |
| Roberts, Isaac, Pt..... | " | 5 "  " | | Omtd in '81 |
| Reasoner, Jno., Pt..... | | 1781 | | Transf'd before Apr. '82 |
| Riles, Wm., Pt......... | Moore's | 28 Apr. " | 12 mo. | Left service 28 Apr. '82 |
| Ricks, Benj., Sergt. Maj. | | 15 "  " | " | Do          15 Apr. '82 |
| Ross, Jas.............. | Lytle's | 1781 | | Do          1 Aug. '82 |
| Roe, Jesse, Musc....... | Sharp's | " | | Do          15 Aug. '82 |
| Roper, Geo., Pt........ | " | " | | Do          6 June '82 |
| Ryan, Corn's, Pt....... | Doherty's | | W | Mustd Jan. '82 |
| Red, Wm., Pt......... | " | " | | Time out 25 May '82 |
| (P. 1150) | | | | |
| Richards, Lewis, Pt..... | " | Jan. '82 | W | Destd 1 Mar. '82 |
| Reves, Fred'k, Pt....... | Rhode's | '81 | 12 mo. | Dischgd 23 Jan. '82 |
| Rhodes, Joseph........ | | 1 Aug. '77 | | |
| Rogers, Dunson, Pt..... | | 1781 | 12 mo. | Time out 1 Dec. '82 |
| Robinson,Willoughby,Pt. | Bailey's | 17 May " | " | Left service 17 May '82 |
| Riggin, Wm., Pt........ | " | 12 Apr. " | " | Do          12 Apr. '82 |
| Roberts, Moses, Pt..... | Brevard's | 1781 | " | Do          21 May '82 |
| Russ, Jno., Pt......... | " | " | " | Do          28 Apr. '82 |
| Raymond, Dan'l, Pt.... | " | | W | Mustd Jan. '82, Destd 23 Jan. '83 |
| Richardson, Elis, Pt..... | Brevard's | 1781 | | Destd before Apr. '82 |
| Reddick, Ab'm, Pt...... | Hall's | " | 12 mo. | Time out 16 Aug. '82 |
| Rhodes, Nath'n, Pt..... | " | " | " | Do          1 Aug. '82 |

| Name and Rank | Company | Dates of Enlistment and Commission | Period of Service | Occurrences |
|---|---|---|---|---|
| Rawson, Dan'l, Sergt.... | Yarborough's | 1781 | 12 mo. | Do 27 Apr. '82 |
| Robertson, Upsher, Pt... | " | " | " | Do 1 June '82 |
| Rittey, Micajah, Pt..... | " | " | " | Do 22 Apr. '82 |
| Roper, Jas., Pt......... | " | " | " | Omtd in '82 |
| Rowland, Wm., Pt..... | " | " | " | Do |
| Richardson, Wm., Pt.... | Carter's | " | " | Time out 25 Apr. '82 |
| Rowlang, Dan'l, Pt.... | " | 12 May " | " | Do 25 Apr. '82 |
| Ramage, Thos., Pt..... | " | 25 May " | " | Died 15 Oct. '81 |
| Runnels, Eph'm, Pt..... | Jones' | 23 Sep. " | " | Pt. Apr. '82 |
| Rogers, Willoughby, Pt.. | " | 3 Oct. " | " | Time out 1 Oct. '82 |
| Rogers, Wm., Pt....... | " | 1 Jan. '82 | " | Died 29 Aug. '82 |
| Riseing, David, Pt..... | " | 4 Jan. | " | |
| Robertson, Jno., Pt.... | Mills' | 6 Feb. " | " | |
| Roberts, Rich'd, Corpl.. | Coleman's | 22 Jan. " | " | Mustd Pt. Dec.'82 for war |
| Richards, Nich'ls, Pt.... | " | 8 " " | " | |
| Rochel, Amos, Pt...... | " | 18 Dec. " | " | |
| Rigsby, Jas., Pt........ | " | 10 Jan. " | " | |
| Railey, Edm'd, Pt...... | " | 1 Feb. " | " | |
| Ray, Arch'd, Pt....... | " | 4 Jan. " | " | |
| Ryall, Wm., Pt......... | Hall's | 1 June " | W | |
| Riggins, Jas., Pt........ | Jones' | 1 Mar. " | 12 mo. | |
| Robins, Jno., Pt........ | Mills' | Apr. " | " | Time out 1 Apr. '83 |
| Roark, Nich's, Pt...... | | Dec. '81 | 12 mo. | |
| Rhinehart, Jacob, Pt.... | Bailey's | | 18 mo. | |
| Ross, Benj., Corpl...... | Hadley's | | | Destd 18 June '83 |
| Richardson, Wm., Pt... | " | | W | Destd 18 Apr. '83 |
| Ryan, Corn'ls, Pt...... | " | | " | |
| Roser, David, Pt....... | " | | 18 mo. | |
| Roe, Jesse, Pt.......... | " | | " | Music Dec. '82 |
| Reynolds, Wm., Pt..... | Bacot's | 1782 | " | Died Nov. 28, '82 |
| Reams, Wm., Pt....... | Carter's | " | " | |
| Rogers, Parker, Pt..... | Raiford's | " | W | |
| Rivers, Benj., Pt....... | " | " | 18 mo. | |
| Roser, Jno., Pt......... | " | " | " | |
| Rasher, Hardy, Pt..... | " | " | " | |
| Roman, Thos., Corpl.... | Sharp's | " | " | |
| Ramsey, Jno., Pt...... | " | " | " | Transf'd 1 Dec. '82 |
| Rown, Henry, Pt...... | " | " | " | Destd 24 June '83 |
| Rutherford, Thos., Pt... | Brevard's | " | " | |
| Roberts, Wm., Pt...... | " | " | " | Dischgd Mar. '83 |
| Rogers, Dan'l, Pt...... | " | " | " | Transf'd Mar. '83 |
| Riley, Wm., Pt........ | " | " | " | |
| Richardson, And'w, Sergt. | Evans' | " | " | Sergt. Mar. '83 |
| Robertson, Jno., Corpl.. | " | " | " | |
| Robinson, Jno., Musc... | " | " | " | |
| Roundtree, Jesse, Pt.... | " | " | " | |
| Reel, Joshua, Pt....... | " | " | " | |
| Rochell, Geo., Pt...... | Evans' | | | Mustd dead '79 |
| Richards, Levy, Pt..... | | | | Mustd in '79 |
| Robido, Peter, Pt...... | | | 3 yrs. | Mustd destd '79 |
| Railey, Isaac, Pt....... | Sharp's | 17 Nov. '78 | | |
| Rutor, Lewis, Pt....... | " | | " | |
| Rogers, David, Pt..... | " | 10 Nov. '78 | 9 mo. | |
| Rogers, Wm., Pt...... | " | " " | " | |
| Roberts, Wm., Pt...... | " | | | |
| Rogers, Wm., Pt....... | Halls' | | 3 yrs. | Mustd Nov. '79 |
| Rees, Jno., Pt......... | Medaris' | | " | Mustd Jan. '79 |

| Name and Rank | Company | Dates of Enlistment and Commission | Period of Service | Occurrences |
|---|---|---|---|---|
| Rees, Roger, Pt........ | Medaris' | | 3 yrs. | Do |
| Reading, Jno., Pt...... | Taylor's | | 2½ yrs. | Do |
| Robertson, Thos., Pt.... | " | | 3 yrs. | Do |
| Richards, Lewis, Pt..... | Eaton's | | W | Do |
| **S** (Pp. 1159-67) | | | | |
| Stokes, Joel, Musc...... | Wilson's | 6 May '77 | 18 mo.W | {Pt. June '78, Corpl. 20 Mar. '79, Pt. Nov. '79 |
| Stearn, Moses, Pt....... | " | 1 Feb. '78 | 3 yrs. W | |
| Simmons, Jno., Sergt.... | " | 15 Aug. '77 | 3 yrs. | Dischgd 21 Aug. '78 |
| Serratt, Sam'l, Pt....... | " | 12 May " | | |
| Shepard, Ab'm, Col..... | | 1777 | | Omtd June '78 |
| Shepard, Wm., Capt.... | | 20 Jan. '78 | | Do |
| Stradley, Jos., Pt....... | Shepard's | 4 May '77 | 3 yrs. | {Pris. 1 June '79, Mustd Nov. '79 |
| Smith, Benj., Pt....... | " | 20 Aug. " | | |
| Stevenson, Hugh, Pt.... | " | 5 May " | | Tr. Nov. '79 to Invalids |
| Smith, Jno., Pt........ | " | 28 July '77 | 3 yrs. | |
| Sweat, David, Pt...... | " | 12 July " | 3 yrs. W | |
| Smith, Bryant, Pt..... | " | 1778 | | |
| Stringer, Jno., Musc..... | " | 3 June '77 | | |
| Stafford, Josiah, Pt..... | " | 5 July " | | |
| Stevenson, Silas, Capt... | | | | Omtd June '78 |
| Shute, Wm., Sergt...... | Stevenson's | 1 May " | 3 yrs. | {Corpl. June '78, Pt. Oct. '78, Omtd Feb. '79 |
| Smith, Wm., Pt........ | " | 13 May " | 3 yrs. W | |
| Simmonds, Sam'l, Corpl. | Jarvis' | 9 May " | 3 yrs. | Pt. June '78 |
| Sanderson, Caleb, Corpl. | " | 6 " " | " | {Pt. June '78, Died 2 Dec. '78 |
| Silvester, Luke, Pt..... | " | 5 " " | " | Dead Dec. '78 |
| Simons, Jno. Jr., Pt..... | " | 7 June " | " | Dischgd 1 Sep. '78 |
| Smith, Jas., Pt......... | " | 17 " " | 3 yrs. W | |
| Scalf, Jno., Corpl....... | Gregory's | 30 May " | 3 yrs. | Pt. June '78 |
| Sanderlin, Isaac, Pt..... | " | 22 " " | " | |
| Shute, Thos., Ensn...... | Heron's | 19 Apr. " | | Omtd June '78 |
| Skeen, Jno., Pt........ | " | 24 July " | 3 yrs. W | |
| Stewart, Jos., Pt........ | " | " " | 3 yrs. | |
| Simmons, Peter, Pt..... | Moore's | 11 May " | " | Died 15 Aug. '77 |
| Snowden, Zebu., Pt..... | " | 22 " " | " | Destd Apr. '78 |
| Sutherland, Jas., Pt..... | " | 1 June " | " | |
| Smith, Benj., Pt....... | " | 3 " " | " | Died 20 Nov. '78 |
| Sears, Jno., Pt.......... | " | 5 Aug. " | " | Omtd Sep. '78 |
| Singleton, Rob, Ensn.... | Vanois' | | " | Omtd June '78 |
| Simmons, Gideon, Corpl. | " | 2 May '77 | " | Pt. June '78 |
| Steward, Jno., Pt...... | " | 20 Aug. '77 | 3 yrs. | |
| Smith, Jno., Pt........ | | 12 July " | " | |
| Stroud, Lott, Pt....... | | 12 May " | 2½ yrs. | Omtd Feb. '79 |
| Steell, Anthony, Pt..... | | Aug. '78 | | Omtd Sep. '78 |
| Sillard, Thos., Pt...... | | 3 May '77 | " | Dischgd 1 June '79 |
| Shaddock, Chas., Pt..... | | 1779 | W | |
| Sisk, Jas., Pt........... | | 1 Oct. '76 | 3 yrs. W | Corpl. Nov. '79 |
| Stertevant, Barnas, Pt.. | | 31 Aug. '77 | 3 yrs. | {Omtd June '79, Mustd Nov. '79 |
| Samples, Wm., Pt...... | Coleman's | 1778 | | Destd 20 Aug. '78 |
| Southall, Stephen, Lt.... | | 1 Apr. " | | Resigned 4 Oct. '78 |
| Story, Caleb, Pt........ | | | | {Joined 5 Apr. '78, died 16 June '78 |

| Name and Rank | Company | Dates of Enlistment and Commission | Period of Service | Occurrences |
|---|---|---|---|---|
| (P. 1160) | | | | |
| Saxton, Wm., Pt....... | | | W | {Joined 5 Apr. '78, Prisner<br>1 June '79, Mustd Nov.'79 |
| Scull, Alex'r, Pt....... | | 20 Apr. '77 | 2½ yrs. | Dischgd 30 Oct. '78 |
| Sharpley, Jno., Pt..... | | | W | Joined Jan. '78 |
| Scott, Adam, Pt....... | | | " | {Mustd Apr. '78, died<br>Oct. '78 |
| Savage, Rans'm, Pt.... | | 2 June '77 | 3 yrs. | Sergt. Feb. '78 |
| Stevens, Jno., Pt...... | | | W | {Mustd Jan, '78,<br>Dischgd 31 Mar. '79 |
| Shute, Jese, Pt........ | | 2 Dec. '78 | 3 yrs. W | {Music Feb. '78,<br>Pt. June '78 |
| Scott, Wm., Pt........ | | 3 May '77 | 2½ yrs. | |
| Schultz, Lewis, Pt..... | | 22 Jan. " | 3 yrs. | |
| Steptoe, Jno., Sergt..... | Colonel's | 20 July '78 | 9 mo. | |
| Scott, Israel, Pt........ | " | " | " | |
| Smith, Thos., Corpl..... | " | " | " | |
| Scurlock, Jas., Pt...... | " | " | " | {Lt. 1 Sep. '81,<br>Deranged 1 Jan. '83 |
| Spear, Joseph, Pt...... | " | " | " | |
| Spear, Sam'l, Pt....... | " | " | " | |
| Smith, Chas., Pt....... | " | " | " | |
| Sweet, Geo., Pt........ | " | " | " | |
| Sentez, Sam'l, Pt...... | " | " | " | |
| Shanks, Jas........... | | | | |
| Smith, Elias, Pt....... | Hogg's | " | W | |
| Smith, Henry, Pt...... | " | " | 9 mo. | |
| Sriven, Jas., Pt....... | | " | " | |
| Sanders, Job, Pt....... | | " | " | |
| Stewart, Jno., Pt...... | | " | " | |
| Simmons, Jas., Pt...... | | " | " | Destd 21 July '78 |
| Selves, David.......... | Quinn's | " | " | |
| Shipman, Toney, Pt.... | " | " | " | |
| Shipman, Asa, Pt...... | " | " | " | |
| Shipman, Jacob, Pt.... | " | " | " | |
| Smith, Platt, Pt....... | " | " | " | |
| Stanton, John, Pt...... | " | " | " | Dischgd 14 July '78 |
| Simpson, Moses, Pt.... | " | " | " | Dischgd 7 Sep. '78 |
| Shadforth, Whittier, Pt.. | " | " | " | |
| Smith, Wm., Pt........ | Lt. Colo's | " | " | |
| Scott, Sterling, Pt..... | " | " | " | |
| Sumner, Rich'd, Pt.... | " | " | " | |
| Scott, Wm., Pt........ | " | " | " | |
| Short, Hardy, Pt...... | " | " | " | |
| Short, Henry, Pt....... | " | " | " | Died 27 Nov. '78 |
| Smith, Nehemh, Musc... | Baker's | 20 July '78 | 9 mo. | |
| Sherrard, Edw'd, Pt..... | " | " | " | |
| Sherrard, Jordon, Pt... | " | " | " | |
| Sykes, Samps., Pt...... | " | " | " | Destd 23 July '78 |
| Stone, Benj., Pt........ | Blount's | " | " | |
| (P. 1161) | | | | |
| Skinner, Thos., Pt..... | " | " | " | |
| Spencer, Solomon, Pt... | " | " | " | |
| Smith, Wm., Pt....... | " | " | " | |
| Skinner, Wm., Pt...... | " | " | " | |
| Sorrel, Thos., Pt....... | " | " | " | Died 16 Sep. '78 |
| Speer, Jno............. | Ballard's | " | " | Omtd Oct. '78 |

| Name and Rank | Company | Dates of Enlistment and Commission | Period of Service | Occurrences |
|---|---|---|---|---|
| Scott, Mich'l, Pt........ | Ballard's | 20 July '78 | 9 mo. | |
| Scott, Wm., Pt......... | " | " | " | |
| Stokes, Henry, Pt...... | " | " | " | Omtd Oct. '78 |
| Skeets, Wm., Pt........ | " | " | " | |
| Scott, Nath'l, Pt....... | " | " | " | |
| Smith, Wm., Pt........ | " | " | " | Omtd Oct. '78 |
| Swales, Enoch, Pt...... | " | 1778 | " | Destd 15 July '78 |
| Surles, Rob., Pt........ | Bradley's | 20 July '78 | " | |
| Sketo, Joseph, Pt...... | " | " | " | |
| Spence, Incell, Pt...... | " | " | " | Omtd Oct. '78 |
| Sutton, Ralph, Pt...... | " | " | " | |
| Smith, Jas., Corpl...... | Childs' | " | " | |
| Smithwick, Wm., Sergt.. | | " | " | |
| Shivers, Jese, Musc..... | | " | " | |
| Shurley, Thos., Pt...... | Childs' | " | " | |
| Sheborn, Wm., Pt..... | " | " | " | |
| Sirmore, Levy, Pt...... | " | " | " | |
| Sanders, Benj., Pt..... | " | " | " | Died Sep. '78 |
| Spellman, Simon, Pt.... | Bradley's | 28 June '79 | W | |
| Stannul, Peter, Pt..... | " | 22 Jan. '80 | | |
| Smith, Jas., Pt......... | " | | | |
| Sug, John, Pt......... | Montfort's | 16 June '79 | | |
| Standley, Jona, Pt...... | " | | | Dischgd Sep. '79 |
| Smith, Wm., Pt....... | " | 1 Mar. " | 9 mo. | Dischgd 1 Dec. '79 |
| Stevenson, Jno., Pt..... | Ballard's | 21 June " | 18 mo. | Omtd Oct. '79 |
| Smith, Wm., Pt....... | " | 1 July " | " | Destd 19 Oct. '79 |
| Savory, Jas., Pt........ | " | 1 " " | " | |
| Smith, Jos., Pt........ | " | 29 " " | W | Destd 22 Aug. '79 |
| Stevens, Jno. Corpl..... | Quinn's | 1 " " | 18 mo. | |
| Short, Chas., Musc...... | " | 24 " " | W | |
| Shivers, Jos., Pt........ | " | " | 3 yrs. | |
| Sandiford, Robt., Pt.... | " | 28 May " | 18 mo. | Omtd Oct. '79 |
| Strange, Eph'm, Pt..... | " | 24 Jan. " | " | Destd Dec. '79 |
| Sanders, Joseph, Corpl.. | Blount's | 1 Mar. " | 3 yrs. | |
| Stranges, Jas., Pt...... | " | 1779 | | |
| Sherrard, Rich'd, Pt.... | " | 7 June " | W | |
| Smith, Jno., Pt........ | " | 27 " " | 18 mo. | |
| Stansberry, Luke, Pt.... | " | 12 " " | 3 yrs. | |
| Scott, Philip, Pt....... | " | 11 " " | 18 mo. | |
| Sutton, Jos., Pt........ | " | 1 Aug. '79 | 12 mo. | Destd Oct. '79 |
| Simkins, Joseph, Pt..... | Ramsay's | '79 | 9 mo. | Omtd Oct. '79 |
| Shoulder, Wm., Pt...... | " | " | " | Destd Sep. '79 |
| Shabshaw, Peter, Pt.... | " | " | " | Dead Sep. '79 |
| Sears, David, Pt....... (P. 1162) | | " | 9 mo. | Omtd Oct. '79 |
| Smethers, Garet, Pt.... | | 1779 | " | Destd Sep. '79 |
| Smith, Wm., Pt....... | | " | " | Omtd Oct. '79 |
| Sugins, Joseph, Pt..... | | " | " | Dead Sep. '79 |
| Searles, Thos., Pt...... | | " | " | Dead Sep. '79 |
| Steed, Jese, Ensn...... | | 1 June '81 | | {And Qr. Mr. 13 July '81, {Lt. 8 Sep. '81 |
| Styrewall, Fred'k, Pt.... | McRee's | 28 Apr. " | 12 mo. | Left service 28 Apr. '82 |
| Stone, Jno., Pt......... | " | " | " | Do Do |
| Searles, Thos., Pt...... | " | " | " | Do Do |
| Sportman, Wm., Pt..... | " | " | " | {Transf'd to the Legion {Aug. '81 |
| Spears, Joseph, Pt..... | " | 9 May " | " | Destd 1 June '81 |

| Name and Rank | Company | Dates of Enlistment and Commission | Period of Service | Occurrences |
|---|---|---|---|---|
| Smith, Thos., Pt. | McRee's | 9 May '81 | 12 mo. | Omtd Jan. '82. Sick |
| Stewart, Sam'l, Pt. | | 26 " " | " | Destd 26 May '81 |
| Senter, Sam'l, Sergt. | Raiford's | 25 Apr. " | | |
| Southhall, Furney, Pt. | " | 5 May " | 2 yrs. W | Pt. Sep. '82 |
| Sanders, Robt., Musc. | " | " | 12 mo. | Left service 3 May '82 |
| Smith, Rich'd, Pt. | " | 2 May " | " | Do 2 Do |
| Starks, Benj., Pt. | " | 17 " " | " | Do 17 Do |
| Spires, Thos., Pt. | " | 25 Apr. " | " | Do 25 Do |
| Scott, Eman'l, Pt. | " | " | | Do 25 Do |
| Sweat, Ab'm, Pt. | | | | |
| Suik, Paul, Pt. | Donaho's | | | See Paul Luek |
| Sykes, Dempsey, Musc. | " | 25 May '81 | 12 mo. | Left service 25 May '82 |
| Stacey, Jno., Pt. | " | 14 June " | " | Time out 14 June '82 |
| Smith, Henry, Pt. | " | " | " | Left service June '82 |
| Step, Jno., Pt. | " | " | " | Omtd in '81 |
| Stevens, Henry, Pt. | " | " | " | Left service 14 June '82 |
| Summers, Geo., Sergt. | Dixon's | 15 May '81 | " | Do 21 May '82 |
| Seers, Asa, Pt. | " | 12 " " | " | Do 21 Do |
| Stilwell, Jacob, Musc. | " | 15 " " | " | {Pt. from 1 Jan. '82, Left service 21 May '82 |
| Shelton, Jos., Pt. | " | 12 " " | " | Do 26 Do |
| Swanson, Jno., Pt. | " | 12 May " | " | Do 26 Do |
| Stricklin, Fred'k, Pt. | " | 12 " " | " | Do 26 Do |
| Smith, Jno., Pt. | " | 25 Apr. " | " | Do 25 Apr. '82 |
| Smith, Thos., Pt. | " | 15 May " | " | Do 21 May '82 |
| Stallions, Moses, Corpl. | Lytle's | 6 June " | " | Do 6 Apr. '82 |
| Simmons, Jno., Pt. | " | " " " | " | Do 12 Apr. '82 |
| Salyers, Martin, Pt. | " | " " " | | Omtd in '81 |
| Scott, Sam'l, Pt. | " | '81 | | Do |
| Syas, Jese, Pt. | " | 1 June " | | Left service 1 June '82 |
| Smith, Aaron, Pt. | " | " | | Do Do |
| Strickland, Jno., Pt. | " | 12 Apr. " | | Do Do |
| Strickland, Marmd'k, Pt. | " | " | | Omtd in '81 |
| Snyder, Chrisn., Pt. | " | 1 June " | | Left service 1 June '82 |
| Sykes, Sampson, Pt. | " | 12 Apr. '81 | | |
| Suet, Sam'l, Pt. | " | 2 Apr. " | | Destd 6 July '81 |
| Stewart, Coldwell, Pt. | " | 2 Apr. " | W | {Destd 5 July '81, Mustd Jan. '82 |
| Sherwood, Jordon, Pt. (P. 1163) | " | 12 " " | | Destd 6 July '81 |
| Styles, Jno., Pt. | " | " | 12 mo. | Left service 12 Apr. '82 |
| Saunders, Jno., Pt. | " | 12 " " | 12 mo. | Do 12 Apr. '82 |
| Spears, Kindred, Pt. | " | 12 " " | " | Do 21 May '82 |
| Solomon, Wm., Pt. | Sharp's | 21 May " | " | Do 21 May '82 |
| Stocks, Joshua | " | | | Omtd in '81 |
| Sherly, Thos. | | 15 " " | | {Sergt. Jan., Left service 5 Apr. '82 |
| Sinclair, Wm. | | 5 " " | " | {Sergt. Jan., Left service 5 Apr. '82 |
| Spelmore, Jacob | | 15 " " | " | Omtd in '81 |
| Smith, Wm. | | 5 " " | | Left service 15 Apr. '82 |
| Spelmore, Aaron | | | | Do 5 Apr. '82 |
| Stringer, Winger | | | | Do 5 Apr. '82 |
| Steward, Dan'l | | | | Do 15 Apr. '82 |
| Spenser, Robt. | | | | Omtd in '81 |
| Sullivan, Jno. | | | | Died 3 Apr. '83 |
| Sherrod, Benj. | | | | Time out 1 Feb. '83 |

| Name and Rank | Company | Dates of Enlistment and Commission | Period of Service | Occurrences |
|---|---|---|---|---|
| Sullivan, Jas., Corpl..... | Walton's | 1781 | | Do      25 May '82 |
| Siddle, Jesse, Pt........ | | | W | |
| Slater, Jas., Pt........ | | | 12 mo. | Time out Dec. '82 |
| Smith, Malachi, Pt..... | | | " | Do      25 Apr. '82 |
| Stringer, Noah, Pt...... | Sharp's | | " | Do      28 Oct. '82 |
| Squires, And'w, Pt..... | " | | " | Do      16 Dec. '82 |
| Spear, Spencer, Pt...... | " | | W | Mustd Jan. '82, Destd 13 June '83 |
| Shepard, Wm., Sergt.... (P. 1163) | Doherty's | 1781 | | Time out 25 May '82 |
| Springs, Micajah, Pt.... | Doherty's | " | | Time out 25 May '82 |
| Simmons, Willis, Pt..... | " | " | | Do      Do |
| Salmon, Vincent, Pt..... | " | | W | Mustd Jan. '82 |
| Sterling, Robt., Pt...... | Rhode's | " | | Time out 25 Apr. '82 |
| Sebril, Joshua, Pt...... | " | " | | Do      24 May '82 |
| Segraves, Jacob, Pt..... | " | " | | Do      25 Apr. '82 |
| Snutman, Wm., Pt...... | " | " | | Do      25 Apr. '82 |
| Stove, Warren, Pt...... | " | " | | Do      14 May '82 |
| Salomon, Lazarus, Pt. .. | " | " | | Do      25 Apr. '82 |
| Scarsey, Asiah, Pt...... | " | " | | Do      24 May '82 |
| Smart, Jno., Pt......... | " | " | | Do      12 Apr. '82 |
| Sterling, Elisha, Pt..... | " | " | | Do      4 June '82 |
| Stevens, Jas., Pt........ | " | 5 Jan. '82 | 12 mo. | Left service 5 Jan. '83 |
| Stevens, Henry, Pt...... | " | " " " | " | Do      5 Jan. '83 |
| Smith, Wm., Sergt...... | Bailey's | 15 Apr. '81 | " | Do      15 Apr. '82, Pt. from 26 Feb. '82 |
| Sykes, Henry, Pt....... | " | 17 May " | " | Left service 17 May '82 |
| Simmons, Jno., Pt..... | " | May | " | Do      17 May '82, Promoted 23 Feb. '82 |
| Still, Jas., Pt.......... | " | May | " | Left service 17 May '82 |
| Smith, Benj., Pt....... | " | 25 May " | " | Do      25 Do |
| Sanderlin, Josiah, Pt.... (P. 1164) | " | 17 " " | " | Do      17 Do |
| Smith, Isaac, Pt........ | " | 17 " " | " | Do      17 Do |
| Santee, Mich'l, Pt...... | " | 9 " " | " | Do      9 Do |
| Sprewell, Godfrey, Pt.... (P. 1164) | " | 3 " " | " | Do      3 Do |
| Scudder, Abner, Pt...... | Brevard's | 1781 | 12 mo. | |
| Scarborough, Sam'l, Pt.. | " | " | " | |
| Sailor, Geo., Pt........ | " | " | " | |
| Spears, Joseph, Pt..... | " | " | " | |
| Swindle, Solomon, Pt.... | " | " | " | |
| Sampson, Isaac, Pt..... | " | " | " | |
| Shoemaker, Randle, Pt.. | " | " | " | |
| Sawyers, Joseph, Pt.... | " | " | " | Dischgd 1 Apr. '82 |
| Sperpoint, Joseph, Pt.... | " | " | " | Transf'd 26 Mar. '82 to Artificers |
| Skinners, Evans, Pt..... | Hall's | " | " | Left service 21 Apr. '82 |
| Shrode, Adam, Pt...... | " | " | " | Time out 27 Dec. '82 |
| Scarborough, Shad'k, Pt. | " | " | " | Do      12 Apr. '82 |
| Snipes, Wm., Pt....... | " | " | " | Do      1 Apr. '82 |
| Scott, Sam'l, Pt....... | " | " | " | Do      13 Dec. '82 |
| Seagroves, Thos., Pt.... | Yarboro's | " | " | Do      22 Apr. '82 |
| Scott, Dennis, Pt...... | " | " | " | Do      1 May '82 |
| Smith, Wm., Pt....... | " | " | " | Do      1 May '82 |
| Scott, Isom, Pt........ | " | " | " | Omtd 1 Apr. '82 |
| Scipio, Hill, Pt........ | " | " | " | Time out 22 Apr. '82 |

| Name and Rank | Company | Dates of Enlistment and Commission | Period of Service | Occurrences |
|---|---|---|---|---|
| Sweeny, Thos., Pt...... | Yarboro's | 1781 | 12 mo. | Do 2 May '82 |
| Stanfield, Jas., Corpl.... | Carter's | 18 July " | " | Do 20 June '82 |
| Stevens, Hugh, Pt...... | " | 25 Apr. " | " | Do 25 Apr. '82 |
| Stevens, Benj., Pt...... | " | 19 May " | " | Do 19 May '82 |
| Sanders, Thos., Pt..... | " | " " " | " | Do 19 May '82 |
| (P. 1164) | | | | |
| Seeburn, Joseph, Pt..... | Carter's | 12 Oct. '81 | 18 mo. | Do 1 Apr. '83 |
| Snead, Zadock, Pt..... | " | 25 Apr. " | 12 mo. | Do 25 Apr. '82 |
| Savage, Moses, Pt..... | " | 19 May " | " | Do 19 May '82 |
| Spelmore, Jacob, Pt..... | " | 3 Apr. " | " | Do 25 Apr. '82 |
| Sandiford, Amos, Pt.... | " | 19 May " | " | Dead Sep. '81 |
| Smith, Rich'd, Pt...... | " | 25 Apr. " | " | Dead 16 Sep. '81 |
| Sneed, Wm., Pt........ | " | 1781 | " | Destd 15 Sep. '81 |
| Sorrell, Lewis, Pt...... | " | 12 Feb. '81 | " | Omtd before '82 |
| Slaughter, Robt., Pt..... | Jones' | 1 Jan. '82 | " | |
| Slaughter, Jno., Pt..... | " | " " | " | |
| Smith, Joab, Pt........ | " | " | " | |
| Smith, Jacob, Pt....... | " | " | " | |
| Smith, Jereh.......... | " | " | " | Died 14 Sep. '82 |
| Screw, Joseph, Pt...... | " | 3 Feb. " | " | |
| Steel, Wm., Pt........ | " | 6 Mar. " | " | |
| Scarlet, Jas., Pt....... | " | 13 Nov. '81 | " | Died 20 Sep. '82 |
| Scarlet, Wm., Pt....... | " | 1 Feb. '82 | " | |
| Stewart, Dan'l, Pt..... | " | 4 Jan. " | " | Died 4 Oct. '82 |
| Stewart, Jno., Pt...... | " | 10 Dec. '81 | " | |
| Sellers, Jno., Pt........ | " | 15 " " | " | |
| Sykes, Jas, Sergt........ | Mill's | 6 Feb. '82 | " | Sergt Maj. Sep. '82 |
| (P. 1165) | | | | |
| Stringer, Jno., Corpl. ... | " | 8 " " | " | Mustd Pt. for W. Dec. '82 |
| Sniles, Anty., Pt........ | " | 7 " " | " | Died 7 Aug. '82 |
| Simpson, Wm., Pt...... | " | 6 " " | " | |
| Simpson, Rich'd, Pt.... | " | 6 " " | " | |
| (P. 1165) | | | | |
| Sullivan, Owen, Pt..... | " | 7 Feb. '82 | 12 mo. | |
| Simmons, Jereh, Pt..... | " | 25 Dec. '81 | " | |
| Simmons, Sander, Pt.... | " | " " | " | |
| Smith, Jno., Pt........ | " | 1 Feb. '82 | " | Died 19 Sep. '82 |
| Sessons, Abel, Pt...... | " | 4 Jan. " | " | |
| Smith, Jas., Pt........ | " | 1 " " | " | |
| Skipper, Jas., Pt....... | " | 18 Dec. '81 | " | |
| Stokeley, Thos., Pt..... | " | 6 Feb. '82 | " | |
| Suggs, Ezk., Pt........ | Coleman's | 1 Jan. " | " | |
| Suggs, Eligood, Pt..... | " | " " | " | |
| Simmons, Jno., Pt..... | " | 18 Dec. '81 | " | |
| Shaw, Duncan, Pt..... | " | 1 Jan. '82 | " | |
| Scarlet, Thos., Pt...... | " | 13 Nov. '81 | " | |
| Slade, Fred'k, Pt....... | Hall's | 1 Mar. '82 | " | |
| Sheffield, Wm., Pt..... | " | " | " | Time out 1 Jan. '83 |
| Smith, Jas., Pt........ | " | 1 Dec. '81 | " | Do 1 Dec. '82 |
| Smith, Peter, Pt........ | " | " " | " | Do 1 Dec. '82 |
| Seayres, Robt., Pt...... | " | 22 Aug. '82 | W | |
| Strawn, Rich'd, Pt..... | " | | " | Mustd Dec. '82, Destd 1 May '83 |
| Stokeley, Peter, Pt...... | Jones' | 1 Mar. '82 | 12 mo. | Corpl. Sep. '82 |
| Silverthan, Robt., Pt.... | Mill's | 10 " " | " | |
| Sterling, Seth, Pt...... | " | 10 Jan. " | " | |
| Smith, Rich'd, Pt...... | " | 1 " " | " | Died 10 Sep. '82 |

| Name and Rank | Company | Dates of Enlistment and Commission | Period of Service | Occurrences |
|---|---|---|---|---|
| Scott, Jas., Pt......... | Bailey's | 1 Aug. '82 | 12 mo. | |
| (P. 1165) | | | | |
| Sowell, Wm., Pt....... | Bailey's | 10 Sep. '82 | 18 mo. | |
| Scurlock, Jas., Pt...... | " | 22 May " | 12 mo. | |
| Strange, Wm., Pt...... | " | 2 Apr. " | " | |
| Sky, Jese, Pt.......... | " | 5 June " | " | |
| Still, Jno., Pt.......... | Hadley's | 1 Aug. " | 18 mo. | |
| Smith, Jno., Corpl..... | " | " | " | |
| Spain, Thos., Musc.... | " | " | " | |
| Smith, Rich'd, Pt...... | " | " | " | |
| Silas, Thos............ | " | " | " | |
| Sturtevant, Chas., Sergt. | Bacot's | 1782 | " | |
| Spears, Willis, Corpl.... | " | " | " | |
| Steptoe, Thos., Musc.... | " | " | " | Destd 18 June '83 |
| Sivet, Allen, Pt........ | " | " | " | |
| Savage, Micaja, Pt..... | " | " | " | |
| Skinner, Jno., Pt...... | " | " | " | |
| Stayway, Jno., Pt...... | " | " | " | |
| Scriggs, Rich'd, Pt..... | " | " | " | |
| Scott, Isaac, Pt........ | " | " | " | |
| Sykes, Jas., Pt........ | " | " | " | |
| Smith, Burrell, Sergt.... | Carter's | " | " | Died 26 Jan. '83 |
| Scott, Dennis, Pt...... | " | " | " | |
| Smith, Peter, Pt....... | " | " | " | |
| (P. 1166) | | | | |
| Sport, Wm., Pt........ | " | " | " | Destd 29 Apr. '83 |
| Smith, Jacob, Pt....... | " | " | " | |
| Stranfield, Pt.......... | " | " | " | Destd 7 Dec. '82 |
| (P. 1166) | | | | |
| Sanderlin, Robt., Pt..... | Raiford's | 1782 | 18 mo. | |
| Shurer, Fred'k, Pt..... | " | " | " | |
| Savage, Thos., Pt...... | " | " | " | |
| Shepard, Valte, Pt..... | " | " | " | |
| Standley, Jas., Pt...... | " | " | " | |
| Spearman, Geo., Pt..... | " | " | " | |
| Shepard, Bird, Pt....... | Sharp's | " | " | |
| Stellard, Peter, Pt..... | " | " | " | |
| Smith, Jno., Pt....... | " | " | " | |
| Simpkins, Josh, Pt..... | " | " | " | |
| Sheets, David, Pt...... | " | " | " | Destd 23 June '83 |
| Scews, Wm., Pt........ | Lytle's | " | " | |
| Sanders, Sam'l, Pt..... | " | " | " | |
| Stevens, Thos., Pt..... | " | " | " | |
| Stewart, Jas., Pt....... | " | " | " | |
| Simmons, Philip, Pt.... | " | " | | |
| Sowell, Isaac, Pt....... | " | " | | Destd 25 Nov. '82 |
| Smith, Peter, Pt....... | " | " | | Do    10 Dec. '82 |
| Smith, Drewry, Pt..... | " | " | | Do    10 Dec. '82 |
| Scaff, Joseph, Pt....... | " | " | | Transf'd Jan. '83 to So. Carolina Line |
| Sanders, Henry, Musc... | Brevard's | " | 18 mo. | |
| Slade, Nath'l, Pt........ | " | " | " | |
| Seagraves, Jno., Pt..... | " | " | " | |
| Stringfield, Aaron, Pt. .. | " | " | " | |
| (P. 1166) | | | | |
| Scrimshire, Jno., Pt..... | " | " | 18 mo. | Destd 27 Nov. '82 |
| Silvester, Nath'l, Pt..... | Rhode's | 1 Dec. '82 | " | |

| Name and Rank | Company | Dates of Enlistment and Commission | Period of Service | Occurrences |
|---|---|---|---|---|
| Smith, Stephen, Pt...... | Rhode's | 1782 | 18 mo. | Died 3 June '83 |
| Scarborough, Nathn, Pt. | " | " | " | |
| Smith, Ez'l, Pt......... | " | " | " | |
| Sullivan, Jno., Pt...... | " | " | " | Destd 21 June '83 |
| Simkins, Jno., Pt...... | " | " | " | |
| Silvester, Nath'l, Pt.... | " | " | " | Omtd Jan. '83, Transf'd |
| Sheppard,Willoughby,Pt. | " | " | " | |
| Stewart, Dempsy, Pt.... | " | " | " | Transf'd Dec. '82 |
| Scott, Thos., Pt........ | " | " | " | |
| Scott, Ab'm, Pt........ | " | " | " | |
| Stringer, Hez'k, Pt...... | Coleman's | | | |
| Scott, Drewry, Pt...... | | 1 Aug. " | 3 yrs. | |
| Sumner, Fran's, Pt..... | Carter's | | | Mustd Dec. '82 |
| Smith, David, Pt....... | Sharp's | | | Do |
| Stewart, Chas., Pt..... | " | | | Do |
| Smith, Sam'l, Pt........ | " | | | Do |
| Smith, Henry, Corpl.... | Walton's | | 12 mo. | Time out 15 June '83 |
| Shoulders, Wm., Pt.... | Sharp's | 21 Oct. '78 | 3 yrs. | |
| Squares, Thos., Pt..... | " | 25 Aug. " | W | |
| Sloan, Wm., Pt........ | " | 10 Nov. " | 9 mo. | |
| Sullivan, Tenig, Pt..... | Tatum's | | W | Mustd Nov. '79 |
| (P. 1167) | | | | |
| Shavers, Jno., Pt...... | Coll. | 1 Feb. '80 | 28 mo. | Mustd Jan. '79, |
| Sersy, Luke, Pt........ | " | | W | Dead May '79 |
| | | | | |
| (P. 1167) | | | | |
| Smith, Jas., Pt......... | Goodman's | | 3 yrs. | Mustd Jan. '79 |
| Skipper, Geo., Pt....... | Doherty's | | " | |
| Skipper, Josh.......... | " | | " | |
| Smith, Josh............ | Lt. Col's | | " | Mustd Mar. '79 |
| Saunders, Josh, Corpl... | Doherty's | | | Mustd Jan. '79 |
| Smith, Reuben, Pt...... | Eaton's | | 9 mo. | Mustd Jan. '79, |
| Summers, Leven, Pt.... | " | | 3 yrs. | Died 20 May '79 |
| | | | | |
| Snowden, Nath'l, Pt.... | | 5 June '78 | | |
| T (P. 1172) | | | | |
| Thomson, Nath'l, Pt.... | Wilson's | 20 May '77 | 3 yrs. | Prisr. 14 Apr. '79 |
| Tyler, Wm., Pt......... | " | 1 Oct. " | " | Destd Jan. '80 |
| Thompson, Willis, Pt.... | Shepard's | 12 July " | | Died Oct. '78 |
| Taylor, Wm., Pt....... | " | 12 Aug. " | | Omtd June '78 |
| Talor, Jese, Pt......... | | 5 May " | | Died 20 Mar. '78 |
| Turner, Robt., Lt....... | Stevenson's | | | Omtd June '78 |
| Thompson, Wm., Sergt.. | Jarvis' | 5 May '77 | 3 yrs. | Pt. June '78 |
| Thompson,Willough'y,Pt | " | 12 Dec. " | " | Died 12 Jan. '79 |
| Taunt, Wm., Sergt..... | Heron's | 26 Apr. " | " | Pt. June '78 |
| Taylor, Elias, Musc..... | " | 25 July " | " | Pt. June '78, |
| | | | | Destd 25 Aug. '78 |
| | | | | |
| Taunt, Jese, Pt......... | " | 26 Apr. " | | |
| (P. 1172) | | | | |
| Tilman, Wm., Pt....... | " | 1 July '77 | 3 yrs. | |
| Tilman, Jno., Pt....... | " | " | " | |
| Tilman, Belitha........ | " | 10 June " | " | Corpl. 10 Oct. '78, Pt. 1 |
| | | | | June '79, Destd 3 July '79, |
| | | | | Mustd Nov. '79 |
| Taunt, Thos., Pt....... | " | 15 Apr. '77 | " | Music, June '78 |
| Tracey, Jno., Pt....... | Vanois' | 24 June " | | Omtd June '78 |

| Name and Rank | Company | Dates of Enlistment and Commission | Period of Service | Occurrences |
|---|---|---|---|---|
| Thomas, Caleb, Pt..... | | 1 May '77 | 3 yrs. W | Music 1 Jan. '78, Pt. Dec. '82 |
| Tradder, Geo., Pt...... | | 20 " '76 | " | Corpl. July '79 |
| Trawl, Jno., Pt........ | | 12 Jan. '78 | 3 yrs. | Destd 8 Mar.'79 |
| Taylor, Aaron, Musc.... (P. 1173) | | 1 Apr. " | W | |
| Taylor, Caleb, Pt....... | Coleman's | 1778 | | Omtd Feb. '79 |
| Tutson, Thos., Pt...... | | | | Mustd July and destd 15 Aug. '78 |
| Thompson, Wm., Pt.... | | 26 Apr. '76 | 2½ yrs. | Dischgd 10 Nov. '78 |
| Thomas, Wm., Pt...... | | | W | Mustd June '78 |
| Terry, David, Pt...... | Montfort's | 20 July '78 | 9 mo. | |
| Turner, Thos., Pt...... | " | " | " | |
| Tippett, Erastus, Musc. | " | " | " | |
| Thompson, Uriah, Pt.... | " | 1778 | | |
| Tann, Jas., Pt.......... | Quinn's | 20 July " | W | Omtd '79 |
| Thompson, Chas., Pt.... | Lt. Col's | " | 9 mo. | |
| Tharp, Jas., Pt........ | " | " | " | |
| Tesley, Jno., Pt........ | " | " | " | Died 24 Oct. '78 |
| Todd, Josiah, Pt........ | Baker's | " | " | |
| Todd, Jno., Pt........ (P. 1173) | " | " | " | |
| Turner, Wm., Pt........ | Baker's | 20 July '78 | 9 mo. | |
| Thomas, Jere, Corpl.... | " | " | " | |
| Tayburn, Allen, Pt...... | " | " | " | Destd 23 July '78 |
| Tann, Eph'm, Pt....... | " | " | " | |
| Thomas, Amos., Pt.... | Blount's | " | " | |
| Tart, Thos., Pt........ | " | " | " | |
| Teder, Thos., Pt........ | Bradley's | " | " | |
| Tinsley, Chas., Pt...... | Child's | " | " | |
| Teal, Eman'l, Pt........ | | " | " | |
| Totteyaine, Winder, Pt.. | Montfort's | | 3 yrs. | Destd Sep. '79 |
| Tharp, Chas., Pt....... | " | 1 June '79 | W | Destd 23 Nov. '79 |
| Tharp, Jno., Pt........ | " | " | " | Do |
| Taylor, Jno., Pt....... | " | 30 " " | " | Destd Sep. '79 |
| Tiney, Jas., Pt........ | Ballard's | 1779 | 9 mo. | Dischgd 1 Dec. '79 |
| Thompkins, Jordan, Pt.. | " | " | " | Do |
| Tucker, Curl, Pt........ | Quinn's | 7 June " | 18 mo. | Sergt. Jan. '80, Corpl. Mar. '80 |
| Taylor, Jese, Pt........ | Blount's | 1 Mar. " | 9 mo. | Dischgd 1 Dec. '79 |
| Tinney, Jno., Pt....... | " | " | " | Do |
| Tunk, Robt., Pt........ | " | 30 May '79 | 18 mo. | Corpl. 1 Dec. '79 |
| Tharp, Eleazer, Pt...... | " | 1 June " | " | Destd Oct. '79 |
| Tomblin, Jno., Pt...... | " | 7 " " | W | Do |
| Turner, Wm., Pt........ | " | 7 " " | " | Do |
| Towel, Ab'm, Pt........ (P. 1173) | " | 5 Aug. " | " | Do |
| Taylor, Sam'l, Pt...... | McRee's | 5 June '81 | 12 mo. | Left service 5 June '82 |
| Tinker, Jno., Pt....... | " | 6 " " | " | Dead Oct. '81 |
| Tysinger, Ad., Pt...... | " | 28 Apr. " | | Destd May '81 |
| Thomas, Philemon, Sergt | Raiford's | 25 May " | " | Left service 18 May '82 |
| Thomas, Thos., Musc... | " | 15 Apr. " | " | Do 15 Apr. '82 |
| Taylor, Jno., Pt....... | " | 4 July " | " | Do 4 July '82 |
| Thomas, Sam'l, Pt...... | " | 19 May " | " | Do 19 May '82 |
| Thomas, Amos., Pt..... | " | 15 Apr. " | " | Do 25 Apr. '82 |
| Tabourne, Joel, Pt...... | Donaho's | 14 June " | " | Mustd for War Jan. '82 |
| Tanner, Jenning, Pt..... | " | " | " | Left service 14 June '82 |

| Name and Rank | Company | Dates of Enlistment and Commission | Period of Service | Occurrences |
|---|---|---|---|---|
| Terrel, Jno., Pt. | Donaho's | 14 June '81 | 12 mo. | Omtd in '81 |
| Thomas, Jas., Pt. (P. 1174) | " | 2 May '81 | " | Left service 2 May '82 |
| Tankesley, Wm., Pt. | Dixon's | 15 May '81 | " | Omtd in '81 |
| Tiffin, Thos., Pt. | " | " | " | Left service 21 May '82 |
| Tipper, Wm., Pt. | " | 12 " " | " | Do 25 May '82 |
| Turpin, Wm., Pt. | Lytle's | 5 Apr. " | " | Omtd in '81 |
| Tabourne, Burrell, Pt. | " | " | " | Left service 5 Apr. '82 |
| Talton, Josiah, Pt. | " | 1 June " | " | Do 1 June '82 |
| Thomaston, Chas., Sergt | Sharp's | 21 May " | | Omtd in '81 |
| Thomas, Stephen, Pt. | " | 2 " " | | Dischgd 1 Feb. '82 |
| Talton, Jas., Pt. | Raiford's | 1781 | | Time out 13 Sep. '82 |
| Thompson, Nichs., Pt. | " | " | | Do Sept. '82 |
| Tillman, Aaron, Pt. (P. 1174) | Moore's | " | | Left service 10 May '82 |
| Teaner, Jas., Pt. | Walton's | 1781 | | Left service 25 May '82 |
| Thomas, Philip, Sergt. | Doherty's | | | |
| Thompson, Sam'l, Corpl. | Rhode's | | | |
| Tucker, Gray, Pt. | Armstrong's | | W | Mustd Jan. '82 |
| Trap, Martin, Pt. | " | | | Mustd War Apr.'82, destd 10 Dec.'82, Joined 14 Dec. '82, Destd 28 May '83 |
| Tims, Jona, Sergt. | Bailey's | 25 May '81 | 12 mo. | Left service 25 May '82 |
| Turner, David, Pt. | Armstrong's | 1781 | | |
| Twigg, Dan'l, Musc. | Bailey's | | 3 yrs. | Mustd Jan. '82 |
| Toxey, Nath'l, Pt. | " | 17 May '81 | 12 mo. | Left service 17 May '82 |
| Thompson, Jese, Pt. | " | 15 Apr. " | " | Do 15 Apr. '82 |
| Turner, Arthur, Pt. | " | 26 July " | " | Do 26 July '82 |
| Thompson, Jno., Sergt. | Brevard's | 1781 | " | Do 21 July '82 |
| Tilley, Jacob, Pt. | " | " | " | Do 21 June '82 |
| Taylor, Emanuel, Pt. | " | " | " | Do 14 Aug. '82 |
| Tucker, Jno., Corpl. | Hall's | " | " | Do 16 Aug. '82 |
| Tice, Henry, Pt. | " | " | " | Time out 15 Apr. '82 |
| Tice, Jas., Pt. | " | " | " | Do 15 Apr. '82 |
| Thompson, Geo., Pt. | " | 1782 | " | Do 15 Jan. '83 |
| Tennison, Absolom, Pt. | Yarboro's | 1781 | " | Do 22 Apr. '82 |
| Thexton, Wm., Pt. | " | " | " | Do 1 May '82 |
| Tucker, Carrel, Pt. | " | " | " | Do 22 Apr. '82 |
| Toney, Jno., Pt. (P. 1174) | " | | | Omtd 1 Apr. '81 |
| Taylor, Benj., Corpl. | Carter's | 3 June '81 | W | |
| Tiller, Thos., Pt. | " | 31 July " | 12 mo. | Time out 28 July '82 |
| Trotman, Thos., Pt. | " | 19 May " | " | Do 19 May '82 |
| Trader, Jona, Pt. | " | " | " | Do 19 May '82 |
| Tomlinson, Aaron, Pt. | Mill's | 3 Jan. '82 | " | |
| Taylor, Lewis, Pt. | " | 22 Oct. '81 | " | |
| Townley, Philemon, Pt. | " | 7 Feb. '82 | " | |
| Tue, Alexr., Pt. | Coleman's | 8 Nov. '81 | W | |
| Trapp, Elijah, Musc. | Hall's | | W | Mustd Apr. '82 |
| Taylor, Benj., Pt. | " | '81 | 12 mo. | |
| Tarlton, Jno., Pt. | Jones' | | W | Mustd 1 Apr. '82, Destd 1 Sep. '82 |
| Taylor, Ab'm, Pt. | " | 1 Mar '82 | 12 mo. | |
| Tice, Thos., Pt. | " | " | " | Sergt. Sep. '82 |
| Thornhill, Benj., Pt. | Mill's | 1 Jan. '82 | " | |
| Tarlton, Josiah, Pt. | Bailey's | 13 Sep. " | 18 mo. | |
| Tranton, Jno., Pt. | " | 10 Sep. " | " | |

| Name and Rank | Company | Dates of Enlistment and Commission | Period of Service | Occurrences |
|---|---|---|---|---|
| **(P. 1175)** | | | | |
| Trader, Jno., Pt....... | Bailey's | 17 Sep. '82 | 18 mo | Destd 21 June '83 |
| Thurston, Wm., Pt..... | " | 10 " " | " | |
| Tennison, Matt'w, Pt... | " | 10 " " | " | Destd 21 June '83 |
| Tan, Drewry, Pt....... | Hadley's | 1 Aug. " | " | |
| Taylor, Jacob, Pt...... | " | " | " | |
| Tarbarra, Sam'l, Pt.... | " | " | " | |
| **(P. 1175)** | | | | |
| Timer, Dan'l, Pt....... | Hadley's | 1 Aug. '82 | 18 mo. | |
| Tippet, Erastus, Musc.. | Bacot's | '82 | " | Destd 15 June '83 |
| Tyson, Ellis, Pt........ | " | " | " | |
| Tyler, Moses, Pt....... | " | " | " | |
| Thompson, Wm., Pt.... | Carter's | " | " | |
| Tobin, Wm., Pt........ | " | " | " | Destd 28 Mar. '82 |
| Tyler, Owen, Pt....... | Raiford's | " | W | |
| Tyner, Wm., Pt....... | " | " | 18 mo. | |
| Trent, Wm., Sergt...... | Sharp's | " | " | |
| Taylor, Chas., Sergt.... | " | " | " | Destd 19 Apr. '83 |
| Taylor, Benj., Corpl.... | " | " | " | Destd 19 Apr. '83 |
| Thompson, Jno., Pt.... | " | " | " | |
| Taylor, Jno., Pt........ | Lytle's | " | " | |
| Taylor, Abel, Pt....... | " | " | " | |
| Taylor, Jas., Pt........ | " | " | " | |
| Tilley, Jacob, Pt....... | " | " | " | |
| Tinney, Sam'l, Pt...... | " | " | " | Omtd Jan. '83 |
| Tucker, Jas., Pt....... | " | " | " | {Destd 10 Dec. '82, Mustd for War Jan. '83 |
| Tucker, Jno., Pt........ | " | " | " | Destd 10 Dec. '82 |
| Thompson, Jno., Pt.... | Brevard's | " | " | |
| Terry, Pompey, Pt..... | " | " | " | Transf'd Mar. '83 |
| Tippet, Geo., Pt........ | " | " | " | |
| Thompson, Wm., Pt... | " | " | " | |
| Talbert, Jno., Pt....... | Evan's | " | " | |
| **(P. 1175)** | | | | |
| Tucker, Jno., Pt....... | " | '82 | 18 mo. | |
| Truett, Wm., Pt....... | " | " | " | Destd 8 June '83 |
| Taylor, Wm., Pt....... | " | " | " | |
| Tyson, Aaron, Pt...... | " | " | " | 21 |
| Turner, Adam, Pt...... | | " | | Mustd '79 |
| Titterton, Jno., Pt..... | | " | | Mustd, destd '79 |
| Tiner, Jesse, Pt........ | Sharp's | 10 Nov. '78 | 9 mo. | Dischgd 13 May '79 |
| Taylor, Sampson, Pt.... | " | " | | |
| Thomas, Jno., Pt....... | " | " | | |
| Thatcher, David, Pt.... | Colonel's | | W | Mustd Jan. '79 |
| Turner, Adam, Pt...... | Major's | | | Do |
| Twigg, Dan'l, Musc..... | Lt. Colo's | | 3 yrs. | Do |
| Tyner, Nich's, Corpl.... | Taylor's | | 2½ yrs. | {Mustd Jan. '79, Dischgd Apr. '79 |
| Tyler, Moses, Musc..... | " | | 3 yrs. | Mustd Jan. '79 |
| Tyner, Arthur, Corpl.... | " | | 2½ yrs. | {Mustd Jan. '79, Dischgd Apr. '79 |
| **V (P. 1179)** | | | | |
| Venters, Dan'l, Pt...... | Stevenson's | 1 Sep. '77 | 3 yrs. | |
| Vanoy, And'w, Capt.... | | | | Omtd June '78 |
| Varcaze, Jas., Lt....... | | 17 Mar. '78 | | {Omtd between Jan. and Sep. '79 |
| Vaughan, Vincent, Pt... | Montfort's | 28 July '76 | 9 mo. | |

| Name and Rank | Company | Dates of Enlistment and Commission | Period of Service | Occurrences |
|---|---|---|---|---|
| Vaisy, Nath'l, Sergt..... (P. 1179) | Hogg's | 28 July '76 | 9 mo. | |
| Vick, Jesse, Sergt....... | " | " | " | |
| Vining, Keeder, Pt...... | Quinn's | " | " | |
| Valentine, Peter, Pt..... | Lt. Colo's | " | " | |
| Van, Nath'n, Pt........ | Blount's | " | " | |
| Vincent, Benj., Pt...... | Ballard's | " | " | |
| Vance, Jas., Pt......... | Child's | " | " | Died 15 Nov. '78 |
| Verrier, Jas., Qr. Mr.... | | Apr. '79 | | Resigned 10 Sep. '79 |
| Vallentine, Dan'l, Pt.... | Bradley's | 7 June " | 18 mo. | |
| Vandergrift, Leonard, Pt | Blount's | " | " | Destd Oct. '79 |
| Vaughn, Wm., Pt....... | McRee's | 9 May '81 | | Destd 1 July '81 |
| Vincen, David, Pt..... | Raiford's | 18 " " | | Died Oct. '81 |
| Vines, Jno., Corpl....... | Sharp's | 15 Apr. " | 12 mo. | Left service 15 Apr. '82 |
| Vollow, Nich's, Pt..... | Doherty's | 1781 | | Time out 25 May '82 |
| Vick, Joseph, Pt........ | Rhode's | " | | Do 16 July '82 |
| Vickny, Jno., Pt....... | Armstrong's | | W | Mustd Jan. '82 |
| Vaughan, Wm., Pt..... | Brevard's | '81 | | Left service 9 May, '82 |
| Varder, David, Pt..... | Hall's | " | 12 mo. | Time out 1 Aug. '82 |
| Vaughan, Dan'l, Corpl. . | Carter's | 19 May " | " | Died 26 Sep. '81 |
| Vines, Jno., Pt........ | Mill's | 19 Dec. " | " | |
| Vines, Sam'l, Pt....... | " | " | " | |
| Vance, David, Pt....... | Carter's | 1782 | 18 mo. | |
| Vaison, Lem'l, Pt...... | " | " | " | |
| Vick, Jacob, Sergt..... | " | " | " | |
| Vicas, Thos., Pt........ | Lytle's | " | " | Music 1 Dec. '82 |
| Vickery, Marma., Pt.... (P. 1179) | " | " | " | Died 14 Dec. '82 |
| Vaughan, Ab'm, Pt..... | " | " | " | |
| Vickery, Luke, Pt....... | Brevard's | | | |
| Vose, Joseph, Pt....... | | 25 May '81 | W | Died 10 July '83 |
| Vaughn, Jno., Pt....... | Goodwin's | | " | Mustd Mar. '79 |
| **W** (P. 1187) | | | | |
| Wilson, Jas., Capt..... | | 19 Apr. '77 | | Resigned 20 May '78 |
| Wilkerson, Jno., Sergt... | Wilson's | 29 May " | 3 yrs. W | Pt. June '78, Destd Apr. '79 |
| Wilkerson, Wm., Pt.... | " | " | " | |
| Wiset, Jas., Pt......... | " | 5 Oct. " | | Omtd June '78 |
| Walker, Wm., Pt....... | Shepard's | 4 Sep. " | 3 yrs. | Destd 24 Mar. '79 |
| Weaver, Jno., Pt....... | | 3 July " | " | |
| White, Jacob, Jr., Musc. | Stevenson's | 21 Apr. " | " | Mustd for War Jan. '82 |
| White, Joseph, Sen'r., Pt. | " | " | " | Prisr. June, '79, Dischged 1 Mar. '80 |
| Webb, Joseph, Pt...... | " | 20 May '77 | " | Omtd June '78 |
| Webb, Jno., Pt........ | " | 1 Sep. " | | |
| Wiggins, Jas., Pt...... | " | 12 Aug. " | | |
| Wareley, Jno., Musc.... | " | 1 " " | " | Drumr. Major 6 Aug. '78, Drum Sep. '78 |
| Wigley, Thos., Sergt. ... | Gregory's | 30 Sep. " | " | Pt. June '78 |
| Williams, Zebede., Pt.... (P. 1187) | " | 30 May " | " | |
| Wright, David, Ensn.... | Moore's | 19 Apr. '77 | | Lt. 15 Feb. '78, Resigned 5 Feb. '80 |
| Williams, Jas., Sergt.... | " | 11 June " | 3 yrs. | Corpl. June '78, Died 24 Sep. '78 |
| Williams, Spencer, Sergt. | " | 20 " " | " | Destd Apr. '78 |
| Woodley, Thos., Pt.... | " | 17 May " | " | Omtd June '78 |

| Name and Rank | Company | Dates of Enlistment and Commission | Period of Service | Occurrences |
|---|---|---|---|---|
| Wood, Edw., Pt........ | Moore's | 1 June '77 | 3 yrs. | Dischgd 1 Aug. '78 |
| Williams, Wm., Pt...... | " | 20 " " | " | Prisr. 14 Apr. '79 |
| Williams, Joseph, Pt.... | " | 20 " " | " | Pris. Apr.'79, Mustd Nov. |
| Williams, Peter, Pt..... | " | 30 " " | " | '79, Mustd 27 Mar. '80 Corpl. Mar. '79, Sergt. 1 Feb. '80 |
| Winham, Jno., Pt....... | " | 30 June '77 | | Destd Apr. '78 |
| Ward, Rich'd, Sergt..... | Vanois' | 28 Apr. " | | Omtd June |
| Wilkins, Andw., Pt...... | " | 2 May " | 3 yrs. | Destd 15 Mar. '79 |
| Wyatt, Jas., Pt........ | | 2 Oct. " | 3 yrs. W | Corpl. Apr. '83, Destd 15 June '83 |
| White, Wm., Pt....... | | 1 Jan. '78 | " | Destd 8 Mar. '79 |
| Waters, Jno., Pt........ | | 15 Nov. '77 | 3 yrs. | Dischgd 1 Feb. '80 |
| Wiggins, Malachi, Pt.... | | 10 Oct. " | " | |
| Willford, Lewis, Pt..... | | 25 Aug. " | 3 yrs. W | |
| Wooten, Jesse, Pt....... | | 4 Apr. '76 | 2½ yrs. | Dischgd 30 Oct. '78 |
| Wallis, Jno., Pt........ | | 4 June '77 | 3 yrs. W | Prisr. 2 June '79 |
| Williams, Wm., Pt...... | | 5 May '76 | 2½ yrs. | Dischgd 10 Nov. '78 |
| (P. 1187) | | | | |
| Wall, Joel, Pt.......... | | 7 Aug. '77 | 3 yrs. | Sergt. Apr.'78, Pt. June'78 |
| Williams, Morson, Pt. .. | | | " | Mustd June '78, Dischgd 30 Oct. '78 |
| Whaley, Ezl., Pt....... | | 20 July '77 | 3 yrs. W | Mustd June '78, Music, Sep. '78 |
| White, Joseph, Cadet... | | 13 Aug. '77 | | Omtd Feb. '78 |
| Wallace, Jas., Lt....... | | 30 Nov. '78 | | Omtd between Jan. and Sep. '79 |
| (P. 1188) | | | | |
| Williams, Jacob, Pt..... | Montfort's | 20 July '78 | 9 mo. | |
| Wheelis, Sion, Pt....... | " | " | " | |
| Worley, Matt'w, Pt..... | " | " | " | |
| Wilkins, Elisha, Pt..... | " | " | " | |
| Watson, Miles, Pt...... | " | " | " | |
| Whites, Batson, Pt...... | Hogg's | " | " | Died 12 Sep. '78 |
| Whatson, Ephm., Pt.... | | " | " | |
| Wiggins, Jas., Pt....... | | " | " | |
| Williams, Alex'r, Pt.... | | " | " | |
| Watson, Solomon, Pt.... | | " | " | |
| Worsley, Thos., Corpl... | Quinn's | " | " | |
| Whaley, John, Musc.... | " | " | " | |
| Whaley, Francis, Musc.. | " | " | " | |
| Watson, Neal, Pt....... | " | " | " | |
| Wood, Aaron, Pt....... | " | " | " | |
| Warwick, Jno., Pt...... | " | " | " | |
| Wilson, Jno., Pt........ | Lt. Col's | " | " | |
| (P. 1188) | | | | |
| Ward, Joseph, Pt...... | " | " | " | |
| Wiggins, Thos., Pt...... | " | " | " | |
| Woodward, Caleb, Pt. .. | " | " | " | |
| Wilkerson, Wm., Pt..... | " | " | " | Died Sep. '78 |
| White, Jno., Pt......... | Baker's | 6 Mar. '77 | 3 yrs. | Omtd '79 |
| Wadkins, Jno., Pt....... | " | 20 July '78 | 9 mo. | |
| White, Wm., Pt........ | Blount's | " | " | |
| Watford, Wm., Pt...... | " | " | " | |
| Weston, Amos., Pt...... | " | " | " | |
| Williams, Jno., Pt...... | " | " | " | |
| White, Peter, Pt........ | " | " | " | |

| Name and Rank | Company | Dates of Enlistment and Commission | Period of Service | Occurrences |
|---|---|---|---|---|
| White, Jas., Pt. | Blount's | 20 July '78 | 9 mo. | |
| Wiggins, Edw'd, Pt. | " | " | " | |
| Wilday, Absolom, Pt. | " | " | " | {Re-enlisted 3 June '79, Corpl. for 18 Mos. |
| White, Burrall, Pt. | " | " | " | Omtd Oct. '78 |
| Whorton, Jacob, Pt. | " | " | " | |
| Wilson, Edw'd, Pt. | " | " | " | |
| Wilkins, Jordon, Corpl. | Ballard's | " | " | |
| Williford, Willis, Pt. | " | " | " | |
| Weather, Jno., Pt. | " | " | " | |
| Ward, Elijah, Pt. | " | " | " | |
| White, Haines, Pt. | " | " | " | {Destd 30 Aug. '78, Mustd Nov. '78 for War |
| Whitley, Thos., Musc... (P. 1188) | Bradley's | " | " | Omtd '79 |
| West, Ciprian, Pt. | " | 20 July '78 | 9 mo. | |
| Webb, Jas., Pt. | " | " | " | |
| Wright, O. Prince, Pt. | Child's | " | " | Omtd '79 |
| Wilson, Jno., Pt. | " | " | " | |
| Worsley, Jno., Pt. | " | " | " | |
| Wailard, Jas., Pt. | " | " | " | |
| Wallace, Rich'd, Pt. | " | " | " | |
| Walker, S. Rich'd, Sgt. Maj... (P. 1189) | | 7 June '79 | " | |
| Wells, Uriah, Pt. | Bradley's | 8 " '78 | 18 mo. | Omtd Oct. '79 |
| Warwick, Shadrach, Cpl. | Montfort's | 1 Nov. " | 3 yrs. | |
| Willoughby, Jas., Pt. | " | 24 June '79 | W | |
| Willoughby, Jno., Pt. | " | " | " | Music 1 Nov. '79 |
| Wiggins, Chs., Pt. | " | 1 " " | 18 mo. | Destd 12 Nov. '79 |
| Wilcox, David, Pt. | " | 15 " " | W | Omtd Oct. '79 |
| Walker, Thos., Pt. | " | 1 July " | 18 mo. | Destd 21 Oct. '79 |
| Ward, Rich'd, Pt. | " | 1 Mar. " | 9 mo. | Dischgd 1 Dec. '79 |
| Wilson, Thos., Sergt. | Ballard's | 15 June " | 18 mo. | Pt. Oct. '79, destd Mar.'80 |
| White, Elisha, Pt. | " | 29 June " | W | Omtd Oct. '79 |
| Ward, Isaac, Pt. | " | 1 July " | 18 mo. | {Pt. 1 Oct. '79 Destd Mar. '80 |
| Wilkins, Wm., Pt. | " | 12 Aug. " | W | Omtd Oct. '80 |
| Ward, Ludwick, Pt. | " | 29 June " | " | Destd 5 Aug. '79 |
| Wilson, Henry, Pt. | " | 1 July " | 12 mo. | Destd Aug. '79 |
| Wodle, Jacob, Sergt. (P. 1189) | Quinn's | 24 June " | 18 mo. | Omtd Oct. '79 |
| Williams, Gilstrap, Cpl. | Quinn's | 22 June '79 | 18 mo. | Pt. Mar. '79 |
| Wheelor, David, Musc. | " | 23 May " | " | |
| Wiggins, Thos., Pt. | " | 26 June " | " | |
| Womble, Jno., Pt. | " | 1 " " | W | |
| Williams, Jas., Pt. | Blount's | 8 " " | 18 mo. | |
| Walker, Wm., Pt. | " | 3 Aug. " | 3 yrs. | |
| Warner, Hardin, Pt. | " | 1 Oct. " | W | |
| Wright, Micaja, Pt. | " | 22 June " | " | Destd Oct. '79 |
| Walker, Jas., Pt. | " | 5 Aug. " | | Do |
| Wood, Jesse, Pt. | " | 14 " " | | Do |
| Wood, Thos., Pt. | " | " | " | Do |
| Walters, Walters, Pt. | | 1779 | 9 mo. | Died 30 Aug. '79 |
| Wells, Isaac, Pt. | | " | " | Destd Sep. '79 |
| Wood, Joseph, Pt. | | " | " | Do |
| White, Geo., Pt. | | " | " | Do |

| Name and Rank | Company | Dates of Enlistment and Commission | Period of Service | Occurrences |
|---|---|---|---|---|
| Wallace, Thos., Pt. | McRee's | 15 Apr. '81 | 12 mo. | Dead Oct. '81 |
| White, Chrisr., Pt. | " | 9 May " | " | Transf'd July '81 to the Legion |
| Wood, Jno., Pt. | " | 28 Apr. " | " | Destd 13 July '81 |
| White, Thos., Pt. | " | " " | " | Omtd Jan. '82, Sick |
| Wilson, Thos., Pt. | " | 11 June " | " | Left service 11 May '82 |
| Woodruff, Jno., Pt. | Raiford's | 5 May " | " | Killed 8 Sep. '81 |
| Ward, Benj., Pt. | " | 1781 | " | Dead, Nov. '81 |
| Wise, Jesse, Pt. | " | | | Time out 1 Apr. '82 |
| Wilkins, Burrel, Pt. | " | 25 Apr. '81 | " | Dead Nov. '81 |
| (P. 1189) | | | | |
| Weaver, Dan'l, Pt. | Raiford's | 26 June '81 | 12 mo. | Left service 26 June '82 |
| Weaver, Benj., Pt. | " | 25 Apr. " | " | Do 25 Apr. '82 |
| Winbern, Philip, Pt. | " | 19 May " | " | Do 19 May '82 |
| Wilson, Joseph, Pt. | " | 17 " " | " | Do 15 Apr. '82 |
| West, Wm., Pt. | " | 18 " " | " | Do 18 May '82 |
| Wildie, Absolom, Pt. | " | 6 " " | " | Do 16 Apr. '82 |
| White, Philip, Pt. | Donoho's | 14 " " | " | Do 14 June '82 |
| Wade, Wm., Pt. | " | 14 " " | " | |
| Wilkins, Elijah, Pt. | " | 14 " " | " | Corpl. Jan., Left service 25 Apr. '82 |
| (P. 1190) | | | | |
| Wallis, Jno., Pt. | " | 25 " " | " | Left service 25 May '82 |
| Warf, Geo., Pt. | " | 14 June " | " | |
| Westbrook, Wm., Pt. | " | " " | " | |
| Wood, Sampson, Pt. | " | 25 May " | " | |
| Wallis, Jas., Pt. | " | " " | " | |
| Williams, Wm., Pt. | Dixon's | 25 Apr. " | " | |
| Womble, Dempy, Pt. | " | | | |
| Walker, Jereh, Sergt. | Lytle's | 7 Apr. " | " | Left service 7 Apr. '82 |
| Ward, Jno., Pt. | " | 1781 | W | |
| Woodert, Henry, Pt. | " | 6 June '81 | 12 mo. | Left service 6 June '82 |
| Williams, Allenby, Pt. | " | 1 " " | " | Do 6 June '82 |
| Wheelow, H. Edw'd, Pt. | " | 2 Apr. " | | Destd 12 July '81 |
| (P. 1190) | | | | |
| Woodrow, H. Edw'd, Pt. | " | 1781 | | |
| Walker, Jno., Pt. | " | 12 Apr. " | 12 mo. | Left service 5 Apr. '82 |
| Wilbourne, Zach., Pt. | " | 5 " " | | Do Do |
| Walden, David, Pt. | Sharp's | 2 May " | | Omtd in '81 |
| Wall, Jno., Pt. | " | 15 Apr. " | | Do |
| Wilson, Wm., Pt. | " | " " | " | Left service 15 Apr. '82 |
| Wilkins, Thos., Pt. | " | " " | | Do Do |
| Watts, Jno., Pt. | Walton's | '81 | | Time out 14 June '82 |
| White, Hampton, Pt. | " | " | " | Do 14 June '82 |
| Wiggins, Jas., Pt. | Lytle's | | " | Do 12 Apr. '82 |
| Wilcox, Benj., Pt. | Sharp's | | " | Do 20 May '82 |
| Wells, Jno., Pt. | " | | W | Mustd Jan. '82 |
| Weaver, Edw'd, Pt. | " | | " | Time out 15 May '82 |
| Wood, Jno., Pt. | " | | " | Do 25 Apr. '82 Waggon Conductor |
| Williford, Theo., Pt. | " | | " | Time out 24 June '82 |
| Williams, Nichs., Corpl. | Doherty's | | " | Do 25 May '82 |
| Waddle, Jas., Corpl. | " | | " | Do 25 May '82 |
| Walden, Jno., Pt. | " | | " | Do Do |
| Warwick, Wyatt, Pt. | " | | " | Do Do |
| Williams, Sam'l, Pt. | " | | " | Do Do |
| Welsh, Theo., Pt. | " | | " | Do Do |

| Name and Rank | Company | Dates of Enlistment and Commission | Period of Service | Occurrences |
|---|---|---|---|---|
| Wiggins, Levy, Musc.... (P. 1190) | Doherty's | '81 | W | Mustd Jan. '82, Pt. Apl. '82 |
| Wilson, Wm., Pt........ | Rhode's | 1781 | | Time out 25 Apr. '82 |
| Woodle, Jos., Pt........ | " | " | | Do    21 July '82 |
| Woodle, Jereh, Pt...... | " | " | | Do    Do |
| Wheelor, Benj., Pt...... | " | " | | Do    14 May '82 |
| Wilder, Wm., Pt........ | " | " | | Do    Do |
| Wood, Jno., Pt......... | " | " | | Do    1 Apr. '82 |
| Williams, Peter, Sergt... | Armstrong's | | W | Mustd Jan. '82 |
| Whiteley, Micajah, Pt... | " | | | Time out 23 Apr. '82 |
| Wells, Isaac, Pt........ | Bailey's | 15 May '81 | 12 mo. | Left service 15 May '82 |
| Ward, Willis, Pt........ | " | 2 Apr.  " | " | Do    2 Apr. '82 |
| Webb, Jacob, Pt........ | " | 12   "   " | " | Do    12 Apr. '82 |
| Webb, Rice, Pt......... (P. 1191) | " | "   "   " | " | Do    12 Apr. '82 |
| Wiley, Jas., Pt......... | " | 2 May  " | " | Left service 2 May '82 |
| Workman, Peter, Pt..... | Brevard's | 1781 | " | Do    28 Apr. '82 |
| Warren, Jno., Pt........ | " | " | " | Do    12 Apr. '82 |
| Warren, Archbd, Pt..... | " | " | " | Do    Do |
| Welch, Wm., Pt........ | " | | W | Mustd Jan. '82 |
| Wilson, Robt., Pt....... | " | | | Left service 20 May '82 |
| Weaks, Dixon, Pt....... | " | | | Do    11 July '82 |
| Winters, Moses, Pt..... | " | | | Do    12 July '82 |
| Williams, Nath'l, Pt..... | Hall's | | | Mustd Jan. '82 |
| Wilcox, Jno., Pt........ | " | | W | {Mustd Jan. '82, {Destd 9 June '83 |
| Warburton, Solomon, Pt. (P. 1191) | " | '81 | 12 mo. | Time out 21 Apr. '82 |
| Williams, Mich'l, Pt.... | " | " | " | Destd 1 Apr. '82 |
| Wilkins, Geo., Pt...... | " | " | " | Time out 13 Dec. '82 |
| Weathers, Philip, Pt.... | " | " | " | Do    12 Apr. '82 |
| Williams, Stephen, Sergt. | Yarboro's | " | " | Do    22 Apr. '82 |
| Wilkerson, Wm., Corpl.. | " | | " | Do    1 May '82 |
| Wood, Isaac, Pt........ | " | | " | Do    22 Apr. '82 |
| Wilkerson, Jno., Pt..... | " | | " | Do    25 May '82 |
| Williamson, Wm., Pt.... | " | | " | Do    16 May '82 |
| Winley, Jas., Sergt...... | Carter's | 15 Apr. '81 | " | Do    25 Apr. '82 |
| White, Church, Pt...... | " | 16 May  " | " | Do    16 May '82 |
| Waggoner, Jas., Pt..... | " | 1781 | " | Died 25 Feb. '82 |
| Whitson, Benj., Pt...... | " | | | Destd 15 Sep. '81 |
| Weaks, Lewis, Sergt..... | Jones' | 1 Jan. '82 | " | |
| Wood, Wm., Pt........ | " | 6 Mar.  " | " | |
| Williams, Jno., Pt...... | " | 10 Jan.  " | " | |
| Weston, Jno., Pt........ | " | 24 Sep. '81 | " | |
| Williamson, Adam, Cpl.. | Mill's | 6 Feb. '82 | " | |
| Waters, Solomon, Musc. | " | "   " | W | Pt. Sep. '82 |
| Wall, Rich'd, Pt........ | " | 4 Jan. '82 | 12 mo. | |
| West, Meredith, Pt.... | " | 22 Dec. '81 | " | |
| Weble, Jno., Pt......... | " | 20 Jan. '82 | " | |
| Williams, Edw'd, Pt..... | " | 25   "   " | " | {Mustd War Sep. '82, {died 28 Mar. '83 |
| Williams, Robt., Pt..... (P. 1191) | " | 25 May '81 | " | |
| Wright, Ab'm, Sergt.... | Coleman's | 1 Dec. '81 | 12 mo. | Pt. Apr. '82 |
| Williams, David, Pt..... | " | 10 Jan. '82 | " | |
| Wiggins, Wm., Pt....... | " | 1 Jan.  " | " | |
| Wheeler, Asa, Pt...... | " | 10 Jan.  " | " | Corpl. Sep. '82 |

| Name and Rank | Company | Dates of Enlistment and Commission | Period of Service | Occurrences |
|---|---|---|---|---|
| Wilson, Jas., Pt......... | Coleman's | 1 June '81 | 12 mo. | |
| Wilkins, Kinchin, Pt.... | " | 27 Nov. " | " | |
| White, Benj., Pt........ | Hall's | | W | Mustd Apr. '82 |
| Williams, Robt., Pt..... | " | 1 Jan. '82 | 12 mo. | Time out 1 Jan. '83 |
| Wilcox, David, Pt...... | " | 10 Oct. " | W | Destd 9 June '83 |
| Watson, Lott, Pt....... | " | 1 Aug. " | " | |
| White, Edw'd, Pt....... | Jones' | 1 Apr. " | 12 mo. | |
| Wallace, Thos., Sergt.... | Bailey's | " | " | |
| White, Wm., Pt........ | " | 22 Oct. '82 | | |
| Wiggins, Matt'w, Pt.... (P. 1192) | " | 10 Sep. " | 18 mo. | |
| Wiggins, Arthur, Pt..... | " | " | " | |
| Woodward, Edward, Pt. | " | 27 Aug. '82 | " | |
| Watson, Alex'r, Pt...... | " | 12 Mar. " | 12 mo. | |
| Watson, Neal, Pt....... | " | 1 Aug. " | " | |
| Walker, Solomon, Pt.... | " | 18 June " | " | |
| Warburton, Thos., Pt... | " | 1 Aug. " | 18 mo. | |
| Welch, C. Noah, Pt..... | Hadley's | " | " | Died 21 Apr. '82 |
| Woodell, Jno., Pt...... | " | " | " | |
| William, Francis, Pt.... | " | " | " | |
| Warren, Sam'l, Pt..... (P. 1192) | " | " | " | |
| Wainwright, Obdh., Pt.. | Hadley's | 1 Aug. '82 | 18 mo. | Died 13 June '83 |
| Watkins, Benj., Pt..... | " | " | " | |
| Wilkins, Thos., Pt..... | " | " | " | |
| Williford Arch'd, Pt.... | " | 10 Sep. " | " | |
| White, Geo., Pt....... | " | " | " | |
| Webb, Sam'l, Pt....... | " | 1 Aug. '82 | " | |
| White, Wm., Pt........ | " | " | " | Died 26 May '83 |
| Williams, Benj., Pt..... | Bacot's | 1782 | " | |
| White, Jno., Pt........ | " | " | " | |
| Williams, Coleden, Pt... | " | " | " | |
| Worsley, Leman, Pt..... | " | " | " | |
| Whitley, Micajah, Pt.... | " | " | " | |
| Wheeler, David, Corpl... | Carter's | " | " | |
| Webb, Lewis, Musc..... | " | " | " | |
| Wade, Elisha, Pt...... | " | " | " | |
| Woodward, David, Pt... | " | " | " | |
| Worrell, Jno., Pt....... | " | " | " | |
| Williams, Wm., Pt..... | " | " | " | |
| Williams, Seth, Pt..... | " | " | " | Destd 20 Jan. '83 |
| Wright, Ewel, Pt...... | " | " | " | |
| Waller, Nath'l, Pt..... | " | " | " | |
| Whittaker, Robt., Pt.... | " | " | " | |
| Witwell, Thos., Pt..... (P. 1192) | " | " | " | Destd 10 Nov. '82 |
| Womble, Benj., Pt..... | Raiford's | 1782 | 18 mo. | Destd 11 June '83 |
| Whitfield, Willis, Pt..... | " | " | " | |
| Walker, Wm., Pt...... | " | " | " | |
| Williams, Stephen, Pt... | " | " | " | |
| West, Sam'l, Pt....... | " | " | " | |
| Wilson, Thos., Pt...... | Sharp's | " | " | {Transf'd to Penna. 8 Feb. '83 |
| Ward, Wm., Pt........ | " | 1782 | " | |
| Wilson, Jno., Pt....... | " | " | " | |
| Whitman, Fred'k, Pt.... | " | " | " | Destd 13 June '83 |

| Name and Rank | Company | Dates of Enlistment and Commission | Period of Service | Occurrences |
|---|---|---|---|---|
| West, Jas., Pt.......... | Sharp's | 1782 | 18 mo. | |
| Wynn, Ezkl., Pt....... | " | " | " | |
| Widener, Sam'l, Corpl... | Lytle's | " | " | |
| Wade, Jno., Pt........ | " | " | " | |
| Wall, Jona, Pt......... | " | " | " | |
| Wallace, Aaron, Pt...... | " | " | " | Destd 15 May '83 |
| Williford, Jas., Pt....... | Hadley's | 10 Sep. " | " | |
| (P. 1193) | | | | |
| Wiggins, Elisha, Pt..... | Lytle's | 1782 | " | |
| Williams, Jereh, Pt..... | " | " | " | |
| Wilton, Jas., Pt........ | " | " | " | |
| Witt, Berge, Pt........ | " | " | " | |
| Williams, Dudley, Pt.... | " | " | " | Omtd Jan. '78, dead |
| Wilford, Arch'd, Pt..... | " | " | " | |
| Wilson, Robt., Pt...... | " | " | " | Destd 25 Nov. '82 |
| (P. 1193) | | | | |
| Whitehead, Jno., Pt..... | Brevard's | 1782 | 18 mo. | |
| Ward, Elijah, Pt........ | Evans' | " | " | |
| White, David, Pt....... | " | " | " | |
| White, Churchill, Pt.... | " | " | " | |
| Walter, Jereh, Pt....... | " | " | " | Omtd Jan, '83, destd |
| Whitehouse, Anty, Pt... | " | " | " | |
| White, Benj., Pt....... | " | " | " | Omtd Jan. '83, dead |
| Wood, Willis, Pt........ | " | 1 Aug. '82 | " | |
| Winborn, Jno., Pt..... | | | | Mustd, destd '79 |
| Wheeler, Emperor, Pt... | | | 3 yrs. | Mustd '79 |
| Wood, Bennett, Pt...... | Bacot's | | 18 mo. | {Mustd Dec. '82, Dischgd 13 Dec. '83 |
| Williams, Nich's, Pt..... | Sharp's | | " | {Mustd Dec. '83, Destd 29 Mar. '83 |
| Wardsworth, Wm., Pt... | Rhode's | | " | Mustd Dec. '82 |
| White, Timothy, Musc.. | Sharp's | '79 | " | Dischgd 20 Mar. '79 |
| Wiggins, Geo., Pt...... | " | 10 Nov. '78 | 9 mo. | |
| Wood, Jas., Pt......... | Coleman's | | | Joined 28 Mar. '80 |
| Williams, Geo., Sergt.... | Colonel's | 1 June '79 | 18 mo. | |
| Williams, Wm., Pt...... | " | " | " | |
| Whitehead, Wm., Pt.... | " | | 2½ yrs. | Mustd Feb. '79 |
| Wicker, Willis, Sergt.... | Lt. Colonel's | | | Mustd Jan. '79 |

The following volumes have been checked.   Some of these being used:

North Carolina Revolutionary Army Accounts, Vol. I.   Old Series Vol. 1, Nos. 1-5.

North Carolina Revolutionary Army Accounts, Vol. II.   Old Series Vol. 1, No. 2-6; Vol. 2, Nos. 7-10.

North Carolina Revolutionary Army Accounts, Vol. III.   Old Series Vol. 3.   Journal of Commissioners.

North Carolina Revolutionary Army Accounts, Vol. IV.   Old Series Vol. 4.   Remarks of Commissioners.

North Carolina Revolutionary Army Accounts, Vol. V.   Old Series Vol. 5-L; Book No. 11 & 175 to 180.

North Carolina Revolutionary Army Accounts, Vol. VI.   Old Series Vol. 6.   Books 21-25.

North Carolina Revolutionary Army Accounts, Vol. VII.   Old Series Vol. 6.   Books 26-90.   Old Series Vol. 7, Books C13, C17, G16, G17.

North Carolina Revolutionary Army Accounts, Vol. VIII.   Old Series Vol. 7, Book 18; Vol. 8, Books E, F; No. 1, F; No. 2, K.

North Carolina Revolutionary Army Accounts, Vol. IX.   Old Series Vol. 9.   Books L, Nos. 1, 2, 3, P. 39, L 26; Vol. 10, Books 12, 14, 17.

North Carolina Revolutionary Army Accounts, Vol. X.   Old Series Vol. 10.   Books 18 and 19; Vol. 14 Commissioners Statements A, B, C.

North Carolina Revolutionary Army Accounts, Vol. XI.   Old Series Vol. 12; Books A1, A2, A11, AM15, AM16.

North Carolina Revolutionary Army Accounts, Vol. XII.   Old Series Vol. 13; Books AA-ZZ.

Three books of Land warrants were also used.   Vols. I, II, III *Military Land Warrants Continental Line.*

NOTE—All 12 volumes were searched.   Some are not used, on account of insufficient explanation.   Only service for militia, and war being used.   A great volume of names had to be omitted, who did receive money for various purposes, but unless the record plainly showed military service it was deemed inexpedient to use them.

NOTE—Spelling of names has been faithfully followed, according to the old books and pamphlets, it may be noted instances occur when a name will be spelled several different ways.   However, it was not deemed wise to change them in any way.

# NORTH CAROLINA REVOLUTIONARY
# ARMY ACCOUNTS

VOL. II. OLD SERIES, VOL. I, No. 6; VOL. II, No. 7-10. BOOK A.A.
VOL. II. PAGES 1-44 INCLUSIVE

[Page 1]
[Folio page 3]
Halifax, July 25th, 1783.

Journal of the proceedings of the Commissioners appointed by Act of Assembly passed in May, 1783, to liquidate and finally settle the accounts of the officers & soldiers of the Continental Line, of the State of North Carolina.

\* \* \* \* \* \*

NOTE—Vol. I, North Carolina Army Accounts, Old Series Vol. I, Nos. 1-5. Paid by John Armstrong. (No remarks to tell the status or service of the persons whose names are within the book, hence it is omitted from the Roster.)

## Vol. II. Book A.A.—Pages 1-44 Inclusive

[Page 2]
[Folio page 1]
Col. John Armstrong
Lt. Anthony Crutcher
Maj. John Nelson
Capt. Howell Tatum (resigned)
Sergt. Peter Dimnneuck (?)
James West Green
Lt. William Hargrove
Capt. Thomas Armstrong
[Folio page 2]
Capt. John Craddock
Col. Thomas Polk
Maj. William Polk
Capt. Edward Yarbrough
Lt. Stephen Slade
Willoughby Jarvis, common soldier
William Witherington, common soldier
[Folio page 3]
Thomas Camphill, common soldier
William Thompson, common soldier
Thomas Moncriefs, common soldier
William Parr, common soldier
Tho. Fletcher, common soldier
Jolly Holstead, common soldier
Jacob Dunn, common soldier
[Page 4]
Richard Flora, common soldier
Absolom Ellis, common soldier
William Farrell, common soldier
Richard Downman, common soldier
Capt. James Brantley
Lt. Howell Gee
[Page 3]
Lt. Alexander Nelson
William Reasons

Capt. John McNees
Henry Horne, common soldier
Henry Overstreet, common soldier
Zachariah Dillard, common soldier
William Bools, common soldier
Jesse Bools, common soldier
Jesse Bools, common soldier
Capt. Thomas Evans
James Bond, common soldier
John Lockhart, Q. M. Sergt.
David Edwards, Sergt.
Lt. James Scurlock
Howell Truman, common soldier
Micajah Hicks, common soldier
Abraham Moses, common soldier
Jesse Camphill, common soldier
Charles Cole, common soldier
Absolom Bibboy, common soldier
Lazarus Solomon, common soldier
[Page 4]
Wm. Barksdale, Sold.
John Guthrie, Sold.
Capt. Joseph Montfort
Phil. Adams, Sold.
James Allen, Sold.
Lenl. Carter, Sold.
William Orange, Sold.
Peter Parker, Sold.
Lt. Richard Andrews
Thomas Holt, Sold.
James Evans, Sold.
William Bynum, Sold.
Capt. Robert Fenner
Isum Scott, Sold.
Robt. Hill, Sold.
Benjamin McCulsury (?), Sold.

John Coleman, Sold.
Andrew Parks, Sold.
James Parker, Sergt.
  [Page 3]
William Bryan, Sold.
William Sweat, Sold.
John Smith, Sold.
Jesse Shutes, Sold.
Joseph Corways, Sold.
Jeptha Parker, Sergt.
Gardner Moy, Sold.
Giles Nelson, Sold.
  [Folio page 4]
Burrell Lucy, Sold.
Thomas Merritt, Sold.
William Riggins, Sold.
William Durham, Sold.
Edmund Griffin, Sold.
Capt. James Gee
Peter Duncan, Sold.
Wm. Graham, Sergt.
Simon Acock, Sold.
  [Page 5]
  [Folio page 1]
William Lomax, Sold.
John Hedgepeth, Sold.
Edward Griffin, Sold.
Jacob Ginn, Sold.
Emanuel Taylor, Sold.
Robt. Brown, Sold.
Francis Westerdhal, Sold.
Ezekiel Whaley, Sold.
Patrick Ryan, Sergt.
  [Folio page 2]
Dempsey Reed, Sold.
James Read, Capt.
Col. James Thackston
John Asply, Sergt.-Majr.
Capt. John Welch
William Kendoll, Sold.
Willam Rowland, Sold.
Philip Shackler, Sold.
  [Folio page 3]
John Etheridge, Sold.
John Wood, Sergt.
John Bertie, Sold.
Jacob White, Sold.
Major Glanders, Sergt.
Jacob White, Drummer
William Anderson, Corpl.
William Parker, Sold.
Griffin Morris, Sold.
  [Folio page 4]
Thomas Hadaway, Sold.
John Mitchell, Sold.

Spencer, Thomas, Sold.
Moses, Mathews, Sold.
Shadrack Scarbrough, Sold.
George Knight, Sold.
Etheldred Owens, Sold.
  [Folio page 6]
  [Page 1]
Simon Edwards, Sold.
Henry Gay, Sold.
Richard Gay, Sold.
John Hanbury, Sold.
George Aron, Sold.
Isaac Aron, Sold.
Isam Scott, Sold.
  [Page 2]
Lt. Thomas Finney, Sold.
Capt. Benjamine Williams
Lt. John Clendennin
Charles Edwards, Sold.
Lt. James Tatum
Joshua Gammon, Sold.
John Strickland, Sold.
  [Page 3]
Willis Hodges, Sold.
Calep (?) Rafield, Sold.
Moses Powers, Sold.
Absolom Powers, Sergt.
James Sykes, Sold.
Thomas Culloms, Sold.
Jesse Alsobrook, Sold.
  [Page 4]
William McCoran, Sold.
Shadrick Midlen, Corpl.
Stephen Arane, Sold.
Reuben Bennett, Sold.
Thomas Swinney, Sold.
Ferney Southall, Sold.
Lewis Ballard, Corpl.
Wm. Smith, Sold.
  [Folio page 1]
  [Page 7]
Wm. Smith, Sold.
John Barrot, Sold.
Samuel Lentex, Sergt.
Robert Harris, Sold.
Richard Smith, Sold.
Wm. Carter, Sold.
Elisha Wilkens, Capt.
Thomas Duffell, Sold.
  [Page 2]
Lt. John Ford
James Jones, Sold.
William Williamson, Sold.
John Archer, Sold.
Emanuel Scott, Sold.

William Vaughan, Sold.
Robert Thompson, Sold.
  [Page 3]
Tobiah Ingram, Sold.
Richard Thompson, Sold.
John Glover, Sold.
Samuel Stringer, Sergt.
Daniel Johnson, Sold.
Mark Browning
John Hill, Sold.
  [Folio page 4]
William Patterson, Sold.
William Dempsey, Sold.
Asa Sircey, Sold.
Capt. John Medearis
Joel Wall, Sergt.
John Simmons, Sold.
Robert Coggins, Sold.
Samuel Weldon, Sold.
  [Page 8]
  [Folio page 1]
Lt. Wynn Dixon
Capt. Robt. Raiford
John Mills, Sergt.
Jacob Johnson, Sold.
Dimpsey Howill, Sold.
John Fitzgarrald
Benjamin Bell, Sold.
William Bird, Sold.
  [Folio page 2]
Samuel Williams, Sold.
Michael Bunkley, Corpl.
Drew Bass, Sold.
Jeremiah Walker, Sergt.
Moses Stallions, Sold.
Thomas Hinds, Sold.
William Pritchet, Sold.
Richard Hill, Sold.
  [Folio page 3]
Jesse Mitchell, Sold.
Thomas Thomas, Sold.
Benj. Smith, Sold.
Edmund Blount, Sold.
James Fawcett, Sold.
Joseph Gurley, Sold.
Joshua Gay, Sold.
Allen Gay, Sold.
Micajah Davis, Sold.
  [Folio page 4]
Paul Machen, Sold.
Capt. John Ingles
George Browning, Sergt.
Henry Smith, Sold.
Lt. Arthur Cotgraves, decsd. (Capt. Thos.
  Evans, administr.)

Capt. James Pearl
David Philips, Sergt.
David Fountain, Sold.
  [Page 9]
  [Folio page 1]
Enoch Flood, Sold.
Kendrid Spears, Sold.
William Howard, Sold.
Wilson Howard, Sold.
Charles Bright, Sergt.
John Calwell, Sold.
Lt. Dixon Marshall
Samuel Chappell, Sergt.
  [Page 2]
  [Folio page 2]
Capt. John Rochell, as supernumery
Thomas Geddy, Sold.
Jesse Brown, Sold.
Samuel Thomas, Sold.
William Jones, Sold.
Roderick, Easley, Sold.
Randolph Rutland, Sold.
George Smith, Sold.
Wm. Taylor Wagh (?) on Col. Long's
  Certificate
  [Folio page 3]
James Dunnan, Sergt.
James Russell, Sergt.
Willis Moor, Sold.
West Warrick, Sold.
William Smith, Sold.
Hardy Ginn or (Gunn) Sold.
James Richardson, Sold.
John Mason, Sold.
Jacob Daughty
  [Folio page 4]
Stephen Williams, Sergt.
John Wood, Sold. and wagon conductor
Conrade Elbert, on Col. Long's Certificate
John Luton, Sold.
Peter Hadsock, Sold.
Elisha Hunt, Sold.
James Turner, Junr. Soldier
Abram Farrel
Bert Ellis, Soldier
  [Page 10]
  [Folio page 1]
Benjamin Starkes, Soldier
Zebulon Gordon, Soldier
Drury Bynum, Sergt.
Samuel Scarborough, Soldier
Noah Stringer, Soldier
James Griffin, Corpl.
John Taylor, Soldier
John Babb, Soldier

Evan Skinner, Soldier
[Folio page 2]
Israel Pearce, Soldier
James Hare, Soldier
John Hill, Soldier
John Padgitt, Soldier
William Mitchell, Soldier
Jacob Webb, Soldier
Moody Ring, Soldier
Zachariah Jones, Soldier
James Willie, Soldier
Daniel Massongale, Soldier
[Folio page 3]
Stephen Hassell, Soldier
Joshua Jones, Soldier
Arthur Turner, Soldier
William Forte, Soldier
Epharaim Davenport, Soldier
Lewis Massy, Sergt.
John Edwards, Soldier
Absolom Wilbie, Soldier
Richard Billops, Soldier
[Page 4]
Capt. Francis Child
Dempsey Underdo, Soldier
Curl Tucker, Soldier
Benjamin Coats, Soldier
Solomon Gordon, Soldier
John Coleman, Soldier
Benjamin Glover, Soldier
James Wiggins, Soldier
[Page 11]
[Folio page 1]
Amos Thomas, Soldier
James Ellum, Soldier
John Josey, Soldier
William Baswell, Sergt.
Peter Williams, Sergt.
Philip White, Soldier
William Arnuld, Soldier
Andrew King, Soldier
Dudley Ballard, Soldier
[Folio page 2]
David King, Soldier
Levi Ginlirie, Soldier
Elisha Petteford, Soldier
Joshua Martin, Soldier
Philip Petiford, Soldier
Moses Winters, Soldier
Hardy Bass, Soldier
William Smith, Soldier
Isaac Ledenham, Soldier
William Smith, Soldier
[Folio page 3]
Edward Bibby, Soldier

Simon Worsley, Soldier
William Wood, Soldier
Malachi Nichins, Soldier
Evan Andrews, Soldier
Rice Webb, Soldier
Absolom Ternison, Soldier
Lt. Charles Dixon
Capt. John Summers
[Folio page 4]
Col. John Patten
Capt. Tilman Dixon
Maj. George Doherty
Capt. Elijah Moore
Lt. William Saunders
William Bryant
Archibald Butts, Drummer
[Page 12]
[Folio page 1]
Samuel Baxter, Sergt.
Holland Johnston, Soldier
James Sisk, Corpl.
Henry Johnston, Corpl.
George Wallis, Fifer
Stephen Golden, Soldier
Joshua Scabriel
Lt. Lewis Cannon (resigned)
[Folio page 2]
William Gallimore, Sold.
Lt. Charles Garrard
William McLure, Surgeon
John Sheppard, Sold.
William Groves, Capt. (resigned)
Col. James Armstrong
Jesse Thompson, Sold.
Reden Rutland, Sold.
[Folio page 3]
Josiah Stafford, Sold.
Colo. James Armstrong
Colo. Archibald Little
Capt. Clement Hall
Maj. Thomas Donohu
Josiah Stringer, Sergt.
Thomas Angle, Soldier
James Griffin, Corpl.
[Folio page 4]
Henry Tison, Soldier
Amos Parcmore, Soldier
Samuel Glover, Sergt.
Jeremiah Smith, Soldier
Joel Whitehurst, Soldier
Thomas Spain, Drummer
Jacob Mathews, Soldier
Etheridge Newsom, Soldier
[Page 13]
[Folio page 1]

Lt. Thomas Pasteur
David Gillaspie, Soldier
Stephen White, Soldier
Zachariah Wilburn, Soldier
Luke Bates, Soldier
Richard Blanton, Soldier
Thomas Wiggins, Soldier
Morgan Murry, Soldier
James Roper, Soldier
[Folio page 2]
Daniel Twigg, Soldier
Dempsey Womble, Soldier
James Summers, Sergt.
James Oram, Soldier
Thomas Land, Soldier
Lt. Col. Henry Dixon, decsd.
Drury Nobles
Joseph Hardy, Soldier
[Folio page 3]
Joseph Hobbs
Jesse Arlack, Soldier
William McClury, Soldier
William Thackston, Soldier
...... Haney, Soldier
John Harney, Corpl.
Thomas Robertson, Soldier
Jeptha Rice, Sergt.
[Folio page 3]
Thomas Smith, Soldier
John Carney, Soldier
William Harrison, Soldier
Capt. James Martin,
Lt. John Granbery
Capt. Clement Hall
John Arelir, Soldier
Joseph Woodland, Soldier
George Duncan, Soldier
[Folio page 4]
Enoch Ferrell, Soldier
Benjamin Hester, Soldier
Robin Morgan, Soldier
Benjamin Morgan, Soldier
Cole Carles, Sergt.
Phil Chance, Corpl.
Lt. Nathaniel Williams
Stephen Ewell, Soldier
Wyatt Ballard
[Folio page 2]
John Vines, Sergt.
Jeremiah Messer, Soldier
Jesse Lane
Lt. Samuel Ashe
John Rand, Soldier in Medicies Troops
William Wilkerion, Soldier
John Edwards, Soldier

David Hunt
[Folio page 3]
William Turner
Benjamin Ricks, Sergt.
Benjamin Ricks
George Fowler, Soldier
Jarvis Forhead, Soldier
Gabriel Long, Soldier
James Amos, Soldier
Capt. William Fawn
George Andrewson
Doct. Joseph Blythe
John Gooch, Soldier
Lt. John Rudpath, decsd.
Capt. Gee Bradley
Surgeon Jonathan Loomiss
Joseph Brann, Soldier
[Page 15]
[Folio page 1]
Lt. Stephen Owens, Supernumery
Lt. Col. Haray Murfree, Supernumery
Capt. William Lythe
Joseph Heartly, Soldier
James Smith, Soldier
William Frim, Soldier
Elisha Boon, soldier & wagoner
Edmund Ganble, Lt. Supernumery
Capt. Nehemiah Long, resigned
Ensn. Richard Mosson, resigned
Nathanl Cooper, Soldier
David Ambrose, Drummer
Micajah Hoard
[Folio page 3]
Thomas Flinn, Soldier
Capt. John Ba(r)ker, resigned
Amos Smart
David Arnold, Soldier
Capt. Kedar Ballard
Robert Huddleston, Soldier
Moses Savage, Soldier
Thomas Spiers
[Folio page 4]
Henry Smith, Soldier
William Pettiferd, Soldier
William Chavus, Soldier
Henry Nichols, Soldier
Thomas Cooper, Soldier
Thomas Billops, Drummer
Buckner Floyd, Soldier
[Page 16]
[Folio page 1]
John Wood, Soldier
Philip Hockanner
Theophilus Hays, Soldier
Lt. ..... Parkmon

Jesse Monger, Soldier
Samuel Williams
Emd. Gaklin
John Gilbert
[Folio page 2]
Jonah Wilson
Archd. Warren
John Warren
James Conners
Jno. Parker
Wm. Marshburn
Daniel Vaughan
John Brickell, Sergt.
James Kelly
James Southerland, Certfn.
[Folio page 3]
John Kelley, Soldier
John Smith, Soldier
Lt. Thomas Clark
William Hathcock, Soldier
Ransom Savage, Soldier
Elias Fort, Sergt.
Theophilus Willeford, Soldier
Thomas Taunt, Soldier
Jonas Lasiter, Soldier
[Page 4]
Asa Sears, Soldier
Warren Stone, Soldier
James Brown, Soldier
Luke Lasiter, Soldier
Lt. John Vance
Thomas Barrott Whitehead, Soldier
John Edwards, Soldier
Capt. Jno. Brickle, Supernumery
Alex. Morrison, Soldier
[Page 17]
[Folio page 1]
William Tear, Gunner
James W. Green, Surgeon for extra service
Ewd. Mitchel, decsd.
Moses Brown, decsd.
Philemon Bristol
James Scurlock, or Will Pendergast,
    Dept. Com. of Purchases Certificate
Arch. Henderson, Drummer
John Richardson, Soldier
Alex Flood, Soldier
[Folio page 2]
Thos. Harrison, Soldier
Joseph Harrison, Soldier
James Taylor, Soldier
Edward Hutchins
John Hartly, Soldier
John Geffery, Soldier
David Sweat, Soldier

Isaac Clark, Soldier
[Folio page 3]
James Barfield, Soldier
James Folcaner, Soldier
Fred Moore, Soldier
Jesse Johnston, Soldier
James Moore, Soldier
Thomas Moore, Soldier
Henry Miller, Sergt.
James Hutchins, Soldier
William Ponder
[Folio page 4]
Capt. Benjamin Coleman
Capt. John Kinsborough, of Artillery
Lt. Curtis Ivey
Col. Gideon Lamb, decsd., the acct. ex-
    hibited by Lt. Abner Lamb, Exectr.
. . . . . . Harris, Soldier
Thomas Tucker, Soldier
Jno. Hargrove, Soldier
Jay or Jeremiah James
[Page 18]
[Folio page 1]
Abraham Taylor, Soldier
Lt. William Bush
James Purdy, Soldier
Lt. Richard Whidbie, decsd.
Samuel Thompson, Corpl.
John Walker, Soldier
William Powell, Soldier
John Wilkirson, Soldier
[Folio page 2]
Bryan Smith, Soldier
Major James Emmitt
Douglas Carrell, Soldier
John Mathews, Corpl.
Enos Bizzel, Soldier
Demsey Archer, Soldier
Jesse Archer, Soldier
Charles Dunston, Corpl.
Reuben Evans, Soldier
[Folio page 3]
William Rutledge, decsd., late Lieut.
Joseph Howard
Benjamin Reed, Soldier
Charles Ellins, Soldier
Isaac Butler, Soldier
George Lisles, Soldier
Wm. Lisles, Soldier
Henry Winburn, Soldier
Jno. White, Soldier
[Folio page 4]
Jno. M. Ashe, Lt. Col., resigned
Crawford Johnston
Samuel Gainer, Soldier

James Flemming, Soldier
William Vance, Corpl.
Hosa Bell, Sergt.
Isaac Smith, Soldier
John Simmons, Sergt.
Henry Gibson, Soldier
     [Page 19]
     [Folio page 1]
William Moorsoldin
James Will, Soldier
Henry Sykes, Soldier
Jno. Butler, Soldier
Nicholas Edwin, Soldier
Lewis Hines, Soldier
John Carter, decsd.
James Brock, Soldier
William Jno. Bryan, Soldier
     [Folio page 2]
Benjamin Flood, Soldier
Jno. Smith, Soldier
Benjamin Smith, Soldier
Briton George, Soldier
Brig. Gen. James Hogan
Robert Hayes
John Smart, Soldier
     [Folio page 3]
Jno. Christmas, Drummer
Jesse Bright, Corpl.
Joseph May, Soldier
Jno. Scott, Sergt.
James Thomas, Soldier
Lt. William Linton
James Baker, Soldier
Henry Porch, Soldier
     [Folio page 4]
Maj. Reading Blount
Martin Cole, Sergt.
Benjamin Sharp, Sergt.
James Gray, Sergt.
John Simpson, Soldier
Joseph Forlice or (Forbee) Capt.
     (deranged)
Capt. Charles Stewart, Brigdr. Qr. Mstr.
     [Folio page 1]
Lt. Col. Peter Dange (deranged)
Lt. John Mercer (resigned)
James Lankon, Soldier
William Wilson, Soldier
Elisha Sterling, Soldier
     [Folio page 2]
Robert Sterling, Soldier
Peter Aluckson
Capt. William Feribee
James Berkes, Soldier
James Simmons, Soldier

Elijah Kedwill, Soldier
Maj. Pinkethmon Eaton
Buckford Garris
     [Folio page 3]
John Stephins, Soldier
Israel Campbell, Soldier
Stephen West, Soldier
Ezekiel White, Soldier
Lt. Kedar Parker
Lt. Walter Allen
Nathaniel Doboy, Soldier
     [Folio page 4]
William Gee, Soldier
Anthony Gerner, Soldier
William Mitchell, Drummer
Simpson West Lewis, Soldier
Thomas Powell, Soldier
Absolom Spears, Soldier
William Rose, Sergt.
William Green, Soldier
William Card, Sergt.
     [Page 21]
     [Folio page 1]
William Burnett, Soldier
Thomas Hardy, Soldier
Jno. Ellis Waggoner
Hezekiah Nobles, Soldier
Vincent Salmon, Corpl.
Lt. William Hilton, decsd.
Hezekiah Nobles, Soldier
Jno. Leech, Soldier
Henry Johnston, decsd.
Malachi Simmons, Soldier
Caleb Jordan, Soldier
Ceaser Saules, Soldier
Daniel Roson, Sergt.
Micajah Whitley, Soldier
Walter Allen, Comis.
     [Folio page 3]
Jesse Richardson, Soldier
George Anderson, Soldier
James Johnston, Soldier
James Swunney or (Swinney), Soldier
Isaac Gregory, Soldier
Jno. Hill, Soldier
Robert Ellis, Soldier
John Stringer
Philip Adams
     [Folio page 4]
Lewis Hardy
Charles Webb, Soldier
James Jones, Soldier
Jno. Thomas, Soldier
Samuel Stringer, Sergt.
Lt. Richard Fenner

Thomas Pitman
[Page 22]
[Folio page 1]
Kadar Coupland, Soldier
James Fountain, Corpl.
Lewis Price, Soldier
Capt. Peter Bacot
Capt. Jno. Pointer
Thomas Shirly, Soldier
Jno. Atkins
Tho. Pearson, Soldier
[Folio page 2]
Benjamin Wamble, Soldier
Jno. Dews, Soldier
Cornelius Callahan, Soldier
Alex Gunn, Sergt.
Isaac Rowell, Sergt.
Lt. Thomas Dudley
Benjamin Roberson, Soldier
Joshua Webb
[Folio page 3]
Jeremiah Perry, Soldier
Capt. Robert Smith (resigned)
Capt. Thomas Callender
Joseph Nichols, Sergt.
Charles Keel, Soldier
Joseph Fox, Sergt.
John McLaughlin, Soldier
[Folio page 4]
Capt. Benjamin Bailey
Capt. William Walton
Lt. Jno. Campbell
Capt. Samuel Jones
Daniel White, Soldier
Joseph Witherington, Soldier
James Whitley, Soldier
[Folio page 23]
William Thompson, Soldier
Capt. Alex. Brevard
Thomas Shearley, Sergt.
Capt. Jas. Thos. Rhodes
Major William Fenner, decsd.
John Enloe, Capt. (resigned)
[Folio page 2]
Jno. Weaver, Soldier
Lt. William Alexander
Capt. William Armstrong ("pretty Billy")
Josiah Talton, Soldier
Jno. Wills, Soldier
George Phillips, Soldier
Richard Daughtry, Soldier
[Folio page 3]
Neil Watson, Soldier
John Lambert, Soldier
Thomas Prior, ?

Benj. Atkins, Corpl.
Robert Meek, Corpl.
James Tison, Sergt.
Abraham Fowler, Soldier
William Smith, Soldier
[Folio page 4]
William Cunningham, Soldier
Thomas Saunders, Soldier
Samuel Thomas, Soldier
Josiah Jones, Drummer
Joseph Bailey, Sergt.
Lt. Levi Gatlin
Capt. Jno. Allen
[Page 24]
[Folio page 1]
Jesse Nelson, Soldier
Isaac Hayes, Soldier
William Pope, Sergt.-Maj.
Lt. Samuel Blythe (resigned)
Anthony Hart, Lt. & Adjutant (resigned)
George Topp, Soldier
John Epps, Soldier
[Folio page 2]
William Epps, Soldier
Lt. Thomas Allen
William Smith, Soldier
Simon Smith, Soldier
Henry Harris, Soldier
Jno. Morris,
William Charlton, Soldier
George Moy, Soldier
[Folio page 3]
Jeremiah Dixon, Soldier
Daniel Stewart, Soldier
Thomas Lytle, Soldier
Jno. Coupland, Soldier
John Liles, Soldier
Gideon Akins, Soldier
Wm. Jones, Soldier
[Folio page 4]
James King, Soldier
Ozburn Clarke, Soldier
Abraham Dennis, Soldier
Richard Johnson, Soldier
Lt. David Vance
Thomas Thow, Soldier
Thomas Wiggins, Soldier
[Page 25]
[Folio page 1]
Moses Deen Soldier
Thomas Smith Soldier
Capt. Anthony Sharp
Lt. Jesse Steed
Mingo Stringer, Soldier
Ursell Goodson, Soldier

Jno. Messer, Soldier
[Folio page 2]
Upshaw Roberson
Francis Williams, Soldier
Finehas Latham, Sergt.
Lt. Philip Jones
Warren Brown, Soldier
David Vance, Soldier
Arthur McDonald, Soldier
[Folio page 3]
James Ives, Soldier
William Boon, Soldier
John Morgan, Soldier
William Powers, Soldier
John Watts, Soldier
Philip Jones, Soldier
Lt. John Carstaphen (resigned)
[Folio page 4]
David Love, Surgeon (resigned)
William Fomes, Soldier
Mathew Creekman, Soldier
Richard Weaver, Soldier
William Drew, Soldier
James Amos, Soldier
Joel Davis, Soldier
[Page 26]
[Folio page 1]
Balaam Bullock, Soldier
George Richards, Soldier
John Yarbrough, Soldier
William Sinclair
Joseph Andrews, Soldier
John Hubbert, Soldier
John Scott, Soldier, decsd.
[Folio page 2]
Lt. John Gambier (Scull)
Jno. King, Soldier
Brig. Gen. Francis Nash, decsd.
John Brantley, Soldier
Col. Thomas Clark
Henry Howell, Soldier
[Folio page 3]
Jno. Maularn, Soldier
James Wilson, Soldier
Corbin Hickson, Soldier
Jesse Taunt, Soldier
Maj. Griffith Jno. McRee
Thomas McCoy, Soldier
David Rishell, Soldier
[Folio page 4]
James McMullen, Soldier
Thomas Jones, Soldier
Jno. Potter, Soldier
William Taunt, Soldier
Francis Lechro, Sergt.

Roger Rice, Soldier
David Pasmore, Soldier
Jacob Brayboy, Soldier
Capt. Christopher Godins
[Page 27]
[Folio page 1]
Lt. Thomas Watson (resigned)
John White, Sergt.
George Williams, Soldier
Edward Weaver, Soldier
Joseph Smith, Soldier
Lt. William Green (resigned)
Absolom Powers, Soldier
Thomas Queen, Soldier
[Folio page 2]
James Church, Soldier
Ephraim Hooks, Soldier
Micajah Davis, Soldier
John Carter, Soldier
Stephen White, decsd. Sergt.
James Robins, Soldier
Elijah Weaver, Soldier
Martin Campbell, Soldier
[Folio page 3]
William Richardson, Soldier
William Williams, Soldier
Peter Trivitts, Soldier
Hardy Garris, Soldier
Thomas Pyatt, Soldier
Thomas Davis, Sergt.
David Hale, Sergt.
Peter Hedpeth, Soldier
[Folio page 4]
Patrick Campbell, field conductor & Sergt.
James Roper, Soldier
David Wheeler, Fifer, decsd.
David Chister, Sergt.
James Lanier, Ensn.
Lt. Jethro Lasiter
John Powell, Soldier
[Page 28]
[Folio page 1]
William Douglass, Soldier
Henry Brenier, Soldier
William Garris, Soldier
Dennes, Scott, Soldier
Capt. John Daves
William Lawrence, Soldier
Jesse Wise, Soldier
[Folio page 2]
John Worsley, Soldier
Lt. Caleb Foreman
Lt. Robert Greear
Lt. Azariah Mackafoy
William Griffin, Soldier

Capt. John Hadley
Daniel Frazell, Soldier
[Folio page 3]
Capt. John Eborn
Jesse Lassiter, Soldier
John Butler, Soldier
Benjamin Sherwood, Soldier
William Mitcheall, Soldier
Robert Combs, Soldier
Dr. Samuel Cooley
[Folio page 4]
William Smith, Sergt., allowed on an
   order of
Wm. Colby, Sergt. Maj. of 1st N. C. Regt.
Hardy Jones, Soldier
Capt. Mathew Wood (resigned)
Lt. Col. Lott Bruster
Lt. Robert Bell
Richard Roberts, Soldier
[Page 29]
[Folio page 1]
Nicholas Long, Esqr., Deputy Quart. Mstr.
John Hall
John Medearis
Abishai Thomas
John Tillery
Jesse Potts
William Pasteur
Edwd. Gamble
Edwd. Hall
Mat. Ramsey
John Rutherford
Bat. Birdsong
John C. Bryan
Mat. McCawley
John Nichols
Charles Saunders
William Howard
Thomas Davis
William Hargrove
Robt. Christie
John Wood
Reubin Smith
Robt. Smith
Jas. Scurlock
Jarrot Edwards
John Selenarvis, gunner of Capt. Kings-
   borough's company of Artillery
Willis Barco, Soldier
William Thompson, Drummer
[Folio page 2]
Lewis Powell, Soldier
Benjamin Wheelar, Soldier
John Jarvis, Soldier
John Ames, Soldier

Willis Weathers
Quinn Little
Lt. Col. Selby Harney
[Folio page 3]
Melone Mullen, Soldier
Maj. Thomas Hogg
Dr. John Ingram
Micajah Blanchard, Soldier
Henry Jacobs, Soldier
Reubin Hobbs
Wm. Madry, Sergt.
[Folio page 4]
Simon Wood, Soldier
Mons Walker, Soldier
Mark Haycroft, Soldier
Caleb Thomas, Drummer
William Westbrook, Soldier
Robert Wilburn, Soldier
William Smith, Sergt.
[Page 30]
[Folio page 1]
Jeremiah Sandelin, Soldier
Benjamin Cooper, Soldier
Joseph Webb, Soldier
John Cockburn, Soldier
William Deffnall, Soldier, decsd.
David Deffnall, Soldier
Capt. Henry Darnald, decsd.
[Folio page 2]
Capt. William Caswell
Mason Philips, Soldier
Thomas Cole, Soldier
David Denny, Soldier
Shadrack Cumming, Soldier
John Harrell, Sergt.
Joseph Philips, Soldier
[Folio page 3]
Sutton Truluck, Soldier
Lawson Arthur, Soldier
Bennett Morgan Sergt.
Thomas Norman, Soldier
John Dial, Soldier
Jeremiah Sutton, Sergt.
Lt. Daniel Shaw
[Folio page 4]
William Baskett, an Indian
William Barnard, Soldier
Lt. William Ferrell
Ensign Davis Grandy
William Mullen, Soldier
Capt. Denny Porterfield, decsd.
Lt. John McNorton
[Page 31]
[Folio page 1]
John Garrell, Forage Marker

Capt. James Mills
Isaack Curlee, Soldier
Capt. Benjamin Mills
John Rogerson, Soldier
Capt. Cosimo Medicie
Jacob Lane, Soldier
[Folio page 2]
Edwd. Gamble, Supernumery Lt.
Thomas Modlin, Soldier
Micajah Parley, Soldier
Capt. Jesse Read
William Lippincott, Fifer
Richard Mullen, Soldier
Lt. William Faircloth (resigned)
[Folio page 3]
Dempsey Jinkins, Soldier
Frederick Davis, Soldier
Lt. Jeremiah Bullock
Ensign Joshua Bullock
Capt. Richard D. Cooke
Lt. Thomas Blount Whitmill
Capt. Ralph Williams
[Folio page 4]
Capt. Allen Ramsey
Capt. Samuel Chapman
Capt. William Goodman, decsd.
William Manly, Soldier
Joshua Stock, Soldier
Joseph Mitchell, Soldier
William Dove, Soldier
[Page 32]
[Folio page 1]
William Morgan, Soldier
John B. Hammond, Sergt.
Zebedee Williams, Soldier
Jesse Harrison, Soldier
William McDonald, Soldier
Thomas Cartright, Soldier
Dempsey Gardner
Robt. Cartwright
[Folio page 2]
James Whorton, Soldier
John Taylor, Soldier
Averry Tillett, Soldier
Thomas Gregory, Soldier
John Ginnings, Soldier
Thomas Atkins, Soldier
Dempsey Capps, Soldier
[Folio page 3]
Thomas Love, Soldier
Mitchell Philips, Soldier
John Scalf, Soldier
Benjamin Davis, Soldier
Samuel Price, Soldier
Caleb Partlock, Soldier

Cornelius Bray, Soldier
[Folio page 4]
Elisha Davis, Soldier
Benjamin Eastman, Soldier
Martin Black, Soldier
Isaack Purkins, Soldier
Samuel Read, Sergt.
Charles Elms, Soldier
Richard Bullock, Soldier
John Bartholomew, Soldier
[Page 33]
[Folio page 1]
James Judge, Soldier
John Watkins, Soldier
Hazzard Creed, Soldier
John Ryon, Corpl.
John Berry, Sergt.
Solomon Berry, Sergt.
Dempsey Harrison, Soldier
Wm. Gray, Soldier
[Folio page 2]
Jonathan Lewis, Soldier
Curtis Clements, Soldier
John Bullock, Soldier
Samuel Mavis, Sergt.
Jacob Watson, Soldier
John McVay, Soldier
Eli McVay, Soldier
John Norwood, Soldier
[Folio page 3]
William White, Soldier
Benjamin Johnson, Corpl.
Lt. William Harrison
Elijah Cotton, Soldier
Thomas Smith, Sergt.
Capt. John Masons
John Reece
[Folio page 4]
John Freas, Soldier
Andrew Boston
Christopher Boston
Francis Gorham, Soldier
James Gay, Sergt.
Christopher Frederick, Soldier
Joel Edwards, Soldier
Peter Workman, Soldier
Ferdenand Gonsolos, Soldier
[Page 34]
[Folio page 1]
Michael Santee, Soldier
Andrew Little, Soldier
Col. William Polk
Capt. Martin Phiffer
Lt. Charles Alexander
Capt. William Timple Coles

John Ward, Soldier
[Folio page 2]
Dock Lancelott Johnson
Maj. Thomas Harris
Capt. Samuel Budd
Capt. Andrew Armstrong
Lt. Thomas Orrell
Capt. Philip Taylor
Andrew Allison, Soldier
[Folio page 3]
Maurice Mooring, Corpl.
Samuel Carter, Soldier
Gibbs Lamb, Soldier
Charles Burk, Soldier
William Faithell, Soldier
Noah James, Soldier
Corbin Westmonth, Soldier
Samuel Rowe, Soldier
Daniel Umphries, Soldier
John Collins, Soldier
[Folio page 4]
John Barco, Soldier
William Jones, Soldier
Charles Dodson, Soldier
The Revd. Adam Boyd
Israel Scott, Soldier
Thomas Means, Sergt.
T. Sykes, Soldier
Thomas Burns, Soldier
Thomas Overton, Soldier
Thomas Shute, Ensn.
[Page 33]
[Folio page 1]
William Pyson, Soldier
Joseph Gathey, Soldier
Angukes Davis, Soldier
John Pughe, Soldier
William Riley, Soldier
Samuel Gilston, Sergt.
William Thomas, Soldier
Henry Costin, Soldier
Drury Ward, Soldier
Robert Lynn, Soldier
[Folio page 2]
William Capps, Soldier
William Shippard, Soldier
Lt. Hardy Holms
Capt. Frederick Haskell
Lt. John Bush
Joseph Sharp, Srgt. of Dragoons &
    express rider.
James Runnells, Soldier
[Folio page 3]
The Revd. James Tate
Thomas Dunegan, Soldier

William Chalk, soldier
William Smith, Soldier
Sampson Dillard, Corpl.
Thomas Hays, Soldier
Isaack Howard, Soldier
Jesse Jeans, Soldier
Thomas Mallet, Soldier
[Folio page 4]
John Bowers, Soldier
Lt. Joseph Johnston
David Philips, Soldier
Benjamin Johnston, Soldier
John Price, Soldier
Jesse Duncan, Soldier
Joseph Bobson, Soldier
Johnston Webb, Soldier
Ensign James Taylor
[Page 36]
[Folio page 1]
Jacob Richards, Soldier
William Campbell, Soldier
Benjamin Mott, Soldier
Miller Sawyer, Soldier
Thomas Bryant, Sergt.
John M. Struker
Brig. Gen. Sumner
[Folio page 2]
John Squires, Soldier
Edw'd. Deal, Soldier
Timothy Miars, Soldier
John Wilson, Soldier
Lt. Robert Galespie
Lt. William T. Lewis
Lt. Joel Lewis
[Folio page 3]
Capt. Micajah Lewis
Capt. Joseph Philips
Miles Knight, Sergt.
Robert Williams, Soldier
James Huckins, Soldier
Elisha Williams, Soldier
Lt. Williams Slade
[Folio page 4]
John Conner, Soldier
Darling Madrey, Soldier
Robert Saunders
Joshua Barber, Soldier
Josiah Davis, Soldier
John Collins, Sergt.
Thomas Hart, Soldier, decsd.
Capt. Thomas White, decsd.
[Page 37]
[Folio page 1]
Richard Davis, Soldier
Anthony Godfrey, Soldier

John Ayer, Soldier
Benjamin Cofield, Lt. and Adjutant
(resigned)
John Pendergast, Soldier
Job. Pendergast, Soldier
[Folio page 2]
Ludwick Strend, Soldier
John Stroud, Soldier
Benjamin Jacobs
Lt. Henry Cannon, supernumery
Aron Hathcock
James Comer, Sergt.
[Folio page 3]
Samuel Simpson, Corpl.
Capt. Simon Jones
James Young, Clerk to the A. C. or Issues,
and Sub. Conductor of Wagons
Lt. James Campen
Capt. Joshua Bowman, decsd.
Lt. Patrick McGibbony (resigned)
[Folio page 4]
Lt. James Coots (supernumery)
Farnath Lucas, Privt.
Capt. Matthew McCawley, supernumery
Lt. William Barber
Spencer Donaldson, Drummer
Richard Bradley, decsd. payms'tr.
Thomas Lucas
[Page 38]
[Folio page 1]
Capt. Charles Allen
Lt. James Powers (resigned)
Lt. John Lowe
Ensign William Washington (resigned)
Lt. John Hodges (resigned)
John Lee, Privt.
Benjamin Hodges, Sergt.
Howell Gillam, Sergt.
Robert Homes, Sergt.
[Folio page 2]
Malachi Towe, Privt.
Spencer Williams, Sergt.
Levi Barker, Privt.
Lt. & Adjutant Miles M. Shebee, decsd.
Richard Ward, Privt.
Wm. Johnston
Samuel Penrice, Sergt.
Jonathan Traider
James Harmon, Corpl.
[Folio page 3]
Jeremiah Collins, Corpl.
William Bacchus
Abram Pharo
Timothy Lane
John Miller, Drummer

Thomas Clarkson, Sergt.
John Bryan, Sergt.
Lt. Col. Robert Mebane, decsd.
[Folio page 4]
Hardy Bird, decsd.
Richard Foster
Robert Nelson, Sergt.
John Carrol
James Sullivan, Sergt.
John Bryan
Peter Pycate, Asst. Commisary of Issues
Duncan Carmical, Soldier
Wm. Ekels, Sergt.
[Page 39]
[Folio page 1]
Silas Linton, Soldier
Jesse Cox, Forage Master
Benjamin Thermady, Soldier
Charles Baker, Soldier
Christopher Wootten, Soldier
Lazarus Jones, Soldier
William Gray, Soldier
Charles Wood, Soldier
James Gambling, Soldier
Dr. Giles Worth
Capt. Armwill Hearon
[Folio page 2]
John Horton, Sergt.
David Jones, Corpl. of Artilley
George Reynolds, Sergt. of Artillery
James Dowell
Charles Butler
William Smith
James Clark, Corpl.
Lt. Reuben Roundtree
Henry Martin, Soldier
Samuel Williams
[Folio page 3]
William Charlton, Soldier
William Davenport, Soldier
Plate Smith, Soldier
Jethro Jones, Soldier
Samuel Pearson, Soldier
Jesse Howe, Soldier
George Rowe, Soldier
James Avery, Soldier
Neal Watson, Soldier
Peter Hobbs, Soldier
[Folio page 4]
Harris Yeoman, Soldier
George Weare, Soldier
Lt. Caleb Coen
Lt. Timothy Jones
Thomas Smith, Soldier
William Wormington, Soldier

Clement Smith
John Scarfe, Soldier
Saunders Cooke, Soldier
[Page 40]
[Folio page 1]
Lemonlation Lamb, Soldier
John Killingsworth, Drummer
Henry Albertson, Soldier
Zachariah Jones, Soldier
Samuel Smith, Soldier
John Roper, Soldier
Micajah Pettaway, Soldier
Marmaduke Hedgepeth
Willis Smith (invalid) Soldier
[Folio page 2]
Joseph Hudlar, junr.
John Hudlar
Samuel Hudlar
Joseph Hudlar
Capt. Thomas McRory, decsd.
Abraham Jenkins, Soldier
William Farmer, Soldier
William Parker, Soldier
[Folio page 3]
James Christian, Soldier
Solomon Manly, Soldier
Mark Manly, Soldier
James Horton, Soldier
Solomon Howard, Soldier
William Bryant, Soldier
Daniel Johnson, Soldier
[Folio page 4]
John Mann, Soldier
Jacob Smith, Soldier
Robert Carter, Soldier
Matthew Wiggins, Soldier
Shadrack Holmes, Sergt.
John Leadone or (M) Soldier
John Williams, Soldier
Andrew Perkins, Soldier
[Page 41]
[Folio page 1]
George Brook, Soldier
John Embry, Soldier
John Elliott, Soldier
George Smith, Sergt.
Francis Fox, Soldier
Wright Bass
Belitha Tilghman
Col. Abraham Sheppard
Capt. Abraham Sheppard
[Folio page 2]
John Tilghman
Bailey Benson
William Noble, Sergt.

Matthew Newby
[Folio page 3]
John Daughtry
William Nelson
Cornelius Ryan
David Wilcocks, Soldier
Jem Davis (?), Soldier
Giles Bowers, Soldier
[Folio page 4]
John Hicks, Soldier
James Hicks, an Indian
Wimoke Charbe, Indian
Sampson Phillips, Soldier
Samuel Pope, Soldier
George Copeland, Soldier
Howell Sawyer, Soldier
Bickwell Chistin, Sergt.
[Page 42]
[Folio page 1]
James Worley, Sergt.
Werly Griffin, Corpl.
John Fowlar, Soldier
James Bryant, Sergt.
Thomas A. Meek, Corpl.
Mason Kelly, Sergt.
James Wittey, Soldier
[Folio page 2]
Henry Sweating, Sergt.
Ensn. & Adjutant William Beck
Isaac Gibdon, Soldier
Jeremiah Beaumount, Soldier
Philemon Thomas, Sergt.
John Johnston, Soldier
Richard Thomas, Soldier
[Folio page 3]
Capt. Samuel Ashe
Randol Newson, Soldier
Sovereign Bloxom, Soldier
Samuel Chappel, Sergt.
Augusta Spain, Sergt.
William Gibson
Lewis Bailey, Soldier
Robert Hicks, Soldier
[Folio page 4]
James Briston, Soldier
David Madborn, Soldier
James Harris, Soldier
James Wiggins, Soldier
Thomas Jamerson, Soldier
John Anderson, Soldier
Robert Roaper, Soldier
[Page 43]
[Folio page 1]
William Bobbs, Soldier
Andrew Wade, Soldier

William Dowell, Soldier
John Tellerton, or Tetterton, Soldier
Robert Fossett, Soldier
Simon Parker
Benjamin Dorton
Solmon Brown
[Folio page 2]
Levi Wiggins
Richard Coupland
James Coupland
William Parham
Isaac Carter
Drewry Parham
James Christian
Richard Coupland
[Folio page 3]
John Barganear, Soldier
Bird Braswell
John Christian, Fife Maj.
William Dillard
Osborn Dillard
Robert Cypert, Sergt.
James Avent
William Bugg
Solomon Seymour
[Folio page 4]
John Hardin
William Seymour
Lt. Jephtha Rice
Etheldred Washington, Fifer
Lt. John Winborn, decsd.

Capt. Nicholas Edmunds
Lt. John L. Hare
[Page 44]
[Folio page 1]
Capt. Manlove Tarrant (resigned)
Josiah Holland
Wilson Liscombe
Arthur Pow
Isaac Rochell
Micajah Price
Henry Dunneloe
Robert Cowan
Theophilus Williams
Allen Manly
Jeffery Garner
[Folio page 2]
Empry Wheeler
Hardy Morgan
Solomon Green
Dempsy Rooks
William Gooden
James Pully
Ladock Williams
Dudley Reardon
John Madray, Corpl.
Jesse Boyce
Miles Ramsey
[Folio page 3]
Arthur Tyner
Nicholas Tyner

## Vol. II.  Pages 46-73.  Book ZZ

An account of allowance made officers and soldiers of the late Continental Line of this State for pay and by the commissioners of Army Accounts at Hillsboro May 1, 1792.

[Page 46]
[Folio page 1]
No.
1. Erastus Tippett, Drummer
2. Micheil Brinkley, Privt.
3. Ezekiel Griffin, Privt.
4. Henry Gray, Sergt.
5. John Long, Privt.
6. Gabriel Ferrill, Privt.
7. John Anderson, Privt.
8. John Russ, Privt.
[Folio page 2]
9. Francis Pridgen, Privt.
10. William Wiseheart, Privt.
11. Edward Jackson, Privt.
12. Benjamin Boyt, Privt.
13. Daniel Williams, Capt.
14. Lewis Lodge, Privt.
15. Thomas Castilloe, Privt.

No.
16. Edward H. Woodrow, Privt.
[Folio page 3]
17. James Danage, Privt.
18. Charles Bright, Sergt.
19. John Jarvis, Capt.
20. Humphrey Molden, Privt.
21. John Hall, Privt.
22. William Boyce, Privt.
23. Loven Phillips, Privt.
24. William H. Bailey, Sergt.
25. Joseph Runnals, Corpl.
[Folio page 4]
26. Samuel Smith, Corpl.
27. Willoughby Rogers, Privt.
28. Matthew Lucas, Privt.
29. Miles Privitt (or Pruitt), Privt.
30. William Haines, Privt.
31. Elisha Jenkins, Privt.

No.
32. Matthias Cates
33. John Smith, Privt.
34. Henry Williamson, Privt.
[Page 47]
[Folio page 1]
35. John Emory, Privt.
36. Job Pendergrass, Privt.
37. David Rothnell, Privt.
38. William Rothnell, Privt.
39. Abraham Finley, Privt.
40. Eli Drake, Privt.
41. Ishmael Roberts, Privt.
42. David Burke, Privt.
[Folio page 2]
43. William Morris, Privt.
44. John Parrimore, Privt.
45. Willis Lewis, Privt.
46. Emanuel Teal, Privt.
47. Reuben Gurganos, Privt.
48. Charles Tinsley, Privt.
49. William Wilson, Privt.
50. Joshua Towsan, Privt.
[Folio page 3]
51. William Brewer, Privt.
52. William Walters, Privt.
53. Elijah Clay, Sergt.
54. James Largan, Privt.
55. Alexander McKinsey, Privt.
56. Thomas McMeans, Sergt.
57. John Gass, Sergt.-Maj.
58. Thomas Hall, Privt.
59. John Rowland, Privt.
[Folio page 4]
60. William Yates, Privt.
61. James Yew, Privt.
62. Thomas Carvin, Privt.
63. James Dobbins, Privt.
64. Jonathan Times, Sergt.
65. John Toney, Privt.
66. John Fields, Privt.
67. John Step, Privt.
[Page 48]
[Folio page 1]
68. Alexander Smith, Privt.
69. Edward Prichell, Privt.
70. Major May, Corpl.
71. John Atkinson, Corpl.
72. Thomas Johnston, Privt.
73. Humphrey Durham, Privt.
74. Thomas Earley, Privt.
75. Robert Shaw, Privt.
[Folio page 2]
76. John Long, Ensn.
77. Alexandra Cole, Corpl.

No.
78. Sylvanius Weeks, Privt.
79. Isaac Walters, Privt.
80. Robert Jordan, Privt.
81. William Cormis, Privt.
82. William Hawkins, Privt.
[Folio page 3]
83. John Vickory, Privt.
84. Joseph Sawyer, Privt.
85. Adam Turner, Privt.
86. Owen Smith, Privt.
87. Zachariah Philips, Privt.
88. James Cronnister, Privt.
89. Levi Coleman, Privt.
[Folio page 4]
90. Edmund Pendleton, Sergt.
91. James Johnston, Privt.
92. Abraham Parish, Privt.
93. Nathan Lewis, Privt.
94. Willis Williford, Privt.
95. Stephen Conger, Sergt.
96. Francis Dezearn, Privt.
[Page 49]
[Folio page 1]
97. Jesse Hutchins, Privt.
98. Jesse Boseman, Privt.
99. Alexander Lemon, Privt.
100. Charles Evans, Privt.
101. Charles Evans, Privt.
102. Bartholomew Curtis, Privt.
103. Joshua Curtis, Ensn.
104. Reuben Curtis, Ensn.
[Folio page 2]
105. John Skinner, Corpl.
106. John Cottle, Privt.
107. David Brodwell, Privt.
108. Edmund Dickins, Privt.
109. Amos Alsobrook, Privt.
110. Thomas Kelly, Privt.
111. William Norton, Music
[Folio page 3]
112. Bush Philips, Privt.
113. James Bennett
114. Joel Ramsey, Privt.
115. William Poor, Privt.
116. Mecajah James, Privt.
117. Josiah Messle, Privt.
118. Isaac Scollar, Privt.
[Folio page 4]
119. John Clemons, Privt.
120. Lawrence Butler, Privt.
121. Richard Martin, Privt.
122. Erasmus Tippett, Trooper
123. Joseph Edwards, Privt.
124. Luke Stansberry, Privt.

*No.*
125. John Grinder, Privt.
[Page 50]
[Folio page 1]
126. John Portress, Privt.
127. Peter Smith, Privt.
128. William Kelly, Privt.
129. Thomas Paylor, Privt.
130. Peter Melone, Privt.
131. Ezekiel Coats, Privt.
132. Cornelius Robeson, Privt.
[Folio page 2]
133. Thomas Wilkins, Privt.
134. James Winley, Sergt.
135. Stephen Arthur, Privt.
136. George Oliver, Privt.
137. Sterling Scott, Privt.
138. Curl Tucker, Corpl.
139. Alfred Andrews, Privt.
[Folio page 3]
140. Frederick Desern, Privt.
141. Burwell Wilkins, Privt.
142. William Pass, Trooper
143. Joseph Alsobrook, Trooper
144. Randal Robertson, Trooper
145. Charles Thompson, Sergt.
146. George McDonald, Drummer
[Folio page 4]
147. Richard Willis, Privt.
148. Christopher Lackey, Lt.
149. Thomas Harris, Corpl.
150. William Godfrey, Privt.
151. Samuel Johnston, Privt.
152. Charles Johnston, Privt.
153. Benjamine Johnston, Privt.
[Page 51]
[Folio page 1]
154. George Pettiford, Privt.
155. John Farmer, Corpl.
156. Gilbert Matthews, Trooper
157. Edward Ferrell, Sergt.
158. *Joseph Singletary, Privt.
159. *William Plummer, Privt.
[Folio page 2]
160. Hardin Warren, Privt.
161. Robert Beech, Privt.
162. Alexander Cherry, Privt.
163. John Everitt, Privt.
164. Daniel Cherry, Privt.
165. James Morriss, Corpl.
166. Benjamin Sanders, Privt.
[Folio page 3]
167. Shadrack Moore, Privt.

*No.*
168. Benjamin Kennedy, Sergt.
169. John Moore, Privt.
170. Ezekiel Habbit, Privt.
171. Elisha Mills, Privt.
172. Samuel Hart, Drummer
173. Arthur Graham, Privt.
[Folio page 4]
174. Thomas Scarlet, Privt.
175. James Orr, Privt.
176. Hugh Forsythe, Privt.
177. Joseph Stewart, Privt.
178. Jacob Porter, Privt.
179. William Watford, Privt.
180. Joab Kail, Privt.
[Page 52]
[Folio page 1]
181. John Hoggard, Privt.
182. Thomas Tart, Privt.
183. Thomas Sorrell, Privt.
184. John Farmer, Privt.
185. John Cooper, Privt.
186. Edward Going, Privt.
187. Caleb Berry, Privt.
[Folio page 2]
188. Lemuel Litten, Privt.
189. Abel Litten, Drummer
190. Willis Spann, Trooper
191. Thomas Germany, Privt.
192. Charles Kight, Privt.
193. Demsey Kight, Privt.
194. Jesse Prichard, Sergt.
[Folio page 3]
195. Caleb Taylor, Privt.
196. Isaac Burges, Privt.
197. John Harrison, Fifer
198. Samuel Chappell, Sergt.
199. Martin Phifer, Privt.
200. Seth Wilson, Privt.
201. John Luttrell, Lt.-Col.
[Folio page 4]
202. Gideon Simons, Corpl & Privt.
203. Henry Medlin, Privt.
204. Jaley Smith, Ensn. & Lt.
205. Abel Miller, Privt.
206. John Dickerson, Privt.
207. Carter Hastings, Fifer
208. Benjamin Ray, Privt.
[Page 53]
[Folio page 1]
209. Solomon Watson, Privt.
210. Ephraim Watson, Privt.
211. Jacob Nichols, Sergt.

* The accounts of Joseph Singletary and William Plummer were settled at Warrenton in the year 1786, as nine months men, etc., consequently not on muster, and reported as such by agents.

*No.*

212. William Sheppard, Privt.
213. Alexander Ballentine, Sergt.
214. Charles Thompson, Privt.
215. Timothy Morgan, Privt.
[Folio page 2]
216. James Tharpe, Privt.
217. Joel Tayborne, Privt.
218. Samuel Taylor, Sergt.
219. Charles Ragan, Privt.
220. Thomas Gransberry, Capt.
221. Joseph Leftyear, Privt.
222. Caleb Greenman, Privt.
[Folio page 3]
223. John Moore, Privt.
224. Levi Jarvis, Privt.
225. Martin Penniger, Privt.
226. Joseph Boyd, Corpl.
227. Jacob Parish, Privt.
228. Gabriel Cooly, Privt.
229. Jacob Ginn, Privt.
[Folio page 4]
230. James Scarlet, Privt.
231. William Alston, Lt. & Col.
232. Aron Odam, Privt.
233. Futrell Hall, Privt.
234. Howell Hearn, Privt.
235. Isaac Jones, Privt.
236. Lemuel Jelkes, Trooper
[Page 54]
[Folio page 1]
237. James Ammons, Privt.
238. William Nicholas, Privt.
239. William Tervathan, Privt.
240. Thomas Johnston, Privt.
241. Richard Sumner, Privt.
242. Jeremiah James, Privt.
243. Thomas Garner, Privt.
[Folio page 2]
244. Benjamin James, Privt.
245. John Glover, Wagoner
246. John Phillips, Privt.
247. James Lenter, Sergt.
248. Robert Wilson, Privt.
249. Thomas Bowers, Privt.
250. Benjamine McGackey
[Folio page 3]
251. James Wosson, Privt.
252. James Shannon, Privt.
253. Roll Matthews, Privt.
254. Stephen Bailey, Privt.
255. John Ashley, Privt.
256. James Campbell, Privt.
257. Nathaniel Farrar, Privt.

*No.*

[Folio page 4]
258. Thomas Garvey, Privt.
259. Thomas Brees, Corpl.
260. Hardy Hughkins, Privt.
261. Ephraim Reynolds, Privt.
262. Absolom Martin, Privt.
263. William Stewart, Privt.
[Page 55]
[Folio page 1]
264. John Polson, Corpl. & Sergt.
265. Willis Wiggins, Corpl. & Sergt.
266. John Warner, Privt.
267. Kader Benton, Privt.
268. Hezekiah Jones, Privt.
269. Josiah Jones, Privt.
270. Jesse Benton, Sergt.
[Folio page 2]
271. Josiah Bowers, Privt.
272. Daniel Peele, Privt.
273. Caleb Archer, Privt.
274. Arthur Monday, Privt.
275. Alexander Martin, Col.
276. Isaac Hicks, Privt.
[Folio page 3]
277. Thomas Erving, Privt.
278. Edward Morris, Privt.
279. Absolem Cameron, Privt.
280. Hance Hamilton, Sergt.
281. William Williams, Privt.
[Folio page 4]
282. Jacob Read, Privt.
283. Barnet March, Privt.
284. James Read, Privt.
285. Nicholas Edenton, Sergt.
286. Samuel Martin, Lt.
[Page 56]
[Folio page 1]
287. Micheil Huggins, Privt.
288. Robert Brownlay, Corpl. & Sergt.
289. Jacob Burke, Privt.
290. John Hamilton, Privt.
291. Burwell Lloyd, Privt.
[Folio page 2]
292. William Bowers, Privt.
293. Henry Short, Privt.
294. Isaac Gumbs, Privt.
295. Charles Gibson, Privt.
296. James Parks, Privt.
[Folio page 3]
297. Henry Dawson, Capt.
298. Isaiah Vick, Privt.
299. Norris Baker, Privt.
300. William Scott, Privt.

*No.*

301. William Griffin, Privt.
302. Thomas Weeks, Privt.
[Folio page 4]
303. John Johnston, Privt.
304. Anthony Hall, Privt.
305. William Singletary, Sergt.
306. William Carrol, Privt.
[Page 57]
[Folio page 1]
307. Asheley Fowler, Privt.
308. Solomon Northern, Privt.
309. Edward Harris, Privt.
310. William McKinney, Wagoner
311. James McKey, Privt.
[Folio page 2]
312. Henry Martin, Privt.
313. Caleb Barr, Privt.
314. Absalom Harvey, Privt.
315. Thomas Hudson, Privt.
316. James Hodges, Privt.
[Folio page 3]
317. Henry Waller, Privt.
318. Jacob Gibson, Privt.
319. Patrick Rogers, Lt.
320. William Douglas, Qr. Mstr.
321. William Douglas, issuing Commissary
[Folio page 4]
322. Jacob Seagreaves, Privt.
323. Benjamin Dickson, Trooper
324. William Wynn, Privt.
325. William Cavender, Privt.
326. Sutton Green, Privt.
[Page 58]
[Folio page 1]
327. Berry Jones, Privt.
328. Benjamine Farmer, Privt.
329. John Pierce, Privt.
330. Lawney Reynord, Privt.
331. David Culbertson, Sergt.
[Folio page 2]
332. Cornelius McGraw, Privt.
333. Elijah Vickers, Privt.
334. Daniel Killian, Privt.
335. William Staggs, Privt.
336. James Hammond, Privt.
[Folio page 3]
337. James Armstrong, Privt.
338. John Sorrell, Privt.
339. David Everheart, Privt.
340. John Lyon, Privt.
341. Thomas Kinney, Privt.
[Folio page 4]
342. William Norris, Privt.
343. William Tilson, Privt.

*No.*

344. John Black, Privt.
345. Jacob Reid, Privt.
346. William Ridley, Privt.
[Page 59]
[Folio page 1]
347. Daniel Smith, Privt.
348. James Spann, Trooper
349. Charles Short, Musician
350. Mason Broom, Privt.
351. James Anderson, Drum Majr.
[Folio page 2]
352. Robert McAlpin, Privt.
353. Samuel Jewell, Privt.
354. Hezekiah Shermantine, Privt.
355. Archibald Murphy, Privt.
356. Timothy Rich, Corpl.
[Folio page 3]
357. John Vance, Capt. Artillery
358. Johns Adams, Privt.
359. Robert Moss, Privt.
360. Daniel Middleton, Privt.
361. Joel Martin, Privt.
[Folio page 4]
362. Daniel Murfree, Privt.
363. Ephraim Lewis, Privt.
364. Michael Scott, Privt.
365. Haynes White, Privt.
366. Stephen Pall, Privt.
[Page 60]
[Folio page 1]
367. Caleb Story, Privt.
368. John Harvey, Privt.
369. Fredick Lucy, Privt.
370. Dempsey Johnston, Privt.
371. Owen Omerry, Privt.
[Folio page 2]
372. Coleman Clayton, Privt.
373. Henry Smith, Privt.
374. Henry May, Privt.
375. Benjamin Brady, Corpl.
376. Noah Robeson, Privt.
377. Issued through mistake and returned.
[Folio page 3]
378. Joshua Pritchet, Privt.
379. Thomas Brown, Privt.
380. Matthias Johnson, Privt.
381. Richard Smith, Privt.
382. Joseph Purser, Privt.
[Folio page 4]
383. William Melton, Privt.
384. Richard Lewis, Sergt.
385. Henry Cooper, Sergt.
386. Hardy Redley, Privt.
387. Caleb Woodward, Privt.

No.
[Page 61]
[Folio page 1]
388. Saul Scott, Privt.
389. Ballenger Lucas, Privt.
390. Malichi Strickland, Privt.
391. Edwin James, Privt.
392. James Sanders, Privt.
393. William James, Privt.
[Folio page 2]
394. William Bennett, Privt.
395. Thomas Pierce, Privt.
396. Charles Morgan, Sergt.
397. Adam Rabby, Privt.
[Folio page 3]
398. John Weston, Privt.
399. Ezekiel Modlin, Privt.
400. Gabriel Cooly, already charged,
    *see 228.*
401. Edward Fossett, Privt.
402. Micajah Watson, Privt.
[Folio page 4]
403. Benjamine Williams, Privt.
404. Henry Chaver, Privt.
405. James Price, Privt.
406. William Eason, Privt.
407. James Wadkins, Privt.
[Page 62]
[Folio page 1]
408. George Murkinock, Privt.
409. Thomas Biby, Privt.
410. William McIntire, Privt.
411. John Weaver, Privt.
412. Robert Moseman, Privt.
[Folio page 2]
413. Phillip Logan, Musician
414. Giles Gaunt, Privt.
415. Miles Castilloe, Privt.
416. William Ryles, Privt.
417. Tekel Rarks, Privt.
[Folio page 3]
418. James Long, Privt.
419. John Patterson, Privt.
420. William Davis, Sergt.
421. James Talton, Privt.
422. William Talton, Privt.
[Folio page 4]
423. John Harper, Privt.
424. John Perry, Privt.
425. James Fike, Privt.
426. Michael McGuire, Privt.
427. Amos Cail, Privt.
[Page 63]
[Folio page 1]
428. John Green, Privt.

No.
429. Noah Wiggins, Privt.
430. David Danley, Corpl.
431. Robert Colchorn, Privt.
432. John Durham, Musician
[Folio page 2]
433. Robert Dennis, Privt.
434. George Campbell, Privt.
435. John Taylor, Privt.
436. John Lacey, Sergt.
437. James Walker, Privt.
[Folio page 3]
438. Baxter Boling, Privt.
439. John Whitaker, Sergt.
440. Shadrack Gallop, Corpl.
441. John Gibson, Privt.
442. Isaac Merrett, Privt.
[Folio page 4]
443. Josiah Dowdy, Sergt.
444. Samuel Barker, Privt.
445. William Gilbert, Privt.
446. Thomas Jarvis, Sergt.
447. John Taylor, Privt.
[Page 64]
[Folio page 1]
448. Andrew Phillips, Privt.
449. Matthias Goodridge, Sergt.
450. George Hargrove, Privt.
451. Johnathan Erexon, Privt.
452. Richard Ward, Sergt.
[Folio page 2]
453. James Dobbins, Privt.
454. James Davis, Privt.
455. Benjamine Davis, Privt.
456. Jordan Ammons, Privt.
457. Stephen Wiley, Privt.
[Folio page 3]
458. Frederick Callum, Privt.
459. Thomas Gregory, Privt.
460. Nicholas Icour, Privt.
461. Francis Tartanson, Capt.
462. David Shores, Privt.
[Folio page 4]
463. Moses Hopper, Privt.
464. Nicholas Hair, Privt.
465. Solomon Fountain, Privt.
466. Absalom Sallenger, Privt.
467. Hardy Hardyson, Sergt.
[Page 65]
[Folio page 1]
468. William Price, Privt.
469. William Smithwick, Privt.
470. Shubal Claghorne, Privt. & Corpl.
471. George Beck, Privt.
472. Joseph Palmer, Privt.

No.
[Folio page 2]
473. William Fox, Privt.
474. Alexander McCarter, Privt.
475. Stephen Charles Craft, Privt.
476. Reuben McCoy, Privt.
477. Edmond Howard, Corpl.
478. George Williams, Sergt.
[Folio page 3]
479. Jacob Brown, Privt.
480. Samuel Webb, Privt.
481. Valentine Beard, Lieut.
482. James Deacon, Trooper
483. Richard Pearson, Privt.
[Folio page 4]
484. John Fry, Privt.
485. Michael Legal, Privt.
486. Jacob Bennett, Privt.
487. George Moore, Privt.
488. John Reason, Privt.
489. William Adams, Privt.
[Page 66]
[Folio page 1]
490. Hezekiah Bryan, Privt.
491. James Orrell, Sergt.
492. Nicholas Blanks, Privt.
493. Michael McMullan, Privt.
494. Nicholas Dunn, Privt.
495. William McDaniel, Privt.
[Folio page 2]
496. Edward Vail, Privt.
497. Jesse Hardyson, Sergt.
498. John Fisher, Privt.
499. Thomas King, Privt.
500. Francis Coston, Privt.
501. John Harris, Privt.
[Folio page 3]
502. Charles Shaddock, Privt.
503. Henry Wiggins, Privt.
504. Stephen Thomas, Privt.
505. Henry Hawstory, Trooper
506. John Willoughby, Musician
507. James Willoughby, Privt.
[Folio page 4]
508. John Howard, Privt.
509. Joshua Elkins, Corpl.
510. William Hardin, Trooper
511. Howell Rowell, Trooper
512. Theopelus Mitchell, Privt.
513. Joseph Tate, Capt.
[Page 67]
[Folio page 1]
514. Thomas Pratt, Privt.
515. Benjamin Solebury, Privt.

No.
516. Hezekiah Cooksey, Privt.
517. Thomas Cooksey, Privt.
518. George Thompson, Privt.
519. Joshua Martin, Privt.
[Folio page 2]
520. William Smith, Privt.
521. John Mars, Trooper
522. William Todd, Privt.
523. James Todd, Privt.
524. Ephraim Todd, Privt.
525. Thomas Todd, Privt.
[Folio page 3]
526. Dempsey Boyce, Privt.
527. James White, Privt.
528. Daniel Weaver, Privt.
529. William Womack, Sergt.
530. Arthur Markum, Sergt.
531. William Pierce, Privt.
[Folio page 4]
532. Lewis Legett, Privt.
533. John Brooks, Privt.
534. Benjamin Almerry, Privt.
535. John Hamilton, Sergt.
536. Blake Rabby, Privt.
537. Solomon Spence, Privt.
[Page 68]
[Folio page 1]
538. Jeremiah Glohon, Sergt.
539. Thomas Pearson, Privt.
540. William Herbert, Sergt.
541. William Moore, Privt.
542. William Lord, Lieut.
543. Absalom Wildey, Privt.
[Folio page 2]
544. Absalom Wildey, Corpl.
545. Hugh Donally, Privt.
546. Isaac Griffin, Sergt.
547. William Jackson, Privt.
548. Francis Penrice, Privt.
549. Edward Howell, Corpl.
[Folio page 3]
550. Joseph Spears, Privt.
551. Samuel Spears, Privt.
552. Daniel Ramsey, Privt.
553. Francis Bennett, Privt.
554. Arthur Corbin, Privt.
555. Isaac Wells, Privt.
[Folio page 4]
556. Frederick Jones, Privt.
557. Oliver Johnston, Privt.
558. James O'Neal, Privt.
559. Jesse Hall, Corpl.
560. Edward Hathcock, Privt.

*No.*
561. Matthew Worley, Privt.
[Page 69]
[Folio page 1]
562. Samuel Davis, Privt.
563. John Wilson, Privt.
564. Thomas Garvey
565. Thomas Sinclair, Privt.
566. Richard Low
[Folio page 2]
567. Alexander Scull, Privt.
568. Joshua Proctor, Privt.
569. William Leighton, Privt.
570. Andrew Simpson, Corpl.
571. John Wood, Privt.
572. Jethro Benton, Ensn.
[Folio page 3]
573. Barnaba Murrill, Privt.
574. John Henry, Privt.
575. Jacob Hafner, Privt.
576. William Collett, Privt.
577. Abraham Kenny, Privt.
578. Daniel Matthews, Privt.
[Folio page 4]
579. Daniel Huggins, Sergt.
580. Thomas Ralph, Privt.
581. John Nutter, Privt.
582. James Low, Privt.
583. Cornelius Love, Privt.
584. John Best, Privt.
[Page 70]
[Folio page 1]
585. Kinneth McKinsey, Privt.
586. Joseph Arthur, Privt.
587. David Clement, Privt.
588. Lewis Guthridge, Privt.
589. Richard Baker, Privt.
590. Timothy Murray, Sergt.
[Folio page 2]
591. Cendall Bootey, Privt.
592. Robert McKay, Privt.
593. Ross Thomas, Privt.
594. Benjamine Neal, Privt.
595. Jeremiah Allen, Privt.
596. Benjamin Mason, Privt.
[Folio page 3]
597. Benjamin Blango, Privt.
598. Moses Blango, Privt.
599. Henry Brady, Privt.
600. James Slaughter, Privt.
601. John Brown, Sergt.
602. Thomas McKeal, Privt.
[Folio page 4]
603. James Abbott, Privt.
604. James Berry, Privt.

*No.*
605. James Chambers, Privt.
606. Henry Dixon, Privt.
607. William Smith, Privt.
608. Abreham Perkin, Privt.
[Page 71]
[Folio page 1]
609. Aaron Wood, Privt.
610. John Whaley, Musician
611. Jesse Freeman, Privt.
612. Lewis Conner, Privt.
613. Hillery Brinson, Privt.
614. Francis Whaley, Privt.
[Folio page 2]
615. Cox Gray, Privt.
616. John Brown, Privt.
617. Isaac Sampson, Privt.
618. Thomas Lee, Privt.
619. James Huggins, Privt.
620. Cox Gray, Privt.
[Folio page 3]
621. Benjamin Wilcox, Privt.
622. Mallachi Jolley, Privt.
623. John Killebrew, Privt.
624. William Duke, Privt.
625. Matthew Garvey, Privt.
[Folio page 4]
626. Seth Eason, Lieut.
627. Cornelius Anglen, Privt.
628. Mathias Belks, Privt.
629. John Hopper, Privt.
630. Edward Bell, Privt.
631. Jonathan Hickman, Privt.
[Page 72]
[Folio page 1]
632. John Mullins, Privt.
633. Aron Smith, Privt.
634. Benjamine Stedman, Capt.
635. Simon Alderson, Capt.
636. William Bailey, Corpl.
637. John Brinn, Privt.
[Folio page 2]
638. William Boomer, Privt.
639. Lewis Taylor, Privt.
640. Joshua Wilkins, Privt.
641. Godfrey Rowland, Privt.
642. Robert Allen, Privt.
643. John Miller, Privt.
[Folio page 3]
644. Joseph Sanders, Privt.
645. Shadrack Medlin, Privt.
646. William Hopper, Sergt.
647. Elijah Garner, Privt.
648. Mack Ferguson, Privt.
649. Charles Upchurch, Trooper

No.
[Folio page 4]
650. Thomas Laughinhouse, Privt.
651. Daniel Neal, Privt.
652. Levi Branton, Privt.
653. Arthur Nelson, Privt.
654. Solomon Molborne, Privt.
655. John Carter, Privt.
[Page 73]
[Folio page 1]
656. John Wall, Privt.
657. Joseph Ward, Privt.
658. James Woolard
659. Brittain Jones, Privt.
660. Brittain Jones, Privt.
661. William Bond, Privt.
[Folio page 2]
662. John Corey, Privt.
663. James Nobles, Privt.

No.
664. Robert Ruff, Privt.
665. Benjamine Cummings, Privt.
666. James Eslick, Privt.
667. Hardy Nelson, Sergt.
[Folio page 3]
668. Noah Bartlett, Privt.
669. Elisha Lewis, Privt.
670. William Cox, Privt.
671. Joseph Cox, Privt.
672. William Deal, Privt.
[Folio page 4]
673. William Corothers, Privt.
674. John Hackleman, Privt.
675. Isaac Rolston, Lt.   Allowed 130
    pounds 5 shillings 2 pence & de-
    livered to Col. R. Hays, of Cum-
    berland, by a resolve of the General
    Assembly at their session in 1792.

Vol. IV.  North Carolina Army Accounts.  Old Series—Vol. IV—
Remarks of Commissioners

No.
[Page 1]
[Folio page 1]
    Officers Accts.
[Folio page 2]
1. James Craven
[Page 2]
[Folio page 1]
2. Butler Cowell
[Folio page 2]
3. Luke Lamb Ferrell, Lt.
4. William Charlton, Lt.
5. Jacob Messick, Lt. mustrd as Lt.
   then Ensn., then Lt.
[Folio page 3]
6. John Dickinson, this should be
   Richard Dickinson who is mustered
   as Ensn, then Lt., then Ensn. & Lt.
7. Lemuel Ely, Capt.
8. John P. Williams, Capt.*
[Page 3]
[Folio page 2]
9. Edward Buncombe, Col.
[Folio page 3]
10. Benj'n. Bryer, Lt., appears on mus-
    ters as Ensn.
[Folio page 4]
11. Acct. withdrawn

No.
12. Eli Ely, Capt.
[Page 4]
[Folio page 1]
13. John Pilly, Ensn.
14. Hugh Dobbins, Lt.
[Folio page 2]
15. Benjamin Dillon
16. Whitfield Wilson, F. M. mustrd. as
    Q. M.
17. John Lessenby, Lt.
[Folio page 3]
18. David Cowan, Lt.
19. Elias Hoell, Lt.
[Folio page 4]
20. William Lord, Lt.
21. Wm. Knott, Lt.
22. Wm. Murray, Lt.
[Page 5]
[Folio page 1]
23. Edward Vail, Capt.
24. John McGlahan, Capt.
25. Isaac Moore, Capt.
[Folio page 2]
26. Frederick Heimburg, Surgeon
27. Jno. Martin Gist, Lt.
[Folio page 3]
28. Zeri Rice, Lt.

* Explanation of defects in musters' Folio pages 7-8-9-10.—In Jan. 1778 a reform in the army
took place, the Junior Regmts. of the N. Car. Lines were reduced; the non. com. officers & privates
were incorporated with those of the elder, & the com. officers of the reduced regiments returned
to the state on the recruiting service and to take charge of such men as they might be appointed
to command by the state, on this principle ten Regiments were reduced to three, etc.

*No.*
29. John Williams, Colo.
[Folio page 4]
30. Josiah Mann, Lt.
31. Robert Singleton, Lt.
[Page 6]
[Folio page 1]
32. William Hancock, Lt.
33. Andrew Vanoy, Capt.
34. James Vaughan, Capt.

*No.*
[Folio page 2]
35. Micajah Ferrell, Lt.
36. James Armstrong, Lt.
37. Lovick Rochell, Lt.
38. David Jones, Lt.
[Folio page 3]
39. James McRory, Ensn.
40. William Corrington, Lt.
41. Joseph John Wade, Capt.

NON COMMISSIONED OFFICERS, PRIVATES & MUSIC

*No.*
[Folio page 4]
1413. Jordan Wilkins
1414. George Wilkins
1416. Peter Williams, enlisted as Corpl., then Sergt.
[Page 7]
[Folio page 1]
1429. Benj'n. Bird
1441. Wm. Cobb, appears on Musters in '77, died Jan. 26th, 1778.
1444. Wm. Pollard
[Folio page 2]
1450. John Stone
1459. John Mills, a musician of this name in Child's Company.
1469. John Pearsey, this name entered in Commissioners book as John Kersey.
[Folio page 3]
1482. John Todd
1483. Jno. Jordan
1485. Peter Poyner
1488. Stephen Truitt
[Page 8]
[Folio page 1]
1489. Abraham Clark
1490. Jacob Clark
1493. Thomas Daniel, deserted 2nd Aug. '78.
[Folio page 2]
1494. Peter Furney
1495. Joshua Larouze
[Folio page 3]
1496. Anthony Cross
1497. John Dean
1498. John Giles, Sergt.
1499. Jesse Aldridge
[Folio page 4]
1500. Jesse Duggan, killed Oct. 4th, 1777.
1501. Andrew Rowell
1504. Isaac Bagley, a 9 mos. Corporal.

*No.*
1506. Wm. Warren
1507. Arthur Tyner, appears on muster also as Arthur Tainer.
1508. Holland Harrel, died Aug. 28th, '77
[Page 9]
[Folio page 1]
1509. Edward Smithwick
1510. Jesse Woolard, pris. June '79, again mustered Nov. '79.
1511. Thomas Aims, deserted 12th Feb. '79.
1514. Thomas Duggin, missing 4th Oct. '77.
1515. Moses Hizzard. A Moses Hissett appears on the muster, we suppose it to be the same man. Hissett died 3rd May, '78. Moses Hizzard does not appear on the musters.
1516. Peter Simmons. Died 15th Aug. '77
1518. William Martin, (2 accts. in this name)
[Folio page 2]
1520. Francis Duggin
1523. Elisha Modlin
1524. James Williams, Sergt. then Corpl. Died Sept. 24th, '78.
1525. Joseph Williams
[Folio page 3]
1527. Zebulon Pratt
1528. Asahel Davenport
[Folio page 4]
1529. Wm. Jenkins
1530. James Harrison
1583. John Norwood
1585. Samuel Bradley
[Page 10]
[Folio page 1]
1589. Daniel Moore
1591. John Hooker
1607. John Lilly (there appears a John Lille on musters who deserted 25th Dec., '77)

*No.*

1608. Wm. Brownen (there is a Wm. Browning on the musters, but we cannot decide on this claim).

1626. Samuel Parker

[Folio page 2]

1636. George Brooks

1739. John Jarvis

1741. Benjamin Brittle

1742. Jesse Baggett. (There appears on the musters *Jesse Badget*, a Corpl.)

[Folio page 3]

1743. John Russell. (3 men of this name appear on the muster, etc.)

1744. Matthew Murrell, appears on muster as Sergt.

1745. John Cannon. (3 men appear of this name)

[Folio page 4]

1749. James Roberts. (2 men of this name appear)

1750. John Bettis

1752. Thomas Green

1753. John Floyd

[Page 11]

[Folio page 1]

1797. John Cummings (died Oct. '78)

1810. Isaac Morrison, deserted 5th Dec. 1777. Appears again in Sept. '78, and again deserts in Dec.

1849. Benjamin Cannon (mustered as musician, Apr. '78. Died 1st May, '78)

1877. David Jones

[Folio page 2]

1894. Wm. Brownen. (2 accts. of this name)

1940. Christopher Dasher

1950. Samuel Morrow, Corpl. then Privt.

1969. Peter Herrendon, Corpl. then Privt.

2018. Sterling Dean. Enlisted July 5, 1777.

2019. Isaac Sanderlin. Enlisted May 22, '77.

2025. Thomas Mann. Deserted Feb. 14, 1780.

[Folio page 3]

2022. Thomas Waldron, music to June 1778.

2021. Levi Right

2024. Isaac Litten, mustered as Sergt., his amount was settled as Privt.

2025. William Sexton

2026. Jabez Spence

*No.*

2031. Thomas Garrett, charges as Sergt., mustered as Privt., then deserted.

2033. Samuel Nichols, never appears on muster, there is a Samuel Nicholas, Sergt. "We know not if this is the same man.

2034. George Burges

2035. Thomas Jennings, Privt. & Corpl.

[Folio page 4]

2037. Thomas Caton, Privt. enlisted, then Corpl.

2039. Levi Sanderlin, enlisted '77, deserted 25th Dec. '77, mustered again Jan. '79, Corpl. June '79.

2040. John Lutt, Corpl. before he died, Nov. '78.

2041. Isaac Herrington, never appears on the musters, his amount charged to soldier serving to the southward, very few of whom ever appear on the musters. See reasons for defects in No. 8 Acct. of J. P. Williams.

2042. The same, etc.

2043. The same, etc.

2044. Willoughby Thompson

[Page 12]

[Folio page 1]

2045. Luke Sylvester

2046. } The same

2047. }

2053. Andrew Rowell

2055. Hillary Crabb

2059. The same.

2061. The same. There are 4 J. Clarkes on muster.

2062. John Morrison

2064. Stephen Powell

2066. Jo. Smith. There are 2 men of this name.

[Folio page 2]

2069. John Blanchard does not appear on musters but John Blanchet, musician appears.

2071. George Harris

2072. Daniel Sevills, we do not find this name on the musters. There is a Daniel Sewells enlisted 77, died 14th Apr. '78.

[Folio page 3]

2073. Willis Upton enlisted 14th Feb. '77, died 1st July '78.

2075. James Bennett. 2 men of this name appear.

*No.*

2076. Lemuel Rowe, served sometime as Corpl.

2079. James Goodson, never appears, there is a James Gotson.

2081. Joshua Lewis, 3 of this name appear.

[Folio page 4]

2095. Noell Clarke, does not appear. A name of Niel Clark appears.

2097. Jordan Wilkins, 2 accts. of this name.

2104. John Davis. We find 4 men of this name.

[Page 13]

[Folio page 1]

2106. John Williams. There are 4 of this name.

2122. Abraham Dean

2131. Abraham Green. 2 of this name on the musters, the account is entered by the Commissioners as Abraham Geen.

2134. Edmund Diggins

[Folio page 2]

2135. John Morgan. 3 of this name appear.

2137. John Dixon.

2153. Nathaniel Cooper. 2 of this name appear.

2157. William Bush, deserted April, '77.

[Folio page 3]

2158. Hardy Keel, mustered as Sergt.

2159. Hardy Robertson

2160. William Hendley

2161. James Davis

2184. Isaac Waters

2193. ⎫ John McCoy, Senr. ⎫ There is 2
2197. ⎰ John McCoy, Junr. ⎰ of this name on the musters—one for the war, settled at Halifax, & one for 2½ yrs. who enlisted in '77 & died 10th Mch. '78

[Folio page 4]

2199. Edmund Hammons, deserted Aug. 1777

2213. Daniel Peale

2214. Moses Venters

2215. Edward Matthews, music

2216. Eli Rogers

[Page 14]

[Folio page 1]

2217. Peter McGee, mustered as privt., as Corpl. & as Sergt.

2218. Caleb Saunders—*Caleb Saunderson* on the musters Corpl.

*No.*

[Folio page 2]

2224. John Campbell

2227. Samuel Burnham

2229. Malachi White

2230. Josiah Miller

2231. Jacob Bennett

2234. George Williamson. Deserted 3rd Sept. '78.

2235. Lemuel Halsted

2237. James Rainey, admitted as Sergt. then Privt., there is another James Rainey.

2240. John Elliott

2241. Wm. Guinn. No such name on the musters. Wm. Ginn appears.

[Folio page 3]

2242. Thomas McDaniel. No such name on the musters, but there are 2 of Thomas McDonall.

2247. Maltiah Turner

2250. John Gibson

2252. Joshua McTeebee, or McCeebe, as in the acct. or McEbbe as in the Commissioner's book. But Joshua McKabe appears in '77, died Feb. '78, and possibly may be the man.

2255. Benjamin Smith. 4 of this name.

[Folio page 4]

2257. Thomas Newberry does not appear on musters, but a Thomas Newbern appears

2259. John Hains, died June '78.

2261. Micajah Savage, Michael Savage on the musters.

2267. Wm. White, several of this name on musters.

2268. Charles Evans. 2 of this name on musters.

2280. John White. Six of this name on musters, but not one corresponding in time with this claim.

2292. Thomas Owns, or Oans. Neither appear on the musters. Thomas Owens appears & there are 2 of this name.

[Page 15]

[Folio page 1]

2296. Lorton Hawkins, mustered Lewerton Hawkins.

2298. Larkin Rogers

2299. John Ketanch (altered in acct. to Cotanch)

2301. James Vance, died 15th Nov. '78.

2305. Thomas Williams. 3 of this name.

2312. Daniel Hopkins

No.
2320. John Canaway, charges as Sergt.
[Folio page 2]
2323. John Wiatt
2324. Emanuel Marshall, enlisted Mch.
'78, died Apr. 5, '78.
2327. Thomas Hendricks
2328. George Lowe, enlisted in '77, deserted 15th Aug. '78.
2329. Robert Staples
[Folio page 3]
2330. Willis Sawyer
2332. Miles Modlin
2334. Job Bright, mustered as Privt., then Corpl.
2335. Wm. Parr, never appears on muster, there is a Wm. Pair.
[Folio page 4]
2336. Malachi Dunn, mustered 3rd Dec. '77, died Dec. '78.
2337. Hillary Parker
2369. Thomas Todd, mustered in '77 for 3 yrs., died Sept. '77.
2370. Jonathan Richards, enlisted 10th May '77, died June '78.
2373. Wm. Lomax
[Page 16]
[Folio page 1]
2374. John Artis
2375. David Davis
2384. John Thornall. A John Thurnell musters but not a John Thornall; he died Nov. '78.
2395. Jonathan Henry
2397. Alexander McCulloch
2400. Wm. Martin, see No. 1518
2402. James Caton, served as Corpl. & Privt.
[Folio page 2]
2406. Peter Allison, no such name on the musters, but Peter Alexon appear.
2409. Frederick Cooper
2410-2415. The same, etc.
2416. Thomas May, died 6th Nov. '81
2417. Wm. Beasly
2418. Moses Venters. (See No. 2214)
[Folio page 3]
2419-2420. The same. Mutalis mutendis.
2421. Abraham Reddick. Inadmissible, but 1 of this name on musters, his amount was settled at Halifax & receipted by himself.
[Folio page 4]
2422. Robert Ferrebee
2424. Wm. Smith

No.
[Page 17]
[Folio page 1]
2425. Another of the same name, etc.
2426. Richard Bailey
2427. Thomas . Brinkley—as Privt. & Sergt.
[Folio page 2]
2428. Nathan Horton
2429. Mark Robertson     ⎫ The vouchers
2430. Anthoney Alexander ⎬ of these 4 ac-
2431. Levi Norman        ⎪ counts are
2432. Stephen Cross      ⎭ missing
2433. John Tucker, served 12 mos. as Corpl.
2434. Thomas Mullen
2435. Benjamin Carroll
[Folio page 3]
2436. Paul Sink
2437. Dempsey Sikes
2438. Wm. Duke       ⎫
2439. James Rogers   ⎪
2440. Henry Tice     ⎬ All similar to
2441. Wm. Campbell   ⎪ preceding
2442. John Kettle    ⎭
2443. Peter Grover (the discharge given in the name of Crover)
2444. Joseph Newman, or Numan did not commence service prior to the year 1782, consequently the U. States admits nothing to our credit for this claim.
[Folio page 4]
2445. Matthias Betts
2446. George Wilkins
2447. Jonathan Case
2448. Anderson Runnery
2449-2453. These amts. are similar to the foregoing, 12 mo. accts., etc.
2454. Wm. Morgan, S.
2455. Wm. Story
[Page 18]
[Folio page 1]
2456. Lewis Shultz
2457. Solomon Thrift
2458. West Hadnot, Sergt. & Privt.
2459. Wm. Low
2461. Peter Roberto (voucher missing)
2462. Uriah Leftyear
2463. John Downs, Privt. & Corpl.
[Folio page 2]
2464. John Keith, Privt. & Music
2465. Samuel Serrett
2466. William Graham. 2 of this name, both Sergts.

No.
2467. John Needham
2469. Charles Rozier
2470. Jesse Goldsmith, Privt. & Fifer
[Folio page 3]
2484. James Maloy
2485. Alexander McGlanghlin
2487. Charles A. Scruggs
2488. James Akins
2489. James Gifford, Sergt., then Privt. when he deserted.
[Folio page 4]
2491. Acey Davis, Privt. & Music.
2492. John Davis (several of same name)
2493. Wm. Davis, Corpl., then Privt., then Corpl. again.
2494. Solomon Jennett, musters as Privt.
[Page 19]
[Folio page 1]
2495. Jonathan Kemmy
2498. James Royal, Privt. & Corpl.
2499. James Fooks
2500. John Fooks
2501. Robert Grisson, Privt., Music
2508. Charles Murray, Sergt.
2512. Richard Atkins
2513. John Avery
[Folio page 2]
2514. John Hill
2515. James Jones
2516-2517. Similar to foregoing
2518. David Brothers
[Folio page 3]
2519. Whitaker Shadforth
2520. Frederick Blount
2521. Charles Roach, never musters but certificate admits his service.
2522. Austin Spain, Sergt.
2523. Wm. Spain, Music
2525. Peter Harrold, Sergt.
2527. Thomas Prescott, died 20th Mch. '78.
[Folio page 4]
2528. William Meeks
2549. John Smith. 13 of the names on the musters.
2551. Willis Curling
2554. Samuel Burnham. 2 of this name on musters.
2561. William Elliott, not mustered, having served in Qr. M's. Department.
2562. Jesse Brown. Similar with foregoing.
[Page 20]
[Folio page 1]
2563. Solomon Brown

No.
2565. Samuel McClelland, never appears on musters, admitted as 9 mo's. man to the Southward.
2566. The same with the foregoing.
2567. Daniel Crawley, mustered in '79 as Sergt.
2568. George Carcher, 9 mos. soldier to the Southward, never appears on musters.
2571. John Madry
2585. William Foster. 2 acts. in this name.
[Folio page 2]
2601. Charles Mannan, there appears a Charles Manning on the musters in '77, deserted same year.
2603. James Tinner, never appears, there is a James Teaner.
[Folio page 3]
2609. David Spears, or Spear or Speir
[Folio page 4]
2613. James Overton
2615. Richard Moss
2616. Isaac Etheridge, never appears, there is an Isaac Everidge, Music.
2618. Uriah Pendleton, never appears on muster, there is Hiram Pendleton mustered.
2620. Wm. Foster. See No. 2585
2637. James Butler
[Page 21]
[Folio page 1]
2645. Arthur Wright, never appears on musters, there is an Arthur Britt.
2666. Willis Johnston, a dragoon. We have no muster of the Cavalry.
2677. Morris Evans
2678. Jesse Bunn
2679. Wm. West
2680-2683. All twelve months accts. similar to above.
2690. John Marr, a dragoon. See No. 2666.
2691. Sampson Morgan
[Folio page 2]
2692. Arington Sheppard
2693. Caleb Wright, does not appear on musters, but acct. is admitted.
2695. Peter Jones
2705. Reubin Ivey
2753 to 2760. Claims of dragoons. See No. 2666.
2761. John May, only one on musters.
[Folio page 3]
2762. Bazil Holland

No.
2763. James Smith, many corresponding with this name on the musters.
2764. Wm. Myers, one of the names in Blount's Co.
2766. George Dunn, name not on the musters, 9 mo's. man to the Southward.
2768. Jesse Fulton
2770. David Gillaspie
[Folio page 4]
2772. Isaac Solomon, 9 mo's. man to the Southward, name does not appear on musters.
2773. Drury Jones, same
2780. James McNatt, never appears on musters, service as 9 mo's. man to the Southward.
2781. Wm. Dennis. We presume this should be Hezekiah Dennis, for the acct. is headed Ezekier Dennis but endorsed Wm. Dennis. The musters bear the name Ezekiah or Hezekiah.
2782. Alexander Patterson, 9 mo's. man to the Southward.
2783 to 2788. The same as above.
[Page 22]
[Folio page 1]
2789. Wm. Thomas. 2 of this name.
2790. Philip Morris
2791. James Sloan
2792. John Holdbrook
both appear as 9 mo's. men to the Southward, names never appear on musters.
2793. Thomas Bond, as above.
2797. Hugh Patterson, same.
[Folio page 2]
2799. Marmaduke Maples
2800. John Stevens, 9 mo's. man to the Southward.
2801. James Stanford, same
2803. John Ingram. 2 of this name on musters, both Sergts.
2808. James Sexton
[Folio page 3]
2817. Wm. Clifton, 9 mo's. man to the Southward, not on musters. 2 of this name appear.
2818. Nehemiah Smith
2819. Wm. Hartgrove, 9 mo's. man to the Southward.
2820. James Bell, same
2822. Joseph Hughes, same. There is a Joseph Hewes. S. enlisted in '81.

No.
2825. Thomas Reddin, 9 mo's. man to the Southward.
2838. George Roper, same
2839. John Adcock, same. There is a Jno. Adcock on musters for 3 yrs., his acct. was settled at Halifax.
2842. Charles Driver, 9 mo's. man to the Southward.
2843. Robert Woodall, same
2844. John Gallimore
[Folio page 4]
2845. John Coats
2888. John Todd
2906. John Roor, 9 mo's. man to the Southward.
2907. Finley Shaw
2908. John Rounsever
Same as before.
2909. John Black, same
2910. David Benton, same, but 1 on musters, that settled at Halifax.
2911. Anthoney Garrett, not on musters, etc.
[Page 23]
[Folio page 1]
2914. David Ivey, appears on musters as Music.
2917. John Blanchard. 2 accts. occur in this name. See No. 2069 for other.
2918. Charles Coleman, Qr. M.
[Folio page 2]
2919. Thomas Barnes, dragoon. See No. 2666.
2922. Peter Ferguson
2923. James Dilliard
2924. Hannes Steiner
2930. Robert Briggs, Privt., then Sergt.
2931. Elisha Parker, 9 mo's. man to the Southward, not on musters.
2932. John West, as above.
2937. John Blair, same.
2968. John Mahoney
[Folio page 3]
2783. John Thompson. Five of this name.
2984. John Henly. 1 appears on musters.
2993. John Morgan
2994. Thomas Green
2995. John Duke
2996. Moses Manley
3007. John Stone. 9 mo's. man to the Southward.
[Folio page 4]
3008-3010. 9 mo's. men.
3011. John Hays, war acct. etc.
3023-3024. 9 mo's. accts. to Southward.

*No.*
3025. Solomon Park, Ensn.
3034. William Trowell
3038. Thomas Manning
3051. Rawleigh Prendergrass
[Page 24]
[Folio page 1]
3055. Hugh Catchem
3056. John Griffis
3057. Wm. Red
3058. Benjamin Brady, Corpl. & Sergt.
3059. Albert Hendricks, Corpl. & Sergt.
3060-3072. All 12 mo's. accts.
3082. John Edwards, several of the name, etc.
3083-3091. 12 mo's. accts.
3097-3098. 9 mo's. men to the Southward.
[Folio page 2]
3099. John Douglass, Sergt.
3100. Maurice Fennel, 9 mo's. Sergt. to the Southward, not on musters.
3103. Arnold Mann, dragoon. See No. 2666.
3104-3105. Both dragoons.
3106. Wm. Miller
3111. David Sayers, this name not on musters, but name David Sears appears.
3114. Richard Stranghan, war soldier, not on musters. Richard Strawn appears but his time of service commenced in 1782.
3127. Zeanus Bawlin, not on musters, but there is a proper discharge, which authorizes the acct.
3128. John O'Neal
[Folio page 3]
3131. Richard Vaughn. Name not on the muster. Richard Vaughn is, etc.
3133. Thomas Mallett. We find Thomas Mollett in '79 for 9 mo's., deserted Sept. '79. This charge is for a 9 mo's. man to the Southward. An acct. was settled at Halifax for a Thomas Mullett, so we cannot decide between them.
3135. John Thompson, several of the name on musters, etc.
3137. Wm. Cole
3141. David Stokes, 9 mo's man to Southward, not on muster.
3152. John Jones, several on musters.
[Folio page 4]
3153. Isham Ferguson, 9 mo's. man to Southward.

*No.*
3154. Jeremiah Norris, same.
3155. Sherwood Harris, dragoon.
3156. John Reeves ⎫ both dragoons
3157. Johnstone Cruise ⎭
3160. Wm. Hall, 9 mo's. man to Southward, not on musters.
3161. Joseph Pack
3162. Elihu Burk
3165. Wm. Hewell, or Ewell, S. Neither Hewell nor Ewell on musters.
3166. Thomas Marston ⎫ nearly the same
3167. Aaron Spilmore ⎭
3168. Thomas Daniel, mustered as Corpl.
[Page 25]
[Folio page 1]
3169 and 3170. 12 mo's. accts.
3171. Larkin McDonald, killed Sept. 8th, '81.
3172. Jesse Liddle
3173. Abraham Harrold, 9 mo's. to the Southward.
3174. Hance Pettigrew, same.
3175. John Brock
3176. Matthew Newby
[Folio page 2]
3177. West Colson
3178. Daniel Gunn
3179. John Ogewin. There is a Jno. Ogiven,. cannot be applied to this name.
3180. Joseph Allen
3181. Francis Huzza. A Francis Husser on musters, etc.
3182. Thomas Morris, 9 mo's. man to Southward.
3183. William Townley, ditto.
3184-3190. Same.
3191. George Rochell, same.
[Folio page 3]
3192-3193. 9 mo's. men, neither on musters.
3194. Jessee Hall, mustered in '79, deserted in Sept. '79.
3195. John Hudson. 2 of same name. See No. 3158.
3196. Matthias Morgan, 9 mo's. to the Southward.
3197. Michael McMullen, 9 mo's. to the Southward.
3198. George Spivey, 9 mo's. Southward, not on muster.
3199. Ricey Oliver, 9 mo's. Southward, not on muster.

No.
3200. Wm. Phimer, 9 mo's. Southward, not on muster.
3201. Joseph Singletory, 9 mo's. Southward, not on muster.
3202. Wm. McClennin, 9 mo's. Southward, not on muster.
3203. Arthur Graham, 12 mo's. man.
3204. Samuel Barber, not on muster.
3205. Francis Hugga. See No. 3181
[Folio page 4]
3206. Ezekiel Hawes, 9 mo's. man to the Southward.
3207. Moses Tyler, Music.
3208. Jessee Flood, 9 mo's. to Southward.
3209. John Titherton, 9 mo's. to Southward.
3211. Stephen Davis
3212. Miles Hudson
3213. Stephen Brady
3217. Person Taylor
3218. Joshua Bruant
3221. James Gaylor
3224. Nehemiah Huggins
3226. Jessee Martin
3228. James Yarborough
3229. Richard Acherson, or Achison, not on musters.
3230. James Savage, not on musters.
3231. Matthias Menson
3232. Gabriel Manley, 9 mo's., not on musters.
3235. Jefferry Cooley
[Page 26]
[Folio page 1]
3237. Robert Lockabar, same.
3239. Benj'n. Banks, same.
3240. John Neilson, same.
3241. William Burgay, same.
3242. Thomas Rickitts, 9 mo's., Music.
3243. George Wiggins, 9 mo's, Corpl.
3244. Thomas Seymour, 9 mo's. Corpl.
3245. James Lesly, 9 mo's., Corpl.
3246. Rich'd. Hopkins, 9 mo's., Privt.
3247. John Bush
[Folio page 2]
3248. Edward Robertson
3250. Matthew Davis
3251-3253. 12 mo's. accts.

No.
3259. Jeremiah Clance, 9 mo's., not on musters.
3262. Richard Brown, same.
3265-3266. Same.
[Folio page 3]
3267. Jacob Eason, dragoon. See No. 2666.
3268. Thomas Everett
3269-3273. All dragoons. See No. 2666.
3274-3281. 9 mo's. not on muster.
3282. James McDonald. May be same as James McDaniel.
3285. Benjamin Boling, 9 mo's., not on muster.
3286. Henry Woodward, 9 mo's., not on muster.
3287. Henry Philips, 9 mo's., not mustered. Died Aug. 10th, '79.
3289. James Beesley, 9 mo's. man, not on muster.
3289. David Holloway, 9 mo's., admitted as Corpl.
3290. David Blalock, 9 mo's. not on musters.
3291-3292. Same.
3293. Joseph Hill, 9 mo's. man, appears on muster.
3294-3300. 9 mo's. man, not on musters.
3306. Thomas Vernon, 9 mo's. man, not on musters.
3307. Archibald Hood, have a claim signed Archibald Wood.
[Folio page 4]
3308-3309. Both 12 mos. accts.
3310-3313. Same.
3314. Hardy Jones
3315. John Hussey
3316. Israel Harding. S. Voucher missing.
3344. John Burus
[Folio page 5]
3357. Bashford Morpass, not on muster.
3361. Hardy Tyner, not on muster.
3364. Wm. Taylor, not on muster. Voucher missing.
3365. Nehemiah Smith, not on muster. Voucher missing. Name found in muster as music.
3366. Wm. Buckley } both 9 mo's. men,
3371. Henry Bailey } not on musters

# NORTH CAROLINA REVOLUTIONARY ARMY ACCOUNTS, VOL. V

OLD SERIES VOL. 5—L BOOK, NO. 11, & 175 TO 180

No. 11. Pages 53-67 inclusive.

Claims allowed and passed by the Board of Auditors for the Dist. of Wilmington, from the 16th of July, 1783 (included) to the 19 of March, 1784, for which certificates are issued from No. 1459 to No. 3348 inclusive, & returned into the Comptroller's office.

Thos. Routledge

W. Dickson

Thos. Sewell

(Because many names of women were included in this list, and there was no way of ascertaining the service of the soldier through whom they received the pay, it was decided best to omit this list.)

## Comptroller's Office Vouchers

| No. | | No. | |
|---|---|---|---|
| 224. | John Baggett | 3055. | Mali'k Bergis, Wilmington Dist. |
| 334. | Alexander Ballentine | 1236. | John Busbey, Wilmington Dist. |
| 362. | Benjamin Bryer | 1235. | Isea Busbey, Wilmington Dist. |
| 422. | William Bowers | 4624. | James Burnsides, Wilmington Dist. |
| 429. | Norris Baker | 4563. | James Bredric—, Salisbury Dist. |
| 388. | Thomas Bre—— | 2363. | William Buffelow, Wilmington Dist. |
| 302. | Caleb Berry | 7704. | James Brandon, Salisbury Dist. |
| 3724. | Cornelius Breas, Wilmington Dist. | 7780. | John Brandon, Salisbury Dist. |
| 5570. | Thos. Bratcher, Wilmington Dist. | 2526. | Wm. Bone, Salisbury Dist. |
| 400. | Josiah Bowers | 1929. | William Boon, Wilmington Dist. |
| 399. | Jesse Ben—— | 2759. | Robert Biggor, Salisbury Dist. |
| 451. | Uriah Burket, Wilmington Dist. | 1691. | James Bland, Wilmington Dist. |
| 1109. | John Boylin, Wilmington Dist. | 2270. | Ezekiah Blizard, Wilmington Dist. |
| 5890. | Robert Brock, Wilmington Dist. | 4061. | Lewis Bowell, Wilmington Dist. |
| 5571. | Wm. Bush, Wilmington Dist. | 4167. | Josiah Baggot, Wilmington Dist. |
| 5653. | Jar—— Bush, Wilmington Dist. | 1411. | John Backhannon, Salisbury Dist. |
| 4095. | John Blue, Salisbury Dist. | 1838. | Joshua B—inton, Wilmington Dist. |
| 2424. | Nicholas Beaver, Salisbury Dist. | 4116. | George Barge, Wilmington Dist. |
| 675. | Josiah Barns, Wilmington Dist. | 438. | Baxter Bohng |
| 1928. | Elijah Bowin, Wilmington Dist. | 5028. | John Gilbert, Wilmington Dist. |
| 3995. | John Bickerstaff, Morgan Dist. | 4200. | James Holmes, Salisbury Dist. |
| 4202. | Joseph Byers, Salisbury Dist. | 654. | Moses Holmes, Halifax Dist. |
| 440. | Caleb Barr | 5614. | Robt. Holmes, Salisbury Dist. |
| 6670. | Joseph Byers, Salisbury Dist. | 2227. | Isaac Holmes, Salisbury Dist. |
| 5852. | Sam'l Bogle, Salisbury Dist. | 2818. | Hardy Holmes, Wilmington Dist. |
| 8446. | Wm. Bishop, Salisbury Dist. | 274. | David Holmes, Fayetteville Dist. |
| 711. | Samuel Bowman, Salisbury Dist. | 1423. | John Holmes, Newbern Dist. |
| 1867. | Josiah Browen, Wilmington Dist. | 97. | Stewart Hambleton, Hilsboro Dist. |
| 3961. | Michael Brocher, Wilmington Dist. | 535. | John Hambleton, Hilsboro Dist. |
| 4985. | John Boon, Wilmington Dist. | 290. | John Hamilton, Hilsboro Dist. |
| 832. | William Beard, Salisbury Dist. | 3708. | John Hamilton, Salisbury Dist. |
| 2642. | Jonathing Boyles, Salisbury Dist. | 280. | Horace Hamilton, Hilsboro Dist. |
| 3777. | Woodmond Bishop, Wilmington Dist. | 5944. | Andrew Hamilton, Salisbury Dist. |
| 4187. | Peter Beaton, Wilmington Dist. | 3036. | Samuel Howard, Wilmington Dist. |
| 681. | Samuel Bowan, Wilmington Dist. | 65. | Patrick Howard |
| 5747. | Frederick Burns, Wilmington Dist. | 886. | Wm. Howard, Wilmington Dist. |
| 6448. | Wm. Boni, Salisbury Dist. | 2407. | Ely Howard, Salisbury Dist. |

No.
2375. Benjamin Howard, Salisbury Dist.
773. Joseph Howard, Wilmington Dist.
477. Edmond Howard
2852. Elias Howard, Salisbury Dist.
4698. Elijah Howard, Salisbury Dist.
935. Barnet Howard, Dobbs Co.
        Newbern Dist.
508. John Howard
2377. Gideon Howard, Salisbury Dist.
7234. Henry Kittering, Salisbury Dist.
167. James Jenkins
1513. Joseph Jordan, Wilmington Dist.
3432. Archibald Jackson, Wilmington Dist.
1477. Israel Joyner, Dobbs Co., Dobbs Dist.
819. —— Jackson
1413. Solomon Jennett, Newbern Dist.
476. Wm. Jernigan, Newbern Dist.
60. Elisha Jenkins
1049. Britton Jarrell, Newbern Dist.
597. William Jackson
9483. John James, Halifax Dist.
440. Thom's Joyner, Newbern Dist.
1070. Edmund Jackson
4998. Matthew Jacobs, Wilmington Dist.
285. Allen Jackney
6. Solo— Jennet
147. Stephen Jessop
149. Josiah Jenkins
156. John Jordan
7372. Moses Jinkens, Salisbury Dist.
4995. Josiah Jacobs, Wilmington Dist.
222. Zachariah Jackson, privt.
3500. —— Jinkings, Wilmington Dist.
7942. Richard Jacks, Salisbury Dist.
7371. Sam'l Jenkins, Salisbury Dist.
6006. Matthew Jacobs, Wilmington Dist.
601. Simon Jeffreys, Halifax Dist.
145. Jacob Jeffreys, Halifax Dist.
1275. John Jeffreys, Newbern Dist.
941. John Jeffreys, Halifax Dist.
2001. William Jam—, Salisbury Dist.
6003. Josiah Jacobs, Wilmington Dist.
2841. John Johnston, Wilmington Dist.
5375. John Johnston, Salisbury Dist.
677. Asa J——kins
806. Mallachi Jolley
6991. Edward Jacobs, Salisbury Dist.
3703. William Jackson, Wilmington Dist.
1259. Frederick James
2177. Joel Johnston, Wilmington Dist.
3790. Elisha Jernigan, Wilmington Dist.
4092. Mills Jourdan, Wilmington Dist.
530. Lewis Jackson, Wilmington Dist.
1132. Benjamin Jackson
2708. Dan'l John, Salisbury Dist.

No.
3290. Benjamin Johnston, Wilmington Dist.
4506. Charles Johnson, Wilmington Dist.
6005. Jo's Johnston, Salisbury Dist.
1763. Charles Johnston, Newbern Dist.
354. Fred. Joh—, Newbern Dist.
1782. Frances Johnston, Wilmington Dist.
474. Sam'l Johnston, soldier
7893. And'w Johnson, Salisbury Dist.
4306. Archibald Johnson, Wilmington Dist.
3266. Robert Johnston, Wilmington Dist.
1810. —— Johnston, Craven Co.,
        Newbern Dist.
3136. Sam'l Johnston, Wilmington Dist.
444. Thomas James, Capt., Wilmington
        Dist.
1318. Fountain Jordan
162. Richard Jarrott, Wilmington Dist.
1241. James Jackson
446. Thomas Jarvis
536. William James
616. Miles Jordan, Warrenton Dist.
545. Willoughby Jarvis, Warrenton Dist.
600. Thomas Jarvis
244. Benjamin James
547. William Jackson
391. Edwin James
793. Robt. Jackson, Newbern Dist.
455. Avan Jordans, Dobbs Co., Newbern
        Dist.
34. John Jarvis
364. Lemuel Jelkes
11. Edward Jackson
151. Robert Jordan
203. Micajah James
26. David Jones, Warrenton Dist.
370. Jeremiah James
351. Levi Jarvis
372. Benjamin Jones
397. Hezekiah Jones
117. Micajah James
11. Edward Jackson
398. Josiah Jones
380. Thomas James, Soldier
393. William James, Soldier
236. Lemuel Jelkes, Soldier
224. Levi Jarvis
1594. Grey Jourdan, Soldier, Pitt Co.
        Newbern Dist.
812. John Pool, Wilmington Dist.
3511. John Jarrett, Wilmington Dist.
545. Leiv—— Jackson, Wilmington Dist.
3701. James Jack, Salisbury Dist.
490. Samuel Jewell
934. James Josey, Craven Co., Newbern
        Dist.

## LOCKE FAMILY

*No.*

884. L—— Lock, Wilmington Dist.
2310. Matthew Lock, Salisbury Dist.
610. Thomas Lock, Wilmington Dist.
4486. John Lock, Wilmington Dist.
1465. David Lock, Jr., Wilmington Dist.
2943. Thomas Lock, Wilmington Dist.
4488. Benj. Lock, Wilmington Dist.
2251. Matthew Lock, Salisbury Dist.
446. William Lock, Salisbury Dist.
3112. Lt. Francis Lock, Salisbury Dist.
3241. David Lock, Wilmington Dist.
1466. Benj. Lock, Wilmington Dist.
4097. Matthew Lock, Salisbury Dist.

*No.*

458. Alexander Lock, Salisbury Dist.
3085. John Lock, Wilmington Dist.
2952. Joseph Lock, Wilmington Dist.
480. Richard Lock, Salisbury Dist.
8954. Wm. Lock, Salisbury Dist.
4214. Capt. John Lock, Salisbury Dist.
871. William Lock, Salisbury Dist.
.... William Lock, Warrenton Dist.
443. George Lock, Salisbury Dist.
3128. David Lock, Jr., Wilmington Dist.
493. Francis Lock, Salisbury Dist.
.... William Lock, Warrenton Dist.
2273. George Lock, Salisbury Dist.

## LAWRENCE FAMILY

*No.*

6346. ——— Lawrance, Salisbury Dist.
4653. Joseph Lawrance, Salisbury Dist.
6933. Abraim Lawrance, Salisbury Dist.
2000. John Lawrance, Salisbury Dist.

*No.*

5053. Adam Lawrance, Salisbury Dist.
1345. Joseph Lawrence, Warrenton Dist.
5895. Adam Lawrance, Salisbury Dist.
2075. John Lawrance, Salisbury Dist.

## LITTLE FAMILY

*No.*

466. Thomas Little, Wilmington Dist.
490. John Little, Wilmington Dist.
108. Abraham Little, Newbern Dist.
172. Capt. William Lytle, Halifax Dist.
1155. Guinn Litle, Sold., Halifax Dist.
245. Col. Archibald Lytle, Halifax Dist.
243. William Lytle, Halifax Dist.

*No.*

5027. Thos. Little, Wilmington Dist.
2741. Th—— Little, Wilmington Dist.
356. William Lytle
4611. James Lyttle, Morgan Dist.
1794. John Little, Wilmington Dist.
344. Will'm Lytle
3005. Duncan Little, Wilmington Dist.

## LASSITER FAMILY

*No.*

545. Jethro Lassiter, Halifax Dist.
42. Thomas Lassiter, Halifax Dist.

*No.*

1120. Jacob Lassiter, Sold., Newbern Dist.
137. James Lassiter, Sergt.

## LARKIN FAMILY

*No.*

377. John Larkins, Wilmington Dist.
378. Roger Larkins, Wilmington Dist.

*No.*

33. John Larkins, Wilmington Dist.

## LAMBERT FAMILY

*No.*

1782. Benj'm Lambert, Newbern Dist.
.... John Lambert, Warrenton Dist.
754. Henry Lambert

*No.*

328. John Lambert, Warrenton, Dist.
2996. John Lambert, Wilmington Dist.

## LOVE FAMILY

*No.*

4225. John Love, Wilmington, Dist.
451. Doct' David Love, Halifax Dist.
767. Cornelius Love, Hillsborough Dist.
3611. Capt. James Love, Wilmington, Dist.

*No.*

.... Sam'l Love, Salisbury Dist.
3677. John Love, Salisbury, Dist.
2668. Alexander Love, Salisbury Dist.

No.

| No. | | No. | |
|---|---|---|---|
| 3904. | James Leonard, Wilmington Dist. | 5. | Alexander Nelson |
| 4644. | Sam Leonard, Wilmington, Dist. | 1238. | James Nichols |
| 7625. | Jacob Leonard, Salisbury Dist. | 211. | Jacob Nichols |
| 3917. | James Leonard, Wilmington Dist. | 4944. | Caleb Nichols, Wilmington Dist. |
| 7511. | Philip Leonard, Salisbury Dist. | 366. | William Nichols |
| 4708. | Henry Leonard, Wilmington Dist. | 193. | Thom's Nelson, Newbern Dist. |
| 828. | Gibbs Lamb, Soldier | 329. | Jacob Nichols |
| 387. | John Marr | 4307. | John Nelson, Salisbury Dist. |
| 846. | William Mantey, Soldier | 14. | Maj. John Nelson |
| 90,088. | Thomas Masters | 70. | Phillip Niles |
| 90,444. | William Mashum | 4944. | Sam'l Nuly, Salisbury Dist. |
| 90,810. | Allen Manley | 295. | Joseph Norton, Newbern Dist. |
| 514. | Henry May | 4943. | David Nuly, Salisbury Dist. |
| 555. | Arnold Mann | 927. | Patrick Newton, Wilmington Dist. |
| 283. | B—— March | 4639. | James Patterson, Wilmington Dist. |
| 2920. | Thomas Mays | 419. | —— Patterson |
| 1593. | Marmaduke Maples | 5291. | Wm. Patterson, Salisbury Dist. |
| 9957. | Absolom Mann | .... | John Patterson |
| 957. | Thomas Mann | .... | Thomas Patterson, Salisbury Dist. |
| 1248. | —— Manly, privt. | 454. | John Patterson, Salisbury Dist. |
| 8999. | William Manley | 3703. | Robert Patterson, Salisbury Dist. |
| 8828. | William Manning, Nash Co., Halifax Dist. | 58. | Elisha Price |
| 9722. | Daniel Massingill, Hampton Co., Halifax Dist. | 7269. | Alexander Porter, Salisbury Dist. |
|  | | 275. | John Price |
| 9..4. | John Markland, Newbern Dist. | 1976. | Richard Price |
| 266. | John Man—— | 552. | James Price |
| 703. | Arthur Markum | 429. | Dixon Price |
| 8985. | William Madra, Halifax Dist. | 217. | Jordan Pitman |
| 681. | Theophilus Mitchell | 485. | William Polk, Maj. |
| 1517. | —— McCullen, Wilmington Dist. | 3740. | John Pollock, Wilmington Dist. |
| 3161. | Joseph McGuo——, Salisbury Dist. | 4609. | John Porterfield, Wilmington Dist. |
| 4948. | David McCall, Salisbury Dist. | 4577. | Den. Porterfield, Wilmington Dist. |
| 712. | James McConnaguhey, Salisbury Dist. | 4605. | George Pricket |
| 5998. | John McCain, Salisbury Dist. | 4433. | William Plummer, Wilmington Dist. |
| 4469. | John McGaughey, Salisbury Dist. | 1455. | Thomas Patton, Salisbury Dist. |
| 6546. | Jno. Nesbett, Salisbury Dist. | 1. | Thomas Polk |
| 791. | John N——, Salisbury Dist. | 181. | Col. John Patten |
| 765. | John Nutter | 1443. | James Portwent, Wilmington Dist. |
| 77. | Jethro Nott | 5180. | Rigdon Pits, Wilmington Dist. |
| 1617. | George Nooles, Wilmington Dist. | 518. | Joshua Pritchet |
| 69. | Thomas Nail | 92. | Isaac Powell, Newbern Dist. |
| 238. | —— Nichols | 154. | George Pettiford |
| 2563. | Joseph Nichols, Salisbury Dist. | 5441. | Lt. Jn'o Pasture, Wilmington Dist. |
| 1658. | Joel Nichols, Newbern Dist. | 7867. | Capt. James Purviance, Salisbury Dist. |
| 3098. | Joshua Nelson, Salisbury Dist. | 3070. | Jerry Plummer, Wilmington Dist. |
| 837. | Arthur Nelson | 236. | Stephen Phillips |
| 488. | David Nelson, Craven Co., Newbern Dist. | 149. | John Pilly, Ensn. |
|  | | 522. | Joseph Purser |
| 851. | Hardy Nelson | 1662. | Eph'm Powers, Newbern Dist. |
| 2132. | Wm. Neathercut, Wilmington Dist. | 594. | James Powers |
| 619. | John Nelson | 656. | John Powers |
| 1775. | James Nevil, Newbern Dist. | 585. | Robert Powers |
| 1101. | Martin Nilson, Newbern Dist. | 3195. | John Powers, Wilmington Dist. |
|  | | 845. | Wm. Pilgrim, Newbern Dist. |

*No.*

1650. William Quin, Soldier, Pitt Co., Newbern Dist.
8748. Charles Quigley, Salisbury Dist.
2739. Jno. Query, Salisbury Dist.
1486. Peter Quilman, Salisbury Dist.
3403. David Quin, Wilmington Dist.
1326. James Quinn, Wilmington Dist.
752. Thomas Reagon, Salisbury Dist.
4871. Lt. Wm. Ross, Salisbury Dist.
4780. John Russel, Wilmington Dist.
3678. Hardy Reaves, Wilmington Dist.
4559. Robert Rosiar, Wilmington Dist.
1968. Silus Register, Wilmington Dist.
281. John Ridgeway
4376. Richard Regan, Wilmington Dist.
210. Isaac Rowell, Sergt.
2037. Joseph Robinson, Salisbury Dist.
1000. John Rigby, Wilmington Dist.
55. Daniel Ruff, Dobbs Co.
5961. James Russ, Wilmington Dist.
172. James Russell, Sergt.
38. William Rothwell
389. John Rigkins
337. Capt. Wm. Thomas Rodes
201. James Roark
4233. Edward Railsback, Salisbury Dist.
598. Reuben Roundtree, Lt.
1606. John Ritter
1422. James Reynolds, Newbern Dist.
3110. Ardi'l Ronaldson, Wilmington Dist.
122. Jordan Rozier
1495. John Ryley, Wilmington Dist.
618. Jesse Robinson
1760. David Roach, Newbern Dist.
966. Isaac Randsome, Newbern Dist.
534. John Ross Dragoon
260. Nehemiah Randolph, Newbern Dist.
1257. Dudley Reardon, private
5950. Capt. Wm. Routledge, Wilmington Dist.
163. John Rayford
528. Hardy Redley
1248. Andrew Ramsey, Salisbury Dist.
69. William Rowl—
3429. Joseph Ricks, Wilmington Dist.
1601. Jesse Rooks, Wilmington Dist.
1221. Shad Riggs, Newbern Dist.
4133. Philip Raiford, Wilmington Dist.
3538. Cornelius Ryan, Wilmington Dist.
512. David Ryal, Wilmington Dist.
891. George Roaper
1174. Robert Roaper, soldier
1101. John Roaper
650. Robt. Reynolds, Newbern Dist.

*No.*

893. Hugh Robinson, Salisbury Dist.
3619. Thomas Ricey, Salisbury Dist.
552. Daniel Ramsey
2397. Isaac Ross, Salisbury Dist.
4314. Philip Robeson, Wilmington Dist.
699. James Robinson, soldier
136. Cornelius Robeson
4471. Rhuben Rosier, Wilmington Dist.
688. Joseph Runnion, Salisbury Dist.
303. John Riggs, Craven Co., Newbern Dist.
1043. George Reynolds, Capt.
493. Timothy Rich
379. William Ramsey, Wilmington Dist.
171. Sergt. Peter Rhem
4877. Lt. Wm. Ross, Salisbury Dist.
20. Mathew Ramsey (formerly Capt.) Salisbury Dist.
3710. Steph— Riche, Wilmington Dist.
7623. Henry Remer, Salisbury Dist.
2958. John Regan, Wilmington Dist.
511. Howell Rowell
647. Sam'l Rowland, Wilmington Dist.
3169. Lt. John Rigan, Wilmington Dist.
17. Francis Ross, Lt.
216. Math Ramsey, Capt.
232. Daniel Roson, Sergt.
696. Wm. Rix
340. Capt. Joseph Thomas Rodes
547. Allen Ramsey, Capt.
452. Thomas Rice, Sergt.
1235. Ruben Raines, Newbern Dist.
116. Mala—— Russell
1982. —————— Robson, Newbern Dist.
940. Ephraim Rice, Newbern Dist.
1505. John Roach, Wilmington Dist.
3031. Nicholas Routledge, Wilmington Dist.
825. Godfrey Rowland
595. George Riggs
276. Frederick R—eingbark, Wilmington Dist.
114. Jesse Rowell, Newbern Dist.
261. Ephraim Reynolds, Newbern Dist.
8111. William Richey, Salisbury Dist.
3994. George Russell, Morgan Dist.
1349. Simon Rowse, Newbern Dist.
257. Lemuel Rowe, Newbern Dist.
611. Joseph Russ, Wilmington Dist.
1898. Joshua Rice, Craven Co., Newbern Dist.
1412. Capt. James Ruse, Salisbury Dist.
1367. —————— Rowse, Soldier, Dobbs Co., Newbern Dist.

No.
5927. Jeremiah Rackley, Wilmington Dist.
5202. Henry Robison, Salisbury Dist.
245. Cornelius Robeson
1436. David R———, Salisbury Dist.
49. Willoughby Rogers
1113. Cornelius Ryan
866. Reason Ricketts
1486. Robert Ramsey, Soldier, Dobbs Co., Newbern Dist.
573. Morris Richards
2059. James Ratliff, Wilmington Dist.
5810. Solomon Roach, Wilmington Dist.
186. Jesse Rickmon, soldier
274. James Rowl———, private
6098. John Redford, Salisbury Dist.
725. Daniel Ramsey
711. Blake Rabby
848. Robert Rust
754. Samuel Ross
8. John Russ
874. Jam's Robson, Newbern Dist.
6259. John Richey, Salisbury Dist.
128. Capt. Robert Raiford
688. John Rice, Craven Co., Newbern Dist.
142. Methusala Roland, Newbern Dist.
190. John Riggs, Craven Co., Newbern Dist.
963. George Robins, Newbern Dist.
1619. Thomas Readon
310. She——— Riggs, Craven Co., Newbern Dist.
1204. Mathas Rolain, Newbern Dist.
2693. Joel Rees, Salisbury Dist.
764. Thomas Ralph
3451. Jeremiah Rackley, Wilmington Dist.
464. Lawney Reynord
5370. John Ross, Salisbury Dist.
603. John Robison, Salisbury Dist.
6483. Wm. Rand, Salisbury Dist.
6461. Daniel Roman, Salisbury Dist.
735. Capt. William Reynolds, Salisbury Dist.
1524. Shadrack Runnels, Wilmington Dist.

**R**

3938. M——— Russel, Wilmington Dist.
716. Samuel Rowan, Wilmington Dist.
1458. Arthur Rodgers, Warrenton Dist.
4675. Lieut. Robston, Salisbury Dist.
4534. John Rutledge, Salisbury Dist.
3286. Rob't. Robison, Salisbury Dist.
2004. Peter Robeson, Wilmington Dist.
842. James Rainey, Hilsboro Dist.
1934. James Ratcleft, Newbern Dist.

No.
1379. Peter Robertson, Warrenton Dist.
279. Henry Rutherford, Salisbury Dist.
192. Charles Right, Hillsboro Dist.
346. William Redley, Hillsboro Dist.
59. John Rowland, Hillsboro Dist.
437. Samuel Ross, Hillsboro Dist.
417. Pekel Roske, Hillsboro Dist.
273. James Royal, Hillsboro Dist.
657. John Reason, Hillsboro Dist.
25. Joseph Runnals, Hillsboro Dist.
115. Joel Ramsey, Hillsboro Dist.
4554. Rubin Rosias, Wilmington Dist.
5910. Joseph Ricke, Wilmington Dist.
476. Howell Redman
4033. Marvin Rouick, Morgan Dist.
275. James Rowland, Halifax Dist.
3234. Janes Robison, Salisbury Dist.
294. Joseph Rich, Newbern Dist.
1438. Thomas Ryan, Warrenton Dist.
3263. Wm. Russ, Wilmington Dist.
2719. George Rusdwas, Salisbury Dist.
7099. Rich'd Randolph, Salisbury Dist.
130. Morris Raiford, Newbern Dist.
481. William Riggins, Halifax Dist.
2154. J——— Rhodes, Wilmington Dist.
1640. William Russ, Wilmington Dist.
1969. Benjamin Register, Wilmington Dist.
547. Cornelius Roomer, Hillsborough Dist.
5869. Benjamin Robeson, Wilmington Dist.
676. Isaac Rolston, Hillsboro Dist.
3027. Jacob Rogers, Wilmington Dist.
1247. David Ramsey, Salisbury Dist.
475. Aaron Ruther, Salisbury Dist.
452. Lieut. Patrick Rogers, Hillsboro Dist.
648. John Rowland, Wilmington Dist.
532. John Radford, Johnston Co., Newbern Dist.
1169. Elecazer Russ, Wilmington Dist.
3285. John Robison, Salisbury Dist.
565. William Ryles
193. Joel Ramsey, Salisbury Dist.
8156. Robt. Robinson, Salisbury Dist.
756. George Rockwell
680. Howell Rowell
7080. Ninian Steel, Salisbury Dist.
2789. Isaiah Sikes, Wilmington Dist.
682. Benjamin Solebury
3419. John Slocumb, Wilmington Dist.
276. John Skeen, private
382. Lt. Jesse Steed

No.
693. John Sykes, Wilmington Dist.
561. William Slade, Lt. Adjt.
433. Lt. Daniel Schaw
2640. Thomas Shelby, Salisbury Dist.
672. Charles Shaddock
174. Thomas Scarlet
578. William Shannon
111. John Step
194. Ephraim Shuffield, Wilmington Dist.
241. Richard Sumner
5320. Andrew Snoddy, Salisbury Dist.
390. Mallachi Strickland
183. Thomas Sorrell
849. Noah Strayhorn, Wilmington Dist.
4689. Fargus Sloan, Salisbury Dist.
2609. James Sloan, Salisbury Dist.
4191. Wm. Sloan, Salisbury Dist.
300. Wm. Sloan, Hilsboro Dist.
575. Wm. Sloan, Wilmington Dist.
4448. Samuel Sloan, Salisbury Dist.
2666. Alexander Sloan, Salisbury Dist.
676. John Sloan, Salisbury Dist.
6301. David Sloan, Salisbury Dist.
1906. Alen Sloan, Wilmington Dist.
.... Arch Sloan, Salisbury Dist.
1285. Alexander Sloan, Wilmington Dist.
3799. Patrick Sloan, Morgan Dist.
1363. Thos. Sloan, Salisbury Dist.
1880. Alexander Sloan, Newbern Dist.
504. Caleb Story
1955. George Scarlo——
533. Mallachi Strickland
342. John Stander
3. Frederick Stricklen
2303. James Sykes, Wilmington Dist.
7531. Wm. Standard, Salisbury Dist.
1970. E—ond Spivey, Wilmington Dist.
5915. Cornelius Sykes, Wilmington Dist.
4808. John Spencer, Morganton Dist.
348. James Spain
5358. Lt. James Todd, Salisbury Dist.
5156. Capt. John Todd, Salisbury Dist.
4198. William Trent, Wilmington Dist.
172. Stephen Titus
191. David Thernton
407. John Titterson
686. Joseph Tate
610. Moses Tyler, Warrenton Dist.
694. William Todd
696. Ephraim Todd
64. Jonathan Times
6678. William Tase, Salisbury Dist.

No.
4575. Patrick Travers, Lt., Wilmington Dist.
403. Moses Tyler
1129. Hezekiah Tyson, Pitt Co., Newbern Dist.
1990. Fredrick Tyson
989. Benja Tanner, Wilmington Dist.
523. James Todd
65. John Toney
1989. Moses Teel
48. Charles Tinsley
2538. Col. —— Thaxon, Wilmington Dist.
1984. Jacob Teale, Newbern Dist.
46. Emanuel Teal
4549. Samuel Thares, Wilmington Dist.
216. James Tharpe
422. William Talton
217. Joel Tayborn
4356. John Tolly, Wilmington Dist.
574. James Talton
1272. John Tinney, Salisbury Dist.
2219. Patrick Traverse, Wilmington Dist.
575. William Talton
209. Erasmus Tippett
239. William Tervathan
142. Solomon Thrift
2012. James Tyson, Newbern Dist.
1287. John Thipps, Newbern Dist.
695. James Todd
697. Thomas Todd
1251. —— Turnage, Dobbs Co., Newbern Dist.
1755. Moses Tyson, Pitt Co. Newbern Dist.
1128. Zachariah Tyson, Newbern Dist.
1974. —— Tyson, Pitt Co., Newbern Dist.
1586. Aaron Tyson, Pitt Co., Newbern Dist.
513. Joseph Tate
3957. M—— Tyrrell, Wilmington Dist.
819. Hezekiah Tyson, Pitt Co., Newbern Dist.
421. James Talton
492. Jesse Teel
98. Benjamin Troublefield
286. Absalom Travis
1075. John Thomas, Salisbury Dis.
5. Amos Thomas, Halifax
529. Reuben Thomas, Newbern Dist.
1897. John Thomas, Newbern Dist.
673. Stephen Thomas, Hillsborough Dist.
2161. Isaac Thomas, Wilmington Dist.

*No.*
329. Thomas Thomas, Hilsboro Dist.
252. Edward Thompson, Hilsboro Dist.
133. William Thomas, Hilsboro Dist.
770. Ross Thomas, Hilsboro Dist.
418. Lemuel Thomas, Halifax Dist.
1453. Remple G. Thomas, Wilmington Dist.
2785. David Thomas, Wilmington Dist.
3594. Luke Thomas, Wilmington Dist.
688. Nathan Thomas, Wilmington Dist.
110. Spincer Thomas, Halifax Dist.
. . . . Philip Thomas, Wilmington Dist.
1034. Thomas Thompson, Wilmington Dist.
1052. Robt. Thompson, Wilmington Dist.
2041. William Toaler, Newbern Dist.
293. Lt. Daniel Teachy
524. Ephraim Todd
88. Henry Tice
5160. Isaac Tissom, Wilmington Dist.
3386. Elisha Ternigan, Wilmington Dist.
1274. Aaron Tilman, Johnston Co., Newbern Dist.
5427. John Umphrey, Wilmington Dist.

*No.*
792. Jonathon Umphrey, Wilmington Dist.
4144. George Underwood, Wilmington Dist.
1433. Robert Upton, Wilmington Dist.
833. Charles Upchurch, Wilmington Dist.
4621. Isaac ——grove, Salisbury Dist.
7538. Lawrence Unger, Salisbury Dist.
5186. John Urell, Wilmington Dist.
3522. James Ulren, Wilmington Dist.
4520. William Underhill, Wilmington Dist.
3751. Wm. Wren, Wilmington Dist.
2100. William Woodcock, Wilmington Dist.
1805. Wm. Williams, Newbern Dist.
834. Jos. Worsley, Newbern Dist.
2947. Wist Waters, Salisbury Dist.
7622. Peter Warlow, Salisbury Dist.
559. Sam'l Williamson, Wilmington Dist.
2262. James Whaley, Wilmington Dist.
1014. Joh— Whitford, Newbern Dist.
1189. Richard Williford, Wilmington Dist.
3559. Wm. Waldron, Wilmington Dist.

HALIFAX SEPT. 3, 1778

A list of men who Inlisted in the Continental Army from "Cartrite County" for 3 yrs.

*Name*
John Howell
Cald. O. White
Isaac X Barrington
Lawful X Daniel
Christ'r X Neal
George X Wair
Wm. Smith
Benj. X Merryhew
Francis X Neale
Thomas X Neale
Joel Meyzick
(Note X his mark.)

*Name*
Ephriam X Runnels
Theoph'l X Norrard
Dannie X Ireland
George Sammson
George Gouder
John X Rivers
John Brayboy
Obid Norwood
Benjamin German
William Forrist
James King

FROM HYDE CO.

*Name*
Abraham Swindell
Benjamin Mason
Robert Mackey X
John Brinn X
Benj'm Neal X
Timothy Murrey X
Solomon Baker X

*Name*
Abel Harris X
Elija Harris X
James Harvey X
Rass Thomas X
Abel Ross
Gabriel Coley X
Pelig Brightman X

ONSLOW COUNTY

*Name*
Major W. Clark
James Orroll
Richard Thompson, Cmpl.
Jonathan Jenkins, Compl.
Thomas Weeds X
Martin Johnston
Elias C. Craig
Henry Mainer
William Clark
John Johnston
Jonathan Elixon
William King

*Name*
Hilleoy Breyon?
David P. Simson
Joseph Wright
Mathew Litman
Mor'l Wood
Sam Webb
———— Sloan
Jacob I. B. Brown
John Wiley
Elijah Smith X
,William Farris
John Thornburn

*No.*
3954. James Burnside, Wilmington Dist.
2126. John Lockhart, Newbern Dist.
1161. ———— Lockhart, Newbern Dist.
1529. Richid Lathinghouse, Newbern Dist.
1353. Obediah Lawson, Newbern Dist.
1658. Young Lathinghouse, Newbern Dist.
188. Lemuel Litten, Hillsboro Dist.
189. Abel Lettan, Hillsboro Dist.
388. Samuel Linton, Salisbury Dist.
244. John Suffman, Hillsborough Dist.
369. Fred'k Lucye, Hillsborough Dist.
3085. Charles Lowrey, Salisbury Dist.
496. James Lynch, Newbern Dist.
1238. David Lippencutt
2265. Ebenezer Loflin, Newbern Dist.
1594. James Lockhart, Wilmington Dist.
54. James Largon, Newbern Dist.
542. William Lord?, Newbern Dist.
327. Frank Lockhard, Newbern Dist.
2125. James Lockhard, Newbern Dist.
1377. Joel Lockhart, Newbern Dist.
1703. Michaul Soper, Wilmington Dist.
1353. Peter Lynce, Salisbury Dist.
413. Philip Logan, Hillsborough Dist.
13. Burrell Lenox?, Halifax
.... James Leech, Salisbury Dist.
463. Hardy Lilley, Newbern Dist.
1579. James Linch, Newbern Dist.
1378. Brit Lockhart, Newbern Dist.
6782. Wm. Leath, Salisbury Dist.
6152. George Leany, Salisbury Dist.
340. John Lyon, Hillsborough Dist.
1244. Geo. Linton, Newbern Dist.
1783. Joseph Lasley, Wilmington Dist.
835. Lemuel Lavender, Newbern Dist.
373. Sam Lavender, Newbern Dist.
474. John Lyon, Hilsboro Dist.
3256. John Lenier, Wilmington Dist.

*No.*
1025. Wm. London, Wilmington Dist.
2535. John Laird, Salisbury Dist.
2517. William Lohrey, Salisbury Dist.
4793. John Luckey, Salisbury Dist.
5468. William Leatch, Salisbury Dist.
2007. Samuel Lusk, Salisbury Dist.
4363. George Lean, Wilmington Dist.
858. Samuel Lusk, Salisbury Dist.
390. Richd Lancaster, Newbern Dist.
7707. David Luckie, Salisbury Dist.
487. Isham Lucy, Halifax Dist.
485. Michael Leagal, Hilsboro Dist.
436. John Lacey, Hilsboro Dist.
1067. George Lott, Halifax Dist.
3086. James Lowry
1551. James Lockerman, Wilmington Dist.
3623. John Lastly, Wilmington Dist.
784. Edward Littleton, Newbern Dist.
4498. David Linsaywhite, Wilmington Dist.
702. Lewis Lilly, Halifax
1090. Moses Lovuk, Halifax Dist.
701. John Lockhart, Halifax Dist.
108. Uriah Leftyear, Newbern Dist.
3669. John Laiton, Wilmington Dist.
446. William Lomax, Halifax Dist.
148. Christopher Lackey, Lieut., Hilsboro Dist.
308. John Lindsy, Craven Co., Newbern Dist.
913. Charles Lowry, Salisbury Dist.
8676. John Lockhart, Salisbury Dist.
173. Walter Lindsey, Warrenton Dist.
2734. Jno. Lowry, Salisbury Dist.
82. James Lockhart, Johnson Co., Newbern Dist.
1757. Joseph Little, Newbern Dist.

No.

1525. Isom Laram, Pitt Co., Newbern Dist.
4797. Robert Livingston, Wilmington Dist.
4416. William Lackey, Salisbury Dist.
5741. James Lister, Wilmington Dist.
6862. John Linsey, Salisbury Dist.
1451. Daniel Loving, Warrenton Dist.
4711. Wm. Larkie, Salisbury Dist.
587. John Lacey, Hillsborough Dist.
654. Micheal Legal, Hillsborough Dist.
506. Frederick Lucy, Hillsborough Dist.
201. John Luttrell, Newbern Dist.
259. William Lomax, Newbern Dist.
221. Joseph Leftyear, Newbern Dist.
6938. Robt. Lucky, Salisbury Dist.
717. William Lord
567. Phillip Logan
100. Stephen Lynch
605. Bennett Loca——
306. Martin Loughry
834. Thomas Laughinhouse
705. Lewis Leggett
4528. Capt. George Lawmon, Salisbury Dist.
1866. Wm. Lawley, Newbern Dist.
532. Lewis Leggitt, Newbern Dist.
2560. Nathaniel Laind, Salisbury Dist.
548. James Longden, Johnston Co., Newbern Dist.
3951. James ——, Wilmington Dist.
778. William Lindal
436. John Luten, Sold., Halifax Dist.
936. George Le——, Warrenton Dist.
3280. Andrew Laws, Wilmington Dist.
1201. Noel Latham, Beaufort Co., Newbern Dist.
268. William Lord, Warrenton Dist.
2495. Robert Leviston, Salisbury Dist.
2110. James Lowry, Salisbury Dist.
415. Christopher Lackey
5735. Thomas Lusk, Salisbury
3981. John Leer, Wilmington Dist.
1082. Vincent Page, Newbern Dist.
807. John Page, Newbern Dist.
683. Lemual Page, Newbern Dist.
1244. Jonathan McFarson, Wilmington Dist.
5159. John McPherson, Wilmington Dist.
4204. Ma—— McFarson, Salisbury Dist.
5798. William McCoy, Salisbury Dist.
2043. Kedar Harrill, Wilmington Dist.
3515. James Harrill, Wilmington Dist.
1213. James Hudson, Warrenton Dist.

No.

448. Thomas Hudson, Hillsboro Dist.
196. John Hudson, Hillsboro Dist.
1657. Miles Hudson, Wilmington Dist.
351. Thomas Hudson, Hilsboro Dist.
1818. Nath'l Hudson, Wilmington Dist.
2208. Lewis Hudson, Wilmington Dist.
2765. Joseph Hudson, Wilmington Dist.
3219. John Houston, Salisbury Dist.
1122. Hugh Huston, Halifax Dist.
6370. Jas Huston, Salisbury Dist.
3218. David Huston, Salisbury Dist.
.... Christopher Houston, Salisbury Dist.
4113. Daniel Houston, Salisbury Dist.
6063. Wm. Houston, Salisbury Dist.
1243. Archibald Houston, Salisbury Dist.
6787. Henry Houston, Salisbury Dist.
1334. Edward Houston, Wilmington Dist.
2333. Samuel Houston, Wilmington Dist.
955. James Reed, Newbern Dist.
4005. Andrew Reed, Salisbury Dist.
3068. Geo. Reed, Salisbury Dist.
.... Robb Reed, Salisbury Dist.
1443. Thomas Reed, Salisbury Dist.
4. Captain James Read, Halifax Dist.
1333. Andrew Reed, Wilmington Dist.
7663. Samuel Reed, Salisbury Dist.
429. Jesse Read, Capt., Halifax Dist.
284. James Read, Hillsborough Dist.
8135. James Reed, Salisbury Dist.
179. William Read, Hillsborough Dist.
7848. Alvin Reid, Salisbury Dist.
457. Jacob Reid, Hillsborough Dist.
1030. Fred'k Reed, Halifax Dist.
4030. Hugh Reed, Morgan Dist.
1085. Joshua Porter, Halifax Dist.
2566. John Porter, Wilmington Dist.
5312. James Porter, Salisbury Dist.
178. Jacob Porter, Hillsborough Dist.
5037. Alexander Porter, Salisbury Dist.
5883. Samuel Porter, Wilmington Dist.
4954. Alex'r Porter, Salisbury Dist.
638. Hugh Porter, Wilmington Dist.
504. James Pugh, Wilmington Dist.
978(?). Stephen Pugh, Newbern Dist.
7. Jeptath Parker, Halifax Dist.
5944. Francis Parker, Wilmington Dist.
5626. Josiah Parker, Wilmington Dist.
707. Samuel Parker, Hillsborough Dist.
.... Kedor Parker, Halifax Dist.
290. James Parker, Hillsborough Dist.
.... Joseph Parker, Halifax Dist.
280. Joseph Parker, Hillsborough Dist.
168. John Parker, Wilmington Dist.
4295. Jacob Parker, Wilmington Dist.

*No.*

1784. Sessoms Parker, Wilmington Dist.
1142. Simon Parker, Halifax Dist.
5908. Daniel Parker, Wilmington Dist.
 151. Hubard Parker, Newbern Dist.
 49?. Thomas Parker, Halifax Dist.
4616. Humphreys Parker, Morgan Dist.
5907. Daniel Parker, Wilmington Dist.
 935. Jonas Parker, Newbern Dist.
1494. Hollida Parker, Wilmington Dist.
 470. Levi Phillips, Salisbury Dist.
  88. Zacheriah Phillips, Hillsborough Dist.
 113. Bush Phillips, Hillsborough Dist.
 601. Andrew Phillips, Hillsborough Dist.
  23. Loven Phillips, Hillsborough Dist.
 608. Abraham Phillips, Hillsborough Dist.
 374. John Phillips, Hillsborough Dist.
 191. Rush Phillips, Hillsborough Dist.
5407. Risbin Phillips, Salisbury Dist.
4082. Stephen Phillips, Wilmington Dist.
8012. Thomas Phillips, Salisbury Dist.
 702. Thomas Phillips, Newbern Dist.
1403. Edward Phillips, Newbern Dist.
1788. Henry Phillips, Warrenton Dist.
 859. William Phillips, Wilmington Dist.
1142. Sampson Phillips, Halifax Dist.
 667. Isaac Perkins, Wilmington Dist.
 797. Abraham Perkins, Hillsborough Dist.
 654. Joshua Perkins, Wilmington Dist.
1417. Isaac Perkins, Wilmington Dist.
.... Addams Purkins, Halifax Dist.
 933. Absalom Powers, Halifax Dist.
2420. Adam Perkins, Salisbury Dist.
 459. ——— Turner, Edenton Dist.
4737. John Tipson, Wilmington Dist.
4385. Henry Taylor, Wilmington Dist.
4394. James Taylor, Wilmington Dist.
5514. Saban Taylor, Wilmington Dist.
3140. John Taylor, Jr., Wilmington Dist.
3396. Capt. Jonathan Taylor, Wilmington Dist.
4472. Aaron Taylor, Wilmington Dist.
4664. Thomas Taylor, Wilmington Dist.
2292. Jacob Taylor, Wilmington Dist.
4798. Michael Taylor, Morgan Dist.
5363. Elijah Taylor, Salisbury Dist.
2678. James Taylor, Salisbury Dist.
 808. John Taylor, Newbern Dist.
 706. Charles Taylor, Newbern Dist.
 742. Jacob Taylor, Newbern Dist.

*No.*

 823. Lewis Taylor, Hillsborough Dist.
 586. John Taylor, Hillsborough Dist.
 130. Thomas Taylor, Hillsborough Dist.
 218. Samuel Taylor, Hillsborough Dist.
 311. Caleb Taylor, Hillsborough Dist.
 168. Morris Taylor
 442. Emanuel Taylor, Halifax Dist.
 860. Thos. Taylor, Halifax Dist.
 537. James
3388. John Turner, Wilmington Dist.
1102. Thomas Turner, Wilmington Dist.
4855. James Turner, Wilmington Dist.
1621. Daniel Turner, Wilmington Dist.
3585. William Turner, Wilmington Dist.
8937. Thos. Turner, Salisbury Dist.
3360. George Turner, Salisbury Dist.
2637. William Turner, Salisbury Dist.
1035. George Turner, Newbern Dist.
 361. David Turner, Newbern Dist.
 447. Jacob Turner, Newbern Dist.
  86. Adam Turner, Hillsborough Dist.
  97. Capt. Jacob Turner, Halifax Dist.
 852. Mattas Turner, Warrenton Dist.
 937. James Thompson, Wilmington Dist.
 283. William Thompson, Wilmington Dist.
5184. Enoch Thompson, Wilmington Dist.
1464. Dugal Thompson, Wilmington Dist.
4006. Thomas Thomson, Wilmington Dist.
1067. Absalom Thompson, Wilmington Dist.
 649. Charles Thompson, Wilmington Dist.
3996. William Thomson, Wilmington Dist.
1157. John Thompson, Halifax Dist.
 224. Nicholas Thompson, Halifax Dist.
 149. Robert Thompson, Halifax Dist.
 638. Nath—— Thompson, Halifax Dist.
2157. Elijah Thompson, Newbern Dist.
4604. William Thompson, Morgan Dist.
4002. Peter Thompson, Morgan Dist.
 197. Daniel Thompson, Hillsborough Dist.
 578. George Thompson, Hillsborough Dist.
 145. Charles Thompson, Hillsborough Dist.
4046. James Prichard, Morgan Dist.

No.

4486. Littleton Pitillo, Morgan Dist.
2964. John Parnal, Wilmington Dist.
1096. Wm. Pollock, Wilmington Dist.
1708. Regdon Pitts, Wilmington Dist.
1711. Lt. Porterwent, Wilmington Dist.
4709. John Potter, Wilmington Dist.
3427. John Peterson, Wilmington Dist.
1776. Brittian Powell, Wilmington Dist.
5771. William Powell, Wilmington Dist.
3644. Capt. Arthur Pipkin, Wilmington Dist.
4112. John Porterfield, Wilmington Dist.
3465. Lieut. James Portivent, Wilmington Dist.
4042. William Pate, Wilmington Dist.
2913. Zachariah Plummer, Wilmington Dist.
3526. William Parradiso, Wilmington Dist.
3741. William Pollock, Wilmington Dist.
2947. James Perdie, Wilmington Dist.
900. J—— Peacock, Wilmington Dist.
1309. Joab Paget, Wilmington Dist.
2372. Aaron Plummer, Wilmington Dist.
1607. John Pormpion, Wilmington Dist.
3144. John Pemberton, Wilmington Dist.
2932. Jeremiah Plummer, Wilmington Dist.
5906. John Peterson, Wilmington Dist.
2934. Moses Plummer, Wilmington Dist.
4725. J—— Pounds, Wilmington Dist.
4730. Miles Potter, Wilmington Dist.
7818. Thomas Patton, Salisbury Dist.
1362. Chas. Polk, Capt., Salisbury Dist.
8116. Sim V. Pitt, Salisbury Dist.
29. Miles Privitt, Hillsborough Dist.
1094. James Passemore, Halifax Dist.
248. Peter Payner, Hillsborough Dist.
720. Francis Pellsie, Hillsborough Dist.
405. James Price, Hillsborough Dist.
250. Zebulon Pratt, Hillsborough Dist.
382. Joseph Purser, Hillsborough Dist.
378. Joshua Pritchet, Hillsborough Dist.
80. Nathaniel Parrott, Hillsborough Dist.
389. Joseph Pack, Hillsborough Dist.
91. Edmund Pendleton, Hillsborough Dist.
376. William Parr, Hillsborough Dist.
298. John Phips, Hillsborough Dist.
225. Martin Penegar, Hillsborough Dist.
366. Stephen Pall, Hillsborough Dist.
69. Edward Prickell, Hillsborough Dist.

No.

159. William Plumer, Hillsborough Dist.
344. Charles Pressley, Hillsborough Dist.
914. Jacob Pollard, Newbern Dist.
1780. Wm. Priestley, Newbern Dist.
1431. Aaron Pickerin, Newbern Dist.
.... Stephen Powell, Newbern Dist.
338. Rich'd Pate, Newbern Dist.
123. Daniel Pate, Newbern Dist.
454. —— Pernal, Newbern Dist.
647. James Pollock, Newbern Dist.
241. William Pilgrim, Newbern Dist.
1266. Ruffin Pridgen, Newbern Dist.
1117. Jno. Parramore, Newbern Dist.
186. John Patten, Halifax Dist.
196. David Poe, Halifax Dist.
298. Thomas Powell, Halifax Dist.
1205. Wm. Parham, Halifax Dist.
393. William Pridgen, Halifax Dist.
12... Peter Powell, Halifax Dist.
1143. Thomas Pedon, Halifax Dist.
219. Noah Parr, Halifax Dist.
692. William Prescott, Halifax Dist.
334. George Plumby
734. Dave James, Wilmington Dist.
747. Moses James, Wilmington Dist.
3400. John Jarman, Wilmington Dist.
5657. Jas. Joiner, Wilmington Dist.
3296. Leanence Jerman, Wilmington Dist.
100. Joshua Jinkins, Wilmington Dist.
757. Joseph Jennet, Wilmington Dist.
4207. John Jackson, Wilmington Dist.
4399. Solomon James, Wilmington Dist.
572. Wm. Jackson, Wilmington Dist.
3590. Elisha Jennings, Wilmington Dist.
3733. John Jinkins, Wilmington Dist.
4957. John James, Wilmington Dist.
7404. James Jinkins, Salisbury Dist.
7616. Wm. Jackson, Salisbury Dist.
4103. Joel Jelton, Salisbury Dist.
4220. John Johnson, Salisbury Dist.
4585. John Johnson, Salisbury Dist.
736. James Jinkins, Salisbury Dist.
5296. Jas—— Jack——, Salisbury Dist.
80. Robert Jordan, Hillsborough Dist.
909. Joshua James, Warrenton Dist.
954. Robt. Jackson, Warrenton Dist.
966. Thomas Jennings, Warrenton Dist.
288. John J——, Newbern Dist.
640. Caleb Jordan, Halifax Dist.
381. Thomas James, Halifax Dist.
895. Nathan Jackson, Halifax Dist.
622. Mallachi Jolley, Hillsborough Dist.
721. Wm. Jackson, Hillsborough Dist.
534. Edwin James

*No.*

4693. William Robison, Morgan Dist.
4991. Hugh Ross, Morgan Dist.
4679. Christain Reinbort, Morgan Dist.
4050. David Robinsa, Morgan Dist.
1826. Wm. Rhodes, Wilmington Dist.
3097. Andrew Ranaldson, Wilmington
        Dist.
4188. David Richards, Wilmington Dist.
1631. Rich'd Rigan, Wilmington Dist.
4637. Philip Raiford, Wilmington Dist.
4743. Amos Renalds, Wilmington Dist.
4738. William Rollo, Wilmington Dist.
7533. Sam'l Richard, Salisbury Dist.
7847. Robert Rankin, Salisbury Dist.
5642. Robert Rolston, Salisbury Dist.
7855. Jas. Robinson, Salisbury Dist.
4861. Wm. Ross, Salisbury Dist.
3321. Moses Robison, Salisbury Dist.
2219. John Red, Salisbury Dist.
 330. Lawney Reynord, Hillsborough Dist.
 479. William Ridley, Hillsborough Dist.
 570. Pekel Rarke, Hillsborough Dist.
 541. Adam Rabby, Hillsborough Dist.
  37. David Rothwell, Hillsborough Dist.
 406. Jacob Rusher, Hillsborough Dist.
  90. John Renton, Hillsborough Dist.
 113. Charles Rosier, Hillsborough Dist.

*No.*

 258. John Richardson, Hillsborough
        Dist.
  69. Anderson Runnery, Hillsborough
        Dist.
 126. Lovick Rockwell, Hillsborough
        Dist.
 390. Ephriam Reynolds, Hillsborough
        Dist.
 218. William Redd, Hillsborough Dist.
 195. Jonathan Richards, Hillsborough
        Dist.
  25. Joseph Rack, Hillsborough Dist.
 200. Constantine Reddick, Hillsborough
        Dist.
108?. John Rowland, Hillsborough Dist.
  83. John Renton, Hillsborough Dist.
  75. Wm. Rothwell, Hillsborough Dist.
  74. David Rothwell, Hillsborough Dist.
  59. Powell Riggins, Hillsborough Dist.
  24. John Reddick, Halifax Dist.
 157. Aron Renn
 135. Solomon Ramsay
 398. Absalom Riggs
 171. Jethro Randolph
 136. Thos. Reddick
 159. Peter Reddick
 251. Benj. Rowland
 425. Geni Rice
 137. Andrew Russell

# NORTH CAROLINA REVOLUTIONARY ARMY ACCOUNTS, VOL. X

OLD SERIES—VOL. 10, BOOKS 18 & 19; VOL. 11, COMMISSIONERS STATEMENTS A. B. C.

The United States.
      To the State of North Carolina Dr.
    [Page 64]
    [Folio page 1]

For the following payments made by said State to officers and Soldiers of the Continental Line for personal services during the late war; which payments having been made in the year 1792, were not acted upon by the General board of Commissioners.

*No.*
- 3. Ezekiel Griffin, Privt.
- 4. Henry Gray, Sergt.
- 5. John Long, Privt.
- 6. Gabriel Ferrell, Privt.
- 7. John Anderson, Privt.
- 8. John Russ, Privt.
- 9. Francis Pridgen, Privt.
- 16. Edward H. Woodrow
  [Folio page 2]
- 20. Humphrey Malden, Privt.
- 21. John Hall, Privt.
- 22. William Bryce, Privt.
- 23. Loven Philips, Privt.
- 27. Willoughby Rogers, Privt.
- 31. Elisha Jenkins, P.
- 32. Matthias Cate, Privt.
- 39. Abraham Finley, Privt.
- 42. David Burke, Privt.
- 49. William Wilson, Privt.
- 59. John Rowland, Privt.
- 60. William Yeates, Privt.
- 63. James Dobbins, Privt.
- 64. Jonathan Thames, Sergt.
  [Folio page 3]
- 65. John Toney, Privt.
- 67. John Step, Privt.
- 69. Edward Pritchett, Privt.
- 75. Humphrey Durham, Privt.
- 82. William Hawkins, Privt.
- 83. John Vickery, Privt.
- 84. Joseph Sawyers, Privt.
- 87. Zachariah Philips, Privt.
- 88. James Chronester, Privt.
- 89. Levi Coleman, Privt.
- 92. Abraham Parrish, Privt.
- 97. Jesse Hutchings, Privt.
- 100. Charles Evans, Privt.
- 108. Edmund Dickins, Privt.
- 115. William Poor, Privt.
- 120. Lawrence Butler, Privt.

*No.*
- [Folio page 4]
- 119. John Clemmons, Privt.
- 124. Luke Stansberry, Privt.
- 127. Peter Smith, Privt.
- 131. Ezekiel Coats, Privt.
- 132. Cornelius Robertson, Privt.
- 133. Thomas Wilkins, Privt.
- 134. James Winley, Sergt.
- 135. Stephen Arthur, Privt.
- 138. Curl Tucker, Privt.
- 139. Alfred Andrews, Privt.
- 141. Burwell Wilkins, Privt.
- 145. Charles Thompson, Sergt.
  [Page 65]
  [Folio page 1]
- 147. Richard Willis, Privt.
- 160. Hardin Warner, Privt.
- 167. Shadrack Moore, Privt.
- 171. Elisha Mills, Privt.
- 173. Arthur Graham, Privt.
- 174. Thomas Scarlet, Privt.
- 187. Caleb Berry, Privt.
- 189. Abel Litten, Drummer
- 191. Tho. Germany, Privt.
- 198. Samuel Chappel, Sergt.
- 202. Gideon Simmons, Privt. & C.
- 203. Henry Medlin, Privt.
- 207. Carter Hastings, Mus.
- 208. Benjamin Ray, Privt.
- 217. Joel Tayborn, Privt.
- 222. Caleb Greenman
- 223. John Moore
  [Folio page 2]
- 225. Martin Penagar, Privt.
- 229. Jacob Ginn, Privt.
- 230. James Scarlet, Privt.
- 234. Howell Hearn, Privt.
- 235. Isaac Jones, Privt., & as Sergt. & as Corpl.
- 238. William Nichols, Privt.

No.
239. William Fernathan, Privt.
243. Thomas Garner, Privt.
244. Benjamin James, Privt.
245. John Glover, Wagoner
248. Robert Willson, Privt.
254. Stephen Bailey, Privt.
258. Thomas Garvey, Privt.
259. Thomas Brees, Corpl.
  [Folio page 3]
261. Ephraim Reynolds, Privt.
262. Absalom Martin, Privt.
283. Barnet March, Privt.
284. James Read, Privt.
287. Michael Huggins, Privt.
288. Robert Brownlay, Corpl. & Sergt.
289. Jacob Burke, Privt.
290. John Hamilton, Privt.
296. James Parks, Privt.
298. Isaiah Vick, Privt.
299. Norris Baker, Privt.
304. Anthony Hall, Privt.
307. Ashley Fowler, Privt.
308. Solomon Northern, Privt.
310. William McKenny, Wagoner
314. Absalom Harvey, Privt.
316. James Hodges, Privt.
  [Folio page 4]
318. Jacob Gibson, Privt.
322. Jacob Seagreaves, Privt.
325. William Cavender, Privt.
326. Sutton Green, Privt.
327. Berry Jones, Privt.
328. Benjamin Farmer, Privt.
341. Thomas Henry, Privt.
349. Charles Short, Musc.
355. Archibald Murphy, Privt.
369. Frederick Lucy, Privt.
372. Coleman Clayton, Privt.
381. Richard Smith, Privt.
382. Joseph Purser, Privt.
383. William Milton, Privt.
  [Page 66]
  [Folio page 1]
384. Richard Lewis, Sergt.
388. Saul Scott, Privt.
390. Malachi Strickland, Privt.
398. John Weston, Privt.
402. Micajah Watson, Privt.
405. James Price, Privt.
408. George Muskenoch, Privt.
410. William McIntire, Privt.
414. Giles Gaunt, Privt.
416. William Riles, Privt.

No.
418. James Long, Privt.
420. William Davis, Sergt.
421. James Talton, Privt.
423. John Harper
430. David Dawley, Corp'l. & Privt.
432. John Durham, Privt.
  [Folio page 2]
437. James Walker, Privt.
447. John Taylor, Privt.
456. Jordan Ammons, Privt.
460. Nicholas Icour, Privt.
463. Moses Hopper, Privt.
470. Shubal Claghurn, Privt. & C.
476. Reuben McKoy, Privt.
478. George Williams, Sergt.
483. Richard Pearson, Privt.
487. George Moore, Privt.
488. John Reasoner, Privt.
489. William Adams, Privt.
490. Hezekiah Bryan, Privt.
493. Michael McMullen, Privt.
494. Nicholas Dunn, Privt.
502. Charles Chaddock, Privt.
504. Stephen Thomas, Privt.
506. John Willebough, Privt.
512. Theophilus Mitchell, Privt.
514. Thomas Pratt, Privt.
516. Hezekiah Cooksey, Privt.
517. Thomas Cooksey, Privt.
522. William Todd, Privt. & Corpl.
526. Dempsey Boyce, Privt. & Corpl.
528. Daniel Weaver, Privt.
542. William Lord, Privt.
544. Absalom Wildey, Corpl.
545. Hugh Donally, Privt.
548. Francis Penrise, Privt.
552. Daniel Ramsey, Privt.
555. Isaac Wells, Privt.
  [Folio page 4]
556. Frederick Jones, Privt.
558. James Oneal, Privt.
559. Jesse Hall, Corpl.
564. Thomas Garvey, Privt.
569. William Leighton, Privt.
570. Andrew Simpson, Prvt., Corp. & Lt.
571. John Wood, Privt.
575. Jacob Hafner, Privt.
577. Daniel Matthews, Privt.
580. Thomas Ralph, Privt.
582. James Low, Privt.
600. James Slaughter, Privt.
604. James Berry, Privt.
605. James Chambers, Privt.

No.
[Page 67]
[Folio page 1]
616. John Brown, Privt.
617. Israel Simpson, Privt.
618. Tho. Lee, Privt.
619. James Huggins, Privt.
620. Cox Gray, Privt.
621. Benjamin Wilcox, Privt.
623. John Killebrew, Privt.
629. John Hopper, Privt.

No.
633. Aaron Smith, Privt.
636. William Bailey, Corpl.
639. Lewis Taylor, Privt.
640. Joshua Wilkins, Privt.
652. Levi Branton, Privt.
656. John Wall, Privt.
659. Britton Jones, Privt.
[Folio page 2]
668. Noah Bartlett, Privt.
673. William Crothers, Privt.

## Volume X

The United States. . . . To the State of North Carolina. For the following payments, made by said State to the officers and soldiers of the late Continental Line, thereof for depreciation and arrears of pay for service prior to the 1st day of January, 1782, in addition to and exclusive of the settlements made at Halifax in the years 1783, 4, & 5 and at Warrenton in the year 1786.

No.
[Page 68]
[Folio page 1]
**A**
7. John Anderson
71. John Atkinson
109. Amos Alsobrook
135. Stephen Arthur
[Folio page 2]
139. Alfred Andrews
143. Joseph Alsobrook
231. William Alston, Lt.-Col.
237. James Ammons
255. John Ashley
273. Caleb Archer
337. James Armstrong
357. James Anderson
358. John Adams
456. Jordan Ammons
489. William Adams
534. Benjamin Almerry
586. Joseph Arthur
[Folio page 3]
595. Jeremiah Allen
603. James Abbot
627. Cornelius Anglen
635. Simon Alderson, Capt.
642. Robert Allen

**B**
2. Michael Brinkley
12. Benjamin Boyt
18. Charles Bright
22. William Boyce
24. William H. Bailey
42. David Burke
51. William Brewer

98. Jesse Bozeman
107. David Brodwell
[Folio page 4]
113. James Bennett
120. Lawrence Butler
161. Robert Beach
187. Caleb Berry
196. Isaac Burgess
213. Alexander Ballentine
226. Joseph Boyd
249. Thomas Bowers
254. Stephen Bailey
259. Thomas Brees
267. Kader Benton
271. Josiah Bowers
[Page 69]
[Folio page 1]
288. Robert Brownley
289. Jacob Burke
292. William Bowers
299. Norris Baker
313. Caleb Barr
344. John Black
350. Mason Broom
375. Benjamin Brady
379. Thomas Brown
394. William Bennett
409. Thomas Biley
438. Baxter Bowling
444. Samuel Baker
471. George Beck
479. Jacob Brown
[Folio page 2]
486. Jacob Bennett
490. Hezekiah Bryan

*No.*
492. Nicholas Blanks
526. Dempsey Boyce
533. John Brooks
572. Jethro Benton
584. John Bert
589. Richard Baker
591. Cendall Booty
597. Benjamin Blango
598. Moses Blango
[Folio page 3]
599. Henry Brady
601. John Brown
604. James Berry
613. Hillary Brinson
616. John Brown
628. Matthias Betts
630. Edward Bell
636. William Bailey
637. John Brinn
638. William Boomer
652. Levi Branton
661. William Bond
668. Noah Bartlett

C

[Folio page 4]
32. Matthias Cates
53. Elijah Clay
62. Thomas Carvin
77. Alexander Cole
81. William Conner
88. James Cronnister
89. Levi Coleman
95. Stephen Conger, Adjt.
102. Bartholomew Curtis
103. Joshua Curtis, Ensn.
104. Reuben Curtis, Ensn.
106. John Cottle
119. John Clemons
[Page 70]
[Folio page 1]
131. Ezekiel Coats
162. Alexander Cherry
164. Dan'l. Cherry
185. John Cooper
198. Samuel Chappell
228. Gabriel Cooley
256. James Campbell
279. Absalom Cameron
300. William Carrol
325. William Cavender
331. David Culbertson
372. Coleman Clayton
385. Henry Cooper

*No.*
400. Gabriel Cooley
[Folio page 2]
404. Henry Chaves
415. Miles Castillo
427. Amos Cail
431. Robert Colchorn
434. George Campbell
458. Frederick Callum
470. Shubal Claghorn
475. Stephen Charlescraft
500. Francis Coston
516. Hezekiah Cooksey
517. Thomas Cooksey
554. Arthur Corban
576. William Collett
587. David Clement
[Folio page 3]
605. James Chambers
612. Lewis Connor
655. John Carter
662. John Carey
665. Benjamin Cummins
670. William Cox
671. Joseph Cox
673. William Carothers

D

17. James Dange
40. Eli Drake
83. James Dobbins
93. Humphrey Duchan
96. Francis Discorn
108. Edmund Dickins
[Folio page 4]
140. Frederick Discern
206. John Disheroon
297. Henry Dawson, Capt.
320. William Douglas, Q. M.
321. William Douglas
323. Benjamin Dickson
420. William Davis
430. David Dawley
432. John Durham
433. Robert Dennis
443. Josiah Dowdy
453. James Dobbins
454. James Davis
[Page 71]
[Folio page 1]
455. Benjamin Davis
482. James Deacon
494. Nicholas Dunn
545. Hugh Donnally
562. Samuel Davis

*No.*
606. Henry Dixon
624. William Duke
672. William Deal

**E**
35. John Emory
74. Thomas Early
100. Charles Evans
123. Joseph Edwards
213. John Everit
277. Thomas Erving
[Folio page 2]
285. Nicholas Edenton
339. David Everhart
406. William Eason
626. Seth Eason, Lt.
666. James Eslick
101. Charley Evans
451. Jonathan Erexon
569. Joshua Elkins

**F**
6. Gabriel Ferrell
39. Abraham Finley
155. John Farmer
157. Edward Ferrell

**H**
21. John Hall
30. William Haines
58. Thomas Hall
82. William Hawkins
97. Jesse Hutchins
[Folio page 3]
149. Thomas Harris
170. Ezekiel Habit
172. Samuel Hart
181. John Hoggard
197. John Harrison
207. Carter Hastings
233. Futrill Hall
234. Howell Hearn
260. Hardy Hukins
276. Isaac Hicks
280. Hance Hamilton, Sur.
287. Michael Huggins
290. John Hamilton
304. Anthony Hall
309. Edward Harris
314. Absalom Harvey
[Folio page 4]
315. Thomas Hudson
316. James Hodges
336. James Hammond

*No.*
368. John Harvey
423. John Harper
450. George Hargrove
463. Moses Hopper
464. Nicholas Hair
467. Hardy Hardison
477. Edw'd. Howard
497. Jesse Hardison
501. John Harris
508. John Howard
[Page 73]
[Folio page 1]
510. William Hardy
535. Jno. Hamilton
540. William Herbert
549. Edward Howell
559. Jesse Hall
560. Edward Hatchcock
574. John Henry
575. Jacob Hafner
579. Daniel Huggins
619. James Huggins
629. John Hopper
631. Jonathan Hickman
646. William Hopper
674. John Hackleman

**J**
11. Edward Jackson

**F**
[Folio page 3]
170. Hugh Forsyth
184. John Farmer
257. Nathaniel Farrar
307. Ashley Fowler
328. Benjamin Farmer
343. William Filson
425. James Fike
465. Solomon Fountain
473. William Fox
484. John Fry
498. John Fisher
611. Jesse Freeman
648. Mack Ferguson
66. John Fields
401. Edward Fossett

**G**
[Folio page 4]
3. Ezekiel Griffin
4. Henry Gray
47. Reuben Gurganos
125. John Grinder
150. William Godfrey
173. Arthur Graham

*No.*
186. Edward Gouing
191. Thomas Germany
220. Thomas Granberry, Capt.
222. Caleb Greenman
229. Jack Ginn
243. Thomas Garner
245. John Glover
     [Page 72]
     [Folio page 1]
258. Thomas Garvey
294. Isaac Gumbs
295. Charles Gibson
301. William Griffin
318. Jacob Gibson
326. Sutton Green
414. Giles Gaunt
428. John Green
440. Shadrack Gallop
441. John Gibson
445. William Gilbert
449. Matthias Goodrich
459. Thomas Gregory
538. Jeremiah Glohorn
546. Isaac Griffin
     [Folio page 2]
564. Thomas Garvey
588. Lewis Guthridge
615. Cox Gray
620. Cox Gray
625. Matthew Garvey
647. Elijah Garner
 57. John Grass
     [Folio page 2]

**J**
 19. John Jarvis
 31. Elisha Jenkins
 72. Thomas Johnston
 80. Robert Jordan
 91. James Johnston
110. Micajah James
151. Samuel Johnston
152. Charles Johnston
153. Benjamin Johnston
224. Levi Jarvis
235. Isaac Jones
236. Lemuel Jelks
240. Thomas Johnston
     [Folio page 3]
242. Jeremiah James
244. Benjamin James
268. Hezekiah Jones
269. Josiah Jones
303. John Johnston
327. Berry Jones
353. Sam'l. Jewell

*No.*
370. Dempsey Johnston
380. Matthias Johnston
391. Edwin James
393. William James
446. Thomas Jarvis
460. Nicholas Icour
547. William Jackson
556. Frederick Jones
557. Oliver Johnston
     [Folio page 4]
622. Malachi Jolly
659. Briton Jones
660. Briton Jones

**K**
110. Thomas Kelly
128. William Kelly
180. Job Kail
192. Charles Kite
193. Dempsey Kite
334. Daniel Killian
344. Thomas Kenny
623. John Killibrew
578. Abraham Kenny
     [Page 74]
     [Folio page 1]
168. Benjamin Kennedy
499. Thomas King

**L**
  5. John Long
 14. Lewis Lodge
 28. Matthew Lucas
 45. Willis Lewis
 54. James Largan
 76. John Long, Ensn.
 93. Nathan Lewis
 99. Alexander Lemon
148. Lemuel Litten
189. Abel Litten
201. John Luttrell, Lt. Col.
     [Folio page 2]
221. Joseph Leftyear
291. Burwell Lloyd
340. John Lyon
363. Ephraim Lewis
369. Frederick Lucy
384. Richard Lewis
389. Ballinger Lucas
413. Philip Logan
418. James Long
436. John Lacy
485. Michael Legal
532. Lewis Leggett
542. William Lord, Lt.

No.

560. Richard Low
[Folio page 3]
569. William Leighton
582. James Low
583. Cornelius Love
618. Thomas Lee
650. Thomas Laughinghouse
669. Elisha Lewis

**M**

20. Humphrey Molden
55. Alexander McKinsey
56. Thomas McMeans
70. Major May
117. Josiah Messle
121. Richard Martin
130. Peter Malone
146. George McDonald
156. Gilbert Matthews
[Folio page 4]
165. James Morris
167. Shadrach Moore
169. John Moore
171. Elisha Mills
203. Harry Medley
205. Abel Miller
215. Timothy Morgan
223. John Moore
250. Benjamin McGackey
253. Roll Matthews
262. Absalom Martin
274. Arthur Monday
275. Alex'r. Martin, Colo.
[Page 75]
[Folio page 1]
278. Edward Morris
283. Barnett March
286. Sam'l. Martin, Lt.
310. William McKinny
311. James McKey
312. Harry Martin
352. Robert McAlpin
355. Archibald Murphey
359. Robert Moss
360. Daniel Middleton
361. Joel Martin
362. Daniel Murphree
374. Henry May
383. Wm. Melton
396. Charles Morgan
[Folio page 2]
399. Ezekiel Modlin
408. George Murkinock
410. William McIntire

No.

412. Robert Moseman
426. Michael McGuire
442. Isaac Merritt
474. Alexander McCarter
478. Reuben McCoy
487. George Moore
493. Michael McMullen
495. William McDaniel
512. Theophilus Mitchell
519. Joshua Martin
[Folio page 3]
521. John Marr
530. Arthur Marcum
541. William Moore
573. Barnaba Murrell
587. Daniel Matthews
585. Kennith McKinsey
590. Timothy Murray
592. Robert McRay
596. Benj'm. Mason
602. Thos. McKiel
632. John Mullins
643. John Mullen
645. Shadrach Medlin
654. Solomon Molborne
332. Cornelius McGraw

**N**

[Folio page 4]
43. William Norris
111. Wm. Norton
211. Jacob Nichols
238. William Nicholas
308. Solomon Norton
342. William Norris
581. John Nutter
594. Benj'n. Neal
651. Daniel Neal
653. Arthur Nelson
663. James Nobles
667. Hardy Nelson
[Page 76]
[Folio page 1]

**O**

136. George Oliver
175. James Orr
232. Aaron Olam
371. Owen Omerry
491. James Orrell
558. James Oneal

**P**

9. Francis Pridgen

*No.*
23. Lovan Philips
29. Miles Pruit
36. Job Pendergrass
44. John Parrimore
69. Edward Pritchell
87. Zachariah Philips
90. Edmund Pendleton
[Folio page 2]
92. Abram Parish
112. Bush Philips
115. William Poor
126. John Portress
142. William Pass
154. George Pettiford
159. Wm. Plummer
178. Jacob Porter
194. Jesse Pritchard
199. Martin Pfifer
225. Martin Panniger
227. Jacob Parish
246. John Philips
264. John Poulson
[Folio page 3]
272. Dan'l. Peal
296. James Parks
329. Jno. Price
366. Stephen Paul
378. John Pritchell
382. Joseph Purser
395. Thomas Pierce
419. John Patterson
424. John Perry
448. Andrew Philips
468. Wm. Price
472. Joseph Palmer
483. Rch'd. Pearson
514. Thos. Pratt
531. Wm. Pierce
[Folio page 4]
539. Thomas Pearson
548. Francis Penrice
608. Abram Perkins
405. James Price
568. Joshua Proctor

R

8. John Russ
25. Joseph Runnols
27. Willoughby Rogers
37. David Rothwell
41. Ishmael Robards
59. John Roland
114. Joel Ramsay

*No.*
[Page 77]
[Folio page 1]
132. Cornelius Robison
144. Randal Robison
208. Benj'n. Ray
219. Charles Ragan
261. Ephraim Reanolds
282. Jacob Reid
319. Patrick Rogers, Lt.
330. Launey Reynord
345. Jacob Reid
346. Wm.Ridley
356. Timothy Rich
376. Noah Robison
386. Hardy Ridley
397. Adam Rabby
416. Wm. Ryles
417. Tekel Rasko
[Folio page 2]
488. John Reason
511. Howell Rowell
536. Blake Rabby
552. Dan'l. Ramsay
641. Godfrey Rowland
664. Robt. Ruff
675. Isaac Ralston, Lt.
284. James Reid
580. Tho. Ralph

S

26. Sam'l. Smith
33. John Smith
67. John Step
68. Alex Smith
[Folio page 3]
75. Robt. Shaw
84. Joseph Sawyer
86. Owen Smith
105. John Skinner
118. Isaac Scollar
124. Luke Stansbury
127. Peter Smith
137. Israel Scott
158. Joseph Singletary
166. Benj'n. Saunders
174. Thos. Scarlet
177. Joseph Stuart
183. Thos. Sorrel
190. Miles Span
202. Gideon Simons or (L)
204. Galey Smith
[Folio page 4]
212. William Shepperd

*No.*
230. James Scarlett
241. Rich'd. Sumner
247. James Senter
252. James Shanon
263. William Stuart
293. Henry Short
300. Wm. Scott
305. William Singletary
322. Jacob Segraves
335. William Staggs
338. John Sorrell
347. Dan'l. Smith
348. James Span
  [Page 78]
  [Folio page 1]
349. Charles Short
354. Hezekiah Shermantine
364. Michael Scott
367. Caleb Story
373. Henry Smith
381. Rich'd. Smith
388. Saul Scott
390. Malechi Strickland
392. James Saunders
462. David Showers
466. Absalom Sallenger
469. Wm. Smithwick
502. Charles Shaddock
505. Henry Haws Story
515. Benj'n. Saulberry
520. William Smith
  [Folio page 2]
537. Solomon Spence
550. Joseph Spears
551. Sam'l. Spears
565. Thomas Sinclair
567. Alex Scull
570. Andrew Simpson
600. James Slaughter
607. Wm. Smith
617. Isaac Sampson
633. Aaron Smith
634. Benj'n. Steadman
644. Joseph Saunders

## T

[Folio page 3]
1. Erastus Tippit
46. Emanuel Tiel
48. Charles Tinsley
50. Joshua Tousan
64. Jonathan Times
65. John Toney
85. Adam Turner

*No.*
122. Erasmus Tippit
129. Thomas Taylor
138. Curl Tucker
145. Charles Thompson
182. Thomas Tart
195. Caleb Taylor
214. Charles Thompson
216. James Tharp
217. Joel Tayborne
  [Folio page 4]
218. Sam'l. Taylor
239. William Tervathan
421. James Tarleton
422. William Tarleton
435. John Taylor
447. John Taylor
461. Francis Tartanson
504. Stephen Thomas
513. Joseph Tate, Capt.
518. George Thompson
522. William Todd
523. James Todd
524. Ephraim Todd
  [Page 79]
  [Folio page 1]
529. Thomas Todd
593. Ross Thomas
639. Lewis Taylor

## V

83. John Vicory
298. Isaah Vick
333. Elijah Vickers
357. John Vance, Capt.
496. Edward Vale
649. Charles Upchurch

## W

10. William Wiseheart
13. Daniel Williams
16. Edward H. Woodroe
34. Henry Williamson
49. Wm. Wilson
  [Folio page 2]
52. William Walters
78. Silvanus Wicks
79. Isaac Walters
94. Willis Williford
133. Thomas Wilkins
134. James Winley
141. Burwell Wilkins
147. Richard Willis
160. Harden Warner

*No.*
199. William Watford
200. Seth Wilson
209. Solomon Watson
210. Ephraim Watson
   [Folio page 3]
248. Robert Wilson
251. James Wosson
265. Willis Wiggins
266. John Warner
281. William Williams
302. Thomas Weeks
317. Henry Waller
324. William Wynn
365. Haynes White
387. Caleb Woodward
398. John Weston
402. Micajah Watson
403. Benjamin Williams
407. James Wadkins

*No.*
411. John Weaver
   [Folio page 4]
555. Isaah Wells
561. Matthew Worley
563. John Wilson
571. John Wood
609. Aaron Wood
610. John Whaley
614. Francis Whaley
621. Benjamin Wilcox
640. Joshua Wilkins
650. John Wall
657. Joseph Ward
507. James Willoughby
658. James Wolard

### Y

60. William Yates
61. James Yene

# MILITARY LAND WARRANTS, CONTINENTAL LINE
## (Part I)
### A LIST OF WARRANTS FOR LANDS GRANTED THE OFFICERS AND SOLDIERS IN THE CONTINENTAL LINE OUT OF THE SECRETARY'S OFFICE

| No. | To whom granted and rank | No. acres | Service in months | Location and to whom deeded and date of warrant. Within the limits of the lands allotted the officers and soldiers of the Continental Line, by Law, 1783, Oct. 14 | | |
|---|---|---|---|---|---|---|
| 1. | Archibald Lytle, Lt. Col. Commdt. | 7,200 | 84 | Oct. 14,'83 | | Self |
| 2. | Alexander Martin, Col. 2nd Reg. ... | 2,314 | 27 | " | | " |
| 3. | Alexander Morrison, Sergt. | 1,000 | 84 | " | | " |
| 4. | William Lytle, Capt. | 3,840 | 84 | " | | " |
| 5. | Demcey Underdue, Privt. | 640 | 84 | " | Col. Long | |
| 6. | John Wilkerson, Matross. | 640 | 84 | " | " | |
| 7. | George Topp, Privt. | 640 | 84 | " | " | |
| 8. | Henry Johnston, Privt. | 640 | 84 | " | " | |
| 9. | Kedar Copeland, Privt. | 640 | 84 | " | " | |
| 10. | Major Glandon, Sergt. | 1,000 | 84 | " | " | |
| 11. | Henry Smith, Privt. | 640 | 84 | Oct. 15 | " | |
| 12. | James Simmons, Privt. | 640 | 84 | " | " | |
| 13. | Milond Mullins, Privt. | 228 | 30 | Oct. 16 | Robt. Goodloe | |
| 14. | John Potter, Privt. | 228 | 30 | " | " | |
| 15. | David Phillips, Privt. | 228 | 30 | " | " | |
| 17. | John Armstrong, Lt. Col. | 5,760 | 84 | " | | Self |
| 16. | Daniel Hilton, Heir at law to William Hilton, Lieut. Decsd.... | 2,560 | 84 | " | " | |
| 18. | George Daugherty, Maj. | 4,800 | 84 | " | " | |
| 19. | John Maderris, Capt. 5th Reg. | 3,290 | 72 | " | " | |
| 20. | Robert Bell, Lieut. | 2,560 | 84 | " | | " |
| 21. | Enoch Ferrell, Privt. | 366 | 48 | Oct. 17 | Col. Moore | |
| 22. | John Yates, Privt. | 640 | 84 | " | " | |
| 23. | James Moore, Heir at law to Brig. Gen. James Moore, decd. | 12,000 | 84 | " | Maj. Tatum | |
| 24. | Charles Allen, Capt. | 1,695 | 37 | " | " | |
| 25. | Martin Pfifer, Capt. | 1,149 | 25 | " | Caleb Pfifer | |
| 26. | Daniel McCoy, Privt. | 549 | 72 | " | David Wilson | |
| 27. | Nathaniel Hughs, Privt. | 316 | 41 | Oct. 18 | Wm. Ross | |
| 28. | Elisha Bond, Privt. | 274 | 36 | " | " | |
| 29. | Richard Davin, Privt. | 274 | 36 | Oct. 20 | | Self |
| 30. | James McRory, Heir at law to Thomas McRory, a Capt. | 3,840 | 84 | " | | " |
| 31. | Charles Wood, Corpl. | 1,000 | 84 | Oct. 20 | | Self |
| 32. | Elijah Moore, Capt. | 3,840 | 84 | " | Alfred Moore | |
| 33. | Nathaniel Williams, Lieut. | 2,560 | 84 | " | David Rice | |
| 34. | Francis Child, Capt. | 3,840 | 84 | " | R. Caswell | |
| 35. | Joshua Martin, Privt. | 274 | 36 | " | Lt. Campbell | |
| 36. | Charles Dodson, Privt. | 640 | 84 | Oct. 21 | | " |
| 37. | John Nelson, Maj. 1st Reg. | 4,800 | 84 | " | | " |
| 38. | John Gee, Heir to Capt. James Gee, desd. | 3,840 | 84 | " | Col. D. Gee | |
| 39. | Nathaniel Dobey, Privt. | 228 | 30 | " | " | |
| 40. | William Gee, Privt. | 228 | 30 | " | " | |
| 41. | John Campbell, Lieut. | 2,560 | 84 | " | | " |
| 42. | James Ferrell, Privt. | 274 | 36 | " | | " |
| 43. | William Tate, Trooper. | 274 | 36 | " | | " |
| 44. | John Christie, Fife Maj. | 358 | 30 | " | | " |
| 45. | John Cyprell, Sergt. | 358 | 30 | " | | " |
| 46. | Tillman Dixon, Capt. | 3,840 | 84 | " | | " |

| No. | To whom granted and rank | No. acres | Service in months | date of warrant | Location and to whom deeded and date of warrant. Within the limits of the lands allotted the officers and soldiers of the Continental Line, by Law, 1783, Oct. 14 | |
|---|---|---|---|---|---|---|
| 47. | William Sanders, Lieut........... | 2,560 | 84 | Oct. 21 | Capt. Dixon | |
| 48. | Winne Dixon, Lieut.............. | 2,560 | 84 | " | " | |
| 49. | John Simpson, Privt............. | 640 | 84 | " | " | |
| 50. | John Christmas, Privt........... | 640 | 84 | " | " | |
| 51. | Anthony Toney, Privt........... | 640 | 84 | " | " | |
| 52. | Anthony Sharp, Capt............ | 3,840 | 84 | " | | Self |
| 53. | Jesse Steed, Lieut............... | 2,560 | 84 | " | | " |
| 54. | William Terrell Lewis, Heir of Micajah Lewis, decsd. Capt....... | 3,840 | 84 | " | | " |
| 55. | William Terrell Lewis, Lieut...... | 1,463 | 48 | " | | " |
| 56. | Joel Lewis, Lieut................ | 1,463 | 48 | " | | " |
| 57 | James Christian, Privt. Infirn..... | 640 | 84 | " | | " |
| 58. | The Reverend Mr. James Tate, Chaplain..................... | 1,553 | 84 | " | | " |
| 59. | Joshua Hadley, Capt............ | 3,840 | 84 | " | | " |
| 60. | Charles Dixon, Exec'r of the last will of Henry Dixon, Lieut Col. in trust for the legatees........ | 5,760 | 84 | " | | " |
| 61. | Charles Dixon, Lieut............ | 2,560 | 84 | " | Chas. Dixon | |
| 62. | William Armstrong, Capt........ | 3,840 | 84 | " | " | |
| 63. | Nathaniel Dickerson, Lieut....... | 949 | 31 | " | " | |
| 64. | Daniel Freeman, Privt. Heir of Nathan Freeman, decsd........ | 640 | 84 | " | " | |
| 65. | John Barginer, Privt............ | 228 | 30 | " | " | |
| 66. | James Witty, Privt.............. | 366 | 48 | " | " | |
| 67. | Benjamin Sharp, Sergt.......... | 1,000 | 84 | " | " | |
| 68. | Morriss Morgan, Privt.......... | 640 | 84 | " | | Self |
| 69. | Drury Hern, Privt.............. | 228 | 30 | " | | " |
| 70. | David Christee, Sergt.......... | 1,000 | 84 | " | | " |
| 71. | Riply Copeland, Privt.......... | 274 | 36 | " | Neil Copeland | |
| 72. | William Douglass, Corpl......... | 1,000 | 84 | " | | Self |
| 73. | Thomas White, Trooper......... | 228 | 30 | " | Maj. Tatum | |
| 74. | James Gray, Sergt.............. | 429 | 36 | " | | " |
| 75. | John Giles, Sergt............... | 358 | 30 | " | Maj. McKinen | |
| 76. | Job Pendergrass, Privt.......... | 274 | 36 | Oct. 22 | Maj. McCauley | |
| 77. | Thomas Clarke, Lieut........... | 2,560 | 84 | " | | Self |
| 78. | Daniel Thompson, Privt......... | 274 | 36 | " | Lt. Clarke | |
| 79. | John Jones, Privt............... | 274 | 36 | " | " | |
| 80. | Ralph Williams, Capt........... | 1,142 | 25 | " | | " |
| 81. | Thomas Armstrong, Capt........ | 3,840 | 84 | " | | " |
| 82. | Charles Gerard, Lieut........... | 2,560 | 84 | " | | " |
| 83. | James Armstrong, Col. 8th Reg.... | 7,200 | 84 | " | Capt. Armstrong | |
| 84. | Francis Williams, Privt. | 640 | 84 | " | " | |
| 85. | Abraham Towler, Privt.......... | 640 | 84 | " | " | |
| 86. | Jephtha Parker, Sergt.......... | 1,000 | 84 | " | " | |
| 87. | Thomas Angel, Privt............ | 274 | 36 | " | " | |
| 88. | John Nash, Sergt............... | 428 | 36 | " | Col. Bledsoe | |
| 89. | Martin Cole, Sergt.............. | 1,000 | 84 | " | | Self |
| 90. | Patrick Campbell, Sergt......... | 428 | 36 | " | | " |
| 91. | James Lott, Privt............... | 274 | 36 | " | Philip Jones | |
| 92. | John Hardin, Privt............. | 228 | 30 | " | Lt. Steed | |
| 93. | John Bowers, Privt............. | 228 | 30 | " | " | |
| 94. | James Avent, Privt............. | 228 | 30 | " | " | |
| 95. | Solomon Seymore, Privt......... | 228 | 30 | " | " | |
| 96. | William Seymore Privt.......... | 274 | 36 | " | " | |
| 97. | Silby Harney, Lt. Col. Commdt.... | 7,200 | 84 | " | Jo. Ferebee | |

| No. | To whom granted and rank | No. acres | Service in months | Location and to whom deeded and date of warrant. Within the limits of the lands allotted the officers and soldiers of the Continental Line, by Law, 1783, Oct. 14 | |
|---|---|---|---|---|---|
| 98. | Pettit Cook, Heir to Geo. Cook, Lt. | 2,560 | 84 | Oct. 21 | Jo. Ferebee |
| 99. | James Porterfield, Heir to Demsey Porterfield, Capt. | 3,840 | 84 | " | John Porterfield |
| 100. | Elizabeth Rudpeth, widow of John Rudpeth, Lieut. Decsd | 2,560 | 84 | Oct. 22 | Self |
| 101. | James White, Heir of Thomas White, Capt. Decsd | 3,840 | 84 | " | " |
| 102. | Richard Copeland, Privt. | 228 | 30 | " | " |
| 103. | Matthew McCauly, Lieut. | 761 | 25 | " | " |
| 104. | John Eborn, Capt. | 1,645 | 36 | " | " |
| 105. | James Comer, Sergt. Troops | 428 | 36 | " | " |
| 106. | Hardy Murphey, Lieut. Col. | 5,760 | 84 | " | Col. Murfree |
| 107. | Thomas Finney, Lieut. | 2,560 | 84 | " | " |
| 108. | Nehemiah Long, Capt. | 1,785 | 39 | " | " |
| 109. | William Walton, Capt. | 3,840 | 84 | " | " |
| 110. | Richard Andrews, Lieut. | 2,200 | 72 | " | " |
| 111. | John Granberry, Lieut. | 792 | 26 | " | " |
| 112. | William Winborn, Heir to John Winborn, Lieut. Decsd | 2,560 | 84 | " | " |
| 113. | James Martin, Capt. | 1,462 | 32 | " | " |
| 114. | John Laurance Hare, Lieut. | 914 | 30 | " | " |
| 115. | John Billops, Privt. | 274 | 36 | " | " |
| 116. | Elisha Hunt, Privt. | 640 | 84 | " | " |
| 117. | Ben. Johnston, Privt. | 390 | 52 | " | " |
| 118. | John Wells, Privt. | 640 | 84 | " | " |
| 119. | David Bizzell, Heir at law to Enus Bizzell | 640 | 84 | " | " |
| 120. | William Mitchell, Drummer | 1,000 | 84 | " | " |
| 121. | Ezehiel White, Privt. | 274 | 36 | " | " |
| 122. | John Butler, Privt. | 228 | 30 | " | " |
| 123. | William Ponder, Privt. | 318 | 42 | " | " |
| 124. | Baker Archer, Heir to Demcey Archer, Privt. | 640 | 84 | " | " |
| 125. | Baker Archer, Heir to Jesse Archer, Privt. | 640 | 84 | " | " |
| 126. | Joseph Howard, Privt. | 274 | 36 | " | " |
| 127. | Absalom Spires, Privt. | 360 | 48 | " | " |
| 128. | John Harris, Privt. | 640 | 84 | " | " |
| 129. | Benjamin Reed, Privt. | 640 | 84 | " | " |
| 130. | Anthony Gaines, Privt. | 640 | 84 | " | " |
| 131. | James Purdy, Privt. | 281 | 37 | " | " |
| 132. | John White, Privt. | 228 | 30 | " | " |
| 133. | William Powell, Privt. | 440 | 55 | " | " |
| 134. | Ransom Savage, Privt. | 560 | 70 | " | " |
| 135. | Douglass Carrol, Fifer. | 4,289 | 36 | " | " |
| 136. | Allen Ramsey, Capt. | 1,097 | 24 | " | " |
| 137. | Henry Winburn, Privt. | 389 | 51 | " | " |
| 138. | Isaac Butler, Privt. | 228 | 30 | " | " |
| 139. | Mary Knight, Relect of Jesse Knight, Decsd. Privt. | 640 | 84 | ' | " |
| 140. | Anna Manley, Relect of Solomon Manley, Decsd. Privt. | 640 | 84 | " | " |
| 141. | Thomas Powell, Privt. | 320 | 42 | " | " |
| 142. | James Christian, Privt. | 640 | 84 | " | " |
| 143. | William Lewis, Privt. | 274 | 36 | " | " |
| 144. | Demcey Jinkins, Privt. | 320 | 42 | " | " |

| No. | To whom granted and rank | No. acres | Service in months | Location and to whom deeded and date of warrant. Within the limits of the lands allotted the officers and soldiers of the Continental Line, by Law, 1783, Oct. 14 | | |
|---|---|---|---|---|---|---|
| 145. | Joseph Mitchell, Privt.......... | 274 | 36 | Oct. 22 | Col. Murfree | |
| 146. | Bryant Smith, Privt............ | 342 | 45 | " | " | |
| 147. | William Manley, Privt.......... | 274 | 36 | " | " | |
| 148. | Giles Webb, Heir to Joseph Webb, Privt................ | 640 | 84 | " | " | |
| 149. | Martha Lewis, Relect of Sampson Lewis, Privt................ | 640 | 84 | " | " | |
| 150. | Mosson Williams, Privt......... | 228 | 30 | " | " | |
| 151. | Thomas Loyd, Heir to Leonard Loyd, Privt............... | 640 | 84 | " | L. C. Armstrong | |
| 152. | James Scurlack, Lieut.......... | 2,560 | 84 | " | Maj. Ramsey | |
| 153. | Matthew Ramsey, Capt......... | 2,697 | 59 | " | " | |
| 154. | The heirs of William Rollen, Pri. . | 640 | 84 | " | Lt. Steed | |
| 155. | Lucky Enloe, Legatee of John Enloe, Capt................ | 1,280 | 28 | " | Col. Glasgow | |
| 156. | Thomas Polk, Ensn. 4th Battln... | 2,191 | 25 | " | Maj. Polk | |
| 157. | William Caswell, Capt.......... | 1,280 | 28 | " | Gen. Caswell | |
| 158. | John Herritage, Capt........... | 1,280 | 28 | " | " | |
| 159. | Nathaniel Jones, Heir of Samuel Jones, Ensn. Decsd........... | 2,560 | 84 | Oct. 22 | | Self |
| 160. | David Gillespie, Privt.......... | 274 | 36 | " | Wm. Gillespie | |
| 161. | Wm. Mebane, Heir of Robert Mebane, Senr. Col. Commandant, Decsd.................. | 7,200 | 84 | Oct. 23 | " | Self |
| 162. | William Polk, Maj. 9th Reg...... | 1,888 | 33 | " | " | " |
| 163. | Thomas Massey, Heir.......... | 640 | 84 | " | Lt. Steed | |
| 164. | Reuben Massey, Heir.......... | 640 | 84 | " | " | |
| 165. | Hon. Brig. Gen. Jethro Sumner... | 12,000 | 84 | " | Capt. Armstrong | |
| 166. | Edward Yarborough, Capt....... | 3,840 | 84 | " | " | Self |
| 167. | Archibald Henderson, Drummer.. | 773 | 65 | " | Col. Murfree | |
| 168. | Samuel Smith, Corpl........... | 429 | 36 | " | S. Smith | |
| 169. | Kedar Parker, Capt., Samuel Parker's Heir................ | 3,840 | 84 | " | Saml. Parker | |
| 170. | Elijah Duncan, Privt........... | 274 | 36 | " | " | " |
| 171. | John Burton, Adjt. 8th N. C. Battln...................... | 1,168 | 36 | " | Col. Murfree | |
| 172. | William Robb, Corpl........... | 357 | 30 | " | " | " |
| 173. | Thomas Dudley, Lieut.......... | 2,560 | 84 | " | Lt. Bush | |
| 174. | William Bush, Lieut............ | 2,560 | 84 | " | " | " |
| 175. | Samuel Jones, Capt............ | 3,840 | 84 | " | " | |
| 176. | Curtis Ivey, Lieut............. | 2,560 | 84 | " | " | " |
| 177. | Hardy Jones, Privt............ | 360 | 48 | " | " | " |
| 178. | Thomas Harriss, Maj........... | 2,057 | 36 | " | | " |
| 179. | Alexander Nelson, Lieut........ | 763 | 25 | " | | " |
| 180. | George Phillips, Privt.......... | 640 | 84 | " | " | |
| 181. | Drury Ward, Privt............. | 274 | 36 | " | " | |
| 182. | Henry Coleston, Privt.......... | 274 | 36 | " | " | |
| 183. | William Jackson, Privt.......... | 274 | 36 | " | " | |
| 184. | Thomas Moore, Privt.......... | 274 | 36 | " | " | |
| 185. | John Macon, Capt............. | 1,097 | 24 | " | | " |
| 186. | Rabon Gibbs, Heir of Joel Gibbs, Privt. Decsd................. | 640 | 84 | Oct. 24 | | " |
| 187. | Robert Smith, Capt............ | 1,828 | 40 | " | Wm. Alexander | |
| 188. | William Alexander, Lieut........ | 2,560 | 84 | " | " | |
| 189. | Sarah Routledge, Heir of William Routledge, Lieut..... | 2,560 | 84 | " | Lt. Ivey | |

| No. | To whom granted and rank | No. acres | Service in months | Location and to whom deeded and date of warrant. Within the limits of the lands allotted the officers and soldiers of the Continental Line, by Law, 1783, Oct. 14 | | |
|---|---|---|---|---|---|---|
| 190. | Nathaniel McCann, Heir of John McCann, Lieut. | 2,560 | 84 | Oct. 24 | Capt. Gillespie | |
| 191. | Hezekiah Linton, Senr. Heir of Hezekiah Linton, Privt. | 640 | 84 | Oct. 24 | Wm. B. Jones | |
| 192. | Philip Taylor, Capt. | 1,759 | 39 | " | | Self |
| 193. | Thomas Donoho, Maj. | 4,800 | 84 | " | | " |
| 194. | Demcey Womble, Privt. | 640 | 84 | " | Maj. Donoho | |
| 195. | Joseph Blythe, Surgeon | 4,800 | 84 | " | | " |
| 196. | James Dowall, Privt. | 274 | 36 | " | | " |
| 197. | John Atkinson, Privt. | 228 | 30 | " | | " |
| 198. | Henry Brewer, Privt. | 360 | 48 | " | | " |
| 199. | Thomas McKessick, Pt. Wounded | 640 | 84 | " | | " |
| 200. | Samuel Gilston, Sergt. Killed, David Gilston, Sergt. | 1,000 | 84 | " | | " |
| 201. | Lawrence Byrum, Privt. | 228 | 30 | " | | " |
| 202. | Edward Howard, Privt. | 228 | 30 | " | | " |
| 203. | James Fogertee, Privt. | 274 | 36 | " | | " |
| 204. | Robert Linn, Privt. | 274 | 36 | " | | " |
| 205. | John Ward, Privt. | 640 | 84 | " | | " |
| 206. | Edward Howell, Heir of John Howell, Privt. Decsd. | 640 | 84 | Oct. 25 | Maj. Cage | |
| 207. | James Thackston, Lt. Col. Comdt. | 4,352 | 48 | " | | " |
| 208. | John Tipper, Privt. | 228 | 30 | " | | " |
| 209. | John Southerland, Privt. | 274 | 36 | " | Maj. Donoho | |
| 210. | Nathaniel Durham, Privt. | 600 | 77 | " | | " |
| 211. | Hardy Holmes, Lieut. | 2,560 | 84 | Oct. 25 | C. Ivey | |
| 212. | Jacob Stillwell, Fifer. | 264 | 39 | " | Mr. Dixon | |
| 213. | Thomas Tiffin, Privt. | 570 | 67 | " | " | " |
| 214. | Libba Archer, Heiress of Mark Manley, Privt. | 640 | 84 | " | Col. Murphy | |
| 215. | John Bush, Lieut. | 914 | 30 | " | Lt. Bush | |
| 216. | Samuel Knight, Privt. | 274 | 36 | Oct. 25 | | Self |
| 217. | Thomas Brannon, Privt. | 274 | 36 | " | | " |
| 218. | Powell Riggins, Privt. | 274 | 36 | " | | " |
| 219. | Richard Phillips, Privt. | 274 | 36 | " | | " |
| 220. | Francis Owen, Privt. | 278 | 30 | " | Capt. Hadley | |
| 221. | David Burnsides, Sergt. | 360 | 30 | " | " | |
| 222. | William McKinsey, Privt. | 640 | 84 | " | " | |
| 223. | William Welch, Corpl. | 1,000 | 84 | " | Capt. Lytle | |
| 224. | John Bryan, Sergt. | 430 | 36 | " | | Self |
| 225. | Frederick Hargitt, Capt. | 1,508 | 33 | " | Lt. Bush | |
| 226. | James Read, Capt. | 3,840 | 84 | " | | " |
| 227. | Jacob Richards, Privt. | 342 | 45 | " | | " |
| 228. | Joseph Smith, Privt. | 604 | 72 | " | Col. Moore | |
| 229. | John Summers, Capt. | 3,840 | 84 | " | " | |
| 230. | William Fawn, Capt. | 3,840 | 84 | " | Capt. Armstrong | |
| 231. | Solomon Bibley, Privt. | 274 | 36 | " | " | |
| 232. | Demcey Moore, Lieut. | 780 | 25 | " | Col. Wm. Moore | |
| 233. | Elijah Moore, Capt. | 3,840 | 84 | " | " | " |
| 234. | John Reese, Privt. | 274 | 36 | " | " | |
| 235. | Roger Reese, Privt. | 274 | 36 | " | " | |
| 236. | William Washington, Ensn. | 1,096 | 36 | " | | Self |
| 237. | Miles Knight, Sergt. | 1,000 | 84 | " | C. Ivey | |
| 238. | Stephen Bowen, Sergt. | 428 | 36 | " | " | |
| 239. | Vincent Salmon, Corpl. | 1,000 | 84 | " | " | |
| 240. | John Bailey Privt. | 640 | 84 | " | " | |

| No. | To whom granted and rank | No. acres | Service in months | Location and to whom deeded and date of warrant. Within the limits of the lands allotted the officers and soldiers of the Continental Line, by Law, 1783, Oct. 14 | | |
|---|---|---|---|---|---|---|
| 241. | Owen Tyler, Privt. | 640 | 84 | Oct. 25 | C. Ivey | |
| 242. | John Hurley, Privt. | 640 | 84 | " | " | |
| 243. | Andrew Phillips, Privt. | 360 | 48 | " | | " |
| 244. | Joseph Phillips, Capt. | 1,280 | 28 | " | | " |
| 245. | Wm. Temple Cole, Capt. | 1,500 | 34 | " | | " |
| 246. | The Rev. Adam Boyd, Chaplain. | 7,200 | 84 | " | | " |
| 247. | William Daves, Lt. Col. | 2,468 | 36 | " | Ad. Boyd | |
| 248. | John Walker, Maj. | 1,709 | 32 | " | " | " |
| 249. | James Parkeson, Lieut. | 2,560 | 84 | " | " | " |
| 250. | Gibbs, Lamb, Privt. | 640 | 84 | " | " | " |
| 251. | Reason Holland, Privt. | 274 | 36 | " | Capt. Cole | |
| 252. | Andrew Allison, Privt. Wounded.. | 640 | 84 | " | " | |
| 253. | William Davidson, Lt. Col. Heir, George Davidson | 5,760 | 84 | " | | Self |
| 254. | Daniel Huston, Heir of Neil Huston, Privt. | 640 | 84 | " | Capt. Cole | |
| 255. | William Reason, Privt. | 412 | 54 | " | M. Nelson | |
| 256. | Benjamin Joyner, Privt. | 640 | 84 | Oct. 27 | C. Ivey | |
| 257. | James McClelland, Sergt. | 429 | 36 | " | Maj. Nelson | |
| 258. | Thomas Clark, Col. | 7,200 | 84 | " | Maj. Boyd | |
| 259. | Phillip Jones, Capt. Lt. Artillery.. | 2,560 | 84 | " | " | Self |
| 260. | Andrew Lytle, Privt. Dead., Wm. Lytle Heir. | 640 | 84 | " | Col. Lytle | |
| 261. | Robert Nelson, Sergt. | 357 | 30 | " | | Self |
| 262. | Adam Hart, Privt. | 640 | 84 | " | | " |
| 263. | Reading Blount, Majr. | 4,800 | 84 | " | | " |
| 264. | Peter Baccote, Capt. | 3,840 | 84 | " | Maj. Blount | |
| 265. | Benjamin Coleman, Capt. | 3,840 | 84 | " | " | |
| 266. | Samuel Baxter, Sergt. | 1,000 | 84 | " | Jno. Haywood | |
| 267. | Joseph Faulks, Privt. | 640 | 84 | " | John Ellet | |
| 268. | Eli McVey, Privt. | 640 | 84 | " | " | |
| 269. | Eli McVey, Heir of John McVey. | 640 | 84 | " | " | " |
| 270. | John Pendergrass, Privt. | 274 | 36 | " | | Self |
| 271. | Joel Lewis, assignee of Peter Rainey, Sergt. Decsd. | 1,000 | 84 | " | Wm. Lewis | |
| 272. | Joel Lewis, assignee of James Rainey, Privt. Decsd. | 640 | 84 | " | " | |
| 273. | Thomas Blount, Lieut. | 853 | 28 | " | Wm. Blount | |
| 274. | Jacob White, Privt. | 274 | 36 | " | " | |
| 275. | Jacob White, Junr. Privt. | 274 | 36 | " | " | |
| 276. | Daniel Rice, Privt. | 640 | 84 | Oct. 28 | David Pasmore | |
| 277. | Ambrose Lowell, Privt. | 640 | 84 | " | " | |
| 278. | The heirs of David Rothwell, Pt. . | 640 | 84 | Oct. 28 | Col. Phillips | |
| 279. | The heir of Henry Brizner, Decsd. | 640 | 84 | " | " | |
| 280. | John Burke, heir of James Burke . | 640 | 84 | " | " | |
| 281. | The heir of Leonard Loyd, Privt.. | 640 | 84 | " | " | |
| 282. | The heir of Levi Eldridge, Privt... | 640 | 84 | " | " | |
| 283. | The heir of Abimelech Cole, Pt. . | 640 | 84 | " | " | |
| 284. | The heir of Richard Gains, Pt.... | 640 | 84 | " | " | |
| 285. | The heir of Andrew Bohn, Privt. . | 640 | 84 | " | " | |
| 286. | The heirs of James Trayner, Pt... | 640 | 84 | " | " | |
| 287. | The heir of William Rothwell, Pt. | 640 | 84 | " | " | |
| 288. | Phillip Halcom, Privt. | 185 | 24 | " | | Self |
| 289. | Benjamon Jacobs, Privt. | 274 | 36 | " | | " |
| 290. | Robert Williams, Privt. | 274 | 36 | Nov. 9,'83 | | " |
| 291. | Elisha Williams, Privt. | 274 | 36 | " | Ro. Williams | |

| No. | To whom granted and rank | No. acres | Service in months | Location and to whom deeded and date of warrant. Within the limits of the lands allotted the officers and soldiers of the Continental Line, by Law, 1783, Oct. 14 | | |
|---|---|---|---|---|---|---|
| 292. | Thomas Hogg, Majr | 4,800 | 84 | Nov. 10 | John Wood | |
| 293. | John Ingles, Capt | 3,840 | 84 | " | " | |
| 294. | John Davis, Capt | 3,840 | 84 | " | " | |
| 295. | Jesse Reed, Capt | 3,840 | 84 | " | " | |
| 296. | Jacob Goodman, Heir of William Goodman, decsd. Capt | 3,840 | 84 | " | " | |
| 297. | John Ford, Lieut | 2,560 | 84 | " | " | |
| 298. | Thomas Pasture, Lieut | 2,560 | 84 | " | " | |
| 299. | Jacob Matthews, Privt | 640 | 84 | " | " | |
| 300. | Patrick Ryan, Sergt | 1,000 | 84 | " | " | |
| 301. | Sion Young, Privt | 640 | 84 | " | " | |
| 302. | Thomas Smith, Privt | 640 | 84 | " | " | |
| 303. | Theophilus Hays, Privt | 411 | 54 | " | " | |
| 304. | John Wood, Privt | 360 | 48 | " | " | |
| 305. | George Wallis, Fife Maj | 857 | 72 | Nov. 24 | Jno. Williams, Esqr. | |
| 306. | Isaac Hudson, Sergt | 357 | 30 | " | | Self |
| 307. | James Bryant, heir of Ambrose Bryant, decsd | 640 | 84 | Nov. 25 | Henry Williams | |
| 308. | John Emmery's heirs | 640 | 84 | " | " | |
| 309. | James Summers, Sergt | 857 | 72 | " | " | |
| 310. | Andrew Haddock, Sergt | 429 | 36 | " | " | |
| 311. | C. William Brooks, heir of George Brooks, Sergt | 1,000 | 84 | " | " | |
| 312. | James Martin, Privt | 274 | 36 | " | " | |
| 313. | William Hargrove, Lieut | 2,560 | 84 | " | | Self |
| 314. | John Hargrove, Privt | 274 | 36 | " | Lt. Hargrove | |
| 315. | Dan Dunbar, Corpl | 688 | 57 | " | " | |
| 316. | Patrick McGibbon, Lieut | 1,920 | 63 | Nov. 27 | P. Pycatt, Com. | |
| 317. | Peter Pycatt, Sergt | 428 | 36 | " | " | |
| 318. | James Coots, Lieut | 853 | 28 | " | " | |
| 319. | William Jackson, Privt | 274 | 36 | " | " | |
| 320. | John Jeffreys, Privt | 274 | 36 | " | Lt. Crutchen | |
| 321. | William Sweat, Privt | 228 | 30 | " | " | |
| 322. | Gee Bradley, Capt | 3,840 | 84 | " | " | |
| 323. | Samuel Hogan, heir of James Hogan, Brig. Gen. decsd | 12,000 | 84 | " | " | " |
| 324. | Samuel Gainer, Privt | 640 | 84 | " | " | |
| 325. | Moses Walker, Privt | 228 | 30 | " | " | |
| 326. | Joseph Hartley, Privt | 383 | 50 | " | " | |
| 327. | Thomas Bryant, Fifer | 595 | 50 | " | " | |
| 328. | John Vance, heir of John Vance, Capt. of Artillery, decsd | 3,840 | 84 | " | " | |
| 329. | John Vance, Lieut. of Artillery | 2,560 | 84 | " | " | |
| 330. | William Davin, Privt | 274 | 36 | " | " | |
| 331. | Hobert Finner, heir of Wm. Finner, Maj. decsd | 2,057 | 36 | " | " | |
| 332. | Hobert Finner, Capt | 3,840 | 84 | " | " | |
| 333. | James Campain, Lieut | 2,560 | 84 | " | " | |
| 334. | James Tatum, Lieut | 2,560 | 84 | " | " | |
| 335. | John McNeese, Capt | 3,840 | 84 | " | " | |
| 336. | Andrew Armstrong, Capt | 1,280 | 28 | " | " | |
| 337. | Miller Sawyer, Fifer | 1,000 | 84 | " | " | |
| 338. | David Love, Surgeon | 2,057 | 36 | Nov. 27 | Lt. Crutches | |
| 339. | Joseph Montford, Capt | 3,840 | 84 | " | " | |
| 340. | Howell Tatum, Capt | 3,565 | 78 | " | " | |
| 341. | Blount Whitmill, Subn | 824 | 28 | " | " | |

| No. | To whom granted and rank | No. acres | Service in months | Location and to whom deeded and date of warrant. Within the limits of the lands allotted the officers and soldiers of the Continental Line, by Law, 1783, Oct. 14 | |
|---|---|---|---|---|---|
| 342. | James Strange, Privt. | 274 | 36 | Nov. 27 | Lt. Crutches |
| 343. | John Sugg, Privt. | 274 | 36 | " | " |
| 344. | Anthony Crutchen, Lieut. | 2,560 | 84 | " | " |
| 345. | Robert Hicks, Privt. | 228 | 30 | " | Sam Parks |
| 346. | Andrew Wade, Privt. | 228 | 30 | Nov. 29 | " |
| 347. | James Brister, Privt. | 228 | 30 | " | " |
| 348. | John Summers, Capt. | 3,840 | 84 | " | Col. Blount |
| 349. | Francis Graves, Lieut. | 2,560 | 84 | " | " |
| 350. | Britain George, Privt. | 640 | 84 | " | " |
| 351. | Nathaniel Lawrence, Lieut. | 2,560 | 84 | " | " |
| 352. | John Eaton, administrator of Pinkeyton Eaton, Majr. | 4,800 | 84 | " | " |
| 353. | John Patton, Col. 2nd N. C. Brigade | 7,200 | 84 | " | " |
| 354. | Thomas Atkins, Privt. | 274 | 36 | Dec. 4 | Jno. Squires |
| 355. | Cornelius Bray, Privt. | 320 | 42 | " | " |
| 356. | William Griffin, Privt. | 640 | 84 | " | " |
| 357. | John Squires, Privt. | 320 | 42 | " | " |
| 358. | Solomon Berry, Sergt. | 1,000 | 84 | " | " |
| 359. | Bennet Morgan, Sergt. | 1,000 | 84 | " | " |
| 360. | John Berry, Sergt. | 1,000 | 84 | " | " |
| 361. | William Jones, Privt. | 274 | 36 | Dec. 6 | " |
| 362. | Thomas Kirvin, Privt. | 274 | 36 | " | Arthur Parker |
| 363. | Arthur Parker, Privt. | 228 | 30 | " | " |
| 364. | James Emmet, Maj. | 1,600 | 28 | " | Capt. Gillespie |
| 365. | Robert Gillespie, Sergt. | 793 | 26 | " | " |
| 366. | James Campbell, Capt. | 2,057 | 45 | " | " |
| 367. | Robert Hays, Lieut. | 2,560 | 84 | " | " |
| 368. | Charles Wood, Privt. | 274 | 36 | " | " |
| 369. | Patrick Murphey, Sergt. | 1,000 | 84 | " | " |
| 370. | Miles Knight, Sergt. | 1,000 | 84 | Dec. 7 | |
| 371. | Isaac Gregory, Privt. | 640 | 84 | " | Phillip Shackler |
| 372. | Frances Westwardhall, Privt. | 640 | 84 | " | |
| 373. | Phillip Shackler, Privt. | 640 | 84 | | |
| 374. | John Jackson, Privt. | 274 | 36 | | |
| 375. | Nathaniel Wooten, heir of Alexr. Wooten, Privt. | 640 | 84 | | Self |
| 376. | William Smith, Privt. | 640 | 84 | Dec. 13 | Majr. Allen |
| 377. | James Clark, Privt. | 274 | 36 | | |
| 378. | William Charlton, Privt. | 274 | 36 | | " |
| 379. | George Moye, Privt. | 228 | 30 | | " |
| 380. | Charley Butler, Privt. | 228 | 30 | | " |
| 381. | Thomas Harrison, Privt. | 274 | 36 | Dec. 13 | |
| 382. | John Kingsbury, Capt. Comdt N. C. Artillery | 4,800 | 84 | Dec. 15 | " " |
| 383. | George Reynolds, Sergt. Comdt N. C. Artillery | 1,000 | 84 | " | " " |
| 384. | David Jones, Corpl. Comdt N. C. Artillery | 1,000 | 84 | " | " " |
| 385. | John Sillinaver, a Gunner. | 640 | 84 | | Wm. Patterson of Warren |
| 386. | John Allen, Capt. | 1,600 | 35 | | " Jas. Gatlent |
| 387. | Reubin Roundtree, Lieut. | 1,144 | 36 | | " " |
| 388. | Cornelius Ryan, Privt. | 640 | 84 | | " Self |
| 389. | John Skeen, Privt. | 640 | 84 | | " " |
| 390. | John Richardson, Privt. | 274 | 36 | | " " |

| No. | To whom granted and rank | No. acres | Service in months | Location and to whom deeded and date of warrant. Within the limits of the lands allotted the officers and soldiers of the Continental Line, by Law, 1783, Oct. 14 | |
|---|---|---|---|---|---|
| 391. | Benjamin Easman, Privt. | 274 | 36 | | Wm. Patterson of Warren     Self |
| 392. | Robert Tossitta, Privt. | 274 | 36 | Jan. 2,'84 | "     " |
| 393. | Henry Martin, Privt. | 640 | 84 | | "     " |
| 394. | Thomas Brickle, Capt. | 10,970 | 24 | Jan. 6 | " Thos. Davis |
| 395. | Shadrach Lasciter, Lieut. | 731 | 24 | Jan. 6 | "     " |
| 396. | Samuel Cooley, Surgeon | 1,428 | 25 | | "     " |
| 397. | Benjamin Coffield, Lieut. | 1,607 | 53 | | "     " |
| 398. | Richard Fenner, Lieut. | 2,560 | 84 | | "     " |
| 399. | Daniel Humphries, Privt. | 228 | 30 | | "     " |
| 400. | Archibald Butt, Drummer | 1,000 | 84 | | "     " |
| 401. | James Rolins, Privt. | 274 | 36 | Jan. 6 | " Thos. Davis |
| 402. | William Vance, Corpl. | 428 | 36 | " | "     " |
| 403. | Cornelius Drake, Sergt. | 571 | 48 | " | "     " |
| 404. | Thomas Lewellin, Privt. | 274 | 36 | " | "     " |
| 405. | Benjamin Flood, Privt. | 640 | 84 | " | "     " |
| 406. | Griffith Donge, Sergt. | 1,000 | 84 | " | "     " |
| 407. | Richard Donge, Privt. | 640 | 84 | " | "     " |
| 408. | Martin Stricker, Privt. | 228 | 30 | " | "     " |
| 409. | Isaiah Parr, Privt. | 274 | 36 | " | "     " |
| 410. | Benjamin Williams, Capt. | 1,828 | 40 | " | "     " |
| 411. | Noah Parr, Privt. | 640 | 84 | " | "     " |
| 412. | William Farmer, Privt. | 228 | 30 | " | "     " |
| 413. | Abram Jinkins, Sergt. | 357 | 30 | " | "     " |
| 414. | Joab Donge, Privt. | 274 | 36 | " | "     " |
| 415. | William Thomas, Privt. | 640 | 74 | Jan. 7 | " Wm. Scott |
| 416. | David Pasmore, Privt. | 365 | 48 | " | " Self |
| 417. | Charles Kelley, Sergt. | 580 | 48 | " | " David Passmore |
| 418. | Jonathan Richards, Privt. | 274 | 36 | " | " Thos. Davis |
| 419. | John Gillum, Heir of Howell Gillum, Sergt. | 1,000 | 84 | | "     " |
| 420. | Andrew Randall, and Caty his heirs, Sergt. | 1,000 | 84 | | Warrant assigned to Green Hill in presence of McWilliams |
| 421. | John Clinton, Privt. | 228 | 30 | " | " Thos. Davis |
| 422. | John Walker, Sergt. | 357 | 30 | " | "     " |
| 423. | Reuben Smith, Privt. | 640 | 84 | | " Wm. Mullen |
| 424. | John Sugg, Privt. | 274 | 36 | Jan. 22 | "     " |
| 425. | James Strange, Privt. | 274 | 36 | " | " John McNeese |
| 426. | William Nelson, Privt. | 640 | 84 | | "     " |
| 427. | Jesse Nelson, Privt. | 640 | 84 | | "     " |
| 428. | William Ewell, Sergt. | 404 | 33 | " | " Self |
| 429. | James West Green, Surgeon | 4,800 | 84 | | " Thos. Davis |
| 430. | William Green, Privt. | 640 | 84 | Jan. 31 | "     " |
| 431. | John Allen, Administrator of Thos. Allen, Sergt. | 2,560 | 84 | Feb. 2 | " Self |
| 432. | Walter Allen, Sergt. | 912 | 30 | | " John Allen |
| 433. | Kedar Phelps, Drummer | 1,000 | 84 | | |
| 434. | James Phelps, Fifer | 1,000 | 84 | | "     " |
| 435. | Drewry Bynum, Sergt. | 1,000 | 84 | Feb. 9 | " Self |
| 436. | John Elliot, Privt. | 365 | 48 | Feb. 12 | Jno. Elliot |
| 437. | Joshua Adcock, Privt. | 274 | 36 | " | "     " |
| 438. | Abraham Hargis, Privt. | 228 | 30 | " | "     " |
| 439. | Cornelius Anglin, Heir, Privt. | 640 | 84 | " | "     " |
| 440. | Edward Deal, Privt. | 640 | 84 | Feb. 16 | " Capt. McNeese |
| 441. | Timothy Mears, Privt. | 640 | 84 | " | "     " |

| No. | To whom granted and rank | No. acres | Service in months | Location and to whom deeded and date of warrant. Within the limits of the lands allotted the officers and soldiers of the Continental Line, by Law, 1783, Oct. 14 | |
|---|---|---|---|---|---|
| | | | | | Jno. Elliot |
| 442. | Joshua Tindal, Heir of Frances Nash | 640 | 84 | | Capt. McNeese |
| 443. | Jesse Donaldson, Privt | 640 | 84 | | " " |
| 444. | Etheldred Nusum, Privt | 640 | 84 | | " Jas. Williams |
| 445. | Marmaduke Barfield, Privt. Decsd. Rch'd Barfield, heir | 640 | 84 | | " I. Glasgow |
| 446. | Wm. Barfield, Heir of Stephen Barfield | 640 | 84 | | " " |
| 447. | The Heirs of Abram Hay, Privt | 640 | 84 | | " " |
| 448. | Peter Haddock, Privt | 640 | 84 | Feb. 19 | " Self |
| 449. | John Mackelway, Drummer | 1,000 | 84 | | Jno. Elliot |
| 450. | The Heir of Robert Chermmy, Pt. | 640 | 84 | Feb. 20 | " |
| 451. | The Heir of John Adcock, Privt | 640 | 84 | | " |
| 452. | James Elliot, Privt | 274 | 36 | | " |
| 453. | John Stewart, Privt | 274 | 36 | | " |
| 454. | Thomas Cole, Privt | 365 | 48 | | " " |
| 455. | Abraham Denny, Privt | 365 | 48 | | " " |
| 456. | David Denny, Privt | 274 | 36 | | " " |
| 457. | Thomas McDonald, Privt | 640 | 84 | | " D. Gardner |
| 458. | Demcey Gardner, Privt | 274 | 36 | | " " |
| 459. | The Heir of James Royal, Privt | 640 | 84 | | " " |
| 460. | John Bullock, Privt | 228 | 30 | Feb. 23 | " James Avera |
| 461. | Drury Bullock, Heir of Balaam Bullock, Privt | 640 | 84 | " | " " |
| 462. | Drewry Bullock, Heir of John Bullock | 640 | 84 | | " " |
| 463. | The Heir of Moses Bullock | 640 | 84 | | " " |
| 464. | Samuel Thomas, Privt | 640 | 84 | | " " |
| 465. | William Richardson, Privt | 640 | 84 | | " Ald. Thomas |
| 466. | Burrell Lucy, Privt | 640 | 84 | | " " |
| 467. | John Kelley, Privt | 640 | 84 | | " " |
| 468. | William Taylor, Privt | 274 | 36 | | " |
| 469. | Hosea Gregory, Privt | 274 | 36 | | " |
| 470. | John Aspley, Dragoon | 640 | 84 | | Thos. Davis |
| 471. | Benjamin Simmons, Sergt | 428 | 36 | Feb. 23 | Self |
| 472. | James Williams, Heir of Thomas Williams | 640 | 84 | Mar. 1, '84 | " Jas. Lanier |
| 473. | Andrew Simpson, Sergt | 1,000 | 84 | | " Self |
| 474. | James Lanier, Wounded, Ensign | 2,560 | 84 | Mar. 3 | " " |
| 475. | William Capps, Privt | 640 | 84 | | " Jas. Lanier |
| 476. | Giles Bowers, Privt | 640 | 84 | | " W. Caswell |
| 477. | John Davis, Privt | 640 | 84 | | " " |
| 478. | David Willcocks, Privt | 640 | 84 | | " " |
| 479. | Joseph Hudler, Privt | 274 | 36 | | " " |
| 480. | Samuel Hudler, Privt | 274 | 36 | | " " |
| 481. | Joseph Hudler, Senr. Privt | 274 | 36 | | " " |
| 482. | John Hudler, Privt | 640 | 84 | | " " |
| 483. | William Gray, Privt | 274 | 36 | | " " |
| 484. | Corbin Weymouth, Privt | 365 | 48 | Mar. 4 | W. Scott |
| 485. | Ezekiel Whaley, Fife Maj | 1,000 | 84 | " | R. White |
| 486. | John Smith, Privt | 640 | 84 | Mar. 17 | " Capt. Barrow |
| 487. | Joseph Gurley, Privt | 640 | 84 | " | " Self |
| 488. | Matthew Wewley, Privt | 640 | 84 | " | Jas. Williams |
| 489. | Isaac Hay, Privt | 365 | 48 | | " " |
| 490. | Stephen Chance, Privt | 365 | 48 | " | Self |
| 491. | Stephen Slade, Lieut | 2,560 | 84 | Mar. 22,'84 | Wm. Street |

| No. | To whom granted and rank | No. acres | Service in months | Location and to whom deeded and date of warrant. Within the limits of the lands allotted the officers and soldiers of the Continental Line, by Law, 1783, Oct. 14 | | |
|---|---|---|---|---|---|---|
| 492. | Arthur Arnold, Privt. | 640 | 84 | | Wm. Street | Self |
| 493. | Richard Johnston, Sergt. | 428 | 36 | | " | " |
| 494. | Luke Bates, Privt. | 640 | 84 | Mar. 25 | Montflorance | |
| 495. | John Baptist Ashe, Lieut. Col. | 4,457 | 65 | | " | " |
| 496. | Thomas Duffell, Privt. | 411 | 54 | | " | Self |
| 497. | Francis Fox, Privt. | 274 | 36 | Mar. 30 | " | " |
| 498. | Sovereighn Blackson, Privt. | 274 | 36 | | " | |
| 499. | John Killingworth, Drummer | 714 | 60 | | " | Is. Wms |
| 500. | James Barfield, Privt. | 342 | 45 | Apr. 2, '84 | Capt. McNees | " |
| 501. | Ephraim Rogers, Privt. | 274 | 36 | | " | " |
| 502. | John Dunagan, Privt. | 640 | 84 | | " | " |
| 503. | Sarah Benson, wife of Bailey Benson, decsd. Privt. | 640 | 84 | | " | " |
| 504. | John Daughtrey, Privt. | 640 | 84 | | " | " |
| 505. | Benjamin Powell, Privt. | 640 | 84 | " | " | " |
| 506. | James Hawkins, Privt. | 640 | 84 | | Jas. Gatlin | |
| 507. | Hardy Hawkins, Privt. | 274 | 36 | | " | " |
| 508. | Stephen Truit, Privt. | 640 | 84 | | | A. Herring |
| 509. | William Shute, Privt. | 640 | 84 | | Jas. Person | |
| 510. | William Slade, Lieut. | 1,607 | 54 | Apr. 11 | " | Jas. Person |
| 511. | Jesse Row, Drummer | 428 | 36 | Apr. 11 | " | Jas. Person |
| 512. | Samuel Pierson, Privt. | 640 | 84 | " | " | " |
| 513. | George Row, Privt. | 640 | 84 | Apr. 20 | " | Eli Robinson |
| 514. | William White, Privt. | 640 | 84 | | " | " |
| 515. | Henry White, Privt. | 228 | 30 | | " | Capt. Armstrong |
| 516. | Solomon Malborn, Sergt. | 1,000 | 84 | | " | " |
| 517. | David Malborn, Privt. | 274 | 36 | | " | " |
| 518. | Martin Trapp, Privt. | 640 | 84 | | " | " |
| 519. | John Benion, Privt. | 640 | 84 | | " | " |
| 520. | John Vickery, Privt. | 640 | 84 | | " | " |
| 521. | William Cason, Privt. | 640 | 84 | | " | " |
| 522. | William Anderson, Privt. | 640 | 84 | | " | " |
| 523. | Robert Meeks, Privt. | 274 | 36 | | " | " |
| 524. | Jacob Robinson, Sergt. | 428 | 36 | | " | " |
| 525. | Jeremiah Smith, Privt. | 274 | 36 | | " | " |
| 526. | Craffor Johnston, Privt. | 640 | 84 | | " | " |
| 527. | Peter Rhem, Sergt. | 428 | 36 | | " | " |
| 528. | John Williams, Sergt. | 1,144 | 36 | | " | " |
| 529. | John Craddock, Capt. | 3,840 | 84 | | " | " |
| 530. | Frederick Blount, Privt. | 640 | 84 | | " | Montflorance |
| 531. | George Browning, Sergt. | 1,000 | 84 | | " | " |
| 532. | Thomas Scott, Privt. | 388 | 51 | | " | " |
| 533. | The Heirs of John White, Sergt. | 1,000 | 84 | | " | " |
| 534. | The Heir of Stephen White, Sgt. | 1,000 | 84 | | " | " |
| 535. | The Heir of Ephraim Simon | 1,000 | 84 | | " | " |
| 536. | The Heirs of William Forrister Pt. | 640 | 84 | | " | " |
| 537. | The Heir of Archibald Craigge, Pt. | 640 | 84 | | " | " |
| 538. | Jesse Duncan, Privt. | 274 | 36 | | " | " |
| 539. | John Handcock, Heir of Isaac Handcock, Sergt. | 1,000 | 84 | | " | Chas. Robinson |
| 540. | Joshua Pruite, Privt. | 274 | 36 | | " | Self |
| 541. | Ransom Prewite, Privt. | 274 | 36 | | " | " |
| 542. | James Ives, Privt. | 640 | 84 | | " | Maj. Blount |
| 543. | John Hill, Lieut. | 2,560 | 84 | | " | " |
| 544. | James Moore, Lieut. | 2,560 | 84 | | " | " |
| 545. | James Mills, Capt. | 3,840 | 84 | | " | " |

| No. | To whom granted and rank | No. acres | Service in months | Location and to whom deeded and date of warrant. Within the limits of the lands allotted the officers and soldiers of the Continental Line, by Law, 1783, Oct. 14 | | |
|---|---|---|---|---|---|---|
| 546. | Levi Wiggins, Privt............ | 640 | 84 | | Jas. Person Maj. Blount | |
| 547. | Simon Parker, Infirm. Privt...... | 640 | 84 | | " | Lt. Steed |
| 548. | Jesse Steed, Sergt.............. | 357 | 30 | | " | " |
| 549. | Isaac Howard, Privt............ | 274 | 36 | | " | " |
| 550. | William Bugg, Privt............ | 228 | 30 | | " | " |
| 551. | Benjamin Bailey, Capt.......... | 3,840 | 84 | | " | M. Blount |
| 552. | Jacob Messick, Heir of Jacob Messick, Lieut............... | 2,560 | 84 | | " | Col. Brown |
| 553. | Griffith John McRee, Maj........ | 4,800 | 84 | Apr. 20 | Capt. Clark | |
| 554. | Clement Hall, Capt............ | 3,840 | 84 | | Capt. Armstrong | |
| 555. | Robert McCullock, Heir of Alexander McCullock, Privt.... | 640 | 84 | | " Robt. McCullock | |
| 556. | John Young, Privt............. | 228 | 30 | | Isaac Hutson | |
| 557. | Jeremiah Perry, Privt.......... | 228 | 30 | | | Self |
| 558. | James Taylor, Sergt............ | 535 | 45 | | Capt. Hensbro | |
| 559. | William Burch, Capt. N. C. Art.. | 1,000 | 84 | | " | " |
| 560. | Manlove Tarrant, Capt......... | 1,371 | 30 | | " | " |
| 561. | William Washington, Heir of Etheldred Washington, Fifer... | 1,000 | 84 | | " | |
| 562. | Samuel Lockheart, Lt. Col. (discharged on account of his indisposition)............... | 5,760 | 84 | | " | " |
| 563. | Thomas Evans, Capt........... | 3,840 | 84 | " | Capt. Craddock | |
| 564. | Richard Martin, Privt.......... | 228 | 30 | | | Jas. Martin |
| 565. | John Douglass, Privt........... | 640 | 84 | | " M. Armstrong | |
| 566. | John Smith, dischged on account of inability, Privt............. | 640 | 84 | | " | " |
| 567. | William Birch, Heir of John Birch, Decsd. Privt........... | 640 | 84 | | " | " |
| 568. | Joseph Sparepoint, Privt........ | 640 | 84 | | " | " |
| 569. | Frederick Desern, Privt........ | 274 | 36 | | " | " |
| 570. | John Lockheart, Q. M. Sergt..... | 321 | 27 | | " Col. Lockheart | |
| 571. | Matthew Wood, Capt.......... | 1,622 | 52 | Apr. 20 | Maj. Montflorance | |
| 572. | John Gouge, Privt. Infirm........ | 640 | 84 | " | Col. Robinson | |
| 573. | Daniel Hargett, Devism? of Dan Miller a Privt........... | 640 | 84 | " | Capt. Hargett | " |
| 574. | Benjamin Messer, Privt......... | 274 | 36 | | " | " |
| 575. | Felix Simmons, Privt.......... | 274 | 36 | | " | " |
| 576. | Phillimon Morriss, Privt........ | 274 | 36 | Apr. 21 | " | " |
| 577. | Thomas Barritt, Heir of William Barrett..................... | 3,840 | 84 | " | Colo. Lockheart | |
| 578. | William Oharion, Privt......... | 274 | 36 | " | Geo. Rowland | |
| 579. | David Benton, Privt............ | 274 | 36 | | " | " |
| 580. | John Matlock, Sergt............ | 428 | 36 | | " | " |
| 581. | Evan Jones, Heir of John Jones, Sergt.................. | 1,000 | 84 | Apr. 21 | B. Jones | " |
| 582. | Evan Jones, Heir of Thomas Jones, Privt................. | 640 | 84 | | " | " |
| 583. | Lazarus Jones, Privt............ | 352 | 46 | | " | " |
| 584. | John Scarf, Privt.............. | 297 | 39 | | " | " |
| 585. | Hezekiah Linton, Heir of John Linton, Privt................ | 640 | 84 | | " | " |
| 586. | Hezekiah Linton, Heir of Jesse Linton, Sergt................ | 1,000 | 84 | | " | " |
| 587. | Thomas Smith, Privt........... | 274 | 36 | | " | " |

| No. | To whom granted and rank | No. acres | Service in months | Location and to whom deeded and date of warrant. Within the limits of the lands allotted the officers and soldiers of the Continental Line, by Law, 1783, Oct. 14 | | |
|---|---|---|---|---|---|---|
| 588. | Thomas Smith, Heir of Clement Smith, Privt. | 640 | 84 | | B. Jones Col. Lockheart | |
| 589. | Zedekiah Sikes, Privt. | 274 | 36 | | " | " " |
| 590. | David Hall, Privt. | 274 | 36 | | " | " " |
| 591. | Demcey Harrison, Privt. | 383 | 50 | | " | " " |
| 592. | Samuel Ashe, Capt. | 1,500 | 33 | Apr. 21 | Colo. McCullock | |
| 593. | Samuel Ashe, Lieut. | 2,560 | 84 | " | " | " |
| 594. | John Tatum, Privt. | 274 | 36 | " | Chas. Parke | |
| 595. | John Lock, Sergt. | 357 | 30 | | " | " |
| 596. | David Cozart, Privt. | 274 | 36 | | " | " |
| 597. | James Dowell, Privt. | 411 | 54 | | " | " |
| 598. | William Burns, Heir of John Burnes, Privt. | 640 | 84 | " | | Self |
| 599. | Edmund Gamble Subalt. | 1,158 | 38 | | " | " |
| 600. | Elijah Kidwell, Privt. | 640 | 84 | " | Subt. Gamble | |
| 601. | Frederick Reeves, Privt. | 228 | 30 | Apr. 21,'84 | | Self |
| 602. | Willoughby Williams, Heir of James Anderson, Privt. Decsd. | 640 | 84 | " | | " |
| 603. | Williams Collins, Privt. Disabled. | 640 | 84 | " | Jno Rice | |
| 604. | William Pate, Privt. | 274 | 36 | " | Capt. Hargett | |
| 605. | Simon Baris, Privt. | 640 | 84 | " | Jno. Rice | |
| 606. | Joseph Thomas Rhodes, Capt. | 3,840 | 84 | " | Capt. Ivey | " |
| 607. | William Laton, Heir of John Laton | 640 | 84 | | " | |
| 608. | William Apperson, Privt. | 228 | 30 | " | Colo. Armstrong | |
| 609. | Stephens Garrison, Privt. | 640 | 84 | | " | Self |
| 610. | James Purkins, Heir of Abraham Purkins | 640 | 84 | | " | Jas. Hutson |
| 611. | Henry Johnston, Privt. | 640 | 84 | " | Jno. Gray Blount | |
| 612. | Holland Johnston, Sergt. | 428 | 36 | Apr. 21 | " | Jno. Gray Johnston |
| 613. | William Faunt, Privt. | 640 | 84 | | " | " |
| 614. | Jesse Taunt, Drummer | 1,000 | 84 | | " | " |
| 615. | Thomas Taunt, Privt. | 640 | 84 | | " | " |
| 616. | Benjamin Chadwick, Privt. | 640 | 84 | | J. Glasgow | " |
| 617. | Benj. Hodge Blount, Privt. | 640 | 84 | " | J. G. Blount | " |
| 618. | Thomas Blount, Privt. | 274 | 36 | | " | " |
| 619. | Cornelius Callyham, Privt. | 274 | 36 | | " | " |
| 620. | Robert Cole, Privt. | 274 | 36 | | " | " |
| 621. | John Segrove, Privt. | 228 | 30 | Apr. 21 | Col. B. Hawkins | |
| 622. | Phinehas Latham, Sergt. | 1,000 | 84 | " | Jno. Gray Blount | |
| 623. | Jesse Shute, Privt. | 640 | 84 | | " | " |
| 624. | William Linton, Capt. | 1,427 | 31 | " | Gen. Person | |
| 625. | Moses Hezard, Privt. Decsd. | 640 | 84 | | Colo. Blount | |
| 626. | Robert Calliham, Decsd. Privt. | 640 | 84 | | " | " |
| 627. | Thomas Fornes, Heir of Jonathan Fornes, Decsd. | 640 | 84 | | " | " |
| 628. | Thomas Fornes, Heir of John Fornes, Decsd. | 640 | 84 | " | " | " |
| 629. | James Wall, Sergt. of Artillery | 2,560 | 84 | " | Capt. Kingsbury | |
| 630. | Robert Douglas, Sergt. of Art. | 2,560 | 84 | | " | " |
| 631. | Richard Douge, Sergt. | 1,000 | 84 | Apr. 21 | Capt. Kingsbury | |
| 632. | Archibald Gray, Sergt. | 1,000 | 84 | Apr. 23 | " | " |
| 633. | Laughlin Campbell, Sergt. | 1,000 | 84 | " | " | " |
| 634. | Stephen Linn, Sergt. | 1,000 | 84 | " | " | " |
| 635. | Joseph Flemin, Privt. | 640 | 84 | " | " | " |
| 636. | Malachi Russell, Privt. | 640 | 84 | | " | " |

| No. | To whom granted and rank | No. acres | Service in months | | Location and to whom deeded and date of warrant. Within the limits of the lands allotted the officers and soldiers of the Continental Line, by Law, 1783, Oct. 14 |
|---|---|---|---|---|---|
| 637. | Kindle Hislip, Privt. | 640 | 84 | | Capt. Kingsbury [John Gray Johnston |
| 638. | David Laws, Privt. | 640 | 84 | | " " |
| 639. | William Campbell, Privt. | 640 | 84 | | " " |
| 640. | Robert Morrison, Privt. | 640 | 84 | | " " |
| 641. | Robert Bradley, Privt. | 640 | 84 | | " " |
| 642. | Phillip Burgess, Privt. | 640 | 84 | | " " |
| 643. | James Jimmison, Privt. | 640 | 84 | | " " |
| 644. | Frances Lewes, Privt. | 640 | 84 | | " " |
| 645. | Hancock Nicholes, Privt. | 640 | 84 | | " " |
| 646. | Philip Cake, Privt. | 640 | 84 | | " " |
| 647. | Michael Bullin, Privt. | 640 | 84 | | " " |
| 648. | John Thomasson, Privt. | 640 | 84 | | " " |
| 649. | John Barnes, Privt. | 640 | 84 | | " " |
| 650. | Michael Smith, Privt. | 640 | 84 | | " " |
| 651. | William Teer, Privt. | 640 | 84 | Apr. 23 | Capt. Kingsburry " |
| 652. | Michael Nash, Privt. | 640 | 84 | | " " |
| 653. | Obadiah Winnor, Privt. | 640 | 84 | | " " |
| 654. | James Row, Fifer. | 1,000 | 84 | | " " |
| 655. | John Wilkerson, Privt. | 640 | 84 | | " " |
| 656. | Peter Dummick, Privt. | 640 | 84 | | " |
| 657. | David Adkins, Privt. | 640 | 84 | | " |
| 658. | William Stewart, Privt. | 640 | 84 | | " |
| 659. | John Francks, Privt. | 640 | 84 | | " |
| 660. | Thomas Farnes, Heir of William Farnes, Privt. | 640 | 84 | " | Col. Blount |
| 661. | William Riardon Dennis, his Heir, Sergt. | 1,000 | 84 | | " Reuben Searey |
| 662. | Benjamin Smith, Sergt. | 428 | 36 | | Self |
| 663. | The heir of Hugh Curren, Decsd. Privt. | 640 | 84 | " | " |
| 664. | The heir of Elisha Curren, Decsd. Privt. | 640 | 84 | " | " |
| 665. | Jonathan Loomes, Surgeon | 3,942 | 69 | Apr. 25 | Jno. Gray Blount |
| 666. | Charles Hood, Privt. | 274 | 36 | | " Self |
| 667. | George Smith, Privt. | 274 | 36 | | " James Coartney |
| 668. | John Foddes, Heir of James Foddes, Privt. | 640 | 84 | Apr. 26 | " Self |
| 669. | Thomas Estridge, Privt. | 640 | 84 | | " Majr. Tatum |
| 670. | Joseph Sharpe, Sergt. | 428 | 36 | | " Self |
| 671. | George Cole, Privt. | 274 | 36 | Apr. 26 | " " |
| 672. | Franklin Truitt, John Eckland his heir | 640 | 84 | " | Capt. Ferebee " |
| 673. | Joshua Forbis, Sergt. | 428 | 36 | | " " |
| 674. | Joseph Ferebee, Capt. | 1,371 | 30 | | " " |
| 675. | Thomas Hambleton, Heir to Hanes Hambleton, Surgeon | 4,800 | 84 | " | Thos. Hamilton |
| 676. | William McIntire, Privt. | 640 | 84 | " | Self |
| 677. | William Cole, Privt. | 274 | 36 | " | Gen. Person |
| 678. | John Collins, Sergt. | 428 | 36 | " | Eli West |
| 679. | Charles Oneal, Lieut. | 853 | 28 | " | Self |
| 680. | Thomas Fletcher, Sergt. | 580 | 48 | " | Capt. Ferebee |
| 681. | John Robinson, Heir of Jesse Robison, Privt. | 640 | 84 | " | Jno. Robeson |
| 682. | Joseph King, Privt. | 274 | 36 | " | Wm. Ward |
| 683. | Adam Tate, Heir of Joseph Tate, Capt. | 3,840 | 84 | " | A. Tate |

| No. | To whom granted and rank | No. acres | Service in months | Location and to whom deeded and date of warrant. Within the limits of the lands allotted the officers and soldiers of the Continental Line, by Law, 1783, Oct. 14 | | |
|---|---|---|---|---|---|---|
| 684. | William Aldridge, Privt. | 228 | 30 | Apr. 26 | Daniel McMahon | |
| 685. | William Gibson, Privt. | 640 | 84 | " | | Self |
| 686. | William Collins, Heir of Charles Collins, Privt. | 640 | 84 | " | Jno. Rice | |
| 687. | William Ferebee, Capt. | 3,062 | 67 | " | Capt. Ferebee | |
| 688. | James Caruthers, Privt. | 274 | 36 | " | Alex. Wilson | |
| 689. | Thomas Caruthers, Privt. | 274 | 36 | Apr. 27 | " | " |
| 690. | James Bradley, Privt. | 274 | 36 | " | " | " |
| 691. | Peggey Hart, Heir of Thomas Hart, Privt. | 640 | 84 | " | Col. McCullock | |
| 692. | William Lomax, Privt. | 274 | 36 | " | Alex. Nelson | |
| 693. | Benjamin Carter, Capt. | 3,840 | 84 | " | Mjr. Nelson | " |
| 694. | Charles Alexander, Lieut. | 914 | 30 | | | |
| 695. | John Reddin, Privt. | 228 | 30 | Apr. 29 | Col. Lewis | |
| 696. | Jesse Boyce, Privt. | 236 | 31 | " | Col. H. Murfree | |
| 697. | John Madry, Corpl. | 333 | 28 | " | " | " |
| 698. | Snoden Johnston, Heir of Richard Johnston | 640 | 84 | " | " | " |
| 699. | Jeremiah Pierce, Heir of Thomas Pierce | 640 | 84 | | " | " |
| 700. | Elizabeth Ray, Heir of Stephen Ray | 640 | 84 | | " | " |
| 701. | William White, Privt. | 274 | 36 | " | Col. Lewis | |
| 702. | Nancey & Elizabeth Reardon, Coheirs of Dudley Reardon | 640 | 84 | | " | " |
| 703. | Zadock Williams, Privt. | 280 | 37 | " | " | " |
| 704. | James Pulley, Privt. | 228 | 30 | " | " | " |
| 705. | Chloe Goodman, Heir of Wm. Goodman | 640 | 84 | " | " | " |
| 706. | Nicholas Tyner, Privt. | 266 | 35 | " | " | " |
| 707. | Arthur Tyner, Privt. | 274 | 36 | " | " | " |
| 708. | Thomas Lassiter, Privt. | 640 | 84 | " | Col. Murfree | " |
| 709. | Elizabeth Underwood & Mourning Wheeler, Coheirs of Empery Wheeler | 640 | 84 | | " | " |
| 710. | John Ramsay, Heir of Mills Ramsay | 640 | 84 | " | " | " |
| 711. | Demcey Lassiter, Heir of Jacob Lassiter | 640 | 84 | | Col. Murfree | |
| 712. | John B. Hammond, Sergt. | 357 | 30 | | " | " |
| 713. | Solomon Howard, Privt. | 228 | 30 | | " | " |
| 714. | Joseph Holland, Heir of Wm. Holland, Privt. | 640 | 84 | | " | " |
| 715. | Joseph Holland, Heir of Josiah Holland, Privt. | 640 | 84 | | | " |
| 716. | John Baker, Capt. | 1,462 | 32 | | " | " |
| 717. | Jane Manley, Heir of Allen Manley | 640 | 84 | | " | " |
| 718. | John Williams, Heir of Theophilus Williams | 640 | 84 | | " | " |
| 719. | Josiah Jones, Drummer | 1,000 | 84 | | " | " |
| 720. | John Williams, Privt. | 274 | 36 | | " | " |
| 721. | James Coalston, Privt. | 274 | 36 | " | Col. Murfree | " |
| 722. | James Smith, Privt. | 640 | 84 | | " | " |
| 723. | Alexander Flood, Privt. | 304 | 40 | | Col. Murfree | " |
| 724. | John Pearce, Heir of James Pearce | 640 | 84 | | " | " |

| No. | To whom granted and rank | No. acres | Service in months | Location and to whom deeded and date of warrant. Within the limits of the lands allotted the officers and soldiers of the Continental Line, by Law, 1783, Oct. 14 | |
|---|---|---|---|---|---|
| 725. | John Pearce, Heir of Hardy Pearce | 640 | 84 | | Col. Murfree | Self |
| 726. | Jacob Rochal, Heir of Isaiah Rochell | 640 | 84 | | " | " |
| 727. | David Pen, Heir of Arthur Pen... | 640 | 84 | | " | " |
| 728. | Samuel Budd, Capt............ | 3,840 | 84 | | " | " |
| 729. | Nathan Mann, Heir of John Mann | 640 | 84 | | " | " |
| 730. | Matthew Wiggins, Privt........ | 274 | 36 | | " | " |
| 731. | Adam Purkins, Privt........... | 640 | 84 | Apr. 29 " | Col. Murfree | " |
| 732. | Sarah Horton, Heiress of James Horton..................... | 640 | 84 | | " | " |
| 733. | William Bryan, Privt.......... | 274 | 36 | | | " |
| 734. | Daniel Johnston, Privt......... | 274 | 36 | | " | " |
| 735. | Robert Carter, Privt.......... | 228 | 30 | | " | " |
| 736. | Anthony Garnes, Heir of Jeffrey Garnes.................... | 640 | 84 | | " | " |
| 737. | Robert Leadon, Heir of John Leadon..................... | 640 | 84 | | " | " |
| 738. | Shadrach Holmes, Privt........ | 228 | 30 | | " | " |
| 739. | Isaac Rhodes, Privt........... | 228 | 30 | | " | " |
| 740. | James Bradley, Capt.......... | 1,280 | 28 | | " | " |
| 741. | James Ferges, Surgeon......... | 4,800 | 84 | | " | " |
| 742. | William McClure, Surgeon...... | 4,800 | 84 | | " | " |
| 743. | The Heir of Philip Whitsell, Drummer.................... | 1,000 | 84 | Apr. 29 | Maj. Nelson | " |
| 744. | The Heir of Peter Duffell, Privt... | 640 | 84 | " | " | |
| 745. | Jeremiah Reardon, Privt........ | 274 | 36 | " | " | |
| 746. | The Heir of John Gunn, Drummer | 1,000 | 84 | " | Alex. Gunn | |
| 747. | Alexander Gunn, Non Commissioned Officer............. | 1,000 | 84 | " | Self | |
| 748. | James Marr, Heir of John Marr, Jun. decsd................. | 640 | 84 | " | " | |
| 749. | John Marr, Senr. Privt......... | 335 | 44 | " | " | |
| 750. | Frederick Rigsbey............. | 274 | 36 | " | " | |
| 751. | Thomas Barnes, Senr. Burwell his heir, Privt.............. | 640 | 84 | " | | |
| 752. | Joel Ramsey, Privt............ | 274 | 36 | " | Col. M. Armstrong | |
| 753. | Fountain Jordan, Privt......... | 640 | 84 | " | W. Williams | |
| 754. | The Heir of Francis Nash, Brig. Gen................... | 12,000 | 84 | " | Montflorance | |
| 755. | James Deal, L. Dragoon........ | 274 | 36 | " | Self | |
| 756. | Daniel Bullock, Sergt.......... | 1,000 | 84 | " | Capt. Sharpe | |
| 757. | Major May, Privt............. | 640 | 84 | " | Thomas May | |
| 758. | Thomas May, Privt............ | 274 | 36 | " | " | " |
| 759. | Mary Pain Elizabeth & Sarah Fenton, Coheirs of Caleb Fenton, dead................ | 640 | 84 | " | Capt. I. Ferebee | |
| 760. | Alexander Brevard, Capt........ | 3,840 | 84 | " | Maj. T. Poke | |
| 761. | Joseph Brevard, Lieut.......... | 2,560 | 84 | | " | " |
| 762. | Peter Duffey, Privt............ | 640 | 84 | " | Is. Pickard | |
| 763. | Nathan Tomson, Privt.......... | 640 | 84 | | " | |
| 764. | Hugh Hueston, Privt.......... | 274 | 36 | " | Maj. Nelson | |
| 765. | David Dodd, Privt............ | 274 | 36 | " | Colo. Love | " |
| 766. | James Britnall, Privt.......... | 274 | 36 | | " | |
| 767. | Hugh McDaniel, Heirs. Sergt..... | 1,000 | 84 | | Self | |
| 768. | Elizabeth & Laughlin Flynn, Coheirs of Thomas Flynn, Privt... | 640 | 84 | | " Maj. Dauherty | |

| No. | To whom granted and rank | No. acres | Service in months | Location and to whom deeded and date of warrant. Within the limits of the lands allotted the officers and soldiers of the Continental Line, by Law, 1783, Oct. 14 | |
|---|---|---|---|---|---|
| 769. | Peter Ferguson, Privt........... | 228 | 30 | | Colo. Love |
| | | | | | Maj. Dauherty |
| 770. | William Whitehead, Privt....... | 228 | 30 | | " " |
| 771. | William Pafford, Privt.......... | 640 | 84 | Apr. 30 | Maj. Dauherty |
| 772. | Nancey Butts, heiress of Wm. Butts, Privt................. | 640 | 84 | " | Capt. Wm. Algood |
| 773. | Thomas Rutler, Heir of Joseph Rutler, Privt................ | 640 | 84 | | " " |
| 774. | Reuben Mitchell, Heir of John Mitchell, ecsd................ | 640 | 84 | | " " |
| 775. | George Elmoure, Privt.......... | 274 | 36 | " | Self |
| 776. | Benjamin Thomas, Privt........ | 640 | 84 | " | T. Thomas |
| 777. | Duncey Campbell, Heir of Solomon Campbell............ | 640 | 84 | " | Is. Phillips |
| 778. | The Heirs of Samuel Nicholos.... | 1,000 | 84 | " | Gen. Gregory |
| 779. | Robert Brownfield, Surgeon of the militia by virtue of an act of Assembly................. | 1,000 | | " | Alexander |
| 780. | Nathan Alexander, Srgt. of Militia by virtue of an act of the assembly | 1,000 | | | |
| 781. | Valentine Lucas, Privt.......... | 228 | 30 | Apr. 30 | Robt. Parker |
| 782. | The heirs of Joseph Copeland, Pt. | 640 | 84 | " | M. Ramsey |
| 783. | Robert King, Heir of George King | 640 | 84 | " | Gen. Person |
| 784. | The heirs of Thomas Sinclear, Pt. | 640 | 84 | " | John Armstrong |
| 785. | Robert Eccart, Fife Majr........ | 297 | 25 | " | Maj. Walker |
| 786. | Martin Cross, Drum Majr........ | 607 | 37 | " | " |
| 787. | John Brown, heir of Clement Brown..................... | 640 | 84 | " | Abm. Brown |
| 788. | James Berry, heir of Robert Berry. | 640 | 84 | " | Col. Brown |
| 789. | Lawrance Thomson, Capt........ | 1,806 | 39 | May 4 | Lt. Gamble |
| 790. | Thomas Robeson, Privt.......... | 274 | 36 | " | Self |
| 791. | John Cockram, Privt........... | 228 | 30 | " | " |
| 793. | John Kirk, Privt............... | 274 | 36 | " | Maj. Nelson |
| 793. | John McCoy, Sergt............. | 1,000 | 84 | " | Col. Thakston |
| 794. | William Campbell, Privt........ | 640 | 84 | " | Capt. Gillespie |
| 795. | Joseph Case, Privt............. | 274 | 36 | May 5 | Jno. Humphrey |
| 796. | William Dillard, Privt.......... | 228 | 30 | " | Col. Robeson |
| 797. | Richard Thomas, Privt.......... | 228 | 30 | " | Gen. Person |
| 798. | Francis Fordene, Sergt.......... | 428 | 36 | " | Self |
| 799. | John Brown, Capt.............. | 317 | 38 | " | Col. Brown |
| 800. | Thomas Right, Privt........... | 274 | 36 | " | Thos. Haires |
| 801. | Osborn Dillard, Privt.......... | 228 | 30 | " | Jno. Dillard |
| 802. | William Starkey, Privt.......... | 640 | 84 | May 6 | Capt. Donohoe |
| 803. | Henry Hicks, Privt............ | 640 | 84 | " | " |
| 804. | John Clendennon, Lt........... | 2,560 | 84 | " | Self |
| 805. | Nathan Orr, heir of Charles Orr.. | 640 | 84 | May 7 | Col. Irwin |
| 806. | James Turner, heir of Jacob Turner, Capt................. | 3,840 | 84 | " | Gen. Person |
| 807. | John Dillard, Sergt............. | 357 | 30 | " | Self |
| 808. | Julius King, heiress of James King | 640 | 84 | " | Col. Armstrong |
| 809. | Charles Bailey, Privt........... | 640 | 84 | May 8 | M. Cole |
| 810. | Randolph Humphress, Privt...... | 640 | 84 | " | This warrant transfer'd to Martin Cole, from Cole to Willoughby Williams, from Williams to Green Hill, the warrant be made in Hill's name |

| No. | To whom granted and rank | No. acres | Service in months | Location and to whom deeded and date of warrant. Within the limits of the lands allotted the officers and soldiers of the Continental Line, by Law, 1783, Oct. 14 | | |
|---|---|---|---|---|---|---|
| 811. | Andrew Bay, Sergt. Maj......... | 357 | 30 | May 8 | Maj. Nelson | |
| 812. | Samuel Burton, Privt........... | 228 | 30 | " | Maj. Brock | |
| 813. | Thomas Stephens, Privt......... | 640 | 84 | " | Maj. Nelson | |
| 814. | Alexander Ramage, Privt....... | 640 | 84 | " | Thos. Thompson | |
| 815. | Thomas Seskon, Privt.......... | 640 | 84 | " | " | |
| 816. | Thomas Thompson, Privt....... | 640 | 84 | " | " | |
| 817. | The heirs of William Thompson, Privt. dcsd................. | 640 | 84 | " | " | |
| 818. | Robert Caper, Sergt........... | 1,000 | 84 | " | " | |
| 819. | Drewry Bass, Privt............. | 243 | 32 | May 10 | Col. Thomas | |
| 820. | David Ivey, Privt............. | 274 | 36 | " | | Self |
| 821. | Benjamin Bridges, Privt........ | 274 | 36 | May 11 | Montflorance | |
| 822. | John Mires, Privt.............. | 274 | 36 | " | | Self |
| 823. | Frances Therrogood, Corpl...... | 773 | 65 | " | | " |
| 824. | Benjamin Davis, Privt.......... | 376 | 51 | " | Lt. Linton | |
| 825. | William Sexton, Privt........... | 640 | 84 | " | " | |
| 826. | Thomas Sawyer, Privt.......... | 274 | 36 | " | " | |
| 827. | John Jinnings, Privt............ | 365 | 48 | May 12 | " | |
| 828. | Silas Linton, Privt............. | 640 | 84 | " | " | |
| 829. | Robert Cartwright, Privt........ | 640 | 84 | " | " | |
| 830. | Joseph Cartwright, Privt........ | 640 | 84 | " | " | |
| 831. | James Gambling, Privt......... | 350 | 46 | " | " | |
| 832. | Caleb Merchant, Privt.......... | 274 | 36 | " | " | |
| 833. | Jeremiah Seston, Privt......... | 640 | 84 | " | " | |
| 834. | James Overton, Privt........... | 365 | 48 | " | " | |
| 835. | Sanders Cook, Privt........... | 640 | 84 | " | " | |
| 836. | Thomas Cartwright, Privt....... | 640 | 84 | " | " | |
| 837. | Elisha Davis, Privt............. | 365 | 48 | " | " | |
| 838. | John Koen, Corpl.............. | 571 | 48 | " | " | |
| 839. | John Barcot, Privt............. | 365 | 48 | " | " | |
| 840. | Jesse Harrison, Privt........... | 274 | 36 | May 12 | Lt. Linton | |
| 841. | Robert Jordan, Privt........... | 640 | 84 | " | " | |
| 842. | Alexander Torrentine & John his heir, Privt................... | 640 | 84 | " | John Turrentine | |
| 843. | John Robinson, Heir of Jesse Robinson, dead, Corpl........ | 1,000 | 84 | " | Col. Lytle | |
| 844. | Abram Jones, Heir of Brinson Jones, Privt................. | 640 | 84 | " | Capt. Jones | |
| 845. | Robert Vernon, Lieut.......... | 1,280 | 42 | " | Robert Rowan | |
| 846. | Charles McKinney, Privt........ | 640 | 84 | " | The Revd. Boyd | |
| 847. | Archibald Martin, Privt......... | 297 | 39 | " | Maj. Willson | Self |
| 848. | John McGlaughlin, Privt........ | 274 | 36 | " | " | |
| 849. | John Umstead, Heir of John Lytterall, Lieut. Col........... | 2,262 | 33 | May 13 | Jno Umsted | |
| 850. | The Heirs of Abel Mosslander.... | 2,560 | 84 | " | Col. Jno. Armstrong | |
| 851. | Elijah Roberson, allowed by the assembly for service as Sergt.... | 960 | | | " | Self |
| 852. | James Russell.................. | 357 | 30 | " | Maj. McGurkin | |
| 853. | John Story, Heir of Caleb Story.. | 640 | 84 | May 14 | Maj. Mays | |
| 854. | The Heirs of William Story...... | 640 | 84 | " | " | " |
| 855. | The Heirs of Luke Searcey, Privt. | 640 | 84 | " | Jno. Searcey | |
| 856. | James Durning, Sergt.......... | 428 | 36 | " | McGeeking | |
| 857. | John English, Privt............ | 640 | 84 | " | Col. Lewis | |
| 858. | Lieut. Col. John Armstrong, Heir of Richard White........ | 327 | 43 | " | Col. Armstrong | |

| No. | To whom granted and rank | No. acres | Service in months | Location and to whom deeded and date of warrant. Within the limits of the lands allotted the officers and soldiers of the Continental Line, by Law, 1783, Oct. 14 | |
|---|---|---|---|---|---|
| 859. | Samuel Glaze, Heir of Jonathan Glaze, Corpl. | 1,000 | 84 | May 14 | M. Hunter |
| 860. | Henry Singleton, Privt. | 640 | 84 | " | Col. Randal |
| 861. | James Williams, Heir of Herbert Williams, non commissioned officer | 1,000 | 84 | May 14,'84 | Jas. Williams |
| 862. | Adam Wright, Fifer | 1,000 | 84 | " | Jas. Mebane |
| 863. | Abner Lamb, Lieut. | 2,560 | 84 | " | Col. Benj. Hawkins |
| 864. | Jesse Lane, Privt. | 640 | 84 | " | " |
| 865. | Morgan Drury, Privt. | 640 | 84 | " | Mijurking |
| 866. | John Drewry, Privt. | 640 | 84 | | "          " |
| 867. | Humphrey Garland, Privt. | 228 | 30 | " | Col. E. Robertson |
| 868. | Anthony Hart, Lieut. | 2,194 | 72 | | Col. Murfree |
| 869. | George Marshall, Privt. | 228 | 30 | | " |
| 870. | Thomas Calender, Capt. | 3,840 | 84 | | " |
| 871. | Gales Carter, Privt. | 274 | 36 | May 14 | " |
| 872. | Lewis Brown, Heir of Benjamin Brown, Privt. | 640 | 84 | | " |
| 873. | James Smith, Heir of Joseph Smith | 640 | 84 | May 18 | Col. A. Lytle |
| 874. | Thomas Jimmason, Privt. | 228 | 30 | | "          Self |
| 875. | William James, Privt. | 640 | 84 | | "          " |
| 876. | John Callahan, Privt. | 640 | 84 | | "          " |
| 877. | John Crabtree, Privt. | 640 | 84 | | " |
| 878. | The Heir of Thomas Brukins | 640 | 84 | | |
| 879. | Samuel Chapman, Capt. | 3,291 | 72 | | Self          " |
| 880. | John McAlister, Privt. | 274 | 36 | May 19 | Wm. Armstrong " |
| 881. | Phileman Bristes, Privt. | 228 | 30 | " | R. Sugg          " |
| 882. | Willis Spann, Privt. | 228 | 30 | | " |
| 883. | Clabern Harris, Privt. | 640 | 84 | | "          " |
| 884. | William Lock, Privt. | 640 | 84 | | "          " |
| 885. | Charles Bright, Non. com. officer. | 1,000 | 84 | | "          " |
| 886. | Gidean Akins, Non. com. officer. | 1,000 | 84 | | "          " |
| 887. | France Law, Non. com. officer. | 1,000 | 84 | | "          " |
| 888. | Benjamin Mott, Non. com. officer | 1,000 | 84 | | "          " |
| 889. | David Ambrose, Non. com. officer | 1,000 | 84 | | "          " |
| 890. | Henry Miller, Non. com. officer | 1,000 | 84 | | "          " |
| 891. | William Cole, Non. com. officer | 1,000 | 84 | May 18 | "          " |
| 892. | Demcey Bryan, Non. com. officer. | 1,000 | 84 | May 19 | Col. A. Lytle " |
| 893. | James Sisk, Privt. | 640 | 84 | | " |
| 894. | Cogerton Motte, Privt. | 640 | 84 | | |
| 895. | Isaac Clark, Privt. | 640 | 84 | " | Colo. A. Lytle |
| 896. | Arthur McDonald, Privt. | 640 | 84 | | "          " |
| 897. | James Hagins, Privt. | 640 | 84 | | " |
| 898. | Shadrach Cummins, Privt. | 640 | 84 | | " |
| 899. | Benjamin Blount, Privt. | 640 | 84 | | " |
| 900. | Samuel Simpson, Privt. | 640 | 84 | | " |
| 901. | Levi Coulter, Privt. | 640 | 84 | May 19,'84 | " |
| 902. | Caleb Jordan, Privt. | 640 | 84 | | " |
| 903. | Cesar Sante, Privt. | 640 | 84 | | " |
| 904. | Richard Hardick, Privt. | 640 | 84 | | " |
| 905. | John Sheppard, Privt. | 640 | 84 | | " |
| 906. | Isaac Lewis, Privt. | 640 | 84 | | " |
| 907. | John Lee, Privt. | 640 | 84 | | " |
| 908. | John Leech, Privt. | 640 | 84 | | " |
| 909. | William Faithfull, Privt. | 640 | 84 | | " |
| 910. | Benjamin Rivers, Privt. | 640 | 84 | | " |
| 911. | Robert Lewis, Privt. | 640 | 84 | | " |

| No. | To whom granted and rank | No. acres | Service in months | Location and to whom deeded and date of warrant. Within the limits of the lands allotted the officers and soldiers of the Continental Line, by Law, 1783, Oct. 14 | | |
|---|---|---|---|---|---|---|
| 912. | John Grayham, Privt............ | 640 | 84 | Colo. A. Lytle | | |
| 913. | Robert Marlo, Privt............ | 640 | 84 | " | | |
| 914. | Lott Watson, Privt............. | 640 | 84 | " | | |
| 915. | William Ryal, Privt.. .......... | 640 | 84 | " | | |
| 916. | Daniel Reymond, Privt......... | 640 | 84 | " | | |
| 917. | Spencer Spiers, Privt.......... | 640 | 84 | " | | |
| 918. | Roger McRaee, Privt........... | 640 | 84 | " | | |
| 919. | Hugh McCann, Privt........... | 640 | 84 | " | | |
| 920. | Solomon Middleton, Privt....... | 640 | 84 | " | | |
| 921. | John Faulks, Privt............. | 640 | 84 | " | | |
| 922. | William Crosley, Privt.......... | 640 | 84 | " | | |
| 923. | Benjamin White, Privt.......... | 640 | 84 | " | | |
| 924. | Joel Paybourn, Privt.......... | 640 | 84 | " | | |
| 925. | John Wilcox, Privt............. | 640 | 84 | " | | |
| 926. | James Bond, Privt............. | 640 | 84 | " | | |
| 927. | John Gill, Privt............... | 640 | 84 | " | | |
| 928. | James Tucker, Privt........... | 640 | 84 | " | | |
| 929. | Abraham Vaughn, Privt........ | 640 | 84 | " | | |
| 930. | Thomas Brown, Privt.......... | 640 | 84 | " | | |
| 931. | John Dowd, Privt............. | 640 | 84 | " | | |
| 932. | Daniel McFalter, Privt......... | 640 | 84 | " | | |
| 933. | Nehemiah Pearcy, Privt........ | 640 | 84 | " | | |
| 934. | John Carter, Privt............. | 640 | 84 | " | | |
| 935. | Robert McKinnie, Privt........ | 640 | 84 | " | | |
| 936. | John Platt, Privt.............. | 640 | 84 | " | | |
| 937. | William Brown, Privt.......... | 640 | 84 | " | | |
| 938. | William Burnet, Privt......... | 640 | 84 | " | | |
| 939. | John Ellis, Privt.............. | 640 | 84 | " | | |
| 940. | John Stringer, Privt.. ......... | 640 | 84 | " | | |
| 941. | Richard Roberts, Privt......... | 640 | 84 | " | | |
| 942. | Caleb Thomas, Privt.......... | 640 | 84 | " | | |
| 943. | Richard Straughon, Privt....... | 640 | 84 | " | | |
| 944. | Sampson Sikes, Privt.......... | 640 | 84 | " | | |
| 945. | David Sweat, Privt............ | 640 | 84 | " | | |
| 946. | Joseph Voss, Privt............. | 640 | 84 | " | | |
| 947. | John Campen, Privt........... | 640 | 84 | " | | |
| 948. | William McKinney, Privt....... | 640 | 84 | " | | |
| 949. | Matthias Egner, Privt......... | 640 | 84 | " | | |
| 950. | William Price, Privt........... | 640 | 84 | " | | |
| 951. | Sykes Garris, Privt............ | 640 | 84 | " | | |
| 952. | Edmund King, Privt........... | 640 | 84 | " | | |
| 953. | Solomon Waters, Privt......... | 640 | 84 | " | | |
| 954. | Cornelius Ryon, Privt.......... | 640 | 84 | " | | |
| 955. | John Etherige, Privt........... | 640 | 84 | Col. A. Lytle | | |
| 956. | William Couch, Privt........... | 640 | 84 | Col. Chas. Robeson | | |
| 957. | Stephen Merritt, Heir of Benjamin Merrit, died......... | 640 | 84 | Maj. R. Searcey | | |
| 958. | The heir of Christopher Gooden, Capt................. | 3,840 | 84 | Colo. Brown C.——— | | |
| 959. | John King, Privt.............. | 274 | 36 | Lt. Clendennen | | |
| 960. | David Kenedy, Privt........... | 640 | 84 | Col. Robt. Rone | | |
| 961. | William Cruise, Privt.......... | 640 | 84 | May 20,'84 | " | |
| 962. | Henry Hughes, Privt........... | 640 | 84 | " | " | |
| 963. | Willis Smith, Privt............ | 640 | 84 | May 21 | | Self |
| 964. | The Heir of James Oneal........ | 640 | 84 | Mr. Dobbins | | |
| 965. | The Heir of William Hurt...... . | 640 | 84 | Chas. Parker | | |

| No. | To whom granted and rank | No. acres | Service in months | Location and to whom deeded and date of warrant. Within the limits of the lands allotted the officers and soldiers of the Continental Line, by Law, 1783, Oct. 14 | |
|---|---|---|---|---|---|
| 966. | The Heir of George Adcock...... | 640 | 84 | | Mr. Parks |
| 967. | The Heir of Richard Vaughan.... | 640 | 84 | | "  Self |
| 968. | The Heir of Gideon Lamb, Colo. . | 6,171 | 72 | | Col. B. Hawkins |
| 969. | John Ferrell, Privt.............. | 274 | 36 | May 21 | Self |
| 970. | James Britain, Privt............. | 274 | 36 | " | " |
| 971. | Phillip Britain, Privt.. ......... | 274 | 36 | | Jas. Brittain |
| 972. | Samuel Chappell, Privt......... | 274 | 36 | | Capt. Lytle |
| 973. | Thomas Gennings, Privt......... | 365 | 48 | | " |
| 974. | Marmaduke Moore, Privt........ | 640 | 84 | | " |
| 975. | Thomas Saydon, Privt.......... | 274 | 36 | | " |
| 976. | Isaac Rolston, Lieut............. | 1,240 | 36 | " | Capt. R. Rolston |
| 977. | John Carter, Heir of Humphrey Carter, Privt................. | 640 | 84 | " | Mourning Anderson |
| 978. | William Hood, Privt............ | 274 | 36 | " | Self |
| 979. | Joshua Harvey, Privt........... | 640 | 84 | | Capt. Budd |
| 980. | William Madry, Sergt.......... | 357 | 30 | | Wm. Manley |
| 981. | Absalom Burgess, Sergt......... | 1,000 | 84 | May 21,'84 | " |
| 982. | John Chumney, Sergt........... | 428 | 36 | | James Brown |
| 983. | Thomas Kelley, Privt........... | 274 | 36 | | "        " |
| 984. | James Douge, Sergt............. | 1,000 | 84 | | Capt. Jas. Ferebee |
| 985. | William Fletcher, Sergt......... | 1,000 | 84 | | "        " |
| 986. | Thomas Monerciff, Privt........ | 274 | 36 | | "        " |
| 987. | Lazarus Flowron, Privt......... | 274 | 36 | | " |
| 988 | Richard Flowron, Privt.......... | 274 | 36 | | " |
| 989. | William Thompson, Sergt....... | 428 | 36 | | " |
| 990. | Willibee Jarvis, Privt........... | 274 | 36 | | " |
| 991. | William Parr, Privt............. | 274 | 36 | | " |
| 992. | Charles Griggs, Privt........... | 274 | 36 | | " |
| 993. | Thomas Campbell, Privt........ | 274 | 36 | | " |
| 994. | Jolley Holstead, Privt.......... | 274 | 36 | | " |
| 995. | Henry Hannus, Privt........... | 274 | 36 | | " |
| 996. | Peter Poyner, Privt............ | 274 | 36 | | " |
| 997. | John Garrell, Sergt............. | 440 | 36 | | " |
| 998. | John Collens, Privt............ | 274 | 36 | | " |
| 999. | Byrd Braswell, Privt........... | 228 | 30 | May 24,'84 | Col. Ramsey |
| 1000. | Isaac Burnham (an invalid) Pt. . | 640 | 84 | | Ben Jones |
| 1001. | William Long, Privt............ | 640 | 84 | May 24 | Thos. Nelson |
| 1002. | James Anthoney, Privt......... | 640 | 36 | | Col. Wm. Lewis |
| 1003. | Robert Rolston, Capt.......... | 1,097 | 24 | " | Self |
| 1004. | The Heir of Leonard Davis, Pt. . | 640 | 84 | " | Lt. Spearpoint |
| 1005. | Jacob Cleon, Sergt............. | 358 | 30 | May 26 | Col. Lytle |
| 1006. | John Boggs, Privt.............. | 274 | 36 | | " |
| 1007. | Hugh Parks, Privt............. | 274 | 36 | | " |
| 1008. | Alexander McCaul, Privt........ | 640 | 84 | | " |
| 1009. | Archibald McCauld, Privt....... | 640 | 84 | | " |
| 1010. | Matthew Cates or (o), Privt..... | 274 | 36 | | |
| 1011. | Edward Woodman, Privt........ | 228 | 30 | May 26 | " |
| 1012. | Burwell Smith, Sergt........... | 1,000 | 84 | | "        " |
| 1013. | David Wheeler, Corpl.......... | 1,000 | 84 | | " |
| 1014. | Asel Nocks, Privt.. ............ | 640 | 84 | May 26 | Col. A. Lytle |
| 1015. | Davey Conner, Privt........... | 640 | 84 | " | " |
| 1016. | Thomas Farrow, Privt......... | 640 | 84 | " | " |
| 1017. | Michael Mullen, Privt......... | 640 | 84 | " | " |
| 1018. | George Ginnis, Privt........... | 640 | 84 | " | " |
| 1019. | Joseph Massey, Privt.......... | 640 | 84 | " | " |
| 1020. | Jeremiah Waters, Privt........ | 640 | 84 | " | " |

| No. | To whom granted and rank | No. acres | Service in months | Location and to whom deeded and date of warrant. Within the limits of the lands allotted the officers and soldiers of the Continental Line, by Law, 1783, Oct. 14 | |
|---|---|---|---|---|---|
| 1021. | Abraham Jones, Privt.......... | 640 | 84 | May 26 | Col. A. Lytle |
| 1022. | Stephen Smith, Privt.......... | 640 | 84 | " | " |
| 1023. | John Blainer, Privt............ | 640 | 84 | " | " |
| 1024. | Edmund Cummins, Privt....... | 640 | 84 | " | " |
| 1025. | Richard Phillips, Privt......... | 640 | 84 | " | " |
| 1026. | Noel Rileet, Privt............. | 640 | 84 | " | " |
| 1027. | Stephen Towell, Privt.......... | 640 | 84 | " | " |
| 1028. | Joseph Baxley, Privt.......... | 640 | 84 | " | " |
| 1029. | William Philips, Privt......... | 640 | 84 | " | " |
| 1030. | Lewis Lowell, Privt............ | 640 | 84 | " | " |
| 1031. | Obadiah Wainwright, Privt...... | 640 | 84 | " | " |
| 1032. | William Reynolds, Privt........ | 640 | 84 | " | " |
| 1033. | William Adams, Privt.......... | 640 | 84 | " | " |
| 1034. | Joseph Baker, Privt........... | 640 | 84 | " | " |
| 1035. | John Colants, Privt........... | 640 | 84 | " | ⎰Deeded to Govr Cherry ⎱of Martin County, 4th ⎰Dec. 1795. |
| 1036. | Dudley Williams, Privt........ | 640 | 84 | " | " |
| 1037. | Marmaduke Vickers, Privt...... | 640 | 84 | " | " |
| 1038. | Samuel Finney, Privt.......... | 640 | 84 | " | " |
| 1039. | Joel Copeland, Privt.......... | 640 | 84 | " | " |
| 1040. | Alexander Gill, Privt.......... | 640 | 84 | " | " |
| 1041. | Jacob Gerrard, Privt.......... | 640 | 84 | May 26 | Col. A. Lytle |
| 1042. | John Killon, Privt............. | 640 | 84 | " | " |
| 1043. | John Gervis, Privt............ | 640 | 84 | " | " |
| 1044. | John Fuller, Privt............. | 640 | 84 | " | " |
| 1045. | John Grimmage, Privt......... | 640 | 84 | " | " |
| 1046. | Edward Newton, Privt......... | 640 | 84 | " | " |
| 1047. | William Dobbins, Privt........ | 640 | 84 | " | " |
| 1048. | Robert Dean, Privt............ | 640 | 84 | " | " |
| 1049. | John McVery, Privt............ | 640 | 84 | " | " |
| 1050. | Edward Williams, Privt........ | 640 | 84 | " | " |
| 1051. | John Sullivan, Privt........... | 640 | 84 | " | " |
| 1052. | James Faulks, Privt........... | 640 | 84 | " | " |
| 1053. | Clemen Ferrell, Privt.......... | 640 | 84 | " | " |
| 1054. | Frederick Flood, Privt......... | 640 | 84 | " | " |
| 1055. | James Scarlet, Privt........... | 640 | 84 | " | " |
| 1056. | David Driskell, Privt.......... | 274 | 36 | | Self |
| 1057. | James Segare, Privt........... | 365 | 48 | May 27,'84 | " |
| 1058. | William Duke, Sergt........... | 357 | 30 | | Brother |
| 1059. | Theophilus Pearce, Privt....... | 640 | 84 | | Capt. A. Lytle |
| 1060. | Thomas Evins, Privt.......... | 640 | 84 | " | " |
| 1061. | William Morgan, Sergt......... | 1,000 | 84 | May 28 | " |
| 1062. | James Johnston, Sergt......... | 1,000 | 84 | " | Capt. Clendennen |
| 1063. | David Pooe, Privt............. | 640 | 84 | | " |
| 1064. | William Morris, Privt.......... | 640 | 84 | | Self |
| 1065. | Isaac Gateley, Privt........... | 640 | 84 | | John Willson |
| 1066. | William Walker, Privt......... | 640 | 84 | | David Pasmore |
| 1067. | Peter Rainey, Privt........... | 640 | 84 | | Wm. T. Lewis |
| 1068. | Thomas Reason, Privt......... | 274 | 36 | | Capt. Alford |
| 1069. | John McCoy, Privt............ | 640 | 84 | | M. Cole |
| 1070. | John Henry, Privt............ | 640 | 84 | | " |
| 1071. | Thomas Buncombe, Heir of Edward Buncombe, Colo...... | 7,200 | 84 | " | Col. Murfree |
| 1072. | Andrew Hoddock, Heir of Henry Hicks................ | 640 | 84 | | A. Haddock |

| No. | To whom granted and rank | No. acres | Service in months | Location and to whom deeded and date of warrant. Within the limits of the lands allotted the officers and soldiers of the Continental Line, by Law, 1783, Oct. 14 | |
|---|---|---|---|---|---|
| 1073. | Joseph Royal, Privt. | 640 | 84 | | M. Cole | |
| 1074. | Joel Joyner, Privt. | 640 | 84 | May 28 | " | |
| 1075. | Andrew Haddock, Sergt. | 1,000 | 84 | | " | Self |
| 1076. | William Ferrell, Heir of Edward Ferrell | 640 | 84 | | Wm. Ferrell | |
| 1077. | John Hall, Heir of Thomas Hall, Lieut. | 2,560 | 84 | | Colo. McClain | |
| 1078. | Thomas Davis, Sergt. | 642 | 52 | | Capt. Davis | |
| 1079. | Benjamin Hodges, Sergt. | 1,000 | 84 | | McGunken | |
| 1080. | Spencer Donaldson, Drummer | 428 | 36 | | " | |
| 1081. | John Deal, P.ivt. | 380 | 50 | | " | |
| 1082. | William Mullen, Privt. | 365 | 48 | | " | |
| 1083. | Richard Meallen, Privt. | 365 | 48 | | " | |
| 1084. | Robert Thomas, Sergt. | 428 | 36 | | " | |
| 1085. | Isaac Moore, Capt. | 3,840 | 84 | | " | |
| 1086. | Miles McShehe, Lieut. | 2,560 | 84 | | " | |
| 1087. | Levi Barker, Privt. | 640 | 84 | | Mr. Jno. Rice | |
| 1088. | Jacob Lane, Privt. | 274 | 36 | | Lt. Nat. Williams | |
| 1089. | William Farrow, Privt. | 228 | 30 | | James Comer | |
| 1090. | Francis Wilks, Privt. | 228 | 30 | | " | |
| 1091. | Samuel Gray, Privt. | 640 | 84 | May 28 | Capt. A. Herring | |
| 1092. | John Tilghman, Privt. | 274 | 36 | " | " | |
| 1093. | William Gray, Privt. | 640 | 84 | " | " | |
| 1094. | James Hutchens, Privt. | 640 | 84 | " | " | |
| 1095. | Simon Totevine, Heir of Coleburn Totevine, Sergt. dcsd. | 1,000 | 84 | " | | Self |
| 1096. | Francis Sumner, Privt. | 274 | 36 | " | | " |
| 1097. | Matthew Hearon, Privt. | 640 | 84 | | | " |
| 1098. | John Smith, Privt. | 640 | 84 | | | " |
| 1099. | Bellitha Tilghman, Sergt. | 1,000 | 84 | | Capt. Shute | |
| 1100. | William Tilghman, Privt. | 640 | 84 | | " | |
| 1101. | Simon Totevine, Heir of Winder Totevine | 640 | 84 | May 28,'84 | Capt. Simon Totevine | |
| 1102. | William Becks, Ensign | 1,096 | 36 | " | | Self |
| 1103. | Mark Haycraft, Privt. | 640 | 36 | | Capt. Herren | |
| 1104. | James Standley, Privt. | 274 | 36 | | " | |
| 1105. | Robert Standley, Sergt. | 428 | 36 | | " | |
| 1106. | Samuel Stringer, Sergt. | 571 | 48 | | " | |
| 1107. | Benjamin Reaves, Privt. | 640 | 84 | | " | |
| 1108. | Silas Gray, Privt. | 640 | 84 | | John McNeese | |
| 1109. | William Feloes, Sergt. | 1,000 | 84 | " | | Self |
| 1110. | Thomas Guinn, Privt. | 365 | 48 | | Mc Williams | |
| 1111. | Azariah Meafee (McAfee) Privt. | 640 | 84 | " | " | |
| 1112. | Isaac Carter, Privt. | 274 | 36 | | Jno. Allen | |
| 1113. | John Caldwell, Privt. | 389 | 51 | | | Self |
| 1114. | John Smith, Privt. | 640 | 84 | | " | |
| 1115. | Benjamin Smith, Privt. | 274 | 36 | | McWilliams | |
| 1116. | Gideon Pettit, Fifer | 428 | 36 | July 14,'84 | | Self |
| 1117. | Joel Whitehouse, Privt. | 274 | 36 | July 17 | | " |
| 1118. | The Heir of Jesse Taylor, Privt. | 640 | 84 | July 22 | Sam Motlady | |
| 1119. | Samuel Pope, Privt. | 274 | 36 | July 25 | Jas. Williams | |
| 1120. | William Pridgeon, Privt. | 274 | 36 | | " | |
| 1121. | John Hodges, Lieut. | 792 | 26 | " | " | |
| 1122. | Daniel White, Privt. | 228 | 30 | | " | |
| 1123. | Anthony Diggs, Lieut. | 1,097 | 36 | July 28 | " | |
| 1124. | Stephen Ewell, Sergt. | 523 | 44 | | " | |

| No. | To whom granted and rank | No. acres | Service in months | Location and to whom deeded and date of warrant. Within the limits of the lands allotted the officers and soldiers of the Continental Line, by Law, 1783, Oct. 14 | |
|---|---|---|---|---|---|
| 1125. | The Heir of John Bratcher, Pt... | 640 | 84 | July 28 | Capt. Wm. Bush Self |
| 1126. | Mason Broom, Privt............ | 274 | 36 | | Sam Holliday |
| 1127. | Philemon Chance, Privt........ | 274 | 36 | | " |
| 1128. | The Heir of James Stradley, Pt.. | 640 | 84 | | " |
| 1129. | John Weaver, Privt............ | 640 | 84 | | " |
| 1130. | Robert Henderson, Pri. & Sergt.. | 307 | 30 | July 31,'84 | Self |
| 1131. | James Harris, Privt............ | 228 | 30 | Aug. 2, '84 | Bartholomew Kelly |
| 1132. | Lewis Bailey, Privt............ | 228 | 30 | " | " |
| 1133. | The Heir of Burwell Collins, Pt.. | 640 | 84 | | Saml. Parker |
| 1134. | The Heir of Dilliard Collins, Pt.. | 640 | 84 | | " |
| 1135. | The Heir of John Stovealls, Pt... | 640 | 84 | | " |
| 1136. | John Berten, Corpl............ | 1,000 | 84 | | " |
| 1137. | Peter Williams, Sergt.......... | 1,000 | 84 | | " |
| 1138. | William Cronister, Privt....... | 640 | 84 | | " |
| 1139. | Patrick Foy, Corpl............ | 1,000 | 84 | | " |
| 1140. | Samuel Johnston, Privt........ | 185 | 24 | | " |
| 1141. | John Psowdford, Privt......... | 640 | 84 | Aug. 2, '84 | " |
| 1142. | William Hudlestone, Privt...... | 640 | 84 | " | " |
| 1143. | Robert Hudlestone, Privt...... | 640 | 84 | " | " |
| 1144. | Britain Johnston, Privt........ | 640 | 84 | | L. Holleday |
| 1145. | Richard Downham, Privt...... | 274 | 36 | | " |
| 1146. | Speakman Downham, Privt..... | 274 | 36 | | " |
| 1147. | Hugh Williamson, Surgeon...... | 4,800 | 84 | | Maj. Blount |
| 1148. | The Heir of Arthur Council, Cpt. | 3,840 | 84 | " | " |
| 1149. | Zadock Sowell, Privt.......... | 228 | 30 | | S. Holleday |
| 1150. | Jesse Woollard, Privt.......... | 228 | 30 | | " |
| 1151. | Thomas Martin, Privt......... | 228 | 30 | " | " |
| 1152. | Thomas Aims, Heir of John Aims, Privt................. | 640 | 84 | " | " |
| 1153. | Thomas Aimes, Privt.......... | 640 | 84 | " | " |
| 1154. | Edward Warren, Privt......... | 228 | 30 | | " |
| 1155. | Jesse Cherry, Heir of John Cherry, Privt.............. | 640 | 84 | | " |
| 1156. | John Smithick, Heir of Edward Smithick, Privt............ | 640 | 84 | | " |
| 1157. | Jesse McColister, Heir of James McColister................. | 640 | 84 | | " |
| 1158. | William Duggin, Heir of Thomas Duggin, Privt....... | 640 | 84 | | " |
| 1159. | William Duggin, Heir of Jesse Duggin, Privt.............. | 640 | 84 | | " |
| 1160. | William Warren, Privt......... | 228 | 30 | | " |
| 1161. | Josiah Stringer, Privt.......... | 274 | 36 | Aug. 13,'84 | Self |
| 1162. | James Griffin, Privt.......... | 274 | 36 | | Jo. Stringer |
| 1163. | Maltiah Turner, Sergt.......... | 1,000 | 84 | Aug. 18 | Jno. Watkins |
| 1164. | Levi West, Drummer.......... | 428 | 36 | " | " |
| 1165. | Benjamin German, Privt....... | 365 | 48 | | " |
| 1166. | John Jordan, Heir of William Jordan.................... | 640 | 84 | | J. Gordan |
| 1167. | William Montgomery, Privt..... | 640 | 84 | | Capt. Gamble |
| 1168. | John Copeland, Sergt.......... | 1,000 | 84 | | " |
| 1169. | Daniel Milton, Privt.......... | 640 | 84 | | " |
| 1170. | John Roberson, Privt.......... | 640 | 84 | | |
| 1171. | Flourance McCathey, Lieut..... | 822 | 27 | Aug. 27,'84 | " |
| 1172. | Sion Barnett, Privt............ | 320 | 42 | | " |
| 1173. | Lewes Shilkes, Privt.......... | 640 | 84 | | Saml. Holladay |

| No. | To whom granted and rank | No. acres | Service in months | Location and to whom deeded and date of warrant. Within the limits of the lands allotted the officers and soldiers of the Continental Line, by Law, 1783, Oct. 14 | | |
|---|---|---|---|---|---|---|
| 1174. | Joshua Rogers, Privt. | 640 | 84 | | Saml. Holladay | |
| 1175. | John Anderson, Privt. | 640 | 84 | | " | |
| 1176. | Edward Adcock, Privt. | 640 | 84 | | Col. Lytle | |
| 1177. | John Hays, Privt. | 640 | 84 | | Saml. Holladay | |
| 1178. | Francis Ross, Heir of Abram Ross, Privt. | 640 | 84 | Sept. 6, '84 | | Self |
| 1179. | William Fryar, Privt. | 228 | 30 | Sept. 13 | | " |
| 1180. | William Fryar, Heir of Josiah Fryar, Privt. | 640 | 84 | | | " |
| 1181. | Elisha Grant, Privt. | 640 | 84 | Sept. 13,'84 | John Price | |
| 1182. | John Nichols, Privt. | 640 | 84 | | " | |
| 1183. | David Defnell, Privt. | 487 | 64 | Sept. 15 | | Self |
| 1184. | The Heirs of William Defnell | 640 | 84 | | | " |
| 1185. | Robert Raiford, Capt. | 3,840 | 84 | | | " |
| 1186. | James Morehead, Lieut. | 944 | 31 | | | " |
| 1187. | John Rees, Privt. | 640 | 84 | Sept. 20,'84 | Col. A. Lytle | |
| 1188. | Samuel Fest, Privt. | 640 | 84 | " | " | |
| 1189. | Andrew Faddes, Privt. | 640 | 84 | " | " | |
| 1190. | George Stringer, Privt. | 411 | 54 | Sept. 20,'84 | Col. A. Lytle | |
| 1191. | Richard Philsby, Privt. | 274 | 36 | " | " | |
| 1192. | John Addlemon, Privt. | 274 | 36 | " | " | |
| 1193. | Isaac Burnum, Privt. | 640 | 84 | " | " | |
| 1194. | John Morreson, Privt. | 640 | 84 | " | " | |
| 1195. | Arthur Kerney, Privt. | 274 | 36 | " | " | |
| 1196. | Thomas Hayse, Privt. | 274 | 36 | " | " | |
| 1197. | William Milton, dec'd, Privt. | 640 | 84 | " | " | |
| 1198. | Benjamin Johnston, Privt. | 228 | 30 | " | " | |
| 1199. | George Woodliff, dec'd, Privt. | 640 | 84 | " | " | |
| 1200. | James Tracey, Privt. | 274 | 36 | " | " | |
| 1201. | Robert Edwards, Sergt. | 1,000 | 84 | " | " | |
| 1202. | Thompson Harris, dec'd, Privt. | 640 | 84 | " | " | |
| 1203. | James Rowland, Privt. | 640 | 84 | " | " | |
| 1204. | Samuel Daven, Drummer | 357 | 30 | " | " | |
| 1205. | Daniel Clifton, Privt. | 640 | 84 | " | " | |
| 1206. | Moses Scathers, Corpl. | 357 | 30 | " | " | |
| 1207. | Ezekiel Boggs, Privt. | 274 | 36 | " | " | |
| 1208. | Robert Marlin, Corpl. | 428 | 33 | " | " | |
| 1209. | Jesse Cole, Privt. | 640 | 84 | " | " | |
| 1210. | Edward Cole, Privt. | 640 | 84 | " | " | |
| 1211. | William Martin, Infirm | 640 | 84 | " | McWilliams | |
| 1212. | John Welch, Capt. | 1,508 | 33 | " | | Self |
| 1213. | Robert Greer, Lieut. | 1,005 | 33 | " | | " |
| 1214. | Daniel Twig, Privt. | 274 | 36 | " | | " |
| 1215. | The heir of John Miller, dec'd, Privt. | 640 | 84 | " | | " |
| 1216. | Lewis Cannon, Lieut. | 1,584 | 57 | " | L. Cannon | |
| 1217. | Hardy Bird & Joseph Hail, heir | 640 | 84 | | Jo. Hail | |
| 1218. | John McCullock, Privt. | 274 | 36 | Sept. 27,'84 | Robt. Hay | |
| 1219. | John Grinder, dec'd, Sergt. | 1,000 | 84 | " | " | |
| 1220. | Joseph Eller, dec'd, Privt. | 640 | 84 | | " | |
| 1221. | Alexander McDaniel, Corpl. | 1,000 | 84 | Sept. 29,'84 | Capt. R. Hays | |
| 1222. | Richard Evans, Privt. | 640 | 84 | " | " | |
| 1223. | David Stillwell, Privt. | 403 | 53 | | " | |
| 1224. | Syrus Daves, Privt. | 228 | 30 | | " | |
| 1225. | Micajah Davis, Privt. | 274 | 36 | | " | |
| 1226. | James Judge, Privt. | 228 | 30 | | Thos. Pridgeon | |

| No. | To whom granted and rank | No. acres | Service in months | Location and to whom deeded and date of warrant. Within the limits of the lands allotted the officers and soldiers of the Continental Line, by Law, 1783, Oct. 14 |
|---|---|---|---|---|
| 1227. | James Powers, Lieut............ | 1,200 | 40 | Self |
| 1228. | John Wise, Privt............... | 274 | 36 | A. Pearce |
| 1299. | John Smith, Privt.............. | 388 | 51 | Noah Woodard |
| 1230. | Redick Smith, Privt............ | 640 | 84 | " |
| 1231. | Thomas Jones, Privt............ | 228 | 30 | " |
| 1232. | James McMullen ,,Drummer..... | 309 | 30 | " |
| 1233. | Nathaniel Cooper, Privt........ | 228 | 30 | " |
| 1234. | Admiral Haddock, Privt........ | 228 | 30 | A. Haddock |
| 1235. | John Raiford, Lieut............ | 635 | — | Self |
| 1236. | Wm. Eckols, Sergt............. | 738 | 63 | Wm. Eckols' Cousin |
| 1237. | Curtis Clemons, Privt.......... | 274 | 30 | Sep. 29,'84 Chance |
| 1238. | John Pond, Privt............... | 274 | 30 | P. Henderson |
| 1239. | Parker Rogers, Pfifer.......... | 319 | 27 | |
| 1240. | Darling Madry, Privt.......... | 228 | 30 | Nath. W. Macon |
| 1241. | Wm. McIlyea, Heir of John Mcyea, Drummer............ | 1,000 | 84 | Self |
| 1242. | John Cox, Heir of Edward Cox, Privt................. | 640 | — | Jno. Cox |
| 1243. | Thomas Cox, Privt............. | 274 | 36 | " |
| 1244. | Richard Lidell, Privt........... | 274 | 36 | Phillips |
| 1245. | William Smith, Privt.......... | 480 | 63 | Self |
| 1246. | James Douge, dec'd, Privt...... | 640 | 84 | Gen. Gregory |
| 1247. | Aquila Macomes, Privt., John Poteat, Heir, dec'd........ | 640 | 84 | Col. Wm. Moore |
| 1248. | Benjamin Robison, Privt........ | 274 | 36 | Wm. Caswell |
| 1249. | Benjamin Stanaland, Junr, Heir of Robt. Stanaland, Sgt. dec'd. | 1,000 | 84 | Capt. W. Bush |
| 1250. | Benjamin Stanaland, Jr. Heir of James Stanaland, a Pt. dec'd. | 640 | 84 | |
| 1251. | The Heir of Nathan Skipper, Privt., dec'd................ | 640 | 84 | Capt. Wm. Beese |
| 1252. | The Heir of Joseph Skipper Privt. dec'd................ | 640 | 84 | " |
| 1253. | The Heir of Richard Freeman, Privt. dec'd................ | 640 | 84 | " |
| 1254. | John Knox, Heir of William Knox, Capt. killed........... | 3,840 | 84 | John Knox |
| 1255. | The Heir of William Barnes Privt. dec'd................ | 640 | 84 | Capt. Joseph Ferebe |
| 1256. | John Brabble, Heir of James Brabble, Privt.............. | 640 | 84 | " |
| 1257. | The Heir of James Caton, Privt.. | 640 | 84 | " |
| 1258. | Jesse Holstead, Heir of Samuel Holstead, Privt............. | 640 | 84 | " |
| 1259. | Zachariah Douge, Privt........ | 274 | 36 | " |
| 1260. | Thomas Lane, Privt........... | 274 | 36 | Chance |
| 1261. | Sarah Hays, Heiress to Richard Clifton, Privt.............. | 640 | 84 | Col. Steward |
| 1262. | John Hays, Privt.............. | 274 | 36 | " |
| 1263. | John Walker, Heir of Robert Barlow, Privt.............. | 640 | 84 | Jno. Walker |
| 1264. | Andrew Cainahan, Heir of Daniel McKinly, Privt........ | 640 | 84 | " |
| 1265. | The Heir of Edward Harris, Pt. | 640 | 84 | " |
| 1266. | The Heir of David Brown, Pt. .. | 640 | 84 | " |
| 1267. | William Saunders, Privt........ | 274 | 36 | And. Saunders |

| No. | To whom granted and rank | No. acres | Service in months | Location and to whom deeded and date of warrant. Within the limits of the lands allotted the officers and soldiers of the Continental Line, by Law, 1783, Oct. 14 |
|---|---|---|---|---|
| 1268. | Solomon Jennet, Privt......... | 274 | 36 | And. Saunders |
| 1269. | Andrew Sanders, Corpl......... | 428 | 36 | Self |
| 1270. | William Godfrey, Privt........ | 274 | 36 | |
| 1271. | John Thomas, Privt........... | 297 | 39 | Self |
| 1272. | Notingham Monk, Privt........ | 274 | 36 | Col. Oliver |
| 1273. | Mary Seeberry, Heiress of Alstone Seeberry, Privt...... | 640 | 84 | John Price |
| 1274. | Mary Campbell, Heiress of James Campbell, Privt........ | 640 | 84 | " |
| 1275. | Eleanor Taylor, Heiress of John Bruton, Privt.......... | 640 | 84 | " |
| 1276. | Lucy Plumley, Heiress of George Plumley, Privt........ | 640 | 84 | " |
| 1277. | Hansel Hicks, Privt............ | 274 | 36 | Jas. Williams |
| 1278. | Phillip Jones, Privt............ | 640 | 84 | " |
| 1279. | Mary Regans, Heiress of John Regans, Privt.......... | 640 | 84 | Jno. Price |
| 1280. | Thomas Anderson, Privt....... | 640 | 84 | |
| 1281. | Ishmael Roberts, Heir of Kinchin Roberts, dec'd....... | 640 | 84 | Ishm. Roberts |
| 1282. | Jonathan Standley, Privt........ | 274 | 36 | Jno. Price |
| 1283. | Thomas Orrell, Lieut.......... | 1,144 | 36 | Col. Johnston (Onslow) |
| 1284. | James Southerland, Privt....... | 274 | 36 | Maj. May |
| 1285. | Charles Nelms, Privt........... | 274 | 36 | N. Macon |
| 1286. | Anthony Dowden, Heir of Samuel Dowden, Privt. dec'd . | 640 | 84 | John Macon |
| 1287. | Solomon Car, Privt............ | 274 | 36 | " |
| 1288. | Daniel Jones, Capt............ | 1,234 | 27 | " |
| 1289. | John Powell, Privt............ | 228 | 30 | " |
| 1290. | John Parrish, Privt............ | 280 | 37 | Benj. Jones |
| 1291. | Joseph Hawley's Heir, Privt..... | 640 | 84 | Gen. Person |
| 1292. | Asa Thomas, Privt............ | 228 | 30 | " |
| 1293. | David Pendergrass, Privt....... | 228 | 30 | " |
| 1294. | The Heir of Robt. Gist. Privt.... | 640 | 84 | " |
| 1295. | Archiles Davis & Augustin Davis, heir, Privt........... | 640 | 84 | Col. Barton |
| 1296. | Benjamin Ray, Privt.......... | 640 | 84 | Maj. Dauherty |
| 1297. | Davis Jones, Lieut............ | 1,096 | 36 | " |
| 1298. | The Heir of Thomas Padgett, Privt. dec'd................. | 640 | 84 | " |
| 1299. | The Heir of Francis Disern, Privt. dec'd................. | 640 | 84 | " |
| 1300. | John Gambier Scull, Lieut....... | 1,127 | 37 | Sept. 29,'84 | " |
| 1301. | Maurice Rayford, Privt........ | 236 | 31 | A. Pearce |
| 1302. | Moses Bird, Privt............ | 274 | 36 | N. Mays |
| 1303. | Joseph Collins, Privt.......... | 274 | 36 | " |
| 1304. | Jacob Braboy, Privt........... | 228 | 30 | " |
| 1305. | Elijah Nance, Privt........... | 228 | 30 | " |
| 1306. | William Church, Privt......... | 228 | 30 | " |
| 1307. | Ephraim Hooks, Privt......... | 228 | 30 | " |
| 1308. | James Bond, Privt............ | 396 | 52 | Genl. Bryan |
| 1309. | The Heir of Thomas Moseley, Pt. | 640 | 84 | |
| 1310. | Bryan Worsley, Privt.......... | 640 | 84 | |
| 1311. | The Heir of Isaac Clark, Privt... | 640 | 84 | |
| 1312. | James Avery, Infirm.......... | 640 | 84 | J. Williams (Pitt) |
| 1313. | The Heir of William Nelson, Pt.. | 640 | 84 | J. Glasgow |

| No. | To whom granted and rank | No. acres | Service in months | Location and to whom deeded and date of warrant. Within the limits of the lands allotted the officers and soldiers of the Continental Line, by Law, 1783, Oct. 14 | |
|---|---|---|---|---|---|
| 1314. | The Heir of Jesse Nelson, Privt.. | 640 | 84 | J. Glasgow | |
| 1315. | The Heir of James Corbin, Pt. .. | 640 | 84 | " | |
| 1316. | The Heir of Francis Corbin, Pt. . | 640 | 84 | " | |
| 1317. | The Heir of Joseph English, .... | 640 | 84 | " | |
| 1318. | The Heir of William Brierly..... | 640 | 84 | " | |
| 1319. | David Vance, Piivt............ | 228 | 30 | " | |
| 1320. | Simon Smith, Heir of William, Privt.............. | 640 | 84 | W. Williams | |
| 1321. | Simon Smith, Privt............ | 274 | 36 | " | |
| 1322. | William Mills, Corpl........... | 285 | 24 | " | |
| 1323. | Elijah Mills, dec'd, William Mills, heir, Privt............ | 640 | 84 | " | |
| 1324. | Gardner Maye, Corpl.......... | 428 | 36 | " | |
| 1325. | Henry Albritton, Privt......... | 640 | 84 | L. Holleday | |
| 1326. | Isaac Gregory, Privt........... | 640 | 84 | Col. Long | |
| 1327. | John Williams and Wm. Williams, Heir, Privt........ | 640 | 84 | W. Williams | |
| 1328. | Joseph Humphries, The U. and to his heirs, Privt........... | 640 | 84 | Col. T. Johnston | |
| 1329. | Jabeth Elliot, Infirm.......... | 640 | 84 | | Self |
| 1330. | The Heiress of Dixson Nolley, dec'd. Privt................ | 640 | 84 | Capt. Wm. Bush | |
| 1331. | The heir of John Milton, dec'd. Privt............... | 640 | 84 | " | |
| 1332. | The heir of Joseph Card, dec'd. Privt............... | 640 | 84 | " | |
| 1333. | The heir of Seth Boyce, dec'd. Privt............... | 640 | 84 | " | |
| 1334. | The heir of John Hart, dec'd. Pt. | 640 | 84 | " | |
| 1335. | The heir of Christopher Folk, dec'd. Privt............... | 640 | 84 | " | |
| 1336. | The heir of William Bond, dec'd. Privt............... | 640 | 84 | " | |
| 1337. | The heir of Richard Broadbent, dec'd. Privt............... | 640 | 84 | " | |
| 1338. | The heir of Jesse Person, Privt... | 640 | 84 | Mary Parsons | |
| 1339. | The heir of Nathan Person, Pt... | 640 | 84 | " | |
| 1340. | The heir of Roger Person, Privt.. | 640 | 84 | " | |
| 1341. | Thomas Dison, Privt.......... | 640 | 84 | Col. Margett | |
| 1342. | William Knox, Heir of Allison Knox, Privt............... | 640 | 84 | " | |
| 1343. | The Heir of Henry Darnald, Cpt. | 1,325 | 29 | W. Darnald | |
| 1344. | Peter Harrell, Sergt........... | 535 | 45 | " | |
| 1345. | Abraham Taylor, Privt........ | 274 | 36 | Jno. Patrick | |
| 1346. | James Peel, Heir of Daniel Peel, Privt................. | 640 | 84 | Maj. Briole | |
| 1347. | David Denny, Privt........... | 274 | 36 | I. G. | |
| 1348. | Malicha White, Privt.......... | 640 | 84 | Capt. Ferebee | |
| 1349. | Reubin Wilkinson, Lieut........ | 2,560 | 84 | | Self |
| 1350. | The Heir of Henry Alligood, Pt.. | 640 | 84 | Capt. Hargett | |
| 1351. | James Gilbert, dec'd. for the Heir, Privt................ | 640 | 84 | " | |
| 1352. | Ann Cox, Heir of Alexander Smith..................... | 640 | 84 | | |
| 1353. | Jacob Bledsoe, Heir of Aron Bledsoe, a Privt............. | 640 | 84 | Capt. Bletcher | |

| No. | To whom granted and rank | No. acres | Service in months | Location and to whom deeded and date of warrant. Within the limits of the lands allotted the officers and soldiers of the Continental Line, by Law, 1783, Oct. 14 | |
|---|---|---|---|---|---|
| 1354. | Peter Alexon, Privt. | 640 | 84 | John Price | |
| 1355. | Charles Ashe, Privt. | 640 | 84 | John Price | |
| 1356. | Michael Quinn, Capt. | 2,102 | 46 | Capt. Marget | |
| 1357. | Richard Hopkins, Privt. | 228 | 30 | D. Wilson | |
| 1358. | The Heir of Barnabas Burns, Pt. | 640 | 84 | John Price | |
| 1359. | The Heir of George Gardner and Lewis, Heir, Privt. | 640 | 84 | " | |
| 1360. | Thomas Eason and Joseph Eason, heir, Privt. | 640 | 84 | Col. John Armstrong | |
| 1361. | Thomas Smith, Privt. Infirm | 640 | 84 | Nov. 8 | Self |
| 1362. | The Heir of Peter Magee, died in service, Sergt. | 1,000 | 84 | Maj. McRee | |
| 1363. | The Heir of Morgan McFarlin, Privt. decsd. | 640 | 84 | " | |
| 1364. | The Heir of Daniel Sellars, Pt. | 640 | 84 | " | |
| 1365. | The Heir of Neil Clark, Privt. | 640 | 84 | " | |
| 1366. | The Heir of Archibald Craike, Privt. killed | 640 | 84 | " | |
| 1367. | The Heir of Dougal McKay, dec'd, Sergt. | 1,000 | 84 | " | |
| 1368. | The Heir of Thomas Essins, dec'd, Privt. | 640 | 84 | {Returned by Maj. Mcree to M. P. May '86 | |
| 1369. | The Heir of William Pierce, Pt. | 640 | 84 | Lt. Grimes | |
| 1370. | The Heir of William Grimes | 640 | 84 | " | |
| 1371. | John Moriss, Heir of James Morris, Privt. | 640 | 84 | Nov. 9 | S. Holliday |
| 1372. | John Morriss, Heir of Benjamin Morris, Privt. | 640 | 84 | " | |
| 1373. | John Harrell, Heir of Holland Harrell, Privt. | 640 | 84 | " | |
| 1374. | Wm. Whitfield, Heir of Jesse Whitfield | 640 | 84 | " | |
| 1375. | William Smith, Sergt. | 1,000 | 84 | Maj. McRee | |
| 1376. | John Smith, (Bladen) dec'd. Pt. | 640 | 84 | | |
| 1377. | Levi Dawson, Lt. Col. | 2,125 | 31 | | Self |
| 1378. | John Turner, Privt. | 274 | 36 | Capt. Jones | |
| 1379. | Thomas Smith, dec'd, Saml Reed Adkins, Sergt. | 465 | 38 | | Self |
| 1380. | The Heir of Stephen Gainey | 640 | 84 | | " |
| 1381. | Levy Weeks, Sergt. | 500 | 36 | | |
| 1382. | John Boyd, Sergt. | 476 | 40 | Maj. Harris | |
| 1383. | Daniel Tolar, Privt. | 640 | 84 | Capt. Coart | |
| 1384. | John Gothrop, Infirm, Privt. | 640 | 84 | Col. B. Sheppard | |
| 1385. | William Moore, wounded, Privt. | 640 | 84 | | Self |
| 1386. | Joseph Reddick, Heir of Isaac Reddick | 640 | 84 | | |
| 1387. | John Macon, Junr. for William Macon | 640 | 84 | Gen. Person | |
| 1388. | John Macon, Junr. for James Macon | 640 | 84 | " | |
| 1389. | Jacob Hawley, Junr. for Benjamin Hawley, Privt. | 640 | 84 | " | |
| 1390. | Jacob Burk's heir, Privt. | 640 | 84 | Maj. Hall | |
| 1391. | The Heir of Michael McGuire, Privt. | 640 | 84 | " | |
| 1392. | The Heir of John White, Privt. | 640 | 84 | " | |

| No. | To whom granted and rank | No. acres | Service in months | Location and to whom deeded and date of warrant. Within the limits of the lands allotted the officers and soldiers of the Continental Line, by Law, 1783, Oct. 14 |
|---|---|---|---|---|
| 1393. | The Heir of Silas McGuire, Pt... | 640 | 84 | Maj. Hall |
| 1394. | Michael McKeel, Privt......... | 342 | 45 | " |
| 1395. | Solomon Williams, Privt....... | 640 | 84 | Levi Weeks |
| 1396. | Benjamin Weeks, Privt........ | 640 | 84 | " |
| 1397. | John Conner, Privt........... | 274 | 36 | Self |
| 1398. | William Morgan, Privt........ | 274 | 36 | Capt. Bush |
| 1399. | Archibald Davis, Privt......... | 274 | 36 | " |
| 1400. | Richard Margan, Privt........ | 640 | 84 | " |
| 1401. | Dixon Marshall, Lieut......... | 2,560 | 84 | Maj. T. Dixon |
| 1402. | William York, Privt........... | 533 | 70 | {This warrant on return to be retained for Col. Wm. Terrel Lewis. |
| 1403. | John Clark, Privt............. | 226 | 30 | |
| 1404. | George Lott, Privt............ | 640 | 84 | |
| 1405. | Peter Jacobs, Privt............ | 640 | 84 | |
| 1406. | Isaac Hancock, Sergt.......... | 1,000 | 84 | |
| 1407. | Robert Obar, Privt............ | 457 | 60 | |
| 1408. | Daniel Obar, Privt............ | 457 | 60 | |
| 1409. | Jones Wynne, Privt........... | 457 | 60 | |
| 1410. | Goldman Harris, Privt......... | 228 | 30 | |
| 1411. | William Stother, Privt......... | 640 | 84 | Maj. T. Dixon |
| 1412. | Joel Robinson, Privt........... | 640 | 84 | |
| 1413. | Ezekiel Turner, Heir of Benjamin Turner, dec'd. Pt. ... | 640 | 84 | Col. Abram Jones |
| 1414. | Zachariah Williams, Heir of Stephen Emmery, Privt. dec'd. | 640 | 84 | |
| 1415. | Abel Edmunds, Privt.......... | 274 | 36 | |
| 1416. | Joseph Seaburn, Privt......... | 274 | 36 | |
| 1417. | The Heir of Samuel Estis, Privt.. | 640 | 84 | Maj. Donohoe |
| 1418. | The Heir of Elijah Olliver, Privt. | 640 | 84 | " |
| 1419. | The Heir of James Sanders, Pt... | 640 | 84 | " |
| 1420. | The Heir of James Earl, Privt... | 640 | 84 | " |
| 1421. | The Heir of Samuel Wilson, Pt. . | 640 | 84 | " |
| 1422. | John Morgan, Privt........... | 274 | 36 | " |
| 1423. | Rubin Roberts, Privt.......... | 228 | 30 | " |
| 1424. | The Heir of James Brown, Privt. | 640 | 84 | " |
| 1425. | The Heir of Henry Guttery, Pt.. | 640 | 84 | " |
| 1426. | Wiley Borough, Privt.......... | 457 | 60 | " |
| 1427. | John Abbitt, Sergt............ | 428 | 36 | " |
| 1428. | The Heir of George Hudson, Pt.. | 640 | 84 | " |
| 1429. | The Heir of Isum Carner, Privt.. | 640 | 84 | " |
| 1430. | Thomas Harris, Maj. allowed by the Gen. assembly | 1,000 | | {Maj. Willson (Mecklenburg) |
| 1431. | "      "      " | 1,000 | | " |
| 1432. | "      "      " | 1,000 | | " |
| 1433. | "      "      " | 1,000 | | " |
| 1434. | Robert Whitlock, Infirm. Privt.. | 640 | 84 | Maj. Donohoe |
| 1435. | James Jones, Privt............ | 274 | 36 | Lieut. Hargett |
| 1436. | Job Branch, Privt............. | 350 | 46 | Capt. Nath'l. Williams |
| 1437. | Elisha Modlin, Privt.......... | 640 | 84 | " |
| 1438. | Zebod Modlin, Privt........... | 640 | 84 | " |
| 1439. | Thomas Modlin, Privt......... | 365 | 48 | " |
| 1440. | Henry Harris, Privt........... | 274 | 36 | |
| 1441. | John Howell, Heir of Frederick Howell, Privt............... | 640 | 84 | Maj. Howell |
| 1442. | John Howell, Privt........... | 640 | 84 | " |

| No. | To whom granted and rank | No. acres | Service in months | Location and to whom deeded and date of warrant. Within the limits of the lands allotted the officers and soldiers of the Continental Line, by Law, 1783, Oct. 14 |
|---|---|---|---|---|
| 1443. | Benj. Hill or Mills, Capt........ | 1,142 | 25 | Apd. a Duplicate Jan. 11th 1792, Maj. Howell Col. A Thomas |
| 1444. | William Waters, Lieut......... | 2,011 | 66 | |
| 1445. | James Moore, Privt........... | 274 | 36 | Lut. S. Truluck |
| 1446. | Sutton Truluck, Privt......... | 274 | 36 | Sutton Truluck |
| 1447. | Wm. Noble, Sergt............. | 500 | 42 | Wm. Noble |
| 1448. | Samuel Wiggins, Heir of Thomas Wiggins, Privt...... | 640 | 84 | Col. McCafferty |
| 1449. | Bedford Garris, Privt.......... | 274 | 36 | " |
| 1450. | Joseph Cossey, Privt.......... | 640 | 84 | " |
| 1451. | The Heir of John Stepp, dec'd, Privt.............. | 640 | 84 | Gen. Person |
| 1452. | The Heir of Nicholas Rogester, Corpl. dec'd............... | 1,000 | 84 | " |
| 1453. | The Heir of Patrick Robinson, Privt............ | 640 | 84 | Col. James Armstrong |
| 1454. | Giles Nelson, Privt........... | 274 | 36 | " |
| 1455. | The Heir of Edward Hatchett, Privt. dec'd................ | 640 | 84 | L. Curtis Ivey |
| 1456. | Samuel Williams, Privt........ | 640 | 84 | " |
| 1457. | William Laighton, Privt........ | 274 | 36 | " |
| 1458. | John Hill, Privt.............. | 365 | 48 | Self |
| 1459. | Samuel Middleton, Sergt....... | 1,000 | 84 | Capt. Gillespie |
| 1460. | George Downing, Privt........ | 274 | 36 | John Price |
| 1461. | James Brown, Privt........... | 274 | 36 | Col. Hargett |
| 1462. | John Webb, Privt............. | 640 | 84 | Self |
| 1463. | Samuel Daves, Drummer...... | 357 | 30 | Col. Lytle |
| 1464. | Chamberlain Hudson, Privt..... | 640 | 84 | " |
| 1465. | Zachariah Cates, Privt........ | 640 | 84 | " |
| 1466. | Thomas Estridge, Privt........ | 640 | 84 | " |
| 1467. | James Brannon, Corpl......... | 1,000 | 84 | " |
| 1468. | John Black, Privt............. | 640 | 84 | " |
| 1469. | Samuel Churchell, Non Com. Officer.................... | 1,000 | 84 | " |
| 1470. | Joseph Smith, Privt........... | 640 | 84 | " |
| 1471. | Wiott Warwick, Privt......... | 640 | 84 | Wm. Faircloth |
| 1472. | Thomas Johnston, Privt....... | 274 | 36 | " |
| 1473. | John Rows (or Ross), Privt..... | 274 | 36 | " |
| 1474. | Shadrach Warwick, Privt...... | 640 | 84 | " |
| 1475. | George Davis, Privt........... | 228 | 30 | |
| 1476. | John Morris, Heir of Benj. Morris, Privt.............. | 640 | 84 | Apt. before Saml. Mallery |
| 1477. | John Morris, Heir of James Morris, Privt.............. | 640 | 84 | |
| 1478. | William Whitfield, Heir of Jesse Whitfield............. | 640 | 84 | " |
| 1479. | John Harrell, Heir of Holland Harrell................... | 640 | 84 | " |
| 1480. | Moses Acock, dec'd. Privt...... | 640 | 84 | Robt. Acock |
| 1481. | William Acock, dec'd. Privt.... | 640 | 84 | " |
| 1482. | Robert Acock, dec'd, Privt..... | 228 | 30 | " |
| 1483. | Josiah Stafford, Privt.......... | 274 | 36 | Dec. 20,'84 Winston Chance |
| 1484. | Elijah Cotton, Privt........... | 274 | 36 | " " |
| 1485. | Amos Lewis, Privt............ | 228 | 30 | Self |

| No. | To whom granted and rank | No. acres | Service in months | date of warrant | Location and to whom deeded and date of warrant. Within the limits of the lands allotted the officers and soldiers of the Continental Line, by Law, 1783, Oct. 14 |
|---|---|---|---|---|---|
| 1486. | William Jones, Heir of John Jones, Privt................ | 640 | 84 | | Capt. A. Herring |
| 1487. | William Jones, Privt........... | 411 | 54 | | " |
| 1488. | James Roberts, Privt.......... | 274 | 36 | | Philip Shackler |
| 1489. | Benjamin Atkins, Privt......... | 308 | 42 | | " |
| 1490. | The Heir of Brantley Davis..... | 640 | 84 | | Capt. T. Dixon |
| 1491. | The Heirs of Ephraim Grant, Pt. | 640 | 84 | Jan. 20, '85 | " |
| 1492. | The Heirs of Joseph Parker, Sgt. | 1,000 | 84 | | " |
| 1493. | The Heirs of James Boon, Privt. | 640 | 84 | | " |
| 1494. | The Heir of John Mewshaw " | 640 | 84 | | " |
| 1495. | The Heir of John Chester, " | 640 | 84 | | " |
| 1496. | The Heir of Nehemiah Bennit " | 640 | 84 | | " |
| 1497. | The Heir of John Grant, " | 640 | 84 | | " |
| 1498. | The Heir of Jeremiah Jackson " | 640 | 84 | | " |
| 1499. | The Heir of Richard Corbert, " | 640 | 84 | | " |
| 1500. | The Heirs of Abraham Page, " | 640 | 84 | | " |
| 1501. | The Heirs of Cyperan West, " | 640 | 84 | | Capt. T. Brown |
| 1502. | The Heirs of Aaron Newshan, " | 640 | 84 | | " |
| 1503. | The Heirs of Caleb Holley, " | 640 | 84 | | " |
| 1504. | The Heirs of John Newall, " | 640 | 84 | | " |
| 1505. | The Heirs of James Blackwell, " | 640 | 84 | | " |
| 1506. | The Heirs of John Bradshaw, " | 640 | 84 | | " |
| 1507. | The Heirs of William Bennett, " | 640 | 84 | | " |
| 1508. | The Heirs of Stephen Pettis, " | 640 | 84 | | " |
| 1509. | The Heirs of Frederick Harper, " | 640 | 84 | | " |
| 1510. | The Heirs of Matthew Pollard, " | 640 | 84 | | " |
| 1511. | The Heirs of Job Sanders, " | 640 | 84 | | Capt. Dixon |
| 1512. | The Heirs of Daniel Elmore, " | 640 | 84 | | " |
| 1513. | The Heirs of John Maning, " | 640 | 84 | | " |
| 1514. | The Heirs of Meredith Berk, " | 640 | 84 | | " |
| 1515. | The Heirs of Benjamin Brewington, Privt........... | 640 | 84 | | " |
| 1516. | The Heirs of Lewis Doughtry,Pt. | 640 | 84 | | " |
| 1517. | The Heirs of James King, Capt. dec'd................ | 3,840 | 84 | | " |
| 1518. | The Heirs of James Vaughn, Pt.. | 640 | 84 | | " |
| 1519. | The Heirs of William Southerland, Privt.......... | 640 | 84 | | " |
| 1520. | George Southerland, Privt...... | 274 | 36 | | " |
| 1521. | Vinson Roberts, Pri........... | 308 | 42 | Jan. 20, '85 | |
| 1522. | The heirs of Elisha Langston, Pt. | 640 | 84 | | Capt. Til. Dixon |
| 1523. | The heirs of James Perrymore, Dcsd. Privt................ | 640 | 84 | | " |
| 1524. | Ezekiah Dennis, a Privt........ | 640 | 84 | | Samuel Hollady |
| 1525. | John Story, Privt............. | 640 | 84 | | " |
| 1526. | Daniel Milton, Privt........... | 640 | 84 | | " |
| 1527. | Richard Bradley, Privt........ | 274 | 36 | | Capt. T. Dixon |
| 1528. | The heirs of Edward Everton, Privt. dcsd................ | 640 | 84 | Feb. 2, '85 | Jo. Grimes |
| 1529. | John Johnston, Privt. died...... | 640 | 84 | | W. Nichols |
| 1530. | Hugh Stevenson, Privt.......... | 365 | 48 | | Col. J. Sheppard |
| 1531. | Esau Bass, Privt.............. | 274 | 36 | Feb. 3, '84 | " |
| 1532. | William Proctor, Privt........ | 228 | 30 | | " |
| 1533. | Silas Weeks' heir,............. | 640 | 84 | | A. Johnson |
| 1534. | The heir of James Allen ........ | 640 | 84 | | Philip Shackler |
| 1535. | Willoughby Prescot, Privt...... | 365 | 48 | | " |

| No. | To whom granted and rank | No. acres | Service in months | Location and to whom deeded and date of warrant. Wi hin the limits of the lands allotted the officers and soldiers of the Continental Line, by Law, 1783, Oct. 14 | |
|---|---|---|---|---|---|
| 1536. | Medaris Abraham, Privt....... | 274 | 36 | Philip Shackler | |
| 1537. | Benjamin Collins, Privt........ | 289 | 34 | " | |
| 1538. | Nathan Ewell, Privt........... | 228 | 30 | " | |
| 1539. | Spencer Rayfield, Privt........ | 228 | 30 | Wm. Forrest | |
| 1540. | Thomas Harris, Privt.......... | 213 | 28 | .............. | |
| 1541. | Micajah Pettyway, Privt....... | 228 | 30 | Wm. Forest | |
| 1542. | George Duncan, Privt.......... | 228 | 30 | T. Parsons | |
| 1543. | George Williams, Privt......... | 228 | 30 | " | |
| 1544. | James Broadstreet, Privt....... | 640 | 84 | Col. B. Sheppard | |
| 1545. | John Darden, Privt............ | 640 | 84 | " | |
| 1546. | William Cron, Privt........... | 640 | 84 | " | |
| 1547. | Robert Newby, Privt........... | 640 | 84 | " | |
| 1548. | Elisha Rogers, Privt........... | 640 | 84 | " | |
| 1549. | Thomas Cox, Privt............ | 640 | 84 | " | |
| 1550. | Nicholas Parrish, Privt........ | 640 | 84 | " | |
| 1551. | Michael Rogers, Privt......... | 274 | 36 | John Price | |
| 1552. | Henry Parrish, Privt.......... | 274 | 36 | " | |
| 1553. | Benjamin Howard, Privt....... | 274 | 36 | " | |
| 1554. | William Wadsworth, Privt...... | 640 | 84 | " | |
| 1555. | The heirs of John Anderson, Pt.. | 640 | 84 | " | |
| 1556. | Thomas Price, Privt........... | 274 | 36 | Wm. Faircloth | |
| 1557. | John Simmons, Privt.......... | 274 | 36 | " | |
| 1558. | Samuel Cooper, Privt.......... | 274 | 36 | " | |
| 1559. | Thomas Winters, Privt......... | 640 | 84 | " | |
| 1560. | Kedar Ballard, Capt........... | 3,840 | 84 | Col. Murfree | |
| 1561. | Jesse Coice, Privt............. | 228 | 30 | Feb. 22, '85 | " |
| 1562. | The heirs of Benjamin Conner,Pt. | 640 | 84 | " | |
| 1563. | William Witherington, Privt..... | 228 | 36 | " | |
| 1564. | Jonathan Hopkins, Corpl........ | 1,000 | 84 | | Self |
| 1565. | Thomas Geddy, Privt.......... | 640 | 84 | Mar. 7, '85 | Wm. Fort |
| 1566. | Samuel Pike, Capt. his heir,..... | 3,840 | 84 | Capt. Evans | |
| 1567. | The heir of Hardy Hodges, Fifer | 1,000 | 84 | Joshua Hodges | |
| 1568. | Francis Harrison, heir of James Harrison, Privt....... | 640 | 84 | J. Glasgow | |
| 1569. | Cornelius Weeks, Sergt........ | 429 | 36 | Capt. Evans | |
| 1570. | Joel Bernent, or (Bermet) Sergt.. | 357 | 30 | " | |
| 1571. | George Gary, Privt............ | 228 | 30 | Mar. 8 | " |
| 1572. | Joseph Gary, Privt............ | 228 | 30 | " | |
| 1573. | John Perry, Privt............. | 228 | 30 | Capt. Evans | |
| 1574. | Hezekiah Barnes, Corpl........ | 357 | 30 | " | |
| 1575. | Abel McPherson, Sergt........ | 1,000 | 84 | " | |
| 1576. | James Charlescraft, Privt...... | 228 | 30 | " | |
| 1577. | Isaac Hopkins, Privt........... | 274 | 36 | " | |
| 1578. | Samuel Styron, Privt.......... | 640 | 84 | " | |
| 1579. | Arthur Colgrave, Lt........... | 2,246 | 78 | " | |
| 1580. | The heir of John Abuck, dcsd.... | 640 | 84 | .............. | |
| 1581. | Amos Baker's heirs........... | 640 | 84 | Jno. Bonde | |
| 1582. | The heirs of Britain Branton,dcsd. | 640 | 84 | " | |
| 1583. | The heirs of Elias Ball, dcsd..... | 640 | 84 | " | |
| 1584. | The heirs of Robert Bailey, dcsd. | 640 | 84 | " | |
| 1585. | The heirs of Ephraim Tann,dcsd. | 640 | 84 | " | |
| 1586. | The heirs of Joseph Tann....... | 640 | 84 | " | |
| 1587. | The heirs of William Gay....... | 640 | 84 | " | |
| 1588. | The heirs of Richard Harris..... | 640 | 84 | " | |
| 1589. | The heirs of Jeremiah Thomas .. | 640 | 84 | " | |
| 1590. | The heirs of Josiah Todd....... | 640 | 84 | " | |

| No. | To whom granted and rank | No. acres | Service in months | Location and to whom deeded and date of warrant. Within the limits of the lands allotted the officers and soldiers of the Continental Line, by Law, 1783, Oct. 14 | |
|---|---|---|---|---|---|
| 1591. | The heirs of Peter Jones, dcsd. . . | 640 | 84 | | Jno. Bonde |
| 1592. | The heirs of Edmund Sherwood . | 640 | 84 | | " |
| 1593. | The heirs of Shadrick Underwood | 640 | 84 | | " |
| 1594. | James Wyatt, Privt. . . . . . . . . . . . | 640 | 84 | | |
| 1595. | The heirs of John Matthews,dcsd. | 640 | 84 | | Capt. Gerrard |
| 1596. | The heirs of Abraham Clark. . . . . | 640 | 84 | | Self |
| 1597. | The heirs of John Black. . . . . . . . | 640 | 84 | Mar. 12 | Jas. Stewart |
| 1598. | John Bartholomew, Privt. . . . . . . | 228 | 30 | " | J. Marshall |
| 1599. | Joel Gunter, Privt. . . . . . . . . . . . . | 274 | 36 | " | " |
| 1600. | Daniel Carrell, Privt. . . . . . . . . . . | 228 | 30 | " | " |
| 1601. | William Dunkin, Privt. . . . . . . . . | 228 | 30 | " | " |
| 1602. | John Glover, Privt. . . . . . . . . . . . | 228 | 30 | " | " |
| 1603. | John Harris, Privt. . . . . . . . . . . . . | 228 | 30 | " | " |
| 1604. | The heirs of Harvel Carrell,    " | 640 | 84 | " | " |
| 1605. | The heirs of Moses Vinson,    " | 640 | 84 | " | " |
| 1606. | The heirs of Zachus Shaw,    " | 640 | 84 | " | " |
| 1607. | The heirs of James Bevers,    " | 640 | 84 | " | " |
| 1608. | The heirs of William Bevers,    " | 640 | 84 | " | " |
| 1609. | The heirs of John Hutson,    " | 640 | 84 | " | " |
| 1610. | The heirs of Francis West,    " | 640 | 84 | " | " |
| 1611. | The heirs of Arthur Rogers,    " | 640 | 84 | " | " |
| 1612. | The heirs of David Hatcher,    " | 640 | 84 | " | " |
| 1613. | The heirs of Charles Floyd,    " | 640 | 84 | " | " |
| 1614. | The heirs of Richard Mathews, " | 640 | 84 | " | " |
| 1615. | The heirs of Newton Striplin, " | 640 | 84 | " | " |
| 1616. | The heirs of Thomas Kent,    " | 640 | 84 | " | " |
| 1617. | The heirs of George White,    " | 640 | 84 | " | " |
| 1618. | The heirs of David Hunt,    " | 640 | 84 | " | " |
| 1619. | The heirs of William Denson, " | 640 | 84 | " | " |
| 1620. | The heirs of Abraham Primm,Sgt. | 1,000 | 84 | " | " |
| 1621. | The heirs of John Ajaton, Sergt.. | 1,000 | 84 | Mch. 12,'85 | Isc. Marshall |
| 1622. | The heirs of Nathan Hall, Drm.. | 1,000 | 84 | " | " |
| 1623. | James Townen, Privt. . . . . . . . . . | 640 | 84 | " | " |
| 1624. | The Heirs of William Bryant,Pt. | 640 | 84 | " | " |
| 1625. | The Heirs of Arthur Boyce, Sgt.. | 1,000 | 84 | " | Philip Miller |
| 1626. | Frederick Moore, Privt. . . . . . . . | 274 | 36 | " | Wm. Moore |
| 1627. | James Bundy, Privt. . . . . . . . . . . | 274 | 36 | Mch. 20,'85 | Jno. Sheppard |
| 1628. | James Williams, Privt. . . . . . . . . | 274 | 36 | " | Ben. Sheppard |
| 1629. | Francis Dugan, Privt. . . . . . . . . . | 274 | 36 | " | " |
| 1630. | Elisha Modlin, Privt. . . . . . . . . . | 274 | 36 | " | " |
| 1631. | Zebulon Pratt, Privt. . . . . . . . . . | 274 | 36 | Mch. 22,'85 | Jno. Price |
| 1632. | Benjamin Smith, (Pasquo.) Pt... | 274 | 36 | " | " |
| 1633. | Joseph Williams, Privt. . . . . . . . | 274 | 36 | " | " |
| 1634. | Woode Jones, Privt. . . . . . . . . . . | 274 | 36 | " | " |
| 1635. | Michael Brannor, Privt. . . . . . . . | 274 | 36 | " | " |
| 1636. | Peter Simmons, Privt. . . . . . . . . | 640 | 84 | " | " |
| 1637. | Thomas Pettyjohn, Privt. . . . . . . | 640 | 84 | " | " |
| 1638. | Enoch King, Privt. . . . . . . . . . . . | 640 | 84 | " | " |
| 1639. | Joshua Cheason, Privt. . . . . . . . . | 274 | 36 | " | " |
| 1640. | James Snell, Privt. . . . . . . . . . . . . | 274 | 36 | " | " |
| 1641. | Jonathan Lewis, Privt. . . . . . . . . | 274 | 36 | " | Maj. Jno. Allen |
| 1642. | Jahlul Smith, Lieut. . . . . . . . . . . . | 914 | 30 | Mch. 30,'85 | Thos. Foreman |
| 1643. | Thomas Templeton, Sergt. . . . . . | 428 | 36 | " | J. Malloy |
| 1644. | The heirs of William Garret, Pt.. | 640 | 84 | " | " |
| 1645. | John Frazier, Privt. . . . . . . . . . . | 640 | 84 | " | Maj. Dixon |
| 1646. | John Kilpatrick, Privt. . . . . . . . . | 298 | 30 | " | Dr. McNeese |

| No. | To whom granted and rank | No. acres | Service in months | Location and to whom deeded and date of warrant. Within the limits of the lands allotted the officers and soldiers of the Continental Line, by Law, 1783, Oct. 14 | |
|---|---|---|---|---|---|
| 1647. | Thomas Hartley, heir of John Hartley, Privt.............. | 640 | 84 | Mch. 30,'85 | Dr. McNeese |
| 1648. | Israel Cullum, Privt........... | 640 | 84 | " | ⎰Sent to Pitt Court by ⎱J. G. |
| 1649. | The heirs of Michael Atkinson,.. | 640 | 84 | " | Maj. Dixon |
| 1650. | The heirs of Trueell Hicks, Sgt. . | 1,000 | 84 | " | " |
| 1651. | The heirs of Spencer Breedlove,Pt | 640 | 85 | " | " |
| 1652. | Lewis Ralph, Privt............. | 228 | 30 | Apr. 22 | " |
| 1653. | The heirs of James Rollen, Privt. | 640 | 84 | " | " |
| 1654. | Robert Warwick, Privt........ | 228 | 30 | " | " |
| 1655. | William Hayse, Sergt.......... | 1,000 | 84 | " | " |
| 1656. | Peter Harriss, Drummer........ | 1,000 | 84 | " | " |
| 1657. | Michael Obarr, Privt........... | 640 | 84 | " | " |
| 1658. | Hardy Peterson, Privt.......... | 640 | 84 | " | " |
| 1659. | Alanson Simmons, Sergt....... | 1,000 | 84 | " | " |
| 1660. | Mardecai Holdman, Privt...... | 640 | 84 | " | " |
| 1661. | John Hedspeth, Privt.......... | 640 | 84 | " | " |
| 1662. | William Spoolman, Sergt....... | 1,000 | 84 | " | " |
| 1663. | Israel McCubbins, Privt....... | 640 | 84 | " | " |
| 1664. | Henry Cole, Drummer......... | 1,000 | 84 | " | " |
| 1665. | Edward Butler, Sergt.......... | 1,000 | 84 | " | " |
| 1666. | Joseph Williford, Privt......... | 640 | 84 | " | " |
| 1667. | Joel Borough, Sergt........... | 1,000 | 84 | " | " |
| 1668. | John Beaver, Sergt............ | 1,000 | 84 | " | " |
| 1669. | Peter Goodwin, Privt.......... | 640 | 84 | " | " |
| 1670. | John Cash, Privt.............. | 640 | 84 | " | " |
| 1671. | Benjamin Lyles, Privt.......... | 640 | 84 | " | " |
| 1672. | Henry Rollen, Sergt........... | 1,000 | 84 | " | " |
| 1673. | Daniel Jacobs, Sergt........... | 1,000 | 84 | " | " |
| 1674. | David Rose, Sergt............. | 1,000 | 84 | " | " |
| 1675. | Ezekiel Riely, Sergt........... | 428 | 36 | " | " |
| 1676. | John Ward, Fifer.............. | 1,000 | 84 | " | " |
| 1677. | Moses Weaver, Privt.......... | 274 | 36 | " | " |
| 1678. | John Dodson, Privt........... | 274 | 36 | " | " |
| 1679. | Jacob Hicks, Privt............ | 228 | 30 | Apr. 22 | Maj. Dixon |
| 1680. | Edmund Wright, Privt......... | 228 | 30 | " | " |
| 1681. | The heirs of John Dukes, Privt.. | 640 | 84 | " | " |
| 1682. | The heirs of Jacob Bickey, Privt. | 640 | 84 | | |
| 1683. | The heirs of Drury Snider....... | 640 | 84 | | |
| 1684. | The heirs of William Davis..... | 640 | 84 | | |
| 1685. | The heirs of Jacob Gwinn....... | 640 | 84 | | |
| 1686. | The heirs of John Stokes, Privt.. | 640 | 84 | | |
| 1687. | William Hopper, Privt......... | 228 | 30 | | |
| 1688. | Isaac Hill, Privt.............. | 228 | 30 | | |
| 1689. | Jennings Brown, Privt......... | 228 | 30 | | |
| 1690. | Henry Holley, Privt........... | 228 | 30 | | |
| 1691. | Fuller Gibson, Privt........... | 228 | 30 | | |
| 1692. | Simon Ford, Privt............. | 228 | 30 | | |
| 1693. | Simeon Bates, Privt........... | 228 | 30 | | |
| 1694. | George Beck, Sergt, for his heirs. | 1,000 | 84 | " | " |
| 1695. | Jacob Burton, Privt........... | 228 | 30 | | |
| 1696. | Andrew Burton, Privt......... | 228 | 30 | | |
| 1697. | David Carter, Privt........... | 640 | 84 | | |
| 1698. | William Clerk, Sergt........... | 1,000 | 84 | | |
| 1699. | Daniel Campbell, Privt........ | 640 | 84 | | |

| No. | To whom granted and rank | No. acres | Service in months | Location and to whom deeded and date of warrant. Within the limits of the lands allotted the officers and soldiers of the Continental Line, by Law, 1783, Oct. 14 | |
|---|---|---|---|---|---|
| 1700. | The heirs of Christopher Conner, Privt............. | 640 | 84 | | |
| 1701. | The heirs of John Corbett, Privt. | 640 | 84 | | |
| 1702. | Thomas Curtis, Privt.......... | 274 | 36 | | |
| 1703. | The heirs of Absalom Clifton, Pt. | 640 | 84 | | |
| 1704. | The heirs of Archibald Ray, Pt. . | 640 | 84 | | |
| 1705. | Joseph Davis, Privt........... | 320 | 42 | | |
| 1706. | The heirs of William Demmitt,Pt. | 640 | 84 | | |
| 1707. | The heirs of Thomas Flemming, Privt.................... | 640 | 84 | | |
| 1708. | The heirs of Anthony Godfrey, Corpl...................... | 1,000 | 84 | | |
| 1709. | The heirs of Daniel Gale, Corpl.. | 1,000 | 84 | | |
| 1710. | The heirs of Howell Warrod, Sgt. | 1,000 | 84 | | |
| 1711. | Sherwood H. Harris, Privt...... | 228 | 30 | | |
| 1712. | The heirs of John Harmon, Pt... | 640 | 84 | | |
| 1713. | Phillip Haines, Pri. wounded in service................. | 640 | 84 | | |
| 1714. | The heirs of John Lamb, Privt... | 640 | 84 | | |
| 1715. | The heirs of Dugald McCoy, Pt.. | 640 | 84 | | |
| 1716. | The heirs of Hugh McKincy, Pt. | 640 | 84 | | |
| 1717. | The heirs of Alexander McCloud, Privt............. | 640 | 84 | | |
| 1718. | The heirs of Hugh McCann, Pt.. | 640 | 84 | | |
| 1719. | The heirs of Alexander McClouskin, Privt.......... | 640 | 84 | | |
| 1720. | The heirs of William Myers, Pt.. | 640 | 84 | | |
| 1721. | The heirs of Joseph McCulloch, Privt..................... | 640 | 84 | | |
| 1722. | Abraham Mitchell, Privt....... | 228 | 30 | | |
| 1723. | The heirs of Enoch Pasmore, Pt. | 640 | 84 | | |
| 1724. | The heirs of Beverley Perkison, Privt............. | 640 | 84 | | |
| 1725. | Adams Perkins, Privt.......... | 274 | 36 | | |
| 1726. | The heirs of David Rison, Privt.. | 640 | 84 | | |
| 1727. | The heirs of William Rochester, Privt............. | 640 | 84 | | |
| 1728. | The heirs of John Riley, Privt... | 640 | 84 | | |
| 1729. | James Rainey, Privt........... | 320 | 42 | | |
| 1730. | Jesse Robins, Privt............ | 274 | 36 | | |
| 1731. | John Reaves, Privt............ | 228 | 30 | | |
| 1732. | Bernard Tatum, Privt......... | 228 | 30 | | |
| 1733. | The heirs of William Weaver, Pt. | 640 | 84 | | |
| 1734. | The heirs of Joseph Wood, Privt. | 640 | 84 | | |
| 1735. | William Wilkinson, Privt....... | 274 | 36 | | |
| 1736. | The heirs of James Gurley, Cpl.. | 1,000 | 84 | | |
| 1737. | The heirs of Daniel Stewart, Pt.. | 640 | 84 | | |
| 1738. | The heirs of John Saunders, Pt. . | 640 | 84 | | |
| 1739. | The heirs of John Scott, Privt. .. | 640 | 84 | | |
| 1740. | James Spence, Privt........... | 228 | 30 | | |
| 1741. | John Andrews, Privt........... | 640 | 84 | Apr. 22 | Is. Sum. Martin |
| 1742. | The heir of James Stallions, Pt. . | 640 | 84 | " | Col. Long |
| 1743. | Moses Bennett, Privt.......... | 304 | 40 | " | " |
| 1744. | The heir of John Morris, Privt... | 640 | 84 | " | " |
| 1745. | The heirs of John Betts, Privt... | 640 | 84 | Apr. 23 | Maj. Dixon |
| 1746. | The heirs of Jesse Beggett, Pt. .. | 640 | 84 | " | " |

| No. | To whom granted and rank | No. acres | Service in months | Location and to whom deeded and date of warrant. Within the limits of the lands allotted the officers and soldiers of the Continental Line, by Law, 1783, Oct. 14 | |
|---|---|---|---|---|---|
| 1747. | The heirs of Benjamin Brittle, Pt. | 640 | 84 | Apr. 23 | Maj. Dixon |
| 1748. | The heirs of John Balmer, Privt. | 640 | 84 | " | " |
| 1749. | The heirs of James Ballard, Pt... | 640 | 84 | " | " |
| 1750. | The heirs of Hillery Crab, Privt.. | 640 | 84 | " | " |
| 1751. | The heirs of Ephraim Cotten, Pt. | 640 | 84 | " | " |
| 1752. | The heirs of John Crawford, Pt.. | 640 | 84 | " | " |
| 1753. | The heirs of William Carrell, Pt.. | 640 | 84 | " | " |
| 1754. | The heirs of Anthony Charter, Pt. | 640 | 84 | " | " |
| 1755. | The heir of James Goodson, Pt. . | 640 | 84 | " | " |
| 1756. | The heirs of John Gallaway, Sgt. | 1,000 | 84 | " | " |
| 1757. | The heirs of Thomas Greene, Pt. | 640 | 84 | " | " |
| 1758. | The heirs of Edmund Hammond, Privt............ | 640 | 84 | | |
| 1759. | The heirs of Hardy Hines, Privt. | 640 | 84 | " | " |
| 1760. | The heirs of Jacob Herring, Pt... | 640 | 84 | " | " |
| 1761. | The heirs of James Hagwood, Pt. | 640 | 84 | " | " |
| 1762. | The heirs of Holladay Hathcock, Privt............ | 640 | 84 | " | " |
| 1763. | The heirs of Isaac Hutson, Pt.... | 640 | 84 | " | " |
| 1764. | The heirs of Samuel Orr, Privt... | 640 | 84 | " | " |
| 1765. | The heirs of John Floyd, Privt... | 640 | 84 | " | " |
| 1766. | The heirs of Jacob Ferrell, Pt.... | 640 | 84 | " | " |
| 1767. | The heirs of George Johnston, Pt. | 640 | 84 | " | " |
| 1768. | The heirs of Hardy Johnston, Pt. | 640 | 84 | " | " |
| 1769. | The heirs of Samuel Jones, Pt. .. | 640 | 84 | " | " |
| 1770. | The heirs of Joshua Jones, Privt. | 640 | 84 | " | " |
| 1771. | The heirs of John Lewis, Privt... | 640 | 84 | " | " |
| 1772. | The heirs of Joshua Lewis, Pt.... | 640 | 84 | " | " |
| 1773. | The heirs of Mathew Murrell, Pt. | 640 | 84 | " | " |
| 1774. | The heirs of James Murry, Pt. .. | 640 | 84 | " | " |
| 1775. | The heirs of William Morton, Sgt. | 1,000 | 84 | " | " |
| 1776. | The heirs of John McCoy, Junr. Privt................ | 640 | 84 | " | " |
| 1777. | The heirs of Samuel Moore, Pt. . | 640 | 84 | " | " |
| 1778. | The heirs of John Morrison, Pt. . | 640 | 84 | " | " |
| 1779. | The heirs of William Phillips, Pt. | 640 | 84 | " | " |
| 1780. | The heirs of Nicholas Powell, Pt. | 640 | 84 | " | " |
| 1781. | The heirs of Francis Powell, Pt. . | 640 | 84 | " | " |
| 1782. | The heirs of Moses Powell, Pt. .. | 640 | 84 | " | " |
| 1783. | The heirs of Stephen Powell, Pt.. | 640 | 84 | " | " |
| 1784. | The heirs of Mark Philips, Pt.... | 640 | 84 | " | " |
| 1785. | The heirs of Benjamin Pollock,Pt. | 640 | 84 | " | " |
| 1786. | The heirs of Charles Smith, Pt... | 640 | 84 | " | " |
| 1787. | The heirs of Stephen Smith, Pt. . | 640 | 84 | " | " |
| 1788. | The heirs of Andrew Rowell, Pt.. | 640 | 84 | " | " |
| 1788. | The heirs of John Russell, Pt.... | 640 | 84 | " | " |
| 1789. | The heirs of James Wilkenson,Pt. | 640 | 84 | " | " |
| 1790. | The heirs of Larkin McDaniel.Pt. | 640 | 84 | Apr. 25 | For Gen. Person |
| 1791. | Giles Driver, Junr., Heir of Charles Driver, Privt. killed in service.................. | 640 | 84 | " | " |
| 1792. | Daniel Shaw, Lieut............ | 2,560 | 84 | Apr. 27 | Self |
| 1793. | The heirs of Philip Exum, Privt.. | 640 | 84 | May 4 | James Thomson |
| 1794. | The heirs of Henry Robinson, Pt. | 640 | 84 | " | " |
| 1795. | The heirs of John Mason, Privt.. | 640 | 84 | " | " |

| No. | To whom granted and rank | No. acres | Service in months | Location and to whom deeded and date of warrant. Within the limits of the lands allotted the officers and soldiers of the Continental Line, by Law, 1783, Oct. 14 | |
|---|---|---|---|---|---|
| 1796. | The heirs of William Beckenham, Privt............ | 640 | 84 | May 4 | James Thomson |
| 1798. | The heirs of Thomas Avery, Pt.. | 640 | 84 | " | " |
| 1799. | The heirs of John Worsley, Privt. | 640 | 84 | | |
| 1800. | The heirs of John Dixon, Privt. . | 640 | 84 | May 11,'85 | Phl. Shaekler |
| 1801. | The heirs of Henry Dixon, Privt. | 640 | 84 | " | " |
| 1802. | Josel Dixon, Privt............ | 274 | 36 | " | " |
| 1803. | The heirs of Sylvanus Weeks, Pt. | 640 | 84 | " | " |
| 1804. | Jonathan Keay, Privt.......... | 228 | 30 | " | " |
| 1805. | Theophelus Weeks, Privt....... | 274 | 36 | " | " |
| 1806. | The heirs of Isaac Bagley, Privt. | 640 | 84 | | |
| 1807. | The heirs of Arthur Tyner, Pt... | 640 | 84 | | |
| 1808. | The heirs of William Green Carpenter, a Privt. ye 2nd. and certify by Thos. Armstrong that there are two of the same. | 640 | 84 | " | Jno. Smith, Surcy or ry. |
| 1809. | Josiah Jackson, Privt.......... | 640 | 84 | " | " |
| 1810. | John Haynes, Privt............ | 228 | 30 | " | |
| 1811. | Richard Omery, heir of Owen Omery, Privt. d'cd in service.. | 640 | 84 | | " |
| 1812. | The heir of Joshua Davis....... | 640 | 84 | | |
| 1813. | The heirs of Ayers Gurley....... | 640 | 84 | June 13, '85 those gran tained | Thos Smith. ts on this side to be re- |
| 1814. | The heirs of James Robertson, son of Jno................... | 640 | 84 | " | " |
| 1815. | The heirs of Capt. Geo. Gray ... | 3,840 | 84 | " | " |
| 1816. | The heirs of William Halcom.... | 1,000 | 84 | " | " |
| 1817. | The heir of Isaac Shockley...... | 640 | 84 | " | " |
| 1818. | The heirs of Henry Mayo....... | 640 | 84 | " | " |
| 1819. | The heirs of William Wadkins... | 640 | 84 | " | " |
| 1820. | John Petty, Privt.............. | 228 | 30 | " | " |
| 1821. | Saml. Dougtey................ | 228 | 30 | " | " |
| 1822. | The heirs of Patrick Martin, Sgt. | 1,000 | 84 | " | " |
| 1823. | The heirs of William Porter..... | 640 | 84 | " | " |
| 1824. | The heirs of Joshua Porter...... | 640 | 84 | June 13, '83 | The 1st issue Thorton Yancey |
| 1826. | John Allen, heir of Thomas Allen, Lieut................ | 2,560 | 84 | | Capt. Craddock |
| 1827. | The heir of William Coventon, Subaltern................... | 2,560 | 84 | | Robt. Webb |
| 1828. | James Richards, Sergt......... | 357 | 30 | | C. H. Hill Frank |
| 1829. | The heir of Holder Hudgin...... | 640 | 84 | June 14 | Capt. Bond |
| 1830. | The heir of William Crawley.... | 640 | 84 | " | " |
| 1831. | The heir of Brittain Thomas.... | 640 | 84 | " | " |
| 1832. | The heir of Aaron Nucum....... | 640 | 84 | " | " |
| 1833. | The heir of Robert Fletcher..... | 640 | 84 | " | " |
| 1834. | The heirs of Charles Lewis...... | 640 | 84 | | " |
| 1835. | The heirs of Joseph Bailey...... | 640 | 84 | " | " |
| 1836. | The heirs of Ephraim Surlock... | 640 | 84 | " | " |
| 1837. | The heirs of Ephraim Rains..... | 640 | 84 | " | John Bond |
| 1838. | The heirs of John Rains........ | 640 | 84 | " | " |
| 1839. | The heirs of William Tucker.... | 640 | 84 | " | " |
| 1840. | The heir of John Yancey........ | 640 | 84 | | |
| 1841, | Abner Everedge, Privt. Infirm... | | | | Col. Joel Lewis |
| 1842. | Williams Clark, Sergt.......... | 357 | 30 | | Col. John Armstrong |

| No. | To whom granted and rank | No. acres | Service in months | Location and to whom deeded and date of warrant. Within the limits of the lands allotted the officers and soldiers of the Continental Line, by Law, 1783, Oct. 14 | |
|---|---|---|---|---|---|
| 1843. | The heirs of Elijah Abbitt...... | 640 | 84 | | Col. John Armstrong |
| 1844. | The heirs of John Hambleton.... | 640 | 84 | June 15 | Col. Lytle |
| 1845. | William Minshaw, heir of Micajah Minshaw........... | 640 | 84 | " | " |
| 1846. | The heirs of Owen Smith....... | 640 | 84 | | " |
| 1847. | John Salter, Pri............... | 457 | 60 | | " |
| 1848. | Jonathan Low, Infirm......... | 640 | 84 | | |
| 1849. | The heir of James Wagoner..... | 640 | 84 | " | " |
| 1850. | The heirs of John Allen Tharpe.. | 640 | 84 | June 18 | Col. Lytle |
| 1851. | William Clark, heir of James Clark.................... | 640 | 84 | " | " |
| 1852. | The heirs of Thomas Paddin.... | 640 | 84 | " | " |
| 8153. | Anthony Godfrey, Jr. Privt...... | 274 | 36 | | |
| 1854. | Thomas Castles, Privt......... | 274 | 36 | | |
| 1855. | The heirs of Daniel Campbell, Jr. | 640 | 84 | | " |
| 1856. | William Clower, wounded....... | 640 | 84 | | " |
| 1857. | Jacob Boston, Pri.............. | 228 | 30 | | " |
| 1858. | Andrew Bostain, Pri........... | 228 | 30 | | " |
| 1859. | William Williams, Capt......... | 3,840 | 84 | | " |
| 1860. | William Goldsburry, wounded... | 640 | 84 | | |
| 1861. | Charles Murry, Sergt.......... | 357 | 30 | June 25, '85 | Self |
| 1862. | John Lawson, Pri.............. | 274 | 36 | " | Col John Sheppard |
| 1863. | John Revill, Pri............... | 274 | 36 | | " |
| 1864. | Thomas Carraway, Privt....... | 640 | 84 | | |
| 1865. | Gardner Jernagan, Privt....... | 274 | 36 | | " |
| 1866. | Abram Wise, Privt............. | 274 | 36 | | Wm. Tho. Love |
| 1867. | Isham Wood, Privt............. | 274 | 36 | | |
| 1898. | Asa Jinkins, Privt............. | 274 | 36 | " | |
| 1869. | The heir of George Bachelor, Pt. | 640 | 84 | " | |
| 1870. | James Tyson, Privt............ | 274 | 36 | | Maj. John Allen |
| 1870. | The heirs of Daniel Vinters...... | 640 | 84 | " | |
| 1871. | William Blake, Heir, Sergt...... | 1,000 | 84 | " | |
| 1872. | William Reads, heir, Privt....... | 640 | 84 | | Jno. Elliott |
| 1873. | John Elliot, Senr. Sergt......... | 642 | 54 | " | |
| 1874. | John Pendergrass, Privt. Infirm.. | 640 | 84 | " | |
| 1875. | The heirs of John Moye........ | 2,560 | 84 | | William Moye |
| 1876. | The heirs of William Walker, Sgt. | 1,000 | 84 | July 11 | Maj. Jno. Nelson |
| 1877. | George Hook, Pri.............. | 274 | 36 | " | " |
| 1878. | The heirs of David Freeman, Pt. | 640 | 84 | " | " |
| 1879. | The heirs of Hugh Patterson.... | 640 | 84 | " | " |
| 1880. | The heirs of David Sloan....... | 640 | 84 | | " |
| 1881. | The heirs of John Holbrooks.... | 640 | 84 | | " |
| 1882. | John Bantley, Privt........... | 640 | 84 | | " |
| 1884. | John Curry, Privt.............. | 640 | 84 | | " |
| 1885. | George Strader, Sergt.......... | 1,000 | 84 | | " |
| 1886. | William Deacon, Privt......... | 182 | 24 | | " |
| 1887. | The heirs of Dencey Marley, Pri. | | | | Jno. Colwell |
| 1888. | John Worseley, Pri............. | 640 | 84 | | Capt. Johnston |
| 1889. | Thomas Avery, Pri............. | 640 | 84 | | " |
| 1890. | The heirs of David Ward, Pri.... | 640 | 84 | July 15 | Sherrwood Barron |
| 1891. | The heir of Abram Dean, Pri.... | 640 | 84 | " | " |
| 1892. | The heir of Morris Moore, Pri... | 640 | 84 | " | " |
| 1893. | The heir of Overstreet Scott, Pri. | 640 | 84 | " | " |
| 1894. | The heir of Demcey Pace, Pri.... | 640 | 84 | " | " |
| 1895. | The heir of Hack Cee, ......... | 640 | 84 | " | " |
| 1896. | The heir of James Ward, Pri..... | 640 | 84 | " | " |

| No. | To whom granted and rank | No. acres | Service in months | Location and to whom deeded and date of warrant. Within the limits of the lands allotted the officers and soldiers of the Continental Line, by Law, 1783, Oct. 14 | |
|---|---|---|---|---|---|
| 1897. | The heir of Ethelred Ecum, Pri.. | 640 | 84 | July 15 | Sherrwood Barron |
| 1898. | The heir of Samuel Scutchins, Pt. | 640 | 84 | " | " |
| 1899. | The heir of Randal Hancock, Pt. | 640 | 84 | " | " |
| 1900. | The heir of Jacob Murrell, Pri... | 640 | 84 | " | " |
| 1901. | The heir of Morgan Lewis, Pri... | 640 | 84 | " | " |
| 1902. | The heir of David Gunn, Pri..... | 640 | 84 | " | " |
| 1903. | The heir of Benjamin Wilkins, Pt. | 640 | 84 | " | " |
| 1904. | The heir of John Phillops, Pri.... | 640 | 84 | " | " |
| 1905. | The heir of James Hair, Pri...... | 640 | 84 | " | " |
| 1906. | The heir of William Hair, Pri.... | 640 | 84 | " | " |
| 1907. | The heir of John Hair, Pri....... | 640 | 84 | " | " |
| 1908. | The heir of Jones Wilkins, Pri. .. | 640 | 84 | | |
| 1909. | The heir of Elisha Wilkins, Pri... | 640 | 84 | " | " |
| 1910. | The heirs of William Merritt, Pt. | 640 | 84 | " | " |
| 1911. | The heir of Francis Ward, Pri. .. | 640 | 84 | | |
| 1912. | The heir of James Daget, Pri.... | 640 | 84 | " | " |
| 1913. | The heir of John Pitnon, Pri..... | 640 | 84 | July 15 | Sherwood Barron |
| 1914. | The heirs of John Aberrian, Pri.. | 640 | 84 | " | " |
| 1915. | The heir of Nathan Harris, Pri. . | 640 | 84 | " | |
| 1916. | The heir of Frederick Jackson,Pt. | | | | |
| 1917. | The heirs of Stephen Joyner, Pri. decsd.................. | 640 | 84 | | ⎰To be retained I Macon ⎱d'd Geo. Jones for ⎰Thomas Smith |
| 1918. | The heirs of James Harrison, Pr. decsd................... | 640 | 84 | | " |
| 1920. | Jehu Stokely, Pri.............. | 228 | 30 | | " |
| 1920. | Simon Frazier, Pri............. | 274 | 36 | " | |
| 1921. | Richard Roper, Pri............ | 228 | 30 | | ⎰To be retained J. Macon ⎱Rec. Thomas Smith |
| 1922. | The heir of Shadrack Cobb, Pri.. | 640 | 84 | | Chas. Gerard |
| 1923. | William Thurston, Pri.......... | 228 | 30 | | William Stone, Bertie |
| 1924. | William Hoggard, Pri.......... | 228 | 30 | " | " |
| 1925. | David Nance, Lieut............ | 1,097 | 36 | | Capt. Grainger |
| 1926. | The heir of Solomon Thrift, Pri.. | 640 | 84 | July 27, '85 | ⎰James Lee in part for ⎱W. Dixon |
| 1927. | Abraham Thrift, Pri........... | 274 | 36 | " | |
| 1928. | James Jackson, Pri............ | 228 | 30 | " | |
| 1929. | The heir of Thomas Blansett, Corpl...................... | 1,000 | 84 | " | |
| 1930. | Frederick Blansett, Pri......... | 274 | 36 | " | |
| 1931. | John Ingram, Ser............. | 797 | 67 | " | |
| 1932. | Nehemiah Reaves, Pri......... | 228 | 30 | " | |
| 1933. | Berriman Redley, Pri.......... | 640 | 84 | " | ⎰James Lee and part for ⎱W. Dixon |
| 1934. | Jacob Wiggins, Ser............ | 1,000 | 84 | " | " |
| 1935. | Drury Burgess, Pri............ | 274 | 36 | " | " |
| 1936. | Micajah Fullington, Pri........ | 228 | 30 | " | " |
| 1937. | Jeremiah McLain, Pri.......... | 640 | 84 | " | " |
| 1938. | James Cunningham, Pri........ | 640 | 84 | " | " |
| 1939. | Burwell Jinkins, Pri........... | 274 | 36 | " | " |
| 1940. | Jones Morton, Pri............. | 274 | 36 | " | " |
| 1941. | Hezekiah Smith, Pri........... | 228 | 30 | | " |
| 1942. | Benjamin Grimes, Pri.......... | 274 | 36 | " | " |
| 1943. | William Jakins, Pri............ | 274 | 36 | " | " |
| 1944. | Benjamin Womwell, Pri........ | 228 | 30 | " | Self |
| 1945. | Jesse Rickeson, Pri............ | 320 | 42 | " | Aaron Lambert |

| No. | To whom granted and rank | No. acres | Service in months | Location and to whom deeded and date of warrant. Within the limits of the lands allotted the officers and soldiers of the Continental Line, by Law, 1783, Oct. 14 | |
|---|---|---|---|---|---|
| 1946. | The heir of Mellica Simmons, Pt. | 640 | 84 | July 27,'85 | Daniel Wilburn |
| 1947. | Charles Burk, Pri.............. | 640 | 84 | " | " |
| 1948. | James Amos, Pri............... | 640 | 84 | | " |
| 1949. | The heir of Ackiss Ellison....... | 640 | 84 | | " |
| 1950. | Joseph West, Ser.............. | 357 | 30 | " | " |
| 1951. | Phillip Hoehamer, Pri.......... | 640 | 84 | " | " |
| 1952. | The heirs of Thomas Thope, Pri. | 640 | 84 | Aug. 6 | Ja. Thompson |
| 1953. | Marmaduke Hedgpeth, Pri...... | 274 | 36 | " | " |
| 1954. | Thomas Phillips, heir of ———— Phillips.......... | 640 | 84 | | Sent to Tig Jones |
| 1955. | The heir of Wodington Abbitt, Pt. | 640 | 84 | Aug. 10 | Col. Lytle for Dugle, Jr. |
| 1956. | Harmon Duke, Non Commis Off. | 439 | 36 | | For " |
| 1957. | The heir of Abraham Low, Pri... | 640 | 84 | " | |
| 1958. | The heir of Peter Melene, Pri.... | 640 | 84 | " | |
| 1959. | William Arthur, wounded....... | 640 | 84 | " | |
| 1960. | Jacob Myers, wounded......... | 640 | 84 | " | |
| 1961. | The heirs of Richard Minshew,Pt. | 640 | 84 | " | |
| 1962. | The heir of Johnson Cruse, Pri... | 640 | 84 | | |
| 1963. | The heir of Henry Vickery, Pri.. | 640 | 84 | " | |
| 1964. | The heir of William Weatherspoon, Pri........... | 640 | 84 | " | |
| 1965. | The heir of John Hester, Pri..... | 640 | 84 | " | |
| 1966. | The heir of David Hester, Pri.... | 640 | 84 | " | |
| 1967. | Granville Davis, Pri.......... | 228 | 30 | " | { Gen. Person to Col. Lytle |
| 1968. | James Rich, wounded......... | 640 | 84 | " | |
| 1969. | Joseph McClammey, Lieut...... | 2,560 | 84 | " | { Maj. Montfloher for Gen. Ashe |
| 1970. | William Williams, Prvt........ | 640 | 84 | | Wm. Faircloth |
| 1971. | T. Howell, Prvt.............. | 640 | 84 | | |
| 1972. | Jacob Setgreaves, Prvt......... | 640 | 84 | | " |
| 1973. | John Setgreaves, Prvt......... | 640 | 84 | | " |
| 1974. | John Curlee, Prvt............. | 640 | 84 | | " |
| 1975. | Thomas Curlee, Prvt.......... | 640 | 84 | | " |
| 1976. | Zachariah Pridgeon, Prvt....... | 640 | 84 | | " |
| 1977. | Jesse Richards................ | 640 | 84 | | B. Sheppard |
| 1978. | Isaac Wheeler................. | 640 | 84 | | |
| 1979. | The Heirs of Robert Sherod..... | 640 | 84 | | Wm. Faircloth |
| 1980. | The heirs of Daniel Howell, Privt | 640 | 84 | | " |
| 1981. | The heirs of John Richards, Pt. . | 640 | 84 | | " |
| 1982. | The heirs of James Gardner, Pt.. | 640 | 84 | | " |
| 1983. | Isaac Dawson, Privt........... | 274 | 36 | " | " |
| 1984. | The heirs of Abraham Really, Pt. | 640 | 84 | " | " |
| 1985. | The heirs of Edward Hail, Privt. | 640 | 84 | | " |
| 1986. | The heirs of Joseph Skeeton, Pt. | 640 | 84 | | " |
| 1987. | The heirs of Francis Beeman, Pt. | 640 | 84 | | " |
| 1988. | The heirs of Arthur Smith, Privt. | 640 | 84 | | " |
| 1989. | The heirs of Arthur Branch, Pt. . | 640 | 84 | | " |
| 1990. | The heirs of Mark Bogue, Privt.. | 640 | 84 | | " |
| 1991. | The heirs of Benj. Blow, Privt... | 640 | 84 | | " |
| 1992. | The heirs of Joshua Fletcher, ... | 640 | 84 | | " |
| 1993. | The heirs of John Langston, Pt. . | 640 | 84 | | " |
| 1994. | The heirs of Joshua Boone, Pt... | 640 | 84 | | " |
| 1995. | The heirs of Thomas Bokin, P:.. | 640 | 84 | | " |
| 1996. | The heirs of Solomon Ward, Pt.. | 640 | 84 | | " |

| No. | To whom granted and rank | No. acres | Service in months | Location and to whom deeded and date of warrant. Within the limits of the lands allotted the officers and soldiers of the Continental Line, by Law, 1783, Oct. 14 | |
|---|---|---|---|---|---|
| 1997. | The heirs of Andrewson Nunnery, Privt............. | 640 | 84 | | Wm. Faircloth |
| 1998. | Runard Jones, Privt........... | 640 | 84 | | " |
| 1999. | Thomas Hursk, Privt.......... | 640 | 84 | | " |
| 2000. | John Hooks, Privt............. | 640 | 84 | | " |
| 2001. | Thomas Viney, Privt.......... | 640 | 84 | | " |
| 2002. | Thomas Finney............... | 274 | 36 | Aug. 10 | " |
| 2003. | Elisha Besall................. | 274 | 36 | | " |
| 2004. | The heirs of John Rhone, Privt.. | 640 | 84 | " | " |
| 2005. | The heirs of John Vinson, Pt. ... | 640 | 84 | | " |
| 2006. | The heirs of John Pool, Privt.... | 640 | 84 | | " |
| 2007. | The heirs of John Grandal, Pt. .. | 640 | 84 | | " |
| 2008. | The heirs of Thomas Dunn, Pt. . | 640 | 84 | | " |
| 2009. | The heirs of John Oxly Harrison.................. | 640 | 84 | | " |
| 2010. | The heirs of Francis Floyd...... | 640 | 84 | | " |
| 2011. | The heirs of Willis Wilson...... | 640 | 84 | | " |
| 2012. | The heirs of Peter Jett........ | 640 | 84 | | " |
| 2013. | The heirs of Elisha Flood....... | 640 | 84 | | " |
| 2014. | The heirs of Edmund Seymore... | 640 | 84 | | " |
| 2015. | The heirs of Jeremiah Jett, Pt... | 640 | 84 | | " |
| 2016. | The heirs of John Marcey, Pt.... | 640 | 84 | | " |
| 2017. | Sterling Deen, Privt........... | 640 | 84 | | Self |
| 2018. | William Meeks................ | 228 | 30 | | James Hearn |
| 2019. | The heirs of Joshua Proctor, Pt.. | 640 | 84 | | " |
| 2020. | Nathaniel Laurance, Lieut....... | 2,560 | 84 | | For Gen. Person |
| 2021. | Samuel Thomson, Piivt........ | 640 | 84 | | |
| 2022. | Hance Pettigrew, a non com. offcr, wounded.............. | 1,080 | 84 | | {For Capt. Nickols {Hilsbro. |
| 2023. | William Cox, Pri.............. | 228 | 30 | | Self |
| 2024. | The heirs of James Williams, Cor. | 1,000 | 84 | | {d'd, Wm. Cox, John {Ponds (?) |
| 2025. | The heirs of Joseph Williams, Pri. | 640 | 84 | | d'd,   " |
| 2026. | John Wood, Sergt.............. | 1,000 | 84 | | John Blount |
| 2027. | Josel Wall, (or Joel) Sergt...... | 1,000 | 84 | Aug. 26 | " |
| 2028. | Robert Ellis, Pri.............. | 274 | 36 | " | " |
| 2029. | The heirs of James Pritchard, | 640 | 84 | | |
| 2030. | The heirs of William Owens, Pri. decd.................. | 640 | 84 | | Capt. McNeese |
| 2031. | The heirs of George Faigan, decsd, Privt............... | 640 | 84 | Aug. 26 | " |
| 2032. | The heirs of George Swagot, decsd. Privt............... | 640 | 84 | " | " |
| 2033. | The heirs of Robert Hutchins, Pt. | 640 | 84 | " | " |
| 2034. | The heirs of John Stephenson, Pt. | 640 | 84 | " | " |
| 2035. | The heirs of John Cameron, Pt. . | 640 | 84 | " | " |
| 2036. | The heirs of Walter White, Pt... | 640 | 84 | " | " |
| 2037. | The heirs of Samuel Griffin, Pt. . | 640 | 84 | " | " |
| 2038. | The heirs of Nathaniel Nelson,Pt. | 640 | 84 | " | " |
| 2039. | The heirs of John Willoughby, Pt. | 640 | 84 | " | " |
| 2040. | The heirs of Solomon Wood, Pt.. | 640 | 84 | " | " |
| 2041. | The heirs of Christopher Wolf, " | 640 | 84 | " | " |
| 2042. | The heirs of Frederick Brown, " | 640 | 84 | " | " |
| 2043. | The heirs of John Hardy, Privt.. | 640 | 84 | " | " |
| 2044. | The heirs of Daniel Morehouse, " | 640 | 84 | " | " |

| No. | To whom granted and rank | No. acres | Service in months | Location and to whom deeded and date of warrant. Within the limits of the lands allotted the officers and soldiers of the Continental Line, by Law, 1783, Oct. 14 | |
|---|---|---|---|---|---|
| 2045. | The heirs of John Bartlie, Privt.. | 640 | 84 | Aug. 26 | Capt. McNeese |
| 2046. | The heirs of Moses Easten, Pt... | 640 | 84 | " | " |
| 2047. | The heirs of Jeremiah Brantley," | 640 | 84 | " | " |
| 2048. | The heirs of Christopher Tryal, " | 640 | 84 | " | " |
| 2051. | The heirs of John Brown, Privt.. | 640 | 84 | " | " |
| 2052. | The heirs of Peter Pratt, Privt... | 640 | 84 | " | " |
| 2050. | The heirs of John Ross, Privt.... | 640 | 84 | " | " |
| 2052. | The heirs of Lewis Grant. Privt.. | 640 | 84 | " | " |
| 2053. | The heirs of Lewis Pen, Privt.... | 640 | 84 | " | " |
| 2054. | The heirs of William Lawson, Pt. | 640 | 84 | " | " |
| 2055. | The heirs of Moses Simpson, Pt.. | 640 | 84 | " | " |
| 2056. | The heirs of William Orange, Pt. | 640 | 84 | " | " |
| 2057. | The heirs of Thomas Sims, Pt.... | 640 | 84 | " | " |
| 2058. | The heirs of John Randall, Pt. .. | 640 | 84 | " | " |
| 2059. | The heirs of Mathew Lawless, Pt. | 640 | 84 | " | " |
| 2060. | The heirs of John Wright, Privt.. | 640 | 84 | " | " |
| 2061. | The heirs of Thomas Warren, Pt. | 640 | 84 | " | " |
| 2062. | The heirs of John Nelson, Privt.. | 640 | 84 | " | " |
| 2063. | James Smithwick, Privt........ | 640 | 84 | " | John Price |
| 2064. | The heirs of William Malebey, " | 640 | 84 | " | |
| 2065. | The heirs of William Jinkins, Pt. | 640 | 84 | " | J. Glasgow |
| 2066. | Phillip Mason, drm. Maj........ | 1,000 | 84 | " | Saml. Holliday |
| 2067 | The heirs of Asabel Davenport, Pt. | 640 | 84 | " | " |
| 2068. | The heirs of John Davis, Sergt... | 1,000 | 84 | " | Thos. Davis |
| 2069. | The heirs of Stephen Harrison, Pt. | 640 | 84 | " | Saml. Holliday |
| 2070. | Ambrose Bull, heir of John Moran, Sergt............. | 1,000 | 84 | " | J. G. Blount |
| 2071. | Simon Alderson, Sergt......... | 1,000 | 84 | " | " |
| 2072. | James Clark, Corpl............ | 428 | 36 | " | " |
| 2073. | The heirs of William Kirkland | 640 | 84 | " | Capt. Lascitur |
| 2074. | The heirs of Hardy Keel, Privt. . | 640 | 84 | Sept. 1, '85 | " |
| 2075. | The heirs of John Wilson, Privt.. | 640 | 84 | | " |
| 2076. | The heirs of Thomas Wallace, Pt. | 640 | 84 | | " |
| 2077. | The heirs of John Wilburn, Pt... | 640 | 84 | | " |
| 2078. | The heirs of Isaac Bently, Pt.... | 640 | 84 | | " |
| 2079. | The heirs of Elias Baker, Privt... | 640 | 84 | | " |
| 2080. | The heirs of James Davis, Privt.. | 604 | 84 | | " |
| 2081. | The heirs of Thomas Jordan, Pt. | 640 | 84 | | " |
| 2082. | The heirs of Henry Lambert, Pt. | 640 | 84 | | " |
| 2083. | The heirs of Francis Rape, Pt.... | 640 | 84 | | " |
| 2084. | The heirs of Daniel Rogers, Pt... | 640 | 84 | | " |
| 2085. | The heirs of Hardy Robeson, Pt. | 640 | 84 | | " |
| 2086. | The heirs of Nathan Cooper, Pt.. | 640 | 84 | | " |
| 2087. | The heirs of John Cole, Privt.... | 640 | 84 | | " |
| 2088. | The heirs of Josiah Clark, Privt.. | 640 | 84 | | |
| 2089. | The heirs of David Pugh, Privt.. | 640 | 84 | | |
| 2090. | The heirs of William Parker, Pt.. | 640 | 84 | | |
| 2091. | The heirs of John Parsmore, Pt.. | 640 | 84 | | |
| 2092. | The heirs of Abram Shoecroft, Pt. | 640 | 84 | | |
| 2093. | The heirs of Willis Metts, Privt.. | 640 | 84 | | |
| 2094. | The heirs of Timothy Mars, Pt. . | 640 | 84 | Sept. 1 | Capt. Lascitur |
| 2095. | The heirs of Randal Greene, Pt.. | 640 | 84 | | |
| 2096. | The heirs of Jacob Griffin, Pt.... | 640 | 84 | | |
| 2097. | The heirs of William Nowell, Pt. | 640 | 84 | | |
| 2098. | The heirs of Joseph Newkins, Pt. | 640 | 84 | | |
| 2099. | The heirs of William Hendly, Pt.. | 640 | 84 | | |

| No. | To whom granted and rank | No. acres | Service in months | Location and to whom deeded and date of warrant. Within the limits of the lands allotted the officers and soldiers of the Continental Line, by Law, 1783, Oct. 14 | |
|---|---|---|---|---|---|
| 2100. | The heirs of William Hamm, Pt.. | 640 | 84 | | |
| 2101. | The heirs of Joseph Heel, Privt.. | 640 | 84 | | |
| 2102. | The heirs of William Buck, Pt... | 640 | 84 | | |
| 2103. | The heirs of Josiah Langston, Pt. | 640 | 84 | Sept. 2 | |
| 2104. | The heirs of John Gibson, Privt.. | 640 | 84 | | John Trousdale, Orange |
| 2105. | The heir of Samuel Warren, Pt. . | 640 | 84 | | James Sanders |
| 2106. | The heirs of Vernon Alhead, Pt.. | 640 | 84 | | |
| 2107. | The heirs of Charles Anderson, Pt. | 640 | 84 | | |
| 2108. | The heirs of Asa Brooks, Corpl.. | 1,000 | 84 | | |
| 2109. | The heirs of William Binnell, Jr. Privt.................. | 640 | 84 | Sept. 9, '85 | John McNees |
| 2110. | The heirs of George Barlow, Pt.. | 640 | 84 | " | |
| 2111. | The heirs of Frederick Bagwell," | 640 | 84 | " | |
| 2112. | The heirs of William Binnell, Jr. Privt................... | 640 | 84 | | |
| 2113. | The heirs of Jesse Brown, fifer... | 1,000 | 84 | | |
| 2114. | The heirs of James Bowler, Pt... | 640 | 84 | | |
| 2115. | The heirs of James Cannady, Pt. | 640 | 84 | | |
| 2116. | The heirs of Thoma. Corne, Pt. . | 640 | 84 | | |
| 2117. | The heirs of Isaac Cornelius, fifer | 1,000 | 84 | | |
| 2118. | The heirs of James Capps, Corp.. | 1,000 | 84 | | |
| 2119. | The heirs of William Cane, Pt... | 640 | 84 | | |
| 2120. | The heirs of Anthony Cross, Pt.. | 640 | 84 | | |
| 2121. | The heirs of Michael Fling, Pt... | 640 | 84 | " | |
| 2122. | The heirs of James Flusher, Senr. Privt................. | 640 | 84 | | |
| 2123. | The heirs of James Flusher, Jr. Privt.................. | 640 | 84 | | |
| 2124. | The heirs of Peter Furney, Pt.... | 640 | 84 | | |
| 2125. | The heirs of James Grace, Pt.... | 640 | 84 | | |
| 2126. | The heirs of Samuel Griffis, Sergt. | 1,000 | 84 | | |
| 2127. | The heirs of William Groves, Pt.. | 640 | 84 | | |
| 2128. | The heirs of Jonathan Harrison, Sergt...................... | 1,000 | 84 | | |
| 2129. | The heirs of Bernard Hilen, Pt... | 640 | 84 | | |
| 2130. | The heirs of William Harris, Pt.. | 640 | 84 | | |
| 2131. | The heirs of Warburton Hubbard, Sergt............. | 1,000 | 84 | | |
| 2132. | The heirs of Richd. Howard, Pt.. | 640 | 84 | | |
| 2133. | The heirs of Abraham Jacobus, " | 640 | 84 | " | |
| 2134. | The heirs of Mathew Lively, Pt.. | 640 | 84 | | |
| 2135. | The heirs of Joshua Larouse, Pt.. | 640 | 84 | | |
| 2136. | The heirs of Mathew Levi, Pt. .. | 640 | 84 | | |
| 2137. | The heirs of Nicholas Moore, Pt.. | 640 | 84 | | |
| 2138. | The heirs of William Mathews, " | 640 | 84 | | |
| 2139. | The heirs of Abraham Mott, Pt.. | 640 | 84 | | |
| 2140. | The heirs of Walter McFarlin, " | 640 | 84 | | |
| 2141. | The heirs of John Martin, Privt.. | 640 | 84 | | |
| 2142. | The heirs of Samuel McConnough, Privt......... | 640 | 84 | | |
| 2143. | The heirs of Dugald McConnough, Privt......... | 640 | 84 | " | |
| 2144. | The heirs of Daniel McCloud, Pt. | 640 | 84 | | |
| 2145. | The heirs of John McKinnis, Pt.. | 640 | 84 | | |
| 2146. | The heirs of George Minory, Pt.. | 640 | 84 | | |
| 2147. | The heirs of James Miller, Pt.... | 640 | 84 | | |

| No. | To whom granted and rank | No. acres | Service in months | Location and to whom deeded and date of warrant. Within the limits of the lands allotted the officers and soldiers of the Continental Line, by Law, 1783, Oct. 14 | |
|---|---|---|---|---|---|
| 2148. | The heirs of Jesse Nelms, Privt.. | 640 | 84 | | |
| 2149. | The heirs of Richd. Oglesbey, Pt.. | 640 | 84 | | |
| 2150. | The heirs of John Polk, Sergt.... | 1,000 | 84 | | |
| 2151. | The heirs of Joseph Persythe, Pt. | 640 | 84 | Sept. 9, '85 | James McNees |
| 2152. | The heirs of Clement Prichard, " | 640 | 84 | | |
| 2153. | The heirs of John Reverr, Privt.. | 640 | 84 | | |
| 2154. | Benjamin Reaves, Sergt......... | 1,000 | 84 | | |
| 2155. | The heirs of Daniel Raymore, Pt. | 640 | 84 | | |
| 2156. | The heirs of Jacob Redy, Privt.. | 640 | 84 | | |
| 2157. | The heirs of James Reel, Privt... | 640 | 84 | | |
| 2158. | The heirs of John Seavron, Pt. .. | 640 | 84 | | |
| 2159. | The heirs of Thomas Wilsh, (Welch) Privt.............. | 640 | 84 | | |
| 2160. | The heirs of William Whitman, " | 640 | 84 | | |
| 2161. | The heirs of John Ventress, Pt... | 640 | 84 | | |
| 2162. | The heirs of John Thompson, " | 640 | 84 | | |
| 2163. | The heirs of John Jones, Privt... | 640 | 84 | | |
| 2164. | The heirs of Thomas Allen, Pt... | 640 | 84 | Sept. 12,'85 | Jno. Price |
| 2165. | The heirs of Thomas Armsworth, Privt........... | 640 | 84 | | " |
| 2166. | The heirs of Thomas Alford, Pt.. | 640 | 84 | | " |
| 2167. | The heirs of Peter Ballard, Pt. .. | 640 | 84 | | " |
| 2168. | The heirs of Samuel Barker, Pt.. | 640 | 84 | | " |
| 2169. | The heirs of Isum Burns, Privt.. | 640 | 84 | | " |
| 2170. | The heirs of Sherrard Britt, Pt... | 640 | 84 | | " |
| 2171. | The heirs of Moses Brumfield, Pt. | 640 | 84 | | " |
| 2172. | The heirs of John Benson, Pt..... | 640 | 84 | | " |
| 2173. | The heirs of John Bradley, Pt.... | 640 | 84 | | " |
| 2174. | The heirs of Obed Bryant, Pt.... | 640 | 84 | | " |
| 2175. | The heirs of Thomas Cannon, Pt. | 640 | 84 | | " |
| 2176. | The heirs of Peter Cobb, Privt... | 640 | 84 | | " |
| 2177. | The heirs of Samuel Collins, Pt.. | 640 | 84 | | " |
| 2178. | The heirs of Solomon Cooper, Pt.. | 640 | 84 | | |
| 2179. | The heirs of Henry Carter, Pt. .. | 640 | 84 | | " |
| 2180. | The heirs of Job Cherry, Privt... | 640 | 84 | | " |
| 2181. | The heirs of Arthur Dukes, Pt... | 640 | 84 | | " |
| 2182. | The heirs of Peter Dillard, Pt.... | 640 | 84 | | " |
| 2183. | The heirs of Charles Flowers, Pt. | 640 | 84 | | " |
| 2184. | The heirs of Edward Griffin, Pt.. | 640 | 84 | | " |
| 2185. | The heirs of Richard Goodnas, " | 640 | 84 | | " |
| 2186. | The heirs of Solomon Groves, Pt.. | 640 | 84 | | " |
| 2187. | The heirs of Joseph Graves, Pt. . | 640 | 84 | | " |
| 2188. | The heirs of James Howell, Pt... | 640 | 84 | | " |
| 2189. | The heirs of James Harrell, Pt... | 640 | 84 | | " |
| 2190. | The heirs of Peter Howell, Pt.... | 640 | 84 | | " |
| 2191. | The heirs of James Holton, Pt... | 640 | 84 | | " |
| 2192. | The heirs of Charles Hickman, " | 640 | 84 | | " |
| 2193. | The heirs of Peter Johnston, Pt.. | 640 | 84 | " | " |
| 2194. | The heirs of Martin Jones, Sergt. | 1,000 | 84 | " | " |
| 2195. | The heirs of Taylor Joperton, Pt.. | 640 | 84 | " | " |
| 2196. | The heirs of Taylor Jones, Privt. | 640 | 84 | | |
| 2197. | The heirs of Philip Jackson, Pt... | | | | |
| 2198. | The heirs of Tanner Jeth, Pt. ... | | | | |
| 2199. | The heirs of Kedar Jones, Privt.. | | | | |
| 2200. | The heirs of Jesse Jones, Privt... | | | | |
| 2201. | The heirs of John James, Privt.. | | | | |

| No. | To whom granted and rank | No. acres | Service in months | Location and to whom deeded and date of warrant. Within the limits of the lands allotted the officers and soldiers of the Continental Line, by Law. 1783, Oct. 14 |
|---|---|---|---|---|
| 2202. | The heirs of Thomas Johnston," | | | |
| 2203. | The heirs of Aaron Jones, Privt.. | | | |
| 2204. | The heirs of Peter Knight, Pt.... | | | |
| 2205. | The heirs of Jesse Lee, Privt..... | | | |
| 2206. | The heirs of Robert Lenier, Pt... | | | |
| 2207. | The heirs of Peter Langford, Pt.. | | | |
| 2208. | The heirs of Abraham Mears, Sgt. | 1,000 | 84 | Sept. 12,'85 Jno. Price |
| 2209. | The heirs of John Mears, Privt.. | 640 | 84 | "              " |
| 2210. | The heirs of Jacob Morgan, Pt... | | | |
| 2211. | The heirs of Abraham May, Sgt.. | 1,000 | 84 | |
| 2212. | The heirs of James Night, Privt.. | 640 | 84 | "              " |
| 2213. | The heirs of Peter Pope, Privt... | | | |
| 2214. | The heirs of John Peters, Privt.. | | | |
| 2215. | The heirs of Solomon Parks, Pt.. | | | |
| 2216. | The heirs of Benjamin Pulley, Pt. | 640 | 84 | Sept. 12,'85 Jno. Price |
| 2217. | The heirs of John Pew, Pri'..... | 640 | 84 | |
| 2218. | The heirs of Richard Phew, Pt... | 640 | 84 | " |
| 2219. | The heirs of Rice Price, Privt.... | 640 | 84 | " |
| 2220. | The heirs of Joshua Parnel, Pt... | 640 | 84 | " |
| 2221. | The heirs of Peter Payne, Privt.. | 640 | 84 | " |
| 2222. | The heirs of Abraham Peter, Pt.. | 640 | 84 | " |
| 2223. | The heirs of Servie Robertson, " | 640 | 84 | " |
| 2224. | The heirs of Gardiner Robertson, Privt............ | 640 | 84 | " |
| 2225. | The heirs of Absolam Rogers,  " | 640 | 84 | " |
| 2226. | The heirs of William Ring, Pt. .. | 640 | 84 | " |
| 2227. | The heirs of Aaren Renn, Privt.. | 640 | 84 | " |
| 2228. | The heirs of Peter Reddick, Pt... | 640 | 84 | " |
| 2229. | The heirs of Jesse Rogers, Pt.... | 640 | 84 | " |
| 2230. | The heirs of Jesse Renn, Privt... | 640 | 84 | " |
| 2231. | The heirs of Stephen Reed, Pt... | 640 | 84 | " |
| 2232. | The heirs of John Skinner, Pt.... | 640 | 84 | " |
| 2233. | The heirs of Joseph Sparks, Pt... | 640 | 84 | " |
| 2234. | The heirs of Samuel Shute, Pt... | 640 | 84 | " |
| 2235. | The heirs of Joshua Searchwell, " | 640 | 84 | " |
| 2236. | The heirs of Isaac Simmons, Pt.. | 640 | 84 | " |
| 2237. | The heirs of John Stinson, Pt.... | 640 | 84 | " |
| 2238. | The heirs of James Shanks, Pt... | 640 | 84 | " |
| 2239. | The heirs of Joseph Surls, Pt.... | 640 | 84 | " |
| 2240. | The heirs of James Smally, Pt... | 640 | 84 | " |
| 2241. | The heirs of Joshua Thompson, " | | | " |
| 2242. | The heirs of Willey Tucker, Pt... | 640 | 84 | " |
| 2243. | The heirs of John Thornall, Pt... | 640 | 84 | " |
| 2244. | The heirs of Henry Taylor, Pt... | 640 | 84 | " |
| 2245. | The heirs of Joseph Toomer, Pt.. | 640 | 84 | " |
| 2246. | The heirs of Charles Tutson, or (J), Privt................ | 640 | 84 | " |
| 2247. | The heirs of Jacob Wells, Pt..... | 640 | 84 | " |
| 2248. | The heirs of Peter Williams, Pt.. | 640 | 84 | " |
| 2249. | The heirs of Solomon Willis, Pt.. | 640 | 84 | " |
| 2250. | The heirs of William Wright, Pt. | 640 | 84 | " |
| 2251. | The heirs of Titus Wood, Pt..... | 640 | 84 | " |
| 2252. | The heirs of James Woolward, " | 640 | 84 | " |
| 2253. | The heirs of Thomas Winstell, " | 640 | 84 | " |
| 2254. | The heirs of Peter Ward, Privt... | 640 | 84 | " |
| 2255. | The heirs of Thomas Wooten,  " | 640 | 84 | " |

| No. | To whom granted and rank | No. acres | Service in months | Location and to whom deeded and date of warrant. Within the limits of the lands allotted the officers and soldiers of the Continental Line, by Law, 1783, Oct. 14 | |
|---|---|---|---|---|---|
| 2256. | The heirs of George Wilkins, Pt.. | 640 | 84 | | Jno. Price |
| 2257. | The heirs of Jordon Wilkins, Pt.. | 640 | 84 | | " |
| 2258. | The heirs of Peter Wright, Pt.... | 640 | 84 | | " |
| 2259. | Thomas Andrews, Privt........ | 640 | 84 | | " |
| 2260. | The heirs of Duncan Ancinclash, Privt............ | 640 | 84 | | " |
| 2261. | William Lowe, fife Maj........ | 427 | 36 | Sept.12,'85 | Self |
| 2261. | The heirs of Arthur Parker, Lt... | 1,000 | 84 | .Sept. 17 | A. Pearce |
| 2263. | The heirs of John Eller, Privt.... | 640 | 84 | " | |
| 2264. | The heirs of David Yarbrough, " | 640 | 84 | | |
| 2265. | The heirs of Jacob Dadrick, Pt. . | 640 | 84 | | |
| 2266. | The heirs of William Hawley, " | 640 | 84 | | |
| 2267. | The heirs of Samuel Hay, Pt..... | 640 | 84 | | |
| 2268. | James Roper, Privt............ | 274 | 36 | | |
| 2269. | James Price, Privt............. | 274 | 36 | | |
| 2270. | The heirs of William Allen, Decsd. Privt............. | 640 | 84 | Sept. 28 | Mr. Marshal |
| 2271. | The heirs of John Baltrip, Pt.... | 640 | 84 | | |
| 2272. | The heirs of William Curk, Pt... | 640 | 84 | | |
| 2273. | The heirs of Shurrod Duke, Pt... | 640 | 84 | | |
| 2274. | James Glover, Privt............ | 228 | 30 | | |
| 2275. | Samuel Harris, Privt.......... | 228 | 30 | | |
| 2276. | The heirs of John Jeffres........ | 640 | 84 | | |
| 2277. | The heirs of William Lithco, Pt.. | 640 | 84 | | " |
| 2278. | The heirs of William Morris, Pt.. | 640 | 84 | Sept. 28,'85 | Mr. Marshal |
| 2279. | The heirs of James Talton, Pt. .. | 640 | 84 | | |
| 2280. | The heirs of Peter Valentine, Pt. | 640 | 84 | | |
| 2281. | The heirs of Uriah Russell, Pt. .. | 640 | 84 | | |
| 2282. | The heirs of Benjamin Ward, Pt. | 640 | 84 | | |
| 2283. | Joel Rigins, Privt............. | 228 | 30 | | |
| 2284. | The heirs of Burrell Wilkins, Pt.. | 640 | 84 | | |
| 2285. | The heirs of John Woodrough, " | 640 | 84 | | |
| 2286. | The heirs of William Young, Pt.. | 640 | 84 | | |
| 2287. | The heirs of John King, Privt.... | 457 | 60 | | |
| 2288. | The heirs of Joshua Barber, Pt... | 274 | 36 | | |
| 2289. | James Roach, Privt............ | 502 | 66 | | |
| 2290. | The heirs of Levi Alexander, Pt.. | 640 | 84 | " | Widow Alexander |
| 2291. | Henry Irwin, Heir of Henry Irwin, Lieut. Col............. | 5,760 | 84 | | Henry Irwin |
| 2292. | Mecaijah Savage, Privt........ | 228 | 30 | | William Sanders |
| 2293. | Abraham Crump, Privt........ | 228 | 30 | " | " |
| 2294. | Ransom Savage, Sergt........ | 357 | 30 | " | " |
| 2295. | George Summers, Sergt........ | 228 | 24 | " | " |
| 2296. | Richard Mount, Privt......... | 274 | 36 | | " |
| 2297. | James Craven, Lt.............. | 1,242 | 42 | | " |
| 2298. | The heirs of James Depreast, Pt. | 640 | 84 | | " |
| 2299. | The heirs of William Vinson, Pt.. | 640 | 84 | | " |
| 2300. | The heirs of Francis Mosir, Pt... | 640 | 84 | | " |
| 2301. | The heirs of Samuel Mosir, Pt... | 640 | 84 | | " |
| 2302. | Jacob Medgett................ | 640 | 84 | Sept. 29,'85 | William Faircloath |
| 2303. | Lewis Jennett, Sergt........... | 1,000 | 84 | | |
| 2304. | Aaron Gaylord................ | 640 | 84 | | |
| 2305. | Jeremiah Gurganus, Privt...... | 640 | 84 | | |
| 2306. | Roger Wildie, Privt........... | 640 | 84 | | |
| 2307. | Absalom Colley, Privt......... | 640 | 84 | | |
| 2308. | Frederick Fairfax, Sergt........ | 1,000 | 84 | | |

| No. | To whom granted and rank | No. acres | Service in months | Location and to whom deeded and date of warrant. Within the limits of the lands allotted the officers and soldiers of the Continental Line, by Law, 1783, Oct. 14 | |
|---|---|---|---|---|---|
| 2309. | The heirs of Peter Mitts, Privt... | 640 | 84 | | |
| 2310. | The heirs of Jonathan Bett, Pt. . | 640 | 84 | | |
| 2311. | The heirs of William Fairfax, Pt. | 640 | 84 | | |
| 2312. | The heirs of Richard Pickle, Pt.. | 274 | 36 | | |
| 2313. | Jonathan Gay, Privt........... | 274 | 36 | | |
| 2314. | Josiah Dove, Privt............. | 274 | 36 | | |
| 2315. | The heirs of Peter Lee, Privt.... | 274 | 36 | | |
| 2316. | The heirs of Jesse Jitt, Corpl.... | 1,000 | 84 | | |
| 2317. | The heirs of Roberson Jackson,Pt. | 640 | 84 | | |
| 2318. | Zachariah Flood, Privt......... | 640 | 84 | | |
| 2319. | Elisha Dukes, Corpl........... | 1,000 | 84 | | |
| 2320. | The heirs of Willoughby Rogerson, Privt............. | 640 | 84 | | |
| 2321. | The heirs of Sampson Batts, Pt.. | 640 | 84 | | |
| 2322. | Crekiel Prigin, Privt........... | 640 | 84 | | |
| 2323. | The heirs of Richard Galloway, " | 640 | 84 | | |
| 2324. | The heirs of John Cator, Privt... | 640 | 84 | | |
| 2325. | Joseph Wilkins, Privt.......... | 640 | 84 | William Faircloath | |
| 2326. | Joseph Flood, Privt........... | 640 | 84 | | |
| 2327. | The heirs of William Bradley, Pt. | 640 | 84 | | |
| 2328. | Willis Mears, Privt............ | 640 | 84 | | |
| 2329. | Enos Goodsoon, Privt......... | 640 | 84 | | |
| 2330. | James Pulley, Privt........... | 640 | 84 | | |
| 2331. | The heirs of Frederick Pugh, Pt.. | 640 | 84 | | |
| 2332. | The heirs of Benjamin Woolard," | 640 | 84 | | |
| 2333. | Jacob Basdel, Privt............ | 640 | 84 | | |
| 2334. | Joseph Candler, Privt.......... | 640 | 84 | | |
| 2335. | John Gaultney, Privt.......... | 640 | 84 | | |
| 2336. | Benjamin Covenan, Privt...... | 640 | 84 | | |
| 2337· | Abraham Hammons, Privt...... | 640 | 84 | | |
| 2338· | Francis Berry, Privt........... | 640 | 84 | | |
| 2339· | Thomas Saunderlin, Privt...... | 640 | 84 | Sept. 29,'85 | Wm. Faircloth |
| 2340· | Lemon Griffin, Privt.......... | | | | |
| 2341. | Isaac Abbott, Privt............ | | | | |
| 2342. | The heirs of Augustine Darnald, Privt.............. | 640 | 84 | " | " |
| 2343. | The heirs of Micajah Smith, Pt.. | 640 | 84 | | |
| 2344. | Willis Humphries, Privt........ | 640 | 84 | | |
| 2345. | Daniel Haston, Privt.......... | 640 | 84 | | |
| 2346. | Peter Jarmany, Privt.......... | 640 | 84 | | |
| 2347. | Demsey Wiggle, Privt......... | 640 | 84 | | |
| 2348. | John Grogan, Fifer............. | 1,000 | 84 | " | " |
| 2349. | Joseph Braner, Privt........... | 640 | 84 | | |
| 2350. | | | | | |
| 2351. | Th heirs of Richard Rose, Privt.. | 640 | 84 | | |
| 2352. | The heirs of Samuel Wigley, Pt.. | 640 | 84 | | |
| 2353. | Joshua Murray, Privt.......... | 640 | 84 | | |
| 2354. | William Charlton, Privt........ | 640 | 84 | " | Maj. R. Blount |
| 2355. | Edmund Tison, Privt.......... | 274 | 36 | " Ec'd | |
| 2356. | Kedar Benton, Privt........... | 228 | 30 | Sept. 30 | Capt. Davis |
| 2357. | George Harris, Privt........... | 640 | 84 | | " |
| 2358. | Hezekiah Jones, Privt.......... | 228 | 30 | | |
| 2359. | John Polson, Privt............ | 228 | 30 | | |
| 2360. | Daniel Guinn, Privt........... | 640 | 84 | | |
| 2361. | Josiah Jones, Privt............ | 228 | 30 | | |
| 2362. | The heirs of James Robins, Pt... | 640 | 84 | | |
| 2363. | The heirs of Francis Speight, Pt. | 640 | 84 | | |

| No. | To whom granted and rank | No. acres | Service in months | Location and to whom deeded and date of warrant. Within the limits of the lands allotted the officers and soldiers of the Continental Line, by Law, 1783, Oct. 14 | |
|---|---|---|---|---|---|
| 2364. | The heirs of Robert Blanshett, " | 640 | 84 | | |
| 2365. | The heirs of Richard Sherwell Walker, Sergt. | 1,000 | 84 | Sept. 30 | Thos. Thompson |
| 2364. | The heir of William Ester, Pt. | 640 | 84 | | " |
| 2365. | The heir of John Carrier, Privt. | 640 | 84 | | |
| 2366. | The heirs of Jonathan Baker, Pt. | 640 | 84 | | B. Sheppard |
| 2367. | Demsey Bunington, Privt. | 274 | 36 | " | John Faircloth |
| 2368. | The heirs of William Benton, Pt. | 640 | 84 | " | " |
| 2369. | The heirs of Hardy Britain, Pt. | 640 | 84 | | |
| 2370. | Isaiah Cooke, Privt. | 640 | 84 | | |
| 2371. | Malachi Crawford, Privt. | 640 | 84 | | B. Sheppard |
| 2372. | The heirs of Jesse Dewet, Pt. | 640 | 84 | " | John Faircloth |
| 2373. | William Fox, Privt. | 640 | 84 | | |
| 2374. | Jacob Grogan, Privt. | 274 | 36 | " | " |
| 2375. | Simon Grimes, Privt. | 640 | 84 | | |
| 2376. | David Ginn, Privt. | 640 | 84 | | |
| 2377. | Samson George, Privt. | 640 | 84 | | |
| 2378. | The heirs of Edward Harrison, " | | | | |
| 2379. | Charles Harrison, Privt. | | | | |
| 2380. | Lewis Hester, Privt. | | | | |
| 2381. | The heirs of Drury Harrington, " | 274 | 36 | | |
| 2382. | The heirs of Reubin Mundine, " | 274 | 36 | | |
| 2383. | The heirs of Phillip Mason, Pt. | 640 | 84 | | B. Sheppard |
| 2384. | Zebulon Mundine, Privt. | 640 | 84 | | John Faircloth |
| 2385. | The heirs of George Martin, Pt. | 640 | 84 | | |
| 2386. | The heirs of Jesse Marbery, Pt. | 640 | 84 | | |
| 2387. | The heirs of Anderson Nolly, Pt. | 640 | 84 | | |
| 2388. | The heirs of Lewis Odam, Pt. | 640 | 84 | | |
| 2389. | The heirs of Benjamin Palmer, " | 640 | 84 | | |
| 2390. | Thomas Piner, Privt. | 640 | 84 | | |
| 2391. | Zachariah Ponds, Privt. | 640 | 84 | | |
| 2392. | Jesse Rowe, Privt. | 640 | 84 | | |
| 2393. | James Savage, Privt. | 640 | 84 | | |
| 2394. | The heirs of Joseph Savage, Pt. | 640 | 84 | | |
| 2395. | Martin Titus, Privt. | 640 | 84 | | B. Sheppard |
| 2396. | The heirs of Joseph Upton, Pt. | 640 | 84 | | John Faircloth |
| 2397. | Demcey Wigley, Privt. | 640 | 84 | | |
| 2398. | Isaiah Wood, Privt. | 640 | 84 | | |
| 2399. | Gabriel Weight, Privt. | 640 | 84 | | |
| 2401. | Robert Willie, Privt. | 640 | 84 | | John Faircloth |
| 2402. | The heirs of Jesse Waughmock, Pt. | 640 | 84 | | |
| 2403. | Jonathan Wyatt, Privt. | 640 | 84 | | |
| 2404. | Jonathan Abbett, Privt. | 640 | 84 | | Capt. J. Davis |
| 2405. | The heirs of Lemon Baker, Pt. | 640 | 84 | | " |
| 2406. | The heirs of William Bryant, Pt. | 640 | 84 | | " |
| 2407. | The heirs of William Bunington, " | 640 | 84 | | " |
| 2408. | The heirs of Michael Braner, Pt. | 640 | 84 | | " |
| 2407. | The heirs of Jeremiah Banks, Pt. | 640 | 84 | | " |
| 2408. | Thomas Baxter, Privt. | 640 | 84 | | " |
| 2409. | The heirs of David Braswell, Pt. | 640 | 84 | | " |
| 2410. | Isaac Cook, Privt. | 640 | 84 | | " |
| 2411. | Joseph Cahoon, Privt. | 640 | 84 | | " |
| 2412. | William Darnald, Privt. | 640 | 84 | | " |
| 2413. | Patrick Darbey, Privt. | 640 | 84 | | " |
| 2414. | Joshua Fowler, Privt. | 640 | 84 | | " |
| 2415. | The heirs of Isaac Griffin, Privt. | 640? | 84 | | " |

| No. | To whom granted and rank | No. acres | Service in months | Location and to whom deeded and date of warrant. Within the limits of the lands allotted the officers and soldiers of the Continental Line, by Law, 1783, Oct. 14 | |
|---|---|---|---|---|---|
| 2416. | James Grogan, Privt........... | 640 | 84 | | Capt. J. Davis |
| 2417. | Josiah Griffin, Privt........... | 640 | 84 | | " |
| 2418. | The heirs of Daniel Ganlor, Pt... | 640 | 84 | | " |
| 2419. | The heirs of John Harrison, Pt... | 640 | 84 | | " |
| 2420. | The heirs of Augustine Harrison, Privt.............. | 640 | 84 | | " |
| 2421. | Willis Hastings, Privt.......... | 640 | 84 | | " |
| 2424. | The heirs of Lazerous Hart, Pt... | 640 | 84 | | " |
| 2425. | Thomas Jermany, Privt........ | 640 | 84 | | " |
| 2426. | Benjamin Lucis, Privt......... | 640 | 84 | | " |
| 2427. | The heirs of Joseph Mundine, Pt. | 640 | 84 | | " |
| 2428. | Robert Mann, Privt........... | 640 | 84 | | " |
| 2429. | George Norris, Privt.......... | 640 | 84 | | " |
| 2430. | Joseph Palmer, Privt.......... | 640 | 84 | | " |
| 2431. | Peter Poyner, Privt........... | 640 | 84 | | " |
| 2432. | Michael Phillips, Privt......... | 365 | 48 | Sept. 30 | " |
| 2433. | Samuel Price, Privt........... | 365 | 48 | | " |
| 2434. | Demsey Rowe, Privt.......... | 640 | 84 | | " |
| 2435. | The heirs of Isaac Sanderlin, Pt.. | 640 | 84 | | " |
| 2436. | Charles Smith, Privt.......... | 640 | 84 | | " |
| 2437. | Edward Sage, Privt............ | 640 | 84 | | " |
| 2438. | The heirs of Thomas Sherrord, Pt. | 640 | 84 | | " |
| 2439. | John Upton, Privt............. | 640 | 84 | | " |
| 2440. | Willis Upton, Privt............ | 640 | 84 | | " |
| 2441. | The heirs of Edward Werton, Pt. | 640 | 84 | | " |
| 2442. | Thomas Wigley, Privt......... | 640 | 84 | | " |
| 2443. | Isaac Ward, Privt............. | 640 | 84 | | " |
| 2444. | Zachariah Williams, Privt...... | 640 | 84 | | " |
| 2445. | The heirs of Joshua Ballard, Pt.. | 640 | 84 | | {Cert'f. delv'd by B. L. {for J. P. issd. |
| 2446. | The heirs of Jonathan Cherry, " | 640 | 84 | | " |
| 2447. | The heirs of Absalom Coward, " | 640 | 84 | | " |
| 2448. | The heirs of John Eastwood, Pt.. | 640 | 84 | | " |
| 2449. | The heirs of Joshua English, Pt.. | 640 | 84 | | " |
| 2450. | The heirs of John Fones, Privt... | 640 | 84 | | " |
| 2451. | The heirs of Augustine Floyd, Pt. | 640 | 84 | | " |
| 2452. | The heirs of Thomas George, Pt.. | 640 | 84 | | " |
| 2453. | The heirs of Henry Ginn, Privt.. | 640 | 84 | | " |
| 2454. | The heirs of Andrew Grimes, Pt.. | 640 | 84 | | " |
| 2455. | The heirs of Henry Griffiths, Pt.. | 640 | 84 | | " |
| 2456. | The heirs of Andrew Homes, Pt.. | 640 | 84 | | " |
| 2457. | The heirs of Henry Humphries, " | 640 | 84 | | " |
| 2458. | The heirs of Andrew Hines, Pt... | 640 | 84 | | " |
| 2459. | The heirs of James Howard, Pt... | 640 | 84 | | " |
| 2460. | The heirs of Jacob Jones, Pt..... | 640 | 84 | | " |
| 2461. | The heirs of Abslom Jones, Pt... | 640 | 84 | | " |
| 2462. | The heir of Elisha Ivy, Privt.... | 640 | 84 | | " |
| 2463. | The heirs of Andrew King, Pt. .. | 640 | 84 | | " |
| 2464. | The heir of Peter Lanier, Privt. . | 640 | 84 | | " |
| 2465. | The heirs of Elias Leggett, Pt.... | 640 | 84 | | " |
| 2466. | The heirs of Henry McFashions, Prit...................... | 640 | 84 | | " |
| 2467. | The heirs of Griffin Morgan, Pt.. | 640 | 84 | | " |
| 2468. | The heirs of Humphrey Morgan, Privt.............. | 640 | 84 | | " |

| No. | To whom granted and rank | No. acres | Service in months | Location and to whom deeded and date of warrant. Within the limits of the lands allotted the officers and soldiers of the Continental Line, by Law, 1783, Oct. 14 |
|---|---|---|---|---|
| 2469. | The heirs of Titus Peters, Pt..... | 640 | 84 | {Cert'f. delv'd by B. L. for J. P. issd. |
| 2470. | The heirs of Peter Powell, Pt.... | 640 | 84 | " |
| 2471. | The heirs of Robert Powers, Pt.. | 640 | 84 | " |
| 2472. | The heirs of George Pulley, Pt... | 640 | 84 | " |
| 2473. | The heirs of Peter Pains, Privt... | 640 | 84 | " |
| 2474. | The heirs of Hardy Roberts, Pt.. | 640 | 84 | " |
| 2475. | The heirs of Henry Richards, Pt. | 640 | 84 | " |
| 2476. | The heirs of Sampson Roberts, " | 640 | 84 | " |
| 2477. | The heirs of Joal Smith, Privt... | 640 | 84 | " |
| 2478. | The heirs of Nathaniel Wood, " | 640 | 84 | " |
| 2479. | The heirs of Ephraim Wyatt, " | 640 | 84 | " |
| 2480. | The heirs of Thomas Wood, Pt. . | 640 | 84 | " |
| 2481. | The heirs of Absalom Wallace, " | 640 | 84 | " |
| 2482. | The heirs of John Applewhite, " | 640 | 84 | {Cert. Colo. John Shepard |
| 2483. | The heirs of Abraham Applewhite, Privt........... | 640 | 84 | " |
| 2484. | The heirs of Marmaduke Brantley, Privt............. | 640 | 84 | " |
| 2485. | The heirs of Randall Cross, Pt... | 640 | 84 | " |
| 2486. | The heirs of Gran Duke, Privt... | 640 | 84 | " |
| 2487. | The heirs of Abraham Gunn, Pt.. | 640 | 84 | " |
| 2488. | The heirs of Demcey Green, Pt.. | 640 | 84 | " |
| 2489. | The heirs of John Hathcock, Pt.. | 640 | 84 | " |
| 2490. | The heirs of John Holloway, Pt.. | 640 | 84 | " |
| 2491. | The heirs of Portis Mulford, Pt.. | 640 | 84 | " |
| 2492. | The heirs of Lewis Morgan, Pt... | 640 | 84 | " |
| 2493. | The heirs of Abraham Short, Pt.. | 640 | 84 | " |
| 2494. | The heirs of John Winoak, Pt.... | 640 | 84 | " |
| 2495. | The heirs of Joseph Abrams, Pt.. | 640 | 84 | Capt. McNees |
| 2496. | John Atchinclash, Privt........ | 640 | 84 | " |
| 2497. | The heirs of Avandal Blackman" | 640 | 84 | " |
| 2498. | The heirs of Nicholass Barber, " | 640 | 84 | " |
| 2499. | The heirs of Peter Baker, Pt..... | 640 | 84 | " |
| 2500. | The heirs of Matthew Braker, " | 640 | 84 | " |
| 2501. | The heirs of Hillery Crook, Pt... | 640 | 84 | " |
| 2502. | The heirs of John Creege, Pt..... | 640 | 84 | " |
| 2503. | The heirs of Joseph Dupont, Pt.. | 640 | 84 | " |
| 2504. | The heirs of John Dunkinson, Pt. | 640 | 84 | " |
| 2505. | The heirs of Abraham Duester, " | 640 | 84 | " |
| 2506. | The heirs of James Duester, Pt.. | 640 | 84 | " |
| 2507. | The heirs of Jesse Dupont, Pt.... | 640 | 84 | " |
| 2508. | The heirs of Christopher Dasher, Privt............... | 640 | 84 | " |
| 2509. | The heirs of John Dugald, Pt.... | 640 | 84 | " |
| 2510. | The heirs of James Ducawin, Pt. | 640 | 84 | " |
| 2511. | The heirs of George Dill, Pt..... | 640 | 84 | " |
| 2512. | The heirs of John Farmer, Pt.... | 640 | 84 | " |
| 2513. | The heirs of Joseph Farden, Pt.. | 640 | 84 | " |
| 2514. | The heirs of George Grantson, " | 640 | 84 | " |
| 2515. | The heirs of Thomas Guist, Pt... | 640 | 84 | " |
| 2516. | The heirs of Frederick Harper, " | 640 | 84 | " |
| 2517. | The heirs of Benberry Hines, Pt. | 640 | 84 | " |
| 2518. | The heirs of Levi Jinkins, Pt..... | 640 | 84 | " |
|  | Anthony King, Privt.......... | 640 | 84 | " |
| 2519. | The heirs of David Kemp, Pt.... | 640 | 84 | " |

| No. | To whom granted and rank | No. acres | Service in months | Location and to whom deeded and date of warrant. Within the limits of the lands allotted the officers and soldiers of the Continental Line, by Law, 1783, Oct. 14 |
|---|---|---|---|---|
| 2520. | The heirs of Andrew Litchworth, Privt............ | 640 | 84 | Capt. McNees |
| 2521. | The heirs of Nathan Lamb, Pt... | 640 | 84 | " |
| 2522. | The heirs of Daniel Lawrecy, Pt. | 640 | 84 | " |
| 2523. | The heirs of James Lambreck, " | 640 | 84 | " |
| 2524. | The heirs of John Lymus, Pt.... | 640 | 84 | " |
| 2526. | The heirs of George Lynch, Pt... | 640 | 84 | |
| 2527. | The heirs of Joseph Mallery, Pt.. | 640 | 84 | |
| 2528. | The heirs of Allen Murdock, Pt.. | 640 | 84 | Capt. J. W. McNees |
| 2529. | The heirs of John Manson, Pt... | 640 | 84 | " |
| 2530. | The heirs of Archebald McDugald, Privt............ | 640 | 84 | " |
| 2531. | The heirs of Samuel Morron, Pt.. | 640 | 84 | " |
| 2532. | The heirs of John McDaniel, Pt.. | 640 | 84 | " |
| 2533. | The heirs of Allen McDaniel, Pt. | 640 | 84 | " |
| 2534. | The heirs of McCloud Murdock, Privt............ | 640 | 84 | " |
| 2535. | The heirs of John Nations, Pt.... | 640 | 84 | " |
| 2536. | The heirs of Mathias O'Neal, Pt. | 640 | 84 | " |
| 2537. | The heirs of Archibald O'Neal, " | | | " |
| 2538. | The heirs of Daniel Oate, Pt..... | 640 | 84 | " |
| 2539. | The heirs of James Orr, Pt...... | 640 | 84 | " |
| 2540. | The heirs of John Reyley, Pt.... | 640 | 84 | " |
| 2541. | The heirs of Andrew Ramsey, " | 640 | 84 | " |
| 2542. | The heirs of James Richardson, " | 640 | 84 | " |
| 2543. | The heirs of Isaih Stedham, Pt... | 640 | 84 | " |
| 2545. | The heirs of Nathaniel Slade, Pt.. | 640 | 84 | " |
| 2546. | The heirs of Joel Smythe, Pt..... | 640 | 84 | " |
| 2547. | The heirs of Joseph Siver, Pt.... | 640 | 84 | " |
| 2548. | The heirs of Henry Shaffer, Pt... | 640 | 84 | " |
| 2549. | The heirs of John Strand, Pt..... | 640 | 84 | " |
| 2550. | The heirs of Richard Talifarro, " | 640 | 84 | " |
| 2551. | The heirs of John Tripp, Pt..... | 640 | 84 | " |
| 2552. | The heirs of David Thompson, " | 640 | 84 | " |
| 2553. | The heirs of William Thust, Pt.. | 640 | 84 | " |
| 2554. | The heirs of Brown Wallace, Pt.. | 640 | 84 | " |
| 2555. | The heirs of Casper Wimer, Pt... | 640 | 84 | " |
| 2556. | The heirs of Goodman Welch, " | 640 | 84 | " |
| 2557. | The heirs of Jacob Willis, Pt..... | 640 | 84 | " |
| 2558. | The heirs of Michael Bazemore," | 640 | 84 | " |
| 2559. | The heir of Robert Bazemore, Pt. | 640 | 84 | " |
| 2560. | The heirs of Stephen Begworth, " | 640 | 84 | " |
| 2561. | The heirs of Jacob Burden, Pt... | 640 | 84 | " |
| 2562. | The heirs of Solomon Benton, " . | 640 | 84 | " |
| 2563. | The heirs of Andrew Burrn, Pt... | 640 | 84 | " |
| 2564. | The heirs of Isaiah Brenkley, " | 640 | 84 | " |
| 2565. | The heirs of David Brooks, Pt... | 640 | 84 | " |
| 2566. | The heirs of John Cockar, Pt.... | 640 | 84 | " |
| 2567. | The heirs of Josiah Collins, Pt... | 640 | 84 | " |
| 2568. | The heirs of Benjamin Daniel, " | 640 | 84 | " |
| 2569. | The heirs of Benjamin Dundelor, Privt............ | 640 | 84 | " |
| 2570. | The heirs of Joel Grant, Privt.... | 640 | 84 | " |
| 2571. | The heirs of David Hughs, Pt.... | 640 | 84 | " |
| 2572. | The heirs of Abraham Henderson, Privt............ | 640 | 84 | " |

| No. | To whom granted and rank | No. acres | Service in months | Location and to whom deeded and date of warrant. Within the limits of the lands allotted the officers and soldiers of the Continental Line, by Law, 1783, Oct. 14 |
|---|---|---|---|---|
| 2573. | The heirs of Job Jackson, Pt..... | 640 | 84 | Capt. J. W. McNees |
| 2574. | The heirs of Willis McDuell, Pt.. | 640 | 84 | " |
| 2575. | The heirs of Peter McCabe, Pt... | 640 | 84 | " |
| 2576. | The heirs of Micajah Muzles, Pt. | 640 | 84 | " |
| 2577. | The heirs of Jacob Mitchell, Pt.. | 640 | 84 | " |
| 2578. | The heirs of Ezekeel Regbey, Pt. | 640 | 84 | " |
| 2579. | The heirs of Amos Raynor, Pt... | 640 | 84 | " |
| 2580. | The heirs of Edward Sparkman " | 640 | 84 | " |
| 2581. | The heirs of Jonas Sharp, Pt..... | 640 | 84 | " |
| 2582. | The heirs of Richard Spruell, Pt.. | 640 | 84 | " |
| 2583. | The heirs of Henry Stephens, Pt. | 640 | 84 | " |
| 2584. | The heirs of Ezekell Slawson, Pt.. | 640 | 84 | " |
| 2585. | The heirs of Obadiah Sorrell, Pt.. | 640 | 84 | " |
| 2586. | The heirs of Semon Stillwell, Pt.. | 640 | 84 | " |
| 2587. | The heirs of Constantine Slaughter, Privt............ | 640 | 84 | " |
| 2588. | The heirs of William Spence, Pt.. | 640 | 84 | " |
| 2589. | The heirs of William Venters, Pt.. | 640 | 84 | " |
| 2590. | The heirs of Hezekiah Warren, " | 640 | 84 | Capt. McNees |
| 2591. | The heirs of Josiah Winkles, Pt.. | 640 | 84 | " |
| 2592. | The heirs of Daniel Wells, Pt.... | 640 | 84 | " |
| 2593. | The heirs of James Wensett, Pt.. | 640 | 84 | " |
| 2594. | The heirs of Zachariah Badwell, Corpl. died................ | 1,000 | 84 | " |
| 2595. | The heirs of Jethro Ballender, Corpl. dcsd................ | 1,000 | 84 | " |
| 2596. | The heir of Casper Browngary, Pri. klld.................... | 640 | 84 | " |
| 2597. | The heirs of Samuel Buffenton, Corpl. desd............... | 1,000 | 84 | " |
| 2598. | The heirs of John Badsley, Sergt. killed............... | 1,000 | 84 | " |
| 2599. | The heirs of John Browines, Sergt. killed............... | 1,000 | 84 | " |
| 2600. | The heirs of George Collins, Pri. klld.................... | 640 | 84 | " |
| 2601. | The heirs of Metrue Castandee, Pri. kild.................... | 640 | 84 | " |
| 2602. | The heirs of William Crook, Corpl. Died............... | 1,000 | 84 | " |
| 2603. | The heirs of Demana Draminas, drum. kild................ | 1,000 | 84 | " |
| 2604. | The heirs of Hugh Frausher, Sergt. dcsd................ | 1,000 | 84 | " |
| 2605. | The heirs of John Fusman, Pri. dcsd.................... | 640 | 84 | " |
| 2606. | The heirs of Henry Fetner, Corpl. kild................ | 1,000 | 84 | " |
| 2607. | The heirs of Peter Gray, Pri..... | 640 | 84 | " |
| 2608. | The heirs of Henry Gray, Corpl. kild................ | 1,000 | 84 | " |
| 2609. | The heirs of Richard Gidean, Fifer, kild................ | 1,000 | 84 | " |
| 2610. | The heirs of David Gowin, Sergt. kild................ | 1,000 | 84 | " |

| No. | To whom granted and rank | No. acres | Service in months | Location and to whom deeded and date of warrant. Within the limits of the lands allotted the officers and soldiers of the Continental Line, by Law, 1783, Oct. 14 |
|---|---|---|---|---|
| 2611. | The heirs of George Ingram, Pri. dcsd.................. | 640 | 84 | Capt. McNees |
| 2612. | The heirs of John Muss, Pri. dcsd.................. | 640 | 84 | " |
| 2613. | The heirs of Duncan McFarson, Pr. kild.................... | 640 | 84 | " |
| 2614. | The heirs of Abraham McConnough, Corpl. decsd.... | 1,000 | 84 | " |
| 2615. | The heirs of John McNeel, Pr. kld..................... | 640 | 84 | " |
| 2616. | The heirs of William McMurtry, Pri. kld................... | 640 | 84 | " |
| 2617. | The heirs of Thomas Melary, fifer, decd.................. | 1,000 | 84 | " |
| 2618. | The heirs of John Niclett, Pri. klld.................... | 640 | 84 | " |
| 2619. | The heirs of Tide Abriam, Corp. dcsd.................. | 1,000 | 84 | " |
| 2620. | The heirs of George Preton, Pri. dcsd.................. | 640 | 84 | " |
| 2621. | The heirs of Francis Peney, Drum. dcsd.................. | 1,000 | 84 | " |
| 2622. | The heirs of David Rusters, Pr. dcsd.................... | 640 | 84 | " |
| 2623. | The heirs of Peter Snither, Cpl. . | 1,000 | 84 | " |
| 2624. | The heirs of Henry Morner, Cpl. | 1,000 | 84 | " |
| 2625. | The heirs of William Templeston, drum. kld........ | 1,000 | 84 | " |
| 2626. | The heirs of Robert Velven, Fifer, dcsd.................. | 1,000 | 84 | " |
| 2627. | The heirs of Isaac Weatherley, Privt. dcsd................. | 640 | 84 | " |
| 2628. | The heirs of Olver Williams, Fifer, dcsd................. | 1,000 | 84 | " |
| 2629. | The heirs of Benjamin Williamson, Sergt. died....... | 1,000 | 84 | " |
| 2630. | The heirs of Benjamin Weathers, Sergt. died......... | 1,000 | 84 | " |
| 2631. | The heirs of John Askins, Pri.... | 640 | 84 | Sherrard Barron |
| 2632. | The heirs of John Admons...... | | | " |
| 2633. | The heirs of David Boon....... | | | " |
| 2634. | The heirs of John Baconham.... | | | " |
| 2635. | The heirs of Elisha Boon....... | | | " |
| 2636. | The heirs of Edward Chappell... | | | " |
| 2637. | The heirs of Burwell Cole....... | | | " |
| 2638. | The heirs of Simon Corson...... | | | " |
| 2639. | The heirs of James Carrom..... | | | " |
| 2640. | The heirs of Aaron Cocks....... | | | " |
| 2641. | The heirs of William Culliseon... | | | " |
| 2642. | The heirs of John Cloyd........ | | | " |
| 2643. | The heirs of John Coumbs...... | | | " |
| 2644. | The heirs of Joel Cross......... | | | " |
| 2645. | The heirs of John Dowdy....... | | | " |
| 2646. | The heirs of John Daffin........ | | | " |
| 2647. | The heirs of William Etheredge.. | | | " |
| 2648. | The heirs of John Edens........ | | | " |

| No. | To whom granted and rank | No. acres | Service in months | Location and to whom deeded and date of warrant. Within the limits of the lands allotted the officers and soldiers of the Continental Line, by Law, 1783, Oct. 14 |
|---|---|---|---|---|
| 2649. | The heirs of David Furlee....... | | | Sherrard Barron |
| 2650. | The heirs of Jeremiah Frasur.... | | | " |
| 2651. | The heirs of William Gilbert.... | | | " |
| 2652. | The heirs of John Howell....... | 640 | 84 | " |
| 2653. | The heirs of Ralph Hammonds.. | 640 | 84 | " |
| 2654. | The heirs of Amos Hathcock.... | 640 | 84 | Sept. 30 " |
| 2655. | The heirs of Samuel Hammock.. | 640 | 84 | " " |
| 2656. | The heirs of Hardy Hart........ | 640 | 84 | " |
| 2657. | The heirs of Henry Harrison.... | 640 | 84 | " |
| 2658. | The heirs of Robert Harrison.... | 640 | 84 | " |
| 2659. | The heirs of Robertson Hill..... | 640 | 84 | " |
| 2660. | The heirs of Robert Hayar...... | 640 | 84 | " |
| 2661. | The heirs of James Hacksaw.... | 640 | 84 | " |
| 2662. | The heir of John Hammett...... | 640 | 84 | " |
| 2663. | The heirs of Joel Hudson....... | 640 | 84 | " |
| 2664. | The heirs of Aaron Hollomon.... | 640 | 84 | " |
| 2665. | The heirs of James Hambleton .. | 640 | 84 | " |
| 2666. | The heirs of James Hammon.... | 640 | 84 | " |
| 2667. | The heirs of Lewis Joynet....... | 640 | 84 | " |
| 2668. | The heirs of John Libbincutt.... | 640 | 84 | " |
| 2669. | The heirs of James Long........ | 640 | 84 | " |
| 2670. | The heirs of Haywood Long..... | 640 | 84 | " |
| 2671. | The heirs of Thomas Locust..... | 640 | 84 | " |
| 2672. | The heirs of Samuel Lassiter.... | 640 | 84 | " |
| 2673. | The heirs of David Lewis....... | 640 | 84 | " |
| 2674. | The heirs of Isham Morgan..... | 640 | 84 | " |
| 2675. | The heirs of Daniel Mills....... | 640 | 84 | " |
| 2676. | The heirs of Morris McCoy..... | 640 | 84 | " |
| 2677. | The heirs of Caleb McFashon... | 640 | 84 | " |
| 2678. | The heirs of David Nevur....... | 640 | 84 | " |
| 2679. | The heirs of David Narress..... | 640 | 84 | " |
| 2680. | The heirs of John Overstreet.... | 640 | 84 | " |
| 2681. | The heirs of Isham Onooles..... | 640 | 84 | " |
| 2682. | The heirs of Isham Oneal....... | 640 | 84 | " |
| 2683. | The heirs of Isham Petman..... | 640 | 84 | " |
| 2684. | The heirs of David Reaves...... | 640 | 84 | " |
| 2685. | The heirs of Lewis Ricks........ | 640 | 84 | " |
| 2686. | The heirs of Elijah Revill....... | 640 | 84 | " |
| 2687. | The heirs of James Sikes........ | 640 | 84 | " |
| 2688. | The heirs of William Short...... | 640 | 84 | " |
| 2689. | The heirs of Isham Short....... | 640 | 84 | " |
| 2690. | The heirs of David Short....... | 640 | 84 | " |
| 2691. | The heirs of Valentine Sheppard. | 640 | 84 | " |
| 2692. | The heirs of Joshua Stevens..... | 640 | 84 | " |
| 2693. | The heirs of Thomas Smart..... | 640 | 84 | " |
| 2694. | The heirs of Jeremiah Thomas... | 640 | 84 | " |
| 2695. | The heirs of Gray Tucker....... | 640 | 84 | " |
| 2696. | The heirs of Thomas Talton..... | 640 | 84 | " |
| 2697. | The heirs of Howell Underwood . | 640 | 84 | " |
| 2698. | The heirs of Thomas Vallentine.. | 640 | 84 | " |
| 2699. | The heirs of Green Waker...... | 640 | 84 | " |
| 2700. | The heirs of James Wellman, or (Winman)............... | 640 | 84 | " |
| 2701. | The heirs of Everitt Wattson.... | 640 | 84 | " |
| 2702. | The heirs of Joseph Walkins..... | 640 | 84 | " |
| 2703. | The heirs of John Zutson....... | 640 | 84 | " |

| No. | To whom granted and rank | No. acres | Service in months | Location and to whom deeded and date of warrant. Within the limits of the lands allotted the officers and soldiers of the Continental Line, by Law, 1783, Oct. 14 |
|---|---|---|---|---|
| 2704. | The heirs of Isaac Benford...... | 640 | 84 | Sherrard Barron |
| 2705. | The heirs of James Bentford.... | 640 | 84 | " |
| 2706. | The heirs of James Bulworth.... | 640 | 84 | " |
| 2707. | The heirs of Solomon Bennett... | 640 | 84 | " |
| 2708. | The heirs of Abraham Buck..... | 640 | 84 | " |
| 2709. | The heirs of James Buntin...... | 640 | 84 | " |
| 2710. | The heirs of Wakor Ballard..... | 640 | 84 | " |
| 2711. | The heirs of Silus Cross......... | 640 | 84 | " |
| 2712. | The heirs of Henry Chaimberlin. | 640 | 84 | " |
| 2713. | The heirs of Frederick Cross.... | 640 | 84 | " |
| 2714. | The heirs of Elijah Cornelus..... | 640 | 84 | " |
| 2715. | The heirs of Joseph Elliott...... | 640 | 84 | " |
| 2716. | The heirs of Matthew Forrest... | 640 | 84 | Sherrod Baron |
| 2717. | The heirs of Burwell Foster..... | 640 | 84 | " |
| 2718. | The heirs of Joshua Garvis...... | 640 | 84 | |
| 2719. | The heirs of Hardy Gun........ | 640 | 84 | |
| 2720. | The heirs of Joshua Griffin...... | 640 | 84 | |
| 2721. | The heirs of Samuel Green...... | 640 | 84 | |
| 2722. | The heirs of Abraham Green.... | 640 | 84 | |
| 2723. | The heirs of Nathan Gardner.... | 640 | 84 | |
| 2724. | The heirs of Anthony Habbett... | 604 | 84 | |
| 2725. | The heirs of Ephraim Harnett... | 640 | 84 | |
| 2726. | The heirs of Charles Hansel..... | 640 | 84 | |
| 2727. | The heirs of Ishum Henry.... | 640 | 84 | |
| 2728. | The heirs of Festor Hammonds.. | 640 | 84 | |
| 2729. | The heirs of Hardy Harris...... | 640 | 84 | |
| 2730. | The heirs of John Hitson....... | 640 | 84 | |
| 2731. | The heirs of Abraham Harris.... | 640 | 84 | |
| 2732. | The heirs of William Hooks..... | 640 | 84 | " |
| 2733. | The heirs of Chester Hickerison . | 640 | 84 | |
| 2734. | The heirs of James Hill......... | 640 | 84 | |
| 2735. | The heirs of Harper Johnston... | 640 | 84 | |
| 2736. | The heirs of Joseph Jordan...... | 640 | 84 | |
| 2737. | The heirs of Pilate Jordan...... | 640 | 84 | |
| 2738. | The heirs of Thophilus Jones.... | 640 | 84 | |
| 2739. | The heirs of Jeremiah Jordan.... | 640 | 84 | |
| 2740. | The heirs of Freeman Joiner..... | 640 | 84 | |
| 2741. | The heirs of Harmon Johnston .. | 640 | 84 | |
| 2742. | The heirs of Daniel Ray........ | 640 | 84 | |
| 2743. | The heirs of Abram Lain....... | 640 | 84 | |
| 2744. | The heirs of John Lille......... | 640 | 84 | |
| 2745. | The heirs of James Lain........ | 640 | 84 | |
| 2746. | The heirs of John Lackey....... | 640 | 84 | Sherrod Baron |
| 2747. | The heirs of Drewry Morgan.... | 640 | 84 | |
| 2748. | The heirs of Febreas March..... | 640 | 84 | |
| 2749. | The heirs of Henry Moveal...... | 640 | 84 | |
| 2750. | The heirs of John Mayo, or (S).. | 640 | 84 | |
| 2751. | The heirs of Henry Murrell.... | 640 | 84 | |
| 2752. | The heirs of Morris McFoy..... | 640 | 84 | |
| 2753. | The heirs of Charles McCree.... | 640 | 84 | |
| 2754. | The heirs of James Nickleson.... | 640 | 84 | |
| 2755. | The heirs of Barnett Purvice.... | 640 | 84 | |
| 2756. | The heirs of John Pursly........ | 640 | 84 | |
| 2757. | The heirs of Isum Parker....... | 640 | 84 | |
| 2758. | The heirs of Ellexana Purton.... | 640 | 84 | |
| 2759. | The heirs of Randal Putman.... | 640 | 84 | |

| No. | To whom granted and rank | No. acres | Service in months | Location and to whom deeded and date of warrant. Within the limits of the lands allotted the officers and soldiers of the Continental Line, by Law, 1783, Oct. 14 | |
|---|---|---|---|---|---|
| 2760. | The heirs of Isaac Robertson.... | 640 | 84 | | |
| 2761. | The heirs of Joshua Roberts..... | 640 | 84 | | |
| 2762. | The heirs of William Rush...... | 640 | 84 | | |
| 2763. | The heirs of Foster Rives....... | 640 | 84 | | |
| 2764. | The heirs of John Sellars........ | 640 | 84 | | |
| 2765. | The heirs of Elick Sneed........ | 640 | 84 | | |
| 2766. | The heirs of Robert Sellars...... | 640 | 84 | | |
| 2767. | The heirs of Applewhite Landers. | 640 | 84 | | |
| 2768. | The heirs of Elias Savage....... | 640 | 84 | | |
| 2769. | The heirs of John Sanders....... | 640 | 84 | | |
| 2770. | The heirs of William Shivers.... | 640 | 84 | | |
| 2771. | The heirs of Meredy Scutchins .. | 640 | 84 | | |
| 2772. | The heirs of Joel Stone......... | 640 | 84 | | |
| 2773. | The heirs of Handcock Standley. | 640 | 84 | | |
| 2774. | The heirs of John Sneed........ | 640 | 84 | | |
| 2775. | The heirs of Ezekiel Skipper..... | 640 | 84 | | |
| 2776. | The heirs of Hardy Skipper..... | 640 | 84 | | |
| 2777. | The heirs of Nehemiah Smith... | 640 | 84 | | |
| 2778. | The heirs of Joel Shafford....... | 640 | 84 | | |
| 2779. | The heirs of John Todd........ | 640 | 84 | Sherrod Barron | |
| 2780. | The heirs of James Underwood.. | 640 | 84 | | |
| 2781. | The heirs of Patrick Venus...... | 640 | 84 | | |
| 2782. | The heirs of George Vinson...... | 640 | 84 | | |
| 2783. | The heirs of Charterite Vinson .. | 640 | 84 | | |
| 2784. | The heirs of Isom Whitton...... | 640 | 84 | | |
| 2785. | The heirs of Solomon Wiloughby | 640 | 84 | | |
| 2786. | Charter Wiggins.............. | 640 | 84 | | |
| 2787. | Edward Hutchens, Sergt........ | 1,000 | 84 | | Self |
| 2788. | The heirs of Hardy Atway, Pri... | 640 | 84 | Capt. McNees | |
| 2789. | The heirs of John Bryan........ | 640 | 84 | " | |
| 2790. | The heirs of William Bryner..... | 640 | 84 | " | |
| 2791. | The heirs of Nathaniel Biggs.... | 640 | 84 | " | |
| 2792. | The heirs of Benjamin Buckhannon............... | 640 | 84 | " | |
| 2793. | The heirs of Silas Biggs......... | 640 | 84 | " | |
| 2794. | The heirs of John Berry........ | 640 | 84 | " | |
| 2795. | The heirs of John Barrott....... | 640 | 84 | " | |
| 2796. | The heirs of William Bushop.... | 640 | 84 | " | |
| 2797. | The heirs of Colden Bushop..... | 640 | 84 | " | |
| 2798. | The heirs of John Carson....... | 640 | 84 | " | |
| 2799. | The heirs of John Capton....... | 640 | 84 | " | |
| 2800. | The heirs of John Duggan...... | 640 | 84 | " | |
| 2801. | The heirs of Jesse Davis........ | 640 | 84 | " | |
| 2802. | The heirs of William Evans..... | 640 | 84 | " | |
| 2803. | The heirs of Samuel Flessur..... | 640 | 84 | " | |
| 2804. | The heirs of Gilbert Grant...... | 640 | 84 | " | |
| 2805. | The heirs of Richard Harrington. | 640 | 84 | " | |
| 2806. | The heirs of Thomas Harwood... | 640 | 84 | " | |
| 2807. | The heirs of John Hopkins...... | 640 | 84 | " | |
| 2808. | The heirs of Stephen Jessop..... | 640 | 84 | " | |
| 2809. | The heirs of Samuel Jaby....... | 640 | 84 | " | |
| 2810. | The heirs of Richard King...... | 640 | 84 | " | |
| 2811. | The heirs of John Mulkey....... | 640 | 84 | " | |
| 2812. | The heirs of Robert Magby..... | 640 | 84 | " | |
| 2813. | The heirs of John Mills......... | 640 | 84 | " | |
| 2814. | The heirs of James Pervie....... | 640 | 84 | " | |

| No. | To whom granted and rank | No. acres | Service in months | Location and to whom deeded and date of warrant. Within the limits of the lands allotted the officers and soldiers of the Continental Line, by Law, 1783, Oct. 14 |
|---|---|---|---|---|
| 2815. | The heirs of John Roberts...... | 640 | 84 | Capt. McNees |
| 2816. | The heirs of William Reaves.... | 640 | 84 | " |
| 2817. | The heirs of James Richardson, Pri.............. | 640 | 84 | " |
| 2818. | The heirs of Tobias Steadham... | 640 | 84 | Sept. 30 " |
| 2819. | The heirs of Drewry Simms..... | 640 | 84 | " |
| 2820. | The heirs of Thomas Thomas.... | 640 | 84 | " |
| 2821. | The heirs of John Tanner....... | 640 | 84 | " |
| 2822. | The heirs of John Thomas...... | 640 | 84 | " |
| 2823. | The heirs of William Vanderfield | 640 | 84 | " |
| 2824. | The heirs of James Willis....... | 640 | 84 | " |
| 2825. | The heirs of Benjamin Whealer.. | 640 | 84 | " |
| 2826. | The heirs of Thomas Williams... | 640 | 84 | " |
| 2827. | The heirs of Samuel Weaver..... | 640 | 84 | " |
| 2828. | The heirs of Jesse Asken........ | 640 | 84 | " |
| 2829. | The heirs of James Albright..... | 640 | 84 | " |
| 2830. | The heirs of Jesse Applewhite... | 640 | 84 | " |
| 2831. | The heirs of Stephen Ash....... | 640 | 84 | " |
| 2832. | The heirs of Jacob Boon........ | 640 | 84 | " |
| 2833. | The heirs of James Belch....... | 640 | 84 | " |
| 2834. | The heirs of William Banns..... | 640 | 84 | " |
| 2835. | The heirs of Jesse Boseman..... | 640 | 84 | " |
| 2836. | The heirs of Absolum Burress... | 640 | 84 | " |
| 2837. | The heirs of Thomas Buckle, Drum............... | 1,000 | 84 | " |
| 2838. | The heirs of Henry Bennet...... | 640 | 84 | " |
| 2839. | The heirs of Drewry Ballard.... | 640 | 84 | " |
| 2840. | The heirs of James Cowens...... | 640 | 84 | " |
| 2841. | The heirs of John Capehart..... | 640 | 84 | " |
| 2842. | The heirs of Zebulon Cobb...... | 640 | 84 | " |
| 2843. | The heirs of William Daws...... | 640 | 84 | Capt. McNees |
| 2844. | The heirs of John Drawhorn.... | 640 | 84 | " |
| 2845. | The heirs of Amos Davison..... | 640 | 84 | " |
| 2846. | The heirs of Solomon Danby, Fifer..................... | 1,000 | 84 | " |
| 2847. | The heirs of Zachariah Durham . | 640 | 84 | " |
| 2848. | The heirs of William Freeman... | | | " |
| 2849. | The heirs of William Fillgon..... | | | " |
| 2850. | The heirs of George Hughs...... | | | " |
| 2851. | The heirs of Nathaniel Holly.... | | | " |
| 2852. | The heirs of James Hall........ | | | " |
| 2853. | The heirs of Josiah Hadsock, Pt.. | 640 | 84 | " |
| 2854. | The heirs of Josiah Jenkins...... | | | " |
| 2855. | The heirs of Archibald Johnston. | | | " |
| 2856. | The heirs of Isaiah Jackson..... | | | " |
| 2857. | The heirs of William Kite....... | | | " |
| 2858. | The heirs of Josiah Laster....... | | | " |
| 2859. | The heirs of James Laster....... | | | " |
| 2860. | The heirs of Joshua Laurence.... | | | " |
| 2861. | The heirs of William Morgan.... | | | " |
| 2862. | The heirs of James Morgan..... | | | " |
| 2863. | The heirs of James Mardera..... | | | " |
| 2864. | The heirs of Isaac McMullin.... | | | " |
| 2865. | The heirs of Jesse Williams, Sgt.. | 1,000 | 84 | " |
| 2866. | The heirs of Solomon Miller, Pt.. | 640 | 84 | " |
| 2867. | The heirs of James Nowell...... | 640 | 84 | " |

| No. | To whom granted and rank | No. acres | Service in months | Location and to whom deeded and date of warrant. Within the limits of the lands allotted the officers and soldiers of the Continental Line, by Law, 1783, Oct. 14 |
|---|---|---|---|---|
| 2868. | Aaron Outlow................ | | | Capt. McNees |
| 2869. | The heirs of Isaac Pelt......... | | | " |
| 2870. | The heirs of John Persey....... | | | " |
| 2871. | The heirs of Isaac Perry....... | | | " |
| 2872. | The heirs of Benjamin Pender... | | | " |
| 2873. | The heirs of Willis Pipkin....... | | | " |
| 2874. | The heirs of Thomas Reddick... | | | " |
| 2875. | The heirs of John Rainer....... | | | |
| 2876. | The heirs of Solomon Ramsey, Sergt..................... | 1,000 | 84 | " |
| 2877. | The heirs of Andrew Russell, Pt.. | 640 | 84 | " |
| 2878. | The heirs of James Lowell...... | 640 | 84 | " |
| 2879. | The heirs of Joseph Scull....... | 640 | 84 | " |
| 2880. | The heirs of Joshua Simons..... | 640 | 84 | " |
| 2881. | The heirs of William Sparkman.. | 640 | 84 | " |
| 2882. | The heirs of John Stone........ | 640 | 84 | " |
| 2883. | The heirs of Andrew Skipton.... | 640 | 84 | " |
| 2884. | The heirs of Zedekiah Stone..... | 640 | 84 | " |
| 2885. | The heirs of Jonathan Smith.... | 640 | 84 | " |
| 2886. | The heirs of William Todd...... | 640 | 84 | " |
| 2887. | The heirs of William Tyner..... | 640 | 84 | " |
| 2888. | The heirs of Absolam Turner.... | 640 | 84 | " |
| 2889. | The heirs of Benjamin Troublefield, Pri............. | 640 | 84 | " |
| 2890. | The heirs of Silas Valentine..... | 640 | 84 | " |
| 2891. | The heirs of Jesse Witherington . | 640 | 84 | " |
| 2892. | The heirs of Jacob Witherington. | 640 | 84 | " |
| 2893. | The heirs of William Watson.... | 640 | 84 | " |
| 2894. | The heirs of Joseph Whitaker ... | 640 | 84 | " |
| 2895. | The heirs of Randol Wilder, Cpl.. | 1,000 | 84 | " |
| 2896. | The heirs of Isum Whealey, Sgt.. | 1,000 | 84 | " |
| 2897. | The heirs of Job Williamson, Pri.. | 640 | 84 | " |
| 2898. | The heirs of John Yearly....... | 640 | 84 | " |
| 2899. | The heirs of Demsey Archer..... | 640 | 84 | " |
| 2900. | The heirs of Isaah Rigleston.... | 640 | 84 | " |
| 2901. | The heirs of Jesse Booth........ | 640 | 84 | " |
| 2902. | The heirs of Ezekiel Burdock.... | 640 | 84 | " |
| 2903. | The heirs of Aaron Baker....... | 640 | 84 | " |
| 2904. | The heirs of Benjamin Brown... | 640 | 84 | " |
| 2905. | The heirs of William Baker..... | 640 | 84 | " |
| 2906. | The heirs of Thomas Billips..... | 640 | 84 | " |
| 2907. | The heirs of Mills Bryan........ | 640 | 84 | " |
| 2908. | The heirs of Peter Clifton....... | 640 | 84 | Capt. McNees |
| 2909. | The heirs of William Cobb...... | 640 | 84 | " |
| 2910. | The heirs of Benjamin Doughlas. | 640 | 84 | " |
| 2911. | The heirs of Hugh Dundele..... | 640 | 84 | " |
| 2912. | The heirs of Jeremiah Fletcher, Pri..................... | 640 | 84 | " |
| 2913. | The heirs of Abraham Finley.... | 640 | 84 | " |
| 2914. | The heirs of Thomas Farmer.... | 640 | 84 | " |
| 2915. | The heirs of Garret Fulks....... | | | " |
| 2916. | The heirs of Jesse Garrett....... | | | " |
| 2917. | The heirs of William Gloughn... | | | " |
| 2918. | The heirs of David Gold........ | | | " |
| 2919. | The heirs of Alexander McFirney | | | " |
| 2920. | The heirs of William Goodwin... | | | |

| No. | To whom granted and rank | No. acres | Service in months | Location and to whom deeded and date of warrant. Within the limits of the lands allotted the officers and soldiers of the Continental Line, by Law, 1783, Oct. 14 |
|---|---|---|---|---|
| 2921. | The heirs of William Gooding... | | | Capt. McNees |
| 2922. | The heirs of John Harris........ | | | " |
| 2923. | The heirs of Job Harris......... | | | " |
| 2924. | The heirs of Samuel Hardenson.. | | | " |
| 2925. | The heirs of Joel Hobbs........ | | | " |
| 2926. | The heirs of Timothy Hunter.... | | | " |
| 2927. | The heirs of Moses Hobbs...... | | | " |
| 2928. | The heirs of Isaac Hobbs....... | | | " |
| 2929. | The heirs of John Hinton....... | | | " |
| 2930. | The heirs of Burwell Hughs..... | | | " |
| 2931. | The heirs of John Hicks........ | | | " |
| 2932. | The heirs of William Hicks...... | | | " |
| 2933. | The heirs of Joel Jefferson..... | | | " |
| 2934. | The heirs of Timothy Lee...... | | | " |
| 2935. | The heirs of Hardy Lee......... | | | " |
| 2936. | The heirs of Jonathan Miller.... | | | " |
| 2937. | The heirs of Stephen McDewell, Pri...................... | 640 | 84 | " |
| 2938. | The heirs of Edge Mott........ | 640 | 84 | " |
| 2939. | The heirs of James Mardera..... | 640 | 84 | " |
| 2940. | The heirs of William Newberry.. | 640 | 84 | " |
| 2941. | The heirs of William Percy...... | 640 | 84 | " |
| 2942. | The heir of Zedekiah Perkins.... | 640 | 84 | " |
| 2943. | The heirs of Stephen Phelps..... | 640 | 84 | " |
| 2944. | The heirs of William Putnell.... | 640 | 84 | " |
| 2945. | The heirs of Samuel Parks...... | 640 | 84 | " |
| 2946. | The heirs of William Perry...... | 640 | 84 | " |
| 2947. | The heirs of Micajah Price...... | 640 | 84 | " |
| 2948. | The heirs of Joseph Reed....... | 640 | 84 | " |
| 2949. | The heirs of John Robbins, a Pt.. | 640 | 84 | " |
| 2950. | The heirs of Hezekiah Ready.... | | | " |
| 2951. | The heirs of James Rogers...... | | | " |
| 2952. | The heirs of Lewis Rodes....... | | | " |
| 2953. | The heirs of Zaddock Risby..... | | | " |
| 2954. | The heirs of Moses Roche....... | | | " |
| 2955. | The heirs of Timothy Rich...... | | | " |
| 2956. | The heirs of Mills Ramsey...... | | | " |
| 2957. | The heirs of Isaac Reddick...... | | | " |
| 2958. | The heirs of Jacob Sumner...... | | | " |
| 2959. | The heirs of Francis Summers ... | | | " |
| 2960. | The heirs of Isaac Saunders..... | | | " |
| 2961. | The heirs of Thomas Sorrel, Pri.. | | | " |
| 2962. | The heirs of Richard Tilton..... | | | " |
| 2963. | The heirs of Josiah Whitaker.... | | | " |
| 2964. | The heirs of Josiah Willis....... | | | " |
| 2965. | The heirs of Jno. Wyns........ | | | " |
| 2966. | The heirs of Jacob Wingfield.... | | | " |
| 2967. | The heirs of Michael Ward...... | | | " |
| 2968. | The heir of John Winborn...... | | | " |
| 2969. | The heirs of Dredd Washington . | | | " |
| 2970. | The heirs of Theophilus Williams................... | | | " |
| 2971. | The heirs of Isaiah Yearly...... | | | " |
| 2972. | The heirs of Martin Doughlass, Sergt..................... | 1,000 | 84 | " |
| 2973. | The heirs of Evan Hooker...... | 1,000 | 84 | " |

| No. | To whom granted and rank | No. acres | Service in months | Location and to whom deeded and date of warrant. Within the limits of the lands allotted the officers and soldiers of the Continental Line, by Law, 1783, Oct. 14 | |
|---|---|---|---|---|---|
| 2974. | The heirs of George Trueluck, Pt. | 640 | 84 | | Capt. McNees |
| 2975. | The heirs of James Beard....... | | | | " |
| 2976. | The heirs of Ephraim Daniel.... | | | | " |
| 2977. | The heirs of Stephen Perkins.... | | | | " |
| 2978. | The heirs of John Colchester.... | | | | " |
| 2979. | The heirs of Ephaphroditus King. | | | | " |
| 2980. | The heirs of Jeremiah Evans.... | | | | " |
| 2981. | The heirs of Elias Dobson...... | | | | " |
| 2982. | The heirs of Joshua Allmand.... | 274 | 36 | | Thos. Butcher |
| 2983. | The heirs of John Balford....... | 640 | 84 | | " |
| 2984. | The heirs of Robert Brooks..... | 428 | 36 | | " |
| 2985. | The heirs of John Balson....... | 640 | 84 | | " |
| 2987. | The heirs of Samuel Bellwood... | | | | " |
| 2988. | The heirs of William Barkley.... | | | | " |
| 2988. | The heirs of Moses Braxton..... | | | | " |
| 2989. | The heirs of Joel Fisher, Pri.... | 640 | 84 | | " |
| 2990. | The heirs of Jacob Freeland..... | | | | " |
| 2991. | The heirs of Francis Fowler..... | | | | " |
| 2992. | The heirs of Thomas Crain...... | | | | " |
| 2993. | Timothy Cavuner............. | | | | " |
| 2994. | Sampson Cullennver.......... | | | | " |
| 2995. | The heirs of George Cook, Corpl.. | 1,000 | 84 | | " |
| 2996. | The heirs of Joseph Chestnut.... | 640 | 85 | | " |
| 2997. | Isaac Dines................. | 274 | 36 | Sept. 30 | " |
| 2998. | Joseph Dilmore............... | 274 | 36 | | " |
| 2999. | The heirs of Louis Deal........ | 640 | 84 | | " |
| 3000. | Benjamin Davison............ | 274 | 36 | | " |
| 3001. | The heirs of Philip Evans....... | 640 | 84 | | " |
| 3002. | Thomas Gannon.............. | 274 | 36 | | " |
| 3003. | The heirs of Luke Head, Corpl... | 1,000 | 84 | | " |
| 3004. | The heirs of George Hopewell... | 640 | 84 | | " |
| 3005. | George Hampton............. | 274 | 36 | | " |
| 3006. | The heirs of Willis Mammons... | 640 | 84 | | " |
| 3007. | The heirs of Robert Hailey...... | 274 | 36 | | " |
| 3008. | The heirs of Oliver Hastin...... | 640 | 84 | | " |
| 3009. | The heirs of Joel Jarvis, Pri. .... | 640 | 84 | | " |
| 3010. | Joseph Kelly................. | 274 | 36 | | " |
| 3011. | The heirs of Mark Lowman, or (Lonman)............... | 640 | 84 | | " |
| 3012. | Lewis Lemare................. | 274 | 36 | | " |
| 3013. | Stephen Newton.............. | 274 | 36 | | " |
| 3014. | Robert Nobles................ | 274 | 36 | | " |
| 3015. | James Owel.................. | 274 | 36 | | " |
| 3016. | The heirs of John Owel........ | 640 | 84 | | " |
| 3017. | The heirs of Solomon Overton, Sergt..................... | 1,000 | 84 | | " |
| 3018. | Daniel Peter................. | 274 | 36 | | " |
| 3019. | The heirs of Mark Parrish, Cpl.. | 1,000 | 84 | | " |
| 3020. | The heirs of John Pervatt, Sgt... | 1,000 | 84 | | " |
| 3021. | The heirs of Stephen Sebaston, Pri............... | 640 | 84 | | " |
| 3022. | The heirs of Edmund Spalding... | | | | " |
| 3023. | John Stedmon................ | | | | " |
| 3024. | The heirs of James Stedmon..... | | | | " |
| 3025. | The heirs of James Scalp....... | | | | " |
| 3026. | The heirs of Peter Stedmon..... | | | | " |

| No. | To whom granted and rank | No. acres | Service in months | Location and to whom deeded and date of warrant. Within the limits of the lands allotted the officers and soldiers of the Continental Line, by Law, 1783, Oct. 14 | |
|---|---|---|---|---|---|
| 3027. | The heirs of John Simons....... | | | Thos. Butcher | |
| 3028. | George Woodward............. | | | " | |
| 3029. | Charles Warldon.............. | | | " | |
| 3030. | Aaron Walker................. | | | " | |
| 3031. | Jonathan Wallard............. | | | " | |
| 3032. | Zebulon Wells................ | | | " | |
| 3033. | John Poynter, Capt............ | 1,508 | 33 | George Wynne | |
| 3034. | Howell Rowell, Pri............ | 228 | 30 | Capt. Tatum | |
| 3035. | The heirs of Robert Bowman.... | 640 | 84 | | |
| 3036. | John Mathews, Pri............ | 274 | 36 | | |
| 3037. | John Bartee, Pri.............. | 640 | 84 | | Self |
| 3038. | James Carmack, Pri........... | 640 | 84 | Austin Prescott | |
| 3039. | James Underhill, Pri.......... | 274 | 36 | " | |
| 3040. | James Wiggens, Pri............ | 640 | 84 | | Self |
| 3041. | The heirs of John Blamer....... | 640 | 84 | Capt. Pearl | |
| 3042. | James Pearl, Capt............. | 3,860 | 84 | " | |
| 3043. | The heirs of Archibald Ray..... | 640 | 84 | | |
| 3044. | The heirs of Thomas Wimpie.... | 640 | 84 | | |
| 3045. | The heirs of Thomas Dring..... | 640 | 84 | Lute Slade | |
| 3046. | Daniel Potter................. | 228 | 30 | Col. Sherrod | |
| 3047. | The heirs of Samuel Ross....... | 640 | 84 | James Mulloy | |
| 3048. | George Wolfenden, the sole legatee of Capt. Chas. Stewart dcsd..................... | 3,840 | 84 | Geo. Wolfender | |
| 3049. | The heirs of William Moore..... | 640 | 84 | Capt. Jarret | |
| 3050. | The heirs of Moses Moore, Pri... | 640 | 84 | " | |
| 3051. | The heirs of Benjamin Moore, Pt. | 640 | 84 | " | |
| 3052. | The heirs of Elisha Harris, Pri... | 640 | 84 | Col. Hinds | |
| 3053. | Bartholomew Curtis, Pri....... | 185 | 24 m o. 10da. | Gov. Martin | |
| 3054. | Joshua Curtis, Ens............ | 741 | 24 m o. 10da. | " | |
| 3055. | Thomas Prescoate, Sergt....... | 1,000 | 84 | Austin Prescote | |
| 3056. | Joshua Webb, Pri............. | 640 | 84 | Jno. Webb | |
| 3057. | Charles Webb................. | 640 | 84 | | |
| 3058. | Benj. Coats, Pri.............. | 365 | 40 | | |
| 3059. | William Williams, Capt........ | 3,840 | 84 | Nov. 30 | Col. Long | |
| 3060. | The heirs of John Swanson...... | 640 | 84 | " | " |
| 3061. | Robert Perry, Pri............. | 640 | 84 | Gen. Ramsay | |
| 3062. | The heirs of William Norton.... | 640 | 84 | " | |
| 3063. | Lewis Stevens, Pri............ | 228 | 30 | " | |
| 3064. | William Pope, Pri............. | 365 | 40 | | Self |
| 3065. | Edward Stradley, Pri.......... | 640 | 84 | " | |
| 3066. | Frederick Cook, Pri........... | 640 | 84 | Col. Wm. Polk | |
| 3067. | The heirs of John McCormick... | 640 | 84 | " | |
| 3068. | The heirs of Anthony Black..... | 640 | 84 | " | |
| 3069. | The heirs of Hance Starr....... | 640 | 84 | " | |
| 3070. | The heirs of Abraham Coltain, Pt. | 640 | 84 | " | |
| 3071. | The heirs of John Poor........ | 640 | 84 | " | |
| 3072. | The heirs of Francis Bird...... | 640 | 84 | " | |
| 3073. | The heirs of John Waters....... | 640 | 84 | " | |
| 3074. | The heirs of Samuel Ross....... | 640 | 84 | " | |
| 3075. | The heirs of Tobias Goodwin.... | 640 | 84 | " | |
| 3076. | Patrick Murphrey, Pri......... | 640 | 84 | Col. Whitaker | |
| 3077. | Elisha Hunter, Pri............ | 640 | 84 | | Self |
| 3078. | Caleb Hawley, Pri............. | 640 | 84 | A. Stern | |
| 3079. | Osborn Clark................. | 640 | 84 | | |
| 3080. | John Delaney................. | 640 | 84 | | |

| No. | To whom granted and rank | No. acres | Service in months | Location and to whom deeded and date of warrant. Within the limits of the lands allotted the officers and soldiers of the Continental Line, by Law, 1783, Oct. 14 | |
|---|---|---|---|---|---|
| 3081. | James Gifford, Sergt. | 428 | 36 | Dec. 2, '95 | Frazs. Greavs |
| 3082. | Matthias Hammon, Pri. Infrm. | 640 | 84 | | Col. Wm. Polk |
| 3083. | Daniel Williams, Capt. | 2,285 | 50 | | Col. C. Ivey |
| 3084. | John Nichols, Privt. dcsd. | 640 | 84 | | Col. Long |
| 3085. | The heirs of Daniel Griffin, Sgt. | 1,000 | 84 | | Aaron Lambert |
| 3086. | The heirs of Daniel McDaniel, Pt. | 640 | 84 | | Col. Jno. Armstrong |
| 3087. | The heirs of Moses Madry, Pri. | 640 | 84 | | Col. Montfort |
| 3088. | Enoch King, Pri. | 640 | 84 | | |
| 3089. | Nathaniel Williams, Pri. | 228 | 30 | | Wm. T. Lewis |
| 3090. | Samuel Guin, Pri. | | | | |
| 3091. | Francis Mosure, Pri. | 640 | 84 | | " |
| 3092. | Matthias Pitt. | 640 | 84 | | " |
| 3093. | William Humphries, Pri. | 640 | 84 | | |
| 3094. | Ephraim Parmaley. | | | | |
| 3095. | Thomas Laine, western country. | 640 | 84 | | " |
| 3096. | Edmund Griffin, Sergt. | 452 | 38 | | " |
| 3097. | William Love, Pri. | 640 | 84 | | |
| 3098. | The heirs of Mallicha Dawe, Pri. | 640 | 84 | | Col. Harney |
| 3099. | The heirs of Jeffrey Dan. | | | | " |
| 3100. | The heirs of Thomas Jackson. | | | | " |
| 3101. | Robert Jackson. | 276 | 34 | | |
| 3102. | The heirs of Willoughby Creef, decsd. | 640 | 84 | | " |
| 3103. | John Ralph. | 640 | 84 | | " |
| 3104. | John Gilbert. | 640 | 84 | | " |
| 3105. | William Ferrell, Lieut. | 2,560 | 84 | " | " |
| 3106. | Isaac Gallop, Pri. | 320 | 42 | | " |
| 3107. | Jesse Prichard, Sergt. | 428 | 36 | | " |
| 3108. | Luke Lamb Ferrell, Lieut. | 2,560 | 84 | | " |
| 3109. | Thomas Mann, Pri. | 640 | 84 | | " |
| 3110. | Levi Sanderlin, Pri. | 228 | 30 | | |
| 3111. | Benjamin Angle, Pri. | 640 | 84 | | Wm. P. Lewis |
| 3112. | The heirs of Jeremiah Clay Sgt. | 1,000 | 84 | | " |
| 3113. | Joshua Rinehart, Pri. | 640 | 84 | | " |
| 3114. | Allisander McKinzey, Pri. | | | | |
| 3115. | David Arnold, Pri. | 274 | 36 | | Maj. Tatum |
| 3116. | James Spann, Pri. | 228 | 30 | | " |
| 3117. | Miles Maudlin's heirs, Pri. | 640 | 84 | Dec. 12, '85 | Capt. Howell Tatum |
| 3118. | Gilbert Matthews, Pri. | 434 | 67 | | " |
| 3119. | The heirs of Christopher Ton. | 640 | 84 | | " |
| 3120. | The heirs of Thomas Woodley. | 640 | 84 | | " |
| 3121. | Thomas Norman. | 365 | 48 | | |
| 3122. | Joseph and James Gray, heirs of John Gray, Capt. | 3,840 | 84 | | J. Macon |
| 3123. | Austin Prescote. | 640 | 84 | | James McCafferty |
| 3124. | The heirs of Jacob Bermit, or (Bennit) Pri. | 640 | 84 | | Isles Simmons Self |
| 3125. | Isles Simmons, Sergt. | 428 | 36 | | |
| 3126. | Benjamin Crabb. | 274 | 36 | | Isles Simmons |
| 3127. | William Thompson. | 228 | 30 | | Howell Tatum, Esq. |
| 3128. | James Barnes. | 274 | 36 | | Wm. Hays |
| 3129. | John Muckleroy, Pri. | 274 | | | " |
| 3130. | David Edwards, Pri. | 573 | 69 | | Col. ........ |
| 3131. | Matthias Bates, infirm. Pri. | 640 | 84 | | W. T. Lewis |
| 3132. | Joel Morrison, Pri. | 640 | 84 | | " |
| 3133. | Jesse Edwards, Pri. | 640 | 84 | | " |

| No. | To whom granted and rank | No. acres | Service in months | Location and to whom deeded and date of warrant. Within the limits of the lands allotted the officers and soldiers of the Continental Line, by Law, 1783, Oct. 14 | |
|---|---|---|---|---|---|
| 3134. | Jesse Williams, Pri............ | 640 | 84 | | W. T. Lewis |
| 3135. | The heirs of Patrick Rogers, Lt.. | 2,560 | 84 | | Capt. Bacote |
| 3136. | The heir of William Lewis...... | 640 | 84 | | Jas. Lewis |
| 3137. | The heirs of John Hartley...... | 1,000 | 84 | | Hartley |
| 3138. | Jacob Gridor, non com. Off...... | 428 | 36 | | ........ Rutherford |
| 3139. | The heirs of John Kelly, decsd... | 640 | 84 | | |
| 3140. | William Parks, Pri............. | 640 | 84 | Dec. 17,'85 | Auga. Wood |
| 3141. | The heirs of Thomas Pedon..... | 640 | 84 | | |
| 3142. | William Mahains, Pri.......... | 274 | 36 | | Isles Simmons |
| 3143. | The heirs of William McDonald. | 640 | 84 | | " |
| 3144. | The heirs of Alexander Cherry... | 640 | 84 | | " |
| 3145. | John Beasley, fifer............. | 357 | 30 | | " |
| 3146. | John Solman, Pri.............. | 274 | 36 | | |
| 3147. | The heirs of Luke Silvester...... | 640 | 84 | | |
| 3148. | The heirs of Joseph Stephens.... | 640 | 84 | | Levi Ivey |
| 3149. | Isaac Hays................... | 640 | 84 | | " |
| 3150. | James Bullock................. | 640 | 84 | | Elijah Robertson |
| 3151. | The heirs of Richard Sanders.... | 640 | 84 | | " |
| 3152. | The heirs of Samuel Ewell...... | 640 | 84 | | " |
| 3153. | The heirs of John Carlton....... | 640 | 84 | | " |
| 3154. | The heirs of Stephen Garriss.... | 640 | 84 | | " |
| 3155. | Estridge Newton, Sergt........ | 1,000 | 84 | | " |
| 3156. | John Overton, Pri............. | 274 | 36 | | " |
| 3157. | Ross Thomas, Pri............. | 274 | 36 | | " |
| 3158. | The heirs of Peter Sanders...... | 640 | 84 | | |
| 3159. | Arthur Corbin, Pri............. | 274 | 36 | | Maj. Tatum |
| 3160. | Francis Harrison, heir of James Harrison, (Bertie) Pri........ | 640 | 84 | | |
| 3161. | The heirs of Charles Adams, Pri. | 640 | 84 | | |
| 3162. | The heirs of Henry Baldwin, Pri. | 640 | 84 | | " |
| 3163. | The heirs of Lewis Beard, Pri.... | 640 | 84 | | " |
| 3164. | The heirs of Joseph Brachen, Pri. | 640 | 84 | | " |
| 3165. | The heirs of John Coram, Pri.... | 640 | 84 | | " |
| 3166. | The heirs of John Clay, Pri...... | 640 | 84 | | " |
| 3167. | The heirs of Zach'h Davis, Pri... | 640 | 84 | | " |
| 3168. | The heirs of Henry Ferrel, Pri. .. | 640 | 84 | | " |
| 3169. | The heirs of John Ferrel, Pri..... | 640 | 84 | | " |
| 3170. | The heirs of Peter Graham, Pri.. | 640 | 84 | | " |
| 3171. | The heirs of Joel Gibson, Pri..... | 640 | 84 | | " |
| 3172. | The heirs of William H....., Pri. | 640 | 84 | | " |
| 3173. | The heirs of .... H......, Pri.. | 640 | 84 | | " |
| 3174. | ......................... | 640 | 84 | | " |
| 3175. | The heirs of Jeremiah Litteral, Pri................ | 640 | 84 | | " |
| 3176. | The heirs of Jacob Miles, Pri.... | 640 | 84 | | " |
| 3177. | The heirs of Henry McClarney, " | 640 | 84 | | " |
| 3178. | The heirs of John Parrot, Pri.... | 640 | 84 | | " |
| 2179. | The heirs of Jesse Perkins, Pri... | 640 | 84 | | " |
| 3180. | The heirs of Will Pendergrass, " | 640 | 84 | | " |
| 3181. | The heirs of Thomas Ponder, " | 640 | 84 | | " |
| 3182. | The heirs of James Paul, Pri..... | 640 | 84 | | " |
| 3183. | The heirs of Moses Richardson, " | 640 | 84 | | " |
| 3184. | The heirs of James Ray, Pri..... | 640 | 84 | | " |
| 3185. | The heirs of Limage Stringer, Pri. | 640 | 84 | | " |
| 3186. | The heirs of Jeremiah Stillwell, " | 640 | 84 | | " |
| 3187. | The heirs of Thomas Swaim, Pri. | 640 | 84 | | " |

| No. | To whom granted and rank | No. acres | Service in months | Location and to whom deeded and date of warrant. Within the limits of the lands allotted the officers and soldiers of the Continental Line, by Law, 1783, Oct. 14 |
|---|---|---|---|---|
| 3188. | The heirs of Joseph Terry, Pri... | 640 | 84 | Maj. Tatum |
| 3189. | The heirs of Oliver Terry, Pri.... | 640 | 84 | " |
| 3190. | The heirs of Garrot Watts, Sgt... | 1,000 | 84 | " |
| 3191. | The heirs ·f John Wisdom, Pri... | 640 | 84 | " |
| 3192. | The heirs oɪ William Whitlock, " | 640 | 84 | " |
| 3193. | The heirs of Thomas Ware, Pri.. | 640 | 84 | " |
| 3194. | The heirs of James Wright, Pri. . | 640 | 84 | " |
| 3195. | The heirs of Thomas Watts, Sgt. | 1,000 | 84 | " |
| 3196. | The heirs of Thomas Waters, Pri. | 640 | 84 | " |
| 3197. | The heirs of William Whitton... | 640 | 84 | " |
| 3198. | The heirs of Micaijah Woodward. | 640 | 84 | " |
| 3199. | The heirs of Thomas Whitehead. | 640 | 84 | " |
| 3200. | William Rose, Sergt.......... | 420 | 36 | Maj. Tatum |
| 3201. | Isham Tulley, Pri............. | 274 | 36 | " |
| 3202. | William Dove................ | 274 | 36 | Self |
| 3203. | Isaac Perkins................ | 274 | 36 | " |
| 3204. | John Artist.................. | 274 | 36 | Ar. Pearce |
| 3205. | William Lomack.............. | 274 | 36 | " |
| 3206. | The heirs of Richard Nash, Pri. dcsd................ | 640 | 84 | " |
| 3207. | John Spence, Pri............. | 274 | 36 | Col. Harney |
| 3208. | George Buges, Pri............ | 274 | 36 | |
| 3209. | William Mains, Pri........... | 274 | 36 | |
| 3210. | The heirs of Hodges Bencham, Pt. | 640 | 84 | |
| 3211. | Willoughby Thompson's heirs, " | 640 | 84 | Jas. Ferebee, esqr. |
| 3212. | Ned Thompson............... | 640 | 84 | " |
| 3213. | Charles Dailey, Pri........... | 274 | 36 | Colo. R. Blount |
| 3214. | The heirs of Arthur Britt, Pri.... | 640 | 84 | " |
| 3215. | Miller Sawyer, Pri............ | 274 | 35 | Colo. L. Harney |
| 3216. | Wm. Barber, Pri............. | 640 | 84 | E. Everingen |
| 3217. | The heirs of Stephen Paul, Pri... | 640 | 84 | Col. Eborn |
| 3218. | Charles Rue, Pri............. | 640 | 84 | " |
| 3219. | Joshua Jacobs............... | 640 | 84 | |
| 3220. | Thomas Germins............. | 640 | 84 | Colo. L. Harney |
| 3221. | Moses Bass................. | 640 | 84 | J. Glasgow |
| 3222. | ........................ | 640 | 84 | " |
| 3223. | John Pugh Williams, Capt...... | 1,371 | 30 | Self |
| 3224. | The heirs of James Craig, Pri.... | 640 | 84 | T. Frohock |
| 3225. | Jacob Cruder, non comd. officer.. | 428 | 36 | Gen. Rutherford |
| 3226. | The heirs of John Patterson, Pr.. | 640 | 84 | " |
| 3227. | Jesse Allen, Pri............. | 228 | 30 | Gen. Person |
| 3228. | The heirs of Abner Dennis, Pri... | 640 | 84 | " |
| 3229. | The heirs of Francis West, Pri... | 640 | 84 | " |
| 3230. | The heirs of Newton Striplin, Pri. | 640 | 84 | " |
| 3231. | Jacob Watson, Pri. disr. infermity................ | 640 | 84 | Saml. Williams |
| 3232. | The heirs of James Barber, Pri... | 640 | 84 | " |
| 3233. | William Zealott, Pri........... | 274 | 30 | " |
| 3234. | Jonathan Zealott, ............. | 274 | 30 | A. Pearce |
| 3235. | John Hughs, Sergt............ | 428 | 36 | Gen. Rutherford |
| 3236. | John Brukins, Pri............. | 274 | 36 | Jno. Price |
| 3237. | John Waseley, Pri............ | 274 | 36 | " |
| 3238. | Arthur Corban, Pri........... | 274 | 36 | " |
| 3239. | The heirs of John Lynch, Pri.... | 640 | 84 | A. Pearce |
| 3240. | Zebulon Masey, Pri........... | 640 | 84 | Jno. Price |
| 3241. | William Brownen, Pri.......... | 640 | 84 | " |

| No. | To whom granted and rank | No. acres | Service in months | Location and to whom deeded and date of warrant. Within the limits of the lands allotted the officers and soldiers of the Continental Line, by Law, 1783, Oct. 14 | |
|---|---|---|---|---|---|
| 3242. | Samuel Brownen, Pri.......... | 640 | 84 | | Jno. Price |
| 3243. | The heirs of Taylor Willis, Pri... | 640 | 84 | | " |
| 3244. | The heirs of Britain Bass, Pri.... | 640 | 84 | | " |
| 3245. | Sampson Collins, Pri.......... | 274 | 36 | | " |
| 3246. | The heirs of William Batley, Pri.. | 640 | 84 | | " |
| 3247. | William Frost, Pri............. | 640 | 84 | | " |
| 3248. | Michael Bockner, Pri.......... | 640 | 84 | | " |
| 3249. | Benjamin Willis, Pri.......... | 640 | 84 | | " |
| 3250. | Samuel Rolan, Pri............. | 640 | 84 | | " |
| 3251. | James Rolan, Pri.............. | 274 | 36 | | " |
| 3252. | Aron Blackmore, Pri.......... | 640 | 84 | | " |
| 3253. | Samuel Tucker, Pri............ | 640 | 84 | | " |
| 3254. | William Brumley, Pri.......... | 640 | 84 | | " |
| 3255. | The heirs of Joseph Hanners, Pri. | 640 | 84 | | " |
| 3256. | The heirs of Christopher Church, Pri................. | 640 | 84 | | " |
| 3257. | The heirs of Thomas Catton, Pri. | 640 | 84 | | Capt. Ferebee |
| 3258. | The heirs of Solomon Truett, Pri. | 640 | 84 | | " |
| 3259. | The heirs of Thomas Trenton, " | 640 | 84 | | " |
| 3260. | The heirs of Malachi Valentine, " | 640 | 84 | | " |
| 3261. | The heirs of William Simmons, " | 640 | 84 | | " |
| 3262. | The heirs of Jonathan Henry, " | 640 | 84 | | " |
| 3263. | The heirs of George Williamson, Pri... ,................. | 640 | 84 | | " |
| 3264. | William Carpenter, Pri......... | 185 | 24 | | " |
| 3265. | The heirs of Joseph Evans, Pri... | 640 | 84 | | " |
| 3266. | The heirs of John Brunt........ | ... | .. | | " |
| 3267. | The heirs of Emanuel Paratree.. | ... | .. | | " |
| 3268. | The heirs of Smith Simpson..... | ... | .. | | " |
| 3269. | Matthew Dawson, Pri.......... | 640 | 84 | Dec. 24,'85 | " |
| 3270. | West Hadnot, Sergt........... | 1,000 | 84 | " | J. Ellis, N. Bern. |
| 3271. | Nimrod Swaim, Sergt.......... | 351 | 30 | " | Butcher Swaim |
| 3272. | James Morgan, Pri............. | 274 | 36 | " | Col. Murfree |
| 3273. | Demsey Capps, Pri............. | 274 | 36 | | R. Redding |
| 3274. | The heirs of Francis Burke, Pri.. | 640 | 84 | | Capt. Hall |
| 3275. | The heirs of Thomas Pettijohn, " | 640 | 84 | | " |
| 3276. | The heirs of Abner Cale, Pri..... | 640 | 84 | | " |
| 3277. | William Morris, Sergt.......... | 1,000 | 84 | | Jno. Hambleton |
| 3278. | Timothy de Monroe, Lieut...... | 1,000 | 84 | | Elish. Roberts |
| 3279. | Wilton Willis, Pri............. | ... | .. | .......... | ............ |
| 3280. | Solomom Whitley,... ......... | 640 | 84 | | |
| 3281. | James McBride, Pri............ | 640 | 84 | | Jno. Price |
| 3282. | James Mallaby, Pri............ | 640 | | | " |
| 3283. | The heirs of Daniel Etheridge, Corpl...................... | 1,000 | 84 | | Capt. Rhoades |
| 3284. | The heirs of Abraham Therrell, Pri........... ... | 640 | 84 | | " |
| 3285. | The heirs of William Rhoads, Sgt. | 1,000 | 84 | | " |
| 3286. | The heirs of Henry Rhoades, Pri. | 640 | 84 | | " |
| 3287. | William Phelps, Pri............ | 640 | 84 | | Colo. Morring |
| 3288. | The heirs of William Casteele, Pri. | 640 | 84 | | Capt. Gelaspie |
| 3289. | The heirs of William Rodgers, " | 640 | 84 | | " |
| 3290. | Colo. Har_____........ | | | | Self |
| 3291. | .............................. | | | | " |
| 3292. | Solomon Parks............... | 236 | 24 | | Col. A. Lytle |
| 3293. | The heirs of John Williams, Pri.. | 640 | 84 | | " |

| No. | To whom granted and rank | No. acres | Service in months | Location and to whom deeded and date of warrant. Within the limits of the lands allotted the officers and soldiers of the Continental Line, by Law, 1783, Oct. 14 | |
|---|---|---|---|---|---|
| 3294. | Thomas McDaniel, Pri......... | 274 | 36 | | Col. A. Lytle |
| 3295. | John Elliot, Pri................ | 277 | 38 | | " |
| 3296. | Thomas Boyd, Pri.............. | 228 | 30 | | " |
| 3297. | William Price, Pri............. | 640 | 84 | | " |
| 3298. | The heirs of Peter Farmer, Sgt... | 1,000 | 84 | | " |
| 3299. | Estrige Avery's Heirs.......... | 640 | 84 | Jan. 7, '86 | Col. Armstrong |
| 3300. | The heirs of Peter Black....... | 640 | 84 | | " |
| 3301. | William Burk................. | 228 | 30 | | " |
| 3302. | Giles Bruce, Pri............... | 228 | 30 | | " |
| 3303. | The heirs of William Caldwell... | 640 | 84 | | " |
| 3304. | The heirs of Lemuel Caldwell.... | 640 | 84 | | |
| 3305. | The heirs of Antony Cobb...... | 640 | 84 | | Col. M. Armstrong |
| 3306. | The heirs of James Dotey...... | 640 | 84 | | |
| 3307. | The heirs of Isaac Dunbar...... | 640 | 84 | | |
| 3308. | The heirs of Bennet Dudley..... | 640 | 84 | | |
| 3309. | The heirs of Matthias Dudley... | 640 | 84 | | |
| 3310. | The heirs of William Duggs..... | 640 | 84 | | |
| 3311. | The heirs of Stephen Gole...... | 640 | 84 | | |
| 3312. | The heirs of William Garrison... | 640 | 84 | | |
| 3313. | The heirs of Haston Gordon.... | 640 | 84 | | |
| 3314. | ............................. | ... | .. | | |
| 3315. | Thomas Hollingsworth......... | ... | .. | | |
| 3316. | ............................. | ... | .. | | |
| 3317. | The heirs of Estridge Nelson.... | 640 | 84 | | |
| 3318. | The heirs of Robert Nixon...... | 640 | 84 | | |
| 3319. | The heirs of Elijah Roberts..... | 640 | 84 | | |
| 3320. | The heirs of Stephen Roger, Sgt.. | 1,000 | 84 | | |
| 3321. | The heirs of Samuel Ricly...... | 640 | 84 | | |
| 3322. | The heirs of Thomas Ricly...... | 640 | 84 | | |
| 3323. | The heirs of Archer Roundtree. | 640 | 84 | | |
| 3324. | The heirs of Alexander Stokely, Sergt.............. | 1,000 | 84 | | |
| 3325. | The heirs of George Smithy..... | 640 | 84 | | |
| 3326. | The heirs of Stephen Williard... | 640 | 84 | | |
| 3327. | The heirs of Evan Watkins..... | 640 | 84 | | |
| 3328. | The heirs of Thompson Chapman | 640 | 84 | | |
| 3329. | The heirs of Etheldred Bailey... | 640 | 84 | | |
| 3330. | The heirs of Charles Osser, Sgt... | 1,000 | 84 | | Capt. W. Shelby |
| 3331. | The heirs of Charles Bowman, " | 1,000 | 84 | | |
| 3332. | The heirs of Peter Barnett...... | 640 | 84 | | |
| 3333. | The heirs of Archibald Beckham. | 640 | 84 | | |
| 3334. | The heirs of Burwell Ballard.... | 640 | 84 | | |
| 3335. | The heirs of Henry Cammell.... | 640 | 84 | | |
| 3336. | Samuel...................... | 640 | 84 | | |
| 3337. | The heirs of_____........ | | | | |
| 3338. | ............................. | | | | |
| 3339. | The heirs of George Carter...... | 640 | 84 | | " |
| 3340. | James Dunning............... | 274 | 84 | | |
| 3341. | The heirs of Thomas Daniel, Sgt. | 1,000 | 84 | | |
| 3342. | The heirs of Joseph Fletcher.... | 640 | 84 | | |
| 3343. | Timothy Fields................ | 274 | 36 | | |
| 3344. | The heirs of John Fuller........ | 640 | 84 | | |
| 3345. | The heirs of William Fuller..... | 640 | 84 | | |
| 3346. | The heirs of George Flanigan.... | 640 | 84 | | |
| 3347. | The heirs of Nicholas Garvis.... | 640 | 84 | | |
| 3348. | The heirs of John Greenway..... | 640 | 84 | | |

| No. | To whom granted and rank | No. acres | Service in months | Location and to whom deeded and date of warrant. Within the limits of the lands allotted the officers and soldiers of the Continental Line, by Law, 1783, Oct. 14 |
|---|---|---|---|---|
| 3349. | The heirs of William Gafford.... | 640 | 84 | |
| 3350. | William Haynes.............. | 320 | 42 | |
| 3351. | The heirs of James Hardgroves.. | 640 | 84 | Capt. M. Shelby |
| 3352. | The heirs of John Huver....... | 640 | 84 | " |
| 3353. | The heirs of Solomon Hunter, Sgt. | 1,000 | 84 | " |
| 3354. | The heirs of Corbin Hickman.... | 640 | 84 | " |
| 3355. | The heirs of Daniel Hackner.... | 640 | 84 | " |
| 3356. | The heirs of John Hitchcock..... | 640 | 84 | " |
| 3357. | The heirs of Lewis Hammond... | 640 | 84 | " |
| 3358. | The heirs of Joseph_____.... | ... | .. | " |
| 3359. | The heirs of Henry Leck........ | ... | .. | " |
| 3360. | .......................... | ... | .. | " |
| 3361. | Samuel Murray............... | 274 | 36 | " |
| 3362. | The heirs of Francis Mann...... | 640 | 84 | " |
| 3363. | The heirs of Patrick McConnical. | 640 | 84 | " |
| 3364. | The heirs of Alex. MacFarland.. | 640 | 84 | " |
| 3365. | The heirs of Joseph Mendenhall. | 640 | 84 | " |
| 3366. | Jacob Martin................. | 620 | 42 | " |
| 3367. | Gray Mabry.................. | 228 | 30 | " |
| 3368. | John Mabry.................. | 228 | 30 | " |
| 3369. | The heirs of William Norwood... | 640 | 84 | " |
| 3370. | The heirs of John Punang....... | 640 | 84 | " |
| 3371. | Jesse Patterson.............. | 320 | 42 | " |
| 3372. | Samuel Porter................ | 320 | 42 | " |
| 3373. | The heirs of Joseph Robertson... | 640 | 84 | " |
| 3374. | The heirs of Mark Rogers....... | | | " |
| 3375. | Joseph Roberts............... | 228 | 30 | " |
| 3376. | The heirs of John Shaw......... | 640 | 84 | " |
| 3377. | The heirs of Thomas Sully...... | | | " |
| 3378. | The heirs of Archibald Smith.... | | | " |
| 3379. | The heirs of Peter Stokes....... | | | " |
| 3380. | The heirs of William Sherwood.. | | | " |
| 3381. | The heirs of Littleberry Stone... | | | " |
| 3382. | The heirs of William Turner..... | ... | .. | " |
| 3383. | .......................... | ... | .. | " |
| 3384. | The heirs of Thomas Tate...... | ... | .. | " |
| 3385. | The heirs of Jesse White........ | 640 | 84 | " |
| 3386. | The heirs of Lewis Webb....... | 640 | 84 | " |
| 3387. | The heirs of George Wilson..... | 640 | 84 | " |
| 3388. | The heirs of William Johnson.... | 640 | 84 | " |
| 3389. | Benjamin Jones............... | 320 | 42 | " |
| 3390. | The heirs of Timothy McKinne . | 640 | 84 | " |
| 3391. | The heirs of William Carr, Sgt... | 1,000 | 84 | " |
| 3392. | The heirs of Abraham Step, Sgt.. | 1,000 | 84 | Colo. M. Armstrong |
| 3393. | The heirs of George Hearn...... | 640 | 84 | Drewry Hearn |
| 3394. | The heirs of Shadrach Zeallott, Pri.................. | 640 | 84 | A. Pearce |
| 3395. | Joshua Zealott............... | | | |
| 3396. | The heirs of Nelson Zealott, Sgt.. | 1,000 | 84 | |
| 3397. | The heirs of Janajah Yarkins, Sgt. | 1,000 | 84 | " |
| 3398. | Timothy Zarlett, Pri........... | 640 | 84 | Jan. 19 " |
| 3399. | Zachariah Zarlett, Pri.......... | 640 | 84 | |
| 3400. | James Zarlett, Pri............. | 640 | 84 | |
| 3401. | Nicholas Tyner the heir of Arthur Pearce Tyner, Pri. dcsd. | 640 | 84 | |
| 3402. | Andrew McAndrews, Pr......... | | | |

| No. | To whom granted and rank | No. acres | Service in months | Location and to whom deeded and date of warrant. Within the limits of the lands allotted the officers and soldiers of the Continental Line, by Law, 1783, Oct. 14 | |
|---|---|---|---|---|---|
| 3403. | Joshua Devenshire, Pri........ | | | | |
| 3404. | Collins Nelson, Pri............ | | | | |
| 3405. | Ambrose Jacobas, Pri.......... | | | | |
| 3406. | Zebulon Thomas............... | ... | .. | | |
| 3407. | Aaron Bush................... | ... | .. | | |
| 3408. | ............................. | ... | .. | | |
| 3409. | ............................. | ... | .. | | |
| 3410. | Andrew Gray.................. | | | | |
| 3411. | Isaiah Weaver, Pri............ | 640 | 84 | | |
| 3412. | Whitaker Neal, Pri............ | 640 | 84 | | |
| 3413. | Abner Lath, Pri............... | 640 | 84 | | |
| 3414. | John Brooks, Pri.............. | 640 | 84 | | |
| 3415. | Mason Bailey, Pri............. | 640 | 84 | | |
| 3416. | The heirs of John Billego, Pri.... | 640 | 84 | | |
| 3417. | Hampton Borden, Pri.......... | | | | |
| 3418. | Jonathan Bass, Pri............ | | | | Thomas Butler |
| 3419. | Morris Bailey, Pri............ | | | | |
| 3420. | The heirs of Baker Braswell, Pt.. | ... | .. | | |
| 3421. | Lawrence Colbert, Pri......... | ... | .. | | |
| 3422. | Obed Colven, Pri............. | ... | .. | | |
| 3423. | Phillip Colden, Sergt........... | 428 | 36 | | |
| 3424. | Allen Crockley, Pri............ | 640 | 84 | | |
| 3425. | Abraham Croker, Pri.......... | 274 | 36 | | |
| 3426. | West Dorman, Pri............. | 640 | 84 | | |
| 3427. | The heirs of Joseph Drummon, Pri.............. | 640 | 84 | | |
| 3428. | George Dilloway, Pri.......... | 274 | 36 | | |
| 3429. | George Ware, Pri.............. | 274 | 36 | | D. Welburn |
| 3430. | Jonas Fluallen, Pri............ | 640 | 84 | | Thos. Butcher |
| 3431. | James Poole, Pri.............. | 640 | 84 | | |
| 3432. | Josiah Lasciter, Pri............ | 640 | 84 | | |
| 3433. | George McCl_____.......... | 640 | 84 | | |
| 3434. | Jeremiah Hughlet............. | 640 | 84 | | |
| 3435. | ............................. | 640 | 84 | | |
| 3436. | Richard Knowles, Pri.......... | 640 | 84 | | M. Armstrong |
| 3437. | Garret Altman, Pri............ | 640 | 84 | | " |
| 3438. | James Bridger................. | 640 | 84 | | |
| 3439. | Abraham Ginalien............. | 640 | 84 | | |
| 3440. | Morgan Elmore............... | 640 | 84 | | |
| 3441. | The heirs of Joseph Alexander, Pt. | 640 | 84 | Feb. 2, '86 | Capt. Shelby |
| 3442. | The heirs of John Best......... | 640 | 84 | | |
| 3443. | The heirs of Robert Beach...... | 640 | 84 | | |
| 3444. | The heirs of Ignatious Beach.... | 640 | 84 | | |
| 3445. | The heirs of Navey Bateman.... | 640 | 84 | | |
| 3446. | The heirs of Edmund Bean...... | 640 | 84 | | |
| 3447. | The heirs of William Bean...... | 640 | 84 | | |
| 3448. | Robert Bean, Pri.............. | 228 | 30 | " | |
| 3449. | The heirs of Jesse Bean........ | 640 | 84 | | |
| 3450. | The heirs of John Cotanch...... | 640 | 84 | | |
| 3451. | The heirs of John Cockburn..... | 640 | 84 | | " |
| 3452. | Charles Cox, Pri.............. | 228 | 30 | | |
| 3453. | Jeremiah Steelley, Pri.......... | 274 | 36 | | |
| 3454. | The heirs of Peter Cotanch...... | 640 | 84 | | |
| 3455. | Abner Carr, Sergt............. | 428 | 30 | | |
| 3456. | Henry Dickinson, Pri.......... | 274 | 36 | | |
| 3457. | The heirs of Numa Davis....... | | | | |

| No. | To whom granted and rank | No. acres | Service in months | Location and to whom deeded and date of warrant. Within the limits of the lands allotted the officers and soldiers of the Continental Line, by Law, 1783, Oct. 14 |
|---|---|---|---|---|
| 3458. | ............................ | | | |
| 3459. | George Dealer................ | 274 | 36 | Feb. 2, '86 |
| 3460. | The heirs of Thomas Everitt.... | 640 | 84 | |
| 3461. | The heirs of Thomas Elliott..... | 640 | 84 | |
| 3462. | The heirs of Martin Griffin...... | 640 | 84 | |
| 3463. | The heirs of William Howard.... | 640 | 84 | Capt. Shelby |
| 3464. | The heirs of Joseph Hill........ | 640 | 84 | " |
| 3465. | The heirs of David Hair........ | 640 | 84 | " |
| 3466. | The heirs of Charles Holland.... | 640 | 84 | " |
| 3467. | The heirs of Hanry Hover...... | 640 | 84 | " |
| 3468. | The heirs of Charles Janus, or (James).................... | 640 | 84 | " |
| 3469. | Samuel Kirkindall............ | 274 | 36 | " |
| 3470. | The heirs of Joshua McKeel..... | 640 | 84 | " |
| 3471. | The heirs of Nicholas Martin.... | | | " |
| 3472. | The heirs of Samuel Mitchell.... | | | " |
| 3473. | The heirs of Charles Marshall... | | | " |
| 3474. | The heirs of Samuel Rose....... | | | " |
| 3475. | The heirs of Jacob Rhodes...... | 640 | 84 | |
| 3476. | The heirs of James Stevenson... | 640 | 84 | |
| 3477. | The heirs of John Steele........ | 640 | 84 | " |
| 3478. | The heirs of Peter Starn........ | 640 | 84 | " |
| 3479. | The heirs of David Sampson.... | 640 | 84 | " |
| 3480. | The heirs of John Smart........ | 640 | 84 | " |
| 3481. | The heirs of Dred Si_____... | ... | .. | " |
| 3482. | ............................ | ... | .. | " |
| 3483. | ............................ | ... | .. | " |
| 3484. | ............................ | .. | .. | " |
| 3485. | The heirs of William Myham.... | 640 | 84 | " |
| 3486. | Hance Whitley, Pri............ | 228 | 30 | " |
| 3487. | The heirs of Benjamin Brewer... | 640 | 84 | " |
| 3488. | Henry Drewery, Pri........... | 228 | 30 | " |
| 3489. | The heirs of Arthur Jones, Pri... | 640 | 84 | " |
| 3490. | Thomas Boyer, Pri............ | 640 | 84 | J. McNees |
| 3491. | Nathan Butler, Privt.......... | 640 | 84 | |
| 3492. | Job Carpenter, Pri............ | 640 | 84 | |
| 3493. | Archibald Burdon, Pri......... | 640 | 84 | |
| 3494. | Jarrell Fitchjarrell............ | 640 | 84 | Ben. Sheppard |
| 3495. | Jacob Sampson, Pri........... | 640 | 84 | |
| 3496. | Arthur Sears, Pri............. | 640 | 84 | |
| 3497. | Joal Stratin, Pri.............. | 640 | 84 | |
| 3498. | Seth Spear, Pri............... | 640 | 84 | |
| 3499. | Baletha Anderson, Pri......... | 640 | 84 | |
| 3500. | William John Alsobon, Pri...... | 640 | 84 | " |
| 3501. | Drewry Fadlock, Pri........... | 640 | 84 | " |
| 3502. | Arthur Jolock, Pri............ | | | " |
| 3503. | Ahab Thompson, Pri.......... | | | " |
| 3504. | The heirs of Thomas Trouter, Pri. | | | " |
| 3505. | Phillip Williams, Pri........... | 640 | 84 | " |
| 3506. | Walter Walker, Pri........... | 640 | 84 | " |
| 3507. | Walter Watkins, Pri........... | 274 | 36 | |
| 3508. | George Zaney, Pri............ | 640 | 84 | |
| 3509. | Isaac Holden................. | 274 | 36 | |
| 3510. | Zacha Hughes................ | 640 | 84 | |
| 3511. | The heirs of Gilbert Harrison, Pt. | 640 | 84 | |
| 3512. | Joshua Pasmore, Pri........... | 640 | 84 | |

| No. | To whom granted and rank | No. acres | Service in months | Location and to whom deeded and date of warrant. Within the limits of the lands allotted the officers and soldiers of the Continental Line, by Law, 1783, Oct. 14 | |
|---|---|---|---|---|---|
| 3513. | George Manshare, Pri. | 640 | 84 | | |
| 3514. | John Mosland, Pri. | 640 | 84 | | |
| 3515. | William Nobleand, Pri. | 640 | 84 | | |
| 3516. | Menoah Jolley, Pri. | 274 | 36 | | |
| 3517. | David Joice | 640 | 84 | | |
| 3518. | Howell Johnston | 640 | 84 | | |
| 3519. | Andrew Lector | 640 | 84 | | |
| 3520. | Jonathan Lockland | 640 | 84 | | |
| 3521. | Patrick Lroper | 274 | 36 | | |
| 3522. | The heirs of Simon Rosean | . . . | . . | | |
| 3523. | George Southerland, Pri. | 274 | 36 | | |
| 3524. | James Stoboth, Pri. | 640 | 84 | | |
| 3525. | Frederick Hathcock, Pri. | 228 | 30 | | {Capt. Hart for Col. {Long |
| 3526. | Robert Wilburn | 320 | 42 | | Capt. Hart for Lt. Ford |
| 3527. | Andrew Nathan, Pri. | 274 | 36 | | Capt. McNees |
| 3528. | Absalom Akinclas, Pri. | 274 | 36 | | |
| 3529. | John Apleton, Sergt. | 1,000 | 84 | | |
| 3530. | John Browner, Pri. | 274 | 36 | | |
| 3531. | Samuel Brooks, Pri. | 274 | 36 | | |
| 3532. | Isaac Bloodgood, Pri. | 274 | 36 | | |
| 3533. | | . . . | . . | | |
| 3534. | | . . . | . . | | |
| 3535. | Sampson Cannon, Pri. | 274 | 36 | | |
| 3536. | Samuel Carry, Pri. | 274 | 36 | | |
| 3537. | Robert Howell, Pri. | 274 | 36 | | |
| 3538. | The heirs of Hugh Joiner | 640 | 84 | | |
| 3539. | Absolom McNeel, Pri. | 274 | 36 | | " |
| 3540. | John McDash | 274 | 36 | | |
| 3541. | Joseph McDilton | 274 | 36 | | |
| 3542. | The heirs of Zebulon McNeel, Corpl. | 1,000 | 84 | | |
| 3543. | Isaiah Story | 274 | 36 | | |
| 3544. | Peter Stephenson | 274 | 36 | | |
| 3545. | Andrew Stewart | . . . | . . | | |
| 3546. | Michael Sugg___ | . . . | . . | | |
| 3547. | Hooker Robertson | 274 | 36 | | John McNees |
| 3548. | Elijah Taylor | 274 | 36 | | " |
| 3549. | Abram Sheppard, Col. | 2,571 | 30 | | Self |
| 3550. | Benjamin Dillon, Lieut. | 2,560 | 84 | | Capt. McShelby |
| 3551. | The heirs of Thomas Joyner, Lt. | 2,560 | 84 | | {The warrants to Co. {retndwtc |
| 3552. | William Sheppard, Capt. | 1,252 | 30 | | Self |
| 3553. | The heirs of William Watts | 640 | 84 | Dec. 27 | Alt. Watts |
| 3554. | Jacob Eason, Pri. | 228 | 30 | | Self |
| 3555. | William Gough, N. C. Officer | 1,000 | 84 | Aug. 1787 | " |
| 3556. | Cornelius Robinson, Pri. | 274 | 36 | | " |
| 3557. | John Womble, Pri. | 640 | 84 | | Capt. Gerrard |
| 3558. | Austin ___, Sergt. | 428 | 36 | | " |
| 3560. | Eps Spain, Sergt. | 1,000 | 84 | | " |
| 3561. | Thomas Spain, Fifer. | 1,000 | 84 | | |
| 3562. | William Spain, Fifer. | 1,000 | 84 | | |
| 3563. | The heirs of John Stewart, Sergt. | 1,000 | 84 | Oct. 20, '87 | {Capt. Nath. Moore {Col. Muffree for John {Baker |
| 3563. | The heirs of Garrett Phelps | 640 | 84 | | |

| No. | To whom granted and rank | No. acres | Service in months | Location and to whom deeded and date of warrant. Within the limits of the lands allotted the officers and soldiers of the Continental Line, by Law, 1783, Oct. 14 | |
|---|---|---|---|---|---|
| 3564. | The heirs of Wm. Hardgroves, Sergt.................... | 1,000 | 84 | | {Col. Muffree {for John Baker |
| 3565. | Samuel Reddit, Pri............ | 366 | 49 | | { do C. for Cons Jas. {Reddit Baker. |
| 3566. | William Nichols, or (Nicholby).. | 640 | 84 | | do C. for Nichols |
| 3567. | Kinchin Holliman, Pri......... | 228 | 30 | | "           Self |
| 3568. | Joseph Bailey, Sergt........... | ... | .. | | C. for Bailey |
| 3569. | Thomas Davidson, Pri. infirm... | 640 | 84 | | |
| 3570. | Wilson Liscomb, Pri........... | 274 | 36 | Oct. 24 | Col. Murfree for soldier |
| 3571. | Alex'r Acquard............... | 274 | 36 | | "          " |
| 3572. | William Knott, Lt............. | 1,882 | 54 | " | Const. Redditt. |
| 3573. | Caleb Portlock............... | 274 | 36 | Dec. 3, '87 | Col. Daugh |
| 3574. | James Barror, drummer....... | 357 | 30 | Dec. 13,'87 | |
| 3575. | Richard Webster, Pri.......... | 640 | 84 | | Self |
| 3576. | Thomson Curry, Sergt......... | 357 | 30 | | " |
| 3577. | Sampson Dillard, Pri.......... | 640 | 84 | Dec. 14,'78 | Capt. Ingles |
| 3578. | Marmaduke Maples........... | 278 | 48 | | Wm. Groves |
| 3579. | Henry F_____............ | | | | McCreecy |
| 3580. | William Alexander............ | 200 | | acres pursuant to a resolve Dec, 21, 1787 | |
| 3581. | "        ............ | 200 | | " Same sent Jno. Slade by Uncle David | |
| 3582. | "        ............ | " | " | " | |
| 3583. | "        ............ | " | " | " | |
| 3584. | "        ............ | " | " | " | |
| 3585. | "        ............ | " | " | " | |
| 3586. | John Stevens................. | 228 | 30 | Mch. 10,'88 | Harrison Bailey |
| 3587. | Tymmothy Manner, Pri....... | 228 | 30 | | {Elias Fort Edgecomb {Co. |
| 3588. | Matthew Collins, Pri.......... | 640 | 84 | | B. Caswell for self. |
| 3589. | The heirs of Samuel Horton, Pri. | 640 | 84 | | |
| | George Loe, Pri............... | 294 | 36 | June 27,'88 | {Wm. Richards, {Perquimans |
| 3590. | Jeremiah Sutton, Sergt......... | 1,000 | 84 | | |
| 3591. | William Boswell, Sergt......... | 1,000 | 84 | | |
| 3592. | Joseph Brown, Pri............. | 640 | 84 | | {William Richards, {Perquimans |
| 3593. | Robert Staples............... | 228 | 30 | | |
| 3594. | The heirs of Willis Gregory, Pri.. | 640 | 84 | | "       " |
| 3595. | Clement Godfrey, Pri.......... | 274 | 36 | | |
| 3596. | The heirs of Thomas Hendricks, Pri.............. | 640 | 84 | | |
| 3597. | John Rogerson, Pri............ | 360 | 48 | June 27,'88 | " |
| 3598. | Samuel Hart................. | 274 | 36 | Apr. 9, '88 | J. Mulloy |
| 3599. | The heirs of John Bowman...... | 640 | 84 | | Stokeley Donaldson |
| 3602. | The heirs of William Wateis, Pri. | 640 | 84 | | " |
| 3603. | William Haire................ | 640 | 84 | | |
| 3604. | ........................... | ... | .. | | Joseph Hardy |
| 3605. | Daniel Notestine.............. | ... | .. | | Maj. Montflorance |
| 3606. | ........................... | ... | .. | | Marmaduke Maples |
| 3607. | Cisimo de Medicies, Capt....... | 1,872 | 41 | Nov. 18, '88 | d'd self |
| 3608. | The heirs of Thomas Jaison, decd. | 640 | 84 | | {Wm. Davis, Moore {County |
| 3609. | The heirs of Jonathan Cahoon, fifer...................... | 1,000 | 84 | Nov. 1788 | Capt. Wm. Bush |
| 3610. | Miles Hudson, Privt........... | 274 | 36 | | Wm. D. Williams |
| 3611. | The heirs of Emanuel Marshall.. | 640 | 84 | | " |
| 3612. | William Hoggs, Heir, Sergt...... | 1,000 | 84 | | Rich'd Fenner |

| No. | To whom granted and rank | No. acres | Service in months | Location and to whom deeded and date of warrant. Within the limits of the lands allotted the officers and soldiers of the Continental Line, by Law, 1783, Oct. 14 | |
|---|---|---|---|---|---|
| 3613. | .......................... | | | | |
| 3614. | Isaac Anderson, Pri............ | 183 | 24 | | Gen. Rutherford |
| 3615. | The heirs of Thomas Eason..... | 640 | 84 | | Maj. Lewis |
| 3616. | John Wood, Privt............. | ... | .. | | |
| 3617. | The heirs of Daniel McCarron... | ... | .. | | |
| 3618. | The heirs of Petor Ordon....... | 640 | 84 | Dec. 10,'88 | Simon Totwine |
| 3619. | The heirs of Patrick Leary...... | 640 | 84 | | |
| 3620. | The heirs of Mills Dourday..... | 640 | 84 | | |
| 3621. | The heirs of Archibald Colbreath. | 640 | 84 | | |
| 3622. | The heirs of Edmon Jackson.... | ... | 42 | | Capt. Faison |
| 3623. | The heirs of William Cheek..... | 640 | 84 | | |
| 3624. | Arthur Adams................ | 274 | 30 | | d'd Col. Armstrong by Wm. Williams Andrew Griffin, do as above. |
| 3625. | Thomas Rutherford........... | 640 | 84 | | |
| 3626. | The heirs of _____........ | | | | d'd to Col. Armstrong, surveyor by W. Williams " |
| 3628. | .......................... | | | | |
| 3629. | The heirs of Thomas Bond...... | 640 | 84 | | Maj. Graham d'd surveyor by Wm. Williams |
| 3630. | Edward Ruth, Infirm.......... | 640 | 84 | | Same as above |
| 3631. | John Kerr, Infirm............. | 640 | 84 | | Same as above |
| 3632. | John Taylor................. | 640 | 84 | | For Howell Tatum, d'd surveyor as above |
| 3633. | Noah Wiggens................ | 228 | 30 | | Same as last above |
| 3634. | Samuel Wheeler.............. | 228 | 30 | | Alx. Nelson, d'd Surveyor by Wm. Williams |
| 3635. | Melcher Fair, Infirm.......... | 640 | 84 | | Same as above |
| 3636. | John Keeth's heirs,........... | 640 | 84 | | " |
| 3637. | Alexander Cameron, Pri....... | 491 | 64 | | "     "     " |
| 3638. | Joseph Cowen, or (Cowan), Pri.. | ... | .. | | " |
| 3639. | The heir of Philip Morris....... | ... | .. | | " |
| 3640. | The heirs of Julius Burton...... | 640 | 84 | | For Col. Lytle, d'd surveyor by Wm. Williams |
| 3641. | William Guinn, Pri............ | 274 | 36 | | Same as above |
| 3642. | The heirs of Micajah Menshen .. | 640 | 84 | | "     " |
| 3643. | The heirs of Henry Howell...... | 640 | 84 | | "     " |
| 3644. | Henry Davis' heirs............ | 640 | 84 | | "     " |
| 3645. | The heirs of Stephen Smith..... | 640 | 84 | " | Simon Tolwine |
| 3646. | The heirs of John Blammer..... | 640 | 84 | | " |
| 3647. | The heirs of Zebulon Phillips.... | | | | " |
| 3648. | The heirs of _____........ | | | | " |
| 3649. | The heirs of John Atkins....... | | | | " |
| 3650. | The heirs of Ayler Thomson..... | | | | " |
| 3651. | .......................... | | | | " |
| 3652. | The heirs of James Dosier....... | 640 | 84 | Dec. 10,'88 | Simon Tolwine |
| 3653. | The heirs of Demsey Stripes..... | 640 | 84 | same | same |
| 3654. | The heirs of Danill McCoy...... | 640 | 84 | " | " |
| 3653. | The heirs of James Lerr........ | 640 | 84 | " | " |
| 3655. | The heirs of Stephen Jones...... | 640 | 84 | " | " |
| 3656. | The heirs of John Dillan........ | 640 | 84 | " | " |
| 3657. | The heirs of Peter Morgan...... | 640 | 84 | " | " |
| 3658. | The heirs of Thomas Morrow.... | 640 | 84 | " | " |
| 3659. | The heirs of Crawford Newsom.. | 640 | .. | " | " |
| 3660. | The heirs of Daniel Quillin...... | ... | .. | " | " |
| 3661. | The heirs of Burwell Herring.... | ... | .. | " | " |

| No. | To whom granted and rank | No. acres | Service in months | Location and to whom deeded and date of warrant. Within the limits of the lands allotted the officers and soldiers of the Continental Line, by Law, 1783, Oct. 14 | |
|---|---|---|---|---|---|
| 3662. | The heirs of Joseph Griffen...... | ... | .. | Dec. 10,'88 | Simon Tolwine |
| 3663. | The heirs of Henry Newton..... | 640 | 84 | | " |
| 3664. | The heirs of Thomas Goodman.. | | | Ditto | " |
| 3665. | The heirs of John Taylor....... | 640 | 84 | " | " |
| 3664. | The heirs of John Pain......... | 640 | 84 | " | " |
| 3665. | The heirs of Armon Pain....... | 640 | 84 | " | " |
| 3666. | The heirs of James Henderson... | 640 | 84 | " | " |
| 3667. | The heirs of Henry Ramsey..... | 640 | 84 | " | " |
| 3668. | The heirs of James Clyer....... | 640 | 84 | " | " |
| 3669. | The heirs of Peter Truit........ | 640 | 84 | " | " |
| 3670. | The heirs of John Dew......... | ... | .. | " | " |
| 3671. | The heirs of John Gardnor...... | ... | .. | " | " |
| 3672. | ............................. | ... | .. | " | " |
| 3673. | The heirs of Aron Tison........ | 640 | 84 | " | " |
| 3674. | The heirs of John Nobles....... | 640 | 84 | " | " |
| 3675. | The heirs of Henry Dickerson... | 640 | 84 | " | " |
| 3676. | The heirs of James Purview..... | 640 | 84 | " | " |
| 3677. | The heirs of Isaac Brown...... | 640 | 84 | " | " |
| 3678. | The heirs of Elisha Palmer...... | 640 | 84 | | |
| 3679. | The heirs of James Sullivan..... | 640 | 84 | | |
| 3680. | The heirs of Francis Newham... | 640 | 84 | | |
| 3681. | The heirs of Elijah Ward....... | 640 | 84 | | |
| 3682. | The heirs of Nathan Scarborough. | ... | .. | | |
| 3683. | The heirs of William Oston...... | ... | .. | | |
| 3684. | The heirs of Nathaniel _____. | ... | .. | | |
| 3685. | The heirs of William L_____.. | ... | .. | | |
| 3686. | The heirs of Edward Robinson,Pt. | 640 | 84 | June 27, '89 | John Buchannon |
| 3687. | John Standen, Pri.............. | ... | 66 | Sept. 12,'89 | d'd Gen. John Moran of Chowan County |
| 3688. | Arnold Mann, Pri.............. | 228 | 30 | | |
| 3689. | Benaiah Turner, Lt............. | 2,560 | 84 | | David Turner, Bertie |
| 3690. | John Roberts, Pri............. | 372 | 49 | | d'd Col. Hardy Murfree |
| 3691. | Daniel Sivel's heirs, Pri........ | 640 | 84 | Nov. 25 | ditto for Walton of Nasheville |
| 3692. | The heirs of John Blanehard.... | 640 | 84 | " | |
| 3693. | Benjamin Dickson............. | 182 | 24 | Dec. 1st | d'd Col. Martin Fifer |
| 3694. | Robert Hardon................ | 182 | 24 | " | " |
| 3695. | George Farr.................. | 182 | 24 | " | |
| 3696. | James Humphries............. | 182 | 24 | " | |
| 3697. | George Carlock............... | 182 | 24 | " | |
| 3698. | ............................. | 182 | 24 | | |
| 3699. | ............................. | 182 | 24 | | |
| 3700. | ............................. | ... | .. | | |
| 3701. | ............................. | ... | .. | | |
| 3702. | Francis Edleman, Pri.......... | 274 | 36 | Nov. 27 | Caleb Fifer, Esqr. |
| 3703. | Peter Seener, Pri.............. | 182 | 24 | " | " |
| 3704. | Henry Carsey, Pri. or (Cersey).. | 182 | 24 | | " |
| 3705. | Jacob Cersey, Pri............. | 182 | 24 | | " |
| 3706. | Francis Seals, Pri.............. | 182 | 24 | | " |
| 3707. | John Ross, Pri................. | 182 | 24 | | |
| 3708. | Henry Nunnery, Pri........... | 228 | 30 | " | Col. Eph. Phillips |
| 3709. | John Smith, trooper.......... | 182 | 24 | " | Caleb Fifer |
| 3710. | Peter Dunnock, Sergt.......... | 360 | .. | | Capt. Medicis |
| 3711. | The heirs of David Owens...... | 640 | .. | " | Rras. Owens |
| 3712. | Hopkins Dye, Pri............. | 274 | 36 | " | _____ Maples |
| 3713. | William Maclain, Surgeons mate. | 640 | 84 | | |

| No. | To whom granted and rank | No. acres | Service in months | Location and to whom deeded and date of warrant. Within the limits of the lands allotted the officers and soldiers of the Continental Line, by Law, 1783, Oct. 14 | |
|---|---|---|---|---|---|
| 3714. | The heirs of David Jones, Corpl.. | ... | .. | | |
| 3715. | Moses Newsom, Pri........... | ... | .. | | |
| 3716. | William Brown............... | 274 | 36 | O. Smith | |
| 3717. | Robert Lypeart, Pri.......... | 228 | 30 | | Self |
| 3718. | William Cail, Pri............. | 640 | 84 | | |
| 3719. | Rice Johnston, Pri........... | 274 | 36 | | |
| 3720. | Abraham Poole, Pri.......... | 640 | 84 | | |
| 3721. | Lewis Lodge................ | 640 | 84 | Wm. T. Taylor | |
| 3722. | Benj. Mott, heir of Daniel Mott, Pri................. | 640 | 84 | Nov. 23, '90 | John Dickson |
| 2723. | The heirs of Jesse Goldsmith.... | 640 | 84 | | Wm. Bethell |
| 3724. | William White, Sergt......... | 357 | 30 | | Murfree |
| 3725. | The heirs of Samuel Serrett..... | 640 | 84 | | Gen. Person |
| 3726. | John Carter, Pri............. | 228 | 30 | | " |
| 3728. | ........................... | 640 | 84 | | " |
| 3729. | Davis Cyrus................ | 762 | .. | | |
| 3730. | ........................... | | | Mch. 25,'91 | {d'd to S. Martin for S. {Halling |
| 3731. | Hezekiah Shoematstine, Pri..... | 228 | 30 | Jan 13, '92 | Thos. Blount |
| 3732. | William McKenzie, Pri........ | 640 | 84 | " | " |
| 3733. | The heirs of Frederick Jones.... | 640 | 84 | | " |
| 3734. | The heirs of Samuel Glover, Sgt.. | 1,000 | 84 | | {John Durand's wife {relect of Glover |
| 3735. | The heirs of Duncan Schaw..... | 640 | 84 | | Singletary |
| 3736. | The heirs of John Anderson, Pri. | 640 | 84 | | Mr. Beard |
| 3737. | The heirs of James Smith....... | 640 | 84 | | " |
| 3738. | Henry Gray, Sergt............ | 1,000 | 84 | | " |
| 3739. | John Taylor, Pri............. | 640 | 84 | | Col. Dange |
| 3740. | Isaac Leadingham, Pri......... | 274 | 26 | | ———— Dawson |
| 3741. | John Raper, Pri.............. | ... | .. | | |
| 3742. | Robert Raper, Pri............ | ... | .. | | |
| 3743. | The heirs of William Wisehart,Pt. | ... | .. | | |
| 3744. | David Wilcox, Pri............ | 274 | 36 | Jan. 18, '92 | Capt. Rhodes, Duplin |
| 3745. | Joel Ramsey, Pri............. | 274 | 36 | | Maj. Jno. McKay |
| 3746. | John Curry, Pri.............. | 640 | 84 | | Maj. Winston |
| 3747. | Nathaniel Bilberry, Pri........ | 228 | 30 | Feb. 22 | A. Johnston |
| 3748. | Samuel Green, Pri............ | 228 | 30 | Mch. 4, '92 | d'd Wm. Martin |
| 3749. | David Clagg, Pri............. | 274 | 36 | May 3,'92 | James Galbraith |
| 3750. | John Sheppard, Maj........... | 1,714 | 30 | May 6 | d. Self |
| 3751. | Peter Dauge................ | 274 | 36 | June 1 | d. Self |
| 3752. | Joab Overton, Pri............. | 640 | 84 | June 8 | d'd Ben Eastman |
| 3753. | Maltire Balantine............. | 640 | 84 | " | |
| 3754. | William Gamewell............ | 640 | 84 | " | |
| 3755. | ........................... | | | " | |
| 3756. | Samuel Jewel............... | 640 | 84 | July 3, '92 | d'd Docky Leigh |
| 3757. | The heirs of William Henry Bailey, Pri................ | 640 | 84 | Aug. 1, '92 | Chs. Mabins |
| 3758. | Joseph Ryals, Pri............ | 640 | 84 | " | |
| 3759. | Edward Pritchet, Pri.......... | 640 | 84 | | Self |
| 3760. | William Smith, Pri........... | 274 | 36 | Aug. 18 | " |
| 3761. | David Grant, Pri............. | 640 | 84 | Sept. 5 | " |
| 3762. | John Eppes, Pri............. | 274 | 36 | | Wm. Hargrove |
| 3763. | Samuel Carter, Pri........... | 228 | 30 | Oct. 1 | Self |
| 3764. | James Moore, Pri............ | 228 | 30 | " | Capt. Coit |
| 3765. | Joseph Spaight, Pri.......... | 640 | 84 | Oct. 20 | " |

| No. | To whom granted and rank | No. acres | Service in months | Location and to whom deeded and date of warrant. Within the limits of the lands allotted the officers and soldiers of the Continental Line, by Law, 1783, Oct. 14 | |
|---|---|---|---|---|---|
| 3766. | The heirs of James Johnston, Pri. | 640 | 84 | | Charity McDaniels, wife of Johnston |
| 3767. | The heirs of Alexander Cole..... | 640 | 84 | | " |
| 3768. | Thomas Garvey, Pri............ | 640 | 84 | | |
| 3769. | Wm. Morgan, Pri.............. | 640 | 84 | Nov. 29, '92 | Mr. Singletary |
| 3770. | Ebenezer Hewit............... | 640 | 84 | " | d'd " |
| 3771. | Theophilus Williams, Ens....... | 1,096 | 36 | Dec. 6, '92 | Self |
| 3772. | Henry Costen, Pri............. | 640 | 84 | Dec. 23, '92 | d'd Capt. Barnes |
| 3773. | Richard Laws, Pri............. | 274 | 36 | " | d'd to Mr. Alexander |
| 3774. | Benj. Kennedy, Sergt.......... | 500 | 42 | " | d'd Jesse Cherry |
| 3775. | Stephen Rogers, Pri........... | 356 | 48 | " | d'd Mr. Jasper |
| 3776. | John Poe's heirs.............. | 640 | 84 | " | James Williams, esqr. |
| 3777. | Richard Morris............... | 228 | 30 | " | d'd to Mr. Grant |
| 3778. | John Richard Lacey........... | 852 | 52 | Dec. 26, '92 | d'd to Col. John Allen |
| 3779. | Thomas Breace................ | ... | .. | ........... | delivered Wm. Russell |
| 3780. | John Reynolds................ | ... | .. | ........... | " " |
| 3781. | The heirs of Ezekiel Modlin..... | 640 | 84 | Dec. 27 | d'd Mr. Cherry |
| 3782. | Henry Cooper, Pri............ | 440 | 36 | | d'd Mr. Cherry |
| 3783. | Peter Dauge, Lt. Col......... | 2,057 | 30 | Dec. 28, '92 | Self |
| 3784. | Stephen Congur, Sergt. Majr.... | 357 | 30 | " | Genl. Mabane |
| 3785. | The heirs of Wm. Reed........ | 640 | 84 | Jan. 22, '93 | d'd Col. Robt. Hays |
| 3786. | Micajah Watson, Pri.......... | 365 | 48 | May 20 | d'd to Col. Murfee |
| 3787. | Alex. Ballentine, Sergt......... | 1,000 | 84 | Nov. 15, '93 | Thos. O'Neil |
| 3788. | The heirs of George Bell....... | 640 | 84 | | Alex McMillan, Salisbury |
| 3788. | The heirs of John Dixon, Sergt... | 1,000 | 84 | " | |
| 3789. | The heirs of John Cummins, Pri. | 640 | 84 | " | |
| 3790. | The heirs of Wm. Lusk, Pri...... | 640 | 84 | | |
| 3791. | The heirs of James Summeral, Sergt...................... | 1,000 | 84 | " | |
| 3792. | The heirs of David Johnson, Pri. | 640 | 84 | " | |
| 3793. | The heirs of James Douglass, Pri. | 640 | 84 | " | |
| 3794. | The heirs of Thomas Flemming, Pri...................... | 640 | 84 | " | |
| 3795. | The heirs of Wm. Houston, Pri. . | 640 | 84 | " | |
| 3796. | The heirs of Moses Davis, Pri. .. | 640 | 84 | " | |
| 3797. | James Worley, Sergt........... | 1,000 | 84 | Dec. 18, '93 | d'd to Jno. Kilby |
| 3798. | The heirs of Willis Sawyer, Pri... | 640 | 84 | | d'd to Caleb Grandy |
| 3799. | William Willoams, Pri.......... | 228 | 30 | | d'd to Edmund Branch |
| 3800. | John Brooks, Pri.............. | 228 | 30 | | d'd to self |
| 3801. | Hopkins Dye, Pri............. | 274 | 36 | | d'd to Mr. Berford of Caswell County |
| 3802. | The heirs of James Honeford.... | 640 | 84 | | d'd to " |
| 3803. | The heirs of Thomas Eason, Pri.. | 640 | 84 | Jan. 1, '94 | d'd to Isaac Broks |
| 3804. | The heirs of Southey Hays, Pri. . | 640 | 84 | | d'd to Josiah Lewis |
| 3805. | Thomas Parker, Pri........... | 640 | 84 | | d'd to Mjr. Ferebee |
| 3806. | Hillary Parker................ | | | | " |
| 3807. | The heirs of James Jenkins...... | | | | " |
| 3808. | The heirs of Joshua Daley, Capt. | 3,840 | 84 | Jan. 6, '94 | d'd to Gen. Gregory |
| 3809. | The heirs of Charles Shaddock .. | 640 | 84 | Jan. 7, '94 | M. Brooks, esqr. |
| 3810. | The heirs of Colin McDonald.... | | | Jan. 8, '94 | d'd to Marma Maples |
| 3811. | Alexander McArthur, Pri....... | 274 | 36 | Jan. 10,'94 | d'd to Mjr. Rhodes |
| 3812. | Stephen Owens, Lieut.......... | 2,097 | 36 | | Mr. Jasper |
| 3813. | The heirs of Tras Discum....... | 640 | 84 | | Arch'd. Hampbell |
| 3814. | Norris Baker, Pri............. | 640 | 84 | | " |
| 3815. | Boston Splendor.............. | 640 | 84 | | Col. Dixon, Lincoln Co. |

| No. | To whom granted and rank | No. acres | Service in months | Location and to whom deeded and date of warrant. Within the limits of the lands allotted the officers and soldiers of the Continental Line, by Law, 1783, Oct. 14 | |
|---|---|---|---|---|---|
| 3816. | The heirs of Ruebin Grady...... | 640 | 84 | Maj. Jno. Nelson | |
| 3817. | William King, Pri.............. | ... | .. | | Self |
| 3818. | Anthony Garret, Pri........... | ... | .. | | |
| 3819. | Jonathan Lain's heirs to Jethro Lain.................... | | | | |
| 3820. | Arch'd Wood, Pri.............. | 228 | 30 | Aug. 21,'94 | d'd to Saml. Davis |
| 3821. | Alexander Cameron, Pri........ | 320 | 42 | Jan. 1795 | d'd to self |
| 3822. | The heirs of Ephraim Lennon... | 640 | 84 | Duncan Stuart, esqr. | |
| 3823. | The heirs of Edmund Jackson... | 640 | | Capt. Fawn | |
| 3824. | Robt. Edwards, Pri............. | 320 | 42 | Phil. Hodges | |
| 3825. | The heirs of Edward Robeson, Sergt.................... | 1,000 | 84 | A. McMullin | |
| 3827. | William Proctor, Sergt......... | 500 | 42 | Phil. Hodges | |
| 3827. | Michael McMullin, Pri......... | 274 | 36 | Bradley | Self |
| 3828. | The heirs of Benj. Dillon, Lt.... | ... | .. | Mr. Spruill | |
| 3829. | Dugald Kelly................. | ... | .. | Jan. 31, '95 | Phil. Hodges |
| 3830. | Jacob Apley.................. | ... | .. | Feb. 2, '95 | " |
| 3831. | ........................ | ... | .. | | |
| 3832. | The heirs of John Lane, Sergt.... | 1,000 | 84 | Feb. 3, '95 | B. Gen McKinne |
| 3833. | James Avery, Pri.............. | 228 | 30 | M. Holliday | |
| 3834. | The heirs of Thos. Forster...... | 640 | 84 | Mr. Lucas, (Luea) | |
| 3835. | The heirs of Wm. Charlton, Lt... | 2,560 | 84 | Jo. Ferebee | |
| 3836. | The heirs of Archibald Murphey. | 640 | 84 | Feb. 7, '95 | Mr. D. Stuart |
| 3837. | The heirs of Michael Delaney... | 640 | 84 | Mch. 16 | Phil Hodges |
| 3838. | The heirs of William Leighton... | 640 | 84 | " | " |
| 3839. | The heirs of Abraham Thurrell.. | 640 | 84 | " | " |
| 3840. | The heirs of Roger McCoy...... | 640 | 84 | | {Jno. Hadley by Mr. Dixon |
| 3841. | The heirs of Duncan Morrison... | 640 | 84 | | " |
| 3842. | The heirs of Arch'd. McDonald.. | ... | .. | | |
| 3843. | The heirs of John Holley, Jr..... | ... | .. | | |
| 3844. | The heirs of Samuel Carter...... | 640 | 84 | Aug. 31,'95 | Philemon Hodge |
| 3845. | The heirs of John McNulty..... | 640 | 84 | " | " |
| 3846. | The heirs of Etheridge Edwards. | 640 | 84 | | " |
| 3847. | The heirs of John McLemore.... | 640 | 84 | | { " for Duncan Stewart |
| 3848. | The heirs of Edward Newman... | 640 | 84 | " | for " |
| 3849. | The heirs of Jordan Ammon..... | 640 | 84 | " | " |
| 3850. | The heirs of Stephen Arthur..... | 640 | 84 | | " for James Carraway |
| 3751. | The heirs of Abell Sessums...... | 640 | 84 | " | " for Duncan Stewart |
| 3852. | The heirs of Theophilus Grice... | 640 | 84 | " | " |
| 3853. | The heirs of Abram Wright..... | ... | .. | " | " |
| 3854. | Williams Carey............... | ... | .. | | d'd to Philemon Hodge |
| 3855. | John Dunbar................. | ... | .. | | " |
| 3856. | The heirs of Robert White..... | 640 | 84 | Sept. 22 | d'd to P. Hodge |
| 3857. | The heirs of James Oram....... | 640 | 84 | " | |
| 3858. | The heirs of Benjamin Johnston. | 640 | 84 | " | |
| 3859. | The heirs of Ephraim Bratcher.. | 640 | 84 | Oct. 12 | {d'd to Duncan Stuart, esqr. |
| 3860. | The heirs of David Williams.... | 640 | 84 | | " |
| 3861. | The heirs of Alexander Few..... | 640 | 84 | | " |
| 3862. | The heirs of Edward Cannon.... | 640 | 84 | | " |
| 3863. | The heirs of Joseph Edge....... | 640 | 84 | | " |
| 3864. | The heirs of Marmaduke Edge .. | 640 | 84 | | " |
| 3865. | The heirs of Henry Malpus..... | 640 | 84 | | " |
| 3866. | The heirs of Richard Lewis..... | ... | .. | | " |

| No. | To whom granted and rank | No. acres | Service in months | Location and to whom deeded and date of warrant. Within the limits of the lands allotted the officers and soldiers of the Continental Line, by Law, 1783, Oct. 14 |
|---|---|---|---|---|
| 3867. | William Ryal................ | ... | .. | {d'd to Duncan Stuart, {esqr. |
| 3869. | Nehemiah Pevy, fifer........... | 1,000 | 84 | Oct. 12 " |
| 3870. | The heirs of Jacob Teal........ | 640 | 84 | " |
| 3871. | The heirs of John Morpus...... | 640 | 84 | " |
| 3872. | The heirs of Marmaduke Larrimore.................. | 640 | 84 | " |
| 3873. | The heirs of Oliver Jones....... | 640 | 84 | Nov. 2 d'd to Wm. Dixon |
| 3874. | The heirs of Moses Looney...... | 640 | 84 | " |
| 3875. | The heirs of John Kerkendawl... | 640 | 84 | " |
| 3876. | The heirs of Henry Step........ | 640 | 84 | " |
| 3877. | Reuben Johnson, Pri........... | 640 | 84 | James Welborn, esqr. |
| 3878. | William Ch_____........... | | 84 | Thomas Banks |
| 3879. | The heirs of Samuel Pope....... | ... | .. | |
| 3880. | ............................ | ... | .. | J. Holladay, esqr. |
| 3881. | The heirs of Richard Evans, Pri.. | 640 | 84 | Nov. 13 {d'd to Phil. Hodges, {esqr. |
| 3882. | Bryan Worsley, Pri............ | 365 | 48 | Capt. Lytle |
| 3883. | Isaac Sanderlin, Pri........... | 640 | 84 | Wm. Snowden |
| 3884. | The heirs of John Calvin....... | 640 | 84 | d'd to Phil. Hodge. |
| 3885. | Harden Warner, Pri........... | 320 | 42 | " |
| 3886. | Job Smith, Sergt.............. | 355 | 30 | Himself |
| 3887. | John Warner, Pri.............. | 320 | 42 | P. Hodges |
| 3888. | The heirs of Richard Warner.... | 640 | 84 | " |
| 3889. | Reubin Knight, fifer........... | 357 | 30 | {Mr. Wolfendon, Bertie {County |
| 3890. | Lewis Jenkins................. | 374 | .. | Self |
| 3891. | Joseph Witherington........... | | | |
| 3892. | Joseph Aldridge............... | | | |
| 3893. | William Epps, Pri............. | 274 | 36 | Nov. 21,'95 |
| 3894. | Charles Upchurch, Pri......... | 228 | 30 | d'd to self |
| 3895. | William Capps, Pri. farmer...... | 274 | 36 | {d'd to Nathan Powell {of Johnston |
| 3896. | Dumon Brown, Pri............ | 228 | 30 | Nov. 25 d'd Benj. FitzRandolph |
| 3897. | Matthew Powell's heirs, Pri..... | 640 | 84 | " |
| 3898. | The heirs of Abel Sullivan...... | 640 | 84 | " |
| 3899. | The heirs of Solomon Martel.... | 640 | 84 | " |
| 3900. | The heirs of Miles Martin...... | 640 | 84 | |
| 3901. | John Dimery.................. | 640 | 84 | |
| 3902. | ............................ | ... | .. | |
| 3903. | Thomas Dodd................. | ... | .. | d'd Wm. Ferrall |
| 3904. | | | | |
| 3905. | The heirs of George Bruce, Pri.. | 640 | 84 | Nov. 26 Mr. P |
| 3906. | Thomas Morriss, Pri........... | 274 | 36 | Nov. 28,'95 Mr. Jones |
| 3907. | The heirs of Andrew Squires.... | 640 | 84 | " |
| 3908. | Joseph Collins, drummer........ | 428 | 36 | " |
| 3909. | Thomas Ansgood's heirs........ | 640 | 84 | " |
| 3910. | John Manifee, Sergt........... | 357 | 30 | d'd Jos. Stuart |
| 3911. | The heirs of Holdin Simmons, Pt. | 640 | 84 | " |
| 3912. | The heirs of Alexander McDaniel, Pri.............. | 640 | | " |
| 3913. | The heirs of William Winbright, Pri.............. | 640 | 84 | " |
| 3914. | The heirs of Caleb Roper, or (Raper) Pri................ | 640 | | Col. Murfree |
| 3915. | Benjamin Dorton, Pri......... | 228 | 36 | Jos. Stuart |
| 3916. | Drury Parham, Pri............ | ... | .. | |

| No. | To whom granted and rank | No. acres | Service in months | Location and to whom deeded and date of warrant. Within the limits of the lands allotted the officers and soldiers of the Continental Line, by Law, 1783, Oct. 14 |
|---|---|---|---|---|
| 3917. | Thomas Shute, Ensn.......... | ... | .. | |
| 3918. | The heirs of Timothy Carter.... | ... | .. | |
| 3919. | The heirs of Dennis Trimnal, Pri. | 640 | 84 | Dec. 8, '95 {Delivered to Duncan Stuarth for |
| 3920. | The heirs of Underhill Jones..... | 640 | 84 | " " |
| 3921. | The heirs of Simmons Jay...... | 640 | 84 | " " |
| 3922. | The heirs of Leonard Keller..... | 640 | 84 | " |
| 3923. | The heirs of Oliver Pasmore.... | | | " |
| 3924. | The heirs of Conrod Halfaker.... | 640 | 84 | " |
| 3925. | The heirs of Stephen Moglin.... | 640 | 84 | " |
| 3926. | Malachi Foke heir of James Foke...................... | 640 | 84 | Self |
| 2927. | The heirs of Duncan McBride... | 640 | 84 | Douglas Lucas |
| 3928. | The heirs of Edmund Bilbey.... | ... | .. | Hodges |
| 3929. | The heirs of David Canddy..... | ... | .. | |
| 3930. | John Cantrell.................. | ... | .. | d'd William Dick |
| 3931. | John Childers................. | ... | .. | " |
| 3932. | Jones Posam.................. | ... | .. | " |
| 3933. | The heirs of Andrew Storm, or (Stonn)................. | 640 | | d'd to Wm. Dick |
| 3934. | The heirs of Miles Jones....... | 640 | | " |
| 3935. | The heirs of Solomon Jones..... | 640 | | " |
| 3936. | The heirs of John Folar........ | 640 | | " |
| 3937. | Isaac Linsney................. | 274 | 36 | " |
| 3938. | The heirs of Jacob Saunders..... | 640 | 84 | Wm. Ferrell |
| 3940. | The heirs of Sylvanus Stone..... | 640 | 84 | " |
| 3941. | Patrick McCoy, Pri........... | 640 | 84 | Ben Sheppard |
| 3942. | Benford Jones, Pri............ | 640 | 84 | " |
| 3943. | Robert Biggs.................. | | | " |
| | The heirs of Eli Marsh........ | ... | .. | |
| 4944. | The heirs of Joseph _____... | ... | .. | |
| 3945. | The heirs of Gideon (Petit)?..... | ... | .. | |
| 3946. | John Mosely, Pri.............. | | | |
| 3947. | The heirs of Matthews Bagley... | 640 | 84 | d'd Stockley Donelson |
| 3948. | The heirs of John R. Stephenson. | 640 | 84 | " " |
| 3949. | The heirs of Reuben McCormack | 640 | 84 | " " |
| 3950. | The heirs of David Davis....... | 640 | 84 | " " |
| 3951. | The heirs of Miles Clayton...... | 640 | 84 | " " |
| 3952. | The heirs of Zedekiah Brock.... | 640 | 84 | " " |
| 3953. | The heirs of Arthur McRory.... | 640 | 84 | " " |
| 3954. | Igntius Chissum, Pri........... | 274 | 36 | " |
| 3955. | James Chissum, Pri............ | 640 | 84 | " |
| 3956. | John McCallister.............. | 274 | 36 | " |
| 3957. | David Manifee................ | ... | .. | " |
| 3958. | ........................... | ... | .. | " |
| 3958. | James McCoy................. | | | " |
| 3959. | Charles McParish............. | 640 | 84 | " |
| 3960. | James R. Whitney, Pri......... | 640 | 84 | " |
| 3961. | The heirs of Thomas Richey, Cpl. | 1,000 | 84 | " " |
| 3962. | The heirs of Watson Andrews,Pt. | 640 | 84 | Mch. 8, '96 | Wm. Ferrell |
| 3963. | Zion Bradley.................. | 228 | 30 | " |
| 3964. | The heirs of Nathaniel Richard Brickle.................... | 640 | 84 | " |
| 3965. | The heirs of Lemuel Bullock.... | 1,000 | 84 | " |
| 3966. | The heirs of Watson Reed, Pri... | 640 | 84 | " |
| 3967. | Nicholas Russell, Pri........... | 228 | 30 | |

## 312 ROSTER OF NORTH CAROLINA SOLDIERS

| No. | To whom granted and rank | No. acres | Service in months | Location and to whom deeded and date of warrant. Within the limits of the lands allotted the officers and soldiers of the Continental Line, by Law, 1783, Oct. 14 | |
|---|---|---|---|---|---|
| 3968. | The heirs of Jonah McAdoe..... | 640 | 84 | Mch. 8,'98 | |
| 3969. | The heirs of John Davis........ | 640 | 84 | " | |
| 3970. | The heirs of Abraham Johnston . | 640 | 84 | | |
| 3971. | The heirs of Gresham T_____ .. | ... | .. | | |
| 3972. | The heirs of John G_____...... | ... | .. | | |
| 3973. | The heirs of Nathan B. Williams. | ... | .. | | |
| 3974. | Thomas Bennet, Pri........... | 228 | 30 | Nov.19,'95 | {delivered Joseph Williams |
| 3975. | William Williamson........... | 228 | 30 | | d'd " |

# VOUCHERS

The following are the usual form of vouchers found in the *Comptroller's Records.*

**(1)**
State of North Carolina.
Salisbury District No. 5727  Agreeable to an act of the General Assembly, passed in Hoke County
the 14th July 1781..................was allowed nine pounds Shillings Specie for Militia Service
by board of Auditors.  Dec. 17th, 1783.
By order.

                                 Harris................................................
                                 Hill Cathey

**(2)**
North Carolina.                                          No. 1622.
Agreeable to Act of Assembly passed in December 1785, the State of North Carolina is indebted
to...............................of the Continental Line of this State.  Thirty-nine
pounds, nineteen Shillings Specie in account of his pay to January 1st, '89, with interest from
the first of Aug. 1783.  Dated at Warrenton the first of May, 1786.
f 36, 19                                               H. Montford.
                         ..............................................
                         .............................................} Commissioners.

**(3)**
North Carolina.
Agreeable to Act of Assembly, passed January, 1792, the State Aforesaid is indebted to........
.........................................of the late Continental Line, the sum of six pounds
Specie, being the fourth in pay and interest to 1st August 1783, for which delivered to.........
.................................payments.
    Hillsborough, 1st May, 1792.
                                         J. M. Binford
                                         B. Sanders     Comns.

**(4)**
North Carolina.                                       No..............
Agreeable to an Act of the Assembly passed in May one thousand seven hundred and eighty-three,
the State of North Carolina is indebted to...................................Capt. of the
Continental Line of this State, one hundred ninety-seven pounds, 5 Shillings, 8 pence, with interest
from the date, account of his pay and subsistance to 1st....................., 177..... Dated
at Halifax the first day of August, 1783.
f 197-5-8.
                                     Willie Jones  }
                                     H. Montford  } Coms.

**(5)**
No.................. State of North Carolina, 21st March 1783.
    As Auditors for the District of Wilmington.  This is to Certify that.......................
...........................is allowed the sum of twenty-five pounds, fifteen shillings specie for
his services in the Militia as returned in pay roll No......................
    Lewis Holmes.             O.K.
f 25, 15.
                                     Hen. Dickson
                                     Thos. Routledge

**(6)**
No..............                                    f.., .., .. Specie.
By virtue of the authority vested in us, by an Act of the General Assembly, passed at Newbern,
January 1792, we hereby certify that the State of North Carolina is indebted to...............
.................................soldier in the Continental Line, of said State.  The sum of
twenty pounds, two shillings, and eight pence specie, with interest from the 1st day of August,
1783, as appears by vouchers lodged in this office.
    Hillsborough 1st May, 1792.
    By order,
................................, Clk.
                       ..............................................
                       ..............................................} Commissioners.

**(7)**
North Carolina.
Newbern District.
This may certify that......................................... of.......................Co.
for Militia duty as per Capt................................pay roll, was allowed the sum of
....................pounds ...................Shillings Specie, this 5th day of March, 1782.
..........................., Clk.
                       ..............................................} Dist.
                       ..............................................} Auditors

The list of names taken from these vouchers follows, with their number and what district.

*No.*

| | | |
|---|---|---|
| 1. Benj'm. Armstrong | 5727 | Salisbury Dist. |
| 2. James Armstrong | 1622 | |
| 3. Andrew Armstrong, Capt. | 477 | |
| 4. Capt. William Armstrong | 358 | |
| 5. Lt. Thomas Armstrong | 2960 | |
| 6. Cha. Armstrong | 3915 | Dist. of Wilmington |
| 7. John Armstrong | 4741 | Salisbury Dist. |
| 8. John Armstrong | 4685 | Salisbury Dist. |
| 9. John Armstrong | 3801 | Morgan Dist. |
| 10. John Armstrong | 4063 | Dist. of Wilmington |
| 11. John Armstrong | 935 | Dist. of Wilmington |
| 12. Lt. John Armstrong | 5786 | Dist. of Wilmington |
| 13. John Armstrong | 2099 | Dist. of Wilmington |
| 14. Capt. John Armstrong | 1743 | Dist. of Wilmington |
| 15. Lt. John Armstrong | 899 | Dist. of Wilmington |
| 16. John Armstrong | 2782 | Dist. of Wilmington |
| 17. Lt. Col. John Armstrong | 28 | |
| 18. Mathew Armstrong | 3736 | Salisbury Dist. |
| 19. Capt. William Armstrong | 5548 | |
| 20. Richard Armstrong | 4822 | Morgan Dist. |
| 21. Lt. Abel Armstrong | 4792 | Salisbury Dist. |
| 22. Jediah Alexander | 9235 | Salisbury Dist. |
| 23. Lt. Abel Armstrong | 5549 | Salisbury Dist. |
| 24. Capt. Wm. Armstrong | 34 | |
| 25. James Armstrong | 471 | |
| 26. Col. Martin Armstrong | 683 | Salisbury Dist. |
| 27. William Armstrong | 132 | Hillsborough Dist. |
| 28. Capt. Able Armstrong | 4727 | Salisbury Dist. |
| 29. Capt. William Armstrong | 359 | |
| 30. Capt. William Armstrong | 360 | |
| 31. James Armstrong | 592 | Salisbury Dist. |
| 32. James Armstrong | 337 | |
| 33. Capt. Able Armstrong | 1977 | Salisbury Dist. |
| 34. James Armstrong | 6196 | Salisbury Dist. |
| 35. John Alston | 320 | Dist. of Wilmington |
| 36. William Alston | 231 | |
| 37. Col. Phil. Alston | 20 | |
| 38. William Alston | 358 | |
| 39. Dan Alexander | 5294 | Salisbury Dist. |
| 40. Elias Alexander | 5293 | Salisbury Dist. |
| 41. Capt. William Alexander | 3054 | Salisbury Dist. |
| 42. Jediah Alexander | 2603 | Salisbury Dist. |
| 43. Andrew Alexander | 3322 | Salisbury Dist. |
| 44. Capt. Thos. Alexander | 8516 | Salisbury Dist. |
| 45. Capt. Charles Alexander | 8672 | Salisbury Dist. |
| 46. Isaac Alexander | 4296 | Salisbury Dist. |
| 47. Anthony Alexander | 1360 | |
| 48. Joseph Alexander | 152 | |
| 49. David Alexander | 3277 | Salisbury Dist. |
| 50. Charles Alexander | 3316 | Salisbury Dist. |
| 51. Moses Alexander | 5105 | Salisbury Dist. |
| 52. Nat. Alexander | 2681 | Salisbury Dist. |

|     |                           | *No.* |                    |
|-----|---------------------------|-------|--------------------|
| 53. | Abram Alexander ............... | 5272 | Salisbury Dist. |
| 54. | Jno. Alexander ................. | 5245 | Salisbury Dist. |
| 55. | Capt. Thomas Alexander ......... | 5099 | Salisbury Dist. |
| 56. | Capt. Thomas Alexander ......... | 5287 | Salisbury Dist. |
| 57. | Capt. William Alexander ........ | 3274 | Salisbury Dist. |
| 58. | Roland Alexander ............... | 3897 |                    |
| 59. | Elias Alexander ................ | 3700 | Salisbury Dist. |
| 60. | Wm. B. Alexander .............. | 1374 | Salisbury Dist. |
| 61. | Capt. Stephen Alexander ......... | 3213 | Salisbury Dist. |
| 62. | Col. George Alexander .......... | 1165 | Salisbury Dist. |
| 63. | William Alexander .............. | 3705 | Salisbury Dist. |
| 64. | Capt. Wm. Alexander ........... | 5242 | Salisbury Dist. |
| 65. | Dan. Alexander ................. | 2598 | Salisbury Dist. |
| 66. | Gabriel Alexander .............. | 7890 | Salisbury Dist. |
| 67. | Isaac Alexander ................ | 6657 | Salisbury Dist. |
| 68. | Benjamin Alexander ............. | 151  |                    |
| 69. | Isaac Alexander ................ | 3287 | Salisbury Dist. |
| 70. | Isaac Alexander ................ | 6665 | Salisbury Dist. |
| 71. | Charles Alexander .............. | 1395 | Salisbury Dist. |
| 72. | William Alexander .............. | 2605 | Salisbury Dist. |
| 73. | Amos Alexander ................ | 2950 | Salisbury Dist. |
| 74. | David Alexander ............... | 5289 | Salisbury Dist. |
| 75. | Ezekiel Alexander .............. | 20   |                    |
| 76. | Ezekiel Alexander .............. | 3717 | Salisbury Dist. |
| 77. | Abner Alexander ............... | 3716 | Salisbury Dist. |
| 78. | Jonah Alexander ............... | 3746 | Salisbury Dist. |
| 79. | Thomas Alexander .............. | 3699 | Salisbury Dist. |
| 80. | Moses Alexander ............... | 2685 | Salisbury Dist. |
| 81. | John Alexander ................ | 2607 | Salisbury Dist. |
| 82. | Thomas Alexander .............. | 2620 | Salisbury Dist. |
| 83. | Capt. Wm. Alexander ........... | 6638 | Salisbury Dist. |
| 84. | Thos. Alexander ............... | 3310 | Salisbury Dist. |
| 85. | Moses Alexander ............... | 596  | Salisbury Dist. |
| 86. | Capt. Stephen Alexander ......... | 2533 | Salisbury Dist. |
| 87. | Ezekiel Alexander .............. | 5674 | Salisbury Dist. |
| 88. | Abram Alexander ............... | 1358 | Salisbury Dist. |
| 89. | John Alexander ................ | 145  | Morgan Dist. |
| 90. | Wm. Alexander ................ | 3294 | Salisbury Dist. |
| 91. | Ezrah Alexander ............... | 6059 | Salisbury Dist. |
| 92. | George Alexander .............. | 1477 | Salisbury Dist. |
| 93. | Wm. Alexander ................ | 8299 | Salisbury Dist. |
| 94. | Elijah Alexander ............... | 5507 | Salisbury Dist. |
| 95. | Elis. Alexander ................ | 3312 | Salisbury Dist. |
| 96. | Abraham Alexander ............. | 3609 | Salisbury Dist. |
| 97. | Mathew Alexander ............. | 5247 | Salisbury Dist. |
| 98. | Edward Alexander ............. | 3711 | Salisbury Dist. |
| 99. | Roland Alexander .............. | 3869 | Salisbury Dist. |
| 100. | John Alexander ............... | 3305 | Salisbury Dist. |
| 101. | Isaac Alexander ............... | 5295 | Salisbury Dist. |
| 102. | ........ Atkins ............... | 27   |                    |
| 103. | Benjamin Atkins .............. | 230  |                    |
| 104. | Silas Atkins ................. | 663  | Dist. of Wilmington |
| 105. | David Adkins ................ | 1170 |                    |
| 106. | John Adkins ................. | 3440 | Dist. of Wilmington |

| | | No. | |
|---|---|---|---|
| 107. | James Atkins | 4881 | Dist. of Wilmington |
| 108. | James Atkins | 645 | Dist. of Wilmington |
| 109. | James Adkins | 3161 | Dist. of Wilmington |
| 110. | Isaac Atkins | 3970 | Dist. of Wilmington |
| 111. | Ese.... Adkins | 8986 | Dist. of Wilmington |
| 112. | Harrison Adkins | 5445 | Dist. of Wilmington |
| 113. | Richard Adkins | 280 | Dist. of Wilmington |
| 114. | Capt. Stafford | 1744 | Newbern Dist. |
| 115. | Lt. John Adams | 7655 | Salisbury Dist. |
| 116. | Benjamin Adams | 2143 | Dist. of Wilmington |
| 117. | Jacob Adams | 792 | Salisbury Dist. |
| 118. | Capt. Fred | 1861 | Newbern Dist. |
| 119. | John Adams | 495 | |
| 120. | Ceasar Adams, of Pitt Co. | 1506 | Newbern Dist. |
| 121. | Thomas Adams | 419 | |
| 122. | William Adams | 658 | |
| 123. | John Adams | 358 | |
| 124. | William Adams | 489 | |
| 125. | James Adams | 1816 | Salisbury Dist. |
| 126. | Bird Adams, of Johnson Co. | 515 | Newbern Dist. |
| 127. | Levi Adams, of Pitt Co. | 1047 | Newbern Dist. |
| 128. | Arthur Adams | 1008 | |
| 129. | Benja. Adams | 242 | |
| 130. | Elisha Adams | 4596 | Salisbury Dist. |
| 131. | William Adams | 3952 | Morgan Dist. |
| 132. | Peter Adams | 1165 | Newbern Dist. |
| 133. | Robert Adams | 4356 | Morgan Dist. |
| 134. | John Adams | 2093 | Salisbury Dist. |
| 135. | Philip Adams | 72 | |
| 136. | Daniel Adams | 4614 | Salisbury Dist. |
| 137. | David Adams | 497 | Newbern Dist. |
| 138. | Elijah Adams | 4237 | Salisbury Dist. |
| 139. | William Averitt | 682 | Dist. of Wilmington |
| 140. | William Averitt | 706 | Dist. of Wilmington |
| 141. | Lewis Averitt | 4558 | Dist. of Wilmington |
| 142. | Benjamin Averitt | 5213 | Dist. of Wilmington |
| 143. | Lewis Averitt | 757 | Dist. of Wilmington |
| 144. | Demsey Archer | 97 | Dist. of Wilmington |
| 145. | Michel Albright | 5362 | Salisbury Dist. |
| 146. | Simon Albright | 410 | Salisbury Dist. |
| 147. | Jacob Albright | 536 | Salisbury Dist. |
| 148. | Peter Albright | 806 | Salisbury Dist. |
| 149. | Thomas Archibald | 6501 | Salisbury Dist. |
| 150. | David Alderman | 1788 | Dist. of Wilmington |
| 151. | Andrew Allison | 4090 | Salisbury Dist. |
| 152. | Thomas Ammons | 994 | |
| 153. | David Allison | 6209 | Salisbury Dist. |
| 154. | Hugh Ayer | 6624 | Salisbury Dist. |
| 155. | John Atkins | 726 | |
| 156. | Col. John Ashe | 183 | |
| 157. | Samuel Ashe | 820 | |
| 158. | Benjamin Arnall | 4355 | Dist. of Wilmington |
| 159. | Henry Alligood, Sold. | 418 | |
| 160. | Theophilus Allison | 7166 | Salisbury Dist. |

|     |                                        | *No.* |                     |
|-----|----------------------------------------|-------|---------------------|
| 161. | John Adcock | 57 | |
| 162. | Rich'd. Allison | 7139 | Salisbury Dist. |
| 163. | James Atkinson | 115 | Dist. of Wilmington |
| 164. | Jos. Allison | 5107 | Salisbury Dist. |
| 165. | Philip Aman | 3749 | Dist. of Wilmington |
| 166. | Richard Alliston, of Pitt Co. | 2815 | Newbern Dist. |
| 167. | David Alphin | 4964 | Dist. of Wilmington |
| 168. | Hardy Adkison | 465 | |
| 169. | Samuel Alis., privt. | 202 | |
| 170. | Moses Adcock | 1212 | |
| 171. | Thomas Aid | 3009 | Dist. of Wilmington |
| 172. | Richard Andrews | 25 | |
| 173. | Reuben Aid. | 3010 | Dist. of Wilmington |
| 174. | Garrett Altman | 842 | |
| 175. | Stephen Anders | 1159 | Dist. of Wilmington |
| 176. | Andrew Andrews | 335 | |
| 177. | Alfred Andrews | 139 | |
| 178. | Joseph Andrews | 889 | |
| 179. | Hugh Andrews | 5076 | Salisbury Dist. |
| 180. | Andrew Andrews | 465 | Dist. of Wilmington |
| 181. | Leonard Andrews | 7509 | Salisbury Dist. |
| 182. | Joseph Andrews | 2791 | Dist. of Wilmington |
| 183. | Capt. Joseph Andrews | 875 | Dist. of Wilmington |
| 184. | Andrew Andrews | 40 | |
| 185. | Joseph Andrews | 878 | Dist. of Wilmington |
| 186. | James Avery | 728 | |
| 187. | John Avery | 25 | |
| 188. | Wm. Avery | 4849 | Dist. of Wilmington |
| 189. | William Avera | 4828 | Dist. of Wilmington |
| 190. | Daniel Avery, of Johnston Co. | 1189 | Newbern Dist. |
| 191. | John Avery, of Craven Co. | 1767 | Newbern Dist. |
| 192. | Capt. Alexander Avera | 4822 | Dist. of Wilmington |
| 193. | Alex. Avera, of Johnston Co. | 661 | Newbern Dist. |
| 194. | John Alban Avera, of Johnston Co. | 34 | Newbern Dist. |
| 195. | Thos. Avery | 5728 | Dist. of Wilmington |
| 196. | Andrew Avery, of Johnston Co. | 1159 | |
| 197. | Alex. Avera, of Johnston Co. | 578 | Newbern Dist. |
| 198. | William Avera, of Johnston Co. | 648 | Newbern Dist. |
| 199. | Jonathan Avera, of Johnston Co. | 479 | Newbern Dist. |
| 200. | John Anderson | 4551 | Morgan Dist. |
| 201. | Charles Anderson | 1774 | |
| 202. | John Anderson | 829 | Dist. of Wilmington |
| 203. | Francis Anderson | 4771 | Dist. of Wilmington |
| 204. | Wm. Anderson | 1208 | Dist. of Wilmington |
| 205. | John Anderson, soldier | 388 | Dist. of Wilmington |
| 206. | George Anderson, soldier | 734 | Dist. of Wilmington |
| 207. | Thos. Anderson, of Craven Co. | 681 | Newbern Dist. |
| 208. | Joseph Anderson, of Craven Co. | 1915 | Newbern Dist. |
| 209. | Wm. Anderson, of Pitt Co. | 414 | Newbern Dist. |
| 210. | David Anderson, of Pitt Co. | 1059 | Newbern Dist. |
| 211. | Lawrence Anderson, of Pitt Co. | 1179 | Newbern Dist. |
| 212. | Thomas Anderson, of Wayne Co. | 2037 | Newbern Dist. |
| 213. | John Anderson, of Pitt Co. | 2014 | Newbern Dist. |
| 214. | Jno. Anderson, of Pitt Co. | 1187 | Newbern Dist. |

| | | No. | |
|---|---|---|---|
| 215. | James Anderson, Soldier ................. | 351 | |
| 216. | John Anderson, Soldier .................. | 7 | |
| 217. | Wm. Anderson, of Pitt Co. .............. | 919 | Newbern Dist. |
| 218. | Frances Anderson, of Pitt Co. ............ | 1223 | Newbern Dist. |
| 219. | Isaac Anderson ........................ | 1132 | |
| 220. | James Anderson ....................... | 448 | |
| 221. | Isaac Anderson, Soldier ................. | 287 | |
| 222. | William Anderson ..................... | 7844 | Salisbury Dist. |
| 223. | Leonard Anderson ..................... | 632 | Salisbury Dist. |
| 224. | William Anderson ..................... | 1249 | Salisbury Dist. |
| 225. | William Anderson ..................... | 5816 | Salisbury Dist. |
| 226. | James Anderson ....................... | 796 | Salisbury Dist. |
| 227. | Dempsey R. Allen, of Pitt Co. ............ | 1579 | Newbern Dist. |
| 228. | Alex'r. Allen ......................... | 2713 | Salisbury Dist. |
| 229. | Ric'd. Allen .......................... | 784 | Dist. of Salisbury |
| 230. | John Allen ........................... | 5108 | Dist. of Salisbury |
| 231. | Capt. Richard Allen ................... | 1029 | Dist. of Salisbury |
| 232. | John Allen, of Craven Co. .............. | 1351 | Newbern Dist. |
| 233. | Capt. Rich'd. Allen ................... | 818 | Dist. of Salisbury |
| 234. | Robt. Allen .......................... | 7244 | Salisbury Dist. |
| 235. | Thomas Allen ........................ | 931 | |
| 236. | Joe Allen ............................ | 4723 | Dist. of Wilmington |
| 237. | Capt. Richard Allen ................... | 751 | Dist. of Salisbury |
| 238. | Alex. Allen .......................... | 8701 | Salisbury Dist. |
| 239. | ...... Allen, Soldier ................. | 434 | |
| 240. | Jeremiah Allen ....................... | 778 | |
| 241. | Robert Allen ......................... | 826 | |
| 242. | Josiah Allen ......................... | 243 | Newbern Dist. |
| 243. | Hugh Allen .......................... | .... | Salisbury Dist. |
| 244. | Thomas Allen ........................ | 4575 | Salisbury Dist. |
| 245. | Alexander Allen ...................... | 4005 | Dist. of Wilmington |
| 246. | Elkanah Allen ........................ | 4713 | Dist. of Wilmington |
| 247. | John Allen ........................... | 4121 | Morgan Dist. |
| 248. | Robert Allen, Soldier .................. | 642 | |
| 249. | Reuben Allen ......................... | 4947 | Salisbury Dist. |
| 250. | Charles Allen, soldier of Pitt Co........... | 1554 | Newbern Dist. |
| 251. | Andrew Allen ........................ | 1451 | Salisbury Dist. |

## REFERENCE, COMPTROLLER'S OFFICE

### Vouchers in Box B-1 follow

| | | No. | |
|---|---|---|---|
| | Moses Branch ................... | 472 | |
| | Moses Branch ................... | 5053 | |
| | Moses Branch ................... | 3359 | |
| | Jesse Branch ................... | 3680 | |
| | Thomas Branch ................ | 3361 | |
| | Jesse Branch ................... | 5808 | |
| Militia | Thos. Battle, Ensn. .............. | 5480 | |
| | Thos. Battle ................... | 3566 | |
| | Ephriam Battle .................. | 157 | |
| | Thos. Battle ................... | 5740 | |
| Militia | Wm. Brown ................... | 7257 | Salisbury Dist. |

|  |  | No. |  |
|---|---|---|---|
|  | Wm. Brown | 8013 | Salisbury Dist. |
|  | Jesse Brown | 2074 |  |
|  | Stephen Brown | 1487 |  |
|  | Daniel Brown | 2651 | Salisbury Dist. |
|  | Dempsey Brown | 1036 | Wilmington Dist. |
|  | Richard Brown | 3114 |  |
| Militia | ......Brown, Wake Co. | .... |  |
|  | Jesse Brown | 5765 |  |
| Militia | Daniel Brown | 2718 | Salisbury Dist. |
|  | James Brown | 5151 |  |
| Continental | Moses Brown, soldier | 633 |  |
| Militia | Charles Brown | 1399 |  |
|  | George Brown | .... | Morgan Dist. |
|  | Edwin Brown | 3900 |  |
| Continental | Bezelys Bowme | 581 | Halifax Dist. |
|  | Ben Brown | 4969 |  |
| Continental | Robert Brown, soldier | 441 | Halifax Dist. |
|  | Samuel Brown, soldier, Pitt Co. | 1633 | Newbern Dist. |
|  | Richard Brown | 6496 | Salisbury Dist. |
|  | James Brown | 1286 |  |
|  | Nathan Brown | 481 |  |
|  | Rich'd. Brown | 1450 |  |
|  | Charles Brown | 5820 |  |
| Continental | George Brown, Sergt. | 104 |  |
|  | Willie Brown | 1190 | Halifax Dist. |
|  | Charles Brown | 1390 |  |
|  | George Brown | 3234 |  |
|  | George Brown | 1430 | Warrenton Dist. |
| Continental | Jesse Brown | .... | Hillsborough Dist. |
|  | Demcy Brown, of Johnston Co. | 1256 | Warrenton Dist. |
| Militia | Francis Brown, of Johnston Co. | .... | Newbern Dist. |
|  | George Brown | 3102 |  |
|  | Charles Brown | 1365 |  |
|  | Peter Brown, in Company of Ashbury, commanded by Col. James Moore | .... | Wilmington Dist. |
| Militia | Thomas Brown | 1288 | Salisbury Dist. |
|  | Thomas Brown | 805 |  |
|  | Thomas Brown | 1474 | Salisbury Dist. |
| Continental | Thomas Brown | 733 | Halifax Dist. |
| Continental | ..... Brown | 1620 | Warrenton Dist. |
|  | Otway Burns | 48 |  |
|  | Jo. Burch | 278 |  |
|  | David Byors | 8017 | Salisbury Dist. |
|  | Stephen Bearfield | 274 |  |
|  | Timothy Bloodworth | 6011 |  |
|  | John Beck | 1834 |  |
|  | Lewis Bruenton | 5559 |  |
|  | Peter Baleman | 6004 |  |
|  | Benjamin Brantley | 3090 |  |
|  | Daniel Bowney | 1695 |  |
|  | Joseph Bivin | 1685 |  |
|  | David Beaty | 6335 | Salisbury Dist. |
| Militia | Ephraim Battle | 157 |  |
| Militia | Richard Bass | 5039 |  |

|  |  | *No.* |  |
|---|---|---|---|
| Continental | Moses Bass | 1405 | |
| | Hardy Bass, (volunteer on back of certificate) | 120 | |
| Militia | Burwell Bass | 5051 | |
| Militia | Richard Bass | 571 | |
| Militia | William Bass | 536 | |
| Militia | Larsin Bennett | 1124 | |
| Continental | James Bennett | 192 | |
| | Francis Bennett | 726 | |
| Militia | D..... Bennett | 3777 | |
| Continental | Jacob Bennett | 655 | |
| Militia | William Bennett, of Dobbs Co. | 2411 | Newbern Dist. |
| | Stephen Bennett | 4096 | |
| Militia | Will Butler, Craven Co. | 885 | Newbern Dist. |
| Continental | Jethro Butler, Militia duty | 982 | |
| Continental | William Butler | 83 | |
| Militia | Arthur Butler, Craven Co. | 500 | |
| Militia | James Butler | 5537 | |
| Continental | Lawrence Butler | 207 | |
| | Elias Butler | 1,5749 | Salisbury Dist. |
| | Simon Butler | 6065 | Halifax Dist. |
| | Christopher Butler | 2590 | Salisbury Dist. |
| | Robert Butler | 74 | Wilmington Dist. |
| | Stephen Butler | 3103 | Halifax Dist. |
| | John Butler | 292 | Halifax Dist. |
| | Laurence Butler | 89-727 | |
| | John Butler | 4315 | Halifax Dist. |
| | William Butler | 90 | Wilmington Dist. |
| | Zachariah Butler | 2940 | Wilmington Dist. |
| | John Butler | 6675 | Halifax Dist. |
| Militia | Joseph Butler | 861 | Wilmington Dist. |
| | James Butler | 817 | Hillsborough Dist. |
| | Stephen Butler | 7198 | Halifax Dist. |
| | Stephen Butler | 7174 | Halifax Dist. |
| | Andrew Butler | 6113 | Halifax Dist. |
| | Willis Butler | 3206 | Edenton Dist. |
| | Charles Butler | 5882 | Wilmington Dist. |
| | Capt. James Butler | 5878 | Wilmington Dist. |
| | Andrew Butler | 6086 | Halifax Dist. |
| | Wm. Butler | 5549 | Wilmington Dist. |
| | Lawrence Butler | 121 | Hillsboro Dist. |
| | Thos. Byam Butler | 392 | |
| | James Butler | 754 | Salisbury Dist. |
| | James Butler | 330 | Wilmington Dist. |
| | Willis Butler | 609 | Edenton Dist. |
| | Samuel Butler | 2424 | Wilmington Dist. |
| | John Butler | 4316 | Halifax Dist. |
| | Samuel Butler | 2922 | Wilmington Dist. |
| | John Butler | 898 | Wilmington Dist. |
| | Stephen Butler | 1534 | Wilmington Dist. |
| | Curry Butler | 851 | Edenton Dist. |
| | Fort Butler | 1348 | Hillsborough Dist. |
| | Zackariah Butler | 2649 | Wilmington Dist. |
| | Capt. James Butler | 5537 | Wilmington Dist. |

| | | *No.* | |
|---|---|---|---|
| | Jethro Butler | 2074 | Edenton Dist. |
| | John Butler | 4273 | Washington & Sulivan Co. |
| | Wm. Butler | 1523 | Wilmington Dist. |
| Militia | Wm. Butler | 1678 | Wilmington Dist. |
| Militia | Wm. Butler | 1684 | Newbern Dist. |
| | John Butler | 9528 | Halifax Dist. |
| | Arthur Butler | 500 | Newbern Dist. |
| | Elisha Butler | 23 | Newbern Dist. |
| Continental | James Butler | 1471 | Warrenton Dist. |
| Continental | William Butler | 83 | Hillsborough Dist. |
| Continental | James Butler | 1471 | Newbern Dist. |
| Militia | Charles Butler | 928 | Newbern Dist. |
| Continental | Jethro Butler | 982 | Halifax Dist. |
| Militia | Wm. Butler | 835 | Newbern Dist. |
| Continental | Hardy Brogden | 1209 | |
| | Hanod Brogden | 2233 | Halifax Dist. |
| | Hardy Brogden | 497 | Halifax Dist. |
| Militia | Thomas Brogden | 2039 | Newbern Dist. |
| | William Brogden | 316 | Halifax Dist. |
| Militia | John Brogden | 2406 | Newbern Dist. |
| | John Bridges | 2644 | Halifax Dist. |
| | Benjamin Bridges | 6729 | Halifax Dist. |
| Militia | David Bridges | 77 | Morgan Dist. |
| | Ben Bridges | 386 | Halifax Dist. |
| | William Bridges | 3408 | Morgan Dist. |
| | David Bridges | 125 | Salisbury Dist. |
| | William Bridges | 2038 | Salisbury Dist. |
| | Thomas Bridges | 719 | Halifax Dist. |
| | Wm. Bridges | 6730 | Halifax Dist. |
| | Benjamin Bridges | .... | |
| Militia | Isaac Bridges | 26 | Morgan Dist. |
| | Will'm. Bridges | 698 | Newbern Dist. |
| | Benjamin Bridges | 2896 | Halifax Dist. |
| | Moses Bridges | 4665 | Morgan Dist. |
| | Nathan Bridges | 5703 | Halifax Dist. |
| | Peter Bennet, Capt. | 309 | Hillsborough Dist. |
| | Peter Bennett | 20 | Hillsborough Dist. |
| | Peter Bennett | 530 | Hillsborough Dist. |
| | Leonard Bradley | 5391 | Salisbury Dist. |
| | Edward Bradley | 4974 | Salisbury Dist. |
| Militia | John Bradley | 3352 | Wilmington Dist. |
| | Richard Bradley | 12 | Rutherford Co. |
| | Richard Bradley | 2850 | Wilmington Dist. |
| | William Bradley | 1261 | Hillsborough Dist. |
| Militia | Thomas Bradley | 4907 | Morgan Dist. |
| | John Bradley | 146 | Salisbury Dist. |
| | Richard Bradley | 6738 | Halifax Dist. |
| | James Bradley | 3378 | Salisbury Dist. |
| | Thomas Bradley | 3640 | Halifax Dist. |
| | John Bradley | 840 | |
| | Capt. James Bradley | 33 | Halifax Dist. |
| | Capt. James Bradley | 34 | Halifax Dist. |
| | Rich'd. Bradley | 8039 | Halifax Dist. |
| | James Bradley | 3971 | Wilmington Dist. |

|  |  | No. |  |
|---|---|---|---|
|  | Wm. Bradley | 2729 | Halifax Dist. |
|  | Capt. Geo. Bradley | 347 | Halifax Dist. |
|  | Stephen Bradley | 6735 | Halifax Dist. |
|  | Enoch Bradley | 2964 | Hillsborough Dist. |
|  | John Bradley | 248 | Morgan Dist. |
|  | James Bradley | 1649 | Salisbury Dist. |
|  | John Bradley | 23 | Rutherford Dist. |
|  | Burrill Bradley | 3810 | Halifax Dist. |
|  | James W. Bradley | 3316 | Salisbury Dist. |
|  | Burnell Bradly | 3941 | Salisbury Dist. |
|  | Walter Bradly | 1642 | Morgan Dist. |
| Continental | Nimrod Bradly | 1949 | Warrenton Dist. |
|  | William Bradly | 2299 | Halifax Dist. |
| Militia | John Bradly | 5110 | Salisbury Dist. |
|  | Benjamin Bradly | 8725 | Halifax Dist. |
|  | Benjamin Bradly | 1947 | Halifax Dist. |
|  | James Bradly | 2867 | Wilmington Dist. |
|  | Walter Bradly | 1530 | Morgan Dist. |
| Militia | Thomas Bradley | 473 | Wilmington Dist. |
|  | Samuel Bradley | 2141 | Halifax Dist. |
|  | Rich'd. Bradley | 7104 | Halifax Dist. |
|  | Ben Bradley | 5320 | Halifax Dist. |
|  | Harton Bradley | 3504 | Morgan Dist. |
|  | Arnold Bradley | 686 | Halifax Dist. |
|  | John Bradley | 2499 | Salisbury Dist. |
|  | James Bradley | 267 | Halifax Dist. |
|  | Jacob Bradley | 66 | Wilmington Dist. |
| Militia | Lieut. Len Bradley | 132 | Salisbury Dist. |
|  | Thomas Bradley | 6673 | Halifax Dist. |
|  | Gee Bradley | 609 | Halifax Dist. |
|  | Samuel Bradley | 529 | Halifax Dist. |
|  | James Bradley | 129 | Hillsborough Dist. |
|  | Wm. Bradley | 2539 | Halifax Dist. |
|  | William Bradley | 1853 | Hillsborough Dist. |
|  | James Bradley | 5829 | Hillsborough Dist. |
|  | James Bradley | 1522 | Hillsborough Dist. |
|  | James Bradley | 346 | Halifax Dist. |
|  | James Bradley | 5754 | Halifax Dist. |
|  | James Bradley | 316 | Halifax Dist. |
|  | Benjamin Bradley | 1066 | Halifax Dist. |
|  | Enoch Bradley | 6797 | Hillsborough Dist. |
|  | Leonard Bradley | 2450 | Salisbury Dist. |
| Militia | John Bradley | 178 | Wilmington Dist. |
| Continental | Capt. James Bradley | 35 | Halifax Dist. |
| Continental | William Bradley | 831 | Warrenton Dist. |
|  | Capt. James Bradley | 36 | Halifax Dist. |
|  | Thomas Bradley | 9358 | Halifax Dist. |
| Continental | Corpl. Richard Bradley | 1043 | Halifax Dist. |
| Continental | Samuel Bradley | 422 | Hillsborough Dist. |
|  | Wm. Bradley | 216 |  |
|  | Capt. Gee Bradley | 346 | Halifax Dist. |
|  | Capt. Gee Bradley | 345 | Halifax Dist. |
| Continental | Robert Bradley | 1174 | Halifax Dist. |
|  | James Bradley | 8 | Halifax Dist. |

|  |  | *No.* |  |
|---|---|---|---|
| Militia | Mathew Ghaston | 4843 | Salisbury Dist. |
| Militia | Jeremiah Gaylord | 1000 | Newbern Dist. |
| Militia | Neil Galbreath | 3839 | Wilmington Dist. |
| Militia | John Galbreath | 1849 | Newbern Dist. |
| Militia | Basil Gaither | 5086 | Salisbury Dist. |
| Militia | Benjamine Gaither | 4634 | Salisbury Dist. |
| Militia | Peter Gaither | 2903 | Wilmington Dist. |
| Militia | Anthony Gilbard | 4956 | Wilmington Dist. |
| Militia | Aaron Gurganus | 1439 | Newbern Dist. |
| Militia | Charles Gorden | 4470 | Salisbury Dist. |
| Continental | Patrick Gaul | 661 |  |
| Continental | James Gutray | 1472 | Warrenton Dist. |
| Continental | Arandall Grant | 260 | Gen. Assembly |
| Continental | Francis Good | 472 | Gen. Assembly |
| Continental | Daniel Gaugh | 618 | Gen. Assembly |
| Continental | John Grinder | 126 | Newbern Dist. |
| Militia | George Gary | 528 | Wilmington Dist. |
| Militia | Burges Gaither | 5089 | Salisbury Dist. |
| Militia | Peter Gates | 3120 | Wilmington Dist. |
| Militia | James Gardner | 2383 | Salisbury Dist. |
| Continental | Thos. Garland | 1289 | Gen. Assembly |
| Continental | Handy Garris | 795 | Gen. Assembly |
| Militia | Henry Garroth | 1945 | Gen. Assembly |
| Militia | Peter Growel | 3174 | Salisbury Dist. |

### CHAPMAN FAMILY

| Militia | James Chapman | 4573 | Salisbury Dist. |
|---|---|---|---|
| Militia | Abner Chapman | 4078 | Wilmington Dist. |
| Militia | David Chapman | 4049 | Wilmington Dist. |

### CUNNINGHAM'S

| Militia | James Cunningham | 2523 | Salisbury Dist. |
|---|---|---|---|
| Militia | Joseph Cunningham | 76.31 | Salisbury Dist. |
|  | Lieut. Joseph Cunningham | 47.77 | Salisbury Dist. |
| Militia | Joseph Cunningham | 2374 | Salisbury Dist. |

### CAINS

| Militia | Wm. Cains | 1257 | Wilmington Dist. |
|---|---|---|---|
| Militia | Wm. Cains | 688 | Wilmington Dist. |
| Militia | Wm. Cains | 715 | Wilmington Dist. |
| Militia | Wm. Cains | 4734 | Wilmington Dist. |
| Militia | Samuel Cains | 2366 | Wilmington Dist. |
| Militia | John Cains | 713 | Wilmington Dist. |
| Militia | Thomas Cains | 4507 | Wilmington Dist. |
| Militia | James Cains | 695 | Wilmington Dist. |
| Militia | John Cains | 2953 | Wilmington Dist. |
| Militia | James Cains | 3265 | Wilmington Dist. |
| Militia | Samuel Cains | 2927 | Wilmington Dist. |
| Militia | James Cains | 714 | Wilmington Dist. |
| Private in State Legion | Elisha Cains | 1025 | Wilmington Dist. |

### CANNON'S

| Militia | David Cannon | 1882 | Wilmington Dist. |
|---|---|---|---|
| Militia | Penn Cannon | 1689 | Newbern Dist. |

| | | No. | |
|---|---|---|---|
| Militia | Caleb Cannon | 378 | Newbern Dist. |
| Militia | Dennis Cannon | 2428 | Wilmington Dist. |
| Militia | Arch Cannon | 1349 | Newbern Dist. |
| Continental | Benjamin Cannon | 277 | Hillsboro Dist. |
| Militia | Benjamin Cameron Cannon | 557 | Newbern Dist. |
| Militia | Henry Cannon | 1067 | Newbern Dist. |
| Continental | Lewis Cannon | 155 | Halifax Dist. |
| Militia | Radford Cannon | 1653 | Newbern Dist. |
| Militia | John Cannon | 1136 | Newbern Dist. |
| State Troops | John Cannon | 2247 | Newbern Dist. |
| State Troops | Reeding Cannon | 2246 | Newbern Dist. |
| Militia | Farnifold Cannon | 1513 | Newbern Dist. |
| Militia | Pugh Cannon | 1059 | Newbern Dist. |

### COLES'

| | | | |
|---|---|---|---|
| Continental | Alexander Cole | 77 | Newbern Dist. |
| Continental | Alexander Cole | 143 | Hillsboro Dist. |
| Continental | George Cole | 96 | Hillsboro Dist. |
| Continental | Robert Cole | 223 | Hillsboro Dist. |
| Continental | Robert Cole | 332 | Hillsboro Dist. |
| Militia | Thomas Cole | 1712 | Newbern Dist. |
| Militia | Willis Cole | .... | Wilmington Dist. |
| Continental | Martin Cole | 252 | |
| Militia | Stephen Cole | 8992 | Salisbury Dist. |
| Continental | George Cole | 96 | Hillsboro Dist. |
| Militia | Joab Cole | 2228 | Salisbury Dist. |

### CARRAWAYS

| | | | |
|---|---|---|---|
| Militia | Lieut. Bed'r. Carraway | 5024 | Wilmington Dist. |
| Militia | James Carraway | 3886 | Wilmington Dist. |
| Militia | Francis Carraway | 1392 | Halifax Dist. |
| Militia | John Carraway | 4909 | Wilmington Dist. |
| Militia | Jessie Carraway | 183 | Newbern Dist. |
| Militia | John Cleveland | 2846 | Salisbury Dist. |
| Militia | Joseph Cowen | 5230 | Salisbury Dist. |
| Militia | Joseph Cowen | 889 | Salisbury Dist. |
| Militia | Joseph Cowen | 6946 | Salisbury Dist. |
| Militia | ...... Clark's | 5667 | Salisbury Dist. |
| Militia | David Clark | 5495 | Wilmington Dist. |
| Militia | David Clark | 5058 | Wilmington Dist. |
| Militia | David Clark | 3346 | Wilmington Dist. |
| Militia | David Clark | 1809 | Wilmington Dist. |

### CARTWRIGHTS

| | | | |
|---|---|---|---|
| Continental | Thomas Cartwright | 851 | Halifax Dist. |
| Line | Heze Cartwright | 933 | Newbern Dist. |

### CORBETT FAMILY

| | | | |
|---|---|---|---|
| Militia | John Corbett | 3468 | Wilmington Dist. |
| Militia | John Corbett | 864 | Newbern Dist. |
| Militia | Thomas Corbett | 3473 | Wilmington Dist. |
| Militia | Thomas Corbett | 1723 | Wilmington Dist. |

### CRAWFORD FAMILY

| | | No. | |
|---|---|---|---|
| Militia | Capt. Charles Crawford | 3987 | Wilmington Dist. |
| Militia | John Crawford | 5789 | Salisbury Dist. |
| Militia | John Crawford | 2096 | Wilmington Dist. |
| Militia | Moses Crawford | 4592 | Wilmington Dist. |
| Militia | John Crawford | 7849 | Salisbury Dist. |
| Militia | John Crawford | 4167 | Salisbury Dist. |
| Militia | James Crawford | 4065 | Salisbury Dist. |
| Militia | Charles Crawford | 4216 | Wilmington Dist. |
| State Troops | Benjamine Crawford | 498 | Newbern Dist. |

### CHAVIS FAMILY

| | | | |
|---|---|---|---|
| Continental Line | C...... Chavis | 699 | Halifax Dist. |
| Militia | Ishamael Chavis | 4808 | Wilmington Dist. |
| Militia | Ishamael Chavis | 4478 | Wilmington Dist. |

### CHERRY

| | | | |
|---|---|---|---|
| Continental | Joshua Cherry | 212 | Hillsboro Dist. |
| Continental | Alexander Cherry | 270 | Hillsboro Dist. |
| Continental | John Cherry | 1146 | Warrenton Dist. |
| Militia | Willis Cherry | 3675 | Wilmington Dist. |
| Continental | Alexander Cherry | 162 | Newbern Dist. |
| | Willis Cherry | 3356 | Wilmington Dist. |
| Militia | Lemuel Cherry | 1737 | Newbern Dist. |
| Militia | Willis Cherry | 3799 | Wilmington Dist. |
| Militia | Daniel Cherry | 164 | Newbern Dist. |

### COOLY FAMILY

| | | | |
|---|---|---|---|
| Continental Line | Gabriel Cooly | 400 | Newbern Dist. |
| Militia | Francis Cooly | 4837 | Wilmington Dist. |
| Militia | Francis Cooly | 5854 | Wilmington Dist. |
| Militia | Francis Cooly | 4768 | Wilmington Dist. |
| Continental | Gabriel Cooly | 255 | Hillsboro Dist. |
| Militia | Francis Cooly | 3929 | Wilmington Dist. |
| Militia | Francis Cooly | 760 | Wilmington Dist. |
| Militia | Frank Cooly | 4588 | Wilmington Dist. |
| Militia | Francis Cooly | 4891 | Wilmington Dist. |

### COTTON FAMILY

| | | | |
|---|---|---|---|
| Continental Line | Sergn't. John Cotton | 399 | Halifax Dist. |
| Continental Line | Capt. Samuel Chapman | 517 | Halifax Dist. |
| Militia | Weeks Chapman | 1823 | Newbern Dist. |

### CATHEY FAMILY

| | | | |
|---|---|---|---|
| Militia | William Cathey | 2305 | Salisbury Dist. |
| Militia | John Cathey | 2775 | Wilmington Dist. |
| Militia | Capt. James Cathey | 869 | Salisbury Dist. |
| Militia | James Cathey | 5461 | Salisbury Dist. |
| Militia | George Cathey | 4560 | Salisbury Dist. |
| Militia | Richard Cathey | 6725 | Salisbury Dist. |

| | | No. | |
|---|---|---|---|
| Militia | James Cathey | 4475 | Salisbury Dist. |
| Militia | Alex Cathey | 8310 | Salisbury Dist. |

CALDWELL FAMILY

| | | | |
|---|---|---|---|
| Militia | David Caldwell | 2717 | Salisbury Dist. |
| Militia | David Caldwell | 7048 | Salisbury Dist. |
| Continental Line | Thos. Caldwell | 94 | Halifax Dist. |
| Militia | James Caldwell | 6506 | Salisbury Dist. |

CAMPBELL

| | | | |
|---|---|---|---|
| Continental Line | Patrick Campbell | 475 | Halifax Dist. |
| Continental Line | Wm. Campbell | 1178 | Halifax Dist. |
| Militia | Hugh Campbell | 4035 | Salisbury Dist. |
| Militia | John Campbell | 4369 | Wilmington Dist. |
| Continental Line | Wm. Campbell | 1420 | |
| Militia | John Campbell | 4281 | Wilmington Dist. |
| Continental | George Campbell | 434 | Hillsboro Dist. |
| Militia | John Campbell | 3245 | Salisbury Dist. |
| Militia | John Campbell | 7392 | Salisbury Dist. |
| | Dugall Campbell | 4113 | Wilmington Dist. |
| | Anguis Campbell | 8437 | |
| Militia | Robert Campbell | 3898 | Morgan Dist. |
| Militia | John Campbell | 4022 | Morgan Dist. |
| Militia | John Campbell | 2776 | Salisbury Dist. |
| Militia | John Campbell | 1402 | Salisbury Dist. |
| Militia | John Campbell | 2985 | Wilmington Dist. |
| Militia | David Campbell | 6436 | Salisbury Dist. |
| Militia | Robert Campbell | 4018 | Wilmington Dist. |
| Militia | Archibald Campbell | 444 | Salisbury Dist. |
| Militia | Duncan Campbell | 4278 | Wilmington Dist. |
| Militia | James Campbell | 256 | Hillsboro Dist. |
| Continental | George Campbell | 585 | Hillsboro Dist. |
| Continental | Solomon Campbell | 82 | Hillsboro Dist. |
| Militia | John Campbell | 7407 | Salisbury Dist. |
| Militia | John Campbell | 4123 | Wilmington Dist. |
| Militia | John Campbell | 4625 | Wilmington Dist. |
| Continental | John Campbell | 204 | Hillsboro Dist. |
| Militia | William Campbell | 1878 | Newbern Dist. |
| | Private William Campbell | 283 | |
| Militia | Neil Campbell | 4447 | Wilmington Dist. |
| Militia | Colin Campbell | 2561 | Salisbury Dist. |
| Militia | Alex Campbell | 5975 | Salisbury Dist. |
| Militia | Daniel Campbell | 4318 | Wilmington Dist. |
| Militia | Charles Campbell | 4982 | Wilmington Dist. |
| Continental | James Campbell | 86 | Halifax Dist. |
| Continental | Thomas Campbell | 24 | Halifax Dist. |
| | Capt. James Campbell | 3820 | Wilmington Dist. |
| Militia | Michel Campbell | 4310 | Wilmington Dist. |
| Militia | Andrew Campbell | 3637 | Salisbury Dist. |

## CARSON

| | | No. | |
|---|---|---|---|
| Militia | Alex Carson | 4481 | Salisbury Dist. |
| Militia | Charles Carson | 3608 | Salisbury Dist. |
| Militia | John Carson | 4003 | Morgan Dist. |
| Militia | Robert Carson | 6515 | Salisbury Dist. |
| Militia | Hugh Carson | 2376 | Salisbury Dist. |

## CHAMBERS

| | | | |
|---|---|---|---|
| Militia | Robert Chambers | 2534 | Salisbury Dist. |
| Militia | Henry Chambers | 4036 | Salisbury Dist. |
| Militia | Arthur Chambers | 2665 | Salisbury Dist. |
| Militia | William Chambers | 857 | Salisbury Dist. |
| Militia | James Chambers | 4799 | Salisbury Dist. |

## COX

| | | | |
|---|---|---|---|
| Continental | John Cox | 171 | Hillsboro Dist. |
| Militia | Solomon Cox | 4074 | Wilmington Dist. |
| Continental | Joseph Cox | 671 | Hillsboro Dist. |
| Continental | William Cox | 670 | Hillsboro Dist. |
| Militia | Caleb Cox | 2986 | Salisbury Dist. |
| Militia | John Cox | 1224 | Newbern Dist. |
| Militia | Joseph Cox | 2987 | Salisbury Dist. |
| Militia | Charles Cox | 3558 | Wilmington Dist. |
| Militia | Simon Cox | 3022 | Wilmington Dist. |
| Militia | Elisha Cox | 47 | Newbern Dist. |
| Militia | Aaron Cox | 3560 | Wilmington Dist. |
| Militia | John Carruth | 7763 | Salisbury Dist. |
| Militia | Stephen Coston | 3532 | Wilmington Dist. |
| Militia | Joab Crage | 3037 | Salisbury Dist. |
| Continental | Ezekiel Coats | 240 | Hillsboro Dist. |
| Continental | James Cronnister | 161 | Hillsboro Dist. |
| Continental | Elijah Clay | 102 | Hillsboro Dist. |
| Continental | Dempsey Carol | 1677 | Wilmington Dist. |
| Continental | Jonmiah Chilos | 4449 | Morgan Dist. |
| Continental | William Clifton | 1929 | Warrenton Dist. |
| Militia | Reuben Cock | 3570 | Wilmington Dist. |
| Militia | Conrad Corneilson | 763 | Salisbury Dist. |
| Militia | Patrick Cannady | 5762 | Wilmington Dist. |
| Militia | Shadrack Carvons | 866 | Wilmington Dist. |
| Continental | Charles Coleman | 217 | Hillsboro Dist. |
| Continental | Israel Cullom | 359 | |
| Militia | Wm. Charlton | 511 | Newbern Dist. |
| Militia | James Cason | 1113 | Wilmington Dist. |
| Continental | Samr Connol | 815 | Warrenton Dist. |
| Militia | Wm. Croswell | 8939 | Salisbury Dist. |
| Continental | Robert Chumley | 987 | Halifax Dist. |
| Militia | Henry Canwas | 7258 | Salisbury Dist. |
| Continental | Thos. Carothers | 427 | Halifax Dist. |
| Continental | John Curls | 757 | |
| Militia | Eleazor Cummins | 8947 | Salisbury Dist. |
| Militia | Wm. Coonie | 4577 | Morgan Dist. |
| Militia | Fredrick Coolock | 679 | Salisbury Dist. |

COOPER'S

| | | No. | |
|---|---|---|---|
| Militia | James Cooper | 977 | Newbern Dist. |
| Continental | Thomas Cooper | 728 | Halifax Dist. |
| Continental | Nathaniel Cooper | 357 | Hillsboro Dist. |
| Militia | Samuel Cooper | 881 | Salisbury Dist. |
| Continental | Joseph Cooper | 1425 | Warrenton Dist. |
| Continental | Frederick Cooper | 159 | Hillsboro Dist. |
| Militia | William Cooper | 2303 | Salisbury Dist. |
| Continental | Henry Cooper | 385 | Hillsboro Dist. |
| Continental | Benjamin Cooper | 840 | Halifax Dist. |
| Continental | James Cooper | 678 | Halifax Dist. |
| Militia | Willis Cooper | 1527 | Wilmington Dist. |
| Militia | John Cooper | 3394 | Wilmington Dist. |
| Continental | William Cooper | 1211 | Warrenton Dist. |
| Continental | John Cooper | .... | Hillsboro Dist. |
| Militia | David Clay | 201 | |
| Militia | Joseph Christie | 5172 | Salisbury Dist. |
| Militia | Gibson Cumbo | 4459 | Wilmington Dist. |
| Continental | Joseph Crief | 544 | |
| Continental | Thomas Cullas | 153 | |
| Continental | William Capps | 131 | Hillsboro Dist. |
| Continental | William Carroll | 306 | Hillsboro Dist. |
| Continental | Thomas Castilloe | 15 | Hillsboro Dist. |
| Continental | James Crounister | 89 | Hillsboro Dist. |
| Militia | John Culp | 1346 | Salisbury Dist. |
| Militia | Frederick Copper | 7691 | Salisbury Dist. |
| Militia | George Clans | 484 | Newbern Dist. |
| Militia | Benjamin Cummings | 524 | Newbern Dist. |
| Militia | William Covington | 1259 | Wilmington Dist. |
| Continental | William Covington | 129 | Hillsboro Dist. |
| Continental | William Clifton | 132 | Hillsboro Dist. |
| Militia | Henry Carrigher | 2490 | Salisbury Dist. |
| Militia | Henry Crasy | 3121 | Salisbury Dist. |
| Militia | Robert Croswell | 6705 | Salisbury Dist. |
| Continental | Johnson Crusse | 1616 | Warrenton Dist. |
| Militia | Amos Catrill | 317 | Newbern Dist. |
| Continental | Peter Cammell | 56 | |
| Continental | William Cavender | 325 | Hillsboro Dist. |
| Continental | Samuel Chappell | 314 | Hillsboro Dist. |
| Continental | John Coats | 248 | Hillsboro Dist. |
| Continental | David Crawley | 174 | Hillsboro Dist. |
| Continental | Stephen Couger | 169 | Hillsboro Dist. |
| Militia | Lieut. Clayton | 8370 | Salisbury Dist. |
| Militia | Shuibal Claghorn | 470 | Hillsboro Dist. |
| Continental | John Carmack | 43 | Halifax Dist. |
| Continental | Thomas Chitten | 209 | Halifax Dist. |
| Continental | Levi Coleman | 90 | Hillsboro Dist. |
| Continental | John Curk | 944 | Halifax Dist. |
| Continental | Georg Claunce | 343 | Hillsboro Dist. |
| Militia | Jos. Causay | 420 | Newbern Dist. |
| Militia | Joseph Crispin | 989 | Newbern Dist. |
| Militia | Michl. Curmon | 998 | Newbern Dist. |
| Militia | Windeth Corbitt | 1596 | Newbern Dist. |
| Continental | Butler Cowell | 170 | Hillsboro Dist. |

| | | No. | |
|---|---|---|---|
| Continental | Job Carlisle | 471 | |
| Militia | Thomas Carrel | 1290 | Salisbury Dist. |
| Militia | Charles Caten | 7325 | Salisbury Dist. |
| Militia | Francis Coston | 3510 | Wilmington Dist. |
| Continental | Elisha Coward | 426 | Halifax Dist. |
| Continental | Wm. Couppels | 8720 | Salisbury Dist. |
| Militia | Joseph Clindinner | 8374 | Salisbury Dist. |
| Militia | John Carson | 3650 | Salisbury Dist. |
| Militia | John Cummins | 5982 | Wilmington Dist. |
| Continental | Searj. John Cake | 255 | |
| Militia | Joseph Cokron | 1242 | |
| Militia | William Cokron | 1240 | |
| Continental | Henry Cobb | 98 | Hillsboro Dist. |
| Continental | Thomas Carvin | 112 | Hillsboro Dist. |
| Continental | Mathias Cates | 63 | Hillsboro Dist. |
| Continental | Levi Coleman | 162 | Hillsboro Dist. |
| Continental | Richard Clifton | 57 | Warrenton Dist. |
| Militia | Lemand Carver | 2505 | Salisbury Dist. |
| Militia | John Conoly | 4150 | Morgan Dist. |
| Continental | Capt. Francis Child | 48 | Halifax Dist. |
| Continental | Stephen Cougar | 96 | Hillsboro Dist. |
| Continental | William Cavender | 459 | Hillsboro Dist. |
| Militia | Richard Caney | 2870 | Wilmington Dist. |
| Continental | Laniel Carroll | 1338 | Halifax Dist. |
| Militia | George Crozine | 1337 | Salisbury Dist. |
| Militia | Stephen Cade | 3789 | Wilmington Dist. |
| Militia | George Croncraft | 2497 | Salisbury Dist. |
| Continental | Joshua Cheason | 846 | Halifax Dist. |
| Continental | William Childers | 138 | Halifax Dist. |
| Continental | Stephen Coock | 1205 | |
| Militia | James Cobb | 827 | Newbern Dist. |
| Militia | Shadrack Cummins | 369 | Halifax Dist. |
| Continental | James Cavender | 141 | Halifax Dist. |
| Continental | John Chester | 243 | Newbern Dist. |
| Militia | Wm. Crylwas | 6080 | Salisbury Dist. |
| Militia | Wm. Cassel | 4213 | Wilmington Dist. |
| Militia | John Carruthors | 4986 | Salisbury Dist. |
| Militia | Peter Currell | 2423 | Salisbury Dist. |
| Militia | Isam Carver | 4495 | Wilmington Dist. |
| Continental | Thomas Chittem | 208 | Halifax Dist. |
| Militia | John Corbett | 1777 | Wilmington Dist. |
| Militia | Henry Cragg | 58 | Wilmington Dist. |
| Militia | Richard Cullom | 5725 | Wilmington Dist. |
| Militia | John Cummins | 4971 | Wilmington Dist. |
| Continental | Zachariah Cates | 599 | Halifax Dist. |
| Militia | John Caru | 7846 | Salisbury Dist. |
| Militia | John Curry | 9249 | Salisbury Dist. |
| Militia | John Corger | 2392 | Salisbury Dist. |
| Continental | James Carothers | 426 | Halifax Dist. |
| Continental | John Cottle | 107 | Hillsboro Dist. |
| Militia | Elias Cragg | 54 | Wilmington Dist. |
| Continental | James Crimor | 1031 | Halifax Dist |
| Militia | James Cason | 1093 | Wilmington Dist. |
| Militia | Philip Coonce | 868 | Newbern Dist. |

| | | No. | |
|---|---|---|---|
| Militia | Wm. Clayton .................. | 942 | Newbern Dist. |
| Militia | Joseph Cansway .............. .... | 81 | Halifax Dist. |
| Continental | Robert Carmicheil .............. | 210 | Hillsboro Dist. |
| Militia | Georg Cusick ................. | 5144 | Salisbury Dist. |
| Militia | Wm. Carrel ................... | 4892 | Wilmington Dist. |
| Militia | George Carcher ............... | 341 | Hillsboro Dist. |
| Continental | Robert Cook .................. | 267 | Hillsboro Dist. |
| Continental | Wm. Corothers ................ | 678 | Hillsboro Dist. |
| Continental | William Clack ................. | 157 | Hillsboro Dist. |
| Continental | Benjamine Cummings ........... | 665 | Hillsboro Dist. |
| Militia | Wm. Chapel .................. | 2930 | Salisbury Dist. |
| Militia | Saml Charlecroft .............. | 1517 | Newbern Dist. |
| Militia | John Corben .................. | 247 | Newbern Dist. |
| Continental | Robert Cates ................. | 598 | Halifax Dist. |
| Militia | Joshua Carbet ................ | 526 | Newbern Dist. |
| Continental | David Crawley ................ | 89 | Hillsboro Dist. |
| Continental | Ephraim Coward .............. | 1478 | Warrenton Dist. |
| Militia | Isaac Cokerwas ............... | 5746 | |
| Militia | John Cone ................... | 1709 | Newbern Dist. |
| Militia | David Carlton ................ | 357 | Newbern Dist. |
| Militia | John Carrell ................. | 1188 | Newbern Dist. |
| Militia | Thomas Chance .............. | 1080 | Newbern Dist. |
| Militia | Abraham Congleton ........... | 795 | Newbern Dist. |
| Continental, | Colonel Thos. Clark ........... | 41 | |
| Militia | William Cash ................ | 3093 | Salisbury Dist. |
| Militia | James Clendinson ............. | 6516 | Salisbury Dist. |
| Militia | John Cunkerton .............. | 5000 | Morgan Dist. |
| Militia | Wm. Cimmon ................ | 5383 | Salisbury Dist. |
| Continental | Wm. Master ................. | 1026 | Halifax Dist. |
| Continental | John Cottle .................. | 183 | Hillsboro Dist. |

### CLARK FAMILY

| | | | |
|---|---|---|---|
| Militia | John Clark ................... | 521 | Newbern Dist. |
| Militia | Nathan Clark ................ | 931 | Newbern Dist. |
| Militia | John Clark ................... | .... | |
| Militia | John Clark ................... | 5577 | Wilmington Dist. |
| Continental | William Clark ................ | 280 | Halifax Dist. |
| Militia | Jessie Clark .................. | 1445 | Salisbury Dist. |
| Militia | Jonas Clark .................. | 681 | Salisbury Dist. |
| Militia | John Clark ................... | 4477 | Wilmington Dist. |
| Militia | Wm. Clark ................... | 1922 | Newbern Dist. |
| Militia | Nathan Clark ................ | 1808 | Wilmington Dist. |
| Militia | Benjamin Clark ............... | 1801 | Wilmington Dist. |
| Militia | Wm. Clark ................... | 1099 | Newbern Dist. |
| Militia | Thos. Clark ................. | 1642 | Wilmington Dist. |
| Continental | Thos. Clark ................. | 286 | Halifax Dist. |
| Militia | Arthur Clark ................. | 4857 | Morgan Dist. |
| Militia | George Clark ................. | 367 | Newbern Dist. |
| Militia | Jesey Clark .................. | 6847 | Salisbury Dist. |
| Militia | Wm. Clark ................... | 2881 | Wilmington Dist. |
| Militia | Benjamine Clark .............. | 2792 | Wilmington Dist. |
| Militia | Wm. Clark ................... | 2103 | Wilmington Dist. |
| Militia | Nathan Clark ................ | 2811 | Wilmington Dist. |
| Militia | Benj. Clark ................. | 5499 | Wilmington Dist. |

| | | No. | |
|---|---|---|---|
| Militia | Wm. Clark | 4608 | Morgan Dist. |
| Continental | Wm. Clark | 231 | Halifax Dist. |
| Militia | Joseph Clark | 6650 | Salisbury Dist. |
| Militia | Wm. Clark | 1451 | Wilmington Dist. |
| Militia | James Clark | 8294 | Salisbury Dist. |
| Militia | Daniel Clark | 5566 | Wilmington Dist. |
| Continental | Benj. Clark | 189 | Halifax Dist. |
| Militia | Jonas Clark | 1446 | Salisbury Dist. |
| Militia | Jonathan Clark | 3742 | Salisbury Dist. |
| Militia | John Clark | 5930 | Salisbury Dist. |
| Militia | Archibald Curry | 5057 | Wilmington Dist. |
| Militia | John Coffen | 3818 | Morgan Dist. |
| Continental | Mathew Cates | 550 | Halifax Dist. |
| Continental | John Coats | 284 | Hillsboro Dist. |
| Continental | Wm. Charton | 312 | Halifax Dist. |
| Continental | Jeremiah Chubbock | 938 | Wilmington Dist. |
| Continental | Johnston Cruise | 564 | Hillsboro Dist. |
| Continental | Fredrick Callum | 625 | Hillsboro Dist. |
| Continental | Arthur Corbin | 554 | Hillsboro Dist. |
| Continental | Stephen Craft | 643 | Hillsboro Dist. |
| Continental | Shubal Claghorn | 638 | Hillsboro Dist. |
| Continental | Henry Cobb | 106 | Hillsboro Dist. |
| Continental | Coleman Clayton | 372 | Hillsboro Dist. |
| Continental | Lieut. Arthur Colgrave | 137 | Halifax Dist. |
| Continental | James Camper | 459 | Halifax Dist. |
| Continental | Hugh Calchnon | 62 | Hillsboro Dist. |
| Continental | Charles Coleman | 47 | Hillsboro Dist. |
| Militia | Michel Centchal | 536 | Salisbury Dist. |
| Continental | John Caven | 950 | Halifax Dist. |
| Continental | Robert Colchorn | 431 | Hillsboro Dist. |
| Continental | William Collett | 576 | Hillsboro Dist. |
| Continental | John Connoway | 371 | Hillsboro Dist. |
| Continental | Henry Chavers | 404 | Hillsboro Dist. |
| Continental | David Culbertson | 331 | Hillsboro Dist. |
| Continental | James Craven | 291 | Hillsboro Dist. |
| Continental | John Chesire | 162 | Hillsboro Dist. |
| Militia | William Caps | 238 | Morgan Dist |
| Continental | Amos Cail | 579 | Hillsboro Dist. |
| Continental | George Conder | 560 | Halifax Dist. |
| Continental | George Carcher | 533 | |
| Continental | John Callas | 30 | |
| Militia | William Caps | 4930 | Morgan Dist. |
| Continental | Henry Chavers | 551 | Hillsboro Dist. |
| Continental | Colemay Clayton | 512 | Hillsboro Dist. |
| Continental | Gabriel Cooly | 539 | Hillsboro Dist. |
| Continental | Cery Curry | 2940 | Salisbury Dist. |
| Continental | Michal Clifford | 4593 | Salisbury Dist. |
| Continental | Thos. Carraway | 391 | Halifax Dist. |
| Militia | Frederick Corlock | 4881 | Salisbury Dist. |
| Militia | Jessie Cock | 3569 | Wilmington Dist. |
| Militia | Henry Chester | 715 | Newbern Dist. |
| Militia | Robert Carver | 4496 | Wilmington Dist. |
| Militia | James Cotterhed | 1091 | Newbern Dist. |
| Militia | James Crandal | 774 | Newbern Dist. |

|  |  | No. |  |
|---|---|---|---|
| Militia | Jacob Clifford | 762 | Salisbury Dist. |
| Militia | Thos. Cabeen | 4630 | Wilmington Dist. |
| Continental | Butler Cowell | 322 |  |
| Continental | Capt. Francis Child | 49 | Halifax Dist. |
| Continental | James Carstapher | 530 | Halifax Dist. |
| Militia | James Crunkleton | 4210 | Salisbury Dist. |
| Militia | William Crumdy | 631 | Wilmington Dist. |
| Continental | John Christmas | 619 | Halifax Dist. |
| Continental | William Chalk | 867 | Halifax Dist. |
| Militia | Archibald Curry | 227 |  |
| Militia | Daniel Calbraith | 2272 | Wilmington Dist. |
| Militia | Lieut. Absolan Cleveland | 2841 | Salisbury Dist. |
| Militia | Capt. Larkin Cleveland | 778 | Salisbury Dist. |
| Militia | William Caton | 310 | Newbern Dist. |
| Militia | John Cornelius | 782 | Newbern Dist. |
| Continental | David Culbertson | 465 | Hillsboro Dist. |
| Militia | David Carney | 6538 | Salisbury Dist. |
| Militia | William Chapel | 602 | Salisbury Dist |
| Militia | Lambert Clay | 7836 | Salisbury Dist. |
| Militia | Thomas Carey | 4013 | Morgan Dist. |
| Militia | John Corothers | 2835 | Salisbury Dist. |
| Continental | Pleasant Childers | 186 | Halifax Dist. |
| Militia | David Carney | 449 | Salisbury Dist. |
| Militia | William Cosse | 4667 | Salisbury Dist. |
| Militia | Lorance Cossen | 4656 | Salisbury Dist. |
| Militia | Philip Christopher | 7574 | Salisbury Dist. |
| Continental | Abel Crump | 1207 | Warrenton Dist. |
| Continental | Peter Conoly | 167 |  |
| Continental | Nicholas Cozime | 628 | Salisbury Dist. |
| Militia | Robert Corothers | 2873 | Salisbury Dist. |
| Continental | Thomas Cookey | 691 | Hillsboro Dist. |
| Continental | West Colson | 609 | Warrenton Dist. |
| Continental | William Collett | 760 | Hillsboro Dist. |
| Continental | Arthur Corbin | 729 | Hillsboro Dist. |
| Militia | David Corlock | 2576 | Salisbury Dist. |
| Continental | Lieut. Benj. Coffield | 571 | Halifax Dist. |
| Militia | Thomas Connor | 8459 | Salisbury Dist. |
| Militia | William Crumdy | 631 | Wilmington Dist. |
| Militia | Stephen Cade | 3039 | Wilmington Dist. |
| Militia | Thos. Creil | 4424 | Wilmington Dist. |
| Militia | J. Cumberland | 7633 | Salisbury Dist. |
| Continental | Capt. Francis Child | 46 | Halifax Dist. |
| Continental | Francis Coston | 669 | Hillsboro Dist. |

ELLIOTTS

| Continental | John Elliott | 1106 | Halifax Dist. |
|---|---|---|---|
| Militia | Zack Elliott | 1046 | Newbern Dist. |
| Militia | Edward Elliott | 3689 | Salisbury Dist. |
| Militia | Alexander Elliott | 7278 | Salisbury Dist. |
| Continental | William Elliott | 706 | Hillsboro Dist. |
| Continental | John Elliott | 845 | Edenton Dist. |
| Militia | Thomas Elliott | 3685 | Salisbury Dist. |
| Militia | Jessie Eliot | 3878 | Wilmington Dist. |
| Militia | Gilbert Ecles | 4604 | Wilmington Dist. |

| | | No. | |
|---|---|---|---|
| Militia | Joseph Edmiston | 3058 | Salisbury Dist. |
| Militia | Lewis Evitt | 4107 | Salisbury Dist. |
| Militia | Thos. Estes | 4583 | Salisbury Dist. |
| Militia | Joseph Gulbarger | 4538 | Salisbury Dist. |
| Militia | Nathaniel Ewing | 3139 | Salisbury Dist. |
| Militia | Jno. Eagle | 4693 | Salisbury Dist. |
| Militia | Peter Edleman | 5336 | Salisbury Dist. |
| Continental | Edward Earp | 304 | Halifax Dist. |
| Militia | John Evers | 3035 | Wilmington Dist. |
| Militia | Russel Earl | 3712 | Wilmington Dist. |
| Militia | Philip Egle | 5369 | Salisbury Dist. |
| Continental | Abner Easton | 1534 | Newbern Dist. |
| Militia | Thomas Edins | 3731 | Wilmington Dist. |
| Militia | James Evers | 3225 | Wilmington Dist. |
| Continental | Noah Eggleston | 1433 | Newbern Dist. |
| Militia | James Eggleston | 3110 | Wilmington Dist. |
| Continental | Caleb Estwood | 577 | |
| Continental | Benj. Eastman | 852 | Halifax Dist. |
| Continental | Ephraim Etheridge | 608 | Halifax Dist. |
| Militia | Benjamin Ellwell | 4487 | Wilmington Dist. |
| Militia | John Erwin | 4409 | Salisbury Dist. |
| Militia | John Evers | 3785 | Wilmington Dist. |
| Militia | Philip Eagle | 5344 | Salisbury Dist. |
| Militia | Mathew Clendennin | 5818 | Salisbury Dist. |
| Militia | William Elkins | 2988 | Wilmington Dist. |
| Militia | Gilbert Eccles | 4104 | Wilmington Dist. |
| Militia | Mial Gwalt | 3202 | Salisbury Dist. |
| Militia | John Eccles | 4124 | Wilmington Dist. |
| Militia | Joshua Elkins | 2989 | Wilmington Dist. |
| Militia | James Evers | 4545 | Wilmington Dist. |
| Militia | Thos. Easton | 1900 | Newbern Dist. |
| Militia | Abner Ecleon | 1891 | Newbern Dist. |
| Militia | Randolph Elmore | 1265 | Newbern Dist. |
| Militia | Wm. Earle | 3942 | Wilmington Dist. |
| Militia | Thomas Edmonson | 1609 | Newbern Dist. |
| Continental | Charles Emes | 261 | Halifax Dist. |
| Continental | Capt. John Enloe | 154 | Halifax Dist. |
| Continental | Capt. John Eborn | 473 | |
| Continental | Capt. Nicholas Edmunds | 630 | Halifax Dist. |
| Militia | Capt. John Eborn | 1635 | Newbern Dist. |
| Continental | Capt. Harrell | 8931 | Halifax Dist. |
| Continental | Maj. Perkethman Eborn | .... | Halifax Dist. |
| Militia | Isaac Eason | 4070 | Wilmington Dist. |
| Militia | Mike Gnott | 2923 | Salisbury Dist. |
| Militia | George Eagle | 5342 | Salisbury Dist. |
| Continental | Charles Ellams | .... | Halifax Dist. |
| Militia | Thomas Enox | 4789 | Wilmington Dist. |
| Militia | Zenos Eborn | 1901 | Newbern Dist. |
| Militia | Col. James Emmitt | 2122 | Wilmington Dist. |
| Militia | Capt. William Owens | 5066 | Wilmington Dist. |
| Militia | Abel Edmunds | 950 | Newbern Dist. |
| Militia | Lum Enzor | 2747 | Wilmington Dist. |
| Militia | Richard Elwell | 796 | Wilmington Dist. |
| Militia | Benjamin Elledge | 876 | Halifax Dist. |

|  |  | *No.* |  |
|---|---|---|---|
| Militia | James Everitt | 1054 | Newbern Dist. |
| Militia | Daniel Eubank | 42 | Newbern Dist. |
| Militia | Samuel Erixon | 1045 | Wilmington Dist. |
| Militia | Kitt Edmonds | 1542 | Wilmington Dist. |
| Militia | A.... Erixon | 1040 | Wilmington Dist. |
| Militia | John Baylus Earl | 31 | Morgan Dist. |
| Militia | Benjamin Eason | 1511 | Wilmington Dist. |
| Continental | Shadrack Elkins | 1955 | Warrenton Dist. |
| Militia | Mal Everidge | 401 | Newbern Dist. |
| Continental | John Ethridge | 35 | Halifax Dist. |

### EDWARDS FAMILY

|  |  |  |  |
|---|---|---|---|
| Continental | John Edwards, Johnston Co. | 2123 | Newbern Dist. |
| Continental | John Edwards | 737 | Halifax Dist. |
| Militia | William Edwards | 1781 |  |
| Militia | Henry Edwards | 2054 | Wilmington Dist. |
| Continental | Simon Edwards | 112 | Halifax Dist. |
| Continental | Joseph Edwards | 124 | Hillsboro Dist. |
| Militia | Micajah Edwards | 1230 | Newbern Dist. |
| Continental | Lemuel Edwards | 239 | Hillsboro Dist. |
| Militia | John Edwards (Jones Co.) | 105 | Newbern Dist. |
| Militia | John Edwards (Wayne Co.) | 1034 | Newbern Dist. |
| Militia | John Edwards (Hampton Co.) | 9611 | Halifax Dist. |
| Continental | Charles Edwards | 19 | Halifax Dist. |
| Militia | Joshua Edwards | 336 | Wilmington Dist. |
| Militia | Stephen Edwards | 1234 | Newbern Dist. |
| Militia | Jacob Edwards, Johnson Co. | 1188 | Newbern Dist. |
| Militia | Israil Edwards, Pitt Co. | 1582 | Newbern Dist. |
| Continental | Ruben Edwards | 1793 | Warrenton Dist. |
| Continental | Joel Edwards | 98 | Halifax Dist. |
| Militia | Andrew Edwards | 1781 | Wilmington Dist. |
| Militia | Solomon Edwards | 903 | Newbern Dist. |
| Continental | Robert Edwards | 9 | Halifax Dist. |
| Militia | Obidiah Edwards | 518 | Wilmington Dist. |

### ELLIS FAMILY

|  |  |  |  |
|---|---|---|---|
| Militia | Capt. Henry Ellis | 1961 | Newbern Dist. |
| Continental | Absalom Ellis | 39 | Halifax Dist. |
| Militia | William Ellis | 219 | Newbern Dist. |
|  | Capt. William Ellis | 701 | Wilmington Dist. |
| Militia | John Ellis | 2434 | Salisbury Dist. |
| Militia | Shadrack Ellis | 1780 | Newbern Dist. |
| Continental | James Ellis | 159 | Hillsboro Dist. |
| Continental | Joseph Ellis | 459 | Newbern Dist. |
| Continental | Robert Ellis | 188 | Halifax Dist. |
| Continental | Ebenezar Ellis | 1464 | Newbern Dist. |

### FLETCHER

|  |  |  |  |
|---|---|---|---|
| Continental | Thomas Fletcher | 30 | Halifax Dist. |
| Militia | Capt. William Fletcher | 1022 | Salisbury Dist. |
| Continental | James Fletcher | 239 |  |
| Continental | Nathan Fletcher | 1231 | Warrenton Dist. |
| Continental | John Fletcher | 581 |  |
| Continental | Reuben Fletcher | 1228 | Warrenton Dist. |

FORDS & FORT FAMILIES

| | | No. | |
|---|---|---|---|
| Militia | Lieut. John Fort | 2401 | Wilmington Dist. |
| Militia | John Ford | 4800 | Wilmington Dist. |
| Militia | Thos. Fort | 479 | Wilmington Dist. |
| Continental | Lieut. John Ford | 110 | Halifax Dist. |
| Continental | Nowel Fort | 229 | Wilmington Dist. |
| Continental | James Ford | 3196 | Wilmington Dist. |
| Continental | John Fort | 2785 | Wilmington Dist. |
| Continental | John Ford | 5116 | Salisbury Dist. |
| Militia | Henry Fesperman | 645 | Salisbury Dist. |
| | ........ Fowler | 83 | |
| Continental | Jacob Freeland | 660 | Wilmington Dist. |
| Militia | Daniel Fowler | 2196 | Wilmington Dist. |
| Militia | Francis Fortner | 5148 | Wilmington Dist. |
| Militia | Thos. Frohack | 8883 | Salisbury Dist. |
| Militia | Lieut. Edmund Fear | 4187 | Morgan Dist. |
| | ...... ...... .......... | 6160 | Salisbury Dist. |
| Military | Capt. George Farragut | 443 | Fayetteville |
| Continental | Abraham Fardwell | 1102 | Halifax Dist. |
| Militia | Aaron Fegan | 4184 | Wilmington Dist. |
| Militia | Kelbey Faison | 3608 | Wilmington Dist. |
| Militia | William Forney | 3707 | Salisbury Dist. |
| Militia | John Faulkner | 4180 | Wilmington Dist. |
| Militia | Isarel Folsom | 4331 | Wilmington Dist. |
| Militia | John Faulkner | 4360 | Wilmington Dist. |
| Militia | John Fraser | 6823 | Salisbury Dist. |
| Militia | William Flowers | 5539 | Wilmington Dist. |
| Militia | Thomas Faircloth | 1249 | Newbern Dist. |
| Continental | William Fann | 733 | Halifax Dist. |
| Continental | James Falconer | 472 | Newbern Dist. |
| Militia | John Flowers, Wayne Co. | 1041 | Newbern Dist. |
| Militia | Cason Fulskir | 322 | Newbern Dist. |
| Militia | Caleb Fautner | 4212 | Wilmington Dist. |
| Militia | James Farnal | 5332 | Wilmington Dist. |
| Militia | William Tonvielle | 594 | Newbern Dist. |
| Continental | John Fooks | 37 | Hillsboro Dist. |
| Continental | Edward Fossett | 407 | Hillsboro Dist. |
| Militia | James Falkner | 1263 | Newbern Dist. |
| Militia | Stephen Fatheroe, Pitt Co. | 394 | Newbern Dist. |
| Militia | Wickliff Frank | 882 | Newbern Dist. |
| Militia | Stephen Fatherly, Pitt Co. | 1540 | Newbern Dist. |
| Militia | John Faulke, Johnson Co. | 1176 | Newbern Dist. |
| Militia | Edward Flanagan | 897 | Newbern Dist. |
| Militia | Stephen Fosterby | 1540 | Newbern Dist. |
| Continental | James Pike | 425 | Hillsboro Dist. |
| Militia | Moses Fox | 3721 | Wilmington Dist. |
| Continental | John Fisher | 498 | Hillsboro Dist. |
| Continental | Peter Ferguson | 354 | Hillsboro Dist. |
| Militia | Flud Foley | 1772 | Wilmington Dist. |
| Militia | Thomas Flowers | 186 | Wilmington Dist. |
| Continental | John Farmer | 184 | Hillsboro Dist. |
| Continental | Timothy Field | 125 | Hillsboro Dist. |
| Continental | John Field | 116 | Hillsboro Dist. |
| Continental | Hugh Forsythe | 289 | Hillsboro Dist. |

|  |  | No. |  |
|---|---|---|---|
| Continental | Philip Fishburn | 392 | Hillsboro Dist. |
| Continental | Ashby Fowler | 440 | Hillsboro Dist. |
| Continental | Nathaniel Farron | 385 | Hillsboro Dist. |
| Militia | Sutton Trueclink | 1788 | Newbern Dist. |
| Militia | Andrew Hemphill | 4819 | Salisbury Dist. |
| Continental | Jotham Felps | 1253 | Warrenton Dist. |
| Militia | Robert Tillingham | 1874 | Newbern Dist. |
| Militia | Uriah Floyed | 2011 | Newbern Dist. |
| Militia | Benjamine Fulcher | 279 | Newbern Dist. |
| Militia | John Faircloth | 5040 | Wilmington Dist. |
| Continental | James Finney | 1463 | Warrenton Dist. |
| Continental | Andrew Franks | 1953 | Warrenton Dist. |
| Continental | William Foster | 1454 | Warrenton Dist. |
| Continental | Capt. William Fawn | 342 | Halifax Dist. |
| Continental | Maj. William Fenner | 180 | Halifax Dist. |
| Militia | Lieut. Jos. Frisor | 6298 | Salisbury Dist. |
| Militia | John Tucker | 621 | Newbern Dist. |
| Militia | Arch Fluelin | 447 | Newbern Dist. |
| Militia | John Fulcher | 199 | Newbern Dist. |
| Militia | Griffin Floyed | 258 | Newbern Dist. |
| Continental | Franklin Truit | 960 | Warrenton Dist. |
| Continental | Mack Ferguson | 648 | Hillsboro Dist. |
| Continental | Nicholas Pennell | 393 | Hillsboro Dist. |
| Militia | Martin Fulch | 1563 | Wilmington Dist. |
| Militia | William Towler | 1572 | Wilmington Dist. |
| Militia | Jacob Fryont | 5069 | Wilmington Dist. |
| Militia | William Farris | 2929 | Wilmington Dist. |
| Militia | Benjamin Fitz | 3173 | Wilmington Dist. |
| Militia | Ed Fogerty | 614 | Wilmington Dist. |
| Continental | Mack Ferguson | 832 | Hillsboro Dist. |
| Continental | Jessie Freeman | 795 | Hillsboro Dist. |
| Continental | William Fox | 641 | Hillsboro Dist. |
| Continental | Benj. Farmer | 462 | Hillsboro Dist. |
| Continental | William Filson | 477 | Hillsboro Dist. |
| Continental | John Farmer | 266 | Hillsboro Dist. |
| Continental | Morris Pennell | 607 | Hillsboro Dist. |
| Militia | Nicholas Fennel | 3210 | Wilmington Dist. |
| Continental | Aaron Freeman | 33 | Newbern Dist. |
| Militia | Thos. Fornes | 908 | Newbern Dist. |
| Continental | Jessie Fulton | 561 |  |
| Continental | William Taunt | 221 | Halifax Dist. |
| Militia | John Faircloth | 5040 | Wilmington Dist. |
| Continental | Thomas Fulcher | .... |  |
| Continental | Isham Ferguson | 172 | Warrenton Dist. |
| Continental | Solomon Fountain | 465 | Hillsboro Dist. |
| Continental | Capt. William Fawn | 342 | Halifax Dist. |
| Continental | Francis Fox | 1131 | Halifax Dist. |
| Continental | James Falconer | 531 | Halifax Dist. |
| Continental | Alexander Flood | 530 | Halifax Dist. |
| Continental | John Franks | 1165 | Halifax Dist. |
| Continental | Richard Fenner | 307 | Halifax Dist. |
| Continental | George Fowler | 736 | Halifax Dist. |
| Continental | William Farell | 40 |  |
| Militia | John Fail | 642 | Newbern Dist. |

|  |  | No. |  |
|---|---|---|---|
| Militia | John Faison | 7021 | Salisbury Dist. |
| Militia | John Frizel | 5372 | Salisbury Dist. |
| Militia | James Findley | 95 | Salisbury Dist. |
| Continental | Nathaniel Farrow | 257 | Hillsboro Dist. |
| Militia | Ephraim Faulkner | 4067 | Wilmington Dist. |
| Militia | John Fuller | 1306 | Newbern Dist. |
| Militia | Capt. Samuel Flemhen | 6023 | Salisbury Dist. |
| Militia | John Towler | 5941 | Wilmington Dist. |
| Militia | James Farmer | 755 | Wilmington Dist. |
| Militia | John Fling | 513 | Wilmington Dist. |
| Continental | Brittain Forster | 755 | Hillsboro Dist. |
| Militia | John Finney | 2756 | Salisbury Dist. |
| Militia | Thad Tuliker | 550 | Newbern Dist. |
| Continental | William Town, Capt. | 168 | |
| Militia | William B. Fonville | 1834 | Newbern Dist. |
| Continental | James Fountain | 207 | Halifax Dist. |
| Militia | Thos. Fergison | 5181 | Salisbury Dist. |
| Militia | Elias Faison | 5562 | Wilmington Dist. |
| Militia | William Forister | 2510 | Salisbury Dist. |
| Militia | William Feamster | 4411 | Salisbury Dist. |
| Militia | John Firgy | 4341 | Salisbury Dist. |
| Continental | James Fawcett | 146 | Halifax Dist. |
| Militia | George Gulham | 1097 | Newbern Dist. |

### GRAY F.

|  |  | | |
|---|---|---|---|
| Continental | Cox Gray | 615 | Hillsboro Dist. |
| Continental | Henry Gray | 4 | Hillsboro Dist. |
| Militia | James Gray | 8719 | Salisbury Dist. |
| Militia | Lodwick Gray | 1497 | |
| Militia | Thomas Gray | 6683 | Salisbury Dist. |
| Militia | Robert Gray | 8709 | Salisbury Dist. |
| Militia | Jonathan Gray | 4659 | Salisbury Dist. |
| Continental | Archabald Gray | 1153 | Halifax Dist. |
| Militia | William Gray | 6241 | Salisbury Dist. |
| Militia | John Gray | 4203 | Salisbury Dist. |
| Militia | Jessic Greer | 734 | Salisbury Dist. |

### GIBSON F.

|  |  | | |
|---|---|---|---|
| Continental | John Gibson | 441 | Hillsboro Dist. |
| Continental | Jacob Gibson | 318 | Hillsboro Dist. |
| Continental | William Gibson | 1182 | Halifax Dist. |
| Militia | George Gibson | 1239 | Salisbury Dist. |
| Militia | Joseph Gibson | 6365 | Salisbury Dist. |
| Continental | Charles Gibson | 295 | Hillsboro Dist. |

### GRAHAM F.

|  |  | | |
|---|---|---|---|
| Continental | James Graham | 558 | |
| Militia | Lieut. John Graham | 7775 | Salisbury Dist. |
| Militia | Robert Graham | 2700 | Salisbury Dist. |
| Militia | Hugh Graham | 6838 | Salisbury Dist. |
| Militia | Benjamine Graham | 4869 | Wilmington Dist. |
| Militia | Samuel Graham | 482 | Salisbury Dist. |
| Militia | Alexander Graham | 4004 | Morgan Dist. |

### GRIFFETH F.

|  |  | No. |  |
|---|---|---|---|
| Militia | Edward Griffeth | 6435 | Salisbury Dist. |
| Continental | John Griffeth | 61 | Hillsboro Dist. |
| Militia | William Griffeth | 646 | Newbern Dist. |
| Continental | Isaac Griffeth | 176 | Halifax Dist. |
| Continental | Henry Griffeth | 586 |  |

### GREER F.

| Militia | John Greer | 2078 | Wilmington Dist. |
|---|---|---|---|
| Continental | Lieut. Robert Greer | 548 | Halifax Dist. |
| Militia | Thomas Greer | 2825 | Salisbury Dist. |
| Militia | David Greer | 1336 | Wilmington Dist. |
| Militia | Joseph Greer | 4569 | Wilmington Dist. |
| Militia | Moses Greer | 2488 | Salisbury Dist. |

### GARNER

| Continental | Thomas Garner | 243 | Hillsboro Dist. |
|---|---|---|---|
| Continental | Elijah Garner | 831 | Hillsboro Dist. |
| Militia | Francis Garner | 2644 | Salisbury Dist. |
| Militia | John Garner | 2692 | Salisbury Dist. |

### GAY

| Continental | Bable Gay | 700 | Halifax Dist. |
|---|---|---|---|
| Militia | Simon Gay | 488 | Wilmington Dist. |
| Militia | Robt. Gay | 7668 | Salisbury Dist. |
| Militia | James Gay | 4730 | Salisbury Dist. |
| Continental | Allen Gay | 155 | Halifax Dist. |

### GILMORE

| Militia | James Gilmore | 3271 | Salisbury Dist. |
|---|---|---|---|
| Militia | Thomas Gilmore | 3888 | Wilmington Dist. |
| Militia | James Gilmore | 3985 | Wilmington Dist. |
| Militia | Thomas Gilmore | 4594 | Wilmington Dist. |
| Militia | Charles Hud Gilmore | 4028 | Wilmington Dist. |
| Militia | John Gilmore | 2973 | Wilmington Dist. |
| Militia | William Gilmore | 5386 | Salisbury Dist. |
| Militia | Stephen Garner | 803 | Wilmington Dist. |

### GAREN

| Militia | Samuel Garen | 3449 | Wilmington Dist. |
|---|---|---|---|
| Militia | ...... Gurley | 1300 | Newbern Dist. |
| Militia | Peter Gates | 4547 | Wilmington Dist. |
| Militia | William Goodfrey | 3137 | Wilmington Dist. |
| Militia | Gideon Gain | 4464 | Wilmington Dist. |
| Militia | Nicholas Gaither | 5081 | Salisbury Dist. |
| Militia | George Gentil | 4665 | Salisbury Dist. |
| Militia | Needham Gause | 4674 | Wilmington Dist. |
| Militia | William Gilbert | 4474 | Wilmington Dist. |
| Militia | Charles Gause | 4661 | Wilmington Dist. |
| Militia | Peter Goble | 2419 | Salisbury Dist. |
| Militia | Jesse Gloscolk | 4598 | Salisbury Dist. |
| Militia | Jacob Gaster | 5416 | Salisbury Dist. |
| Militia | Joseph Guest | 4350 | Wilmington Dist. |
| Militia | James Gilbert | 5032 | Wilmington Dist. |
| Militia | Needham Gardner | 1269 | Newbern Dist. |

| | | No. | |
|---|---|---|---|
| Militia | Josiah Godwin ................. | 500 | Newbern Dist. |
| Militia | James Guy .................... | 5481 | Salisbury Dist. |
| Militia | Dugald Gillis ................. | 3028 | Wilmington Dist. |
| Militia | Lazarus Gatlin ................ | 1341 | Newbern Dist. |
| Continental | Samuel Glover ................ | 518 | Halifax Dist. |
| Continental | Capt. Christopher Gooden ........ | 408 | Halifax Dist. |
| Continental | Thomas Geddie ................ | 107 | Halifax Dist. |
| Continental | Jonathan Gebbins .............. | 5777 | Wilmington Dist. |
| Continental | Henry Gamileon ............... | 4947 | Wilmington Dist. |
| Militia | Thos. Gains .................. | 5288 | Wilmington Dist. |
| Militia | Joseph Guest ................. | 4302 | Wilmington Dist. |
| Continental | Joseph Gurley ................ | 151 | Halifax Dist. |
| Militia | James Geddie ................. | 1587 | Wilmington Dist. |
| Militia | Lieut. Thomas Gooden .......... | 1036 | Salisbury Dist. |
| Militia | T.... Gauff .................. | 3650 | Wilmington Dist. |
| Militia | Lieut. Denis Glisson ........... | 1204 | Wilmington Dist. |
| Militia | John Gordon ................. | 737 | Salisbury Dist. |
| Militia | John Gore ................... | 1322 | Wilmington Dist. |
| Militia | Thomas Gauff ................ | 1977 | Wilmington Dist. |
| Militia | Francis Gloss ................. | 1406 | Salisbury Dist. |
| Militia | Thos. Gedding ............... | 1556 | Wilmington Dist. |
| Militia | Lewis Grantham .............. | 653 | Wilmington Dist. |
| Militia | Hugh Goloher ............... | 642 | Salisbury Dist. |
| Militia | William Gilbert .............. | 96 | Newbern Dist. |
| Militia | William Gulley .............. | 482 | Newbern Dist. |
| Militia | Thomas Gardner ............. | 1045 | Newbern Dist. |
| Militia | Anthony Curley .............. | 1237 | Newbern Dist. |
| Militia | Mathew Ganey ............... | 1287 | **Wilmington Dist.** |
| Militia | Nicholas Gargan ............. | 3285 | Wilmington Dist. |
| Militia | William Guy ................. | 1754 | Wilmington Dist. |
| Militia | Henry Goff .................. | 1131 | Newbern Dist. |
| Militia | Lewis Gurly ................. | 1171 | Newbern Dist. |
| Militia | Denis Gladson ............... | 799 | Newbern Dist. |
| Militia | Michael Gurley .............. | 547 | Newbern Dist. |
| Militia | Lenard Garver ............... | 616 | Salisbury Dist. |
| Militia | Arthur Gurley ............... | 1237 | Newbern Dist. |
| Continental | William Goldsberry ........... | 1425 | Halifax Dist. |
| Militia | David Gargainus ............. | 756 | Newbern Dist. |
| Militia | Fisher Gaston ............... | .... | Newbern Dist. |
| Militia | Stephen Gargainus ........... | 804 | Newbern Dist. |
| Continental | Samner Gainer ............... | 229 | Assembly |
| Militia | Lewis Gurley ................ | 1291 | Newbern Dist. |
| Militia | Thos. Girens ................ | 44 | Newbern Dist. |
| Militia | George Gurley ............... | 1226 | Newbern Dist. |
| Militia | Fisher Gaskin ................ | 289 | Newbern Dist. |
| Militia | Jacob Godwin ................ | 1830 | Wilmington Dist. |
| Militia | John Goff ................... | 1774 | Wilmington Dist. |
| Continental | William Gaskin .............. | 21 | Newbern Dist. |
| Militia | Reeding Grist ................ | 2000 | Newbern Dist. |
| Militia | John Gardner ................ | 374 | Newbern Dist. |
| Militia | Benjamine Garriss ............ | 1496 | Newbern Dist. |
| Militia | Wm. Barry Grove ............ | 5165 | Wilmington Dist. |
| Militia | Daniel McGoodwin ........... | 3615 | Salisbury Dist. |
| Militia | Edward Gaither .............. | 960 | Newbern Dist. |

| | | No. | |
|---|---|---|---|
| Militia | Abner Goodwine | 3728 | Wilmington Dist. |
| Militia | Moses Granberry | 1507 | Newbern Dist. |
| Militia | Joseph Galbreath | 4272 | Salisbury Dist. |
| Militia | Capt. Bazel Grant | 5279 | Wilmington Dist. |
| Militia | Capt. Thomas Givens | 3606 | Salisbury Dist. |
| Continental | Thomas Geddy | 106 | Halifax Dist. |
| Continental | John Gilbert | 201 | Halifax Dist. |
| State Troops | John Garner | 525 | Newbern Dist. |
| Militia | Samuel Ginton | 4510 | Wilmington Dist. |
| Militia | Cornelius Grainjer | 5115 | Wilmington Dist. |
| Militia | John Gates | 2962 | Wilmington Dist. |
| Militia | Benjamine Gaylord | 1928 | Newbern Dist. |
| Militia | Francis Glass | 4261 | Salisbury Dist. |
| Militia | Will Grant | 5092 | Wilmington Dist. |
| Continental | Searj. Samuel Gilston | 804 | Halifax Dist. |
| Militia | Douglas Geater | 5571 | Salisbury Dist. |
| Militia | James Gaylard | 1872 | Newbern Dist. |
| Continental | Isaac Gallop | 32 | Hillsboro Dist. |
| Militia | Edwards Gates | 2961 | Wilmington Dist. |
| Militia | Elias Grantham | 652 | Wilmington Dist. |
| Militia | James Gaddy | 4263 | Wilmington Dist. |
| Militia | Winfield Gaylard | 1437 | Newbern Dist. |
| Militia | William Gurley | 1295 | Newbern Dist. |
| Continental | Thomas Garrott | 1457 | Warrenton Dist. |
| Continental | George Glenn | 1482 | Warrenton Dist. |
| Continental | James Glasco | 1431 | Warrenton Dist. |
| Militia | John Gates | 2931 | Wilmington Dist. |
| Continental | Samuel Gainer | 538 | Halifax Dist. |
| Militia | James Gee | 4631 | Wilmington Dist. |
| Militia | Elias Garrison | 5117 | Salisbury Dist. |
| Continental | Lieut. Edmund Gamble | 96 | Halifax Dist. |
| Militia | John Galbraith | 4267 | Salisbury Dist. |
| Continental | Joseph Gurley | 151 | Halifax Dist. |
| Militia | James Gilbert | 5032 | Wilmington Dist. |
| Militia | Thomas Gains | 4288 | Wilmington Dist. |
| Militia | Henry Gamilson | 4947 | Wilmington Dist. |
| Militia | Jonathan Gibbins | 5777 | Wilmington Dist. |
| Continental | Christopher Goodin | 408 | Halifax Dist. |
| Continental | Sergt. Sam Glover | 518 | Halifax Dist. |
| Militia | Dugald Gillis | 3028 | Wilmington Dist. |
| Militia | James Guy | 5481 | Salisbury Dist. |
| Militia | Lieut. Dennis Glissom | 1204 | Wilmington Dist. |
| Militia | John Gordon | 737 | Salisbury Dist. |
| Militia | John Gore | 1322 | Wilmington Dist. |
| Militia | Thos. Gauff | 1977 | Wilmington Dist. |
| Militia | Francis Glass | 1406 | Salisbury Dist. |
| Militia | Thos. Gedding | 1556 | Wilmington Dist. |
| Militia | Lewis Grantham | 653 | Wilmington Dist. |
| Militia | William Gilbert | 96 | Newbern Dist. |
| Continental | John Godett | 6 | Newbern Dist. |
| Continental | Capt. John Granger | 1306 | Newbern Dist. |
| Militia | James Gatlin | 329 | Newbern Dist. |
| Militia | Capt. Joshua Guest | 1227 | Wilmington Dist. |
| Militia | John Grantham | 650 | Wilmington Dist. |

| | | *No.* | |
|---|---|---|---|
| Militia | Jeblick Gitstrape | 855 | Newbern Dist. |
| Continental | Q. M. Edmund Gamble | 423 | Halifax Dist. |
| Militia | Nathan Grantham | 1038 | Newbern Dist. |
| Militia | William Gowers | 153 | Newbern Dist. |
| Militia | Frederick Grady | 2138 | Wilmington Dist. |
| Militia | Joshua Gist | 1841 | Wilmington Dist. |
| Militia | Andrew Gurley | 545 | Newbern Dist. |
| Militia | Jeremiah Gurley | 155 | Newbern Dist. |
| Militia | James Gattin | 925 | Newbern Dist. |
| Militia | Edward Gattin | 1013 | Newbern Dist. |
| Militia | Hardy Gattin | 466 | Newbern Dist. |
| Militia | Stephen Gattin | 1886 | Newbern Dist. |
| Militia | Levi Gattin | 1811 | Newbern Dist. |
| Militia | | 745 | Newbern Dist. |
| Militia | Levi Gattin | .... | |
| Militia | William Gattin | 412 | Newbern Dist. |
| Militia | John Gattin | 934 | Newbern Dist. |
| Militia | Abel Gober | 127 | Newbern Dist. |
| Continental | Samuel Gilston | 803 | Halifax Dist. |
| Militia | John Gilmon | 1243 | Wilmington Dist. |
| Militia | James Gayley | 590 | Salisbury Dist. |
| Militia | William Glover | 4555 | Wilmington Dist. |
| Militia | Peter Gates | 4547 | Wilmington Dist. |
| Militia | William Godfren | 3137 | Wilmington Dist. |
| Militia | Gideon Gain | 4464 | Wilmington Dist. |
| Militia | Nicholas Gaither | 5081 | Salisbury Dist. |
| Militia | George Gentil | 4665 | Salisbury Dist. |
| Militia | Needham Gause | 4674 | Wilmington Dist. |
| Militia | Peter Gobble | 2419 | Salisbury Dist. |
| Militia | Jessie Glascock | 4598 | Salisbury Dist. |
| Militia | Jacob Garster | 5416 | Salisbury Dist. |
| Militia | Joseph Guest | 4350 | Wilmington Dist. |
| Militia | Jonas Goodwin | .... | Newbern Dist. |
| Militia | Benjamine Harden | 5035 | Wilmington Dist. |
| Militia | Thomas Harden | 86 | Hillsboro Dist. |
| Militia | Isarael Harding | 307 | Hillsboro Dist. |
| Militia | Joshua Hill | 1563 | Newbern Dist. |
| Militia | Isaac Hill | 5475 | Wilmington Dist. |
| Militia | Solomon Harden | 522 | Wilmington Dist. |
| Continental | John Harden | 542 | Wilmington Dist. |
| Continental | William Harden | 679 | Hillsboro Dist. |
| Continental | Jonas Hinton | 108 | Wilmington Dist. |
| Militia | Noah Hinton | 1238 | Edenton Dist. |
| Militia | Isaac Hinton | 2167 | Newbern Dist. |
| Continental | William Hilton | 125 | Halifax Dist. |
| Continental | Arnold Hilton | 1343 | Halifax Dist. |
| Militia | Philip Hewitt | 4693 | Wilmington Dist. |
| Militia | John Hewitt | 4703 | Wilmington Dist. |
| Militia | Richard Hewitt | 4732 | Wilmington Dist. |
| Militia | John Hewitt | 5606 | Wilmington Dist. |
| Militia | Sam House | 3327 | Wilmington Dist. |
| Militia | Isam House | 3555 | Wilmington Dist. |
| Continental | Archabald Hood | 171 | Hillsboro Dist. |
| Militia | John Hood | 2934 | Salisbury Dist. |

|  |  | No. |  |
|---|---|---|---|
| Militia | Edward Harris | 1179 | Wilmington Dist. |
| Continental | Edward Harris | 442 | Hillsboro Dist. |
| Continental | James Hicks | 1137 | Halifax Dist. |
| Militia | Lewis Hicks | 3819 | Wilmington Dist. |
| Continental | Serj. James Harrison | 366 | Hillsboro Dist. |
| Militia | Richard Harrison | 2490 | Wilmington Dist. |
| Continental | John Harrison | 313 | Hillsboro Dist. |
| Militia | James Harrison, Jones Co. | 2 | Newbern Dist. |
| Militia | Shadrack Hill | 3016 | Wilmington Dist. |
| Militia | James Hill | 5475 | Salisbury Dist. |
| Militia | George Hill | 4724 | Wilmington Dist. |
| Militia | John Hill | 3280 | Salisbury Dist. |
| Militia | Robert Hill | 3024 | Salisbury Dist. |
| Continental | John Hill | 190 | Halifax Dist. |
| Militia | Thos. Hill | 5448 | Wilmington Dist. |
| Continental | William Hill | 321 | Hillsboro Dist. |
| Militia | Edward Hall | 3920 | Wilmington Dist. |
| Continental | Q. M. Edward Hall | 119 | Halifax Dist. |
| Militia | Thomas Harper | 689 | Newbern Dist. |
| Continental | Frederick Harper | 827 | Halifax Dist. |
| Continental | John Harper | 423 | Hillsboro Dist. |
| Militia | William Harper | 1520 | Wilmington Dist. |
| Militia | James Harper | 5737 | Wilmington Dist. |
| Militia | Lieut. Robert Hicks | 3720 | Wilmington Dist. |
| Militia | John Hicks | 1063 | Wilmington Dist. |
| Militia | Lieut. Thomas Hicks | 3634 | Wilmington Dist. |
| Continental | Charles Hicks | 294 | Hillsboro Dist. |
| Continental | Corbin Hicks | 1167 | Halifax Dist. |
| Continental | Trubal Hicks | 8797 | |

### HAWKINS

|  |  |  |  |
|---|---|---|---|
| Militia | Ezekiel Hawkins | 5595 | Wilmington Dist. |
| Militia | Uriah Hawkins | 5461 | Wilmington Dist. |
| Militia | Joseph Hawkins | 4637 | Salisbury Dist. |
| Militia | John Hawkins | 5594 | Wilmington Dist. |
| Continental | Lofton Hawkins | 1245 | Warrenton Dist. |
| Militia | M.... Hawkins | 4658 | Wilmington Dist. |
| Militia | John Hawkins | 4909 | Morgan Dist. |
| Militia | William Hawkins | 153 | Hillsboro Dist. |

### HOLDEN

|  |  |  |  |
|---|---|---|---|
| Militia | Job Holden | 4653 | Wilmington Dist. |
| Militia | Moses Hicks | 10.. | Wilmington Dist. |
| Militia | Robert Hall | 7104 | Salisbury Dist. |
| Militia | Joseph Hall | 6464 | Salisbury Dist. |
| Militia | Wm. Hall | 6300 | Salisbury Dist. |
| Continental | Wm. Hall | 380 | Warrenton Dist. |
|  | Capt. Wm. Hall, Nash Co. | 8808 | Halifax Dist. |
| Continental | James Hall | 221 | Hillsboro Dist. |
| Militia | James Hall | 698 | Halifax Dist. |
| Continental | Thomas Hall | 55 | Hillsboro Dist. |
| Militia | Thomas Hall | 4266 | Salisbury Dist. |
| Militia | Drury Hall | 802 | Newbern Dist. |
| Militia | Sam Hall | 2159 | Wilmington Dist. |
| Continental | Anthony Hall | 304 | Hillsboro Dist. |
| Continental | Jessie Hall | 292 | Hillsboro Dist. |

## HALLS

| | | No. | |
|---|---|---|---|
| Continental | Abner Hall | 1416 | Newbern Dist. |
| Continental | Joshua Hall | 1430 | Warrenton Dist. |
| Continental | Capt. Clement Hall | 230 | Halifax Dist. |
| Militia | Capt. Hugh Hall | 6997 | Salisbury Dist. |
| Militia | Morgan Hall | 1259 | Salisbury Dist. |
| Militia | Alexander Hall | 7180 | Salisbury Dist. |
| Continental | Futrell Hall | 233 | Hillsboro Dist. |
| Militia | David Hall | 1903 | Wilmington Dist. |
| Militia | Martin Hall | 923 | Newbern Dist. |

## HENRY

| | | | |
|---|---|---|---|
| Continental | John Henry | 574 | Hillsboro Dist. |
| Militia | Hugh Henry | 3026 | Salisbury Dist. |
| Militia | John Henry | 5945 | Salisbury Dist. |
| Continental | John Henry | 30 | Halifax Dist. |
| Militia | James Henry | 5885 | Salisbury Dist. |
| Continental | Jonathan Henry | 388 | Warrenton Dist. |
| Militia | Joseph Humphry | 5423 | Wilmington Dist. |

## HOWELLS

| | | | |
|---|---|---|---|
| Continental | Edward Howell | 724 | Hillsboro Dist. |
| Continental | Dempsey Howell | 433 | Halifax Dist. |
| Continental | Silas Howell | 257 | Assembly |
| Militia | Hopkins Howell | 1260 | Newbern Dist. |

## HUGHES

| | | | |
|---|---|---|---|
| Continental | Joseph Hughes | 16 | Warrenton Dist. |
| Militia | Samuel Hughes | 3269 | Salisbury Dist. |
| Militia | James Hughes | 4773 | Wilmington Dist. |
| Continental | Willis Hughes | 1404 | Halifax Dist. |
| Militia | Thomas Hughes | .... | Newbern Dist. |
| Continental | John Hughes | 144 | Warrenton Dist. |

## COMPTROLLER'S OFFICE CERTIFICATES
### 1780-1782

| Pages | | (Miscellaneous) |
|---|---|---|
| 192. | Frederick Haimburg | Wilmington Dist. |
| 5616. | Cap. Phil. Hodge | Wilmington Dist. |
| 7687. | Capt. James Holstan (?) | Salisbury Dist. |
| 5038. | Nathan Jackson | Wilmington Dist. |
| 957. | James Raulens | Wilmington Dist. |
| 1724. | Nicholas Richards | Wilmington Dist. |
| 4935. | Henry Rooks | Wilmington Dist. |
| 642. | Solomon Rose | Wilmington Dist. |
| 205. | Patrick Ryan | Halifax Dist. |
| 2997. | Capt. John Regan | Wilmington Dist. |
| 425. | John Rutherford | Halifax Dist. |
| 1627. | William Ridley | Warrenton Dist. |
| 777. | John Knight | |
| 1066. | Obadiah Roundtree | |
| 339. | Thomas Reason, Sold. | Halifax Dist. |
| 3573. | John Roach | Wilmington Dist. |

*Pages*                                                    (Miscellaneous)
3261. David Templeton ..........................      Salisbury Dist.
 304. John Tinsley, Johnson Co. ..................     Newbern Dist.
 633. Amos Tilton .............................
1183. Hardy Tyner .............................       Warrenton Dist.
 130. Wm. Tilman .............................        Halifax Dist.
2865. Hailey Tatum ............................       Salisbury Dist.
1704. Thomas Tyson ............................
 336. Capt. John Thomas .......................       Halifax Dist.
1061. James Waltom ............................       Wilmington Dist.
 201. Arthur Tony, privt. ......................      Halifax Dist.
 522. William Todd, Sold. .....................       Hillsborough Dist.
  85. Henry Trice, Sold. ........................      Warrenton Dist.
  99. Joshua Towsan ...........................       Hillsborough Dist.
 114. Jonathan Times ..........................       Hillsborough Dist.
 115. John Toney .............................        Hillsborough Dist.
 104. Howell Tatum, Capt. ......................       Halifax Dist.
1027. Allen Tayburn ...........................       Halifax Dist.
1267. Benj. Tedderton .........................       Newbern Dist.
1124. Aron Tyson .............................        Newbern Dist.
1435. Thomas Thornton, Jones Co. .................     Newbern Dist.
   1. Erastus Tippett ..........................      Hillsborough Dist.
1578. Milchar Tar .............................       Warrenton Dist.
 304. William Thornton, Hyde Co. .................     Newbern Dist.
2233. ...... Thulley ...........................      Wilmington Dist.
1180. Amos Traverse ...........................       Newbern Dist.
 461. Francis Tartauson ........................      Hillsborough Dist.
 629. Francis Tartauson ........................      Hillsborough Dist.
 118. R'd Tumberlic, Sen, Wayne Co. ..............    Newbern Dist.
5158. David Torry .............................       Wilmington Dist.
3250. Thomas Tawnsend .........................       Wilmington Dist.
6636. Adam Todd .............................         Salisbury Dist.
5459. Parnel Truet ............................       Wilmington Dist.
 249. Curl Tucker .............................       Hillsborough Dist.
 138. Curl Tucker .............................       Hillsborough Dist.
  30. John Tucker .............................       Hillsborough Dist.
 948. Matthew Tuckers .........................       Wilmington Dist.
 378. Richard Tucker ..........................       Warrenton Dist.
 548. Richard Tucker ..........................       Warrenton Dist.
7606. Wm. Tucker .............................        Salisbury Dist.
9252. Wm. Tockker ............................        Salisbury Dist.
2726. George Tucker ...........................       Salisbury Dist.
1655. Joshua Tucker ...........................       Newbern Dist.
 873. Wright Tucker ...........................       Newbern Dist.
1757. Matthew Tucker ..........................       Wilmington Dist.
1211. Matthew Tucker ..........................       Wilmington Dist.
  50. Joshua Towsan ...........................       Hillsborough Dist.
 536. Blake Rabby .............................       Hillsborough Dist.
 331. Phillip Fishburn .........................
 456. Jesse Fountain ...........................
  55. Moses Frost .............................
 484. John Fry ...............................        Hillsborough Dist.
1064. Sutten Freeluck, Craven Co. .................    Newbern Dist.
1651. George Fowler ...........................       Newbern Dist.
 916. Daniel Frizle, Sold. .......................     Halifax Dist.

*Pages*
1044. George Frisher .............................. Newbern Dist.
810. Peter Fries ................................. Salisbury Dist.
6340. Wm. Falls ................................. Salisbury Dist.
2302. Arthur Fosque, Craven Co. ................... Newbern Dist.
4415. James Fast ................................. Wilmington Dist.
5423. Jacob Frisher, or (Fischer) ................. Salisbury Dist.
43. Jesse Fulton ............................... Warrenton Dist.
4335. John Faulkner ............................. Wilmington Dist.
5913. John Finney ............................... Salisbury Dist.
359. Thomas Fenton ............................ Warrenton Dist.
4908. Ebenezer Frilson .......................... Wilmington Dist.
233. Simon Fitspatrick ..........................
12. John Fookes ...............................
191. Francis Fowler .............................
71. James Fookes .............................
593. William Fluellen .......................... Halifax Dist.
195. John Fusman ..............................
1853. Calap Folkner ............................ Wilmington Dist.
951. Isham Forge ............................... Halifax Dist.

## VOUCHERS FOR SOLDIERS IN CONTINENTAL LINE 1783-92

| | | |
|---|---|---|
| Continental | Durham Hall ......................... | Franklin Co. |
| Continental | Francis Harrison ..................... | Tyrell Co. |
| Continental | Nelson Harris ....................... | Warren Co. |
| Continental | Joseph Hopkins ...................... | State of N. C. |
| Continental | Edward Hutchins ..................... | Dobbs Co. |
| Continental | Josiah Holmes ....................... | Brunswick Co. |
| Continental | Griffin Hammontree .................. | Craven Co. |
| Continental | Robert Hardy ........................ | Pitt Co. |
| Continental | Capt Richard Hadock ................. | Hillsboro |
| Continental | John Hayse .......................... | N. C. Co. |
| Continental | Wilson Howard ....................... | Martin Co. |
| Continental | John Hewey .......................... | Burk Co. |
| Continental | Micajah Heard ....................... | Bertie Co. |
| Continental | Thomas Halaway ..................... | Halifax Co. |
| Continental | Isaac Hayes ......................... | Dobbs Co. |
| Continental | Sonthy Hayes ........................ | Bladen Co. |
| Continental | Joshua Hayes ........................ | |
| Militia | Solomon Hills ....................... | Wilmington Co. |
| Continental | John Holmes ......................... | Brunswick Co. |
| Continental | Richard Hardewick .................. | Bertie Co. |
| Continental | Joshua Hall ......................... | Abbeville Co. |
| Continental | John Hassey ......................... | New Hanover Co. |
| Continental | Alexander Hatch ..................... | Orange Co. |
| Continental | Henry Hicks ......................... | Randolph Co. |
| Continental | John Arnold ......................... | Randolph Co. |
| Continental | Thomas Hill ......................... | |
| Continental | Peter Hedgepeth ..................... | Wake Co. |
| Continental | William Haynes ...................... | Surry Co. |
| Continental | Willis Howard ....................... | Edgecomb Co. |
| Continental | Joseph Hassel ....................... | Tyrell Co. |
| Continental | John Hinds .......................... | Burk Co. |
| Continental | Lewis Hinds ......................... | Wayne Co. |

| | | | |
|---|---|---|---|
| Continental | Benjamine Holley | | Greenville Co. |
| Continental | Thomas Harrison | | Dobbs Co. |
| Continental | Samuel Hill | | Rockingham Co. |
| Continental | Jessie Hanberry | | Edgecomb Co. |
| Continental | Nicholas Helderman | | Lincoln Co. |
| Continental | William Hodges | | Wake Co. |
| Continental | Richard Hill | | Franklin Co. |
| Continental | Asa Hunter | | Onslow Co. |
| Continental | Henry Harris | | Randolph Co. |
| Continental | Hezekiah Hargrove | | Wilkes Co. |
| Continental | Israel Hardway | | Beaufort Co. |
| Continental | Abbot Hendricks | | Rockingham Co. |
| Continental | James Hall | | Franklin Co. |
| Continental | James Hedgepeth | | Burtie Co. |
| Continental | Jessie Hill | | Tyrell Co. |
| Continental | Stewart Hamilton | | Warrenton Co. |
| Continental | Jessie Hall | | Wake Co. |
| Continental | John Holly | | Sampson Co. |
| Continental | James Hollis | | Tyrell Co. |
| Continental | Joseph Handley | | Granville Co. |
| | | *No.* | |
| Continental | Richard Atchison | 627 | Warrenton Dist. |
| Continental | Jerekirah Ashley | 1203 | Halifax Dist. |
| Continental | Amos Ashbrook | 110 | Hillsboro Dist. |
| Continental | Capt. Samuel Ashe | 618 | Halifax Dist. |
| Continental | Lieut. Richard Andrews | 26 | Halifax Dist. |
| Continental | John Adcock | 1799 | Warrenton Dist. |
| Continental | Benjamine Almerry | 709 | Hillsboro Dist. |
| Continental | Joseph Arthur | 770 | Hillsboro Dist. |
| Continental | Jordan Ammonds | 623 | Hillsboro Dist. |
| Continental | Drury Anthony | 680 | N. C. A. |
| Continental | John Anderson | 7 | Hillsboro Dist. |
| Continental | James Adkins | 55 | Hillsboro Dist. |
| Continental | Joseph Allen | 288 | Hillsboro Dist. |
| Continental | James Ammons | 385 | Hillsboro Dist. |
| Continental | Joseph Alsobrook | 253 | Hillsboro Dist. |
| Continental | Alfred Andrews | 250 | Hillsboro Dist. |
| Continental | Benjamine Angle | 402 | Hillsboro Dist. |
| Continental | John Ashley | 383 | Hillsboro Dist. |
| Continental | Amos Alsobrooke | 186 | Hillsboro Dist. |
| Continental | Philip Axum | 818 | Halifax Dist. |
| Continental | Thomas Aldridge | 1089 | Halifax Dist. |
| Continental | John Athison | 137 | Hillsboro Dist. |
| Continental | Cornelius Anglen | 627 | Hillsboro Dist. |
| Continental | Thomas Abbot | 482 | Newbern Dist. |
| Continental | Caleb Archer | 273 | Hillsboro Dist. |
| Continental | James Abbot | 787 | Hillsboro Dist. |
| Continental | James Adkins | 45 | Hillsboro Dist. |
| Continental | Jordan Ammons | 450 | Hillsboro Dist. |
| Continental | John Abbot | 498 | Halifax Dist. |
| Continental | John Andrews | 1175 | Halifax Dist. |
| Continental | James Amos | 514 | Halifax Dist. |
| Continental | Joseph Arthur | 586 | Hillsboro Dist. |
| Continental | Stephen Arthur | 135 | Hillsboro Dist. |
| Continental | John Atkison | 71 | Hillsboro Dist. |

| | | *No.* | |
|---|---|---|---|
| Continental | Elias Ashburne | 179 | N. C. |
| Continental | Simon Alderson | 819 | Hillsboro Dist. |
| Continental | Robert Adcock | 318 | N. C. |
| Continental | Robert Acock | 126 | Hillsboro Dist. |
| Continental | Moses Acock | 128 | Hillsboro Dist. |
| Continental | Joseph Aldridge | 558 | Hillsboro Dist. |
| Continental | William Acock | 1200 | Warrenton Dist. |
| Continental | Nathan Arrindal | 1471 | Newbern Dist. |
| Continental | Benjamine Angle | 164 | Hillsboro Dist. |
| Continental | Jessie Aldridge | 272 | Hillsboro Dist. |
| Continental | David Arnold | 551 | Halifax Dist. |
| Militia | Thomas Atherson | 2760 | Wilmington Dist. |
| Militia | Joshua Davis | 976 | Halifax Dist. |
| Militia | John Deal | 907 | Newbern Dist. |
| Militia | David Hill | 1030 | Newbern Dist. |
| Militia | Richard Hill | 1072 | Newbern Dist. |
| Militia | .... Dubberly | 925 | Newbern Dist. |
| Militia | Epsilom Dimont | 654 | Newbern Dist. |
| Militia | John Dubberly | 978 | Newbern Dist. |
| Militia | Thomas Downs | 377 | Newbern Dist. |
| Militia | Paul Deale | 1671 | Newbern Dist. |
| Militia | Colin Enson | 893 | Newbern Dist. |
| Militia | Abner Easton | 1694 | Newbern Dist. |
| Militia | Sanders Easton | 593 | Newbern Dist. |
| Militia | Joshua Chestnutt | 2770 | Wilmington Dist. |
| Militia | Samuel Cromose | 805 | Newbern Dist. |
| Militia | Robert Croswell | 8786 | Salisbury Dist. |
| Continental | Thuball Cleghorn | 287 | N. C. Assem. |
| Militia | John Cade | 1201 | Wilmington Dist. |
| Militia | Stephen Cade | 915 | Wilmington Dist. |
| Militia | Henry Alberton | 729 | Newbern Dist. |
| Militia | Jessie Ashlock | 150 | Halifax Dist. |
| Militia | Nelson Allcock | 654 | Newbern Dist. |
| Militia | Joel Champin | 1432 | Wilmington Dist. |
| Militia | Howel Ammons | 1515 | Wilmington Dist. |
| Militia | Dempsey Ammons | 791 | Wilmington Dist. |
| Militia | Charles Gasin | 1484 | Wilmington Dist. |
| Militia | Charles Gilkey | 5223 | Salisbury Dist. |
| Militia | Sam Granger | 971 | Newbern Dist. |
| Continental | Stephen Cross | 1362 | Warrenton Dist. |
| Militia | Thomas Crumpton | 1787 | Wilmington Dist. |
| Militia | Waggoner Robert Christie | 436 | Halifax Dist. |
| Continental | ..... ..... ........•••••• | .... | |
| Militia | Cullen Connely | 2776 | Wilmington Dist. |
| | ..... ..... ............... | 656 | Wilmington Dist. |
| Continental | James Christian | 1099 | Halifax Dist. |
| Militia | Abso Carrell | 475 | Newbern Dist. |
| Militia | Isaac Charlecraft | 1019 | Wilmington Dist. |
| Militia | William Crosby | 7996 | Salisbury Dist. |
| Militia | William Kincade | 4258 | Wilmington Dist. |
| Militia | Lazrus Creel | 656 | Wilmington Dist. |
| Militia | James Chilley | 29 | Newbern Dist. |
| Continental | Drummer, John Killingsworth | 1076 | Halifax Dist. |
| Militia | Jessie Rouse | 1254 | Newbern Dist. |
| Militia | Charles King | 5631 | Wilmington Dist. |

|  |  | *No.* |  |
|---|---|---|---|
| Militia | William Keen | 2991 | Wilmington Dist. |
| Militia | Thomas Bishop | 3706 | Wilmington Dist. |
| Militia | Daniel Blue | 1462 | Wilmington Dist. |
| Militia | William Conn | 1331 | Salisbury Dist. |
| Militia | William Kilson | 5857 | Salisbury Dist. |
| Militia | George Kerr | 5502 | Salisbury Dist. |
| Militia | Joseph Bland | 5108 | Wilmington Dist. |
| Militia | John Bighorn | 5005 | Salisbury Dist. |
| Militia | Robt. Beaty | 5066 | Salisbury Dist. |
| Militia | Mark Brum | 4436 | Wilmington Dist. |
| Militia | George Barge | 4782 | Wilmington Dist. |
| Militia | George Blocker | 3959 | Wilmington Dist. |
| Militia | William Blocker | 3947 | Wilmington Dist. |
| Militia | John Busby | 4790 | Wilmington Dist. |
| Continental | Levi Barker | 999 | Halifax Dist. |
| Militia | Joshua Barron | 1281 | Newbern Dist. |
| Continental | Joseph Robsen | 888 | Halifax Dist. |
| Militia | James Brantly | 1859 | Wilmington Dist. |
| Militia | Robert Bannerman | 4946 | Wilmington Dist. |
| Militia | Michael Blacker | 3945 | Wilmington Dist. |
| Militia | Mathias Bever | 2705 | Salisbury Dist. |
| Militia | James Beats | 3733 | Salisbury Dist. |
| Militia | Elias Bost | 2572 | Salisbury Dist. |
| Continental | Taylor Bowles | 636 | N. C. Assem. |
| Continental | William Brickle | 609 | Halifax Dist. |
| Continental | Lieut. Samuel Budd | 437 | Halifax Dist. |
| Militia | William Baldin | 1505 | Newbern Dist. |
| Continental | Daniel Barrow | 813 | Halifax Dist. |
| Militia | Capt. John Brownfield | 4896 | Salisbury Dist. |
| Militia | Jonathan Bryan, Ens. | 5281 | Wilmington Dist. |
| Continental | William Brownen | 122 | N. C. Assem. |
| Continental | Horress Barker | 40 | N. C. Assem. |
| Continental | Thomas Bedford | 46 | Halifax Dist. |
| Continental | Thomas Bane | 247 | Halifax Dist. |
| Militia | William Boldwin | 2662 | Wilmington Dist. |
| Militia | Abram Barrow | 5208 | Wilmington Dist. |
| Militia | John Brinson | 3723 | Wilmington Dist. |
| Militia | William Blue | 4422 | Wilmington Dist. |
| Militia | John Balch | 5506 | Salisbury Dist. |
| Militia | Jacob Bean | 5334 | Salisbury Dist. |
| Militia | John Burnes | 4959 | Wilmington Dist. |
| Militia | Thomas Burnet | 5199 | Wilmington Dist. |
| Militia | Thomas Killon | 3715 | Wilmington Dist. |
| Militia | Jacob Karray | 4481 | Wilmington Dist. |
| Militia | Michael Kenan | 4943 | Wilmington Dist. |
| Militia | Samuel Kelongh | 5263 | Salisbury Dist. |
| Militia | John Kemp | 3123 | Wilmington Dist. |
| Militia | William Kineade | 3964 | Wilmington Dist. |
| Militia | David Kenadye | 3303 | Salisbury Dist. |
| Militia | Andrew Kilpatrick | 2659 | Salisbury Dist. |
| Militia | Joseph Kerr | 2445 | Salisbury Dist. |
| Militia | John Kemp | 3254 | Wilmington Dist. |
| Militia | Joseph Kennedy | 5937 | Salisbury Dist. |
| Militia | Capt. Nathan King | 2967 | Wilmington Dist. |

|        | | No. | |
|--------|------------------------|------|------------------|
| Militia | Joseph Knox | 5889 | Salisbury Dist. |
| Militia | Samuel Kinston | 4890 | Salisbury Dist. |
| Militia | Owen Kenan | 5107 | Wilmington Dist. |
| Militia | William Kineade | .... | Wilmington Dist. |
| Militia | James Knowles | 3253 | Wilmington Dist. |
| Militia | Jessie Braur | 4359 | Wilmington Dist. |

## COMPTROLLER'S VOUCHERS

### Mc's.

No.

| | | |
|------|--------------------------------|--------------------------------|
| 208. | Archibald McDougall | |
| 1027. | James McDogal | Halifax Dist. |
| 2111. | Donald McDugald | Wilmington Dist. |
| 198. | John McDugal | Salisbury Dist. |
| 2098. | Alexander McDugald | Wilmington Dist. |
| 1572. | Anguish McDugald | Wilmington Dist. |
| 101. | Charles McHenry | |
| 466. | Isaac McHenry | Fayetteville, Office of Compt's. |
| 2664. | John McHenry | Salisbury Dist. |
| ..7. | John McCarty | |
| 4197. | Thomas McClendon | Wilmington Dist. |
| 4195. | Isaac McClendon | Wilmington Dist. |
| 3823. | Alexander McKay | Wilmington Dist. |
| 7246. | Sam'l McCollom | Salisbury Dist. |
| 7154. | Daniel McCollom | Salisbury Dist. |
| 3956. | John McCay | Wilmington Dist. |
| 1566. | Daniel McKinney | Halifax Dist. |
| 4931. | Florince McCarthy | Wilmington Dist. |
| 2963. | Jno. McKein | Salisbury Dist. |
| 2939. | Sam'l McLure | Salisbury Dist. |
| 8913. | John McConnel, Sergt. | Salisbury Dist. |
| 7881. | William McKnight | Salisbury Dist. |
| 205. | Thomas Mackey | Edenton Dist. |
| 8363. | John McMullen | Salisbury Dist. |
| 3620. | Robert McCachran | Salisbury Dist. |
| 4688. | John McConnar | Salisbury Dist. |
| 6284. | Thos. McCullock | Salisbury Dist. |
| 6236. | Wm. McCain | Salisbury Dist. |
| 4078. | Alexander Mackay | Salisbury Dist. |
| 4507. | Daniel MacNeil | Wilmington Dist. |
| 3237. | William McRee | Wilmington Dist. |
| 3235. | William McRee | Wilmington Dist. |
| 2784. | William McRee | Wilmington Dist. |
| 3238. | Samuel McRee | Wilmington Dist. |
| .... | Maj. Griffith John McRee | |
| 2783. | Samuel McKee | Salisbury Dist. |
| 4402. | Turpin McRee | Wilmington Dist. |
| 3451. | Ambrose McKee | Salisbury Dist. |
| 4760. | John McFarson | Wilmington Dist. |
| 2345. | Neil McNier | Wilmington Dist. |
| 1760. | Duncan McIntire | Wilmington Dist. |
| 4797. | Neill McCrainey | Wilmington Dist. |
| 6535. | Jno. McCord | Salisbury Dist. |

*No.*
2610. Murdock McIntire ........................ Wilmington Dist.
.... Chas. McClane .......................... Salisbury Dist.
5621. Dan'l McCraine ......................... Wilmington Dist.
6457. John McIntosh .......................... Salisbury Dist.
3025. Robert McBride ......................... Salisbury Dist.
5174. Robert McBride ......................... Salisbury Dist.
4498. Alex McConnel .......................... Salisbury Dist.
5193. David McBride .......................... Salisbury Dist.
1469. James McCall ........................... Salisbury Dist.
 730. James McCracken ........................ Salisbury Dist.
3652. Nathan'l McCann ........................ Wilmington Dist.
7751. Dan'l McCloud .......................... Salisbury Dist.
6208. Samuel McCleary ........................ Salisbury Dist.
3248. Francis McC..... ....................... Salisbury Dist.
1377. Wm. McClearie .......................... Salisbury Dist.
6.... Wm. McCawn ............................. Salisbury Dist.
2028. Adom McNeely ........................... Salisbury Dist.
3307. Andrew McCombs ......................... Salisbury Dist.
1572. John McGinty ........................... Salisbury Dist.
1254. James McGown ........................... Salisbury Dist.
7466. Roger McPeak ........................... Salisbury Dist.
6042. Thos. McClure .......................... Salisbury Dist.
5681. D.... McCord ........................... Salisbury Dist.
1387. Dinskin McCown ......................... Salisbury Dist.
3667. David McKinley ......................... Salisbury Dist.
3247. David McCullot ......................... Salisbury Dist.
4259. Capt. N.... McCrany .................... Wilmington Dist.
3932. William McKinzie ....................... Wilmington Dist.
3093. Wm. McRee .............................. Wilmington Dist.
3247. Moses Skirpir .......................... Salisbury Dist.
 313. Isam Sellers ........................... Wilmington Dist.

## COMPTROLLER'S OFFICE CERTIFICATES
### 1785

**B.**
3374. J.... iah Blackman ..................... Wilmington Dist.
1765. Right Base ............................. Wilmington Dist.
 703. Patrick Barr ........................... Salisbury Dist.
2939. James Beard ............................ Wilmington Dist.
 309. Joseph Britton ......................... Wilmington Dist.
1497. Clifton Bowen .......................... Wilmington Dist.
  14. Batte Birdsong, Lt. ....................
5327. John Beck, Junr. ....................... Wilmington Dist.
2094. John Bowman ............................ Salisbury Dist.
4021. Thomas Beaty ........................... Salisbury Dist.
3479. John Bland ............................. Wilmington Dist.
3072. Wm. Buffelow ........................... Wilmington Dist.
4778. David Bray ............................. Salisbury Dist.
1959. Benj. Brandon .......................... Salisbury Dist.
2077. Hugh Barr .............................. Salisbury Dist.
2720. Rice Blackman .......................... Wilmington Dist.
2067. James Bowman ........................... Wilmington Dist.
4904. Wm. Barnett ............................ Salisbury Dist.
2130. John Bennet ............................ Wilmington Dist.
1525. John Boykin ............................ Wilmington Dist.

*No.*

| No. | Name | District |
|---|---|---|
| 1576. | James Burdox | Wilmington Dist. |
| 3243. | Richard Bruen | Wilmington Dist. |
| 1417. | Richard Bolton | Halifax Dist. |
| 1627. | John Brabham | Wilmington Dist. |
| 1246. | John Bored | Wilmington Dist. |
| 7598. | William Bodenhammer | Salisbury Dist. |
| 3350. | Robert Bratney | Salisbury Dist. |
| 3224. | Samuel Br. | Salisbury Dist. |
| 321. | James Blanton | Wilmington Dist. |
| 4481. | Daniel Brannon | Wilmington Dist. |
| 2006. | William Ballinger | Salisbury Dist. |
| 5550. | Frederick Boykin | Wilmington Dist. |
| 2547. | Thomas Bone | Salisbury Dist. |
| 447. | Jacob Boston | Salisbury Dist. |
| 5231. | Neil Braley | Salisbury Dist. |
| 722. | William Bucke, Craven Co. | Newbern Dist. |
| 794. | Jno. Boing, Pitt Co. | Newbern Dist. |
| 1081. | Isaac Bowen, Pitt Co. | Newbern Dist. |
| 1300. | Wm. Bush | |
| 261. | Tom Borring | Wilmington Dist. |
| 1759. | Huston Beesley | Wilmington Dist. |
| 3659. | Barnet Brock | Wilmington Dist. |
| 3601. | Joshua Bruenlon | Wilmington Dist. |
| 3838. | Wm. Belew | Morgan Dist. |
| 5154. | Thomas Bishop | Salisbury Dist. |
| 20166. | Thomas Brinkley | Salisbury Dist. |
| 5787. | Hezekiah Burns | Wilmington Dist. |
| 1032. | Benjamin Biggs | Salisbury Dist. |
| 3850. | Robt. Boyle | Salisbury Dist. |
| 1239. | Stephen Beton | Wilmington Dist. |
| 3530. | John Berryman | Wilmington Dist. |
| 3503. | Nat. Burrap | Wilmington Dist. |
| 3605. | William Bush | Wilmington Dist. |
| 343. | Capt. Wm. Fawn | Halifax Dist. |
| 433. | Isham Finch | Newbern Dist. |
| 1203. | Daniel Frissell | Warrenton Dist. |
| 354. | Patrick Foy | Halifax Dist. |
| 3755. | James Foy | Wilmington Dist. |
| 3186. | James Foy | Wilmington Dist. |
| 5134. | Thos. Flere or (Flen) | Wilmington Dist. |
| 1849. | John Folkner | Wilmington Dist. |
| 756. | David Forster | Halifax Dist. |
| 1201. | John Floyd | Halifax Dist. |
| 4839. | John Foster | Salisbury Dist. |
| 5327. | Jacob Frick | Salisbury Dist. |
| 214. | Benjamin Fordice | Salisbury Dist. |
| 4815. | Binga Freeman | Wilmington Dist. |
| 6942. | Thos. Ferguson | Salisbury Dist. |
| 194. | Hugh Frasier | |
| 259. | Henry Fitner | |
| 1180. | Isham Finch | |
| 5875. | Elisha Faison | Wilmington Dist. |
| 3166. | Joshua Faroah | Wilmington Dist. |

*No.*
1455. Edmond Fogetty .......................... Wilmington Dist.
  50. Peter Foster ...............................
  68. Peter Foster ...............................
3245. James Farr ...............................
3643. Lt. John Farrior .......................... Wilmington Dist.
1105. Lt. John Fillyan .......................... Wilmington Dist.
7830. Capt. Galeth Falls ........................ Salisbury Dist.
1648. John Fields .............................. Newbern Dist.
 847. John Fields .............................. Newbern Dist.
  66. John Fields .............................. Hillsborough Dist.
 392. Morris Fennell ........................... Warrenton Dist.
 341. John Flend, Sold. ......................... Halifax Dist.
5855. Will Falls ............................... Salisbury Dist.
4597. Mich'l Ferrel ............................. Wilmington Dist.
2063. Francis Fox .............................. Wilmington Dist.
5265. Rich'd Farr .............................. Wilmington Dist.
 781. J..... Fox ............................... Wilmington Dist.
5234. John Fryar .............................. Wilmington Dist.
7630. Peter Fry ............................... Salisbury Dist.
 408. Enoch Flood, Sold. ....................... Halifax Dist.
 432. Henry Frinch ............................ Newbern Dist.
1153. John Fowler ............................. Halifax Dist.
4315. James Finney ............................ Salisbury Dist.
2471. Jacob Fifer ............................. Salisbury Dist.
 481. Newsom Faircloth, Johnson Co. .............
1395. Samuel Freeman ......................... Warrenton Dist.
4475. John Flowers ............................ Wilmington Dist.
5337. Frederick Fennel ......................... Salisbury Dist.
 598. Backner Floyd ...........................
 343. William Filson .......................... Newbern Dist.
 328. Benjamin Farmer ......................... Newbern Dist.
2092. James Fisher ............................ Salisbury Dist.
9275. John Fichpatrick ......................... Salisbury Dist.
 140. James Foods ............................. Newbern Dist.
 352. John Flowers ............................ Wilmington Dist.

|  |  | *No.* |  |
|---|---|---|---|
| Continental | Holland Johnson | 628 | Halifax Dist. |
| Continental | James Johnson | 939 | Halifax Dist. |
| Continental | Benjamine Johnson | 844 | Halifax Dist. |
| Continental | Archibald Johnson | 148 | Assem. |
| Continental | Oliver Johnson | 557 | Hillsboro Dist. |
| Continental | Mathias Johnson | 380 | Hillsboro Dist. |
| Continental | Thomas Johnson | 72 | Hillsboro Dist. |
| Militia | Charles Johnson | 3088 | Wilmington Dist. |
| Militia | Travis Johnson | 1161 | Newbern Dist. |
| Militia | Adam Johnson | 7910 | Salisbury Dist. |
| Militia | Nathaniel Johnson | 450 | Salisbury Dist. |
| Militia | Joseph Johnson | 4969 | Salisbury Dist. |
| Militia | Alexander Johnson | 4788 | Wilmington Dist. |
| Militia | Crafford Johnson | 3630 | Wilmington Dist. |
| Militia | William Johnson | 3831 | Wilmington Dist. |
| Continental | Isaac Johnson | 635 | Assem. |
| Militia | Thomas Nobles | 901 | Newbern Dist. |
| Militia | James Nobles | 663 | Hillsboro Dist. |

|  |  | *No.* |  |
|---|---|---|---|
| Militia | Levi Nobles | 1193 | Newbern Dist. |
| Militia | Philemon Nobles | .... | Newbern Dist. |
| Militia | Hezekia Nobles | 239 |  |
| Militia | Francis Nelms | 5909 | Wilmington Dist. |
| Continental | Aron Newsom | 350 | Hillsboro Dist. |
| Continental | Colo. John Patten | .... | Halifax Dist. |
| Continental | John Nelson | 401 | Hillsboro Dist. |
| Militia | James Ramsey | 3950 | Wilmington Dist. |
| Militia | William Ross | 1424 | Salisbury Dist. |
| Militia | William Register | 1983 | Wilmington Dist. |
| Militia | Alex Newberry | 7247 | Salisbury Dist. |
| Militia | William Naile | 1246 | Salisbury Dist. |
| Militia | Philip Wolf | 7653 | Salisbury Dist. |
| Militia | Moses Winsley | 8918 | Salisbury Dist. |
| Militia | John Wason | 5597 | Salisbury Dist. |
| Militia | Joseph Robinson | 2648 | Salisbury Dist. |
| Militia | John Richardson | 4800 | Morgan Dist. |
| Militia | Thos. Robison | 2945 | Wilmington Dist. |
| Militia | Samuel Robison | 6924 | Salisbury Dist. |
| Continental | Thomas Richardson | 134 | N. C. Assem. |
| Militia | Lewis Johnson | 541 | Newbern Dist. |
| Continental | Barnaby Johnson | 1830 | Warrenton Dist. |
| Continental | Daniel Johnson | 1093 | Halifax Dist. |
| Continental | Charles Johnson | 263 | Hillsboro Dist. |
| Continental | Samuel Johnson | 262 | Hillsboro Dist. |
| Continental | Reuben Johnson | 12 | Hillsboro Dist. |
| Continental | Benjamine Johnson | 264 | Hillsboro Dist. |
| Continental | Amos Johnson | 246 | Hillsboro Dist. |
| Continental | John Johnson | 433 | Hillsboro Dist. |
| Continental | Dempsey Johnson | 507 | Hillsboro Dist. |
| Militia | Robert Johnson | 59 | Newbern Dist. |
| Militia | Absolom Johnson | 507 | Newbern Dist. |
| Militia | Jeremiah Johnson | 1435 | Newbern Dist. |
| Militia | Jacob Johnson | 4175 | Wilmington Dist. |
| Militia | Joseph Johnson | 5059 | Salisbury Dist. |
| Militia | Richard Johnson | 537 | Wilmington Dist. |
| Militia | Ambrose Johnson | 1698 | Newbern Dist. |
| Militia | Solomon Johnson | 77 | Wilmington Dist. |
| Militia | Starling Johnson | 502 | Newbern Dist. |
| Militia | John Robinson | 5580 | Salisbury Dist. |
| Militia | David Robinson | 4717 | Salisbury Dist. |
| Militia | George Robinson | 6941 | Salisbury Dist. |
| Militia | Andrew Richardson | 1792 | Newbern Dist. |
| Militia | Benjamine Richardson | 22 | Newbern Dist. |
| Militia | Moses Johnston | 1218 | Newbern Dist. |
| Continental | Arthur Pew | 1242 | Halifax Dist. |
| Continental | William Jackson | 268 | Halifax Dist. |
| Continental | Edward Howard | 645 | Hillsboro Dist. |
| Continental | Samuel Serrett | 111 | Hillsboro Dist. |
| Continental | James Spann | 481 | Hillsboro Dist. |
| Continental | Alexander Scull | 744 | Hillsboro Dist. |
| Militia | William Pickrin | 31 | Newbern Dist. |
| Militia | James Barson | 546 | Newbern Dist. |
| Militia | David Richardson | 4171 | Wilmington Dist. |

|  |  | *No.* |  |
|---|---|---|---|
| Militia | Silvenus Phumphry | 823 | Newbern Dist. |
| Militia | John Patrick | 936 | Newbern Dist. |
| Militia | Bazil Preater | 6907 | Salisbury Dist. |
| Militia | Asher Pipkin | 2820 | Wilmington Dist. |
| Militia | Joseph Paltan | 2448 | Salisbury Dist. |
| Militia | Levy Pharies | 6325 | Salisbury Dist. |
| Militia | Edmund Ricks | 1962 | Newbern Dist. |
| Militia | Adam Williams | 1144 | Wilmington Dist. |
| Militia | Joseph Silver | 6984 | Salisbury Dist. |
| Continental | Benjamine Robeson | 754 | Halifax Dist. |
| Continental | Caleb Parr | 1302 | Halifax Dist. |
| Continental | Jacob Parett | 477 | Newbern Dist. |
| Continental | John Pollard | 1770 | Warrenton Dist. |
| Continental | James Pollard | 1772 | Warrenton Dist. |
| Continental | John Padgett | 1215 | Warrenton Dist. |
| Continental | James Paxton | 522 | N. C. A. |
| Continental | Joshua Pelt | 287 | N. C. |
| Continental | Colo. John Patton | 891 | Halifax Dist. |
| Continental | Jeremiah James | 242 | Hillsboro Dist. |
| Continental | Isaac Joy | 479 | N. C. |
| Continental | Elisha Jenkins | 31 | Hillsboro Dist. |
| Militia | Joshua Johnson | 217 | Wilmington Dist. |
| Militia | Andrew Snoddy | 8946 | Salisbury Dist. |
| Militia | Dinnard James | 353 | Newbern Dist. |
| Militia | Edward Pearsall | 2109 | Wilmington Dist. |
| Militia | Jeremiah Pearsall | 3645 | Wilmington Dist. |
| Militia | James Pearsall | 1007 | Wilmington Dist. |
| Militia | William Peterson | 2207 | Wilmington Dist. |
| Militia | William Harbison | 4489 | Morgan Dist. |

## SUNDRY NAMES

|  |  |  |  |
|---|---|---|---|
| Continental | John Norwood | 982 | Halifax Dist. |
| Continental | John Webb | 752 | Halifax Dist. |
| Continental | Samuel Webb | 648 | Hillsboro Dist. |
| Militia | Fred Mills | 1743 | Newbern Dist. |
| Militia | Nahor Norris | 1303 | Newbern Dist. |
| Militia | Sepean Sheppard | 2246 | Wilmington Dist. |
| Continental | Benjamine Williams | 550 | Hillsboro Dist. |
| Continental | George Wilkie | 582 | Halifax Dist. |
| Militia | John Bartlett | 220 | Newbern Dist. |
| Continental | Benjamine Womble | 211 | Halifax Dist. |
| Militia | John Ward | 2990 | Wilmington Dist. |
| Militia | Nathan Norris | 1370 | Newbern Dist. |
| Continental | Arthur Nelson | 653 | Hillsboro Dist. |
| Militia | Benjamine Swan | 3734 | Wilmington Dist. |
| Militia | William Swan | 3083 | Salisbury Dist. |
| Continental | Pugh Williams | 350 |  |
| Continental | Georg Williams | 646 | Hillsboro Dist. |
| Continental | Robert Williams | 950 | Halifax Dist. |
| Militia | Samuel Walker | 3034 | Salisbury Dist. |
| Militia | Joel Williams | 7742 | Newbern Dist. |
| Militia | William Williams | 1205 | Newbern Dist. |
| Continental | Capt. Ralph Williams | 463 | Halifax Dist. |

| | | No. | |
|---|---|---|---|
| Continental | Colo. Samuel Williams | 4214 | Halifax Dist. |
| Continental | Capt. Samuel Williams | 9 | |
| Militia | Richard Williams | 3727 | Wilmington Dist. |
| Militia | Nicholas Williams | 1761 | Wilmington Dist. |
| Militia | Jeremiah Williams | 2051 | Wilmington Dist. |
| Continental | Clayborn Williams | 182 | N. C. Assm. |
| Militia | James Williams | 3614 | Wilmington Dist. |
| Continental | Zeb Williams | 330 | Hillsboro Dist. |
| Continental | John Williams | .... | Halifax Dist. |
| Continental | Harper Johnson | 1171 | Warrenton Dist. |
| Militia | Robert Walker | 1438 | Salisbury Dist. |
| Militia | Isaac Williams | 6043 | Salisbury Dist. |
| Militia | Thomas Williams | 3496 | Wilmington Dist. |
| Militia | Absolom Johnson | .... | Newbern Dist. |
| Militia | Robt. Johnson | 6929 | Salisbury Dist. |
| Continental | Samuel Johnson | 352 | Halifax Dist. |
| Militia | Jeremial Malpas | 1599 | Wilmington Dist. |
| Militia | Daniel Magell | .... | Wilmington Dist. |
| Militia | James Malpas | 1583 | Wilmington Dist. |
| Militia | Robert Magee | 1526 | Wilmington Dist. |
| Militia | William Magee | 2830 | Wilmington Dist. |
| Militia | Thos. Marsh | 1508 | Wilmington Dist. |
| Militia | John Manor | 1020 | Wilmington Dist. |
| Militia | James Marlow | 5460 | Salisbury Dist. |
| Militia | Josiah Maples | 4158 | Wilmington Dist. |
| Militia | Peter Mallard | 1500 | Newbern Dist. |
| Continental | Dempsey Marlow | 245 | Hillsboro Dist. |
| Continental | Charles Mannan | .... | N. C. A. |
| Continental | Isham Macklin | 361 | N. C. A. |
| Continental | John Manning | 810 | Halifax Dist. |
| Continental | Joseph May | 241 | Halifax Dist. |
| Continental | Daniel Mapenjale | 101 | Halifax Dist. |
| Continental | ..... Morris | 837 | Halifax Dist. |
| Militia | John Marlow | 695 | Salisbury Dist. |
| Militia | John Massey | 2986 | Wilmington Dist. |
| Militia | Jeremiah Maples | 4036 | Wilmington Dist. |
| Militia | Donnal Mackay | 4077 | Salisbury Dist. |
| Militia | Philip Magee | 1547 | Wilmington Dist. |
| Militia | Daniel Maxwell | 40 | Salisbury Dist. |
| Continental | John Marr | 69 | Hillsboro Dist. |
| Continental | Samuel Marrow | 278 | Hillsboro Dist. |
| Militia | Amos Richardson | 4801 | Morgan Dist. |
| Continental | Jacob Robinson | 1207 | Halifax Dist. |
| Continental | William Richardson | 389 | Halifax Dist. |
| Continental | Powell Riggan | 76 | Hillsboro Dist. |
| Militia | James Ruthledge | 2445 | Salisbury Dist. |
| Militia | John Rop | 614 | Salisbury Dist. |
| Militia | Mark Runnals | 4419 | Wilmington Dist. |
| Militia | William Runnals | 4430 | Wilmington Dist. |
| Militia | Searjt. Peter Robel | 5402 | Salisbury Dist. |
| Militia | Simon Rivenbark | 2224 | Wilmington Dist. |
| Militia | George Quick | 1877 | Wilmington Dist. |
| Militia | Thos. Quinn | 2328 | Wilmington Dist. |
| Militia | Mark Prigion | 2169 | Wilmington Dist. |

| | | No. | |
|---|---|---|---|
| Militia | Will Peters | 1063 | Newbern Dist. |
| Militia | Nathan Prine | 1862 | Wilmington Dist. |
| Militia | William Ramsey | 4258 | Salisbury Dist. |
| Militia | Argulas Pointer | 3059 | Wilmington Dist. |
| Militia | John Parrimore | 1976 | Newbern Dist. |
| Militia | Everit Pollard | 885 | Newbern Dist. |
| Militia | Robert Purser | 693 | Newbern Dist. |
| Militia | James Purser | 697 | Newbern Dist. |
| Continental | Henry Pythrus | 48 | Warrenton Dist. |
| Continental | John Platt | 1039 | Halifax Dist. |
| Continental | Colburn Solevine | 322 | Halifax Dist. |
| Continental | William Pollard | 117 | N. C. A. |
| Continental | William Proctor | 1155 | Halifax Dist. |
| Continental | John Potter | 824 | Haifax Dist. |
| Continental | John Pond | 1359 | Halifax Dist. |
| Continental | Drury Parham | 1208 | Halifax Dist. |
| Continental | Jessie Pritchard | 194 | Hillsboro Dist. |
| Continental | Francis Pridgen | 9 | Hillsboro Dist. |
| Continental | Martin Phifer | 199 | Hillsboro Dist. |
| Continental | Augustin Prescoll | 91 | Hillsboro Dist. |
| Continental | John Peekman | 439 | N. C. A. |
| Continental | Abraham Prim | 358 | Halifax Dist. |
| Continental | John Parr | 90 | N. C. A. |
| Continental | John Poor | 93 | Hillsboro Dist. |
| Continental | Joshua Pelt | 49 | |
| Militia | Thomas Pittman | 4253 | Wilmington Dist. |
| Militia | Charles Payn | 400 | Salisbury Dist. |
| Militia | Joshua Pharough | 4534 | Wilmington Dist. |
| Militia | James Patterson | 5430 | Salisbury Dist. |
| Militia | Samuel Phariss | 850 | Wilmington Dist. |
| Militia | Balam Peoples | 1125 | Newbern Dist. |
| Militia | John Porterfield | 4058 | Wilmington Dist. |
| Militia | James Jackson | 4545 | Salisbury Dist. |
| Militia | Cary Jernigan | 160 | Newbern Dist. |
| Militia | John Jonas | 7782 | Salisbury Dist. |
| Militia | William Norkett | 1575 | Newbern Dist. |
| Militia | Nicholas Norkett | 1963 | Newbern Dist. |
| Militia | Joseph Jackson | 382 | Newbern Dist. |
| Militia | Richard Carson | 803 | Newbern Dist. |
| Militia | Michael Petteway | 837 | Newbern Dist. |
| Militia | Thomas Jenkins | 3760 | Newbern Dist. |
| Militia | John Yates | 928 | Morgan Dist. |
| Militia | Joseph Young | 5256 | Salisbury Dist. |
| Militia | James Young | 5152 | Wilmington Dist. |
| Militia | William Gandle | 6050 | Salisbury Dist. |
| Militia | S..... Young | 257 | Wilmington Dist. |
| Continental | Joel Yelverton | 790 | N. C. |
| Continental | John Yelverton | 217 | N. C. |
| Continental | Nathan Yammons | 1462 | Warrenton Dist. |
| Continental | Jame Forgarty | 28 | Halifax Dist. |
| Continental | Capt. Edward Yarborough | 92 | Halifax Dist. |
| Continental | James Yew | 61 | Hillsboro Dist. |
| Continental | Martin Young | 13 | Hillsboro Dist. |
| Continental | James Young (Waggoner) | 581 | Halifax Dist. |

| | | No. | |
|---|---|---|---|
| Continental | John Yearley | 143 | N. C. A. |
| Militia | Archibald Young | 6635 | Salisbury Dist. |
| Militia | Benjamine Yates | 3317 | Wilmington Dist. |
| Militia | Joseph Young | 4781 | Wilmington Dist. |
| Militia | James Yandle | 6045 | Salisbury Dist. |
| Militia | Dobbs Young | 5651 | Wilmington Dist. |
| Militia | Andrew Yandle | 5526 | Salisbury Dist. |
| Militia | John Young | 4528 | Wilmington Dist. |
| Militia | Russel Yunt | 7583 | Salisbury Dist. |
| Continental | William Yates | 60 | Hillsboro Dist. |
| Continental | Leon Young | 1863 | Warrenton Dist. |
| Continental | Searjnt. James Gray | 616 | Halifax Dist. |
| Continental | James Yew | 110 | Hillsboro Dist. |
| Continental | William Yates | 109 | Hillsboro Dist. |
| Continental | Joshua Yealott | 1403 | Warrenton Dist. |
| Continental | Shadrick Yealott | 1404 | Warrenton Dist. |
| Continental | Robert Ruff | 664 | Hillsboro Dist. |
| Continental | Charles Reese | 18 | Warrenton Dist. |
| Continental | Johnathan Richards | 154 | Hillsboro Dist. |
| Militia | John Register | 1975 | Wilmington Dist. |
| Militia | Nicholas Richards | 586 | Wilmington Dist. |
| Militia | Hardy Richards | 1676 | Newbern Dist. |
| Militia | Leonard Rue | 8472 | Salisbury Dist. |
| Militia | John Raford | 1293 | Newbern Dist. |
| Militia | Peter Riggan | 5615 | Salisbury Dist. |
| Militia | Jessie Rowe | 309 | Newbern Dist. |
| Militia | Robert Russel | 67 | Salisbury Dist. |
| Militia | George Robinson | 5187 | Salisbury Dist. |
| Militia | Bartram Robinson | 2946 | Wilmington Dist. |
| Militia | Archibald Ranaldson | 4927 | Wilmington Dist. |
| Militia | Mether'on Roland | 520 | Newbern Dist. |
| Continental | Ralph Thomas | 580 | Hillsboro Dist. |
| Continental | Cornelius Ryan | 1126 | Halifax Dist. |
| Continental | Capt. Hezekiah Rice | 20 | Halifax Dist. |
| Continental | Daniel Rhodes | 755 | N. C. A. |
| Militia | Benja. Tiby Randolph | 606 | Wilmington Dist. |
| Militia | Thomas Russ | 4954 | Wilmington Dist. |
| Militia | Robert Ross | 8624 | Salisbury Dist. |
| Militia | John Reford | 5520 | Salisbury Dist. |
| Militia | Philip Raeford | 3922 | Wilmington Dist. |
| Militia | John Ron | 1451 | Newbern Dist. |
| Militia | Absolem Rouse | 7566 | Salisbury Dist. |
| Militia | Conrad Reather | 4583 | Morgan Dist. |
| Militia | James Rolston | 2257 | Salisbury Dist. |
| Militia | Edward Robeson | 4094 | Wilmington Dist. |
| Militia | Joseph Rooks | 772 | Wilmington Dist. |
| Militia | William Russell | 3939 | Wilmington Dist. |
| Continental | William Reason | 18 | Halifax Dist. |
| Continental | Cornelius Roomer | 377 | Hillsboro Dist. |
| Continental | William Reason | 16 | Halifax Dist. |
| Continental | John Reason | 488 | Hillsboro Dist. |
| Continental | William Red | 330 | Warrenton Dist. |
| Continental | Samuel Rowland | 111 | N. C. A. |
| Continental | John Russ | 8 | Hillsboro Dist. |

| | | *No.* | |
|---|---|---|---|
| Militia | Sonthy Ren | 603 | Newbern Dist. |
| Militia | Joseph Ross | 4873 | Salisbury Dist. |
| Militia | Hugh Royal | 5557 | Wilmington Dist. |
| Militia | B Reding | 896 | Newbern Dist. |
| Militia | Alex Reed | 7186 | Salisbury Dist. |
| Militia | Nat Reives | 3077 | Wilmington Dist. |
| Militia | Robert Ross | 3857 | Salisbury Dist. |
| Militia | Isaac Rich | .... | Salisbury Dist. |
| Militia | Benjamine Randall | 3257 | Wilmington Dist. |
| Militia | Robert Rollings | 2170 | Wilmington Dist. |
| Militia | Ruben Raiser | 4393 | Wilmington Dist. |
| Militia | Jacob Roachel | 1044 | Newbern Dist. |
| Militia | William Runnels | 82 | Wilmington Dist. |
| Militia | William Roach | 3747 | Wilmington Dist. |
| Militia | Thomas Rowland | 2951 | Wilmington Dist. |
| Militia | Thomas Ragines | 1258 | Wilmington Dist. |
| Militia | Sat Rich | 3430 | Wilmington Dist. |
| Militia | James Roe | 706 | Newbern Dist. |
| Militia | Peter Riggon | 7570 | Salisbury Dist. |
| Militia | Thomas Rowe | 1025 | Newbern Dist. |
| Militia | Young Ryal | 516 | Wilmington Dist. |
| Militia | Dredge Runnels | 823 | Halifax Dist. |
| Militia | John Register | 3579 | Wilmington Dist. |
| Militia | John Rand | 7100 | Salisbury Dist. |
| Militia | Peter Rape | 1497 | Salisbury Dist. |
| Continental | William Ryles | 416 | Hillsboro Dist. |
| Continental | Jacob Richards | 900 | Halifax Dist. |
| Continental | John King | 823 | Halifax Dist. |
| Continental | James Roach | 706 | Newbern Dist. |
| Continental | Timothy Rich | 1337 | Halifax Dist. |
| Continental | Elijah Rodwell | 612 | Halifax Dist. |
| Continental | Daniel Rice | 227 | Halifax Dist. |
| Continental | Isaac Reddick | 780 | Halifax Dist. |
| Continental | William Robbs | 1346 | Halifax Dist. |
| Continental | Rowland Godfrey | 641 | Hillsboro Dist. |
| Militia | L. (?) Roe | 824 | Newbern Dist. |
| Militia | William Murrell | 3314 | Morgan Dist. |
| Militia | James Murrow | 2034 | Wilmington Dist. |
| Continental | Georg Muskinock | 408 | Hillsboro Dist. |
| Continental | John Mullins | 876 | Hillsboro Dist. |
| Continental | Barabas Murrill | 750 | Hillsboro Dist. |
| Militia | Alex Bigham | 5153 | Wilmington Dist. |
| Militia | David Murdough | 2036 | Wilmington Dist. |
| Militia | Joseph McKinney | 9 | Salisbury Dist. |
| Militia | Duncan McLelland | 4750 | Wilmington Dist. |
| Militia | Robert McCloud | 4797 | Salisbury Dist. |
| Militia | Joseph McDowel | 403 | Wilmington Dist. |
| Militia | Hugh McCracken | 8631 | Salisbury Dist. |
| Militia | Daniel McKetham | 4370 | Wilmington Dist. |
| Militia | L.... McCullen | 3576 | Wilmington Dist. |
| Militia | Reuben Small | 12 | Newbern Dist. |
| Militia | Wm. McKinsey | 4756 | Wilmington Dist. |
| Militia | Alex Steel | 1495 | Newbern Dist. |
| Militia | Aaron McWhorter | 6102 | Salisbury Dist. |

| | | No. | |
|---|---|---|---|
| Militia | Alexander McCurday | 4473 | Salisbury Dist. |
| Militia | Capt. C. N. McCrany | 428 | Wilmington Dist. |
| Militia | John McCoy | 721 | Wilmington Dist. |
| Militia | Daniel McMillan | 3366 | Wilmington Dist. |
| Militia | Neil McMullan | 4265 | Wilmington Dist. |
| Militia | Edward McKay | 4324 | Wilmington Dist. |
| Militia | Francis McKay | 4842 | Wilmington Dist. |
| Militia | William McCleary | 6044 | Salisbury Dist. |
| Militia | Daniel McLevd | 3838 | Wilmington Dist. |
| Militia | Danel McDuffy | 4293 | Wilmington Dist. |
| Militia | Thomas Johnson | 617 | Newbern Dist. |
| Militia | Joseph Johnson | 1235 | Newbern Dist. |
| Militia | Isaac Johnson | 7340 | Salisbury Dist. |
| Militia | James Johnson | 5603 | Salisbury Dist. |
| Militia | Robert Johnson | 4638 | Salisbury Dist. |
| Militia | John Brumley | 4041 | Morgan Dist. |
| Militia | Chesley Dobbs | 4852 | Morgan Dist. |
| Continental | William King | 288 | Halifax Dist. |
| Militia | David Dudley | 5901 | Wilmington Dist. |
| Militia | Jacob Dry | 8633 | Salisbury Dist. |
| Militia | Abram Hill | 78 | Salisbury Dist. |
| Continental | Henry Hill | 921 | Halifax Dist. |
| Militia | Richard Hill | 2374 | Newbern Dist. |
| Militia | Simon Eagles | 8397 | Salisbury Dist. |
| Militia | Thomas Eakens | 8395 | Salisbury Dist. |
| Militia | John Edmonson | 449 | Newbern Dist. |
| Militia | Daniel Earely | 6447 | Salisbury Dist. |
| Militia | S.... Engor | 5876 | Wilmington Dist. |
| Militia | Martin Ekhard | 4212 | Morgan Dist. |
| Continental | Thomas Biby | 409 | Hillsboro Dist. |
| Continental | Benjamine Braddy | 72 | Hillsboro Dist. |
| Continental | Caleb Berry | 187 | Hillsboro Dist. |
| Continental | Michael Buckner | 123 | Assembly |
| Continental | P.... Burch | 79 | Assembly |
| Militia | Henry Bates | 1535 | Newbern Dist. |
| Militia | Edward Blinton Johnson | 1944 | Newbern Dist. |
| Continental | Archibald Butts | 399 | Halifax Dist. |
| Continental | Epharim Bullock | 1659 | Newbern Dist. |
| Militia | Nathan Bullock | 898 | Newbern Dist. |
| Militia | Nathan Barranton | 2248 | Newbern Dist. |
| Militia | Artila Burnett | 891 | Newbern Dist. |
| Militia | Cornelius Bray | 324 | Assembly |
| Militia | John Beasley | 342 | Newbern Dist. |
| Militia | Peter Banks | 943 | Newbern Dist. |
| Militia | Edward Baldwin | 2128 | Newbern Dist. |
| Militia | Thomas Boyakan | 1050 | Newbern Dist. |
| Militia | Thomas Blango | 1187 | Newbern Dist. |
| Militia | ...... Barfield | 1029 | Newbern Dist. |
| Militia | Edward Blurton | 1187 | Newbern Dist. |
| Militia | Joseph Berwick | 1236 | Newbern Dist. |
| Militia | John Barllett | 1058 | Newbern Dist. |
| Militia | Georg Blackbourne | 1061 | Newbern Dist. |
| Militia | James Bosworth | 140 | Newbern Dist. |
| Militia | Edward Blurton | 1157 | Newbern Dist. |

| | | No. | |
|---|---|---|---|
| Continental | Levi Branton .................. | 836 | Hillsboro Dist. |
| Continental | Austin Bilfort .................. | 173 | Assembly |
| Continental | Jessie Bunn .................... | 7 | Hillsboro Dist. |
| Continental | Noah Bartlett .................. | 852 | Hillsboro Dist. |
| Continental | George Beck ................... | 632 | Hillsboro Dist. |
| Continental | Michael Brinkley ............... | 2 | Hillsboro Dist. |
| Continental | Mathew Brickell ............... | 64 | Halifax Dist. |
| Continental | Capt. Thomas Brickett .......... | 90 | Halifax Dist. |
| Continental | Isaac Burges .................. | 196 | Hillsboro Dist. |
| Against | | | |
| Cherokees | | | |
| | James Burnes .................. | .... | Hillsboro Dist. |
| Against | | | |
| Cherokee Ind. | | | |
| | Benjamine Blackburn ..................... | 1132 | Hillsboro Dist. |
| | Samuel Brownen ............... | 457 | Assembly |
| | James Burbage ................. | 904 | Warrenton Dist. |
| Continental | David Brodnell ............... | 108 | Hillsboro Dist. |
| Continental | Alexander Balentine ............. | 213 | Hillsboro Dist. |
| Continental | Bailey Benzor ................. | 1120 | Halifax Dist. |
| Continental | Thomas Bowers ............... | 249 | Hillsboro Dist. |
| Continental | Ezekial Boggs ................. | 270 | Halifax Dist. |
| Continental | Luke Bates .................... | 539 | Halifax Dist. |
| Continental | Jacob Bright ................. | 1433 | Warrenton Dist. |
| Continental | John Bolton .................. | 1464 | Warrenton Dist. |
| Continental | William Banks ................ | 1424 | Warrenton Dist. |
| Continental | William Bobs ................. | 1173 | Halifax Dist. |
| Continental | Benjamin Boutton .............. | 1954 | Warrenton Dist. |
| Continental | Arthur Bright ................ | 1479 | Warrenton Dist. |
| Continental | James Burley ................. | 1489 | Warrenton Dist. |
| Continental | Solomon Borough .............. | 1795 | Warrenton Dist |
| Continental | David Blalock ................ | 1791 | Warrenton Dist. |
| Continental | Navey Bateman ................ | 1222 | Warrenton Dist. |
| Continental | William Boyce ................. | 22 | Hillsboro Dist. |
| Continental | Thomas Brinkley ............... | 586 | Warrenton Dist. |
| Continental | William Boomer ............... | 638 | Hillsboro Dist. |
| Continental | John Blanchard ................ | 234 | Hillsboro Dist. |
| Continental | Hillery Brinson .............. | 797 | Hillsboro Dist. |
| Continental | Thomas Biby .................. | 560 | Hillsboro Dist. |
| Continental | Jessie Benton ................. | 270 | Hillsboro Dist. |
| Continental | Drury Binum .................. | 425 | Halifax Dist. |
| Continental | Charles Burk ................. | 987 | Halifax Dist. |
| Continental | ...... Giles .................. | 1134 | Halifax Dist. |
| Continental | Charles Butlar ............... | 1047 | Halifax Dist. |

### JOHN WRIGHT FAMILY

| | | | |
|---|---|---|---|
| Militia | John Wright .................. | 4695 | Morgan Dist. |
| Continental | John Wright .................. | 1618 | Warrenton Dist. |
| Militia | James Wright ................. | 2835 | Assembly |
| Continental | Job Wright ................... | 76 | Assembly |
| Continental | Jacob Wright ................. | 60 | Assembly |

### ROBERTS' FAMILY

| | | | |
|---|---|---|---|
| Continental | Shadrick Roberts ............... | 435 | Hillsboro Dist. |
| Continental | Ishmael Roberts ............... | 41 | Hillsboro Dist. |

|  |  | *No.* |  |
|---|---|---|---|
| Militia | Jessie Roberts | 5902 | Wilmington Dist. |
| Militia | Richard Roberts | 5925 | Wilmington Dist. |
| Continental | Vincent Roberts | 1064 | Halifax Dist. |
| Continental | Binchen Roberts | 1298 | Halifax Dist. |
| Militia | Briton Roberts | 435 | Newbern Dist. |
| Continental | Samson Roberts | 584 | Assembly passed |
| Militia | William Roberts | 632 | Newbern Dist. |
| Militia | Henry Roberts | 939 | Newbern Dist. |
| Continental | Ruben Roberts | 1194 | Halifax Dist. |
| Militia | Rowl'd Roberts | 1270 | Newbern Dist. |

### PARTIN FAMILY

| Continental | Benjamine Partin | 553 | N. C. Assem. |
|---|---|---|---|

### HAYS FAMILY

| Militia | William Hays | 8677 | Salisbury Dist. |
|---|---|---|---|
| Mil. & Cont. | David Hays | 453 | Salisbury Dist. |
| Militia | Adam Hays | 1435 | Salisbury Dist. |
| Continental | Lieut. Robert Hays | 188 | N. C. Assem. |
| Militia | John Hays | 8998 | N. C. Assem. |
| Militia | Henry Hays | 5120 | Salisbury Dist. |
| Militia | Jacob Hays | 4554 | Salisbury Dist. |
| Continental | Thomas Hays | 903 | Halifax Dist. |
| Militia | Robert Patrick Hays | 7739 | Salisbury Dist. |

### WRIGHT FAMILY

| Militia | Capt. Thomas Wright | 5021 | Wilmington Dist. |
|---|---|---|---|
| Militia | Capt. William Wright | 3464 | Wilmington Dist. |
| Continental | Peter Wright | 84 | N. C. Assem. |
| Continental | Levi Wright | 952 | Warrenton Dist. |
| Militia | Archibald Wright | 3470 | Wilmington Dist. |
| Militia | Abraham Wright | 5912 | Wilmington Dist. |
| Continental | Caleb Wright | 238 | Hillsboro Dist. |
| Militia | Jo Wright | 3483 | Wilmington Dist. |

### SIMS FAMILY

| Continental | Drury Sims | 154 | Assem. N. C. |
|---|---|---|---|
| Militia | James Sims | 4162 | Wilmington Dist. |
| Militia | William Sims | 1644 | Wilmington Dist. |
| Militia | Isaac Sims | 3074 | Wilmington Dist. |
| Continental | Joseph Sims | 1304 | Newbern Dist. |

### LANE FAMILY

| Continental | Benjamine Lane | 1109 | Halifax Dist. |
|---|---|---|---|
| Militia | James Lane | 3759 | Wilmington Dist. |
| Continental | Jethro Lane | 1401 | Halifax Dist. |
| Continental | Jacob Lane | 761 | Halifax Dist. |

### SHAW FAMILY

| Continental | Robert Shaw | 141 | Hillsboro Dist. |
|---|---|---|---|
| Militia | Neil Shaw | 3176 | Wilmington Dist. |
| Continental | Zacecheus Shaw | 1403 | Halifax Dist. |
| Militia | John Shaw | 4471 | Salisbury Dist. |
| Militia | James Shaw | 1571 | Wilmington Dist. |
| Continental | Finley Shaw | 433 | Hillsboro Dist. |
| Militia | Thomas Shaw | 1263 | Salisbury Dist. |

## LEE FAMILY

| | | No. | |
|---|---|---|---|
| Continental | Thomas Lee | 618 | Hillsboro Dist. |
| Militia | Solomon Lee | 1739 | Wilmington Dist. |
| Continental | Richard Lee | 135 | Hillsboro Dist. |
| Militia | James Lee | 1145 | Wilmington Dist. |
| Militia | Jessie Lee | 4707 | Wilmington Dist. |
| Militia | Sampson Lee | 2774 | Wilmington Dist. |
| Militia | Joseph Lee | 4476 | Wilmington Dist. |
| Militia | William Lee | .... | Newbern Dist. |
| Continental | Abraham Lee | 201 | Hillsboro Dist. |
| Continental | Major Lee | 265 | N. C. Assem. |
| Continental | Noah Lee | 5900 | Wilmington Dist. |
| Continental | Hardy Lee | 96 | N. C. Assem. |
| Continental | Timothy Lee | 97 | N. C. Assem. |
| Continental | John Lee | 989 | Halifax Dist. |
| Militia | David Lee | 5792 | Wilmington Dist. |
| Militia | C.... Lee | 3369 | Wilmington Dist. |

## LAMB FAMILY

| | | | |
|---|---|---|---|
| Militia | Arthur Lamb | 4465 | Wilmington Dist. |
| Militia | Nudy Lamb | 4814 | Wilmington Dist. |
| Militia | William Lamb | 5868 | Wilmington Dist. |
| Continental | Colonel Gideon Lamb | 95 | Halifax Dist. |
| Militia | Thomas Lamb | 1595 | Wilmington Dist. |
| Continental | Abner Lamb | 299 | N. C. Assem. |

## POOL FAMILY

| | | | |
|---|---|---|---|
| Militia | Samuel Pool | 1190 | Newbern Dist. |
| Continental | Elisha Pool | 347 | N. C. Assem. |
| Continental | Andrew Pool | 39 | N. C. Assem. |
| Militia | Levi Pool | 1421 | Newbern Dist. |
| Militia | Joshua Pool | 813 | Wilmington Dist. |

## LEWIS FAMILY

| | | | |
|---|---|---|---|
| Continental | Nathan Lewis | 167 | Hillsboro Dist. |
| Continental | Willis Lewis | 90 | N. C. Assem. |
| Militia | John Lewis | 5425 | Wilmington Dist. |
| Continental | Edward Lewis | 139 | Hillsboro Dist. |
| Continental | Hardy Lewis | 1314 | Halifax Dist. |
| Militia | Richard Lewis | 4443 | Wilmington Dist. |
| Militia | Amos Lewis | 829 | Newbern Dist. |
| Militia | Elisha Lewis | 1838 | Newbern Dist. |
| Militia | Jessie Lewis | 526 | Newbern Dist. |
| Militia | Joseph Lewis | 321 | Newbern Dist. |
| Militia | Aaron Lewis | 1622 | Wilmington Dist. |
| Continental | Ephraim Lewis | 363 | Hillsboro Dist. |
| Militia | Joshua Lewis | 549 | Newbern Dist. |
| Continental | Charles Lewis | 1016 | Halifax Dist. |
| Continental | Thomas Lewis | 589 | N. C. Assem. |
| Militia | Walter Lewis | 7226 | Salisbury Dist. |
| Continental | Frances Lewis | 1168 | Halifax Dist. |
| Continental | Joel Lewis | 555 | Halifax Dist. |
| Continental | William Lewis | 704 | Halifax Dist. |
| Militia | Abraham Lewis | 3000 | Salisbury Dist. |
| Militia | Frederick Lewis | 940 | Wilmington Dist. |
| Continental | William Lewis | 764 | N. C. Assem. |

## RAY FAMILY

| | | No. | |
|---|---|---|---|
| Militia | Duncan Ray | 1269 | Wilmington Dist. |
| Militia | Isaac Ray | 7025 | Salisbury Dist. |
| Continental | Benjamin Ray | 326 | Hillsboro Dist. |
| Militia | John Ray | 3840 | Wilmington Dist. |
| Militia | Thomas Ray | 4245 | Salisbury Dist. |
| Militia | James Ray | 4850 | Salisbury Dist |

## WHITAKER FAMIILY

| | | | |
|---|---|---|---|
| Salisbury | Mark Whitaker | 7056 | Salisbury Dist. |
| Continental | Joseph Whitaker | 109 | N. C. Assem. |
| Continental | John Whitaker | 593 | |

## MISCELLANEOUS

| | | | |
|---|---|---|---|
| Continental | William Waddenton | 17 | Hillsboro Dist. |
| Continental | George Williamson | 360 | Hillsboro Dist. |
| Continental | Daniel Weston | 904 | Halifax Dist. |
| Continental | Mathew Worley | 561 | |
| | John Whaley | 796 | |
| Continental | John Weir | 872 | Halifax Dist. |
| Militia | Capt. Patrick Watson | 440 | Salisbury Dist. |
| Continental | Mathew Lucas | 50 | Hillsboro Dist. |
| Continental | John Woodward | 174 | Hillsboro Dist. |
| Continental | John Windom | 220 | Hillsboro Dist. |
| Militia | Johnson Womack | 4069 | Morgan Dist. |
| Militia | William Winehiston | 2762 | Salisbury Dist. |
| Militia | Elisha Woodward | 3660 | Wilmington Dist. |
| Continental | John Swanson | 531 | Hillsboro Dist. |
| Continental | Dempsey Sikes | 23 | Hillsboro Dist. |
| Continental | Henry Short | 293 | Hillsboro Dist. |
| Continental | James Strange | 136 | Halifax Dist. |
| Militia | Daniel Rayman | 620 | Salisbury Dist. |
| Militia | Demsey Taylor | 258 | Wilmington Dist. |
| Militia | Joseph Williams | 1176 | Newbern Dist. |
| Militia | Joseph Williams | 5503 | Wilmington Dist. |
| Militia | Capt. George Walker | 452 | Salisbury Dist. |
| Militia | William Taylor | 43 | Wilmington Dist. |
| Continental | Henry White | 1035 | Salisbury Dist. |
| Militia | William Turner | 1502 | Wilmington Dist. |

## WILEY AND WILDER FAMILY

| | | | |
|---|---|---|---|
| Continental | Philip Wilder | 1149 | Warrenton Dist. |
| Continental | Stephen Wiley | 624 | Hillsboro Dist. |
| Continental | James Wiley | 686 | Halifax Dist. |
| Militia | Elijah Wiley | 265 | Wilmington Dist. |
| Militia | Capt. Oliver Wiley | 2729 | Salisbury Dist. |
| Continental | Hardy Wiley | 1328 | Halifax Dist. |
| Militia | Alexander Wiley | 120 | Wilmington Dist. |
| Militia | John Wiley | 84 | Wilmington Dist. |
| Militia | Drummer, Hardy Wiley | 3309 | Wilmington Dist. |

## WIGGENS FAMILY

| | | | |
|---|---|---|---|
| Continental | Willis Wiggens | 394 | Hillsboro Dist. |
| Militia | James Wiggens | 905 | Newbern Dist. |
| Continental | James Wiggens | 1178 | Halifax Dist. |

| | | **No.** | |
|---|---|---|---|
| Militia | William Wiggens | 1672 | Wilmington Dist. |
| Continental | Henry Wiggens | 671 | Hillsboro Dist. |
| Continental | George Wiggens | 302 | Hillsboro Dist. |
| Continental | Noah Wiggens | 429 | Hillsboro Dist. |

## WARREN FAMILY

| | | | |
|---|---|---|---|
| Militia | Abram Warren | 304 | Newbern Dist. |
| Militia | Jeremiah Warren | 708 | Newbern Dist. |
| Militia | Henry Warren | 679 | Newbern Dist. |
| Militia | Horsonton Warren | 237 | Newbern Dist. |
| Militia | Robert Warren | 3229 | Morgan Dist. |
| Continental | William Warren | 229 | Hillsboro Dist. |

## WALLACE FAMILY

| | | | |
|---|---|---|---|
| Militia | John Wallace | 4192 | Wilmington Dist. |
| Militia | William Wallace | 2699 | Salisbury Dist. |
| Continental | Fifer George Wallace | 412 | Halifax Dist. |
| Militia | Joseph Wallace | 5134 | Salisbury Dist. |

## WEST FAMILY

| | | | |
|---|---|---|---|
| Continental | William West | 239 | Hillsboro Dist. |
| Continental | Drummer Levi West | 5446 | Wilmington Dist. |
| Militia | John West | 529 | Wilmington Dist. |
| Militia | James West | 932 | Wilmington Dist. |
| Militia | Samuel West | 2229 | Wilmington Dist. |
| Militia | Lieut. William West | 4183 | Wilmington Dist. |
| Militia | Joseph West | 889 | Newbern Dist. |
| Continental | Riva West | 189 | Halifax Dist. |

## WILLIS FAMILY

| | | | |
|---|---|---|---|
| Militia | Samuel Willis | 956 | Newbern Dist. |
| Continental | Richard Willis | 147 | Hillsboro Dist. |
| Militia | Benjamine Willis | 2935 | Filmington Dist. |
| Militia | James Willis | .... | Newbern Dist. |
| Militia | Lieut. Stephen Willis | .... | Wilmington Dist. |
| Militia | Robert Willis | 2936 | Wilmington Dist. |
| Militia | George Willis | 1789 | Wilmington Dist. |
| Militia | Ephraim Willis | 716 | Newbern Dist. |
| Militia | Jeremiah Willis | 1796 | Newbern Dist. |
| Militia | Caleb Willis | 714 | Newbern Dist. |
| Militia | Agerton Willis (may mean Adjutant) | 2906 | Newbern Dist. |
| Militia | William Willis | 637 | Salisbury Dist. |
| Militia | Capt. John Willis | 4374 | Wilmington Dist. |
| Militia | William Wiley | 2684 | Salisbury Dist. |

## WHITE FAMILY

| | | | |
|---|---|---|---|
| Continental | James White | 979 | Halifax Dist. |
| Continental | William White | 431 | Warrenton Dist. |
| Militia | Robert White | 8912 | Salisbury Dist. |
| Militia | Moses White | 8931 | Salisbury Dist. |
| Continental | Drummer Jacob White | 8016 | Halifax Dist. |
| Militia | Thomas White | 4014 | Salisbury Dist. |
| Militia | John White | 2556 | Salisbury Dist. |
| Continental | Malichi White | 373 | Hillsboro Dist. |

|  |  | No. |  |
|---|---|---|---|
| Militia | George White | 576 | Newbern Dist. |
| Militia | James White | 3096 | Wilmington Dist. |
| Continental | Haines White | 502 | Hillsboro Dist. |
| Militia | G.... White | 3083 | Wilmington Dist. |
| Militia | Mathew White | 3175 | Wilmington Dist. |
| Militia | Joseph White | 3060 | Wilmington Dist. |
| Militia | Andrew White | .... | Salisbury Dist. |
| Continental | George White | 446 | Halifax Dist. |
| Militia | Benjamine White | 362 | Newbern Dist. |
| Continental | Stephen White | 363 | Halifax Dist. |
| Militia | Samuel White | ..04 | Salisbury Dist. |
| Militia | David White | 2395 | Wilmington Dist. |
| Continental | Daniel White | 217 | Halifax Dist. |
| Continental | Hampton White | 1053 | Halifax Dist. |

### WALKER FAMILY

| Militia | Thomas Walker | 4954 | Morgan Dist. |
|---|---|---|---|
| Militia | John Walker | 3252 | Wilmington Dist. |
| Militia | William Walker | 1465 | Wilmington Dist. |
| Militia | Baker Walker | 5940 | Wilmington Dist. |
| Continental | Moab Walker | 175 | |
| Militia | Andrew Walker | 5948 | Salisbury Dist. |
| Militia | David Walker | 5660 | Wilmington Dist. |
| Militia | Henry Walker | 807 | Salisbury Dist. |
| Continental | James Walker | 437 | Hillsboro Dist. |
| Continental | Savin Walker | 285 | Halifax Dist. |
| Continental | Richard Walker | 286 | Halifax Dist. |
| Militia | Hugh Walker | 4974 | Wilmington Dist. |
| Militia | Robert Walker | 678 | Salisbury Dist. |
| Militia | Michael Walker | 1349 | Salisbury Dist. |

These were found in the box of W's.

### HARVEYS

| Continental | Joshua Harvey | 753 | Halifax Dist. |
|---|---|---|---|
| Continental | Absalom Harvey | 447 | Hillsboro Dist. |
| Continental | John Harvey | 505 | Hillsboro Dist. |
| Continental | James Harvey | 293 | Hillsboro Dist. |
| Continental | Hugh Harvey | 4208 | Salisbury Dist. |
| Militia | Solnum Carter | 2146 | Wilmington Dist. |
| Militia | Mack Carter | 4408 | Wilmington Dist. |
| Militia | Mack Carter | 657 | Wilmington Dist. |
| Militia | John Carter | 1209 | Newbern Dist. |
| Militia | Bozin Brock Carter | 1200 | Wilmington Dist. |
| Continental | Giles Carter | 41 | Halifax Dist. |
| Continental | John Carter | 839 | Hillsboro Dist. |
| Continental | Sergt. John Carter | 569 | Halifax Dist. |
| Militia | Solman Carter | 2274 | Wilmington Dist. |
| Militia | Joseph Carter | 923 | Wilmington Dist. |
| Militia | John Carter | 4086 | Wilmington Dist. |
| Militia | Daniel Carter | 4003 | Salisbury Dist. |
| Continental | John Carter, Soldier | 655 | Hillsborough Dist. |
| Militia | Thomas Carter | 1149 | Wilmington Dist. |
| Militia | Joseph Carter | 2972 | Wilmington Dist. |
| Militia | John Carter | 704 | Newbern Dist. |

| | | No. | |
|---|---|---|---|
| Militia | Stephen Carter | 5542 | Wilmington Dist. |
| Militia | Isaac Carter | 4409 | Wilmington Dist. |
| Militia | Solomon Carter | 245 | Wilmington Dist. |
| Continental | Willis Carter | 1429 | Warrenton Dist. |
| Militia | William Carter | 4633 | Salisbury Dist. |
| Militia | Joseph Carter | 1747 | Wilmington Dist. |
| Continental | John Carter | 636 | Halifax Dist. |
| Continental | John Carter, Soldier | 61 | Hillsborough Dist. |
| Militia | Joseph Carter | 6319 | Salisbury Dist. |
| Militia | John Carter | 918 | Wilmington Dist. |
| Militia | Thomas Carter | 4117 | Morgan Dist. |
| Continental | Abraham Carter | 166 | Hillsborough Dist. |
| Militia | Abraham Carter | 4069 | Wilmington Dist. |
| Continental | Abraham Carter, Soldier | 150 | Hillsborough Dist. |
| Militia | Richard Creech, Lt. | 1842 | Wilmington Dist. |
| Militia | Joseph Croker | 8460 | Salisbury Dist. |
| Militia | James Ceilain | 41 | Morgan Dist. |
| Militia | Benj. Cochranuas | 8756 | Salisbury Dist. |
| Continental | John Crabb | 469 | Halifax Dist. |
| Continental | John Clay | 1951 | Warrenton Dist. |
| Continental | Benjamin Carroll | 807 | Halifax Dist. |
| | Lieut. Samuel Casnell | 225 | |
| Continental | James Crabb, Soldier | 1626 | Warrenton Dist. |
| Continental | John Carey | 622 | Hillsborough Dist. |
| Continental | Frederick Callem | 456 | Hillsborough Dist. |
| Militia | Brittin Carroll | 629 | Newbern Dist. |
| Continental | John Carroll, Soldier | 1018 | Halifax Dist. |
| Militia | Britian Carol | 535 | Newbern Dist. |
| Continental | Elijah Clay, Soldier | 53 | Hillsborough Dist. |
| Militia | Thos. Croley | 4544 | Salisbury Dist. |
| Militia | Francis Canfield | 4462 | Wilmington Dist. |
| Militia | Nathaniel Cook | 3741 | Salisbury Dist. |
| Militia | Wm. Curathorus | 6641 | Salisbury Dist. |
| Militia | Cullen Crumly | 445 | Wilmington Dist. |
| Continental | Brettor Carroll | 804 | Halifax Dist. |
| Continental | Abselom Cameron | 410 | Hillsborough Dist. |
| Continental | Abselom Cameron | 279 | Hillsborough Dist. |
| Militia | John Cameron | 4870 | Wilmington Dist. |
| Continental | Alexander Cameron | 100 | Warrenton Dist. |
| Militia | Daniel Cameron | 1832 | Wilmington Dist. |
| Continental | John Cameron | 113 | |
| Militia | Charles Copeland | 630 | Newbern Dist. |
| | Kedar Copeland, Soldier | 810 | Hillsborough Dist. |
| Continental | Richard Coupland, Private | 200 | Halifax Dist. |
| | George Coupland, Soldier | 1141 | Halifax Dist. |
| Militia | David Copelin | 3638 | Salisbury Dist. |
| Militia | Dennis Copelin | 3621 | Salisbury Dist. |
| Militia | Daniel Copeland | 174 | Hillsborough Dist. |
| Continental | William Carpenter | 1939 | Warrenton Dist. |
| Militia | Christian Carpenter | 4634 | Morgan Dist. |
| Militia | James Conner | 2337 | Wilmington Dist. |
| Continental | James Conner, Soldier | 662 | Halifax Dist. |
| Militia | James Conner | 2258 | Wilmington Dist. |
| Militia | Docias Conner | 2749 | Wilmington Dist. |

| | | No. | |
|---|---|---|---|
| Militia | Docia Conner | 2431 | Wilmington Dist. |
| Militia | James Conner | 2930 | Salisbury Dist. |
| Continental | William Conner | 152 | Hillsborough Dist. |
| Militia | James Conner | 5742 | Salisbury Dist. |
| Militia | Theodolius Conner | 1810 | Wilmington Dist. |
| Militia | James Conner | 2153 | Wilmington Dist. |
| Militia | D.... Conner | 2823 | Wilmington Dist. |
| Militia | James Conner | 3667 | Wilmington Dist. |
| Continental | James Conner | 610 | Halifax Dist. |
| Continental | William Conner, Soldier | 81 | Hillsborough Dist. |
| Continental | Leuis Conner | 612 | Hillsborough Dist. |
| Continental | Leuis Conner | 796 | Hillsborough Dist. |
| | Samul Chapman, Capt. | 520 | Halifax Dist. |
| Militia | Joseph Champin | 5007 | Wilmington Dist. |
| Militia | Joseph Chevess | 1035 | Wilmington Dist. |
| Militia | Charles Chevess | 70 | Wilmington Dist. |
| Militia | Archibald Carr | 1375 | Wilmington Dist. |
| Militia | John Carr | 985 | Wilmington Dist. |
| Continental | James Carr | 198 | Hillsborough Dist. |
| Militia | William Carr | 3036 | Salisbury Dist. |
| Militia | Jonathan Carr | 3373 | Wilmington Dist. |
| Continental | James Carr, Soldier | 225 | Warrenton & Hillsboro D. |
| Militia | Thomas Coor | 2063 | Newbern Dist. |
| Militia | James Coor | 348 | Newbern Dist. |
| Continental | James Coor, Soldier | 21 | Warrenton Dist. |
| Militia | James Crno | 2002 | Salisbury Dist. |
| Continental | James Craig | 120 | Hillsboro Dist. |
| Militia | John Craig | 4865 | Wimington Dist. |
| Continental | James Craig, Soldier | 331 | Warrenton Dist. |
| Militia | Alexander Craig | 4619 | Salisbury Dist. |
| Militia | Thomas Cook | 1042 | Wilmington Dist. |
| Militia | Thos. Cook | 1091 | Wilmington Dist. |
| Continental | John Cook | 2956 | Warrenton Dist. |
| Militia | Archibald Cook | 17 | Wilmington Dist. |
| Militia | Robert Cook | 1391 | Salisbury Dist. |
| Militia | Jacob Cook | 2568 | Salisbury Dist. |
| Militia | Nathaniel Cook | 4651 | Morgan Dist. |
| Militia | Lazarus Cook | 1937 | Wilmington Dist. |
| Militia | Sergt. John Cook | 3780 | Wilmington Dist. |
| Militia | William Cook | 3232 | Wilmington Dist. |
| Militia | Henry Cook | 2202 | Wilmington Dist. |
| Militia | William Cook | 2218 | Wilmington Dist. |
| Continental | George Cook | 653 | |
| Continental | Rich'd D. Cook | 461 | |
| Militia | William Cook | 4407 | Wilmington Dist. |
| Militia | James Cook | 7 | Morgan Dist. |
| Militia | John Cook | 6375 | Salisbury Dist. |
| Militia | Wm. Cook | 1789 | Wilmington Dist. |
| Militia | John Cook | 4619 | Morgan Dist. |
| Militia | Philip Cook | 7621 | Salisbury Dist. |
| Militia | John Cook | 2232 | Wilmington Dist. |
| Militia | Adam Crine | 8336 | Salisbury Dist. |
| Militia | Benjamin Cray | 5233 | Wilmington Dist. |
| Militia | David Cinmore | 5359 | Salisbury Dist. |

| | | *No.* | |
|---|---|---|---|
| Militia | James Coltrin ................... | 6433 | Salisbury Dist. |
| Militia | David Calhorn .................. | 2454 | Salisbury Dist. |
| Militia | Jos. Calahan ................... | 4696 | Salisbury Dist. |
| Militia | Philip Christopher .............. | 7591 | Salisbury Dist. |
| Militia | Abraham Colleh ............... | 4495 | Morgan Dist. |
| Militia | Elisha Carroll ................. | 3356 | Wilmington Dist. |
| Militia | Patrick Conely ................. | 4539 | Salisbury Dist. |
| Militia | John Crinkleton ................ | 15 | Morgan Dist. |
| Militia | David Coswel ................... | 2394 | Salisbury Dist. |
| Continental | Thomas Chestnutt .............. | 587 | |
| Continental | Solman Casey .................. | 65 | |
| Continental | Elias Crockley ................. | 681 | |
| Militia | John Critchett ................. | 616 | |
| Continental | Philip Cakes ................... | 734 | Halifax Dist. |
| Continental | Hezekiah Cooksey, Soldier ........ | 576 | Hillsborough Dist. |
| Continental | William Cobb ................. | 114 | |
| Continental | Thomas Cooksey, Soldier .......... | 517 | Hillsborough Dist. |
| Continental | James Crain ................... | 320 | |
| Continental | Richard Clifton, Soldier .......... | 50 | Hillsborough Dist. |
| Continental | Thomas Costilloe ............... | 30 | |
| Continental | Thil. Chance, Soldier ............ | 741 | Halifax Dist. |
| Continental | Stephen Craft, Soldier ........... | 475 | Hillsborough Dist. |
| Militia | Joseph Charlton ................ | 543 | Newbern Dist. |
| Militia | Thomas Cirlwas ................ | 7505 | Salisbury Dist. |
| Continental | John Christopher .............. | 500 | |
| Militia | Charles Council ................ | 2391 | Wilmington Dist. |
| Militia | Wm. Cash .................... | 4181 | Salisbury Dist. |
| Militia | Timothy Clayborn .............. | 740 | Wilmington Dist. |
| Militia | James Cadborn ................. | 4735 | Salisbury Dist. |
| Militia | John Cliban ................... | 3163 | Wilmington Dist. |
| Militia | Samson Caern .................. | 4491 | Wilmington Dist. |
| Militia | John Callihan .................. | 2538 | Salisbury Dist. |
| Militia | John Coones ................... | 7517 | Salisbury Dist. |
| Continental | John Caeson, Sergt. ............. | 689 | Halifax Dist. |
| Continental | John Carey ................... | 846 | Hillsborough Dist. |
| Militia | Ezekiel Cliftin ................ | 274 | Newbern Dist. |
| Continental | Benjamin Cumings .............. | 849 | Hillsborough Dist. |
| Continental | Daniel Cellaes ................. | 346 | |
| Continental | Francis Coston, Soldier .......... | 500 | Hillsborough Dist. |
| Militia | Rich'd. Chanfield .............. | 58 | Newbern Dist. |
| Militia | Sam'l Chard... ................ | 236 | Newbern Dist. |
| Militia | Patrick Connely ................ | 1479 | Salisbury Dist. |
| Militia | Moses Cuthbasm ............... | 4302 | Salisbury Dist. |
| Militia | Alexander Chestnutt ............. | 5898 | Wilmington Dist. |
| Militia | Nathan Clirk .................. | 221 | Wilmington Dist. |
| Militia | Cullen Connely ................ | 2838 | Wilmington Dist. |
| Militia | Robt. Ceosnellner .............. | 6676 | Salisbury Dist. |
| Continental | Absalom Costander ............. | 56 | |
| Militia | Michal Cride .................. | 8331 | Salisbury Dist. |
| Militia | Gunley Cor.... ................ | 3523 | Wilmington Dist. |
| Militia | John Carouthers ................ | 292 | Newbern Dist. |
| Militia | James Creemore ................ | 1660 | Newbern Dist. |
| Continental | Danil Carroll .................. | 506 | Halifax Dist. |
| Militia | Jas. Campain .................. | 694 | Newbern Dist. |

|  |  | *No.* |  |
|---|---|---|---|
| Continental | Anthony Critcher, Lieut. .......... | 118 | Halifax Dist. |
| Continental | John Campton ................. | 153 |  |
| Militia | Wm. Chanie ................... | 921 | Newbern Dist. |
| Militia | James Cason ................... | 1985 | Newbern Dist. |
| Militia | James Cariegan ................ | 2999 | Salisbury Dist. |
| Militia | Richard Creech ................ | 4835 | Wilmington Dist. |
| Militia | Isaac Currin .................. | 6901 | Salisbury Dist. |
| Militia | Thomas Crinne ................ | 3736 | Wilmington Dist. |
| Militia | Elisha Carroll ................ | 1192 | Wilmington Dist. |
| Militia | James Canes .................. | 972 | Wilmington Dist. |
| Militia | Cullan Connly ................ | 1653 | Wilmington Dist. |
| Militia | Hugh Connoly ................ | 3842 | Morgan Dist. |
| Militia | John Cuthberson ............... | 4301 | Salisbury Dist. |
| Militia | Wm. Calahan ................. | 5093 | Salisbury Dist. |
| Continental | Lieut. Anthony Critcher ......... | 117 | Halifax Dist. |
| Militia | Jacob Caemack ................ | 1828 | Newbern Dist. |
| Militia | Robt. Caeswell ................ | 7839 | Salisbury Dist. |
| Militia | Robert Canneth ............... | 2506 | Salisbury Dist. |
| Militia | Alexander Canneth ............. | 2025 | Salisbury Dist. |
| Militia | James Canneth ............... | 2790 | Salisbury Dist. |
| Militia | Archibald Clinton ............. | 4844 | Morgan Dist. |
| Continental | Burnell Collins ................ | 1469 | Warrenton Dist. |
| Continental | Dillard Collins ................ | 1468 | Warrenton Dist. |
| Continental | Corporal Jeremiah Collins ....... | 1006 | Halifax Dist. |
| Militia | Henry Collins ................. | 1710 | Newbern Dist. |
| Militia | John Collins .................. | 4980 | Wilmington Dist. |
| Continental | Burnell Collins ................ | 469 |  |
| Militia | Josiah Collins ................. | 868 | Newbern Dist. |
| Militia | M.... Collins ................ | 3853 | Wilmington Dist. |
| Continental | John Collins .................. | 981 | Halifax Dist. |
| Continental | William Collins ............... | 1782 | Warrenton Dist. |
| Continental | John Collins .................. | 952 | Halifax Dist. |
| Militia | Stephen Collins ................ | 4039 | Wilmington Dist. |
| Militia | Dele Collins .................. | 1162 | Newbern Dist. |
| Militia | George Collins ................ | 581 | Newbern Dist. |
| Militia | ?...... Collins ............... | 1783 | Wilmington Dist. |
| Militia | Stephen Collins ............... | 3862 | Wilmington Dist. |
| Continental | Samson Collins ................ | 443 |  |
| Militia | John Collins .................. | 5987 | Wilmington Dist. |
| Militia | William Collins ............... | 3861 | Wilmington Dist. |
| Militia | Philip Collins ................ | 5243 | Wilmington Dist. |
| Militia | Stephens Collins .............. | 4099 | Wilmington Dist. |
| Militia | Nicholas Cook ................ | 2721 | Salisbury Dist. |
| Militia | Nathan Cook ................. | 3499 | Wilmington Dist. |
| Militia | Jno. Cook .................... | 7842 | Salisbury Dist. |
| Militia | Wm. Cook ................... | 1414 | Wilmington Dist. |
| Militia | William Cook ................ | 325 | Wilmington Dist. |
| Militia | Joseph Cook .................. | 311 | Wilmington Dist. |
| Continental | S..... Cook .................. | 690 | Halifax Dist. |
| Continental | Sanders Cook, Soldier ........... | 1070 | Halifax Dist. |
| Militia | Ruben Cook .................. | 1092 | Wilmington Dist. |
| Militia | Henry Cook .................. | 2186 | Wilmington Dist. |
| Continental | Lieut George Cook ............. | 71 | Halifax Dist. |
| Militia | Cornelius Cook ................ | 484 | Wilmington Dist. |

|  |  | No. |  |
|---|---|---|---|
| Militia | Thom's. Clements ................ | 1855 | Newbern Dist. |
| Militia | Cornelius Clements .............. | 104 | Morgan Dist. |
| Continental | John Clemons, Soldier ........... | 120 | Hillsborough Dist. |
| Continental | David Clement ................. | 771 | Hillsborough Dist. |
| Militia | Jno. Clemmons ................. | 4189 | Salisbury Dist. |
| Continental | Jno. Clemmons, Soldier .......... | 373 | Halifax Dist. |
| Militia | Mathew Clements .............. | 1232 | Newbern Dist. |
| Continental | John Clemmons ................ | 206 | Hillsborough Dist. |
| Militia | Charles Coplin ................. | 135 | Newbern Dist. |
| Continental | Capt. Francis Child ............. | 47 | Halifax Dist. |
| Continental | John Craddock, Capt. B. & M....... | 365 |  |
| Continental | Sergt. Bricknel C.... ........ | 1139 | Halifax Dist. |
| Continental | Lt. James Couper ............... | 457 | Halifax Dist. |
| Militia | Moses Cogan .................. | 1225 | Newbern Dist. |
| Continental | Thomas Donoho ............... | 439 |  |
| Continental | Thomas Donoho ............... | 435 |  |
| Continental | Thomas Donoho ............... | 440 |  |
| Continental | Thomas Donoho ............... | 433 |  |
| Continental | Thomas Donoho ............... | 434 |  |
| Continental | Thomas Donoho ............... | 443 |  |
| Continental | Thomas Donoho ............... | 432 |  |
| Continental | Thomas Donoho ............... | 436 |  |
| Continental | Thomas Donoho ............... | 442 |  |
| Continental | Thos. Donoho ................. | 269 |  |
| Militia | John Daniels ................... | 734 | Newbern Dist. |
| Militia | John Daniels .................. | 2633 | Newbern Dist. |
| Militia | Charles Doeherty .............. | 1268 | Salisbury Dist. |
| Continental | Alxander Daugherty ............ | 751 |  |
| Continental | Absalom Daugherty ............. | 247 |  |
| Continental | Richard Daugherty ............. | ..21 |  |
| Continental | John Daugherty, Soldier ......... | 1121 | Halifax Dist. |
| Militia | Benjamin Daugherty ............ | 278 | Wilmington Dist. |
| Continental | Richard Daugherty, Soldier ....... | 24 | Hillsboro Dist. |
| Militia | John Doherty .................. | 3714 | Salisbury Dist. |
| Continental | James Damport ................ | 656 |  |
| Continental | Giles Damport ................. | 181 |  |
| Militia | John Damport ................. | 728 | Wilmington Dist. |
| Militia | John Damport ................. | 3421 | Wilmington Dist. |
| Militia | Patrick Davis ................. | 4849 | Salisbury Dist. |
| Militia | John Davis .................... | 539 | Wilmington Dist. |
| Militia | David Davis ................... | 1689 | Wilmington Dist. |
| Militia | David Davis ................... | 1782 | Wilmington Dist. |
| Militia | John Lahir Davis ............... | 4993 | Salisbury Dist. |
| Militia | Jacob Davis ................... | 2130 | Newbern Dist. |
| Continental | Jonah Davis ................... | 2 |  |
| Militia | Jonathan Davis ................ | 2854 | Salisbury Dist. |
| Militia | Joseph Davis .................. | 7503 | Salisbury Dist. |
| Militia | Jonah Davis ................... | 2237 | Wilmington Dist. |
| Militia | John Davis .................... | 2853 | Salisbury Dist. |
| Militia | John Davis .................... | 80 | Newbern Dist. |
| Militia | Joseph Davis .................. | 1466 | Salisbury Dist. |
| Militia | Thomas Davis ................. | 1919 | Newbern Dist. |
| Militia | Joseph Davis .................. | 1783 | Wilmington Dist. |
| Militia | Jonathan Davis ................ | 1779 | Wilmington Dist. |

| | | No. | |
|---|---|---|---|
| Militia | Thom's. Davis | 1672 | Newbern Dist. |
| Militia | James Davis | 1042 | Newbern Dist. |
| Continental | Samuel Davis | 562 | Hillsborough Dist. |
| Continental | James Davis, Soldier | 454 | Hillsborough Dist. |
| Continental | Archelius Davis | 426 | Hillsborough Dist. |
| Continental | Joshua Davis | 147 | Hillsborough Dist. |
| Continental | William Davis | 573 | Hillsborough Dist. |
| Continental | William Davis, Soldier | 420 | Hillsborough Dist. |
| Continental | Benjamin Davis | 455 | Hillsborough Dist. |
| Continental | Benjamin Davis | 621 | Hillsborough Dist. |
| Continental | Thomas Davis | 434 | Halifax Dist. |
| Continental | Frederick Davis, Soldier | 833 | Halifax Dist. |
| Continental | ...... Davis | 961 | Halifax Dist. |
| Continental | John Davis | 1135 | Halifax Dist. |
| Continental | ..cajah Davis | 253 | Halifax Dist. |
| Militia | Thomas Davis | 4237 | Morgan Dist. |
| Continental | William Davis | 5 | |
| Militia | William Davis | 4859 | Morgan Dist. |
| Militia | Capt.Myrick Davis | 7473 | Salisbury Dist. |
| Militia | Myrid Davis | 7441 | Salisbury Dist. |
| Militia | Wm. Davis | 5113 | Salisbury Dist. |
| Militia | Andrew Davis | 683 | Salisbury Dist. |
| Militia | Brisco Davis | 913 | Newbern Dist. |
| Militia | Raf. Davis | 1239 | Wilmington Dist. |
| Militia | Matthis Davis | 1267 | Wilmington Dist. |
| Continental | Acey Davis | 3 | |
| Continental | Matthew Davis | 67 | Hillsborough Dist. |
| Continental | Matthew Davis | 187 | Hillsborough Dist. |
| Continental | Joshua Davis | 452 | Newbern Dist. |
| Militia | Joshua Davis | 1241 | Newbern Dist. |
| Militia | James Davis | 528 | Wilmington Dist. |
| Militia | Robb. Davis | 5947 | Salisbury Dist. |
| Continental | James Davis, Soldier | 1315 | Newbern Dist. |
| Continental | John Davis | 461 | |
| Continental | James Davis | 1317 | Newbern Dist. |
| Continental | James Davis, Soldier | 429 | Hillsborough Dist. |
| Continental | James Davis | 620 | Hillsborough Dist. |
| Continental | Samul Davis | 739 | Hillsborough Dist. |
| Militia | Wm. Davis | 8462 | Salisbury Dist. |
| Militia | Jacob Davis | 1298 | Salisbury Dist. |
| Continental | Hugh Davis, Soldier | 183 | Hillsborough Dist. |
| Militia | Samuel Davis | 5112 | Salisbury Dist. |
| Militia | George Davis | 7825 | Salisbury Dist. |
| Militia | Wm. Davis | 5903 | Salisbury Dist. |
| Militia | John Davis | 1443 | Newbern Dist. |
| Militia | James Davis | 2824 | Salisbury Dist. |
| Militia | Daniel Davis | 4570 | Salisbury Dist. |
| Continental | Joshua Davis | 324 | |
| Militia | Abner Davis | 9250 | Salisbury Dist. |
| Militia | John Davis | 2121 | Newbern Dist. |
| Militia | Hugh Davis | 5323 | Salisbury Dist. |
| Militia | Hugh Davis | 2989 | Salisbury Dist. |
| Militia | Wm. Davis | 830 | Wilmington Dist. |
| Militia | Ephraim Davidson | 8436 | Salisbury Dist. |

|  |  | *No.* |  |
|---|---|---|---|
| Militia | Jno. Davidson | 8366 | Salisbury Dist. |
| Militia | Joseph Davidson | 3400 | Wilmington Dist. |
| Militia | John Davidson | 4480 | Morgan Dist. |
| Continental | Thomas Davidson | 1829 | Warrenton Dist. |
| Militia | Joseph Davidson | 5033 | Wilmington Dist. |
| Continental | John Davidson, Soldier | 78 | Hillsborough Dist. |
| Continental | James Davidson | 1303 | Halifax Dist. |
| Continental | William Davie, Soldier | 825 | Halifax Dist. |
| Continental | Hemphrey Durham | 139 | Hillsborough Dist. |
| Continental | John Durham | 584 | Hillsborough Dist. |
| Continental | John Durham, Soldier | 432 | Hillsboro Dist. |
| Continental | Hemphrey Durham | 73 | Hillsborough Dist. |
| Militia | William Durham | 138 | Newbern Dist. |
| Militia | William Durham | 130 | Newbern Dist. |
| Continental | William Durham, Soldier | 482 | Halifax Dist. |
| Continental | Nathanel Durham | 1291 | Halifax Dist. |
| Militia | John Durham | 1311 | Newbern Dist. |
| Militia | Robert Dixson | 924 | Newbern Dist. |
| Continental | Lieut.-Col.-Brig. Henry Dixon | 204 | |
| Militia | Edward Dickson | 998 | Wilmington Dist. |
| Militia | John Dixon | 1980 | Newbern Dist. |
| Continental | Charles Dixon | 270 | Hillsboro Dist. |
| Continental | Henry Dixon, Soldier | 606 | Hillsboro Dist. |
| Militia | Edw'd. Dickson | 5502 | Wilmington Dist. |
| Militia | James Dickson | .... | Morgan Dist. |
| Militia | John Dickson | 915 | Newbern Dist. |
| Militia | Edward Dickson | 4046 | Wilmington Dist. |
| Militia | James Dickson | 995 | Wilmington Dist. |
| Continental | Benjamin Dickson | 323 | Hillsborough Dist. |
| Continental. | Lieut. Col. Brig. Henry Dickson | 202 | |
|  | Col. Joseph Dickson | 260 | |
| Continental | Benjamin Dickson | 456 | Hillsborough Dist. |
| Militia | John Dixon | 6621 | Salisbury Dist. |
| Militia | Robt. Dickson | 4228 | Salisbury Dist. |
| Continental | Tilman Dixon | 310 | |
| Militia | William Dodd | 1371 | Newbern Dist. |
| Militia | David Dodd | 1472 | Wilmington Dist. |
| Militia | William Dunn | 787 | Newbern Dist. |
| Militia | George Dunn | 8454 | Salisbury Dist. |
| Militia | William Dunn | 2292 | Newbern Dist. |
| Militia | David Dunn | 294 | Newbern Dist. |
| Militia | George Dunn | 4531 | Salisbury Dist. |
| Militia | John Dunn | 1639 | Wilmington Dist. |
| Militia | Isaac Dunn | 5711 | Wilmington Dist. |
| Militia | Samul Dunn | 1745 | Wilmington Dist. |
| Militia | Robt. Dunn | 6082 | Salisbury Dist. |
| Militia | Samul Dunn | 901 | Wilmington Dist. |
| Continental | James Dillard | 168 | Hillsborough Dist. |
| Continental | Christopher Dorhn | 101 | Hillsborough Dist. |
| Continental | Robert Dennis | 589 | Hillsborough Dist. |
| Continental | James Deacon | 651 | Hillsborough Dist. |
| Continental | Ere Dego, Soldier | 384 | Hillsborough Dist. |
| Continental | Hugh Darally | 738 | Hillsborough Dist. |
| Militia | John Deer | 1137 | Newbern Dist. |

|  | | No. | |
|---|---|---|---|
| Continental | John Donas | 109 | Hillsborough Dist. |
| Continental | Timothy Decent | 632 | |
| Continental | Isaac Davis | 626 | |
| Militia | James Doty | 5000 | Wilmington Dist. |
| Militia | Arthur Donelly | 4240 | Wilmington Dist. |
| Militia | Francis Donelly | 4085 | Wilmington Dist. |
| Continental | Morgan Ducey | 1311 | Halifax Dist. |
| Continental | Martin Dickerson | 945 | Halifax Dist. |
| Continental | William Den.., Soldier | 438 | |
| Militia | William Dowdle | 1530 | Wilmington Dist. |
| Militia | Corp. Thos. Drish | 7656 | Salisbury Dist. |
| Militia | Martin Dye | 4100 | Wilmington Dist. |
| Militia | Ranol Dorning | 2993 | Wilmington Dist. |
| Militia | James Dyer | 3941 | Wilmington Dist. |
| Militia | Edward Everage | 4334 | Wilmington Dist. |
| Militia | William Dancey | 3009 | Salisbury Dist. |
| Militia | Jacob Dewalt | 2500 | Salisbury Dist. |
| Militia | Clayton Dunfield | 4786 | Wilmington Dist. |
| Continental | Sergt. James Dunnar | 171 | Halifax Dist. |
| Militia | George Davenport | 1931 | Newbern Dist. |
| Militia | George Davenport | 1949 | Newbern Dist. |
| Continental | Giles Davenport | 255 | |
| Militia | Joel Davenport | 1887 | Newbern Dist. |
| Militia | Joel Davenport | 1932 | Newbern Dist. |
| Militia | Wm. Davenport | 984 | Newbern Dist. |
| Continental | Ephriam Davenport, Soldier | 681 | Halifax Dist. |
| Militia | John Dobbin | 703 | Salisbury Dist. |
| Militia | John Dobbins | 4111 | Wilmington Dist. |
| Militia | Andrew Dobbins | 2539 | Salisbury Dist. |
| Militia | James Dobbins | 3921 | Wilmington Dist. |
| Continental | James Dobbins | 606 | Hillsborough Dist. |
| Militia | James Dobbins | 699 | Salisbury Dist. |
| Militia | James Dobbins | 113 | Hillsborough Dist. |
| Militia | James Dobbins | 453 | Hillsborough Dist. |
| Militia | Hugh Dobbins | 5219 | Salisbury Dist. |
| Militia | James Dobbins | 4769 | Wilmington Dist. |
| Continental | James Dobbins, Soldier | 63 | Hillsborough Dist. |
| Militia | John Dobbins | 759 | Salisbury Dist. |
| Militia | John Dobbins | 5217 | Salisbury Dist. |
| Militia | James Dobbins | 6912 | Salisbury Dist. |
| Militia | James Dobbins | 3893 | Wilmington Dist. |
| Militia | Capt. Alexander Dobbins | 178 | Halifax Dist. |
| Militia | Sergt. James Dobbins | 6913 | Salisbury Dist. |
| Continental | Sergt. Hugh Dobbins | 1985 | Warrenton Dist. |
| Continental | William Deal, Soldier | 672 | Hillsborough Dist. |
| Continental | John Deal | 764 | Halifax Dist. |
| Militia | Anthony Dean | 796 | Newbern Dist. |
| Militia | ...ham Dees | 1535 | Wilmington Dist. |
| Continental | Col. Levi Dauson | 34 | Halifax Dist. |
| Militia | Nehemiah Dorms | 1087 | Newbern Dist. |
| Militia | ....arfoot Dorch | 1039 | Newbern Dist. |
| Militia | Anthony Dean | 359 | Newbern Dist. |
| Continental | Isaiah Denis | 613 | |
| Continental | Robert Dawling | 77 | |

| | | No. | |
|---|---|---|---|
| Continental | Sterling Dean | 949 | Warrenton Dist. |
| Militia | Avery Dze | 3854 | Wilmington Dist. |
| Militia | John Dennis | 5974 | Salisbury Dist. |
| Militia | Sergt. Tho. Devane | 5170 | Wilmington Dist. |
| Militia | John Donald | 4275 | Salisbury Dist. |
| Continental | Ephraim Dorning | 349 | |
| Continental | Absolom Durkins | 254 | |
| Continental | Holland Deek | 237 | |
| Continental | Jesse Donan | 309 | |
| Continental | John Drury | 1310 | |
| Continental | .... Diel | 37 | Halifax Dist. |
| Continental | Joshua Dunigan | 223 | Warrenton Dist. |
| Militia | Tho. Devane | 348 | Wilmington Dist. |
| Militia | Martin Dye | 3851 | Wilmington Dist. |
| Continental | Dempsey Daughtry | 1402 | Warrenton Dist. |
| Continental | Frances Delong, Soldier | 177 | Hillsborough Dist. |
| Continental | Isham Dyches, Soldier | 178 | Hillsborogh Dist. |
| Militia | Sugar Dulin | 275 | Newbern Dist. |
| Militia | Rue Duling | 1481 | Newbern Dist. |
| Continental | Sam Dozier | 230 | |
| Militia | John Dumbesh | 6490 | Salisbury Dist. |
| Militia | Edward Dofferty | 4523 | Morgan Dist. |
| Militia | ..... Durkworth | 6309 | Salisbury Dist. |
| Militia | John Durkins | 904 | Newbern Dist. |
| Militia | Henry Davis | 538 | Wilmington Dist. |
| Militia | Archil. Duhemple | 4298 | Wilmington Dist. |
| Militia | William Dudley | 63 | Wilmington Dist. |
| Militia | Absolom Demont | 517 | Newbern Dist. |
| Militia | Charles Duart | 812 | Salisbury Dist. |
| Continental | Peter Delight | 1423 | Warrenton Dist. |
| Militia | Edward Doty | 23 | Wilmington Dist. |
| Militia | Mack Dedman | 3029 | Salisbury Dist. |
| Continental | Peter Duffee | 637 | Halifax Dist. |
| Continental | Charles Dodson, Soldier | 793 | Halifax Dist. |
| Continental | Henry Dunnehe | 1245 | Halifax Dist. |
| Militia | Thomas Deel | 131 | Newbern Dist. |
| Continental | John Dean | 285 | Hillsborough Dist. |
| Continental | ..... Duncan | 240 | |
| Militia | John Delisslin | 2118 | Wilmington Dist. |
| Militia | William Deros | 3848 | Morgan Dist. |
| Militia | A.... Diggo | 1160 | Newbern Dist. |
| Militia | Aulling Dean | 1090 | Newbern Dist. |
| Continental | Lieut. Hugh Dobbins | 473 | |
| Militia | Lieut. Wm. Dobbins | 7050 | Salisbury Dist. |
| Militia | James Dobbins | 4344 | Wilmington Dist. |
| Continental | William Duncan | 1339 | Halifax Dist. |
| Militia | Isaac Duncan | 3414 | Wilmington Dist. |
| Militia | Edward Duncan | 1196 | Wilmington Dist. |
| Militia | Elias Duncan | 5014 | Wilmington Dist. |
| Continental | Jeremiah Duncan | 166 | |
| Militia | Wm. Dunkan | 4536 | Salisbury Dist. |
| Militia | George Davison | 7861 | Salisbury Dist. |
| Militia | Lieut. Geo. Davison | 8359 | Salisbury Dist. |
| Militia | Ruban Davison | 831 | Wilmington Dist. |

| | | No. | |
|---|---|---|---|
| Militia | James Davison ................. | 896 | Hillsborough Dist. |
| Militia | Ephriam Davison ............... | 8381 | Salisbury Dist. |
| Militia | Lt. Jos. Davison ............... | 3645 | Wilmington Dist. |
| Militia | Wm. Davison .................. | 3136 | Salisbury Dist. |
| Militia | Joseph Davison ............... | 1475 | Wilmington Dist. |
| Militia | Alexander Davidson ............ | 5962 | Salisbury Dist. |
| Militia | James Davidson ............... | 6263 | Salisbury Dist. |
| Militia | George Davidson ............... | 4196 | Salisbury Dist. |
| Militia | Major George Davidson ......... | 427 | Salisbury Dist. |
| Militia | Wm. Davidson ................. | 6314 | Salisbury Dist. |
| Continental | John Davidson ................. | 231 | Hillsborough Dist. |
| Militia | John Davidson ................. | 4496 | Morgan Dist. |
| Militia | ..... Dellamar ................ | 932 | Newbern Dist. |
| Militia | Francis Delamar ............... | 1761 | Newbern Dist. |
| Militia | Thomas Delamar ............... | 312 | Newbern Dist. |
| Militia | Dempsey Delamar ............. | 1222 | Newbern Dist. |
| Militia | Dempsey Delamar ............. | 1071 | Newbern Dist. |
| Militia | Francis Dauson ................ | 967 | Newbern Dist. |
| Continental | Matthew Dauson .............. | 1846 | Warrenton Dist. |
| Militia | Bartholam Dauson ............. | 4985 | Morgan Dist. |
| Continental | Isaac Dauson ................. | 239 | |
| Militia | Capt. Levi Dauson ............. | 275 | Newbern Dist. |
| Continental | Capt. Henry Dauson ........... | 297 | Hillsborough Dist. |
| Continental | James Dickins ................. | 135 | Hillsborough Dist. |
| Continental | Edmund Dickins .............. | 185 | Hillsborough Dist. |
| Continental | Edmund Dickins, Soldier ........ | 109 | Hillsborough Dist. |
| Militia | Abram Duck .................. | 4616 | Salisbury Dist. |
| Militia | Jacob Duck ................... | 4646 | Morgan Dist. |
| Militia | James Duck ................... | 4623 | Wilmington Dist. |
| Continental | Peter Dandy .................. | ...3 | |
| Continental | Josiah Dandy ................. | 597 | Hillsborough Dist. |
| Militia | Obadiah Dandy ............... | 2991 | Salisbury Dist. |
| Continental | Josiah Dandy, Soldier ........... | 443 | Hillsborough Dist. |
| Continental | William Dunston .............. | 479 | Halifax Dist. |
| Continental | Holland Delk ................. | 163 | |
| Militia | Francis Doowely .............. | 5858 | Wilmington Dist. |
| Militia | John Dofson .................. | 4211 | Wilmington Dist. |
| Continental | Isaac Dean ................... | 705 | |
| Continental | Am.... Dodley ............... | 1192 | Warrenton Dist. |
| Militia | Isaac Davie .................. | 3654 | Salisbury Dist. |
| Militia | Abraham Dickey .............. | 2653 | Salisbury Dist. |
| Militia | Henry Diller ................. | 7240 | Salisbury Dist. |
| Militia | Jacob Deal ................... | 5406 | Salisbury Dist. |
| Militia | Michal Dillard ............... | 5324 | Salisbury Dist. |
| Continental | Ephraim Downing ............. | 54 | |
| Militia | James Diver .................. | 4197 | Morgan Dist. |
| Militia | John Deer, Soldier ............. | 1550 | Newbern Dist. |
| Militia | Daniel Dees .................. | 2155 | Newbern Dist. |
| Continental | Sherrod Duke ................ | 19 | Hillsborough Dist. |
| Continental | William Duke ................ | 119 | Hillsborough Dist. |
| Continental | Samuel Darden ............... | 72 | Hillsborough Dist. |
| Continental | William Dennis ............... | 122 | Hillsborough Dist. |
| Continental | Frederick Desern .............. | 251 | Hillsborough Dist. |
| Continental | Francis Desern ................ | 172 | Hillsborough Dist. |

|  |  | No. |  |
|---|---|---|---|
| Continental | Henry Dauson, Capt. | 427 | Hillsborough Dist. |
| Continental | John Desheron | 323 | Hillsborough Dist. |
| Militia | Ahaseur Dzar | 4538 | Morgan Dist. |
| Militia | William Dieskel | 2875 | Salisbury Dist. |
| Militia | Edward Dudley | 2011 | Wilmington Dist. |
| Militia | Thos. Dudley | 148 | Wilmington Dist. |
| Continental | Zachariah Douge | 788 | Halifax Dist. |
| Continental | Griffieth Douge | 36 | Hillsborough Dist. |
| Continental | Griffieth Douge | 35 | Hillsborough Dist. |
| Continental | James Douge | 32 | Hillsborough Dist. |
| Continental | Griffieth Douge | 38 | Hillsborough Dist. |
| Continental | Griffieth Douge | 37 | Hillsborough Dist. |
| Continental | Richard Douge | 1156 | Halifax Dist. |
| Continental | Joab Douge, Soldier | 363 | Hillsborough Dist. |
| Continental | Griffieth Douge, Soldier | 271 | Hillsborough Dist. |
| Continental | James Douge | 17 | Hillsborough Dist. |
| Militia | John Daniel | 611 | Halifax Dist. |
| Militia | Jephtha Daniel | 1901 | Wilmington Dist. |
| Militia | Shadrack Daniel | 193 | Wilmington Dist. |
| Militia | Benj. Daniel | 8989 | Salisbury Dist. |
| Militia | Shaderick Daniel | 2284 | Wilmington Dist. |
| Militia | Francis Daniel | 3978 | Wilmington Dist. |
| Militia | Enoch Daniel | 462 | Newbern Dist. |
| Militia | Elias Daniel | 568 | Wilmington Dist. |
| Militia | Wm. Daniel | 5926 | Wilmington Dist. |
| Militia | Thomas Daniel | 1943 | Newbern Dist. |
| Militia | Enoch Daniel | 1964 | Newbern Dist.· |
| Militia | Hezekiah Dunn | 5710 | Wilmington Dist. |
| Militia | Bartho'm. Dunn | 4202 | Wilmington Dist. |
| Militia | Simon Dunn | 1348 | Wilmington Dist. |
| Militia | James Dunn | 5481 | Wilmington Dist. |
| Militia | Bamhos Dunn | 904 | Salisbury Dist. |
| Continental | Jacob Dunn, Soldier | 36 | Halifax Dist. |
| Militia | James Dunn | 141 | Wilmington Dist. |
| Continental | Nicolas Dunn, Soldier | 494 | Hillsborough Dist. |
| Militia | Jno. D.... Dunn | 952 | Newbern Dist. |
| Militia | Andrew Dunn | 1473 | Salisbury Dist. |
| Militia | George Dunn | 2626 | Salisbury Dist. |
| Militia | Drury Dunn | 1056 | Wilmington Dist. |
| Militia | Wm. Dum | 5713 | Wilmington Dist. |
| Militia | Neheniah Dum | 2359 | Wilmington Dist. |
| Continental | Malachi Dum | 34 | Hillsborough Dist. |
| Militia | Robert Dum | 1475 | Salisbury Dist. |
| Continental | Nicolas Dum | 663 | Hillsborough Dist. |
| Continental | Jeffrey Dum, Soldier | 35 | Hillsborough Dist. |
| Continental | William Douglas, Soldier | 320 | Hillsborough Dist. |
| Continental | William Douglas | 321 | Hillsborough Dist. |
| Continental | Hezekiah Douglas | 134 | Halifax Dist. |
| Militia | Solomon Douglas | 5728 | Salisbury Dist. |
| Continental | William Douglas | 454 | Hillsborough Dist. |
| Continental | William Douglas | 453 | Hillsborough Dist. |
| Continental | William Drew, Soldier | 355 | Halifax Dist. |
| Continental | Jesse Donaldson | 1287 | Halifax Dist. |
| Militia | Capt. Abraham Demoss | 747 | Salisbury Dist. |

|  | | No. | |
|---|---|---|---|
| Continental | William Duvall, Soldier .......... | 1171 | Halifax Dist. |
| Militia | Lieut. George Draughon .......... | 4149 | Wilmington Dist. |
| Militia | Capt. James Devane .............. | 573 | Wilmington Dist. |
| Continental | Sergt. John Dilliard ............. | 111 | Halifax Dist. |
| Continental | Spencer Donaldson .............. | 936 | Halifax Dist. |
| Militia | James Duson .................. | 6052 | Salisbury Dist. |
| Militia | George Duckett ............... | 3634 | Salisbury Dist. |
| Militia | William Dorton ............... | 622 | Salisbury Dist. |
| Continental | Richard Dean .................. | 1033 | Halifax Dist. |
| Militia | John Davie ................... | 3655 | Salisbury Dist. |
| Continental | Absolom Durkins ............... | 180 | |
| Continental | Isaac Dauson .................. | 165 | |
| Militia | Daniel Dees ................... | 2101 | |
| Militia | Alize Denny .................. | 4556 | Salisbury Dist. |
| Militia | Samuel Denont ................ | 498 | Newbern Dist. |
| Continental | Lieut. Benjamin Dillon .......... | 1986 | Warrenton Dist. |
| Militia | Sterling Dupree ............... | 1639 | Newbern Dist. |
| Militia | Obadiah Doddy ............... | 5177 | Salisbury Dist. |
| Militia | David Davie .................. | 313 | Newbern Dist. |
| Militia | Joseph Demster ............... | 3077 | Salisbury Dist. |
| Militia | William Dollis ................ | 1285 | Salisbury Dist. |
| Continental | John Duggan .................. | 133 | |
| Militia | William Duce ................. | 4902 | Morgan Dist. |
| Militia | Joshua Daughtery ............. | 5688 | Wilmington Dist. |
| Militia | John Dumond ................. | 6031 | Salisbury Dist. |
| Militia | John Dearmon ................ | 1400 | Salisbury Dist. |
| Militia | Martin Die ................... | 4034 | Wilmington Dist. |
| Militia | John Denoho ................. | 1646 | Wilmington Dist. |
| Militia | John Devane ................. | 6022 | Wilmington Dist. |
| Continental | S.... Daughtry ............... | 821 | Halifax Dist. |
| Militia | Jacob Dulose ................. | 3474 | Wilmington Dist. |
| Continental | Charles Dailey ............... | 1217 | Halifax Dist. |
| Continental | John Desheson, Soldier .......... | 206 | Hillsborough Dist. |
| Continental | William Duke ................. | 624 | Hillsborough Dist. |
| Militia | John Durn.... ............... | 1273 | Salisbury Dist. |
| Militia | Joseph Dobson ................ | 5004 | Morgan Dist. |
| Continental | John Duckingham .............. | 354 | |
| Militia | Bazel Dosey .................. | 1252 | Salisbury Dist. |
| Militia | Jacob Dollar .................. | 5535 | Wilmington Dist. |
| Militia | John Durdan ................. | 1258 | Newbern Dist. |
|  | **Bird** Dupree, Soldier ........... | 1644 | Newbern Dist. |
| Militia | Benj. Dorsey ................. | 5730 | Salisbury Dist. |
| Continental | Capt. Geo. Dudley ............. | 344 | Halifax Dist. |
| Militia | Capt. Dubos ................. | 5140 | Wilmington Dist. |
| Militia | **David Dickey** ................ | 5480 | Salisbury Dist. |
| Militia | Wm. Danoldson ............... | 7245 | Salisbury Dist. |
| Continental | Benjamin Dean ............... | 236 | Hillsborough Dist. |
| Continental | Francis Dezearn ............... | 97 | Hillsborough Dist. |
| Continental | David Danley ................. | 582 | Hillsborough Dist. |
| Militia | Avery Dye ................... | 3847 | Wilmington Dist. |
| Militia | Samuel Deans ................ | 739 | Wilmington Dist. |
| Militia | Elijah Dudley ................ | 392 | Newbern Dist. |
| Continental | Samuel Dowden, Soldier .......... | 57 | Hillsborough Dist. |
| Militia | John Davie ................... | 4533 | Salisbury Dist. |

|  |  | *No.* |  |
|---|---|---|---|
| Militia | A. Haukins, Durkworth .......... | 8619 | Salisbury Dist. |
| Militia | Joseph Dobson .................. | 4464 | Morgan Dist. |
| Continental | David Deffnall, Soldier .......... | 924 | Halifax Dist. |
| Continental | John Duckingham ............... | 59 |  |
| Militia | Martin Dye ................... | 3849 | Wilmington Dist. |
| Militia | Robert Davie .................. | 6228 | Salisbury Dist. |
| Militia | Patrick Davie ................. | 6453 | Salisbury Dist. |
| Militia | John Durkworth ............... | 4994 | Morgan Dist. |
| Militia | William Dykes ................. | 1518 | Newbern Dist. |
| Militia | Jacob Dardin .................. | 266 | Newbern Dist. |
| Militia | James Dyck ................... | 3962 | Wilmington Dist. |
| Militia | John Drayhan ................. | 4285 | Wilmington Dist. |
| Continental | Ispin Dorran .................. | 235 |  |
| Continental | John Dawson .................. | 560 |  |
| Militia | George Devhan ................ | 1844 | Wilmington Dist. |
| Militia | John Devane .................. | 5171 | Wilmington Dist. |
| Continental | Isham Dyches .................. | 448 |  |
| Continental | David Douby, Soldier ........... | 430 | Hillsborough Dist. |
| Continental | Hugh Donally ................. | 545 | Hillsborough Dist. |
| Continental | William Duke ................. | 808 | Hillsborough Dist. |
| Militia | Daniel Dillahunt ............... | 1151 | Newbern Dist. |
| Militia | George Dudley ................ | 3896 | Wilmington Dist. |
| Militia | Hopkins Dye .................. | 4046 | Wilmington Dist. |
| Militia | Barton Dyson ................. | 5613 | Salisbury Dist. |
| Continental | Frederick Desern .............. | 140 | Hillsborough Dist. |
| Continental | Eli Drake .................... | 77 | Hillsborough Dist. |
| Continental | Eli Drake, Soldier ............. | 39 | Hillsborough Dist. |

### ERWIN FAMILY

|  |  |  |  |
|---|---|---|---|
| Militia | Jarrald Erwin ................. | 3182 | Wilmington Dist. |
| Militia | Jarrel Erwin .................. | 2256 | Wilmington Dist. |
| Militia | Gaevin Erwin ................. | 7137 | Salisbury Dist. |
| Militia | Arthur Erwin ................. | 7368 | Salisbury Dist. |
| Militia | Wm. Erwin ................... | 6770 | Salisbury Dist. |
| Militia | John Erwin ................... | 7184 | Salisbury Dist. |
| Militia | Wm. Erwin ................... | 6935 | Salisbury Dist. |
| Militia | Jared Erwin .................. | 3215 | Wilmington Dist. |
| Militia | Wm. Erwin ................... | 5499 | Salisbury Dist. |
| Militia | Nath'l. Erwin ................. | 5137 | Salisbury Dist. |
| Militia | Jarod Erwin .................. | 4548 | Wilmington Dist. |
| Militia | Arthur Erwin ................. | 2285 | Salisbury Dist. |
| Militia | William Erwin ................ | 5793 | Salisbury Dist. |
| Militia | Thos. Erwin .................. | .... | Salisbury Dist. |
| Militia | Jno. Erwin ................... | 5881 | Salisbury Dist. |
| Militia | John Erwin ................... | 7058 | Salisbury Dist. |
| Militia | Robert Erwin ................. | 886 | Salisbury Dist. |
| Militia | John Erwin ................... | 6419 | Salisbury Dist. |
| Militia | John Erwin ................... | 6903 | Salisbury Dist. |
| Militia | John Erwin ................... | 2286 | Salisbury Dist. |
| Militia | John Erwin ................... | 5811 | Salisbury Dist. |
| Militia | John Erwin ................... | 7211 | Salisbury Dist. |

### EVANS FAMILY

|  |  |  |  |
|---|---|---|---|
| Militia | Edward Evans ................. | 4654 | Salisbury Dist. |
| Militia | Samuel Evans ................. | 1925 | Wilmington Dist. |

| | | No. | |
|---|---|---|---|
| Continental | Charles Evans | 177 | Hillsborough Dist. |
| Continental | Charles Evans, Soldier | 358 | Hillsborough Dist. |
| Militia | David Evans | 3491 | Wilmington Dist. |
| Militia | George Evans | 4054 | Wilmington Dist. |
| Militia | Samul Evans | 2217 | Wilmington Dist. |
| Militia | Ephm. Evans | 358 | Newbern Dist. |
| Militia | James Evans | 207 | Newbern Dist. |
| Militia | Samuel Evans | 316 | Wilmington Dist. |
| Militia | David Evans | 5143 | Wilmington Dist. |
| Militia | George Evans | 1647 | Newbern Dist. |
| Militia | James Evans | 3744 | Wilmington Dist. |
| Continental | Rubin Evans, Soldier | 590 | Halifax Dist. |
| Continental | Charles Evans | 101 | Hillsborough Dist. |
| Continental | Charles Evans | 178 | Hillsborough Dist. |
| Militia | Benja Evans | 1339 | Wilmington Dist. |
| Militia | Benja Evans | 964 | Wilmington Dist. |
| Continental | Morris Evans, Soldier | 315 | Hillsborough Dist. |
| Continental | Joseph Evans | 784 | Halifax Dist. |
| Continental | David Evans | 55 | Wilmington Dist. |
| Continental | Saml' Evans | 1088 | Wilmington Dist. |
| Continental | William Evans | 139 | |
| Continental | Phillip Evans | 655 | |
| Continental | Capt. Thomas Evans | 61 | Halifax Dist. |
| Continental | Capt. Thomas Evans | 64 | Halifax Dist. |
| Militia | Thos. Evans | 4581 | Wilmington Dist. |
| Militia | Theopilis Evans | 4568 | Wilmington Dist. |
| Militia | John Ferrel | 30 | Wilmington Dist. |
| Militia | John Ferrel | 2054 | Newbern Dist. |
| Militia | Wm. Ferrel | 6379 | Salisbury Dist. |
| Continental | Nathan Ferrel | 903 | Halifax Dist. |
| Continental | Edward Ferrel, Soldier | 157 | Hillsborough Dist. |
| Continental | James Ferrel | 1081 | Halifax Dist. |
| Continental | Enoch Ferrel, Soldier | 490 | Halifax Dist. |
| Continental | Micajah Ferrel | 194 | Hillsborough Dist. |
| Continental | James Ferrel | 143 | Halifax Dist. |
| Continental | Edward Ferrel | 269 | Hillsborough Dist. |
| Continental | Gabriel Ferrel | 6 | Hillsborough Dist. |
| Continental | Robert Ferebee, Soldier | 240 | Hillsborough Dist. |
| Continental | Capt. Wm. Ferebee | 129 | Halifax Dist. |
| Continental | Abraham Finley, Soldier | 40 | Hillsborough Dist. |
| Militia | James Finley | 2590 | Salisbury Dist. |
| Militia | George Finley | 3223 | Salisbury Dist. |
| Militia | James Finley | 3055 | Salisbury Dist. |
| Militia | James Finley | 3251 | Salisbury Dist. |
| Militia | Joseph Findley | 3226 | Salisbury Dist. |
| Militia | Joseph Findley | 8383 | Salisbury Dist. |
| Continental | Abraham Findley | 78 | Hillsborough Dist. |
| Militia | George Finley | 2733 | Salisbury Dist. |
| Militia | John Finley | 1241 | Salisbury Dist. |
| Militia | Wm. Finley | 592 | Salisbury Dist. |
| Militia | George Finley | 670 | Salisbury Dist. |
| Militia | John Fleming | 2080 | Salisbury Dist. |
| Militia | John Fleming | 1294 | Wilmington Dist. |
| Militia | Mitchell Fleming | 3076 | Salisbury Dist. |

|  |  | *No.* |  |
|---|---|---|---|
| Militia | John Fleming | 3111 | Salisbury Dist. |
| Militia | Alison Fleming | 2023 | Salisbury Dist. |
| Militia | Mitchell Fleming | 2555 | Salisbury Dist. |
| Continental | James Fleming, Soldier | 567 | Halifax Dist. |
| Militia | James Fleming | 4417 | Morgan Dist. |
| Continental | Joseph Fleming | 1164 | Halifax Dist. |
| Militia | John Fleming | 909 | Salisbury Dist. |
| Continental | John Fleming | 825 | Warrenton Dist. |
| Militia | Gideon Freeman | 4306 | Salisbury Dist. |
| Militia | David Foster | 803 | Salisbury Dist. |
| Militia | William Falls | 4076 | Salisbury Dist. |
| Militia | Jermiah Fonville | 5743 | Wilmington Dist. |
| Militia | Zacheriah Field | 3326 | Wilmington Dist. |
| Continental | Timothy Fields | 1927 | Warrenton Dist. |
| Militia | Luke Fosque | 792 | Newbern Dist. |
| Militia | James Findall | 1990 | Newbern Dist. |
| Continental | Benjam. Flood, Soldier | 599 | Halifax Dist. |
| Militia | Jef Florees | 1021 | Newbern Dist. |
| Militia | Alex Ferguson | 2696 | Salisbury Dist. |
| Militia | James Faenal | 5753 | Wilmington Dist. |
| Militia | Richard Fair | 3568 | Wilmington Dist. |
| Continental | Nicholas Frazir | 73 |  |
| Continental | Willis Floyd | 927 | Warrenton Dist. |
| Militia | ...... Foley | 5978 | Salisbury Dist. |
| Militia | Arthur Forbes | 46 | Salisbury Dist. |
| Continental | Moses Frost | 350 |  |
| Continental | Frederick Frances | 440 |  |
| Militia | Frances Forks | 3668 | Wilmington Dist. |
| Militia | Joseph Foster | 5241 | Salisbury Dist. |
| Militia | John Fespeman | 644 | Salisbury Dist. |
| Continental | Hugh Forsyth, Soldier | 176 | Hillsborough Dist. |
| Continental | Cornelius Futrell | 477 |  |
| Militia | James Floyd | 2289 | Wilmington Dist. |
| Militia | Hugh Fillips | 2627 | Salisbury Dist. |
| Militia | James Frazer | 8392 | Salisbury Dist. |
| Militia | Elizabeth Fry | 4567 | Morgan Dist. |
| Continental | David Fort, Soldier | 1661 | Newbern Dist. |
| Militia | Jacob Fingle | 1852 | Newbern Dist. |
| Militia | Elisha Faison | 1521 | Wilmington Dist. |
| Militia | Lieut. S... Fisher | 526 | Wilmington Dist. |
| Continental | Robert Fosett | 1189 | Halifax Dist. |
| Continental | Jesse Freeman, Soldier | 611 | Hillsborough Dist. |
| Militia | Mich. Freeman | 8149 | Salisbury Dist. |
| Militia | Peter Franklin | 1780 | Newbern Dist. |
| Continental | Wm. Fryar | 1259 | Halifax Dist. |
| Continental | Maj. Wm. Fen.... | 181 | Halifax Dist. |
| Continental | Richard Fenn | 305 | Halifax Dist. |
| Militia | Capt. Gilbreth Falls | 6686 | Salisbury Dist. |
| Militia | Felix Fredrick | 1180 | Wilmington Dist. |
| Militia | James Gee | 4631 | Wilmington Dist. |
| Continental | Samul Gaines, Soldier | 532 | Halifax Dist. |
| Continental | Gilbert Grant | 214 |  |
| Militia | John Gates | 2931 | Wilmington Dist. |
| Continental | James Glasco | 1431 | Warrenton Dist. |

| | | *No.* | |
|---|---|---|---|
| Continental | George Glenn | 1482 | Warrenton Dist. |
| Continental | Thomas Ganott | 1457 | Warrenton Dist. |
| Militia | John Gardun | 374 | Newbern Dist. |
| Militia | David Gargainus | 756 | Newbern Dist. |
| Militia | Joshua Guard | 500 | Newbern Dist. |
| Continental | William Goldsbury | 1421 | Halifax Dist. |
| Militia | Arthur Gurley | 1237 | Newbern Dist. |
| Continental | Thomas Gamet, Soldier | 962 | Warrenton Dist. |
| Militia | Thos. Gardun | 1045 | Newbern Dist. |
| Militia | John Goff | 1774 | Wilmington Dist. |
| Militia | Jacob Gordin | 1830 | Wilmington Dist. |
| Militia | Fisher Gaskins | 289 | Newbern Dist. |
| Militia | George Gurley | 1226 | Newbern Dist. |
| Militia | Leuis Gurley | 1291 | Newbern Dist. |
| Militia | Hardy Galtin | 990 | Newbern Dist. |
| Continental | Thomas Girin | 44 | Halifax Dist. |
| Militia | Jos. Guilford | 364 | Newbern Dist. |
| Continental | Wm. Gaskins | 21 | Newbern Dist. |
| Militia | Jacob Gorley | 1210 | Newbern Dist. |
| Militia | William Gaskill | 689 | Newbern Dist. |
| Militia | Reeding Giest | 2000 | Newbern Dist. |
| Militia | Fisher Gaston | .... | Newbern Dist. |
| Militia | Benjamin Grayson | 4239 | Morgan Dist. |
| Continental | Jenkins Goin | 919 | Halifax Dist. |
| Militia | Henry Gilbert | 7611 | Salisbury Dist. |
| Militia | Elias Garrison | 6288 | Salisbury Dist. |
| Militia | Stephen Griffud | 5543 | Wilmington Dist. |
| Continental | John Gautheop | 802 | Halifax Dist. |
| Militia | Wm. Gauff | 5501 | Wilmington Dist. |
| Continental | Benjamin Gorman | 658 | Halifax Dist. |
| Continental | George Gary | 655 | Halifax Dist. |
| Continental | Joseph Gawburn | 978 | Halifax Dist. |
| Continental | William Gooch | 12 | Halifax Dist. |
| Continental | Leuis Goodrich | 1244 | Halifax Dist. |
| Continental | Abraham Gamilion | 817 | Halifax Dist. |
| Continental | James Gilbert, Soldier | .... | Halifax Dist. |
| Continental | Zachariah Gofoth | 848 | Halifax Dist. |
| Militia | Jacob Grindstaff | 4452 | Morgan Dist. |
| Militia | Isaac Grindstaff | 4964 | Morgan Dist. |
| Militia | John Gebbs | 4958 | Morgan Dist. |
| Militia | Wm. Goodrich | 5785 | Wilmington Dist. |
| Miltia | Robt. Givene | 6706 | Salisbury Dist. |
| Militia | James Greenlee | 4486 | Morgan Dist. |
| Militia | Wm. Glais | 7085 | Salisbury Dist. |
| Militia | Matthew Gordir | 4629 | Morgan Dist. |
| Militia | John Goas | 6828 | Salisbury Dist. |
| Militia | James Gordin | 5788 | Wilmington Dist. |
| Militia | Alexander Gunn | 6871 | Salisbury Dist. |
| Militia | Joseph Gilbroth | 7041 | Salisbury Dist. |
| Militia | John Gilbroth | 7040 | Salisbury Dist. |
| Militia | Henry Gougar | 7218 | Salisbury Dist. |
| Militia | John Gibbs | 4795 | Morgan Dist. |
| Militia | Frederick Grady | 5780 | Wilmington Dist. |
| Continental | Thomas Green | 1821 | Warrenton Dist. |

| | | No. | |
|---|---|---|---|
| Militia | John Green | 2223 | Wilmington Dist. |
| Militia | Richard Green | 5346 | Salisbury Dist. |
| Militia | B..... Green | 3311 | Wilmington Dist. |
| Continental | Sutton Green, Soldier | 326 | Hillsborough Dist. |
| Continental | Randall Green | 758 | |
| Continental | Abraham Green, Soldier | 218 | Hillsborough Dist. |
| Militia | Soet Green | 1688 | Wilmington Dist. |
| Militia | Benj. Green | 5269 | Wilmington Dist. |
| Continental | William Green, Soldier | 127 | Hillsborough Dist. |
| Militia | John Green | 1948 | |
| Militia | Ruben Green | 1701 | Wilmington Dist. |
| Militia | James Green | 858 | Wilmington Dist. |
| Militia | James Green | 691 | Salisbury Dist. |
| Militia | Samul Green | 3693 | Wilmington Dist. |
| Militia | John Green | 3310 | Wilmington Dist. |
| Militia | Wm. Green | 824 | Wilmington Dist. |
| Continental | J. H. Green, Surgeon | 239 | Halifax Dist. |
| Continental | John Green, Soldier | 428 | Hillsborough Dist. |
| Continental | Solomon Green | 1252 | Halifax Dist. |
| Continental | Thomas Green | 843 | Halifax Dist. |
| Militia | Capt. Thomas Givens | 3606 | Salisbury Dist. |
| Militia | Capt. Bazel Grant | 5279 | Wilmington Dist. |
| Militia | Joseph Galbreath | 4272 | Salisbury Dist. |
| Militia | Moses Granbeay | 1507 | Newbern Dist. |
| Militia | Abner Goodrine | 3728 | Wilmington Dist. |
| Continental | John Gilbert, Soldier | 201 | Halifax Dist. |
| Continental | Thomas Geddy | 106 | Halifax Dist. |
| Militia | Edwd. Gather | 960 | Newbern Dist. |
| Militia | Daniel McGoodwin | 3615 | Salisbury Dist. |
| Militia | Wm. Bony Gene | 5165 | Wilmington Dist. |
| Militia | Saml Ginton | 4510 | Wilmington Dist. |
| Militia | Francis Glass | 3584 | Salisbury Dist. |
| Militia | John Guebbs | 1815 | Newbern Dist. |
| Militia | Cornelius Granger | 5115 | Wilmington Dist. |
| Militia | John Gates | 2962 | Wilmington Dist. |
| Militia | Benjamin Gaylard | 1873 | Newbern Dist. |
| Militia | Will Garnet | 5092 | Wilmington Dist. |
| Continental | Sergt. Samuel Gilston | 804 | Halifax Dist. |
| Militia | ....as Geater | 5571 | Salisbury Dist. |
| Continental | Jeffrey Games | 1249 | Halifax Dist. |
| Continental | Isaac Gallop, Soldier | 32 | Hillsborough Dist. |
| Militia | Edward Gates | 2961 | Wilmington Dist. |
| Continental | Charles Grinesley | 333 | |
| Militia | James Gheen | 4348 | Salisbury Dist. |
| Militia | John Gallraith | 4267 | Salisbury Dist. |
| Continental | Lieut. Edward Gamble | 96 | Halifax Dist. |
| Militia | Eias Garrison | 5117 | Salisbury Dist. |
| Militia | Capt. Richard Graham | 7364 | Salisbury Dist. |
| Militia | Richard Graham | 4684 | Salisbury Dist. |
| Militia | Richard Graham | 229 | Salisbury Dist. |
| Militia | Col. William Graham | 2741 | Salisbury Dist. |
| Continental | James Gregory | 1486 | Warrenton Dist. |
| Militia | Lt. Hardy Gregory | 3487 | Wilmington Dist. |
| Continental | Thomas Gregory | 626 | Hillsboro Dist. |

|  |  | No. |  |
|---|---|---|---|
| Militia | Thomas Gregory | 5147 | Salisbury Dist. |
| Militia | John Gregory | 127 | Wilmington Dist. |
| Continental | Adam Gregory | 863 | Halifax Dist. |
| Militia | Lott Gregory | 589 | Newbern Dist. |
| Militia | Jacob Gill | 681 | Newbern Dist. |
| Militia | John Gunter | 774 | Newbern Dist. |
| Continental | Lieut. Francis Graves | 297 | Halifax Dist. |
| Militia | Solomon Goodman | 5639 | Wilmington Dist. |
| Militia | Luke Goodman | 5695 | Wilmington Dist. |
| Militia | Job Goodman | 4914 | Wilmington Dist. |
| Continental | Samul Goodman | 1460 | Warrenton Dist. |
| Militia | Lt. Henry Goodman | 3397 | Wilmington Dist. |
| Continental | Joeb Green | 438 |  |
| Militia | Foster Green | 1040 | Newbern Dist. |
| Militia | Thomas Green | 653 | Newbern Dist. |
| Militia | Thomas Giles | .... | Salisbury Dist. |
| Militia | Hugh Giles | 382 | Newbern Dist. |
| Militia | Wm. Giles | 8824 | Salisbury Dist. |
| Militia | James Giles | 7725 | Salisbury Dist. |
| Continental | Henry Guthrie | 1196 | Halifax Dist. |
| Militia | Ebenz. Guthey | 531 | Newbern Dist. |
| Continental | Howel Gillam | 992 | Halifax Dist. |
| Militia | Isaac Gillispie | 2103 | Salisbury Dist. |
| Militia | Robert Gillispie | 5140 | Salisbury Dist. |
| Militia | John Gilispie | 815 | Salisbury Dist. |
| Militia | Thomas Gillispie | 708 | Salisbury Dist. |
| Militia | George Gillispie | 5205 | Salisbury Dist. |
| Militia | Capt. Robert Gillispie | 8449 | Salisbury Dist. |
| Continental | Mathew Gillispie | 293 |  |
| Continental | David Gillispie | 563 |  |
| Militia | Borthick Gillispie | 1283 | Wilmington Dist. |
| Militia | David Gillispie | 3959 | Wilmington Dist. |
| Militia | William Gillispie | 4172 | Wilmington Dist. |
| Militia | Capt. James Gillispie | 2014 | Wilmington Dist. |
| Continental | Isaac Griffin | 719 | Hillsborough Dist. |
| Militia | Jacob Griffin | 1284 | Newbern Dist. |
| Militia | John Griffin | 232 | Wilmington Dist. |
| Militia | John Griffin | 1802 | Wilmington Dist. |
| Militia | Ezekiel Griffin | 2857 | Salisbury Dist. |
| Continental | Edward Griffin, Soldier | 444 | Halifax Dist. |
| Continental | Ezekiel Griffin | 3 | Hillsborough Dist. |
| Continental | Lawrence Griffin | 554 | Hillsborough Dist. |
| Continental | Corpl. James Griffin | 711 | Halifax Dist. |
| Continental | Capt. Hurley Griffin | 1143 | Halifax Dist. |
| Continental | Jacob Griffin | 769 |  |
| Militia | John Griffin | 5568 | Wilmington Dist. |
| Militia | Ezekiel Griffin | 3030 | Salisbury Dist. |
| Continental | William Griffin, Soldier | 353 | Halifax Dist. |
| Continental | Henry Griffin | 252 | Halifax Dist. |
| Continental | Isaac Griffin | 546 | Hillsborough Dist. |
| Continental | Sergt. Edmund Griffin | 62 | Halifax Dist. |
| Militia | Wm. Griffin | 2363 | Newbern Dist. |
| Militia | Simon Griffin | 2352 | Newbern Dist. |
| Militia | Zeckal Griffin | 2384 | Salisbury Dist. |

|  |  | *No.* |  |
|---|---|---|---|
| Militia | Benj. Griffin | 857 | Newbern Dist. |
| Militia | Stephen Gurganis | 804 | Newbern Dist. |
| Continental | Samul Gainer | 229 | |
| Militia | Henry Goff | 1131 | Newbern Dist. |
| Militia | Wm. Guy | 1754 | Wilmington Dist. |
| Militia | Nicholas Gorgan | 3285 | Wilmington Dist. |
| Militia | Matthew Gainey | 1287 | Wilmington Dist. |
| Militia | Mich'l. Gurley | 547 | Newbern Dist. |
| Militia | Dennis Gladson | 799 | Newbern Dist. |
| Militia | John Gadett | 1 | Newbern Dist. |
| Militia | Frederick Gofs | 1917 | Salisbury Dist. |
| Militia | Alexander Gordon | 1035 | Salisbury Dist. |
| Militia | Leonard Gaever | 616 | Salisbury Dist. |
| Militia | John Gilmon | 1243 | Wilmington Dist. |
| Militia | James Gayley | 590 | Salisbury Dist. |
| Continental | Sergt. Samul Gilston | 803 | Halifax Dist. |
| Militia | Abel Goner | 1217 | Newbern Dist. |
| Militia | James Gatlin | 727 | Newbern Dist. |
| Militia | John Gatlin | 934 | Newbern Dist. |
| Militia | William Gatlin | 412 | Newbern Dist. |
| Militia | Levi Gatlin | 225 | Newbern Dist. |
| Militia | Hardy Gatlin | 888 | Newbern Dist. |
| Militia | Stephen Gatlin | 1886 | Newbern Dist. |
| Militia | Edwd. Gatlin | 1013 | Newbern Dist. |
| Militia | Frederick Grady | 2138 | Wilmington Dist. |
| Militia | Joshua Gist | 1841 | Wilmington Dist. |
| Militia | Matthew Gurley | 595 | Newbern Dist. |
| Militia | John Gardem | 1652 | Salisbury Dist. |
| Militia | Peter Gronel | 3174 | Salisbury Dist. |
| Militia | Henry Garrott | 1945 | Newbern Dist. |
| Continental | Hardy Garies, Soldier | 795 | Halifax Dist. |
| Continental | Thos. Garland | 1289 | |
| Militia | James Gardner | 2383 | Salisbury Dist. |
| Militia | Peter Gates | 3120 | Wilmington Dist. |
| Militia | Burges Gaitlin | 5089 | Salisbury Dist. |
| Militia | George Gary | 5281 | Wilmington Dist. |
| Militia | Charles Gorden | 4470 | Salisbury Dist. |
| Continental | John Grinder, Soldier | 126 | Hillsborough Dist. |
| Continental | Daniel Gaugh | 618 | |
| Continental | Francis Gord | 472 | |
| Continental | Arandell Grant | 260 | |
| Continental | Patrick Gaul | 661 | |
| Continental | Ephraim Genley | 322 | |
| Militia | Anthony Gillard | 4956 | Wilmington Dist. |
| Militia | Jeremiah Gaylard | 1894 | Newbern Dist. |
| Militia | Sergt. William Gilbert | 1249 | Newbern Dist. |
| Militia | Benjamin Gether | 4634 | Salisbury Dist. |
| Militia | Peter Gates | 2903 | Wilmington Dist. |
| Militia | John Gabriel | 1849 | Newbern Dist. |
| Militia | Basil Gaither | 5086 | Salisbury Dist. |
| Militia | Mathew Ghaston | 4843 | Salisbury Dist. |
| Militia | Neil Galbreath | 3839 | Wilmington Dist. |
| Militia | Capt. Nathaniel Gorden | 857 | Salisbury Dist. |
| Militia | Capt. William Green | 4915 | Wilmington Dist. |

| | | No. | |
|---|---|---|---|
| Militia | Andrew Gurley | 545 | Newbern Dist. |
| Militia | Jeremiah Gurley | 155 | Newbern Dist. |
| Militia | Jessie Gurley | 1169 | Newbern Dist. |
| Militia | William Goner | 153 | Newbern Dist. |
| Militia | Nathan Granthan | 1038 | Newbern Dist. |
| Militia | ...... Gaskins | 1008 | Newbern Dist. |
| Continental | Edmund Gamble | 423 | Halifax Dist. |
| Militia | John Grant | 650 | Wilmington Dist. |
| Militia | Idlick Gilitrape | 855 | Newbern Dist. |
| Militia | Capt. Joshua Guest | 1227 | Wilmington Dist. |
| Militia | Nathan Godley | 1643 | Newbern Dist. |
| Continental | John Godet | 6 | Newbern Dist. |
| Militia | Thomas Gilbreth | 476 | Salisbury Dist. |
| Militia | Wm. Gurley | 1295 | Newbern Dist. |
| Militia | J. Gaddy | 4363 | Wilmington Dist. |
| Militia | George Gurley | 2112 | Newbern Dist. |
| Militia | Elias Granehan | 652 | Wilmington Dist. |
| Continental | ...... Hadrock | 114 | |
| Continental | ...... Harjers | 1771 | Warrenton Dist. |
| Continental | Elisha Hirth, Soldier | 114 | Halifax Dist. |
| Continental | Nathanil Hughes | 129 | Halifax Dist. |
| Continental | Satterfield Holstein | 1857 | Warrenton Dist. |
| Continental | Joseph Hail | .... | Halifax Dist. |
| Continental | William Haines, Soldier | 30 | Hillsborough Dist. |
| Militia | Samuel Hatch | 446 | Newbern Dist. |
| Militia | George Hauser | 362 | Salisbury Dist. |
| Militia | Zezidee Hancock | 1084 | Wilmington Dist. |
| Militia | John Hansley | 110 | Wilmington Dist. |
| Militia | Joel Holbert | 475 | Salisbury Dist. |
| Militia | Conrad Hennigar | 544 | Salisbury Dist. |
| Militia | Hugh Harris | 5934 | Salisbury Dist. |
| Continental | Thomas Harris | 260 | Hillsborough Dist. |
| Continental | John Hag | 1838 | Warrenton Dist. |
| Continental | John Hearn, Soldier | 221 | Hillsborough Dist. |
| Continental | Isaac Hunter | 332 | Hillsborough Dist. |
| Continental | William Hubbs, Soldier | 1394 | Newbern Dist. |
| Continental | Major Thomas Hogg | 164 | |
| Continental | John Hains | 1208 | Warrenton Dist. |
| Continental | Lieut. Samuel Hollowell | 26 | Halifax Dist. |
| Continental | Everit Huntington | 278 | |
| Continental | Joshua Hodges | 465 | Newbern Dist. |
| Continental | Howell Hearn, Soldier | 234 | Hillsborough Dist. |
| Continental | Keirchen Holomon | 185 | Hillsborough Dist. |
| Militia | Samuel Harison | 364 | Newbern Dist. |
| Continental | Jonathan Hopkins | 40 | Hillsborough Dist. |
| Continental | Daniel Hopkins | 202 | Hillsborough Dist. |
| Continental | Absalum Hopkins | 68 | |
| Continental | Joseph Hopkins | 39 | Halifax Dist. |
| Militia | William Harris | 7024 | Salisbury Dist. |
| Militia | William Harris | 1670 | Newbern Dist. |
| Militia | Josiah Harris | 788 | Wilmington Dist. |
| Militia | James Harris | 4705 | Salisbury Dist. |
| Militia | James Harris | 1179 | Halifax Dist. |
| Continental | Hugh Harris, Soldier | 35 | Halifax Dist. |

| | | No. | |
|---|---|---|---|
| Continental | Willie Harris | 171 | Hillsborough Dist. |
| Militia | Major Harris | 863 | Wilmington Dist. |
| Militia | Elisha Harris | 1939 | Newbern Dist. |
| Militia | Daniel Harris | 1623 | Newbern Dist. |
| Militia | Capt. William Harris | .... | Salisbury Dist. |
| Militia | Chas. Harris | 6246 | Salisbury Dist. |
| Militia | Jeremia Harris | 8601 | Salisbury Dist. |
| Militia | Jonathan Harris | 8261 | Salisbury Dist. |
| Militia | Major James Harris | 428 | Salisbury Dist. |
| Militia | J. Lewis Harris | 3644 | Salisbury Dist. |
| Continental | S..... Harris | 563 | Hillsborough Dist. |
| Continental | Nathan Harris | 555 | Hillsborough Dist. |
| Continental | Gibson Harris, Soldier | 132 | Halifax Dist. |
| Continental | Abraham Harris | 1177 | |
| Continental | Henry Harris, Soldier | 310 | Halifax Dist. |
| Militia | Stephen Harris | 1076 | Newbern Dist. |
| Militia | Thomas Harris | 93 | Newbern Dist. |
| Militia | Samul Harris | 1228 | Newbern Dist. |
| Militia | Laird Harris | 2797 | Salisbury Dist. |
| Militia | Benjamin Harris | 2760 | Wilmington Dist. |
| Militia | Daniel Harris | 1628 | Newbern Dist. |
| Militia | Samul Harris | 948 | Salisbury Dist. |
| Militia | Robert Harris | 2836 | Salisbury Dist. |
| Militia | George Harris | 7045 | Salisbury Dist. |
| Militia | Thomas Harris | 8525 | Salisbury Dist. |
| Continental | ....ah Harris | 79 | Hillsborough Dist. |
| Continental | William Hopper | 646 | Hillsborough Dist. |
| Continental | John Hooker | 105 | |
| Militia | Sam Hogshead | 3059 | Salisbury Dist. |
| Militia | Nath'l Hawthorne | 4654 | Wilmington Dist. |
| Militia | Thomas Hooks | 2422 | Wilmington Dist. |
| Militia | John Hansley | 3737 | Wilmington Dist. |
| Militia | Henry Hoghen | 1338 | Salisbury Dist. |
| Militia | Charles Hardyson | 3726 | Wilmington Dist. |
| Militia | John Hutchinson | 6172 | Salisbury Dist. |
| Militia | John Henn | 1596 | Wilmington Dist. |
| Militia | William Henley | 12 | Wilmington Dist. |
| Militia | Samul Hemphill | 1470 | Salisbury Dist. |
| Militia | Allen Herron | 5912 | Salisbury Dist. |
| Militia | James Hodges | 925 | Newbern Dist. |
| Militia | William Hurst | 197 | Wilmington Dist. |
| Militia | Majr. Francis Hailgrace | 834 | Salisbury Dist. |
| Militia | William Hantley | 5200 | Wilmington Dist. |
| Continental | Lt. Aron Hatchcock | 1078 | |
| Continental | Ezekiel Habbitt, Soldier | 170 | Hillsborough Dist. |
| Continental | John Happer | 813 | Hillsbrough Dist. |
| Militia | Wm. Hatchet | 5477 | Wilmington Dist. |
| Militia | Natl. Hensley | 4353 | Wilmington Dist. |
| Militia | John Hamblin | 4470 | Wilmington Dist. |
| Militia | Joseph Hail | 2372 | Newbern Dist. |
| Militia | William Hooks | 902 | Wilmington Dist. |
| Militia | John Head | 2943 | Salisbury Dist. |
| Militia | Jacob Hoots | 4651 | Salisbury Dist. |
| Militia | Samuel Hemphill | 3347 | Salisbury Dist. |

| | | No. | |
|---|---|---|---|
| Militia | Laban Heartley | 2979 | Salisbury Dist. |
| Militia | John Hollis | 4780 | Salisbury Dist. |
| Militia | William Heans | 2876 | Wilmington Dist. |
| Militia | Hardy Holmes | 1658 | Wilmington Dist. |
| Militia | John Hires | 6013 | Wilmington Dist. |
| Continental | Hardy Hardison | 467 | Hillsborough Dist. |
| Continental | Thomas Hays, Soldier | 905 | Halifax Dist. |
| Continental | Edward Hathcock | 737 | Hillsborough Dist. |
| Continental | Jonathan Hickman | 815 | Hillsborough Dist. |
| Continental | William Hubert | 715 | Hillsborough Dist. |
| Continental | George Hargrove | 603 | Hillsborough Dist. |
| Continental | William Happer | 830 | Hillsborough Dist. |
| Continental | Francis Huyze | 296 | Hillsborough Dist. |
| Continental | Thomas Hadaway | 153 | Halifax Dist. |
| Continental | James Hodges, Soldier | 316 | Hillsborough Dist. |
| Continental | Ezekiel Haws | 612 | Hillsborough Dits. |
| Continental | James Huggins | 803 | Hillsborough Dist. |
| Militia | Basil Holland | 5143 | Salisbury Dist. |
| Militia | Dan'l Hocton | 4851 | Morgan Dist. |
| Militia | Simon Horse | 4415 | Morgan Dist. |
| Militia | William Hooker | 1110 | Newbern Dist. |
| Militia | Valentine Hipp | 1372 | Salisbury Dist. |
| Militia | Gabriel Hardy | 1058 | Wilmington Dist. |
| Militia | Malichi Herford | 683 | Newbern Dist. |
| Militia | John Holloway | 558 | Newbern Dist. |
| Militia | James Hollingsnath | 2743 | Wilmington Dist. |
| Militia | J...... Herrington | 822 | Newbern Dist. |
| Militia | Zacariah Hollis | 1797 | Newbern Dist. |
| Militia | Joseph Horsenas | 1850 | Newbern Dist. |
| Militia | Charles Halton | 8014 | Salisbury Dist. |
| Militia | Lemul Hatch | 642 | Newbern Dist. |
| Militia | John Hemesy | 1725 | Wilmington Dist. |
| Militia | Simeon Hussey | 2002 | Wilmington Dist. |
| Militia | Wm. Holloway | 884 | Newbern Dist. |
| Militia | Thomas Hooks | 2751 | Wilmington Dist. |
| Militia | Henry Herring | 787 | Newbern Dist. |
| Continental | John Happer | 629 | Hillsborough Dist. |
| Continental | William Hewill | 94 | Hillsborough Dist. |
| Continental | John Hobgood | 65 | Hillsborough Dist. |
| Miltia | Allen Herron | 4915 | Salisbury Dist. |
| Militia | Wm. Hay | 3891 | Wilmington Dist. |
| Militia | Hambleton Hilbon | 1671 | Wilmington Dist. |
| Militia | Jacob Hofner | 3739 | Salisbury Dist. |
| Militia | Dan'l Hargett | 1416 | Newbern Dist. |
| Militia | Bazal Hollon | 2224 | Salisbury Dist. |
| Militia | Ab... Honey | 3425 | Wilmington Dist. |
| Militia | Thomas Huskinson | 1480 | Salisbury Dist. |
| Militia | Josiah Holton | 3860 | Wilmington Dist. |
| Militia | Colins Hardy | 4050 | Wilmington Dist. |
| Militia | John Horse | 45 | Morgan Dist. |
| Militia | Valentine Hip | 3646 | Salisbury Dist. |
| Militia | John Hawthorne | 4410 | Wilmington Dist. |
| Militia | Geo. Hobbs | 3642 | Wilmington Dist. |
| Militia | Adam Hedrick | 7500 | Salisbury Dist. |

| | | No. | |
|---|---|---|---|
| Continental | John Heffeman | 203 | |
| Continental | Albert Hendricks | 84 | Hillsborough Dist. |
| Continental | Capt. James Harman | 1005 | |
| Militia | Jene Hickman | 1574 | Newbern Dist. |
| | ........ Hodge | 6037 | Salisbury Dist. |
| Militia | Henry Hollingsworth | 1482 | Wilmington Dist. |
| Militia | Hillary Hooks | 914 | Wilmington Dist. |
| Militia | John Herring | 897 | Wilmington Dist. |
| Militia | Danil Highsmith | 5002 | Wilmington Dist. |
| Militia | Jacob Hainey | 1074 | Wilmington Dist. |
| Militia | Selathan Holson | 671 | Newbern Dist. |
| Militia | Hugh Herron | 5007 | Salisbury Dist. |
| Militia | Samul Hollyworth | 4490 | Wilmington Dist. |
| Militia | Sam Haphiel | 3067 | Salisbury Dist. |
| Militia | Richard Hoffum | 1648 | Wilmington Dist. |
| Militia | John Holley | 4744 | Wilmington Dist. |
| Militia | Philmon Hodge | 4246 | Wilmington Dist. |
| Militia | James Huggins | 2072 | Salisbury Dist. |
| Militia | James Henry | 4209 | Salisbury Dist. |
| Militia | John Hibbs | 137 | Newbern Dist. |
| Militia | Emit House | 1116 | Newbern Dist. |
| Militia | Phil Hodges | 4341 | Wilmington Dist. |
| Militia | Jno. Hysmith | 1183 | Newbern Dist. |
| Militia | David Holton | 936 | Newbern Dist. |
| Militia | Enos Harrold | 178 | Newbern Dist. |
| Militia | Robt. Holton | 384 | Newbern Dist. |
| Militia | Henry Holland | 5778 | Wilmington Dist. |
| Militia | David Hendry | 4676 | Salisbury Dist. |
| Militia | Leuis Henry | 4222 | Salisbury Dist. |
| Militia | John Hensy | 5005 | Wilmington Dist. |
| Militia | Uzzell Herring | 5874 | Wilmington Dist. |
| Militia | Geo. H. | 1558 | Wilmington Dist. |
| Militia | Beacham Helton | 4786 | Salisbury Dist. |
| Militia | William Hooks | 2756 | Wilmington Dist. |
| Militia | Stephen Hollins | 2908 | Wilmington Dist. |
| Militia | Thomas Hooks | 3042 | Wilmington Dist. |
| Militia | Philip Hoos | 2727 | Salisbury Dist. |
| Militia | John Huffam | 1740 | Wilmington Dist. |
| Militia | Hill Hulbert | 6001 | Wilmington Dist. |
| Militia | Gasper Humpberrier | 4581 | Morgan Dist. |
| Continental | James Harpoon | 222 | |
| Militia | Wm. Hargrove | 5682 | Wilmington Dist. |
| Militia | Isaac Hughey | 4206 | Salisbury Dist. |
| Militia | James Hamilton | 8235 | Salisbury Dist. |
| Militia | Saml. Hemphill | 5301 | Salisbury Dist. |
| Militia | James Hanken | 6017 | Salisbury Dist. |
| Militia | Jonathan Thims | 4239 | Wilmington Dist. |
| Militia | Phil. Hodges | 4348 | Wilmington Dist. |
| Militia | Nathaniel Henseley | 1870 | Wilmington Dist. |
| Militia | George Hooks | 5650 | Wilmington Dist. |
| Militia | Hudnall Huffham | 1431 | Wilmington Dist. |
| Militia | John Hurley | 2069 | Newbern Dist. |
| Continental | Anthony Haney | 559 | Halifax Dist. |
| Continental | Joseph Hodges | 466 | |

| | | No. | |
|---|---|---|---|
| Continental | Caleb Holly | 839 | |
| Continental | David Hass | 185 | Halifax Dist. |
| Continental | Brig. Gen. James Hogun | 143 | Halifax Dist. |
| Continental | Jacob Hanks | 777 | |
| Continental | William Hubert, Soldier | 540 | Hillsborough Dist. |
| Continental | Hardy Hardison | 635 | Hillsborough Dist. |
| Continental | Daniel Huggins | 763 | Hillsborough Dist. |
| Continental | Luke Heard | 540 | |
| Continental | Abien Halbe | 491 | |
| Continental | George Hargrove | 450 | Hillsborough Dist. |
| Continental | John Hacklemar | 857 | Hillsborough Dist. |
| Continental | Carter Hastings | 325 | Hillsborough Dist. |
| Continental | Moses Hopper | 631 | Hillsborough Dist. |
| Continental | Nicholas Hair | 632 | Hillsborough Dist. |
| Continental | Joseph Hayman | 731 | Halifax Dist. |
| Continental | Peter Hadcock, Soldier | 449 | Halifax Dist. |
| Continental | Corbin Hickman | 261 | Halifax Dist. |
| Continental | Ezekie Hans, Soldier | 395 | Hillsborough Dist |
| Continental | Steener Hannis, Soldier | 5 | Hillsborough Dist. |
| Continental | Francis Hugga, Soldier | 396 | Hillsborough Dist. |
| Continental | Jacob Hafner, Soldier | 575 | Hillsborough Dist. |
| Continental | Francis Hubbard | 1204 | Halifax Dist. |
| Continental | John Hobgood | 127 | Hillsborough Dist. |
| Continental | William Haines | 52 | Hillsborough Dist. |
| Continental | Joseph Harp | 17 | Hillsborough Dist. |
| Continental | Matthew Herring | 1095 | Halifax Dist. |
| Continental | Peter Hobbs | 1060 | Halifax Dist. |
| Continental | Joseph Harp | 8 | Hillsborough Dist. |
| Continental | John Headright, Soldier | 7 | Halifax Dist. |
| Continental | Nathan Horton | 44 | Hillsborough Dist. |
| Continental | Jacob Horton | 1474 | Warrenton Dist. |
| Continental | Everitt Hunter | 204 | |
| Continental | Solomon Hunter | 454 | Halifax Dist. |
| Militia | John Hunter | 5276 | Salisbury Dist. |
| Militia | Thomas Hunter | 4203 | Morgan Dist. |
| Militia | Wm. Hunter | 4530 | Salisbury Dist. |
| Militia | Nicolas Hunter | 1767 | Wilmington Dist. |
| Militia | Thomas Hunter | 3772 | Wilmington Dist. |
| Continental | Isaac Hunter | 314 | Hillsborough Dist. |
| Continental | Andrew Hunter | 549 | Halifax Dist. |
| Continental | Peter Herndon | 217 | |
| Continental | Luke Huggins | 18 | |
| Continental | Mark Haycraft, Soldier | 382 | Halifax Dist. |
| Continental | Jesse Hardyson, Soldier | 497 | Hillsborough Dist. |
| Continental | William Harrington | 558 | Warrenton Dist. |
| Continental | Willis Hastings | 365 | Hillsborough Dist. |
| Continental | William Hargrove | 1613 | Warrenton Dist. |
| Militia | Aldridge Hadnot | 101 | Wilmington Dist. |
| Militia | John Hinson | 1540 | Wilmington Dist. |
| Militia | Stephen Hipp | 6307 | Salisbury Dist. |
| Continental | Isham Hatchcock | 1382 | Halifax Dist. |
| Continental | Jonathan Hickman | 631 | Hillsborough Dist. |
| Militia | Benjamin Herndon | 858 | Salisbury Dist. |
| Continental | Jesse Hapiel | 468 | |

| | | No. | |
|---|---|---|---|
| Continental | Micheil Huggins ............... | 287 | Hillsborough Dist. |
| Continental | James Huggins ................. | 619 | Hillsborough Dist. |
| Continental | Griffin Hanmontree, Soldier........ | 138 | Hillsborough Dist. |
| Militia | Christian Hisler ................ | 7518 | Salisbury Dist. |
| Militia | Major Hurst ................... | 3800 | Wilmington Dist. |
| Militia | George Hamilton ............... | 1119 | Newbern Dist. |
| Continental | Frederick Hathcock ............. | 15 | Halifax Dist. |
| Militia | Rubin Hobly .................. | 639 | Newbern Dist. |
| | Joseph Hinson, Soldier ........... | 1450 | Newbern Dist. |
| Militia | Peter Hargett .................. | 1508 | Newbern Dist. |
| Militia | William Harp ................. | 158 | Newbern Dist. |
| Militia | Michael Hook ................. | 3824 | Morgan Dist. |
| Militia | John Headright ................ | 9170 | Salisbury Dist. |
| Militia | Albert Hendrick ................ | 7222 | Salisbury Dist. |
| Militia | John Haggans ................. | 6094 | Salisbury Dist. |
| Militia | Roger Ha..ock ................ | 797 | Newbern Dist. |
| Continental | Major Thomas Hogg ............ | 422 | Halifax Dist. |
| Continental | Philip Hochamm ............... | 184 | Halifax Dist. |
| Continental | John Hirchey .................. | 1250 | Halifax Dist. |
| Continental | Corpl. John Honey ............. | 564 | Halifax Dist. |
| Continental | Patrick Haggard, Soldier ......... | 4 | Halifax Dist. |
| Continental | James Hearn .................. | 1137 | Halifax Dist. |
| Continental | Philip Hochaman ............... | 183 | Halifax Dist. |
| Continental | Lieut. William Harrison .......... | 515 | Halifax Dist. |
| Continental | Abel Highman ................. | 621 | |
| Continental | Samul Hurson ................. | 345 | |
| Continental | Asa Hunter ................... | 303 | Hillsborough Dist. |
| Continental | Hardy Hugbkins ............... | 260 | Hillsborough Dist. |
| Continental | William Hawkins ............... | 83 | Hillsborough Dist. |
| Continental | James Hiffeman ................ | 39 | |
| Militia | Robert Hair ................... | 5477 | Salisbury Dist. |
| Militia | Amos Holder .................. | 6005 | Wilmington Dist. |
| Militia | James Hopkins ................. | 880 | Newbern Dist. |
| Militia | ..... Hunter ................. | 5123 | Salisbury Dist. |
| Militia | William Holleman .............. | 604 | Newbern Dist. |
| Militia | Joseph Hadnot ................. | 5238 | Wilmington Dist. |
| Militia | William Hannot ................ | 1539 | Wilmington Dist. |
| Continental | Hielry Hooks .................. | 1184 | Warrenton Dist. |
| Continental | Michial Huggins ............... | 417 | Hillsborough Dist. |
| Continental | John Hannord ................. | 420 | Hillsborough Dist. |
| Continental | Howell Hoearn ................ | 361 | Hillsborough Dist. |
| Continental | Michiel Hooks ................. | 466 | |
| Continental | Stewart Hamberton, Soldier ....... | 97 | Hillsborough Dist. |
| Continental | Shad'r. Hornes, Soldier ........... | 1088 | Halifax Dist. |
| Continental | James Hodges ................. | 449 | Hillsborough Dist. |
| Continental | Ezekiel Halbitt ................ | 283 | Hillsborough Dist. |
| Continental | Major Thomas Heagg ........... | 423 | Halifax Dist. |
| Militia | Jacob Hurst ................... | 3796 | Wilmington Dist. |
| Militia | William Hancock .............. | 5223 | Wilmington Dist. |
| Militia | Col. Frederick Hambright ......... | 273 | Salisbury Dist. |
| Militia | S..... Herring ................ | 260 | Wilmington Dist. |
| Militia | Henry Hodges ................. | 1977 | Newbern Dist. |
| Militia | Whitfield Herring .............. | 247 | Wilmington Dist. |
| Militia | Jacob Hysmith ................ | 1182 | Newbern Dist. |

| | | No. | |
|---|---|---|---|
| Militia | Gasper Hinkel | 7582 | Salisbury Dist. |
| Militia | Jesse Holton | 287 | Newbern Dist. |
| Militia | Floyd Hodges | 1663 | Newbern Dist. |
| Continental | Selly Harney | 301 | Hillsborough Dist. |
| Continental | John Hoggard | 294 | Hillsborough Dist. |
| Continental | John Hupsey | 229 | Hillsborough Dist. |
| Continental | Hance Hamilton | 411 | Hillsborough Dist. |
| Militia | William Harbert | 1781 | Wilmington Dist. |
| Militia | William Hooks | 3788 | Wilmington Dist. |
| Militia | John Herring | 370 | Wilmington Dist. |
| Militia | James Ho.... | 1191 | Newbern Dist. |
| Militia | Will Hammonds | 1198 | Newbern Dist. |
| Continental | William Hargrave | 74 | Halifax Dist. |
| Continental | Capt. Joshua Hadly | 439 | Halifax Dist. |
| Continental | Michiel Higgins | 46 | Newbern Dist. |
| Continental | Sergt. Benjamin Hodges | 491 | Halifax Dist. |
| Continental | West Hadnot, Soldier | 430 | Hillsborough Dist. |
| Continental | Lemuel Halstead | 242 | Hillsborough Dist. |
| Militia | James Hethman | 8021 | Salisbury Dist. |
| Militia | Patrick Hughey | 6998 | Salisbury Dist. |
| Militia | Oneuphonis Hunt | 5314 | Wilmington Dist. |
| Militia | Benjamin Herndon | 852 | Salisbury Dist. |
| Militia | Sala.. Holson | 1455 | Newbern Dist. |
| Militia | Arthur Herring | 5541 | Wilmington Dist. |
| Militia | William Hagard | 564 | Newbern Dist. |
| Continental | John Holdbrooks | 325 | Hillsborough Dist. |
| Continental | John Hogan | 878 | Halifax Dist. |
| Continental | Robert Haley | 544 | |
| Militia | John Huske | 5074 | Wilmington Dist. |
| Militia | Francis Holloway, Soldier | 1569 | Newbern Dist. |
| Militia | Paul Hamilton | 966 | Newbern Dist. |
| Militia | Joshua | 675 | Newbern Dist. |
| Militia | Seth Hovey | 1869 | Newbern Dist. |
| Militia | Simon Heel | 1666 | Newbern Dist. |
| Militia | Parker Hutchinson | 1894 | Newbern Dist. |
| Militia | Peter Horsends | 958 | Newbern Dist. |
| Militia | Albert Henderson | 7564 | Salisbury Dist. |
| Militia | Joseph Hodges | 257 | Newbern Dist. |
| Militia | William Hay | 2913 | Salisbury Dist. |
| Militia | Duglas Hudin | 7307 | Salisbury Dist. |
| Militia | ....... Haney | 1034 | Wilmington Dist. |
| Militia | Lieut. Thomas Hedley | 1228 | Wilmington Dist. |
| Militia | Capt. William Hooks | 3037 | Wilmington Dist. |
| Militia | Capt. Thomas Hadley | 4896 | Wilmington Dist. |
| Militia | Samuel Hollingsworth | 2889 | Wilmington Dist. |
| Militia | Robt. Hodge | 8345 | Salisbury Dist. |
| Militia | John Hank | 4574 | Morgan Dist. |
| Militia | Capt. Benjamin Herndon | 864 | Salisbury Dist. |
| Militia | Lieut. Joseph Hickman | 5395 | Salisbury Dist. |
| Militia | Lieut. Phil. Hodges | 1783 | Wilmington Dist. |
| Militia | George Holton | 1218 | Newbern Dist. |
| Militia | Philip Hose | 1488 | Salisbury Dist. |
| Militia | Aldridge Hadnot | 5207 | Wilmington Dist. |
| Continental | Micheal Harkley | 480 | |

| | | No. | |
|---|---|---|---|
| Continental | John Heffeman | 277 | |
| Continental | Lieut. Speir Holland | 32 | Halifax Dist. |
| Continental | David Henson | 1243 | Warrenton Dist. |
| Militia | William Hargrove | 268 | Wilmington Dist. |
| Militia | Zebedee Hancock | 86 | Wilmington Dist. |
| Militia | Will Hullib | 4993 | Wilmington Dist. |
| Militia | Zedock Humford | 5583 | Wilmington Dist. |
| Militia | Elijah Herndon | 4599 | Salisbury Dist. |
| Militia | John Harris | 269 | Wilmington Dist. |
| Militia | Joseph Hejgit | 1289 | Salisbury Dist. |
| Militia | Moses Hnonan | .... | Salisbury Dist. |
| Militia | Isaac Hosin | 1261 | Wilmington Dist. |
| Militia | Henry Haddock | 1266 | Wilmington Dist. |
| Militia | Capt. John Hambright | 310 | Salisbury Dist. |
| Continental | Major Thomas Hogg | 421 | Halifax Dist. |
| Continental | John Hamilton | 710 | Hillsborough Dist. |
| Continental | Joseph Hardison | 1084 | Halifax Dist. |
| Continental | William Hancock, Soldier | 188 | Hillsborough Dist. |
| Militia | Capt. Pendleton Isbell | 882 | Salisbury Dist. |
| Militia | Col. Elijah Isaacs | 900 | Salisbury Dist. |
| Militia | Curtis Ivey | 2786 | Wilmington Dist. |
| Militia | Wm. Irvinson | 5726 | Salisbury Dist. |
| Militia | John Isleeson | 450 | Newbern Dist. |
| Militia | John Irwin | 5759 | Salisbury Dist. |
| Militia | Shadrack Inman | 4959 | Morgan Dist. |
| Militia | James Ivey | 4766 | Wilmington Dist. |
| Militia | Jacob Iarrel | 944 | Newbern Dist. |
| Militia | Christ.. Ipock | 880 | Newbern Dist. |
| Militia | Jacob Ipock | 852 | Newbern Dist. |
| Militia | S..... Ipock | 912 | Newbern Dist. |
| Militia | Wm. Ireland | 6425 | Salisbury Dist. |
| Militia | Jacob Idel | 7600 | Salisbury Dist. |
| Militia | John Innis | 3142 | Salisbury Dist. |
| Militia | Hardin Ives | 2301 | Newbern Dist. |
| Militia | William Ives | 1795 | Newbern Dist. |
| Militia | Joseph Ingram | 2152 | Newbern Dist. |
| Militia | Joseph Irvin | 1312 | Newbern Dist. |
| Militia | Daniel Innes | 3890 | Wilmington Dist. |
| Militia | Isaac Irwin | 5706 | Salisbury Dist. |
| Militia | Edward Ingram | 5139 | Wilmington Dist. |
| Militia | John Stener | 4482 | Wilmington Dist. |
| Militia | Thomas Ivey | 1293 | Wilmington Dist. |
| Militia | Peter Ipock | 1029 | Newbern Dist. |
| Militia | Wm. Irnin | 5307 | Salisbury Dist. |
| Militia | James Isham | 1412 | Wilmington Dist. |
| Militia | Peter Irons | 4718 | Salisbury Dist. |
| Militia | Samuel Ipock | 1771 | Newbern Dist. |
| Militia | Ruben Isey | 662 | Wilmington Dist. |
| Militia | Hith Ipock | 847 | Newbern Dist. |
| Militia | Saml Irwin | 2359 | Salisbury Dist. |
| Continental | Elishai Ivey | 588 | |
| Continental | Samul Iggby | 220 | |
| Continental | Nicholas Icour | 628 | Hillsborough Dist. |
| Continental | Nicholas Isler | 1131 | Halifax Dist. |

|  |  | *No.* |  |
|---|---|---|---|
| Continental | Jacob Ivey | 558 |  |
| Continental | John Ingles | 80 |  |
| Continental | Reuben Ivey | 153 | Hillsborough Dist. |
| Continental | James Ives, Soldier | 333 | Halifax Dist. |
| Continental | I.... Ingram | 421 |  |
| Militia | Thomas Ivey | 2998 | Wilmington Dist. |
| Militia | Henry Ikard | 4442 | Morgan Dist. |
| Militia | John Irwin | 2444 | Salisbury Dist. |
| Militia | John Isler | 87 | Newbern Dist. |
| Militia | Jacob Ipock | 730 | Newbern Dist. |
| Militia | Robert Irwin | 2698 | Salisbury Dist. |
| Militia | John Ingram | 4615 | Wilmington Dist. |
| Militia | Capt. Pendleton Isbell | 83 | Salisbury Dist. |
| Militia | Lieut. Thomas Isbell | 693 | Salisbury Dist. |
| Militia | Col. Elijha Isaacs | 901 | Salisbury Dist. |
| Militia | William Ingram | 2119 | Newbern Dist. |
| Militia | James Ireland | 7871 | Salisbury Dist. |
| Continental | Lieut. Adj. Curtis Ivey | 293 | Halifax Dist. |
| Continental | John Ingram | 443 | Halifax Dist. |
| Militia | Hugh Jorist | 6415 | Salisbury Dist. |
| Militia | Thomas Jordan | 883 | Newbern Dist. |
| Militia | John Jones | 1308 | Salisbury Dist. |
| Militia | John Jones | 2004 | Newbern Dist. |
| Militia | John Jones | 2248 | Wilmington Dist. |
| Militia | James Jones | 426 | Newbern Dist. |
| Militia | James Jones | 6945 | Salisbury Dist. |
| Militia | James Jones | 806 | Wilmington Dist. |
| Militia | William Jones | 687 | Newbern Dist. |
| Militia | Hardy Jones | 1245 | Newbern Dist. |
| Militia | Silvanus Jones | 2365 | Newbern Dist. |
| Militia | Matthew Jones | 1983 | Newbern Dist. |
| Militia | David Jones | 4644 | Salisbury Dist. |
| Militia | Joshua Jones | 4321 | Wilmington Dist. |
| Militia | David Jones, Soldier | 1488 | Newbern Dist. |
| Militia | Henry Jones | 3159 | Wilmington Dist. |
| Militia | Sampson Jones | 2249 | Wilmington Dist. |
| Militia | Peter Jones | 3514 | Wilmington Dist. |
| Militia | Stephen Jones | 187 | Wilmington Dist. |
| Militia | Edward Jones | 3233 | Wilmington Dist. |
| Militia | Robt. Jones | 6465 | Salisbury Dist. |
| Militia | Thomas Jones | 5161 | Salisbury Dist. |
| Militia | Insgrove Jones | 3247 | Wilmington Dist. |
| Militia | Fred Jones | 1720 | Newbern Dist. |
| Militia | Anthony Jones | 2336 | Wilmington Dist. |
| Militia | William Jones | 810 | Newbern Dist. |
| Militia | Elias Jones | 1790 | Wilmington Dist. |
| Continental | William Jones | 1627 | Warrenton Dist. |
| Continental | Drury Jones, Soldier | 179 | Halifax Dist. |
| Continental | Freman Jones | 135 | Halifax Dist. |
| Continental | Dempsey Jones | 1205 | Halifax Dist. |
| Continental | Elisha Jones | 107 |  |
| Continental | Brittain Jones | 1391 | Halifax Dist. |
| Continental | Nathan Jones | 1323 | Halifax Dist. |
| Continental | Isham Jones | 225 | Halifax Dist. |

| | | *No.* | |
|---|---|---|---|
| Continental | Josiah Jones | 269 | Hillsborough Dist. |
| Continental | Capt. Lieut. Phil Jones | 393 | |
| Continental | William Jones | 423 | Halifax Dist. |
| Continental | Lieut. Timothy Jones | 602 | Halifax Dist. |
| Continental | Richard Jones | 215 | Hillsborough Dist. |
| Continental | James Jones | 274 | Hillsborough Dist. |
| Continental | Fred Jones | 601 | |
| Continental | Thomas Jones | 923 | Halifax Dist. |
| Continental | Zachariah Jones, Soldier | 1103 | Halifax Dist. |
| Continental | David Jones | 700 | |
| Continental | Benjamin Jones | 407 | Hillsborough Dist. |
| Continental | David Jones | 25 | Hillsborough Dist. |
| Continental | Brillain Jones | 660 | Hillsborough Dist. |
| Continental | Benj. Jones | 461 | Hillsborough Dist. |
| Continental | Isaac Jones | 363 | Hillsborough Dist. |
| Continental | Frederick Jones | 556 | Hillsborough Dist. |
| Continental | Hezekiah Jones | 268 | Hillsborough Dist. |
| Militia | Elisha Jones | 5781 | Wilmington Dist. |
| Militia | William Jones | 3052 | Salisbury Dist. |
| Militia | Thomas Jones | 4064 | Wilmington Dist. |
| Militia | Bridger Jones | 5212 | Wilmington Dist. |
| Militia | Isaac Jones | 1280 | Newbern Dist. |
| Militia | David Jones | 1553 | Wilmington Dist. |
| Militia | Francis Jones | 4076 | Wilmington Dist. |
| Militia | Lieut. Samul Jones | 147 | Wilmington Dist. |
| Militia | Jacob Jones | 382 | Newbern Dist. |
| Militia | Capt. Kelber Jones | 5578 | Wilmington Dist. |
| Militia | Rich'd. Jones | 1502 | Newbern Dist. |
| Militia | Nuesh Jones | 4406 | Wilmington Dist. |
| Militia | Edward Jones | 4241 | Wilmington Dist. |
| Militia | Ant. . . . Jones | 3665 | Wilmington Dist. |
| Militia | William Jones | 894 | Wilmington Dist. |
| Militia | Isaac Jones | 2774 | Wilmington Dist. |
| Militia | Arthur Jones | 122 | Newbern Dist. |
| Militia | Nicholas Jones | 4595 | Salisbury Dist. |
| Militia | Shadrack Jones | 612 | Newbern Dist. |
| Militia | Edward Jones | 2388 | Wilmington Dist. |
| Militia | Peter Jones | 5028 | Salisbury Dist. |
| Militia | David Jones | 1635 | Salisbury Dist. |
| Militia | Solomon Jones | 6833 | Salisbury Dist. |
| Militia | Sampson Jones | 2335 | Wilmington Dist. |
| Militia | Handy Jones | 114 | Newbern Dist. |
| Militia | Nathaniel Jones | 946 | Wilmington Dist. |
| Militia | Abel Johnston | 4137 | Wilmington Dist. |
| Militia | Jesse Jones | 262 | Wilmington Dist. |
| Militia | Charles Jones | 3561 | Wilmington Dist. |
| Militia | Peter Kitner | 7205 | Salisbury Dist. |
| Militia | Lewis Kellar | 1800 | Salisbury Dist. |
| Militia | John Killian | 4893 | Morgan Dist. |
| Militia | John Knott | 1036 | Newbern Dist. |
| Militia | John King | 1005 | Wilmington Dist. |
| Militia | Anthony Keimore | 918 | Newbern Dist. |
| Militia | Michael Kenan | 2806 | Wilmington Dist. |
| Militia | Isaac Kemp | 1047 | Newbern Dist. |

| | | *No.* | |
|---|---|---|---|
| Militia | Joshua Kree | 1557 | Newbern Dist. |
| Militia | William King | 740 | Newbern Dist. |
| Militia | George Kisbrough | 4569 | Salisbury Dist. |
| Militia | Absalom Kurx | 4211 | Salisbury Dist. |
| Militia | Nathaniel John Kerr | 2004 | Salisbury Dist. |
| Militia | George Kilner | 1317 | Salisbury Dist. |
| Militia | Joshua Kurx | 552 | Newbern Dist. |
| Militia | Nathaniel Kellar | 1420 | Newbern Dist. |
| Militia | Jno. Killinworth | 647 | Newbern Dist. |
| Militia | Absalom Kirby | 445 | Newbern Dist. |
| Militia | Joshua Kemp | 467 | Newbern Dist. |
| Militia | Thomas Kemp | 678 | Newbern Dist. |
| Militia | Joseph King | 971 | Newbern Dist. |
| Militia | Robert Kurx | 1018 | Newbern Dist. |
| Militia | George Killum | 1028 | Wilmington Dist. |
| Militia | Joseph Karr | 2278 | Salisbury Dist. |
| Militia | James Kellum | 796 | Newbern Dist. |
| Militia | Micajah King | 3497 | Wilmington Dist. |
| Militia | Capt. John Kees | 844 | Salisbury Dist. |
| Militia | Elepha. King | 1686 | Newbern Dist. |
| Militia | James King | 970 | Newbern Dist. |
| Militia | John Kiney | 1069 | Wilmington Dist. |
| Militia | Sharp Key | 83 | Newbern Dist. |
| Militia | James Murphey | 8732 | Salisbury Dist. |
| Militia | James Murray | 3649 | Wilmington Dist. |
| Continental | Isaac Parker | 909 | Halifax Dist. |
| Continental | William Price | 636 | Hillsborough Dist. |
| Militia | Jene Peacock | 1744 | Wilmington Dist. |
| Militia | William Price | 4526 | Morgan Dist. |
| Continental | Martin Penegar | 352 | Hillsborough Dist. |
| Continental | Daniel Peel | 401 | Hillsborough Dist. |
| Continental | John Polson | 393 | Hillsborough Dist. |
| Continental | Jacob Parish | 254 | Hillsborough Dist. |
| Continental | William Pervotham | 367 | Hillsborough Dist. |
| Continental | John Portress | 213 | Hillsborough Dist. |
| Continental | Erastus Peppett | 1 | Hillsborough Dist. |
| Continental | Miles Privitt | 51 | Hillsborough Dist. |
| Continental | Edward Prichett | 134 | Hillsborough Dist. |
| Continental | Daniel Peal | 131 | Hillsborough Dist. |
| Continental | George Pettiford | 265 | Hillsborough Dist. |
| Continental | Martin Phifer | 310 | Hillsborough Dist. |
| Continental | Thomas Pet | 295 | Hillsborough Dist. |
| Continental | William Poor | 194 | Hillsborough Dist. |
| Continental | Rainleigh Pendergrass | 73 | Hillsborough Dist. |
| Continental | Joel Pa...borne | 340 | Hillsborough Dist. |
| Continental | Noah Parr | 213 | Halifax Dist. |
| Continental | ...... Pender, Soldier | 967 | Halifax Dist. |
| Continental | Micajah Pettaway | 247 | Hillsborough Dist. |
| Continental | Joseph Palmer | 640 | Hillsborough Dist. |
| Continental | Stephen Pall | 503 | Hillsborough Dist. |
| Continental | William Pea | 511 | Hillsborough Dist. |
| Continental | Lieut. Thomas Pastiere | 268 | Halifax Dist. |
| Continental | Philip Peterford, Soldier | 428 | Halifax Dist. |
| Continental | Col. John Pattin | 180 | Halifax Dist. |

| | | No. | |
|---|---|---|---|
| Continental | Peter Piland | 1373 | Halifax Dist. |
| Continental | Kedar Phelps | 731 | Halifax Dist. |
| Militia | Robert Parks | 3281 | Salisbury Dist. |
| Continental | Peter Parks, Soldier | 622 | Halifax Dist. |
| Continental | James Parks | 426 | Hillsborough Dist. |
| Continental | Thomas Parks | 580 | |
| Militia | John Parks | 1253 | Salisbury Dist. |
| Militia | Jesse Pollock | 337 | Newbern Dist. |
| Militia | Col. Calib Phifer | 499 | Salisbury Dist. |
| Militia | Lieut. Thomas Polk | 5100 | Salisbury Dist. |
| Militia | Lieut. James Purdee | 4412 | Wilmington Dist. |
| Militia | Lieut. James Philco | 5960 | Wilmington Dist. |
| Militia | John Padget | 766 | Wilmington Dist. |
| Militia | A.... Plummer | 2892 | Wilmington Dist. |
| Militia | Amos Pitman | 5894 | Wilmington Dist. |
| Militia | William Pharis | 711 | Wilmington Dist. |
| Militia | Moses Peterson | 1932 | Wilmington Dist. |
| Militia | Levi Peacock | 2034 | Newbern Dist. |
| Militia | Abraham Perry | 4351 | Wilmington Dist. |
| Continental | Job. Pendergrass | 71 | Hillsborough Dist. |
| Continental | William Parr | 348 | Hillsborough Dist. |
| Continental | William Plumer | 272 | Hillsborough Dist. |
| Continental | Jesse Prichard | 310 | Hillsborough Dist. |
| Continental | Edward Pendleton | 163 | Hillsborough Dist. |
| Continental | John Parrimore | 89 | Hillsborough Dist. |
| Continental | Francis Pridgen | 9 | Hillsborough Dist. |
| Continental | William Parr | 255 | Hillsborough Dist. |
| Continental | Abraham Parish | 165 | Hillsborough Dist. |
| Continental | Benjamin Sharp | .... | Halifax Dist. |
| Militia | Ezekiel Sharpe | 5252 | Salisbury Dist. |
| Militia | Capt. Joseph Sharpe | 4460 | Salisbury Dist. |
| Militia | John Sharpe | 4006 | Salisbury Dist. |
| Militia | Charles Sharpe | 5998 | Wilmington Dist. |
| Militia | John Sharpe | 6002 | Wilmington Dist. |
| Militia | James Sharpe | 8604 | Salisbury Dist. |
| Continental | Capt. Anthony Sharpe | 377 | Halifax Dist. |
| Continental | Sergt. Ransom Savage | 523 | Halifax Dist. |
| Militia | Arthur Savage | 2026 | Wilmington Dist. |
| Militia | Jacob Savage | 2287 | Wilmington Dist. |
| Militia | Francis Savage | 3399 | Wilmington Dist. |
| Militia | Henry Savage | 6724 | Salisbury Dist. |
| Continental | Micajah Savage | 1210 | Warrenton Dist. |
| Continental | Luke Stansbury | 125 | Hillsborough Dist. |
| Continental | Joseph Seaburn | 141 | Hillsborough Dist. |
| Continental | Joseph Sketer | 261 | Hillsborough Dist. |
| Continental | John Smart | 1053 | Halifax Dist. |
| Militia | Absalom Sessions | 4700 | Wilmington Dist. |
| Militia | Ivey Smith | 1299 | Wilmington Dist. |
| Militia | Noah Smith | 3628 | Wilmington Dist. |
| Militia | Elisha Smith | 4420 | Wilmington Dist. |
| Militia | Abner Smith | 204 | Wilmington Dist. |
| Militia | Hardy Smith | 4878 | Wilmington Dist. |
| Militia | Zachariah Smith | 551 | Wilmington Dist. |
| Militia | Nathaniel Smith | 4573 | Morgan Dist. |

| | | No. | |
|---|---|---|---|
| Militia | Nathan Smith | 150 | Newbern Dist. |
| Militia | Col. Robert Smith | 1178 | Salisbury Dist. |
| Militia | Duncan Smith | 5619 | Wilmington Dist. |
| Militia | Capt. Archibald Smith | 4174 | Wilmington Dist. |
| Militia | Josiah Smith | 3543 | Wilmington Dist. |
| Militia | Lieut. David Smith | 7809 | Salisbury Dist. |
| Militia | Jeremiah Smith | 666 | Newbern Dist. |
| Militia | Alex. Smith | 534 | Newbern Dist. |
| Militia | Benjamin Smith | 1265 | Newbern Dist. |
| Militia | Frederik Smith | 2350 | Wilmington Dist. |
| Militia | Peter Smith | 2326 | Newbern Dist. |
| Militia | Peter Smith | 3029 | Wilmington Dist. |
| Militia | Andrew Smith | 385 | Salisbury Dist. |
| Militia | Francis Smith | 4882 | Wilmington Dist. |
| Militia | Caleb Smith | 5588 | Wilmington Dist. |
| Militia | Charles Smith | 737 | Newbern Dist. |
| Militia | Ezekiel Smith | 1294 | Newbern Dist. |
| Militia | Capt. George Smith | 5046 | Morgan Dist. |
| Militia | Thomas Smith | 807 | Wilmington Dist. |
| Militia | Thomas Smith | 8352 | Salisbury Dist. |
| Militia | Thomas Smith | 1072 | Halifax Dist. |
| Militia | Capt. Daniel Smith | 223 | Salisbury Dist. |
| Militia | Daniel Smith | 4196 | Morgan Dist. |
| Militia | John Smith | 3002 | Wilmington Dist. |
| Militia | John Smith | 117 | Salisbury Dist. |
| Continental | John Smith | 33 | Hillsborough Dist. |
| Continental | Daniel Smith | 480 | Hillsborough Dist. |
| Continental | Thomas Smith | 1338 | |
| Continental | Peter Smith | 128 | Hillsborough Dist. |
| Continental | Arm Smith | 633 | Hillsborough Dist. |
| Continental | Lieut. Joley Smith | 204 | Hillsborough Dist. |
| Continental | Benjamin Smith, Soldier | 595 | Halifax Dist. |
| Continental | Richard Smith | 381 | Hillsborough Dist. |
| Continental | Charles Smith | 1256 | Halifax Dist. |
| Continental | Jeremiah Smith, Soldier | 519 | Halifax Dist. |
| Continental | Oren Smith | 87 | Hillsborough Dist. |
| Continental | Samuel Smith | 48 | Hillsborough Dist. |
| Continental | William Smith | 219 | Hillsborough Dist. |
| Continental | Peter Smith | 214 | Hillsborough Dist. |
| Continental | Willis Smith | 1263 | Halifax Dist. |
| Continental | Nathaniel Smith | 1187 | Warrenton Dist. |
| Militia | George Smith | 5931 | Wilmington Dist. |
| Militia | David Smith | 4854 | Wilmington Dist. |
| Militia | David Smith | 449 | Newbern Dist. |
| Militia | Alexander Smith | 4104 | Morgan Dist. |
| Militia | Archibald Smith | 4817 | Wilmington Dist. |
| Militia | Joseph Smith | 1909 | Newbern Dist. |
| Militia | Richard Smith | 2639 | Wilmington Dist. |
| Militia | Enridge Smith | 2231 | Wilmington Dist. |
| Militia | Malcom Smith | 2583 | Wilmington Dist. |
| Militia | Jeremiah Smith | 3672 | Wilmington Dist. |
| Militia | Ezekiel Smith | 1045 | Newbern Dist. |
| Militia | William Smith | 3035 | Salisbury Dist. |
| Militia | Lieut. William Smith | 8220 | Salisbury Dist. |

|  |  | No. |  |
|---|---|---|---|
| Militia | Alexander Smith | 4138 | Wilmington Dist. |
| Militia | David Smith | 2258 | Salisbury Dist. |
| Militia | Lewis Smith | 1535 | Newbern Dist. |
| Militia | Frederik Smith | 3872 | Wilmington Dist. |
| Militia | Tulligh Smith | 754 | Newbern Dist. |
| Militia | Lewis Smith | 733 | Newbern Dist. |
| Militia | Solomon Smith | 838 | Newbern Dist. |
| Militia | Clemm Smith | 785 | Wilmington Dist. |
| Militia | Nathaniel Smith | 1322 | Newbern Dist. |
| Militia | Ezekiel Smith | 4900 | Wilmington Dist. |
| Militia | Camm Smith | 1023 | Newbern Dist. |
| Militia | Stephen Smith | 4522 | Wilmington Dist. |
| Militia | Lurdu Smith | 5637 | Salisbury Dist. |
| Militia | Josiah Smith | 3507 | Wilmington Dist. |
| Militia | Nathan Smith | 5719 | Wilmington Dist. |
| Militia | Gasper Smith | 764 | Salisbury Dist. |
| Militia | Jesse Smith | 1739 | Newbern Dist. |
| Militia | Richard Smith | 2665 | Wilmington Dist. |
| Militia | Ezekiel Smith | 4139 | Wilmington Dist. |
| Militia | Moses High Smith | 769 | Newbern Dist. |
| Militia | Ivey Smith | 1377 | Wilmington Dist. |
| Militia | Joshua Smith | 4477 | Morgan Dist. |
| Continental | Mitchell Smith | 1173 | Halifax Dist. |
| Continental | Benjamin Smith | 1204 | Warrenton Dist. |
| Continental | Nehemiah Smith | 1612 | Warrenton Dist. |
| Continental | Simon Smith | 309 | Halifax Dist. |
| Continental | Samuel Smith, Soldier | 1102 | Halifax Dist. |
| Continental | Joseph Smith | 444 |  |
| Continental | Nicholas Smith | 457 |  |
| Continental | Alexander Smith | 68 | Hillsborough Dist. |
| Continental | Reuben Smith | 438 | Halifax Dist. |
| Militia | Arthur Smith | 272 | Newbern Dist. |
| Continental | George Smith | 501 | Halifax Dist. |
| Militia | James Smith | 3682 | Salisbury Dist. |
| Militia | James Smith | 2060 | Newbern Dist. |
| Militia | James Smith | 4958 | Wilmington Dist. |
| Continental | James Smith | 493 | Halifax Dist. |
| Militia | William Smith | 2362 | Newbern Dist. |
| Continental | John Smith | 66 | Hillsborough Dist. |
| Militia | John Smith | 1506 | Wilmington Dist. |
| Militia | John Smith | 1208 | Newbern Dist. |
| Militia | John Smith | 4952 | Morgan Dist. |
| Militia | William Smith | .... | Salisbury Dist. |
| Militia | William Smith | 5161 | Wilmington Dist. |
| Militia | William Smith | 1001 | Newbern Dist. |
| Continental | John Smith | 1427 | Warrenton Dist. |
| Continental | Willis Sawyer | 31 | Hillsborough Dist. |
| Continental | Joseph Sawyer | 156 | Hillsborough Dist. |
| Militia | Henry Sewell | 7401 | Salisbury Dist. |
| Militia | Christopher Sewell | 2265 | Salisbury Dist. |
| Militia | Samuel Sewell | 236 | Wilmington Dist. |
| Militia | Wm. Sewell | 7375 | Salisbury Dist. |
| Militia | James Sewell | 125 |  |
| Continental | Thomas Sewell | 202 |  |

| | | No. | |
|---|---|---|---|
| Militia | Peter Shrup | 4578 | Morgan Dist. |
| Continental | Jonathan Smiter | 120 | |
| Militia | John Stephens | 3879 | Wilmington Dist. |
| Militia | Soammey Stephens | 3365 | Wilmington Dist. |
| Militia | Moab Stephens | 2919 | Wilmington Dist. |
| Militia | Asa Stephens | 5309 | Wilmington Dist. |
| Militia | Benja. Stephens | 5601 | Wilmington Dist. |
| Militia | Nath'l. Stephens | 5600 | Wilmington Dist. |
| Militia | John Stephens | 8985 | Salisbury Dist. |
| Militia | Mathew Stephens | 696 | Newbern Dist. |
| Militia | Jesse Stephens | 5602 | Wilmington Dist. |
| Militia | Asa Stephens | 5439 | Wilmington Dist. |
| Militia | Robert Stephens | 4194 | Wilmington Dist. |
| Militia | William Stephens | 5864 | Wilmington Dist. |
| Militia | Abrien Stephens | 591 | Wilmington Dist. |
| Militia | Mathew Stephens | 2184 | Wilmington Dist. |
| Militia | William Stephens | 27 | Newbern Dist. |
| Militia | Samuel Stevenson | 6266 | Salisbury Dist. |
| Militia | Wm. Stevenson | 8707 | Salisbury Dist. |
| Militia | James Stevenson | 4468 | Salisbury Dist. |
| Militia | John Stevenson | .... | Salisbury Dist. |
| Militia | William Stevenson | 2255 | Salisbury Dist. |
| Militia | John Stevenson | 586 | Newbern Dist. |
| Militia | Henry Stevenson | 5625 | Wilmington Dist. |
| Continental | James Stevenson | 1455 | Warrenton Dist. |
| Continental | Andrew Stevenson | 93 | |
| Continental | Abraham Stevenson | 258 | |
| Continental | John Sternes | 1594 | Warrenton Dist. |
| Continental | John Sternes, Soldier | 300 | Halifax Dist. |
| Continental | Henry Sternes | 600 | Halifax Dist. |
| Continental | Jesse Stancil | 1283 | Newbern Dist. |
| Continental | Jesse Stancil | 1778 | Warrenton Dist. |
| Continental | James Sexton | 6197 | Salisbury Dist. |
| Continental | James Sexton | 180 | Hillsborough Dist. |
| Continental | Henry Smith | 513 | Hillsborough Dist. |
| Continental | Henry Smith, Soldier | 591 | Halifax Dist. |
| Militia | Henry Smith | 5936 | Wilmington Dist. |
| Militia | Capt. Henry Smith | 968 | Newbern Dist. |
| Militia | Henry Smith | 2905 | Salisbury Dist. |
| Continental | Capt. Charles Stewart | 301 | Halifax Dist. |
| Militia | Joshua Sorrell | 7377 | Salisbury Dist. |
| Militia | Walton Sorrell | 5015 | Morgan Dist. |
| Continental | John Sorrell | 472 | Hillsborough Dist. |
| Continental | Thomas Sorrell | 299 | Hillsborough Dist. |
| Militia | John Sanders | 1426 | Newbern Dist. |
| Militia | Robert Sanders | 371 | Newbern Dist. |
| Militia | William Sanders | 1369 | Newbern Dist. |
| Militia | Charles Sanders | 375 | Newbern Dist. |
| Militia | Jesse Sanders | 779 | Newbern Dist. |
| Militia | Joseph Sanders | 1415 | Newbern Dist. |
| Militia | Jesse Sanders | 3185 | Wilmington Dist. |
| Continental | Benjamin Sanders | 280 | Hillsborough Dist. |
| Continental | James Sanders | 392 | Hillsborough Dist. |
| Continental | Joseph Sanders | 828 | Hillsborough Dist. |

| | | No. | |
|---|---|---|---|
| Continental | Lieut. William Sanders | 214 | Halifax Dist. |
| Continental | Charles Sanders | 430 | Halifax Dist. |
| Continental | Andrew Sanders | 3 | |
| Continental | Joseph Sanderson | 162 | Newbern Dist. |
| Militia | David Sheppard | 3964 | Wilmington Dist. |
| Militia | Cyprian Sheppard | 1038 | Wilmington Dist. |
| Militia | John Sheppard | 4864 | Wilmington Dist. |
| Militia | Joseph Sheppard | 3746 | Wilmington Dist. |
| Militia | George Sheppard | 1064 | Wilmington Dist. |
| Militia | Benjamin Sheppard | 5294 | Wilmington Dist. |
| Continental | William Sheppard | 330 | Hillsborough Dist. |
| Continental | John Sheppard | 210 | Hillsborough Dist. |
| Continental | Col. Abraham Sheppard | 611 | Halifax Dist. |
| Continental | John Sheppard | 499 | |
| Continental | Arrington Sheppard | 39 | Hillsborough Dist. |
| Continental | Majr. John Sheppard | 40 | Halifax Dist. |
| Continental | Samuel Stewart | 4269 | Salisbury Dist. |
| Continental | Capt. William Stewart | 4703 | Salisbury Dist. |
| Continental | Jas. Stewart | 6526 | Salisbury Dist. |
| Continental | Matthew Stewart | 4260 | Salisbury Dist. |
| Continental | Samuel Stewart | 3843 | Morgan Dist. |
| Continental | David Stewart | 1403 | Salisbury Dist. |
| Continental | John Stewart | 1962 | Wilmington Dist. |
| Continental | Robert Stewart | 445 | |
| Continental | Dan. Stewart | 5298 | Salisbury Dist. |
| Continental | James Stewart | 4803 | Morgan Dist. |
| Continental | Alexander Stewart | 3296 | Salisbury Dist. |
| Continental | William Stewart | 1167 | Halifax Dist. |
| Continental | Joseph Stewart | 177 | Hillsborough Dist. |
| Continental | Gideon Simmons | 319 | Hillsboro Dist. |
| Continental | John Simmons | 624 | |
| Militia | Absolom Simmons, Jones Co. | 770 | Newbern Dist. |
| Militia | Benjamin Simmons, Jones Co. | 1482 | Newbern Dist. |
| Militia | John Simmons | 2496 | Salisbury Dist. |
| Continental | Samuel Simmons | 368 | Hillsboro Dist. |
| Continental | Peter Simmons | | Assembly passed |
| Militia | Isaac Simmons | 4910 | Wilmington Dist. |
| Militia | Thomas Simmons | 2503 | Salisbury Dist. |
| Militia | Capt. Richard Simmons | 2623 | Salisbury Dist. |
| Militia | James Simmons, Jones Co. | 456 | Newbern Dist. |
| Militia | Elijah Simmons | 3338 | Wilmington Dist. |
| Militia | Willis Simmons | 73 | Wilmington Dist. |
| Continental | Felix Simmons | 412 | Halifax Dist. |
| Continental | Isles Simmons | 347 | Warrenton Dist. |
| Continental | Martin Simmons | 42 | Assembly |
| Militia | George Simmons | 104 | Newbern Dist. |
| Continental | James Simmons | 285 | Assembly |
| Continental | William Stuart | 688 | Halifax Dist. |
| Continental | Joseph Stuart | 290 | Hillsborough Dist. |
| Continental | William Stuart | 386 | Hillsborough Dist. |
| Militia | Felly Hearn | .... | Salisbury Dist. |
| Militia | John Hearn | 557 | Hillsborough Dist. |
| Continental | Lieut. Thomas Watson | 458 | Halifax Dist. |
| Continental | Philip Watson | 195 | Hillsborough Dist. |

| | | No. | |
|---|---|---|---|
| Continental | Ephraim Watson | 210 | Hillsborough Dist. |
| Continental | Solomon Watson | 209 | Hillsborough Dist. |
| Continental | Micajah Watson | 402 | Hillsborough Dist. |
| Continental | Cain Watson | 4687 | Salisbury Dist. |
| Militia | Sol'm. Watson | 438 | Newbern Dist. |
| Militia | James Watson | 3676 | Salisbury Dist. |
| Continental | Jacob Watson, Soldier | 948 | Halifax Dist. |
| Militia | Benj. Watson | 4479 | Wilmington Dist. |
| Militia | John Watson | 684 | Newbern Dist. |
| Militia | Reuben Wise | 5148 | Salisbury Dist. |
| Militia | Reuben Wise | 4016 | Wilmington Dist. |
| Militia | Abel Wise | 4015 | Wilmington Dist. |
| Continental | Abraham Wise | 631 | Halifax Dist. |
| Militia | Daniel Wise | 1846 | Newbern Dist. |
| Militia | Saven Wadkins | 5811 | Wilmington Dist. |
| Continental | James Wadkins | 407 | Hillsborough Dist. |
| Militia | John Rogers | 3682 | Wilmington Dist. |
| Militia | Jos. Rogers | 833 | Newbern Dist. |
| Militia | Stephen Rogers | 1002 | Wilmington Dist. |
| Militia | Thomas Rogers | 3484 | Wilmington Dist. |
| Militia | Benj. Rogers | 1687 | Newbern Dist. |
| Militia | Thos. Rogers | 1714 | Wilmington Dist. |
| Militia | Hugh Rogers | 3242 | Salisbury Dist. |
| Militia | James Rogers | 8406 | Salisbury Dist. |
| Militia | Dant Rogers | 417 | Newbern Dist. |
| Militia | Joseph Rogers | 1418 | Salisbury Dist. |
| Continental | David Rogers | 299 | Hillsborough Dist. |
| Continental | Ephraim Rogers | 1099 | Halifax Dist. |
| Continental | Jesse Rogers | 160 | |
| Continental | Eli Rogers | 753 | Hillsborough Dist. |
| Continental | James Rogers | 124 | Hillsborough Dist. |
| Continental | Stephen Rogers | 371 | Halifax Dist. |
| Continental | Lieut. Patrick Rogers | 319 | Hillsborough Dist. |
| Continental | Willoughby Rogers | 27 | Hillsborough Dist. |
| Continental | Samuel Wheeler | 98 | Hillsborough Dist. |
| Continental | David Wheeler, Soldier | 933 | Halifax Dist. |
| Continental | Emprey Wheeler | 1250 | Halifax Dist. |
| Continental | Batron Wheeler | 1387 | Halifax Dist. |
| Militia | Col. John Wilson | 3017 | Salisbury Dist. |
| Militia | Joseph Wilson | 2897 | Salisbury Dist. |
| Militia | Geo. Wilson | 2788 | Wilmington Dist. |
| Militia | John Wilson | 6398 | Salisbury Dist. |
| Militia | Saml. Wilson | 4500 | Wilmington Dist. |
| Militia | Saml. Wilson | 2965 | Salisbury Dist. |
| Militia | John Wilson | 2519 | Wilmington Dist. |
| Militia | Absolam Wilson | 5644 | Salisbury Dist. |
| Militia | Alexander Wilson | 3482 | Wilmington Dist. |
| Militia | David Wilson | 3240 | Salisbury Dist. |
| Militia | John Wilson | .... | Newbern Dist. |
| Militia | Seth Wilson | 1163 | Newbern Dist. |
| Militia | James Wilson | 4417 | Wilmington Dist. |
| Militia | Alexander Wilson | 4007 | Salisbury Dist. |
| Militia | James Wilson | 7649 | Salisbury Dist. |
| Militia | Willis Wilson | 1171 | Newbern Dist. |

|          |                       | *No.* |                   |
|----------|-----------------------|-------|-------------------|
| Militia | Robert Wilson | 5624 | Salisbury Dist. |
| Militia | Daniel Wilson | 823 | Newbern Dist. |
| Militia | Alsolm Wilson | 7658 | Salisbury Dist. |
| Militia | Alexander Wilson | 2426 | Wilmington Dist. |
| Militia | George Wilson | 5103 | Salisbury Dist. |
| Militia | Zacheus Wilson | 3221 | Salisbury Dist. |
| Militia | Matthew Wilson | 4468 | Morgan Dist. |
| Militia | William Wilson | 1422 | Wilmington Dist. |
| Militia | Capt. William Wilson | 3015 | Salisbury Dist. |
| Militia | David Wilson | 3429 | Salisbury Dist. |
| Militia | Timothy Wilson | 583 | Wilmington Dist. |
| Militia | William Wilson | 1094 | Newbern Dist. |
| Continental | Robert Wilson | 376 | Hillsborough Dist. |
| Continental | John Wilson, Soldier | 939 | Halifax Dist. |
| Continental | Whitfield Wilson | 145 | Hillsborough Dist. |
| Continental | Capt. James Wilson | 75 | Halifax Dist. |
| Continental | Seth Wilson | 200 | Hillsborough Dist. |
| Continental | Amos Wilson | 211 | Hillsborough Dist. |
| Continental | Edward Wilson | 980 | Halifax Dist. |
| Continental | Joshua Wilson | 486 | Halifax Dist. |
| Continental | Randolph Wilson | 112 |  |
| Continental | Samuel Wilson | 99 | Hillsborough Dist. |
| Continental | John Wilson | 563 | Hillsborough Dist. |
| Continental | William Wilson | 49 | Hillsborough Dist. |
| Continental | John Wilson | 1169 | Halifax Dist. |
| Militia | Isaac Baldred, Soldier | 1522 | Newbern Dist. |
| Militia | Pengrine Buning | 1903 | Newbern Dist. |
| Militia | Thos. Barrow | 544 | Newbern Dist. |
| Militia | John Becton | 625 | Newbern Dist. |
| Militia | John Banks | 297 | Newbern Dist. |
| Militia | David Bang | 455 | Newbern Dist. |
| Militia | John Steele Beeton | 1499 | Newbern Dist. |
| Militia | Edw'd. Blachehead | 376 | Newbern Dist. |
| Militia | John Beeton | 73 | Newbern Dist. |
| Militia | Rub. Bullock | 540 | Newbern Dist. |
| Militia | Abel B....... | 1863 | Newbern Dist. |
| Militia | Thomas Barrow | 325 | Newbern Dist. |
| Militia | John Ba.... | 1645 | Newbern Dist. |
| Militia | John Balton | .... | Newbern Dist. |
| Militia | Ambors Britt | 359 | Newbern Dist. |
| Militia | Rich'd. Barrinton | 736 | Newbern Dist. |
| Militia | Will'm. Blakey | 285 | Newbern Dist. |
| Militia | Rich'd. Bullock | 565 | Newbern Dist. |
| Continental | David Brodnell | 184 | Hillsborough Dist. |
| Continental | Michiel Brinkley | 2 | Hillsborough Dist. |
| Continental | Leanus Barolin | 148 | Hillsborough Dist. |
| Continental | Robert Buck | 275 | Hillsborough Dist |
| Continental | James Barnhill | 79 | Hillsborough Dist. |
| Continental | Christian Barnhart | 24 | Hillsborough Dist. |
| Continental | William Boyce | 43 | Hillsborough Dist. |
| Continental | David Burke | 86 | Hillsborough Dist. |
| Continental | Charles Bright | 33 | Hillsborough Dist. |
| Continental | Jesse Burn | 16 | Hillsborough Dist. |
| Continental | Nathaniel Belbuy | 117 | Hillsborough Dist. |

| | | No. | |
|---|---|---|---|
| Continental | Joshua Brington | 18 | Hillsborough Dist. |
| Continental | Jacob Borean | 121 | Hillsborough Dist. |
| Continental | Mason Brown | 350 | Hillsborough Dist. |
| Continental | John Bradshaw | 822 | Halifax Dist. |
| Continental | Joseph Barrett | 95 | Hillsborough Dist. |
| Continental | Aaron Barham | 619 | |
| Continental | Baitham Bohannon | 639 | |
| Continental | Thomas Barnes | 377 | Hillsborough Dist. |
| Continental | Benjamin Buyer | 247 | Hillsborough Dist. |
| Continental | Luke Bates | 542 | Halifax Dist. |
| Continental | William Barket | 374 | Halifax Dist. |
| Continental | Album Bruce | 327 | Warrenton Dist. |
| Continental | Charles Burke | 289 | |
| Continental | Thomas Brees | 259 | Hillsborough Dist. |
| Continental | Mack Benson | 246 | |
| Continental | James Banon | 221 | |
| Continental | Nicolas Blanks | 661 | Hillsborough Dist. |
| Continental | Samuel Barkley | 416 | Hillsborough Dist. |
| Continental | Stephen Bowen | 293 | Halifax Dist. |
| Continental | James Besley | 5 | |
| Continental | Charles Bright | .... | Hillsborough Dist. |
| Continental | Davis Benton | 862 | Warrenton Dist. |
| Continental | John Bullock, Soldier | 919 | Halifax Dist. |
| Continental | James Brittain | 117 | Halifax Dist. |
| Continental | Samuel Baxter | 396 | Halifax Dist. |
| Continental | William Boomer | 822 | Hillsborough Dist. |
| Continental | John Brinn | 821 | Hillsborough Dist. |
| Continental | Matthias Belts | 628 | Hillsborough Dist. |
| Continental | Plier Barber | .... | Newbern Dist. |
| Continental | Job Benbo | 46 | |
| Continental | Robert Berry | 344 | |
| Continental | Stephen Beanfield | 423 | Halifax Dist. |
| Continental | White Bernick | 398 | Hillsborough Dist |
| Continental | William Bysom, Soldier | 124 | Halifax Dist. |
| Continental | John Brian | .... | Halifax Dist. |
| Continental | Lieut.-Col. Lott Breuster | 188 | Halifax Dist. |
| Continental | Col. Wm. Blount | 470 | Halifax Dist. |
| Continental | James Bundy, Soldier | 398 | Halifax Dist. |
| Continental | Norma Bruce | 14 | |
| Continental | William Barkley | 654 | |
| Continental | Simon Braxton | 216 | |
| Continental | Simm Broadstreet | 231 | |
| Continental | Samuel Bulenton | 197 | |
| Continental | Henry Brady | 599 | Hillsborough Dist. |
| Continental | William Blake | 202 | Hillsborough Dist. |
| Continental | Dempsey Boyce | 698 | Hillsborough Dist. |
| Militia | William Bulls | 2139 | Newbern Dist. |
| Militia | John Burnet | 16 | Newbern Dist. |
| Militia | James Bayworth | 1307 | Newbern Dist. |
| Militia | Thomas Barrow | 501 | Newbern Dist. |
| Militia | Ramey Butts | 1219 | Newbern Dist. |
| Militia | John Barley | 218 | Newbern Dist. |
| Militia | John Broadstreet | 1180 | Newbern Dist. |
| Militia | John Ballinger | 2146 | Newbern Dist. |

| | | No. | |
|---|---|---|---|
| Militia | Edward Blurton | 1157 | Newbern Dist. |
| Militia | James Bosworth | 140 | Newbern Dist. |
| Militia | Rubin Binn | .... | Newbern Dist. |
| Militia | George Blackbourne | 1061 | Newbern Dist. |
| Militia | Edw'd. Blurton | 1380 | Newbern Dist. |
| Militia | Jno. Barttell | 1058 | Newbern Dist. |
| Militia | John Bernick | 1236 | Newbern Dist. |
| Militia | .... Barfield | 1029 | Newbern Dist. |
| Militia | Thomas Blango | 1406 | Newbern Dist. |
| Militia | Thomas Boyakan | 1050 | Newbern Dist. |
| Militia | Edward Baldwin | 2128 | Newbern Dist. |
| Militia | Peter Banks | 943 | Newbern Dist. |
| Militia | Nathan Barrington | 998 | Newbern Dist. |
| Militia | Artily Burnett | 891 | Newbern Dist. |
| Militia | Nathan Bullock | 898 | Newbern Dist. |
| Militia | Ephraim Bullock | 1659 | Newbern Dist. |
| Militia | Henry Bates | 1535 | Newbern Dist. |
| Militia | John Beasley | 345 | Newbern Dist. |
| Continental | Cornelius Bray | 324 | |
| Continental | Archibald Butts | 399 | Halifax Dist. |
| Continental | Michael Buckran | 123 | |
| Continental | Caleb Berry | 187 | Hillsborough Dist. |
| Continental | Benjamin Braddy | 72 | Hillsborough Dist. |
| Continental | Thomas Biby | 409 | Hillsborough Dist. |
| Continental | William Blunby | 449 | |
| Continental | Soloman Bandy | 430 | |
| Continental | ....mon Briton | 628 | Halifax Dist. |
| Continental | John Balford | 204 | |
| Continental | Randall Britting | 73 | |
| Continental | Coldon Bashop | 103 | |
| Continental | Silas Bromfield | 243 | |
| Continental | Jesse Boseman | 99 | Hillsborough Dist. |
| Continental | Benjamin Brady | 375 | Hillsborough Dist. |
| Continental | Capt. Alex Buvard | 191 | |
| Continental | Lieut. Maj. Andrew Bay | 236 | Halifax Dist. |
| Continental | Sergt. Charles Bright | 92 | Halifax Dist. |
| Continental | Moses Blango | 598 | Hillsborough Dist. |
| Continental | Capt. Peter Bacot | 375 | Halifax Dist. |
| Continental | Roger Bratchen | 1955 | |
| Continental | Capt. Joel Brevard | 108 | Halifax Dist. |
| Militia | Jos. B.... | 514 | Newbern Dist. |
| Continental | Edward Buncomb | 224 | Hillsborough Dist. |
| Continental | Hillery Brinson | 613 | Hillsborough Dist. |
| Continental | Josiah Benton | 1230 | Halifax Dist. |
| Continental | Benjamin Brady | 515 | Hillsborough Dist. |
| Continental | James Boon | 823 | Halifax Dist. |
| Continental | Frederick Bagurtt | 99 | |
| Continental | Noah Barttell | 668 | Hillsborough Dist. |
| Continental | Lt. Valentine Beard | 650 | Hillsborough Dist. |
| Continental | Matthew Betts | 56 | Hillsborough Dist. |
| Continental | Joshua Brennington | 156 | Hillsborough Dist. |
| Continental | Thomas Bulhard | 289 | Hillsborough Dist. |
| Continental | Mason Bims | 487 | Hillsborough Dist. |
| Continental | White Bennick | 615 | Hillsborough Dist. |

| | | No. | |
|---|---|---|---|
| Continental | Josiah Bowers | 271 | Hillsborough Dist. |
| Continental | John Bradshaw | 417 | Halifax Dist. |
| Continental | Henry Burton | 128 | Hillsborough Dist. |
| Continental | George Binbow | 262 | Halifax Dist. |
| Continental | James Brock, Soldier | 635 | Halifax Dist. |
| Continental | Burgain Booles, Soldier | 59 | Halifax Dist. |
| Militia | Henry Blurton | 2159 | |
| Militia | Joshua Baltin | 523 | Newbern Dist. |
| Militia | Mathew Brinson | 292 | Newbern Dist. |
| Militia | William Bull | 493 | Newbern Dist. |
| Militia | Sanders Burnet | 1189 | Newbern Dist. |
| Militia | Baezella Blossom | 643 | Newbern Dist. |
| Militia | Edmund Becton | 63 | Newbern Dist. |
| Militia | Charles Bullock | 1248 | Newbern Dist. |
| Militia | Thomas Barrow, Soldier | 1228 | Newbern Dist. |
| Militia | T..... Braswell | 474 | Newbern Dist. |
| Militia | John Bedscot | 1028 | Newbern Dist. |
| Militia | Noah Barttell | 1688 | Newbern Dist. |
| Militia | Hopkins Bateman | 302 | Newbern Dist. |
| Militia | John Brothers | 699 | Newbern Dist. |
| Militia | Lt. Wm. Bryan | 1620 | Wilmington Dist. |
| Militia | George Baning | 1055 | Newbern Dist. |
| Continental | Dr. Robert Brownfield | 90 | |
| Continental | Sergt. Thomas Brickell | 337 | |
| Continental | Joseph Bedgood | 1837 | Warrenton Dist. |
| Continental | Drury Baggett | 149 | Halifax Dist. |
| Continental | Wm. Bedditt | 1147 | Warrenton Dist. |
| Continental | John Barco | 1304 | Halifax Dist. |
| Continental | James Brady | 222 | Hillsborough Dist. |
| Continental | Lewis Boon, Soldier | 379 | Halifax Dist. |
| Continental | Archibald Butts | 400 | Halifax Dist. |
| Continental | Thomas Barie | 248 | Halifax Dist. |
| Continental | Thomas Billops | 727 | Halifax Dist. |
| Continental | Isaac Bagby | 1406 | Halifax Dist. |
| Continental | Benjamin Bremington | 826 | |
| Continental | James Bootery, Soldier | 1436 | |
| Continental | Capt. Wm. Brinkley | 120 | Halifax Dist. |
| Continental | Daniel Bullock | 1239 | Halifax Dist. |
| Continental | Lieut. Samuel Budd | 435 | Halifax Dist. |
| Continental | Reuben Bullock, Soldier | 910 | Halifax Dist. |
| Continental | John Barnhill | 584 | Halifax Dist. |
| Continental | William Bond | 845 | Hillsborough Dist. |
| Militia | Wm. Boing | 6669 | Salisbury Dist. |
| Militia | Jno. Bullocke | 785 | Newbern Dist. |
| Militia | Mica.... Bull | 1790 | Newbern Dist. |
| Militia | Frances Beaseley | 717 | Newbern Dist. |
| Militia | John Bush | 524 | Newbern Dist. |
| Militia | Benj'm. Broolein | 1189 | Newbern Dist. |
| Militia | David Blackshear | 380 | Newbern Dist. |
| Militia | Ephraim Bullock | 739 | Newbern Dist. |
| Militia | George Bradley | 738 | Newbern Dist. |
| Militia | John Biggs | 185 | Newbern Dist. |
| Militia | David Barnhill | 1576 | Newbern Dist. |
| Indians | John Branden | 1140 | Hillsboro Dist. |

|  |  | *No.* |  |
|---|---|---|---|
| Indians | James Blake | 1154 | Hillsboro Dist. |
| Militia | Ambross Bull | 591 | Newbern Dist. |
| Militia | John Burn | 2038 | Newbern Dist. |
| Militia | William Barrow | 1204 | Newbern Dist. |
| Militia | Zollas Bucke | 748 | Newbern Dist. |

## MISCELLANEOUS

|  |  |  |  |
|---|---|---|---|
| Militia | Frederick Mims | 326 | Warrenton Dist. |
| Militia | Jacob Rochelle | 2017 | Newbern Dist. |
| Militia | David Kornegay | 435 | Newbern Dist. |
| Militia | Capt. Joseph Wood | 776 | Wilmington Dist. |
| Militia | James Wood | 3319 | Wilmington Dist. |
| Militia | Cornelius Wood, Soldier | 1680 | Salisbury Dist. |
| Militia | Robert Wood | 3444 | Salisbury Dist. |
| Militia | Samuel Wood | 4029 | Morgan Dist. |
| Militia | Zadack Wood | 138 | Wilmington Dist. |
| Militia | Philip Wood | 3075 | Wilmington Dist. |
| Militia | Simon Wood | 1946 | Wilmington Dist. |
| Militia | Joseph Wood | 2088 | Salisbury Dist. |
| Militia | Wm. Wood | 7391 | Salisbury Dist. |
| Militia | Frederick Wood | 3320 | Wilmington Dist. |
| Militia | Aaron Wood | 18 | Newbern Dist. |
| Militia | Capt. Samuel Wood | 1022 | Salisbury Dist. |
| Militia | Charles Wood | 7946 | Salisbury Dist. |
| Militia | Samuel Wood | 3906 | Morgan Dist. |
| Militia | Fred'k. Wood | 5592 | Wilmington Dist. |
| Militia | Matthew Wood | 5707 | Salisbury Dist. |
| Militia | Suvey Wood | 2317 | Wilmington Dist. |
| Militia | James Wood | 7396 | Salisbury Dist. |
| Continental | Joseph Wood | 579 | Halifax Dist. |
| Continental | John Wood, Soldier | 546 | Halifax Dist. |
| Continental | Charles Wood, Soldier | 1032 | Halifax Dist. |
| Continental | John Wood | 571 | Hillsborough Dist. |
| Continental | Sampson Wood, Soldier | 391 | Halifax Dist. |
| Continental | John Wood | 394 | Halifax Dist. |
| Continental | Aron Wood | 793 | Hillsboro Dist. |
| Continental | Nathaniel Wood | 557 |  |
| Continental | Samuel Wood | 102 |  |
| Continental | John Wood | 748 | Hillsborough Dist. |
| Militia | William Langston | 553 | Wilmington Dist. |
| Militia | John Langston | 1246 | Newbern Dist. |
| Continental | Josiah Langston | 753 |  |
| Militia | John Lowe | 4386 | Wilmington Dist. |
| Militia | James Lowe | 661 | Wilmington Dist. |
| Militia | William Lowe | 725 | Wilmington Dist. |
| Militia | Matthew Lowe | 6473 | Salisbury Dist. |
| Militia | Robt. Lowe | 5707 | Wilmington Dist. |
| Continental | George Lowe | 372 | Hillsborough Dist. |
| Continental | Richard Lowe | 566 | Hillsborough Dist. |
| Continental | William Lowe | 282 | Hillsborough Dist |
| Continental | James Lowe | 766 | Hillsborough Dist. |
| Continental | Abraham Lowe | 154 | Hillsborough Dist. |
| Continental | William Lowe | 496 |  |
| Continental | Drury Ledbetter | 1166 | Salisbury Dist. |

| | | *No.* | |
|---|---|---|---|
| Continental | William Lannis | 1528 | Newbern Dist. |
| Continental | B.... Lanin | 3646 | Wilmington Dist. |
| Continental | Ensign J..... Lanin | 3644 | Wilmington Dist. |
| Continental | Corpl. Lewis Lanin | 3613 | Wilmington Dist. |
| Continental | Isham Lanin | 1652 | Newbern Dist. |
| Militia | Jesse Lanier | 3647 | Wilmington Dist. |
| Militia | Benjamine Lanier | 3615 | Wilmington Dist. |
| Continental | James Lanier | 947 | Halifax Dist. |
| Militia | John Pierce | 1285 | Newbern Dist. |
| Militia | ....... Pierce | .... | Newbern Dist. |
| Militia | John Pierce | 2075 | Newbern Dist. |
| Militia | William Pierce | 763 | Wilmington Dist. |
| Militia | Theophilus Pierce | 161 | Newbern Dist. |
| Militia | Snowden Pierce | 2116 | Wilmington Dist. |
| Continental | Ephraim Pierce | 9 | Newbern Dist. |
| Continental | Arthur Pierce | 319 | |
| Continental | William Pierce | 551 | Hillsborough Dist. |
| Continental | Thomas Pierce | 395 | Hillsborough Dist. |
| Continental | John Pierce | 329 | Hillsborough Dist. |
| Continental | Israel Pierce | 666 | Halifax Dist. |
| Militia | Daniel McDonald | 408 | Salisbury Dist. |
| Militia | Zachariah McDonald | 784 | Wilmington Dist. |
| Continental | Thomas Hines | 463 | Halifax Dist. |
| Continental | Jordan Hines | 791 | |
| Militia | James Hines | 1655 | |
| Continental | Hardy Hines | 269 | Hillsboro Dist. |
| Militia | Nathaniel Reeves | 4497 | Wilmington Dist. |
| Militia | Richard Reeves | 1570 | Newbern Dist. |
| Militia | Robert Reeves | 1643 | Newbern Dist. |
| Continental | John Reeves | 160 | Warrenton Dist. |
| Continental | John Reeves | 562 | Hillsboro Dist. |
| Continental | David Reeves | 1199 | Warrenton Dist. |
| Continental | Frederick Reeves | 732 | Hillsborough Dist. |
| Militia | Benj'm. Robertson | 1273 | Newbern Dist. |
| Militia | Capt. James Robertson | 95 | Salisbury Dist. |
| Militia | John Robertson | 112 | Wilmington Dist. |
| Militia | John Robertson | 7069 | Salisbury Dist. |
| Militia | Capt. Peter Robertson | 2352 | Wilmington Dist. |
| Militia | Moses Robertson | 3627 | Salisbury Dist. |
| Militia | David Robertson | 4453 | Morgan Dist. |
| Militia | Richard Robertson | 2694 | Salisbury Dist. |
| Militia | William Robertson | 1984 | Wilmington Dist. |
| Continental | Noah Robertson | 516 | Hillsborough Dist. |
| Continental | Mack Robertson | 1359 | Warrenton Dist. |
| Continental | Randal Robertson | 144 | Hillsborough Dist. |
| Continental | Edward Robertson | 86 | Hillsborough Dist. |
| Continental | Henry Robertson | 726 | Halifax Dist. |
| Continental | David Robertson | 1130 | Halifax Dist. |

## MISCELLANEOUS

| | | | |
|---|---|---|---|
| Militia | Adam Williamson | 4249 | Wilmington Dist. |
| Militia | Henry Whitener | .... | Salisbury Dist. |
| Continental | John Wilcocks | 670 | |
| Continental | John Worsley | 1252 | Warrenton Dist. |

| | | No. | |
|---|---|---|---|
| Militia | Richard Williford .............. | 2878 | Wilmington Dist. |
| Militia | Cleverly Wetherinton ............ | 1267 | Newbern Dist. |
| Militia | George Whealy ................. | 4542 | Morgan Dist. |
| Militia | Dewey Westbrook .............. | 5540 | Wilmington Dist. |
| Militia | Muhager Williford ............. | 1188 | Wilmington Dist. |
| Militia | William Wills ................. | 2861 | Salisbury Dist. |
| Militia | James Wallace ................. | 5630 | Salisbury Dist. |
| Militia | John Wadsworth ............... | 4048 | Wilmington Dist. |
| Militia | Thomas Walton ................ | 5328 | Wilmington Dist. |
| Militia | Fendell Whitworth ............. | 7688 | Salisbury Dist. |
| Continental | James Winley ................. | 134 | Hillsborough Dist. |
| Continental | Isaac Wells ................... | 730 | Hillsborough Dist. |
| Continental | Absalom Wildey ............... | 727 | Hillsborough Dist. |
| Militia | Anthony Willoughby ............ | .... | Newbern Dist. |
| Militia | Needham Whitley .............. | 3154 | Newbern Dist. |
| Militia | Richard Williamson ............. | 1488 | Newbern Dist. |
| Continental | John Whaley .................. | 796 | Hillsborough Dist. |
| Continental | Francis Whaley ................ | 614 | Hillsborough Dist. |
| Continental | Daniel Walden ................ | 317 | Warrenton Dist. |
| Continental | Job. Williamson ............... | 184 | |
| Continental | Holland Woolard .............. | 91 | |
| Continental | Isaac Wells ................... | 555 | Hillsborough Dist. |
| Continental | James Wenley ................. | 242 | Hillsborough Dist. |
| Continental | William Walters ............... | 52 | Hillsborough Dist. |
| Continental | William Wiseheart ............. | 10 | Hillsborough Dist. |
| Continental | William Williamson ............ | .... | Halifax Dist. |
| Continental | Francis Werderhall, Soldier........ | 77 | Halifax Dist. |
| Continental | Sergt. Joel Wall ............... | 98 | Halifax Dist. |
| Continental | Whitley ..................... | 699 | Halifax Dist. |
| Continental | Joshua Weirdon ............... | 640 | |
| Continental | George Woodard .............. | 627 | |
| Continental | Francis Wilkerson ............. | 961 | Halifax Dist. |
| Continental | Thomas Wilkins ............... | 241 | Hillsborough Dist. |
| Continental | Joshua Wilkins ............... | 824 | Hillsborough Dist. |
| Continental | Benjamin Wilcox .............. | 805 | Hillsborough Dist. |
| Continental | Cobb Woodward .............. | 529 | Hillsborough Dist. |
| Continental | William Wynn ................ | 458 | Hillsborough Dist. |
| Continental | Henry Whillis ................ | 530 | Hillsborough Dist. |
| Militia | George Williamson ............. | 344 | Newbern Dist. |
| Militia | Jesse Woodward ............... | 5521 | Wilmington Dist. |
| Militia | Michael Wadkin ............... | 3622 | Wilmington Dist. |
| Militia | John Wilkins ................. | 3139 | Wilmington Dist. |
| Militia | Benjamin Windure ............. | 1486 | Newbern Dist. |
| Militia | Lieut. T.... Worthy ........... | 4217 | Wilmington Dist. |
| Militia | Micajah Windun ............... | 1803 | Wilmington Dist. |
| Militia | .... Worthun ................. | 1372 | Newbern Dist. |
| Militia | Sorin Watkins ................ | 3798 | Wilmington Dist. |
| Militia | Joseph Wade ................. | 3437 | Wilmington Dist. |
| Militia | Robert Whitington ............. | 662 | Newbern Dist. |
| Militia | David Williamson ............. | 35 | Newbern Dist. |
| Militia | John Wash ................... | 1293 | Salisbury Dist. |
| Militia | John Week ................... | 4495 | Salisbury Dist. |
| Militia | Joel Wells ................... | 1439 | Wilmington Dist. |
| Militia | William Wilkins .............. | 5947 | Wilmington Dist. |

|  |  | *No.* |  |
|---|---|---|---|
| Militia | John Wolum .................. | 136 | Wilmington Dist. |
| Militia | William Whitager ............... | .011 | Salisbury Dist. |
| Indians | Phillip Waggoner ............... | .... |  |
| Militia | John Wilkinson ................. | 1519 | Newbern Dist. |
| Militia | Isaac Whaley .................... | .... | Newbern Dist. |
| Militia | John Whitley .................. | 1009 | Newbern Dist. |
| Militia | Jno. White...... ............. | 1088 | Newbern Dist. |
| Militia | Thomas Wilkins ............... | 408 | Newbern Dist. |
| Continental | Caleb Woodward ............... | 387 | Hillsborough Dist. |
| Continental | Willis Weathers ................ | 930 | Halifax Dist. |
| Continental | James Wiggins, Soldier .......... | 162 | Halifax Dist. |
| Continental | James Willoughby .............. | 676 | Hillsborough Dist. |
| Continental | Thomas Woodley ............... | 254 | Hillsborough Dist. |
| Continental | Thomas Wilkins ............... | 133 | Hillsborough Dist. |
| Continental | Thomas Worsley ............... | 305 | Hillsborough Dist. |
| Continental | John Weston .................. | 542 | Hillsborough Dist. |
| Continental | Edward Woodrow .............. | 16 | Hillsborough Dist. |
| Continental | William Hatford .............. | 179 | Hillsborough Dist. |
| Continental | James Willoughby ............. | 507 | Hillsborough Dist. |
| Continental | John Willoughby .............. | 506 | Hillsborough Dist. |
| Continental | William Wharton .............. | 1409 | Newbern Dist. |
| Continental | John Ware .................... | .... | Newbern Dist. |
| Continental | Daniel Witherington ............ | .... | Newbern Dist. |
| Continental | William Womack .............. | 529 | Hillsborough Dist. |
| Continental | Henry Wallen ................. | 317 | Hillsborough Dist. |
| Continental | John Wade ................... | 159 | Hillsborough Dist. |
| Continental | Thomas Wigley ............... | 230 | Hillsborough Dist. |
| Continental | Capt. John Welch ............. | 69 | Halifax Dist. |
| Continental | Hopkins Witley ................ | 457 | Hillsboro Dist. |
| Continental | Matthew Wesley ............... | 738 | Hillsboro Dist. |
| Continental | John Wood ................... | 437 | Halifax Dist. |
| Continental | Richard Whedbee .............. | 84 | Halifax Dist. |
| Militia | Capt. Richmond Pierson ......... | 2840 | Salisbury Dist. |
| Militia | John Pierson ................. | 5335 | Wilmington Dist. |
| Militia | John Pierson ................. | 547 | Newbern Dist. |
| Militia | James Pierson ................ | 4754 | Morgan Dist. |
| Militia | Thomas Pierson .............. | 5218 | Wilmington Dist. |
| Militia | James Pierson ................ | 1992 | Wilmington Dist. |
| Continental | Richard Pierson ............... | 483 | Hillsborough Dist. |
| Continental | Roger Pierson ................ | 1213 | Halifax Dist. |
| Continental | Thomas Pierson ............... | 539 | Hillsborough Dist. |
| Continental | Peter Payne .................. | 556 |  |
| Militia | Wm. Potts ................... | 8554 | Salisbury Dist. |
| Militia | John Potts ................... | 60.. | Salisbury Dist. |
| Militia | Capt. Jon't. Potts .............. | 2895 | Salisbury Dist. |
| Continental | Alexander Potts ............... | 164 |  |
| Continental | Abraham Parrish .............. | 93 | Hillsborough Dist. |
| Continental | Jacob Parrish ................. | 227 | Hillsborough Dist. |
| Militia | Charles Parrish ............... | 605 | Newbern Dist. |
| Militia | Jacob Parrish ................. | 5917 | Wilmington Dist. |
| Militia | Seth Pearce .................. | 1856 | Newbern Dist. |
| Militia | Shad'r. Pearce ............... | 1295 | Newbern Dist. |
| Militia | Laza. Pearce ................. | 1632 | Newbern Dist. |
| Continental | Israel Pierce .................. | 1456 | Warrenton Dist. |

| | | No. | |
|---|---|---|---|
| Continental | Hopkin Puree | 622 | |
| Continental | M.... Prevett | 46 | Halifax Dist. |
| Continental | Micajah Prevett | 734 | Hillsborough Dist. |
| Continental | John Prevett | 1393 | Halifax Dist. |
| Militia | Sion Picket | 2948 | Wilmington Dist. |
| Militia | James Picket | 3538 | Wilmington Dist. |
| Militia | Abraham Perry | 4852 | Wilmington Dist. |
| Militia | William Perry | ..65 | Newbern Dist. |
| Militia | Wavel Perry | 176 | Newbern Dist. |
| Militia | John Perry | 1230 | Wilmington Dist. |
| Militia | Robert Perry | 4784 | Wilmington Dist. |
| Militia | Hardy Perry | 1556 | Newbern Dist. |
| Militia | Demsey Perry | 509 | Newbern Dist. |
| Continental | Robert Perry | 1308 | Halifax Dist. |
| Continental | John Perry | 577 | Hillsborough Dist. |
| Continental | Isaac Perry | 116 | |
| Continental | Jeremiah Perry, Soldier | 209 | Halifax Dist. |
| Continental | Needum Perry | 935 | Halifax Dist. |
| Militia | John Marshall | .... | Wilmington Dist. |
| Continental | Lieut. Dixon Marshall | 146 | Halifax Dist. |
| Continental | George Marshall | .... | |
| Militia | Edmund Mattheis | 2198 | Wilmington Dist. |
| Militia | Mirsentine Matthews | 7074 | Salisbury Dist. |
| Militia | Hardy Mattheus | 4843 | Wilmington Dist. |
| Militia | Tho. Mattheus | 4866 | Wilmington Dist. |
| Militia | Hardy Mattheus | 4902 | Wilmington Dist. |
| Militia | Joseph Mattheus | 4140 | Wilmington Dist. |
| Militia | John Mattheus | 1872 | Wilmington Dist. |
| Continental | Moses Mattheus | 114 | Halifax Dist. |
| Continental | Bolin Mattheus | 1625 | Warrenton Dist. |
| Continental | Roll Mattheus | 253 | Hillsborough Dist. |
| Continental | Daniel Mattheus | 701 | Hillsborough Dist. |
| Continental | Gilbert Mattheus | 267 | Hillsborough Dist. |
| Continental | James Mattheus | 1369 | Salisbury Dist. |
| Continental | Richard Martin | 122 | Salisbury Dist. |
| Continental | Absalom Martin | 262 | Salisbury Dist. |
| Continental | Benjamin Martin | 1631 | Newbern Dist. |
| Continental | John Martin | 424 | |
| Continental | Christopher Martin | .... | |
| Continental | Hosea Martin | 1885 | |
| Continental | Baron Martin | 707 | |
| Continental | Benjamin Mason | 780 | Hillsborough Dist. |
| Continental | Benjamin Mason | 1420 | Newbern Dist. |
| Militia | Richard Mason | 1366 | Wilmington Dist. |
| Militia | Wm. Mason | 5889 | Wilmington Dist. |
| Militia | Matthew Mason | 1516 | Wilmington Dist. |
| Militia | Kemp Herritt | 144 | Wilmington Dist. |
| Militia | Philip Hurst | 3795 | Wilmington Dist. |
| Militia | Wm. Honeycutt | 5548 | Wilmington Dist. |
| Militia | Wm. Handon | 3064 | Wilmington Dist. |
| Militia | John Holley | 3442 | Wilmington Dist. |
| Militia | Wm. Hansley | 3515 | Wilmington Dist. |
| Militia | Hillary Hooks | 2796 | Wilmington Dist. |
| Militia | Beason Holland | 4540 | Salisbury Dist. |

| | | *No.* | |
|---|---|---|---|
| Militia | Alexander Hutchinson | 1442 | Salisbury Dist. |
| Militia | Leuis Hurvey | 4026 | Salisbury Dist. |
| Militia | James Herrin | 1276 | Newbern Dist. |
| Militia | John Hobbs | 2032 | Newbern Dist. |
| Militia | John Hennard | 426 | Newbern Dist. |
| Militia | Isam Holmes | 2215 | Wilmington Dist. |
| Militia | Reuben Hargrove | 1507 | Wilmington Dist. |
| Militia | Jeremiah Holland | 1592 | Wilmington Dist. |
| Militia | George Hobbs | 3574 | Wilmington Dist. |
| Militia | William Hansley | 105 | Wilmington Dist. |
| Militia | Abraham Honey | 83 | Wilmington Dist. |
| Militia | Thomas Haines | 1471 | Wilmington Dist. |
| Militia | Henry Hulet | 2156 | Wilmington Dist. |
| Militia | Matthew Holland | 772 | |
| Militia | Joshua Headley | 1045 | Salisbury Dist. |
| Militia | Samuel Hutchison | 5055 | Salisbury Dist. |
| Militia | Joseph Headen | 2864 | Salisbury Dist. |
| Militia | John Hutchison | 6002 | Salisbury Dist. |
| Militia | Simon Horse | 4444 | Morgan Dist. |
| Militia | Benj. Hickman | 4095 | Salisbury Dist. |
| Militia | Peter Hay | 2175 | Wilmington Dist. |
| Militia | Isaac Hortler | 5754 | Wilmington Dist. |
| Militia | Robt. Hogston | 8914 | Salisbury Dist. |
| Militia | John Handcock | 2314 | Newbern Dist. |
| Militia | Barzella Holtin | 947 | Newbern Dist. |
| Militia | James Hodges | 1526 | Newbern Dist. |
| Militia | Hardy Hargrove | 5683 | Wilmington Dist. |
| Militia | Lieut. John Hawthorne | 4454 | Wilmington Dist. |
| Militia | Gabriel Hardyson | 1119 | Wilmington Dist. |
| Militia | Josiah Hendon | 3104 | Wilmington Dist. |
| Militia | James Hurt | 2230 | Salisbury Dist. |
| Militia | Peter Hedrick | 5152 | Salisbury Dist. |
| Militia | William Hurst | 3677 | Wilmington Dist. |
| Militia | William Hodge | 5627 | Wilmington Dist. |
| Militia | Joseph Hardnot | 5272 | Wilmington Dist. |
| Militia | Thos. Hooks | 5498 | Wilmington Dist. |
| Militia | John Holley | 5880 | Wilmington Dist. |
| Militia | Ezekiel Hallimand | 2048 | Newbern Dist. |
| Militia | James Hyman | 300 | Newbern Dist. |
| Militia | James Handcock | 2312 | Newbern Dist. |
| Militia | Samuel Harrisday | 1360 | Salisbury Dist. |
| Militia | Jno. Hanna | 2908 | Salisbury Dist. |
| Militia | John Hollis | 2978 | Salisbury Dist. |
| Militia | John Head | 958 | Wilmington Dist. |
| Continental | Joseph Hodges | 1319 | Newbern Dist. |
| Continental | Edward Hathcock | 560 | Hillsborough Dist. |
| Continental | James Hoseford | 121 | Hillsborough Dist. |
| Continental | Joshua Halton | 309 | Hillsborough Dist. |
| Continental | James Hailey | 241 | |
| Continental | Willis Hodges, Soldier | 134 | Halifax Dist. |
| Continental | Jolly Holstead | 33 | Halifax Dist. |
| Continental | Thomas Harris, Soldier | 954 | Halifax Dist. |
| Continental | William Hamb | 1091 | Halifax Dist. |
| Continental | Lieut. William Hargrove | 72 | Halifax Dist. |

| | | No. | |
|---|---|---|---|
| Continental | Ephriam Hooks | 972 | Halifax Dist. |
| Continental | David Holoway | 790 | Warrenton Dist. |
| Continental | James Hayward | 582 | |
| Continental | William Howerton | 763 | Halifax Dist. |
| Continental | John Harrell | 1928 | Warrenton Dist. |
| Continental | Zachariah Henly | 322 | Warrenton Dist. |
| Continental | Stephen Hamer | 71 | |
| Continental | Drury Hyme | 843 | Warrenton Dist. |
| Continental | James Hines | 378 | Warrenton Dist. |
| Continental | Henry Honess | 134 | |
| Continental | William Hancock | 429 | |
| Continental | Griffin Harmontree | 29 | |
| Continental | Joseph Hudnell | 70 | |
| Continental | George Hopenell | 658 | |
| Continental | James Heartfield | 450 | |
| Continental | Elisha Hogg | 352 | |
| Continental | Hert Hadnot | 337 | |
| Continental | Carter Hastings | 207 | Hillsborough Dist. |
| Continental | Daniel Harrison | 1453 | Warrenton Dist. |
| Continental | William Harrison | 516 | Halifax Dist. |
| Continental | Nicholas Hair | 761 | Halifax Dist. |
| Militia | John Walters | 700 | Newbern Dist. |
| Militia | George McWhorter | 5960 | Salisbury Dist. |
| Militia | Isaac Whitaker | 1566 | Newbern Dist. |
| Militia | Thomas Worsley | 853 | Newbern Dist. |
| Militia | Joseph Worsley | 994 | Newbern Dist. |
| Militia | George Wolfinden | 1735 | Newbern Dist. |
| Militia | John Whitaker | 3042 | Salisbury Dist. |
| Militia | Robarib Wick | 2231 | Wilmington Dist. |
| Militia | Lieut. Samuel Wason | 5703 | Salisbury Dist. |
| Militia | James Wasson | 7685 | Salisbury Dist. |
| Militia | James Walt | 6906 | Salisbury Dist. |
| Militia | William Wills | 2267 | Salisbury Dist. |
| Militia | Frederick Wills | 3630 | Wilmington Dist. |
| Militia | Joseph Whitley | 3413 | Wilmington Dist. |
| Militia | Savin Watkins | 177 | Wilmington Dist. |
| Militia | Joseph Whitney | 3582 | Wilmington Dist. |
| Militia | Daniel Wheaton | 1713 | Wilmington Dist. |
| Militia | John Wilkings | 4571 | Wilmington Dist. |
| Militia | William Whiten | 4907 | Wilmington Dist. |
| Militia | Joseph Whitley | 3392 | Wilmington Dist. |
| Militia | Nicolas Worley | 3663 | Wilmington Dist. |
| Militia | Richard Wilkinson | 4538 | Wilmington Dist. |
| Militia | Alex Whitley | 1192 | Newbern Dist. |
| Militia | William Whitley | 1857 | Newbern Dist. |
| Militia | Jno. Whaley | 374 | Newbern Dist. |
| Militia | Wm. Williamson | 2164 | Wilmington Dist. |
| Continental | John Wade | 1449 | Newbern Dist. |
| Continental | Obadiah Winson | 1166 | Halifax Dist. |
| Continental | Wyatt Warnick, Soldier | 163 | Halifax Dist. |
| Continental | David Welch | 1145 | Warrenton Dist. |
| Continental | Willis Whitehead | 1407 | Halifax Dist. |
| Continental | Hardin Warnese | 160 | Hillsborough Dist. |
| Continental | Absolm Woodard | 325 | |

| | | *No.* | |
|---|---|---|---|
| Militia | Robt. Withington | 976 | Newbern Dist. |
| Militia | Wm. Williamson | 53 | Newbern Dist. |
| Militia | Charles Wilkerson | 606 | Newbern Dist. |
| Militia | Wm. Wellington | 555 | Newbern Dist. |
| Militia | Samuel Wade | 2367 | Newbern Dist. |
| Militia | Wm. Whealler | 501 | Newbern Dist. |
| Militia | Angus Warsdon | 1269 | Newbern Dist. |
| Militia | Jno. Whitford | 1038 | Newbern Dist. |
| Militia | Needham Whitley | 1293 | Newbern Dist. |
| Militia | William Whitley | 2087 | Newbern Dist. |
| Militia | William Wayne | 321 | Newbern Dist. |
| Militia | James Weirkle | 1703 | Newbern Dist. |
| Militia | Thomas Wharton | 1216 | Newbern Dist. |
| Militia | Joseph Whalfud | 1595 | Newbern Dist. |
| Militia | Benj. Windon | 407 | Newbern Dist. |
| Militia | Alex. Whitley | 1756 | Newbern Dist. |
| Militia | Jeremiah Watson | 458 | Newbern Dist. |
| Militia | James Williamson | 789 | Newbern Dist. |
| Militia | John Windham | 888 | Newbern Dist. |
| Militia | Andrew Willoby | 699 | Newbern Dist. |
| Militia | Wm. Wilkinson | 1546 | Newbern Dist. |
| Militia | Willis Whitehead | 800 | Newbern Dist. |
| Militia | Nehemiah Woolin | 1558 | Newbern Dist. |
| Militia | Joseph Whatford | 387 | Newbern Dist. |
| Militia | Jesse Walton | 701 | Newbern Dist. |
| Militia | William Wilkinson | 1784 | Wilmington Dist. |
| Militia | David Witherspoon | 4585 | Morgan Dist. |
| Militia | Alex. McWheartor | 7128 | Salisbury Dist. |
| Militia | Moses Winsley | 8949 | Salisbury Dist. |
| Militia | John Westrope | 4579 | Salisbury Dist. |
| Militia | David Wm | 2884 | Salisbury Dist. |
| Militia | Philip Woolf | 3190 | Salisbury Dist. |
| Militia | John Watson | 882 | Salisbury Dist. |
| Militia | Theadale Whitnith | 4699 | Salisbury Dist. |
| Militia | Joseph McWrath | 6928 | Salisbury Dist. |
| Militia | Richard Womack | 7448 | Salisbury Dist. |
| Militia | Kader Warrick | 3433 | Wilmington Dist. |
| Militia | Wm. Westbrook | 5784 | Wilmington Dist. |
| Militia | Hugh Watson | 2978 | Wilmington Dist. |
| Militia | Edward Wingate | 4910 | Wilmington Dist. |
| Militia | John Wade | 3676 | Wilmington Dist. |
| Militia | Arthur Whitehouse | 1656 | Newbern Dist. |
| Militia | Andrew Willsby | 595 | Newbern Dist. |
| Continental | William Withington | 22 | Halifax Dist. |
| Continental | Lieut. John Winborn | 632 | Halifax Dist. |
| Continental | Willis Wicker | 266 | Hillsborough Dist. |
| Continental | Richard Wallace | 130 | Hillsborough Dist. |
| Continental | William Watford | 292 | Hillsborough Dist. |
| Continental | Harden Warner | 273 | Hillsborough Dist. |
| Continental | Burnick Wilkins | 252 | Hillsborough Dist. |
| Continental | Willis Williford | 168 | Hillsborough Dist. |
| Continental | James Wasson | 379 | Hillsborough Dist. |
| Continental | John Warner | 395 | Hillsborough Dist. |
| Continental | Isaac Walters | 146 | Hillsborough Dist. |

|  |  | No. |  |
|---|---|---|---|
| Continental | William Worton | 112 | Hillsborough Dist. |
| Continental | William Walters | 101 | Hillsborough Dist. |
| Continental | Henry Williamson | 68 | Hillsborough Dist. |
| Continental | James Woolard | 842 | Hillsborough Dist. |
| Continental | William Womack | 702 | Hillsborough Dist. |
| Continental | John Weaver | 411 | Hillsborough Dist. |
| Continental | John Whaley | 610 | Hillsborough Dist. |
| Continental | Daniel Winchester | 14 | Hillsborough Dist. |
| Continental | Burnell Wilkins | 141 | Hillsborough Dist. |
| Continental | John Weston | 398 | Hillsborough Dist. |
| Continental | Absalom Wildey | 718 | Hillsborough Dist. |
| Continental | Abner Winns | 19 | Hillsborough Dist. |
| Continental | John Willoughby | 700 | Hillsborough Dist. |
| Continental | Thomas Winters | 707 | Halifax Dist. |
| Continental | James Woodard | 93 |  |
| Continental | George Warnick | 72 |  |
| Continental | William Welch | 37 | Halifax Dist. |
| Continental | Chaverly Witherington | 469 | Halifax Dist. |
| Continental | Frances Westduhall, Soldier | 73 | Halifax Dist. |
| Continental | Nathan Withington | 463 | Halifax Dist. |
| Continental | Moses Winters, Soldier | 462 | Halifax Dist. |
| Continental | Jno. Wills | 630 | Halifax Dist. |
| Continental | William Wilkerson, Soldier | 738 | Halifax Dist. |
| Continental | Corbin Weymonth | 381 | Halifax Dist. |
| Continental | Job Williamson | 110 |  |
| Continental | Lieut. John Winborn | 631 | Halifax Dist. |
| Continental | Wm. Williamson | 118 | Halifax Dist. |
| Continental | Thomas Walden | 953 | Warrenton Dist. |
| Continental | Alexander Walch | 238 |  |
| Continental | James Willace | 107 |  |
| Continental | Daniel Woodland | 1655 |  |
| Continental | Solomon Warbutton | 1045 | Halifax Dist. |
| Continental | Benj. Wilcocks | 12 | Halifax Dist. |
| Continental | Bryan Worsley | 729 | Halifax Dist. |
| Continental | Robert Woodland | 830 | Warrenton Dist. |
| Continental | Henry Williamson | 34 | Hillsborough Dist. |
| Continental | John Wood | 591 | Halifax Dist. |
| Continental | Charles Wincock, Soldier | 778 | Halifax Dist. |
| Continental | John Wrenn | 476 | Halifax Dist. |
| Continental | Joel Whiteherst | 720 | Halifax Dist. |
| Continental | Wyatt Warnick | 793 | Halifax Dist. |
| Continental | Elija Windley | 1415 | Halifax Dist. |
| Continental | Willis Williford | 95 | Hillsborough Dist. |
| Continental | Alexander Walsh | 312 |  |
| Continental | James Woodard | 167 |  |
| Militia | John Weeks | 159 | Wilmington Dist. |
| Militia | William Worsley | 1298 | Newbern Dist. |
| Militia | Aliga Wise | 1170 | Newbern Dist. |

### FOUND IN ANOTHER BOX

|  |  |  |  |
|---|---|---|---|
| Militia | Robert Allison | 5064 | Salisbury Dist. |
| Militia | Theophilus Allison | 5652 | Salisbury Dist. |
| Militia | Fordman Gunzalus | 2231 | Salisbury Dist. |
| Militia | Richard Godwin | 495 | Wilmington Dist. |

| | | No. | |
|---|---|---|---|
| Militia | Joseph Gorden | 3452 | Wilmington Dist. |
| Militia | James Gauncey | 4567 | Salisbury Dist. |
| Militia | Charles Garin | 3423 | Wilmington Dist. |
| Militia | Sam'l. Gauff | 259 | Wilmington Dist. |
| Militia | John Glenn | 3553 | Wilmington Dist. |
| Militia | Charles Goff | 506 | Wilmington Dist. |
| Militia | John Charlescraft | 411 | Wilmington Dist. |
| Militia | Isaac Cornnerlin | 3372 | Wilmington Dist. |
| Militia | Joseph Chears | 3325 | Wilmington Dist. |
| Militia | Alexander Chestnut | 549 | Wilmington Dist. |
| Militia | Jas. Guy | 345 | Wilmington Dist. |
| Militia | William Gaff | 446 | Wilmington Dist. |
| Militia | James Gailor | 3436 | Wilmington Dist. |
| Militia | Gillis Murphey | 548 | Wilmington Dist. |
| Militia | Thomas Graulton | 521 | Wilmington Dist. |
| Militia | Thomas Goff | 3578 | Wilmington Dist. |
| Militia | Joshua Armous | 5691 | Wilmington Dist. |
| Militia | John Akell | 7,690 | Salisbury Dist. |
| Militia | John Alcoun | 8795 | Salisbury Dist. |
| Militia | Henry Archibald | 4635 | Salisbury Dist. |
| Militia | Capt. Matthew Albitton | 1049 | Wilmington Dist. |
| Militia | William Atkinson | 59 | Wilmington Dist. |
| Militia | William Alphen | 4965 | Wilmington Dist. |
| Militia | James Atkinson | 5986 | Wilmington Dist. |
| Militia | James Alburton | 727 | Newbern Dist. |
| Militia | Nathan Archibald | 692 | Newbern Dist. |
| Militia | Benj. Almory | 7743 | Salisbury Dist. |
| Militia | Enoch Arnett | 3336 | Wilmington Dist. |
| Militia | Joseph Arthur | 880 | Salisbury Dist. |
| Militia | Thomas Archibald | 1759 | Salisbury Dist. |
| Militia | Benjamin Alferd | 1200 | Newbern Dist. |
| Militia | John Arthur | 1109 | Newbern Dist. |
| Militia | Nathan Atkinson | 2145 | Newbern Dist. |
| Militia | Amos Atkinson | 1221 | Newbern Dist. |
| Militia | Arch'd. Artis | 511 | Newbern Dist. |
| Militia | Jesse Agreston | 765 | Wilmington Dist. |
| Militia | Arnal Adkins | 8997 | Salisbury Dist. |
| Militia | Joseph Artis | 3445 | Wilmington Dist. |
| Militia | Adam Allison | 7078 | Salisbury Dist. |
| Militia | Wm. Adcock | 4552 | Salisbury Dist. |
| Militia | Sam'l. Archibald | 4811 | Salisbury Dist. |
| Militia | Sam'l. Aud | 6528 | Salisbury Dist. |
| Continental | Henry Harrison, Mecklenburg Co.... | 1780 | |
| Continental | Anthony Haynes, Caswell Co. | .... | |
| Continental | John Hall, Wake Co. | 1791 | |
| | Micajah Hicks, Wayne Co. | 1791 | |
| Continental | John Hooker, Granville Co. | 1791 | |
| Continental | William Hall, Rowan Co. | 1791 | |
| Continental | Peter Clifton | 1158 | Warrenton Dist. |
| Continental | Josiah Ellis | 1159 | Warrenton Dist. |
| Continental | Jeremiah Ellis | 1658 | Warrenton Dist. |
| Continental | William Nurckell | 1849 | Warrenton Dist. |
| Continental | Curtis Whitley | 1817 | Warrenton Dist. |
| Continental | John Christopher | 1979 | Warrenton Dist. |

| | | No. | |
|---|---|---|---|
| Continental | Abraham Ballard | 1156 | Warrenton Dist. |
| Continental | Nathan Dees | 1816 | Warrenton Dist. |
| Continental | Robert Singleton | 1997 | Warrenton Dist. |
| Continental | Josiah Stevenson | 1630 | Warrenton Dist. |
| Continental | David Stokes | 1645 | Warrenton Dist. |
| Continental | Josiah Nunn | 1996 | Warrenton Dist. |
| Continental | Joseph Smith | 1857 | Warrenton Dist. |
| Continental | David Davis | 1326 | Warrenton Dist. |
| Continental | John Outlaw | 1157 | Warrenton Dist. |
| Continental | David Arnold | 551 | Halifax Dist. |
| Militia | Capt. Able Armstrong | 4674 | Salisbury Dist. |
| Militia | Enoch Arnold | 2012 | Wilmington Dist. |
| Continental | William Aldridge | 1340 | Halifax Dist. |
| Continental | James Ammons | 237 | Hillsborough Dist. |
| Militia | John Allison | 2270 | Salisbury Dist. |
| Militia | Nathan Askew | 3307 | Wilmington Dist. |
| Militia | James Atkinson | 4979 | Wilmington Dist. |
| Militia | John Askew | 3520 | Wilmington Dist. |
| Militia | Capt. Thomas Ard | 4798 | Wilmington Dist. |
| Militia | Alexander Afton | 1996 | Salisbury Dist. |
| Militia | John Arthur | 1134 | Newbern Dist. |
| Militia | Jesse Aldridge | 1275 | Newbern Dist. |

### ANOTHER BOX

| | | | |
|---|---|---|---|
| Militia | Lieut. Thomas Grantham | 464 | Wilmington Dist. |
| Militia | Jeremiah Groon | 6886 | Salisbury Dist. |
| Militia | James Garrison | 7571 | Salisbury Dist. |
| Militia | Jesse Gullet | 761 | Salisbury Dist. |
| Militia | Andrew George | 1287 | Salisbury Dist. |
| Militia | John Gardner | 5019 | Salisbury Dist. |
| Militia | John Gather | 6980 | Salisbury Dist. |
| Militia | Peter Glascock | 4230 | Salisbury Dist. |
| Militia | Samuel Calhoon | 5444 | Salisbury Dist. |
| Militia | Abraham Childers | 2226 | Salisbury Dist. |
| Militia | Alexander Carruth | 3064 | Salisbury Dist. |
| Militia | John Collum | 4549 | Salisbury Dist. |
| Militia | Lambeth Clayton | 5833 | Salisbury Dist. |
| Militia | Britton Cobb | 832 | Newbern Dist. |
| Militia | Peter Callmay | 111 | Newbern Dist. |
| Continental | James Gifford | 1 | |
| Militia | John Jenkins | 4620 | Salisbury Dist. |
| Militia | John Durrill | 1099 | Wilmington Dist. |
| Militia | Patrick Smith | 5618 | Wilmington Dist. |
| Continental | John Hill | 14 | Newbern Dist. |
| Continental | Moses Elmore | 1246 | Halifax Dist. |
| Continental | Spencer Donaldson | 937 | Halifax Dist. |
| Continental | Joseph Hill | 1794 | Warrenton Dist. |
| Militia | Joshua Devall | 1116 | Wilmington Dist. |
| Militia | David Dudley | 1094 | Wilmington Dist. |
| Militia | Jacob Daughtery | 756 | Wilmington Dist. |
| Militia | Edward Debruhl | 1755 | Wilmington Dist. |
| Militia | Joseph Eickilberg | 781 | Salisbury Dist. |
| Militia | Philip Eaple | 2221 | Salisbury Dist. |
| Militia | John Edmiston | 3302 | Salisbury Dist. |

| | | No. | |
|---|---|---|---|
| Militia | Thomas Eakires | 1382 | Salisbury Dist. |
| Militia | Henry Eaple | 2233 | Salisbury Dist. |
| Militia | Joshua Eclin | 1828 | Newbern Dist. |
| Militia | Daniel Delle | 1222 | Newbern Dist. |
| Militia | Edmon Perkins | 180 | Newbern Dist. |
| Militia | Peter Gordun | 5356 | Salisbury Dist. |
| Militia | James Blanton | 2228 | Wilmington Dist. |
| Continental | Selby Harney | 313 | |
| Continental | James Kellun | 32 | |
| Continental | George Brownrigg | 105 | Halifax Dist. |
| Continental | John Bertie | 11 | Halifax Dist. |
| Continental | Welian Barkley | 64 | Halifax Dist. |
| Continental | Mundell Burke | 831 | Halifax Dist. |

## NORTH CAROLINA PENSION ROLL

(Copied from U. S. War Department, Report on Pensions, 1835)

NAMES, RANK, &c. OF INVALID PENSIONERS RESIDING IN ANSON COUNTY, NORTH CAROLINA

| Names | Rank | Sums received | Description of service | Commencement of pension | Ages | Laws under which they were formerly inscribed on the Pension Roll and remarks |
|---|---|---|---|---|---|---|
| Josiah Abshier | Corporal | $ 345.97 | 3rd Regt. U.S. rifle | Dec. 20, 1826 | 64 | Ex. mil. est. |
| Thomas Childs* | Captain | 4,085.26 | Army of Revolution | Mar. 4, 1795 | — | Died Sept. 15, 1820 |
| Alston Fort | Private | 1,873.03 | — | Sept. 16, 1814 | — | Act Apr. 30, 1816 |
| James Redfern | Do | 277.08 | Revolutionary Army | Sept. 5, 1808 | — | |
| Do | Do | 596.93 | Do | Apr. 24, 1816 | 76 | Act Apr. 24, 1816 |
| Richard Russell | Private | 228.63 | Va. Cont'l line | Mar. 4, 1831 | 73 | Died Jan. 13, 1834 |
| James Ross | Do | 202.50 | N. C. Militia | Do | 86 | |
| William Ricketts | Do | 210.00 | S. C. Cont'l line | Do | 86 | |
| Richard Tomlinson | Pri. and Ser. | 78.99 | N. C. Militia | Do | 84 | |
| John Threadgill | Private | 120.00 | Do | Do | 77 | |
| Thomas Terry | Do | 240.00 | Do | Do | 82 | |
| William Vaughan | Do | 90.00 | Do | Do | 78 | |
| Leven Watson | Pri. Cav. | 259.05 | Georgia Militia | Do | 82 | |
| Edlyne Willoughby | Private | 240.00 | Va. Cont'l line | Do | 74 | |
| Jourdan Woodward | Do | 60.00 | N. C. Militia | Do | 83 | |
| William Wood | Do | 240.00 | Do Cont'l line | Do | 77 | |
| Robert Wilson | Do | 66.99 | Do Militia | Do | | |

Above found in North Carolina Pension Roll pages 2 and 60.

ASHE COUNTY, NORTH CAROLINA

| Names | Rank | Sums received | Description of service | Commencement of pension | Ages | Laws under which they were formerly inscribed on the Pension Roll and remarks |
|---|---|---|---|---|---|---|
| David Johnson* | Private | $1,628.45 | Army of the U. S. | Mar. 4, 1789 | — | Died Feb. 18, 1829 |
| Do | Do | 1,327.00 | Do | Apr. 24, 1816 | — | Act Apr. 24, 1816 |
| Francis Johnson | Do | 310.08 | Do | Sept. 5, 1808 | | Do |
| Do | Do | 1,044.91 | Do | Apr. 24, 1816 | | |
| Nathan Blevins | Private | 40.00 | Va. Militia | Mar. 4, 1831 | 71 | |
| John Baldwin | Do | 240.00 | N. C. Militia | Do | 74 | |
| Landrine Eggers | Do | 104.15 | N. York Militia | Do | 77 | |

| | | | | | | |
|---|---|---|---|---|---|---|
| Jeremiah Green............ | Do | 134.42 | N. C. Militia | Do | 78 | |
| Francis Johnston............ | Pri. Ser. & Lieut. | 196.32 | Do Militia | Do | 73 | |

Above found in North Carolina Pension Roll pages 2 and 60.

## BEAUFORT COUNTY, NORTH CAROLINA

| | | | | | | |
|---|---|---|---|---|---|---|
| Isaac Buck...... | Private | $ 180.00 | N. C. Militia | Mar. 4, 1831 | 73 | |
| Joseph Campen, Sen...... | Do | — | Do | Do | 80 | Died May 10, 1833 |
| James Creemer, Sen...... | Do | — | Do | Do | 79 | |
| Joseph Guilford...... | Do | 207.00 | Do | Do | 72 | |
| Joshua Hill...... | Do | 60.00 | Do | Do | 77 | |
| Anthony Kinnin...... | Do | 129.99 | Do | Do | 71 | |
| Jacob O. Merry...... | Do | 104.97 | Do | Do | 72 | Died Oct. 20, 1833 |
| John Nobles...... | Do | 159.99 | Do | Do | 70 | |
| Israel Pierce...... | Seaman & Private | 264.00 | Do | Do | 76 | |
| Joseph Wall...... | Private | 169.98 | Do | Do | | |

Above found in North Carolina Pension Roll page 65.

## BLADEN COUNTY, NORTH CAROLINA

| | | | | | | |
|---|---|---|---|---|---|---|
| Caleb Berry......... | Private | $ 575.48 | 1st Regt. U. S. Inf. | May 29, 1816 | — | {Act mil. est. / Died May 25, 1825 |
| Robert Johnston...... | Private | 87.48 | N. C. Militia | Mar. 4, 1831 | 72 | |
| Aaron Lewis, Sen...... | Do | 60.00 | Do | Do | 73 | |
| Duncan McCullock...... | Do | 54.25 | Do | Do | 70 | |
| Hugh Murphey...... | Do | 166.65 | N. C. Cont'l Line | Do | 82 | Died Aug. 27, 1833 |
| William Pridgeon...... | Do | 94.98 | N. C. Militia | Do | 102 | |
| Samuel Pharis...... | Do | 99.99 | Do | Do | 73 | |
| John Parker...... | Do | 134.64 | Do | Do | 81 | |
| Joseph Russ...... | Do | 150.00 | Do | Do | 71 | |
| Jeremiah Rackley...... | Private and Ser. | 75.00 | N. C. Cont'l line | Do | 74 | |
| James Shipman...... | Captain | 1,440.00 | N. C. Militia | Do | 82 | |
| Josiah Singletary...... | Private | 129.99 | Do | Do | 71 | |
| Sanders Simmons...... | Do | 120.00 | Do | Do | 71 | |
| William Smith...... | Do | 73.32 | Do | Do | 76 | |
| Henry Wheeler...... | Do | 53.32 | S. C. | Do | 72 | |

Above found in North Carolina Pension Roll pages 3 and 64.

BUNCOMBE COUNTY, NORTH CAROLINA

| Names | Rank | Sums received | Description of service | Commencement of pension | Ages | Laws under which they were formerly inscribed on the Pension Roll and remarks |
|---|---|---|---|---|---|---|
| Adam Cooper | Private | $ 418.29 | — | Dec. 20, 1825 | — | (Died Apr. 27, 1830 (Act Mar. 3, 1827 |
| James Alexander | Do | 222.48 | N. C. Cont'l line | Mar. 4, 1831 | 77 | |
| Daniel Ball | Private and Ser. | 120.00 | N. C. Militia | Do | 71 | |
| William Brittian | Private | 60.00 | Do Do | Do | 72 | |
| Edward Decoine | Ser. & Ser. Major | 425.88 | Va. Cont'l line | Do | 77 | (Act Mar. 18, 1818 Dropped and inscribed under Act6/7/1832 Died Feb. 1, 1834 |
| Do | Private | 300.00 | Do | Do | 79 | |
| Clement Davis | Private | 240.00 | N. C. Militia | Mar. 4, 1831 | 70 | |
| William Deaver | Do | 120.00 | Va. Militia | Do | 80 | |
| William Erwin | Pri. Inf. and Cal. | 132.48 | N. C. Militia | Do | 84 | |
| Thomas Foster | Private | 240.00 | Va. Cont'l line | Do | 78 | |
| Reuben Fletcher | Do | 120.00 | N. C. Militia | Do | 69 | |
| Alexander Fuller | Do | — | Do | Do | 70 | |
| Joseph Henry | Do | 60.00 | Do | Do | 70 | |
| Elijah Henson | Do | 240.00 | Va. Cont'l line | Do | 73 | |
| James F. Jester | Do | 60.00 | N. C. Cont'l line | Do | 72 | |
| James Jennings | Do | 240.00 | N. C. Militia | Do | 77 | |
| John Lanning | Do | — | N. C. Cont'l line | Do | 77 | |
| John Merrill | Pri. Inf. and Cal. | 112.47 | N. C. Militia | Do | 77 | |
| Benj. Merrill | Private | 73.93 | Do | Do | 82 | |
| James Owenbey | Do | — | Do | Do | 73 | |
| Jess Palmer, Sen. | Do | 60.00 | Va. Militia | Do | 71 | |
| Thomas Payne | Do | 53.32 | N. C. Militia | Do | 71 | |
| Edmond Palmer | Do | 60.00 | N. C. Cont'l line | Do | 86 | |
| Samuel Patton | Pri. Inf. and Calv. | 187.50 | N. C. Militia | Do | 75 | |
| Jonathan Prestwood | Pri. & Ser. Drag's | 133.95 | N. C. Cont'l line | Do | 75 | |
| John Roberts | Pri. Inf. and Art. | 275.00 | N. C. Militia | Do | 76 | |
| Thomas Reid | Private | — | Do | Do | 77 | |
| William Robinson | Do | — | Do | Do | 74 | |
| Thomas Sharp | Pri. Cal. and Inf. | 67.50 | N. C. Cont'l line | Do | 80 | |
| Michael Tanner | Private | 129.99 | Va. Militia | Do | 74 | |

| | | | | | |
|---|---|---|---|---|---|
| Valentine Thrash.......... | Do | — | N. C. Militia | Do | 85 |
| Elijah Williamson.......... | Pri. Inf. and Calv. | 135.00 | S. C. Militia | Do | 79 |
| Charles Williamson.......... | Private | 240.00 | N. C. Militia | Do | 80 |

Above found in North Carolina Pension Roll pages 3, 65, 66 and 67.

## BURKE COUNTY, NORTH CAROLINA

| | | | | | | |
|---|---|---|---|---|---|---|
| Samuel Alexander......... | Private | $ 60.00 | N. C. Militia | Mar. 4, 1831 | 75 | |
| John Arwood............. | Do | 150.00 | Do | Do | 72 | |
| Benjamin Austin......... | Do | 120.00 | Do | Do | 74 | |
| David Baker............. | Corporal | 264.00 | V. Cont'l line | Do | 85 | |
| Sherwood Bowman......... | Private | 60.00 | N. C. Militia | Do | 76 | |
| Steven Ballen........... | Do | 79.98 | Do | Do | 72 | |
| William Crawley......... | Private of Art. | 250.00 | V. Cont'l line | Do | 75 | |
| Jonathan Curtes......... | Private | 230.40 | N. C. Militia | Do | 87 | Died Jan. 22, 1834 |
| George Clontz........... | Sergeant......... | 135.00 | N. C. Cont'l line | Do | 74 | |
| Conrad Crump........... | Private | 139.98 | N. C. Militia | Do | 81 | |
| William Culberson, Sen... | | 117.00 | Do | Do | 94 | |
| Samuel Davis........... | Do | 99.99 | V. Militia | Do | 81 | |
| John Duckworth......... | Do | 183.99 | N. C. Militia | Do | 76 | |
| Joseph Dovson........... | Do | 199.98 | Do | Do | 78 | |
| William Freeman......... | Do | 150.00 | Do | Do | 76 | |
| John Fox, Sen........... | Do | 79.98 | Do | Do | 70 | |
| John Green.............. | Do | 99.99 | Do | Do | 72 | |
| Solomon Good........... | Do | 90.00 | Do | Do | 74 | |
| William Gragg........... | Do | 69.99 | Va. Militia | Do | 76 | |
| Charles Haney........... | Do | 93.30 | Penna. Militia | Do | 86 | |
| George Hodge........... | Do | 76.98 | N. C. Militia | Do | 74 | |
| David Hays.............. | Pri. Inf. and Calv. | 114.99 | Do | Do | 74 | |
| Adam Hoppis........... | Private | 90.00 | Va. Cont'l line | Do | 80 | |
| Leonard Hise........... | Do | — | Do | Do | 78 | |
| Robert Kincaid......... | Do | 79.98 | N. C. Militia | Do | 70 | |
| James Kincaid......... | Do | 99.99 | S. C. Militia | Do | 80 | |
| David Montgomery...... | Do | 73.89 | N. C. Militia | Do | 79 | |
| Daniel Moore, Sen...... | Do | 100.00 | Do | Do | 69 | |
| William Morris, Sen..... | Do | 86.64 | N. C. Militia | Do | 84 | |
| Lewis Powell........... | Do | 150.00 | Do | Do | 75 | |
| George Poplin......... | Do | 139.98 | Do | Do | 81 | |
| John Presnell......... | Do | — | Do | Do | 83 | |

| Names | Rank | Sums received | Description of service | Commencement of pension | Ages | Laws under which they were formerly inscribed on the Pension Roll and remarks |
|---|---|---|---|---|---|---|
| Joseph Pyett | Private | $ 183.99 | N. C. Militia | Mar. 4, 1831 | 79 | |
| Samuel Reed | Do | 139.98 | Do | Do | 79 | |
| George Silver | Do | 240.00 | Md. Cont'l line | Do | 83 | |
| Daniel Sullivan | Do | 60.00 | Pa. Militia | Do | 71 | |
| Aaron Stacy | Do | 83.32 | N. C. Militia | Do | 74 | |
| Joseph Starnes | Do | 139.98 | Va. Cont'l line | Do | 78 | |
| George Sigman | Do | 75.00 | N. C. Militia | Do | 78 | |
| Thomas Smith | Do | — | S. C. Militia | Do | 70 | |
| Benjamin Spencer | Do | — | Do | Do | 73 | |
| John Stewart | Do | — | N. C. Militia | Do | 72 | |
| John Swink | Do | 120.00 | Do | Do | — | |
| Isaac Thompson | Do | 90.00 | Do | Do | 79 | |
| Jacob Tipps | Do | 90.00 | Do | Do | 86 | |
| Samuel Turner | Do | 69.99 | S. C. Militia | Do | 72 | |
| Lawrence Unger | Do | 178.35 | N. C. Cont'l line | Do | 78 | |
| Reuben Walker | Do | 120.00 | N. C. Militia | Do | 74 | |
| Henry Woods | Do | 90.00 | Do | Do | 81 | |

Above found in North Carolin Pension Roll pages 61 and 62.

## BRUNSWICK COUNTY, NORTH CAROLINA

| Names | Rank | Sums received | Description of service | Commencement of pension | Ages | Laws under which they were formerly inscribed on the Pension Roll and remarks |
|---|---|---|---|---|---|---|
| John Cason | Private | $ 150.00 | N. C. Militia | Mar. 4, 1831 | 82 | |
| Sedgwick Springs | Do | 240.00 | N. C. Cont'l line | Do | 79 | |
| Steven Williams | Do | 96.65 | Do | Do | 71 | |

Above found in North Carolina Pension Roll page 63.

## CABARRUS COUNTY, NORTH CAROLINA

| Names | Rank | Sums received | Description of service | Commencement of pension | Ages | Laws under which they were formerly inscribed on the Pension Roll and remarks |
|---|---|---|---|---|---|---|
| John Gellon | Private | $ 275.07 | Army of Revolution | Sept. 4, 1808 | — | |
| Do | Do | 1,000.13 | Do | Apr. 24, 1816 | — | Act Apr. 24, 1816 |
| Abraham Alexander | | — | N. C. Militia | Mar. 4, 1831 | 72 | Died Dec. 17. 1832 |

| Name | Rank | Amount | Line | Date | Age | Notes |
|---|---|---|---|---|---|---|
| George Barnhardt | Do | 38.33 | Do | Do | 73 | Died Feb. 5, 1833 |
| James Bradford | Do | 79.98 | N. C. Cont'l line | Do | 72 | |
| Charles Blackwelder | Do | 66.30 | Do | Do | 73 | Died Mar. 31, 1833 |
| Thomas Campbell | Do | 53.32 | N. C. Militia | Do | 73 | |
| William Carrigan | Do | 210.00 | Do | Do | 74 | |
| Henry Furrer | Private and Sergt. | 114.99 | Do | Do | 73 | |
| James Hamilton | Private | 133.32 | Do | Do | 71 | |
| Thomas Irwin | Do | 103.98 | Do | Do | 75 | |
| Samuel Killough | Do | 90.00 | Pa. Militia | Do | 78 | |
| Thomas McLure | Do | 77.34 | N. C. Militia | Do | 69 | |
| Jacob Miller | Do | 120.00 | Do | Do | 86 | |
| Archibald McCurdy | Private and Lt. | 339.99 | N. C. Cont'l line | Do | 82 | |
| Martin Phifer | Capt. of Drag. | 1800.00 | N. C. Militia | Do | 79 | |
| Martin Stough | Private | 75.00 | Do | Do | 80 | |
| William Stow | Do | 79.98 | V. Cont'l line | Do | 81 | |
| Henry Smith | Captain | 583.92 | N. C. Cont'l line | Do | 92 | |
| Caleb Toup | Private | 139.98 | N. C. Militia | Do | 77 | |
| William Walker | Do | — | Pa. Militia | Do | 73 | |
| Paul Walker | Do | 157.50 | N. C. Militia | Do | 79 | |
| Reuben Parrott | Do | — | Do | Do | 72 | |

Above found in North Carolina Pension Roll pages 6 and 72.

## CARTERET COUNTY, NORTH CAROLINA

| Name | Rank | Amount | Line | Date | Age | Notes |
|---|---|---|---|---|---|---|
| Richard Arthur, Sen. | Private | $ 79.93 | N. C. Militia | Mar. 4, 1831 | 74 | |
| John Brook | Do | 89.41 | N. C. Cont'l line | Do | 83 | Died Mar. 29, 1833 |
| James Fulford | Do | 240.00 | N. C. Militia | Do | 79 | |
| Steven Fulford | Sergeant | 200.42 | Do | Do | 86 | Died Feb. 4, 1834 |
| James G. Briel | Private and Sergt. | 322.50 | Do | Do | 75 | |
| John Hancock | Private | 66.99 | Do | Do | 71 | |

Above found in North Carolina Pension Roll page 73.

## CAMDEN COUNTY, NORTH CAROLINA

| Name | Rank | Amount | Line | Date | Age | Notes |
|---|---|---|---|---|---|---|
| Robert Darrah | Sergeant | $1,077.06 | 1st Regt. U. S. Rifle | June 16, 1815 | — | Ex. mil. est. trans. from Va. 9/4/1826 |
| Thomas Linton | Private | 99.99 | N. C. Militia | Mar. 4, 1831 | 79 | |
| Thomas Walston | Do | 129.99 | Do | Do | 72 | |

Above found in North Carolina Pension Roll pages 5 and 68.

CASWELL COUNTY, NORTH CAROLINA

| Names | Rank | Sums received | Description of service | Commencement of pension | Ages | Laws under which they were formerly inscribed on the Pension Roll and remarks |
|---|---|---|---|---|---|---|
| Thomas Belsaih* | Private | $ 428.28 | U. S. Army | Mar. 4, 1809 | — | Died May 10, 1829 |
| Do | Do | 1,250.79 | — | Apr. 24, 1815 | — | Act Apr. 24, 1816 |
| Braxton Carter | Do | 119.36 | Do | Jan. 1, 1813 | — | Vide Act Aug. 2, 1813 |
| Do | Do | 1,000.13 | Do | Apr. 24, 1816 | — | Act Apr. 24, 1816 |
| William Norman | Do | 481.71 | Donohoe's U.S. Art. | Feb. 20, 1824 | 90 | Ex. mil. est. |
| Jacob A. Hart | Do | 75.00 | N. C. Militia | Mar. 4, 1831 | 76 | |
| William Adkins, Sen. | Do | 109.98 | N. C. Cont'l | Do | 72 | |
| William Badget | Do | 78.99 | N. C. Militia | Do | 74 | |
| David Baker | Do | 120.00 | Do | Do | 74 | |
| Peter Badget | Private and Ens. | 240.00 | Do | Do | 77 | |
| Jeremial Beaver | Private | 75.00 | Do | Do | 70 | |
| Robert Browning | Do | 64.98 | Do | Do | 72 | |
| Charles Cock | Do | 60.00 | Va. Militia | Do | 71 | |
| Joseph Dameron | Do | 66.99 | N. C. Militia | Do | 77 | |
| John Davis | Do | 87.50 | Do | Do | 75 | |
| John Dill | Do | 90.00 | Do | Do | 74 | |
| Elisha Evans, Sen. | Pri. Inf. and Cav. | 157.98 | Do | Do | 67 | |
| John Ferrell | Private | 60.00 | Do | Do | 70 | |
| Starling Gunn | Do | 90.00 | Do | Do | 86 | |
| Dudley Gatewood | Do | 109.98 | Va. Militia | Do | 83 | |
| Zacharia Hastings | Do | 69.99 | Do | Do | 79 | |
| Berry Hunt | Do | 240.00 | N. C. Militia | Do | 72 | |
| William Harvile | Do | 60.00 | Do | Do | 75 | |
| Benjamin Long | Do | 79.98 | Do | Do | 78 | |
| John McMullen | Lt. and Capt. | 379.98 | N. C. Cont'l | Do | 79 | |
| Richard Martin | Private | 240.00 | Md. Militia | Do | 72 | |
| John Mathins | Do | 90.00 | N. C. Militia | Do | 72 | |
| Daniel Merrit | Do | 150.00 | Do | Do | 74 | |
| John Marlan | Do | 240.00 | Do | Do | 73 | |
| William McMennamy | Do | 69.99 | Va. Cont'l | Do | 78 | |
| William Pleasant | Do | 180.00 | N. C. Militia | Do | 79 | |
| William Parker | Do | 120.00 | Do | Do | 73 | |
| Thomas Roan | Pri. and Musc. | 132.00 | | | | |

| Name | Rank | Service | Amount | Age | |
|---|---|---|---|---|---|
| William Roberts | Private | Va. Militia | 180.00 | 72 | Do |
| Elisha Rowark | Do | N. C. Militia | 60.00 | 76 | Do |
| William Roberts | Do | Va. Militia | 40.00 | 72 | Do |
| Samuel Stevens | Do | N. C. Militia | 73.32 | 72 | Do |
| William Slad, Sen | Do | Do | 90.00 | 76 | Do |
| Jonothan Starkey | Pri. Inf. and Cav. | Do | 117.99 | 74 | Do |
| Richard Smith | Private | Do | 69.99 | 90 | Do |
| William Ware | Do | Do | 159.99 | 75 | Do |
| John Ware, Sen | Do | Do | 120.00 | 79 | Do |

Above found in North Carolina Pension Roll pages 4, 70 and 71.

## CHATHAM COUNTY, NORTH CAROLINA

| Name | Rank | Service | Amount | | Age | | Remarks |
|---|---|---|---|---|---|---|---|
| Joshua Adcock | Private | N. C. Cont'l line | $ 240.00 | Mar. 4, 1831 | 74 | Do | |
| Jesse Ausley | Do | N. C. Militia | 129.99 | Do | 79 | Do | |
| James Burns | Do | Do | 60.00 | Do | 71 | Do | |
| John Burgess | Do | Do | 75.00 | Do | 73 | Do | |
| Rackford Boon | Do | Do | — | Do | 71 | Do | |
| Nathaniel Clark | Pri. Inf. and Cav. | N. C. Cont'l | 109.98 | Do | 72 | Do | |
| James Clark | Private | Do | 137.49 | Do | 74 | Do | |
| Richard Drake | Do | N. C. Militia | 90.00 | Do | 72 | Do | |
| William Drake | Do | Do | 180.00 | Do | 79 | Do | |
| Daniel Ellington | Do | Do | 85.54 | Do | 73 | Do | |
| James Heathcock | Do | Do | 60.00 | Do | 91 | Do | |
| Jospeh Hackney | Capt. and Lt. | Do | 744.99 | Do | 82 | Do | Died Jan. 4, 1833 |
| Edmund Jones | Private | Do | 56.25 | Do | 84 | Do | |
| Herbert Lewis | Do | Va. Militia | 204.00 | Do | 75 | Do | |
| Hardy Lewter | Do | N. C. Militia | 90.00 | Do | 90 | Do | |
| John Lawrence | Do | Do | 174.99 | Do | 72 | Do | |
| William Marsh | Do | N. C. Cont'l | 109.98 | Do | 75 | Do | |
| John Moring | Private and Capt. | Va. Militia | 63.30 | Do | 70 | Do | |
| John Mebane | Private | N. C. Militia | 308.32 | Do | 77 | Do | |
| Richard Pope | Do | Do | 129.99 | Do | 73 | Do | |
| Charles Roe | Do | Do | 210.00 | Do | 80 | Do | |
| Bias Rogers | Do | Do | 87.50 | Do | 79 | Do | |
| John Rossen | Do | Do | 60.00 | Do | 85 | Do | |
| Abner Sasater | Do | Do | 50.00 | Do | 81 | Do | |
| Lewis Tyson | Do | Do | 72.52 | Do | 77 | Do | Died Dec. 27, 1832 |
| Nathan Yarborough | Do | Do | — | Do | 84 | Do | |

| Names | Rank | Sums received | Description of service | Commencement of pension | Ages | Laws under which they were formerly inscribed on the Pension Roll and remarks |
|---|---|---|---|---|---|---|
| Joseph Bridges............ | Lt. and Sergt. | $ 300.00 | N. C. Militia | Mar. 4, 1831 | 84 | |
| Thomas May.............. | Private | — | Do | Do | 73 | |
| John Fooshee............. | Private and Lt. | 330.00 | Do | Do | 75 | |

Above found in North Carolina Pension Roll page 69.

## CHOWAN COUNTY, NORTH CAROLINA

| Names | Rank | Sums received | Description of service | Commencement of pension | Ages | Laws under which they were formerly inscribed on the Pension Roll and remarks |
|---|---|---|---|---|---|---|
| Benjamin Bolton.......... | Private | $ 800.17 | 20th Regt. U.S. Inf. | July 24, 1814 | — | Act. mil. est. |
| Benjamin Vickery......... | Do | 283.08 | — | | — | Act. Mar. 3, 1809 |
| Do | Do | 20.28 | — | Apr. 24, 1816 | — | Act. Apr. 24, 1816 |
| John Avery............... | Do | 64.98 | N. C. Militia | Mar. 4, 1831 | 83 | |
| William Ford............. | Do | 60.00 | Do | Do | 90 | |
| Henry Halsey............. | Do | 60.00 | Do | Do | 77 | |
| Malache Halsey........... | Do | 60.00 | Do | Do | 75 | |
| Jonathan Overton......... | Do | 93.95 | N. C. Cont'l line | Do | 81 | |
| John Pettijohn............ | Do | 63.32 | N. C. Militia | Do | 82 | |
| Thomas Smith............ | Do | — | Do | Do | 81 | |

Above found in North Carolina Pension Roll pages 5 and 75.

## COLUMBUS COUNTY, NORTH CAROLINA

| Names | Rank | Sums received | Description of service | Commencement of pension | Ages | Laws under which they were formerly inscribed on the Pension Roll and remarks |
|---|---|---|---|---|---|---|
| Simon Bright............. | Private | $ — | N. C. Cont'l line | Mar. 4, 1831 | 70 | |
| John Butler.............. | Do | 79.98 | N. C. Militia | Do | 75 | |
| Joseph Cartwright......... | Do | 120.00 | Do | Do | 72 | |
| Theophilus Coleman....... | Pri. Inf. and Cav. | 144.99 | Do | Do | 72 | |
| Edward Davis............. | Private | 164.99 | Do | Do | 73 | |
| John Fowler.............. | Do | 60.00 | Do | Do | 87 | |
| Pierce Goodwin........... | Do | 50.00 | Do | Do | 74 | |
| Ezekiel Hawes............ | Do | 125.00 | N. C. Cont'l line | Do | 75 | |
| Samuel Hickman.......... | Do | 99.99 | S. C. Militia | Do | 73 | |
| Elias Jeannret............ | Do | 293.29 | N. C. Militia | Do | 74 | Died Sept. 28, 1833 |

| Name | Rank | Amount | Service | Date | Age |
|---|---|---|---|---|---|
| John Mooney | Do | 60.00 | Do | Do | 77 |
| Absalom Powell | Pri. Ens. & Sergt. | 594.99 | Do | Do | 82 |
| David Ross | Private | 79.15 | Do | Do | 73 |
| Benjamin Sasser | Do | 54.15 | Do | Do | 79 |
| John Simmons | Pri. Cav. and Inf. | 262.50 | N. C. Cont'l line | Do | 71 |
| John Mills | Private | 120.00 | Do | Do | 75 |

Above found in North Carolina Pension Roll page 74.

## CRAVEN COUNTY, NORTH CAROLINA

| Name | Rank | Amount | Service | Date | Age | Remarks |
|---|---|---|---|---|---|---|
| Thomas Broughton | Private | $ 192.00 | 6th Regt. U. S. Inf. | Apr. 23, 1815 | — | {Act. mil. est. trans. from {N. Y. Sept. 4, 1821 |
| Do | Do | 280.00 | Do | Do | — | |
| Herman Gaskins* | Do | 906.75 | U. S. Army | Sept. 4, 1793 | — | Act. Apr. 24, 1816 |
| Do | Do | 663.28 | Do | Apr. 24, 1816 | — | |
| Wiat Hinckley* | Do | 559.35 | Army of Rev. | Dec. 28, 1806 | — | Do |
| Do | Do | 1,522.89 | Do | Apr. 24, 1816 | — | |
| Peter Banks | Private | 99.99 | N. C. Militia | Mar. 4, 1831 | 80 | Act. Mar. 18, 1818 |
| Michael Ellis | Fifer | 69.29 | Md. Cont'l line | June 15, 1819 | 74 | Died Dec. 9, 1833 |
| Do | Do | 143.15 | Do | Mar. 4, 1831 | | {Act. Mar. 18, 1818. Suspended under Act May 1, 1820 restored commencing Aug. 10, 1829. |
| Samuel Gerock | Lieut. | 360.00 | German Regt. | Apr. 15, 1818 | 78 | |
| Do | Do | 919.81 | Do | Mar. 4, 1831 | 80 | {Died 9/8/1833 |
| John P. Ives | Private | 120.00 | N. C. Militia | Do | 75 | |
| Samuel Ipoch | Do | 240.00 | Do | Do | 74 | |
| Daniel Lane | Private and Sergt. | 84.99 | N. C. Cont'l line | Do | 76 | |
| Enoch Masters | Private | 40.00 | N. C. Militia | Do | 74 | |
| Edward Nelson | Do | 84.99 | Do | Do | 72 | |
| Jacob Pollard | Do | 40.00 | Do | Do | 73 | |
| Peter Vendrick | Do | 75.20 | Do | Do | 72 | |
| Benjamin White | Do | 60.00 | Do | Do | 73 | |
| Solomon Witherington | Do | 113.28 | Do | Do | 69 | |
| Rufus Wiley | Do | 60.00 | Do | Do | | Died Dec. 30, 1833 |

Above found in North Carolina Pension Roll pages 4 and 71.

## CUMBERLAND COUNTY, NORTH CAROLINA

| Names | Rank | Sums received | Description of service | Commencement of pension | Ages | Laws under which they were formerly inscribed on the Pension Roll and remarks |
|---|---|---|---|---|---|---|
| James Christian* | Private | $1,628.45 | Army of Revolution | Mar. 4, 1789 | — | {Act. Sept. 29, 1789 / Died Oct. 11, 1826} |
| Do | Do | 1,004.79 | Do | Apr. 24, 1816 | — | Act. Apr. 24, 1816 |
| John Spears* | Do | 275.07 | Revolutionary Army | Sept. 4, 1808 | | Died June 19, 1828 |
| Do | Do | 572.85 | Do | Apr. 24, 1816 | | Act. Apr. 24, 1816 |
| Consider Bushee | Private and Corpl. | 258.00 | R. I. Cont'l line | Mar. 4, 1831 | 71 | |
| Lawrence Byrun | Private of Cav. | 300.00 | N. C. Cont'l line | Do | 75 | |
| John Cameron, Sen. | Pri. Cav. and Inf. | 77.49 | N. C. Militia | Do | 70 | |
| William Cutts, Sen. | Private | 79.98 | Do | Do | 81 | |
| William Carver, Sen. | Do | 120.00 | Do | Do | 81 | |
| Sherwood Fort | Musician | 186.99 | Do | Do | 75 | |
| William Grice | Private | 150.00 | Do | Do | 70 | |
| James Guy | Do | 60.00 | Do | Do | 76 | |
| Alexander Johnson | Do | 99.99 | Do | Do | 74 | |
| John Lumsden | Private and Ensn. | 259.98 | Do | Do | 75 | |
| Nathan King | Captain | 900.00 | N. C. Cont'l line | Do | 83 | Died Dec. 1, 1833 |
| Daniel McClellan | Private | 150.00 | N. C. Cont'l line | Do | 75 | |
| Edward McKay | Do | 60.00 | N. C. Militia | Do | 75 | |
| Hardy Mathews | Pri. Inf. and Cav. | 144.99 | Do | Do | 79 | |
| Malcolm McClellan | Private | 60.00 | Do | Do | 73 | |
| Malcolm Monroe | Private of Cav. | 124.98 | Do | Do | 73 | |
| Amos Nunnery | Pri. Cav. and Inf. | 249.99 | Do | Do | 76 | |
| Richard Plummer | Private | 120.00 | R. I. Cont'l line | Do | 76 | |
| James Reardon | Do | 60.00 | Md. Militia | Do | 83 | |
| John Small | Do | 109.98 | N. C. Militia | Do | 77 | |
| Robert Scoggins | Do | 90.00 | N. C. Cont'l line | Do | 73 | |
| Wm. L. Walker alias Needham Walker | Private of Inf. | 74.16 | N. C. Militia | Do | 76 | |
| John Wilson | Private | 231.70 | Do | Do | 77 | Died Jan. 27, 1833 |

Above found in North Carolina Pension Roll pages 6, 67 and 68.

## CURRITUCK COUNTY, NORTH CAROLINA

| Name | Rank | Amount | Service | Date | Age | Remarks |
|---|---|---|---|---|---|---|
| Leven Balance | Private | — | N. C. Militia | Mar. 4, 1831 | 72 | |
| Hosea Ball | Private and Ensn. | 293.32 | Do | Do | 77 | |
| Joshua Ball | Private | 132.65 | Do | Do | 75 | |
| Samuel Ferebee | Ensign | 210.00 | Do | Do | 73 | |
| Charles Riggs | Private | — | Do | Do | 76 | |
| Thomas Ives | Do | 180.00 | Do | Do | 81 | |
| Thomas Jarvis | Capt. Lt. and Pri. | 919.98 | N. C. Cont'l line | Do | 79 | |
| David Lindsey | Private | 240.00 | N. C. Militia | Do | 82 | |
| Thomas Poyner | Private and Capt. | 462.39 | Do | Do | 74 | |
| Thomas Williams | Private | 180.00 | Va. Militia | Do | 62 | |
| John Williams | Do | 240.00 | N. C. Cont'l line | Do | 83 | |
| Willoughbly West, Sen. | | — | | | 77 | Pension Suspended |

Above found in North Carolina Pension Roll page 73.

## DAVIDSON COUNTY, NORTH CAROLINA

| Name | Rank | Amount | Service | Date | Age |
|---|---|---|---|---|---|
| John Beck | Private | $ 180.00 | N. C. Troops | Mar. 4, 1831 | 74 |
| Jonothan Barrett | Do | 120.00 | Md. Militia | Do | 77 |
| Isaac Barrett | Do | 120.00 | Do | Do | 75 |
| Buckner Daniel | Do | 90.00 | Va. Militia | Do | 74 |
| Benj. Dillen | Do | 90.00 | Do | Do | 79 |
| Peter Everhart | Do | 90.00 | N. C. Militia | Do | 77 |
| Joseph Essig alias Essick or Essix | Ind. Spy | 90.00 | N. C. Ind. Spy | Do | 72 |
| George Fritts | Private | 159.99 | N. C. Cont'l line | Do | 81 |
| James Gordon | Do | 90.00 | N. C. Militia | Do | 86 |
| John Gillian | Do | 66.65 | N. C. Cont'l line | Do | 80 |
| Jacob Goss | Do | 240.00 | N. C. Militia | Do | 71 |
| Peter Headrick | Do | 240.00 | Do | Do | 72 |
| Sherwood Kennedy | Private and Sergt. | 94.93 | Do | Do | 74 |
| John Koonts | Private | 90.00 | Do | Do | 79 |
| Moses Lambeth | Do | 141.65 | Do | Do | 77 |
| David Lookebee | Do | 129.99 | S. C. Militia | Do | 72 |
| Jacob Leonard | Do | — | N. C. Militia | Do | 75 |
| Lewis Mullikin | Do | 69.99 | Md. Militia | Do | 73 |
| Jacob Miller | Do | 240.00 | N. C. Militia | Do | 74 |

| Names | Rank | Sums received | Description of service | Commencement of pension | Ages | Laws under which they were formerly inscribed on the Pension Roll and remarks |
|---|---|---|---|---|---|---|
| Joseph Nothern | Private | $ 69.59 | N. C. Cont'l line | Mar. 4, 1831 | 72 | |
| Steven Osborne | Do | 240.00 | N. C. Cont'l line | Do | 81 | |
| John Paine | Do | 94.68 | Del. Militia | Do | 80 | |
| John Richard | Do | 60.00 | N. C. Militia | Do | 81 | |
| John Scott | Do | 75.00 | Pan. Militia | Do | 79 | |
| Philip Sanders | Private and Lt. | 150.00 | N. C. Militia | Do | 78 | |
| Abraham Stoner | Private | 90.00 | Va. Cont'l line | Do | 75 | |
| Clairborne Spaine | Do | 90.00 | Va. Militia | Do | 69 | |
| Peter Smith | Do | 240.00 | N. C. Militia | Do | 71 | |
| Alexander Thomas | Do | 235.00 | N. J. Militia | Do | 76 | |
| George Thompson | Do | 150.00 | N. C. Cont'l line | Do | 71 | Dead |
| Melcher Tar or Dorr | Do | 100.00 | Do | Do | 82 | |
| William Thompson | Do | 90.00 | N. J. Militia | Do | 85 | |
| William Waddsworth | Do | 109.98 | N. C. Militia | Do | 72 | |
| John White | Do | 40.00 | Do | Do | | |

Above found in North Carolina Pension Roll pages 77 and 78.

DUPLIN COUNTY, NORTH CAROLINA

| Names | Rank | Sums received | Description of service | Commencement of pension | Ages | Laws under which they were formerly inscribed on the Pension Roll and remarks |
|---|---|---|---|---|---|---|
| William Alfin, Sen. | Private | $ — | N. C. Militia | Mar. 4, 1831 | 73 | |
| Bezzant Brock | Pri. Inf and Cav. | 97.50 | Do | Do | 76 | |
| Burrell Branch | Private | 120.00 | Do | Do | 77 | |
| Jesse Brown | Pri. Inf. and Cav. | 97.50 | Do | Do | 71 | |
| Joshua Blake | Private | 144.96 | Do | Do | 99 | |
| Hilira Brinson | Do | 149.45 | Do | Do | 76 | |
| David Carlton | Do | 125.00 | Do | Do | 77 | |
| William Carr | Do | 60.00 | N. C. Cont'l line | Do | 79 | Died Feb. 27, 1834 |
| John Davis | Do | 120.00 | N. C. Militia | Do | 70 | |
| Joshua Goodson | Do | 75.00 | N. C. Militia | Do | 80 | |
| Samuel Goff | Do | — | N. C. Cont'l line | Do | 75 | |
| Kidder Harrell | Pri. Inf. and Cav. | 75.00 | N. C. Militia | Do | 85 | |
| James Holland | Private | 270.00 | Do | Do | 89 | |
| Elisha Jones | | 69.99 | Do | Do | 73 | |

| Name | Rank | Amount | Service | Pension Date | Age | Notes |
|---|---|---|---|---|---|---|
| Thomas Keneday | Do | — | N. C. Cont'l line | Do | 72 | |
| Merrit Murrel | Do | — | N. C. Troops | Do | 86 | |
| John Page | Private of Cav. | 250.00 | N. C. Militia | Do | 75 | |
| David Quinn | Private | 150.00 | N. C. Cont'l line | Do | 79 | |
| John Rigby | Pri. Inf. and Cav. | 232.50 | N. C. Militia | Do | 71 | |
| Frederick Rivenbark | Private | 90.00 | Do | Do | 87 | |
| William Robert, Sen. | Do | 75.00 | N. C. Cont'l line | Do | 77 | Died Apr. 17, 1834 |
| Jesse Swinson | Private and Musc. | 134.58 | N. C. Militia | Do | 75 | Died May 17, 1833 |
| Samuel Stanford, Sr. | Private | 103.32 | Do | Do | 69 | |
| Robert Sloan | Do | 150.00 | Do | Do | 82 | |
| John Stuart | Do | 150.00 | Do | Do | 100 | |
| Theophilus Swinson | Do | 62.20 | Do | Do | 80 | |
| William Taylor | Pri. Inf. and Cav. | 135.00 | Do | Do | 77 | |
| James Wallis | Private | — | S. C. Militia | Do | 73 | |
| Thomas Wright | Do | 129.99 | N. C. Militia | Do | 79 | |
| James Wright | Pri. Inf. and Cav. | 112.50 | Do | Do | 75 | |
| Jacob Wells | Private | — | Do | Do | 91 | |
| James Wallis | Do | — | N. C. Cont'l line | Do | | |

Above found in North Carolina Pension Roll pages 75 and 76.

EDGECOMBE COUNTY, NORTH CAROLINA

| Name | Rank | Amount | Service | Pension Date | Age |
|---|---|---|---|---|---|
| George Anderson | Private | $ 139.98 | N. C. Militia | Mar. 4, 1831 | 77 |
| William Anderson | Do | 240.00 | N. C. Cont'l line | Do | 77 |
| Jacob Braswell | Do | 79.98 | N. C. Militia | Do | 71 |
| Burrel Bradley | Do | 79.98 | Do | Do | 80 |
| Nathaniel Bilbrey | Do | 240.00 | Do | Do | 76 |
| Nichols Dunn | Do | 64.98 | Do | Do | 80 |
| David Forehand | Do | 50.00 | Do | Do | 80 |
| Hardy Howard | Private Inf. | 87.48 | Do | Do | 74 |
| Wilson Howard | Private | 120.00 | Do | Do | 81 |
| Isaac Jackson | Do | 240.00 | Va. Cont'l line | Do | 79 |
| Thomas Jenkins | Do | 99.99 | N. C. Cont'l line | Do | 76 |
| Henry Kea | Pri. Inf. and Cav. | 75.00 | N. C. Militia | Do | 81 |
| Shadrach Langley | Private | 60.00 | Do | Do | 71 |
| Henry Lancaster | Sergeant | 300.00 | Do | Do | 82 |
| William Morgan | Private | 60.00 | Do | Do | 70 |
| Enos Norwell | Do | 199.98 | Md. Militia | Do | 75 |
| Micajah Pettaway | Private and Adj. | 389.97 | N. C. Cont'l line | Do | 74 |

| Names | Rank | Sums received | Description of service | Commencement of pension | Ages | Laws under which they were formerly inscribed on the Pension Roll and remarks |
|---|---|---|---|---|---|---|
| Joseph Pippin. | Ensign | — | N. C. Militia | Mar. 4, 1831 | 82 | Died Apr. 10, 1833 |
| James Scarborough. | Sergt. and Capt. | 675.00 | Do | Do | 85 | |
| Richard Taylor. | Private | 69.99 | Do | Do | 87 | |
| Gillead Thigphen. | Do | 189.99 | N. C. Cont'l line | Do | 74 | |
| Lewis Todd. | Pri. Cav. and Inf. | 147.48 | N. C. Militia | Do | 71 | |
| John Webb. | Private | 79.98 | Do | Do | 71 | |

Above found in North Carolina Pension Roll pages 78 and 79.

## FRANKLIN COUNTY, NORTH CAROLINA

| Names | Rank | Sums received | Description of service | Commencement of pension | Ages | Laws under which they were formerly inscribed on the Pension Roll and remarks |
|---|---|---|---|---|---|---|
| James Collins. | Private | $ 90.00 | N. C. Militia | Mar. 4, 1831 | 72 | |
| Moses Carr. | Do | 50.00 | Va. Militia | Do | 92 | |
| Ephriam Conyers. | Do | 108.32 | N. C. Militia | Do | 78 | |
| Miles Hicks. | Do | 60.00 | Do | Do | 70 | |
| William Jones. | Private and Sergt. | 212.64 | Do | Do | 76 | |
| Moses Joiner. | Private | 99.99 | Do | Do | 75 | |
| William Leonard. | Do | 60.00 | Do | Do | 74 | |
| James Murray. | Do | 200.00 | Do | Do | 79 | |
| John Piper. | Private and Lt. | 139.98 | Do | Do | 79 | |
| Richard Peppen. | Private | 60.00 | Do | Do | 77 | |
| Richard Reeves. | Do | 60.00 | Do | Do | 74 | |
| Jonathan Stone. | Do | 53.33 | Do | Do | 80 | |
| John Stone. | Pri., Corpl. & Ser. | 85.00 | Do | Do | 75 | |
| William Sanders. | Private | 63.66 | Do | Do | 88 | |
| Jesse Webb. | Do | 159.99 | Do | Do | 78 | |
| Green Walker. | Do | 62.50 | Do | Do | 74 | |
| Daniel Westray. | Do | 90.00 | Do | Do | 81 | |

Above found in North Carolina Pension Roll pages 79 and 80.

## GATES COUNTY, NORTH CAROLINA

| Names | Rank | Sums received | Description of service | Commencement of pension | Ages | Laws under which they were formerly inscribed on the Pension Roll and remarks |
|---|---|---|---|---|---|---|
| John Wilson* | Private | $ 208.15 | — | Sept. 4, 1808 | — | Died Aug. 11, 1815 |

| Name | | Amount | | | Age | |
|---|---|---|---|---|---|---|
| William Brooks | Do | 60.00 | N. C. Militia | Mar. 4, 1831 | 80 | |
| Do | Do | — | Do | Do | 80 | |
| Amos Dildee | Do | 60.00 | Do | Do | 73 | |
| William Pearce | Do | 180.00 | Do | Do | 80 | |
| Kider Parker | Do | 53.32 | Do | Do | 75 | |
| Uriah Ure | Do | 60.00 | Do | Do | 75 | |

Above found in North Carolina Pension Roll pages 7 and 82.

## GRANVILLE COUNTY, NORTH CAROLINA

| Name | Rank | Amount | Service | Date | Age | Remarks |
|---|---|---|---|---|---|---|
| Richard Grissom* | Private | $ 222.49 | — | Sept. 14, 1808 | — | Act. May 3, 1815 |
| Do | Do | 87.63 | — | Nov. 8, 1814 | — | Do |
| Do | Do | 1,474.89 | — | Apr. 24, 1816 | — | Act. Apr. 24, 1816 |
| Thomas Goodrum* | Do | 164.18 | — | Mar. 14, 1810 | — | Act. Apr. 27, 1810 |
| Do | Ser. of Inf. & Cav. | 430.86 | Va. Militia | Apr. 24, 1816 | — | Act. Apr. 24, 1816 |
| William Allen | Private | 240.00 | Va. Cont'l line | Mar. 4, 1831 | 74 | |
| Thomas Blackwell | Pri. Ser. and Capt. | 461.33 | N. C. Militia | Do | 74 | Died June 27, 1833 |
| Lewis Bledsoe | Private | 125.00 | N. C. Militia | Do | 76 | |
| Charles Bullock | Do | 180.00 | Va. Militia | Do | 74 | |
| Charles Barnett | Do | 90.00 | N. C. Militia | Do | 71 | |
| Peter Cash | Sergeant | 105.63 | N. C. Cont'l line | Do | 78 | |
| Lemuel Goodwin | Private | 169.98 | N. C. Militia | Do | 82 | |
| James Grisham, Sr. | Do | 120.00 | Do | Do | 75 | |
| Richard Glassgow | Do | 120.00 | Va. Cont'l line | Do | 79 | |
| William Guy | Do | 159.99 | 5th Rgt. Col. Eaton | Do | 71 | |
| Edward Going | Do | 240.00 | N. C. Cont'l line | Do | 92 | |
| Zacharih Hester | Major | 382.08 | Do | Do | 73 | |
| Benj. Hester | Private | 99.99 | N. C. Troops | Do | 74 | |
| William Hunt | Do | 60.00 | N. C. Militia | Do | 76 | Died Mar. 8, 1833 |
| James Haskins | Do | 240.00 | Do | Do | 83 | |
| Allen Howard | Do | 160.00 | Do | Do | 71 | |
| Harris Hicks | Do | 184.98 | Va. Cont'l line | Do | 75 | (Cert. issued Anderson Paschall, guardian |
| John Lemay | Do | 180.00 | N. C. Militia | Do | 73 | Died Jan. 5, 1834 |
| Shadrach Owen | Pri. Inf. and Cav. | 60.00 | Do | Do | 72 | |
| Thomas Parham | Private | 75.41 | Va. Militia | Do | 76 | |
| John Philips | Pri. Inf. and Cav. | 79.98 | Do | Do | 72 | |
| Samuel Smith | Private | | N. C. Militia | Do | 74 | Died Apr. 4, 1833 |

| Names | Rank | Sums received | Description of service | Commencement of pension | Ages | Laws under which they were formerly inscribed on the Pension Roll and remarks |
|---|---|---|---|---|---|---|
| John Taylor, Sr. | Private and Capt. | $ 319.98 | N. C. Cont'l line | Mar. 4, 1831 | 78 | |
| William Taburn, Sr. | Private | 103.32 | N. C. Militia | Do | — | |
| Thomas Ussery | Do | 87.50 | Va. Militia | Do | 75 | |
| Vincent Vaughan | Do | 150.00 | N. C. Militia | Do | 73 | |

Above found in North Carolina Pension Roll pages 7, 83 and 84.

GREENE COUNTY, NORTH CAROLINA

| Names | Rank | Sums received | Description of service | Commencement of pension | Ages | Laws under which they were formerly inscribed on the Pension Roll and remarks |
|---|---|---|---|---|---|---|
| William Forrest | Private | $ — | N. C. Militia | Mar. 1, 1831 | 73 | |
| John Taylor | Do | 50.00 | N. C. Cont'l line | Do | 73 | |

Above found in North Carolina Pension Roll page 82.

GUILFORD COUNTY, NORTH CAROLINA

| Names | Rank | Sums received | Description of service | Commencement of pension | Ages | Laws under which they were formerly inscribed on the Pension Roll and remarks |
|---|---|---|---|---|---|---|
| Thomas Smith, 2nd* | Private | $ 60.57 | — | Apr. 18, 1814 | — | Act. mil. est. |
| Do | Do | 401.44 | — | Apr. 24, 1816 | — | Act. Apr. 24, 1816 |
| Do | Do | 342.00 | N. C. Militia | Sept. 4, 1824 | — | Act. Mar. 3, 1819 |
| William Albright | Do | 340.00 | Do | Mar. 4, 1831 | 83 | |
| Daniel Apple | Do | 50.00 | Do | Do | 73 | |
| Jonathan Brooks | Do | 75.54 | Do | Do | 72 | |
| John Boon | Do | 79.98 | Do | Do | 79 | |
| Thomas Cummings | Pri. Cav. and Inf. | 67.50 | N. C. Cont'l line | Do | 76 | |
| Leo Derick Clapp | Private | 160.00 | N. C. Militia | Do | 92 | |
| Jeremiah Cunningham | Do | 99.99 | Va. Militia | Do | 74 | |
| Lee Clark | Do | 60.00 | N. C. Militia | Do | 78 | |
| Daniel Donnell | Do | 79.98 | Do | Do | 78 | |
| Andrew Donnell | Do | 69.99 | Do | Do | 77 | |
| Joseph Denny | Do | 79.98 | Do | Do | 76 | |
| John Findley | Sergeant | 360.00 | | Do | 69 | Died Jan. 20, 1834 |
| James Findley | Private | 66.99 | | Do | 74 | |
| William Fitzgerald | Do | 240.00 | Md. Cont'l line | Do | 73 | |

| Name | Rank | Amount | Service | Date | Age | Remarks |
|---|---|---|---|---|---|---|
| Thomas Grear | Do | 90.00 | Pa. Militia | Do | 78 | |
| Fieldman Harris | Do | 63.00 | Va. Militia | Do | 75 | |
| James Henderson | Do | 65.64 | N. C. Militia | Do | 74 | |
| Philip Jean | Pri. Inf. and Cav. | 64.98 | Do | Do | 72 | |
| Reuben Land | Private | 180.00 | Do | Do | 75 | |
| John McBride | Private, Sergt. | 504.99 | Do | Do | 78 | |
| John Montgomery | Ensn. and Lt. | 60.00 | Do | Do | 71 | |
| William Maxwell | Private | 55.25 | Do | Do | 72 | |
| Josiah McBride | Do | 41.29 | Do | Do | — | Died Sept. 26, 1832 Cert. issued in favor of Jos. McBride, heir |
| Thomas McCuister | Do | 86.25 | Do | Do | 71 | |
| Joseph McLane | Do | 146.16 | Do | Do | 82 | Died Dec. 23, 1832 |
| Massy C. Medaris | Do | 120.00 | N. C. Cont'l line | Do | 79 | |
| Philip Mason | Do | 129.99 | N. C. Militia | Do | 81 | |
| Jacob Newson | Do | 75.96 | Do | Do | 72 | |
| George Neese | Do | 240.00 | N. C. Cont'l line | Do | 88 | |
| Ezekiel Nolen | Do | 120.00 | Pa. Militia | Do | 74 | |
| William Riley | Pri. Inf. Cav. and Sergt. | 318.54 | N. C. Cont'l line | Do | 75 | |
| William Ryan | Private | 180.00 | N. C. Militia | Do | 71 | |
| Mathew Roe | Do | 69.99 | Do | Do | 80 | |
| James Stewart | Do | 139.98 | Do | Do | 74 | |
| William Smith | Do | 182.85 | Do | Do | 88 | |
| Mathias Swing | Do | 240.00 | N. C. Cont'l line | Do | 86 | Died June 17, 1833 |
| Frederick Soots | Do | 105.00 | N. C. Militia | Do | 77 | |

Above found in North Carolina Pension Roll pages 8, 80 and 81.

## HALIFAX COUNTY, NORTH CAROLINA

| Name | Rank | Amount | Service | Date | Age |
|---|---|---|---|---|---|
| Levi Browning | Private | $ 69.99 | N. C. Militia | Mar. 4, 1831 | 76 |
| William Dickens | Do | 69.99 | Do | Do | 73 |
| Solomon Drew | Do | 84.99 | Do | Do | 80 |
| Joshua Drew | Do | 79.98 | Do | Do | 83 |
| William Edmundson | Do | 79.98 | Do | Do | 70 |
| George Green | Do | 79.98 | Do | Do | 75 |
| Reuben Griffin | Private Art. | — | Do | Do | 73 |
| John Harper | Pri. Cav. and Inf. | 124.98 | — | — | — |

| Names | Rank | Sums received | Description of service | Commencement of pension | Ages | Laws under which they were formerly inscribed on the Pension Roll and remarks |
|---|---|---|---|---|---|---|
| Joseph Johnson. | Private | $ 90.00 | N. C. Militia | Mar. 4, 1831 | 70 | |
| Shadrach Merritt. | Do | 40.00 | Do | Do | 78 | |
| George Powell. | Do | 60.00 | Do | Do | 72 | |
| William Perkins. | Private and Lt. | 150.00 | Do | Do | 78 | |
| William Riggan. | Private | 60.00 | Do | Do | 73 | |
| Robert L. Whitaker. | Do | 120.00 | N. C. Cont'l line | Do | 69 | |
| William Wood. | Do | — | N. C. Militia | Do | 83 | |
| John Lee. | Do | 175.00 | N. C. Cont'l line | Do | 72 | Dropped and Inscribed under Act May 15, 1828 at Treas. Dept. |
| James Lock, Sen. | Do | 120.00 | N. C. Militia | Do | 75 | |

Above found in North Carolina Pension Roll pages 84 and 85.

### HAYWOOD COUNTY, NORTH CAROLINA

| Names | Rank | Sums received | Description of service | Commencement of pension | Ages |
|---|---|---|---|---|---|
| Thomas Davis. | Private | $ 60.00 | N. C. Militia | Mar. 4, 1831 | 73 |
| Abraham Hooper. | Do | 240.00 | S. C. Militia | Do | 69 |
| Daniel Hinson. | Do | 180.00 | Va. Militia | Do | 70 |
| John Hood. | Do | — | N. C. Militia | Do | 84 |
| Robert Love. | Sergeant | 255.00 | Va. Militia | Do | 74 |
| Samuel Monteath. | Private | — | N. C. Militia | Do | 79 |
| John Massey. | Do | 240.00 | Do | Do | 76 |
| Louis Smith. | Do | 53.65 | Va. Cont'l line | Do | 71 |
| Andrew Shook. | Do | 60.00 | N. C. Militia | Do | 79 |
| Jacob Shook. | Do | 60.00 | Do | Do | 85 |

Above found in North Carolina Pension Roll page 86.

### HERTFORD COUNTY, NORTH CAROLINA

| Names | Rank | Sums received | Description of service | Commencement of pension | Ages |
|---|---|---|---|---|---|
| Mitchell Britton. | Private | $ 50.00 | N. C. Militia | Mar. 4, 1831 | 71 |
| Joseph Dilday. | Do | 120.00 | Va. Militia | Do | 79 |

| Name | Rank | Amount | Service | Date | Age | Notes |
|---|---|---|---|---|---|---|
| Charles Powell | Do | 60.00 | N. C. Militia | Do | 77 | |
| Nathaniel Saunders | Musician | 66.00 | Do | Do | 78 | |
| James Weston | Private | 120.00 | Do | Do | 75 | |
| Waring Williams | Do | 90.00 | Do | Do | 71 | |

Above found in North Carolina Pension Roll page 85.

## HYDE COUNTY, NORTH CAROLINA

| Name | Rank | Amount | Service | Date | Age | Notes |
|---|---|---|---|---|---|---|
| William Spencer | Private | $ 90.00 | N. C. Militia | Mar. 4, 1831 | 81 | |
| Robert Silverthorn | Do | 98.58 | Do | Do | 81 | |
| George Williams | Do | — | Do | Do | 77 | |

Above found in North Carolina Pension Roll page 85.

## IREDELL COUNTY, NORTH CAROLINA

| Name | Rank | Amount | Service | Date | Age | Notes |
|---|---|---|---|---|---|---|
| Thomas Harris* | Major | $2,627.82 | Army of Revolution | Oct. 3, 1806 | — | Died Aug. 31, 1826 |
| Do | Do | 1,185.51 | Do | May 25, 1821 | — | |
| Zachariah Linney | Private | 489.75 | — | May 16, 1818 | — | Act Apr. 24, 1816 |
| James Potts* | Do | 197.05 | Army of Revolution | Sept. 5, 1808 | — | Died Feb. 16, 1826 |
| Do | Do | 282.75 | Do | Apr. 24, 1816 | | Act Apr. 24, 1816 |
| Do | Do | 97.73 | Do | Sept. 4, 1823 | | Do |
| John Patterson* | Do | 832.00 | Revolution Army | Sept. 18, 1815 | — | Act Apr. 30, 1816 |
| Do | Do | 41.18 | Do | Jan. 18, 1833 | — | Act Apr. 24, 1816 |
| Adams Terrence* | Do | 227.33 | N. C. Militia | Oct. 5, 1824 | — | Act Feb. 4, 1822 |
| Do | Do | 563.16 | Do | Apr. 23, 1828 | — | Act Apr. 24, 1816 |
| Hugh Andrews | Do | 134.97 | Do | Mar. 4, 1831 | 80 | |
| Shadrach Allen | Do | 240.00 | Do | Do | 83 | |
| George Allen | Do | 60.00 | Do | Do | 91 | |
| James Alexander | Do | 75.00 | Va. Militia | Do | 85 | |
| Jacob Boston | Private Cav. | 300.00 | N. C. Cont'l line | Do | 77 | |
| David Beaty | Private | 62.64 | N. C. Militia | Do | 72 | |
| William Brown | Do | 60.00 | Do | Do | 73 | |
| Andrew Carson | Do | 180.00 | Do | Do | 78 | |
| John Cavin | Pri. Cav. and Inf. | 122.29 | Do | Do | 73 | |
| James Carter | Private | 69.99 | Md. Militia | Do | 73 | |
| Philip Drum | Do | 79.98 | Va. Militia | Do | 74 | |
| David Dickey | Pri. Inf. and Cav. | 150.00 | N. C. Cont'l line | Do | 74 | |
| William Falls | Do | 193.38 | N. C. Militia | Do | 71 | |

| Names | Rank | Sums received | Description of service | Commencement of pension | Ages | Laws under which they were formerly inscribed on the Pension Roll and remarks |
|---|---|---|---|---|---|---|
| William Frenister | Pri. Inf. and Cav. | $ 122.49 | N. C. Militia | Mar. 4, 1831 | 76 | |
| John Grant | Private | 135.00 | N. C. Cont'l line | Do | 79 | |
| Robert Gracey | Pri. Cav. and Inf. | 229.98 | N. C. Militia | Do | 70 | |
| James Gunston | Private | 90.00 | Do | Do | 73 | |
| Alexander Hall | Do | 90.00 | Do | Do | 79 | |
| Abraham Hill | Pri. Inf. and Cav. | 244.98 | Do | Do | 76 | |
| James Holmes | Private | 68.34 | Do | Do | 72 | |
| Robert Hair | Do | 180.99 | N. C. Cont'l line | Do | 82 | |
| David Hair | Do | 150.00 | N. C. Militia | Do | 72 | |
| Claiborne Howard | Do | — | Va. Militia | Do | 70 | |
| Nicholas Jones | Pri. Cav. and Inf. | 98.40 | N. C. Militia | Do | 86 | Died June 14, 1833 |
| Daniel Lewis | Private | 60.00 | N. Y. Militia | Do | 79 | |
| Thomas Lawson | Do | 99.99 | Do | Do | 80 | |
| John Luck | Do | 109.98 | Va. Militia | Do | 74 | |
| George Lackey | Pri. Cav. and Inf. | 188.76 | N. C. Militia | Do | 78 | |
| Thomas Lackey | Private | 129.99 | Do | Do | 87 | |
| Lawrence Maiden, Sen. | Do | 60.00 | N. C. Cont'l line | Do | 80 | |
| Alexander McKee | Do | 64.65 | Do | Do | 71 | |
| Robert McLeod | Do | 90.00 | Do | Do | 78 | |
| Benjamin Mays | Do | 61.65 | Va. Militia | Do | 77 | |
| John Morrison | Do | 99.99 | N. C. Militia | Do | 91 | |
| William Mason | Do | 69.99 | Va. Cont'l line | Do | 82 | |
| Mathew McPherson | Do | 79.76 | N. C. Militia | Do | 76 | |
| James Mitchell | Do | 109.98 | Do | Do | 75 | |
| John Mayhew | Do | 58.32 | Va. Militia | Do | 77 | |
| James Murphy | Lieutenant | 169.98 | N. C. Militia | Do | 87 | |
| Gilbreath Neill | Private | 942.10 | Do | Do | 82 | Died Jan. 29, 1834 |
| John Norwood | Do | 139.98 | Do | Do | 76 | |
| Benjamin Recktor | Pri. Inf. and Cav. | 60.00 | Do | Do | 73 | |
| Andrew Ramsay | Private | 82.21 | Do | Do | 79 | |
| John Rounsavill | Pri. Cav. Inf. | 75.00 | S. C. Militia | Do | 77 | |
| Joseph Sharpe | Lt. and Capt. | 528.48 | N. C. Militia | Do | 82 | |
| Jeremiah Scroggs | Private | 168.18 | Do | Do | 79 | |

| Name | Rank | Amount | Service | Date | Age | Remarks |
|---|---|---|---|---|---|---|
| John Scrogs | Do | 69.99 | Do | Do | 72 | Died Mar. 12, 1834 |
| John Stewart | Do | 112.50 | Do | Do | 78 | |
| John Stevenson | Pri. Inf. and Cav. | 53.32 | Do | Do | 76 | |
| William Smith | Private | 240.00 | Do | Do | 72 | |
| John Scott | Do | 90.00 | Do | Mar. 4, 1831 | 75 | |
| John Studthem | Pri. Inf. and Cav. | 268.87 | N. C. Cont'l line | Do | 82 | |
| John Thomas | Private | 60.00 | Va. Cont'l line | Do | 72 | |
| Mathew Vendivier | Do | 105.99 | N. C. Militia | Do | 81 | |
| James Watts | Pri. Inf. and Cav. | 107.67 | Do | Do | 77 | |
| William Woodsides | Do | 229.98 | N. C. Cont'l line | Do | 79 | |
| David White | Private and Sergt. | 69.99 | Va. Militia | Do | 79 | |

Above found in North Carolina Pension Roll pages 8, 86, 87 and 88.

## JONES COUNTY, NORTH CAROLINA

| Name | Rank | Amount | Service | Date | Age | Remarks |
|---|---|---|---|---|---|---|
| Hugh Stanley* | Private | $ 305.63 | U. S. Army | Sept. 4, 1808 | — | Died Aug. 26, 1823 |
| Do | Do | 469.85 | Do | Apr. 24, 1816 | 75 | Act Apr. 24, 1816 |
| Samiel Davis | Do | — | N. C. Militia | Mar. 4, 1831 | 68 | |
| Frederick Foscue | Do | 50.00 | Do | Do | 73 | |
| Lawson Mallard | Do | 141.65 | Do | Do | 86 | |
| Ambrose Whitledge | Do | 69.99 | Do | Do | | |

Above found in North Carolina Pension Roll pages 9 and 90.

## JOHNSTON COUNTY, NORTH CAROLINA

| Name | Rank | Amount | Service | Date | Age |
|---|---|---|---|---|---|
| Amos Atkinson | Private | $ 221.99 | N. C. Militia | Mar. 4, 1831 | 81 |
| William Capps | Do | 240.00 | N. C. Cont'l line | Do | 83 |
| James Carrell | Do | 99.99 | N. C. Militia | Do | 69 |
| Benjamin Edwards | Do | 90.00 | Do | Do | 70 |
| Dixon Faile | Do | 180.00 | S. C. Cont'l line | Do | 78 |
| Jesse Green | Do | 90.00 | N. C. Militia | Do | 70 |
| Chapman Hayles | Do | 60.00 | Do | Do | 73 |
| James Holt | Corpl. and Ensn. | 156.00 | Do | Do | 80 |
| Elijah Lassiter | Private | 60.00 | Do | Do | 72 |
| Joel Nichols | Do | 60.00 | Do | Do | 82 |
| James Odon | Do | 40.00 | Do | Do | 82 |
| Richard Pilkinton | Do | 79.98 | N. C. Cont'l line | Do | 72 |
| Britton Roberts | Do | 60.00 | N. C. Militia | Do | 72 |

| Names | Rank | Sums received | Description of service | Commencement of pension | Ages | Laws under which they were formerly inscribed on the Pension Roll and remarks |
|---|---|---|---|---|---|---|
| Valentine Sheppard......... | Private | $ 148.41 | N. C. Cont'l line | Aug. 19, 1818 | 76 | Act Mar. 18, 1818 |
| Do | Do | 120.00 | Do | Mar. 4, 1831 | | |
| Robert Sterling............ | Do | 210.00 | N. C. Militia | Do | 74 | |
| Abel Sassen................ | Do | — | Do | Do | 71 | |
| William Tarlton............ | Do | 240.00 | Do | Do | 79 | |
| Charles Willons............ | Do | 57.77 | Va. Cont'l line | Do | 72 | |

Above found in North Carolina Pension Roll page 89.

### LENOIR COUNTY, NORTH CAROLINA

| Names | Rank | Sums received | Description of service | Commencement of pension | Ages | Laws under which they were formerly inscribed on the Pension Roll and remarks |
|---|---|---|---|---|---|---|
| Elisha Hunt................ | Private | $1,628.45 | Army of Revolution | Mar. 4, 1789 | — | Act Sept. 29, 1789 |
| Do | Do | 1,041.80 | Do | Apr. 24, 1816 | | Act Apr. 24, 1816 |
| Benjamin Cox.............. | Private | 141.65 | N. C. Militia | Mar. 4, 1831 | 80 | |
| John Cox.................. | Do | 120.00 | Do | Do | 72 | |
| William Davenport......... | Do | 150.00 | Do | Do | 80 | |
| John Hartsfield............ | Do | 120.00 | Do | Do | 77 | |
| Stephen Parish............. | Do | 229.98 | S. C. Cont'l line | Do | 77 | |
| Charles Tull............... | Do | 60.00 | N. C. Militia | Do | 81 | |
| Marclin Wooters........... | Do | 69.99 | Do | Do | 76 | |

Above found in North Carolina Pension Roll pages 10, 92 and 93.

### LINCOLN COUNTY, NORTH CAROLINA

| Names | Rank | Sums received | Revolutionary War | | Ages | |
|---|---|---|---|---|---|---|
| John Chittin............... | Private | $ 286.73 | Jan. 1, 1815 | | — | {Act Apr. 30, 1816 {Died Dec. 24, 1818 |
| Samuel Espey*............. | Do | 125.90 | — | Sept. 4, 1808 | | |
| Do | Do | 777.44 | — | Apr. 24, 1816 | | Act. Apr. 24, 1816 |
| Do | Do | 200.00 | Army U.S. | July 4, 1832 | | July 14, 1832 |
| David Miller*............. | Do | 332.63 | Do | Sept. 4, 1808 | | Died Mar. 18, 1832 |
| Do | Do | 537.01 | Do | Apr. 24, 1816 | | Act Apr. 24, 1816 |
| Do | Do | 383.30 | | Sept. 4, 1824 | | Act Mar. 3, 1819 |

| Name | Rank | Amount | Revolutionary Army | (Pension Act date) | Act July 5, 1812 / Act Apr. 24, 1816 |
|---|---|---|---|---|---|
| Mitchell Reep | Do | 150.00 | Do | Apr. 20, 1811 | 82 |
| Do | Do | 857.07 | Do | Apr. 24, 1816 | 78 |
| Robert Abernathy | Do | 40.00 | N. C. Militia | Mar. 4, 1831 | 85 |
| Vincent Allen | Do | 240.00 | Va. Militia | | 71 |
| Christian Arney | Do | 169.98 | N. C. Militia | | 78 |
| Mathew Armstrong | Do | 99.99 | N. C. Militia | | 75 |
| Casper Bolick | Do | 109.98 | Do | | 72 |
| Jonas Bradshaw | Do | 120.00 | N. C. Cont'l line | | 75 |
| Robert Berry | Do | 60.00 | N. C. Militia | | 74 |
| Samuel Baldwell | Do | 160.00 | N. C. Cont'l line | | 73 |
| Martin Coulter | Pri. Inf. and Cav. | 64.68 | N. C. Militia | | 82 |
| Mitchell Cline | Private | 88.02 | Do | | 87 |
| William Carrol | Do | 120.00 | Do | | — |
| Thomas Costner | Do | 64.98 | Do | | 75 |
| Samuel Collins | Pri. Inf. and Cav. | 78.48 | Md. Militia | | 69 |
| William Elmore | Private | 114.99 | N. C. Cont'l line | | 76 |
| Peter Edleman | Pr. Corp. & Capt. | 94.98 | N. C. Militia | | 76 |
| Samuel Espey | Pri. Sergt. & Capt. | 296.16 | Do | | 77 |
| Abraham Forney | Private | 436.80 | Do | Mar. 4, 1831 | |
| William Gregory | Sergt. Adg. Capt. and Maj. | 60.00 | Do | | |
| Joseph Graham | | | Do | | |
| Robinson Goodwin | Private | 870.00 | N. C. Cont'l line | Do | 75 |
| Simeon Hager | Do | 139.98 | Do | Do | 69 |
| James Hill | Lieut. | 99.99 | Do | Do | 71 |
| James Henry | Private | 360.00 | N. C. Militia | Do | 75 |
| Nicholas Hofner | Do | 210.00 | S. C. Cont'l line | Do | 81 |
| John Harmon | Do | 90.00 | N. C. Militia | Do | 78 |
| John Helm | Do | 117.00 | Do | Do | 72 |
| Simeon Hager | Do | 120.00 | Va. Cont'l line | Do | 73 |
| John Kid | Do | 79.32 | N. C. Militia | Do | 79 |
| Robert Knox | Do | 159.99 | N. C. Cont'l line | Do | 76 |
| John Kinkaid | Do | 80.00 | N. C. Militia | Do | 92 |
| Alexander Moore | Do | 229.98 | S. C. Militia | Do | 85 |
| Tapley Mahanas | Do | 101.64 | N. C. Militia | Do | 80 |
| William Moore | Pri. and Capt. | 240.00 | Va. Cont'l line | Do | 72 |
| Samuel Martin | Do | 210.00 | N. C. Militia | Do | 83 |
| John Moore | Private | 750.00 | S. C. Militia | Do | 100 |
| George Oliver | Do | 66.65 | N. C. Militia | Do | 75 |
| Jacob Plunk | Do | 150.00 | Do | Do | 74 |
| Do | Do | 90.00 | Do | Do | 85 |

| Names | Rank | Sums received | Description of service | Commencement of pension | Ages | Laws under which they were formerly inscribed on the Pension Roll and remarks |
|---|---|---|---|---|---|---|
| Hiram Pendleton | Private | $ 197.27 | N. C. Cont'l line | Mar. 4, 1831 | 84 | Died Aug. 27, 1833 |
| William Potter | Pri. and Corpl. | 74.49 | N. C. Militia | Do | 84 | |
| Humphrey Parker | Private | 99.99 | Do | Do | 72 | |
| Adam Reep | Do | 163.29 | Do | Do | 79 | |
| James Robeson | Do | 99.99 | Do | Do | 71 | |
| William Rankin | Do | 148.90 | Do | Do | 73 | |
| Joshua Roberts | Do | 69.99 | Do | Do | 74 | |
| Charles Regan | Do | 150.00 | N. C. Cont'l line | Do | 76 | |
| Peter Scrum | Do | 136.66 | N. C. Militia | Do | 72 | |
| John Stamey | Do | 210.00 | Do | Do | 72 | |
| Conrad Tippong | Do | 90.00 | Do | Do | 89 | |
| John Turbyfill | Do | 120.00 | Va. Militia | Do | 93 | |
| Bartholomew Thompson | Do | 199.98 | Ga. Militia | Do | 72 | |
| Charles Thompson | Private Cav. | 124.98 | N. C. Militia | Do | 72 | |
| Philip Tilman | Private | 90.00 | N. J. Militia | Do | 87 | |
| Joseph Willis | Do | 76.98 | N. C. Militia | Do | 79 | Died Dec. 28, 1833 |
| Charles Whit | Do | 225.24 | S. C. Militia | Do | 70 | |
| Elisha Weathers | Pri. Cav. and Inf. | 137.49 | N. C. Militia | Do | 75 | |
| John Woolfong | Private | 112.62 | Do | Do | 72 | |
| James Wilkinson | Do | 84.63 | Va. Militia | Do | 71 | |
| Nathan Mendenhall | Do | 109.98 | Pa. Militia | Do | 88 | |
| William McCarthy | Do | 199.98 | S. C. Militia | Do | 76 | |

Above found in North Carolina Pension Roll pages 9, 90, 91 and 92.

## MACON COUNTY, NORTH CAROLINA

| Names | Rank | Sums received | Description of service | Commencement of pension | Ages |
|---|---|---|---|---|---|
| Amos Brown | Private | $ 75.00 | Ga. Militia | Mar. 4, 1831 | 68 |
| Samuel Broadway | Do | 90.00 | Va. Cont'l line | Do | 71 |
| Isham Davis | Do | 120.00 | N. C. Militia | Do | 76 |
| William Fortune | Do | 60.00 | Do | Do | 78 |
| David Fulton | Do | 199.98 | N. C. Cont'l line | Do | 84 |
| William Garret | Pri. Inf. and Cav. | 204.96 | Do | Do | 81 |

| Name | Rank | Service | Amount | Date | Age | Remarks |
|---|---|---|---|---|---|---|
| Peter Ledford, Sen. | Private Cav. | N. C. Militia | 79.56 | Do | 85 | |
| William McLeod | Private | N. C. Militia | 99.99 | Do | 73 | |
| William L. Queen | Do | N. C. Cont'l line | 120.00 | Do | 85 | |
| Samuel Rose | Do | N. C. Militia | 90.00 | Do | 79 | |
| Aaron Thomas | Do | Do | 69.99 | Do | 74 | |
| Samuel Vermillion | Do | Md. Militia | 240.00 | Do | 79 | |
| Thomas Williams | Pri. Inf. and Cav. | N. C. Militia | 264.96 | Do | 74 | |

Above found in North Carolina Pension Roll page 97.

## MARTIN COUNTY, NORTH CAROLINA

| Name | Rank | Service | Amount | Date | Age | Remarks |
|---|---|---|---|---|---|---|
| John Pulley | Private | Crane's Co. of Art'y | $1,506.36 | June 26, 1818 | — | Act Jan. 11, 1812 |
| John Bonner | Pri. and Sergt. | N. C. Militia | 129.71 | Mar. 4, 1831 | 76 | Died Oct. 8, 1833 |
| John Clark | Private | Do | 147.36 | Do | 76 | |
| Abraham Johnson | Do | Do | 60.00 | Do | 73 | |
| William May | Do | Do | 125.00 | Do | 87 | |
| James Medford | Do | Do | 66.65 | Do | 76 | |
| William Mizell, Sen. | Sergeant | Do | 132.48 | Do | 77 | |
| Thomas Price | Pri. of Cav. | Do | 62.50 | Do | 78 | |
| Raleigh Robuck | Private | Va. Militia | 200.00 | Do | 77 | |
| Daniel Robason | Do | N. C. Militia | 79.98 | Do | 76 | |
| John Smithwick, Sen. | Pri. Cav. | Do | 58.32 | Do | 76 | |

Above found in North Carolina Pension Roll pages 11 and 98.

## MECKLENBURG COUNTY, NORTH CAROLINA

| Name | Rank | Service | Amount | Date | Remarks |
|---|---|---|---|---|---|
| Charles Elam* | Private | U. S. Army | $ 351.44 | Sept. 4, 1808 | Act Apr. 24, 1816 |
| Do | Do | Do | 324.96 | Apr. 24, 1816 | Act Mar. 3, 1819 |
| Do | Do | Do | 625.03 | Mar. 4, 1831 | Died Sept. 26, 1826 |
| David Flannigan* | Do | — | 250.90 | Sept. 4, 1808 | Act Apr. 24, 1816 |
| Do | Do | — | 497.44 | Apr. 24, 1816 | Died Aug. 16, 1815 |
| Mathew Pitman | Do | — | 249.93 | Sept. 5, 1808 | Act Apr. 24, 1816 |
| Do | Do | — | — | Apr. 24, 1808 | Died Aug. 3, 1827 |
| John Wentz* | Do | U. S. Army | 283.08 | Sept. 4, 1808 | Act Apr. 24, 1816 |
| Do | Do | Do | 649.57 | Apr. 14, 1816 | Ex. mil. est. Transferred from Mo. from Sept. 4, 1832 |
| Jeptha Yarborough | Do | 6th Inf. | 167.73 | Dec. 6, 1830 | |

| Names | Rank | Sums received | Description of service | Commencement of pension | Ages | Laws under which they were formerly inscribed on the Pension Roll and remarks |
|---|---|---|---|---|---|---|
| Jeremiah Adams............. | Private | $ 83.64 | N. C. Cont'l line | Mar. 4, 1831 | 78 | |
| William Alexander........... | Captain | 1,440.00 | N. C. Militia | Do | 85 | |
| Charles Alexander........... | Pri. Inf. and Cav. | 84.15 | Do | Do | 72 | Died Sept. 2, 1833 |
| Isaac Alexander............. | Pri. and Ser. | 177.92 | N. C. Cont'l line | Do | 77 | |
| Thomas Alexander........... | Private | 125.00 | Do | Do | 81 | Died May 4, 1834 |
| Samuel Bootwright.......... | Do | 75.54 | Va. Militia | Do | 70 | |
| Andrew Barry............... | Do | 63.99 | N. C. Militia | Do | 75 | |
| James Byrum............... | Do | 73.98 | Va. Cont'l line | Do | 78 | |
| Steven Billeu............... | Do | 240.00 | N. C. Cont'l line | Do | 77 | |
| Ezekiel Black............... | Do | 64.98 | Do | Do | 76 | |
| Thomas Barnett............. | Pri. and Sergt. | 165.00 | Do | Do | 75 | |
| Reuben Boswell............. | Private | 240.00 | Va. Militia | Do | 77 | |
| Alexander Cathey........... | Do | 162.00 | N. C. Militia | Do | 74 | |
| James Connor.............. | Pr. Ser. & Qur. M. | 819.96 | Do | Do | 80 | |
| Jeremiah Clontz............ | Private | 90.00 | N. C. Cont'l line | Do | 79 | |
| Burwell Cashone............ | Do | 129.99 | N. C. Militia | Do | 75 | |
| Thomas Cashone............ | Do | 240.00 | Va. Militia | Do | 76 | |
| John Carrothers............ | Do | 210.00 | N. C. Militia | Do | 80 | |
| Hezekiah Dewise............ | Do | 223.98 | Do | Do | 74 | |
| Thomas Downs............. | Pri. and Lt. | 199.98 | Do | Do | 78 | |
| John Elliott................ | Pri. and Ser. | 255.00 | Do | Do | 71 | |
| Charles Finley............. | Private | 50.00 | Do | Do | 76 | |
| Hugh Forbus............... | Do | 240.00 | Do | Do | 78 | |
| Gabriel Ferrell............. | Do | 120.00 | Do | Do | 74 | |
| Nathaniel Farrar........... | Do | — | Do | Do | 75 | |
| James Gillespie............. | Pr. and Ser. | 200.00 | N. C. Militia | Do | 74 | |
| John Gardner.............. | Private | 204.63 | Do | Do | 74 | |
| Richard Griffin............. | Do | 90.00 | Do | Do | 78 | |
| Bedford Garris.............. | Do | 240.00 | N. C. Cont'l line | Do | 71 | |
| Samuel Givens.............. | Do | 134.64 | N. C. Militia | Do | 72 | |
| William Hutchison.......... | Pri. and Capt. | 647.67 | Do | Do | 83 | |
| George Howey.............. | Private | 90.00 | Do | Do | 72 | |
| Allen Herron............... | Do | 74.34 | Do | Do | 76 | Died Nov. 23, 1833 |
| William Howard............ | Do | 66.65 | Do | Do | 71 | |

| Name | Rank | Line | Amount | Date | Age | Notes |
|---|---|---|---|---|---|---|
| Henry Hunter............ | Do | Va. Militia | 70.82 | Do | 83 | Died Mar. 10, 1833 |
| Robert Huddleston........ | Do | Do | 90.00 | Do | 75 | |
| Alexander Hodge......... | Pri. and Lt. | N. C. Militia | 266.64 | Do | 71 | |
| Valentine Hipp.......... | Private | N. C. Cont'l line | 102.15 | Do | 74 | |
| James Knox............. | Do | Do | 66.65 | Do | 74 | |
| Samuel Knox............ | Do | S. C. Militia | 80.54 | Mar. 4, 1831 | 71 | |
| George Kiher........... | Private | N. C. Militia | 99.09 | Do | 80 | |
| Robert Kerr............ | Do | Do | 60.00 | Do | 84 | |
| John McCain........... | Do | N. C. Cont'l line | 108.66 | Do | 81 | |
| John Mulwee........... | Do | N. C. Militia | 88.68 | Do | 88 | |
| Mitchell McLeary........ | Do | Do | 90.00 | Do | 72 | |
| George McWhorter...... | Do | Do | 124.65 | Do | 72 | |
| Ephraim Martin........ | Pri. and Sergt. | N. J. Militia | — | Do | 74 | |
| James Orr............. | Private | N. C. Militia | 69.99 | Do | 84 | |
| Robert Robinson........ | Do | N. C. Militia | 104.64 | Do | 84 | |
| Hugh Rogers........... | Do | S. C. Militia | 69.66 | Do | 75 | |
| David Rea............. | Pri. Inf. and Cav. | N. C. Cont'l line | 71.54 | Do | 77 | |
| William Smith......... | Private | Do | 159.99 | Do | 76 | |
| Richard Spring........ | Pr. Lt. and Capt. | N. C. Militia | 466.32 | Do | 79 | Died Dec. 20, 1833 |
| James Sloan........... | Private | Do | 159.99 | Do | 73 | |
| John Stinson.......... | Do | Do | 78.91 | Do | 75 | |
| George Thomason...... | Pri. Cav. | Do | 75.00 | Do | 85 | |
| William Thompson..... | Private | Do | 219.99 | Do | 76 | |
| Samuel Wilson........ | Pri. and Capt. | Do | 469.98 | Do | 84 | |
| William Weatherspoon.. | Private | Do | 141.96 | Do | 75 | Died Sept. 6, 1833 |
| Andrew Walker........ | Do | N. C. Cont'l line | — | | 77 | |

Above found in North Carolina Pension Roll pages 11, 93, 94 and 95.

## MONTGOMERY COUNTY, NORTH CAROLINA

| Name | Rank | Line | Amount | Date | Notes |
|---|---|---|---|---|---|
| George Bledsoe........... | Private | — | $1,298.45 | Sept. 4, 1794 | {Act Apr. 20, 1796 / {Died July 1, 1831 |
| Do | Do | — | 466.89 | Apr. 24, 1816 | Act Apr. 24, 1816 |
| Do | Do | 4th Va. Regt. | 655.48 | Mar. 4, 1821 | Act Mar. 3, 1819 |
| John Frazier............. | Do | | 64.85 | Nov. 16, 1814 | {Act Mar. 3, 1815 / {Died Aug. 5, 1816 |
| Do | Do | Do | 20.36 | Apr. 24, 1816 | Act Apr. 24, 1816 |
| William Moore........... | Do | 10th Regt. U.S. Inf. | 40.08 | Dec. 24, 1814 | {Ex. mil. est. Transferred / {from S. C. from Mar. / {4, 1826 |

| Names | Rank | Sums received | Description of service | Commencement of pension | Ages | Laws under which they were formerly inscribed on the Pension Roll and remarks |
|---|---|---|---|---|---|---|
| William Moore | Private | $ 473.44 | 10th Regt. U.S. Inf. | Apr. 24, 1816 | | Act Apr. 24, 1816 |
| Do | Do | 368.00 | Do | Mar. 4, 1826 | | |
| Mattiah Turner | Do | 1,628.45 | U. S. Army | Mar. 4, 1789 | | {Act Sept. 20, 1789 / Died May 25, 1831 / Act Apr. 24, 1816 |
| Do | Do | 1,448.25 | Do | Apr. 24, 1816 | 74 | |
| Nathan Almond | Do | 199.98 | N. C. Militia | Mar. 4, 1831 | 69 | |
| Edward Allman | Do | 90.00 | N. C. line | Do | 73 | |
| Benjamin Bell | Do | 60.00 | Do | Do | 81 | |
| Thomas Biles | Do | 120.00 | Do | Do | 88 | |
| Thomas Blake | Do | 100.00 | Va. line | Do | 79 | |
| Solomon Burris | Do | 180.00 | N. C. Cont'l line | Do | 82 | |
| John Barmer | Do | 240.00 | Va. Militia | Do | 87 | |
| George Crowell, Sen. | Do | 90.40 | N. C. Militia | Do | 70 | |
| James Duke | Do | 73.98 | Do | Do | 80 | |
| Daniel Easley | Do | 240.00 | Va. Militia | Do | 76 | |
| Samuel Hancock | Pri. Inf. and Cav. | 94.40 | N. C. line | Do | 72 | |
| Joshua Hurley | Private | 142.50 | Do | Do | 73 | |
| Ebenezer Hearne | Do | 120.00 | Do | Do | 76 | |
| Jesse Jones | Do | 120.00 | Do | Do | 74 | |
| Kinchen Pennington | Do | 180.00 | Do | Do | 85 | |
| William Poplin | Do | 90.00 | Do | Do | 73 | |
| Joseph Parsons | Pri. and Capt. | 259.98 | N. C. Militia | Do | 74 | |
| Williamson Ross | Private | 75.00 | N. C. Cont'l line | Do | 79 | |
| George Shankle | Do | 90.00 | N. C. line | Do | 85 | |
| Robert Surls | Do | 120.00 | Do | Do | 72 | |
| Philip Sell | Do | 129.99 | Do | Do | 72 | |
| Hudston Taylor | Do | 120.00 | Do | Do | 76 | |
| Edward Wright | Do | 60.00 | N. C. Militia | Do | 85 | |
| Andrew Stough | Do | — | N. C. line | Do | | |

Above found in North Carolina Pension Roll pages 10, 95 and 96.

## MOORE COUNTY, NORTH CAROLINA

| | $ | | | | | |
|---|---|---|---|---|---|---|
| Solomon Arnold | 60.00 | Private | N. C. Militia | Mar. 4, 1831 | 76 | |
| John Baker | 50.00 | Do | N. C. Cont'l line | Do | 74 | |
| William Barratt | 178.29 | Do | N. C. Militia | Do | 79 | |
| Jacob Gaster | 69.99 | Do | Do | Do | 69 | |
| James Gaines, Sen. | 90.00 | Do | Va. Militia | Do | 72 | |
| George Horner | 219.99 | Pri. Ensn. & Lt. | N. C. Militia | Do | 73 | |
| Howell Lashley | 60.00 | Private | Va. Militia | Do | 73 | |
| Morris Morrison | 60.00 | Do | N. C. Militia | Do | 70 | |
| Samuel Martindale | 99.99 | Do | N. C. Cont'l line | Do | 82 | |
| John Morgan | 120.00 | Do | N. C. Militia | Do | 73 | |

Above found in North Carolina Pension Roll page 96.

## NASH COUNTY, NORTH CAROLINA

| | $ | | | | | |
|---|---|---|---|---|---|---|
| William Hall* | 226.15 | Captain | N. C. Militia | Nov. 28, 1804 | — | Died June 3, 1835 |
| Do | 361.86 | Do | Do | Sept. 5, 1808 | 73 | Act Mar. 3, 1819 |
| Do | 428.00 | Do | Do | Apr. 24, 1816 | 70 | |
| Do | 32.60 | Do | Do | Mar. 25, 1825 | 80 | |
| Josiah Davis | 84.99 | Private | Do | Mar. 4, 1831 | 78 | |
| Thomas Griffin | 60.00 | Do | Do | Do | 73 | |
| Thomas Hamilton | 60.00 | Do | N. C. Cont'l line | Do | 82 | |
| Jacob Rice, Sen. | 270.00 | Pri. and sergt. | N. C. Militia | Do | 77 | |
| Jordon Sherod | 120.00 | Private | Do | Do | | |
| William Turner | 149.97 | Do | Do | Do | | |
| Benjamin Williams | 79.98 | Do | Do | Do | | |

Above found in North Carolina Pension Roll pages 12 and 89.

## NEW HANOVER COUNTY, NORTH CAROLINA

| | $ | | | | | |
|---|---|---|---|---|---|---|
| James Collins | 90.00 | Private | N. C. Militia | Mar. 4, 1831 | 77 | |
| Robert Cook | 64.65 | Do | Do | Do | 80 | |
| James Devane | 550.00 | Pri. and Capt. | Do | Do | 77 | |
| James Downing | 189.96 | Pri. Inf. and Cav. | Do | Do | 90 | |
| Stephen Felyan | 64.59 | Pri. Inf. and Cav. | Do | Do | 72 | |
| Taylor Halloway | 124.38 | Private | Va. Militia | Do | 63 | Died Sept. 24, 1832 |

| Names | Rank | Sums received | Description of service | Commencement of pension | Ages | Laws under which they were formerly inscribed on the Pension Roll and remarks |
|---|---|---|---|---|---|---|
| Zachariah Jacobs | Private | $ 169.98 | N. C. Militia | Mar. 4, 1831 | 81 | Died May 12, 1833 |
| James Lee | Do | 240.00 | N. C. Cont'l line | Do | 74 | |
| Benjamin Larkins | Pri. Cav. and Inf. | — | N. C. Militia | Do | 75 | |
| James Lewis | Private | 117.90 | Do | Do | 77 | |
| James Malpass | Do | 90.00 | Do | Do | 74 | |
| James Moore, Sen. | Do | 79.98 | Do | Do | 85 | |
| William New | Do | 162.47 | Do | Do | 77 | |
| Ephraim Powersm | Do | 62.20 | N. C. Cont'l line | Do | 77 | |
| Francis Pridgeon | Do | 120.00 | N. C. Militia | Do | 74 | |
| Josiah Sykes | Do | 210.00 | Do | Do | 94 | |
| John Taylor | Do | 180.00 | Do | Do | 89 | |
| John Wheeden | Do | — | Do | Do | 77 | |
| George Bannerman | Pri. Inf. and Cav. | — | Do | Do | 73 | |

Above found in North Carolina Pension Roll page 98.

## NORTHAMPTON COUNTY, NORTH CAROLINA

| Names | Rank | Sums received | Description of service | Commencement of pension | Ages | Laws under which they were formerly inscribed on the Pension Roll and remarks |
|---|---|---|---|---|---|---|
| William Liles | Private | $ 91.39 | 20th Regt. U. S. Inf. | May 30, 1814 | — | Act Apr. 24, 1816 |
| Do | Do | 859.07 | Do | Apr. 24, 1816 | | Act Mar. 3, 1819 |
| Do | Do | 56.78 | Do | June 30, 1827 | 78 | |
| Christopher Cook | Do | 69.99 | N. C. Militia | Mar. 4, 1813 | 78 | |
| Henry Garriss | Do | 60.00 | Do | Do | 74 | |
| Kedar Parker | Do | 62.50 | Do | Do | 72 | |
| James Roper | Do | 160.00 | N. C. Cont'l line | Do | 81 | |
| James Seat | Musc. and Pri. | 90.00 | N. C. Militia | Do | 72 | |
| Drury Walden | Private | 114.99 | Do | Do | 73 | Died Feb. 19, 1833 |
| Samuel Wilson | Do | 78.84 | Do | Do | 72 | |
| Samuel Williams | Do | 180.00 | Do | Do | 70 | |
| John Winborne | Pri. and Adj. | 133.32 | Do | Do | 79 | |
| Buckner Williams | Private | 50.00 | Do | Do | | |

Above found in North Carolina Pension Roll pages 12 and 100.

## ONSLOW COUNTY, NORTH CAROLINA

| Name | Rank | Amount | Service | Date | Age | Remarks |
|---|---|---|---|---|---|---|
| Reuben Arnold | Pri. Art. and Inf. | $225.00 | R. I. Militia | Mar. 4, 1831 | 71 | |
| Stephen Costen | Do | 90.00 | N. C. Militia | Do | 79 | |
| John Corbett | | — | Va. Militia | Do | 79 | |
| Samuel Evans | Pri. Inf. and Cav. | 82.21 | N. C. Militia | Do | 71 | |
| Purnell Marshall | Do | | Do | Do | 73 | |
| John Riggs | Private | 200.00 | N. C. Cont'l line | Do | 90 | |
| Daniel Rodgers | Do | 200.00 | N. C. Militia | Do | 74 | |
| William Reed | Do | | Do | | 70 | Died Jan. 29, 1834 |

Above found in North Carolina Pension Roll page 103.

## ORANGE COUNTY, NORTH CAROLINA

| Name | Rank | Amount | Service | Date | Age | Remarks |
|---|---|---|---|---|---|---|
| Thomas Jacobs | Private | $30.86 | 10th Regt. U. S. Inf. | Oct. 9, 1814 | — | Act mil. est. |
| Do | Do | 571.62 | Do | Apr. 24, 1816 | | Act Apr. 24, 1816 |
| Jesse Rigsby* | Do | 305.63 | Army of Rev. | Sept. 5, 1808 | — | Died Oct. 6, 1827 |
| Do | Do | 736.52 | N. C. line | Apr. 24, 1816 | 73 | Act Apr. 24, 1816 |
| James Allison | Pri. Inf. and Cav. | 193.59 | Do | Mar. 4, 1831 | 73 | |
| Samuel Allen | Pri. and Con. | 150.00 | Do | Do | 75 | |
| Henry Albright | Sergeant | 137.50 | Do | Do | 77 | |
| John Boudy | Private | 240.00 | Do | Do | | {Act June 27, 1834 / Dropped and Inscribed / under Act May 15, 1834 |
| George Carrington | Pri. Inf. and Cav. | 137.49 | N. C. Militia | Do | 79 | |
| William Cumming | Qr. Mr, and Lt. | 360.00 | Do | Do | 76 | |
| William Crabtree | Private | 50.00 | Do | Do | 76 | |
| James Cheek | Pri. Cav. and Inf. | 56.25 | Va. Cont'l line | Do | 72 | |
| James Carter | Private | 240.00 | N. C. Militia | Do | 75 | |
| Richard Christmas | Pri. and Capt. | 213.32 | Do | Do | 81 | {Died Mar. 18, 1833. / Cert. issued to A. Craig, / ex. &c. |
| Hardeman Duke | Private | 240.00 | N. C. Cont'l line | Do | 74 | |
| William Duke | Pri. and Sergt. | 237.50 | Do | Do | 80 | |
| Christopher Daniel | Private | 240.00 | Va. Militia | Do | 75 | |
| Elijah Dollars | Do | 75.00 | N. C. Cont'l line | Do | 75 | |
| Lewis Dishon, alias Dishong | Do | 50.00 | N. C. Militia | Do | 71 | |
| William Dollar | Do | 79.98 | N. C. Militia | Do | 71 | |

| Names | Rank | Sums received | Description of service | Commencement of pension | Ages | Laws under which they were formerly inscribed on the Pension Roll and remarks |
|---|---|---|---|---|---|---|
| John Dolley | Private | — | N. C. Militia | Mar. 4, 1831 | 81 | |
| John Efland | Do | $ 100.00 | Do | Do | 72 | |
| Joseph Fennel | Do | 96.99 | Do | Do | 89 | |
| Alexander Gattis | Pri. Cav. and Inf. | 67.50 | N. C. Cont'l line | Do | 73 | |
| Isaac Griffith | Private | 91.65 | Do | Do | 67 | |
| Thomas Horner | Sergeant | 180.00 | N. C. Militia | Do | 74 | |
| James Hart | Private | 90.00 | Do | Do | — | |
| George Holt | Pr. and sergt. | 62.50 | Do | Do | 78 | |
| Alexander Hatch | Private | 150.00 | Do | Do | 69 | |
| William Hopkins | Do | 60.00 | Do | Do | 75 | Died Mar. 28, 1833 |
| John Hudgins | Pri. Inf. and Cav. | 87.21 | Do | Do | 72 | |
| John Jeffreys | Private | 66.66 | Do | Do | 69 | |
| Abner James | Do | 131.25 | Do | Do | 70 | |
| Thomas King | Do | 50.00 | Do | Do | 86 | |
| Gasper Long | Pri. Inf. and Cav. | 87.50 | N. C. Cont'l line | Do | 80 | |
| Barnabas Laskley | Private | 50.00 | Do | Do | 82 | |
| Thomas Marcum | Do | 60.00 | N. C. Militia | Do | 82 | |
| James McCullock | Do | — | N. C. Cont'l line | Do | 96 | Died |
| Ludwick May | Do | 150.00 | N. C. Militia | Do | 70 | |
| Andrew McBroom | Do | 76.65 | N. C. Cont'l line | Do | 79 | |
| Nathan Mann | Do | — | N. C. Militia | Do | 77 | |
| George Nease | Pri. Inf. and Cav. | 164.60 | S. C. Militia | Do | 75 | |
| Martin Nease | Private | 95.82 | N. C. Cont'l line | Do | 73 | |
| Samuel Nelson | Pri. and Ensn. | 224.97 | Do | Do | 79 | |
| John Pool | Pri. Inf. | 77.49 | N. C. Militia | Mar. 4, 1831 | 72 | |
| Thomas Patterson | Private | 75.99 | Do | Do | 72 | |
| William Ray, Sen. | Captain | 540.00 | Do | Do | 91 | |
| Peter Stone, Sen. | Private | 144.00 | N. C. Cont'l line | Do | 78 | |
| Reuben Smith | Pri. Serg. & Cornet | 125.60 | Do | Do | 85 | |
| John Steader | Private | 52.75 | Do | Do | 76 | |
| William Strayhorn | Do | 66.65 | N. C. Militia | Do | 77 | |
| John Southard | Do | 70.00 | Va. Cont'l line | Do | 75 | |
| Lazarus Tilley | Do | 69.99 | N. C. Militia | Do | 74 | |
| Samuel Thompson | Do | 159.99 | Do | Do | 83 | |

| Name | Rank | Service | Amount | Date | Age |
|---|---|---|---|---|---|
| Henry Trolinger | Do | Do | — | | 71 |
| Robert Tinner | Do | Do | 50.00 | | 71 |
| Thomas Tate | Do | N. C. Cont'l line | 60.66 | | 78 |
| James Turner | Do | Do | 166.65 | | 71 |
| Benjamin Tutterton | Do | N. C. Militia | 75.00 | | 82 |
| John Underwood | Com. Ass't. Qr. M. | Del. Cont'l line | 102.00 | | 79 |
| John Watson | Private | N. C. Militia | 187.47 | | 83 |
| Johnson Webb | Do | N. C. Militia | 129.99 | | 89 |
| William Warren | Do | S. C. Militia | 73.98 | | 89 |
| George Wright | Do | Pa. Militia | — | | 73 |
| Brittian Bowers | Do | Va. Militia | — | | 71 |

Above found in North Carolina Pension Roll pages 13, 100, 101 and 102.

## PASQUOTANK COUNTY, NORTH CAROLINA

| Name | Rank | Service | Amount | Date | Age |
|---|---|---|---|---|---|
| John Koen | Ser. Drum | N. C. Cont'l line | $ 307.98 | Mar. 4, 1831 | 77 |
| Jesse Perry | Private | N. C. Militia | 240.06 | Do | 74 |
| William Palmer | Do | N. C. line | 105.00 | Do | 71 |
| Cornelius Rhodes | Do | Do | 60.00 | Do | 76 |

Above found in North Carolina Pension Roll page 106.

## PERQUIMANS COUNTY, NORTH CAROLINA

| Name | Rank | Service | Amount | Date | Age |
|---|---|---|---|---|---|
| John Dail | Private | N. C. Cont'l line | $ 200.00 | Mar. 4, 1831 | 79 |
| John Goodwin, Sen | Do | N. C. Militia | — | Do | 81 |

Above found in North Carolina Pension Roll page 105.

## PERSON COUNTY, NORTH CAROLINA

| Name | Rank | Service | Amount | Date | Age |
|---|---|---|---|---|---|
| Colman Clayton | Private | N. C. line | $ 210.00 | Mar. 4, 1831 | 74 |
| John Clayton | Do | Do | 75.00 | Do | 76 |
| Thomas Hargis | Pri. Ser. and Capt. | Do | 145.50 | Do | 82 |
| Ephraim Hawkins | Private | N. C. Militia | 210.00 | Do | 73 |
| Archibald Lipscome | Do | Va. Militia | 195.00 | Do | 76 |
| Isaac Lint | Do | N. C. Militia | 120.00 | Do | 79 |
| Richard Pullian | Do | Do | 50.00 | Do | 71 |

| Names | Rank | Sums received | Description of service | Commencement of pension | Ages | Laws under which they were formerly inscribed on the Pension Roll and remarks |
|---|---|---|---|---|---|---|
| Bennett Williams | Private | $ 79.98 | N. C. Militia | Mar. 4, 1831 | 81 | |
| Solomon Whitlow | Do | 75.00 | N. C. Cont'l line | Do | 72 | |
| Buckley Walker | Do | 134.97 | N. C. Militia | Do | 72 | |

Above found in North Carolina Pension Roll Pages 103 and 104.

## PITT COUNTY, NORTH CAROLINA

| Names | Rank | Sums received | Description of service | Commencement of pension | Ages | Laws under which they were formerly inscribed on the Pension Roll and remarks |
|---|---|---|---|---|---|---|
| John Anderson | Private | $ 69.03 | N. C. Cont'l line | June 16, 1819 | 74 | (Act Mar. 18, 1818 Dropped under Act May 1, 1820. |
| Do | Do | 240.00 | N. C. Militia | Mar. 4, 1831 | | |
| Henry Barnhill | Do | 69.03 | Do | June 16, 1819 | 75 | (Act Mar. 18, 1818 Dropped under Act May 1, 1820. |
| Do | Do | 240.00 | Do | Mar. 4, 1831 | | |
| Thomas Bently | Do | 150.00 | Do | Do | 75 | |
| William Cooper | Do | 60.00 | Do | Do | 71 | |
| Thomas Davis | Do | 109.98 | N. C. Cont'l line | Do | 76 | |
| Moses Highsmith | Do | 54.15 | Do | Do | 74 | |
| Benjamin Hope | Do | 85.03 | N. C. Militia | Do | 79 | |
| Richard Jordan | Pri. Inf. and Cav. | 147.48 | N. C. Cont'l line | Do | — | Died Jan. 7, 1834 |
| Simon Keel | Do | 101.82 | N. C. Militia | Do | 70 | |
| David Kennedy | Private | — | Do | Do | 77 | |
| Noah Nathan (L) | Do | 79.98 | Do | Do | 75 | |
| Nasby Mills | Do | 60.00 | Do | Do | 71 | |
| Giles Mathews | Do | 184.98 | Do | Do | 80 | |
| Giles Nelson | Do | 125.03 | N. C. Cont'l line | Nov. 16, 1818 | 87 | (Act Mar. 18, 1818 Dropped under Act May 1, 1820. |
| Do | Do | 240.00 | Do | Mar. 4, 1831 | | |
| Clarborne Parrish | Do | 60.00 | N. C. Militia | Do | 73 | |
| John Rice | Do | 60.00 | N. C. line | Do | 81 | |
| Edmund Ricks | Pri. and Sergt. | 75.00 | Va. line | Mar. 4, 1818 | 76 | |

| Name | Rank | Amount | Service | Date | Age | Remarks |
|---|---|---|---|---|---|---|
| William Spain | Musc. | 128.53 | N. C. Cont'l line | Nov. 3, 1818 | 73 | Act Mar. 18, 1818 Dropped under Act May 1, 1820 |
| William Spain | Do | 240.00 | Do | Mar. 4, 1831 | 73 | |
| Charles Smith | Private | 90.00 | Do | Do | 76 | |
| William Weaver | Do | 60.00 | N. C. Militia | Do | 73 | |
| Willis Wilson | Pri. Cav. | 75.00 | Do | Do | 82 | |
| Arthur Whitehurst, Sen. | Private | 121.32 | Do | Do | 73 | |
| Robert Williams | Sergeant | 720.00 | Do | Do | 75 | |

Above found in North Carolina Pension Roll pages 104 and 105.

## RANDOLPH COUNTY, NORTH CAROLINA

| Name | Rank | Amount | Service | Date | Age |
|---|---|---|---|---|---|
| Richard Bell | Pri. Cav. and Inf. | $177.48 | N. C. Militia | Mar. 4, 1831 | 76 |
| Sterling Cooper | Private | 109.98 | Do | Do | 70 |
| John Graham | Pri. Cav. | 83.34 | Do | Do | 73 |
| Lemuel Glasgow | Private | 240.00 | N. C. Cont'l line | Do | 81 |
| Edmund Hays | Do | 75.00 | S. C. Militia | Do | 75 |
| William Hall | Do | 46.66 | Va. Militia | Do | 87 |
| Joseph Johnston | Pri. Cav. | 124.98 | N. C. Militia | Do | 81 |
| Thomas Jones, 2nd | Private | 76.65 | N. C. Militia | Do | 82 |
| Mitchell Luther | Do | 199.98 | Md. Militia | Do | 84 |
| George Luther | Do | 100.00 | Do | Do | 80 |
| Dan Merrel | Do | 58.32 | N. C. Militia | Do | 79 |
| Anthony Rains | Do | 79.98 | N. C. Cont'l line | Do | 77 |
| Thomas Yeargan | Do | 102.00 | Va. Militia | Do | 71 |
| Manring Brookshire | Lt. Cav. | 600.00 | N. C. Militia | Do | 77 |
| Burwell Barns | Private | 90.00 | Do | Do | 77 |

Above found in North Carolina Pension Roll page 109.

## RICHMOND COUNTY, NORTH CAROLINA

| Name | Rank | Amount | Service | Date | Age | Remarks |
|---|---|---|---|---|---|---|
| William Brown | Pri. Cav. | $112.50 | N. C. line | Mar. 4, 1831 | 71 | |
| John Curry | Q. M. Sergt. | 80.00 | N. C. Cont'l line | May 4, 1819 | 85 | Mar. 18, 1818. Dropped under Act May 1, 1820 |
| Do | Do | 169.98 | Do | Mar. 4, 1831 | | |
| John Clemmens | Private | — | Md. line | Do | 83 | |
| John Dawkins | Pri. Inf. and Cav. | 67.50 | N. C. Militia | Do | 83 | |

| Names | Rank | Sums received | Description of service | Commencement of pension | Ages | Laws under which they were formerly inscribed on the Pension Roll and remarks |
|---|---|---|---|---|---|---|
| Thomas Everitt | Pri. Inf. and Cav. | $ 187.50 | N. C. Militia | Mar. 4, 1831 | 92 | |
| Elias Gardner | Do | 127.50 | Do | Do | 70 | |
| James Hasty, Sen. | Do | 180.00 | Va. Militia | Do | 82 | |
| Edwin Ingram | Pri. and Ensn. | 173.28 | N. C. Militia | Do | 84 | |
| Walter Leah | Private | 240.00 | Do | Do | 73 | |
| Richard Morgan | Drummer | 264.00 | Do | Do | 77 | |
| John McAllister | Pri. Inf. and Cav. | 180.00 | Do | Do | 68 | |
| Isham Norton, Sen. | Private | 75.00 | Do | Do | 82 | |
| Tillitson O'Brien | Do | 90.00 | Do | Do | 73 | |
| Lot Stricklin | Do | 240.00 | Do | Do | 75 | |
| John Surgenor | Do | 109.98 | Do | Do | 83 | |
| William Thomas | Pri. Inf. and Cav. | 105.00 | S. C. Cont'l line | Do | 72 | |
| Isaac Williamson, Sen. | Private | 240.00 | N. C. Cont'l line | Do | 76 | |
| Thomas P. Williams | Pri. Inf. and Cav. | 97.58 | | Do | 72 | |

Above found in North Carolina Pension Roll page 108.

ROBESON COUNTY, NORTH CAROLINA

| Names | Rank | Sums received | Description of service | Commencement of pension | Ages | Laws under which they were formerly inscribed on the Pension Roll and remarks |
|---|---|---|---|---|---|---|
| Isaac Kennedy* | Private | $ 301.08 | Army Revolution | Sept. 4, 1808 | — | Act Apr. 24, 1816 |
| Do | Do | 510.53 | Do | Apr. 24, 1816 | 85 | |
| Samuel Bell | Do | 109.98 | N. C. Cont'l line | Mar. 4, 1831 | 70 | |
| James Kersey | Do | 120.00 | N. C. Militia | Do | 75 | |
| James McNatt | Sergeant | 135.00 | Do | Do | 80 | |
| Nathan Musselwhite | Private | 109.98 | Do | Do | 83 | |
| Milbed Musselwhite | Do | 90.00 | Do | Do | 76 | |
| Nazareth Mitchell | Do | 99.99 | Do | Do | 91 | |
| Benjamin Tyner | Pri. Cav. and Inf. | 97.50 | Do | Do | 73 | |
| John Wooddill | Private | 180.00 | Do | Do | | |

Above found in North Carolina Pension Roll pages 14 and 110.

## ROCKINGHAM COUNTY, NORTH CAROLINA

| Name | Rank | $ | Service | | Age | Remarks |
|---|---|---|---|---|---|---|
| Robert Burton | Private | 60.00 | Va. Militia | Mar. 4, 1831 | 70 | |
| Chesley Barnes | Do | 90.00 | N. C. Militia | Do | 74 | |
| Elijah Brown | Do | 64.98 | Do | Do | 82 | |
| Peter Crawford | Do | 79.98 | Va. Militia | Do | 70 | |
| Thomas Carter | Do | 60.00 | Do | Do | 88 | |
| Henry Delap, Sen. | Do | 48.88 | Do | Do | 96 | |
| John Fields | Sergeant | 180.00 | N. C. Cont'l line | Do | 81 | |
| William Godsey | Private | 60.00 | Va. Militia | Do | 70 | |
| Samuel Gann, Sen. | Do | 120.00 | Do | Do | 83 | |
| Samuel Hill | Do | 240.00 | Do | Do | 71 | |
| Henry Knight | Do | — | Do | Do | 74 | |
| Thomas Lowe | Sergeant | 360.00 | Va. Cont'l line | Do | 79 | |
| Alexander Lemonds | Private | 90.00 | N. C. Cont'l line | Do | 73 | |
| Elijah Lynch | Do | 240.00 | Va. line | Do | 79 | |
| John May | Sergt. and Ensn. | 540.00 | Do | Do | 77 | |
| Nicholas McCubbin | Private | 210.00 | N. C. Militia | Do | 74 | |
| Josiah Morton | Do | 100.00 | Va. Militia | Do | 73 | |
| Abner Powell | Private | 79.98 | Va. Cont'l line | Do | 87 | |
| Irby Phillips | Do | 195.00 | Va. Militia | Do | 71 | |
| William H. Rice | Pri. Ser. and Lt. | 214.98 | N. C. Militia | Do | 73 | |
| John Stegall | Private | 120.00 | Va. Cont'l line | Do | 76 | |
| Philip Rose | Ensign | 600.00 | | Do | 73 | |
| Adam Sharp | Do | 210.00 | N. C. Militia | Do | 69 | |
| William Smith | Pri. and Sergt. | 251.64 | Do | Do | 71 | |
| James Scales | Private | 66.94 | Do | Do | 80 | Died Sept. 6, 1833 |
| Samuel Smith | Do | 120.00 | Do | Do | 75 | |
| Shadrach Tucker | Do | 75.00 | Do | Do | 84 | Died |
| Samuel Woodall | Do | 60.00 | Va. Militia | Do | 75 | |
| William Williams | Do | 60.00 | Do | Do | 72 | |

Above found in North Carolina Pension Roll pages 110 and 111.

## ROWAN COUNTY, NORTH CAROLINA

| Name | Rank | $ | Service | | Date | Remarks |
|---|---|---|---|---|---|---|
| George Smitteel | Private | 37.50 | — | — | June 9, 1814 | Act mil. est. |
| Do | Do | 315.12 | — | — | Apr. 24, 1816 | Act Apr. 24, 1816 |
| John Wilfong* | Do | 152.81 | Army U. S | | Sept. 4, 1808 | |

| Names | Rank | Sums received | Description of service | Commencement of pension | Ages | Laws under which they were formerly inscribed on the Pension Roll and remarks |
|---|---|---|---|---|---|---|
| John Wilfong | Private | $ 571.59 | Army U. S. | Apr. 24, 1816 | — | Act Apr. 24, 1816 |
| Henry Williams | Do | 205.82 | — | June 14, 1809 | — | {Act Mar. 16, 1802 |
| Do | | 632.92 | | | | {Died July 1, 1829 |
| John Blue | Do | 53.32 | N. C. Militia | Apr. 24, 1816 | 75 | Act Apr. 24, 1816 |
| Andrew Bostain | Pri. Cav. | 300.00 | Do | Mar. 4, 1831 | 81 | |
| James Bell | Private | 90.00 | Do | Do | 74 | |
| Andrew Boston | Do | 90.00 | Do | Do | 74 | |
| Thomas Benson | Do | 240.00 | Do | Do | 79 | |
| George Clodfelter | Do | 53.32 | Do | Do | 77 | |
| George Campbell | Do | 120.00 | Do | Do | 76 | |
| Edmund Etchison | Do | 79.98 | Do | Do | 77 | |
| John M. Eller | Do | 63.30 | Do | Do | 78 | |
| Allison Flemming | Do | 50.00 | Do | Do | 75 | |
| Joseph Gibson | Do | 48.20 | Do | Do | 85 | |
| James Graham | Do | 111.65 | Do | Do | 76 | Died Feb. 9, 1834 |
| Zaddock Griffith | Do | 210.00 | Md. Cont'l line | Do | 79 | |
| George Godby, alias Godley | Do | 240.00 | Va. Militia | Do | 74 | |
| Martin Hoffner | Do | 62.20 | N. C. Militia | Do | 74 | |
| Robert Horn | Do | 129.99 | Do | Do | 74 | |
| James Houston | Do | 108.32 | N. C. Cont'l line | Do | 83 | |
| Abraham Irick | Pri. Inf. and Cav. | 79.98 | N. C. Militia | Do | 75 | Died Nov. 11, 1834 |
| Aaron Jenkins | Private | 103.04 | Do | Do | 72 | |
| Benjamin Knox | Pri. Cav. | 50.00 | Do | Do | 74 | |
| Henry Lee | Private | 67.50 | Do | Do | 82 | |
| William Luckie | Do | 60.00 | N. C. Cont'l line | Do | 77 | |
| Jonas Leib | Do | 50.00 | N. C. Militia | Do | 75 | |
| George Monroe | Do | 240.00 | Va. Cont'l line | Do | 74 | |
| John Myers | Do | 90.00 | Md. Cont'l line | Do | 78 | |
| Nathan Morgan | Do | 83.97 | N. C. Militia | Do | 78 | |
| Philip Miller | Pri. Inf. and Cav. | 99.99 | Do | Do | 75 | |
| John McLaughlin | Private | 172.47 | Pa. Cont'l line | Do | 81 | |
| John McNeely | Do | 69.99 | N. C. Militia | Do | 77 | |
| Frederick Menius | | 120.00 | Do | Do | 76 | |

| Name | Rank | Service | Amount | Date | Age | Remarks |
|---|---|---|---|---|---|---|
| William Moore | Do | Do | 172.62 | Do | 70 | |
| John Reaves | Do | Do | 60.00 | Do | 74 | |
| Thomas Rogers | Do | Va. Militia | 54.15 | Do | 71 | |
| Frederick Steigerwaldt | Do | N. C. Militia | 120.00 | Do | 72 | |
| Edward Stewart | Pri. Inf. and Cav. | Va. Cont'l line | 247.50 | Do | 74 | |
| Richard Smith | Private | N. C. line | 240.00 | Do | 79 | |
| Joseph Sawyer | Do | Va. Cont'l line | 99.99 | Do | 69 | |
| William Steelman | Do | N. C. Cont'l line | 159.99 | Do | 84 | |
| Jacob Trout | Do | | 50.00 | Do | 85 | |
| Archibald Woodside | Do | Do | 141.65 | Do | 79 | |

Above found in North Carolina Pension Roll pages 14, 106 and 107.

## RUTHERFORD COUNTY, NORTH CAROLINA

| Name | Rank | Service | Amount | Date | Age | Remarks |
|---|---|---|---|---|---|---|
| Joshua Gordon* | Private | | $ 275.07 | Sept. 4, 1808 | — | Died Aug. 7, 1816 |
| Do | Do | | 16.60 | Apr. 14, 1816 | — | Act Apr. 24, 1818 |
| Miles Goforth | Do | U. S. Rifle | 1,784.25 | Aug. 5, 1815 | — | Act mil. est. |
| Elijah Kidwell | Do | Army Rev. | 814.22 | Mar. 4, 1789 | — | {Act Sept. 29, 1789 / Died Nov. 19, 1831 |
| Do | Do | Do | 747.42 | Apr. 24, 1816 | — | Act Apr. 24, 1816 |
| Do | Do | | 29.63 | Nov. 1, 1814 | — | Act mil. est. |
| Charles McClain | Do | | 43.73 | Apr. 24, 1816 | — | Act Apr. 24, 1816 |
| Do | Do | | 64.98 | Mar. 4, 1831 | — | |
| Bracy Bowen | Do | Va. Militia | 91.25 | Do | 72 | |
| George W. Bradley | Private Inf. | N. C. Militia | 89.99 | Do | 80 | |
| Edward Cook | Private | N. C. Militia | 150.00 | Do | 74 | |
| Andrew Bankston | Pri. Cav. | Ga. Militia | 124.98 | Do | 80 | |
| William Crane | Private | Va. Militia | 90.00 | Do | 85 | |
| Cornelius Clemments | Do | S. C. Militia | 240.00 | Do | 77 | |
| William Dalton | Do | Va. Militia | 60.00 | Do | 80 | |
| James Dobbins | Do | S. C. Militia | 184.98 | Do | 72 | |
| William Depreist | Do | N. C. Militia | 132.48 | Do | 77 | |
| Patrick Downey | Do | | 75.00 | Do | 75 | |
| John Ellison | Do | Va. Militia | 72.30 | Do | 72 | |
| Liford French | Do | S. C. Militia | 116.65 | Do | 82 | |
| Joseph Forbes | Private and Capt. | | 614.97 | Do | 78 | |
| James Gray | Colonel | N. C. Militia | 1,800.00 | Do | 79 | |
| William Graham | Pri. Inf. and Cav. | Do | 194.97 | Do | 93 | |
| Thomas Hutchins | Do | Do | 180.00 | Do | 81 | |
| Robert Haney | Private | S. C. Militia | | Do | 77 | |

| Names | Rank | Sums received | Description of service | Commencement of pension | Ages | Laws under which they were formerly inscribed on the Pension Roll and remarks |
|---|---|---|---|---|---|---|
| William Hastin.......... | Private | $ 84.00 | Va. Gont'l line | Mar. 4, 1831 | 75 | |
| William Holland......... | Pri. and Ensn. | 165.00 | N. C. Cont'l line | Do | 87 | |
| James Irvin............. | Private | 60.00 | S. C. Cont'l line | Do | 69 | |
| James Largent.......... | Pri. Inf. and Cav. | 168.46 | N. C. Cont'l line | Do | 82 | Died Mar. 7, 1833 |
| William Lucas.......... | Private | 79.98 | N. C. Cont'l line | Do | 80 | |
| Drury Logan............ | Do | 240.00 | Do | Do | 72 | |
| John Laquire........... | Do | 180.00 | Do | Do | 79 | |
| Richard Ledbetter....... | Do | 75.00 | Do | Do | 96 | |
| Robert Lemonds......... | Do | 64.65 | Do | Do | 73 | |
| Jesse Mills............. | Do | 240.00 | Do | Do | 72 | |
| William Mayhew........ | Do | 90.00 | Do | Do | 74 | |
| Richard McCleiver...... | Do | 169.32 | Do | Do | 77 | |
| Alexander McFadden.... | Pri. Ser. and Capt. | 570.00 | Do | Do | 74 | |
| Danza Metcalf.......... | Private | 199.98 | Do | Do | 75 | |
| Warner Metcalf......... | Do | 210.00 | Do | Do | 72 | |
| William McKinney...... | Do | — | Do | Do | 70 | |
| John Padgett........... | Pri. Inf. and Cav. | 159.99 | N. C. Militia | Do | 72 | |
| Humphrey Parish....... | Private | 60.00 | Do | Do | 70 | |
| Joseph Pittman......... | Do | 90.00 | Do | Do | 76 | |
| Henry Petit, Sen........ | Do | 180.00 | S. C. Militia | Do | 71 | |
| John Searcy............ | Do | 90.00 | Va. Militia | Do | 66 | |
| Thomas Stovall......... | Do | 90.00 | N. C. Militia | Do | 75 | |
| Thomas Smith.......... | Do | 150.00 | N. C. Cont'l line | Do | 77 | |
| Reuben Treadwell....... | Do | 148.19 | N. C. Militia | Do | 82 | Died May 29, 1833 |
| Jacob Tack............. | Do | 90.00 | Va. Cont'l line | Do | 78 | |
| William Williams....... | Pri. Cav. and Inf. | 214.98 | N. C. Militia | Do | 77 | |
| Jonathan Wall.......... | Private | 81.00 | Do | Do | 90 | |
| Moses Waters.......... | Do | 150.00 | Do | Do | 73 | |
| William Weathers...... | Do | 150.00 | Do | Do | 76 | |
| James Withron.......... | Lt. and Capt. | 979.98 | Do | Do | 88 | |
| William Watson, Sen.... | Private | 94.65 | Do | Do | 75 | |

Above found in North Carolina Pension Roll pages 13, 111, 112 and 113.

## SAMPSON COUNTY, NORTH CAROLINA

| Name | Rank | Amount | Service | Date | Age | Notes |
|---|---|---|---|---|---|---|
| John Boykin | Pri. Inf. and Cav. | $ 56.25 | N. C. Militia | Mar. 4, 1831 | 70 | |
| Joseph Carter, Sen. | Private | 99.99 | N. C. Cont'l line | Do | 72 | |
| William Graney | Do | 50.00 | Va. Militia | Do | 76 | |
| William Hobbs | Do | 120.00 | N. C. Militia | Do | 92 | |
| William Hay | Do | 133.29 | N. C. Cont'l line | Do | 71 | |
| H. Hollingsworth, Sen. | Do | 238.74 | N. C. Militia | Do | 77 | |
| Zebedee Hollingsworth | Do | 127.50 | Do | Do | 73 | |
| Charles Jones | Do | 53.66 | Do | Do | 91 | Died Nov. 10, 1833 |
| Westbrook Lee | Do | 60.00 | Do | Do | 75 | |
| William Lewis | Private and Sergt. | 167.31 | N. C. Cont'l line | Do | 73 | |
| Christopher Manuel | Private | 66.65 | N. C. Militia | Do | 82 | |
| Daniel Merrett | Pri. Inf. and Cav. | 222.48 | Do | Do | 70 | |
| Bryan McCullen | Private | 90.00 | Do | Do | 78 | |
| John Peterson | Do | 51.10 | Do | Do | 84 | |
| Jeremiah Pope | Do | 90.00 | Do | Do | 85 | |
| John Register | Do | 30.82 | Do | Do | 81 | {Died Sept. 19, 1832 Cert. issued to the widow |
| Lot Rich | Do | 60.00 | N. C. Militia | Do | 79 | |
| John Register, Jr. | Do | — | Do | Do | 78 | |
| Peter Ryan | Do | — | Md. Militia | Do | 76 | |
| John Smith | Pri. Inf. and Cav. | 206.70 | N. C. Militia | Do | 84 | |
| Jeremiah Simmons | Private | 120.00 | Do | Do | 73 | |
| Joshua Tatom | Do | 53.32 | Do | Do | 77 | |
| Thomas Tart | Do | 90.00 | Do | Do | 73 | |
| James Thompson | Do | 169.98 | Do | Do | 80 | |
| Arthur D. Young | Do | 97.50 | Do | Do | 75 | |
| William Ward | Do | 240.00 | Do | Do | 81 | |
| John Wright, Sen. | Do | 169.98 | Do | Do | 75 | |
| Jacob Lockerman | Do | 60.00 | Do | Do | 76 | |

Above found in North Carolina Pension Roll pages 117 and 118.

## STOKES COUNTY, NORTH CAROLINA

| Name | Rank | Amount | Service | Date | Age | Notes |
|---|---|---|---|---|---|---|
| William Eaton | Sergeant | $ 95.74 | 1st Regt. U. S. Rifle | Jan. 15, 1814 | — | Act Mar. 16, 1802 |
| Do | Do | 933.65 | Do | Apr. 24, 1816 | — | Act Apr. 24, 1816 |
| Do | Do | 286.23 | Do | Mar. 12, 1830 | — | |

| Names | Rank | Sums received | Description of service | Commencement of pension | Ages | Laws under which they were formerly inscribed on the Pension Roll and remarks |
|---|---|---|---|---|---|---|
| James Larremore* | Private | $ 280.90 | Army of U. S. | Sept. 4, 1808 | 70 | Act Apr. 24, 1816 |
| Do | Do | 849.44 | Do | Apr. 24, 1816 | 84 | |
| Hezekiah Arnold | Do | 120.00 | N. C. Cont'l line | Mar. 4, 1831 | 81 | |
| Noah Bailey | Do | 240.00 | Va. Militia | Do | 84 | |
| Benjamin Banner | Do | 60.00 | N. C. Militia | Do | 81 | |
| Joseph Banner, Sen. | Do | 120.00 | Do | Do | 81 | |
| Ephriam Banner | Do | 139.98 | Do | Do | 76 | |
| Frederick Binkley | Do | 120.00 | Do | Do | 78 | |
| William Beck | Do | 69.99 | Do | Do | 72 | |
| Benjamin Clements | Private Cav. | 250.00 | Va. Militia | Do | 73 | |
| Ephraim Carter | Private | 75.00 | S. C. Militia | Do | 71 | |
| James Cox | Do | 60.00 | Va. Militia | Do | 82 | |
| Charles Davis | Do | 60.00 | N. C. Cont'l line | Do | 84 | |
| Joseph Darnall | Do | 60.00 | N. C. Militia | Do | 80 | |
| James Davis, Sen. | Pri. Inf. and Cav. | 56.66 | Do | Do | 70 | |
| Thomas Fears | Private Cav. | 200.00 | Va. Cont'l line | Do | 79 | |
| Mitchell Fulp, Sen. | Private | 74.64 | N. C. Militia | Do | 70 | |
| Lowell Frazier | Do | 60.00 | Do | Do | 70 | |
| Jacob Hilsabeck | Pri. Inf. and Cav. | 135.00 | S. C. Militia | Do | 73 | |
| Robert Hill, Sen. | Pri. Lt. and Capt. | 519.99 | Do | Do | 83 | |
| Howell Hartgrove | Private | 105.00 | Va. Militia | Do | 70 | |
| Edwin Hickman | Do | 87.99 | N. C. Militia | Do | 72 | |
| Edward Jones | Do | 240.00 | Va. Cont'l line | Do | 75 | |
| Thomas Jones | Do | 69.99 | Va. Militia | Do | 71 | |
| Samuel Jackson | Do | 60.00 | N. C. Militia | Do | 75 | |
| Jacob Idol | Do | 69.99 | Do | Do | 72 | |
| Benjamin Jones | Do | 139.98 | Va. Militia | Do | 81 | |
| George Kreger | Do | 43.32 | Cont'l line | Do | 75 | |
| Ephraim Lands | Do | 200.00 | Va. Militia | Do | 102 | |
| Jacob Lochenour | Do | 50.00 | N. C. Cont'l line | Do | 83 | |
| George Lochenour | Do | 50.00 | Do | Do | 78 | |
| James Larrimore | Ser. Pri. and Corp. | 250.00 | N. C. Militia | Do | 75 | |
| James Martin | Colonel | 1,209.90 | Do | Do | 92 | |
| Harmon McGee | Private | 83.32 | Va. Militia | Do | 74 | |

| Name | Rank | Annual Allowance | Description of Service | Commenced | Age | Remarks |
|---|---|---|---|---|---|---|
| Bryant Medley | Private and M's | 110.00 | N. C. Militia | Do | 84 | |
| Benjamin Marshall | Private | 180.00 | Va. Militia | Mar. 4, 1831 | 74 | |
| William Merritt | Pri. Inf. and Cav. | 76.65 | N. C. Cont'l line | Do | 71 | |
| John Maib, Sen. | Private | 63.33 | N. C. Militia | Do | 76 | |
| John Nicholson | Private and Lt. | 210.00 | Do | Do | 77 | |
| Henry Powers, Sen. | Pri. Inf. and Cav. | 144.48 | N. C. Cont'l line | Do | 98 | |
| David Poindexter | Private | 109.98 | Va. Cont'l line | Do | 71 | |
| James Patterson | Private and Sergt. | 104.16 | N. C. Militia | Do | 74 | |
| John Quillin | Private | 68.64 | Do | Do | 77 | |
| Stephen Ryerson | Do | 120.00 | N. Y. Militia | Do | 71 | |
| Thomas Ring, Sen. | Do | 64.98 | N. C. Cont'l line | Do | 76 | |
| John Riddle | Do | 74.54 | N. C. Militia | Do | 84 | |
| William Sands | Do | 83.32 | Va. Militia | Do | 80 | |
| John Snow | Do | 84.99 | N. C. Militia | Do | 74 | |
| Peter Smith | Do | 109.98 | Do | Do | 84 | |
| Christopher Stanley | Sergeant | 300.00 | Md. Cont'l line | Do | 76 | Died Oct. 25, 1832 Cert. issued in favor of widow |
| Casper Stultz, Sen. | Private | 83.32 | N. C. Militia | Do | 81 | |
| Samuel Stupe | Do | 76.56 | Do | Do | 77 | |
| Francis Steele, Sen. | Do | 200.00 | Va. Militia | Do | 76 | |
| William Southern, Sen. | Do | 81.00 | N. C. Militia | Do | 76 | |
| John Shaffer | Do | 109.98 | N. C. Cont'l line | Do | 72 | |
| Henry Tilling | Do | 56.95 | Do | Do | 80 | |
| William Young | Do | 90.00 | S. C. Militia | Do | 81 | Died Aug. 13, 1833 |
| Leonard Ziglar | Do | 106.32 | Va. Militia | Do | 72 | |
| John Venable | Do | 150.00 | N. C. Militia | Do | 72 | |
| John Ward | Do | 190.62 | Va. Militia | Do | 78 | |
| Joseph Welch | Do | 120.00 | N. C. Militia | Do | 85 | |
| John Whitworth | Do | 99.99 | Do | Do | 74 | |
| Lewis Wolf | Private and Fif. | 96.48 | Do | Do | 76 | |
| John Wilkins | Private | 74.64 | Do | Do | 93 | |

Above found in North Carolina Pension Roll pages 15, 113, 114 and 115.

## SURRY COUNTY, NORTH CAROLINA

| Name | Rank | | Annual Allowance | Description of Service | Commenced | | Acts |
|---|---|---|---|---|---|---|---|
| Edmund McKinney | Private | $ | 96.80 | 4th Regt. U. S. Rifle | Jan. 5, 1814 | — | Act Mar. 16, 1802 |
| Do | Do | | 562.02 | Do | Apr. 24, 1816 | | Act Apr. 24, 1816 |
| Do | Do | | 608.00 | Do | Sept. 4, 1824 | | Act Mar. 3, 1819 |

| Names | Rank | Sums received | Description of service | Commencement of pension | Ages | Laws under which they were formerly inscribed on the Pension Roll and remarks |
|---|---|---|---|---|---|---|
| John Pierce | Private | $ 137.68 | — | Jan. 7, 1814 | 71 | Act Mar. 16, 1802 |
| John Angel | Do | 1,666.92 | — | Apr. 24, 1816 | 77 | Act Apr. 24, 1816 |
| James Anthony | Pri. Inf. Cav. and Sergt. | 126.99 | N. C. Militia | Mar. 4, 1831 | 76 | |
| Thomas Bryant | Private | 240.00 | N. C. Cont'l line | Do | 88 | |
| William Barber | Private Art. | 250.00 | Va. Cont'l line | Do | 91 | |
| David Bray | Private | 60.00 | Va. Militia | Do | 81 | |
| David Cockerham | Private and Ensn. | 156.75 | N. C. Militia | Do | 76 | |
| Daniel Cockerham | Private | 60.00 | N. C. Militia | Do | 71 | |
| Peter Chinn | Do | 90.00 | Do | Do | 79 | |
| Robert Davis | Do | 60.00 | Va. Militia | Do | 72 | |
| Frederick Danner | Do | 160.00 | Va. Cont'l line | Do | 77 | |
| Christopher Eaton | Do | — | N. C. Cont'l line | Do | 71 | {Dropped from the roll Aug. 13, 1833 |
| James Forrester | Do | 62.64 | N. C. Militia | Do | 72 | |
| William Going | Do | — | Do | Do | 74 | |
| Daniel Hunt | Do | 120.00 | Do | Do | 86 | |
| Carter Hudspeth | Pri. of Artificers | 100.00 | N. C. Cont'l line | Do | 74 | |
| William Jean | Private | 70.00 | N. C. Militia | Do | 72 | |
| William Jenkins | Do | 240.00 | Va. Militia | Do | 72 | |
| William Lewis | Do | 129.99 | Do | Do | 78 | |
| Laban Lindsay | Sergeant | 90.00 | N. C. Militia | Do | 78 | |
| Bartholomew Marrion | Private | 59.06 | Do | Do | 94 | |
| Patrick McGuire | Do | — | N. C. Cont'l line | Do | 79 | Died July 10, 1833 |
| George Nix | Do | 240.00 | Va. Militia | Do | 74 | |
| Overton Phoenix | Do | 61.98 | Va. Cont'l line | Do | 70 | |
| Hezekiah Rhodes | Do | 50.00 | Va. Militia | Do | 86 | |
| John Riggs | Pri. Inf. and Cav. | 240.00 | Do | Do | 73 | |
| Morris Richards | Private | 240.00 | N. C. Cont'l line | Do | 75 | |
| John D. Reeves | Do | 206.64 | N. C. Militia | Do | 84 | |
| John Rose | Do | 120.00 | Do | Do | 74 | |
| Edward Smith | Pri. Inf. and Mar. | 60.33 | Do | Do | | Died Sept. 9, 1833 |

| Name | Rank | Amount | Service | Date | Age | Remarks |
|---|---|---|---|---|---|---|
| Barnabas Binzant | Private | 72.99 | N. J. Militia | | 79 | |
| Samuel Wallace | Do | 159.99 | N. C. Militia | Do | 94 | |
| Thomas Wright | Do | 210.00 | N. C. Cont'l line | Do | 75 | |
| Stephen Wood | Do | 50.00 | Va. Cont'l line | Do | 73 | |

Above found in North Carolina Pension Roll pages 15, 116 and 117.

## TYRRELL COUNTY, NORTH CAROLINA

| Name | Rank | Amount | Service | Date | Age | Remarks |
|---|---|---|---|---|---|---|
| Uriah Hudson | Private | $ 51.20 | 10th Regt. U.S. Inf. | Oct. 2, 1813 | — | Act Ex. mil. est. |
| Do | Do | 267.70 | Do | Apr. 24, 1816 | — | Act Apr. 24, 1816 |
| Aleazor Craddock | Do | 150.00 | N. C. Militia | Mar. 4, 1831 | 73 | |

Above found in North Carolina Pension Roll pages 16 and 118.

## WAKE COUNTY, NORTH CAROLINA

| Name | Rank | Amount | Service | Date | Age | Remarks |
|---|---|---|---|---|---|---|
| James Ames | Private | $1,628.29 | Army Rev. | Mar. 4, 1789 | — | Act Sept. 29, 1789; Died Jan. 8, 1828 |
| Do | Do | 1,138.89 | Do | Apr. 24, 1816 | — | Act Apr. 24, 1816 |
| James Christian | Do | 780.00 | — | Mar. 4, 1789 | — | Act Sept. 29, 1789; Died Mar. 28, 1815 |
| John Swenney | Do | 1,530.00 | — | Mar. 4, 1790 | — | Act Sept. 29, 1789 |
| Do | Do | | | Apr. 24, 1816 | — | Act Apr. 24, 1816 |
| Joel Terrell | Do | 94.04 | U. S. Army | Dec. 18, 1813 | 77 | Act Apr. 18, 1814 Dead |
| Do | Do | 87.25 | Do | Apr. 24, 1816 | 78 | Act Apr. 24, 1816 |
| Berthett Allen | Do | 66.00 | N. C. Militia | Mar. 4, 1831 | 75 | |
| James Adams | Do | 240.00 | Do | Do | 73 | |
| Philip Adams | Do | 240.00 | Do | Do | — | |
| Jacob Byrum | Do | 105.00 | Do | Do | 97 | |
| James Brown | Do | 130.32 | Do | Do | 76 | |
| Christopher Babb | Do | 60.00 | Do | Do | 73 | |
| Jesse Bryant | Pri. Inf. and Cav. | 165.38 | Va. Militia | Do | 68 | |
| William H. Burton | Private | 109.75 | N. C. Militia | Do | 83 | |
| William Clifton | Do | 69.99 | Do | Do | 72 | |
| John Green | Private | 100.00 | Do | Do | 78 | |
| James Hughes | Do | 240.00 | Va. Cont'l line | Do | 82 | |
| Vincent King | Pri. Inf. and Cav. | 184.98 | N. C. Militia | Do | 76 | |
| David Mabry | Private | 114.99 | Do | Do | — | |
| Naaman Mills | Do | 66.65 | Do | Do | — | |

| Names | Rank | Sums received | Description of service | Commencement of pension | Ages | Laws under which they were formerly inscribed on the Pension Roll and remarks |
|---|---|---|---|---|---|---|
| James Nance, Sen. | Pri. and Fif. | $ 105.99 | Va. Cont'l line | Mar. 4, 1831 | 72 | Died Jan. 14, 1834 |
| William Polk | Major | 1,566.44 | S. C. Cont'l line | Do | 76 | |
| Elisha Pope | Private | — | Va. Militia | Do | 73 | |
| James Rigsby | Do | 120.00 | N. C. Militia | Do | 71 | |
| Thomas Ross | Do | 120.00 | Do | Do | — | |
| John Rhodes | Do | 66.00 | Do | | 81 | |
| Aaron Roberts | Private | 144.00 | N. C. Militia | Mar. 4, 1831 | 79 | |
| Robert Sneed | Private Art. | 120.00 | Va. Cont'l line | Do | 75 | |
| Joseph Shaw | Private | 80.00 | Pa. Militia | Do | 77 | |
| Isaac Smith | Do | 90.00 | N. C. Militia | Do | 74 | |
| Samuel Standeford | Do | 79.98 | Va. Cont'l line | Do | 84 | |
| Sam'l Scarborough, Sen. | Do | 259.42 | Ca. Militia | Do | 74 | |
| Jonathan Smith, Sen. | Pr. and Capt. | 129.99 | N. C. Militia | Do | 81 | |
| John Sherron | Private | 153.56 | Do | Do | 91 | |
| William Tate | Private Cav. | 79.98 | Do | Do | 79 | Died Oct. 17, 1832 |
| Nathan Upchurch | Private | 120.00 | Do | Do | 74 | |
| William Wilder | Do | 135.00 | Do | Do | 86 | |
| Burrell Whitehead | Pri. Cav. and Inf. | 117.66 | Do | Do | 82 | |
| John Walker | Private | 300.00 | Do | Do | 77 | |
| John Williams | Private Cav. | 112.33 | Do | Do | 89 | |
| Jesse Wall | Pri. Inf. and Cav. | | Do | Do | 80 | Died Feb. 1, 1834 |

Above found in North Carolina Pension Roll pages 16, 122 and 123.

WARREN COUNTY, NORTH CAROLINA

| | | | | | | |
|---|---|---|---|---|---|---|
| Elijah Brainard | Private | $1,663.72 | Col. Sage'sm. Regt. | Nov. 6, 1809 | — | Act Apr. 27, 1810 Trans from Mass. from Mar. 4, 1827 Died May 23, 1828 |
| Do | Do | 96.00 | Do | Mar. 4, 1827 | 95 | |
| William Askew | Do | 69.99 | N. C. Militia | Mar. 4, 1831 | 74 | |
| Augustas Balthrop | Do | — | Do | Do | | |

| | | | | | | |
|---|---|---|---|---|---|---|
| William Casey | Do | Do | 240.00 | Do | 73 | |
| Burrell Davis | Do | Do | 53.32 | Do | 78 | |
| John Dawton | Do | Do | 60.00 | Do | 74 | |
| Thomas Hilliard, 1st | Do | Do | 60.00 | Do | 72 | |
| Roben Harris | Do | Do | 60.00 | Do | 75 | |
| Thomas Hilliard, 2d | Do | Do | — | Do | 72 | |
| David King | Do | Do | 51.35 | Aug. 23, 1819 | 72 | {Mar. 18, 1818 Dropped under Act May 1, 1820 |
| Do | Do | N. C. Cont'l line | 120.00 | Mar. 4, 1831 | 72 | |
| Nathaniel Laffoon | Do | Do | 73.59 | Do | 88 | |
| Francis Riggan | Do | N. C. Militia | 60.00 | Do | 70 | |
| Jesse Stegal | Do | Do | 180.00 | Do | 78 | |
| Henry Southall | Do | Do | 90.00 | Do | 71 | |
| Frederic Shearin | Do | Do | 69.99 | Do | 73 | |
| Joseph Wren | Do | Do | 41.53 | Do | 76 | Died Apr. 1, 1833 |
| William Williamson | Private | N. C. Militia | 147.35 | Aug. 23, 1819 | 78 | {Mar. 18, 1818 Dropped under Act May 1, 1820 |
| Do | Do | N. C. Cont'l line | 240.00 | Mar. 4, 1831 | 78 | |
| John Wadkins | Do | Do | 99.99 | Do | 72 | |
| John L. Ward | Do | N. C. Militia | 139.98 | Do | 71 | |

Above found in North Carolina Pension Roll pages 17 and 119.

## WASHINGTON COUNTY, NORTH CAROLINA

| | | | | | |
|---|---|---|---|---|---|
| Nathaniel Everett | Private | N. C. Cont'l line | $ 90.00 | Mar. 4, 1831 | 71 |

Above found in North Carolina Pension Roll page 123.

## WAYNE COUNTY, NORTH CAROLINA

| | | | | | |
|---|---|---|---|---|---|
| David Edwards | Private | N. C. Militia | $ 120.00 | Mar. 4, 1831 | 71 |
| William Farrell | Do | N. C. Cont'l line | 90.00 | Do | 79 |
| John Howell | Private Cav. | N. C. Militia | 171.00 | Do | 80 |
| George Jerningan | Pri. Inf. Ser. Drag. | Do | 100.50 | Do | 73 |
| Jethro Odon | Private | Do | 60.00 | Do | 87 |
| Mitchell Revell | Do | S. C. Militia | 50.00 | Do | 74 |
| Ezekiel Slocumb | Private and Sergt. | N. C. Militia | 237.40 | Do | 74 |
| Benjamin Smith | Private | Do | 240.00 | Do | 75 |

| Names | Rank | Sums received | Description of service | Commencement of pension | Ages | Laws under which they were formerly inscribed on the Pension Roll and remarks |
|---|---|---|---|---|---|---|
| Jesse Spencer | Private | $ 105.00 | Va. Militia | Mar. 4, 1831 | 73 | |
| Nehimiah Tolar | Pri. Inf. and Cav. | 72.90 | N. C. Militia | Do | 95 | |
| John Wiggs | Do | 92.13 | Do | Do | 76 | |

Above found in North Carolina Pension Roll page 121.

## WILKES COUNTY, NORTH CAROLINA

| Names | Rank | Sums received | Description of service | Commencement of pension | Ages | Laws under which they were formerly inscribed on the Pension Roll and remarks |
|---|---|---|---|---|---|---|
| Samuel Johnson* | Private | $ 438.94 | Army Rev. | Jan. 1, 1809 | — | Act Apr. 24, 1816 |
| Do | Do | 1,738.89 | Do | Apr. 24, 1816 | 82 | (Died Oct. 10, 1832 Cert. issued in favor of the heirs. |
| William Alexander | Do | 90.00 | N. C. Militia | Mar. 4, 1831 | 92 | |
| Richard Allen | Private and Capt. | — | N. C. Cont'l line | Do | | |
| John Bryan | Sergt. Ensn. Lt. and Capt. | 210.99 | Pa. Militia | Do | 81 | |
| Jasper Billings | Private | 74.64 | N. C. Militia | Do | 75 | |
| Robert Bryant | Do | 111.10 | Do | Do | 79 | |
| Thomas Bratherton | Pri. Inf. and Cav. | 247.50 | Do | Do | 78 | |
| Job Cole | Private | 114.00 | Md. Militia | Do | 90 | |
| Joseph Chapman | Do | 180.00 | N. C. Militia | Do | 84 | |
| John Church | Do | — | Do | Do | 74 | |
| Amos Church | Do | — | Do | Do | 76 | |
| Isham Dickeson | Do | 90.00 | Do | Do | 70 | |
| Anthony Foster | Private and Sergt. | 118.68 | Va. Cont'l line | Do | 75 | |
| Thomas Fletcher | Private | 240.00 | Va. Militia | Do | 74 | |
| Alexander Gilbreath | Private and Sergt. | 107.31 | N. C. Militia | Do | 78 | |
| James Gray | Private | 63.32 | Do | Do | 70 | |
| William Gilbreath | Private and Capt. | 390.00 | Va. Cont'l line | Do | 81 | |
| Benjamin Hammons | Private | 65.54 | N. C. Militia | Do | 78 | |
| William Johnson | Do | 69.33 | Do | Do | 83 | |
| William Johnson | Pri. and Ensn. | 146.97 | Va. Militia | Do | 80 | |
| George Johnson, Sen. | Private | 63.30 | Do | Do | 85 | |

| Name | Rank | Amount | Service | | Age | Remarks |
|---|---|---|---|---|---|---|
| David Laws | Do | 50.00 | N. C. Cont'l line | Do | 79 | |
| William Lenoir | Pri. Lt. and Capt. | 699.27 | N. C. Cont'l line | Do | 83 | |
| John Love | Private | 79.98 | Do | Do | 73 | |
| John Montgomery | Do | 60.00 | Va. Militia | Do | 78 | |
| William Powell | Do | 90.00 | N. C. Militia | Do | 74 | |
| Elisha Reynolds | Private and Lt. | 226.65 | Do | Do | 80 | |
| Sterling Rose | Corpl. and Sergt. | 178.17 | N. C. Cont'l line | Do | 77 | |
| William Spicer | Private | 175.35 | Va. Militia | Do | 79 | |
| Joel Stamper | Do | 96.99 | N. C. Militia | Do | 78 | |
| John Swanson | Do | 159.99 | Do | Do | 73 | |
| James Smoot | Do | 129.99 | Va. Cont'l line | Do | 70 | |
| John Sparks | Do | 87.00 | N. C. Militia | Do | 81 | |
| Winburn Sumerlin | Do | 79.99 | Do | Do | 72 | |
| Elijah Vickes | Do | 206.75 | Do | Do | 75 | |
| Moses Watters | Do | 79.98 | Do | Do | 81 | |
| Jacob Wall | Do | 121.98 | N. C. Cont'l line | Do | 85 | Died Feb. 26, 1834 |

Above found in North Carolina Pension Roll pages 17, 120 and 121.

## YANCEY COUNTY, NORTH CAROLINA

| Name | Rank | Amount | Service | | Age | Remarks |
|---|---|---|---|---|---|---|
| Zephaniah Horton | Private | $ 60.00 | N. J. Militia | Mar. 4, 1831 | 74 | |
| Jonathan McPeters | Do | 240.00 | N. C. Militia | Do | 78 | |

Above found in North Carolina Pension Roll page 123.

A list of the Invalid Pensioners who have been inscribed on the roll of North Carolina Agency, and whose residence, and other information called for by the Resolution of the Senate, cannot be ascertained, in consequence of the destruction of the papers in the War Office, in 1801 and 1814.

| Name | Rank | Amount | | | Remarks | |
|---|---|---|---|---|---|---|
| John Beaty | Private | $ — | | Mar. 4, 1789 | | Dead |
| William Caps | Do | 320.00 | | Do | | Act Sept. 29 1789 Dead |
| James Carrigan | Do | 36.00 | | | | |
| Do | Do | 57.60 | | | | |
| Samuel Carter | Do | 24.00 | | | | |
| Do | Do | 38.40 | | | | |
| James Campin | Lieut. | 551.48 | | Mar. 21, 1809 | | Act Mar. 3, 1811 Dead |
| Samuel Freeman | Private | 125.00 | | Sept. 4, 1808 | | |
| Do | Do | 38.40 | | — | | |

| Names | Rank | Sums received | Description of service | Commencement of pension | Ages | Laws under which they were formerly inscribed on the Pension Roll and remarks |
|---|---|---|---|---|---|---|
| Robert Harris............ | Private | $ 392.13 | — | Sept. 4, 1797 | — | Died Mar. 16, 1804 |
| Daniel Houston.......... | Do | 36.00 | — | — | — | |
| Do | Do | 86.40 | — | — | — | Dead, time unknown |
| William Kersey......... | Do | 60.00 | — | — | — | Died Jan. 15, 1804 |
| John Knowles.......... | Do | 591.97 | — | Mar. 4, 1794 | — | Dead |
| William Moor.......... | Do | 189.00 | — | Mar. 4, 1789 | — | Dead |
| Paul Mecham........... | Do | 187.50 | — | Mar. 4, 1790 | — | |
| Daniel McKissick........ | Captain | 2,760.00 | — | Mar. 4, 1795 | — | |
| Robert Robinson........ | Private | 60.00 | — | — | — | Dead |
| Daniel Shaw........... | Do | 390.00 | — | Mar. 4, 1789 | — | Dead |
| Joseph Singletary....... | Lieut. | 160.00 | — | — | — | |
| Joseph Sapp........... | Private | 60.00 | — | — | — | Died 1797 |
| Richard Treasure....... | Do | 120.00 | — | — | — | {Trans. from Md. {Died 1803 |
| Philip Thomas.......... | Sergeant | 180.00 | — | Sept. 4, 1793 | — | |
| Do | Do | 96.00 | — | — | — | |
| Benjamin Ward......... | Do | 136.72 | — | Aug. 22, 1814 | — | |

*William Avis. Remarks—No information respecting the residence of this man can be had. He has never drawn any money and is probably dead.

Above found in North Carolina Pension Roll page 18.

The residence of the following named persons was not ascertained until after the list embracing the counties in which they reside had been prepared for the press.

| Names | Rank | Sums received | Description of service | Commencement of pension | Ages | Laws under which they were formerly inscribed on the Pension Roll and remarks |
|---|---|---|---|---|---|---|
| Warren Benton............. | Private | $ 148.52 | 7th Regt. U. S. Inf. | May 29, 1816 | — | Act mil. est. Resided in Wilkes Died July 1, 1819 |
| John Guthrie............. | Do | 649.22 | U. S. Army | Sept. 4, 1794 | — | Act June 7, 1785. Trans. from Ga. Sept. 4, 1821 |
| Do | Do | 257.42 | Do | Apr. 24, 1816 | — | Act Apr. 24, 1816. Resided in Buncombe Co. No. Car. |

| Name | Rank | Amount | Regiment | Date | | Remarks |
|---|---|---|---|---|---|---|
| James Houston........... | Captain | 2,310.00 | Do | Oct. 3, 1806 | — | {Act Mar. 3, 1807 / Died Aug. 2, 1819} |
| David Holton........... | Private | 46.00 | N. C. Militia | July 1, 1818 | — | Resided in Craven Co. |
| William Lefever........ | Do | 27.71 | 10th Regt. U.S. Inf. | Sept. 5, 1815 | — | Act mil. est. Resided in Burke Co. |
| Do | Do | 151.25 | Do | Apr. 24, 1816 | — | Act Apr. 24, 1816 |
| Alexander Morrison......... | Sergeant | 941.07 | — | Mar. 4, 1790 | — | Act Sept. 29, 1789. Resided in Cumberland Co. |
| Do | Do | 178.89 | — | Apr. 24, 1816 | — | Act Apr. 24, 1816 |
| Sullivan Newell........... | Private | 139.28 | 2d Regt. U. S. Inf. | Sept. 28, 1815 | — | {Act mil. est. Resided in Currituck County} |
| Humphrey Rogers........... | Do | 461.88 | — | Sept. 5, 1808 | — | {Act mil. est. Resided in Anson Co. Dead} |
| Do | Do | 130.92 | — | Apr. 24, 1816 | — | Act Apr. 24, 1816 |
| Ithamer Singletary.......... | Do | 317.10 | — | Mar. 4, 1795 | — | Act June 7, 1785 |
| Do | Do | 92.72 | — | Apr. 24, 1816 | — | {Act Apr. 24, 1816. Resided in Bladen Co.} |

Above found in North Carolina Pension Roll page 19.

A statement of names, &c. of heirs of non-commissioned officers, privates, &c. who died in the
United States Service; who obtained five years' half pay in lieu of Bounty Land under the
Second Section of the Act of April 16, 1816, and who resided in the County of Anson in the
State of North Carolina.

| Names of the original claimants | Rank | Description of service | Time of decease | Names of heirs |
|---|---|---|---|---|
| Eli Brooks.......... | Private | 10th Regt. Inf. | June 1814 | Abraham and Ruthy Brooks.......... |

### COUNTY OF CHATHAM, NORTH CAROLINA

| Name of the original claimants | Rank | Description of service | Time of decease | Names of heirs |
|---|---|---|---|---|
| Azel or Asel Myrick . | Private | 10th Regt. Inf. | Nov. 1813 | Wm. Tyson and Eliz. Myrick...... |

Above found in North Carolina Pension Roll page 20.

### COUNTY OF CUMBERLAND, NORTH CAROLINA

| Names of the original claimants | Rank | Description of service | Time of decease | Names of heirs |
|---|---|---|---|---|
| Timothy Bass....... | Private | 3d Regt. Rifle | Feb. 28, 1815 | Lovedy and Wm. Madison Bass..... |
| Francis Potts....... | Do | 20th Regt. Inf. | Oct. 31, 1814 | Lenan, Eliz., and Francis Potts..... |
| William Ramsay.... | Do | 3d Regt. Rifle | Mar. 19, 1815 | Thos, John and Mary Ramsay.... |

Above found in North Carolina Pension Roll page 21.

### COUNTY OF HALIFAX, NORTH CAROLINA

| Name of the original claimants | Rank | Description of service | Time of decease | Names of heirs |
|---|---|---|---|---|
| James Amos........ | Private | 35th Regt. Inf. | Feb.  1, 1815 | Martha and Chas. Amos........... |
| Claiborne Baker..... | Do | 10th Regt. Inf. | Nov. 30, 1814 | Wm., Maria Lucretia & Claiborne Baker |
| Robert Freear...... | Do | Do | Jan. 18, 1814 | Henry and Jas. Freear........... |
| John Hardy........ | Corporal | 35th Regt. Inf. | Feb. 18, 1815 | Louisa, Henrietta, Whitwell, Carolina, Lavinia and Fanny Hardy........... |
| Miles Zills or Sills... | Private | Do | Dec. 16, 1814 | Thos., Joseph and Everit Zills....... |

Above found in North Carolina Pension Roll page 21.

A statement of names, &c. of heirs of non-commissioned officers, **Privates, &c. who died in the** United States Service; who obtained five years' half pay in lieu of **Bounty Land under the** Second Section of the Act of April, 16 1816, and who resided in the **County of Anson in the** State of North Carolina.

| Annual allowance | Sums received | When placed on roll | Commencement of pension | Ending of pension |
|---|---|---|---|---|
| $48.00 | $240.00 | Jan. 6, 1819 | Feb. 17, 1815 | Feb. 17, 1820 |

## COUNTY OF CHATHAM, NORTH CAROLINA

| Annual allowance | Sums received | When placed on roll | Commencement of pension | Ending of pension |
|---|---|---|---|---|
| $48.00 | $240.00 | Mar. 14, 1820 | Feb. 15, 1820 | Feb. 15, 1825 |

Above found in North Carolina Pension Roll page 20.

## COUNTY OF CUMBERLAND, NORTH CAROLINA

| Annual allowance | Sums received | When placed on roll | Commencement of pension | Ending of pension |
|---|---|---|---|---|
| $48.00 | $240.00 | May  1, 1818 | Feb. 17, 1815 | Feb. 17, 1820 |
| 48.00 | 240.00 | Jan. 14, 1822 | Dec.  7, 1821 | Dec.  7, 1826 |
| 48.00 | 240.00 | Apr. 18, 1818 | Feb. 17, 1815 | Feb. 17, 1820 |

Above found in North Carolina Pension Roll page 21.

## COUNTY OF HALIFAX, NORTH CAROLINA

| Annual allowance | Sums received | When placed on roll | Commencement of pension | Ending of pension |
|---|---|---|---|---|
| $40.00 | $240.00 | Mar.  5, 1819 | Feb. 17, 1815 | Feb. 17, 1820 |
| 48.00 | 240.00 | Jan. 18, 1820 | Dec. 24, 1819 | Dec. 24, 1824 |
| 48.00 | 240.00 | Mar. 16, 1818 | Feb. 17, 1815 | Feb. 17, 1820 |
| 60.00 | 300.00 | Feb. 16, 1819 | Do | Do |
| 48.00 | 240.00 | Jan. 25, 1819 | Do | Do |

Above found in North Carolina Pension Roll page 21.

## COUNTY OF HERTFORD, NORTH CAROLINA

| Names of the original claimants | Rank | Description of service | Time of decease | Names of heirs |
|---|---|---|---|---|
| Roderick Boon...... | Private | 20th Regt. Inf. | Jan. 29, 1815 | Betsey, Cynthia, Patterson, Mary, Martha Boone.... |
| Benjamin Weston... | Do | Do | Mar. 1, 1814 | Uriah and Nancy Weston.......... |

Above found in North Carolina Pension Roll page 22.

## COUNTY OF LINCOLN, NORTH CAROLINA

| Name of the original claimants | Rank | Description of service | Time of decease | Names of heirs |
|---|---|---|---|---|
| John German....... | Private | 10th Regt. Inf. | Nov. 5, 1814 | Fanny, Levi and Betsy German.... |

## PERSON COUNTY, NORTH CAROLINA

| Names of the original claimants | Rank | Description of service | Time of decease | Names of heirs |
|---|---|---|---|---|
| Lewis Frederick..... | Private | 10th Regt. Inf. | 1814 | Betsy, Jane, Polly, Sally, Susanna & Lewis Frederick... |

Above found in North Carolina Pension Roll page 22.

## WAKE COUNTY, NORTH CAROLINA

| Name of the original claimants | Rank | Description of service | Time of decease | Names of heirs |
|---|---|---|---|---|
| Benjamin Deberry... | Private | 25th Regt. Inf. | Dec. 2, 1814 | Jemmy, Judy and Benj. Deberry.... |
| Abingdon Wade..... | Do | 2d Regt. Art. | Aug. 18, 1813 | Esther and Isham Wade............ |

Above found in North Carolina Pension Roll page 23.

## WAYNE COUNTY, NORTH CAROLINA

| Name of the original claimants | Rank | Description of service | Time of decease | Names of heirs |
|---|---|---|---|---|
| Noah Hedgepeth.... | Private | 11th Regt. Inf. | June 2, 1814 | Henry, Chilly, Noah, and Arcadia Hedgepeth....... |

## COUNTY UNKNOWN, NORTH CAROLINA

| Names of the original claimants | Rank | Description of service | Time of decease | Names of heirs |
|---|---|---|---|---|
| Thomas Gregory.... | Private | 1st Regt. Rifle | 1814 | Isaac, Samuel, Noah, and Benj. H. Gregory.......... |

Above found in North Carolina Pension Roll page 23.

## COUNTY OF HERTFORD, NORTH CAROLINA

| Annual allowance | Sums received | When placed on roll | Commencement of pension | Ending of pension |
|---|---|---|---|---|
| $48.00 | $240.00 | July 31, 1818 | Feb. 17, 1815 | Feb. 17, 1820 |
| 48.00 | 240.00 | Do | Do | Do |

Above found in North Carolina Pension Roll page 22.

## COUNTY OF LINCOLN, NORTH CAROLINA

| Annual allowance | Sums received | When placed on roll | Commencement of pension | Ending of pension |
|---|---|---|---|---|
| $48.00 | $240.00 | Dec. 12, 1820 | Feb. 17, 1820 | Feb. 17, 1825 |

## PERSON COUNTY, NORTH CAROLINA

| Annual allowance | Sums received | When placed on roll | Commencement of pension | Ending of pension |
|---|---|---|---|---|
| $48.00 | $240.00 | Mar. 5, 1818 | Feb. 17, 1815 | Feb. 17, 1820 |

Above found in North Carolina Pension Roll page 22.

## WAKE COUNTY, NORTH CAROLINA

| Annual allowance | Sums received | When placed on roll | Commencement of pension | Ending of pension |
|---|---|---|---|---|
| $48.00 | $240.00 | Mar. 31, 1820 | Feb. 24, 1820 | Feb. 27, 1825 |
| 48.00 | 240.00 | May 12, 1820 | May 17, 1820 | May 17, 1825 |

Above found in North Carolina Pension Roll page 23.

## WAYNE COUNTY, NORTH CAROLINA

| Annual allowance | Sums received | When placed on roll | Commencement of pension | Ending of pension |
|---|---|---|---|---|
| $48.00 | $240.00 | Dec. 11, 1819 | Feb. 17, 1815 | Feb. 17, 1820 |

## COUNTY UNKNOWN, NORTH CAROLINA

| Annual allowance | Sums received | When placed on roll | Commencement of pension | Ending of pension |
|---|---|---|---|---|
| $48.00 | $240.00 | Sept. 18, 1819 | Feb. 17, 1815 | Feb. 15, 1820 |

Above found in North Carolina Pension Roll page 23.

## REFERENCE PAGES

| Counties | Manuscript Pages | N. C. Pension Roll Pages |
|---|---|---|
| Anson.................................... | 1 | 2 and 60 |
| Ashe..................................... | 1 | 2 and 60 |
| Beaufort................................. | 2 | 65 |
| Bladen................................... | 2 | 3 and 64 |
| Brunswick................................ | 5 | 63 |
| Buncombe................................. | 3 | 3, 65, 66 and 67 |
| Burke.................................... | 4 and 5 | 61 and 62 |
| Cabarrus................................. | 5 and 6 | 6 and 72 |
| Carteret................................. | 6 | 73 |
| Camden................................... | 5 | 5 and 68 |
| Caswell.................................. | 6 and 7 | 4, 70 and 71 |
| Chatham.................................. | 7 and 8 | 69 |
| Chowan................................... | 8 | 5 and 75 |
| Columbus................................. | 8 and 9 | 74 |
| Craven................................... | 9 | 4 and 71 |
| Cumberland............................... | 10 | 6, 67 and 68 |
| Currituck................................ | 11 | 73 |
| Davidson................................. | 11 and 12 | 77 and 78 |
| Duplin................................... | 12 and 13 | 75 and 76 |
| Edgecombe................................ | 13 | 78 and 79 |
| Franklin................................. | 14 | 79 and 80 |
| Gates.................................... | 14 | 7 and 82 |
| Granville................................ | 14 and 15 | 7, 83 and 84 |
| Greene................................... | 15 | 82 |
| Guilford................................. | 16 and 17 | 8, 80 and 81 |
| Halifax.................................. | 17 | 84 and 85 |
| Haywood.................................. | 17 | 86 |
| Hertford................................. | 18 | 86 |
| Hyde..................................... | 18 | 85 |
| Iredell.................................. | 18, 19 and 20 | 8, 86, 87 and 88 |
| Jones.................................... | 20 | 9 and 90 |
| Johnston................................. | 20 | 89 |
| Lenoir................................... | 21 | 10, 92 and 93 |
| Lincoln.................................. | 21 and 22 | 9, 90, 91, and 92 |
| Macon.................................... | 23 | 97 |
| Martin................................... | 23 | 11 and 98 |
| Mecklenberg.............................. | 23, 24 and 25 | 11, 93, 94 and 95 |
| Montgomery............................... | 25 and 26 | 10, 95 and 96 |
| Moore.................................... | 26 | 96 |
| Nash..................................... | 27 | 12 and 98 |
| New Hanover.............................. | 27 | 98 |
| Northampton.............................. | 28 | 12 and 100 |
| Onslow................................... | 28 | 103 |
| Orange................................... | 28 and 29, 30 | 13, 100, 101 and 102 |
| Pasquotank............................... | 30 | 106 |
| Perquimans............................... | 30 | 105 |
| Person................................... | 31 | 103 and 104 |
| Pitt..................................... | 31 and 32 | 104 and 105 |
| Randolph................................. | 32 | 109 |
| Richmond................................. | 32 and 33 | 108 |
| Robeson.................................. | 33 | 14 and 110 |
| Rockingham............................... | 33 and 34 | 110 and 111 |
| Rowan.................................... | 34 and 35 | 14, 106 and 107 |
| Rutherford............................... | 35, 36 and 37 | 13, 111, 112 and 113 |
| Sampson.................................. | 37 | 117 and 118 |
| Stokes................................... | 38 and 39 | 15, 113, 114 and 115 |

| Counties | Manuscript Pages | N. C. Pension Roll Pages |
|---|---|---|
| Surry............................. | 40 and 41 | 15, 116 and 117 |
| Tyrrell............................ | 41 | 16 and 118 |
| Wake............................. | 41 and 42 | 16, 122 and 123 |
| Warren............................ | 42 and 43 | 17 and 119 |
| Washington........................ | 43 | 123 |
| Wayne............................ | 43 | 121 |
| Wilkes............................ | 43 and 44 | 17, 120 and 121 |
| Yancey............................ | 44 | 123 |

Miscellaneous

| Counties | Manuscript Pages | N. C. Pension Roll Pages |
|---|---|---|
| Invalid Pensioners..................... | 45 and 46 | 18 and 19 |
| Names and heirs of non-commissioned officer.... | 47 and 48 | 20, 21, 22 and 23 |
|  | 49 50 |  |

# APPENDIX

# THE KING'S MOUNTAIN MEN

Katherine Keogh White.

*"I recommend the use of this list in your roster"*

Mrs. Van Orsdell, Registrar Gen., Washington, D. C.

* Fincastle and Tryon counties no longer exist; each named in honor of a royal Governor, but as these governors sided with Great Britain, in the war for American Independence, the names were abolished, by the expedient of subdividing the two counties. Fincastle was divided into the counties of Montgomery, Washington and Kentucky. Tryon being divided into Lincoln and Rutherford.

*Pages*

157. John Childers   } From Wilkes Co.
157. Mitchell Childers
158. John Chittim, pensioned in Lincoln Co., N. C.
158. James Clark, pensioned in Lincoln Co., N. C.
158. Michael Clark, pensioned in Lincoln Co., N. C.
159. Benjamin Cleveland, commanded the men from Surry and Wilkes Co., at King's Mtn.
159. Robert Cleveland, died in Wilkes Co. in 1812
159. Samuel Clowney, settled on the Catawba
161. James Collins, from Lincoln Co.
161. Samuel Collins, from Lincoln Co.
162. William Cook, in the Surry troops under Cleveland
162. Charles Cook   } pensioned in N. C., claimed by descendants
162. Edward Cook     to have served at King's Mtn.
162. Robert Cook
162. Thomas Costner, received pension in Lincoln Co., 1833
162. Martin Coulter, of Surry Co., pensioned in Lincoln Co., 1833
162. Thomas Cowan, born in Rowan Co.
162. William Cox, living on Watauga in 1775.
163. James Cozby (or Cosby), regimental surgeon under Sevier
164. Joseph Crockett, Capt. of militia
164. Walter Crockett, Maj.   } of Fincastle County
164. William Crockett, in militia
164. John Crockett, father of Davy Crockett, was with the militia from Lincoln Co.
166. John Crow, commanded a company from Fincastle at Point Pleasant
166. George Dameron, pensioned in Lincoln Co.
166. Lawrence Darnell, surveyor, went to Fincastle in 1774.
167. Benjamin Davidson   } home at Davidson's Fort, in the
167. William Davidson     extreme west of Burke Co.
167. John Davis, Capt.
167. Nathaniel Davis
167. Samuel Davis   }
167. Robert Davis     all owned land in Fincastle Co. in 1774
167. Joel Davis   }
167. Nathan Davis   pensioned by N. C.
168. Joseph Dickson, commanded a company of Lincoln Co. men
168. Joseph Dickson, of Rowan Co., a Major at King's Mtn.
169. Joseph Dixon (Dickson)   }
169. John Dixon (Dickson)     of the N. C. Line
169. Joel Dixon (Dickson)   }
169. Rev. Samuel Doak of Watauga   }
169. Jesse Duncan, in Cleveland's Regt.   } Watauga County
169. Joseph Duncan, Sevier's
169. John Duncan
170. Peter Eddlemon, in Lincoln Co. regiment and pensioned in Lincoln Co., 1835
170. William Elmore, pensioned in N. C.
171. Benjamin Estill, one of the first justices of Fincastle
171. Samuel Espey, living in Lincoln Co., in 1770; wounded at King's Mountain
171. James Ewart   } in N. C. Line
171. Robert Ewart
171. James Farewell, with Lincoln Co. men
172. Edmund Fear, from Burke Co.
172. Thomas Fear, of N. C. Line, pensioned but name does not appear in the battle roll

*Pages*
173. James Gaines, Sr., pensioned in N. C., in 1833
174. Harris Gammon, in militia of Washington Co., N. C.
174. John Goss, of militia, Washington Co., N. C., Sergt. under Sevier
174. Thomas Gillespie } settled on Watauga in 1772
174. George Gillespie }
175. Devereux Gilliam, early settler in the fork at the mouth of the French Broad
175-176. Enoch Gilmer } brothers from Lincoln Co.
175-176. William Gilmer }
176. Benjamin Gist, a justice of Washington Co., in 1778, Capt. in its militia in 1780
177. Joseph Godwin } from Lincoln Co.,
177. Robinson Godwin } pensioned in Lincoln in 1833
177. Samuel Godwin }
177. Preston Goforth, in the Rutherford troops under Col. Hampton and was killed by brother who was on tory side.
177. Charles Gordon, native of Va., who moved to Wilkes Co., N. C., where he became a Maj. of militia.
178. Chapman Gordon } in the N. C. troops
178. George Gordon }
178. Thomas Gourley (also Gorly and Gorely) early settler on the Watauga
178. Col. William Graham, born in Va., moved to Shelby Co., N. C., where he died in 1835
178. James Gray, from Rutherford
178. Jesse Green, early settler in Watauga
178. Alexander Greer, early settler in Watauga
179. John Gregory } of Lincoln Co., pensioned there in 1833
179. William Gregory }
179. Nathan Gwaltney, from Lincoln, pensioned in 1833
180. Nicholas Hafner (Hofner), pensioned in Lincoln, 1833
180. Simon Hager, pensioned in Lincoln, 1833
180. John Haile, early settler at Watauga
180-181. Frederick Hambright, before the Revolution, moved to Long Creek in Tryon County
182. Andrew Hampton, born in England, but in 1751 was living in Rutherford Co., N. C.; Capt. in 1776; Col. in 1779
182. Edward Hampton, a brother and a Capt.
182. Jonathan Hampton, with Rutherford troops
182. Capt. Samuel Handly, born in N. C.
184. Robert Hansley, in N. C. militia
184. William Hansley, in Albemarle militia, was not at King's Mtn.
184. John Harrell }
184. Joseph Harrell } pensioned by North Carolina
184. Kidder Harrell }
184. James Harris, born in N. C., 1736
186. John Helm, in Lincoln militia, pensioned in Lincoln in 1833. It is a family tradition that he was in the battle of King's Mtn.
186. Abraham Helton, of N. C. militia
186. Conrad Henniger, on the Middle Fork of Hokton in Fincastle in 1774
186. Henry Henry }
186. James Henry } brothers living in Gaston Co., N. C.
186. Moses Henry }
188. James Hill, from Lincoln
189. Daniel Horton }
189. Henry Horton } early Watauga settlers
189. Joshua Horton }

*Pages*

189. Zephaniah Horton, pensioned in N. C., but his application does not say whether he was in the battle of King's Mtn.
191. David Hughes ⎫
191. Francis Hughes ⎬ early Watauga settlers
191. Thomas Hughes ⎭
191. Thomas Hunter, from Gaston Co.
192. Zachary Isbell, early Watauga settler
192. Jeremiah Jack, Watauga settler
193. William Jackson, Capt.
193. George Jarnigan (Jernigan), Lt., pensioned by N. C. in 1844
194. James Johnson, born in Lincoln Co., 1742.
194. Robert Johnston (Johnstone), pensioned by N. C., 1835, privt.
194. Capt. William Johnstone, pensioned in N. C.
195. Daniel Jones, of N. C.
195. John Jones, a Watauga rifleman
195. Robert Karr (Carr), lived in what is now Greene Co., N. C.
196. Robert Kennedy, mentioned by Heitman as a Capt. in the N. C. service
196. Henry Kerby, in N. C. militia
196. Joseph Kerr, born in Pennsylvania, the family moved to N. C. when he was very young.
197. John Kidd, with the Lincoln men and was pensioned
198. Robert Knox, in militia of Lincoln Co., N. C., pensioned in 1833
198. Benjamin Knox
198. James Knox ⎱
198. Samuel Knox ⎰ on N. C. pension list
198. Tidence Lane, born 1764, was in N. C. Line
199. George Ledbetter, Capt. of Rutherford troops
199. James Lee, born in Va., settled at High Shoals, N. C.
199. James Leeper, moved to Davidson Co. in the the winter of 1780-81, and was a Capt. on the border.
200. Shadrach Lefy, Lincoln Co. man, and pensioner
200. Maj. Micajah Lewis, born in Va., 1755, moved to Surry Co., N. C.
200. Capt. Joel Lewis, born in Va., 1760, moved to Surry Co., N. C.
201. Joseph Logan ⎱
201. William Logan ⎰ Lincoln Co. men in the Company of Mattocks
201. Robert Lucas, on the Watauga in 1772, at King's Mtn. A Capt. under Sevier
201. Major Isaac Lucas, brother of Robert; in 1781 moved to Davidson Co.
201. Capt. Joseph Lucas, an early Watauga settler.
201. Capt. Joseph Lusk, was on the Watauga in 1776.
202. John McAdoo, early settler on Watauga
202. William McCafferty, Irish merchant, near Charlotte, who turned the British army into a wrong road to protect the whigs on their way to King's Mtn.
203. William McCarthy, was under Cleveland, pensioned in Lincoln in 1833
203. Francis McCorkle, in 1774 on the Committee of Safety for Rowan Co., N. C.
204. Magnus McDonald, in the N. C. militia
204. Charles McDowell, Col., born in Va. 1743, did at Morganton, N. C., 1811
204. Maj. Joseph McDowell, brother to the colonel, commanded a regt. at King's Mountain
204. James McElwee, a native of N. C.
204. Robert McFarland, Lt. in the battle; moved from N. C. to Wythe Co.
205. McKee———, the mother of Maj. William Chronicle, first married a McKee in Penn. He died in Lincoln Co., N. C. The Maj. was the only son by her first marriage
205. Capt. David McKessick, wounded at Ramseur's Mill; it is claimed that he was present at King's Mtn.

*Pages*

205. Alexander McLain, came from Ireland to N. C.
206. Tapley Mahannas, from Lincoln Co., N. C., pensioned there
207. Josiah Manor, in the N. C. troops, is said to have been in the battle, pension application does not give it
207. Salathiel Martin, in the N. C. troop
208. Patrick Mason } of Lincoln Co., pensioned in 1833
208. Thomas Mason
208. Capt. John Mattocks, of the Lincoln Co. men
209. William Mayes, a N. C. Soldier, pensioned in Lincoln as a privt., 1833
209. Adam Meek, came from Ireland while young, settled in Mecklenburg Co., N. C., and was a signer of the Mecklenburg petition. Lt. at King's Mtn.
209. Nathan Mendenhall, said to have been with the Lincoln men; pensioned in Lincoln, 1833
210. Elijah Mitchell, born in Mecklenburg Co., N. C.
211. Alexander Moore, in the Lincoln militia, pensioned in Lincoln, 1833. Tradition says he was at King's Mtn.
211. John Moore, born in Lincoln in 1759.
211. Alexander Moore } brothers of John, in Rev., and all claimed as
211. James Moore } King's Mtn. men
211. William Moore
211. John Morehead, born in Richmond Co., Va., 1766, moved to Rockingham Co., N. C., where he died 1832
211. Peter Morrison } of Burke Co., N. C.
211. William Morrison
211. Jeremiah Munday, a Lincoln Soldier, pensioned there in 1833
212. Henry Murfree, claimed as a N. C. participant
212. Teeler Nave, one of the first settlers of the Watauga
212. Abraham Nave } Sons of Teeler Nave
212. Conrad Nave } Tradition is that they were under Shelby
212. Henry Nave
212. John Neal, of N. C. militia
212. John Nelson, N. C. private
213. Isaac Newman, in the militia from Guilford
213. John Newman, early immigrant to the Watauga
214. Eli Overton, of the N. C. militia
214. George Parke, born in Amherst Co., Va., when a boy went with his father to the Yadkin
215. Humphrey Parker, from Lincoln Co., where he was pensioned
215. Arthur Patterson, native of Ireland, settled near King's Mtn.
215. Arthur Patterson, Jr. }
215. Thomas Patterson } sons of Arthur, all in the battle
215. William Patterson
215. William Patterson of Patterson's Mill on the Watauga was in the battle
216. Elias Peebar, one of the early Watauga settlers, signed the Halifax petition
216. Adam Peck came from Botetourt, one of the first pioneers on Mossy Creek
217. Jesse Perry, pensioned in Knox, 1833, for service in the N. C. militia; tradition is that he was in the battle
217. Joseph Phillips, served under Cleveland; moved from Surry Co., N. C., to Clairborne Co., Tenn.
217. Ezekiel Polk, signed the Mecklenburg declaration
218. William Potter, of the Lincoln militia, pensioned in N. C.; claimed he was in the battle
218. Thomas Preston, commanded a company under Sevier. In the Watauga purchase of 1775, his name appears, etc

*Pages*
219. William Rankin, with the N. C. troops
219. Benjamin Reed  ⎫
219. James Reed
219. Thomas Reed
219. William Reed          pensioned
219. John Reed              at King's Mountain
219. Joseph Reed
219. Samuel Reed  ⎭
        The above seven names are those of James Reed's seven sons; all were at
        King's Mountain
219. Adam Reep, lived on west bank of Catawba
219. Michael Reep, pensioned in Lincoln Co., N. C., name does not appear as a
        King's Mtn. man
219. Charles Regan, pensioned in Lincoln; it is the tradition that he was in the battle
219. Henry Remfeldt, pensioned in Lincoln, 1833, not known whether he was at
        King's Mtn.
219. James Reese, lived in Greene Co., noted for the state of Franklin; the others
        from the county in the same convention being Daniel Kennedy, Joseph
        Hardin, John Newman, and James Roddy.  All were King's Mtn. soldiers
219. David Reese, a signer of the Mecklenburg resolutions
219. William Reeves, on Watauga in 1775, signed the Halifax petition of 1776
220. Elisha Reynolds, born in Wilkes 1755; became a Lt.
221. William Robertson, of the Rutherford men, under Hampton, was wounded
221. William Robinson, lived in Rutherford Co.
221. Thomas Robinson, brother to William
221. William Robinson, a Lt. under Sevier; signed of the Halifax petition
221. James Roddy, early settler on the Watauga
222. John Ross, born 1764; served in the N. C. militia; said to have been at King's
        Mountain
223. Samuel Scott, Sr., a minute man under Campbell, born in N. C.
223. Thomas Scott, brother to Samuel, in militia
223. William Scott, brother to Samuel, in militia
223. Gen. John Sevier lived at fort on Watauga, the first built on that river
223. Valentine Sevier, Capt., born in London, settled first in Va., then came with his
        brother and father to Watauga where he settled
223. Robert Sevier, another brother, also a Capt.
223. Abraham Sevier, another brother, a privt.
223. Joseph Sevier  ⎱  sons of the General
223. James Sevier  ⎰
223. Robert Shannon, Capt. of Lincoln Co.
224. Adam Sherrill, born on the Yadkin, 1758
225. John Shirley, under Cleveland, probably from Watauga
225. John Sigman, of Burke Co., a Capt. under McDowell
225. Daniel Siske, of Wilkes Co., was killed
225. John Smart, a Rutherford soldier
225. David Smith, born in Anson Co., N. C.
226. John Stamey, said to have been in the battle, pensioned in Lincoln Co., N. C.,
        1833
227. Matthew Talbot, Sr., early Watauga settler
228. James Tatum, in the battle, pensioned in Watauga Co., N. C.
228. Andrew Taylor, Jr., in the N. C. troops
229. Major ——— Temple, moved to Mecklenburg Co. in 1766
229. Philip Tillman, a Lincoln man, pensioned in Lincoln Co., N. C., 1833
230. James Todd, probably of Watauga Co.

*Pages*
230. David Vance, born in Frederick Co., Va., 1748, early removed to N. C. In 1797, he was living in Buncombe, a Col. of militia
231. John Waddell, a settler on Watauga, 1775
231. Martin Waddell, also early settler
231. William Walker, of Rutherford Co., pensioned in N. C.
232. George Webb, a man of affairs on Watauga
232. John Weir, born in Ireland 1743, settled at Weir's Bridge in Gaston Co., N. C. In the Revolution a scout, then a Capt.
232. Charles Whit, of Lincoln Co., N. C., pensioned there
232. Isaac White, Lt. ⎫ born in Pennsylvania, moved to Lincoln Co., N. C.,
232. James White, Capt. ⎬ in 1779
232. Thomas White, Lt. ⎭
233. Daniel Williams, Capt. under Marion; he was born in Wilmington Co., N. C.
234. Samuel Williams, born in N. C. 1733; a Capt. under Sevier
234. Joseph Wilson ⎫ in the N. C. Line
234. Robert Wilson ⎭
234. Zaccheus Wilson, signer of Mecklenburg Declaration of Independence; member of provincial Congress of 1776, etc.
235. Maj. Joseph Winston, born in Louisa Co., Va., 1746; moved to Stokes Co., N. C., 1769, etc.
235. Elisha Wither, of the Lincoln Co. men, pensioned in N. C.
235. John Witherspoon, born in 1760, a privt. under Cleveland; after the war, represented Stokes two years in the legislature
235. James Withrow, born in Va., 1746, died 1836; moved to Rutherford Co., served under Hampton
236. Jacob Womack, on the Watauga, 1772; signed the Halifax petition

ADDITIONAL

*Pages*
237. James Alexander, born in Rowan Co., N. C., 1756; entered the army from Lincoln
237. William Carr, enlisted from Mecklenburg Co., N. C., 1775
237. Pharoah Cobb, born in Northampton Co., N. C., 1752; enlisted in Watauga settlement, 1776
238. Robert Culbertson, born in Penn., enlisted from Caswell Co., N. C., 1780
238. John Duckworth, born in Va., 1759; died in Burke Co., N. C., 1843; enlisted 1776
238. William Feinster, born in S. C.; died in Iredell Co., N. C.
238. John Floyd, born in Mecklenburg Co., N. C., 1758; enlisted 1776
238-239. Nicholas Gibbs, said to have been at King's Mountain, received a land grant from North Carolina for services in the Continental line
239. James Gray, born in Va., 1755, enlisted in the "Liberty Men," from Rutherford Co., N. C., applied for pension in Rutherford, 1832
239. Joel Hampton, enlisted from Wilkes Co., N. C., 1779; in service till 1783
239. John Helms, born in Botetourt, 1761, applied for pension in Lincoln Co., N. C., 1833
239. Joseph Henry, pensioned in Buncombe Co., 1832
239. Joseph Henry, enlisted from Lincoln Co., N. C.
239. John Henry ⎫ brothers of second Joseph, were killed at King's Mtn.
239. Moses Henry ⎭
240. Samuel Johnson, Lt. at King's Mtn., and was wounded, pensioned by North Carolina about 1798.
240-241. John Love, born in Va., pensioned 1832, when living in Wilkes Co., N. C., at King's Mtn., a substitute for his father, James

*Pages*

241. Francis McCorkle, born in Scotland 1740; died in Salisbury, N. C., 1802
241. Henry Massengale, born in 1758, enlisted in N. C.
241. Michael Massengale, born in Northampton Co., N. C., 1756
241. Samuel Martin, born in Ireland, 1752; died in Lincoln Co., N. C., 1836.
241. Benjamin Newton, born in Va., enlisted from Caswell Co., N. C.
242. Asher Reeves, enlisted from Wilkes Co., N. C.
242. Elisha Reynolds, died in Wilkes Co., N. C., 1836, in service 1776-81
242. Bethiel Riggs, moved to Wilkes Co., N. C., and took Cleveland's place at
King's Mtn. when the latter was wounded
242. David Smith, born in Anson Co., N. C., 1753
242. James Taylor, substituted in Surry Co., N. C., serving in the Third N. C.;
moved to Blount Co., where pension was allowed in 1832.
242. William Utterly, born in Connecticut, died in Wilkes Co., N. C., 1794
244. William Walton, enlisted in Wilkes Co.
245. James Wyley, born in Mecklenburg Co., N. C., 1762., pensioned in Blount
Co., 1833

## APPENDIX

We are indebted to Mrs. A. G. Barnett of Asheville for her fine interest, in supplying the following items:

Capt. James Johnson (or Johnston) fought under Colonel Hambright in the battle of King's Mountain. After Major Chronicle fell mortally wounded, James Johnson was one of the men given orders such as the occasion demanded.

He was of the same company as "Hambright's party "The South Fork Boys."

Reference: "Commanders at Kings Mountain," by J. D. Bailey, page 196.

Tom Rutledge (Routledge) of Duplin County, North Carolina, was an officer in North Carolina troops of Continental Army.

Reference: History of North Carolina Colonial Records.

Major George Rutledge was sent by Governor Blount, 1793, to fight the Creek and lower Cherokee Indians.

Indians were seen at the Warm Springs (now Hot Springs, N. C.) Guards were stationed at four block houses at Hough's. At the Burnt Cane-brake. At the Painted Rock, and at the Warm Springs.

Reference: Ramseys Annals of Tennessee, pp. 569, 621, 624, 625, 626, 657, 658, 667, 668, 704.

George Rutledge was elected Brigadier General in General Sevier's place when Sevier was made Governor of Tennessee.

Records show George Rutledge helped protect the western frontier of North Carolina from Indian invasion.

He was a descendant of George Rutledge who was a member of Sam Corbin's Company in the "Spanish Alarm" in 1747; whose Company protected the coast of North Carolina in 1742 from the Spaniards.

William Rutledge, made Lieut. Jan. 25, '77 of 4 Regiment North Carolina troops, Continental line.

Reference: "Saunders North Carolina State Records," "North Carolina, 1780-81," Schenck, Appendix B., p. 478, gives the name of Wm. Rutledge (or Routledge of Lincoln County, North Carolina. The name in England was spelled Rootledge, also Routhledge.

Colonel James Brown, a Revolutionary officer, was killed by Indians as he was emigrating to Cumberland to enter into possession of lands alloted him for military services in the North Carolina army of the Revolution.

Reference: "Ramseys Annals of Tennessee, with Faries' Index, pp. 508-10-15-16-17-550.

His descendants were first settlers in Jefferson County, Alabama, where Birmingham is now situated.

Isaac Thomas, Indian fighter and defender of western frontier for many years prior and during the Revolution. Isaac Thomas of Watauga Settlement is one of the three men not killed at the fall of Fort London, 1760.

He sounded the warnings of Indian raids planned, and saved them many times from death. A monument to his memory is standing at Sevierville, Tennessee, in Sevier County, which was once part of North Carolina.

The Nancy Ward Chapter of Chattanooga, Tennessee, D. A. R., was named for the beautiful Indian maiden who furnished him valuable information which protected the settlers of the western boundaries of North Carolina.

Reference: "Gilmores Rear Guard of the Revolution," pp. 82-83.

Reference: "Ramsays Annals of Tennessee," p. 755; "Appleton's Cyclopedia of American Biography," Vol. VI, pp. 82-83.

Major Joseph Dickson (or Dixon) fought at the Battle of Kings Mountain. After Major Chronicle was killed he was one of the men who took charge of the Company.

Reference: "Commanders at Kings Mountain," by J. D. Bailey, p. 196.

William Brown, Regulator, captured by Governor Wm. Tryon 1771, after the Battle of Alamance. He was one of the twelve men condemned to death by Governor Tryon. Six were executed but William Brown with the other six men were condemned at Hillsborough to Court Martial, and respited to await the Kings pleasure.

Reference: "Some Neglected History of North Carolina," by William Edwards Fitch, M. W., p. 242. Also "Colonial Records," Vol. VIII, p. 635; Vol. IX, pp. 36-37-274-311.

\* \* \* \* \* \*

## WAR DEPARTMENT
### THE ADJUTANT GENERAL'S OFFICE
#### WASHINGTON, D. C., MARCH 10, 1917

Respectfully returned to Mrs. J. J. Eaton, 1327 South 20th Street, Birmingham, Alabama, with the information that the records show that James Rutledge served in the Revolutionary War as a private in Captain John Johnston's Company, Colonel John Collier's Regiment, North Carolina Militia. His name appears on a company pay roll dated December 22, 1780; showing that he was paid for service from September 3, to December 22, 1780; and on a receipt roll dated July 29, 1783 showing that he was paid for one tour of duty in said Company on December 16, 1780.

[Signed] N. T. McCLAIN,
The Adjutant General.

James Rutledge is buried at a Presbyterian Church Cemetery near Belmont, Gaston County, North Carolina. Gaston County was cut off from Lincoln County in 1845.

### (APPENDIX)
## REVOLUTIONARY WAR SOLDIERS LIVING IN RUTHERFORD COUNTY, NORTH CAROLINA, 1831-1837.

From County Court Minute Book:

| | |
|---|---|
| Cook, Edward, b. Orange Co. N. C., 1760. | Lucas, Wm., '78 |
| Davis, John, age 74 | Marmy, David b. Pa., age 77 |
| Dalton, Wm., age 78 | Metcalf, Danzn, age 73 |
| Depriest, Wm. | Metcalf, Warren, age 70 |
| Dicky, Anthony, age 87 | McFadden, Alexander |
| Gray, James, age 77 | Newton, Benf. Sr., age 84 |
| Harvy, Robert, age 75 | Padgett, John, age 70 |
| Holland, Wm., age 85 | Sargent, James |
| Hutchens, Thomas, 79 | Williams, John, age 79 |

NOTE: These names furnished by Lily Doyle Dunlap, Ansonville, N. C.

(APPENDIX)

GASTON COUNTY—REVOLUTIONARY SOLDIERS WHO PARTICIPATED IN
THE BATTLE OF KING'S MOUNTAIN, OCTOBER 7, 1780

1. COL. FREDERICK HAMBRIGHT—At time of battle was near Long Creek. Wheeler
   157—Draper 476, & on—Hunter 325—Schenck 159, 168.
2. MAJ. FREDERICK HAMBRIGHT—Family records.
3. JOHN H. HAMBRIGHT—Col. F. Hambright's son—Hunter 325.
4. MAJ. WILLIAM CHRONICLE—South Fork—Draper 477, 551, 214, 219, 225, 231,
   232, 207, 278, 222, 477, 521, 547—Wheeler 158, Schenck 167, 168, 175—Hunter
   158.
5. DR. WILLIAM MCLEAN—South Fouk—Draper 322 (footnote) Hunter 285, 286.
6. ALEXANDER MCLEAN, JR.—moved to Missouri after the war. Hunter 285, 286.
7. GEORGE MCLEAN—moved to Tennessee—Hunter 285, 286.
8. JOHN MCLEAN—Hunter 286.
9. MATTHEW LEEPER—Family Bible and tomb. Fought in the Battle of King's
   Mountain and was buried in Smith's Graveyard near Belmont.
10. CAPT. JOHN MATTOCKS—Wheeler 158, Draper 257, 322, 479—Hunter 291, 295.
11. CAPT. CHARLES MATTOCKS—Wheeler 158—Draper 257, 322, 479—Hunter 291,
    295.
12. LIEUT. WILLIAM RABB—Wheeler 158—Draper 302, 322—Hunter 291.
13. JAMES MCKEE—Half brother of Maj. Chronicle. Wheeler 158, II Section.
14. COL. WILLIAM DAVENPORT—Draper 333, 334, 340, 473.
15. ROBERT HENRY—Draper 119, 122, 150, 198, 214, 224, 226, 228, 232, 257, 279,
    280, 285, 292, 303, 365, 367, 473, 366, 258.
16. WILLIAM CALDWELL—Draper 258—Hunter 294, 291—Wheeler 158.
17. CAPT. SAMUEL CALDWELL—Draper 258—Hunter 294, 291—Wheeler 158.
18. HUGH ERVIN—Draper 365, 367.
19. ANDREW BARRY—Draper 365, 367.
20. ENOCH GILMER—Draper 225, 226, 228, 231—Schenck 158.
21. WILLIAM GILMER—Brother of Enoch Gilmer—Draper 257, 258.
22. JOHN CHITTIM—Draper 258, 303.
23. CAPT. SAMUEL MARTIN—Draper 86, 257, 303, 478—Hunter 291 to 294.
24. LIEUT. JOHN BOYD—Draper 302, 322.
25. JOHN GLENN—Family Bible. Fought in Battle of King's Mountain and buried at
    Goshen.
26. WILLIAM GREGORY—Family Bible. Fought in Battle of King's Mountain and
    buried in Bethel Section.
27. CAPT. SAMUEL ESPEY—Draper 100, 102, 157, 303, 478—Schenck 167.
28. CAPT. ISAAC WHITE—Draper 476 (White & Jenkins Mill).
29. LIEUT. JAMES WHITE—Draper 476 (White & Jenkins Mill).
30. CAPT. JAMES JOHNSTON—Draper 85, 86, 257, 577, 78—Hunter 244, 246, 247.
31. MOSES HENRY—Draper 302, 319, 320.
32. JAMES HENRY—Draper 319.
33. ISAAC HOLLAND, JR.—Hoffman's "Our Kin," page 521.
34. FELIX WALKER—Draper 325, 326 footnote.
35. JACOB HOFFMAN } Born in Germany, emigrated to America, settled in Gaston
36. JOHN HOFFMAN } County, fought at King's Mountain, died 1860, buried on
    "Earl Summey's Place."
37. MAJ. JOSEPH DICKSON—Draper 85, 257, 477—Hunter 29—Schanck 107, 108.
38. MATTHEW ARMSTRONG—From records in Court House, he fought at King's Moun-
    tain and is buried in Smith's graveyard near Belmont.
39. CAPT. JOHN KINCAID—Family Bible record shows he was in the Battle of King's
    Mountain and is buried at Olney Cemetery.
40. ADAM BAIRD—An officer, unable to find out his rank. Mrs. W. E. Weatherly of

Gastonia, Granddaughter of Adam Baird, has in her possession the gun with which he fought in the Battle of King's Mountain. Baird was with Martin.

41. JAMES BAIRD—Adam Baird's brother, records in family history.

42. JESSE LANE—Records in family history.

NOTE: Some Histories spell "Hambright" and others "Hambrite." However, his tombstone says "Hambright."

These muster rolls are presented to the North Carolina Society, Daughters of the American Revolution by Mrs. Edwin C. Gregory, to whom we are greatly indebted for this service.

## DR. THE PROVINCE OF NORTH CAROLINA TO CAPT. CHARLES POLK AND COMPANY OF FOOT SERVICES DONE

1. Charles Polk, Capt.
2. William Ramsay, Lt.
3. John Lemmond, Ensn.
4. John McGinty, Sgt.
5. Hugh Lindsey, Drumr.
6. William Lemmond, Clk. & Surgn.
7. William Gallbreath ⎫
8. John Doneldson
9. John Hall
10. John Queriey
11. John Purser
12. John Findly
13. John Stansell
14. John Gallbreath          Foot
15. John Lowrey            Soldiers
16. John Polk, Senr.
17. Jonathan Queriey
18. James Maxwell
19. James Orr, Junr.
20. James McQuirt
21. James McGinty ⎭

Isaac Burilson ⎫
23. David Orr
24. Thomas Hall, Junr.
25. Thomas Martindale
26. Tumas Hood
27. William Maxwell
28. William Alexander, Junr.
29. William Morgain
30. William Blair
31. William Shields
32. Windsor Pearce          Foot
33. Moses Cubberson        Soldiers
34. Matthew Miller
35. Robert Gallbreath
36. Richard Turnbull
37. Robert Donaldson
38. Richard Kain
39. Daniel Wynchaster
    John Corruthers
40. Benjamin Cochran
41. Charles Polk, Junr.
42. Zabulon Robinet ⎭

The above acct. was duly proven according to Law before me
. . . . . . . . . . Alex,
George Mitchal,

July the A Domini 1776.

The List of Capt. Polks Foot Co. 1776.

(On the side of the sheet is inscribed "No. Carolina Mecklenburg Co., &c.")

Dr.—The Public of North Carolina to Capt. Charles Polk, for services done by him & Company of Light Horse to Brunswick in the service from March '76 to May 1776.

Capt. Charles Polk
1st. Lt. Wm. Ramsey
2nd Lt. John Lemonds
1st Sergt. John McGinty
2nd Sergt. Wm. Gelbreath
John Smith
Hugh Linsey
John Wyly
John Findley

John Gilbreath
Jos. Hall
John Stansel
Wm. McGowen
Humphrey Hunter
Henry Carter
John Miller
Jos. Maxwell
Robert Galbreath

John McCauley
Nicholas Iler
Sam'l. Linton
Thos. Shelby
Jas. Alexander
Robert Harris
Joseph Harris
John Ford
Jonathan Buckbee
Henry Powel
Charles Alexander
Wm. Ross
Sam'l. Hughs

Wm. Shields
John Purser
Charles Alexander, Jr.
Eph. Alexander
Geo. Mitchel
Jos. Jack
Wm. Lemens
Geo. Wilson
A copy
    John Hunt
Halifax 15, Jan. 1779
    Charles Polk's
      Light Horse Com'y.

## THE STATE OF NORTH CAROLINA TO CAPT. CHARLES POLK AND HIS COMPANY TO CROSS CREEK

Capt. Charles Polk
Lt. William Ramsey
Ensn. John Lemonds
Sergt. John McGinty
Do. Wm. Galbreath
Drummer, Hugh Linsey
Clerk, William Lemonds
John Hall
John Donaldson
John Query
John Purser
John Stansel
John Findly
Jonathan Query
John Curethers
Tumas Hood

John Galbreath
Robert Donaldson
James McGinty
Benj'n. Cochran
Wm. Blair
James Maxwell
Daniel Winchester
Mathew Miller
Zebulon Robinet
Robert Galbreath
Charles Polk, Junr.
R'd. Timbell
Wm. Shields
James Ro......
Moses Culberson
John Lowrey

James McGuirt
Tho's. Martindel
(On back of roll)
Wm. Alexander, Junr.
Wm. Maxwell
Winsor Pearce
Isaac Burleson
R'd. Cain
Wm. Morgan
David Orr
Tho's. Hall
A copy
    John Hunt CP. H. C.
Halifax 15 Jan. 1779
    Capt. Polk's Foot Claim.

## THE PUBLIC OF NORTH CAROLINA FOR SERVICES DONE CAPT. CHARLES POLK'S COMP'Y OF MILITIA FOOT SOLDIERS, ETC.

Capt. Charles Polk to services done.
Lt. William Ramsey
Ensn. John Lemmond
Sergt. John Meginty
Drummer, Hugh Lindsey
Surgeon, William Lemmond
John Queriey
J...... Parker
......Stansal
John Findly
Jonathan Queriey
Tumas Hood
Robert Donaldson
James Meginty
Benjamin Cochran
William Blair
Daniel Wynchaster
Matthew Miller

Zebulon Robinett
Charles Polk, Junr.
Richard Turnbull
William Shields
(on the side is written "To the Congress")
James Orr
John Lowry
James McGuirt
Thomas Martindale
William Alexander, Junr.
William Maxwell
Windsor Pearce
Isaac Burlison
Richard Cain
William Morgan
David Orr
Thomas Hall

"The enclosed sheets are exact copies of the 4 Muster Rolls sent by George W. Polk or, his attorney, to prove the truth of his claim that Charles was a Captain, and not merely a Lieutenant, as the North Carolina Rolls seemed to indicate."

The rolls are much disfigured, and show signs of careless handling before they were sent to the Department, Etc. The names have been spelled as in the original, Etc.

Dr. The Province of North Carolina
To Capt. Charles Polk and Company of foot for services Done

| | | Days | per | £ | S | d |
|---|---|---|---|---|---|---|
| Capt. | 1 Charles Polk | 25 | 10 | 12 | 10 | 0 |
| Leuetant | 2 William Ramsay | 25 | 7–6 | 10 | 1 | 6 |
| Ensign | 3 John Lemmond | 25 | 5–4 | 6 | 13 | |
| Sexgant | 4 John McGinty | 25 | 3–9 | 4 | 13 | 9 |
| Drummer | 5 Hugh Lindsey | 25 | 4–6 | 5 | 12 | |
| Clk & Churgeon | 6 William Lemmond | 25 | 9 | 22 | 5 | |
| Foot soldiers | 7 William Gallbreath | 25 | 2–6 | 3 | 2 | 6 |
| | 8 John Doneldson | 25 | 2–6 | 3 | 2 | 6 |
| | 9 John Hall | 25 | 2–6 | 3 | 2 | 6 |
| | 10 John Queriey | 25 | 2–6 | 3 | 2 | 6 |
| | 11 John purser | 25 | 2–6 | 3 | 2 | 6 |
| | 12 John Findly | 25 | 2–6 | 3 | 2 | 6 |
| | 13 John Stansell | 25 | 2–6 | 3 | 2 | 6 |
| | 14 John Gallbreath | 25 | 2–6 | 3 | 2 | 6 |
| | 15 John Lowrey | 25 | 2–6 | 3 | 2 | 6 |
| | 16 John Polk Senr | 25 | 2–6 | 3 | 2 | 6 |
| | 17 Jonathan Queriey | 25 | 2–6 | 3 | 2 | 6 |
| | 18 James Maxwell | 25 | 2–6 | 3 | 2 | 6 |
| | 19 James Orr Jun | 25 | 2–6 | 3 | 2 | 6 |
| | 20 James Mcguirt | 25 | 2–6 | 3 | 2 | 6 |
| | 21 James Mcginty | 25 | 2–6 | 3 | 2 | 6 |
| | 22 Isaac Burilson | 25 | 2–6 | 3 | 2 | 6 |
| | 23 David orr | 25 | 2–6 | 3 | 2 | 6 |
| | 24 Thomas Hall Junr | 25 | 2–6 | 3 | 2 | 6 |
| | 25 Thomas Martindale | 25 | 2–6 | 3 | 2 | 6 |
| | 26 Tumas Hood | 25 | 2–6 | 3 | 2 | 6 |
| | 27 William Maxwell | 25 | 2–6 | 3 | 2 | 6 |
| | 28 William Alexander Junr | 25 | 2–6 | 3 | 2 | 6 |
| | 29 William Morgain | 25 | 2–6 | 3 | 2 | 6 |
| | 30 William Blair | 25 | 2–6 | 3 | 2 | 6 |
| | 31 William Shields | 25 | 2–6 | 3 | 2 | 6 |
| | 32 Windsor Pearce | 25 | 2–6 | 3 | 2 | 6 |
| | 33 Moses Cubberson | 25 | 2–6 | 3 | 2 | 6 |
| | 34 Matthew Miller | 25 | 2–6 | 3 | 2 | 6 |
| | 35 Robert Gallbreath | 25 | 2–6 | 3 | 2 | 6 |
| | 36 Richard Turnbull | 25 | 2–6 | 3 | 2 | 6 |
| | 37 Robert Donaldson | 25 | 2–6 | 3 | 2 | 6 |
| | 38 Richard Kain | 25 | 2–6 | 3 | 2 | 6 |
| | 39 Daniel Wynchaster | 25 | 2–6 | 3 | 2 | 6 |
| | 40 Benjamin Cochran | 25 | 2–6 | 3 | 2 | 6 |
| | 41 Charles Polk Junr | 25 | 2–6 | 3 | 2 | 6 |
| | 42 Zabulon Robinet | 25 | 2–6 | 3 | 2 | 6 |
| | John Corruthers | 15 | 2–6 | | | |
| | 3 Waggons | 25 | 16 | 60 | 0 | 0 |
| | d r 1210 Rashions at 8 p | | | 35 | 0 | 0 |
| | | | £ | 258 | 6 | 4 |

The above acct was Duly Proven according
To Law Before Me
............Alex
George Mitchal
July the          A Domini 1776
The List of Capt. Polks
Foot Company 1776
(On the side of the sheet is inscribed "No Carolina Mecklenburg County &c. ")

Dr. The Publick of North Carolina to Capt. Charles Polk for services done by him & Company of Light Horse to Brunswick in the service from March 76 to May 1776.

|            | Name                    | Days | per | £   | S   | d |
|------------|-------------------------|------|-----|-----|-----|---|
| Capt.      | Charles Polk            | 53   | 12  | 31  | 16  | 0 |
| Ist. Liut. | Wm. Ramsey              | 53   | 10  | 26  | 10  |   |
| 2 Do       | John Lemonds            | 53   | 10  | 26  | 10  |   |
| 1 Sargt    | John McGinty            | 53   | 6   | 15  | 16  |   |
| 2 Sargt    | Wm. Gelbreath           | 53   | 6   | 15  | 16  |   |
|            | John Smith              | 53   | 5   | 13  | 5   |   |
|            | Hugh Linsey             | 28   | 5   | 7   |     |   |
|            | John Wyly               | 58   | 5   | 14  | 0   |   |
|            | John Findley            | 53   | 5   | 13  | 5   |   |
|            | John Gilbreath          | 53   | 5   | 13  | 5   |   |
|            | Jos Hall                | 53   | 5   | 13  | 5   |   |
|            | John Stansel            | 53   | 5   | 13  | 5   |   |
|            | Wm. McGowen             | 53   | 5   | 13  | 5   |   |
|            | Humphrey Hunter         | 53   | 5   | 13  | 5   |   |
|            | Henry Carter            | 53   | 5   | 13  | 5   |   |
|            | John Miller             | 53   | 5   | 13  | 5   |   |
|            | Jas Maxwell             | 53   | 5   | 13  | 5   |   |
|            | Robert Galbreath        | 53   | 5   | 13  | 5   |   |
|            | John McCauley           | 53   | 5   | 13  | 5   |   |
|            | Nicholas Iler           | 53   | 5   | 13  | 5   |   |
|            | Saml Linton             | 53   | 5   | 13  | 5   |   |
|            | Thos Shelby             | 53   | 5   | 13  | 5   |   |
|            | Jas Alexander           | 53   | 5   | 13  | 5   |   |
|            | Robert Harris           | 53   | 5   | 13  | 5   |   |
|            | Joseph Harris           | 53   | 5   | 13  | 5   |   |
|            | John Ford               | 62   | 5   | 15  | 10  |   |
|            | Jonathan Buckbee        | 48   | 5   | 12  | 0   | 0 |
|            | Henry Powel             | 53   | 5   | 13  | 5   |   |
|            | Charles Alexander       | 53   | 5   | 13  | 5   |   |
|            | Wm. Ross                | 53   | 5   | 13  | 5   |   |
|            | Saml Hughs              | 53   | 5   | 13  | 5   |   |
|            | Wm. Shields             | 53   | 5   | 13  | 5   |   |
|            | John Purser             | 53   | 5   | 13  | 5   |   |
|            | Charles Alexander Junr  | 53   | 5   | 13  | 5   |   |
|            | Eph. Alexander          | 53   | 5   | 13  | 5   |   |
|            | Geo. Mitchel            | 46   | 2   | 4   | 12  |   |
|            | Jas. Jack               | 46   | 2   | 4   | 12  |   |
|            | Wm. Lemens              | 53   | 6   | 15  | 16  |   |
|            | Clark                   |      |     |     |     |   |
|            | Geo Wilson              | 53   | 2   | 4   | 12  |   |

(On opposite side of sheet)

|                              | £   | S  | d |
|------------------------------|-----|----|---|
| Brought over                 | 539 | 11 | 0 |
| 3 Waggons 53 Days at 15ᵈ each | 119 | 5  | 0 |
| 2005 Rations at 8ᵈ           | 66  | 15 |   |
|                              | 725 | 11 |   |
| deducted                     | 6   | 12 | 4 |
| £                            | 718 | 18 | 8 |

A Coppy
John Hunt C1HC
Halifax 15 January 1779

£ 665   7

       Charles Polks
     Light Horse Comy.

The State of North Carolina to Capt. Charles Polk and his Company to Cross Creek

|  |  | Days | per | £ | S | d |
|---|---|---|---|---|---|---|
| Capt. | Charles Polk | 26 | 7–6 | 9 | 15 | |
| Lieut. | William Ramsey | 26 | 5– | 6 | 10 | |
| Ensign | John Lemonds | 26 | 4–6 | 5 | 17 | |
| Sergt | John McGinty | 26 | 4– | 5 | 4 | |
| Do. | Wm. Galbreath | 26 | 4– | 5 | 4 | |
| Drummer | Hugh Linsey | 26 | 3–6 | 4 | 11 | |
| Clerk | William Lemonds | 26 | 4– | 5 | 4 | |
| | John Hall | 26 | 2– | 2 | 12 | |
| | John Donaldson | 26 | 2 | 2 | 12 | |
| | John Query | 26 | 2 | 2 | 12 | |
| | John Purser | 26 | 2 | 2 | 12 | |
| | John Stansel | 26 | 2 | 2 | 12 | |
| | John Findly | 26 | 2– | 2 | 12 | |
| | Jonathan Query | 26 | 2 | 2 | 12 | |
| | John Curethers | 26 | 2– | 2 | 12 | |
| | Tumas Hood | 26 | 2– | 2 | 12 | |
| | John Galbreath | 26 | 2– | 2 | 12 | |
| | Robert Donaldson | 26 | 2 | 2 | 12 | |
| | James McGinty | 26 | 2– | 2 | 12 | |
| | Benjn Cochran | 26 | 2 | 2 | 12 | |
| | Wm. Blair | 26 | 2– | 2 | 12 | |
| | James Maxwell | 26 | 2 | 2 | 12 | |
| | Daniel Winchester | 26 | 2– | 2 | 12 | |
| | Mathew Miller | 26 | 2 | 2 | 12 | |
| | Zebulon Robinet | 26 | 2– | 2 | 12 | |
| | Robert Galbreath | 26 | 2 | 2 | 12 | |
| | Charles Polk Junr | 26 | 2 | 2 | 12 | |
| | Rd Trimbell | 26 | 2– | 2 | 12 | |
| | Wm. Shields | 26 | 2– | 2 | 12 | |
| | James Ro.. | 26 | 2– | 2 | 12 | |
| | Moses Culberson | 26 | 2– | 2 | 12 | |
| | John Lowrey | 26 | 2– | 2 | 12 | |
| | James McGuirt | 26 | 2– | 2 | 12 | |
| | Thos Martindel | 26 | 2– | 2 | 12 | |
| | (On back of roll) | | | | | |
| | Wm Alexander Junr | 26 | 2– | 2 | 12 | |
| | Wm. Maxwell | 26 | 2– | 2 | 12 | |
| | Winsor Pearce | 26 | 2– | 2 | 12 | |
| | Isaac Burleson | 26 | 2– | 2 | 12 | |
| | Rd Cain | 26 | 2– | 2 | 12 | |
| | Wm Morgan | 26 | 2– | 2 | 12 | |
| | David Orr | 26 | 2– | 2 | 12 | |
| | Thos Hall | 26 | 2– | 2 | 12 | |
| | 3 Waggons | 26 | 15 | 58 | 1 | |
| | | | t d | | | |
| | Rations for | 26  at | 8 | 39 | 0 | |
| | Total  £ | | | 239 | 15 | |

A Coppy
John Hunt C1HC
Halifax 15 January 1779

Capt. Polks
Foot Claim

The Publick of North Carolina for services Done Capt. Charles Polks Compy of Militi foot soilders &c.

| | Days | per | £ | S | d |
|---|---|---|---|---|---|
| Capt Charles Polk to services done | 25 | 10 | 12 | 10 | 0 |
| Leutanent William Ramsey | 25 | 7–6 | 9 | 7 | 6 |
| Insigs John Lemmond | 25 | 5–4 | 6 | 13 | 4 |
| Sergt John Meginty | 25 | 4– | 5 | 0 | 0 |
| Sergt William Gallbreath* | 25 | 3– | 3 | 15 | |
| Drummer Hugh Linsey | 25 | 3 | 3 | 15 | |
| Churgeon William Lemmond | 25 | 3– | 11 | 5 | |
| John Hall* | 25 | 2–6 | 2 | 2 | 6 |
| John Donaldson* | 25 | 2–6 | 3 | 2 | 6 |
| John Queriey | 25 | 2–6 | 3 | 2 | 6 |
| J........ Parker | 25 | 2–6 | 3 | 2 | 6 |
| ........ Stansal | 25 | 2–6 | 3 | 2 | 6 |
| John findly | 25 | 2–6 | 3 | 2 | 6 |
| Jonathan Queriey | 25 | 2–6 | 3 | 2 | 6 |
| x John Carithers* | 25 | 2–6 | 3 | 2 | 6 |
| Tumas Hood* | 25 | 2–6 | 3 | 2 | 6 |
| x John Gallbreath* | 25 | 2–6 | 3 | 2 | 6 |
| Robert Donaldson | 25 | 2–6 | 3 | 2 | 6 |
| James Meginty | 25 | 2–6 | 3 | 2 | 6 |
| Benjamin Cochran | 25 | 2–6 | 3 | 2 | 6 |
| William Blair | 25 | 2–6 | 3 | 2 | 6 |
| James Maxwell* | 25 | 2–6 | 3 | 2 | 6 |
| Daniel Wynchaster | 25 | 2–6 | 3 | 2 | 6 |
| Matthew Miller | 25 | 2–6 | 3 | 2 | 6 |
| Zebulon Robinett | 25 | 2–6 | 3 | 2 | 6 |
| (On the side is written "To the Congress") | | | | | |
| Robert Collbreath* | 25 | 2–6 | 3 | 2 | 6 |
| Charles Polk Junr. | 25 | 2–6 | 3 | 2 | 6 |
| Richard Turnbull | 25 | 2–6 | 3 | 2 | 6 |
| William Shields | 25 | 2–6 | 3 | 2 | 6 |
| James orr | 25 | 2–6 | 3 | 2 | 6 |
| Moses Culberson* | 25 | 2–6 | 3 | 2 | 6 |
| John Lowry | 25 | 2–6 | 3 | 2 | 6 |
| James McGuirt | 25 | 2–6 | 3 | 2 | 6 |
| Thomas Martingdale | 25 | 2–6 | 3 | 2 | 6 |
| William Alexander Junr | 25 | 2–6 | 3 | 2 | 6 |
| William Maxwell | 25 | 2–6 | 3 | 2 | 6 |
| x John Polk senr* | 25 | 2–6 | 3 | 2 | 6 |
| Windsor Pearce | 25 | 2–6 | 3 | 2 | 6 |
| Isaac Burlison | 25 | 2–6 | 3 | 2 | 6 |
| Richard Cain | 25 | 2–6 | 3 | 2 | 6 |
| William Morgan | 25 | 2–6 | 3 | 2 | 6 |
| David orr | 25 | 2–6 | 3 | 2 | 6 |
| Thomas Hall | 25 | 2–6 | 3 | 2 | 6 |

| | £ | 152 | o | 10 |
|---|---|---|---|---|
| | | D | S | £ |
| 3 Waggons | | 25 | 16 | 60 |
| Rashons for 43 Men at 8 p<sup>d</sup> <sup>r</sup> | | 25 | | 35/6 |

| | £ | 95 | 17 | 1 |
|---|---|---|---|---|
| Carried Down | | 152 | 0 | 1 |
| | £ | 247 | 18 | 2 |

NOTE—*In the Original Copy these names were marked through.

## NORTH CAROLINA'S RECORD IN WAR—VOL. 4, 1904-1905

### By Chief Justice Walter Clark

Vol. IV., Oct. 1904, No. 6. The North Carolina Booklet. Pages 19-20-21.

In the Revolution, 1775-1783. North Carolina had in the "Continental Line":
One Maj. Gen., Robert Howe; four Brig. Gens., (1) James Moore, died in service, Feb. 1777; (2) Francis Nash, killed at Germantown, Oct. 4, 1777; (3) Jethro Sumner; (4) James Hogun, died a prisoner of war at Charlestown, S. C., Jan. 4, 1781.

Besides these who were regular or Cont. officers the following Genl's. of militia, commanded troops in action: Gen. John Ashe, at Briar Creek, Ga., Mch. 3, 1779.

Gen. Rich'd Caswell, at Camden, S. C., Aug. 16, 1780.

Gen. Isaac Gregory, at Camden, S. C., Aug. 16, 1780, where he was wounded, and the conduct of his men highly praised by the British Gen. Griffith Rutherford, at Stono., 20 June, 1779, and at Camden, S. C., 16 Aug., 1780; where he was wounded and captured. (He commanded also in the expeditions against the Scovillite Tories and the Overhill Indians.

Gen. Wm. Lee Davison, killed at Cowan's Ford, Feb. 1, 1781. (He had been a Lt. Col. in the Cont. Line.)

Gen. John Butler, at Stono, 20th June, 1779; at Camden, 16th Aug., 1780, and at Guilford Court House, 15th Mch., 1781.

Gen. Thomas Eaton, at Guilford Court House, 15th Mch., 1781.

North Carolina furnished 10 regt's. of regulars, to the Cont. Line; 1 battery of artillery, (Kingsbury's) and 3 companies of Cavalry.

Besides this, her militia were frequently ordered out on "tours of duty."

Alone and unaided, they won the brilliant victory of Moore's Creek, Ramseur's Mill, and King's Mountain, and helped the Regulars lose the battles of Camden and Guilford Court House.

Under Rutherford's leadership, early in 1776, they so crushed the Scovillite tories in S. C. and in July of that year the Overhill Indians in Tenn., that neither gave further trouble during the entire year.

In the later expedition 2,400 N. C. militia were engaged. They also shared in the Battles of Stono, Briar Creek, Cowpens and the defense and surrender of Charleston.

The N. C. Continentals rendered efficient service at Brandywine, Germantown, Monmouth, at the capture of Stony Point (where they had a conspicuous part), at Hobkirks Hill, Eutaw, at both sieges of Charleston and Savannah, and elsewhere; and formed a part of the garrison of West Point, when our Maj. Gen. Howe succeeded Arnold in command there, upon his treason.

# MECKLENBERG DECLARATION OF INDEPENDENCE

References—The Colonial Records of North Carolina, 1771 to 1775. Saunders, Vol. IX. Pages 1263-1264 and 1265.

The Mecklenberg Declaration of Independence, May 20, 1775. And Lives of its Signers. George W. Graham, M.D.

[P. 81]

References in the above book to Martin's History of North Carolina, which contains a minute description and detailed account of the proceedings.

The above history proven authentic in as much that the book was written during the years 1791 to 1829—Martin's opportunities for ascertaining the truth, are that with the exception of Major Garden, he is the only historian who personally knew eye-witnesses and participants in the Mecklenburg Convention, etc.

### Page 1236, Vol. IX

### THE MECKLENBURG DECLARATION OF 20TH MAY, 1775—DECLARATION

*Names of the Delegates Present*

[P. 1264]

| | |
|---|---|
| Col. Thomas Polk | John McKnitt Alexander |
| Ephraim Brevard | Hezekiah Alexander |
| Hezekiah J. Balch | Adam Alexander |
| John Phifer | Charles Alexander |
| James Harris | Zacheus Wilson, Sen. |
| William Kennon | Waightstill Avery |
| John Ford | Benjamin Patton |
| Richard Barry | Mathew McClure |
| Henry Downs | Neil Morrison |
| Ezra Alexander | Robert Irwin |
| William Graham | John Flenniken |
| John Quary | David Reese |
| Abraham Alexander | Richard Harris, Sen. |

[P. 1265]

Abraham Alexander was appointed chairman, and John McKintt Alexander, clerk. Resolutions were then drawn up, and "after discussing the resolves, and arranging by-laws and regulations for the government of a Standing Committee of Public Safety who were selected from these delegates the whole proceedings were unanimously adopted and signed. A select committee was then appointed.

The names of the signers follow:

*Reference*
*Pages*

27. Ephraim Brevard (drew the week.bg Dec'n Indpndce.
27-28. John McKintt Alexander (secretary)
  81. Major John Davidson (signer)
  20. James Harris
  20. Robert Irwin
          delegates & signers
  20. Col. Adam Alexander, member of Convention
115. Rev. Hezekiah Balch (voted)
117. Hezekiah Alexander served in the Mecklenburg Convention
118. Capt. Zacheus Wilson, member of the Mecklenburg Convention

# COLONIAL RECORDS OF NORTH CAROLINA

Saunders, Vol. X—1775-1776                                    Pages 164 to 169

The Journal of the Proceedings of the Provincial Congress of North Carolina, held at Hillsboro, N. C., 20th of Aug. A. D. 1775.

Pursuant to a resolve of the late Convention, Mr. Samuel Johnston sommoned a meeting of the delegates, at Hillsborough on the 20th day of August, 1775, at which time the members from a majority of the counties and towns not appearing, he adjourned the Congress till tomorrow morning at ten o'clock.

### MONDAY, AUG. 21ST., 1775

At the general meeting of the Delegates of the Inhabitants of this Province, at Hillsborough, the twenty-first day of August, A. Dom, 1775, aforesaid.

ANSON COUNTY—Thomas Wade, Samuel Spencer, William Thomas, David Love, William Pickett.

BEAUFORT COUNTY—Roger Ormond, Thomas Respass, jr., John Patten, John Cooper.

BLADEN COUNTY—William Salter, Walter Gibson, Thomas Owen, Thomas Robinson, jr., Nathaniel Richardson.

BERTIE COUNTY—William Gray, Johnathan Jaycocks, Charles Jaycocks, William Brimage, William Bryan, Jedekiah Stone, Thomas Ballard, Peter Clifton, David Standley, John Campbell, Johnston (John).

BRUNSWICK COUNTY—Robert Howe, Robert Ellis, Parker Quince, Thomas Allon, Roger Moore.

BUTE COUNTY—Green Hill, William Person, Thomas Eaton, Rev. Henry Patillo, Jethro Sumner, Josiah Reddick.

CRAVEN COUNTY—James Coor, William Bryan, Richard Cogdell, Joseph Leech, Jacob Blount, Edmund Hatch.

CARTERET COUNTY—John Easton, William Thomson, Brice Williams, Solomon Sheppard, Enoch Ward.

CURRITUCK COUNTY—Thomas Jarvis, Gideon Lamb, James Ryan, James White, Solomon Perkins.

CHOWAN COUNTY—Samuel Johnston, Thomas Jones, Thomas Benbury, James Blount, Thomas Hunter, Josiah Granbery.

CUMBERLAND COUNTY—Farquard Campbell, Thomas Rutherford, Alexander McKay, Alexander McAlister, David Smith.

CHATHAM COUNTY—Elisha Cain, Richard Kennon, Matthew Jones, Jeduthan Harper, John Birdsong, Ambrose Ramsey, Joshua Rosser, Robert Rutherford, John Thompson, William Clark.

DUPLIN COUNTY—James Kenan, William Dixon, Thomas Gray, Richard Clinton, Thomas Hicks.

DOBBS COUNTY—Richard Caswell, Simon Bright, James Glasgow, Abraham Sheppard, Spyers Singleton, George Miller, Andrew Bass.

EDGECOMBE COUNTY—Robert Bignal, Henry Irwin, Duncan Lamon, Thomas Hunter, Thomas Harminson Hall.

GRANVILLE COUNTY—Thomas Person, John Penn, John Williams, John Taylor, Memucan Hunt.

GUILFORD COUNTY—Alexander Martin, Ransom Southerland, James Park Farley, Thomas Henderson, William Dent, George Cortmer, Nathaniel Williams.

HYDE COUNTY—Joseph Hancock, John Jordan.

HERTFORD COUNTY—William Murfree, Lawrence Baker, Matthias Brickle, Dan Ridley, George Wynns.

HALIFAX COUNTY—Nicholas Long, James Hogan, David Sumner, John Webb, John Geddy.

JOHNSTON COUNTY—Benjamine Williams, Samuel Smith, Needham Bryan, William Bryan, John Smith.

MECKLENBURG COUNTY—Thomas Polk, John Phifer, Waightstill Avery, Samuel Martin, James Houston, John McNitt Alexander.

MARTIN COUNTY—Kenneth McKenzie, Whitmill Hill, John Everett, William Slade, John Stuart, William Williams.

NEW HANOVER COUNTY—George Moore, Alexander Lillington, Samuel Ashe, William Hooper, James Moore, John Ashe.

NORTHAMPTON COUNTY—Jeptha Atherton, Allen Jones, Howell Edmunds, Drewry Gee, Samuel Lockhart.

ONSLOW COUNTY—Isaac Guion, Henry Rhodes, Edward Starkey, John Spicer, John King.

ORANGE COUNTY—Thomas Bourk, John Kinchen, Thomas Hart, John Atkinson, John Williams.

PERQUIMANS COUNTY—Benjamin Harvey, Andrew Knox, Miles Harvey, Thomas Harvey, William Skinner.

PASQUOTANK COUNTY—Joseph Jones, Thomas Boyd, Devotion Davis, Edward Everigin, Demsey Burgess.

PITT COUNTY—John Simpson, Robert Salter, William Bryan, James Gorham, James Latham.

ROWAN COUNTY—Matthew Locke, James Smith, Moses Winslow, Samuel Young, William Kennon, William Sharpe, Robert Lanier.

SURREY COUNTY—Joseph Williams, William Hill, Martin Armstrong, Joseph Winston.

TYRRELL COUNTY—Joseph Spruell, Jeremiah Frazier, Peter Wynne, Stevens Lee, Thomas Hoskins.

TRYON COUNTY—John Walker, Robert Alexander, Joseph Hardin, William Graham, Frederick Hambright, William Kennon.

WAKE COUNTY—Joel Lane, John Hinton, Theophilus Hunter, Michael Rodgers, Tignal Jones, John Rand, Thomas Hines.

BATH TOWN COUNTY—William Brown.

EDENTON COUNTY—Joseph Hewes, Jasper Charlton.

NEWBERN COUNTY—Abner Nash, James Davis, William Tisdale, Richard Ellis.

WILMINGTON COUNTY—Cornelius Harnet, Archibald Maclain.

BRUNSWICK COUNTY—Maurice Moore.

HALIFAX COUNTY—Willie Jones, Francis Nash.

HILLSBOROUGH COUNTY—William Armstrong, Nathaniel Nash.

SALISBURY COUNTY—Hugh Montgomery, Robert Rowan.

COMBLETON COUNTY—James Hepburn.

The respective counties and towns having certified that the preceding persons were only elected delegates to represent said counties, and towns in General Congress, to be held at Hillsborough, the 20th day of August Inst. pursuant to which the following persons appeared, to wit:

| | | |
|---|---|---|
| Thomas Respess | Lawrence Baker | Nicholas Long |
| John Patten | Methias Brickle | Roger Moore |
| William Gray | Alexander Martin | Green Hill |
| Charles Jaycocks | Thomas Henderson | William Pearsons |
| William Bryan | Nathaniel Williams | Robert Alexander |
| Zedekiah Stone | Joseph Hancock | William Graham |
| John Johnston | William Sharp | Frederick Hambright |
| Robert Howe | Robert Lanier | William Kennon |
| John Jordan | Joseph Williams | Josiah Reddick |

James Coor
William Bryan
Richard Cogdell
Richard Ellis
Cornelius Harnett
Archibald Maclain
Thomas Benbury
James Blount
James Kennon
William Dickson
Thomas Gray
Jacob Blount
John Easton
Brice Williams
Solomon Shepherd
Enoch Ward
Samuel Johnston
Thomas Jones
Thomas Person
John Penn
John Taylor
Memucan Hunt
Thomas Hart
John Williams
Benjamin Harvey
Andrew Knox
Miles Harvey
Thomas Harvey
William Skinner
John Simpson
James Hogan
Thomas Eston
Henry Patillo
Jethro Sumner
Kenneth McKinzie
Whitmill Hill
William Williams
George Moore
Alexander Lillington
Samuel Ashe
William Hooper
James Moore
John Ashe
Allen Jones
Isaac Guion
James Gorham
James Latham
Matthew Locke
James Smith
Moses Winslow
Samuel Young
William Kennon

Robert Ellis
Parker Quince
Thomas Allon
Day Ridley
Richard Clinton
Thomas Hicks
Richard Caswell
Simon Bright
James Glasgow
Abraham Sheppard
Spyers Singleton
Robert Bignal
Duncan Lamon
William Bryan
Josiah Granberry
John Webb
John Geddy
John Atkinson
William Salter
Walter Gibson
Thomas Owen
Thomas Roberson, jr.
Nathaniel Richardson
Thomas Wade
Samuel Spencer
David Love
William Picket
Elisha Cain
Richard Kennon
Matthew Jones
Robert Salter
Drewry Gee
Howell Edmunds
Samuel Lockhart
Jeremiah Frasier
Joseph Spruill
Peter Wynne
Robert Rowan
James Hepburn
Thomas Rutherford
Alexander McAlister
Farquard Campbell
Alexander McKay
Joseph Jones
Demsey Burgess
John Thompson
Samuel Martin
James Houston
James H. Hall
William Hill
Jasper Charlton
Joseph Leech
Maurice Moore

Willie Jones
Francis Nash
William Armstrong
John Walker
Joseph Hardin
David Sumner
Benjamin Williams
William Bryan
John Smith
Joel Lane
John Hinton
John Rand
William Brown
Joseph Hewes
James Davis
William Tisdale
Michael Rogers
Tignal Jones
John Cooper
Needham Bryan
Ambrose Ramsey
Robert Rutherford
William Clark
Theophilus Hunter
Thomas Polk
Thomas Boyd
Devotion Davis
Edward Everigin
Henry Rhodes
Edward Starkey
Thomas Burke
John King
John Kinchen
Gideon Lamb
Waightstill Avery
Martin Armstrong
Nathaniel Rochester
Hugh Montgomery
David Smith
John Williams
Henry Irwin
Thomas Hines
John Phifer
John McNitt Alexander
James White
Ransom Southerland
James Parke Farley
William Dent
George Courtner
Joshua Rosser
Joseph Winston
John Birdsong

[Page 186]

FRIDAY, SEPTEMBER 1ST, 1775

The Congress met according to adjournment. Taking into consideration the arrangement of the Military troops—(A resolution having been made the day before, to raise a body of forces, consisting of a thousand men, to be done immediately) and the appointment of Officers to command the said troops. Resolved: That they be divided into 2 Regiments consisting of 500 men each, and that 400, part of the first Regiment, be stationed in the District of Wilmington, 200 in the District of Salisbury, 200 in the District of New Bern, and 200 in the District of Edenton—etc.

[Page 187]

Resolved that the following officers be and they are hereby appointed to command the first Regiment, viz:

James Moore, Esq., Colonel             Thomas Clark, Esq., Major
Francis Nash, Esq., Lt. Col.            Mr. William Williams, Adjutant

### CAPTAINS IN 1ST REGIMENT

| | |
|---|---|
| William Davis | Robert Rowan |
| Thomas Allon | John Walker |
| Alfred Moore | Henry Dickson |
| Caleb Grainger | George Davidson |
| William Picket | William Green |

### LIEUTENANTS

| | |
|---|---|
| John Lillington | Hector McNeill |
| Joshua Bowman | Absolom Tatum |
| Lawrence Thompson | Hezekiah Rice |
| Thomas Hogg | William Brandon |
| William Berryhill | William Hill |

### ENSIGNS

| | |
|---|---|
| Neill McAlister | Howell Tatum |
| James Childs | Henry Neill |
| George Graham | Berryman Turner |
| Maurice Moore, Jr. | Robert Rolston |
| John Taylor | Henry Pope |

Doctor Isaac Guion is appointed Surgeon of the First Regiment.

### OFFICERS FOR THE 2ND REGIMENT

[Pages 187-188]

Robert Howe, Esq., Colonel           John Pattern, Esq., Major
Alexander Martin, Lt. Col.          Dr. John White, 1st. Capt. and Adjutant

### CAPTAINS IN SECOND REGIMENT

| | |
|---|---|
| James Blount | Hardy Murphree |
| Michael Payne | Charles Crawford |
| Simon Bright | Nathaniel Keais |
| John Armstrong | John Walker |
| Henry Irwin Toole | |

### LIEUTENANTS, 2ND REGIMENT

| | |
|---|---|
| John Grainger | Edward Vail, Jr. |
| Clement Hall | John Herritage |
| William Fenner | John Williams |
| Benjamin Williams | Joseph Tate |
| Robert Smith | James Gee |

ENSIGNS OF 2ND REGIMENT

Henry Vipson
Whitmell Pugh
John Olliver
Philip Low
James Cook

John Woodhouse
William Gardner
William Caswell
Benjamin Cleveland
Joseph Clinch

Dr. William Pastuer, Surgeon to 2nd Regiment.

[Pages 204-5-6-7]

SATURDAY, SEPTEMBER 9TH, 1775

The Congress met according to adjournment. The House taking into consideration the appointment of the Field Officers of the Minute Men, came to the following Resolution:

Resolved, That the following persons be appointed to wit:

*Edenton District*—Edward Vail, Col.; Caleb Nash, Major; Andrew Knox, Lt. Col.

*Halifax District*—Nicholas Long, Col.; Jethro Sumner, Major; Henry Irwin, Lt. Col.

*Salisbury District*—Thomas Wade, Col.; Joseph Hardin, Major; Adlai Osburn, Lt. Col.

*Hillsboro District*—Jones Thackston, Col.; James Moore, Major; John Williams, Lt. Col.

*New Bern District*—Richard Caswell Col.; James Gorham, Major; William Bryan, Lt. Col.

*Wilmington District*—Alexander Lillington, Col.; Samuel Swann, Major; Robert Ellis, Lt. Col.

And that the following persons be Field Officers of the Militia.

CURRITUCK COUNTY—1 Company. Samuel Jarvis, Col.; Taylor Jones, 1st Major; Dennis Dauge, Lt. Col.; John Nicholson, 2nd Major.

PASQUOTANK COUNTY—1 Company. John Lowery, Col.; Demsey Burgess, Major; Isaac Gregory, Lt. Col.; Joshua Campbell, 2nd Major.

PERQUIMANS COUNTY—1 Company. Miles Harvey, Col.; Thomas, 1st Maj.; William Skinner, Lt. Col.; Richard Clayton, 2nd Major.

CHOWAN COUNTY—Two Companies. Thomas Bonner, Col.; James Blount, Lt. Col.; Thomas Benbury, 1st Major; Jacob Hunter, 2nd Major.

BERTIE COUNTY—2 Companies. Thomas Whitmill, Col.; Thomas Pugh, Lt. Col.; James Moore, 1st Major; Arthur Brown, 2nd Major.

HERTFORD COUNTY—1 Company. Benjamin Wynns, Col.; Matthias Brickle, Lt. Col.; Lawrence Baker, 1st Major; George Lyttle, 2nd Major.

TYRRELL COUNTY—1 Company. Edward Buncombe, Col.; Benjamin Blount, Lt. Col.; James Long, 1st Major; Joseph Spruill, 2nd Major.

MARTIN COUNTY—1 Company. William Wiliams, Col.; Whitmell Hill, Lt. Col.; Thomas Wiggins, 1st Major; Kenneth McKenzie, 2nd Major.

HALIFAX COUNTY—3 Companies. John Bradford, Col.; William Alston, Lt. Col.; David Sumner, 1st Major; Egbert Haywood, 2nd Major.

NORTHAMPTON COUNTY—2 Companies. Allen Jones, Col.; William Eaton, Lt. Col.; Jeptha Atherton, 1st Major; Howell Edmunds, 2nd Major.

EDGECOMBE COUNTY—3 Companies. William Haywood, Col.; Sherwood Haywood, Lt. Col.; Joseph Moore, 1st Major; Henry Horne, 2nd Major.

BUTE COUNTY—2 Companies. Williams Person, Col.; Phil Hawkins, Lt. Col.; William Alston, 1st Major; Thomas Sherwood, 2nd Major.

ANSON COUNTY—2 Companies. Samuel Spencer, Col.; Charles Medlock, Lt. Col.; James Auld, 1st Major; David Love, 2nd Major.

MECKLENBURG COUNTY—2 Companies. Thomas Polk Col.; Adam Alexander, Lt. Col.; John Phifer, 1st Major; John Davidson, 2nd Major.

GUILFORD COUNTY—1 Company. Ransom Sutherland, Col.; James Martin, Lt. Col.; John Paisley, 1st Major; John Tate, 2nd Major.

TRYON COUNTY—2 Companies—William Graham, Col.; Charles Maclaine, Lt. Col.; Thomas Beatty, 1st Major; Frederick Hambright, 2nd Major.

SURRY COUNTY—1 Company. Martin Armstrong, Col.; Joseph Williams, Lt. Col.; William Hall, 1st Major; Joseph Winston 2nd Major.

ROWAN COUNTY—2 Companies—Griffith Rutherford, Col.; Francis Locke, Lt. Col.; John Dobbin, 1st Major; James Brandon, 2nd Major.

CRAVEN COUNTY—2 Companies. Joseph Leech, Col.; John Bryan, Lt. Col.; John Benners, 1st Major; Frederick Becton, 2nd Major.

CARTERET COUNTY—1 Company. William Thomas, Col.; Solomon Shepherd, Lt. Col.; Thomas Chadwick, 1st Major; Malichi Bell, 2nd Major.

BEAUFORT COUNTY—1 Company. James Bomer, Col.; Thomas Bomer, Lt. Col.; Roger Ormond, 1st Major; William Brown, 2nd Major.

HYDE COUNTY—1 Company. Rotheas Latham, Col.; Benj. Parmerlin, Lt. Col.; William Russell, 1st Major; Thomas Jones, 2nd Major.

JOHNSTON COUNTY—1 Company. Needham Bryan, Col.; William Bryan, Lt. Col.; John Smith, 1st Major; Samuel Smith, Jr., 2nd Major.

DOBBS COUNTY—3 Companies. Abraham Sheppard, Col.; Thomas Torrans, Lt. Col.; Martin Caswell, 1st Major; William McKinnie, 2nd Major.

PITT COUNTY—1 Company. John Simpson, Col.; Robert Salter, Lt. Col.; George Evans, 1st Major; James Armstrong, 2nd Major.

BRUNSWICK COUNTY— 1 Company. John Davis, Col.; Thomas Davis, Lt. Col.; Richard Quince, Jr., 1st Major; Parkr Quince, 2nd Major.

ONSLOW COUNTY—2 Companies. William Cray, Col.; Henry Rhodes, Lt. Col.; Thomas Johnston, 1st Major; James Howard, 2nd Major.

DUPLIN COUNTY—2 Companies. James Kenon, Col.; Richard Clinton, Lt. Col.; Thomas Routledge, 1st Major; James Moore, 2nd Major.

CUMBERLAND COUNTY—1 Company. Thomas Rutherford, Col.; Alexander McAlister, Lt. Col.; Duncan McNeill, 1st Major; Alexander McDonald, 2nd Major.

NEWHANOVER COUNTY—2 Companies. William Purirance, Col.; Sampson Moseley, Lt. Col.; William Moseley, 1st Major; John Devane, 2nd Major.

BLADEN COUNTY—2 Companies. Thomas Roberson, Jr., Col.; Thomas Brown, Lt. Col.; Thomas Owens, 1st Major; James Richardson, 2nd Major.

ORANGE COUNTY—3 Companies. John Hogan, Col.; John Butler, Lt. Col.; William Moore, 1st Major; Nathaniel Rochester, 2nd Major.

GRANVILLE COUNTY—3 Companies. Joseph Taylor, Col.; Charles R. Eaton, Lt. Col.; Samuel Smith, 1st Major; William Williams, 2nd Major.

WAKE COUNTY—2 Companies. John Hinton, Col.; Theophilus Hunter, Lt. Col.; John Hinton, Jr., 1st Major; Thomas Hines, 2nd Major.

CHATHAM COUNTY—2 Companies. Ambrose Ramsey, Col.; Jeduthan Harper, Lt. Col.; Mial Scurlock, 1st Major; Elisha Cain, 2nd Major.

Pages 189-263, inclusive.
Abstract of the Army Accounts, of the N. C. Line. Settled by the Commissioners at Halifax, from 1st Sept. 1784 to the 1st Feb. 1785, and at Warrenton in the year 1786, designating by whom the claims were receipted for respectively.

| No. | Name & Rank | By Whom Received | Remarks |
|---|---|---|---|
| 29. | Charles Allen ................ | H. Montfort | for Charles Allen |
| 33. | N. Alexander, M. G. H. ......... | John Nelson | |
| 36. | Charles Alexander, Lt. .......... | do | |
| 44. | Thos. Armstrong, Capt. ......... | Tho. Armstrong | |
| 25. | James Anthony ............... | Ab. Thomas | |
| 32. | William Aldridge ............. | do | |
| 51. | John Adcock ................. | Robt. Fenner | |
| 52. | Joshua Adcock ............... | do | |
| 97. | Daniel Alderman ............. | Henry Montford | for D. Alderman |
| 102. | Thomas Anderson ............. | Philip Fishburn | |
| 140. | Jesse Ashlock ................ | Henry Montfort | for J. Ashlock |
| 147. | William Adams ............... | Alex Brevard | |
| 222. | Thomas Ammons .............. | J. Bradley | |
| 414. | Samuel Ates ................. | Ab Thomas | |
| 450. | John Alcorn, Lt. .............. | John Craven | |
| 496. | John Addleman ............... | Ardi Lytle | |
| 503. | Joseph Aldridge .............. | do | |
| 518. | John Allen .................. | Charles Dixon | |
| 577. | Arthur Arnold ............... | John McNees | |
| *589. | Philip Adams ................ | William Sanders | |
| 770. | Thomas Anderson ............. | John Shepard | |
| 771. | John Anderson ............... | do | |
| 799. | John Atkinson ................ | Henry Montfort | for Atkinson |
| 823. | Thomas Aldridge ............. | John McNees | |
| 862. | Charles Ashe ................ | John Shepard | |
| 870. | Henry Alligood .............. | Fred Harget | |
| 887. | David Allen ................. | Will Sanders | |
| 891. | John Abbett ................. | Thomas Donoho | |
| 926. | John Allison ................ | Arch. Lytle | |
| 944. | Simon Alderson, Lt. ........... | | |
| 1055. | Jeremiah Ashley ............. | John Craven ☞ | for Hance Bond |
| 1074. | William Anderson ............ | Tho. Armstrong | |
| 1096. | Garrett Altman .............. | B. McCullock | |
| 1102. | Philip Axum ................ | do | |
| 1104. | James Avery ................ | Nich. Long | |
| 1124. | David Adkins ............... | Henry Montfort | for D. Adkins |
| 1133. | John Alrick ................. | John Bonds | |
| 1166. | Arthur Adams ............... | Robt. Fenner | |
| 1197. | Cornelius\Allison ............. | James X Simmon's | |

* The black number ceases and the red begins. Observe that blanks left in the receipt column opposite the name denotes that it was drawn by himself.

| No. | Name & Rank | By Whom Received | Remarks |
|-----|-------------|------------------|---------|
| 1329. | Thomas Allen ................. | Charles Dixon | |
| 1351. | Michael Adkinson .............. | do | |
| 1374. | James Aulton .................. | do | |
| 1381. | John Abbute .................. | William X Griffis | |

[Page 190]

## ABSTRACT. THE ARMY ACCTS. OF THE N. C. LINE
### [Warrenton Settlements]

| No. | Name & Rank | By Whom Received | Remarks |
|-----|-------------|------------------|---------|
| 36. | James Armstrong, Lt. ........... | | not receipted for |
| 1421. | Dempsey Archer ............... | William Faircloth | |
| 1422. | Hardy Atway .................. | do | |
| 1499. | Jesse Aldridge ................. | John McNees | |
| 1511. | Thomas Aims ................. | B. McCulloch | for Jas. Glasgow |
| 1614. | Thomas Ashley ............... | John Price | |
| 1639. | Hardy Atkinson ............... | do | |
| 1783. | Emanuel Asbett .............. | William Faircloth | |
| 1788. | Charles Atbett ............... | do | |
| 1824. | Zachariah Atbett ............. | do | |
| 1842. | Mark Allen ................... | do | |
| 1857. | Drury Anthony ............... | Thomas Butcher | |
| 1931. | Elias Ashburn ................ | William Faircloth | |
| 2094. | Mills Anderson .............. | Thomas Butcher | |
| 2116. | John Applewhite ............. | Sherd. Barrow | |
| 2123. | Abraham Applewhite .......... | do | |
| 2172. | Anthony Abbett .............. | do | |
| 2251. | William Adcock .............. | William Sanders | |
| 2263. | Moses Adcock ............... | do | |
| 2285. | John Airs, Senr. ............. | do | |
| 2286. | John Airs, Junr. ............. | do | |
| 2314. | Robert Acock ................ | M. D. Johnston | for Robt. Acock |
| 3715. | Moses Acock ................ | do | |
| 2357. | Thomas Adams .............. | Philip Fishburn | |
| 2361. | Peter Albright ............... | do | |
| 2363. | Simon Albright .............. | do | |
| 2374. | John Artis ................... | Benj. McCulloch | for Arthur Pearce |
| 2406. | Peter Allison ............... | James Tatum | |
| 2430. | Alexander Anthony ........... | William Sanders | |
| 2488. | James Atkins ................ | "Paid to J. Macon" | receipt not signed |
| 2512. | Richard Atkins .............. | John Daves | |
| 2513. | John Avery ................. | do | |
| 2537. | Jesse Allen, Lt. .............. | Sam'l. Parker | |
| 2544. | Benjamin Alexander .......... | Wm. Sanders | |
| 2550. | Joseph Alexander ............ | do | |
| 2574. | Andrew Andrews ............. | John Price | |
| 2707. | Philip Askew ................ | Charles X Serugg his mark | |
| 2708. | Serugg Askew ............... | do | |
| 2786. | Nathaniel Alexander ......... | Philip Fishburn | |
| 2828. | James Armstrong ............ | Tho. Donoho | |
| 2839. | John Adcock ................ | do | |
| 2903. | George Adcock .............. | Sam'l. Parker | |
| 3045. | Solomon Avery .............. | Thomas Armstrong | |

| No. | Name & Rank | By Whom Received | Remarks |
|---|---|---|---|
| 3078. | John Aycock .................. | H. Montfort | |
| 3126. | Benjamin Angel ............... | J. Estes | for A. Tatum |
| 3180. | Joseph Allen ................. | John Marshall | The orders in |
| 3210. | Isaac Anderson ............... | do | fav. Charles Dixon |
| 3229. | Richard Atchison .............. | John Marshall | |
| 3273. | Charles Anderson .............. | do | for Wm. Sanders |
| 3330. | Isaac Anderson ............... | Timothy McCarthy | |
| 3331. | Jacob Albritton ............... | do | |
| 3341. | John Ashburn ................ | do | |

[Page 191]

ABSTRACT. THE ARMY ACCTS. OF THE N. C. LINE

B

| No. | Name & Rank | By Whom Received | Remarks |
|---|---|---|---|
| 2. | Matthias Brickell, Ens. ........... | H. Murfree | |
| 6. | John Burton, Adjt. ............. | do | |
| 7. | T. Bedford, Clk. H. C. I. ........ | Ab. Thomas | |
| 16. | Joel Brevard, Capt. ............. | N. Montfort | for J. Brevard |
| 20. | Thomas Blount, Lt. ............. | Ab. Thomas | |
| 21. | Joseph Brevard, Lt. ............. | Alex. Brevard | |
| 25. | R. Brownfield, M. G. H. ........ | Joe Nelson | |
| 40. | Robert Blackwell, Lt. ........... | Ab. Thomas | |
| 41. | John Brevard, Capt. ............. | Alex. Brevard | |
| 73. | Wm. Brinkley, Col. ............. | H. Montfort | for W. Brinkley |
| 89. | William Boddington ............. | Ab. Thomas | |
| 96. | Council Bass .................. | do | |
| 97. | Uriah Bass .................... | do | |
| 108. | Drury Bass .................... | do | |
| 112. | John Boggs ................... | Arch'd. Lytle | |
| 135. | David Burnsides, Lt. ............ | Jos. Hadley | |
| 156. | Aaron Bledsoe ................. | H. Montfort | for A. Bledsoe |
| 189. | Absalom Burgess, Lt. ........... | do | A. Burgess |
| 191. | James Bradley ................. | John Nelson | |
| 192. | James Britnal ................. | H. Montfort | for J. Britnal |
| 194. | Daniel Bocker ................. | J. Nelson | |
| 196. | James Britain ................. | H. Montfort | for J. Britain |
| 198. | Benjamin Bridgers ............. | J. Hunt | |
| 211. | James Barnett ................. | H. Montfort | for J. Barnett |
| 228. | Drury Baggett ................. | Jos. Hadley | |
| 245. | David Benton ................. | H. Montfort | for D. Benton |
| 251. | John Baker ................... | Edward Partee | |
| 256. | Philip Brittain ................ | H. Montfort | for P. Brittain |
| 259. | Samuel Burton ................ | James Bristow | |
| 267. | Daniel Bullock ................ | H. Montfort | for D. Bullock |
| 268. | Isaac Barbaree ................ | J. Craven | for Rob. Hulme |
| 286. | Adam Brevard ................ | Alex. Brevard | |
| 294. | Edward Blurton ............... | H. Montfort | for E. Blurton |
| 305. | Stephen Blarfield .............. | John Sheppard | |
| 309. | Marmaduke Barfield ............ | do | |
| 315. | William Brown ................ | H. Montfort | for W. Brown |
| 331. | Moses Bishop ................. | Jer Nelms | |
| 356. | David Barnhill ................ | H. Montfort | for D. Barnhill |
| 359. | Josiah Benton ................ | do | for J. Benton |
| 360. | John Best .................... | do | for J. Best |
| 363. | Isaac Baker .................. | do | for J. Baker |

| No. | Name & Rank | By Whom Received | Remarks |
|---|---|---|---|
| 368. | John Burress | Thomas Vickers | |
| 376. | Stephen Bowen | H. Montfort | |
| 402. | Joseph Bird | Arch'd. Lytle | |
| 403. | Thomas Bane | do | |
| 410. | George Bristow | do | |
| 414. | Ezekiel Boggs | do | |
| 425. | Abraham Beaverhouse | Alex Brevard | |
| 429. | Thomas Brannan, 3 yrs. | do | |
| 431. | Thomas Brannan, 12 mos. | do | |
| 450. | Edward Bradley, Lt. | J. Craven | |
| 5B. | | | |
| | [Page 192] | | |
| 457. | Moses Bird | H. Montfort | for M. Bird |
| 468. | Thomas Brickle, Sergt. | | |
| 483. | William Barnes | Selbey Harney | |
| 485. | Thos. Billups, Drummer | | |
| 507. | Joseph Boon | Ab. Thomas | |
| 508. | Andrew Bay, S. M. | do | |
| 512. | William Baxter | J. Faulkner | |
| 530. | Thos. Brown, Waggr. | John Ingles | for Maj. McRee |
| 538. | John Barco | H. Montfort | for J. Barco |
| 555. | Jones Breach | H. Montfort | for H. Hunt |
| 559. | Darby Bryan | John Allen | |
| 594. | Spencer Breedlove | Charles Dixon | |
| 598. | James Bryan | do | |
| 600. | Abner Barnes | do | |
| 604. | William Bryant | do | |
| 610. | Henry Burton | do | |
| 634. | James Barton, Corpl. | do | |
| 640. | James Barrow | J. Felts | |
| 643. | John Boyd | H. Montfort | for J. Boyd |
| 649. | Richard Bolton, Lt. | John McNees | |
| 651. | William Boyd | H. Montfort | for W. Boyd |
| 657. | Thomas Beotherton | Alex McMillan | |
| 673. | Leonard x Brady x K. | | |
| 682. | Matthew Banks | William Sanders | |
| 694. | John Bevars, Lt. | | |
| 708. | James Beaver | do | |
| 720. | Sion Barnett | do | |
| 724. | Osborn Ball | do | |
| 728. | William Buckham | do | |
| 729. | William Bevers | do | |
| 737. | John Bailey | H. Montfort | for Jno. Bailey |
| 742. | John Burnett | do | for J. Burnett |
| 751. | Joseph Babb | Robt. Fenner | |
| 766. | Barnabas Burns | John Sheppard | |
| 769. | John Bruton | do | |
| 780. | Esau Bass | do | |
| 781. | James Bundy | do | |
| 805. | Frederick Burns | H. Montfort | for F. Burns |
| 840. | Hardy Brogden | Thomas Armstrong | |
| 847. | Jethro Butler | David Collins | |
| 850. | Joel Burmont | John Daves | |
| 858. | Lewis Boon | Sampson Hays | |

| No. | Name & Rank | By Whom Received | Remarks |
|---|---|---|---|
| 865. | Thomas Bently | John Sheppard | |
| 869. | John Bradsher | F. Hargett | |
| 874. | James Brown | do | |
| 893. | William Brown, War | H. Montfort | |
| 906. | Wm. Brown, 9 mos. | Arch'd. Lythe | |
| 913. | Bazely Bourne | do | |
| 916. | John Barnhill | do | |
| 937. | William Brickell | do | |
| 942. | Thomas Bowles | do | |
| 957. | James Brannon | do | |
| 958. | Phil'n Bristow, Drag. | do | |
| 974. | Moses Bennett | Nich. Long | |
| 985. | James Broadstreet | J. Craven | |
| 995. | Hezekiah Barnes | Tho. Evans | |
| | [Page 193] | | |
| 998. | William Bell | do | |
| 1001. | George Bachelor | Jesse Reed | |
| 1018. | Benjamin Baker | H. Murfree | |
| 1025. | David Boon | do | |
| 1030. | Arthur Boice | H. Montfort | |
| 1033. | James Brown | do | |
| 1045. | William Barber | | |
| 1069. | William Bailey | do | for W. Bailey |
| 1075. | William Brown | E. Gamble | |
| 1089. | Joel Butler | B. McCulloch | |
| 1099. | Daniel Barrow | do | |
| 1111. | William Burch, Corpl. | John Kingsbury | |
| 1112. | Michael Bullen | H. Montfort | for M. Bullen |
| 1125. | John Burns | do | for J. Burns |
| 1128. | Robert Bradley | do | for R. Bradley |
| 1131. | Benjamin Brewer | Jere Nelms | |
| 1132. | Robert Bailey | John Bonds | |
| 1134. | Amos Baker | do | |
| 1140. | Alias Bell | do | |
| 1145. | John Brantly | do | |
| 1146. | Elijah Boon | do | |
| 1155. | Thomas Barco | T. Dixon | |
| 1158. | George Bruce | Charles Dixon | |
| 1183. | Bristow Brantley | John Bonds | |
| 1185. | William Buckingham | Henry Overstreet | |
| 1187. | James Blackwell | John Sheppard | |
| 1193. | Thomas Blount | J. Craven | for Rob. Huhne |
| 1196. | Henry Barnhill | H. Montfort | for Barnhill |
| 1221. | John Bradshaw | John Sheppard | |
| 1224. | William Bennett | do | |
| 1225. | Benjamin Brewington | do | |
| 1230. | Meredith Burke | do | |
| 1240. | Arthur Brown | Tho. Armstrong, Junr. | |
| 1256. | Stancell Barbree | H. Montfort | |
| 1261. | Richard Bradley | John Grimes | |
| 1279. | Isaac Bagby | H. Montfort | for Bagby |
| 1299. | Richard Bolton | do | for Bolton |
| 1305. | James Bradley | B. McCulloch | |
| 1307. | Nehemiah Bennett | do | |

| No. | Name & Rank | By Whom Received | Remarks |
|---|---|---|---|
| 1330. | William Baker ................. | Charles Dixon | |
| 1342. | Charles Baker ................. | do | |
| 1347. | James Baultrip ................. | do | |
| 1356. | John Bailey .................... | do | |
| 1369. | John Black .................... | do | |
| 1376. | Ambrose Bryan ................. | do | |
| 1382. | Wyllie Barrow ................. | T. Dixon | |
| 1383. | James Brown ................... | do | |
| 1404. | Frederick Brigsby .............. | John Reachell | |
| 1222. | James Boon ................... | John Sheppard | |
| | [Page 194] | | |

[WARRENTON]

| No. | Name & Rank | By Whom Received | Remarks |
|---|---|---|---|
| 9. | Edwd. Buncombe, Col. ........... | | not rec'd. for |
| 10. | Benjamin Bryer, Lt. ............. | | |
| 1426. | Frederick Bagwell .............. | | |
| 1427. | George Barlow ................. | | |
| 1428. | Silas Biggs .................... | | |
| 1429. | Benjamin Bird ................. | William Faircloth | |
| 1430. | Colden Bushop ................. | | |
| 1431. | John Balford .................. | | |
| 1432. | William Bushop ................ | | |
| 1504. | (Isaac Bagley, C.) .............. | B. McCulloch | for Art. Pearce |
| 1505. | William Burley ................ | do | for J. Glasgow |
| 1521. | Michael Branner ............... | John Price | |
| 1532. | Arthur Britt ................... | B. McCulloch | for Red Blount |
| 1535. | Solomon Bandy ................ | John Price | |
| 1565. | Philip Burch .................. | do | |
| 1578. | Josiah Black .................. | do | |
| 1585. | Samuel Bradley ............... | do | |
| 1605. | William Babley ............... | do | |
| 1608. | William Brownen .............. | do | |
| 1609. | Michael Buckner .............. | do | |
| 1613. | Peter Brumfield ............... | do | |
| 1618. | Britain Bass .................. | do | |
| 1621. | Benjamin Blow ................ | do | |
| 1623. | William Blumby .............. | do | |
| 1625. | Samuel Brownen .............. | do | |
| 1636. | George Brooks, Lt. ............ | do | |
| 1641. | Shadrach Bosman ............. | do | |
| 1656. | Lewis Brooks ................. | do | |
| 1660. | Benjamin Bloodworth .......... | do | |
| 1682. | Stephen Barber ............... | do | |
| 1684. | Absalom Barnett .............. | do | |
| 1705. | Joel Bargeram ................ | William Faircloth | |
| 1712. | Wilkinson Barfield ............ | do | |
| 1715. | Taylor Bowling ............... | do | |
| 1741. | Benjamin Brittle .............. | do | |
| 1742. | Jesse Baggett, C. ............. | do | |
| 1750. | John Bettis, P. ............... | do | |
| 1786. | Booling Brimmer ............. | do | |
| 1796. | Aaron Barham ............... | do | |
| 1812. | Bart'w. Bohannan ............ | do | |
| 1823. | Willis Basdell ................ | do | |
| 1825. | Moses Braxton ............... | do | |

| *No.* | *Name & Rank* | *By Whom Received* | *Remarks* |
|---|---|---|---|
| 1827. | William Barkley ............... | William Faircloth | |
| 1832. | John Bolson ................... | do | |
| 1840. | Allen Brook .................. | do | |
| 1856. | Taylor Bowles ................ | Thomas Butcher | |
| 1862. | Taylor Brockley .............. | do | |
| 1863. | Aaron Breda ................. | do | |
| 1865. | Aaron Bendom ................ | do | |
| 1866. | David Bolston ............... | do | |
| 1879. | Gillam Baily ................ | do | |
| 1835. | Samuel Belward .............. | William Faircloth | |
| 1887. | Joel Bolson ................. | do | |
|  | [Page 195] | | |
| 1889. | William Brumbly ............. | Thomas Butcher | |
| 1894. | William Browner ............. | do | |
| 1906. | David Brittle ............... | do | |
| 1925. | Austin Belford .............. | William Faircloth | |
| 1926. | Arthur Brandum .............. | do | |
| 1935. | John Bradsley ............... | do | |
| 1941. | Peter Baker ................. | do | |
| 1949. | Samuel Buffington ........... | do | |
| 1968. | Simon Braxton ............... | do | |
| 1970. | Samuel Blackman ............. | do | |
| 1973. | James Barrow ................ | do | |
| 1981. | Anthony Barnes .............. | do | |
| 1983. | Simon Broadstreet ........... | do | |
| 1995. | Simon Brady ................. | do | |
| 1998. | Bark Benson ................. | do | |
| 2000. | Silas Bromfield ............. | do | |
| 2002. | James Britt ................. | do | |
| 2012. | Alexander Bentford .......... | do | |
| 2034. | George Burgess .............. | B. McCulloch | for S. Harney |
| 2047. | Hodges Benshaw .............. | do | do |
| 2065. | James Ballard ............... | John Sheppard | |
| 2069. | John Blanchard, M. .......... | Joshua Davis | |
| 2074. | Amariah Blanchard ........... | do | |
| 2075. | James Bennett ............... | do | |
| 2084. | Stephen Bans ................ | Thomas Butcher | |
| 2088. | James Belford ............... | do | |
| 2096. | William Bartea .............. | do | |
| 2098. | John Baconham ............... | Serrod Barrow | |
| 2107. | David Rook (?) .............. | do | |
| 2113. | Meredith Brantley ........... | do | |
| 2157. | William Bush ................ | Thomas Butcher | |
| 2176. | Isaac Bentford .............. | Sherrod Barrow | |
| 2186. | James Butworth .............. | do | |
| 2189. | Robert Biggs ................ | do | |
| 2192. | John Balmer, C. ............. | John Sheppard | |
| 2203. | William Burke ............... | Thomas Butcher | |
| 2225. | John Brunt .................. | Isle Simmons | |
| 2227. | Samuel Burnham .............. | do | |
| 2231. | Jacob Bennett ............... | do | |
| 2245. | William N. Burton ........... | William Lytle | |
| 2249. | Thomas Boyd ................. | do | |
| 2270. | Ignatius Beech .............. | William Sanders | |

| No. | Name & Rank | By Whom Received | Remarks |
|---|---|---|---|
| 2273. | Navy Bateman | William Sanders | |
| 2306. | Robert Beech | John Marshall | |
| 2308. | Samuel Boyett | do | |
| 2333. | Job Branch, C. | Nathaniel Williams | |
| 2334. | Job Bright | do | |
| 2338. | John Brown, Lt. | Philip Fishburn | |
| 2349. | Samuel Barkley | do | |
| (?)2366. | George Bell | do | |
| 2392. | James Brabble | Griffith Dange | |
| 2401. | Jacob Borean, Lt. | | not receipted for |
| 2417. | William Beasley | Benj. McCulloch | for Selby Harney |
| 2420. | James Brown | Nath'l. Williams | |
| 2426. | Richard Bailey | Coseno Medeci | |
| 2437. | Thomas Brinkley | Robert Fenner | |
| | [Page 196] | | |
| 2445. | Matthias Betts | William Lytle | |
| 2450. | James Barnhill | Thomas Pearson | |
| 2452. | William Bushop | Robt. Alexander | |
| 2468. | John Bentley | T. Dixon | |
| 2502. | Thomas Breece | John Daves | |
| 2518. | David Brothers | do | |
| 2520. | Frederick Blount | do | |
| 2526. | Archibald Bogle | Charles Guerard | |
| 2531. | William Bochner | John McNees | |
| 2543. | Thomas Best | William Sanders | |
| 2546. | William Banks | do | |
| 2554. | Samuel Burnham | do | |
| 2555. | Jacob Bright | do | |
| 2562. | Jesse Brown | Benjamin McCulloch | |
| 2563. | Solomon Brown | | not receipted for |
| 2566. | Christian Barnhunt | Philip Fishburn | |
| 2577. | Robert Bartlett | John Price | |
| 2578. | James Barton | do | |
| 2582. | Joseph Bartlett | do | |
| 2592. | Isham Branch | do | |
| 2595. | Solomon Bruton | do | |
| 2612. | Randall Britting | John McNees | |
| 2630. | John Bolton | William Sanders | |
| 2637. | James Butler | do | |
| 2639. | James Blanchitt | do | |
| 2642. | James Ballard | do | |
| 2645. | Arthur Bright | do | |
| 2646. | Thomas Brooks | do | |
| 2656. | Morris Barker | Thomas Butcher | |
| 2662. | Job Benbow | do | |
| 2678. | Jesse Bunn | Jesse Hammond | |
| 2688. | Henry Blurton | | not receipted for |
| 2704. | Robert Berry, Jr. | John McRee | |
| 2716. | Henry Butcher | John Price | |
| 2735. | Aaron Butler | do | |
| 2747. | Elisha Britt | do | |
| 2749. | Joshua Bennett | do | |
| 2758. | Jacob Bostian | Philip Fishburn | |
| 2759. | Andrew Bostian | do | |

| No. | Name & Rank | By Whom Received | Remarks |
|---|---|---|---|
| 2775. | William Bradley | John Garland, Junr. | |
| 2788. | Jonas Beechey | Philip Fishburn | |
| 2793. | Thomas Bond | do | |
| 2816. | William Baker | John Sommers | |
| 2820. | James Bell, C. | Thomas Donoho | |
| 2826. | Thomas Brown, S. | do | |
| 2863. | Clarel Barrs | William Faircloth | |
| 2882. | Zebedee Baker | do | |
| 2897. | Alberson Bruce | do | |
| 2909. | John Black | William Lytle | |
| 2910. | David Benton | do | |
| 2917. | John Blanchard, M. | Charles Guerard | |
| 2919. | Thomas Barnes, Drag. | Dems Spier | |
| 2926. | Thomas Belbury | | |
| 2927. | Thomas Bekiah | John Armstrong | |
| 2930. | Robert Biggs | Ben. Johnson | |
| 2937. | Thomas Blair | | |
| | [Page 197] | | |
| 2940. | James Burbage | James Homes | |
| 2941. | Baker Brand | do | |
| 2977. | David Bryan | Simon Totevine ... ⎧ | for Maxwell, Jno. |
| 3004. | William Butler | H. Murfree ..... ⎨ | Garland, Junr., |
| 3008. | Charles Briggs | Nathaniel Williams. ⎩ | Jas. Holmes |
| 3010. | Joseph Bedgood | do | |
| 3013. | Maltier Ballentine | Benj. Easman | |
| 3018. | Thomas Brown | Robert Fenner | |
| 3021. | William Blake | John Sommers | |
| 3023. | Peter Baker | do | |
| 3026. | James Barnes | do | |
| 3040. | John Betts | Thomas Armstrong | |
| 3047. | Benjamin Bickings | do | |
| 3054. | James Brady | Thomas Person | |
| 3058. | Benjamin Brady, Lt. | ⎫ | not receipted for |
| 3068. | John Baggett | ⎬ | |
| 3070. | Joseph Barrott | ⎭ | do |
| 3072. | Benjamin Boulton | | |
| 3077. | Moses Bass | H. Montfort | |
| 3088. | Burrell Branch | Curtis Ivey | |
| 3091. | Joseph Baker | | |
| 3127. | Zenas Bawlin | J. Estes | for A. Tatum |
| 3145. | Simon Blackman | | ⎫ |
| 3146. | Robinson Bradstreet | | ⎬ no receipt |
| 3150. | Joseph Bradley | John Sheppard | for Asa Croom |
| 3162. | Elihu Burke | | no receipt |
| 3175. | John Brock | John Marshall | order in fav. C. Dixon |
| 3190. | White Berwick | do | do |
| 3204. | Samuel Barber | do | do |
| 3213. | Stephen Brady | do | do |
| 3214. | Joseph Baker | do | do |
| 3218. | Joshua Bruant | do | do |
| 3223. | Joshua Brewington | Andrew Armstrong | for Jas. Pearl |
| 3236. | Thomas Bullard | John Marshall | |
| 3238. | Warren Blount | do | |
| 3239. | Benjamin Banks | do | |

| No. | Name & Rank | By Whom Received | Remarks |
|---|---|---|---|
| 3241. | William Burgay | John Marshall | |
| 3247. | John Bush | Philip Fishburn | |
| 3262. | Richard Brown | do | |
| 3285. | Benjamin Bowling | John Marshall | for W. Sanders |
| 3288. | James Busby | do | do |
| 3290. | David Blalock | do | do |
| 3294. | Solomon Boroughs | do | do |
| 3295. | Nimrod Bradley | do | do |
| 3296. | Joshua Brusfield | do | do |
| 3300. | Benjamin Boulton | do | do |
| 3312. | Thomas Blount | James Armstrong | |
| 3329. | George Benton | Timothy McCarthy | |
| 3334. | Abraham Ballard | do | |
| 3344. | John Burus, L. | do | |
| 3345. | Michael Bond | do | |
| 3348. | Waker Ballard | do | |
| 3356. | Abraham Beck | do | |
| 3366. | William Buckley | do | |
| 3367. | Benjamin Braswell | do | |
| 3371. | Henry Bailey | do | |
| 3373. | Joseph Bentley | do | |

## C

[Page 198]

| No. | Name & Rank | By Whom Received | Remarks |
|---|---|---|---|
| | Benjn. Carter, Capt. | Alex Brevard | |
| 15. | George Cook, Lt. | Selby Hearney | |
| 102. | Thomas Cook | Ab. Thomas | |
| 106. | Martin Cross, Fifer | do | |
| 120. | Giles Carter | H. Murfree | |
| 136. | William Carrol | Jos. Hadley | |
| 137. | John Carr | Jno. Nelson | |
| 138. | John Curry | Jno. Ingles | |
| 143. | Shadrach Curry | do | |
| 162. | William Cole | J. Craven | |
| 172. | Elijah Cotton | Ephraim X Cotton<br>mark | |
| 118. | Benjamin Crabb | Selby Harney | |
| 218. | William Cogdell | Alex. Brevard | |
| 220. | James Cavendar | John Atkinson | |
| 243. | Andrew Canker | John Nelson | |
| 277. | William Collins | William X Harrison<br>mark | |
| 279. | Charles Collins | do | |
| 283. | Robert Christie | H. Montfort | for R. Christie |
| 284. | Joshua Cheason | | |
| 285. | Stephen Chance | James Cobb | |
| 330. | Solomon Chavers | Jer. Nelms | |
| 337. | William Childers | Thomas Armstrong | |
| 393. | John Cochran | C. Dixon | |
| 396. | Jonathan Clower | Eli McVey | |
| 401. | James Clark | Archo. Lytle | |
| 423. | John Conn | do | |

| No. | Name & Rank | By Whom Received | Remarks |
|---|---|---|---|
| 428. | Lambert Clayton, Lt. | A. Brevard | |
| 443. | Pleasant Childers | J. Craven | |
| 445. | William Childers | do | |
| 446. | Benjamin Clark | do | |
| 460. | Nathan Cobb | H. Montfort | for N. Cobb |
| 469. | Bird Cornett | do | for B. Cornett |
| 471. | James Cain | Willie Jones | but not receipted |
| 477. | James Carothers | William Lytle | |
| 478. | Thomas Carothers | do | |
| 490. | John Collins | David Collins | |
| 492. | John Chester | Ab. Thomas | |
| 493. | Thomas Chittim | do | |
| 511. | Francis Capps | J. Faulcon | |
| 518. | Thompson Curry, Sgt. | Thomas Armstrong | |
| 528. | George Cathy | J. Craven | |
| 531. | Philip Cakes | John Ingles | for Major McRee |
| 542. | John Cornelius | Thomas Stewart | for J. Cornelius |
| 560. | David Cozart | H. Montfort | for M. Hunt |
| 564. | James Copeland | A. Lytle | |
| 572. | Matthew Cates | do | |
| 575. | Jacob Cliever | do | |
| 582. | George Conder | do | |
| 624. | Benjamin Conner | do | |
| | [Page 199] | | |
| 646. | William Clifton | do | for W. Clifton |
| 704. | Osborn Crabb | William Sanders | |
| 705. | Garrett Crabb | do | |
| 707. | John Crabb | do | |
| 734. | Drury Chavers | Thomas Person | |
| 752. | John Callaham | H. Montfort | for J. Callahan |
| 753. | William Callaham | do | for W. Callahan |
| 755. | James Carmack | J. McNees | |
| 762. | Daniel Carroll | H. Montfort | for D. Carroll |
| 768. | James Cammell | J. Sheppard | |
| 774. | Thomas Carraway | do | |
| 782. | John Cotton, Lt. | do | |
| 793. | James Cockburn | Ab. Thomas | |
| 800. | George Coombs | H. Montfort | for G. Coombs |
| 829. | Thomas Cocks or Cox | John Price | |
| 839. | James Coomer | Jesse Reed | |
| 851. | Benjamin Collins | John Daves | |
| 854. | John Clemmons | do | |
| 885. | Drury Cook | William Sanders | |
| 886. | Daniel Carroll | do | |
| 899. | Thomas Carpenter | William King | |
| 921. | Daniel Camble | A. Lytle | |
| 924. | Absalom Clifton | do | |
| 930. | Robert Cates | do | |
| 931. | Zachariah Cates | do | |
| 938. | James Conner | do | |
| 945. | John Coupland | do | |
| 961. | Levi Coulter | do | |
| 963. | Thomas Castles | do | |
| 970. | Edward Cole | do | |

| No. | Name & Rank | By Whom Received | Remarks |
|---|---|---|---|
| 972. | Jesse Cole | A. Lytle | |
| 983. | William Crow | J. Craven | |
| 991. | James Charlescraft | Tho. Evans | |
| 1004. | Samuel Cooper | Jesse Reed | |
| 1015. | John Cason | Robert Fenner | |
| 1016. | Stephen Cook | do | |
| 1024. | Cesar Chavers | H. Murfree | |
| 1027. | Robert Churmmer | H. Montfort | |
| 1028. | John Conner | do | |
| 1049. | William Cox | Nicholas Long | |
| 1088. | Britton Carrol | B. McCulloch | |
| 1091. | Benjamin Carroll | do | |
| 1092. | Richard Corbert | do | |
| 1107. | Lan'lin Campbell, Lt. | H. Montfort | for L. Campbell |
| 1116. | Wm. Campbell, Art. | John Kingsbury | |
| 1148. | James Cremor | John Bonds | |
| 1156. | John Clark | T. Dixon | |
| 1160. | Robert Chumley | Charles Dixon | |
| 1170. | John Curls | Henry Overstreet | |
| 1191. | Isaac Cornelius | Willie Jones | |
| 1216. | John Clinton | H. Montfort | for J. Clinton |
| 1232. | John Chester | John Sheppard | |
| 1243. | Francis Carraway | H. Montfort | for Carraway |
| 1302. | Richard Corbett | B. McCulloch | |
| 1311. | Joseph Case | H. Montfort | for Case |
| 1313. | William Campbell | do | |
| | [Page 200] | | |
| 1321. | John Cole | C. Dixon | |
| 1327. | Edmund Cole | do | |
| 1336. | William Cavender | do | |
| 1344. | John Curk | do | |
| 1349. | James Cleveland | John Jones | |
| 1352. | John Caven | C. Dixon | |
| 1361. | Samuel Carey | do | |
| 1365. | Frederick Coock | do | |
| 1367. | Absalom Clifton | do | |
| 1370. | Peter Curtis | do | |
| 1372. | John Cutty | do | |
| 412. | William Clower | Arch'd. Lytle | |
| 419. | William Clark | do | |

[WARRENTON]

| No. | Name & Rank | By Whom Received | Remarks |
|---|---|---|---|
| 1. | James Craven, Lt. | T. Dixon | |
| 2. | Butler Crowell, Lt. | | |
| 4. | William Charleton, Lt. | B. McCulloch | for Col. Harney |
| 18. | David Cowen, Lt. | Philip Fishburn | |
| 70. | Wm. Coventon, Lt. | | ☞ no receipt |
| 1406. | Thomas Cullas | William Faircloth | |
| 1407. | John Cullas | do | |
| 1440. | John Cameron | do | |
| 1441. | Wm. Cobb | do | |
| 1479. | Sampson Culliner | do | |
| 1480. | John Campton | do | |
| 1489. | Abraham Clark | J. McNees | |

| No. | Name & Rank | By Whom Received | Remarks |
|---|---|---|---|
| 1490. | Jacob Clark .................... | J. McNees | |
| 1496. | Anthony Cross .................. | do | |
| 1546. | Jesse Cann .................... | John Price | |
| 1551. | Solomon Casey ................. | do | |
| 1583. | Joel Conigy ................... | do | |
| 1617. | Sampson Collins ............... | do | |
| 1637. | Brittain Culver ............... | do | |
| 1643. | Burwell Collins ............... | do | |
| 1645. | Job Carlisle .................. | do | |
| 1667. | Andrew Clark .................. | do | |
| 1676. | Elisha Cove ................... | do | |
| 1678. | Taylor Cole ................... | do | |
| 1680. | Dempsey Cain .................. | do | |
| 1687. | West Coley .................... | do | |
| 1700. | Malachi Crockley | William Faircloth | |
| 1713. | Azariah Casey ................. | do | |
| 1716. | Thomas Crain .................. | do | |
| 1727. | Sampson Covenor ............... | do | |
| 1736. | Thomas Cain ................... | do | |
| 1745. | John Conner ................... | do | |
| | [Page 201] | | |
| 1764. | Thomas Chestnut ............... | do | |
| 1766. | Joseph Chestnutt .............. | do | |
| 1781. | Etheldred Carter .............. | do | |
| 1793. | John Crichet .................. | do | |
| 1797. | John Cummins .................. | do | |
| 1799. | Coleman Cliavat ............... | do | |
| 1807. | Timothy Covener ............... | do | |
| 1811. | Oliver Clay ................... | do | |
| 1814. | Allen Clifton ................. | do | |
| 1826. | George Cook ................... | do | |
| 1841. | Dennis Corbett ................ | do | |
| 1844. | George Copewell ............... | do | |
| 1848. | Archibald Clary ............... | do | |
| 1849. | Benjamin Cannon, M. ........... | do | |
| 1858. | Elias Crockley ................ | Thomas Butcher | |
| 1881. | George Carby .................. | do | |
| 1888. | George Cockburn ............... | do | |
| 1912. | Elias Cand .................... | do | |
| 1919. | Peter Canaly .................. | do | |
| 1921. | Anthony Cheshire .............. | do | |
| 1965. | Willis Chandler ............... | do | |
| 1994. | Benjamin Cade ................. | do | |
| 2001. | Peter Calvin .................. | do | |
| 2037. | Thomas Caton .................. | B. McCulloch | for Selby Harvey |
| 2048. | Willoby Crief ................. | do | do |
| 2050. | Christopher Church ............ | do | do |
| 2055. | Hillary Crabb ................. | John Sheppard | do |
| 2058. | Anthony Charlton .............. | do | |
| 2061. | John Clark .................... | do | |
| 2091. | Arthur Cross .................. | Thomas Butcher | |
| 2095. | Noel Clark .................... | do | |
| 2108. | Edward Chappel ................ | Sherd. Barrow | |
| 2124. | Hick Cee ...................... | do | |

| No. | Name & Rank | By Whom Received | Remarks |
|---|---|---|---|
| 2129. | Randall Cross | Sherd. Barrow | |
| 2153. | Nathaniel Cooper | Tho. Butcher | |
| 2155. | John Cate | do | |
| 2173. | Silas Cross | Sherd. Barrow | |
| 2183. | Henry Chamberlin | do | |
| 2200. | John Crawford | John Sheppard | |
| 2202. | William Carrell | do | |
| 2219. | Solomon Campbell | Isles Simmons | |
| 2224. | John Campbell | do | |
| 2256. | Stephen Corch | William Sanders | |
| 2258. | Abel Crump | do | |
| 2262. | William Cooper | do | |
| 2269. | Nathaniel Cooper | do | |
| 2302. | Robert Cook | John Marshall | |
| 2317. | John Christopher | Will Lytle | |
| 2320. | John Connoway, Lt. | Griffith Dange | |
| 2356. | James Caylachen | Philip Fishburn | |
| 2402. | James Caton, C. | Griffith Dange | |
| 2409. | Frederick Cooper | A. Nelson | |
| 2411. | John Cheshire | do | |
| 2432. | Stephen Cross | William Sanders | |
| 2435. | Benjamin Carroll | Will Lytle | |
| 2441. | William Campbell [Page 202] | Philip Fishburn | |
| 2447. | Jonathan Case | Isles Simmons | |
| 2453. | James Craig | | no receipt |
| 2472. | William Clark | T. Dixon | |
| 2533. | Malachi Chamberlin | Joshua Davis | |
| 2534. | David Conway | J. Craven | for J. Ingles |
| 2547. | Joseph Cooper | William Sanders | |
| 2551. | Willis Curling | do | |
| 2567. | David Crawley | No. 174 new D. Bills for Clark where Ptolemy Powile has rec'd. it who Smith owed. H. | no receipt |
| 2568. | George Carcher | Philip Fishburn | |
| 2570. | Richard Clifton | | no receipt |
| 2590. | Absalom Castander | John Price | |
| 2608. | Peter Cammell | John McNees | |
| 2634. | Dillard Collins | Wm. Sanders | |
| 2635. | Burwell Collins | do | |
| 2643. | Zadock Coward | do | |
| 2644. | Ephraim Coward | do | |
| 2650. | Caleb Collins | do | |
| 3281. | William Collins | do | J. Marchal for W. Sanders |
| 2667. | Solomon Carr | John Macon | |
| 2689. | Joseph Crief | George Scurlock | |
| 2702. | Daniel Cellars | Griffith I. McRee | |
| 2714. | Clement Cleverill | John Price | |
| 2719. | Harris Coon | do | |
| 2730. | John Chaflin | do | |
| 2754. | Jacob Cersey | Philip Fishburn | |
| 2755. | Henry Cersey | do | |

| No. | Name & Rank | By Whom Received | Remarks |
|---|---|---|---|
| 2778. | Israil Cullon | Peter Cullom | |
| 2795. | Joseph Cowan | Phillip Fishburn | |
| 2798. | Alexander Cameron | do | |
| 2804. | Robert Carmichael | Jno. Sommers | |
| 2817. | William Clifton | Thos. Donoho | |
| 2832. | James Crabb | do | |
| 2845. | John Coats | J. Craven | |
| 2862. | Valentine Cherry | William Faircloth | |
| 2879. | Richard Claresp | do | |
| 2884. | Hardy Coward | do | |
| 2885. | Lawrence Connelly | do | |
| 2918. | Chas. Coleman, Q. M. | | |
| 2920. | Wm. Capps | | |
| 2925. | Wm. Clack | Jno. Armstrong | |
| 2958. | Jesse Caldwell | James Horner | |
| 2965. | Morgan Coker | do | |
| 2976. | Francis Caesar | Simon Toterine, Fra. Maxwell, John Garland, Sr., James Homes, Benj. Eastman | |
| 3016. | Chas. Chamberlain | | |
| 3053. | John Carter | Thomas Person | |
| 3055. | Hugh Catchem | William X Griffis his mark | |
| 3084. | James Carr, Lt. | Curtis Ivey | |
| 3085. | Henry Cobb | Andrew Armstrong | |
| | [Page 203] | | |
| 3090. | Thomas Canady | Curtis Ivey | |
| 3102. | Abram Carter | Alexr. Carter | |
| 3109. | William Clifton | John Marshall | |
| 3117. | George Cole | | not receipted for assigned to N. Jones |
| 3120. | Wm. Carpenter | Timothy McCarthy | |
| 3121. | Jonathan Carrell | do | |
| 3137. | Wm. Cale, M. | Nathan Lassiter | |
| 3157. | Johnson Cruise | James Bristow | |
| 3177. | West Colson | John Marshall | or for C. Dixon |
| 3237. | Jeffery Coley | do | |
| 3259. | Jeremiah Claunce | Phillip Fishburn | |
| 3265. | George Claunce | do | |
| 3284. | Joshua Cherry | John Marshall | for W. Sanders |
| 3297. | John Clay | do | do |
| 3302. | John Cook | do | do |
| 3308. | James Crow | Phillip Fishburn | |
| 3313. | John Cox | Philip Miller | |
| 3318. | Robert Cole | | no receipt |
| 3324. | John Cherry | Timothy McCarthy | |
| 3328. | John Cousan | do | |
| 3336. | Peter Clifton | do | |
| 3343. | Andrew Cox | do | |
| 3346. | John Coffuld | do | |

D

[Page 204]
34. Levi Dawson, Lt.-Col. ............ John Daves

| No. | Name & Rank | By Whom Received | Remarks |
|---|---|---|---|
| 38. | Nathaniel Dickerson, Lt. | Chas. Dixon | |
| 57. | William Dennis, Capt. | H. Montfort | for W. Dennis |
| 63. | Wm. Davis, Lt.-Col. | do | |
| 69. | Joshua Dailey, Capt. | Selby Harney | |
| 70. | James Dupree, Armorer | H. Montfort | for J. Dupre |
| 71. | Anthony Diggs, Lt. | Thos. Armstrong, Jr. | |
| 190. | John Dillard, Lt. | A. Ramsey | |
| 197. | David Dodd | John Nelson | |
| 214. | Exum Drake | H. Montfort | for E. Drake |
| 238. | John Davis | Jno. Nelson | |
| 321. | Hezekiah Dewert | H. Montfort | for H. Dewert |
| 327. | Nicholas Duboise | B. McCulloch | |
| 350. | Jacob Debusk | H. Montfort | for Debusk |
| 388. | Corn's Drake, Q. M. S. | J. Craven | |
| 395. | Nathaniel Durham | H. Montfort | for Durham |
| 441. | Hezekiah Douglass | J. Craven | |
| 533. | James Davidson | H. Montfort | for Davidson |
| 548. | Jonathan Dollar | David Pasmore | |
| 550. | John Drury | H. Montfort | for Drury |
| 551. | Morgan Drury | do | do |
| 553. | Charles Dailey | John Allen | |
| 568. | Edward Douglass | A. Lytle | |
| 576. | Samuel Davis | do | |
| 589. | Robert Deweze | Chas. Dixon | |
| 592. | Zachariah Deweze | do | |
| 597. | Wm. Davis | do | |
| 608. | Wm. Donoho | do | |
| 615. | Thomas Dobbins | do | |
| 616. | Jesse Duncan | do | |
| 678. | Waugh Darnell | Wm. Sanders | |
| 681. | Matthew Davis | do | |
| 702. | Wm. Darnell | do | |
| 716. | John Dickerson | do | |
| 717. | Wm. Daustan | do | |
| 759. | John Dailey | Selby Harney | |
| 763. | Wm. Duncan | H. Montfort | for Duncan |
| 783. | Thomas Dison | John Sheppard | |
| 808. | Wm. Denson | Wm. Sanders | |
| 888. | James Dupreart | do | |
| 889. | Robert Dane | do | |
| 917. | Wm. Demmett | Archd. Lytle | |
| 967. | Peter Duffee | do | |
| 984. | John Durdan | J. Craven | |
| 1044. | George Duncan | Thomas Person | |
| 1090. | Benjamin Durdan | B. McCulloch | |
| 1109. | Richard Douge | H. Montfort | for Douge |
| 1171. | Jesse Donaldson | do | |
| 1174. | John Doherty | Tho. Tison | |
| 1180. | Richard Dean | John Bonds | |
| 1219. | Lewis Daughtry | John Sheppard | |
| 1229. | Bartley Davis | do | |
| 1242. | Allen Denmey | Phillip Fishburn | |
| 1258. | John Delaney | H. Montfort | for Delaney |
| 1270. | Zachariah Douge | Selby Harney | |

| No. | Name & Rank | By Whom Received | Remarks |
|---|---|---|---|
| 1282. | John Dunnegan ................ | | |
| 1309. | Cornelius Durdan .............. | B. McCulloch | |
| 1315. | Wm. Dodd .................... | Charles Dixon | |
| 1324. | Bird Driver ................... | do | |
| 1332. | Jacob Dean ................... | do | |
| 1345. | Martin Dickerson .............. | do | |
| 1357. | Jeremiah Dickson .............. | do | |
| 1360. | James Daughtry ................ | do | |
| 1379. | Obadiah Doddy ................ | do | |
| 1302. | James Douge .................. | Selby Harney | |
| 1398. | George Dowing ................ | George Claus | |
| 1405. | James Dyal ................... | John Rochel | |

### [WARRENTON]

| No. | Name & Rank | By Whom Received | Remarks |
|---|---|---|---|
| 6. | John Dickerson, Lt. ............. | | no receipt |
| 14. | Hugh Dobbins, Lt. ............. | John Marshall | |
| 15. | Benjamin Dillon, Lt. ........... | do | |
| 1455. | John Duggan .................. | William Faircloth | |
| 1493. | Thomas Daniel ................ | John McNees | |
| 1497. | John Dean .................... | do | |
| 1500. | Jesse Duggan ................. | B. McCulloch | for Glasgow |
| 1514. | Thomas Duggan ............... | do | do |
| 1520. | Francis Duggan ............... | John Price | |
| 1528. | Asahel Davenport ............. | B. McCulloch | do |
| 1533. | Chas. Dailey .................. | do | for R. Blount |
| 1563. | Robert Dowling ............... | John Price | |
| 1573. | Joel Deel .................... | do | |
| 1668. | Louis Denn ................... | do | |
| 1670. | Charles Deake ................ | do | |
| 1686. | Abraham Dobbs ............... | do | |
| 1809. | Timothy Discent .............. | William Faircloth | |
| 1829. | James Davenport .............. | do | |
| 1864. | Joel McDowell ................ | Thomas Butcher | |
| 1872. | Peter Damon ................. | do | |
| 1882. | Isaac Dean ................... | do | |
| F 21. | | | |
| 1896. | Benjamin Dawson ............. | do | |
| 1897. | Joseph Delmore .............. | do | |
| 1901. | Albert Davis ................. | do | |
| 1905. | Chas. Dowden ................ | do | |
| 1910. | Joel Doxton ................. | do | |
| 1915. | Holland Dilk ................. | William Faircloth | |
| 1917. | Isaac Dowsam ................ | do | |
| 1918. | Jeremiah Duncan ............. | do | |
| 1932. | Absalom Dinkins .............. | do | |
| 1933. | Giles Davenport .............. | do | |
| 1940. | Christopher Dasher ........... | do | |
| 1979. | Anthony Douglass ............. | do | |
| 1987. | Jesse Donan .................. | do | |
| 1999. | Absalom Daughtry ............ | do | |
| 2015. | Alexander Daughtry ........... | do | |
| 2018. | Sterling Dean ................ | Selby Harney | B. McCulloch for Selby Harney |
| 2104. | John Davis ................... | Sherd. Barrow | |

| No. | Name & Rank | By Whom Received | Remarks |
|-----|-------------|------------------|---------|
| 2122. | Abraham Dean | Sherd. Barrow | |
| 2127. | Gran. Duke | do | |
| 2134. | Edmund Diggins | do | |
| 2137. | John Dixon | do | |
| 2142. | Joseph Davis | do | |
| 2161. | James Davis | Tho. Butcher | |
| .... | Matthew Dawson | | |
| 2271. | Aquilla | Will Sanders | |
| 2318. | Griffith Douge, Lt. | | |
| 2319. | Joab Douge, Dr. | Griffith Douge | |
| 2336. | Malachi Dean | do | |
| 2339. | David Dobbins | Phillip Fishburn | |
| 2358. | James Douglass | do | |
| 2359. | Moses Davis | do | |
| 2360. | Henry Davis | do | |
| 2375. | David Davis | B. McCulloch | for Art Pearce |
| 2399. | George Dunn | | no receipt |
| 2403. | Samuel Dowden | William Weldon | |
| 2408. | Jeffery Dean | Griffith Dange | |
| 2438. | William Duke | | not receipted for |
| 2460. | Eve Dego | William Sanders | |
| 2463. | John Downs | T. Dixon | |
| 2490. | Zachariah Davis | John Davis | |
| 2491. | Acey Davis | do | |
| 2492. | John Davis | do | |
| 2493. | Wm. Davis, Corpl. | do | |
| 2509. | Richard Daughtry | do | |
| 2539. | William Dennis | Sam'l. Parker | |
| 2545. | Peter Delight | Will Sanders | |
| 2588. | Ephraim Downing | John Price | |
| 2593. | John Duchingham | do | |
| 2607. | Peter Downing | John McNees | |
| 2668. | Joshua Davis | John Macon | |
| 2676. | Sharrod Duke | J. Craven | for Mary Duke |
| 2694. | Benjamin Dean | Mar. Johnson | for Ch. Guerard |
| 2724. | Moses Dodd | John Price | |
| 2726. | David Durkett | do | |
| 2733. | Presley Davis | do | |
| 2766. | George Dunn, Lt. | Phillip Fishburn | |
| 2767. | John Dawson | James Pearl | |
| 2781. | Hezekiah Dennis | | not receipted for |
| 2809. | James Duke | John Sommers | |
| 2811. | Francis Delong | do | |
| 2815. | Hugh Davis | do | |
| 2821. | Elizah Duncan | Tho. Donoho | |
| 2842. | Charles Driver | Tho. Person | |
| 2865. | Lewis Denkins | William Faircloth | |
| 2871. | Julius Dover | do | |
| 2876. | Nathan Deaver | do | |
| 2878. | Dempsey Debusk | do | |
| 2880. | Bartholomew Deloach | Wm. Faircloth | |
| 2893. | Joshua Dunnagan | do | |
| 2900. | Granville Davis | Sam'l. Parker | |
| 2901. | Cyrus Davis | do | |

| No. | Name & Rank | By Whom Received | Remarks |
|---|---|---|---|
| 2902. | Archelaus Davis | Sam'l. Parker | |
| 2923. | James Dillard | John Armstrong | |
| 2951. | Cornelius Durdan | James Homes | |
| 2988. | Josiah Dennis | S. Totervine, F. Macwell, J. Garland Jr., J. Holmes | |
| 2990. | Nathan Dees | do | |
| 2995. | John Duke | H. Murfree | |
| 3002. | Thomas Davidson | do | |
| 3019. | Matthew Dawson | Robt. Fenner | |
| 3035. | Isham Dyches | John Sommers | |
| 3044. | Joel Dinbury | Tho. Armstrong | |
| 3046. | William Daursey | do | |
| 3071. | John Davidson | | not receipted for |
| 3074. | Dempsy Daughtry | H. Montfort | |
| 3099. | John Douglas, Lt. | Curtis Ivey | |
| 3113. | Solomon Debury | Neh. Long | for S. Debury |
| 3123. | Emanuel Daniel | Timo. McCarthy | |
| 3168. | Thomas Daniel, Lt. | John Davis | for James Coore |
| 3169. | James Dickson | Tho. Person | |
| 3211. | Stephen Davis | John Marshall | for C. Dixon |
| 3250. | Matthew Davis | | |
| 3276. | Stephen Denkins | John Marshall | for W. Sanders |
| 3370. | Ambrose Dudley | Timo. McCarthy | |
| 3376. | Ethelred Daniel | do | |
| 1708. | Julius Dowd | William Faircloth | |
| 1790. | Isaiah Digns | do | |
| 1803. | Isaac Digns | do | |

### E

[Page 208]

| No. | Name & Rank | By Whom Received | Remarks |
|---|---|---|---|
| 88. | Robert Edward | Ab Thomas | |
| 105. | John English | do | |
| 132. | George Elmore | Rob. Fenner | |
| 158. | Brown Edwards | | |
| 177. | Joel Edwards | H. Montfort | |
| 217. | Francis Endeakin | Wm. King | |
| 223. | James Elmore | do | |
| 253. | William Eldear | Alexander Brevard | |
| 263. | Michal Ewait | John Nelson | |
| 281. | Morgan Elmore | H. Montfort | |
| 289. | Zachariah Elliot | Ab Thomas | |
| 369. | John Earnhart | Philip Fishburn | |
| 427. | George Ewing | Alex Brevard | |
| 482. | Joseph Evans | Selby Harney | |
| 513. | Edward Earp | J. Craven | |
| 596. | Samuel Estes | Chas. Dixon | |
| 664. | Stephen Edwards | William Sanders | |
| 675. | Richard Earp | do | |
| 718. | James Elms | do | |
| 738. | Edward Everton | H. Montfort | |
| 898. | John Egerton, Sergt. | J. Craven | |
| 936. | Ephraim Etheridge | Arch Lytle | |
| 973. | James Earl | do | |

| No. | Name & Rank | By Whom Received | Remarks |
|---|---|---|---|
| 978. | Robert Eccard, F. M. | Ab Thomas | |
| 1009. | Nathan Ewell | Robb Fenner | |
| 1051. | Thomas Endless | J. Craner ☞ | for Hance Bond |
| 1165. | Ackes Ellison | do | for Robb Hulane |
| 1206. | Robert Edwards | John Price | |
| 1228. | Daniel Elmore | J. Sheppard | |
| 1283. | Daniel Ellis | H. Montfort | for Ellis |
| 1303. | Absolom Elist | B. McCulloch | |
| 1348. | Burwell Evans | John Jones | |
| 1373. | John Elliot | Chas. Dixon | |

[WARRENTON]

| | | | |
|---|---|---|---|
| 7. | Lemuel Ely, Capt. | H. Montfort | |
| 12. | Eli Ely, Capt. | | no receipt |
| 1466. | William Evans | William Faircloth | |
| 1691. | Caleb Eastwood | John Price | |
| 1821. | Josiah Ebb | William Faircloth | |
| 1828. | Philip Evans | do | |
| 2011. | Edmund Everitt | do | |

## F

[Page 210]

| | | | |
|---|---|---|---|
| 2042. | Samuel Etheridge | B. McCulloch | for Selby Harney |
| 2040. | John Elliot | William Lytle | |
| 2068. | Charles Evans | Will Sanders | |
| 2347. | Frederick Exell | Philip Fishburn | |
| 2353. | Peter Egnor | do | |
| 2362. | John Earnhart | do | |
| 2451. | George Eagle | | assign'd to J. Misinhina |
| 2503. | Stephen Emmery | John Davis | |
| 2506. | Abel Edmunds | do | |
| 2561. | William Elliott | B. McCulloch | |
| 2610. | Isaac Etheridge | William Sanders | |
| 2672. | Moses Estes | John Macon | |
| 2677. | Morris Evans | Dan Hunter | |
| 2752. | Ralph Edmundson | John Price | |
| 2934. | Lemuel Edwards | Rich'd. Ship | |
| 3082. | John Edwards | Isaac Gregory | |
| 3089. | James Ellis | Curtis Ivey | |
| 3184. | James Edwards | J. Marshall | for C. Dixon |
| 3189. | Jesse Evars | do | do |
| 3267. | Jacob Eason | | |
| 3268. | Thomas Everitt | James Armstrong | |
| 3292. | Reuben Edwards | J. Marshall | for Sanders |
| 3301. | Shadrach Elkin, M. | do | do |
| 3337. | Josiah Ellis | Timothy McCarthy | |
| 3353. | Josiah Enmor | do | |
| 3369. | John Evans | | |
| 3372. | Benjamin Eavin | Timo. McCarthy | |
| 82. | Joseph Futrill | H. Montfort | |
| 107. | James Fogarty | Ab Thomas | |
| 175. | Edward Farrell | H. Montfort | for Ferrell |
| 227. | James Ferrell, 12 mo. | do | for J. Ferrell |

| No. | Name & Rank | By Whom Received | Remarks |
|---|---|---|---|
| G23. | | | |
| 246. | John Ferrell | T. Dixon | |
| 310. | William Fryer | H. Montfort | for W. Fryer |
| 311. | Josiah Fryer | do | for J. Fryer |
| 328. | George Fuller | do | for G. Fuller |
| 335. | John Flind | Thomas Armstrong | |
| 407. | David Fulton | Arch Lytle | |
| 467. | James Ferrell, 3 yrs. | J. Craven | for J. Croom |
| 486. | Patrick Foy, Corpl. | Thos. Armstrong | |
| 567. | Samuel Fist | A. Lytle | |
| 583. | Mack Furguson | do | |
| 591. | Robert Fletcher | Chas. Dixon | |
| 656. | Thos. Foley | Alexander McMillin | |
| 661. | John Foley | do | |
| 741. | Robert Furguson | H. Montfort | for Robt. Ferguson |
| 754. | Nathan Freeman | Rob. Fenner | |
| 759. | Abraham Fardwell | John McNees | |
| 790. | William Fulcher | C. Dixon | |
| 797. | Francis Fortney | H. Montfort | for Fortney |
| 802. | William Filmon | do | do |
| 809. | Nathan Farrell | C. Dixon | |
| 868. | Richard Freeman | F. Harget | |
| 884. | William Ferrill | Wynn Dixon | |
| 933. | Gabriel Ferrill | A. Lytle | |
| 949. | Thomas Flenning | do | |
| 1050. | Thomas Frashier | J. Craven | for Hance Bond |
| 1053. | John Floyd | do | do |
| 1062. | William Farror | H. Montfort | for W. Farror |
| 1118. | Joseph Fleming | do | for J. Flenning |
| 1119. | John Franks | do | for J. Franks |
| 1167. | Jonathan Fornes | do | for J. Fornes |
| 1177. | David Foster | Henry Overstreet | |
| 1213. | William Fornes | | |
| 1214. | John Fornes | H. Montfort | for W. & J. Fornes |
| 1266. | Lazarus Flora | Selby Harney | |
| 1295. | Joshua Forbes | do | |
| 1353. | Isham Forge | C. Dixon | |
| 1354. | James Flack | do | |

[WARRENTON]

| No. | Name & Rank | By Whom Received | Remarks |
|---|---|---|---|
| 3. | Luke Ferrill, Lt. | B. McCulloch | for Col. Harney |
| 35. | Micajah Ferrill, Lt. | J. Marshal | |
| 1468. | Francis Fowler | William Faircloth | |
| 1494. | Peter Farney | J. McNees | |
| | [Page 211] | | |
| 1534. | George Flood | J. Price | |
| 1545. | Frederick Francis | do | |
| 1559. | Nicholas Frasier | do | |
| 1568. | Ambrose Fonton | do | |
| 1602. | Thos. Fulcher | do | |
| 1615. | William Frost | do | |
| 1651. | Cornelius Futrell | do | |
| 1711. | Lawrence Floyd | Wm. Faircloth | |
| 1737. | Joel Fisher | do | |

| No. | Name & Rank | By Whom Received | Remarks |
|---|---|---|---|
| 1753. | John Floyd | Wm. Faircloth | |
| 1758. | John Fletcher | do | |
| 1833. | Jacob Freeland | do | |
| 1900. | Abel Fowler | Thomas Butcher | |
| 1937. | Henry Fitner | William Faircloth | |
| 1939. | Ambrose Fisher | do | |
| 1946. | Hugh Frasier | do | |
| 1947. | John Fusman | do | |
| 1966. | Benjamin Fordice | do | |
| 1985. | Simon Fitzpatrick | do | |
| 1991. | James Fletcher | do | |
| 1992. | Jacob Fitzgerald | do | |
| 2032. | Thomas Fenton | Selby Harney | By B. McCulloch |
| 2043. | Edon Fuller | do | do |
| 2054. | Jacob Ferrell | John Sheppard | |
| 2087. | Isaac Fisher | Thos. Butcher | |
| 2103. | David Furbee | Sher'd. Barrow | |
| 2205. | Peter Flood | Thos. Butcher | |
| 2279. | Reuben Fletcher | William Sanders | |
| 2282. | Nathan Fletcher | do | |
| 2304. | Jotham Felps | John Marshall | |
| 2396. | William Fletcher, S. | Griffith Dange | |
| 2432. | Robert Ferrebee | do | |
| 2477. | Samuel Freeman | T. Dixon | |
| 2499. | James Fooks | John Dares | |
| 2581. | Britain Foster | John Price | |
| 2589. | Moses Frost | do | |
| 2602. | Peter Foster | John McNees | |
| 2585. | William Foster | John Price | |
| 2629. | James Fenney | William Sanders | |
| 2706. | Thomas Forrester | G. J. McKee | |
| 2717. | John Fannen | John Price | |
| 2722. | Patrick Flannegan | do | |
| 2723. | Charles Forrest | do | |
| 2751. | Sampson Forehand | do | |
| 2768. | Jesse Fulton | Philip Fishburn | |
| 2855. | Levi Forehand | William Faircloth | |
| 2861. | Briggs Fitzpatrick | do | |
| 2873. | William Filyan | do | |
| 2891. | John Fitzflemming | do | |
| 2922. | Peter Furguson | John Armstrong | |
| 2963. | Willis Floyd | James Holmes | |
| 3041. | Abner Fletcher | Thomas Armstrong | |
| 3065. | Isham Furguson | William Peay | |
| 3097. | Arthur Fennell | C. Ivy | |
| 3098. | Nicholas Fennell | do | |
| | [Page 212] | | |
| 2500. | John Fooks | John Daves | |
| 3100. | Maurice Fennell | C. Ivy | |
| 3107. | Timothy Fields | John Marshall | |
| 3129. | Jesse Fountain | | |
| 3136. | George Florence | Thos. Butcher | |
| 3144. | Rich'd. Foslerlin | | no receipt |
| 3153. | Isaac Furguson | William Peay | |

| No. | Name & Rank | By Whom Received | Remarks |
|-----|-------------|------------------|---------|
| 3208. | Jesse Flood | J. Marshall | for C. Dixon |
| 3299. | Andrew Franks | do | for Wm. Sanders |
| 3358. | Isham Finch | Timothy McCarthy | |
| 2620. | William Foster | Wm. Sanders | |

**G**

[Pages 213-15]

| No. | Name & Rank | By Whom Received | Remarks |
|-----|-------------|------------------|---------|
| 48. | Deniy Gregory, Capt. | Selby Harney | |
| 59. | Isaac Guion, P. M. | John Daves | |
| 68. | Thomas Gibson, Lieut. | Thos. Pasteur | |
| 80. | Elisha Grant | H. Montfort | |
| 85. | John Gooden, Lt. | do | |
| 91. | William Gouch | Ab Thomas | |
| 155. | Isaac Griffith | Elisha Foot | |
| 201. | John Gunn, Drummer | Alexander Gunn | |
| 250. | Hosea Gregory | J. Craven | for R. Hulme |
| 254. | Joseph Graham, Q. M. S. | J. Nelson | |
| 262. | George Goodman | do | |
| 276. | Lewis Goodrich | H. Montfort | |
| 308. | Sylvanus Gray | J. McNees | |
| 378. | Thos. Garland | H. Montfort | for Garland |
| 405. | Henry Griffin | Arch Lytle | |
| 426. | Nicholas Grindstaff | A. Brevard | |
| 458. | William Grant | William Grant | |
| 543. | William Goin | H. Montfort | |
| 544. | Samuel Garrett | J. Craven | |
| 566. | Christopher Grantz | A. Lytle | |
| 579. | Conrad Goodner | do | |
| 588. | Zachariah Goforth | C. Dixon | |
| 590. | William Guttery | do | |
| 603. | Adam Gregory | do | |
| 609. | John Gibbs | do | |
| 670. | John Glover | Wm. Sanders | |
| 680. | William Gail | do | |
| 692. | Michael Goin | do | |
| 713. | John Glaze | do | |
| 715. | William Gray | do | |
| 721. | Joshua Greenage | do | |
| 777. | James Gilbert | J. Sheppard | |
| 784. | Sikes Garris | Ben Manatkin | |
| 786. | Isaac Gaskin | Chas. Dixon | |
| 789. | John Gutlery | do | |
| 863. | George Gardiner | John Sheppard | |
| 877. | Peter Graham | Wynn Dixon | |
| 880. | John Graham | do | |
| 934. | Simon Gauslin | Arch Lytle | |
| 955. | Daniel Gale, Corpl. | A. Lytle | |
| 976. | Ephraim Grant | Ab Thomas | |
| 990. | Benjamin German | James Armstrong | |
| 997. | George Garey | Thos. Evans | |
| 1010. | William Gray | Jesse Read | |
| 1011. | Samuel Gray | do | |
| 1020. | Bobie Gay | H. Murfree | |
| 1041. | Robert Griest | Thos. Person | |

| No. | Name & Rank | By Whom Received | Remarks |
|---|---|---|---|
| 1086. | John Gonthrop | B. McCulloch | |
| 1101. | Abraham Gamelion | do | |
| 1106. | Archibald Gray, Lt. | H. Montfort | |
| 1159. | Joel Gunter | Chas. Dixon | for A. Gray |
| 1161. | Elisha Gibson | do | |
| | [Page 214] | | |
| 1223. | John Grant | John Sheppard | |
| 1260. | William Grimes | John Grimes | |
| 1263. | Richard Gardner | H. Montfort | for R. Gardner |
| 1275. | William Good | do | W. Goode |
| 1287. | Jones Glover | do | Glover |
| 1310. | Thomas Green | B. McCulloch | |
| 1314. | William Grimes | C. Dixon | |
| 1317. | Jenkins Goin | do | |
| 1378. | Willis Gray | do | |
| 1380. | Joseph Gollehorn | do | |
| 1388. | Henry Guthrie | T. Dixon | |
| 1393. | Alexander Gunn | | |
| 1397. | William Goldsbury | H. Montfort | for Goldsbury |
| 1135. | William Gay | J. Bonds | |
| 593. | James Guttery | C. Dixon | |

[+ 4.29]
[WARRENTON]

| No. | Name & Rank | By Whom Received | Remarks |
|---|---|---|---|
| 27. | John Gist, M. Lt. | Thomas Donoho | |
| 1467. | Gilbert Grant | William Faircloth | |
| 1498. | John Giles, Q. M. S. | John McNees | |
| 1537. | Anthony Griss | John Price | |
| 1543. | Joab Green | do | |
| 1549. | Peter Giles | do | |
| 1562. | Josiah Grimes | do | |
| 1627. | William Goodman | do | |
| 1646. | Francis Good | do | |
| 1675. | George Greenwood | do | |
| 1706. | Solomon Griffin | William Faircloth | |
| 1731. | Thomas George | do | |
| 1732. | Willis Griffith | do | |
| 1752. | Thomas Green, C. | do | |
| 1763. | Henry Griffith | do | |
| 1795. | Daniel Gaugh | do | |
| 1834. | Patrick Gaul | do | |
| 1838. | Jonathan Gray | do | |
| 1938. | Arandall Grant | do | |
| 1942. | Richard Gideon | do | |
| 1976. | Mathew Gillespie | do | |
| 1996. | Moses Greerson | do | |
| 1997. | Simon Gibson | do | |
| 2030. | Isaac Gollop | B. McCulloch | Selby Harney |
| 2031. | Thomas Garrett, Lt. | do | do |
| 2046. | John Gilbert | do | do |
| 2076. | James Goodson | John Sheppard | |
| 2102. | John Garvin | Sherd Barrow | |
| 2126. | Dempsey Green | do | |
| 2131. | Abraham Green | do | |

| No. | Name & Rank | By Whom Received | Remarks |
|---|---|---|---|
| 2150. | Randall Green | Tho. Butcher | |
| 2162. | Jacob Griffin | do | |
| 2174. | Joshua Garvis | Sherd Barrow | |
| 2209. | George Griffin | Thos. Butcher | |
| | [Page 215] | | |
| 2441. | William Gwinn | William Lytle | |
| 2250. | John Gibson | do | |
| 2288. | Martin Griffin | William Sanders | |
| 2316. | Joel Gibbs | John Macon | |
| 2321. | Willis Gregory | Griffith Dange | |
| 2322. | Clement Godfrey | do | |
| 2344. | John Gerritt | Philip Fishburn | |
| 2352. | John Goose | do | |
| 2377. | Ephraim Gurley | Burwell Mourning | |
| 2393. | Charles Greggs | Griffith Dange | |
| 2443. | Peter Grover | Will Lytle | |
| 2466. | William Graham, S. | T. Dixon | |
| 2476. | Jesse Goldsmith, M. | do | |
| 2480. | John Griffis | do | |
| 2489. | James Gifford, Lt. | John Daves | |
| 2501. | Robert Grissum, M. | do | |
| 2504. | Ambrose Goslin | do | |
| 2532. | Arthur Glesson | Joshua Davis | |
| 2536. | James Greenlaw | J. Craven | for J. Ingles |
| 2553. | James Glasco | Wm. Sanders | |
| 2572. | Charles Grimsley | John Price | |
| 2587. | Robert Greer | do | |
| 2604. | George Gilhampton | John McNees | |
| 2614. | Isaac Gately | William Sanders | |
| 2623. | Thomas Garrott | do | |
| 2625. | James Garrott | do | |
| 2626. | Samuel Goodeman, C. | do | |
| 2638. | James Gutray | do | |
| 2711. | Hyman Gardner | John Price | |
| 2748. | Simon Giles | do | |
| 2770. | David Gillaspie | James Pearl | |
| 2844. | John Gallimore, C. | Thomas Person | |
| 2870. | Arthur Groves | William Faircloth | |
| 2911. | Anthony Garrett | William Lytle | |
| 2912. | James Gunn | do | |
| 2954. | Sherrod Granger | James Holmes | |
| 2961. | Reading Gamble | do | |
| 2962. | Lawrence Graddy | do | |
| 2994. | Thomas Green | Hardy Murfree | |
| 3014. | William Gamewell | Benjamin Eastman | |
| 3030. | David Grant | | Paid to J. Macon |
| 3050. | William Green, Lt. | | no receipt |
| 3056. | John Griffis | William Griffis | X his mark |
| 3090. | Thomas Gregory | Curtis Ivey | |
| | | his | |
| 3104. | Lawrence Griffin | Nathan X Harris | |
| | | mark | |
| 3178. | Daniel Gunn | J. Marshall | |
| 3185. | Peter Gates | do | |

| No. | Name & Rank | By Whom Received | Remarks |
|---|---|---|---|
| 3188. | Joseph Garner | Tho. Butcher | |
| 3203. | Arthur Graham | do | |
| 3221. | James Gaylor | do | |
| 3303. | John Griffin, Lt. | do | |
| 2648. | George Glenn | William Sanders | |
| 2652. | James Gregory | do | |

**H**

[Pages 216-21]

| No. | Name & Rank | By Whom Received | Remarks |
|---|---|---|---|
| 3. | Samuel Hotwell, Lt. | J. Craven | |
| 8. | William Hilton, Lt. | H. Montfort | |
| 32. | Lewis Hicks, Ensn. | do | |
| 58. | Spier Holland, Lt. | Tho. Armstrong | |
| 83. | Patrick Hoggard | H. Montfort | |
| 86. | John Headwright | do | |
| 92. | Henry Hewes | Ab Thomas | |
| 94. | Fred'k. Hathcock | do | |
| 109. | John Henry | A. Lytle | |
| 110. | Randolph Humphries | do | |
| 114. | Hugh Harris | do | |
| 134. | Andrew Haddock | | |
| 144. | Patrick Howard | John Ingles | |
| 153. | Henry Hawkins | H. Montfort | |
| 165. | William Hoggard | J. Craven | |
| 185. | Isaac Hancock, Lt. | Thomas Person | |
| 193. | Elisha Hiott | J. Craven | |
| 204. | Reason Holland | E. Gamble | |
| 208. | Nathaniel Hughes | do | |
| 209. | Isaac Hudson | | |
| 213. | John Harmon | Philip Fishburn | |
| 221. | Henry Hancock | H. Montfort | |
| 232. | James Hewes | Joshua Hadley | |
| 237. | Hugh Huston | John Nelson | |
| 244. | Vetch Holdsbrooks | do | |
| 247. | Joshua Harney | John Jones | |
| 288. | Jacob Hobbs | H. Montfort | |
| 290. | John Hinchey, Sen. | do | |
| 316. | Ebenezer Huit | do | |
| 338. | Corbin Hickman | Thomas. Armstrong | |
| 362. | Isaac Hammons | H. Montfort | for Hammons |
| 370. | Joshua Hall | Philip Fishburn | |
| 387. | Thomas Hill | Nicholas Long | |
| 408. | David Harris | Arch Lytle | |
| 409. | Corbin Hickman | do | |
| 415. | Thomas Hayes | do | |
| 435. | John Harton, Drum. | J. Craven | |
| 439. | Gibson Harris | do | |
| 442. | David Hass | do | |
| 451. | James Hester | do | |
| 502. | Chamblin Hudson | J. Davis | |
| 537. | Francis Harrison | Thomas Stewart | for F. Harrison |
| 541. | Henry Harris | Nath. William | |
| 571. | Andrew Hunter | A. Lytle | |
| 581. | Turner Harrod | do | |

| No. | Name & Rank | By Whom Received | Remarks |
|---|---|---|---|
| 584. | Thompson Harris | A. Lytle | |
| 585. | Tucker Harris | do | |
| 587. | Alexander Hammond | C. Dixon | |
| 607. | George Hudson | do | |
| 612. | John Hughes | H. Montfort | |
| 619. | John Hogan | C. Dixon | |
| 628. | William Hall | do | |
| | [Page 217] | | |
| 658. | William Hughes | Alex. McMillin | |
| 659. | Sampson Hillis | do | |
| 660. | Robert Hair | do | |
| 667. | Goalman Harris | A. Lytle | |
| 669. | John Harris | Wm. Sanders | |
| 684. | John Hunt | do | |
| 686. | David Hatches | do | |
| 691. | Solomon Hunter | do | |
| 693. | Nathan Hull, Dr. | do | |
| 725. | James Hall | do | |
| 732. | Benjamin Hester | do | |
| 735. | Edward Howard | Thomas Person | |
| 740. | John Hart | H. Montfort | |
| 746. | John Howell | Robt. Fenner | |
| 765. | Daniel Hunt | H. Montfort | |
| 787. | Moses Hudson | C. Dixon | |
| 795. | Arnold Hilton | H. Montfort | |
| 801. | William Hodges | do | |
| 826. | William Hamb | J. McNees | |
| 827. | Elijah Hinson | do | |
| 828. | Joseph Hart | do | |
| 881. | James Humphrey | Wynn Dixon | |
| 897. | William Hurt | H. Montfort | |
| 907. | William Harris | A. Lytle | |
| 915. | Henry Hayes | do | |
| 922. | Thomas Hopkins | do | |
| 969. | Hugh Hill | do | |
| 980. | Thomas Henry | do | |
| 982. | Isaac Hopkins | J. Craven | |
| 987. | Moses Holmes | do | |
| 1023. | James Hall | H. Murfree | |
| 1034. | Joseph Hall | Thos. Person | |
| 1056. | Francis Hubbard | J. Craven | for H. Bond |
| 1059. | William Howerton | Jas. Thompson | |
| 1064. | David Hall | H. Montfort | |
| 1072. | Joseph Hayman | Thos. Pasteur | |
| 1176. | Fred'k. Howell | B. McCulloch | |
| 1095. | Moses Hill | do | |
| 1115. | Kendall Hislep | H. Montfort | |
| 1149. | Benjamin Heirn | do | |
| 1175. | William Hair | Henry Overstreet | |
| 1179. | Joseph Hardison | Thos. Armstrong, Jr. | |
| 1189. | Henry Hicks | T. Dixon | |
| 1199. | Nicholas Hair | Henry Overstreet | |
| 1200. | Isham Hatchcock | H. Montfort | |
| 1226. | Fred'k. Harper | John Sheppard | |

| No. | Name & Rank | By Whom Received | Remarks |
|---|---|---|---|
| 1234. | John Haskins | J. Craven | |
| 1238. | Jesse Haggerton | H. Montfort | |
| 1249. | Nathan Harper | Philip Miller | |
| 1254. | Henry Holland | H. Montfort | |
| 1267. | James Heans | Philip Causey | |
| 1277. | Willis Hughes | H. Montfort | |
| 1280. | John Hare | do | |
| 1281. | Mathew Herring | Jno. McNees | |
| 1290. | Hicks Hansell | H. Montfort | |
| | [Page 218] | | |
| 1806. | Caleb Holley | B. McCulloch | |
| 1319. | Henry Hill | C. Dixon | |
| 1320. | Hugh Hill | do | |
| 1326. | William Hill | do | |
| 1358. | Jesse Henderson | do | |
| 1364. | Enos Hopper | do | |

[WARRENTON]

| No. | Name & Rank | By Whom Received | Remarks |
|---|---|---|---|
| 19. | Elias Hoell, Lieut. | M. Duke Johnston | |
| 26. | E. Heimberg, Surg. | Thos. Donoho | |
| 32. | William Hancock, Lt. | do | |
| 1508. | Holland Harrell | B. McCulloch | for Jas. Glasgow |
| 1515. | Moses Heggard | John Price | |
| 1530. | James Harrison | Benj. McCulloch | |
| 1531. | Stephen Harrison | do | |
| 1541. | Lemuel Hawley | John Price | |
| 1554. | Absolom Hopkins | do | |
| 1556. | Joseph Hudnell | do | |
| 1557. | Stephen Howell | do | |
| 1561. | Peter Hooks | do | |
| 1575. | Jasper Hood | do | |
| 1580. | Joel Hubbard | do | |
| 1581. | Edward Hawley | do | |
| 1591. | John Hooker | do | |
| 1594. | Benjamin Harrell | do | |
| 1600. | Solomon Hadcock | do | |
| 1601. | Simon Henderson | do | |
| 1610. | Robert Huff | do | |
| 1611. | Henry Herring | do | |
| 1619. | Daniel Holmes | do | |
| 1624. | James Hartfield | do | |
| 1640. | Micharl Hocks | do | |
| 1642. | Jesse Hassell | do | |
| 1654. | Micharl Hockley | do | |
| 1665. | Abner Hable | do | |
| 1679. | Daniel Horney | do | |
| 1688. | Arthur Hudson | do | |
| 1693. | Willis Houby | William Faircloth | |
| 1717. | Lake Heard | do | |
| 1720. | James Howard | do | |
| 1721. | Robert Haley | do | |
| 1724. | George Hampton | do | |
| 1725. | Andrew Holmes | do | |
| 1729. | Joshua Hindes | do | |

| No. | Name & Rank | By Whom Received | Remarks |
|---|---|---|---|
| 1759. | James Hayward | William Faircloth | |
| 1767. | Andrew Hinden | do | |
| 1780. | George Holton | do | |
| 1791. | Harman Harrison | do | |
| 1798. | Abel Highman | do | |
| 1830. | Willis Hammon | do | |
| | [Page 219] | | |
| 1831. | George Hopewell | do | |
| 1836. | Oliver Hostin | do | |
| 1846. | Zebulon Hunter | do | |
| 1876. | Christopher Haley | Thos. Butcher | |
| 1887. | Dennis Holt | do | |
| 1891. | Jesse Hardin | do | |
| 1893. | Dobson Hooks | do | |
| 1955. | John Hifferman | William Faircloth | |
| 1956. | Everett Huntingdon | do | |
| 1969. | Peter Herrenden | do | |
| 1974. | James Harpoon | do | |
| 1993. | James Hailey | do | |
| 2007. | Stephen Hampton | do | |
| 2009. | Silas Hollowell | do | |
| 2027. | William Harrington | Selby Harney | for B. McCulloch |
| 2041. | Isaac' Herrington | do | |
| 2052. | Joseph Hanner | do | |
| 2059. | Holiday Hathcock | John Sheppard | |
| 2063. | Isaac Hutson | do | |
| 2070. | William Harris | Joshua Davis | |
| 2071. | George Harris | do | |
| 2083. | Joshua Hermit | Thomas Butcher | |
| 2086. | William Harmas | do | |
| 2132. | John Hathcock | Sherd Barrow | |
| 2133. | Ralph Hammons | do | |
| 2136. | John Howell | do | |
| 2139. | John Hallaway | do | |
| 2143. | Amos Hathcock | do | |
| 2160. | William Hendley | Thos. Butcher | |
| 2170. | Ephriam Harnett | Sherd Barrow | |
| 2175. | Charles Hansell | do | |
| 2185. | Isham Henry | do | |
| 2194. | John Haygood | John Sheppard | |
| 2195. | Job Herring | do | |
| 2199. | Edward Hammon | do | |
| 2210. | Mathew Heath | Thos. Butcher | |
| 2212. | Jonas Hinton | | |
| 2223. | Caleb Hanna | Isler Simmons | |
| 2235. | Lemuel Halstead, C. | do | |
| 2236. | Adam Hart | William Lytle | |
| 2238. | Drury Hyme | do | |
| 2248. | Howell Harrod | do | |
| 2259. | John Hains | William Sanders | |
| 2260. | Samuel Harris | do | |
| 2264. | James Hudson | do | |
| 2274. | John Harrison, M. | do | |
| 2294. | David Henson | John Marshall his mark | |

| No. | Name & Rank | By Whom Received | Remarks |
|---|---|---|---|
| 2296. | Locton Hawkins | Thomas X Fenn | |
| 2297. | John Hamson | John Marshall | |
| 2312. | Daniel Hopkins, C. | Const Redditt | |
| 2313. | Francis Harris | John Marshall | |
| 2325. | Willis Hastings | Nathaniel Williams | |
| 2326. | Lemuel Horton | do | |
| | [Page 220] | | |
| 2327. | Thomas Hendricks | Nath'l. Williams | |
| 2341. | William Huston | Philip Fishburn | |
| 2378. | Sanders Hodges | Burwell Moening | |
| 2379. | Right Howell | do | |
| 2383. | Hardy Hines | do | |
| 2385. | Lewis Hines | do | |
| 2386. | Rich'd. Hines | do | |
| 2387. | Joseph Herring | do | |
| 2388. | William Hawley | Benjamin McCulloch, | for Arthur Pearce |
| 2390. | Caleb Hawley | do | do |
| 2391. | Samuel Hayes | do | do |
| 2395. | Jonathan Henry | Isler Simmons | |
| 2398. | John Hobgood | | |
| 2404. | John Hewes, Lt. | A. Nelson | |
| 2428. | Nathan Horton | Warren Alford | |
| 2458. | West Hadnot, Sergt. | Abraham Bush | X his mark |
| 2481. | James Horsford | T. Dixon | |
| 2514. | John Hill | John Davis | |
| 2577. | Griffin Hammontree | do | |
| 2525. | Peter Harrill, Lt. | Charles Gerrard | |
| 2529. | William Hill | John Daves | |
| 2541. | Miles Halfred | Wm. Sanders | |
| 2552. | Joshua Hall | do | |
| 2584. | Samuel Hurson | John Price | |
| 2591. | Elisha Hogg | do | |
| 2619. | Daniel Harrison | William Sanders | |
| 2627. | William Hinton | Will Sanders | |
| 2640. | Jacob Horton | do | |
| 2647. | William Hooten, Lt. | do | |
| 2655. | James Hifferman | Thomas Butcher | |
| 2660. | Daniel Hendley | do | |
| 2669. | James Harrison, L. | John Macon | |
| 2670. | Paul Harrod | Tho. Butcher | |
| 2671. | Travis Harper | Cosimo Medici | |
| 2680. | Asa Hunter | And. Armstrong | |
| 2681. | Joseph Harp | | not receipted for |
| 2698. | William Hedgepeth | Simon Tolevine | |
| 2700. | Edwd. Hammonds, C. | do | |
| 2709. | Isaac Hunter | William Hunter | |
| 2713. | Abner Hobbs | John Price | |
| 2718. | Sampson Hodsock | do | |
| 2729. | Diah Henning | do | |
| 2750. | John Hadlock | do | |
| 2760. | Philip Hance | Philip Fishburn | |
| 2762. | Bazel Holland | do | |
| 2779. | John Henderson | James Pearl | |
| 2787. | James Hutchinson | Philip Fishburn | |

| No. | Name & Rank | By Whom Received | Remarks |
|---|---|---|---|
| 2792. | John Holdsbrook | Philip Fishburn | |
| 2819. | William Hartgrove | Tho. Donoho | |
| 2822. | Joseph Hewes, L. | do | |
| 2823. | Anthony Howell | do | |
| 2837. | Trubel Hicks | do | |
| 2840. | Mathew Hubbard | do | |
| 2841. | Alexander Hays | do | |
| 2857. | Jordan Hines | William Faircloth | |
| | [Page 221] | | |
| 2859. | Jacob Hawks | do | |
| 2883. | Daniel Hooks | do | |
| 2889. | James Howe | do | |
| 2892. | Zachariah Houby | do | |
| 2953. | Jonathan Hays | James Holmes | |
| 2957. | Russel Harper | do | |
| 2979. | Stephen Henry | Sim Totevine, Fra. | |
| 2984. | John Hurley | Maxwell, John Garland | |
| 2985. | Arthur Henry | James Holmes | |
| 2987. | Thomas Hall | do | |
| 2989. | Francis Holmes | do | |
| 2999. | Kinchen Holomon | H. Murfree | |
| 3011. | John Hayes | Simon Totevine | |
| 3024. | Satterfield Holstein | John Sommers | |
| 3059. | Albert Hendricks, C. | William Peay | |
| 3063. | Elijah Harris | do | |
| 3066. | Stewart Hambleton | | |
| 3094. | Miles Hutson | Curtis Ivey | |
| 3105. | Nathan Harris | | |
| 3108. | John Harrell | John Marshall | |
| 3115. | Jonathan Hopkins, C. | Philip Miller | |
| 3155. | Sherwood Harris | James Bristow | |
| 3158. | John Hudson | do | |
| 3160. | William Hall | Philip Fishburn | |
| 3165. | William Hewell | John Daves | |
| 3173. | Abraham Harrold | C. Dixon | by Marshall |
| 3182. | Francis Huzza | do | do |
| 3194. | Jesse Hall | do | do |
| 3195. | John Hudson | do | do |
| 3205. | Francis Huzza | do | do |
| 3206. | Ezekial Haws | John Marshall | for C. Dixon |
| 3212. | Miles Hudson | do | do |
| 3219. | James Harvey | do | do |
| 3224. | Nehemiah Huggins | do | |
| 3225. | George Hedgeman | do | |
| 3233. | Lewis Hedgeman | do | |
| 3234. | Charles Hicks | do | |
| 3246. | Richard Hopkins | do | |
| 3257. | Joshua Hatten | James Armstrong | |
| 3253. | John Hearn | do | |
| 3270. | Abraham Hargis | John Marshall | for Wm. Sanders |
| 3280. | John Hickman, C. | do | do |
| 3289. | David Holeway | do | do |
| 3291. | Benjamin Haywood | do | do |
| 3293. | Joseph Hill | do | do |

| No. | Name & Rank | By Whom Received | Remarks |
|---|---|---|---|
| 3304. | Thomas Hudson | John Marshall | for Wm. Sanders |
| 3307. | Archibald Hood | William Burt | |
| 3310. | James Hall | | no receipt |
| 3315. | John Hussey | | do |
| 3316. | Israel Harding, L. | James Armstrong | |
| 3317. | Abraham Harding | do | |
| 3339. | Hezekiah Hart | Tmo. McCarthy | |
| 3354. | George Hackney | do | |
| 3355. | Abraham Harris | do | |
| 3362. | Willoby Hooks | do | |
| 3375. | William Hizzard | do | |
| 1628. | John Hare | John Price | |
| 1634. | Stephen Hedgepeth | do | |
| 3264. | David Hays | Philip Fishburn | |

## I & J

[Page 222]

| No. | Name & Rank | By Whom Received | Remarks |
|---|---|---|---|
| 43. | Samuel Jones, Ensn. | Nat Jones | |
| 56. | Henry Irwin, Lt. Col. | H. Montfort | for H. Irwin |
| 77. | Daniel Jones, Capt. | | |
| 119. | Richard Johnston | H. Murfree | |
| 145. | Jonathan Jones | Selby Harney | |
| 191. | Thomas Jeffries | H. Montfort | |
| 210. | Freeman Jones | do | |
| 224. | Jacob Jeffries | William King | |
| 269. | Isham Jones | A. Thomas | |
| 271. | James Jackson | H. Montfort | |
| 334. | Eli Joiner | Jer. Nelms | |
| 344. | William Inman | T. Armstrong | |
| 355. | Henry Jones | H. Montfort | |
| 384. | Samuel Johnston | Thos. Armstrong | |
| 413. | William Jackson | Arch Lytle | |
| 436. | Drury Jones | J. Craven | |
| 454. | Charles Jones | Isaac Kenedy | |
| 456. | David Journikin | | |
| 461. | John Jones | H. Montfort | |
| 464. | Thomas Jones | do | |
| 466. | John Jones | do | |
| 497. | Bazel Jackson | Ab Thomas | |
| 498. | Zachariah Jackson | do | |
| 500. | Robert Jenkins | H. Montfort | |
| 638. | Nathan Jean | C. Dixon | |
| 652. | Fountain Jourdan | H. Montfort | |
| 739. | Nathan Jones | do | |
| 745. | Henry Jones | do | |
| 773. | John Johnston | J. Sheppard | |
| 817. | Nicholas Isler | William Polk | |
| 818. | Benjamin Jackson | do | |
| 846. | Fred'k. Jones | John Bonds | |
| 859. | Thomas James | Sampson Hays | |
| 860. | David James | do | |
| 929. | William Jackson | Arch Lytle | |
| 1003. | Asa Jenkins | Jesse Read | |
| 1032. | John Jones | H. Montfort | |

| No. | Name & Rank | By Whom Received | Remarks |
|---|---|---|---|
| 1057. | Dempsey Jones | J. Craven | for Hance Bond |
| 1061. | Fred'k. Jackson | James Thompson | |
| 1084. | Thomas Johnston | B. McCulloch | |
| 1126. | James Jameson | H. Montfort | |
| 1150. | Peter Jones | John Bonds | |
| 1157. | Edmund Jackson | T. Dixon | |
| 1186. | Jeremiah Jackson | John Sheppard | |
| 1237. | Briton Jones | H. Montfort | |
| 1325. | Thomas Jenks | C. Dixon | |
| 1337. | James Johnston | do | |
| 1341. | John Jeffries | do | |
| 1375. | Jacob Jones | do | |
| 1394. | John Johnston | Thos. Person | |
| 1153. | Peter Jacobs | T. Dixon | |

[WARRENTON]

| 38. | David Jones, Lieut. | C. Ivey | |
| 1473. | Samuel Igby | William Faircloth | |
| | [Page 223] | | |
| 1474. | Stephen Jessop | do | |
| 1475. | Archibald Johnston | do | |
| 1476. | Josiah Jenkins | do | |
| 1483. | John Jordan | do | |
| 1522. | Wood Jones | John Price | |
| 1529. | William Jenkins | Benj. McCulloch | Glasgow |
| 1293. | Elisha Jones | John Price | |
| 1603. | James Jenkins | do | |
| 1631. | Daniel Joiner | do | |
| 1632. | Arthur Johnston | do | |
| 1653. | Isaac Joy | do | |
| 1657. | Hickling Joiner | do | |
| 1703. | Isaiah Johnston | William Faircloth | |
| 1723. | Thomas Jarman | do | |
| 1735. | Jacob Ivey | do | |
| 1739. | John Jarvis | do | |
| 1740. | Joshua Jones | do | |
| 1747. | Hardy Johnston | do | |
| 1765. | Elisha Ivey | do | |
| 1855. | Isaac Johnston | Thos. Butcher | |
| 1877. | David Jones | do | |
| 2023. | Robt. Jackson | B. McCulloch | |
| 2035. | Thomas Jennings | do | |
| 2056. | Samuel Jones | John Sheppard | |
| 2068. | Taylor Jones | Thos. Butcher | |
| 2082. | George Johnston | John Sheppard | |
| 2141. | Fredrick Jackson | Sherd. Barrow | |
| 2221. | James Jenkins | Isler Simmons | |
| 2310. | David James | John Marshall | |
| 2311. | Frederick James | do | |
| 2369. | David Johnson | Phillip Fishburn | |
| 2382. | Gardner Jernigan | Burwell Moring | |
| 2494. | Solomon Jennett, Lt. | John Daves | |
| 2515. | James Jones | do | |
| 2636. | William Johnston | William Sanders | |

| No. | Name & Rank | By Whom Received | Remarks |
|---|---|---|---|
| 2659. | Dennis Jordan | Thos. Butcher | |
| 2663. | Allen Jackway | do | |
| 2666. | Willis Johnston, drag.: | | |
| 2673. | Richard Jones | John Macon | |
| 2695. | Peter Jones | Simon Totevine | |
| 2705. | Ruben Ivey | G. Ino. McRee | |
| 2725. | Bartlett Jenes | John Price | |
| 2840. | William Johnston | do | |
| 2742. | James Isler | do | |
| 2773. | Drury Jones | | Pd. to W. Sandry no receipt |
| 2803. | John Ingram, L. | John Sommers | |
| 2833. | William Jones | Thos. Donoho | |
| 2899. | Neil Joiner | William Faircloth | |
| 2914. | David Ivey, M. | William Lytle | |
| 2929. | Reuben Johnston | Ben Johnston | |
| 2945. | Joshua James | James Homer | |
| 2949. | Needum James | do | |
| 3303. | | | |
| 3095. | Benjamin Joiner | C. Ivey | |
| 3116. | Willoby Jarvis | Iles Simmons | |
| 3152. | John Jones | William Peay | |
| 3187. | Miles Jordan | C. Dixon | by J. Marshall |
| 3314. | Hardy Jones | | no receipt |
| 3349. | Harper Johnston | Timo. McCarthy | |
| 3352. | Jacob Inn | do | |

K

| No. | Name & Rank | By Whom Received | Remarks |
|---|---|---|---|
| 65. | James King, Capt. | Robt. Fenner | |
| 148. | John King | John Ingles | |
| 169. | Samuel Knight | James King | |
| 183. | Jesse Knight | H. Murfree | |
| 215. | James Kith | H. Montfort | for James Kith |
| 325. | William King | Benjamin McCulloch | |
| 326. | James King | do | |
| 514. | Benjamin Kitchen, Lt. | H. Montfort | |
| 536. | Isaac Kennedy | | |
| 579. | Arthur Kerney | A. Lytle | |
| 626. | Hugh Kelly | C. Dixon | |
| 671. | Thomas Kent | William Sanders | |
| 747. | Jonathan Keay | H. Montfort | for Jon. Keay |
| 760. | Joseph King | do | for J. King |
| 857. | Edward King | John Daves | |
| 909. | John Killian | Arch Lytle | |
| 1008. | Malachi Ketanch | Jesse Reed | |
| 1085. | John Killpatrick | B. McCulloch | |
| 1093. | Richard Knobbs | do | |
| 1241. | Hardy Keel | Thomas Armstrong | |
| 1273. | William Keeter | Samuel Pitman | |
| 1396. | Enoch King | H. Montfort | |

[WARRENTON]

| No. | Name & Rank | By Whom Received | Remarks |
|---|---|---|---|
| 21. | William Knott | | |
| 1469. | John Kearsy | | |

| No. | Name & Rank | By Whom Received | Remarks |
|---|---|---|---|
| 1540. | Phillip Kelly | John Price | |
| 1606. | Blake Kearney | do | |
| 1648. | Bartholomew King | do | |
| 1714. | Patrick Kelby | William Faircloth | |
| 1754. | Andrew King | do | |
| 1772. | Joseph Kelly | do | |
| 1789. | Peter Kelly | do | |
| 1989. | James Knowland | | |
| 2148. | William Kirkland | Thomas Butcher | |
| 2158. | Hardy Keel, L. | do | |
| 2299. | John Ketanch | John Marshall | |
| 2442. | John Kettle, C. | William Lytle | |
| 2464. | John Keeth | T. Dixon | |
| 2495. | Jonathan Kinimy | John Daves | |
| 2651. | Richard Kennady | William Sanders | |
| 2738. | Saucer Keen | John Price | |
| 2836. | James Kemp | Thos. Donoho | |
| 3049. | Frederick Killian | Thomas Armstrong | |
| 3321. | Allison Knox | Phillip Miller | |

### L

| No. | Name & Rank | By Whom Received | Remarks |
|---|---|---|---|
| 37. | John Lowe, Lieut. | Thos. Donoho | |
| 51. | James Luken, Lieut. | H. Montfort | for Jas. Luten |
| 64. | Nath'l. Lawrence, Lt. | Robt. Fenner | |
| 67. | William Luten, Capt. | Thos. Person | |
| 76. | S. Lockhart, Lt. Colo. | | |
| 98. | James Legare | H. Montfort | for M. Hunt |
| 121. | Thomas Lassiter | H. Murfree | |
| 124. | James Lett | H. Montfort | for J. Lett |
| 133. | John Liddy | John Nelson | |
| 147. | Jesse Linton | H. Montfort | for Linton |
| 149. | Lemuel Litten | John Ingles | |
| 151. | Abel Litten | do | |
| 167. | John Lewis | | |
| 168. | Morgan Lewis | | |
| 206. | Jacob Lasseter | H. Murfree | |
| 216. | James Lasseter | Austin Cicaty | |
| 222. | Thomas Lucas | H. Montfort | for T. Lucas |
| 320. | James Lewis | do | |
| 385. | Valentine Lucas | Thomas Armstrong | |
| 459. | William Lewis, Dr. | H. Murfree | |
| 484. | Thomas Lewellen | Nicholas Long | |
| 539. | Citizen Lane | H. Montfort | |
| 540. | Benjamin Lane | Nath. Williams | |
| 554. | Isaac Lilly | Benjamin Perry | |
| 558. | John Lock | H. Montfort | for M. Hunt |
| 569. | Moses Leathers | A. Lytle | |
| 586. | John Logue | do | |
| 645. | Hardy Lewis | H. Montfort | for H. Lewis |
| 663. | William Lougby | Alexander McMillan | |
| 699. | John Lefoy | William Sanders | |
| 710. | Jesse Laneford | do | |
| 719. | John Laneford | do | |
| 727. | Isham Lucy | do | |

| No. | Name & Rank | By Whom Received | Remarks |
|---|---|---|---|
| 803. | Frederick Lewis | H. Montfort | for F. Lewis |
| 825. | Moses Lovick | John McNees | |
| 853. | Aaron Lambert | John Daves | |
| 883. | William Leak | Wynn Dixon | |
| 1019. | Lewis Lilly | H. Murfree | |
| 1108. | Stephen Linn, Lt. | H. Montfort | for S. Linn |
| 1113. | David Laws | do | for D. Laws |
| 1122. | Francis Lewis | do | do |
| 1143. | Chas. Lewis | John Bond | |
| 1154. | George Lott | T. Dixon | |
| 1173. | Amos Lewis | H. Montfort | for A. Lewis |
| 1203. | William Lawson | John McNees | |
| 1205. | Elisha Lanston | John Price | |
| 1215. | William Leathgo | John Jones | |
| 1235. | John Laughinghouse | Thomas Armstrong, Jr. | |
| 1244. | Phillip Lee | H. Montfort | for Lodwick Alford |
| 1269. | Jethro Lane | do | for Lane |
| 1288. | Thomas Leyden | do | for Leyden |
| 1289. | John Lambert | do | for Lambert |
| 1331. | Arthur Leekon | C. Dixon | |
| 1339. | Adam Lawrence | Alexander McMillan | |

[WARRENTON]

| No. | Name & Rank | By Whom Received | Remarks |
|---|---|---|---|
| 17. | John Lissenby, Lt. | | no receipt |
| 20. | William Lord | James Pearl | |
| 1424. | Timothy Lee | William Faircloth | |
| 1423. | Hardy Lee | do | |
| 1495. | Joshua Larouse | Jno. McNees | |
| 1526. | John Lawson | John Price | |
| 1586. | Stephen Lynch | do | |
| 1587. | Reubin Lolly | do | |
| 1607. | John Lilly | do | |
| 1612. | Stephen Larking | do | |
| 1698. | Zechariah Lofton | William Faircloth | |
| 1770. | Lewis Lemare | do | |
| 1779. | Henry Lane | do | |
| 1782. | Bennet Localare | do | |
| 1794. | Stephen Lake | do | |
| 1800. | Mark Lawson | do | |
| 1839. | Timothy Lewis | do | |
| 1850. | Drury Langston | do | |
| 1869. | Isaac Lambkin | Thomas Butcher | |
| 1890. | Francis Lolly | do | |
| 1892. | Patrick Lancaster | do | |
| 1902. | Joel Landom | do | |
| 1980. | Robt. Langton | William Faircloth | |
| 1984. | Martin Loubry | do | |
| 2024. | Isaac Litter | B. McCulloch | for Selby Harney |
| 2040. | John Litt | do | do |
| 2081. | Joshua Lewis | Joshua Lewis | (say John Sheppard) |
| 2101. | James Long | Sherd Barrow | |
| 2109. | John Lippencut | do | |
| 2145. | Jonah Langston | Thomas Butcher | |
| 2146. | Henry Lambert | do | |

| No. | Name & Rank | By Whom Received | Remarks |
|-----|-------------|------------------|---------|
| 2154. | William Lewis | Thomas Butcher | |
| 2228. | John Luffman | Isles Simmons | |
| 2289. | David Lippencut | William Sanders | |
| 2293. | William Loyd | James Armstrong | |
| 2307. | John Linn | John Marshall | |
| 2309. | Abraham Lee | Const. Redditt | |
| 2328. | George Low | Nathaniel Williams | |
| 2340. | William Lurk | Phillip Fishburn | |
| 2346. | William Loyd | do | |
| 2351. | George Lareman | do | |
| 2371. | Abraham Low | Andrew Armstrong | |
| 2373. | William Lomas | Benjamin McCulluck | for Art Pearce |
| 2413. | Joseph Lawrence | Nathaniel Williams | |
| 2459. | William Low | George Shurlock | |
| 2462. | Uriah Leftyear | T. Dixon | |
| 2475. | John Landers | do | |
| 2411. | Edward Lewis | John Davis | |
| 2617. | Daniel Leving | William Sanders | |
| 2653. | Isaac Letter | do | |
| 2683. | Thomas Lewis | J. Craven | |
| 2727. | Joshua Lacup | John Price | |
| 2771. | Richard Lee | John Sheppard | |
| 2802. | Walter Lindsey | John Sommers | |
| 2928. | Patrick Lyon | John Armstrong | |
| 2933. | Jesse Lee | Richard Ship | |
| 2935. | Charles Lee, Sr. | do | |
| 3009. | Moses Lain | Nathaniel Williams | |
| 3081. | John Linton | Isaac Gregory | |
| 3096. | John Laighton | C. Ivey | |
| 3119. | John Lambert | | not receipted for |
| 3132. | William Lock | Samuel Parker | |
| 3193. | Jesse Langston | C. Dixon | |
| 3237. | Robert Locaber | B. McCulloch | |
| 3245. | Joseph Lesly | John Marshall | |
| 3274. | William Lynn | do | for Wm. Sanders |
| 3283. | Jesse Loyd | do | |
| 3368. | John Lacey | Timothy McCarthy | |

## M

| No. | Name & Rank | By Whom Received | Remarks |
|-----|-------------|------------------|---------|
| 1. | Fl'r'nce McCarthy, Lt. | Ab. Thomas | for F. McCarthy |
| 9. | Jas. Morehead, Lt. | H. Montfort | for Jas. Moorehead |
| 13. | Abel Mosslander, Lt. | do | |
| 19. | Robt. McRennals, Ens. | John Adkinson | |
| 27. | John Moore, A. D. Q. M. | I. B. Ashe | |
| 50. | Dempsy Moore | William Sanders | |
| 66. | H. Murfree, Lt. Col. | H. Murfree | |
| 87. | Jacob Morton | Ab. Thomas | |
| 90. | John Morrison | do | |
| 93. | Alex McDonald, C. | do | |
| 95. | John McCulloch | do | |
| 100. | John McCoy | Archd. Lytle | |
| 127. | Thomas Moore | H. Montfort | for Thos. Moore |
| 128. | John Mires | | |
| 195. | Jas. McClellan, Sr. | John Nelson | |

| No. | Name & Rank | By Whom Received | Remarks |
|---|---|---|---|
| 203. | Bartlett Moreland, Lt. | J. Craven | for H. Montfort |
| 236. | Daniel McCay | Thomas Frahock | |
| 239. | Robert Martin, Corpl. | Phillip Fishburn | |
| 242. | Thomas Metisick | Isaac Hudson | |
| 293. | George Mitchell | H. Montfort | for Geo. Mitchell |
| 304. | Lemuel Moore | George Falconer | |
| 313. | John Mitchell | Ab. Thomas | |
| 322. | Andrew McNight | H. Montfort | for And. McKnight |
| 332. | William Myham | Jer. Nelms | |
| 336. | William Morris | Thomas Armstrong | |
| 343. | John Morrison | do | |
| 346. | Daniel Miller | F. Harget | |
| 352. | Patrick Mason | C. Dixon | |
| 354. | Josiah Mainor | H. Montfort | for Joe Mainor |
| 366. | William Mooney, Lt. | C. Dixon | |
| 371. | Benedict Miller | Phillip Fishburn | |
| 375. | Benjamin Messer | F. Harget | |
| 377. | J. Middlebrook, Corpl. | H. Montfort | (Say Chas. Nixon) |
| 386. | George Marshall | | |
| 411. | John Mehaffy | Arch. Lytle | |
| 417. | Andrew McBride, St. | do | |
| 418. | Joseph McCalister | do | |
| 420. | Wm. McCarthy, St. | do | |
| 433. | Robt. McKinny | Alex Brevard | |
| 470. | James Mitchell | Willie Jones | |
| 479. | Reuben Moore | his<br>Hazord X Creed<br>mark | |
| 506. | Agerton Mott | Ab. Mott | |
| 515. | Benjamin Morris | J. Craven | for R. Holme |
| 516. | John McElvea, Dr. | H. Montfort | |
| 549. | Jethro Miltier | do | for Miltier |
| 563. | John Mattock | A. Lytle | |
| 577. | Jacob Myers | do | |
| 614. | Andrew McClary | C. Dixon | |
| 620. | William McClary | do | |
| 622. | Hugh McClary | do | |
| 623. | William McIntosh | do | |
| 625. | Daniel Melton | C. Dixon | |
| 654. | John Mabury | Tho. Armstrong | |
| 666. | William Morris | William Sanders | |
| 688. | John Madry | do | |
| 695. | Frances Moser, Lt. | do | |
| 696. | Samuel Moser | do | |
| 703. | Thomas Minor | do | |
| 723. | John Morris | Nicholas Long | |
| 749. | Abraham Meadows | Robert Fenner | |
| 758. | Philemon Morris | F. Harget | |
| 792. | Patrick Murfree | J. Whitaker | |
| 813. | Samuel Middleton | H. Montfort | for Middleton |
| 819. | John Moseley | do | for Moseley |
| 833. | William Madrid | | Signed Wm. Madray<br>Should be Wm. Madrid |
| 844. | Abraham Moses | | for A. Moses |

| No. | Name & Rank | By Whom Received | Remarks |
|---|---|---|---|
| 892. | Hugh McRory ................. | Ab. Thomas | |
| 901. | John Montgomery .............. | A. Lytle | |
| 904. | William Melton ................ | do | |
| 920. | James Mullen ................. | do | |
| 932. | J. Mabry & H. Stephens ......... | do | |
| 940. | John Mitchell ................. | do | |
| 956. | Abraham Mitchell .............. | do | |
| 1000. | Thomas Massey ................ | Upshaw Robinson | |
| 1026. | Abel McPherson, Lt. ........... | H. Montfort | |
| 1029. | William Morgan ............... | do | |
| 1031. | Richard Morgan ............... | do | |
| 1048. | John Mason, Dd. .............. | Ab. Thomas | |
| 1065. | Richard Martin ............... | H. Montfort | for Martin |
| 1066. | Gilbert Matthews .............. | do | do |
| 1071. | John May .................... | Philip Fishburn | |
| 1073. | John Mason .................. | Tho. Armstrong, Jr. | |
| 1087. | John Mitchell ................ | B. McCulloch | |
| 1094. | John Manning ................ | do | |
| 1114. | Robert Morrison .............. | John Kingsbury | |
| 1139. | Caleb McPherson ............. | John Bonds | |
| 1141. | John Mooneham ............... | do | |
| 1176. | Jeremiah Mount .............. | Robert Fenner | |
| 1188. | Jacob Mitchell ................ | H. Montfort | for Jacob Mitchell |
| 1194. | Shadrach Mays ................ | do | for Mays |
| 1251. | Malcolm McDormid ............ | Anthony Sharp | Signed by J. Craven |
| 1263. | William Maleby .............. | John Price | |
| 1272. | Joel Merritt ................. | Sen. Pitman | |
| 1284. | Peter Marrisetti .............. | H. Montfort | for Morrisette |
| 1316. | John Matthews ............... | C. Dixon | |
| 1340. | Alexander McMullen ........... | | for McMillan |
| 1384. | John Morgan ................. | T. Dixon | |
| 1385. | Richard Mount ............... | do | |
| 1391. | Thomas McClannen ............ | Alexander McMillan | |
| 1395. | Benjamin Morris .............. | Thos. Armstrong, Jr. | |
| 1402. | Edward Malloy ............... | William Sanders | |

[WARRENTON]

| No. | Name & Rank | By Whom Received | Remarks |
|---|---|---|---|
| 5. | Jacob Messick, Lt. ............. | G. J. McRee | |
| 22. | William Murray, Lt. ........... | H. Murfree | |
| 24. | John McGlahon, Capt. .......... | | |
| 25. | Isaac Moore, Capt. ............ | Nathaniel Williams | |
| 30. | Josiah Mann, Lieut. ........... | Thomas Donoho | |
| 39. | James McRory, Ensn. .......... | H. Montfort | for W. Lytle |
| 1455. | Stephen McDowel ............. | William Faircloth | |
| 1456. | John Mulky .................. | do | |
| 1457. | Jonathan Miller .............. | do | |
| 1458. | Robert Magby ................ | do | |
| 1459. | John Mills, M. ............... | do | |
| 1460. | James Myrick ................ | do | |
| 1492. | George Morgan ............... | John McNees | |
| 1512. | Jesse McCalester .............. | B. McCulloch | for J. Glasgow |
| 1518. | William Martin ............... | John Price | |
| 1523. | Elisha Medlin ................ | do | |
| 1538. | Peter McFhagan .............. | do | |

| No. | Name & Rank | By Whom Received | Remarks |
|---|---|---|---|
| 1550. | Joel Monk | John Price | |
| 1560. | Henry Malleby | do | |
| 1564. | Elisha Modley | do | |
| 1566. | Taylor Manning | do | |
| 1569. | Elisha McCaw | do | |
| 1571. | James Modlan | do | |
| 1589. | Daniel Moore | do | |
| 1590. | Samuel Martin | do | |
| 1599. | Daniel McKenzie | do | |
| 1594. | Patrick McKnight | do | |
| 1620. | Levi Martin | do | |
| 1630. | Reuben Mannin | do | |
| 1638. | Thomas McFarmer | do | |
| 1655. | Willis Melt | do | |
| 1662. | George McGarret | do | |
| 1674. | Job Morris | do | |
| 1683. | Ephraim Mirrer | do | |
| 1690. | Charles Mulden | do | |
| 1695. | Josiah McLendon | William Faircloth | |
| 1719. | Henry McFarshion | do | |
| 1744. | Matthew Burwell, Lt. | do | |
| 1755. | Lewis McNeal | do | |
| 1787. | John Moss | do | |
| 1810. | Isaac Morrison | do | |
| 1851. | Jacob Molton | do | |
| 1859. | Elisha Musa | Thomas Butcher | |
| 1884. | Aaron Martin | do | |
| 1913. | Charles McKelt | William Faircloth | |
| 1944. | John Mauson | do | |
| 1950. | Samuel Marrow | do | |
| 1951. | George Muss | do | |
| 1952. | Andrew McDonald | do | |
| 1960. | Archibald McDougall | do | |
| 1963. | Daniel McMoor | do | |
| 1964. | David McGoin | do | |
| 1967. | Marmaduke McCoy | do | |
| 1971. | Theophilus Maxwell | do | |
| 1977. | Samuel Mansfield | William Faircloth | |
| 1982. | Simon McPhater | do | |
| 1986. | Miles McCarthy | do | |
| 2004. | John Miles | do | |
| 2008. | John Markalmant | do | |
| 2014. | Stephen McCarthy | do | |
| 2020. | Thomas Mann | Benjamin McCulloch | for S. Harney |
| 2062. | John Morrison | John Sheppard | |
| 2078. | Jeremiah Modlin | Joshua Davis | |
| 2090. | Stephen McPhadan | Thomas Butcher | |
| 2092. | Isaac Milberry | do | |
| 2115. | Lewis Morgan | Sherd. Barrow | |
| 2125. | Morris Moore | do | |
| 2135. | John Morgan | do | |
| 2144. | Isham Morgan | do | |
| 2149. | William Melts | Thomas Butcher | |
| 2163. | Drury Morgan | Sherd. Barrow | |

| No. | Name & Rank | By Whom Received | Remarks |
|---|---|---|---|
| 2166. | Tiberius March | C. Nixon | |
| 2181. | Henry Noveal | do | |
| 2191. | James Murray | John Sheppard | |
| 2193. | John McCoy Senr. | do | |
| 2197. | John McCoy, Junr. | do | |
| 2207. | Josiah Moore | Thomas Butcher | |
| 2215. | Edward Matthews | | no receipt |
| 2217. | Peter McGee | G. J. McRee | |
| 2222. | William Manes | Isles Simmons | |
| 2226. | Henry Morriset | do | |
| 2230. | Josiah Miller | do | |
| 2242. | Thomas *McDonald | William Lytle | *McDaniel |
| 2243. | Micajah Menhew | do | |
| 2252. | Joshua McEbbe | William Sanders | |
| 2324. | Emanuel Marshall | Griffith Dange | |
| 2331. | Zebulin Modlin | Nath'l. Williams | |
| | (Wrong) Elish Modlin | | |
| 2332. | Miles Modlin | Nath'l. Williams | |
| 2350. | John McNary | Phillip Fishburn | |
| 2355. | John McWhorter | do | |
| 2365. | Phillip Myers | do | |
| 2397. | Alexander McCulloch | William Lytle | |
| 2400. | William Martin | | no receipt |
| 2410. | George Mattison, C. | A. Nelson | |
| 2414. | Richard Mohaves | Griffith Douge | |
| 2416. | Thomas May | B. McCulloch | |
| 2419. | John McGound | | no receipt |
| | Lemuel Moore.  See No. 304, Halifax Settlements | | |
| 2434. | Thomas Mullen | | |
| 2454. | William Morgan | | |
| 2470. | James McCaleb | | |
| 2471. | Joseph McCalister | | |
| 2478. | Duncan McBride | | |
| 2484. | James Maloy | | |
| | Edward Maloy.  See No. 1402, Halifax Settlements | | |
| 2485. | Alexr. McGlanglin | | |
| 2508. | Charles Murray, L. | John Daves | |
| 2516. | William Midget | do | |
| 2528. | William Meeks | | no receipt |
| 2565. | Samuel McClelland | Phillip Fishburn | |
| 2569. | Moland Maibry | H. Montfort | for Mrs. Mabry |
| 2571. | John Madry | Will Johnston | |
| 2579. | Britain Moore | John Price | |
| 2583. | Job Mayo | do | |
| 2596. | Shadrach Mency | do | |
| 2600. | Isham Macklin | do | |
| 2601. | Charles Mannan | do | |
| 2606. | Solomon Mosely | John McNees | |
| 2615. | Richard Moss | William Sanders | |
| 2631. | William Macon | do | |
| 2632. | James Macon | do | |
| 2651. | Henry Monk | Thomas Butcher | |
| 2658. | John McCalop | do | |
| 2674. | Timothy Mauning | | |

| No. | Name & Rank | By Whom Received | Remarks |
|-----|-------------|------------------|---------|
| 2690. | John Marr, Senr. | John Rochell | |
| 2691. | Sampson Morgan | Nichos. Long | |
| 2696. | Peter McClain | Simon Totevine | |
| 2699. | William Martins | do | |
| 2710. | Moses Morris | John Price | |
| 2715. | Caleb McMoor | do | |
| 2721. | Gilbert Mitchell | do | |
| 2741. | Andrew Moorham | do | |
| 2746. | Simon McFoster | do | |
| 2761. | John May | Phillip Fishburn | |
| 2764. | William Myers | do | |
| 2765. | Alexander McCoy | do | |
| 2769. | Ferrell Moss | Benj. Moss | |
| 2780. | James McNatt | James Pearl | |
| 2783. | Thomas McCormack | Phillip Fishburn | |
| 2790. | Phillip Morris | do | |
| 2799. | Marmaduke Maples | Thomas Donoho | |
| 2827. | Bolen Matthews | do | |
| 2829. | William McCormack | do | |
| 2830. | John McCormack | do | |
| 2848. | William Millage | William Faircloth | |
| 2851. | Richard Naughton | do | |
| 2868. | John McMurphy | do | |
| 2894. | Sanders Michals | do | |
| 2913. | Arthur McDonald | William Lytle | |
| 2916. | William Morris | do | |
| 2936. | Dempsey Marlow | Rich'd. Ship | |
| 2944. | Lewis Martin | James Homer | |
| 2950. | Benjamin Mound | do | |
| 2959. | Griffin Michal | do | |
| 2968. | John Mahoney | B. McCulloch | |
| 2971. | Thomas Mosely | Nichos. Long | |
| 2993. | John Morgan | H. Murfree | |
| 2996. | Moses Manley | do | |
| 2997. | Michael McKeel | do | |
| 2998. | Nottingham Monk | do | |
| 3000. | Southam Manly | do | |
| 3005. | Marmaduke Moore | do | |
| 3006. | James Morgan | do | |
| 3022. | William Muckle | John Sommers | |
| 3036. | John Murray | do | |
| 3038. | Thomas Manning | Thomas Armstrong | |
| 3080 | Caleb Merchant | Isaac Gregory | |
| 3103. | Arnold Mann | his<br>Nathan X Harris<br>mark | |
| 3106. | William Miller | J. Marshal | |
| 3133. | Thomas Mallett | | not receipted |
| 3148. | Aaron Medlin | | do |
| 3159. | John Lacolin | James Bristow | |
| 3164. | John Mooring | John Daves | |
| 3166. | Thomas Marstern | do | |
| 3171. | Larkin McDonald | Thomas Person | |
| 3182. | Thomas Morris | C. Nixon | |

| No. | Name & Rank | By Whom Received | Remarks |
|---|---|---|---|
| 3196. | Matthias Morgan | C. Nixon | |
| 3197. | Michael McMullen | do | |
| 3202. | William McLellen | do | |
| 3226. | Jesse Martin | John Marshall | |
| 3231. | Matthias Menson | do | |
| 3232. | Gabriel Manly | do | |
| 3249. | William Moseley | James Armstrong | |
| 3258. | Jacob Milles | Phillip Fishburn | |
| 3282. | James McDonald | John Marshall | for W. Sanders |
| 3357. | Bachford Morpass | Timothy McCarthy | |

**N**

| No. | Name & Rank | By Whom Received | Remarks |
|---|---|---|---|
| 42. | William Neill, Lt. | Alexander Brevard | |
| 161. | John Nicholson | J. Craven | |
| 182. | Isaac Nicholson | Jos. Hadley | |
| 207. | Shadrach Nettles | H. Montfort | for Shad Nettles |
| 266. | James Nichols | do | for James Nichols |
| 347. | Patrick Newton | do | for P. Newton |
| 353. | William Neithercut | do | for Neithercut |
| 463. | Boothe Newsom | | |
| 837. | Robert Newsom | his<br>Boothe X Newsom<br>mark | |
| 873. | Dickson Nelly | F. Harget | |
| 939. | Christopher Neale | Christopher Neale | Say H. Montfort<br>for Neale |
| 1040. | Joseph Nicks | Thomas Person | |
| 1130. | Hancock Nichols | H. Montfort | for Nichols |
| 1181. | Jeremiah Nichols | John Bonds | |
| 1207. | Robert Newbry | John Price | |
| 1212. | Enos Norwell | Phillip Causey | |
| 1227. | John Newall | John Sheppard | |
| 1264. | Francis Nash | William Faircloth | |
| 1362. | John Nicholson | C. Dixon | |
| 1368. | Jeremiah Nicholson | do | |
| 876. | John Nichols | H. Montfort | for Nichols |

[WARRENTON]

| No. | Name & Rank | By Whom Received | Remarks |
|---|---|---|---|
| 1548. | William Neal | John Price | |
| 1582. | John Norwood | do | |
| 1722. | Robert Nobles | William Faircloth | |
| 1847. | Willoby Nobles | do | |
| 1889. | Stephen Newton | Thomas Butcher | |
| 1904. | Jesse Nate | do | |
| 1908. | Allen Near | do | |
| 1922. | Phillip Niles | William Faircloth | |
| 1929. | Jethro Nott | do | |
| 2033. | Samuel Nichols, L. | B. McCulloch | for Selby Harney |
| 2156. | William Norwell | Thomas Butcher | |
| 2257. | Thomas Newberry | William Sanders | |
| 2277. | Drury Nann | do | |
| 2245. | Samuel Nothern | Phillip Fishburn | |
| 2389. | Richard Nash | B. McCulloch | for Art Pearce |
| 2415. | Benjamin Nobles | do | Selby Harney |
| 2431. | Levi Norman | William Sanders | |

| No. | Name & Rank | By Whom Received | Remarks |
|---|---|---|---|
| 2444. | Joseph Newman | William Lytle | |
| 2467. | John Needham | T. Dixon | |
| 2558. | David Neakins | William Sanders | |
| 2598. | Thomas Nail | John Price | |
| 2633. | Nathaniel Nann | William Sanders | |
| 2686. | Aaron Newsom | J. Craven | for B. McCulloch |
| 2846. | Drury Nevill | William Faircloth | |
| 2890. | Joseph Nunn | do | |
| 2896. | Frederick Norris | do | |
| 2942. | Darby Newsom | James Homes | |
| 3027. | John Nixon, C. | John Sommers | |
| 3154. | Jeremiah Norris | William Peay | |
| 3176. | Matthew Newby | C. Nixon | by J. Marshall |
| 3192. | Jesse Night | do | do |
| 3240. | John Nelson, St. | John Marshall | |
| 3333. | Daniel Nowell | Timo. McCarthy | |

### O

| No. | Name & Rank | By Whom Received | Remarks |
|---|---|---|---|
| 14. | Chas. O'Neill, Lt. | Ab. Thomas | |
| 179. | Jacob Omerry | Thos. Armstrong | |
| 184. | Francis Owens | Jos. Hadley | |
| 200. | William O'Bannon | Thos. Person | |
| 280. | David Owens, dd | H. Montfort | for D. Owens |
| 358. | John Olive | do | J. Olive |
| 438. | Bailey Owens | J. Craven | |
| 472. | John Onen | "Pd. Willie Jones" | but not receipted |
| 535. | William Orange | Henry Overstreet | |
| 641. | Charles Orr, Corpl. | H. Montfort | for Orr |
| 925. | William Overby | A. Lytle | |
| 1047. | Enoch Owens | Ab. Thomas | |
| 1163. | Daniel Obarr | Wynn Dixon | |
| 1164. | Robert Obarr | do | |
| 1291. | John Oliver | William Oliver | |
| 1403. | John Overby | William Sanders | |

### 053 [WARRENTON]

| No. | Name & Rank | By Whom Received | Remarks |
|---|---|---|---|
| 1652. | John Oakland | John Price | |
| 1672. | Isaac Owell | do | |
| 1699. | Josiah Oakland | William Faircloth | |
| 1738. | Samuel Orr | do | |
| 1771. | James Owell | do | |
| 1785. | Henry Oliver | do | |
| 1805. | Solomon Overton | do | |
| 1806. | Thomas Owel | do | |
| 1907. | Isaac Obedson | Thomas Butcher | |
| 1911. | John Obedson | do | |
| 1928. | Darby O'bryan | William Faircloth | |
| 1945. | Archibald O'Neill | do | |
| 1948. | Tide O'Bryan | do | |
| 1953. | Daniel Oate | do | |
| 2085. | Michael O'Phegan | Thomas Butcher | |
| 2093. | William Oxby | do | |
| 2100. | John Overstreet | Sherd Barrow | |
| 2112. | Prince Orange | do | |

| No. | Name & Rank | By Whom Received | Remarks |
|-----|-------------|------------------|---------|
| 2138. | Isham O'Neil | Sherd. Barrow | |
| 2283. | Benjamin O'Hassel | Wm. Sanders | |
| 2292. | Thomas Owens | do | |
| 2556. | Daniel Overton | do | |
| 2613. | James Overton | do | |
| 2854. | Rowland Oliver | William Faircloth | |
| 3017. | Joab Overton, C. | Benj. Easman | |
| 3128. | John O'Neal | | no receipt |
| 3179. | John O'Guinn | John Marshall | for C. Nixon |
| 3199. | Ricey Oliver | do | do |
| 3335. | John Outlaw | Timo. McCarthy | |

## P

| No. | Name & Rank | By Whom Received | Remarks |
|-----|-------------|------------------|---------|
| 113. | Hugh Parks | Arch'd. Lytle | |
| 122. | Thomas Pierce | H. Murfree | |
| 125. | Ransom Prewet | Tho. Armstrong | |
| 126. | Joshua Prewet | do | |
| 129. | John Peasley | H. Montfort | for J. Peasley |
| 141. | William Proctor | John Ingles | |
| 146. | John Parish | H. Montfort | for Parish |
| 166. | John Pritchet | J. Craven | |
| 174. | Isham Pully | B. McCulloch | |
| 187. | Isaiah Parr, St. | Selby Harney | |
| 225. | Phil Paul | H. Montfort | for Paul |
| 229. | George Powell | A. Brevard | |
| 252. | James Pierce | Thomas Stokes | |
| 257. | James Powell | Samuel Petman | |
| 265. | Richard Phillips | H. Montfort | for Phillips |
| 270. | Daniel Patter | do | |
| 278. | Gideon Pettit, Fifer | Thos. Armstrong | |
| 292. | Edward Pate | H. Montfort | for Pate |
| 296. | Kedar Phelps | James Cobb | |
| 301. | Hardman Portoise | H. Montfort | for Portoise |
| 306. | William Parks | do | for Parks |
| 339. | Robert Pierson | Thomas Armstrong | |
| 342. | James Passons | do | |
| 373. | John Platt | John Grimes | |
| 374. | William Pate | F. Harget | |
| 383. | John Proudford | Tho. Armstrong | |
| 434. | James Prim, Corpl | J. Craven | |
| 437. | Tilman Patterson, St. | do | |
| 465. | David Poe | H. Montfort | |
| 481. | Emanuel Partree | Selby Harney | |
| 487. | Reubin Pierce | Tho. Armstrong | |
| 496. | Noah Parr | Ab Thomas | |
| 520. | Abraham Prim | Tho. Armstrong | |
| 523. | James Pierce | (See No. 273 forward) | |
| 523. | Caleb Parr | H. Montfort | for Parr |
| 526. | Thomas Parker | | |
| 547. | Robert Perry | H. Montfort | for Perry |
| 557. | Thomas Pryor | John McNees | |
| 574. | Richard Philsby | A. Lytle | |
| 647. | Tobias Purvis | H. Montfort | for Purvis |
| 687. | Absolom Powers | William Sanders | |

| No. | Name & Rank | By Whom Received | Remarks |
|---|---|---|---|
| 709. | John Patterson | William Sanders | |
| 711. | Nathaniel Pharo | do | |
| 733. | Benjamin Page | Thomas Person | |
| 748. | Willoby Prescott | Robert Fenner | |
| 767. | George Plumby | John Sheppard | |
| 775. | Joseph Parker | do | |
| 976. | William Pridgen | do | |
| 812. | Charles Porter | Benj. Atkins | |
| 820. | John Platt | H. Montfort | for John Platt |
| 821. | John Pond | do | J. Pond |
| 830. | James Paramore | John McNees | |
| 841. | James Powers | H. Montfort | for Powers |
| 875. | Thomas Pedon | David Passmore | |
| 912. | Thomas Parks | A. Lytle | |
| 941. | William Parrum | do | |
| 943. | John Parks | do | |
| 952. | Thophilus Pierce | do | |
| 953. | Thomas Paddin | do | |
| 954. | Adam Perkins | do | |
| 960. | Beverly Parkinson | do | |
| 986. | Henry Parish | J. Craven | |
| 996. | John Perry | Thos. Evans | |
| 1021. | Axum Powell | H. Murfree | |
| 1035. | David Pendergrass | Thos. Person | |
| 1036. | James Porch | do | |
| 1060. | John Phillips | James Thompson | |
| 1080. | Thomas Price | B. McCulloch | |
| 1142. | Needum Perrit | John Bonds | |
| 1169. | Peter Piland | H. Montfort | for Piland |
| 1172. | Abraham Page | do | Page |
| 1204. | Benjamin Powell | Tho. Tison | |
| 1208. | Nicholas Parish | John Price | |
| 1211. | William Proctor | Philip Causey | |
| 1223. | Mathew Pollard | John Sheppard | |
| 1231. | Stephen Pettis | do | |
| 1239. | Wm. & Joshua Porter | Thos. Armstrong, Jr. | |
| 1247. | John Privett | Thos. Armstrong, Jr. | |
| 1259. | William Pierce | H. Montfort | for Privett |
| 1292. | Roger Parsons | John Grimes | |
| 1293. | Jesse Parsons | William Oliver | |
| 1294. | Nathan Parsons | Rich'd. Crutchfield | X his mark |
| 1296. | Samuel Pope | John McNees | |
| 1298. | James Phelps, Fifer | William Faircloth | |
| 1301. | George Plumby | John Price | |
| 1318. | Thomas Prewet | Charles Dixon | |
| 1333. | Needum Perry | do | |
| 1400. | Jacob Pendergrass | Wm. Sanders | |
| 1401. | William Petteford | do | |
| 273. | James Pierce | H. Murfree | |

[WARRENTON]

| 13. | John Pilly, P. M. | Cosimo Medici | |
| 1442. | Joseph Purvie | William Faircloth | |
| 1443. | Isaac Perry | do | |

| No. | Name & Rank | By Whom Received | Remarks |
|---|---|---|---|
| 1444. | William Pollard ............... | William Faircloth | |
| 1445. | Willis Pipkin .................. | do | |
| 1485. | Peter Poyner .................. | do | |
| 1517. | Thomas Pettijohn .............. | John Price | |
| 1519. | William Phelps ................ | do | |
| 1527. | Zebulon Pratt ................. | do | |
| 1544. | John Pickman ................. | do | |
| 1576. | John Parr .................... | do | |
| | [Page 240] | | |
| 1592. | Reuben Pope .................. | do | |
| 1596. | Francis Potter ................ | do | |
| 1626. | Samuel Parker ................ | do | |
| 1658. | Noah Phelps ................... | do | |
| 1659. | Moses Phelps ................. | do | |
| 1681. | Jesse Patterson ............... | do | |
| 1685. | Vinson Pope .................. | do | |
| 1696. | James Paxton ................. | William Faircloth | |
| 1701. | Cornelius Paynter ............. | do | |
| 1707. | Arm Proctor .................. | do | |
| 1733. | Peter Payne .................. | do | |
| 1748. | Francis Powell ................ | do | |
| 1751. | Nicholas Powel ................ | do | |
| 1762. | Robert Powers ................ | do | |
| 1769. | Mark Parish .................. | do | |
| 1773. | Peter Powel .................. | do | |
| 1774. | Titus Petty ................... | do | |
| 1775. | Daniel Pettis ................. | do | |
| 1792. | James Phillips ................ | do | |
| 1822. | Stephen Pelock ............... | do | |
| 1898. | Joshua Parnall ................ | Thos. Butcher | |
| 1909. | Aaron Poon ................... | do | |
| 1914. | David Pernalt ................ | William Faircloth | |
| 1916. | Alexander Potts ............... | do | |
| 1958. | Stephen Putnam ............... | do | |
| 1961. | Anthony Powel ................ | do | |
| 1988. | Stephen Philips ............... | do | |
| 2013. | Augustine Price ............... | do | |
| 2060. | Benjamin Pollock .............. | John Sheppard | |
| 2064. | Stephen Powell ............... | do | |
| 2080. | Moses Powel .................. | do | |
| 2117. | Mulford Portes ................ | Sherd. Barrow | |
| 2119. | Demsey Pace ................. | do | |
| 2140. | Isham Pitman ................. | do | |
| 2152. | David Pew .................... | Tho. Butcher | |
| 2167. | John Pusley .................. | Sherd. Barrow | |
| 2171. | Barnett Purvis ................ | do | |
| 2188. | Isham Parker ................. | do | |
| 2190. | Joseph Parker, Lt. ............ | John Sheppard | |
| 2196. | Mark Philips ................. | do | |
| 2201. | William Phillips .............. | do | |
| 2206. | William Patrick .............. | Tho. Butcher | |
| 2213. | Daniel Peal .................. | | no receipt Endorsed Will Barksdale |

| No. | Name & Rank | By Whom Received | Remarks |
|---|---|---|---|
| 2244. | John Pennel | Will Lytle | |
| 2266. | John Padget | William Sanders | |
| 2295. | James Price | John Marshall | |
| 2335. | William Parr | Griffith Dange | |
| 2337. | Hillary Parker | Isles Simmons | |
| 2394. | Austin Prescott | | ☞ no receipt |
| 2497. | William Phelps, Senr. | J. Craven | for B. McCulloch |
| 2527. | Tho. Prescott, Ser. | John Daves | |
| 2530. | Elisha Phelps | John McNees | |
| 2564. | Micajah Petaway | Nath'l. Belberry | |
| 2573. | Andrew Pool | John Price | |
| 2575. | Elisha Peters | do | |
| 2580. | William Perdue | do | |
| 2586. | Elisha Pool | do | |
| 2597. | Elisha Price | do | |
| 2599. | Joseph Phelps | do | |
| 2605. | Peter Paul | John McNees | |
| 2618. | Uriah Pendleton | William Sanders | |
| 2622. | Israel Pierce | do | |
| 2665. | Joshua Pelt | Thomas Butcher | |
| 2687. | Micajah Prewet | Thomas Person | |
| 2720. | Jethro Piper | John Price | |
| 2743. | Andrew Parrot | do | |
| 2777. | Thomas Potter | John Garland, Jr. | |
| 2782. | Alexander Patterson | Philip Fishburn | |
| 2797. | Hugh Patterson | do | |
| 2867. | Parl Perry | William Faircloth | |
| 2872. | Patrick Peal | do | |
| 2881. | Willoby Proctor | do | |
| 2886. | David Paul | do | |
| 2906. | John Poor | William Lytle | |
| 2931. | Elisha Parker | Richard Ship | |
| 2943. | Barnaba Pate | James Homes | |
| 2952. | Nathaniel Pledges | do | |
| 3025. | S. Park, Lt. & Ensn. | John Sommers | |
| 3048. | Martin Patterson | Thomas Armstrong | |
| 3051. | Rawlei'h Pendergrass | | Pd to Macon no receipt |
| 3062. | Nathaniel Parrot | | no receipt |
| 3101. | Jacob Powel | Curtis Ivey | |
| 3142. | Benjamin Partin | B. McCulloch | |
| 3161. | Joseph Pack | Phillip Fishburn | |
| 3174. | Hance Pillegrew | J. Marshall | for C. Dixon |
| 3200. | William Plumer | do | do |
| 3220. | John Phips | do | do |
| 3266. | Charles Presley | Phillip Fishburn | |
| 3269. | John Pollard | J. Marshall | for Saunders |
| 3271. | James Pollard | do | do |
| 3287. | Henry Phillips | do | do |
| 3305. | John Powers | Absalom Powers | |
| 3326. | Henry Pythrus | Timothy McCarthy | |
| 3332. | Aaron Patt | do | |
| 3342. | Jacob Parker | do | |
| 3351. | Elliott Pass | do | |
| 349. | David Quinn | H. Montfort | for Quinn |

[Page 242]

R

| No. | Name & Rank | By Whom Received | Remarks |
|---|---|---|---|
| 4. | Francis Ross, Lt. | Ab Thomas | |
| 12. | John Raiford, Lt. | H. Montfort | for Raiford |
| 23. | Joseph Richardson | do | for Richardson |
| 24. | John Richardson, Ensn. | do | |
| 39. | Hezekiah Rice, Capt. | Ab. Thomas | |
| 99. | James Rainey | do | |
| 101. | Peter Rainey, Lt. | do | |
| 103. | John Reddin | do | |
| 115. | Thos. Robinson | Arch Lytle | |
| 117. | Stephen Ray | H. Murfree | |
| 140. | Nathaniel Roper | John Ingles | |
| 150. | Jesse Rickson | do | |
| 212. | John Reel | Alex Brevard | |
| 235. | Jacob Robinson, Lt. | Thos. Armstrong | |
| 248. | Andrew Randall, Lt. | David Passmore | |
| 249. | Isaac Rhodes | H. Murfree | |
| 255. | Jesse Reeves | Sam'l. Pitman | |
| 264. | David Robinson | John Nelson | |
| 272. | Abraham Reddick | | |
| 275. | Samuel Reeves | H. Montfort | for S. Revons |
| 287. | Joshua Reams | do | |
| 295. | Maurice Raiford | do | |
| 302. | Peter Rheims | Richard Fenner | |
| 307. | Benjamin Reeves | John McNees | |
| 318. | Thomas Reasons | H. Bond | |
| 324. | James Riddle | H. Montfort | |
| 394. | Lewis Ralph | C. Dixon | |
| 397. | Moses Roberts | H. Montfort | |
| 399. | William Rowland | Arch Lytle | |
| 400. | Robert Rowland | do | |
| 406. | Thos. Robinson | do | |
| 416. | James Rowland | do | |
| 424. | James Ross | A. Brevard | |
| 448. | Joel Robinson | J. Craven | |
| 473. | Thomas Roberts | "pd Willie Jones" | not receipted |
| 505. | Daniel Rice | Ab Thomas | |
| 552. | Thomas Richardson | H. Montfort | |
| 566. | John Rice | A. Lytle | |
| 475. | Kinchen Roberts | H. Montfort | |
| 611. | Joseph Robinson | C. Dixon | |
| 627. | William Randall | do | |
| 633. | Thomas Richardson | do | |
| 642. | Isaac Reddick | Benj. Perry | |
| 644. | James Rawls | H. Montfort | for Barksdale |
| 655. | William Randolph | Alex. McMillin | |
| 689. | Thomas Rice | Wm. Sanders | |
| 701. | James Rigsby | do | |
| 706. | Charles Rowe | do | |
| 761. | Benjamin Revons | H. Montfort | for Reeves |
| 772. | John Rigkins | J. Sheppard | |
| 798. | William Robb | H. Montfort | |
| 831. | Ephriam Rogers | J. McNees | |

| No. | Name & Rank | By Whom Received | Remarks |
|---|---|---|---|
| | [Page 243] | | |
| 838. | James Richards | Thomas Armstrong | |
| 842. | Nathan Rhodes | B. McCulloch | |
| 852. | Stephen Rogers | John Daves | |
| 856. | Ephraim Reynolds | do | |
| 861. | John Revills | John Sheppard | |
| 894. | Frederick Reeves | H. Montfort | for M. Hunt |
| 905. | Morris Richards | A. Lytle | |
| 927. | George Reggs | do | |
| 948. | Jesse Robinson | do | |
| 977. | John Ross, Dag | Ab Thomas | |
| 979. | Hudson Ray | A. Lytle | |
| 993. | Jas. Rowe, F. Arty. | Thos. Evans | |
| 999. | Reubin Robinson | Upshaw Robinson | |
| 1012. | James Roberts | Robert Fenner | |
| 1022. | William Rix | H. Murfree | |
| 1077. | John Rowe | B. McCulloch | |
| 1098. | William Russell | do | |
| 1103. | Henry Robinson | B. Adkins | |
| 1117. | Malachi Russell | H. Montfort | for M. Russell |
| 1147. | Frederick Reed | John Bonds | |
| 1151. | Vincent Roberts | T. Dixon | |
| 1209. | Michael Rogers | John Price | |
| 1236. | John Right | H. Montfort | for Right |
| 1255. | Lazarus Revell | do | for L. Revell |
| 1268. | William Rollins | do | for W. Rollins |
| 1271. | Eli Rogers | John Price | |
| 1297. | Jeremiah Reardon | H. Montfort | for J. Reardon |
| 1346. | Joel Riggins | C. Dixon | |
| 1350. | Samuel Rooks | do | |
| 1359. | John Ross | do | |
| 1371. | Peter Rame | do | |
| 1386. | Reubin Roberts | T. Dixon | |

[WARRENTON]

| 28. | Zeri Rice, Lieut. | Thos. Donoho | |
|---|---|---|---|
| 37. | Lovick Rochell, Lt. | John Marshall | |
| 1461. | Thomas Richardson | William Faircloth | |
| 1462. | Solomon Ramsey | do | |
| 1463. | Thomas Reddick | do | |
| 1464. | Andrew Russell | do | |
| 1484. | Aaron Renn | do | |
| 1486. | Peter Reddick | do | |
| 1487. | Jesse Rogers | do | |
| 1501. | Andrew Rowel | John Sheppard | |
| 1502. | Samuel Rowel | do | |
| 1536. | Samuel Rutledge | John Price | |
| 1579. | William Robins | do | |
| 1597. | Samuel Rowland | do | |
| 1622. | James Robins | do | |
| 1633. | Andrew Rose | do | |
| 1649. | Aron Ruther | do | |
| 1650. | Howell Redman | do | |
| 1689. | Moses Raley | do | |

| No. | Name & Rank | By Whom Received | Remarks |
|---|---|---|---|
| 1692. | Jonas Riddick | William Faircloth | |
| 1728. | Henry Richards | do | |
| 1743. | John Russell | do | |
| 1749. | James Roberts | do | |
| 1761. | Sampson Roberts | do | |
| 1815. | Solomon Robinson | do | |
| 1903. | Elisha Roke | Thomas Butcher | |
| 1923. | Jethro Randolph | William Faircloth | |
| 1962. | David Ruster | do | |
| 2003. | Benjamin Rowland | do | |
| 2038. | John Ralph | Benjamin McCulloch | for S. Harvey |
| 2053. | Andrew Rowell | John Sheppard | |
| 2076. | Samuel Rowe, C. | Joshua Davis | |
| 2077. | John Richardson | do | |
| 2147. | Daniel Rhodes | Thomas Butcher | |
| 2159. | Hardy Robertson | do | |
| 2204. | Henry Ruff | do | |
| 2216. | Eli Rogers | Robt. Fenner | |
| 2237. | James Rainey | William Lytle | |
| 5239. | Nicholas Rochester | do | |
| 2272. | Buckner Rooks | William Sanders | |
| 2298. | Larkin Rogers | John Marshall | |
| 2343. | Jacob Rusher | Phillip Fishburn | |
| 2370. | Jonathan Richards | James Bristow | |
| 2421. | Abraham Reddick | | no receipt |
| 2429. | Mark Robertson | William Sanders | |
| 2439. | James Rogers | | no receipt |
| 2448. | Anderson Runnery | | do |
| 2461. | Peter Roberts | William Sanders | |
| 2469. | Charles Rosier | T. Dixon | |
| 2473. | Jesse Rowel | do | |
| 2482. | Jordan Rosier | do | |
| 2486. | Samuel Ross | William Gowdy | |
| 2498. | James Royall | John Davis | |
| 2521. | Charles Roach | Charles Gerrard | |
| 2535. | John Ridgeway | J. Craven | for J. Ingles |
| 2558. | Shadrach Roberts | Samuel Parker | |
| 2560. | Thomas Ryan, M. | William Sanders | |
| 2624. | Arthur Rogers | do | |
| 2675. | William Rogers | James Williams | |
| 2745. | Andrew Right | John Price | |
| 2805. | William Read | John Sommers | |
| 2815. | John Roberts | H. Murfree | |
| 2825. | Thomas Reddin | Thos. Donoho | |
| 2834. | William Ridley | do | |
| 2838. | George Roaper | do | |
| 2853. | Ebenezer Rasberry | William Faircloth | |
| 2866. | Jeremiah Reynolds | do | |
| 2908. | John Ronniefer | Will Lytle | |
| 2915. | Reason Rickets | do | |
| 2938. | Constantine Reddit, C. | | |
| 2946. | Jarvis Raines | James Holmes | |
| 2973. | Anthony Rogers | Sim Totevine, Fran | |
| 2974. | Joseph Ritter | Maxwell, J. Garland & | |

| No. | Name & Rank | By Whom Received | Remarks |
|---|---|---|---|
| 2982. | James Rickerson | James Homes | |
| 2992. | Absolom Riggs | do | |
| 3020. | James Roark | John Sommers | |
| 3042. | Daniel Rowson, S. | Tho. Armstrong | |
| 3057. | William Red | | no receipt |
| 3066. | Powell Riggins | | |
| 3087. | John Renton | B. Sanders | |
| 3110. | Powell Riggins | | |
| 3114. | William Rogers | Samuel Parker | |
| 3138. | Cornelius Roomer | Isles Simmons | |
| 3156. | John Reeves | James Bristow | |
| 3191. | George Rochell | C. Dixon | J. Marshall |
| 3216. | William Roberts | John Marshall | for C. Dixon |
| 3227. | David Rogers | do | |
| 3242. | Thomas Rickets, M. | do | |
| 3248. | Edward Robertson | | no receipt |
| 3261. | Charles Russ | Phillip Fishburn | |
| 3311. | Frederick Reeves | Warren Alford | |
| 3325. | William Redit | Timothy McCarthy | |
| 3347. | David Ryan | do | |
| 3363. | Daniel Ray | do | |
| 3377. | David Reeves | do | |

S

| No. | Name & Rank | By Whom Received | Remarks |
|---|---|---|---|
| 61. | James Spicer, P. M. | John Daves | |
| 5. | John Sheppard, Major | | |
| 17. | John G. Scull, Lieut. | J. Leonard | |
| 18. | Wm. Sheppard, Capt. | John Sheppard | |
| 30. | Silas Stephenson, Cap. | Rich'd. Fenner | for J. Court |
| 55. | Sedg'k. Springs, Armr. | H. Montfort | for S. Springs |
| 60. | John Spicer, P. M. | John Daves | |
| 74. | James Shine, Lieut. | M. Eelbeck, Junr. | |
| 81. | Robert Sears, pri. | H. Montfort | |
| 118. | Joseph Spearpoint | do | for Spearpoint |
| 142. | Caleb Smith | John Ingles | |
| 157. | Lewis Stephens | J. Craven | |
| 180. | John Smith | John Bonds | |
| 186. | Isles Simmons, Sergt. | Selby Harney | |
| 205. | James Strange | John McNees | |
| 230. | James Smith, Wag. | J. Craven | for R. Holme |
| 233. | Christain Snider | A. Brevard | |
| 234. | William Sheppard, St. | H. Montfort | for W. Sheppard |
| 345. | William Snipes | do | for Will Snipes |
| 357. | Willis Simmons | do | for W. Simmons |
| 364. | William Sneatman | do | for W. Sneatman |
| 365. | Frederick Stewalk | do | for Stewalk |
| 367. | Thomas Searts | Thomas Vicars | |
| 372. | Filix Simmons | F. Harget | |
| 379. | George Simmons | C. Dixon | |
| 381. | Jacob Stilwell | do | |
| 382. | John Southerland | do | |
| 389. | Thomas Scott | J. Craven | |
| 392. | Robert Searts | H. Montfort | for R. Searts |
| 421. | George Streider | Arch. Lytle | |

| No. | Name & Rank | By Whom Received | Remarks |
|---|---|---|---|
| 432. | Thomas Stephens | Alexander Brevard | |
| 440. | Christopher Strother | J. Craven | |
| 494. | Francis Sumner | Ab Thomas | |
| 495. | William Sketo | do | |
| 522. | John Steptoe, St. | Henry Overstreet | |
| 529. | Joseph Speight | John Ingles | Maj. McRee |
| 545. | Benjamin Stephens | H. Montfort | for B. Stephens |
| 804. | Micajah Springs | do | for Springs |
| 806. | Hugh Stephenson | do | for Stephenson |
| 811. | George Scurlock | do | for Scurlock |
| 822. | Benjamin Simmons, Lt. | Thomas Evans | |
| 824. | James Surrivan | | Drawn by J. Sheppard no receipt |
| 836. | Augustine Sabury | H. Montfort | |
| 864. | Jonathan Stanley | John Sheppard | |
| 866. | Robert Stranaland | F. Harget | |
| 871. | Joseph Skipper | do | |
| 872. | Nathan Skipper | do | |
| 910. | William Shannon | Arch Lytle | |
| 918. | Asa Searcey | do | |
| 928. | John Sanders | do | |
| 932. | H. Stephens & J. Maibry | do | |
| 959. | James Spence, Drag. | do | |
| 967. | James Stranaland | F. Harget | |
| 962. | William Steele, Corpl. | Archd Lytle | |
| 964. | Jesse Spilliards | do | |
| 965. | William Spiers | do | |
| 971. | John Scott | do | |
| 1002. | John Simmons | Jesse Read | |
| 1014. | William Stewart | Robert Fenner | |
| 1042. | John Stepp | Thomas Person | |
| 1076. | David Stillwell | E. Gamble | |
| 1099. | James Scriven | B. McCulloch | |
| 562. | James Sellers | A. Lytle | |
| 601. | Robert Sanders, Senr. | C. Dixon | |
| 602. | Robert Sanders, Junr. | do | |
| 605. | Jesse Shy | do | |
| 606. | James Shadden | do | |
| 631. | Francis Standback | do | |
| 632. | John Stilwell | do | |
| 635. | Thomas Swann | do | |
| 639. | Henry Singleton | Benjamin McCulloch | |
| 668. | John Seagraves | William Sanders | |
| 672. | Littleberry Stone | do | |
| 676. | John Seagraves, SENR. | do | |
| 677. | John Seagraves, JUNR. | do | |
| 679. | Thomas Striplin | do | |
| 685. | Newton Striplin | do | |
| | [Page 247] | | |
| 700. | William Skeborn | H. Montfort | |
| 712. | William Scott | William Sanders | |
| 722. | James Stallions | Nichos Long | |
| 730. | John Smith | William Sanders | |
| 731. | Aaron Springfield | do | |

| No. | Name & Rank | By Whom Received | Remarks |
|---|---|---|---|
| 756. | William Shute | John McNees | |
| 779. | Hugh Stephenson | John Sheppard | |
| 791. | William Smith | William Muir | |
| 794. | Benjamin Smith | H. Montfort | for Smith |
| 796. | Joseph Spearpoint | H. Montfort | for Spearpoint |
| 1100. | Insell Spence | do | |
| 1121. | William Stewart | H. Montfort | for W. Stewart |
| 1127. | Mitchell Smith | do | for Smith |
| 1152. | Jeremiah Sexton | T. Dixon | |
| 1182. | James Smith | H. Montfort | for J. Smith |
| 1195. | Jesse Shevers | do | for Shevers |
| 1210. | William Smith | Phillip Causey | |
| 1218. | John Sullivan | H. Montfort | for Sullivan |
| 1220. | James Scurlock | do | for Scurlock |
| 1245. | Caldwell Stewart | do | for Stewart |
| 1250. | James Slater | do | for Slater |
| 1257. | Edward Stradley | do | for Stradley |
| 1265. | John Suggs | William Faircloth | |
| 1276. | Zaccheus Shaw | H. Montfort | for Shaw |
| 1278. | Job Sanders | do | for Sanders |
| 1286. | William Spires | do | for Spears |
| 1304. | Joseph Sutton | Benjamin McCulloch | |
| 1322. | James Swiney | C. Dixon | |
| 1328. | Jordan Sherrod | B. McCulloch | Says Charles Dixon |
| 1335. | George Southerland | C. Dixon | |
| 1338. | William Starkey | do | |
| 1377. | Robert Simms | do | |
| 1389. | Jacob Spilmore | F. Dixon | |

[WARRENTON]

[Page 248]

| No. | Name & Rank | By Whom Received | Remarks |
|---|---|---|---|
| 31. | Robert Singleton, Lt. | Thos. Donoho | |
| 1446. | William Sparkman | William Faircloth | |
| 1447. | Jonathan Smiler | do | |
| 1448. | Andrew Skipton | do | |
| 1449. | Joseph Scull | do | |
| 1450. | John Stone | do | |
| 1451. | Joshua Simons | do | |
| 1452. | James Sowell | do | |
| 1453. | Zedekiah Stone | do | |
| 1454. | Edward Spalding | do | |
| 1481. | Drury Simms | do | |
| 1491. | Solomon Swift | John McNees | |
| 1509. | Edward Smithwick | B. McCulloch | for Jas. Glascow |
| 1516. | Peter Simmons | John Price | |
| 1539. | Andrew Stadley | do | |
| 1567. | Peter Sirls | do | |
| 1570. | Samuel Spaun | do | |
| 1572. | Edward Sordon | do | |
| 1584. | Andrew Stephenson | do | |
| 1598. | Thomas Spiers | do | |
| 1644. | John Sprigg | do | |
| 1697. | Joseph Samford | William Faircloth | |
| 1704. | Jesse Stradley | do | |

| No. | Name & Rank | By Whom Received | Remarks |
|---|---|---|---|
| 1756. | William Studman | William Faircloth | |
| 1757. | James Steadmore | do | |
| 1778. | James Scalf | do | |
| 1784. | Joshua Steal | do | |
| 1801. | John Simmons | do | |
| 1802. | Joseph Steadmore | do | |
| 1808. | Stephen Sobarton | do | |
| 1817. | Joel Shubatton | do | |
| 1819. | John Southall | do | |
| 1861. | Garrett Still | Thomas Butcher | |
| 1867. | Evenezer Smith | do | |
| 1874. | John Stobo | do | |
| 1875. | Jeptha Smith | do | |
| 1878. | Thomas Singleton | do | |
| 1880. | Andrew Sills | do | |
| 1936. | Henry Stomer | William Faircloth | |
| 1954. | Thomas Sewell | do | |
| 1957. | Peter Smither | do | |
| 1972. | Elias Skilar | do | |
| 1975. | Peter Stealman | do | |
| 2005. | Thomas Skipton | do | |
| 2010. | Abraham Stephenson | do | |
| 2019. | Isaac Sanderlin | B. McCulloch | for Selby Harney |
| 2025. | William Sexton | do | do |
| 2026. | Jabez Spence | do | do |
| 2028. | Jonathan Sextons | do | do |
| 2039. | Levi Sanderlin | do | do |
| 2045. | Luke Sylvester | do | do |
| 2059. | Charles Smith | John Sheppard | |
| 2066. | Joseph Smith | do | |
| 2067. | John Sollings | Thomas Butcher | |
| 2072. | Daniel Swills | Joshua Davis | |
| 2099. | William Short | Sherd Barrow | |
| 2105. | David Short | do | |
| 2110. | James Sikes | do | |
| 2111. | Isham Short | do | |
| 2118. | Overstreet Scott | do | |
| 2120. | Samuel Scutchins | do | |
| 2128. | Abraham Short | do | |
| 2164. | Applewhite Sanders | do | |
| 2165. | Elleck Sneed | do | |
| 2168. | John Sanders | | |
| 2169. | William Shevers | | |
| 2177. | Lyas Savage | | |
| 2178. | John Sneed | | |
| 2180. | Merideth Scutchins | | |
| 2182. | Hancock Stanly | | |
| 2187. | Joel Stone | | |
| 2198. | Stephen Smith | John Sheppard | |
| 2218. | Caleb Sanders, C. | Isles Simmons | |
| 2232. | Cullen Sanderson | do | |
| 2255. | Benjamin Smith | William Sanders | |
| 2261. | Micajah Savage | do | |
| 2265. | Myatt Stiley | do | |

| No. | Name & Rank | By Whom Received | Remarks |
|---|---|---|---|
| 2275. | Thomas Skinner | William Sanders | |
| 2278. | John Smithers | do | |
| 2281. | Moses Smithers | do | |
| 2284. | Jacob Simpson | do | |
| 2287. | Isaac Simpson | do | |
| 2300. | Jonathan Simpson | John Marshall | |
| 2329. | Robert Staples, M. | Nathaniel Williams | |
| 2330. | Willis Sawyer | do | |
| 2342. | John Silliman | Phillip Fishburn | |
| 2348. | James Simsell | do | |
| 2364. | Robert Skipton | do | |
| 2368. | Samuel Sloan | do | |
| 2412. | Randall Shoemaker | Alex. Nelson | |
| 2424. | William Smith | William Sanders | |
| 2425. | William Smith | | no receipt |
| 2436. | Paul Sink | William Lytle | |
| 2437. | Dempsy Sikes, M. | do | |
| 2449. | John Swanson | James Hinton | |
| 2455. | William Story | his Abram X Bush mark | |
| 2456. | Lewis Sholt | do | |
| 2465. | Samuel Serret | T. Dixon | |
| 2487. | Charles N. Scrugg | John Macon | |
| 2496. | Andrew Sanders | John Daves | |
| 2497. | William Sanders | do | |
| 2505. | Levi Surman | do | |
| 2510. | Joseph Seaburn | do | |
| 2519. | Whitak'r Shadforth, St. | do | |
| 2522. | Austin Spain, St. | Charles Gerrard | |
| 2523. | William Spain, F. | do | |
| 2524. | Epps, Spain, Lt. C. | do | |
| 2540. | William Stephenson | William Sanders | |
| 2542. | Dred Simpson | do | |
| 2548. | John Stealman | William Sanders | |
| 2549. | John Smith | do | |
| 2557. | Josiah Smith | do | |
| 2576. | Martin Simmons | John Price | |
| 2609. | David Spear, S. | John McNees | |
| 2611. | John Smallwood | do | |
| 2621. | James Steverston | William Sanders | |
| 2641. | William Skinner | do | |
| 2657. | Watson Stringer | Thomas Butcher | |
| 2661. | Burwell Salls | do | |
| 2662. | Frederick Stricklin | J. Craven ☞ | |
| 2685. | Joseph Sketar | Thomas Butcher | |
| 2692. | Arrington Sheppard | Phillip Miller | |
| 2697. | Daniel Sullivan | Simon Totevine | |
| 2731. | Ebenezer Stalling | John Price | |
| 2732. | John Stegall | do | |
| 2734. | Abner Shuffeld | do | |
| 2737. | William Spivey | do | |
| 2753. | Peter Seaner | Phillip Fishburn | |
| 2756. | Frances Seals | do | |

| No. | Name & Rank | By Whom Received | Remarks |
|---|---|---|---|
| 2757. | John Smith | Phillip Fishburn | |
| 2763. | James Smith | do | |
| 2772. | Isaac Solomon | John Sheppard | |
| 2791. | James Sloan | Phillip Fishburn | |
| 2800. | John Stephens, C. | Thomas Donoho | |
| 2801. | James Standford | do | |
| 2806. | William Spinney | John Sommers | |
| 2808. | James Sexton, L. | do | |
| 2812. | John Soulter | do | |
| 2818. | Nehemiah Smith | Thomas Donoho | |
| 2831. | William Symms | do | |
| 2835. | Peter Stansell | do | |
| 2849. | Raymond Solomons | William Faircloth | |
| 2850. | Bartholomew Saul | do | |
| 2852. | Allen Stringer | do | |
| 2858. | Lamon Sionyeas | do | |
| 2860. | William Sendal | do | |
| 2864. | Jolly Sparkman | do | |
| 2875. | James Sholders | do | |
| 2877. | Calburn Saunders | do | |
| 2895. | Benjamin Singleton | do | |
| 2907. | Finley Shaw | William Lytle | |
| 2921. | John Sandin, Lt. | | |
| 2929. | Hannah Steiner | John Armstrong | |
| 2929. | Obadiah Sullivan | James Homes | |
| 2955. | Uriah Sugg | do | |
| 2966. | Samuel Sarlf | do | |
| 2969. | John Swanson | Nicholas Long | |
| 2970. | George Sweat | do | |
| 2978. | William Snead | (Simon Totevine | |
| 2981. | Curtis Sommers | Frau Maxwell, J. Garland | |
| 2986. | Edmond Strange | Jr., J. Homes | |
| 3007. | John Stone | Nathaniel Williams | |
| 3012. | James Sutton | Robert Raiford | |
| 3028. | Boston Splendar | John Sommers | |
| 3029. | John Sheppard | do | |
| 3031. | Joseph Smith | Thomas Donoho | |
| 3033. | Alexander Simmons | do | |
| 3039. | Skidmore Squires | Thomas Armstrong | |
| 3064. | Jesse Syrus | William Peay | |
| 3086. | James Skelton | Britain Sanders | |
| 3092. | Joseph Stephens | C. Ivey | |
| 3111. | David Sayers | | |
| 3114. | Richard Straughan | James Bristow | |
| 3112. | Smith Simpson | Timothy McCarthy | |
| 3124. | John Street | John Estes | for A. Tatom |
| 3130. | Joseph Stephenson | Thomas Butcher | |
| 3139. | Samuel Simmons | Selby Harney | |
| 3141. | David Stokes | Solomon Green | |
| 3147. | James Shaw | | no receipt |
| 3167. | Aaron Spilmore | John Daves | for Jas. Coor |
| 3172. | Jesse Siddle | Thomas Person | |
| 3186. | John Sluthers | J. Marshal | for C. Dixon |
| 3198. | George Spivey | do | do |

| No. | Name & Rank | By Whom Received | Remarks |
|---|---|---|---|
| 3201. | Joseph Singletary | J. Marshal | for C. Dixon |
| 3215. | William Sloan | do | do |
| 3222. | William Shoulders | do | do |
| 3230. | James Savage | do | |
| 3244. | Thomas Seamore | do | |
| 3257. | Adam Seawalt | Phillip Fishburn | |
| 3277. | Jesse Stancell | John Marshall | for Will Sanders |
| 3279. | John Simpkins | do | do |
| 3309. | John Swink | Phillip Fishburn | |
| 3338. | Obediah Sewell | Timo McCarthy | |
| 3350. | Ezekiel Skipper | do | |
| 3360. | Edward Shirrod | do | |
| 3365. | Nehemiah Smith | do | |

## T

[Page 252]

| No. | Name & Rank | By Whom Received | Remarks |
|---|---|---|---|
| 28. | L. Thompson, Capt. | Ab Thomas | |
| 53. | Jacob Turner, Capt. | Thomas Turner | |
| 62. | H. Toomer, A. D. Q. M. | Nicholas Long | |
| 78. | Howell Tatum, Capt. | H. Montfort | |
| 84. | Amos Thomas | do | |
| 152. | F. Thorgood, Corpl. | John Daves | |
| 154. | Wm. Tate, Far. | H. Montfort | |
| 164. | William Thurston | J. Craven | |
| 170. | Samuel Thompson | John Jones | |
| 178. | Thomas Trotman | Benjamin Perry | |
| 240. | William Townson | John Nelson | |
| 303. | James Tice | Geo. Falconer | |
| 333. | Thomas Turner | Jer. Nelms | |
| 351. | James Tinnen | H. Montfort | |
| 361. | Philip Thomas | do | |
| 380. | Olive Terry | C. Dixon | |
| 391. | Thomas Tiffin | do | |
| 404. | Alexander Tinnin | A. Lytle | |
| 403. | Thomas Templeton | Alex Brevard | |
| 462. | Arthur Toney | Ab Thomas | |
| 476. | William Tipper | H. Montfort | |
| 499. | Nicholas Thompson | Ab Thomas | |
| 501. | William Tilghman | H. Montfort | |
| 503. | Eredick Threel | John Daves | |
| 517. | William Turpin | Thos. Armstrong | |
| 521. | Jas. Taylor, S. M. | Rich'd. Fenner | |
| 524. | Ambrose Towl | David Pasmore | |
| 534. | William Thompson | J. Craven | |
| 556. | John Tatum | H. Montfort | |
| 561. | James Tracey | A. Lytle | |
| 618. | James Tinnen | C. Dixon | |
| 637. | Thomas Thockston | do | |
| 690. | Merriman Thorn, Lt. | William Sanders | |
| 764. | Willis Truner | H. Montfort | |
| 834. | Coleburn Totevine | do | |
| 835. | Winder Totevine | do | |
| 900. | George Templin | A. Lytle | |
| 902. | Zaccheus Tate | do | |

| No. | Name & Rank | By Whom Received | Remarks |
|---|---|---|---|
| 903. | John Tate ..................... | A. Lytle | |
| 966. | Bernard Tatum ................ | do | |
| 968. | Nathan Thompson .............. | do | |
| 989. | Maltiah Turner ................ | James Armstrong | |
| 1013. | William Thompson ............. | Robb Fenner | |
| 1037. | Richard Thomas ............... | Thomas Person | |
| 1043. | Asa Thomas ................... | do | |
| 1110. | J. Thompson, Corpl. ........... | H. Montfort | |
| 1136. | Jeremiah Thomas .............. | John Bonds | |
| 1137. | James Taun ................... | do | |
| 1138. | Ephraim Taun ................. | do | |
| 1144. | Allen Tayburn ................ | do | |
| 1168. | Abraham Tyson ............... | George Falconer | |
| 1190. | Tom Thomas .................. | Willie Jones | |
| 1198. | Thomas Tedor ................ | Robb Fenner | |
| | [Page 253] | | |
| 1274. | Elijah Tindall ................. | John McNees | |
| 1285. | Archibald Tunin .............. | H. Montfort | |
| 1312. | James Towning ............... | do | |
| 1390. | David Teary .................. | J. Craven | |

[WARRENTON]

| No. | Name & Rank | By Whom Received | Remarks |
|---|---|---|---|
| 1409. | Charles Tutson ............... | William Faircloth | |
| 1425. | Benjamin Troublefield .......... | do | |
| 1477. | William Tinner ............... | do | |
| 1482. | John Todd ................... | do | |
| 1488. | Stephen Truitt Jr. ............. | John McNees | |
| 1507. | Arthur Tyner (S. C.) ........... | B. McCulloch | |
| 1547. | Spencer Towler ............... | John Price | |
| 1552. | Job Tipps .................... | do | |
| 1595. | Martin Tiner ................. | do | |
| 1647. | Simeon Tyar ................. | do | |
| 1666. | Jesse Tiel ................... | do | |
| 1694. | Amos Tellonson ............... | William Faircloth | |
| 1702. | Barthomew Thigpen ........... | do | |
| 1709. | Belitha Tate ................. | do | |
| 1726. | Joel Traverse ................ | do | |
| 1818. | Absolom Turner .............. | do | |
| 1820. | Abel Tope ................... | do | |
| 1853. | Amos Tilton ................. | Thomas Butcher | |
| 1860. | Patrick Titley ................ | do | |
| 1868. | Osburn Temple ............... | do | |
| 1883. | Paul Toter .................. | do | |
| 1886. | Sampson Tilmon .............. | do | |
| 1920. | Morris Taylor ................ | William Faircloth | |
| 1924. | Stephen Tilus ................ | do | |
| 1943. | David Thirnton ............... | do | |
| 1978. | Aaron Tuttle ................. | do | |
| 2017. | Alexander Toop .............. | do | |
| 2029. | Franklin Truitt ............... | B. McCulloch | for S. Harney |
| 2044. | Willoby Thompson ............ | do | do |
| 2049. | Solomon Truitt .............. | do | do |
| 2051. | Edward Thompson ............ | do | do |
| 2247. | Malliah Turner, C. ............ | William Lytle | |

| No. | Name & Rank | By Whom Received | Remarks |
|---|---|---|---|
| 2253. | John Tipper | William Sanders | |
| 2254. | Trusel Daniel* | do | odd names to appear at the end of the Army Accts. |
| 2354. | Michael Tilto | Philip Fishburn | |
| 2369. | Thomas Todd, M. | do | do |
| 2380. | Henry Taylor | Simon Totevine | |
| 2381. | Joseph Toomer | Burl Moering | |
| 2384. | John Thornal | | |
| 2433. | John Tucker, C. | Nathaniel Williams | |
| 2440. | Henry Tice | John Sheppard | |
| 2457. | Solomon Thrift | Abraham Bush | X his mark |
| 2474. | Lewis Tilley | Tilman Dixon | |
| 2479. | Abraham Thrift | do | |
| | [Page 254] | | |
| 2603. | James Tenar | Jno. McNees | |
| 2664. | Absalom Travis | Thomas Butcher | |
| 2703. | Richmond Terrill | G. J. McRee | |
| 2712. | Vinson Taylor | John Price | |
| 2739. | James Talton | do | |
| 2784. | Melchar Tar | Philip Fishburn | |
| 2789. | William Thomas | do | |
| 2796. | Thomas Thompson | do | |
| 2813. | Miles Thrift | John Sommers | |
| 2847. | Jacob Ternage | William Faircloth | |
| 2888. | John Todd | do | |
| 2898. | Turner Turnage | do | |
| 2964. | Travis Tyson | James Homes | |
| 2967. | Joab Tart | do | |
| 2972. | John Titterson | Simon Totevine, Fra. | |
| 2980. | George Tree | Maxwell, John Garland, Jr. | |
| 2983. | John Thompson | J. Holmes | |
| 3140. | Richard Tucker | Isles Simmons | |
| 3163. | John Turner, L. | John Daves | |
| 3183. | William Townley | John Marshall | for C. Dixon |
| 3207. | Moses Tyler | do | do |
| 3209. | John Titherton | do | do |
| 3217. | Parson Taylor | do | do |
| 3298. | Menchy Taylor | do | Sanders |
| 3359. | Josiah Todd | Timothy McCarthy | |
| 3361. | Hardy Tyner | do | |
| 3364. | William Taydor | do | |
| 1871. | Isaac Tiplet | Thos. Butcher | |
| 1873. | Osborn Taylor | do | |
| 10. | Robert Varner, Lt. | H. Montfort | |

U AND V

| | [Page 255] | | |
|---|---|---|---|
| 312. | Shadrach Underwood | H. Montfort | for S. Underwood |
| 650. | James Underhill | John McNees | |
| 744. | Joseph Umphrey | H. Montfort | for Umphrey |
| 648. | Daniel Venters | John Allen | |
| 202. | Benjamin Vinson | Thomas Tabb | |
| 599. | Thomas Vernon | C. Dixon | |
| 807. | Moses Vinson | do | |

| No. | Name & Rank | By Whom Received | Remarks |
|---|---|---|---|
| 890. | William Vincent | William Sanders | |
| 1202. | Paul Vanboreas | H. Montfort | for Vanboreas |
| 1252. | David Varden | do | for D. Varden |
| 1343. | Peter Valentine | C. Dixon | |
| 994. | Kedar Vincing | Thomas Evans | |
| 1068. | James Vaughn | Charles Dixon | |
| 1201. | Vincent Vaughan | Montfort Eelbert, Jr. | |

[WARRENTON]

| | | | |
|---|---|---|---|
| 22. | Edward Vail, Capt. | H. Murfree | |
| 33. | Andrew Venoy, Capt. | Thos. Donoho | |
| 34. | James Vaughan, Capt. | H. Murfree | |
| 1471. | Arthur Venters | William Faircloth | |
| 1472. | Silas Valentine | do | |
| 1671. | Absalom Venson | John Price | |
| 1845. | Arthur Vanpelt | William Faircloth | |
| 1885. | Aaron Volls | Tho. Butcher | |
| 1959. | Robert Velvin | William Faircloth | |
| 2036. | Malachi Valentine | B. McCulloch | for S. Harney |
| 2073. | Willis Upton | Joshua Davis | |
| 2179. | James Underwood | Sherd. Barrow | |
| 2214. | Moses Venters | Robert Fenner | |
| 2290. | Nathaniel Vasey | William Sanders | |
| 2301. | James Vance | John Marshall | |
| 2418. | Moses Venters | Griffith Dauge | |
| 2810. | William Vowel | John Sommers | |
| 3083. | Joseph Vicks | C. Ivey | |
| 3131. | Richard Vaughn | Sam'l. Parker | |
| 3278. | Hezekiah Vickory | John Marshall | for W. Sanders |
| 3306. | Thomas Vernon | Phillip Fishburn | |
| 3320. | Ezekiel Vicory | | no receipt |
| 3374. | Patrick Vinson | Timothy McCarthy | |

W

| | | | |
|---|---|---|---|
| 11. | John Walker, Major | Ab. Thomas | |
| 22. | John Williams, Lt. | Thomas Armstrong | |
| 26. | Thomas White, Capt. | Austin Cicaty | |
| 35. | Theo'l's. Williams, Lt. | H. Montfort | for T. Williams |
| 45. | James Wilson, Capt. | C. Dixon | |
| 46. | W. Williams, A. C. J. | B. McCulloch | |
| 47. | Will Walters, Lt. | do | |
| 49. | Solomon Walker, Lt. | William Sanders | |
| 52. | Reub'n. Wilkinson, Lt. | B. McCulloch | |
| 54. | Richard Whedbee, Lt. | Natl. Williams | |
| 72. | David Wright, Lt. | T. Dixon | |
| 75. | W. Williams, Capt. B. M. | Ab. Thomas | |
| 116. | William Welch | William Lytle | |
| 123. | Thomas Wright | John Nelson | |
| 139. | John White | John Ingles | |
| 159. | Thomas White | Phillip Fishburn | |
| 160. | John Wilson | J. Craven | |
| 163. | Alexander Williams | do | |
| 173. | John Ward | John Nelson | |
| 231. | James Wallis, St. | H. Montfort | for Jas. Wallace |
| 260. | Joseph West | J. Craven | for Rob. Holme |

| No. | Name & Rank | By Whom Received | Remarks |
|---|---|---|---|
| 297. | Absalom Wildie | H. Montfort | for A. Wildie |
| 314. | Augustine Willis | do | |
| 317. | Gillstrap Williams | do | |
| 329. | Hansford Whitley | Jer. Nelms | |
| 341. | Thomas Woodson | Thos. Armstrong | |
| 348. | John Walden | H. Montfort | for J. Walker |
| 390. | Robinson Williamson | J. Craven | |
| 398. | Augustine Woodliffe | Arch. Lytle | |
| 444. | James Williams, St. | J. Craven | |
| 447. | Jeremiah Walker, St. | do | |
| 449. | George Woodley | do | |
| 452. | Benjamin Weaver | H. Montfort | for B. Weaver |
| 453. | Arthur Whitley | Isaac Kennedy | |
| 455. | William Whitley | do | |
| 480. | Isaac Wood | H. Montfort | for J. Wood |
| 488. | James White | David Collins | |
| 489. | Edward Wilson | do | |
| 504. | William Wilkinson | Ab. Thomas | |
| 509. | John Walker, Q. M. S. | do | |
| 510. | Richard Walker, S. | do | |
| 519. | William Williamson | Thomas Armstrong | |
| 525. | William Walker | David Passmore | |
| 532. | James Wyatt | Robert Ward | |
| 546. | Solomon Warburton | J. Craven | for Jas. Jones |
| 578. | Edward Woodman | A. Lytle | |
| 613. | John Willis | C. Dixon | |
| 621. | Johnston Webb | do | |
| 629. | William Walker, St. | do | |
| 636. | Asa Wright | do | |
| 662. | William Woodside | Alexander McMillan | |
| 674. | Samuel Warnock | Wm. Sanders | |
| 683. | George White | do | |
| 697. | Francis West | do | |
| 698. | James Ward | William Sanders | |
| 714. | John Williams | do | |
| 726. | Joshua Wilson | do | |
| 736. | Thomas Welch, St. | H. Montfort | for J. Welch |
| 743. | Hardy Wiley | do | |
| 750. | Silas Weeks | John Daves | |
| 778. | William Walker | John Sheppard | |
| 785. | Thomas Waddle | C. Dixon | |
| 788. | Samuel Wilson | do | |
| 810. | Daniel Webster | do | |
| 814. | Solomon Williams | John Daves | |
| 815. | Benjamin Weeks | do | |
| 816. | Levi Weeks, St. | do | |
| 832. | Sion Wheelus | H. Montfort | |
| 843. | Phillip Winburn | do | for P. Winburn |
| 845. | Dixon Weeks | John Daves | |
| 848. | Theophilus Weeks | do | |
| 849. | John Walters | do | |
| 855. | Levi Weeks, St. | do | |
| 878. | John Wright | Wynn Dixon | |
| 879. | Thomas Wynn | do | |
| 882. | Thomas Wall | do | |

| No. | Name & Rank | By Whom Received | Remarks |
|---|---|---|---|
| 895. | William White | H. Montfort | for M. Hunt |
| 896. | Henry White | do | |
| 908. | Richard Williams | A. Lytle | |
| 911. | Joseph Wood | do | |
| 914. | George Wilkie | do | |
| 923. | John Wood | do | |
| 935. | James Waggoner | do | |
| 947. | Adam Wright, Fifer | do | |
| 950. | George Woodliff | do | |
| 951. | Thomas White, drag. | do | |
| 981. | William Wadsworth | J. Craven | |
| 988. | Levi West, Dr. | James Armstrong | |
| 992. | Cornelius Weeks, St. | Thomas Evans | |
| 1005. | Isham Woods | Jesse Read | |
| 1006. | John Wells | do | |
| 1007. | Abraham Wires | do | |
| 1017. | Mosson, Williams | H. Murfree | |
| 1038. | Hampton White | Thomas Person 2 accts 1 as 12 Mos. man & his other as 9 mos. | |
| 1046. | W. Witherington, St. | H. Murfree | |
| 1052. | Cyprean West | Will Jackson | |
| 1054. | Peter White | J. Craven ☞ | for Hance Bond |
| 1058. | Miles Woodward | do ☞ | do |
| 1063. | Francis Wilks | H. Montfort | for Wilkes |
| 1067. | Malachi Wiggins | Malachi Wiggins | for Wiggins |
| 1070. | John Wamble | Robt. Fenner | |
| 1078. | William Williams | B. McCulloch | |
| 1081. | Thomas Winters | do | |
| 1082. | Wyatt Warwick | do | |
| 1105. | Bryan Worley | Nicholas Long | |
| 1120. | Obediah Winnon | H. Montfort | |
| 1123. | John Wilkerson | John Kingsbury | |
| 1129. | John Walters | H. Montfort | for Walters |
| 1178. | James Webb | Robert Fenner | |
| 1184. | Mial Watson | H. Montfort | for Watson |
| 1192. | Charles Wincoak | Willie Jones | |
| 1217. | Butson Wheelas | H. Montfort | for Wheelas |
| 1246. | William Wilder | John Bonds | |
| 1248. | Samuel Williams | B. McCulloch | |
| 1253. | Jeremiah Woodall | John Bonds | |
| 1300. | Edward Williams | Phillip Miller | |
| 1308. | Moses Williams | B. McCulloch | |
| 1333. | Robert Woodward | C. Dixon | |
| 1334. | Jones Wynn | do | |
| 1335. | Robert Warwick | do | |
| 1363. | Francis Wilkerson | do | |
| 1366. | John Waggoner | do | |
| 1387. | Robert Whitlock | T. Dixon | |
| 1399. | George Waff | William Gar ☞ | We suppose |
| 241. | Richard White | ☞ John Armstrong | |

[WARRENTON]

| 8. | J. Williams, P. Capt. | H. Montfort |

| No. | Name & Rank | By Whom Received | Remarks |
|---|---|---|---|
| 16. | Whitfield Wilson, F. M. | Robt. Fenner | |
| 29. | John Williams, Col. | Thos. Donoho | |
| 41. | John Wade, Capt. | John Marshall | |
| 1408. | Thomas Winstell | William Faircloth | |
| 1410. | William Wright | do | |
| 1411. | Peter Wright | do | |
| 1412. | Titus Wood | do | |
| 1413. | Jordan Wilkins | do | |
| 1414. | Giorge Wilkins | do | |
| 1415. | Solomon Willis | do | |
| 1416. | Peter Williams | do | |
| 1417. | Jacob Wells | do | |
| 1418. | Thomas Wooten | do | |
| 1419. | Peter Ward | do | |
| 1420. | James Woodward | do | |
| 1433. | Jesse Witherington | do | |
| 1434. | James Willace | do | |
| 1435. | Jacob Witherington | do | |
| 1436. | Joseph Whitaker | do | |
| 1437. | Job Williamson | do | |
| 1438. | Samuel Weaver | do | |
| 1439. | Randolph Wilder | do | |
| 1478. | Benjamin Willis | do | |
| 1503. | Obadiah Watson | John Sheppard | |
| 1506. | William Warren | B. McCulloch | for Jas. Glasgow |
| 1510. | Jesse Woolard | do | do |
| 1513. | Jesse Whitfield | do | do |
| 1524. | James Williams | John Price | |
| 1525. | Joseph Williams | do | |
| 1542. | Benjamin Winston | do | |
| 1553. | Jeremiah Wyatt | do | |
| 1555. | Jeremiah West | do | |
| 1558. | George Warwick | do | |
| 1574. | Josiah Whitney | do | |
| 1577. | Holland Woolard | do | |
| 1588. | Samuel Wood | do | |
| 1616. | Sampson Wright | do | |
| 1629. | Taylor Willis | do | |
| 1635. | Stephen Webb | do | |
| 1661. | Malachi Wier | do | |
| 1663. | Etheldred Woodam | do | |
| 1664. | Francis Woodruff | do | |
| 1669. | Ebenezer West | do | |
| 1673. | Emanuel Wright | do | |
| 1677. | Alexander Worrel | do | |
| 1710. | Josiah Wimberty | William Faircloth | |
| 1718. | Ephraim Wyatt | do | |
| 1730. | Absalom Wallace | do | |
| 1734. | Nathaniel Wood | do | |
| 1746. | James Wilkinson | do | |
| 1760. | Jonathan Woolard | do | |
| 1768. | Nathan Wood | do | |
| 1776. | Zebulon Wells | do | |
| 1777. | Charles Wardon | do | |
| 1804. | George Woodard | do | |

| No. | Name & Rank | By Whom Received | Remarks |
|---|---|---|---|
| 1813. | Joshua Windom | William Faircloth | |
| 1816. | Joshua Wabbleton | do | |
| 1843. | John Wilcocks | do | |
| 1852. | Etheldred Watson | do | |
| 1854. | Richard Wilkinson | Thomas Butcher | |
| 1870. | Ignatius Watts | do | |
| 1927. | Moab Walker | do | |
| 1930. | Aaron Welch | do | |
| 1934. | Clayborn Williams | do | |
| 1990. | Alexander Walsh | do | |
| 2006. | Samuel Waller | do | |
| 2021. | Levi Wright | B. McCulloch | for Selby Harney |
| 2022. | Thomas Walden | do | do |
| 2089. | Ambrose Whaley | Thomas Butcher | |
| 2097. | Jordan Wilkins | Sherd. Barrow | |
| 2106. | John Williams | do | |
| 2114. | David Ward | do | |
| 2121. | James Wade | do | |
| 2130. | John Wincoak | do | |
| 2184. | Isaac Walters | do | |
| 2208. | Levi Westbrook | Thomas Butcher | |
| 2211. | Joseph Wyatt | do | |
| 2220. | Timothy Ward | Isles Simmons | |
| 2229. | Malachi White | do | |
| 2234. | George Williamson | do | |
| 2246. | Robert West | William Lytle | |
| 2267. | William White | William Sanders | |
| 2276. | Amos Wilson | do | |
| 2280. | John White | do | |
| 2303. | John Worsley | John Marshall | |
| 2305. | Thomas Williams | do | |
| 2323. | John Wyatt | Griffith Dauge | |
| 2376. | Absalom Woodward | Burwell Moring & Simon Totevine | |
| 2405. | Thomas Woodley | Griffith Dauge | |
| 2446. | George Wilkins | William Lytle | |
| 2507. | John Whitehead | John Daves | |
| 2559. | John Winbury | Wm. Sanders | |
| 2594. | Jacob Wright | John Price | |
| 2610. | Job Wright | John McNees | |
| 2649. | Willis Wickar, S. | William Sanders | |
| 2679. | Andrew West | Andrew Armstrong | |
| 2693. | Caleb Wright | M. Duke Johnson | for Charles Gerrard |
| | Isaac Waters | | Error |
| 2728. | Moses Waddle | John Price | |
| 2736. | Ezekiel Watson | do | |
| 2744. | Peter Wilford | do | |
| 2774. | Robert Woodland | John Garland, Junr. | |
| 2776. | John Woodland | do | |
| 2785. | James Wilson | Phillip Fishburn | |
| 2794. | Samuel Wheeler | do | |
| 2807. | John Woodward | John Sommers | |
| 2824. | John Wright | Thos. Donoho | |
| 2843. | Robert Woodall | Thomas Person | |
| 2869. | Mason Weatherington | William Faircloth | |

| No. | Name & Rank | By Whom Received | Remarks |
|---|---|---|---|
| 2874. | Anthony Williamson | William Faircloth | |
| 2887. | Daniel Walden | do | |
| 2904. | Richard Wallace | | no receipt |
| 2905. | Phillip Watson | | |
| 2932. | John West | John West | |
| 2947. | Elias Walston | James Homes | |
| 2948. | John Wine | do | |
| 2956. | Darlin West | do | |
| 2960. | Zebulon Wasdon | do | |
| 2991. | Curtis Whitley | Sim. Totevine, Trau Maxwell Jno. Garland, Jr. & J. Homes | |
| 3001. | William White | H. Murfree | |
| 3015. | Isaac Ward | Benjamin Easman | |
| 3043. | Joseph Walters | Thomas Armstrong | |
| 3061. | Kinchen Wilkins | George X King his mark | |
| 3069. | Nicholas Williams, C. | | no receipt |
| 3073. | Elijah Ward, C. | H. Montfort | |
| 3079. | Thomas Wigley, S. | Isaac Gregory | |
| 3112. | George White | Alexander Carter | |
| 3118. | *Thomas Wiggins | J. Craven | |
| 3252. | John Windom | James Armstrong | |
| 3255. | Daniel Winchester | Philip Fishburn | |
| 3256. | Samuel Wilson | do | |
| 2125. | Nathaniel Williams | John Estes | |
| 2143. | Peter Warden | | |
| 2149. | John Walker | John Sheppard | |
| 3151. | Daniel Woodland | do | |
| 3170. | Allenby Williams | Thomas Person | |
| 3243. | George Wiggins | J. Marshall | |
| 3260. | William Waddenton | Philip Fishburn | |
| 3263. | Abner Wines | do | |
| 3272. | Nathaniel Waddle | J. Marshall | for Sanders |
| 3275. | Stephen Wright | do | do |
| 3286. | Henry Woodard | do | do |
| 3319. | Thomas Worsley | Jas. Armstrong | |
| 3322. | Mundy White | Timothy McCarthy | |
| 3323. | David Welch | do | |
| 3327. | Philip Wilder | do | |
| 3340. | Hillery Ward | do | |

### Y AND Z
[Page 262]

| 199. | John Young | Isaac Hudson | |
|---|---|---|---|
| 274. | Richard Yarborough | H. Montfort | for Yarborough |
| 946. | John Yeates | Arch. Lytle | |
| 1162. | William York | Wynn Dixon | |

### [WARRENTON]

| 1470. | John Yearby | William Faircloth | |
|---|---|---|---|
| 2628. | Nathan Yammons | William Sanders | |
| 2684. | William Young | | not receipted for |
| 2856. | Joel Yelverton | Wm. Faircloth | |

| No. | Name & Rank | By Whom Received | Remarks |
|---|---|---|---|
| 3037. | Sion Young .................... | Thomas Armstrong | |
| 3228. | James Yarborough ............. | John Marshall | |
| 3254. | Martin Young ................. | Philip Fishburn | |

[WARRENTON]

| | | | |
|---|---|---|---|
| 2291. | Peter Zuly .................... | William Faircloth | |
| 3075. | Shadrack Zealot ............... | H. Montfort | |
| 3076. | Joshua Zealot ................. | do | |
| * | Miscellaneous names, for explanation | see Vol. XVII, P. 263. | |
| 1050. | Thomas Frasier ............... } | J. Craven | for H. Bond |
| 1051. | Thomas Endless ............... | | |
| 1055. | Jeremiah Ashley ..............⎤ | | |
| 1053. | John Floyd ...................| | |
| 1054. | Peter White ..................| | |
| 1056. | Francis Hubbard .............| | |
| 1059. | Dempsey Jones ...............| | |
| 1058. | Miles Woodward ............. | See Vol. 17, State Records |
| 2394. | Austin Prescott ...............| | P. 263 |
| 2682. | Fred'k. Strickland ...........| | |
| 2683. | Thos. Lewis ..................| | |
| 241. | Richard White ...............⎦ | | |
| 1399. | George Waff .................. | | |
| 3032. | Daniel Thomas ...............⎤ | Thomas Donoho | |
| 3034. | William Trotwell .............| | John Sommers | |
| 3067. | Thomas Thomas .............| | J. Craven | |
| 3135. | John Thompson .............⎦ | Isles Simmons | |

EXTRACT FROM THE MORNING CHRONICLE AND LONDON ADVERTISER,
JAN. 16, 1775—ASHE'S HIST., P. 429

Edonton women who refused to use tea imported through Great Britain.

1. Abagail Charlton
2. Elizabeth Creacy
3. Anne Johnstone
4. Mary Woolard
5. Jean Blair
6. Frances Hall
7. Mary Creacy
8. Mary Blount
9. Margaret Cathcart
10. Jane Wellwood
11. Penelope Dawson
12. Susanna Vail
13. Elizabeth Vail
14. Elizabeth Vail
15. J. Johnstone
16. Elizabeth Patterson
17. Margaret Pearson
18. Sarah Beasley
19. Grace Clayton
20. Mary Jones
21. Mary Creacy
22. Anne Hall
23. Sarah Littlejohn
24. Sarah Haskins
25. M. Payne
26. Elizabeth Cricket
27. Lydia Bonner
28. Anne Horniblow
29. Marion Wells
30. Sarah Mathews
31. Elizabeth Roberts
32. Rebecca Bondfield
33. Sarah Howcott
34. Elizabeth P. Ormond
35. Sarah Valentine
36. Mary Bonner
37. Lydia Bennett
38. Tresia Cunningham
39. Anne Houghton
40. Elizabeth Roberts
41. Ruth Benbury
42. Penelope Barker
43. Mary Littledle
44. Elizabeth Johnstone
45. Elizabeth Green
46. Sarah Howe
47. Mary Hunter
48. Anne Anderson
49. Elizabeth Bearsley
50. Elizabeth Roberts

# THE STATE RECORDS OF NORTH CAROLINA
## (CLARK)
### Vol. XXII—Miscellaneous

Pages 55 to and including 92.

North Carolina Revolutionary pensioners under the Acts of 1818 and 1832, as reported by Secretary of State to Congress in 1835

*Name—Rank*

1. Adcock, Joshua, Privt.
2. Apple, Daniel, Privt.
3. Allison, Burch, Privt.
4. Allen, John, Privt.
5. Anderson, James (decsd)
6. Alexander, Stephen, Lt. & Capt.
7. Alexander, William, Capt. of Infantry & Cavalry
8. Amos, John, Privt.
9. Allen, Benjamin, Privt.
10. Archer, Evans, Privt.
11. Allgood, William, Privt.
12. Albright, Henry, Privt. & Sergt.
13. Adkins, William, Senr., Privt.
14. Allen, Richard, Privt. & Capt.
15. Ansley, Jesse, Privt.
16. Arnold, Reuben, Privt., Artillery & Infantry
17. Austin, Benjamin, Privt.
18. Alexander, Abram, Privt.
19. Arnold, Solomon, Privt.
20. Arney, Christian, Privt.
21. Allen, Bartlett, Corpl.
22. Adams, James, Privt.
23. Alfin, William, Privt.
24. Avery, John, Privt.
25. Adams, Philip, Privt.
26. Alexander, James, Privt.
27. Arnold, Hezekiah, Privt.
28. Armstrong, Matthew, Privt.
29. Anders, James, Privt.
30. Addington, William, Privt.
31. Arrand, Peter, Privt.
32. Adams, Bryant, Privt.
33. Allen or Alston, Joseph J., Privt.
34. Armistead, Westwood, Privt.
35. Adams, Jeremiah, Privt.
36. Ahart, Jacob, Privt.
37. Andrews, Hugh, Privt.
38. Abernathy, Robert, Privt.
39. Albright, William, Privt.
40. Allen, Paul, Privt. & Ensign
41. Alexander, Samuel, Privt.
42. Atkinson, Amos, Privt.

*Name—Rank*

43. Allen, Vincent, Privt.
44. Anderson, John, Privt.
45. Alexander, Charles, Privt., Infantry & Cavalry
46. Alexander, Thomas, Privt.
47. Anderson, George, Privt.
48. Askew, William, Privt.
49. Alley, Shadrick, Privt.
50. Arthur, Richard, Privt.
51. Allen, George, Privt.
52. Angel, John, Cavalry, Infantry & Sergt.
53. Allen, William, Cavalry, Infantry & Sergt.
54. Arwood, John, Privt.
55. Almond, Nathan, Privt.
56. Anthony, James, Privt., Infantry & Cavalry
57. Allen, Samuel, Privt. & Commissary
58. Allison, James, Privt., Infantry & Cavalry
59. Allman, Edward, Privt.
60. Alexander, Isaac, Privt. & Sergt.
61. Anderson, William, Privt.
62. Alexander, James, Privt.
63. Brooks, John, Privt.
64. Bradshaw, Robert (decsd.) Privt.
65. Brown, Robert, (decsd.) Privt.
66. Bryan, Hardy (decsd.), Capt. & Adjutant Commanding
67. Burton, Robert, Privt.
68. Badget, William, Privt.
69. Byrum, Jacob, Privt.
70. Byrum, Lawrence, Privt. (of Cavalry)
71. Brown, James, Privt.
72. Bell, Richard, Privt. (Cavalry & Infantry)
73. Brown, William, Privt. (of Cavalry)
74. Buck, Isaac, Privt.
75. Ballow, Stephen, Privt.
76. Boston, Andrew, Privt.
77. Barmer, John, Privt.
78. Bentley, Thomas, Privt.

*Name—Rank*

79. Blanton, James, Privt. (Infantry & Cavalry)
80. Bird, Bonner, Privt. & Sergeant
81. Brady, James, Privt. & Corporal
82. Bailey, John (decsd.), Privt.
83. Bright, Simon (decsd.), Privt.
84. Brookshire, Mannering (decsd.), Lt. of Cavalry
85. Brasfield, John, Privt.
86. Bertie, John, Privt.
87. Bamble, Hackett, Privt.
88. Brewer, William, Privt.
89. Bowles, Benjamin, Privt.
90. Baker, Isaac, Privt.
91. Barr, Isaac, Privt.
92. Butler, Jethro, Privt.
93. Barrott, Peter, Privt.
94. Baswell, William, Privt.
95. Benton, Elkanak, Privt.
96. Boyd, Daniel, Privt.
97. Bartholomew, John, Privt.
98. Barham, Hartwell, Privt.
99. Bryan, Reuben, Privt.
100. Barrington, Joseph Billings, Corporal
101. Burch, William, Privt.
102. Bletcher, Jacob, Privt.
103. Bailey, Stephen, Privt.
104. Bartlett, Haston, Privt.
105. Baker, John, Privt.
106. Browning, Francis, Privt.
107. Bledsoe, Lewis, Privt., Sergeant & Captain
108. Brown, Elijah, Privt.
109. Browning, Levi, Privt.
110. Burns, James, Privt.
111. Billings, Jasper, Privt.
112. Beck, William, Privt.
113. Bushee, Consider, Privt. & Corpl.
114. Ball, Hosea, Privt. & Ensign
115. Brown, Amos, Privt.
116. Biles, Thomas, Privt.
117. Browning, Robert, Privt.
118. Bowman, Sherwood, Privt.
119. Bryan, Robert, Privt.
120. Barnes, Burwell, Privt.
121. Braswell, Jacob, Privt.
122. Ball, Joshua, Privt.
123. Bradley, Burrell, Privt.
124. Bowen, Bracey, Privt.
125. Bullock, Charles, Privt.
126. Bryant, Thomas, Privt. of Artillery
127. Bell, James, Privt.
128. Bilby, Nathaniel, Privt.
129. Blake, Thomas, Privt.

*Name—Rank*

130. Bevan, William, Privt.
131. Bell, Richard, Privt., Cavalry & Infantry
132. Brewington, Joshua (decsd.), Privt.
133. Bradshaw, Jonas, Privt.
134. Ball, Daniel, Privt. & Sergeant
135. Banks, Peter, Privt.
136. Berry, Robert, Privt.
137. Bradley, George W., Privt.
138. Bradford, James, Privt.
139. Barber, William, Privt.
140. Bullard, Thomas, Privt.
141. Beaver, Jeremiah, Privt.
142. Black, Ezekiel, Privt.
143. Babb, Christopher, Privt.
144. Bright, Simon, Privt.
145. Brotherton, Thomas, Privt., Infantry & Cavalry
146. Bell, Samuel, Privt.
147. Boston, Jacob, Privt. of Cavalry
148. Bryant, Jesse, Privt.
149. Burris, Solomon, Privt.
150. Branch, Burrell, Privt.
151. Brown, Jesse, Privt., Infantry & Cavalry
152. Bonner, John, Privt. & Sergeant
153. Burton, William H., Privt., Infantry & Cavalry
154. Burgess, John, Privt.
155. Britton, Michael, Privt.
156. Butler, John, Privt.
157. Beaty, David, Privt.
158. Barnett, Charles, Privt.
159. Bray, David, Privt. & Ensign
160. Boon, John, Privt., Infantry & Cavalry
161. Brock, Bezzant, Privt., Infantry & Cavalry
162. B., George
163. Bean, Jesse, Privt.
164. Bridges, Joseph, Lt. & Sergeant
165. Blake, Joshua, Privt.
166. Brittain, William, Privt.
167. Benson, Thomas, Privt.
168. Broadway, Samuel, Privt.
169. Beck, John, Privt.
170. Brinson, Hillary, Privt.
171. Barnett, Thomas, Privt. & Sergeant
172. Bondy, John, Privt.
173. Boswell, Reuben, Privt.
174. Barrett, William, Privt.
175. Barrett, Jonathan, Privt.
176. Barrett, Isaac, Privt.
177. Bankston, Andrew, Privt.

*Name—Rank*

178. Brooks, William, Privt.
179. Blackwelder, Charles, Privt.
180. Balthrop, Augustine, Privt.
181. Boon, Raeford, Privt.
182. Bowers, Brittain, Privt.
183. Blackwelder, Isaac, Privt. & Sergeant
184. Brooks, James, Privt.
185. Benton, Job, Privt.
186. Brown, Willis, Privt.
187. Barker, David, Privt.
188. Brookshire, William, Privt. & Infantry
189. Bowels, Thomas, Privt.
190. Bryson, Daniel, Privt.
191. Boon, Lewis, Privt.
192. Boney, Daniel, Privt.
193. Brown, Joseph, Privt.
194. Bibbie, Solomon, Privt.
195. Byrd, Thomas, Privt.
196. Bingham, Joseph, Privt.
197. Blalock, John, Lieutenant
198. Bryan, John, Privt.
199. Burrow, Dobson, Privt.
200. Beville, Robert, Privt.
201. Beck, John (decsd.), Privt.
202. Bryan, William (decsd.), Privt.
203. Blackwell, Thomas, Privt.
204. Bailey, Noah, Privt.
205. Brookes, Jonathan, Privt.
206. Banner, Benjamin, Privt.
207. Barker, David, Privt.
208. Badget, Peter, Privt. & Ensign
209. Banner, Joseph, Privt.
210. Banner, Ephraim, Privt.
211. Binkley, Frederick, Privt.
212. Boykin, John, Privt., Infantry & Cavalry
213. Brooks, William, Privt.
214. **Benson, John, Privt.**
215. Barnhardt, George, Privt.
216. Braswell, Richard, Privt.
217. Barnes, Chesley, Privt.
218. Blevins, Nathan, Privt.
219. Boyt, Jacob B., Privt.
220. Bastain, Andrew, Privt. of Cavalry
221. Blue, John, Privt.
222. Bolick, Casper, Privt.
223. Baldwin, John, Privt.
224. Burnhill, Henry, Privt.
225. Boatwright, Samuel, Privt.
226. Berry, Andrew, Privt.
227. Bell, Benjamin, Privt.
228. Byrum, James, Privt.
229. Ballance, Leven, Privt.

*Name—Rank*

230. Cheshire, Richard, Privt.
231. Cockerham, David, Privt.
232. Coulter, Martin, Privt.
233. Cumming, William, Quartermaster Sergeant
234. Carrington, George, Privt. (Infantry & Cavalry)
235. Costen, Stephen, Privt.
236. Chinn, Perry, Privt.
237. Campbell, George, Privt.
238. Clark, James, Privt. (Infantry & Cavalry
239. Clements, Cornelius, Privt.
240. Currey, Hugh, Privt.
241. Carter, James, Privt.
242. Capps, William, Privt.
243. Chapman, Nicholas, Privt.
244. Chapel, Samuel, Privt. & Sergeant
245. Carson, John (decsd.), Privt. & Ensign
246. Cate, Robert, Privt.
247. Combs, George, Privt.
248. Chatham, John, Privt.
249. Cox, John, Privt.
250. Carmical, Duncan, Privt.
251. Clark, Isaac, Privt.
252. Childers, Miller, Privt.
253. Cassel, Thomas, Privt.
254. Cowen, Joseph, Privt.
255. Crabb, Jarrott, Privt.
256. Coggin, Robert, Privt.
257. Carter, Landon, Privt.
258. Crysel, Jeremiah, Privt.
259. Carmack, John, Privt.
260. Carter, Henry, Privt.
261. Cathey, Alexander, Privt.
262. Cook, Edward, Privt. (Infantry & Cavalry)
263. Carroll, William, Privt.
264. Carrell, James, Privt.
265. Carter, Josiah, Sr., Privt.
266. Cox, Benjamin, Privt.
267. Clark, Lee, Privt.
268. Cole, Job, Privt.
269. Collins, James, Privt.
270. Clark, Nathaniel, Privt.
271. Cook, Christopher, Privt.
272. Creemer, James, Senr., Privt.
273. Cox, James, Privt.
274. Curry, John, Privt. & Sergeant
275. Craddick, Eleazer, Privt.
276. Crabtree, William, Privt.
277. Cheek, James, Privt. (Cavalry & Infantry)

*Name—Rank*

278. Cavin, John, Privt.
279. Clayton, Coleman, Privt.
280. Clayton, John, Privt.
281. Costner, Thomas, Privt.
282. Crump, Conrad, Privt.
283. Cameron, John, Privt., Cavalry & Infantry
284. Carr, Moses, Privt.
285. Cutts, William, Senr., Privt.
286. Clodfelter, George, Privt.
287. Clontz, George, Sergeant
288. Collins, James, Privt.
289. Cartwright, Joseph, Privt.
290. Cole, Joseph, Privt.
291. Conner, James, Privt, Seargeant & Qr. Master
292. Carlton, David, Privt.
293. Coson, John, Privt.
294. Crane, William, Privt., Cavalry
295. Crowell, George, Senr., Privt.
296. Congers, Ephraim, Privt.
297. Corbett, John, Privt.
298. Carver, William, Senr., Privt.
299. Cook, Robert, Privt.
300. Chapman, Joseph, Privt.
301. Clontz, Jeremiah, Privt.
302. Coleman, Theophlus, Privt. (Infantry & Cavalry)
303. Carr, William, Privt.
304. Cashon, Burwell, Privt.
305. Cashon, Thomas, Privt.
306. Christmas, Richard, Privt. & Captain
307. Culberson, William, Senr., Privt.
308. Cain, James, Senr., Privt.
309. Cooper, William, Privt.
310. Carrothers, John, Privt.
311. Clemmons, John, Privt.
312. Collins, Samuel, Privt.
313. Church, John, Privt.
314. Church, Amos, Privt.
315. Campbell, John, Privt.
316. Carroll, Benjamin, Privt.
317. Cross, Joseph, Privt.
318. Corn, Peter John, Privt.
319. Crittendin, William, Privt. of Artillery
320. Caldwell, James, Privt.
321. Castle, Samuel, Privt.
322. Childress, William (decsd.), Privt. & Captain
323. Cunningham, George, Privt.
324. Cash, Peter, Privt.
325. Clements, Benjamin, Privt. of Cavalry

*Name—Rank*

326. Campbell, Thomas, Privt.
327. Cockerham, Daniel, Privt.
328. Cummings, Thomas, Privt. (Infantry & Cavalry)
329. Carson, Andrew, Privt.
330. Cock, Charles, Privt.
331. Clapp, Ludwick, Privt.
332. Carpenter, Isaac, Privt.
333. Carrigan, William, Privt.
334. Caldwell, Samuel, Privt.
335. Candel, Absalom, Privt.
336. Cason, John, Privt.
337. Crawford, Peter, Privt.
338. Carter, Thomas, Privt.
339. Crawley, William, Privt. of Artillery
340. Curtis, Jonathan, Privt.
341. Clifton, William, Privt.
342. Casey, William, Privt.
343. Clarke, John, Privt.
344. Cunningham, Jeremiah, Privt.
345. Cline, Michael, Privt., Infantry & Cavalry
346. Carter, Ephraim, Privt.
347. Cooper, Sterling, Privt.
348. Campen, Joseph, Senr., Privt.
349. Daniel, Christopher, Privt.
350. Dalton, William, Privt.
351. Davis, Robert, Privt.
352. Deaver, William, Privt.
353. Dollar, William, Privt.
354. Duke, James, Privt.
355. Dolley, John, Privt.
356. Deal, Jacob, Privt.
357. Dollar, James, Privt.
358. Davis, Simon, Privt.
359. Davis, David, decsd., Privt.
360. Drury Henry, Privt.
361. Dickson, John, Privt.
362. Dickson, Joel, Privt.
363. Dickson, Joseph, Privt.
364. Duncan, George, Privt.
365. Denton, John, Privt.
366. Decone, Edward, Sergeant
367. Davis, Cyrus, Privt.
368. Dickens, Thomas, Privt.
369. Danner, Frederick, Privt.
370. Dilday, Joseph, Privt.
371. Dollars, Elijah, Privt.
372. Daniel, Buckner, Privt.
373. Davis, Edward, Privt.
374. Davis, Isham, Privt.
375. Devane, James, Privt. & Captain
376. Duckworth, John, Privt.
377. Davis, Clement, Privt.

*Name—Rank*

378. Dishon (alias Deshong) Lewis, Privt.
379. Drake, Richard, Privt.
380. Dickerson, Isham, Privt.
381. Davis, Josiah, Privt.
382. Dillen, Benjamin, Privt.
383. Davis, Samuel, Privt.
384. Dunn, Nicholas, Privt.
385. Downing, James, Privt. (Infantry & Cavalry)
386. Depriest, William, Privt.
387. Dobson, Joseph, Privt.
388. Davis, Francis, Privt. & Captain
389. Davis, Thomas, Privt.
390. Dewise, Hezekiah, Privt.
391. Drake, William, Privt.
392. Downes, Thomas, Privt. & Lieutenant
393. Downey, Patrick, Privt.
394. Dickson, John, Privt.
395. Dollar, Jonathan, Privt.
396. Dalton, Thomas, Privt.
397. Dedmon, Mark, Privt.
398. Deveney, Aaron, Lieutenant & Captain
399. Davis, Sampson, Privt.
400. Durham, James, Privt.
401. Duke, William, Privt.
402. Davis, William, Privt.
403. Davis, Charles, Privt.
404. Dail, John, Privt.
405. Dildey, Amos, Privt.
406. Darrach, John, Privt.
407. Duke, Hardernan, Privt.
408. Duke, Williams, Privt. & Sergeant
409. Decoine, Edward, Privt. & Lieutenant Major
410. Donnell, Daniel, Privt.
411. Dowtin, John, Privt.
412. Davis, Burrell, Privt.
413. Denney, Joseph, Privt.
414. Donnell, Andrew, Privt.
415. Demeson, Joseph, Privt.
416. Davis, John, Privt.
417. Delap, Henry, Sr., Privt.
418. Drum, Philip, Privt.
419. Davenport, William, Privt.
420. Dickey, David, Privt. (Infantry & Cavalry)
421. Dicken, William, Privt.
422. Dobbins, James, Privt.
423. Davis, James, Senr., Privt. (Infantry & Cavalry)
424. Darnall, Joseph, Privt.
425. Dawkins, John, Privt. (Infantry &

*Name—Rank*

Cavalry)
426. Drew, Solomon, Privt.
427. Drew, Joshua, Privt.
428. Dill, John, Privt.
429. Evans, Elisha, Senr., Privt., Infantry & Cavalry
430. Edleman, Peter, Privt.
431. Epps, John, Privt.
432. Elms, Charles, decsd., Privt.
433. Emery, William, decsd., Privt.
434. Emerson, Henry, Privt.
435. Ellis, Robert, Privt.
436. Evans, Reuben, Privt.
437. Edwards, David, Privt.
438. Eggers, Landricee, Privt.
439. Easly, Daniel, Privt.
440. Etchison, Edmund, Privt.
441. Everhart, Peter, Privt.
442. Edmundson, William, Privt.
443. Easly, Daniel, Privt.
444. Ellis, Michael, Fifer
445. Edwards, Benjamin, Privt.
446. Everitt, Thomas, Privt. (Infantry & Cavalry)
447. Evans, Samuel, Privt.
448. Eller, John M., Privt.
449. Elfand, John, Privt.
450. Elmore, William, Privt.
451. Ellison, John, Privt.
452. Eaton, Christopher, Privt.
453. Everitt, Nathaniel, Privt.
454. Erwin, William, Privt. (Infantry & Cavalry)
455. Ellington, Daniel, Privt.
456. Essig (alias Essick or Essix) Joseph, Indian Spy
457. Elliott, John, Privt. & Sergeant
458. Espey, Samuel, Privt., Corporal & Captain
459. Earp, Abednego, Privt.
460. Foster, Anthony, Privt. & Sergeant
461. Forney, Abraham, Privt., Sergeant & Captain
462. Furrer, Henry, Privt. & Sergeant
463. Fort, Turner, Privt.
464. Fort, Sherwood, Musician
465. Frost and Snow, Privt.
466. Fergus, John, Wagon master of Infantry & Cavalry
467. Fountain, Soloman, Privt.
468. Felmott, Dorus, Privt.
469. Fox, Francis, Privt.
470. Flinn, John, Privt.
471. Foster, Edmund, Privt.

*Name—Rank*

472. Forehand, David, Privt.
473. Freeman, William, Privt.
474. Forbes, Hugh, Privt.
475. Farrell, William, Privt.
476. Fletcher, Thomas, Privt.
477. Fuller, Alexander, Privt.
478. Ferebee, Samuel, Privt. & Ensign
479. Ferrell, Gabriel, Privt.
480. Fooshee, John, Privt. & Lieutenant
481. Frazer, Sowell, Privt.
482. Fox, John, Senr., Privt.
483. Farrar, Nathaniel, Privt.
484. Forrest, William, Privt.
485. Forney, Peter, Privt.
486. Fry, Nicholas, Privt.
487. Frederick, Felix, decsd., Privt.
488. Fight, Conrad, decsd., Privt.
489. Frey, Philip M., decsd., Drummer
490. Forster, Thomas, Privt.
491. Fuller, Arthur, Privt.
492. Findley, John, Sergeant
493. Ferrell, John, Privt.
494. Fears, Thomas, Privt. of Cavalry
495. Fields, John, Sergeant
496. Fowler, John, Privt.
497. Findley, James, Privt.
498. Fitzgerald, William, Privt.
499. Findley, Charles, Privt.
500. French, Liafford, Privt. of Cavalry
501. Fortune, William, Privt.
502. Ford, William, Privt.
503. Fulford, James, Privt.
504. Fennel, Joseph, Privt.
505. Foscue, Frederick, Privt.
506. Fletcher, Reuben, Privt.
507. Forrester, James, Privt.
508. Fulp, Michael, Senr., Privt.
509. Fulford, Stephen, Sergeant
510. Falls, William, Privt. of Cavalry
511. Fulton, David, Privt.
512. Felyaw, Stephen, Privt. (Infantry & Cavalry)
513. Fritts, George, Privt.
514. Frenister, William, Privt. (Infantry & Cavalry)
515. Faile, Dixon, Privt.
516. Fleming, Allison, Privt.
517. Forbes, Joseph, Privt.
518. Green, Jesse, Privt.
519. Gunn, Starling, Privt.
520. Godsey, William, Privt.
521. Green, John, Privt.
522. Green, George, Privt.
523. Griffith, Isaac, Privt.

*Name—Rank*

524. Gracey, Robert, Privt. (Cavalry & Infantry)
525. Gilbreath, Alexander, Privt. & Sergeant
526. Griffin, Richard, Privt.
527. Godwin, Pierce, Privt.
528. Garret, William, Privt. (Infantry & Cavalry)
529. Gaster, Jacob, Privt.
530. Going, William, Privt.
531. Gaines, James, Senr., Privt.
532. Gulley, John, decs'd., Privt.
533. Gibson, Thomas, decsd., Privt. of Cavalry
534. Gouch, Rowland, Privt.
535. Gregory, Abraham, Privt.
536. Griffin, John, Privt.
537. Grigsby, Moses, Privt.
538. Gatten, Jesse, Privt.
539. Gregory, Thomas, Privt.
540. Glanden, Major, Privt.
541. Gerock, Samuel, Lieutenant
542. Guilford, Joseph, Privt.
543. Graham, James, Privt.
544. Good, Solomon, Privt.
545. Gray, James, Privt.
546. Graham, Joseph, Sergt. Adjt. Capt. & Major
547. Gilreath, William, Privt. & Captain
548. Gragg, William, Privt.
549. Gimston, James, Privt.
555. Garris, Bedford, Privt.
556. Griffith, Zaddock, Privt.
557. Goodwin, Robinson, Privt.
558. Griffis, Reuben, Privt. of Artillery
559. Going, Edward, Privt.
560. Grice, William, Privt.
561. Griffin, Thomas, Privt.
562. Ganey, William, Privt.
563. Glasgow, Lemuel, Privt.
564. Guy, James, Privt.
565. Graham, William, Colonel
566. Goss, Jacob, Privt.
567. Goff, Samuel, Privt.
568. Godby (alias Godley), George, Privt.
569. Givens, Samuel, Privt.
570. Griggs, Charles, Privt.
571. Goodwin, John, Privt.
572. Gibbs, John, Privt.
573. Green, David, Privt.
574. Gudger, William, Privt.
575. Gurganus, Reuben, Privt.
576. Gargis, Job, Privt.
577. Green, William, Privt.

*Name—Rank*

578. Grider, Job, Privt.
579. Gillespie, James, Privt. & Sergeant
580. Gatewood, Dudley, Privt.
581. Green, Jeremiah, Privt.
582. Gardner, John, Privt.
583. Graham, John, Privt. of Cavalry
584. Gann, Samuel, Senr. Privt.
585. Goodwin, Samuel, Sergeant
586. Graves, Richard, Privt.
587. Grear, Thomas, Privt.
588. Gorden, James, Privt.
589. Gibson, Joseph, Privt.
590. Gregory, William, Privt.
591. Gardner, Elias, Privt. (Infantry & Cavalry)
592. Grisham, James, Senr., Privt.
593. Glasgow, Richard, Privt.
594. Gabriel, James, Privt. & Sergeant
595. Garriss, Henry, Privt.
596. Goodson, Joshua, Privt.
597. Gilliam, John, Privt.
598. Guy, William, Privt.
599. Grant, John, Privt.
600. Gettis, Alexander, Privt. (Cavalry & Infantry)
601. Hilsabeck, Jacob, Privt. of Infantry
602. Hays, Edmund, Privt.
603. Hickman, Edwin, Privt.
604. Hilliard, Thomas, Privt.
605. Hatch, Alexander, Privt.
606. Harmon, John, Privt.
607. Hair, David, Privt.
608. Holeman, Yancy, Privt.
609. Hammond, John, Privt.
610. Hood, Charles, Privt.
611. Holdway, Henry, Privt.
612. Harris, William, Privt.
613. Hickman, Jacob, Privt.
614. Harris, Jesse, Privt.
615. Harrison, John, 2nd., Privt.
616. Harrison, William, Privt.
617. Hayes, Thomas, Privt.
618. Hall, John, Privt.
619. Hembre (alias Emery), Abraham, Privt.
620. Hicks, Micajah, Privt.
621. Harrison, Joseph, Privt.
622. Hart, James, Privt.
623. Hutchins, Thomas, Privt. (Infantry & Cavalry)
624. Howard, Hardy, Privt.
625. Hall, Alexander, Privt.
626. Harris, Robin, Privt.
627. Hager, Simon, Privt.

*Name—Rank*

628. Hall, William, Privt.
629. Halsey, Henry, Privt.
630. Halsey, Malchi, Privt.
631. Howell, John, Privt. of Cavalry
632. Hasty, James, Senr., Privt.
633. Hayles, Chapman, Privt.
634. Heathcock, James, Privt.
635. Hough, John, Privt.
636. Hooper, Absolam, Privt.
637. Horton, Zephaniah, Privt.
638. Hanille, William, Privt.
639. Holt, George, Privt. & Sergeant
640. Hudgins, John, Privt. (Infantry & Cavalry)
641. Hay, William, Priv.
642. Hill, Abraham, Privt.
643. Hargis, Thomas Privt., Sergeant & Cavalry
644. Houston, James, Privt.
645. Hill, James, Lieutenant
646. Henry, James, Privt.
647. Hofner, Nicholas, Privt.
648. Haney, Charles, Privt.
649. Harper, John, Privt. (Cavalry & Infantry)
650. Hicks, Miles, Privt.
651. Holmes, James, Privt.
652. Hodge, George, Privt.
653. Howard, Wilson, Privt.
654. Harrell, John, Privt. (Cavalry & Infantry)
655. Hamilton, Thomas, Privt.
656. Hodges, Joseph, Privt. of Cavalry
657. Haney, Robert, Privt.
658. Hair, Robert, Privt.
659. Hays, David, Privt. (Infantry & Cavalry)
660. Hoppis, Adam, Privt.
661. Highsmith, Moses, Privt.
662. Hopkins, William, Privt.
663. Howard, William, Privt.
664. Hinson, Charles, Privt.
665. Handcock, John, Privt.
666. Hammons, Benjamin, Privt.
667. Hunter, Henry, Privt.
668. Hackney, Joseph, Captain & Lieutenant
669. Hastin, William, Privt.
670. Hanson, Daniel, Privt.
671. Hendrickson, Isaac, Privt.
672. Helm, John, Privt.
673. Hollinan, James, Privt.
674. Hagar, Simeon, Privt.
675. Haggard, John, Privt.

*Name—Rank*

676. Hancock, Samuel, Privt. (Infantry & Cavalry)
677. Hope, Benjamin, Privt.
678. Horner, George, Privt., Ensign & Lieutenant
679. Huddleston, Robert, Privt.
680. Haskins, James, Privt.
681. Hollingsworth, Henry, Jr., Privt.
682. Hollingsworth, Zebedee, Privt.
683. Henry, Joseph, Privt.
684. Holland, William, Privt. & Ensign
685. Holly, Osborne, Privt.
686. Hawkins, Philemon, decs'd., Colonel
687. Hopkins, Isaac, Privt.
688. Hartman, Philip, Privt.
689. Herndon, James, Privt. (Cavalry & Infantry)
690. Hopson, William, Privt. of Cavalry
691. Hudgins, James, F., Privt.
692. Hart, James, Privt.
693. Hill, Reuben, Privt.
694. Hood, Reuben, Privt.
695. Hyde, William, Privt.
696. Hughes, John, Senr., Privt.
697. Hedgepeth, Abraham, Privt.
698. Howard, Allen, Privt.
699. Henderson, James, Privt.
700. Hodge, Alexander, Privt. & Lieutenant
701. Headrick, Peter, Privt.
702. Holland, James, Privt. (Infantry & Cavalry)
703. Holt, James, Privt., Corporal & Ensign
704. Hise, Leonard, Privt.
705. Hipp, Valentine, Privt.
706. Harrell, Josiah, Privt.
707. Howard, Claiborne, Privt.
708. Henson, Elijah, Privt.
709. Hicks, Harris, Privt.
710. Hood, John, Privt.
711. Hawkins, Ephraim, Privt.
712. Hurley, Joshua, Privt.
713. Hearne, Ebenezer, Privt.
714. Henry, John, Privt. & Captain
715. Harwood, James, Privt.
716. Hollingsworth, Stephen, Privt.
717. Hester, Zachariah, Privt.
718. Hester, Benjamin, Privt.
719. Hill, Robert, Senr., Privt., Lieutenant & Captain
720. Hester, Thomas, Privt.
721. Hunt, Daniel, Privt.
722. Hutchinson, William, Privt. & Captain

*Name—Rank*

723. Hartgrove, Howell, Privt.
724. Hawes, Ezekiel, Privt.
725. Hastings, Zachariah, Privt.
726. Hobbs, William, Privt.
727. Harthsfield, John, Privt.
728. Howrey, George, Privt.
729. Hamilton, James, Privt.
730. Harris, Fieldman, Privt.
731. Hughes, James, Privt.
732. High, Gardner, Privt.
733. Hunt, William, Privt., Ensign & Major
734. Hoffner, Martin, Privt.
735. Hickman, Samuel, Privt.
736. Hill, Samuel, Privt.
737. Hunt, Berry, Privt.
738. Harrell, Kidder, Privt.
739. Halloway, Taylor, Privt.
740. Hudspeth, Carter, Privt.
741. Hill, Joshua, Privt.
742. Horner, Thomas, Privt.
743. Herron, Allen, Privt.
744. Horn, Robert, Privt.
745. Idole, Jacob, Privt.
746. Ipock, Samuel, Privt.
747. Ingram, Edwin, Privt. & Ensign
748. Ives, John P., Privt.
749. Irwin, Thomas, Privt.
750. Irly, John, Privt. & Captain
751. Irick, Abraham, Privt.
752. Irvin, James, Privt.
753. Ives, Thomas, Privt.
754. Jones, Musgrove, Privt.
755. Jean, Philip, Privt. (Infantry & Cavalry)
756. Jeffreys, John, Privt.
757. Jones, William, Privt.
758. James, Abner, Privt.
759. Johnston, Francis, Privt., Sergeant & Lieutenant
760. Jones, Francis, Captain of Cavalry
761. Jones, Moses, Privt.
762. Johnson, Samuel, decs'd., Privt. of Infantry & Capt. of Cavalry
763. Johnson, Joseph, Lieutenant
764. Jenkins, Charles, Privt.
765. Jacobs, Primus, Privt.
766. Jean, Nathan, Privt.
767. Jinks, Thomas, Corporal
768. Jones, Peter, Captain
769. Jones, Britain, Privt.
770. Johnson, James, Privt.
771. Jones, Benjamin, Privt.
772. Johnston, George, Sr., Privt.
773. Johnston, Joseph, Privt.

*Name—Rank*

774. Jones, Edmund, Privt.
775. Joiner, Moses, Privt.
776. Jones, Charles, Privt.
777. Jones, Thomas, Privt.
778. Jamison, Williams, Privt.
779. Jones, John, Privt.
780. Joiner, Thomas, Privt.
781. Jackson, William, decs'd., Privt.
782. Jackson, Isaac, Privt.
783. Jones, Edward, Privt.
784. Johnston, Robert, Privt.
785. Jean, William, Privt.
786. Jernigan, George, Privt. & Lt. Drag'n.
787. Johnson, Abram, Privt.
788. Jeannet, Elias, Privt.
789. Jones, Elisha, Privt.
790. Jordan, Richard, Privt. (Cavalry & Infantry)
791. Jacobs, Zachariah, Privt.
792. Johnson, William, Privt., Sergeant & Lieutenant
793. Johnson, Alexander, Privt.
794. Jester, James, T., Privt.
795. Jenkins, Thomas, Privt.
796. Jackson, Samuel, Privt.
797. Jarvis, Thomas, Privt., Lieutenant & Captain
798. Jenkins, William, Privt.
799. Johnson, William, Privt.
800. Jones, Jesse, Privt.
801. Jenkins, Aaron, Privt. (Cavalry & Infantry)
802. Jones, Nicholas, Privt.
803. Jennings, James, Privt.
804. Kidds, John, Privt.
805. Kennedy, Thomas, Privt.
806. King, Henry, Privt.
807. King, John, Privt.
808. Keen, William, Privt.
809. King, David, Privt.
810. King, Nathan, Captain
811. Knox, Robert, Privt.
812. Kreger, George, Privt.
813. Kennire, Anthony, Privt.
814. Kea, Henry, Privt. (Cavalry & Infantry)
815. Killough, Samuel, Privt.
816. Knox, Benjamin, Privt.
817. Kennedy, Sherwood, Privt. & Sergeant
818. Karcher (alias Karraher), George, Privt.
819. Kincaid, John, Privt.

*Name—Rank*

820. Koonts, John, Privt.
821. Kincaid, Robert, Privt.
822. Kincaid, James, Privt.
823. Keel, Simon, Privt. (Infantry & Cavalry)
824. Knox, James, Privt.
825. King, Vincent, Privt. (Infantry & Cavalry)
826. Keon, John, Sergeant, Drummer & Corporal
827. King, Thomas, Privt.
828. Knox, Samuel, Privt.
829. Kiher, George, Privt.
830. Kersey, James, Privt.
831. Kerr, Robert, Privt.
832. Kennedy, David, Privt.
833. Knight, Henry, Privt.
834. Kinncair, John, Privt.
835. Kensaul, John, Privt.
836. Limonds, Alexander, Privt.
837. Leonard, William, Privt.
838. Ledford, Peter, Senr., Privt. of Cavalry
839. Lint, Isaac, Privt.
840. Lassiten, Elijah, Privt.
841. Lee, James, descd., Privt.
842. Lewis, Charles, descd., Privt. of Cavalry
843. Leiper, Matthew, descd., Privt.
844. Lloyd, William, descd., Privt.
845. Loughry, William, Privt.
846. Lyttle, Thomas, decsd., Lieutenant & Captain
847. Lane, John, Privt.
848. Lewis, Willis, Privt.
849. Lomack, William, Privt.
850. Lock, John, Privt.
851. Love, Thomas, Privt.
852. Lovett, Joseph, Privt.
853. Lyon, Jacob, Privt.
854. Lewis, John, Privt.
855. Lomax, William, Privt.
856. Luck, John, Privt.
857. Love, John, Privt.
858. Latham, Noah, Privt.
859. Lackey, George, Privt. (Cavalry & Infantry)
860. Lashley, Barnabas, Privt.
861. Lipscomb, Archibald, Privt.
862. Lambreth, Moses, Privt.
863. Logan, Drury, Privt.
864. Lookebee, David, Privt.
865. Lewis, William, Privt.
866. Lumsden, John, Privt. & Ensign

580ROSTER OF NORTH CAROLINA SOLDIERS

*Name—Rank*

867. Lackey, Thomas, Privt.
868. Lindsey, David, Privt.
869. Linton, Thomas, Privt.
870. Lednum, John, Privt.
871. Luckie, William, Privt.
872. Leib, Jonas, Privt.
873. Lindsay, Laban, Sergeant
874. Lee, John, Privt.
875. Laquire, John, Privt.
876. Lee, Wstbrook, Privt.
877. Ledbitter, Richard, Privt.
878. Long, Benjamin, Privt.
879. Lemonds, Robert, Privt.
880. Lashley, Howell, Privt.
881. Love, Robert, Sergeant & Lieutenant
882. Lanning, John, Privt.
883. Lewis, William, Privt.
884. Lewis, James, Privt.
885. Lancaster, Henry, Sergeant
886. Lawrence, John, Privt.
887. Lomax, William, Privt.
888. Leonard, Jacob, Privt.
889. Lewis, Thomas, Privt.
890. Lowe, Nathan, Privt.
891. Lasater, William, Privt. of Cavalry
892. Lasater, Abner, Privt.
893. Lumpkin, Joseph, Privt.
894. Langley, Miles, decs'd., Dragoon
895. Lindsey, Walter, decs'd., Privt.
896. Lands, Ephraim, Privt.
897. Lewis, Aaron, Privt.
898. Lachenour, Jacob, Privt.
899. Lowe, Thomas, Sergeant
900. Lachenour, George, Privt.
901. Land, Reuben, Privt.
902. Lockhart, John, Privt.
903. Lockerman, Jacob, Privt.
904. Laffoon, Nathaniel, Privt.
905. Lee, Henry, Privt., of Cavalry
906. Larrimore, James, Privt., Sergeant & Corporal
907. Leman, John, Privt.
908. Lane, Daniel, Privt. & Sergeant
909. Lucas, William, Privt.
910. Largent, James, Privt. (Cavalry & Infantry)
911. Leak, Walter, Privt.
912. Lewis, Daniel, Privt.
913. Lawson, Thomas, Privt.
914. Lock, James, Senr., Privt.
915. Langley, Shadrach, Privt.
916. Lewis, David, Privt.
917. Laws, David, Privt.
918. Lynch, Elijah, Privt.

*Name—Rank*

919. Lenoir, William, Lieutenant & Captain
920. Luther, Michael, Privt.
921. Luther, George, Privt.
922. Long, Gasper, Privt. (Infantry & Cavalry)
923. Larkins, Benjamin, Privt. (Infantry & Cavalry)
924. Lewter, Hardy, Privt. (Infantry & Cavalry)
925. McLellan, Daniel, Privt.
926. Marsh, William, Privt.
927. McCuister, Thomas, Privt.
928. Masters, Enoch, Privt.
929. May, Ludwick, Privt.
930. Money, John, Privt.
931. McBroom, Andrew, Privt.
932. McAllister, John, Privt. (Infantry & Cavalry)
933. McKinney, William, Privt.
934. Myrick, Moses, Privt.
935. Marshbourne, Daniel, Privt.
936. Mitchell, David, decs'd., Privt.
937. McDaniel, James, decs'd., Privt. (Calvary)
938. Montrose, Elijah, decs'd., Privt.
939. McIntosh, Murdock, decs'd., Privt.
940. McNeill, Laucklin, decs'd., Privt.
941. McNeill, Archibald, decs'd., Privt.
942. Munk, James, Privt.
943. Medlin, Shadrack, Privt.
944. Moore, James, Privt.
945. Mainor, Josiah, Privt.
946. Moony, William, Sergeant
947. McDaniel, Arthur, Privt.
948. Maples, Marmaduke, Privt.
949. Marshall, Isaac, Privt.
950. Manley, Moses, Privt.
951. Manuel, Jesse, Privt.
952. Main, Henry, Privt.
953. Matthews, James, Privt.
954. Matlock, John, Sergeant
955. Munday, Jeremiah, Privt.
956. Mason, Patrick, Privt.
957. Martin, Robert, Privt.
958. Mitchell, Jacob, Privt.
959. Mitchell, George, Privt.
960. Morris, Micajah, Privt.
961. Mayes, William, Privt.
962. McKeithan, John, Privt.
963. Morgan, Richard, Drummer
964. Mulikin, Lewis, Privt.
965. Monroe, George, Privt.
966. McKee, Alexander, Privt.

*Name—Rank*

967. McNatt, James, Sergeant
968. McKay, Edward, Privt.
969. Marcum, Thomas, Privt.
970. Morgan, William, Privt.
971. Merrill, John, Privt. (Infantry & Cavalry)
972. Myers, John, Privt.
973. McLeod, Robert, Privt.
974. Matthews, Hardy, Privt. (Infantry & Cavalry)
975. Mallard, Lawson, Privt.
976. Merritt, William, Privt.
977. Mabry, David, Privt.
978. McClellan, Malcolm, Privt.
979. Morrison, Morris, Privt.
980. McPeters, Jonathan, Privt.
981. Musselwhite, Nathan, Privt.
982. Musselwhite, Millen, Privt.
983. Merril, Daniel, Privt.
984. McCullock, James, Privt.
985. Mays, Benjamin, Privt.
986. Morrison, John, Privt.
987. Mebane, John, Privt. & Captain
988. Malpass, James, Privt.
989. Mason, William, Privt.
990. McPherson, Matthew, Privt.
991. Medaris, Masy C., Privt.
992. Mitchell, James, Privt.
993. Mayhew, John, Privt.
994. Moore, Alexander, Privt.
995. McNeely, John, Privt.
996. Morgan, Nathan, Privt.
997. Miller, Philip, Privt.
998. Merritt, Shadrach, Privt.
999. Marshall, Purnell, Privt. (Cavalry & Infantry)
1000. Miller, John, Privt.
1001. Marshall, Jesse, Privt.
1002. Monteath, Samuel, Privt.
1002. May, William, Privt.
1004. Medford, James, Privt.
1005. Merritt, Daniel, Privt. (Infantry & Cavalry)
1006. Mills, Jesse, Privt.
1007. McLaughlin, John, Privt. (Infantry & Cavalry)
1008. Moore, Daniel, Senr., Privt.
1009. Mulivee, John, Privt.
1010. Mills, John, Privt.
1011. McCurdy, Archibald, Privt. & Lieutenant
1012. Mahanes, Tapley, Privt.
1013. Moore, William, Privt. & Captain
1014. Moore, John, Privt.

*Name—Rank*

1015. Martin, Kinchen, Privt.
1016. Mayhew, William, Privt.
1017. Monroe, Malcolm, Privt. of Calvary
1018. Morris, William, Privt.
1019. Mizell, William, Sergeant
1020. Maib, John, Senr., Privt.
1021. Menius, Frederick, Privt.
1022. Martindale, Samuel, Privt.
1023. Merrill, Benjamin, Privt.
1024. Marlar, John, Privt.
1025. McClewer, Richard, Privt.
1026. McLadden, Alexander, Privt., Lieutenant & Captain
1027. Mitchell, Nazareth, Privt.
1028. McLeary, Michael, Privt.
1029. Moore, James, Sr., Privt.
1030. Mills, Naaman, Privt.
1031. Metcalf, Danga, Privt.
1032. Metcalf, Warner, Privt.
1033. Massey, John, Privt.
1034. Martin, Samuel, Privt. & Captain
1035. Murphy, James, Privt.
1036. McWhorter, George, Privt.
1037. Miles, Narby, Privt.
1038. Matthews, Giles, Privt.
1039. McMennamy, William, Privt.
1040. McLeod, William, Privt.
1041. Murrel, Merritt, Privt.
1042. Miller, Jacob, Privt.
1043. Moore, William, Privt.
1044. Murphy, Hugh, Privt.
1045. Mason, Philip, Privt.
1046. McCullen, Bryan, Privt.
1047. Mendenhall, Nathan, Privt.
1048. Martin, Ephraim, Privt. & Sergeant
1049. Mann, Nathan, Privt.
1050. May, Thomas, Privt.
1051. McGuire,. Patrick, Privt.
1052. McNeill, Hector, Privt.
1053. Mabrey, Matthew, Privt.
1054. Morgan, James, Privt.
1055. Murrill, George, Privt.
1056. Minnis, John, Privt. & Sergeant
1057. McCorkle, Archibald, Privt.
1058. McFalls, Arthur, Privt.
1059. McEller, John, Privt.
1060. Maybin, Mathew, Privt.
1061. Mathis, Arthur, Privt. of Cavalry
1062. Miller, George, decs'd., Privt.
1063. McDonald, James, decs'd., Dragoon
1064. Martin, Jacob, Privt.
1065. McSwain, William, decs'd., Privt.
1066. Matthews, John, decs'd., Corporal
1067. Martin, James, Colonel

*Name—Rank*

1068. Montgomery, John, Privt.
1069. Marion, Bartholomew, Privt.
1070. May, John, Sergt. & Ensign
1071. McGee, Harmon, Privt.
1072. McCullock, Duncan, Privt.
1073. McMulline, John, Lieutenant & Captain
1074. Martin, Richard, Privt.
1075. Medley, Bryant, Privt. & Musician
1076. Matkins, John, Privt.
1077. Manuel, Christopher, Privt.
1078. McBride, John, Privt., Sergeant, Ensign & Lieut.
1079. Maxwell, William, Privt.
1080. McClure, Thomas, Privt.
1081. McBride, Josiah, Privt.
1082. McLane, Joseph, Privt.
1083. Morton, Josiah, Privt.
1084. Merrett, Daniel, Privt.
1085. Montgomery, David, Privt.
1086. Marshall, Benjamin, Privt.
1087. Maidere, Laurence, Sr., Privt.
1088. Moring, John, Privt.
1089. McCubbin, Nicholas, Privt.
1090. Miller, Jacob, decs'd., Privt.
1091. Murphy, Daniel, Privt.
1092. Messer, Jeremiah, Privt.
1093. McCain, John, Privt.
1094. Murray, James, Privt.
1095. Northern, Joseph, Privt.
1096. Nix, George, Privt.
1097. Nichelston, James, Privt.
1098. Nowell, Josiah, Privt.
1099. Nailor, Joshua, Privt.
1100. Newsome, Jacob, Privt.
1101. Neese, George, Privt.
1102. Nolen, Ezekiel, Privt.
1103. Nance, James, Senr., Privt. & Fifer
1104. Nicholson, John, Privt. & Lieutenant
1105. Nelson, Giles, Privt.
1106. Nease, George, Privt. (Cavalry & Infantry)
1107. Nichols, Joel, Privt.
1108. Nobles, John, Privt.
1109. Nease, Martin, Privt.
1110. Neill, Gilbraith, Lieutenant
1111. Nunnery, Amos, Privt. (Cavalry & Infantry)
1112. Nelson, Samuel, Privt.
1113. New, William, Privt.
1114. Nelson, Edward, Privt.
1115. Nash, Michael, Privt.
1116. Norwood, John, Privt.
1117. Norvill, Enos, Privt.

*Name—Rank*

1118. Norton, Isham, Senr., Privt.
1119. Newton, Benjamin, decs'd., Lieutenant
1120. Overton, Jonathan, Privt.
1121. Ownby, James, Privt.
1122. Oliver, James, decs'd., Privt.
1123. Osborn, Jesse, Privt.
1124. Overton, Samuel, Privt.
1125. Overton, James, Privt.
1126. Odom, James, Privt.
1127. Orr, James, Privt.
1128. Osborn, Jonathan, Privt.
1129. Oliver, George, Privt.
1130. Owen, Shadrach, Privt. (Infantry & Cavalry)
1131. Osborn, Stephen, Privt.
1132. O'Merry, Jacob, Privt.
1133. O'Brien, William, Privt.
1134. O'Bryan, Tillotson, Privt.
1135. Odom, Jethro, Privt.
1136. Pettaway, Micajah, Privt.
1137. Poplin, George, Privt.
1138. Pope, Richard, Privt.
1139. Pippin, Richard, Privt.
1140. Patton, Samuel, Privt. (Infantry & Cavalry)
1141. Pyron, William, Privt.
1142. Payne, Thomas, Privt.
1143. Previtt, John, decs'd., Privt.
1144. Powell, John, Privt.
1145. Phillips, Adam, Privt.
1146. Parks, Samuel, decs'd., Privt.
1147. Palmer, Jesse, decs'd., Privt.
1148. Pettiford, Drury, Privt.
1149. Philips, Mark, Privt.
1150. Pettiford, William, Privt.
1151. Petit, Gideon, Privt.
1152. Pratt, Zebulon, Privt.
1153. Patterson, Tilman, Privt.
1154. Pafford, William, Privt.
1155. Privet, John, Privt.
1156. Penninger, Martin, Privt.
1157. Pettiford, George, Privt.
1158. Peterson, James, Privt.
1159. Paylor, William, Privt.
1160. Powers, Ephraim, Privt.
1161. Parker, William, Privt.
1162. Parham, Thomas, Privt.
1163. Powell, Abner, Privt.
1164. Phillips, Irby, Privt.
1165. Potter, William, Privt. & Corporal
1166. Piper, John, Privt. & Lieutenant
1167. Pendleton, Hiram, Privt.

*Name—Rank*

1168. Perkins, William, Privt. & Lieutenant
1169. Poplin, William, Privt.
1170. Powell, Lewis, Privt.
1171. Parson, Joseph, Privt. & Captain
1172. Pharis, Samuel, Privt.
1173. Page, John, Privt. of Cavalry
1174. Pittman, Joseph, Privt.
1175. Petit, Henry, Senr., Privt.
1176. Price, Thomas, Privt. of Cavalry
1177. Peterson, John, Privt.
1178. Pope, Jeremiah, Privt.
1179. Parker, Humphrey, Privt.
1180. Parker, John, Privt.
1181. Poyner, Thomas, Privt. & Captain
1182. Parrot, Reuben, Privt.
1183. Palmer, Edmond, Privt.
1184. Parker, Elisha, Privt.
1185. Parker, Kidar, Privt.
1186. Palmer, William, Privt.
1187. Prestwood, Jonathan, Privt. & Sergeant
1188. Presnell, John, Privt.
1189. Patterson, James, Privt. & Sergeant
1190. Pridgeon, Francis, Privt.
1191. Phillips, John, Privt.
1192. Patterson, Thomas, Privt.
1193. Pyatt, Joseph, Privt.
1194. Plummer, Richard, Privt.
1195. Pope, Elisha, Privt.
1196. Potts, Thomas, Privt.
1197. Pippen, Joseph, Ensign
1198. Penby, John, Privt.
1199. Powell, Elijah, Privt.
1200. Pone, David, Privt. (Infantry & Cavalry)
1200. Paris, William, Prit.
1202. Pope, Harwood, Privt.
1203. Peter-Corn, John, Privt.
1204. Peddy, Andrew, Privt.
1205. Porterfield, John, Privt.
1206. Phillips, John, Privt.
1207. Painter, George, Privt.
1208. Powell, Britton, decs'd., Privt.
1209. Pass, Holloway, Privt.
1210. Pierce, John, Privt.
1211. Parrish, Claiborne, Privt.
1212. Powell, Charles, Privt.
1213. Padgett, John, Privt. (Infantry & Cavalry)
1214. Plunk, Jacob, Privt.
1215. Porter, Charles, Privt.
1216. Powell, Absalom, Privt., Ensign, Sergt. & C. A.

*Name—Rank*

1217. Pleasants, William, Privt.
1218. Pulliam, Richard, Privt.
1219. Pridgeon, William, Privt.
1220. Pool, John, Privt. (Infantry & Cavalry)
1221. Perry, Jesse, Privt.
1222. Paine, John, Privt.
1223. Phifer, Martin, Captain Dragoons
1224. Powers, Henry, Senr., Privt. (Infantry & Cavalry)
1225. Pearce, William, Privt.
1226. Pollard, Jacob, Privt.
1227. Pennington, Kincher, Privt.
1228. Parrish, Stephen, Privt.
1229. Polk, William, Major
1230. Peonix, Oberton, Privt.
1231. Pennil (alias Penrose), Reuben, Privt.
1232. Powell, George, Privt.
1233. Pilkenton, Richard, Privt.
1234. Powell, William, Privt.
1235. Parker, Kedar, Privt.
1236. Pierce, Israel, Prvt. & Sergeant
1237. Poindexter, David, Privt.
1238. Pettijohn, John, Privt.
1239. Palmer, Jesse, Senr., Privt.
1240. Payne, Thomas, Privt.
1241. Parish, Humphrey, Privt.
1242. Quillin, John, Privt.
1243. Quinn, David, Privt.
1244. Quinn, William, L., Privt.
1245. Ryerson, Stephen, Privt.
1246. Rice, William H., Privt., Sergt. & Lt.
1247. Ross, James, Privt.
1248. Rigsby, James, Privt.
1249. Rector, Benjamin, Privt.
1250. Rankin, William, Privt.
1251. Reed, Samuel, Privt.
1252. Roe, Charles, Privt.
1253. Reid, Thomas, Privt.
1254. Roberts, Aaron, Privt.
1255. Ripley, Edward, Privt. of Cavalry
1256. Riggs, James, Privt.
1257. Rocket, John, Privt.
1258. Roberts, James, decs'd., Privt.
1259. Roach, James, decs'd., Privt.
1260. Richardson, David, decs'd., Privt.
1261. Rippy, Edward, Privt.
1262. Roberts, George, Privt.
1263. Roberts, Martin, Forage Master
1264. Robinson, Lambert, Privt.
1265. Reaves, Zachariah, Privt.
1266. Rigsby, Frederick, Privt.

*Name—Rank*

1267. Raper, Robert, Privt.
1268. Riggins, Joel, Privt.
1269. Rhodes, Nathan, Privt.
1270. Redding, John, Privt.
1271. Revell, Michael, Privt.
1272. Ross, Thomas, Privt.
1273. Rhodes, John, Privt.
1274. Rose, Sterling, Corporal & Sergeant
1275. Roberts, John, Privt. (Infantry & Cavalry)
1276. Ring, Thomas, Senr., Privt.
1277. Rodgers, Hugh, Privt.
1278. Rounsavall, John, Privt.
1279. Rigsby, John, Privt. (Cavalry & Infantry)
1280. Ross, Williamson, Privt.
1281. Reavis, John, Privt.
1282. Robeson, Daniel, Privt.
1283. Robeson, James, Privt.
1284. Rodgers, Daniel, Privt.
1285. Ray, Jesse, Privt.
1286. Roberts, Joshua, Privt.
1287. Ricks, Edmund, Privt.
1288. Rogers, Thomas, Privt.
1289. Register, John, Privt.
1290. Rea, David, Privt. (Infantry & Cavalry)
1291. Rhodes, Cornelius, Privt.
1292. Regan, Charles, Privt.
1293. Revenback, Frederick, Privt.
1294. Roberts, William, Senr., Privt.
1295. Rogers, Bias, Privt.
1296. Redd, William, Privt.
1297. Riddle, John, Privt.
1298. Rice, John, Privt. & Sergeant
1299. Ricketts, William, Privt.
1300. Reardon, James, Privt.
1301. Rackley, Jeremiah, Privt. & Sergeant
1302. Rose, Samuel, Privt.
1303. Robinson, William, Privt.
1304. Ray, William, Senr., Captain
1305. Raines, Anthony, Privt.
1306. Rich, Lot, Privt.
1307. Rowark, Elisha, Privt.
1308. Roe, Matthew, Privt.
1309. Rosen, John, Privt.
1310. Reeves, Richard, Privt.
1311. Register, John, Junr., Privt.
1312. Ryan, Peter, Privt.
1313. Rogers, Randall, Privt.
1314. Reeves, John, Privt.
1315. Rudd, John, Senr., Privt.
1316. Rector, Lewis, Privt.
1317. Rayner, Amos, Privt.

*Name—Rank*

1318. Ray, Francis, decs'd., Privt.
1319. Rhodes, Hezekiah, Privt.
1320. Roper, James, Privt.
1321. Riggs, John, Privt.
1322. Ross, David, Privt.
1323. Russ, Joseph, Privt.
1324. Roan, Thomas, Privt. & Musician
1325. Rose, Philip, Ensign
1326. Riley, William, Privt. (Infantry & Cavalry)
1327. Ryan, William, Privt.
1328. Russell, Richard, Privt.
1329. Riggan, Francis, Privt.
1330. Richard, John, Privt.
1331. Roebuck, Raleigh, Privt.
1332. Reynolds, Elisha, Privt.
1333. Riggs, John, Privt. (Infantry & Cavalry)
1334. Reep, Adam, Privt.
1335. Richards, Morris, Privt.
1336. Reeves, John D., Privt.
1337. Robinson, Robert, Privt.
1338. Rose, John, Privt.
1339. Reynolds, Elisha, Privt.
1340. Riggan, William P., Privt.
1341. Robert, Brittain, Privt.
1342. Ramsay, Andrew, Privt. (Infantry & Cavalry)
1343. Swanson, John, Privt.
1344. Strader, John, Privt.
1345. Stoner, Abraham, Privt.
1346. Smith, Lewis, Privt.
1347. Swink, John, Privt.
1348. Shipp, Thomas, Privt.
1349. Snow, Frost and, Privt.
1350. Stephenson, James, Privt.
1351. Sessoms, Solomon, decs'd., Privt. & Lieut.
1352. Stillwell, John, decs'd., Privt.
1353. Smith, Sihon, decs'd., Privt.
1354. Shaw, Michael, Privt.
1355. Springs, Micajah, Privt.
1356. Stratten, William, Privt.
1357. Salmon, Vincent, Privt.
1358. Smith, Peter, Privt.
1359. Seagrove, John, Privt.
1360. Spain, Thomas, Musician
1361. Smith, Charles, Privt.
1362. Sampson, Isaac, Privt.
1363. Spelmore, Asa, Privt.
1364. Steely, Jeremiah, Privt.
1365. Scott, Isham, Privt.
1366. Stephens, John, Privt.
1367. Sullivant, Owen, Privt.

*Name—Rank*

1368. Shipe, Philip, Privt.
1369. Shank, Manus, Privt.
1370. Stokes, Richard, Privt.
1371. Sexton, John, Privt.
1372. Sterling, Seth, Privt.
1373. Shoemaker, Randal, Privt.
1374. Shenault, Benjamin, Privt.
1375. Stiles, John, Privt.
1376. Spain, William, Privt.
1377. Searcy, John, Privt.
1378. Steel, Francis, Senr., Privt.
1379. Simmons, Sanders, Privt.
1380. Simmons, Jeremiah, Privt.
1381. Scroggs, John, Privt.
1382. Stewart, John, Privt.
1383. Stevenson, John, Privt. (Infantry & Cavalry)
1384. Surgener, John, Privt.
1385. Stewart, Edward, Privt. (Infantry & Cavalry)
1386. Scarborough, James, Sergeant & Captain
1387. Sullivan, Daniel, Privt.
1388. Sykes, Josiah, Privt.
1389. Smith, Richard, Privt.
1390. Smith, Benjamin, Privt.
1391. Sasser, Benjamin, Privt.
1392. Smith, Jonathan, Senr., Sergeant & Captain
1393. Sherron, John, Privt.
1394. Surls, Robert, Privt.
1395. Stacy, Aaron, Privt.
1396. Smith, William, Privt.
1397. Sumerlin, Winburn, Privt.
1398. Starns, Joseph, Privt.
1399. Spencer, Jesse, Privt.
1400. Sasater, Abner, Privt.
1401. Sussen, Abel, Privt.
1402. Sigmon, George, Privt.
1403. Strayhorn, William, Privt.
1404. Southard, John, Privt.
1405. Stuart, John, Privt.
1406. Stamey, John, Privt.
1407. Swearingen, Richard C., Privt.
1408. Stovall, Thomas, Privt.
1409. Southern, William, Sr., Privt.
1410. Shaffer, John, Privt.
1411. Sawyer, Joseph, Privt.
1412. Smith, Louis, Privt.
1413. Scott, John, Privt.
1414. Swinson, Theophilus, Privt.
1415. Sanders, Philip, Privt. & Sergeant
1416. Scoggins, Robert, Privt.
1417. Smith, Thomas, Privt.

*Name—Rank*

1418. Shooks, Andrew, Privt.
1419. Shooks, Jacob, Privt.
1420. Springs, Sedgwick, Privt.
1421. Spencer, Benjamin, Privt.
1422. Spring, Richard, Privt., Lieut. & Capt.
1423. Smith, Samuel, Privt.
1424. Sterling, Robert, Privt.
1425. Stow, William, Privt.
1426. Simmons, John, Cavalry & Infantry
1427. Soots, Frederick, Privt.
1428. Spain, Claiborne, Privt.
1429. Studthern, John, Privt. (Infantry & Cavalry)
1430. Smith, Henry, Captain
1431. Sloan, James, Privt.
1432. Sell, Philip, Privt.
1433. Stough, Andrew, Privt.
1434. Stinson, John, Privt.
1435. Steelman, William, Privt.
1436. Stroup, Adam, Privt.
1437. Sellars, Jordan, Privt.
1438. Springfield, Moses, Privt.
1439. Sillaven, William, Privt.
1440. Steele, Thomas, Privt.
1441. Samuel, Andrew, Corporal of Artillery
1442. Scarlet, Thomas, Privt.
1443. Strickland, Lot, Privt.
1444. Smith, Daniel, Privt.
1445. Steele, William, Privt.
1446. Strayhorn, John, Privt.
1447. Slade, Nathan, Privt.
1448. Stanly, Christopher, Sergeant
1449. Stegall, John, Privt.
1450. Stevens, Samuel, Privt.
1451. Sanders, William, Privt.
1452. Stultz, Casper, Senr., Privt.
1453. Smith, Edward, Privt.
1454. Slade, William, Senr., Privt.
1455. Starkey, Jonathan, Privt. (Infantry & Cavalry)
1456. Sharp, Adam, Privt.
1457. Strape, Samuel, Privt.
1458. Smith, William, Privt. & Sergeant
1459. Swing, Matthias, Privt.
1460. Saunders, Nathaniel, Musician
1461. Seat, James, Privt.
1462. Stanford, Samuel, Senr., Privt.
1463. Stough, Martin, Privt.
1464. Scales, James, Senr., Privt.
1465. Smith, Isaac, Privt.
1466. Sandiford, Samuel, Privt.
1467. Scarborough, Samuel, Senr., Privt.

*Name—Rank*

1468. Silverthorn, Robert, Privt.
1469. Smith, John, Privt. (Infantry & Cavalry)
1470. Sherod, Jordan, Privt.
1471. Sawthall, Henry, Privt.
1472. Stegall, Jesse, Privt.
1473. Shearin, Frederick, Privt.
1474. Steigerwaldt, Frederick, Privt.
1475. Singletary, Josiah, Privt.
1476. Shipman, James, Captain
1477. Smithwick, John, Privt. of Cavalry
1478. Slocum, Ezekiel, Privt. & Sergeant
1479. Sheppard, Valentine, Privt.
1480. Small, John, Privt.
1481. Stone, John, Privt., Corporal & Sergeant
1482. Stone, Jonathan, Privt.
1483. Sneed, Robert, Privt. & Artif'r.
1484. Shaw, Joseph, Privt.
1485. Spicer, William, Privt.
1486. Stone, Peter, Senr., Privt.
1487. Stamper, Joel, Privt.
1488. Spencer, William, Privt.
1489. Snow, John, Privt.
1490. Sands, William, Privt.
1491. Sharp, Thomas, Privt. (Cavalry & Infantry)
1492. Shankle, George, Privt.
1493. Silver, George, Privt.
1494. Stewart, James, Privt.
1495. Swinson, Jesse, Senr., Privt. & Musician
1496. Striklin, Lot, Privt.
1497. Smith, Reuben, Privt., Sergt. & Cornet
1498. Sharpe, Joseph, Privt. Cavalry, Lt. & Capt.
1499. Smoot, James, Privt.
1500. Scrum, Peter, Privt.
1501. Sloane, Robert, Privt.
1502. Sparks, John, Privt.
1503. Scroggs, Jeremiah, Privt.
1504. Turner, James, Privt.
1505. Todd, Lewis, Privt. (Cavalry & Infantry)
1506. Thomason, George, Privt.
1507. Tart, Thomas, Privt.
1508. Thomas, Aaron, Privt.
1509. Tyner, Nicholas, Privt.
1510. Thompson, Jarrell, Corporal
1511. Toney, Arthur, decs'd., Privt.
1512. Tankard, John, Surgeon
1513. Topp, George, Privt.
1514. Tarney, Gilbert, Privt.

*Name—Rank*

1515. Taburn, Joel, Privt.
1516. Tyler, Moses, Privt.
1517. Tucker, Robert, Privt.
1518. Tirford, George, Privt.
1519. Tharp, Jonathan, Privt.
1520. Tate, James, Privt.
1521. Taylor, Richard, C.
1522. Thigpen, Gilead, Privt.
1523. Taylor, Isaac, Privt.
1524. Taylor, John, Privt.
1525. Tipps, Jacob, Privt.
1526. Tack, Jacob, Privt.
1527. Tutterton, Benjamin, Privt.
1528. Thompson, Charles, Privt. of Cavalry
1529. Titman, Philip, Privt.
1530. Tyson, Lewis, Privt.
1531. Terry, Thomas, Privt.
1532. Trolinger, Henry, Privt.
1533. Thompson, William, Privt.
1534. Thompson, James, Privt.
1535. Taburn, William, Senr., Privt.
1536. Thrash, Volintine, Privt.
1537. Tilley, Edmund, Senr., Privt.
1538. Thomason, George, Privt. of Cavalry
1539. Taylor, Hudston, Privt.
1540. Toliner, Jesse, Privt.
1541. Turner, Samuel, Privt.
1542. Thompson, William, Privt.
1543. Taylor, William, Privt. (Infantry & Cavalry)
1544. Tuttle, John, Privt. & C. A.
1545. Tallow, Thomas, Privt.
1546. Taborvin, Burwell, Privt.
1547. Trammell, William, decs'd., Privt.
1548. Tarlton, William, Privt.
1549. Turbyfill, John, Privt.
1550. Tomlinson, Richard, Privt. & Sergeant
1551. Toap, Caleb, Privt.
1552. Threadgill, John, Privt.
1553. Taylor, John, Senr., Privt., Capt. & Adj't. Commissary
1554. Turner, William, Privt.
1555. Tucker, Shadrack, Privt.
1556. Thompson, Isaac, Privt.
1557. Thomson, Bartholomew, Privt.
1558. Tar, Melcher, Privt.
1559. Thomas, John, Privt.
1560. Thomas, Alexander, Privt.
1561. Trout, Jacob, Privt.
1562. Taylor, Richard, Privt.

*Name—Rank*

1563. Thomas, William, Privt. (Infantry & Cavalry)
1564. Tull, Charles, Privt.
1565. Tate, William, Privt. of Cavalry
1566. Tolar, Nehemiah, Privt. (Infantry & Cavalry)
1567. Tatom, Joshua, Privt.
1568. Tanner, Michael, Privt.
1569. Tippong, Conrad, Privt.
1570. Tilley, Henry, Privt.
1571. Tilley, Lazerous, Privt.
1572. Thompson, Samuel, Privt.
1573. Treadwell, Reuben, Privt.
1574. Tinnen, Robert, Privt.
1575. Tyner, Benjamin, Privt. (Cavalry & Infantry)
1576. Tate, Thomas, Privt.
1577. Upchurch, Moses, Privt.
1578. Utley, Burwell (or Burrell), Privt.
1579. Ure, Uriah, Privt.
1580. Upchurch, Nathan, Privt.
1581. Ussery, Thomas, Privt.
1582. Unger, Lawrence, Privt.
1583. Underwood, John, Privt.
1584. Vandiver, Matthew, Privt.
1585. Vinzant, Barnabas, Privt.
1586. Vick, Jesse, Privt.
1587. Viars, William, Privt.
1588. Vendrick, Peter, Privt.
1589. Vermillion, Samuel, Privt.
1590. Vickes, Elijah, Privt.
1591. Venable, John, Privt.
1592. Vaughan, Vincent, Privt.
1593. Vaughan, William, Privt.
1594. Wooters, Marclin, Privt.
1595. Williamson, Alexander, Privt.
1596. Watson, William, Privt.
1597. Williams, Thomas, Privt. (Infantry & Cavalry)
1598. Warner, Harden, decs'd., Privt.
1599. Wallace, John, decs'd., Privt. of Cavalry
1600. Woods, William, decs'd., Privt.
1601. Wood, William, Privt. of Cavalry
1602. Wood, Charles, Privt.
1603. West, William, Privt.
1604. Wiles, Abraham, Privt.
1605. White, John, Privt.
1606. White, Peter, Privt.
1607. Whaley, Ezekial, Privt.
1608. Wallis, John, Privt.
1609. Waller, Nathaniel, Privt.
1610. Whitley, Micajah, Privt.

*Name—Rank*

1611. Walker, Tandy, Privt.
1612. Wise, John, Privt.
1613. Wood, William, Privt.
1614. Widgburr (alias Underwood) William, Privt.
1615. Woosley, William, Privt.
1616. Wiley, James, Privt.
1617. Worsley, Thomas, Privt.
1618. Wood, Sampson, Privt.
1619. Williamson, Elijah, Privt. of Infantry & Cavalry
1620. Wilson, Robert, Privt.
1621. Whitaker, Robert L., Privt.
1622. Wooddill, John, Privt.
1623. Winborne, John, Privt. & Adjutant
1624. Williams, Buckner, Privt.
1625. Wiggs, John, Privt., Cavalry & Infantry
1626. Watts, James, Privt.
1627. Wall, Jonathan, Privt.
1628. Wright, Thomas, Senr., Privt.
1629. Whitledge, Ambrose, Privt.
1630. Wilson, James, Privt.
1631. Williamson, Isaac, Senr., Privt.
1632. Wright, James, Privt., Infantry & Cavalry
1633. Witherington, Solomon, Privt.
1634. Witherington, William, Privt.
1635. Walker, Green, Privt.
1636. Waters, Moses, Privt.
1637. Woodsides, William, Privt.
1638. Whitehursh, Arthur, Sr., Privt.
1639. Walker, Reuben, Privt.
1640. Woodside, Archibald, Privt.
1641. Ware, John, Senr., Privt.
1642. White, David, Privt.
1643. Wells, Jacob, Privt.
1644. Weathers, Willis, Privt.
1645. Withrow, James, Lieutenant & Captain
1646. Warren, William, Privt.
1647. Woods, Henry, Privt.
1648. Williams, Benjamin, Privt.
1649. Wellons, Charles, Privt.
1650. Westray, Daniel, Privt.
1651. Wilson, Robert, Privt.
1652. Whetmore, Charles, Privt.
1653. Ward, James, Privt.
1654. Wilson, Samuel, Privt. & Captain
1655. Williams, Robert, Surgeon
1656. Wilkinson, James, Privt.
1657. Williams, Thomas P., Privt., Infantry & Cavalry

*Name—Rank*

1658. Walston, Thomas, Privt.
1659. Wall, Jesse, Privt., Infantry & Cavalry
1660. Ward, William, Privt.
1661. Wilkins, John, Privt.
1662. Wiley, Rufus, Privt.
1663. Wagg, John, Artificer
1664. Witherspoon, William, Privt.
1665. Ward, John L., Privt.
1666. Whitlow, Solomon, Privt.
1667. Wright, John, Senr., Privt.
1668. Weedon, John, Privt.
1669. Walden, John, Privt.
1670. Williamson, Charles, Privt.
1671. Wallis, James, Privt.
1672. Walker, Buckley, Privt.
1673. Walker, Andrew, Privt.
1674. Wright, George, Privt.
1675. Williams, George, Privt.
1676. West, Willoughby, Senr., Privt.
1677. Wardrope, Edward, Privt.
1678. Wilhings, John, Privt. of Cavalry
1679. Wilkerson, John, Privt.
1680. Winingham, James, Privt.
1681. Witherington, Daniel, Privt. of Infantry
1682. West, Alexander, Privt.
1683. Williams, Job, Privt.
1684. Williams, William, Privt.
1685. Weaver, William, Privt.
1686. Wilson, John, Privt.
1687. Wadsworth, William, Privt.
1688. Ward, John, Privt.
1689. Walden, Drury, Privt. & Musician
1690. Weston, James, Privt.
1691. Williams, Waring, Privt.
1692. Woodall, Samuel, Privt.
1693. Welch, Joseph, Privt.
1694. Whit, Charles, Privt.
1695. Ware, William, Privt.
1696. Whitworth, John, Privt.
1697. Willoughby, Edlyne, Privt.
1698. Williams, Samuel, Privt.
1699. Wallace, William, Privt.

*Name—Rank*

1700. Wheeler, Henry, Privt.
1701. Walter, Paul, Privt. (Infantry & Cavalry)
1702. Williams, Bennett, Privt.
1703. Woodward, Jourdan, Privt.
1704. Wren, Joseph, Privt.
1705. Watson, John, Privt. (Infantry & Cavalry)
1706. Williamson, William, Privt.
1707. Wadkins, John, Privt.
1708. Williams, John, Privt.
1709. Wilson, Willis, Privt. of Cavalry
1710. Wolf, Lewis, Privt. & Fifer
1711. Wright, Edward, Privt.
1712. Wall, Joseph, Privt.
1713. Willis, Joseph, Privt.
1714. Watford, William, Privt.
1715. Webb, Jesse, Privt.
1716. Watson, Levin, Privt.
1717. Wiggins, Arthur, Privt.
1718. Wilfong, John, Privt.
1719. Wallace, Samuel, Privt.
1720. Wilder, William, Privt.
1721. Whitehead, Burrel, Privt. (Cavalry & Infantry)
1722. Walker, John, Privt.
1723. Wood, Stephen, Privt.
1724. Weathers, Elisha, Privt. (Cavalry & Infantry)
1725. Walters, Moses, Privt.
1726. Wall, Jacob, Privt.
1727. White, Benjamin, Privt.
1728. Webb, Johnson, Privt.
1729. Walker, William L., Privt. (Infantry & Cavalry)
1730. Webb, John, Privt.
1731. Williams, Stephen, Privt.
1732. Yates, John, Privt.
1733. Yarborough, Joseph, Privt.
1734. Yeargan, Thomas, Privt.
1735. Young, William, Privt.
1736. Young, Arthur D., Privt.
1737. Yarborough, Nathan, Privt.
1738. Ziglar, Leonard, Privt.

## DECLARATIONS FOR PENSIONS

*Page*

93. John Abbott, enlisted June 1st, 1781, Guilford County.
93. Joshua Adcock, of Caswell County.
94. Daniel Alexander, of Mecklenburg County.
95. Jesse Alsobrook, enlisted in Halifax County.
97. Col. Richard Allen, Sr., of Rowan County (now Wilkes), entered the services in 1775.

101. **William Allen,** volunteered Sept. 1781.
102. **John Allison,** entered the service in 1778, in Orange County, under Capt. William Lytle.
104. **Francis Antrican,** entered the service in April 1781, under Capt. Thomas Donohough.
106. **Westwood Armistead,** of Northampton County. In battle of Guilford Courthouse his company having to flee to Troublesome Iron Works, he then was returned a soldier under his brother Anthony Armistead.
107. **William Armstrong,** of Lincoln County.
111. **Wyatt Ballard,** entered the service in 1781, in Warren County, in Capt. Carter's Company in the Regt. of Col. Dixon.
111. **John Butler,** enlisted in Windsor, N. C., in 1776.
112. **John Denny,** of Guilford County.
113. **Andrew Carson,** of Iredell County.
126. **William Graham,** of Rutherford County.
128. **Pleasant Henderson,** born in Granville County, Jan. 9, 1756.
131. **Benjamin Hester,** of Granville County, joined Capt. Taylor's Company at Troublesome Iron Works the day after the Battle of Guilford Court House.
132. **William Hunt,** of Granville County.
133. **John P. Ives,** volunteered in the Militia about the beginning of the Revolutionary War.
133. **James Jones** of Daviess County, Ky., born in York County, Penn. in yr. 1760, moved to Rowan County, where he resided during the Revolutionary War. A volunteer in 1778 in Rowan County, under Capt. Wm. Wilson.
135. **William Lenoir,** a volunteer from Surry County (now Wilkes).
142. **Daniel Lane,** in 17th year, drafted to guard the jail in New Bern, volunteered in 1779.
143. **James McBride,** of Guilford County.
145. **James Martin,** of Guilford County.
150. **Salathiel Martin,** in the Battle of King's Mtn. & Guilford C. H.
151. **John Montgomery** of Guilford County.
152. **William Polk,** of Wake County.
154. **Austin Prescott,** private N. C. Artillery in the Continental Line, in Rev. War.
154. **John Taylor, Senr.,** of Granville County.
158. **John Wilfong,** of Lincoln County, enlisted in 1780.

# BOX OF MILITIA RETURNS, 1770-1779

Field return of the Regt. of Militia for Hyde Co., at a general muster the 24th day of May, 1780, by Wm. Russel, Colo.

### COMMISSIONED OFFICERS

1. Caleb Forman, Captn.
   Lt.
   William Wright, Ensn.
2. Thomas Smith, Capt.
   John Fortescue, Lt.
   Reuben Bartee, Ensn.
3. Steph'n Gaylard, Capt.
   William Saterthwait, Lt.
   Jeremiah Gaylard, Ensn.

4. Solomon Rew, Capt.
   Christopher Mason, Lt.
   Ensn.
5. Joseph Gibbs, Capt.
   Benjamin Gibbs, Lt.
   William Gibbs, Ensn.
6. Solomon Jones, Capt.
   Ezekiel Turner, Lt.
   Case Gibbs, Ensn.

### ONSLOW FIELD RETURNS

| | | |
|---|---|---|
| Capt. John Boston | Ensn. Jno. Beeseley | Lt. Jno. Starkey |
| Lt. En. Battle | Capt. Geo. Mitchell | Ensn. Jos. Wharton |
| Ensn. John Marrill | Lt. Thos. Farnell | Capt. Moses Fox |
| Capt. Reuben Grant | Ensn. Jno. Cooper | Lt. Solomon Ward |
| Lt. Stanton Spooner | Capt. James Gray | Ensn. Wm. Jenkins |
| Ensn. Geo. Hazzard | Lt. James Foy | Capt. Rich'd. Brack |
| Capt. John Spicer | Ensn. Jer'h. Furwelle. | Ensn. Thos. Godly |
| Lt. John Spicer, Junr. | Capt. Stu Grant | |

(Commissions filled as for the above eight Comp's.)
Aug. 1, 1777.

Wm. Cray.

| No. 1 | No. 2 | No. 3 | No. 4 |
|---|---|---|---|
| Ezek'l Creech | Jos'a Barwick. | Wm. Vining | Simon Herring |
| John Heartsfield | John Kennedy | Joseph Smith | David Williams |
| Clint Wine | Moses Lovick | Aaron Pool | Shadrach Campbell |
| John Aldridge | Jacob Ingram | Sanders Bush | John Cox |
| . . . . . . . . . . . . . . | Jacob Thompson | Jesse Smith | Sam'l Pool |
| John Hodges | Fra's Hill | Thos. Daniel, Jr. | Benj. Bruton, Jr. |
| John Tull | Nathan Arrendale | John Woodland | Stanton Smith |
| Sam'l Caswell | John Brown, Jr. | John Fontaine | John Heartsfield, Jr. |
| Gray Westbrook | David Heartsfield | Job Williams | Reuben Freeman |
| Benj. Creech, Jr. | James Smith | James Pool | Paul Heartsfield, Jr. |
| John Grant, Jr. | Jesse Aldridge | Wm. Woodland | Wm. Ferrill |
| Fra's. Freeman | Thos. Byrd | Wm. Ayler | Wm. Skinner |
| John Parrot | Jas'a Williams | John Creech | Wm. Tull |
| Wm. Arrendale | Benj. Byrd | Moses Westbrook | Robert Bird |
| Jas. Ingram | Jude Walters | William Berwick | Robert Woodland |
| Wm. Berwich, Jr. | Stringer Potts | Walter Kennedy | Jos'a Croom |
| Benj. Risher | John Barrs | Fra's Hodges. | Abra. Bush |
| | Wm. Aldridge | Jesse Cobb | Wm. Brown |

(Drafted in Capt. Kennedy's Company, 26th July, 1777.)

# A LIST OF CAPT. SHEPPERD'S COMP., MAY THE 18TH, 1777

1. Isaac Bass
2. Luke Bates
3. Thos. Fail
4. Thos. Potter
5. Benj. Davis
6. Edward Evens
7. William Martin
8. Abr. Hay
9. John Faircloth
10. Marmaduke Barfield
11. John Ward
12. James Martin
13. Samuel Pope, Sr.
14. Samuel Pope, Jr.
15. Shadrach Barfield
16. Richard Suddell
17. Jesse Taylor
18. Abraham Denny
19. David Denny
20. John Weaver
21. Wm. Jackson
22. Benj. Coleson
23. Thos. Price
24. James Jorden
25. John Jorden
26. John Goodson
27. Philip Dean
28. Thos. Caraway
29. Hugh Stephenson
30. Peter Harrell
31. Jesse Nelson
32. Sam'l Sanford
33. Waddel Cade
34. John Jackson
35. Kador Phelps
36. James Phelps
37. James Campbell
38. George Downing
39. William Fulkes
40. Ismeal Semons
41. Frederick Eckles
42. John Mitchell
43. George Turnage

# A JUST AND TRUE RETURN OF SOLDIERS ENLISTED IN THE CONTINENTAL SERVICE FOR THE TERM OF 3 YEARS IN THE 6TH N. C. BATTALION

1777.
June 12th. John Willibough enlisted.
Sept. 3rd. Anthoney Wiles, enlisted.
Sept. 6th., Francis Delong, enlisted.
Sept. 20th., Thomas Cartwright, enlisted.
Oct. 4th., Samuel Prise, enlisted.
Nov. 10th., Robert Cartwright, enlisted.
(Returned by Joseph Richardson, Ensn.)

Agreeable to the Orders of the Day the officer of the 3rd Regt. of N. C. Continental Troops met at Mrs. William Martins in Halifax in order to ascertain and settle the Rank of said Regt. which appears to be as follows:

Apl. ye 16th. 77.
Jethro Summer, Col., Wm. Alston Lt. Col., and Saml. Lockhart, Major Comr. dates 15 Apl. 1776.

| | |
|---|---|
| Jacob Turner, 1st. Capt. | |
| Pinkethman Eaton, 2nd Capt. | |
| James Emmet, 3rd Capt. | Appointed by Congress, Apr. |
| Thos. Granbury, 4th Capt. | 16th, 1776. |
| Wm. Brinkley, 5th Capt. | Recommended and approved of |
| Gabriel Jones, 6th Capt. | by Gen. Lee, 24 July, '76. |
| James Bradley, 7th Capt. | |
| Nich's Edmonds, 8th Capt. | Recomd'd by ye officers 16th April, '77. |

| | |
|---|---|
| 1st Lts. | |
| 1. Kador Ballard, 1st. Lt. | |
| 2. Math. Wood, Lt. | Appointed by Congress, 16th Apr., 1776. |
| 3. John Medows, Lt. | Recommended and approved of by |
| 4. Gee Bradley, Lt. | Gen. Lee, 24 July, '76. |
| 5. John Granbury, Lt. | |
| 6. Christ'r. Lackey | Recommended by ye officers, |
| 7. Edward Yarborough | 16th Apr., 1777. |
| 8. Jos. Montfort | |

| | |
|---|---|
| 2nd Lts. | |
| 1. Wm. Linton, 2nd Lt. | |
| 2. John Morphes | Rec'm'd. & Apprd. of by Genl. Lee |
| 3. Wm. Fawn | 24 July '76 |
| 4. Wm. Rushworms | |
| 5. Harry Vincents | Rec'm'd. by ye officers ye 16 Apr. '77. |
| 6. John Fellows | John Clendenning 1st Ensn. |
| 7. Anthony Hart | Rec'm'd. Chas. O'Neal, 2nd Ensn. |
| 8. Oliver Hodgson | 16 Apl., '77. |

Endorsed: Return of 3rd Battalion. All Continental Coms. made out & dd to Col. John Williams, 11 May, 1777.

# A LIST OF THE VOLUNTEERS AND DRAFTED MEN, HALIFAX RETURN, MCH. 1779

| | | | |
|---|---|---|---|
| William Jackson | John Caine | John Ford | William Reed |
| James Brewer | Isaac Aaron | John Bishops | John Sullivent |
| William Dicken | James Streaker | Fredrick Jones | James Henley |
| Volentine Garner | Jorden Baker | James Alsobrook | Joshua Sikes |
| William Yerbrough | John Richardson | John Channel | Littleberry Overbay |
| John Powell | Joseph Worley | Isom Good | William Gurley |
| Rodrick Easley | William Purkins | Samuell Porter | Mark Browning |
| Henry Harper, Junr. | Josias Lock | Samuell Smith | Walton Vaughters |
| James Baker | Jonathan Lock | Jones Stevens | Jos. Hadley |
| Rily Walker | Joseph Whealor | Burrell Long | Jessy Heath |
| John Thompson | Josiah Smith | William Dunkin | Jorden Powell |
| John Kilpatrick | Tobias Ingram | (37 volunteers) | Nicholas Prince |
| John Garlond | Henry Nunnery | Drafted men (13) | Jessey Wyatt |

Here returned by me Jas. Allen, Colo. Co.

Several of the above men taken for wagoners by the request of Col. Long; their names to (wit) William Barksdell, Isaac Aaron, John Garland, James Brewer, Vol. Garnor, Mark Browning, John Cane, John Martin.

Roll of Officers and private Soldiers detached from the first or Southern Battalion of the Militia of the County of Orange to march against the hostile Indians under the command of Col. Ambrose Ramsey.

| | |
|---|---|
| Maj. Hugh Tinnian | Lt. Joseph Thompson |
| Capt. William Williams | —— Peter Oneal |
| —— William Murray | Ensn. Edward Gwin |
| | —— Elias Powel |

John Murray ⎫
Robert Powel ⎬  Sgts. of Capt. Murrays Co.

George Holt ⎫
John Williams ⎬  Corporals of Capt. Murrays Co.

Jacob Albright, Drummer of Capt. Murrays Co.

| | | | |
|---|---|---|---|
| Rank & | Robert Paysly | James McCall | Charles McClury |
| File | Amariah Reeves | Howel Harwood | John McAdams |
| Hugh Muhulum | John Abbot | Major May | Arch'd Mahon |
| Joseph Thompson | John Strowd | Charles Williams | Dan'l Hoffman |
| William Car | Rich'd Williams | Arnold Bruce | William Thrift |
| James Car | Robert Mains | John Paris | Isaac Earthen |
| Walter Ellis | Andrew Hopkins | John Allison | Hezekiah Purdum |
| Morris Richards | William Hawkins | Solomon Swift | Jesse George |
| John Pogue | Aquilla Darlohside | Frederick Davis | David Horton |
| William Graves | (Dollahide) | Thomas Flemming | Nowel Mercer |
| John Pugh | William Rayny | Thomas Minor | Stephen Seagraves |
| Anthony Godfree | John Logue | Richard Webb | Thomas May |

Non-commissioned officers and private soldiers of Capt. William Williams' Co., as appear by Roll returned to Brig. Gen. Persons.

Aug. 20th, 1776.                    Col. Butlers' Detachment.

A list of the officers that served in the 2nd Battalion since Jan. 9, 1778.

Sept. 9, 1778.

| Names | Date of Commission | Remarks |
|---|---|---|
| Field Officers. | | |
| 1. Alexander Martin, Col.......... | 1777 | Resigned Nov. 22nd, 1777 |
| 2. John Patten, (Sic) Lt. Col....... | Nov. 22, 1777 | Promoted Nov. 22, 1777 |
| 3. John White, Maj............... | Feb. 1, " | Promoted to command a Regt. in Georgia |
| 4. Hardy Murfree, Capt........... | " | Promoted to Maj. |
| 5. Selby Harney, Maj............. | Nov. 22 | Promoted Lt. Col. from 8th to 2nd Regt. |
| 6. John Armstrong, Capt.......... | Oct. 4 | Promoted Maj. to 4th Regt. |
| Captains. | | |
| 7. James Gee.................... | | Died Nov. 12, 1777 |
| 8. John Heritage................. | | Resigned May 15, 1777 |
| 9. Wm. Fenner.................. | Oct. 24 | Promoted Maj. of 7th Regt. |
| 10. Edward Veal, (Sic)............ | | Cashiered Dec. 21, 1777 |
| 11. Benjamin Williams............. | July 19, 1776 1777 | |
| 12. Clement Hall.................. | Apr. 24 | |
| 13. James Martin................. | | Transferred to 5th Regt. |
| 14. Joseph Tate.................. | | Died 2nd June 1777 |
| 15. Charles Allen................. | | Trans. to 5th Regt. |
| 16. Benj'm Coleman............... | Apr. 30 | Trans. from 5th Regt. |
| 17. Robert Fenner................ | | Date of Commission in dispute |
| 18. John Ingles.................. | Oct. 24 | |
| 19. Thos. Armstrong.............. | Oct. 25 | Trans. from 5th Regt. |
| 20. Manlove Tarrant.............. | | Sent to N. C. agreeable to arrangement |
| 21. John Craddock................ | Dec. 21 | |
| 22. Thomas Standiss.............. | | Resigned May 15, 1777 |
| 1st Lieuts. | | |
| 23. Joseph Worth................. | | Died Apr. 6, 1777 |
| 24. Phillip Lowe................. | | Resigned Feb. 1, 1777 |
| 25. Clement Nash................. | | Resigned Feb. 1, 1777 |
| 26. Isaac Rolston................. | | Sent to N. C. agreeable to arrangement |
| 27. David Vance................. | | "    "    "    "    "    " |
| 28. Charles Steward, (t) (?)........ | | Trans. from 5th Regt. |
| 29. Thomas Evans................ | May 15 | |
| 30. John Jacobs.................. | | Resigned Mch. 1, 1778 |
| 31. John Daves.................. | Oct. 4 | |
| 32. James Parkerson.............. | | Died 26 Mch. 1778 |
| 33. Samuel Budd................. | Nov. 11 | |
| 34. John Williams................ | | Sent to N. C. agreeable to arrangement |
| 35. James Campen................ | Dec. 21 | |
| 36. Arthur Colgrove.............. | Mch. 26 | |
| 37. Chas. Gerrard............... | June 1st | Trans. to 5th Regt. |
| 2nd Lts. | | |
| 38. William Killeby............... | | Died Apr. 6, 1777 |
| 39. Sam'l McKlewaine............. | | Resigned Oct. 24, 1777 |
| 40. John Radford................. | | Resigned Feb. 1, 1778 |
| 41. James Luton................. | | Resigned Mch. 10, 1778 |
| 42. Levi Sawyer................. | | Resigned Mch. 16, 1778 |
| Ensigns. | | |
| 43. William Ferrill............... | Sept. 8 | |
| 44. Samuel Jones................ | | Died July 1778 |

| Names | Date of Commission | Remarks |
|---|---|---|
| 45. Richard Andrews.............. | Nov. 1 | |
| 46. Thomas Finney................ | Nov. 12 | |
| 47. Levi Gatling................. | | Cashiered Aug. 26, 1778 |
| 48. Stephen Southall............. | Apr. 1st | |
| 49. Nath. Lawrence............... | June 1st | |
| 50. James Verrier................ | June 1st | John Patton, Col. |

N. B.—This return is not dated in the original, but other records show it to have been Sept. 9, 1778.

| | Appt. | |
|---|---|---|
| 51. Richard Bradley, Paymaster..... | Mch. 5, 1777 | Dismissed June 1, 1778. Agreeable to the new arrangement |
| 52. Lehancius Dekeyser, adjutant.... | Nov. 15, 1775 | Resigned Dec. 10, 1776 |
| 53. John Rice, Adjutant........... | Dec. 10, 1776 | 1st prom. Mch. 28, 1777 |
| 54. Stephen Conger, Adjutant....... | Jan. 29, 1778 | Dismissed June 1, 1778 |
| 55. Yelverton Fowkes, Quar. Mr..... | Feb. 3, 1776 | Resigned Aug. 1st, 1776 |
| 56. Patrick Rogers, Quar. Mr........ | Nov. 1776 | 1st promtn. Mch. 28, 1777 |
| 57. William Womack, Quar. Mr...... | Jan. 1778 | Resigned June 1st, 1777 |
| 58. William Kennon, Comissary...... | Sept. 1777 | Resigned Apr. 1777 |

(N.B.—The Ensigns first promotion was to 2nd Lieut.)

# LIST OF MEMBERS OF CAPT. WILLIAM WILLIAMS' CO., 7TH ORANGE MILITIA

Capt. Williams

1. Jno. Griffy
2. Jas. Allison
3. Andrew McBroom
4. Th's Curtess
5. Jno. Clark
6. Ja's Rutherford
7. Jno. Rutherford
8. David Pinkerton
9. Jas. McCallister
10. Wm. Woods
11. Wm. Clinton
12. Jas. Clark
13. Jno. Makor
14. Jno. Disharoon
15. Wm. Clenny
16. Benj. Jones
17. Dan'l Andrew
18. Abijah Massey
19. Nath'l Newman
20. Elijah Green
21. John Rhodes
22. Joshua Horn
23. Wm. Rhodes
24. Jas. Turner
25. Dan'l Chissenhall
26. Henry Wood
27. Isaac Forrest
28. Rich'd. Nichols
29. Beverly Perkinson
30. Jeremiah Harris
31. Jno. Strayhorn
32. Jno. Gess
33. Aquilla Rhodes
34. Abraham Nelson
35. Jno. Wilkinson
36. Sam'l Aken
37. Wm. Talbie
38. Jas. McColloch
39. Jas. Hartt
40. And'w Reed
41. Thos. Baker
42. Hugh Currothers
43. Jno. Gee
44. Jno. Mitchell
45. George Hightower
46. Wm. Jones
47. John Parton
48. John McBride
49. Jno. Minnis
50. Thos. Capper

The foregoing is a list lodged with me at Hillsborough by Capt. Williams of Col. Butler's Battalion.

Thos. Person, Br. Gen.
22nd. Aug., 1776.

# PAY ROLL OF CAPT. TURNER'S COMPANY

From Caswell Co. and Chatham Co., N. C., under the command of Col. McDowell, from 15 of Mch. to the 30 day of July, 1779.

1. Berryman Turner, Capt.
2. John Taylor, Lt.
3. Josiah Shumaker, Sgt.
4. William Holiness
5. Abraham Fuller, Sgt.
6. Benjamin Abbot, Ensn.
7. John Taylor, Corpl.
8. John Williams, Sergt.
9. Calep Carman, Drum
10. Colman Claton
11. David Barnet
12. John Stone
13. Carter Lee
14. Richard Boyd
15. Thermon Hicks
16. Daniel Merrit
17. Shadrick Adkins
18. John Swiney
19. Charles Brooks
20. Joseph Walker
21. Edmon Haggard
22. Michal Burk
23. Daniel Walker
24. William Thackston
25. Robert Childers
26. David Lee, died 20th June
27. William Slade
28. John Meadows
29. John Floyd
30. James McCollister
31. Peter Skeen
32. William Mason
33. Stephen Hamblin
34. Benjeman Melton
35. David Enouch
36. Joel Corder
37. John Ransol
38. William Parr
39. John Summers
40. Richard Jones
41. William Worthy
42. Thos. Mason

## THE MEN FROM CHATHAM CO.

43. Jerdon Williams, Ensn.
44. John Malown
45. Jimes Coplin, Corpl.
46. Mack Osborne
47. Samuel Brazeal
48. William Jones
49. Stephen Poe
50. William Leperd
51. William Poe
52. John Poe
53. John Roson
54. Richard Copland
55. Aron Terrel
56. Thos. Henry
57. Stephen Powel
58. Denis Phillips
59. Moses Terrel

Caswell Richard Boyd, Corpl.
John Swiney, Corpl.

# A LIST OF CAPT. JOSHUA BOWMANS COMP., FEB. 19, 1778

*Names—When Inlisted*

Edw'd Robinson, Compl., 1776
Wm. Locke, 1776
Zach' Jackson, 1777
Wm. Wood, 1777
Jesse Pritchard, 1777
William Morgan, Compl., 1776
Daniel Potter, 1776
Geo. Williams, 1776
Duncan McBride
Wm. Waters, 1776
Wm. Bell, 1777
Jacob Norton, 1777
Geo. Richards
James Strange?
Shadrick Atkins, 1777
Wm. Gaudy, 1777
Wm. Norton
Thos. Bozer, 1776
Joel Martin, 1777

Joseph Spikes, 1776
Thos. Edge, 1776
Duncan McBride
Wm. Henry, 1776
Wm. Henry Bayley, 1776
Rich'd Walton, 1776
Thom's Jones, 1776
Hubart Carter, 1776
Dan'l McCoy, 1777
Wm. Brantley, 1776
Alex. McDauval, 1777
Wm. Themnel, 1776
Geo. Lote, 1777
Wm. Kincaid, 1776
James Irvin, 1777
Jordan Rozer
James Young, 1777
Thos. Ward, 1777
Hugh McDonnell, 1776

Peter Jacobs, 1777
Joseph Keys
Robt. Berry
Benj. Stevens
Wm. Gipson
Benj. Tomson, 1777
Thos. Jones, 1777
Sam'l Whitley
Simon Christopher
Chas. ———zer
Jesse Rowel
Benj. Davis, 1776
James Davis, 1776
Thos. Higgins
Wm. Goref, 1776
Neal Blue
Peter Biznard
Arthur McDonald, 1776
Sylus Dotterhide

### Box 1770-1779

Roll of Capt. Joshua Bowmans Light Infantry Co. of the N. C. Battalion, Commanded by Col. Thomas Clark, Sept. 8, 1778

1. William Smith
2. Daniel Potter
3. ————
4. William Morgan
5. Demean McBride
6. John Cook
7. Isaac Manchester
8. John Walters
9. Shadrick Elkin
10. Peter Biznard
11. Arthur McDonald
12. William Kincaid
13. John Hendry
14. John Gaudy
15. Daniel Sellers
16. John Riggins

17. John McKay
18. Jesse Spittards
19. James Young
20. Alex. Morrison
21. Daniel Motte
22. Thomas Bozer
23. Rich'd McKay
24. John Turner
25. Edgerton Mott
26. Dan'l McKay
27. Alex'r McDonald
28. William H. Bagley
29. John Wilkeson
30. Henry Cocker
31. James ONeal
32. Samuel Simmons
33. Edw'd Crump

34. Solomon Carr
35. Sam'l Rowe
36. Thomas Sawyer
37. James Almonds
38. Hugh McDonald
39. John Stradford
40. Timothy Rich
41. Francis Owens
42. William Gibson
43. Richard Mounte
44. William Apperson
45. David Benton
46. Alex. Gordon
47. Benj. Smith
48. James Raney
49. Samuel Smith

# MUSTER ROLL OF PART OF THE 6TH N. C. REG'T.

Commanded by Col. Gideon Lamb, Dec. 1778

| Commissioned or Appointed | { | Benj Baley, Lieut., Oct. 20, 1777<br>John S. Hare, Oct. 12, 1777<br>Benj. Coffield, Adj't., May 17, 1777 |
| --- | --- | --- |
| Lieutenants | { | Gideon Bonney<br>Blake Chace |
| Drum & fife | { | William Miller |

| | |
| --- | --- |
| 1. Joseph Borchnes, pt. | 12. Daniel Ballance |
| 2. ——— ——— | 13. Hirim Pendlon |
| 3. Wm. Barber | 14. James Tiland |
| 4. John Winburry | 15. Willoughby Weaver |
| 5. ——— Davis | 16. Willis Bright |
| 6. Peter Brean | 17. William Fular |
| 7. Thomas Staples | 18. Joseph Haymon |
| 8. Lewis | 19. Daniel Leggitt |
| 9. Malachi M'Coy | 20. James ——— |
| 10. Isaac Herrington | 21. Jothan Morrisett |
| 11. Leven Sumers | 22. Peter Morrisett |

COPY OF THE ENLISTMENT OF H. TATUM, COMPT., FEB. 26, 1778

| | |
| --- | --- |
| 1. Alex Morryson | 27. Benj. Modlin |
| 2. Jim Standen | 28. Jeremiah Modlin |
| 3. Joshua Forbes | 29. Christ'er Low |
| 4. Wm. White | 30. James Wharton |
| 5. Isaac' Griffith | 31. Wm. Conner |
| 6. Samuel Roberts | 32. David Gold |
| 7. Thos. Billops | 33. Nottingham Mont |
| 8. Etheldred Washington | 34. John White |
| 9. Joseph Howard | 35. Robt. Moss |
| 10. Elias Ford | 36. Josiah Cooper |
| 11. Jos. Miller | 37. Thos' Ames |
| 12. Willie Burrows | 38. John Williams |
| 13. Fred'k. Lucey | 39. John Jones |
| 14. Christson Wooten | 40. Mills Ramsey |
| 15. Joseph Stephens | 41. Robert Wilbourn |
| 16. John Williams | 42. Simon Lumbby |
| 17. Tho. Williams | 43. Henry Bartley |
| 18. Jim Chinn | 44. Wm. Holland |
| 19. George Top | 45. Thomas Lader |
| 20. Chas. Conner | 46. Tickle Thomson |
| 21. Henry Smith | 47. Stephen Ray |
| 22. Lawrence Lyner | 48. Daniel Tise |
| 23. Christ'v Bardon | 49. Eph'm Todd |
| 24. Joshua Fenton | 50. Wm. Todd |
| 25. Eph'm Branton | 51. Arthur Corbin |
| 26. Bazzell Jackson | |

MAY 25, 1778

A Discriptive list of men raised under the present Act of Assembly, in Companies 1-15
Inclusive.  Signed by Capt. Ralph Williams, 9-N.B.

(The yellowed sheets tell the age, height, color eyes and hair and trade.)

Capt. Richard Taylor's Co.
    John Beavor, shoemaker
    John Williams, planter
    Jeffrey Garus, planter in the room of
        Wm. Edwd. Cock
    Edmund Kelly, planter
Capt. Sam'l Fowler's Company
    John Smith, planter
    Charles Floid, planter
    John Langford, planter
    Jesse Landford, planter
    Henry Hays, planter
    Corben Hickmen, planter
Capt. John Rush
    Abraham Jones
    Jonathan Jones
    Bird Driver
    Isaac Anderson, planter
    Jenkens Gowan (mulatto)
Capt. Abraham Pollard
    James Gallemore, planter
    Luke Searsey, planter
    Henry Nowlin, planter
    John Henry Singen, in the room of
        Joseph Okey
Capt. Samuel Walker's Company
    George Woodlift, planter
    David Hunt, planter
    Gibson Harris, planter
    David Hatcher, planter
    Tolbert Tucker ( several trades)
    John Kennedy, trader
Capt. Benjamine Wade's Company
    Drusy Cook, planter
    John Emery, planter
    Edmund Emery, planter
    John Taylor, planter
    Thomas Taylor, planter
Capt. James Langston's Company
    William Langston, planter
    Thomas Merryweather, shoemaker
        and planter
    Thomas Bressie, planter
    George Reaves, planter

Capt. Bartlet Searsey's Co.
    Benjamin Hester, planter
    Francis Stainback, card maker by trade
    William Beaver, planter
    Thomas Miner, planter
Capt. William Gibb's Company
    Buckner Rooks, carpenter
    Joseph Allen, (mulatto) planter
    John Glaze, planter
    Francis Wilkerson, planter
Capt. Thomas Bradford
    Salkens Nauts, planter
    Elisha Lunceford
    John Hooker
    William Pettiford (mulatto)—Thomas
        Bradford
Capt. Richard Searsey's Co.
    Asa Searsey, planter
    David Harris, planter
    Oswell Searsey, carpenter
    Lewis Simms, planter
Capt. William Knight's Co.
    John Martin, wheelwright for Col.
        Sam'l Smith
    Fulvill Hall, planter
    Augustus Woodliff, planter
    David Allen, planter
    James Beaver
Capt. James Currins' Co.
    John Hopkins, planter
    George Bristoe, planter
    Aaron Sprinkfield, blacksmith
    Alex. Hamilton, blacksmith
    John Hudson, planter
Capt. Thomas Saleswhites' Co.
    John Pharoah, carpenter
    Arthur Marcum, carpenter
    Charles Regan, planter
    Thomas Mullet, planter
    Richard Edwards, blacksmith
    William Tabor, planter
Capt. James Jones' Co.
    William Cox, planter
    Hempton White, planter
    James Jones, planter
    Joshua Greenwitch, planter

# IN THE AMERICAN REVOLUTION

601

## RETURN OF THE AID VOLUNTEERS AND DRAFTS FROM WILKES CO., JAN. 19, 1779

William Combs, Rec'd. his Bounty of—
John Oakley, Rec'd. his Bounty of—
John Morris, Rec'd. his Bounty of—
Abejah Bickas, Rec'd. his Bounty of—
William Gray, Rec'd. his Bounty of
John Gray, Rec'd. his Bounty of—
Maj'r Grissom, Rec'd. his Bounty of—
Bhences Cox, Rec'd. his Bounty of—
William Walters, Rec'd. his Bounty of—
William Brewer, Rec'd. his Bounty of—
Menoah Crais, Rec'd his Bounty of—
William Rhodes, Rec'd. his Bounty of—
Thomas Watts, Rec'd. his Bounty of—

John Thrasher, Rec'd. his Bounty of—
Robt. Boyd, Rec'd. his Bounty of—
Edward Bell, Rec'd his Bounty of—
John Marlen, Rec'd. his Bounty of—
Jesse Hains, Rec'd. his Bounty of—
Thos' Hall, Rec'd. his Bounty of—
Jonathan Hickman, Rec'd. his Bounty of—
Joshua Ware, Rec'd. his Bounty of—
Lewas Baldwin, Rec'd. his Bounty of—
Joshua Touson, Rec'd. his Bounty of—
Alex'r. Renard?, Rec'd. his Bounty of—
Elijah Cay, Rec'd. his Bounty of—

## A LIST OF MEN DRAFTED IN CAPT. THOS. WILLIAMS CO., 30TH OCT., 1778

Arthur Smith, farmer
Daniel Howell, farmer

John Peacock, farmer
Lewis Hutchings

## PAY ROLL OF CAPT. SAMUEL REID, AUG. 9, 1780—NAME AND RANK

Samuel Reid, Capt. (Rowan Co.)
Robert Allison, Lieut.
Robert Rawlston, 1st Lt.
Boston Dyson, 2nd Lt.
Allen MacCaboy, Ensn.
Peter Reggen, 1st Corpl.
James Marlow, 2nd Corpl.
Arch McCoerade, pt.
William Whitfield, pt.
James Norris, pt.
William Dobbins, pt.
James McHargers, pt.
Patrick Hamers, pt.
Aaron Laranison, pt.
Robt. Wilson, pt.
James Weil, pt.
R. D. Walker, pt.
James I. Boostax, pt.
James H. Ware, pt.
James Ware, pt.
James Walton, pt.
William Taylor, pt.
Arch Smith, pt
William Anderson, pt.
Robert Holmes, pt.

Thos. Bailey, pt.
Philip Dyson, pt.
Robt. Barley, pt.
Leander Smith, pt.
James Kidd, pt.
Ebenezer Dickey, pt.
Alexander Patterson, pt.
Michael Kinleven, pt.
Tarden Ann Hollow, pt.
William Patterson, pt.

Note, copied from an original record, by
Miss Virginia Alexander of Charlotte.
Record is owned by a former N. C. family
now living in Montecello, Ga.

## PENSION ROLL OF INVALIDS

Omitted to have been reported by the Comptroller of N. C. to the War Office of the
United States, Nov. 1, 1782 (Raleigh Archives)

William Kersey, Caswell Co.
Harman Gaskins, Craven Co.

Robert Robertson, Mecklenburg Co.

# STATE RECORDS

[Vol. XIII, Pages 343-44]

## U. S. PENSION OFFICE—NORTH CAROLINA MISCELLANEOUS ROLLS

[Not paged. No Dates.]

Names of commissioned and non-commissioned officers belonging to the 3rd, N. C. Battalion, copied from the orderly book of Sergt. Isaac Rowel of North Carolina.

James Hogan, Col.
William L. Davidson, Lt. Col.
Thomas Hogg, Major
Anthy Hart, Adjt.
John Horton
Humphy McEnberg
Wm. Shadford
Charles Rhodes
Andrew Rowan
Richard Holes
S. Bolten

S. Brown
Francis Graves, Q. M.
John Baker, S. M.
Jonathan Lumos, Surg'n.
John Godwin
Wm. Johson
Benjamin Kitchen
Moses Bishop
J. Beasly
Joseph Parker
S. Miller

### CAPTAINS

Blount
Baker
Childs
Montford
Farterson
Thomas Roberds, S. M.
Henry Miller, D. M.

Ballard
Bradley
Hart
Quinn
John Fleming, Q. M. S.
Thomas Endlys, F. M.

### LIEUTENANTS

Yarborough
Mackney
Clendennin
Fawn
Graves
Verrier
Powers

Allen
Conniel
Campbell
Ford
Tatum
Wallace
Wilkinson

### ORDERLY SERGEANTS

John Steptoe
John Reddie
Jesse Hardison
Saul Reed
Isaac Rowel

Henry Cooper
Elijah Hinson
John Hall
Bryant Lee

STATE RECORDS—CLARK'S.  U. S. PENSION OFFICE

P. 479, Vol. XIII

| Name and Rank | Date of Com. Ecb. | Remarks |
|---|---|---|
| Thos. Clark, Capt.. | 1 Jan. '77 | |
| Thos. J. Carnes, Lt.. | 1  "    " | Resigned Mar. 8, '79 |
| John Van Duyck, 1 Lt.. | 1 Feb.  " | |
| Wm. Clark, Sergt.. | 1 Jan.  " | |
| Wm. Pennington, Sergt.. | 7 Mar.  " | |
| Wm. Johnston, Corpl.. | 1  "    " | |
| Isaac Lawrence, Corpl.. | 1  "    " | |
| Major Scudder, Bombadies.. | 7 Jan.  " | Resigned 31 Oct. '78 |
| Nathaniel Ross, Bombadies.. | 1  "    " | Resigned 30 Apr. '79 |
| Daniel Whitehead, Gunner.. | 1  "    " | |
| Ezekial DeCamp, Gunner.. | 1  "    " | |
| Hamblen Robinson, Gunner.. | 2  "    " | |
| Joseph Chase, Music.. | | {A deserter sent to his Regt. June '78 |
| Thos Clark, Matross.. | | |
| John Fletcher, Matross.. | 26 May '78 9 mo. | Destd 1 Dec. '78. Dischg 28 Feb '79 |
| Oliver Kelly, Matross.. | 1 Jan. '77 | |
| Nathaniel Little, Matross.. | 1  "    " | |
| John Mitchell, Matross.. | 1  "    " | |
| James Miller, Matross.. | 6 Feb. '78 | |
| Daniel Southerland, Matross.. | 2 Jan. '77 | |

No date nor signature. Probably 9 Sep. '78.
U. S. Pension Office, in a dilapidated old book, entitled N. C. Rolls, not paged.
(This return is more complete than that in the Army Returns, No. 27, P. 80.)

STATE RECORDS OF N. C.—CLARK'S

(Pages 475-476, Vol. XIII)
A list of officers of the 1st N. C. Continental Battalion from its first Establishment Sep. 1, 1775 to Sep. 1, 1778. For detailed information of their appointment, promotions, deaths, resignations, etc., see Vol. XIII.

| Name and Rank | When Appointed | Remarks |
|---|---|---|
| James Moore, Col.. | Sep.   1, 1775 | Died Apr. 22, 1777 |
| Francis Nash, Lt. Col.. | "    "    " | {Wounded Oct. 4, '77, And died Oct. 7, '77 |
| Thomas Clark, Maj'r.. | "    "    " | |
| William Davis, Capt.. | "    "    " | {Transf'd to one of the 4 Regts in Carolina |
| George Davidson, Capt.. | "    "    " | Resigned Feb. 5, '77 |
| Caleb Grainger, Capt.. | "    "    " | Resigned Apr. 26, '77 |
| John Walker, Capt.. | "    "    " | Dec. 22, '77 |
| Alfred Moore, Capt.. | "    "    " | March 8, '77 |
| Henry Dixon, Capt.. | "    "    " | To a Majority in ye 3rd Regiment |
| Robert Rowan, Capt.. | "    "    " | Resigned 29 June '76 |
| Thomas Allen, Capt.. | "    "    " | Resigned Aug. 15, '76 |
| (No. first name) Pickett, Capt.. | | {These two Cos. reduced by order of the Council of Safety of the State of N. C. Jan. 4, 1776 |
| William Green, Capt.. | "    " | |
| John Lillington, Lieut.. | Sep. 1, 1775 | Resigned May '76 |
| William Brannon, Lieut.. | " | |
| Thomas Hogg, Lieut.. | " | To a Majority in 5th Regt. |
| Absolom Tatum, Lieut.. | " | Resigned Sep. 19, '76 |
| Lawrence Thompson, Lieut.. | | {Transf'd to one of the 4 Regts in Carolina. |
| Hector McNeil, Lieut.. | " | {Destd to ye Torys Feb. 3, '76 Condemed by a Court Mar- tial, March '76. Escaped |

| Name and Rank | When Appointed | Remarks |
|---|---|---|
| Joshua Bowman, Lieut.............. | Sept. 1, 1775 | |
| Tilman Dixon, Lieut................ | Nov. 15  " | |
| Henry Neal, Ensign................. | Sep.   1, 1775 | Resigned Apr. 3, '77 |
| Robert Rolston, Ensign............. | " | Resigned Aug. 29, '77 |
| Howell Tatum, Ensign.............. | " | |
| George Grayham, Ensign............ | " | Resigned Apr. 15, '76 |
| Neil McAllister, Ensign............. | " | Resigned Jan. 20, '77 |
| Maurice Moore, Ensign............. | " | Killed Jan. 18, '76 |
| Lebancius DeKeyser, Ensign........ | Nov. 15  " | Resigned 10 Dec. '76 |
| John Brown, Ensign................ | " | {Transfd to one of the 4 Regts in Carolina |
| Joseph McLemmy, Ensign........... | Jan.   4, 1776 | Died July '76 |
| Wm. Crawford, Ensign.............. | " | Resgn'd Aug. 15, '76 |
| Adam Boyd, Ensign................ | " | Resgn'd May '76 |
| James Read, Ensign................ | " | |
| Wm. Armstrong, Ensign............ | " | {Transfd to one of the 4 Regts in Carolina |
| Stephen Daniel, Ensign............. | " | Resgn'd 3 June '76 |
| Joseph Eagle, Ensign............... | " | Resgn'd 20 March '76 |
| Robert Council, Ensign............. | " | Resgn'd 10 Sep. '76. Ill health |
| Edmunds Gambell, Ensign.......... | Mar. 28  " | {Transfd to one of the 4 Regts in Carolina |
| Samuel Blyth, Ensign.............. | " | Resgn'd May 16, '78 |
| John Summers, Ensign.............. | " | |
| Robt. Varner, Ensign............... | " | |
| Septimus Robinson, Ensign......... | June  1, 1776 | Resgn'd Oct. 10, '76 |
| James King, Ensign................ | " | |
| John Gambier Scull, Ensign........ | June  6   " | |
| Thos. Collender, Ensign............ | June 12   " | |
| James Craven, Ensign.............. | " | |
| John Cheese, Ensign............... | Sep. 19, 1776 | Resgn'd April 1, '77 |
| (P. 475) | | |
| Charles Triflet, Ensign............. | Sep. 19   " | Died Dec. '76 |
| William Walters, Ensign........... | " | {Transfd to one of the 4 Regts in Carolina |
| Peter Bacot, Ensign................ | " | |
| Thomas Hall, Ens'n................ | Dec. 24, 1776 | Resgn'd April 3, '77 |
| Samuel Walters, Ens'n............. | " | Resgn'd April 23, '77 |
| Patrick Rogers, Ens'n.............. | Mar. 28, 1777 | Died Apr. 19, '78 |
| John Rice, Ens'n.................. | " | {Transfd to one of the 4 Regts in Carolina |
| John Erwin, Ens'n................. | " | Resgn'd Aug. 28, '77 |
| James Milligan, Ens'n............. | " | {In N. C. Never joined. Broke by a Court Martial 13 July '78 |
| Dixon Marshall, Ens'n............. | " | |
| Robert Council, Ens'n............. | " | {Transfd to one of the 4 Regts in Carolina |
| James Tate, Staff Chaplain......... | Oct. 13, 1775 | {Transfd to one of the 4 Regts in Carolina |
| Isaac Guion, Surgeon.............. | Sep.   1   " | Resgn'd Dec. '75 |
| James GaKee, Surgeon............. | Dec. 1775 | Resgn'd May '76 |
| John Fergus, Surgeon.............. | May 1776 | Resgn'd Apr. '77 |
| Fred'k Heimburg, Surgeon.......... | Mar. 13, 1778 | |
| Sam'l Ashe, Paymaster............. | Sep.   1, 1775 | Resgn'd Apr. 16, '76 |
| William Lord, Paymaster........... | Dec. 1776 | Resgn'd Mar. 5, '77 |
| Rich'd Bradley, Paymaster......... | Mar.   5, 1777 | {Dismissed June 1, '78. Agreeable to the new arrangement |
| Lehancius DeKeyser, Adjt.......... | Nov. 15, 1775 | Resgn'd 10 Dec. '76 |
| John Rice, Adjt.................... | Dec. 10, 1776 | |
| Stephen Conger, Adjt.............. | Jan. 29, 1778 | Dismissed June 1, '78 |
| Nelverton Folkes, Qr. Mr.......... | Feb.   3, 1776 | Resgn'd Aug. 1, '76 |
| Patrick Rogers, Qr. Mr............ | Nov. 1776 | |
| Wm. Wommack, Qr. Mr........... | Jan. 1778 | Dismissed June 1, '78 |
| Wm. Kennon, Commissary......... | Sep. 1777 | |

## CLARK'S

(Pages 504-505, Vol. XIII)

Roll of Capt. Benjamin Coleman's Company, in 2nd N. C. Battalion, commanded by Col. John Patton, White Plains, Sept. 9, 1778.

| Name and Rank | Time Enlisted | War | Yrs. | Remarks |
|---|---|---|---|---|
| 1. Stephen Carman, Sgt......... | | 1 | | |
| 2. Peter Rhem, Sgt............. | Feb. 10, '77 | | | |
| 3. Abram Burgess, Sgt......... | | 1 | 3 | |
| 4. James Christian, Pri......... | May 19, '77 | | 3 | |
| 5. Mala Cotouch, Pri........... | Jan. 11, '77 | | 3 | |
| 6. William Harriss, Pri......... | Nov. 7, '76 | | | |
| 7. Akis Ellison, Pri............ | | 1 | | |
| 8. Josiah Lilley, Pri............ | Nov. 7, '76 | | 3 | On Light Infantry |
| 9. Jessy Wollard, Pri........... | | 1 | | |
| 10. John Squars, Pri............ | May 22, '77 | | 3 | |
| 11. Samuel Gainer, Pri.......... | | | 3 | |
| 12. Wallace White, Pri.......... | | 1 | | |
| 13. David Smith, Pri............ | Nov. 20, '76 | | 3 | |
| 14. Silas Linton, Pri............ | Aug. 7, '76 | | 3 | |
| 15. Thomas Jones, Pri.......... | Sept. 28, '77 | | 3 | |
| 16. Dudley Reardon, Pri........ | Aug. 25, '77 | | 3 | |
| 17. Charles Peters, Pri......... | | 1 | | |
| 18. Lewis Wilford, Pri.......... | Aug. 25, '77 | | 3 | |
| 19. Thomas Gaddy, Pri......... | Mch. 21, '76 | | 3 | |
| 20. Thomas Reasons, Pri........ | Aug. 5, '77 | | 3 | |
| 21. Osborn Clark, Pri........... | June 1, '77 | | 3 | |
| 22. Gardner Moy, Pr............ | May 22, '77 | | 3 | |
| 23. James Clark, Pri............ | Feb. 7, '77 | | 3 | |
| 24. Benjamin Aged, Pri......... | May 11, '76 | | 2½ | |
| 25. Norris Baker, Pri........... | Apr. 18, '76 | | 2½ | |
| 26. Thomas Campain, Pri....... | Apr. 18, '76 | | 2½ | |
| 27. John Garland, Pri.......... | Apr. 29, '76 | | 2½ | |
| 28. Fred'k Smith Pri............ | Dec. 5, '76 | | 3 | |
| 29. John Lewis, Pri............. | Aug. 1, '77 | | 3 | |
| 30. William Handley, Pri........ | July 28, '77 | | 3 | |
| 31. Richard Johnson, Pri........ | Feb. 9, '77 | | 3 | |
| 32. William Smith, Pri.......... | May 13, '77 | | 3 | |
| 33. James King, Pri............ | Aug. 1, '77 | | 3 | |
| 34. James Hughkins, Pri........ | Dec. 4, '76 | | 3 | |
| 35. Elijah Hunt, Pri............ | | 1 | | |
| 36. Charles Bright, Pri.......... | Aug. 7, '77 | | 3 | |
| 37. John Killingsworth, Pri...... | | 1 | | |
| 38. Abram Fowler, Pri.......... | | 1 | | |
| 39. Hardy Hukins, Pri.......... | May 1, '76 | | 2½ | |
| 40. William Richards, Pri........ | | 1 | | |
| 41. David Sweat, Pri........... | Sept. 5, '77 | | 3 | |
| 42. Job Branch, Pri............ | | 1 | | |
| 43. Stephen Truet, Pri.......... | July 1, '77 | | 3 | |
| 44. Thomas Lane, Pri.......... | May 1, '77 | | 3 | |
| 45. James Brasfield, Pri........ | July 5, '77 | | 3 | |
| 46. Joseph Cooper, Pri.......... | Nov. 17, '77 | | 3 | |
| 47. John O'Neal, Pri............ | Feb. 18, '77 | | 3 | |
| 48. James Pierce, Pri........... | Aug. 24, '77 | | 3 | |
| 49. James Richard, Pri.......... | Apr. 23, '77 | | 2½ | |
| 50. David Riskey, Pri.......... | Aug. 9, '77 | | 3 | |
| 51. Samuel Williams, Pri........ | Nov. 10, '77 | | 3 | |
| 52. Edward Magell, Pri......... | July 28, '77 | | 3 | |
| 53. Sikes Garress, Pri.......... | May 4, '77 | | | |
| 54. Moses Reed, Pri............ | " | | 3 | |

| Name and Rank | Time Enlisted | War | Yrs. | Remarks |
|---|---|---|---|---|
| 55. Edward Lucas, Pri............ | | 1 | | |
| 56. Marmaduke, Moor, Pri....... | Nov. 1, '77 | | 3 | |
| 57. Ben Atkins, Pri............. | Dec. 10, '77 | | 3 | |
| 58. Caleb Taylor, Pri........... | Nov. 5, '77 | | 3 | |
| 59. Burrell Loyd, Pri........... | | 1 | | |
| 60. John Jeffries, Pri............ | | | | |
| 61. William *.................. | | | | |
| 62. Thomas *.................. | | | | |

Ben. Coleman, Capt.   Sam'l Budd, 1st Lt.   Stephen Southall, Lt.
* (Surnames illegible) apparently erased.

Roll of Capt. Clement Hall's Company, in the 2nd Battalion, commanded by Col. John Patten, White Plains, Sept. 9, 1778. (Pages 506-507)

| Names | Time Enlisted | War | Yrs. | Remarks |
|---|---|---|---|---|
| 1. Bennet Morgan.............. | | | | |
| 2. John Hammon.............. | May 9 | | 2½ | |
| 3. John Dudley................ | Apr. 7 | | 3 | |
| 4. Henry Johnston............ | | 1 | | |
| 5. Robert Brownley........... | | 1 | | |
| 6. George Brownrigg.......... | July 7 | | 3 | |
| 7. Josiah Douge............... | | 1 | | |
| 8. Kader Phelps............... | May 1, '77 | | 3 | |
| 9. William Davis.............. | | 1 | | |
| 10. Franklin Truit.............. | | 1 | | |
| 11. Thomas Thomas............. | May 14, '76 | | 2½ | |
| 12. Clement Godfrey........... | | 1 | | |
| 13. James Harris................ | | 1 | | |
| 14. Eleamus Quinby............ | May 4, '76 | | 2½ | |
| 15. James Echols............... | | 1 | | |
| 16. John Delaney............... | Apr. 1, '76 | | 3 | |
| 17. James Amos................ | May 25, '77 | | 2½ | |
| 18. Hezekiah Shirmentine....... | Dec. 20, '76 | | 3 | |
| 19. James Martin............... | May 4, '77 | | 3 | |
| 20. Isaac Pivikins.............. | May 16, '77 | | 3 | |
| 21. Martin Black.............. | " | | 3 | |
| 22. John Steward.............. | | | 3 | |
| 23. Nicholas Irwin............. | Oct. 7, '76 | 1 | | |
| 24. Robert Watson............. | | 1 | | |
| 25. Demsey Marlow............ | July 1, '77 | | 3 | |
| 26. William Banks............. | | 1 | | |
| 27. Archibald Butes............ | | | 3 | |
| 28. James Martin............... | July 15, '76 | | 2½ | |
| 29. Robert Carter.............. | | | 2½ | |
| 30. Isaac Cornelius............. | May 14, '76 | | 2½ | |
| 31. Edward Lewis.............. | May 7, '76 | | 3 | |
| 32. Cadar Copeland............ | | | 3 | |
| 33. Thomas Davis.............. | | | 3 | |
| 34. Henry Martin.............. | Nov. 7, '76 | | 3 | |
| 35. John Smith................ | | | 3 | |
| 36. Asa Thomas............... | Apr. 29, '76 | | 2½ | |
| 37. Levi Right................. | May 7 | | 3 | |
| 38. William Gaskins........... | | 1 | | |
| 39. Joseph Casway............. | Mch. 26, '76 | | | |

| | Names | Time Enlisted | War | Yrs. | Remarks |
|---|---|---|---|---|---|
| 40. | William Caps | May 27, '77 | | 3 | |
| 41. | John Howell | June 17 | | 3 | |
| 42. | Demsey Jarkins | June 19 | | 3 | |
| 43. | Richard Morgan | July 26 | | 3 | |
| 44. | Charles Ellums | Oct. 28, '76 | | 2½ | |
| 45. | William Boon | | | 3 | |
| 46. | William Burnett | | | 3 | |
| 47. | Isaac Carter | | | 3 | |
| 48. | Willis Thompson | | | 3 | |
| 49. | Thomas Cox | June 1 | | 3 | |
| 50. | Douglas Carroll | | | 3 | |
| 51. | Peter McDougal | | 1 | | |
| 52. | John Weaver | | | 3 | |
| 53. | James Coggin | | 1 | | |
| 54. | Matthew Dawson | | 1 | | |
| 55. | Jacob Burke | | 1 | | |
| 56. | James Gifford | | | 3 | |
| 57. | Asa Davis | | 1 | | |
| 58. | Hardy Pierce | | | | ⎰Orderly at the Valley ⎱Forge |
| 59. | Adam Scott | | 1 | | ⎰Orderly at the Valley ⎱Forge |
| 60. | William Bryan | | | | |
| 61. | Marmaduke Maples | Jan. 1, '77 | | 3 | |
| 62. | John Carter | | 1 | | |
| 63. | John Sharpley | | 1 | | |
| 64. | William Butts | | | 3 | |
| 65. | James Saunders | | | 2½ | Sick, Yellow Swamp |
| 66. | David Vance | | | 2½ | "      "        " |
| 67. | Elijah Vance | | | 2½ | "      "        " |
| 68. | John Conner | | | 3 | Sick Valley Forge |
| 69. | Isaac Deal | | 1 | | |
| 70. | Sesar Santee | | | 3 | |
| 71. | John Hambleton | | 1 | | Sick Brunswick |
| 72. | Samuel Simpson | | | 2½ | Sick Valley Forge |
| 73. | Wm. Bugg | | | 2½ | Sick Yellow Swamp |
| 74. | John Mann | | | 3 | Sick Lancaster |
| 75. | Jacob Owens | | | 3 | |

Clem Hall, Capt.   Jesse Reed, Lieut.

## CLARK'S STATE RECORDS

Roll of Capt. John Ingles' Company, 2nd N. C. Battalion, commanded by Col. John Patton. Sept. 9, 1778.
(Pages 509, 510, 511. Vol XIII)

| | Names | Time Enlisted | War | Yrs. | Remarks |
|---|---|---|---|---|---|
| 1. | Solomon Berry, Sergt. | | 1 | | |
| 2. | Ransom Savage, Sergt. | June 7, '77 | | 3 | |
| 3. | Matthew Gallop, Sergt. | | 1 | | |
| 4. | Sampson Dillard, Corpl. | | 1 | | |
| 5. | Noah James, Corpl. | Nov. 7, '76 | | | |
| 6. | Dan Dunbarr, Corpl. | Jan. 12 | | | |
| 7. | Isaac Geldin Fifer | Nov. 7 | | | |
| 8. | Abell Littin, Drummer | Dec. 1 | | | |
| 9. | Thomas Anderson, Privt. | Dec. 18 | | | |
| 10. | John Berry, Privt. | Nov. 9 | 1 | | |
| 11. | Joseph Brown, Privt. | " | | | |

| Names | Time Enlisted | War | Yrs. | Remarks |
|---|---|---|---|---|
| 12. Balam Bullock.............. | | 1 | | |
| 13. John Curry................. | | 1 | | |
| 14. John Collings.............. | Mch. 18 | | 2½ | |
| 15. Shade Cowny............... | May 30, '77 | | | |
| 16. Richard Coddle............. | Nov. 1, '76 | | | |
| 17. Frederick Davis............ | Dec. 18 | | 3 | |
| 18. John Ember................. | July 26, '77 | | 3 | |
| 19. John Ellett................. | June 16 | | | |
| 20. Thomas Grigory............ | | 1 | | |
| 21. William Griffin............ | | 1 | | |
| 22. John Glover................ | Apr. 22, '76 | | 2½ | |
| 23. Kinchin Hollomon.......... | May 4 | | 2 | |
| 24. Samuel Littin............... | Dec. 18 | | 3 | |
| 25. John Lynch................. | | 1 | | |
| 26. Frederick Moore............ | | 1 | | |
| 27. Phillip Pinkum............. | Aug. 12, '77 | | 3 | |
| 28. John Ridgway.............. | | 1 | | |
| 29. James Rooper.............. | Apr. 7 | | 3 | |
| 30. John Stevens............... | | 1 | | |
| 31. Gideon Simmons............ | May 2 | | 3 | |
| 32. Benjamin Smith............ | Aug. 20 | | 3 | |
| 33. Corbin Waymouth.......... | Dec. 18, '76 | | 3 | |
| 34. William Williams........... | May 5 | | 2½ | |
| 35. William Thompson.......... | Apr. 26 | | 2½ | |
| 36. Hopkins Dye............... | Jan. 4, '77 | | 3 | |
| 37. Robert Fosett.............. | Nov. 20, '77 | | 3 | |
| 38. Nathan Ewell.............. | Aug. 29 | | 3 | |
| 39. Jeremiah Beamon........... | | 1 | | |
| 40. Giles Carter............... | Mch. 1 | | 3 | |
| 41. Malachi Malbone........... | | 1 | | |
| 42. Thomas Moore............. | | 1 | | |
| 43. Jeremiah Perrey............ | Apr. 29, '76 | | | |
| 44. Samuel Rowe.............. | Aug. 9, '76 | | | |
| 45. Caleb Smith............... | | 1 | | |
| 46. Darling Madree............ | Apr. 26, '76 | | | |
| 47. Josiah Stafford............ | July 5, '77 | | 3 | |
| 48. John Toxa................. | | 1 | | |
| 49. Henry Johnson............. | May 29 | | 3 | |
| 50. Thomas Spain.............. | Feb. 10 | | 3 | |
| 51. Isom Pulley................ | May 5, '76 | | 2½ | |
| 52. John Paterson.............. | | 1 | | |
| 53. Jacob Matthews............ | | 1 | | |
| 54. Thomas Brown............. | | 1 | | |
| 55. John Brooks............... | May 15 | | 2½ | |
| 56. William Drew.............. | | 1 | | |
| 57. Thomas Danagan........... | | 1 | | |
| 58. William Ferus............. | June 28, '77 | | 3 | |
| 59. Daniel Humphries.......... | Mch. 18, '76 | | 2½ | |
| 60. William Proctor............ | May 15 | | 2½ | |
| 61. William Seaborn........... | | 1 | | |
| 62. John Sheppard............. | | 1 | | |
| 63. John Taylor................ | | 1 | | |
| 64. Avery Tillet............... | | 1 | | |
| 65. Joseph Taylor.............. | | 1 | | |
| 66. John Young................ | May 3 | | 2¼ | |
| 67. Phillip Burges............. | | 1 | | |
| 68. Samuel Pope............... | May 5, '77 | | 3 | |
| 69. Thomas Daffell............ | Feb. 10 | | 3 | |
| 70. William Tryer............. | May 3, | | 2½ | |
| 71. Thomas Quin.............. | May 5, '77 | | 3 | |

John Ingles, Capt.   Arthur Cotgraves, Lieut.

[Pages 512, 513, 514]

Roll of Capt. Fenner's Company—2nd Battalion, commanded by Col. John Patton.
Camp White Plains—9 Sept., 1778

James Scandrett
Patrick Campbell
Thomas Smith

John Mathews ⎫
Jonathan Hopkins ⎬ Corporals
John Parkerson ⎭

Samuel Grey ⎫
Thomas Taunt ⎬ Drums and fifes

1. James Barnes
2. George Nichols
3. John Pond
4. John Thomas
5. Aaron Wilson
6. George Brooks
7. Jesse Taunt
8. William Taunt
9. Edward Hutchins
10. Isaiah Vick
11. Jesse Nelson
12. Thomas Cole
13. William Pate
14. James Brown
15. James Paramore
16. Jesse Rickerson
17. William Grey
18. Stephen Rogers
19. William Stewart
20. Michael Watson
21. Stephen Cook
22. Abraham Taylor
23. James Taylor
24. Charles Williamson
25. Thomas Blanchett
26. John Smith
27. John Lawson Arthur
28. Bagley Benson
29. David Dawley
30. Felix Simons
31. Thomas Tiffen
32. James Herrard
33. Thomas Angle
34. John Moseley
35. Benjamin Davis

36. Aaron Lambert
37. Joseph Babb
38. Daniel Johnston
39. Jordan Ammons
40. Thomas Carraway
41. Richard White
42. John Fook
43. Benjamin Womble
44. Hansford Whitley
45. William Peoples
46. Arthur Parker
47. Samuel Wheeler
48. Brazil Welsh
49. Ebenezer Hoskins
50. Isaac Carter
51. Elisha Lewis
52. Jesse McDowel
53. James Pierce
54. Henry Spill
55. Hardy Hines
56. David Grant
57. John Ellis
58. John Clark
59. William Baker
60. Francis Fox
61. Roger Parson
62. John Wallis
63. William Baker
64. Isascl Gregory
65. James Gilbert

⎧ Wm. Baker (59) sick at Georgetown
⎪ Wm. Baker (63) sick at Valley Forge
⎨ Robt. Fenner, Capt.
⎪ James Campen, Lieut.
⎩ Nathan Lawrence, 2nd Lieut.

## CLARK'S STATE RECORDS

[Page 515]

Roll of Col. John Patton's Company in the 2nd Battalion, commanded by Col. Patton. Sept. 9, 1778.

1. David Spiers, Sergt. Majr.
2. Authur Boice, Qr. M. Sergt.
3. John Lacy, Sergt.
4. Phinehas Latham, Sergt.

5. Reuben Yerberry, Sergt.
6. Phillip Mason, Drum Majr.
7. Thomas Tiack, Fife Majr.
8. John Worsley, Drummer

9. John Darren, Fifer
10. James Tisen, Corpl.
11. Benjamin Johnson, Corpl.
12. Peter Dunnick, Corpl.
13. Epps Spain, privt.
14. Joseph Nash, privt.
15. Joseph Messick
16. Francis Williams
1˘. John King
18. Thomas Garrott
19. Noah Fair
20. Thomas Waldren
21. Simon Alderson
22. William Sexton
23. John Davis
24. James Erven
25. James Gamberlin
26. Eli Rogers
27. Miles Privett
28. Joseph Bailey
29. John Clements
30. Joseph Hartley
31. Thomas Bryant
32. James Underhill
33. Daniel Venters
34. William King
35. Henry Singleton
36. William Caps
37. Benjamin Messer
38. William Charlton
39. William Smith
40. John Conner, Sr.
41. Elisha Williams

42. Robert Meeks
43. William Meeks
44. Isaac Gallop
45. Abraham Hays
46. Joseph Aldridge
47. Cornelas Bray
48. Frederick Blanchet
49. James Reade
50. William Dove
51. Henry Tison
52. Hugh Stephenson
53. James Phelps
54. James Ives
55. Enos Bizzel
56. James Nicholas
57. Arthur Tayner
58. James Townen
59. John Myers
60. William Cox
61. Bryant Worsley
62. John Cooke
63. John Peacock
64. James Simons
65. George Moye
66. Josiah Davis
67. Alexander Scull
68. James Barron
69. David Poe
70. Jesse Wooten
71. John Striker
{ John Craddock, Capt.
{ William Terrell, Lieut.

## CLARK'S STATE RECORDS

[Pages 517, 518, 519, 520]

Roll of Lieut. Col. Harney's Company, 2nd N. C. Battalion, commanded by Col. John Patton. Sept. 9, 1778.

1. John Wood
2. Abel McPherson
3. William Robinson
4. Shubal Claghorn
5. James Griffin
6. James Bundy
7. William Spain
8. Jacob White, Jr.
9. William Boyd
10. Mason Broom
11. Willis Barrow
12. Robert Chumner
13. Zachariah Davis
14. Abraham Denny
15. Robt. Ellis
16. Fred'k. Hathcock
17. Jesse Lane

18. Melone Mullen
19. Wm. Nichols
20. James Purdie
21. James Moore
22. John Raiper
23. Phillip Shackly
24. John Thomas
25. Sutton Truheek
26. Francis Westerdale
27. Joel Wall
28. George Willis
29. Duncan Curry
30. Jabesh Elliot
31. John Wallace
32. Shad'k. Cummins
33. Thos. Harrison
34. Jacob White, Senr.

35. Ben Collins
36. Dan'l. Miller
37. Moses Brown
38. Joseph Phillips
39. Isaac Fonville
40. Major Glanders
41. John Little
42. Elijah Cotton
43. Jo. Bartholomew
44. Rich'd. Webster
45. Thos. Jones
46. John Dew
47. Michael McKeel
48. Valentine Lucas
49. William Reason
50. Jesse Shute
51. Absalom Spires
52. Josiah Stringer
53. William Thomas
54. Phillip Jones
55. Zachariah Hathcock
56. Major Russell
57. William Pope

58. David Dufnel
59. Wm. Dufnel
60. Willis Hastings
61. Arch. Hood
62. John Hill
63. James Stewart
64. Jacob Hewling
65. William Smith
66. Henry Miller
67. John Warner
68. Robt. Raiper
69. Joseph Alexander
70. Charles Burke
71. Ben Bridges
72. Thos. Davidson
73. Joseph McGraw
74. Amos Lewis
75. Michael Delaney
76. Ben Simmons
77. Edmund Griffin
{ Chas. Stewart, Lt.
{ Stephen Slade, Ensign.

## CLARK'S STATE RECORDS

[Vol. XIII. Pages 521-23]
Roll of Major Hardy Murfree's Company in 2nd North Carolina Battalion, commanded by Col. John Patton. Sept. 9, 1778.

1. Anthony Crutcher, Sergt.
2. John Poulson, Sergt.
3. Samuel Stringer, Sergt.
4. John Mardsay, Corpl.
5. Willis Wiggins, Corpl.
6. Pearson Peal, Corpl.
7. William Ponder, Drummer
8. Ezekiel Whaley, Fifer
9. Kadar Blanton, privt.
10. Thomas Metisuck
11. Hardy Bird
12. William Saunderson
13. Samuel Baxter
14. James Pulley
15. John Harvey
16. Balitha Tilmon
17. Miles Knight
18. William Scott
19. Andrew Wilkins
20. James Roberts
21. Arthur Foorms
22. Reuben Knight
23. William Sweat
24. William Thurston
25. Robert Jinkins
26. William Mitchell
27. Abel Edmunds

28. Jacob Brabsy
29. William Farmer
30. Spinencoy Raifield
31. John Skinner
32. Thomas Dyson
33. John Harigrooves
34. Humphrey Callahan
35. Thomas Scott
36. John Husk
37. William Goggard
38. Samuel Carter
39. William Church
40. Hezekiah Jones
41. Arthur Whilley
42. Mathew Herring
43. John Skean
44. Nathaneal Cooper
45. Ephriam Hooks
46. Alexander Flood
47. John Tilmon
48. Theophilus Hays
49. Andrew Saunders
50. William Swinson
51. Francis Copes
52. Robert Williams
53. Richard Roberts
54. Morson Williams

55. William Powell
56. Brien Smith
57. John Parrish
58. John Stringer
59. Stephen Emery
60. Francis Sumner
61. Archib'd. Henderson
62. Mark Waycroft
63. Joseph Seaborn
64. Isaac Rhoads
65. Michael Bull

66. David Wall
67. Elisha Mills
68. Thomas Pierce
69. Thomas Pridgen
70. Abraham Therrell
71. William Jones
72. William Tilman
73. John Cummins
74. Solomon Jinnett
{ Thos. Evans, Lieut.
{ Rich'd. Andrews, Ensn.

## CLARK'S STATE RECORDS

[Pages 524, 525, 526]

Roll of Capt. Thomas Armstrong's Company, 2nd N. C. Battalion, commanded by Col. John Patton. Sept. 10, 1778.

1. Arch'd. Boyle
2. Sam'l. Gover
3. Charles Webb
4. John Richardson
5. Edward Stradley
6. Thomas Best
7. Thomas McDaniel
8. John Smith
9. David Ambrose
10. Frederick Bates
11. Caleb Dolly
12. Joshua Harvey
13. Skidmore Squires
14. George Phillips
15. Wm. Brian
16. Francis Thorogood
17. George Cole
18. Jeremiah Smith
19. Hezekiah Linton
20. Peter Harrell
21. Bigford Garriss
22. Drury Binham
23. Thomas Jirmins
24. John Upton
25. Benjamin Dun
26. Robert Jackson
27. James Jones
28. James Sirks
29. Molaha Wiggins
30. Isaac Hays
31. Joshua Webb
32. William Flood
33. John Webb
34. James Wiggins
35. Sterling Dun
36. John Anderson

37. Stephen Chance
38. John Cotton
39. Philamon Chance
40. Holland Johnston
41. Henry Albertson
42. David Haulborn
43. Jacob Jones
44. Amose Passmore
45. John Colwell
46. John Atkinson
47. James Bond
48. Thomas Smith
49. Sovereign Blokam
50. Daniel White
51. Marmaduke Barfield
52. Barnabas Davant
53. Peter Bateman
54. Abraham Tison
55. William Green
56. Richard Downams
57. Thompson Curry
58. John Blanchard
59. Nath'l. Dobey
60. George Marshall
61. Drury Ham
62. Robert Acock
63. William Williamson
64. Charles Butler
65. John Bullock
66. Henry Starke
67. John Barganiear
68. Simon Smith
69. Elijah Hanish
{ Thos. Armstrong, Capt.
{ Chas. Gerrard, 1 Lieut.
{ James Verrier, Ensign.

## CLARK'S STATE RECORDS

[Page 527, Vol. 13]

Return of the Soldiers of the 2nd. N. C. Battalion reinlisted during the war agreeable to Resolve of Congress and General orders. March 12, 1779.

### Col. Patton's Company

1. James Ives
2. James Simmons
3. James Read
4. John Durremfiss

### Lt. Col. Harney's Company

5. George Willis
6. James Stewart
7. Zachariah Hatchcock
8. Shad'k. Cummins
9. Joel Wall
10. Jesse Lane
11. John Wallace
12. Charles Burke
13. John Gunnell

### Maj. Murfree's Company

14. Pearson Peal
15. Miles Knight
16. John Stringer
17. Thomas Dyson
18. Mathew Herrin
19. Mark Haycraft
20. Ezekial Wheely
21. Belisha Tilman
22. William Swinson
23. Patrick Brown
24. Andrew Wilkins
25. Samuel Baxter
26. Hardy Bird
27. John Skien

### Capt. William's Company, L. I.

28. Elisha Grant
29. Thomas Geddy
30. John Howell
31. John Smith
32. William King
33. Moses Brown
34. John Clemmons
35. Joseph Lilley
36. Henry Martin
37. Jesse Shute
38. John Parkerson
39. Abraham Houston
40. James Ansley
41. Henry Singleton
42. Bryant Worsley

### Capt. Hall's Company

43. William Burnett
44. Joseph Causway
45. Caesar Santee
46. Kadar Copeland
47. Dempsey Marlo
48. John Delany
49. Bennett Morgan
50. George Browning
51. John Stewart
52. Marmaduke Malpes
53. Levi Wright

### Capt. Coleman's Company

54. Thomas Jones
55. Arch. Butts
56. James Hukins
57. Lewis Wilford
58. James King
59. David Sweat
60. George Wallace
61. Edward Majett
62. James Pearce
63. William Handley
64. Marmaduke Moore
65. Stephen Trent
66. William Harris
67. Malachi Cotanch
68. David Smith
69. William Smith
70. David Riskey

### Capt. Fenner's Company

71. Richard White
72. Thomas Carraway
73. William Stewart
74. Jesse Nelson

*Capt. Ingle's Company*

75. Philip Pinkum                        76. Thomas Anderson

*Capt. Armstrong's Company*

77. Drury Bynum                          79. John Upton
78. Thomas Smith                         80. John Adkerson
[Page 530]
81. James Wiggins                        83. Robt. Jackson
82. Sterling Dean

[Page 532, Vol. XIII]

## CLARK'S STATE RECORDS—SENATE JOURNAL
### 19th January, 1779

When the following members appeared:

James Coor                          William Thompson
Elisha Battle                       Henry Rhodes
Robert Harris                       Mr. Speaker
Edward Jones                        Thomas Respass
Kenneth McKenzie                    James Kenan
Ben Exum                            Alexius Mson Forster
Jeremiah Frazier                    Charles Robeson
John Brown                          Alexander Martin
John Ashe                           Robert Sumner
William Russell                     William Graham
Thomas Owen                         Nathan Boddie
Thomas Harvey                       Ebenezer Folsom
Michael Rogers                      John Kinchen
Robert Salter                       Robert Irwin
William Shepherd                    John Birdsong
Luke Sumner                         John Chiles

[Page 784, Vol. XIII]

## CLARK'S STATE RECORDS—HOUSE JOURNAL
### State of North Carolina.   In the House of Commons, May, 1779

At a General Assembly begun and held at Smithfield, on the Third Day of May, in the year of our Lord One Thousand seven Hundred and Seventy-Nine, and in the third year of the Independence of the said State, being the first Session of this Assembly.

The Sherriff's and other returning officers within this State certified that the following persons were duly Elected as members of the Commons House of Assemby for the respective Counties and Towns as follows, Viz.:

Anson—Stephen Miller, Charles Medlock.
Brunswick—
Beaufort—Robert Trip, John Kennedy.
Bladen—Thomas Brown, Samuel Cain.
Bertie—
Burke—Thomas Whitson, William Morrison.
Craven—Hardy Bryan, Benjamin Williams.
Chowan—Thomas Benbury, William Boyd.
Cumberland—Robert Cochran, Robert Rowan.
Chatham—Jonathan Harper, John Luttrell.
Currituck—
Camden—Willis Bright, Caleb Grandy.

Carteret—
Caswell—William Moore, Peter Farrow.
Dobbs—Thomas Gray, Jesse Cobb.
Duplin—Richard Clinton, James Gillespie.
Edgecombe—William Haywood, Ethelred Exum.
Franklin—Thomas Sherrod, Green Hill.
Granville—Thomas Person, Philemon Hawkins, Jr.
Guilford—James Hunter, Daniel Gillespie.
Gates—Jacob Hunter, William Baker.
Hertford—William Wynns, Authur Cotton.
Hyde—
Halifax—
Johnston—Lewis Bryan, Phillip Raiford.
Jones—Frederick Harget, Samuel Hill Lincoln.
[Page 785]
Martin—Samuel Smithwick, Samuel Williams.
Montgomery—John Kimbrough, Solomon Gross.
Mechlinburg, Caleb Phifer, David Wilson.
New Hanover, John A. Campbell, Timothy Bloodworth.
Northampton—Robert Peebles, James Vaughan.
Nash—William Horn, Thomas Hunter.
Orange—William M. Crawley, Mark Patterson.
Onslow—James Howard, Edward Starkey.
Perquimans—
Pasquotank—
Pitt—James Gorham, John Williams.
Rowan—
Randolph—
Rutherford—
Surrey—Gray Bynum, Frederick Miller.
Tyrrell—Benjamin Spruill, Joshua Swain.
Wilkes—
Washington—
Warren—Joseph Hawkins, John Macon.
Wake—Thomas Hines, John Hunter, Jr.

### Towns

Wilmington—William Hooper, Gray Bynum.
New Bern—Richard Cogdell, Green Hill.
Edenton—Robert Smith, Thomas Sherrod.
Halifax—Henry Montford, John Macon.
Hillsborough—Robert Rowan.
Salisbury—Robert Cochran.

Pursuant to which the following members appeared and qualified by taking the several Oaths by Law appointed for the qualification of Members of the General Assembly, subscribed the same and took their seats, to wit, Messrs.,

| | | |
|---|---|---|
| William Haywood | William Horn | Fred Harget |
| William McCrawley | Thomas Hunter | Samuel Hill |
| Mark Patterson | Richard Cogdell | Thomas Person |
| Wiliam Morrison | Lewis Bryan | Samuel Cain |
| David Wilson | Thomas Hines | Thomas Gray |
| Caleb Phifer | John Hinton | Gray Bynum |
| Stephen Miller | Timothy Bloodworth | Green Hill |
| [Page 786] | Jesse Cobb | Thomas Sherrod |
| Charles Medlock | Thomas Benbury | John Macon |

Robert Rowan
Robert Cochran
[Page 399, Vol. XV]
Henry Montford
John Williams
Joseph Hawkins
James Gorham
Daniel Gillespies
James Hunter
Jonathan Harper
Thomas Brown

Samuel Williams
Authur Cotton
Hardy Bryan
Phil Hawkins
John Kennedy
James Howard
Philip Raiford
James Gillespie
John Luttrell
John A. Campbell

Robert Tripp
Willis Bright
Richard Clinton
Solomon Gross
James Vaughan
Peter Farrow
Joshua Swain
Benjamin Spruill
Jacob Hunter
William Boyd

## CLARK'S STATE RECORDS

Extract from Pay Roll of Capt. Elisha Rhodes' Company of the 1st N. C. Regiment of Militia, commanded by Col. Samuel Jarves.  June 5, '80.

1. Elisha Rhodes, Capt.
2. James Swinhow Grover, Lieut.
3. Stephen Buck, Ensn.
4. Joseph Sanderson, Ensn.
5. Peter Pilant, Corpl.
6. Thomas Thomas, Fifer
7. John Doers, privt.
8. Jas. Wilks, privt.
9. Jacob Bass, privt.
10. Geo. Harrison, privt.
11. Edw'd Wilson, privt.
12. Henry Holland, privt.
13. John Cockran, privt.
14. Ben. Sorrel, privt.
15. Christ Harrell, privt.
16. Levi Johnson, privt.
17. Fred'k. Holland, privt.
18. Blake Raby, privt.
19. Shadh. Harrell, privt.
20. St. McDuel

### GATES COUNTY MEN

21. Edw'd Pilant, privt.
22. Jesse Jones, privt.
23. Bray Jones, privt.
24. Elisha Osborne, privt.
25. Jos. Carter, privt.
26. Tilberias Purvis, privt.
27. Elisha Ellis, privt.
28. Uriah Ure, privt.
29. Samuel Williams, privt.
30. Reub. Sparkman, privt.
31. Asa Harrell, privt.
32. John Hamilton, privt.
33. Josiah Harrell, privt.
34. Arthur Williams, privt.

[Page 400]

## CLARK'S STATE RECORDS

Pay Roll of Capt. John Harvey's Company of the 1st Regiment of Militia, commanded by Col. Samuel Jarvis.

1. John Harvey, Capt.
2. John Creery, Lieut.
3. Frederick Nixon, Ensn.
4. John Ming, Sergt.
5. John Davis, Sergt.
6. Alexander Stafford, Corpl.
7. Thomas Penrice, Corpl.
8. James Chew, privt.
9. John Bains, privt.
10. Benjamin Baterman, privt.
11. William Turner, privt.
12. Benjamin Turner, privt.
13. Miles Turner, privt.
14. James Harman, privt.
15. William Winget, privt.
16. Joseph Theach, privt.
17. James Goodwin, privt.
18. John Ellis, privt.
19. Green Thach, privt.
20. Jas. Boush, privt.
21. Ezekiel Ears, privt.
22. David Overton, privt.
23. John Tucker, privt.
24. Charles Jones, privt.
25. Francis Sutton, privt.
26. John Leming, privt.
27. Richard Hatfield, privt.
28. Thos. Ray, privt.

[Page 509, Vol. XV, 1780-1781]

A list of Capt. Wood's Horse in Colo. Malmedy's Regiment.

1. Solomon Wood, Capt.
2. Mark Myatt, Lt.
3. Thomas Gray, Cornet
4. Bryant McCullers, Sergt.
5. Amos Wheeler, Sergt.
6. Charles Johnson, Corpl.
7. Bolen Liphot, Corpl.
8. Charles Lane
9. Rich'd. Lane
10. John Myatt
11. Russell Jones
12. John Mallaby
13. James Tate
14. Thos. Wilmoth
15. Thos. Driver
16. John Orr
17. Charles Cardin
18. Abraham Lumbley
19. Ezekiah Utley, deserted
20. John Humphries
21. Benjamin Pullum
22. Elijah Pope
23. Joseph Ward
24. Nicholas Atkins
25. Elisha Railey
26. Traves Johnson
27. James Lewis
28. Michael Tedrick
29. Ephraim Williams (Quit camp, sent a substitute who was accepted)
30. David McCullers
31. Andrew McKleroy
32. Reubin McKleroy
33. John McKleroy
34. Ford Butler
35. John Hunt
36. William Ambrose
37. Robt. Humphries
38. Benjamin House
39. Nimrod House
40. Joseph Gray
41. William Wheeler
42. John Armstrong
43. Runnell Allen
44. Thomas Barns
45. Robert Martin
46. Frederick Beesley
47. Sion Perry
48. Gideon Allen
49. John Pool
50. Robert Johnson
51. William Hazewood
52. Roland Williams
53. Griffin Hazewood
54. James Sexton
55. Samuel Sexton
56. Alexander Boling, in the comp. of Capt. Patterson quit the camp without leave.
57. Thomas Greene, in the comp. of Capt. Patterson quit the camp without leave, but returned 3 weeks after.
58. John Watson, of Capt. Moore's comp., sent on errand and never returned.
59. Henson Utter, a light horse, of Orange County, left camp without leave.

*Aug. 23, 1781*

60. John Fitz Garrold ⎫
61. Jesse Lane ⎪
62. Peter Roberson ⎬ Gunstockers
63. Thomas Neal ⎭
64. Zachariah Dillard ⎫
65. Icham Scott ⎪ Timbergetters for
66. William Curlew ⎬ Wagons, Etc.
67. Jesse Rowan ⎭
68. John Barrot ⎫
69. James Fawcett ⎬ Wagon Makers
70. Rich'd. Thompson ⎭
71. James Amis
72. William Stephinson ⎫
73. Thomas Collom ⎪
74. Thomas Tuchor ⎪
75. Joseph Hawkins ⎬ Saddlers
76. William Watson ⎪
77. David Pugh ⎪
78. John Hews ⎪
79. William Sikes ⎭
80. Joshua Jones ⎫
81. Joshua Gammon ⎬ Canteen Makers
82. Henry Overstreet ⎭
83. William Trewathan ⎫
84. Thomas Bird ⎪ Shoe makers to
85. Robert Thompson ⎪ furnish shoes
86. James Turner ⎬ clear of expense
87. James Carlisle ⎪ to the public.
88. John Knight ⎪
89. Willis Halyon ⎭
90. Geo. Ware ⎫
91. Nickolas Bryant ⎪
92. Benj. Bell ⎬ Taylors
93. Joel Wooten ⎪
94. William Campbell ⎭
95. Thomas Hines, express rider for 12 months.

[Page 638]

Names of the officers who were killed and wounded in the action of the Eutaw Springs. Sept. 8, 1781.

NORTH CAROLINA BRIGADE

Capt. Goodman  ⎫
Capt. Goodwin  ⎬ Killed
Lieut. Porterfield ⎪
Lieut. Dillain ⎭

Capt. Hadley  ⎫
Lieut. Dixon  ⎪
Lieut. Andrews ⎬ Wounded
Lieut. Dudley ⎪
Ensn. Moore   ⎪
Ensn. Lamb    ⎭

CLARK'S STATE RECORDS

[Pages 718, 719.  Vol. XV]

Roll of Col. Thomas Clark's Company, 1st N. C. Battalion, commanded by Col. Thomas Clark.  Sept. 8, 1778.  (Book of "Army Returns" No. 27, P. 21).

1. Isaiah Pare, Sergt.
2. William Stanfast
3. Benj. Crab
4. Edward Howell, Corpl.
5. Henry Barksdale
6. Caleb Thomas, Drummer
7. William Howe, Fifer
8. Isle Simmons
9. Clement Smith
10. John Boggs
11. George Burges
12. Joseph King
13. Thomas Castle
14. Joseph McDonald
15. Joel Ramsey
16. William Maines
17. Richard Martin
18. David Basmore
19. John Barnes
20. Robt. Herman (?)
21. Patrick Scantling
22. Henry Mires
23. John Lafferty
24. John Hughes
25. John Ross
26. John Call
27. Jesse Boice
28. George White
29. Richard Tucker
30. Hugh Harris
31. John Davis
32. John Needham
33. John Clinton
34. Jacob Pearce
35. William Dillard
36. Thomas Kelly
37. John Lufman
38. Jesse Doughty
39. Geo. Raibourn
40. Joseph Davidson
41. William Cooper
42. Ezekiel White
43. John Barrow
44. Thomas Newburn
45. Cornelius Larry
46. Josiah Miller
47. Thomas Smith
48. Solomon Seymore
49. Thomas Moore
50. Peter Burges
51. Wilson Liscombe
52. John McLaughlan
53. Josiph Mitchell
54. John Bryant
55. Lewis Ralph
56. Samoul Morrow
57. Hugh Parks
58. Thomas Parker
59. William Auldridge
60. Richmond Terryl
61. Martin Campbell
62. Ezekiel Bogs
63. Osborn Dillard
64. Daniel Freeman
65. Lewis Beddlehizer
66. James Raney
67. Powell Riggans
68. George Glenn
69. John Pendergrass
70. Thomas Degnum
71. John Downes
72. Jeremiah Dailey
73. Charles Murray
74. Thomas Gilmore
75. Hugh Huston
76. John Evans
77. Jesse Cox
78. John Tipper

## CLARK'S STATE RECORDS

[Page 724. Vol. XV]

Roll of Lt. Colonel Mebane's Company of 1st N. C. Battalion, commanded by Colonel Thomas Clark. (Army Returns, Book 27, P. 22.) Sept. 8, 1778.

1. Benjamin Hodge, Sergt.
2. Rob Homes, Sergt.
3. Peter Raney, Sergt.
4. Thomas Modling, Corpl.
5. Thomas Pittyjohn, Corpl.
6. James Williams, Corpl.
7. William Lippincott, Drum
8. John Midsleya, Fife
9. Thomas Fee
10. Samuel Chappel
11. Phillip Britton
12. William Logan
13. James Britton
14. James Willey
15. Jacob Lane
16. Francis Dugan
17. Zebulon Pratt
18. Joseph Williams
19. William Brown
20. John Rogers
21. John Bartee
22. Elisha Modlin
23. Thomas May
24. William Williams
25. Isaac Howard
26. Isaac Reddick
27. Thomas Hendricks
28. William Boswell
29. Caleb Overton
30. Samuel Overton
31. Zebulon Modlin
32. William Mullin
33. Proctor Hogan
34. John Deal
35. Martin Miller
36. William Epps
37. Thomas Brannon
38. Mallica Chew
39. Peter Williams
40. Samuel Price
41. William Roberts
42. James Ferrill
43. David Corzzorte
44. Ebenezer Hewitt
45. Howell Gilliam
46. Joseph Keys
47. William Hawkins
48. James Britnell
49. David Donaldson
50. Elisha Bond
51. George Bruce
52. William Poore
53. John Conneway
54. Richard Mullen
55. Michael Scantling (?)
56. John Lock
57. Arthur Rogers
58. David Brown
59. Henry Harris
60. Peter Hatrock
61. Spencer Donaldson
62. David Bullock
63. Ripley Copeland
64. James Sutherland
65. Phillip Watson
66. Chas. Rozer
67. Thomas Norman
68. Edward Harris
69. Enoch King
70. Miller Modling
71. John Bane (?)
72. James Anthoney
73. William Seamore
74. John Carter
75. William Stumm
76. William Gough
77. Jarreed Craig

Robert Nicholson, Lieut.
Thomas Pasteur, 2nd Lt.
Acting Ensign.

## CLARK'S STATE RECORDS

Roll of Captain Griffith John McRee's Company of the 1st N. C. Battalion, commanded by Col. Thomas Clark. ("Army Returns," Book 27, P. 23).

1. James McLelland, Sgt.
2. John Jones, Sgt.
3. Geo. Ammins, Sgt.
4. William Campbell, Corp.
5. Hezekiah Barns, Corp.
6. John Matlock, Corp.
7. Daniel Thompson, Drummer
8. Robert Gessum, Fifer
9. Martin Bullock
10. George Gasey
11. Levi Weeks
12. Joel Dixon

13. Benj. Ray
14. Peter McGee
15. Edward Kelly
16. John Perry
17. Frederick Desern
18. William Jackson
19. John Kirk
20. Nathan Durham
21. John Carter
22. Theophilus Weeks
23. John Wood
24. Alex Ballentine
25. Thomas Baker
26. Miles Thrift
27. William Rose
28. James Lezar
29. Ransom Prewitt
30. David Pendergrass
31. John Jackson
32. Thomas Garey
33. Joel Gunter

34. William Parr
35. John Carter, Sr.
36. Joshua Prewitt
37. Thomas Breece
38. John Conner
39. John Nash
40. Sylas Dollerhide
41. Willobey Prescote
42. Robert Lynn (?)
43. Henry Colston
44. Drury Ward
45. Richard Rabsby
46. Benj. Johnson
47. James Caruthers
48. Thomas Caruthers
49. Robert Nelson
50. John Donaldby
51. Nathan Freeman
52. Joseph Reynolds
53. William Dennis

## CLARK'S STATE RECORDS

[Page 671. Vol. XVI]

List of officers, prisoners of war, Nov. 26, 1782.
Col. Thomas Clark, N. C., taken 12, May, 1780.
Col. John Patten, N. C., taken 12, May, 1780.
Maj. John Nelson, N. C., taken 12, May, 1780.
Capt. Kedar Ballard, N. C., taken 12, May, 1780.
Capt. John Ingles, N. C., taken 12, May, 1780.
Capt. John Craddock, N. C., taken 12, May, 1780.
Capt. John Summers, N. C., taken 12, May, 1780.
Capt. George Bradley, N. C., taken 12, May, 1780.
Capt. Joseph Montford, N. C., taken 12, May, 1780.
Capt. James Reed, N. C., taken Sept. 12, 1781.
Capt. Lieut. Phil Jones, N. C., taken May 12, 1780.
Capt. Lieut. Charles Stewart, N. C., taken May 12, 1780.
Capt. Lieut. William Fawn, N. C., taken May 12, 1780.
Capt. Lieut. Thos. Callender, N. C., taken May 12, 1780.
Lieut. James Tatum, N. C., May 12, 1780.
Lieut. Wm. Hargrove, N. C., taken May 12, 1780.
Lieut. Jesse Reed, N. C., taken 8 Sept., 1781.
Lieut. John Clendennin, N. C., taken 8 Sept., 1781.
Lieut. Samuel Budd, N. C., taken 8 Sept., 1781.
Surgeon James N. Greene, N. C., taken 13 May, 1780.
Note: (Those captured 12 May, 1780, were surrendered at fall of Charleston, and those on Sept. 8, 1781 in the Battle of Eutaw Springs.)

## CLARK'S STATE RECORDS

[Page 1054. Vol. XVII]

Pay Roll of Capt. Alexander Whitehall's Co. of the 1st N. C. Reg'd. of militia, commanded by Col. Sam'l. Jarvis. 1780.

1. Alexander Whitehall, Capt.
2. Thos. Jarvis, Lieut.
3. Hezekiah Wordley, Lieut.

4. Thos. Davis, Lt.
5. Griffin Doug, Ens'n.
6. Randall Jones, Sergt.

7. Charles Diar, Sergt.
8. Hilary Hanars, Corpl.
9. Jacob Dowdy, Corpl.
10. Jacob Gregory, Dmr.
11. Cornelius Gregory, Fifer

1. Henry Woodhouse, pt.
2. John Bacon, pt.
3. Thomas Sanderson, pt.
4. David Hill, pt.
5. Joshua Ball, pt.
6. Joshua Tabor, pt.
7. Elisha Kite, pt.
8. Joseph Jones, pt.
9. Wm. McKoy, pt.
10. William Williams, pt.
11. Samuel Gregory, pt.
12. Jarris Allen, pt.
13. James Parker, pt.
14. Colin Cook, pt.
15. Peter Camp, pt.
16. Jacob Smith, pt.
17. Jonathan Case, pt.
18. John Fourband, pt.
19. John Sally, pt.
20. Adam Seemore, pt.
21. Jos. White, pt.
22. Devotion White, pt.
23. Thos. Sawyer, pt.
24. Robb Bell, pt.
25. Amos Upton, pt.

26. Henry Upton, pt.
27. Nathan Bell, pt.
28. Jos. Michel, pt.
29. John Sicks, pt.
30. Caleb Gregory, pt.
31. Henry Keeton, pt.
32. Hez'kl. Cartwright, pt.
33. Robb Lowry, pt.
34. James Spence, pt.
35. Samuel Spence, pt.
[Page 1055]
36. John Wooten, pt.
37. Thos. Wooten, pt.
38. Joel Leek, pt.
39. Timothy Meeds, pt.
40. Thos. Casey, pt.
41. Daniel Lister, pt.
42. William Boyd, pt.
43. Reuben Davis, pt.
44. Joab Simson, pt.
45. Benj. Lanyard, pt.
46. David Harris, pt.
47. Clabb Glasgow, pt.
48. Devotion Davis, pt.
49. Jos. Banks, pt.
50. Meeds White, pt.
51. William Deel, pt.
52. Nicholas Jordan, pt.
53. Sam'l. Ray, pt.
54. Severn Scott, pt.

## CLARK'S STATE RECORDS

[Pages 1057-8, Vol. XVII]

Pay Roll, 2nd N. C. Reg't. of militia, Capt. Augustus Spain's Co., formerly under command of Col. Benj. Exum, now under Col. Sam'l. Jarvis of 1st Reg.

Augustus Spain, Capt.
Jno. Reddick, Lieut.
Nathan Godfrey, Ensn.
William Spencer, Ensn.
1. Thos. Worsley, Sergt.
2. David Everett, Sergt.
3. Peter Stephens, Corpl.
4. Micajah Savage, Corpl.
5. Joel Nichols, Corpl.
6. Stephen Cader, Corpl.
7. Isaac Stocks, Corpl.
8. Bailey Munger, Corpl.
9. Amos Mayo, Corpl.
10. John Smith, Corp.
11. Elijah Moore, Corpl.
12. Micajah Bull, Corpl.
13. Timothy Collins, Corpl.
14. Wm. Norton, Corpl.
15. Jno. King, Corpl.

16. Jno. Nelson, Corpl.
17. Samuel Spook, Corpl.
18. Henry Warren, Corpl.
19. Joshua Gard, Corpl.
20. Thos. Richardson, Corpl.
21. Thos. Ammons, Corpl.
22. Wm. Smith, Corpl.
23. Wm. Justice, Corpl.
24. David Justice, Corpl.
25. Allen Glover, Corpl.
26. Lemuel Parker, Corpl.
27. Benj. Glover, Corpl.
28. Benj. Salisbury, Corpl.
29. Solomon Jackson, Corpl.
30. Philip Jean, Corpl.
31. Augustin Caltrip, Corpl.
32. Jas. Caltrip, Corpl.
33. Gideon Pegram, Corpl.
34. Aaron Cox, Corpl.

35. Moses Cox, Corpl.
36. Jacob Wiliferd, Corpl.
37. Nathan Brake, Corpl.
38. Wm. Gad, Corpl.
39. Roan Spicer, Corpl.
40. Samuel Moore, Corpl.
41. Isac Coyed, Corpl.
42. James Briemfield, Corpl.
43. Jonah Sunderlin, Corp.
44. John Hugo Mannen, Corpl.
45. Abraham Johnston, Corpl.
[Page 1058]

46. Jesse Riden, Corpl.
47. Micajah Heard, Corpl.
48. Rich'd. Timberlake, Corpl.
49. Jesse Crown, Corpl.
50. Henry Kelly, Corpl.
51. Jno. Omet, Corpl.
52. Francis Mundine, Corpl.
53. Wright Bass, Corpl.
54. William Caleb, Corpl.
55. Peter Smith, Corpl.
56. Isom Norton, Corpl.
57. Wm. Norton, Corpl.

N. B.—Faithfully copied from State Records, all names from 2 to 57, Corpls., we venture this is a misprint, from 4 to 57 probably privates.

## CLARK'S STATE RECORDS

[Page 1059, Vol. XVII]

Pay Roll, of Wm. Earl's of the 1st N. C. Regt., commanded by Col. Sam'l. Jarvis.

William Earl, Capt.
Earl Venelson, Lieut.
John Smithers, Ensn.
Thomas Barnes, Ensn.
James Dalmer, Ensn.
1. Aaron Harkins, Sergt.
2. John McDaniel, Sergt.
3. John Griffin, Sergt.
4. Rich'd. Stubbs, Corpl.
5. Jesse Holt, Corpl.
6. Daniel Richardson, Corpl.
7. Edward Hazell, Drum'r.
8. Thomas Johnson, Fifer
9. William Matthews, private
10. Rich'd Davis, private
11. John Clifton, private
12. Josiah Telph, private
13. John Davis, private
14. Richard Frazier, private
15. Isaac Alexander, private
16. Joseph Hassel, private
17. Adkins Mosey, private

18. James Davenport, private
19. Fred'k. McNeil
20. William Dartreck
21. Stephen Long, private
22. Miles Hatfield, private
23. Thomas Roberts, private
24. Colin Bouch, private
25. Henry Milers, private
26. William Burch, private
27. Wm. Simons, private
28. Finch Terry, private
29. Thomas Terry, private
30. Benjamin James, private
31. Wm. Mills, private
32. Wm. Cole, private
33. Samuel Brothers, private
34. Wm. Briggs, private
35. Joseph Terrell
36. Joshua Armes
37. Stephen Barnes
38. Thomas Allen
39. James Onion

## CLARK'S STATE RECORDS

[Pages 1056, Vol. XVII]

Sundry Rolls Militia. Light Horse Service.

1. Joseph Sharpe, Capt.
2. Arch. Sloan, Lieut.
3. James Sharpe, private
4. Richard Homes, private
5. Hugh Andrew, private
6. John Shaw, private
7. John McGagbey, private
8. Edward Griffith, private
9. Solomon Shelby
10. William Cowan
11. Alexander McUrday
12. James Stevenson

13. Samuel Sloan
14. Francis Queen
15. Alexander Carson
16. Arch'd Wasson
17. Joseph Milsaps
18. Samuel Billingsbe
19. John McCoy
20. Arch'd Hogstone
21. William McHorgul
22. George Laskey
23. John White
24. John Smith

STATE RECORDS, VOL. XVII

Pay Roll Capt. Wm. Brinkley's Co. of the 1st Reg. of N. C. Commanded by Col. Sam'l Jarvis.

[Page 1060]

William Brinkley, Capt.
John Pitts, Capt.
Davis Bagby, Lieut.
James Judge, Lieut.
Samuel Long, Lieut.
Arthur Long, Ensn.
Robb Benn, Ensn.
William Sikes, Q. M.
1. Abraham Johnson, Sergt.
2. John Cone, Sergt.
3. Jacob Michel, Sergt.
4. Stephen Edwards, Sergt.
5. David Mathis, Corpl.
6. David Lewis, Corpl.
7. Randal Newsom, D. Ma'r.
8. Luke Senter, D. Ma'r.
9. Sam'l. Senter, private
10. William Senter, private
11. Mathew Killeworth, private
12. John Smith, private
13. William Jones
14. William Shepherd, private
15. Caleb Etheridge
16. Wm. Dickens, private
17. Charles Sturdivant, private
18. Wm. Yarborough, private
19. Samuel Williams, private
20. James Shaw, private
21. Jeremiah Brinkley, private
22. Wm. Coneway, private
23. Thos. Young, private
24. Rich'd. Drake, private
25. Nelson Kelley, private
26. James Gilbert, private
27. James Scott, private
28. Mart Killeworth, private
29. Mark Rickmon, private
30. John Hall, private
31. William Kelly, private
32. Wm. Marshal, private
33. James Butt, private
34. Jesse Powers, private
35. John Edwards, private
36. Wm. Jordan, private
37. Wm. Bynum, private
38. Daniel Merritt, private
39. James Kitchen, private
40. Moses Battloy, private
41. Benj. Whitehead, private
42. Joseph Crief, private
43. Robert West, private
44. George Night, private
45. Stephen Merritt, private
46. Benj. Greene, private
47. Spencer Rosfield, private
48. Sutton Roe, private
49. Daniel Thomson, private
50. John Barrott, private
51. Traves Weaver, private
52. William Burt, private
53. Joseph Perry, private
54. Higdon Roberson, private
55. Bennet Whitehead, private
56. Henry Ealbeck
57. David Crowley, private
58. Mathew Howell, private
59. William Edmonds, private
60. Wm. Morean, private
61. Absolom Moreland, private
62. Starling Daniel, private
63. Benjamin Hines, private
64. Wm. Gilbert, private
65. Aaron Ethridge, private
66. Abraham Wood, private
67. John Brown, private
68. Abraham Dean, private
69. Nathaniel Sledge, private
70. Colin Brown, private
71. Robb. Etheridge, private
72. Arnold Bradley, private
73. Arthur Merritt, private
74. John Stulker, private
75. John Wallis, private
76. Jeremiah Sullivant, private
77. Thos. Bose, private
78. John Turner, private
79. Thos. Heath, private

STATE RECORDS

[Page 1042, Vol. 17]

(From Pension Office, N. C. Miscellaneous Rolls)
Roll endorsed by Capt. Bynum N. C. Militia. 7 April, 1781.

Turner Bynum, Capt.
Isaac Rowell, Lieut.
Wm. Sykes, Ensign
Nich's Lane, Surgt.

John Louday, Sergt.
Seth Harrison, Corpl.
Nath'l. Woodroof, Corpl.
Nath'l Tatum, Sergt. Major
Wm. McKendree, Q. M., Sergt.

Cordell Dupree, Serg't.
John Blick, Serg't.
Thos. Yeargin, Corp'l.
Frs. Foggerson, Corp'l.

*Privates*

Thomas Garris
Peter Smith
James London
Elijah Harrison
James Going
Rich'd. Mason (destd.)
John Hamour
Anth'y. Sweet
Jno. Williamson
Geo. Graham
Joseph Graham
Hugh Lambert
Charles Bailey
Jno. Singleton
Robon Ingall
Alex'r. Stewart
John White
Wm. Dupree
Arch'd. Wood
Avent Massey
Peter Avent
Robt. Hill
Daniel Harrison
Jno. Edwards
Henry Jones

Thos. Goin
Benj. Harris
Thos. Johnson
Wm. Wright
Charles Avery
Ainsworth Harrison
Rice Rollins (dischgd.)
Peter Williams (dischgd.)
Edw'd. Wallis
Lewis Williams
John Jordan (dischgd.)
Michael Gwaltney (dischgd.)
Lewis Brewer
John Rivers (destd.)
Clifton Harrison
John Thompson
Peter Willis
Britain Bynum
Drury Bynum
Peter Wyche (dischgd.)
Peter Clark
James Thompson
Burnwell Jordan
Rich'd. Mason (dest'd.)

## CLARK'S STATE RECORDS

[Vol. XVII]

Roll of Militia Prisoners on board Forbay Prison Ship, 18 May, 1781.

Axson, Williams, Jun'r.
Ash, Sam'l.
Arthur, George
Anthony, John
Atmore, Ralph
Barnwell, John, Major
Baddily, John, Major
Barnwell, Edwd., Capt.
Bonnethean, Peter, Capt. Lt.
Bembridge, Henry
Black, John, Lieut.
Branford, William
Ball, Joseph
Barnwell, Robt.
Blumdell, Nath'l.
Bricken, James
Bailey, Francis
Baoqum, William
Clarke, Jonathan

Cockran, Thomas
Cooke, Thomas
Calhoon, John (protection)
Cray, Joo. Capt. 16 Aug. '80
Conyers, Norwood
Cox, James
Cummins, Rich'd.
Cohen, Jacob
Dorsins, John
Dewar, Robt.
Desaussure, William
Dunlap, Joseph
Edmunds, Rever
Eveleigh, Thomas
Edwards, John, Jr.
Edwards, John Warren
Elliott, Thomas, Sen'r.
Elliot, Joseph, Junior
Evans John

Eberly, John
Ezan, John (protection)
Elliott William
Guerard, Benjamin
Gibbons, John
Grayson, Thomas
Guerard, Peter
Graves, William
Geir, Christain
Gadsden, Philip
Graves, John
Glover, Joseph
Grott, Francis
George, Mitchel
Holmes, William
Hughes, Thomas
Heward, James
Harris, Thomas
Hornby, William
Harvey, Wm., Lieut.
Henry, Jacob
Hamilton, David
Holmes, John B.
Jones, George
Jacobs, Daniel
Kent, Charles
Kain, John
Lockhart, S., Capt. 16 Aug. 80
Libby, Nathaniel
Liston, Thomas
Lee, Stephen, Lieut.
Legare, Thomas
Lessesne, John
Legbert, Henry
Meyers, Philip
Miche, John
Minott, John, Sen'r.
Moncrief, John
Prioleau, Samuel, Sen'r.
Prioleau, Philip
Pinkney, Charles, Jun'r.
Pogas, James
Palmer, Job
Robinson, Joseph
Revin, Thomas

Rhodes, Daniel
Righton, Joseph
Scott, John, Sen'r.
Snelling, William
Stephenson, John, Jun'r.
Stephens, Daniel
Snyder, Paul
Smith, Samuel
Seavers, Abraham
Singleton, Rippily
Scotton, Samuel
[Page 1044]
Magdalen, Charles
Minoth, John, Jr.
Miller, Samuel
Moore, St'n., Col. 16 Aug. '80
Murphy, William
Monks, George
Jonathan, Morgan
Moss, George, Doctor
Marriett, Abraham
Miller, Solomon, Lieut.
Neufville, John, Jun'r.
Owen John
Sayle, William (protection 61 yrs. of age
    does not mean to be exchanged)
Shrewsbury, Stephen
Tonsiger, James
Tanders, John
Tayloe, Paul
White, Sime., Lieut.
Wigg, William
Williams, James
Warham, Charles, Adjt.
Waring, Thomas, Sen'r.
Waring, Rich'd.
White, Isaac
Welch, George
Wheller, Benjamin
Watirs, John, Jr.
Wilcocks, William
Warham, David
Wilkie, William
Yore, Thomas
Yeadon, Richard

CLARK'S STATE RECORDS—ARTILLERY

| Name and Rank | Dates of Commission and Enilstment | Period of Service | Occurrences |
|---|---|---|---|
| John Kingsbury, Capt............ | | | |
| Phillip Jones, Capt. Lt........... | | | |
| James Wall, 1st Lt............. | | | |
| Jno. Curlew Vance, 2nd Lt....... | | | |
| Robt. Douglas, 3rd Lt.......... | | | |
| Geo. Reynolds, Sergt............. | 17 Nov. '77 | W | |
| Geo Reynolds, Sergt............. | 17 Nov. '76 | W | |
| Rich'd Douge, Sergt............. | 13 Aug. " | | Pt. July 1778 |
| Arch'd Gray, Sergt.............. | 17 Dec. " | | |
| Laughlin Campbell, Sergt........ | 4 June '77 | | Destd 1 Apl. 1779 |
| Stephen Lynn, Sergt............. | 25 Nov. '76 | | |
| Jeremiah Sutton, Sergt........... | 13 Aug. " | | |
| Philip Cake, Corpl.............. | 17 Apl. '77 | | |
| Wm. Ross Vance, Corpl.......... | 10 June " | 3 yrs. | Dischgd 11 Mar. 1779 |
| David Jones, Corpl............. | 15 June '76 | W | |
| Mich'l Bullen, Corpl............. | 17 May " | " | Pt. Julv 1778 |
| Wm. Burk, Corpl................ | 15 July " | W | |
| John Thomason, Corpl........... | 20 Mar. '77 | " | |
| Joseph Fleming, Bombr.......... | 12 Aug. '76 | " | Omtd Jan. 177 |
| Malachi Russell, Bombr......... | 17 Nov. '77 | " | Destd 1 Apl. 1779 |
| Kendle Hislip, Bombr........... | 22 Aug. '77 | " | |
| David Laws, Bombr............. | 22 Nov. '76 | " | |
| William Campbell, Bombr........ | 12 Aug. " | " | Pt. Oct. 1778 |
| Robert Morrison, Bombr......... | 26 Aug. '77 | " | Sergt. July 1778 |
| John Barnes, Gunner............ | 1 Oct. '76 | " | Sergt. 1 Apl. 1779 |
| Mich'l Smith, Gunner........... | 1 June '77 | | |
| John Sullanaver, Gunner........ | 9 May '76 | W | |
| William Fear, Gunner............ | " | " | Pt. Oct. 1778 |
| Mich'l Nash, Gunner............ | 28 Aug. '77 | " | Destd 1 Apl. '79 |
| Obadiah Wynnon, Gunner....... | 20 May '76 | " | Omtd Jan. '79 |
| Benjn Mott, Drumr.............. | 19 July " | " | |
| James Rowe, Fifer............. | 17 Aug. " | " | |
| John Babtists, Matioss.......... | 5 June '77 | " | Destd 8 Apl. '78 |
| Robert Bradley, Matross........ | 9 May '76 | | |
| Philip Burgess, Matross......... | | | Omtd May '78 |
| Wm. Cornelius, Matross......... | 15 July '76 | W | Omtd June '78 |
| James Jamison, Matross......... | 2 Aug. '77 | " | |
| Francis Lewis, Matross.......... | 30 Mar. " | " | |
| Thos. Morrison, Matross......... | 12 Aug. '76 | " | {Mustd not fit for duty and {Omtd May '78 |
| Hancock Nickolas, Matross...... | " " " | " | |
| Austin Prescott, Matross........ | 19 " " | " | |
| John Wilkinson, Matross........ | 13 " " | " | |
| Peter Dunnick, Matross......... | | | Omtd May '78 |
| Wm. Stewart, Matross.......... | 1 Dec. '76 | W | Destd 1 Apl. '79 |
| John Franks, Cadet............. | 20 Oct. '77 | " | |
| Jno. Walters, Mats............. | 11 Apl. '78 | 3 yrs. | |
| Duncan Read, Mats............. | 19 Nov. '76 | W | Destd 18 Jan. '78 |
| Francis Ogeline, Mats........... | 24 Dec. " | " | Destd 16 Jan. '78 |
| Joseph Calaway, Mats........... | 12 Aug. " | " | Destd 16 Jan. '78 |
| John Robison, Mats............. | 1 Aug. '77 | " | Died 12 Feb. '78 |
| John Hawks, Mats.............. | 12 May '76 | 3 yrs. | Died 19 Feb. '78 |
| James Toliver, Mats............. | 26 Aug. '77 | W | {Mustd Sept. '78, destd 18 {Dec. '78 |
| James Kelve, Mats............. | 7 July '79 | 3 yrs. | |
| William Swords, Mats.......... | 17 Apl. '76 | W | |
| David Adkins.................. | 24 Aug. " | " | Destd 1 Apl. '79 |

STATE RECORDS (Cont.)

The following names were entered in book containing the North Carolina Register but do not belong to the line of the State, they are therefore not to be attended to, they would not have been entered here had it been previously ascertained.

(Page 1197)

| Name and Rank | Dates of Commission and Enlistment | Period of Service | Occurrences |
|---|---|---|---|
| Thos. Clark, Capt............... | 1 Jan. '77 | | |
| Thos. J. Carnes, Capt. Lt......... | " | | Resigned 8 Mar. '79 |
| John Van Duyck, 1st Lt.......... | 1 Feb. '77 | | |
| Wm. Clark, Sergt............... | 1 Jan. " | 3 yrs. | |
| Wm. Pennington, Sergt.......... | 7 Mar. " | " | |
| Wm. Johnson, Corpl............. | 1 Jan. " | " | |
| Isaac Lawrence, Corpl........... | " | " | |
| Maj. Scudder, Bombr............ | 7 " " | " | Pt. 31 Oct. '78 |
| Nath'l Ross, Bombr............. | 1 Jan. '77 | 3 yrs. | Pt. 31 Apl. '79 |
| Dan'l Whitehead, Gunner........ | 1 " " | " | |
| Ezekiel DeCamp, Gunner......... | 1 " " | " | |
| Haml'n Robinson, Gunner........ | 2 " " | " | |
| Jos. Chase, Muss............... | | | {A deserter sent to his Regt. {June '78 |
| Thos Clark, Mats............... | 1 Jan. '77 | " | |
| Jno. Fletcher, Mats............. | 26 May '78 | 9 Mo. | {Destd 1 Dec. '78, dischgd 28 {Feb. '79 |
| Oliver Kelly, Mats.............. | 1 Jan. '77 | 3 yrs. | |
| Nath'l Little, Mats............. | " | " | |
| John Mitchell, Mats............ | " | " | |
| James Miller, Mats............. | 6 Feb. '78 | " | |
| Dan'l Sullivan, Mats........... | 2 Jan. " | " | |

United States,

Office of Accounts.

We do certify, that the preceding is a true Register of the North Carolina Line of the late Army of the United States, taken from Official Documents.

Philadelphia, 20th July 1791.

Lynde Catlin
Benja. Mifflin.

# INDEX

Baker, Zebedee, 512
Bakot, Peter, 111
Balance, Leven, 429[2]
Balantine, Maltire, 307
Balch, Hezekiah, 496
Balch, J. Hezekiah, 496
Balch, John, 348
Baldin, William, 348
Baldred, Isaac, 402
Baldwell, Samuel, 441
Baldwin, Edward, 4, 112, 359, 404
Baldwin, Henry, 296
Baldwin, John, 418, 573
Baldwin, Lewas, 601
Baleman, Peter, 319
Baler, Norris, 66
Baley, Benj., 599
Balford, John, 293, 404, 509
Ball, Daniel, 420, 572
Ball, Elias, 265
Ball, Hasea, 4, 28, 110, 429, 572
Ball, Joshua, 429, 572, 621
Ball, Joseph, 624
Ball, Osborn, 507
Ballance, Daniel, 599
Ballard, 602
Ballard, Abraham, 416, 513
Ballard, Burwell, 299
Ballard, Drewry, 290
Ballard, Dudley, 4, 109, 182
Ballard, Jacob, 4
Ballard, James, 269, 510, 511
Ballard, Joal, 111
Ballard, Joshua, 282
Ballard, Kedar, 4[2], 28, 66, 183, 265, 592, 620
Ballard, Lewis, 4, 110
Ballard, Peter, 277
Ballard, Thomas, 498
Ballard, Waker, 513
Ballard, Wakor, 288
Ballard, Wyatt, 4, 110, 183
Ballen, Steven, 421
Ballender, Jethro, 285
Ballentine, Alex, 106, 196, 210, 225, 308, 360, 620
Ballentine, Jas., 70
Ballentine, Malachi, 105
Ballentine, Maltier, 512
Ballinger, John, 403
Ballinger, William, 351
Ballow, Stephen, 571
Balmer, John, 269, 510
Balson, John, 293
Balstaff, Frederick, 4
Balthrop, Augustas, 464
Balthrop, Augustine, 573
Baltin, Joshua, 405
Baltloy, Moses, 623
Balton, John, 402
Baltrip, John, 279
Bamble, Hackett, 572
Bandy, Soloman, 404
Bane, John, 619
Bane, Thomas, 348, 507
Baney, Lyon, 107
Bang, David, 402
Bandy, Solomon, 509
Baning, George, 405
Banks, Benj'n., 209
Banks, Jeremiah, 281
Banks, John, 402
Banks, Joseph, 111, 621
Banks, Matthew, 507
Banks, Peter, 359, 404, 427, 572
Banks, William, 78, 110, 360, 511, 606
Bankston, Andrew, 457, 572
Banner, Benjamin, 460, 573
Banner, Ephriam, 460, 573
Banner, Joseph, 460, 573
Bannerman, George, 448

Bannerman, Robert, 348
Banns, William, 290
Banon, James, 403
Banot, Peter, 4
Bans, Stephen, 510
Bantley, John, 271
Baoqum, William, 624
Barbaree, Isaac, 506
Barber, James, 297
Barber, John, 28, 107
Barber, Joshua, 190, 279
Barber, Nicholass, 283
Barber, Plier, 403
Barber, Samuel, 209, 512
Barber, Stephen, 509
Barber, William, 28, 51, 108, 191, 297, 462, 508, 572, 599
Barbere, Isaac, 107
Barbree, Stancell, 508
Barce, John, 4
Barco, John, 106, 190, 405, 507
Barco, Leaman, 106
Barco, Thomas, 508
Barco, Willis, 188
Barco, Wyllis, 106
Barcot, John, 250
Bardon, Christ'v., 599
Barfield, 359, 404
Barfield, Jas., 105, 184, 243
Barfield, Marmaduke, 242, 506, 591, 612
Barfield, Marmask, 105
Barfield, Rich'd., 242
Barfield, Shadroch, 591
Barfield, Stephen, 242
Barfield, Wm., 242, 509
Barganiear, John, 612
Barge, George, 210, 348
Bargeram, Joel, 509
Barginer, John, 234
Bargoner, Jno., 66
Barham, Aaron, 403, 509
Barie, Thomas, 405
Baris, Simon, 245
Barker, David, 573[2]
Barker, Dan'l., 85
Barker, Horress, 348
Barker, Isaac, 4
Barker, Jas., 92
Barker, Jesse, 85
Barker, John, 183
Barker, Joseph, 109
Barker, Levi, 191, 255, 348
Barker, Morris, 511
Barker, Penelope, 570
Barker, Samuel, 198, 277
Barker, Wm., 106
Barket, William, 403
Barley, John, 403
Barley, Robt., 601
Barlow, Christ, 92
Barlow, George, 276, 509
Barlow, Robert, 258
Barmer, John, 446, 571
Barolin, Leanus, 402
Barkley, Samuel, 403, 511
Barkley, William, 293, 403, 417, 510
Barksdale, Henry, 71, 179, 618
Barksdell, William, 593
Barko, Leyman, 4[2], 92, 110
Barko, Wyllis, 92
Barnard, Peter, 51
Barnard, William, 188
Barner, Abner, 507
Barnes, Anthony, 510
Barnes, Britton, 51
Barnes, Burwell, 248, 572
Barnes, Chesley, 455, 573
Barnes, Hezekiah, 265, 508
Barnes, Hez'l., 85
Barnes, Jas., 59, 295, 512, 609
Barnes, John, 246, 618, 626

Barnes, Moses, 4, 112
Barnes, Stephen, 622
Barnes, Thomas, 28, 108, 207, 248, 403, 512, 622
Barnes, Wm., 77, 108, 258, 507
Barnet, David, 597
Barnet, Jas., 108
Barnet, Jno., 108
Barnett, Absolom, 509
Barnett, Charles, 433, 572
Barnett, James, 506
Barnett, Peter, 299
Barnett, Sion, 4, 256, 507
Barnett, Thomas, 474, 572
Barnett, Wm., 350
Barnhardt, Christian, 402
Barnhardt, George, 423, 573
Barnhill, David, 4, 109, 405, 506
Barnhill, Henry, 107, 452, 508
Barnhill, James, 109, 402, 511
Barnhill, John, 405, 508
Barnhunt, Christian, 511
Barnwell, Edw., 624
Barnwell, John, 624
Barns, Burwell, 453
Barns, Hezekiah, 619
Barns, Josiah, 210
Barns, Thomas, 617
Barnwell, Robt., 624
Barr, Caleb, 197, 210, 225
Barr, Hugh, 350
Barr, Isaac, 572
Barr, Patrick, 350
Barranton, Nathan, 359
Barrett, Isaac, 429, 572
Barrett, Jonathan, 429, 572
Barrett, Joseph, 4, 403
Barrett, William, 28, 244, 447, 572
Barrer, Moses, 111
Barrington, Isaac, 217
Barrington, Joseph B., 572
Barrington, Nathan, 404
Barrington, Rich'd., 402
Barritt, Thomas, 244
Barrlow, Robt., 101
Barron, James, 610
Barron, Joshua, 348
Barror, James, 304
Barrot, Joseph, 109, 512
Barrott, John, 180, 289, 617, 623
Barrott, Peter, 572
Barrow, John, 71, 618
Barrow, Samuel, 28
Barrow, Thomas, 402[2], 403, 405
Barrow, James, 66, 106, 507, 510
Barrow, Jacob, 28
Barrow, Dan'l., 107, 348, 508
Barrow, Abram, 348
Barrow, William, 406
Barrow, Willis, 610
Barrow, Wyllie, 509
Barrs, Clarel, 512
Barrs, John, 590
Barry, Andrew, 444, 488
Barry, Richard, 496, 497
Barson, James, 353
Bartea, William, 510
Bartee, John, 294, 619
Bartee, Reuben, 590
Bartholomew, John, 66, 189, 266, 572, 611
Bartie, John, 106
Bartlett, Haston, 572
Bartlett, John, 354, 359, 404
Bartlett, Joseph, 511
Bartlett, Noah, 201, 225, 226, 360, 404, 405
Bartlett, Robert, 511
Bartley, Henry, 92, 599
Bartlie, John, 275
Barton, James, 507, 511
Barton, John, 28, 479

Blevins, Nathan, 418, 573
Blick, John, 624
Blizard, Ezekiah, 210
Block, James, 4²
Blocker, George, 348
Blocker, William, 348
Blocksom, Sovvain, 78
Blockwell, James, 107
Blokam, Sovereign, 612
Bloodgood, Isaac, 303
Bloodworth, Benjamin, 509
Bloodworth, Timothy, 319, 615²
Blossom, Baezella, 405
Blount, —— 602
Blount, Benj., 109, 251, 502
Blount, Benj. Hodge, 245
Blount, Edmond, 109, 181
Blount, Frederick, 4³, 111, 206, 243, 511
Blount, Jacob, 29, 498, 500
Blount, James, 29, 78, 498, 500, 501, 502
Blount, Jess, 29
Blount, Jno. 85
Blount, Mary, 570
Blount, Reading, 4⁵, 25, 26, 29, 78, 185, 238
Blount, Thomas, 4, 29, 78, 108, 109, 238, 245, 506, 508, 513
Blount, Warren, 112, 512
Blount, William, 29, 403
Blow, Benj., 273, 509
Bloxoni, Sovereign, 192
Blue, Daniel, 348
Blue, John, 210, 456, 573
Blue, Neil, 51, 598
Blue, William, 348
Blumdell, Nath'l., 624
Blunby, William, 404, 509
Blunt, Benjamin, 4
Blunt, Thos., 106
Blunt, Whitmal, 29
Blurton, Edw'd., 78, 359², 404², 506
Blurton, Henry, 78, 405, 511
Blyth, Joseph, 29
Blyth, Samuel, 29, 604
Blythe, Joseph, 4⁵, 108, 183, 237
Blythe, Samuel, 51, 186
Boatwright, Samuel, 573
Bobason, Daniel, 443
Bobs, William, 360
Bobbs, William, 192
Bobson, Joseph, 190
Bochner, William, 511
Bocker, Daniel, 506
Bockner, Michoel, 298
Boddie, Nathan, 614
Boddington, William, 506
Bodenhammer, William, 351
Boga, Benjamin, 4
Bogas, Benajab, 112
Bogart, Tunis, 106
Boggs, Ezekiel, 70, 257, 507, 360
Boggs, Jno., 70, 253, 506, 618
Bogle, Archibald, 58, 11
Bogle, Sam'l., 226
Bogs, Ezekiel, 618
Bogue, Mark, 273
Bohannan, Bart'w., 509
Bohannon, Baitham, 403
Bohn, Andrew, 238
Bohng., Baxter, 210
Boice, Arthur, 508, 609
Boice, Jesse, 618
Boid, Benjamin, 4
Boing, Jno. 351
Boing, Wm., 405
Bokin, Thomas, 273
Boldwin, William, 348
Bolick, Casper, 441, 573
Boling, Alexander, 617

Boling, Baxter, 198
Boling, Benjamin, 209
Boling, Thomas, 4, 112
Bolson, Joel, 510
Bolson, John, 510
Bolston, David, 510
Bolten, S., 602
Bolton, Benj., 110, 426
Bolton, John, 360, 511
Bolton, Richard, 107, 351, 507, 508
Bomer, James, 503
Bomer, Thomas, 503
Bond, Elisha, 100, 233, 619
Bond, James, 4², 179, 252, 259, 612
Bond, Michael, 513
Bond, Richard, 4, 78, 111
Bond, Thos., 100, 207, 305, 512
Bond, William, 201, 226, 260, 405
Bondfield, Rebecca, 570
Bondy, John, 572
Bone, Jas., 58
Bone, Thomas, 351
Bone, Wm., 210
Boney, Daniel, 573
Boni, Wm., 210
Bonner, John, 443, 572
Bonner, Lydia, 570
Bonner, Mary, 570
Bonner, Thomas, 502
Bonner, Wm., 109
Bonnethean, Peter, 624
Bonney, Gideon, 599
Bonny, Gideon, 70
Booles, Burgain, 405
Booling, Wm., 109
Bools, Jesse, 179²
Bools, William, 179
Boomer, William, 112, 200, 226, 360, 403
Boon, David, 4, 107, 109, 286, 508
Boon, Elisha, 4, 107, 109, 183, 286, 508
Boon, Jacob, 290
Boon, Jas., 107, 264, 404, 509
Boon, John, 112, 210, 434, 572
Boon, Joseph, 71, 507
Boon, Lewis, 107, 405, 507, 573
Boon, Rackford, 425
Boon, Raeford, 573
Boon, Roderick, 472
Boon, Whylis, 78
Boon, Wm., 97, 187, 210, 607
Boone, Joshua, 273
Boons, Wm., 112
Boostax, James, 601
Bootery, James, 405
Bootey, Cendall, 200
Bootey, Caudel, 107
Bootle, Thos., 70
Booth, Jesse, 291
Boothe, Jno., 97
Bootwright, Samuel, 444
Booty, Cendall, 226
Borchnes, Joseph, 599
Borden, Hampton, 301
Borean, Jacob, 403, 511
Borganeor, John, 193
Borough, Joel, 267
Borough, Solomon, 360
Borough, Wiley, 262
Boroughs, Solomon, 513
Borows, John, 59
Borring, Tom, 351
Bored, John, 351
Bose, Thos., 623
Boseman, Jesse, 194, 290, 404
Bosen, Jacob, 59
Bosman, Shadroch, 509
Bost, Elias, 348

Bostain, Andrew, 271, 456, 511
Bostian, Jacob, 511
Boston, Andrew, 4, 108, 189, 456, 57r
Boston, Chrisn., 108
Boston, Christopher, 4, 189
Boston, Jacob, 271, 351, 437, 572
Boston, John, 590
Boswell, Reuben, 444, 572
Boswell, Wm., 106, 304, 619
Bosworth, James, 359, 404
Bouch, Colin, 622
Boudy, John, 449
Boulton, Benjamin, 512, 513
Bourk, Thomas, 499
Bourke, Chas., 97
Bourne, Bozely, 508
Boush, Jas., 616
Boutton, Benjamine, 360
Bowan, Samuel, 201
Bowell, Lewis, 210
Boweles, Benjamin, 4, 572
Bowels, Thomas, 573
Bowen, Bracy, 457, 572
Bowen, Clifton, 350
Bowen, Isaac, 351
Bowen, Jas., 112
Bowen, Stephen, 112², 237, 403, 507
Bowers, Brittian, 451, 573
Bowers, Giles, 107, 111, 192, 242
Bowers, Jiles, 4²
Bowers, John, 190, 234
Bowers, Josiah, 196, 210, 225, 405
Bowers, Solomon, 4, 109
Bowers, Thomas, 196, 225, 360
Bowers, Wm., 77, 196, 210, 225
Bowler, James, 276
Bowles, Taylor, 348, 510
Bowles, Thomas, 508
Bowlin, Baxter, 51
Bowlin, Jereh, 51
Bowling, Baxter, 225
Bowling, Benjamin, 225
Bowling, Taylor, 509
Bowman, Charles, 299
Bowman, James, 350
Bowman, John, 304, 350
Bowman, Joshua, 29, 51, 191, 501, 598, 604
Bowman, Rob't., 51, 294
Bowman, Samuel, 210
Bowman, Sherwood, 421, 572
Bowin, Elijah, 210
Bowney, Daniel, 319
Boya, Dempsey, 110
Boya, Wm., 110
Boyakan, Thomas, 359, 404
Boyaken, Jas., 111
Boyakin, James, 4
Boyce, Arthur, 106, 266
Boyce, Dempsey, 199, 224, 226, 403
Boyce, Jesse, 247
Boyce, John, 4, 109
Boyce, Seth, 97, 260
Boyce, William, 225, 360, 402
Boyce, Jesse, 193
Boyce, William, 193
Boyd, Adam, 29, 51, 77, 190, 238, 488, 572, 604
Boyd, Benj., 111
Boyd, Hugh, 29
Boyd, Jas., 107
Boyd, John, 85, 105, 261, 507
Boyd, Joseph, 107, 196, 225
Boyd, Richard, 597²
Boyd, Robt., 601
Boyd, Sam'l, 107
Boyd, Thomas, 4, 299, 499, 500, 510

666                    INDEX

670

INDEX

INDEX INDEX     691

Stephenson, Andrew, 557
Stephenson, Hugh, 556, 557, 591, 610
Stephenson, James, 584
Stephenson, John, 274, 625
Stephenson, John, R., 311
Stephenson, Joseph, 560
Stephenson, Peter, 303
Stephenson, Silas, 555
Stephins, James, 185
Stepp, John, 263, 556
Steptoe, Thos., 166
Sterling, Elisha, 164, 185
Sterling, Elihu, 20
Sterling, Isaac, 64
Sterling, Robt., 164, 185, 440, 585
Sterling, Seth., 165, 585
Sternes, Henry, 399
Sternes, John, 399²
Stertevant, Barnas, 160
Stevens, Benj., 165, 598
Stevens, Henry, 20, 163, 164
Stevens, Hugh, 165
Stevens, James, 20, 164
Stevens, Jno., 161², 162, 207, 304, 556, 584, 602, 608
Stevens, Jones, 593
Stevens, Joseph, 56
Stevens, Joshua, 287
Stevens, Lewis, 69, 294
Stevens, Samuel, 425, 585
Stevens, Thomas, 20, 56, 166
Stevenson, Abraham, 399
Stevenson, Andrew, 399
Stevenson, Benj'n, 90
Stevenson, Henry, 399
Stevenson, Hugh, 160, 264
Stevenson, James, 302, 399², 622
Stevenson, Joseph, 100, 162, 399², 439, 585
Stevenson, Josiah, 416
Stevenson, Samuel, 399
Stevenson, Silas, 47, 160
Stevenson, William, 64, 399² 559, 617
Steverston, James, 559
Stewalk, Frederick, 555
Steward, Charles, 594
Steward, Dan'l, 163
Stewart, Alexander, 400, 624
Stewart, Andrew, 303
Stewart, Charles, 20⁵, 47, 56, 83, 167, 185, 294, 399, 611, 620
Stewart, Coldwell, 163, 557
Stewart, Daniel, 20, 165, 186, 268, 400
Stewart, David, 400
Stewart, Dempsey, 20²
Stewart, Dempsy, 167
Stewart, Edward, 457, 585
Stewart, George, 47, 100
Stewart, James, 20, 166, 400², 435, 586, 611, 613
Steward, Jno., 160, 161, 165, 242, 303, 400, 422, 439, 585, 606, 613
Stewart, Joseph, 47, 103, 160, 195, 400
Stewart, Matthew, 400
Stewart, Nicholas, 47
Stewart, Robert, 400
Stewart, Sam'l, 163. 400²
Stewart, William, 57, 64, 196, 246, 400², 556, 557, 609, 613, 626
Stiles, John, 585
Stiley, Myatt, 558
Still, Garrett, 558
Still, Jas., 164
Still, John, 20, 166

Stilliard, Peter, 20
Stillwel, Jacob, 20
Stillwell, David, 57, 257, 556
Stillwell, Jacob, 56, 237
Stillwell, Jeremiah, 296
Stillwell, John, 584
Stillwell, Semon, 285
Stilwell, Jacob, 163, 555
Stilwell, John, 556
Stinson, James, 47
Stinson, John, 278, 445, 585
Stiwoll, Frederick, 21
Stobath, James, 303
Stobo, John, 558
Stock, Joshua, 189
Stockley, Jehu, 273
Stocks, Benjamin, 20
Stocks, Isaac, 621
Stocks, Joshua, 163
Stokely, Alexander, 299
Stokely, Peter, 165
Stokeley, Thos., 165
Stokely, Peter, 21²
Stokes, David, 208, 416, 560
Stokes, Drury, 76
Stokes, Henry, 162
Stokes, Joel, 160
Stokes, John, 267
Stokes, Peter, 300
Stokes, Richard, 585
Stokes, Young,
Stomer, Henry, 558
Stone, Benj., 161
Stone, Jedekiah, 498
Stone, Joel, 289, 558
Stone, Jno., 21, 162, 202, 207, 291, 432, 557, 560, 586, 597
Stone, Jonathan, 432, 586
Stone, Littleberry, 300, 556
Stone, Peter, 450, 586
Stone, Sylvanus, 311
Stone, Warren, 184
Stone, Zedkiah, 291, 499, 557
Stoner, Abraham, 430, 584
Stonn, Andrew, 311
Storm, Andrew, 311
Storry, Wm., 100
Story, Caleb, 160, 197, 216, 231, 250
Story, Henry Haws, 231
Story, Isaiah, 303
Story, John, 250, 264
Story, Wm., 205, 250, 559
Stother, Williams, 262
Stough, Andrew, 446, 585
Stough, Martin, 423, 585
Stovall, Thomas, 458, 585
Stove, Warren, 164
Stovealls, John, 256
Stow, William, 423, 585
Stphens, Asa, 399
Strader, Geoe., 57
Strader, George, 271
Strader, John, 584
Stradford, John, 598
Stradley, Edward, 64, 294, 557, 612
Stradley, James, 256
Stradley, Jesse, 557
Stradley, Jos., 160
Strahorn, Noah, 216
Stranaland, James, 556
Stranaland, Robert, 556
Strand, John, 24
Stranfield, ———, 166
Strange, Edmond, 560
Strange, Eph'm, 162
Strange, James, 240, 241, 363, 555, 598
Strange, William, 21, 166
Stranges, Jas., 90, 162
Stranghan, Richard, 208
Strape, Samuel, 585

Stratin, Joal, 302
Stratten, William, 584
Straughon, Richard, 252, 560
Strawn, Rich'd, 165, 208
Strayhorn, John, 585, 596
Strayhorn, William, 450, 585
Streaker, James, 593
Street, John, 76, 560
Streider, George, 555
Strend, Ludwick, 191
Stricker, Martin, 241
Stricking, Frederick, 21
Strickland, Fred'k, 570
Strickland, John, 21, 163, 180
Strickland, Lot, 585
Strickland, Malachi, 224
Strickland, Malechi, 231
Strickland, Malichi, 198
Strickland, Mallachi, 216²
Strickland, Marm'k, 163
Stricklen, Frederick, 216
Strickler, Jno., 69
Stricklin, Frederick, 163, 559
Stricklin, Lot, 454, 586
Striker, John, 610
Stringer, Allen, 560
Stringer, George, 257
Stringer, Hezekiah, 21, 167
Stringer, John, 21⁴, 160, 165, 185, 252, 612, 613
Stringer, Josiah, 83, 182, 256, 611
Stringer, Limage, 296
Stringer, Mingar, 21
Stringer, Mingo, 186
Stringer, Noah, 21, 164, 181
Stringer, Potts, 590
Stringer, Sam'l, 83, 181, 185, 255, 611
Stringer, Watson, 559
Stringer, Winger, 163
Stringfied, Aaron, 166
Stripes, Demsey, 305
Striplin, Newton, 266, 297, 556
Striplin, Thomas, 556
Strother, Christopher, 556
Stroud, Jno., 57, 191
Stroud, Lott, 160
Stroup, Adam, 585
Strowd, John, 593
Struker, John, M., 190
Stuart, Daniel, 21
Stuart, John, 21, 431, 499, 585
Stuart, Joseph, 230, 400
Stuart, William, 231, 400²
Stubbs, Rich'd, 622
Studman, William, 558
Studthem, John, 439
Studthern, John, 585
Stulker, John, 623
Stultz, Casper, 461, 585
Stumm, William, 619
Stupe, Samuel, 461
Sturdevant, Charles, 21
Sturdivant, Charles, 623
Sturt, Henry, 69
Sturtevant, Chas., 166
Styles, Jno., 163
Styrewall, Fred'k, 162
Styron, Samuel, 265
Subalt, Edmund, Gamble, 245
Suddell, Richard, 591
Suet, Sam'l, 163
Suffman, John, 218
Sug, John, 162
Sugins, Joseph, 162
Sugg, John, 240, 241
Sugg, Uriah, 560
Suggs, Aleygood, 21
Suggs, Eligood, 165
Suggs, Ezekial, 21, 165
Suggs, John, 557
Suggs, George, 48